AutoCAD® 2011 & AutoCAD LT® 2011 Bible

AutoCAD® 2011 & AutoCAD LT® 2011 Bible

Ellen Finkelstein

WILEY

Wiley Publishing, Inc.

AutoCAD® 2011 & AutoCAD LT® 2011 Bible

Published by
Wiley Publishing, Inc.
10475 Crosspoint Boulevard
Indianapolis, IN 46256
www.wiley.com

Copyright © 2010 by Wiley Publishing, Inc., Indianapolis, Indiana

Published by Wiley Publishing, Inc., Indianapolis, Indiana

Published simultaneously in Canada

ISBN: 978-0-470-60823-4

Manufactured in the United States of America

10 9 8 7 6 5 4 3 2 1

For general information on our other products and services or to obtain technical support, please contact our Customer Care Department within the U.S. at (877) 762-2974, outside the U.S. at (317) 572-3993 or fax (317) 572-4002.

Library of Congress Control Number: 2010928466

To MMY, for teaching me that there's more to life than meets the eye and that the deeper levels of life are the most intelligent, powerful, and blissful.

About the Author

Ellen Finkelstein learned AutoCAD in Israel, where she always got to pore over the manual because it was in English. After returning to the United States, she started consulting and teaching AutoCAD as well as other computer programs, including Microsoft Word, Excel, and PowerPoint. She has also taught courses on Web writing and usability. Her Web site, www.ellenfinkelstein.com, contains tips and techniques for AutoCAD, PowerPoint, and presenting, and she publishes the AutoCAD Tips Blog and the AutoCAD Tips Newsletter. Ellen has written extensively on AutoCAD, including articles for Autodesk's Web site and features for AutoCAD's Help system. Ellen's first book was *AutoCAD For Dummies Quick Reference*. Since then, she has written books on PowerPoint, OpenOffice.org (*OpenOffice.org For Dummies*), Flash (such as *Flash CS4 For Dummies*), and Web technologies (*Syndicating Web Sites with RSS Feeds For Dummies*). You're holding the eleventh edition (wow!) of this book, which previously appeared for AutoCAD releases 14, 2000, 2002, 2004, 2005, 2006, 2007, 2008, 2009, and 2010.

Credits

Senior Acquisitions Editor
Stephanie McComb

Project Editor
Jade L. Williams

Technical Editors
Lee Ambrosius
Richard Donald Gladfelter III

Copy Editor
Marylouise Wiack

Editorial Director
Robyn Siesky

Business Manager
Amy Knies

Senior Marketing Manager
Sandy Smith

**Vice President and Executive Group
Publisher**
Richard Swadley

Vice President and Executive Publisher
Barry Pruett

Project Coordinator
Kristie Rees

Graphics and Production Specialists
Andrea Hornberger
Ronald G. Terry

Quality Control Technician
Melissa Cossell

Proofreading
Shannon Ramsey

Indexing
BIM Indexing & Proofreading Services

Media Development Project Manager
Laura Moss

**Media Development Assistant
Project Manager**
Jenny Swisher

Media Development Associate Producer
Marilyn Hummel

Contents

Table of Contents

Contents

Contents

Contents

Contents

Contents

Contents

Contents

Contents

Part III: Working with Data   529

Chapter 18: Working with Blocks and Attributes 531

Contents

Contents

Contents

Contents

Part V: Organizing and Managing Drawings 883

Chapter 26: Keeping Control of Your Drawings 885

Contents

Contents

Contents

Contents

Contents

Contents

Foreword

Congratulations!

Whether you are an experienced AutoCAD user or a newer member of the community, you have just made a very worthwhile investment with the AutoCAD 2011 & AutoCAD LT 2011 Bible. This book will be a valuable reference and guide that we expect you will use on a regular basis to help you become more proficient and more productive with AutoCAD.

The AutoCAD Bible is an excellent resource for learning and getting up to speed quickly on the power of this new AutoCAD release. Everything from the basics of AutoCAD drafting and documentation tools to 3D modeling and design to programming is covered in this book. You have access to real-world examples and AutoCAD drawings that will help you learn and understand new concepts through hands-on exercises. The step-by-step examples include drawing files so you can follow along and continue your learning at any time.

Ellen has been writing books about AutoCAD for many years and has established herself as a true AutoCAD contributor, both at Autodesk and in the AutoCAD community. She is an active member of our beta community and helps shape the future of AutoCAD. You are truly learning from one of the finest and most experienced professionals in this field.

While the depth of content in this book may seem intimidating, I encourage you to jump right in. Pick out a topic or tool you want to learn about, or choose one each week to expand your knowledge. In no time, you'll be learning new and better ways of working with AutoCAD.

Thank you, Ellen, for delivering another amazing edition of the AutoCAD Bible. I know our customers will appreciate your guidance and benefit greatly from your AutoCAD expertise.

Diane Li
Senior Product Manager, AutoCAD
Autodesk, Inc.

Acknowledgments

I would like to offer special thanks to Stephanie McComb, my acquisitions editor, who was very supportive throughout the writing of this book.

A huge thank-you goes to Jade Williams, whose infinite organizing power kept the book on track. Jade kept up with a seemingly infinite number of versions of text documents and images, coordinating the writing, editing, and production of the entire book. She's been doing it for years, an amazing accomplishment!

My thanks to Lee Ambrosius (www.hyperpics.com), the highly knowledgeable technical editor for most of the book. Lee's comments improved the book throughout. In addition, Lee also took on about a quarter of the chapters to update; his expert help made this huge project a lot easier. He completely rewrote Chapter 37 to cover programming AutoCAD with VB.NET, which unfortunately had to go on the DVD due to page overruns. Finally, Donnie Gladfelter (www.thecadgeek.com/blog) did the technical editing for Lee's chapters. They are both AutoCAD authorities and you, the reader, benefit.

I also thank Marylouise Wiack for her precise editing of this very technical book, and all of the people at Wiley who helped with the production of this book and its DVD.

Thanks to Diane Li, AutoCAD Product Manager at Autodesk, Inc., for the excellent Foreword for this book. I also want to express my great appreciation to the members of Autodesk's beta and product teams who were very supportive throughout the beta period. Specifically, I want to thank Guillermo Melantoni, who "owns" the 3D features of AutoCAD, for answering my many questions. Many people contributed drawings and software for this book. I'd like to thank all of them. They have helped to make this book the most comprehensive book on AutoCAD and AutoCAD LT available.

Finally, I would like to thank my husband, Evan, who helped out around the house while I was writing, writing, and writing. Without his support, I could not have completed this book.

Introduction

Welcome to the *AutoCAD 2011 and AutoCAD LT 2011 Bible*. Whether you use AutoCAD or AutoCAD LT, you'll find complete explanations of all the powerful features that you need to know about to design and draw anything. This book is designed to be your comprehensive guide to both the AutoCAD and AutoCAD LT programs.

This book covers every significant AutoCAD and AutoCAD LT feature. If you're a beginning user, you'll find everything you need to start out; if you're already using AutoCAD or AutoCAD LT regularly, the book covers advanced material as well. Although you can use this book as a tutorial if you're just just starting out or learning a new set of features, it also provides a solid reference base to come back to again and again. The short tutorials on almost every topic will quickly have you creating professional-level drawings. The DVD is chock-full of drawings, a trial version of both AutoCAD 2011 and AutoCAD LT 2011, and add-in programs (which are for AutoCAD only). This book is all that you need to make full use of either program.

For AutoCAD 2011, the emphasis is on a wide range of new features, including transparency, a new interface for hatches, and new 3D surfaces.

Is This Book for You?

The *AutoCAD 2011 and AutoCAD LT 2011 Bible* covers all of the essential features of AutoCAD and AutoCAD LT and includes clear, real-life examples and tutorials that you can adapt to your needs.

Although I fully cover the basics, I have also included material on the many advanced features, such as AutoLISP, 3D modeling, rendering, and customization. (Most of the advanced features apply to AutoCAD only.) The following categories should help you decide whether this book is for you.

If you are a new AutoCAD or AutoCAD LT user

If you are new to AutoCAD or AutoCAD LT, the *AutoCAD 2011 and AutoCAD LT 2011 Bible* guides you through all that you need to know to start drawing effectively, whatever your field. Just start at the beginning.

If you are upgrading to AutoCAD 2011 or AutoCAD LT 2011

This book highlights all of the new features and helps you to make the upgrade transition as seamless as possible. Look for the New Feature icons.

If you are switching from another CAD program

You already know what CAD is all about. This book clearly explains the AutoCAD and AutoCAD LT way of drawing the models that you have already been drawing. In addition, you'll find a great deal of essential information about transferring files and data from other formats.

How This Book Is Organized

This book is divided into eight parts.

Part I: AutoCAD and AutoCAD LT Basics

Part I provides the background information that you need to start drawing. It starts with a "quick tour" that has you drawing right away and then covers how to start a drawing, use commands, specify coordinates, and set up a drawing.

Part II: Drawing in Two Dimensions

Part II covers all of the commands and procedures for drawing and editing in two dimensions. In addition, I discuss how to control the drawing process with layers, zooming, and panning. Also included in this part is information about dimensioning, plotting, and printing.

Part III: Working with Data

Part III covers many ways to organize and share data, including blocks, attributes, external references, and external databases.

Part IV: Drawing in Three Dimensions

Part IV explains everything that you need to know to draw in three dimensions. It also discusses how to present 3D drawings using shading and rendering techniques.

Part V: Organizing and Managing Drawings

Part V helps you to incorporate AutoCAD and AutoCAD LT into your work world by explaining how to set standards, manage drawings, and work with other applications. It concludes with a chapter on creating electronic output.

Part VI: Customizing AutoCAD and AutoCAD LT

Part VI introduces the tools that you need to customize commands, toolbars, linetypes, hatch patterns, shapes, fonts, and the ribbon. You'll also find a chapter on creating macros with script files as well as the Action Recorder.

Part VII: Programming AutoCAD

Part VII introduces you to programming AutoCAD. It includes three chapters on AutoLISP and Visual LISP, and one chapter on VB.NET (on the DVD). This part applies to AutoCAD only.

Part VIII: Appendixes

Part VIII provides additional information for AutoCAD and AutoCAD LT users. Appendix A gives instructions for installing and configuring AutoCAD and AutoCAD LT. Appendix B covers additional resources for AutoCAD and AutoCAD LT users. Appendix C explains what you'll find on the DVD.

How to Use This Book

You can use this book in two ways: as a tutorial and learning tool, or as a reference.

As a tutorial

The overall organization of the book goes from simple to complex, and each chapter has several step-by-step exercises. This enables you to use the book as a tutorial, from beginning to end. You can always go back and redo any exercise when you need to refresh your memory on a particular feature.

For newcomers to AutoCAD or AutoCAD LT, Parts I (AutoCAD and AutoCAD LT Basics) and II (Drawing in Two Dimensions) are essential. After that, you can refer to chapters that interest you. Parts III (Working with Data) and V (Organizing and Managing Drawings) are also useful for beginners. Intermediate users will probably be familiar with most of the material in Part I and will be more likely to skip around, looking for the specific topics that they need. However, don't forget that many new features are introduced in Part I. Enough material appears in this book to bring intermediate users up to a fairly advanced level.

I have designed this book to be comprehensive and to include every significant feature of AutoCAD and AutoCAD LT. Therefore, do not be concerned if some of the material seems too advanced. It will be there when you are ready for it.

As a reference

The *AutoCAD 2011 and AutoCAD LT 2011 Bible* is organized as a reference that you can refer to whenever you are stuck, or when you try to do something for the first time. Each chapter covers a topic completely, making it easy to find what you're looking for. Each Steps exercise (with a few exceptions) can be done on its own without doing the other exercises in the chapter. You can easily look up a topic and complete a related exercise without having to go through the entire chapter. A complete index at the back of the book can also help you to find features and topics.

Using the Kindle version

The *AutoCAD 2011 and AutoCAD LT 2011 Bible* is available in a Kindle version. Unfortunately, the DVD doesn't come with this version. Therefore, you need to access the drawings from www.wiley.com/go/autocad2011bible. In addition, you can download a 30-day trial of AutoCAD from www.autodesk.com/autocad-trial. For AutoCAD LT, go to www.autodesk.com/autocadlt-trial.

Doing the Exercises

AutoCAD is a very customizable program. To a lesser extent, AutoCAD LT can also be customized in many ways. This book assumes that you are working with the default setup. However, a number of changes may have been made to your system that could result in the user interface and drawings appearing or even functioning differently from those shown in this book. If you installed AutoCAD or AutoCAD LT yourself and made some adjustments, you know what changes you have made. However, if you are using a computer that was set up by someone else, it may help to talk to that person first, to see what changes they made.

In addition, as you work through some of the exercises in this book, you will make certain changes in the program's setup. Most of these are minor changes that any user would make while drawing. For safety, Cautions and Tips accompany all changes that could have serious consequences, such as customizing the menu. For example, when customizing the menu, you will be instructed to copy the menu file under a new name, and you will then work with the new menu file, not the original one. Nevertheless, if you are working on a network or sharing your computer with someone else, it is important to consult with others who may be affected by the changes that you make.

If you do the exercises, I recommend that you do them from the beginning. Important instructions are given during earlier exercises that may affect your system later. For example, one of the first exercises is to create a new folder to hold your drawings from the exercises. This folder keeps your exercise drawings separate from other drawings that have been created in your office. However, each exercise stands on its own so that you can go back and do only the exercise that you need.

Cross-Reference

You can create your own configuration to help ensure that some changes that you make will not affect others. Instructions for doing this appear in Appendix A under the heading "Creating Multiple Configurations." ■

The exercises in the *AutoCAD 2011 and AutoCAD LT 2011 Bible* have been carefully checked by a technical editor to ensure accuracy. However, we cannot anticipate all situations, due to either varying hardware and software configurations or customization. If you have a problem with an exercise, contact me at the e-mail address listed at the end of this Introduction so that I can correct the problem in the book's next edition. I will also try to give you the information that you need to complete the exercise.

Conventions Used in This Book

Given all the ways in which you can execute a command in AutoCAD and AutoCAD LT, you'll find it useful to read this section, which describes this book's typographical conventions. You will find this section helpful for doing the step-by-step exercises as well.

Using commands

AutoCAD and AutoCAD LT offer workspaces (covered fully in Appendix A) that provide very different ways of executing commands. The default workspace, 2D Drafting & Annotation, uses the ribbon and Application menu, whereas the Classic workspace uses more traditional menus and toolbars. I use this default workspace (or the 3D Modeling workspace for 3D drawing in AutoCAD) throughout the book. All workspaces offer a command line, where you can execute a command by entering its name.

When I explain how to execute a command, I give the instructions for doing so on the ribbon. In addition, I almost always provide the name of the command so that you can enter it on the command line.

The new ribbon created a quandary for me, because I know that some people, especially those upgrading from earlier releases, don't use it; instead, they will prefer to use the Classic workspace with its familiar menus and toolbars. However, I felt that explaining how to execute each command in three ways (the ribbon, the menu/toolbar, and on the command line) would be awkward, perhaps confusing, and space-consuming. What should you do if you are using this book with the Classic workspace?

In many cases, especially if you're upgrading, you'll already know where to find familiar commands. For new commands, it's easy to find their location in the Classic workspace by going to the Help system. Follow these steps:

1. Press F1 to open the Help window.
2. Click the Contents tab on the left.
3. Expand the Command Reference and then the Commands item.
4. Expand the listing of the command's first letter and click the command.
5. Look at the top of the right-hand pane, where you'll find instructions for all the available methods of executing the command.

When referring to the ribbon, I might say, "Choose Home tab ➪ Draw panel ➪ Line," which means to click the Home tab if it's not already displayed, look for the Draw control panel, and click the Line button in that panel. If you're not sure which button to click, hover the mouse cursor over a button to see its tooltip, which provides more information. You can expand many control panels by clicking their title at the bottom of the ribbon; if a command is on the expanded section, I indicate that in the instruction.

A few of the ribbon panels have drop-down lists (or flyouts), which are equivalent to sub-menus. Therefore, to indicate which button to choose, I may need to tell you to choose View tab ➪ Navigation panel ➪ Zoom drop-down list ➪ Zoom Extents. Although I haven't found a good alternative, this is not completely satisfactory for two reasons. First, it's a mouthful! Second, the flyout names do not appear, making it hard to know which is the Zoom drop-down list. However, in most cases, the button icon will make it obvious which drop-down list I'm talking about.

To indicate that you should choose a command from the Application menu, for example, I say, "Choose Application Button ➪ Save," which means that you should click the Application Button at the upper-left corner of the application window (which opens the Application menu), and then click the Save item.

Every command also has a command name that you can type on the command line, which appears at the bottom of your screen. Command names are shown in capital letters, as in CIRCLE. AutoLISP functions (which apply to AutoCAD only) are shown in small capital letters, as in COMMAND.

Figures

In order to create clear, legible figures, I have used a white background in AutoCAD. However, many people use a black drawing area. In Appendix A, I explain how to change this color. As you read through the book, you should be aware that you may see on your screen a negative image of what I show in the figures — a dark background and light-colored objects. Once you get used to this difference, you'll easily recognize what you see in the figures.

In AutoCAD, the 3D environment further changes what you see on your screen. The default 3D background is gray. Again, I have sometimes changed the background color to white for the purpose of creating a clear figure.

Prompts, your input, and instructions

In the step-by-step exercises, most instructions are presented in the same font and style that you are reading now. However, when I reproduce the command line, the prompts appear in a nonproportional font. Other instructions (such as "*Type the first coordinate*") are shown in italic. In any context, input that you need to type appears in **bold**.

The Dynamic Input feature shows prompts near your cursor, but additional options only appear if you click the down arrow on your keyboard. To make clear all of the available options, I use the command line format of prompts.

Here's a sample step-by-step section. In this exercise, you click the proper ribbon button (which is shown in the margin), type the number shown in bold, press Enter where indicated by the bent arrow (↵) symbol, and follow the instructions that appear in italic.

8. To create a second rectangle inside the first one, choose the Home tab⇨Modify panel⇨Offset. (I cover this and other editing commands in Chapters 9 and 10.) Follow these prompts:

```
Specify offset distance or [Through/Erase/Layer] <Through>: 4 ↵
Select object to offset or [Exit/Undo] <Exit>: Click the rectangle
    to select it.
Specify point on side to offset or Exit/Multiple/Undo] <Exit>:
    Click anywhere inside the rectangle.
Select object to offset or [Exit/Undo] <Exit>: ↵
```

Often I refer to specific elements in a drawing. References to these elements appear in the text as numbers in circles, such as **①**, **②**, **③**, and so on. You'll find the corresponding number in the figure to which the text refers.

Mouse and keyboard terms

You can draw using a mouse or a puck. The mouse is familiar to all users. A puck (or sometimes a stylus) is used with a digitizing tablet. Because most users do not have a digitizing tablet, I do not directly refer to it in this book. If you have one, follow the instructions for using the mouse in the same way but using your puck.

A mouse can have two or more buttons. Many users like using a mouse with at least three buttons because you can customize the buttons to suit your needs. However, because many mice have only two buttons, I assume only two. The left mouse button is used to choose commands and toolbar buttons and to pick points in your drawing. For this reason, it is sometimes called the *pick button*. The right button usually opens a shortcut menu.

The time-sensitive right-clicking feature enables you to use the right button either to open a shortcut menu or as the equivalent of pressing Enter. Because this feature is not on by default, I do not assume that you have turned it on. I use the term *right-click* when you need to access a shortcut menu. If you have time-sensitive right-clicking turned on, you need to hold down the right mouse button more than 250 milliseconds (by default) to display the shortcut menu. See Chapter 3 and Appendix A for more details.

If I say one of the following

- Choose Application Button⇨Options
- Choose Home tab⇨Draw control panel⇨Line
- Select the circle in your drawing

it means that you need to use the left button of your mouse.

When I say to press Enter, it means that you need to press the key that is marked Enter, Return, or ↵ on your keyboard. Often I use the bent arrow symbol (↵) that you see on your Enter key to indicate that you should press Enter.

I also use the mouse terms listed in the following table.

Mouse Terms

Term	Description
Cursor	The shape on your screen that shows you where the mouse is pointed. It can take a number of shapes, such as crosshairs, pickbox, or arrow. It is also known as the mouse pointer.
Pickbox	A type of cursor consisting of a small box, used to select drawing objects.
Crosshairs	A type of cursor consisting of intersecting lines, sometimes with a pickbox at their center.
Pick	Point to a drawing object and click the left mouse button.
Click	Press the left mouse button once and release it.
Double-click	Press the left mouse button twice in rapid succession.
Click and drag	Click the left mouse button and hold it down while you move the mouse, dragging an object on your screen with it.
Choose	Click a ribbon item, menu item, toolbar button, or dialog box item. You can sometimes choose an item using the keyboard, as well. I also use this word when you need to choose a command option, which you can do by choosing from a shortcut menu with a mouse, as well as by typing the option's abbreviation on the keyboard.
Right-click	Press the right mouse button once and release it. If you have turned on time-sensitive right-clicking, hold the right mouse button at least 250 milliseconds (by default) before releasing it.
Shift and click	While holding down the Shift key, press the left mouse button once and release it.
Shift and right-click	While holding down the Shift key, press the right mouse button once and release it.
Shift and mouse wheel	Press the Shift key and hold down the mouse wheel, using it like a button.
Select	Highlight an object in a drawing by picking it or by using another object selection method, or highlight text in a dialog box or text document.

What the Icons Mean

AutoCAD 2011 and AutoCAD LT 2011 Bible is liberally sprinkled with icons — symbols in the left margin that call your attention to noteworthy points.

AutoCAD Only
This icon means that the feature that I am discussing is not available in AutoCAD LT. ■

Caution
The Caution icon means that you should pay special attention to the information or instructions because a possibility exists that you could cause a problem otherwise. ■

Cross-Reference

Cross-references refer you to a related topic elsewhere in the book. Because you may not read this book straight through from cover to cover, you can use cross-references to quickly find just the information you need. ■

New Feature

The New Feature icon means that a feature is new to AutoCAD 2011 or AutoCAD LT 2011 or has been significantly changed. ■

Note

A Note icon alerts you to some important point that requires special attention, or additional information that may be helpful. ■

On the DVD

The On the DVD icon highlights references to related material on the DVD. ■

Tip

A Tip shows you a way to accomplish a task more efficiently or quickly. You'll find plenty of practical advice here. ■

About the DVD

The DVD contains all of the drawings that you need to do the exercises in this book. These drawings are a great resource to help you learn using real-world drawings. In addition, the DVD includes the drawings that result after you finish an exercise or tutorial. In this way, you can check whether you have done an exercise correctly. If you lose the DVD, you can get the drawings at www.wiley.com/go/autocad2011bible.

The DVD also contains many add-on programs that I hope you will find useful. I am especially pleased to include 30-day trial versions of AutoCAD 2011 and AutoCAD LT 2011 on the DVD, as well as this entire book in (nonprintable) PDF format. For more information, read Appendix C. Finally, I have created three videos to help you follow along with the Quick Start tutorial and two other exercises on hatching and creating blend surfaces.

Other Information

This book assumes that you know the basics of Windows, although the instructions that you'll read here are usually detailed enough to get you through any task.

AutoCAD 2011 and AutoCAD LT 2011 Bible covers AutoCAD 2011 and AutoCAD LT 2011. However, most of the information also applies to the 2010 release of both programs. I have used AutoCAD in Windows Vista, but almost everything also applies to Windows XP and Windows 7, although some of the screens will look different. If you are using AutoCAD LT 2011, again, some of the screens will look different. Where there is a significant difference between AutoCAD and AutoCAD LT, I explain the difference.

Contacting the Author

I would be happy to hear any comments that you have about this book. The best way to contact me is by e-mail at ellen@ellenfinkelstein.com. You can also use the United States Postal Service (a.k.a. snail mail) and write to me in care of Wiley. Please note that I can't provide technical support for my readers. The publisher maintains a page on its site that includes the drawings used in the exercises (in case you lose your DVD) and any errata at www.wiley.com/go/autocad2011bible. I have my own Web site at www.ellenfinkelstein.com that contains information on my books, errata (at www.ellenfinkelstein.com/autoCAD.html#errata), and AutoCAD, including many AutoCAD tips. I invite you to sign up there for my free AutoCAD Tips Newsletter, so that you can continue the learning process. Go to www.ellenfinkelstein.com/acad_submit.html.

Part I

AutoCAD and AutoCAD LT Basics

The five chapters in Part I provide all of the basics that you need to know to start drawing in AutoCAD or AutoCAD LT. These chapters are essential for the beginner, but even current users can find some new tips and pointers, especially related to features that are new to AutoCAD 2011 and AutoCAD LT 2011. The Quick Start chapter is a beginner's tutorial to get you up and running immediately. You'll draw a window and have the opportunity to use many of the 2D features of AutoCAD and AutoCAD LT. This tutorial will provide a firm basis for the knowledge in the rest of this book.

Chapter 1 introduces you to AutoCAD and AutoCAD LT and surveys the main screen, including the ribbon, command line, and status bar. You'll learn how to launch the program, execute a command in a variety of ways, save a drawing, close a drawing, and exit the program. Chapter 2 explains how to create and open drawings. Chapter 3 covers the many ways to use commands, while Chapter 4 discusses how to specify coordinates. Chapter 5 concludes Part I with an explanation of how to set up a drawing.

If you feel that you know enough to skip to Part II, skim this part for New Feature icons to find out about the latest developments in AutoCAD and AutoCAD LT.

Drawing a Window

Learning AutoCAD or AutoCAD LT is a bit like trying to decide which came first — the chicken or the egg. On one hand, you need to know the basics before you can start drawing. On the other hand, understanding the basics can be very difficult if you haven't had the experience of drawing something. In this Quick Start chapter, you resolve this problem by drawing, dimensioning, and printing a simple window in AutoCAD or AutoCAD LT.

This Quick Start chapter is meant for beginners. You get the feel of AutoCAD's precision drawing tools and experience how to build a drawing. The AutoCAD/AutoCAD LT interface is very customizable. Note that the instructions for the exercise in this chapter assume that no one has made major changes to the default settings.

Chapters 1–5 fill you in on basic information that you need to move on to drawings that are more complex. By experiencing the drawing process first, you will find the initial learning curve to be easier and smoother.

Don't worry if you don't immediately understand everything you're doing. It all becomes clear as you progress through this book. If you haven't read the Preface, now is a good time to go back and read the part that explains how to follow the exercises. When you type the X and Y coordinates (shown in bold), type the first number, a comma, and then the second number, with no spaces between them. The ↵ symbol means to press Enter on your keyboard.

Note

When you start AutoCAD 2011 for the very first time, the Migrate Custom Settings dialog box may appear, asking you to migrate your custom settings from a previous release of AutoCAD. You'll also see a Welcome Screen with options to see videos on basic drawing skills and new features. ■

On the DVD

The file used in this exercise on drawing a window, `abqs-a.dwt`, is a template located in the `Drawings` folder on the DVD. ■

1. Start AutoCAD or AutoCAD LT.

   You see a new drawing. (If you are prompted for a template, skip to Step 2, third sentence.)

2. Choose Application Button ⇨ New. (The Application Button is the red A at the upper-left corner of your screen.) The Select Template dialog box opens. Navigate to the `Drawings` folder of the DVD of this book, choose `abqs-a.dwt`, and click Open. You see a blank drawing. (I explain more about templates and opening drawings in Chapter 2.)

Caution

Don't use the default drawing. You need to open this template for the rest of the exercise to work properly. ■

3. To save the drawing and give it a name, choose Application Button ⇨ Save. In the Save Drawing As dialog box, use the Save In drop-down list to navigate to any convenient folder, such as the `My Documents` folder. Type **abqs-01** in the File Name text box and click Save. (I go into more detail about saving a drawing in Chapter 1.)

Note

In Chapter 1, I provide instructions for creating a special `AutoCAD Bible` folder for all the exercises in this book. If you want to create this folder now, do so and save the drawing in that folder. ■

4. To free up the drawing area, close any windows or palettes that are open by clicking their Close (X) button, so that your screen looks like Figure QS.1. I've changed the background color to white, but yours will probably be dark gray or black.

Note

This chapter assumes that you're using the default 2D Drafting & Annotation Workspace. If the 2D Drafting & Annotation workspace isn't shown in the drop-down list located in the upper-left corner of your screen, click the Workspace drop-down arrow and choose 2D Drafting & Annotation. ■

5. At the top of the screen, you see a tabbed area filled with buttons, called the *Ribbon*, which contains the Layers *panel* (section) on the Home tab, as shown in Figure QS.1. From the Layer drop-down list in the Layers panel, click the down arrow and choose WINDOW, as shown in Figure QS.2. (Layers help you organize the objects in your drawing; I cover them in detail in Chapter 11.) Anything you draw will now be on the WINDOW layer. (If you don't see the WINDOW layer, you may not have started with the `abqs-a.dwt` template. This template contains the layers that you need to use.)

6. With your left mouse button (also called the *pick button*), choose Home tab ⇨ Draw panel ⇨ Rectangle. (Using the Ribbon is only one way to give AutoCAD and AutoCAD LT commands. I explain other ways in Chapter 3. You can find more about drawing lines and rectangles in Chapter 6.)

   Move your mouse so that the cursor is in the main drawing area. Your screen should look like Figure QS.1, but without the grid. If you don't see the tooltip bar — also called the Dynamic Input tooltip — near the cursor, then click the Dynamic Input button on the status bar at the bottom of your screen.

FIGURE QS.1

The AutoCAD screen, as shown while drawing a rectangle.

Application button   Crosshairs cursor   Layers panel   Dynamic Input tooltip

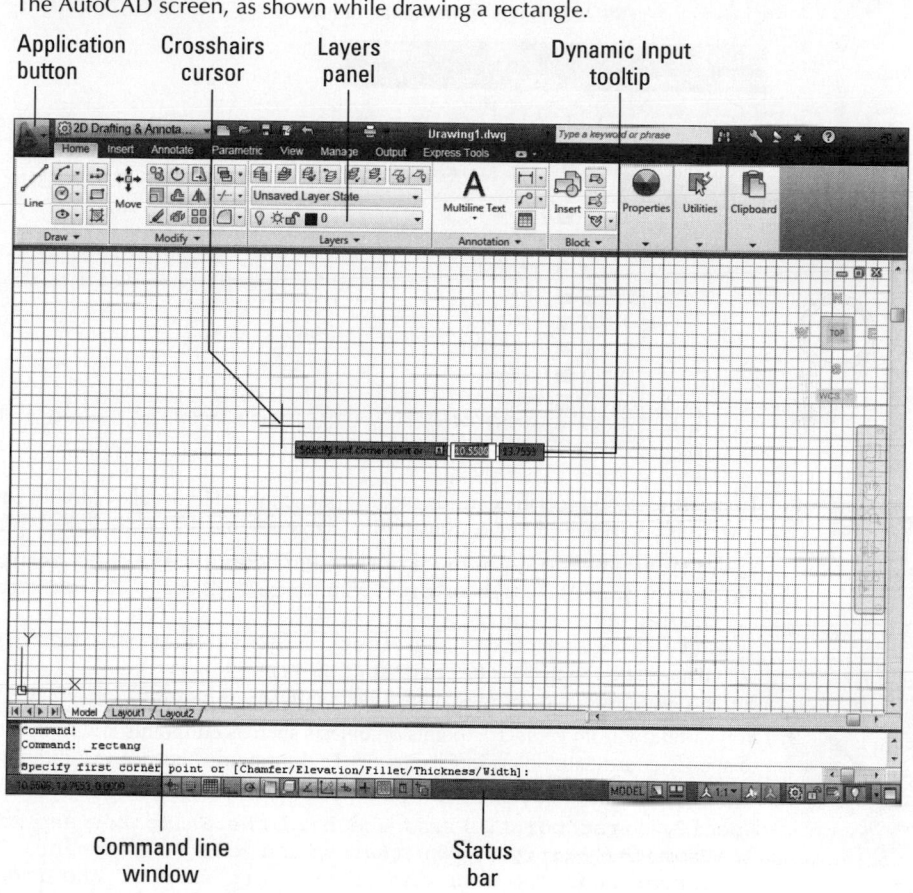

Command line window   Status bar

7. Follow these prompts to draw a rectangle that is 44" wide and 80" high.

   Specify first corner point or [Chamfer/Elevation/Fillet/Thickness/Width]: **0,0** ↵
   Specify other corner point or [Area/Dimensions/Rotation]: **44,80** ↵

Note

In an architectural drawing, distances are assumed to be in inches, so you don't need to specify a unit (although you can if you want). ■

Notice that the text that you type appears next to the cursor in the Dynamic Input tooltip. When you press Enter, the text that you typed is echoed in the Command Line window at the bottom of the screen.

FIGURE QS.2

Choose the WINDOW layer from the list of layers.

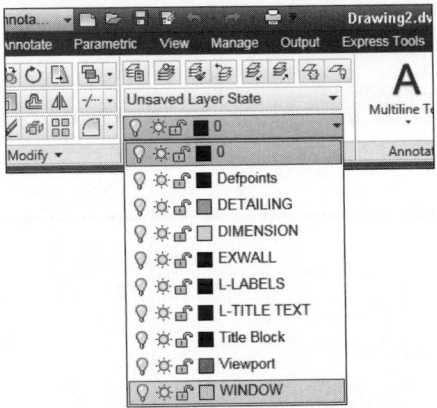

 8. To create a second rectangle inside the first one, choose Home tab ⇨ Modify panel ⇨ Offset. (I cover this and other editing commands in Chapters 9 and 10.) Follow these prompts:

```
Specify offset distance or [Through/Erase/Layer] <Through>: 4 ↵
Select object to offset or [Exit/Undo] <Exit>: Click the rectangle's
    border to select it.
Specify point on side to offset or [Exit/Multiple/Undo] <Exit>: Click
    anywhere inside the rectangle.
Select object to offset or [Exit/Undo] <Exit>: ↵
```

 9. You can draw from geometric points on objects such as endpoints and midpoints. (I explain how to specify coordinate points in Chapter 4.) To draw a line between the midpoints of the inner rectangle, choose Home tab ⇨ Draw panel ⇨ Line, and follow these prompts:

```
Specify first point: Press and hold the Shift key and right-click.
    From the shortcut menu that opens, choose Midpoint. Place the
    cursor near the midpoint of the left side of the inner rectangle.
    When you see a triangle and the Midpoint tooltip, click.
Specify next point or [Undo]: Press and hold the Shift key and right-
    click. From the shortcut menu that opens, choose Midpoint. This
    time, place the cursor near the midpoint of the right side of the
    inner rectangle. When you see the Midpoint tooltip and triangle,
    click.
Specify next point or [Undo]: ↵
```

Your drawing should now look like Figure QS.3. (Your window should be green.)

FIGURE QS.3

The beginning of a window.

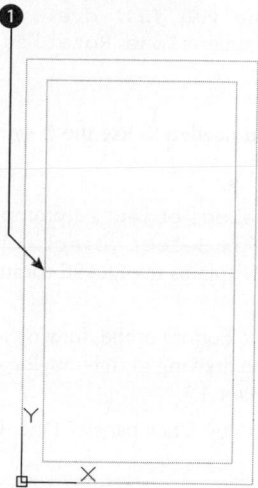

 10. You will now draw a temporary construction line to help you find a starting point for the pane in the top of the window. Again, choose Home tab⇨Draw panel⇨Line. Follow these prompts:

```
Specify first point: Press Shift and right-click. Choose Endpoint
    from the shortcut menu. Pick the left endpoint of the last line
    you drew at ❶ in Figure QS.3.
Specify next point or [Undo]: 4,4 ↵. (This notation specifies that
    the endpoint of the line is 4 units above and to the right of the
    first point. Chapter 4 explains more about specifying coordinates
    in this manner.)
Specify next point or [Undo]: ↵
```

Note

You should see a short diagonal line going up and to the right of ❶. If you don't, it may be because you have a non-default setting that uses absolute coordinates instead of relative coordinates. I explain this setting in Chapter 4. Meanwhile, the easiest way to solve the problem is to type u ↵ to undo the line you drew. You'll still see the prompt to specify the next point. Then type @4,4 ↵. (Adding the @ symbol ensures that you use relative coordinates.) ∎

11. Again, choose Home tab ⇨ Draw panel ⇨ Rectangle. Follow these prompts:

```
Specify first corner point or [Chamfer/Elevation/Fillet/Thickness/
     Width]: Press Shift and right-click. Choose Endpoint and pick the
     final endpoint of the diagonal line you just drew.
Specify other corner point or [Area/Dimensions/Rotation]: 2'4",2'4" ↵
```

Note

This notation specifies 2 feet, 4 inches in the X and Y directions. If you needed to use the @ symbol for Step 10, then use it again here, typing @2'4",2'4" ↵. ■

 12. Choose Home tab ⇨ Modify panel ⇨ Erase. At the Select objects: prompt, click the short, diagonal construction line that you drew in Step 9. The Select objects: prompt appears again. Press Enter to end the command. (Chapter 9 explains the ERASE command as well as other simple editing commands.)

13. Click the Ortho Mode button on the status bar at the bottom of the drawing area if it is not already selected (blue). The Ortho feature constrains drawing to right angles — either horizontal or vertical. (You can find more about Ortho in Chapter 4.)

14. To finish the bottom of the window, choose Home tab ⇨ Draw panel ⇨ Line. Follow these prompts:

```
Specify first point: 8",3'4" ↵
Specify next point or [Undo]: Move the mouse cursor down from the
     start point of the line. You see a temporary drag line. Then type
     the following length of the line. 2'8-7/16 ↵
```

Tip

You can see what you type in the Dynamic Input tooltip as you are typing. Therefore, you can check that you've typed the right numbers before you press Enter. ■

```
Specify next point or [Undo]: Move the cursor horizontally to the
     right and type 28 ↵.
Specify next point or [Close/Undo]: Now try entering the distance
     using decimal notation, rather than feet and inches. Move the
     cursor up and type 32.4375 ↵
Specify next point or [Close/Undo]: ↵
```

15. To draw shutters, first change the layer. Choose Home tab ⇨ Layers panel, click the Layer drop-down list, and choose EXWALL.

 16. Choose Home tab ⇨ Draw panel ⇨ Line. Follow the prompts:

```
Specify first point: Press Shift and right-click. Choose Endpoint
     from the shortcut menu. Click the upper-left corner of the window.
Specify next point or [Undo]: Move the cursor to the left. Type 1'6"
     ↵
Specify next point or [Undo]: Move the cursor down. Type 6'8" ↵
Specify next point or [Close/Undo]: Type #0,0 ↵. (The pound sign
     ensures that your line goes to 0,0 no matter where you are.)
Specify next point or [Close/Undo]: ↵
```

17. To draw the opposite shutter, you'll mirror the first shutter that you just drew. (I cover the MIRROR command and many other editing commands in Chapter 10.) Choose Home tab ⇨ Modify panel ⇨ Mirror, and follow these prompts:

```
Select objects: Click the three lines that make up the shutter.
Select objects: ↵
Specify first point of mirror line: Press Shift and right-click.
    Choose Midpoint from the shortcut menu.
Place the cursor near the middle of the top horizontal line of the
    window. Click when you see the triangle and Midpoint tooltip.
Specify second point of mirror line: (The Ortho Mode button should
    still be blue. If it isn't, click it.) Move the cursor downward
    and pick any point.
Erase source objects? [Yes/No] <N>: ↵
```

The window should look like Figure QS.4.

FIGURE QS.4

The completed window.

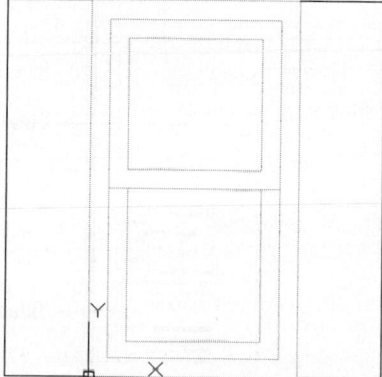

18. To add a dimension to the bottom of the window, you should first change the layer. Choose Home tab ⇨ Layers panel ⇨ Layer drop-down list, and choose DIMENSION. (Chapters 14 and 15 explain how to create and format all types of dimensions.)

⊢─┤ **19.** To place the dimension, choose Home tab ⇨ Annotation panel, and click the Dimension drop-down list. Choose Linear from the list of dimension types. Follow the prompts.

```
Specify first extension line origin or <select object>: ↵ (Pressing
    Enter lets you select an object to dimension.)
Select object to dimension: Pick the bottom horizontal line of the
    window (the bottom of the rectangle).
Specify dimension line location or [Mtext/Text/Angle/Horizontal/
    Vertical/Rotated]: Move the cursor down until the dimension is
    nicely spaced below the window. Click to place the dimension line.
```

Note

If you don't have enough room to place the dimension below the window, type pan and press Enter. Click and drag upward a bit. Press the Esc key to end panning. ■

 20. Click Save on the Quick Access Toolbar at the upper-left corner of the window to save your work.

21. To prepare for printing, click the A Title Block-Landscape tab just above the Command line, on the left. (If you don't see a tab, click the A title Block-Landscape button, which is the second button from the left in the right-hand group of buttons on the status bar at the bottom of your screen.) You then see the window inside a titleblock and border, as shown in Figure QS.5. This titleblock and border come with the template to help you easily prepare the drawing for printing. (Chapter 17 explains how to lay out and print/plot a drawing.)

FIGURE QS.5

The window with a titleblock as it appears on the Layout tab.

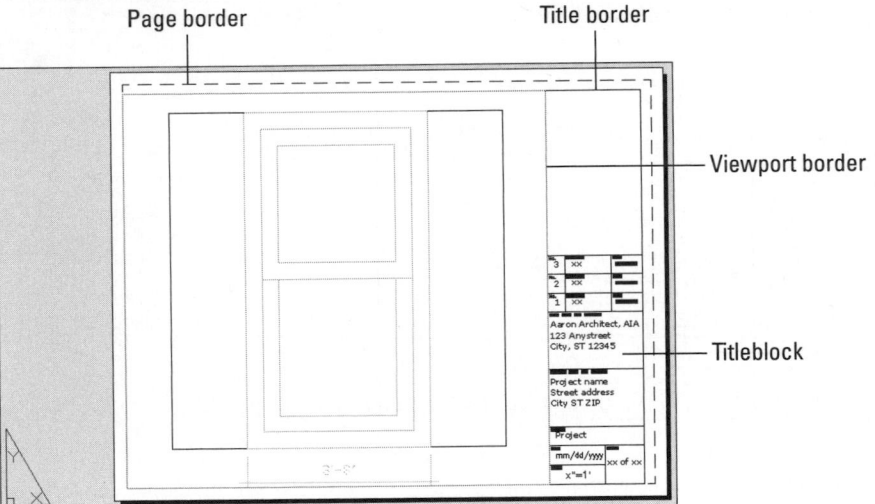

22. To set the scale for printing, click the magenta Viewport border (labeled in Figure QS.5). Choose View tab ⇨ Palettes panel ⇨ Properties. In the Properties palette's Misc. section, click the Standard Scale item. (To see this item, you may have to scroll down in the Properties palette or enlarge it by dragging on its bottom and right edges. If the palette collapses to a thin bar, pass your cursor over the bar to expand it.) Click the down arrow that appears to the right of this item and check that the scale is set to 1" = 1'-0". Click the Close button at the top of the Properties palette. (I explain more about scales in Chapter 5.)

 23. If the window and its dimension are not centered in the viewport window, double-click inside the viewport border. Then choose View tab ⇨ Navigate panel ⇨ Pan. Click and drag as necessary to center the window in the viewport. Press Esc to exit Pan mode. Double-click outside the viewport border to return to the layout.

24. To add some text to the titleblock, you need to zoom in. (I explain zooming in more detail in Chapter 8.) Choose View tab ⇨ Navigate panel ⇨ Zoom drop-down arrow (the bottom button in the panel) ⇨ Window. At the first prompt, click slightly above and to the left of the words Project Name. At the next prompt, click slightly below and to the right of the words City ST ZIP.

These words should now appear very large in the drawing area. They are already placed and formatted, so all you need to do is replace them. (I explain all about how to create and edit text in Chapter 13.)

25. Double-click the `Project name` text. A Text Editor tab appears, along with a ruler, as shown in Figure QS.6.

FIGURE QS.6

Editing text for a drawing.

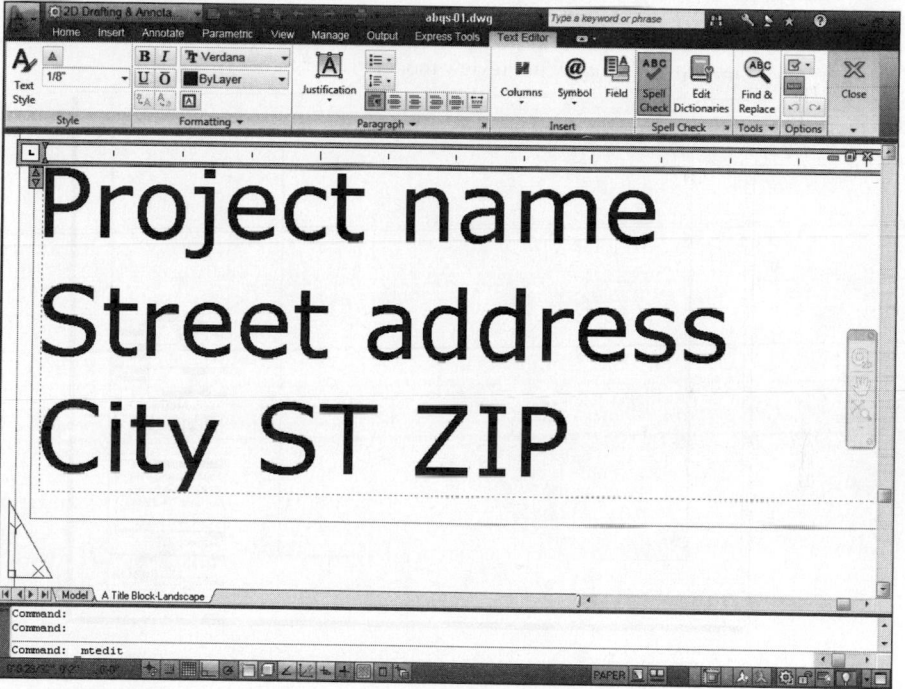

26. Select the text by dragging from the upper-left corner to the lower-right corner. Type the following:

Double-hung window ↵

2010 Coral Lane ↵

Anytown, IA 12345

Click the Close button at the right end of the Text Editor tab, and then choose Close Text Editor to close the In-Place Text Editor.

27. To return to your previous view, choose View tab ⇨ Navigate panel ⇨ Zoom drop-down arrow ⇨ Previous.

28. Click Save on the Quick Access Toolbar to save your drawing.

29. You're ready to print your drawing! Depending on your setup, either you can print directly to your printer, or if you have a plotter available, you can use that. (The layout is set up to fit on an 81/2-x-11-inch or A-size sheet of paper.) Choose Plot on the Quick Access Toolbar. The Plot dialog box opens. (I cover printing and plotting in Chapter 17. Appendix A explains how to configure a printer or plotter.)

30. In the Printer/Plotter section of the Plot dialog box, click the Name drop-down list and choose the printer or plotter that you want to use. In the Plot Area section, make sure that the What To Plot drop-down list reads Layout; if not, choose Layout from the list.

31. Click the Preview button to open the preview window. You should see the window and its title-block laid out, as shown in Figure QS.7.

FIGURE QS.7

Viewing the window in Preview mode.

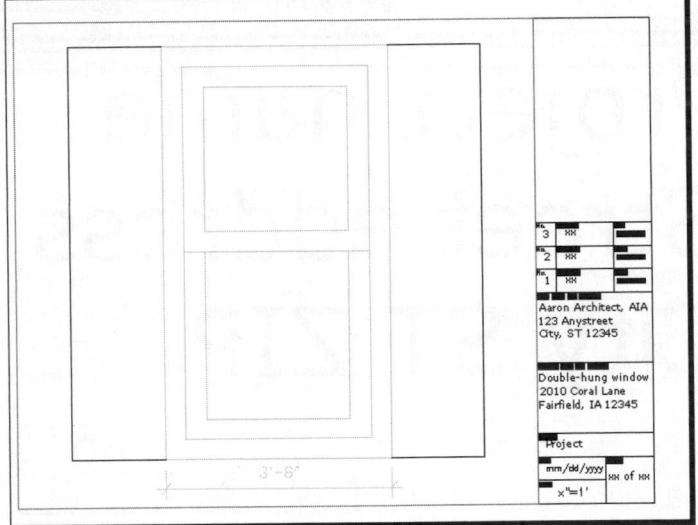

Note

If things don't seem right, click the Close Preview Window button and review the previous steps to see if you can find the problem. Also, see the sidebar, "Help! My drawing doesn't look like the figure." ∎

 32. Make sure that your printer or plotter has an 81/2-x-11-inch or A-size sheet of paper, and click the Plot button on the Preview window's toolbar. Congratulations! You've just created and printed your first drawing!

33. Click the Close button at the upper-right corner of the AutoCAD application window to close both AutoCAD and the drawing. Click Yes to save your changes.

Help! My drawing doesn't look like the figure

If your drawing doesn't look like the image shown in Figure QS.7, there could be several reasons. To fix the problem, try one of the following solutions:

- You may have made a mistake when creating the drawing. If you think that's the case, start over and follow the prompts again.

- You may have started AutoCAD or AutoCAD LT based on a template with different properties from the default. Be sure to use the template on the *AutoCAD 2011 and AutoCAD LT 2011 Bible* DVD, as explained in Step 2 of the preceding exercise. Then follow the prompts again.

- If your drawing still seems wrong, put the DVD that accompanies this book in your DVD drive. Choose Application Menu ⇨ Open and use the Open dialog box to find `abqs-01.dwg` in the `Results` folder on the DVD. This drawing contains the end result of the exercise. You can try to find the difference between this drawing and yours. You can also copy `abqs-01.dwg` from the DVD to your hard drive and print or plot it.

One of the preceding options should solve your problem.

On the DVD

If you're still having problems with the exercise, view QS-Drawing_a_Window.avi, a video of the exercise. ∎

Note

It's important to understand that this Quick Start tutorial uses techniques that are easiest to understand for beginners; as a result, the techniques were sometimes a little awkward. AutoCAD and AutoCAD LT have many capabilities that make drawing easier and faster. You learn all these features in this book. ∎

Summary

In this exercise, you practiced many of the skills that you need to use AutoCAD or AutoCAD LT effectively. Most of your work in AutoCAD or AutoCAD LT builds on these basic skills. The rest of the chapters in this book explain these procedures in more detail as well as many features not covered in this Quick Start exercise.

Starting to Draw

I n this chapter, I explain the essentials that you need to start drawings. After a little background, I discuss the basics of the screen that you see when you open AutoCAD or AutoCAD LT, and how to use it. If you've never used AutoCAD before, do the "Quick Start: Drawing a Window" chapter first.

AutoCAD and its younger sister, AutoCAD LT, are both created by Autodesk. Together they are the most widely used technical drawing programs anywhere. AutoCAD alone has more than 6,000,000 registered users. According to Autodesk, CAD stands for *computer-aided design,* but it can also stand for computer-aided *drafting* or *drawing.*

The first version of AutoCAD, running under DOS, came out in 1982. AutoCAD was the first significant CAD program to run on a desktop computer. At the time, most other technical drawing programs ran on high-end workstations or even mainframes. AutoCAD LT was introduced in 1993, as a less expensive alternative to AutoCAD, for people who don't need all of AutoCAD's advanced features.

AutoCAD's Advantages

AutoCAD's success has been attributed to its famous *open architecture* — the flexibility that the end user has to customize the program by using source code files in plain text (ASCII) format — and programming languages (such as AutoLISP, VB.NET, C#, and C++).

As a result, AutoCAD is an extremely flexible drafting program, applicable to all fields. AutoCAD's support for languages other than English, including those using other alphabets, is unparalleled, making AutoCAD highly popular abroad. As a result, AutoCAD is used in all disciplines and in more than 150 countries.

Through a high level of technical innovation and expertise, Autodesk has created a program with advanced features and capabilities, including 3D surface and solid modeling and visualization, access to external databases, intelligent dimensioning, importing and exporting of other file formats, Internet support, and much more.

The major disciplines that use AutoCAD are:

- Architectural, Engineering, and Construction (AEC)
- Mechanical
- Geographic Information Systems (GIS)
- Surveying and Civil Engineering
- Facilities Management
- Electrical/electronic
- Multimedia

However, AutoCAD has many other lesser-known uses, such as pattern making in the garment industry, sign making, and so on. In this book, I provide examples from several fields. The world of AutoCAD is very broad, and you can learn from seeing the many approaches that AutoCAD makes possible.

Comparing AutoCAD and AutoCAD LT

AutoCAD LT's advantages are its lower cost and its compatibility with AutoCAD. The programming code that is used to create AutoCAD LT is a subset of the code used in AutoCAD. Here are the major differences between AutoCAD and AutoCAD LT:

- AutoCAD includes features that enable CAD managers to hold drawings to certain standards, such as for layer names and text styles. AutoCAD LT doesn't contain these features.
- AutoCAD LT is not as customizable as AutoCAD, which is both programmable and fully customizable. It also doesn't include the Action Recorder.
- AutoCAD LT includes minimal options for 3D; AutoCAD includes a full-featured 3D capability.
- AutoCAD LT has fewer presentation features than AutoCAD, which includes visual styles and 3D rendering.
- AutoCAD LT is deployable on a network but does not have AutoCAD's network license management feature that includes reporting and flexible licensing.
- AutoCAD LT does not offer the database connectivity feature, but you can use tables to connect to data in a Microsoft Office Excel file; AutoCAD offers the flexibility to connect to other types of databases, create labels from the data, and so on.
- AutoCAD LT does not come with Express Tools, a set of additional routines that ship with AutoCAD.
- AutoCAD LT does not include parametric constraints, which allow you to constrain the relationships among objects, but you can use the parametric constraints that are in a drawing that was created with AutoCAD.
- AutoCAD LT does not include the sheet set feature, which was introduced in AutoCAD 2005.

AutoCAD and AutoCAD LT have a few other minor differences, as well. Some of these differences are only in the user interface, so you can accomplish the same task but the procedure is slightly different.

Starting AutoCAD and AutoCAD LT

This section starts a quick tour of AutoCAD and AutoCAD LT. The first step is to start the program.

On the DVD

The DVD contains a 30-day trial version of AutoCAD 2011 and AutoCAD LT 2011. ∎

This book covers AutoCAD 2011 and AutoCAD LT 2011 running on Windows XP Home/Professional, Windows Vista, or Windows 7. (The figures were taken in Windows Vista.) Every computer is set up somewhat differently, so you may need to adjust the following steps slightly. If you didn't install the software yourself and are unfamiliar with the folders (also called *directories*) on your computer, get help from someone who is familiar with your computer system.

Cross-Reference

If you need information on installing AutoCAD or AutoCAD LT, see Appendix A. Appendix A also covers configuring the software and printers or plotters. ∎

By default, installing AutoCAD or AutoCAD LT places a shortcut on your desktop. You can double-click one of the shortcuts to launch the program that is installed on your machine, or use the Windows Start menu to choose one of the following:

- **For AutoCAD.** Start ⇨ (All) Programs ⇨ Autodesk ⇨ AutoCAD 2011 ⇨ AutoCAD 2011 – English (or as appropriate for your language)
- **For AutoCAD LT.** Start ⇨ (All) Programs ⇨ Autodesk ⇨ AutoCAD LT 2011 ⇨ AutoCAD LT 2011

Creating a New Drawing

After you launch AutoCAD or AutoCAD LT, it automatically opens a new drawing named Drawing1.dwg. You can see the drawing name on the title bar. You can start drawing immediately. In Chapter 2, I explain how to start a drawing based on a template and how to open an existing drawing.

STEPS: Starting AutoCAD or AutoCAD LT

1. Click Start on the Windows task bar at the bottom of your screen.
2. Choose one of the following:
   - **For AutoCAD.** Start ⇨ (All) Programs ⇨ Autodesk ⇨ AutoCAD 2011 ⇨ AutoCAD 2011 – English
   - **For AutoCAD LT.** Start ⇨ (All) Programs ⇨ Autodesk ⇨ AutoCAD LT 2011 ⇨ AutoCAD LT 2011

   You see a blank drawing named Drawing1.dwg.

If you are continuing with this chapter, keep this drawing open. I cover exiting from AutoCAD and AutoCAD LT later in this chapter.

Using the AutoCAD and AutoCAD LT Interface

AutoCAD offers four quite different preset *workspaces*, depending on how you want to work. For example, these workspaces determine the Ribbon components, toolbars, and other interface items that you see. AutoCAD offers both 2D and 3D environments. AutoCAD LT has only 2D environments, and the 2D environments for AutoCAD and AutoCAD LT are similar. In this section, I discuss the 2D environment. Both AutoCAD and AutoCAD LT offer two 2D workspaces: 2D Drafting & Annotation and AutoCAD (or AutoCAD LT) Classic. The 2D Drafting & Annotation workspace is the default workspace and displays the Ribbon for executing commands. The AutoCAD Classic and AutoCAD LT Classic workspaces display toolbars and a menu instead.

Note

AutoCAD's 3D Modeling and 3D Basics workspaces create a 3D environment including the drawing templates acad3D.dwt **and** acadiso3D.dwt. **(I cover templates in Chapter 2.) I cover this 3D environment in Part IV, "Drawing in Three Dimensions."** ■

Figure 1.1 shows the default screen that appears when you first open AutoCAD or AutoCAD LT. Your screen may look somewhat different — remember that AutoCAD and AutoCAD LT can be customized in many ways — but the general features will be the same. If you see other items open on your screen, you can close all these items by clicking their Close (X) button.

New Feature

By default, you see a grid when you open AutoCAD. The new grid contains smaller boxes of light lines along with larger boxes of darker lines. I explain how to turn off the grid in Chapter 4. ■

Note

The default screen color is dark gray. You can leave it that way or change the drawing area color, as I explain in Appendix A. I use a white background for the figures in this book for clarity. ■

If you find yourself in a 3D environment in AutoCAD, you'll see a gray background and a perspective view. To work in 2D in AutoCAD, switch to a 2D environment, following these steps in AutoCAD:

1. From the Workspace drop-down list, choose 2D Drafting & Annotation. This displays the Ribbon with 2D commands.

2. Choose Application Button ⇨ New. From the Select Template dialog box, choose acad.dwt and click Open. This places you in a 2D view.

The AutoCAD and AutoCAD LT screens consist of four important areas. These are discussed in the following sections.

The drawing area

The blank area in the middle of the screen, called the *graphics window* or *drawing area*, is where you draw. You can think of this as a sheet of drafting paper, except that this piece of paper can be any size — even the size of a huge factory or an entire county!

FIGURE 1.1

The AutoCAD and AutoCAD LT screens are very similar. The AutoCAD LT screen doesn't include the Express Tools tab on the Ribbon.

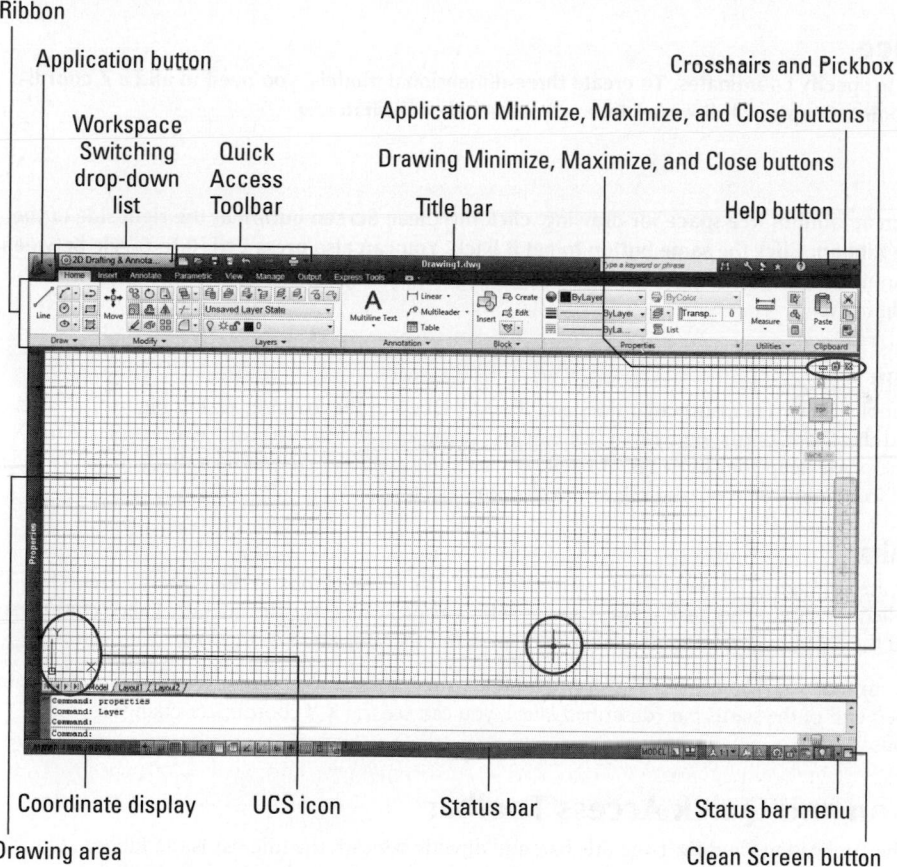

By default, you draw in *model space,* so called because that's where you draw your models. When you create a new drawing, by default, you are in model space, so you can just start drawing. You can lay out your drawings for plotting in *paper space,* also called a *layout.* To switch from model space to a layout, you use the Layout tab at the bottom of the drawing area. You click the Model tab to switch back to model space. (See Chapter 17 for details.)

Note

Rather than the model and layout tabs, you may see Model **and** Layout1 **buttons on the status bar. You can switch between the buttons and tabs by right-clicking either feature and choosing from the shortcut menu.** ∎

When you start to draw, you need to specify where to start drawing. One way is to use coordinates. To specify a coordinate, the universally accepted convention is to put the X coordinate first, followed by a comma, and then the Y coordinate. Examples are –3,5, 3,2, 6,–2, and –1,–1. These coordinates specify points in the drawing area.

Cross-Reference
Chapter 4 explains how to specify coordinates. To create three-dimensional models, you need to add a Z coordinate when specifying a point. Chapter 21 discusses three-dimensional coordinates. ∎

Tip
If you want the maximum amount of free space for drawing, click the Clean Screen button at the right side of the status bar to remove the Ribbon. Click the same button to get it back. You can also press Ctrl+0 to toggle between the two displays. You can double-click the active tab to cycle through three display states of the Ribbon that collapse and expand the Ribbon. ∎

The UCS icon
Notice the symbol with two perpendicular lines and X and Y labels in the drawing area in Figure 1.1. This symbol is called the User Coordinate System (UCS) icon. The lines point to the positive directions of the X and Y axes to help you keep your bearings. (In a 3D environment, you see a Z axis as well.) You can change the look of this icon, and turn it on and off, as I explain in Chapter 8.

The crosshairs
In the drawing area of Figure 1.1, notice the intersecting lines with a small box at their intersection. The small box is called the *pickbox* because it helps you to select, or pick, objects. The lines are called *crosshairs*. They show you the location of the mouse cursor in relation to other objects in your drawing.

As you move your mouse around, the pickbox and crosshairs move with your mouse. At the bottom of your screen, at the left end of the status bar (described later), you can see the X,Y coordinates change as you move your mouse.

The Ribbon and Quick Access Toolbar
At the top of the application window is the title bar, and directly beneath the title bar is the Ribbon. On the left side of the title bar is the Quick Access Toolbar. The Ribbon has tabs, and each tab is divided into control panels (usually called just panels), which are sections of related commands. I explain how to work with the Ribbon and the Quick Access Toolbar in Chapter 3.

Note
The AutoCAD Classic and AutoCAD LT Classic workspaces do not show the Ribbon; instead, you see nine toolbars in AutoCAD and eight in AutoCAD LT, which are usually docked along the left, top, and right sides of the screen. From the Workspace drop-down list (just to the left of the Quick Access Toolbar), try switching between the 2D Drafting & Annotation workspace and the AutoCAD or AutoCAD LT Classic workspace to see which one you prefer. In Appendix A, I explain how to customize workspaces. ∎

On the Home tab, in the Draw panel of the Ribbon, hover the mouse cursor over the leftmost button. You see a tooltip that says Line, as shown in Figure 1.2. Below the tooltip, a description tells you that this button creates straight-line segments. If you continue to hover the cursor over the Line button, the tooltip expands to provide more information about the command.

You use buttons on the Ribbon to execute commands. For example, to draw a line, you click the Line button on the Draw panel of the Ribbon's Home tab. You get some practice drawing lines in the exercise that follows. (In the AutoCAD Classic or AutoCAD LT Classic workspace, you would click the Line button on the Draw toolbar to draw a line.)

FIGURE 1.2

Hovering the cursor over the Line button displays a tooltip that shows the command and a description of its function.

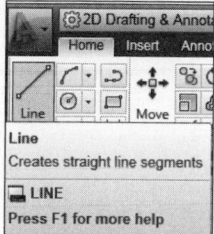

Note

If you inadvertently start a command that you don't want to use, press Esc. ■

The Quick Access Toolbar contains a few often-used commands that are useful to have available all the time. Examples are commands to start a new drawing, open an existing drawing, and save a drawing.

Because you can customize the Ribbon and the Quick Access Toolbar to suit your needs, your screen may appear somewhat different. (See Chapter 29 for information on customizing the Quick Access Toolbar, and see Chapter 33 for information on customizing the Ribbon.) Remember that if the current workspace is AutoCAD Classic or AutoCAD LT Classic, you won't see the Ribbon or Quick Access Toolbar; instead, you'll see a menu bar at the top and several toolbars.

Tip

You can lock the position of Ribbon panels (if they're not docked), toolbars, and windows (palettes). On the right side of the status bar, at the bottom of the screen, is a Lock icon. Click this icon to open a menu allowing you to individually lock specific window, panel, or toolbar components. You can also choose the All option and lock or unlock everything. Locking these interface components prevents you from moving them inadvertently. ■

Using the Application menu

When you click the Application Button, a menu opens (the Application menu), giving you access to file-related commands, as shown in Figure 1.3.

Tip

You can display the menu bar along with the Ribbon. Type menubar ↵ on the command line, and then enter 1 ↵. To hide the menu bar, enter 0 ↵. Alternatively, you can click the down arrow at the right end of the Quick Access Toolbar, and choose Show Menu Bar. Choose Hide Menu Bar to hide it. ■

FIGURE 1.3

The Application Button offers file-related commands, recently opened drawings, access to other open drawings, and a Search box.

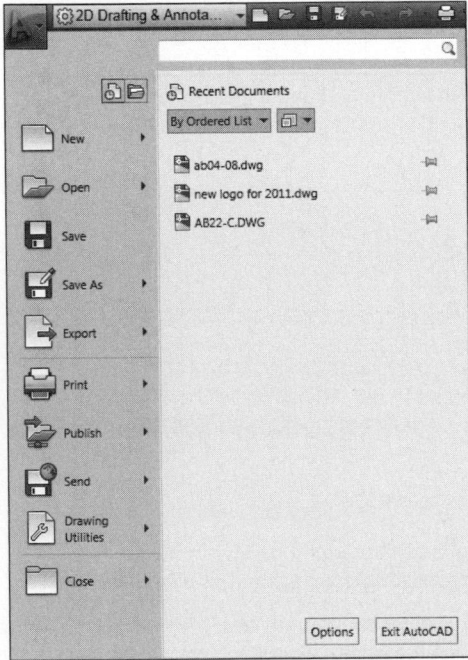

When you open the Application menu, you can type a search term in the Search text box to find a command. On the right, you see a list of drawings that you opened recently. At the top of the list of drawings, you can click a drop-down arrow to choose to display them alphabetically *(ordered list)*, by date, or by type. To the right, you can click a drop-down arrow to display the drawings as icons, or as small, medium, or large images. However, even if you display just icons, if you hover the cursor over any drawing name, an image of the drawing appears.

Tip

Click the Open Documents button to show open drawings rather than recently used drawings. ■

The Options button, at the bottom of the Application menu, opens the Options dialog box where you can specify many settings that affect how AutoCAD works. I explain the Options dialog box in detail in Appendix A.

The command line and dynamic input tooltip

At the bottom of the drawing area, you see a separate window showing approximately three lines of text. (You can change it to show as many lines as you like by dragging the top edge of the window up or down.) Notice the word Command:. This is the *command line*. You can execute any command by typing it on the command line.

Even if you use a menu item or the Ribbon to execute a command, you may see a response on the command line. AutoCAD and AutoCAD LT often provide options that you must type on the keyboard. Text that you type appears on the command line. For example, when you type coordinates specifying a point, they appear on the command line.

The Dynamic Input tooltip allows you to see the text that you type at the cursor. This tooltip doesn't appear until you start typing a command. You can also choose options near the tooltip. (For more information, see Chapter 3.)

To see more of the command line, press F2 to open the AutoCAD or AutoCAD LT Text Window. You can scroll back through previous commands. Press F2 again to close the window. You can also simply hide the Text window by clicking in the AutoCAD or AutoCAD LT window for easy access to the Text window later from the Windows task bar.

The status bar

At the very bottom of the screen is the *status bar* (refer to Figure 1.1). At the left are the X,Y coordinates. As you move your mouse, these coordinates change. (If they don't change, click them and move your mouse again.) The status bar also contains several buttons that I explain later in this book.

At the right side of the status bar is a small down arrow. Click it to open the status bar menu. This menu determines which buttons appear on the status bar. If you don't use a certain button, choose it on the menu to remove its checkmark and make it disappear. You can always go back and choose the item again to redisplay the button.

Creating a New Folder

For your work with this book, you should create a new folder so that you can save your exercise drawings where they won't get mixed up with other drawings. The following directions leave it up to you where to create this new folder. Each computer system is organized differently. If you aren't sure what to do, choose the drive (not the folder) where AutoCAD or AutoCAD LT is installed and create a new folder there.

Caution

I do not recommend creating a subfolder in the AutoCAD 2011 or AutoCAD LT 2011 folder. This folder contains the files that make up the program. If you keep your drawings here, it is too easy to make a mistake and delete necessary program files. Some people create a subfolder in the My Documents or Documents folder. ■

STEPS: Creating a New Folder

1. Move the mouse cursor to the Windows task bar at the bottom of your screen and right-click the Start button.
2. Choose Explore.
3. On the left pane of Windows Explorer, click the drive where you want to create the new folder. If you don't know where to create the folder, choose the drive where AutoCAD or AutoCAD LT is installed. If you're on a network, choose the drive that represents your computer. If you keep your work in subfolders of the My Documents (Documents in Windows Vista and Windows 7) folder, click that folder.
4. If you want to make a *subfolder* (a folder within a folder), choose the folder where you want to create the subfolder.

5. From the Explorer menu, choose File ⇨ New ⇨ Folder. (In Windows Vista, click Organize ⇨ New Folder or New Folder in Windows 7.) A new, highlighted folder, named New Folder, appears in the right pane. You may have to scroll down to see it.

6. Type **AutoCAD Bible** for the folder name and press Enter. (If you did the exercises from a previous edition of this book, such as *AutoCAD 2010 and AutoCAD LT 2010 Bible,* and you already have a folder named AutoCAD Bible, first rename the original folder to something such as ACAD2010Bible.)

Save all drawings that you create for this book in your AutoCAD Bible folder.

Caution
Creating a folder for your drawings as described in the previous steps is essential before you go on to exercises in the rest of this book. ■

Using the Interface

If you did the Quick Start exercise, you had the experience of drawing a window, but I chose the simplest method of completing each task because I had not yet described the AutoCAD and AutoCAD LT application window. In the following exercise, you draw some simple objects, but experiment with all the features of the user interface to get a feel for how they work. (Chapter 3 explains in more detail how to use commands.)

For this exercise, simply follow the instructions exactly. When you type the X and Y coordinates (shown in bold), type the first number, a comma, and then the second number, with no spaces between them.

Tip
Don't worry if you don't understand everything you're doing. It all becomes clear as you progress through this book. If you haven't read the Preface, now is a good time to go back and read the part that explains how to follow the exercises. ■

Follow the prompts shown next. As explained in the Preface, you type what appears in **bold**.

STEPS: Drawing a Line in Four Ways

1. Start AutoCAD or AutoCAD LT.

   You see a new drawing. If you are prompted for a template, choose acad.dwt (for AutoCAD) or acadlt.dwt (for AutoCAD LT).

2. From the Ribbon, choose Home tab ⇨ Draw panel ⇨ Line.

3. Move your mouse to move the crosshairs cursor around the screen. Notice the Dynamic Input tooltip that follows the cursor around, as shown in Figure 1.4. (For this figure, I turned off the grid.) If you don't see the Dynamic Input tooltip, click the Dynamic Input button on the status bar. At the same time, notice the coordinates changing on the left side of the status bar.

4. Anywhere on the screen, stop moving the mouse and click the left mouse button to pick a point. When you move the mouse again, the Dynamic Input bar changes to prompt you to specify the next point and to show you the angle and length of the cursor from the original point you picked, as shown in Figure 1.5.

5. Pick any point to create a line segment. You see the same Dynamic Input tooltip as before, which means that you can continue to create more line segments. (Chapter 6 explains all about drawing lines.)

FIGURE 1.4

When you move the mouse around, the Dynamic Input bar follows the cursor, displaying the current coordinates.

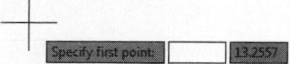

FIGURE 1.5

After specifying the first point of a line, the Dynamic Input bar prompts you for the next point.

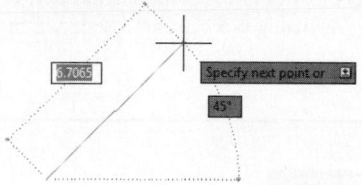

6. Press Enter to end the command and finish your line.

7. For your second line, type **menubar** ↵ and then type **1** ↵ on the command line. The menu bar appears at the top of the screen. From the menu, choose Draw ➪ Line. Again, pick any point on the screen.

8. Move your mouse so you can see the length and angle tooltips. Notice the value for the length. Now type a different value and press Enter. For example, if the Length tooltip says 13.7638, type **5** ↵.

9. Press Enter to end the command. The line's length is based on what you typed, not where the cursor was, but the line's angle is the same as it was before you typed in the length.

10. To hide the menu bar, click the down arrow at the right end of the Quick Access Toolbar and choose Hide Menu Bar near the bottom of the list of menu items.

11. For your third line, type **line** ↵. Notice that the text appears in the Dynamic Input tooltip as you type, but not in the command line area.

12. Press Enter. You now see the command that you typed in the command line area, as well as the Dynamic Input prompt to specify the first point.

13. Click in two places to pick a start point and an endpoint.

14. This time, to end the line, right-click anywhere in the drawing area. By default, this opens a shortcut menu, but it may end the command. If so, you're done. If you see the shortcut menu, choose Enter from the shortcut menu to end the command.

15. For your fourth line, click the Workspace drop-down list at the upper-left corner of your screen, and choose AutoCAD Classic or AutoCAD LT Classic. The entire interface changes: The Ribbon is gone, and in its place you see a menu bar at the top, and several toolbars. If you don't see the Draw toolbar (it's usually docked vertically on the left side of the application window), right-click any toolbar that is already displayed and choose Draw from the list of toolbars. Click the Line button on the Draw toolbar. Move the mouse so that the cursor is in the drawing area. Pick two different points and press Enter.

16. Use the Workspace drop-down list to return to the 2D Drafting & Annotation workspace. Leave the drawing on your screen and complete the next exercise to save the drawing.

You should now have four lines on the screen. You can see how the interface offers several ways to work. You can use the method that suits you best.

Saving a Drawing

Saving a drawing is similar to saving any other file in Windows. You should get in the habit of saving your work every few minutes to avoid losing your work in case the software or your computer system crashes. Saving a drawing for the first time is different from saving it subsequently because you have to name the drawing.

 To save a drawing, click Save on the Quick Access Toolbar or choose Application Button ⇨ Save. If you're saving a drawing for the first time, the Save Drawing As dialog box appears, as shown in Figure 1.6.

FIGURE 1.6

The Save Drawing As dialog box.

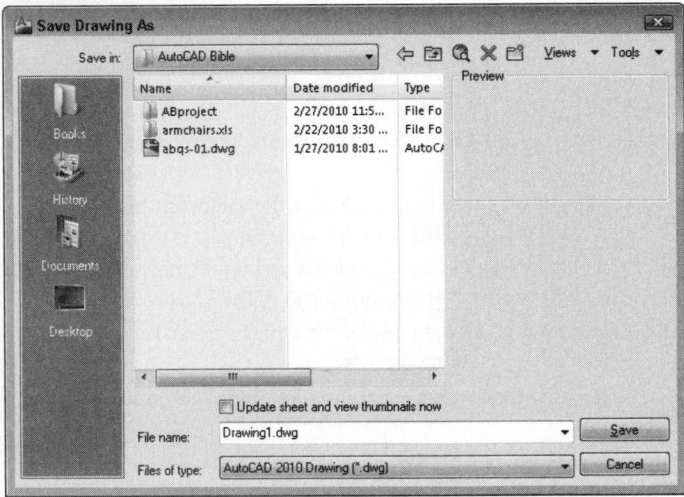

Down the left side of the dialog box are several buttons, called the *Places list*, to help you find a location to save drawings more quickly.

Tip

Conveniently, you can reorder the buttons in the Places list. Just drag any button to a new location. ■

Of course, you can also choose a location from the Save In drop-down list to which you want to save the file. To save a file, type a filename in the File Name text box and click Save to save the file.

Use the Views drop-down list of the dialog box to specify how you want to display files in this dialog box, such as List, Details, Thumbnails, or Preview.

Use the Tools drop-down list of the Save Drawing As dialog box to do the following:

- **Add or Modify FTP Locations.** FTP sites are locations on the Internet for transferring files. To add or modify FTP locations, choose Tools➪Add/Modify FTP Locations. You need to list the name of the FTP site, choose a logon type (Anonymous or User), and specify your user name and password if you're logging on as a User. You can then save drawings (called *uploading*) to FTP locations by clicking the Save In drop-down list and choosing FTP Locations. This feature makes an intranet or any server with FTP capability as accessible as your own computer system.

- **Add Current Folder to Places.** If you save to a specific folder often, you can navigate to that folder and then choose Tools➪Add Current Folder to Places. The Places Bar then displays a new button for that folder so that you can easily click the button to go straight to the folder.

- **Add to Favorites.** When you have navigated to a folder, you can add it to the Favorites folder by choosing Tools➪Add to Favorites. You can also select a file in a folder and add it to the Favorites folder.

- **Options.** The Options dialog box opens, where you can specify certain settings relating to saving drawings. I discuss these options in Chapter 8 and Appendix A.

- **Security Options.** Choose this setting to set a password or attach a digital signature. I discuss these features in Chapter 26.

AutoCAD Only

The SAVEALL command of the Express Tools saves all open drawings, without closing them. Type saveall ↵ on the command line. If a drawing hasn't been saved, you are prompted for a filename. For information on installing Express Tools, see Appendix A. ■

On the DVD

The DVD includes a small program, save2d.lsp, that automatically backs up your drawing to the CD/DVD drive after you've saved it on your hard drive. If you use this drive for backups, this program can be useful. Look in \Software\Chapter 01\Save2d. The file contains instructions for changing the drive to any letter you use (AutoCAD only). ■

STEPS: Saving a Drawing for the First Time

1. The four lines you created earlier in this chapter should still be on your screen. Click Save on the Quick Access Toolbar. The Save Drawing As dialog box opens.

2. Click the Save In drop-down list. If necessary, choose the drive where you created your AutoCAD Bible folder for this book.

3. Double-click the AutoCAD Bible folder.

4. In the File Name text box, select the default filename that appears. Type **ab01-01** and press Enter (or click Save).

5. Keep your drawing on the screen and go to the next exercise.

AutoCAD saves your drawing under the name ab01-01.dwg. This numbering system will help you organize your drawings from this book and find equivalent drawings on the DVD more easily. It just means that this is the first drawing from Chapter 1 of *AutoCAD 2011 and AutoCAD LT 2011 Bible*.

Closing a Drawing and Exiting from AutoCAD and AutoCAD LT

You can close your drawing and keep AutoCAD or AutoCAD LT open. The simplest way to do this is to use the Drawing Close button at the upper-right corner of the drawing. You can also choose Application Button ⇨ Close.

Tip
You can choose Application Button ⇨ Close ⇨ Close All to close all open drawings. If any of the open drawings have unsaved changes, AutoCAD or AutoCAD LT prompts you to save the changes. If you have AutoCAD, you can type qquit ↵ on the command line (an Express Tools command), which closes all open drawings (prompting you to save if necessary) and then exits the program. ■

To exit AutoCAD or AutoCAD LT, click the Close (X) box at the top-right corner of your screen. You can also exit out of AutoCAD or AutoCAD LT by typing **quit** ↵ on the command line. If you've made any changes to your drawing since last saving it, AutoCAD or AutoCAD LT asks you if you want to save your changes. Choose Yes or No as your situation requires. Choosing Cancel returns you to your drawing. If you have opened more than one drawing to which you have made changes, you have a chance to save each drawing in turn so that you don't exit AutoCAD or AutoCAD LT without saving all the changes you've made in your open drawings.

Tip
You can double-click the Application button to close AutoCAD. This is equivalent to typing quit. ■

STEPS: Closing Your Drawing and Exiting AutoCAD or AutoCAD LT

1. Your drawing should still be on your screen. Choose Application Button ⇨ Close. You now see a gray screen with no drawing. (Repeat this process if you have other drawings open. Save or cancel the changes to these extra open drawings as you like.)

2. Click the Close button in the upper-right corner to exit AutoCAD or AutoCAD LT. The program closes immediately.

Summary

In Chapter 1, I explained how to start AutoCAD and AutoCAD LT and create a new drawing. I gave you a tour of the screen and explained how to save a drawing. This chapter provided the basis for all your work in AutoCAD and AutoCAD LT.

In this chapter, you learned the following:

- A brief history of AutoCAD and AutoCAD LT
- Some of the different disciplines that use AutoCAD and AutoCAD LT
- How to start AutoCAD and AutoCAD LT
- How to start a new drawing

- The user interface and its various sections, including the drawing area, the UCS icon, the cross-hairs, the Ribbon, the Quick Access Toolbar, the command line, and the status bar
- How to start a command from the Ribbon
- How to start a command from the menu bar
- How to start a command from the command line
- How to start a command from the Draw toolbar in the AutoCAD Classic or AutoCAD LT Classic workspace
- How to save a drawing for the first time
- How to close a drawing
- How to exit AutoCAD and AutoCAD LT

You may have several questions at this point, but "well begun is half done." The next chapter explains all the ways to start a new drawing as well as how to open an existing drawing.

2

Opening a Drawing

AutoCAD and AutoCAD LT offer a number of options for opening new and existing drawings. These options create a great deal of flexibility and save you time as well. You can create complex templates to avoid doing the same basic setup and drawing over and over.

Creating a New Drawing from a Template

A *template* is a special file that contains drawing settings and often objects (such as a titleblock and text). A template has a DWT filename extension. When you use a template as the basis for a new drawing, the drawing takes on all the settings and objects contained in the template. Use templates to avoid re-creating settings and redrawing objects for new drawings. AutoCAD and AutoCAD LT come with many templates that you can use as is or customize. You can also create your own templates.

Cross-Reference

You can use Initial Setup to make certain setting changes to your drawing environment. These settings affect the default template. For more information, see Appendix A. ∎

To create a new drawing based on a template, choose Application Button ⇨ New to open the Select Template dialog box, which lists all the available templates, as shown in Figure 2.1. Select a template to see its preview, if any. Double-click a template to create a new drawing based on that template. Because AutoCAD or AutoCAD LT opens with Drawing1.dwg, the new drawing is named Drawing2.dwg. When you save and name your drawing, the original template file is unaffected.

The QNEW command is useful if you always start a new drawing based on the same template. You set a default template and then click New on the Quick Access Toolbar to start a new drawing immediately, based on that default template. To set the default template, follow these steps:

1. Choose Application Button ⇨ Options, and click the Files tab.
2. Double-click the Template Settings item.
3. Double-click the Default Template File Name for QNEW item.
4. Click the listing under the Default Template File Name for QNEW item (which says None by default).
5. Click Browse to choose the template that you want.
6. Click OK to close the Options dialog box.

You can specify whether this default template uses metric or imperial measurements by setting the MEASUREINIT system variable. (System variables are discussed further in Chapter 5.) On the command line, type **measureinit** ↵. Enter **0** ↵ for imperial units and **1** ↵ for metric units.

The default template is `acad.dwt` for AutoCAD and `acadlt.dwt` for AutoCAD LT. Another default template is `acad -Named Plot Styles.dwt` or `acadlt -Named Plot Styles.dwt`, which refers to named plot styles. (See Chapter 17 for more information.)

FIGURE 2.1

Choose a template from the Select template dialog box.

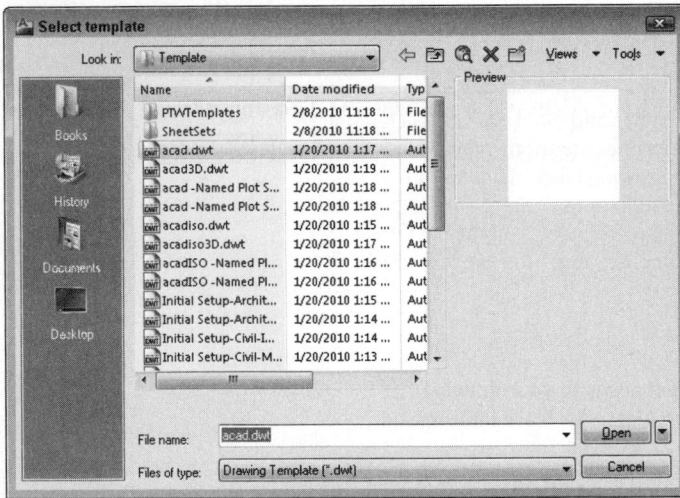

STEPS: Opening a Drawing Based on the Default Template

1. Start AutoCAD or AutoCAD LT.
2. Choose Application Button ⇨ New.

3. From the Select Template dialog box, choose acad.dwt (for AutoCAD) or acadlt.dwt (for AutoCAD LT) from the list.

4. Click Open. You now have a blank drawing named Drawing2.dwg, as shown in Figure 2.2.

FIGURE 2.2

When you create a drawing based on a template, AutoCAD or AutoCAD LT creates a new drawing.

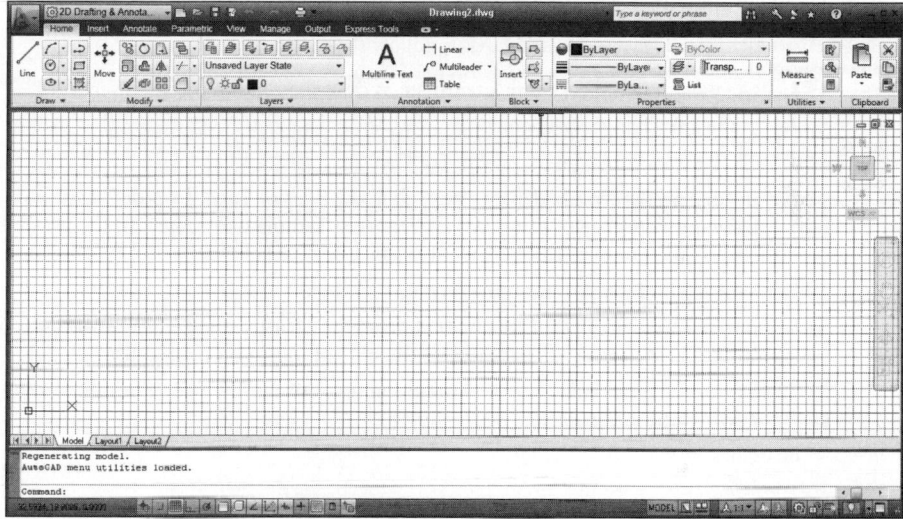

Note

The default workspace is 2D Drafting & Annotation. However, you can choose another 2D workspace, AutoCAD Classic (for AutoCAD) or AutoCAD LT Classic (for AutoCAD LT), from the Workspace drop-down list just to the right of the Application button or from the Workspace Switching button on the right side of the status bar. For 2D drawing in AutoCAD only, make sure that you're not in the 3D Modeling workspace. I discuss workspaces in Appendix A.

In both AutoCAD and AutoCAD LT, you may see palettes (windows) open that you don't want to use right now. You can close these by clicking their Close (X) buttons. ■

Working with Templates

A template contains ready-made settings to get you started drawing quickly. These settings include the size of the drawing (called *limits*), the unit type (such as *decimal* or *feet and inches*), and others. An important part of setting standards in an office where people work together on drawings is the creation of a template so that all users work with an identical setup. Templates may contain more than just settings — they often contain a complete titleblock, for example, and may include *boilerplate* (standardized) text as well.

Cross-Reference

In Chapter 5, I explain the options available for setting up a drawing. In Chapter 26, I cover the process of setting standards for drawings. ∎

Customizing the default template

Most people customize the default template to create one or more templates that suit their particular needs. After your templates are created, you don't have to worry about most settings; they are already available for you, and you can quickly start to draw.

To customize `acad.dwt` or `acadlt.dwt`, follow these steps:

1. Create a drawing based on a template as described in the previous section.
2. Make any changes you want.
3. Click Save on the Quick Access Toolbar.
4. In the Save Drawing As dialog box, click the Files of Type drop-down list box. Choose AutoCAD Drawing Template or AutoCAD LT Drawing Template (`*.dwt`). In the list of template files, choose the template that you want to customize. Click Save.
5. When asked if you want to replace it, click Yes.
6. In the Template Options dialog box, from the Measurement drop-down list, choose English (Imperial) or Metric, depending on the type of units you plan to use.
7. Revise the description in the Description text box as you like. (For information about the New Layer Notification option, see Chapter 26.)
8. Click OK.

Caution

If you're using someone else's computer, don't change the templates that come with AutoCAD or AutoCAD LT without first checking with the computer's owner. Also, if you create new templates, put them in their own folder to avoid losing them when you upgrade or reinstall AutoCAD. ∎

Creating your own templates

You may want several templates to choose from on a regular basis. For example, you may create drawings of several sizes. AutoCAD and AutoCAD LT let you create as many templates as you want. To create your own templates, either start a drawing based on a template and make the changes you want, or open an existing drawing that already has some of the settings you want and make any further changes you need. Follow these steps:

1. If you start a new drawing based on a template, choose Save from the Quick Access Toolbar. If you open an existing drawing, choose Save As from the Quick Access Toolbar.
2. Make any changes you want.
3. In the Save Drawing As dialog box, click the Files of Type drop-down list. Choose AutoCAD Drawing Template or AutoCAD LT Drawing Template (`*.dwt`).
4. In the File Name text box, type a name for your template. Click Save.
5. In the Template Options dialog box, enter the description as you want. From the Measurement drop-down list, choose English (Imperial) or Metric, depending on the type of units you plan to use. (I discuss the New Layer Notification option in Chapter 26.) Click OK.

Tip

Name your templates in a way that clearly differentiates them from regular drawings. You may want drawings set up for each of the standard paper sizes (A through E), with a titleblock in each. Useful names might be `tb-a.dwt`, `tb-b.dwt` **(tb meaning titleblock), and so on.** ■

Most AutoCAD and AutoCAD LT users take advantage of these techniques as a standard practice. You can usually make profitable use of a template as the basis for a new drawing.

Creating a Drawing with Default Settings

Occasionally, you may want to create a drawing without any settings. It is actually impossible for a drawing to have no settings at all, but you can create a drawing with the minimum possible presets. You might want to do this if you're working on someone else's computer and don't want to take the time to get rid of a large number of complex settings that aren't helpful for your work.

To create a drawing with the fewest possible settings, choose Application Button ⇨ New. Instead of choosing a template, click the arrow to the right of the Open button (see Figure 2.1). Choose one of the following options:

- Open with No Template — Imperial
- Open with No Template — Metric

Opening an Existing Drawing

Often you need to open an existing drawing, either to complete it or to make changes. Opening a drawing in AutoCAD or AutoCAD LT is like opening a file in any Windows program. You can find existing drawings by name or by viewing a thumbnail (preview image) of the drawing.

 Choose Open from the Quick Access Toolbar, or choose Application Button ⇨ Open. The Select File dialog box appears, as shown in Figure 2.3. In the Look In drop-down list box, choose the drive where your drawing resides. In the main box, double-click the folder you need. Then choose your drawing. You can also use the Places list at the left side of the dialog box to find drawings. The Preview box enables you to quickly look at the drawing to see if it's the one you want. (If you don't see a preview, choose Preview from the Views drop-down list in the dialog box.) Click Open. The drawing opens.

If you have opened the drawing recently, click the Application Button and look at the Recent Documents list on the right. At the top of the file list, click the arrow button to choose By Ordered List (alphabetical — the default), By Access Date, By Size, or By Type (file type). To the right is a small drop-down list that you can click to view small or large icons or images of the files. When you hover the cursor over any drawing, a tooltip displays, showing you a preview of the drawing, the full path location, the last date it was modified, the release version, the last person who saved the drawing, and who has the drawing currently open, if anyone. Finally, you can click the Pin icon next to a drawing to stick it to the list; the file remains there until you "unpin" it. All these features can help you easily find the drawing you want.

Tip

You can change the number of drawings that appear on the list. Choose Application Button ⇨ Options and click the Open and Save tab. Under the Application Menu section, in the Number of Recently Used Files text box, enter a number from 0 to 50. ■

FIGURE 2.3

The Select File dialog box is equivalent to the Open dialog box in most Windows programs.

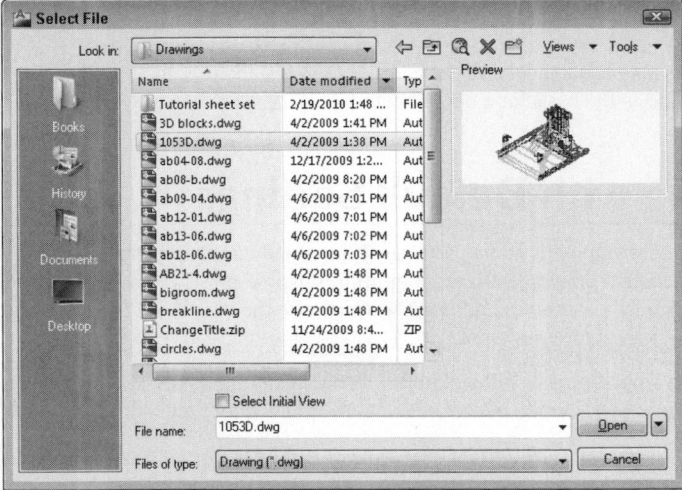

Using other ways to open drawings

You can double-click a drawing in Windows Explorer to open it. If AutoCAD or AutoCAD LT is not running, Windows loads the program and the drawing as well. If AutoCAD or AutoCAD LT is running and a drawing is active, the drawing opens as a second drawing within the program.

 You can also open a drawing from the DesignCenter — a feature for managing both drawing files and many of their components. First, choose View tab ⇨ Palettes panel ⇨ DesignCenter from the Ribbon. The DesignCenter palette opens, displaying an Explorer-like list of drawings in the left pane. (If you don't see the list of drawings, click the Tree View Toggle button on the DesignCenter toolbar.) Navigate to the folder containing the drawing and choose the drawing's folder in the left pane. The drawings in the folder are listed in the right pane. Right-click the drawing of your choice and choose Open in Application Window. For more information on the DesignCenter, see Chapter 26.

You can open a drawing using the Sheet Set Manager (AutoCAD only). I cover sheet sets in Chapter 26.

Switching among open drawings

When you open more than one drawing, by default, AutoCAD and AutoCAD LT display only one button on the Windows task bar. If you want to display a separate task bar button for each drawing, type **taskbar** ↵ on the command line. At the Enter new value for Taskbar <0>: prompt, type **1** ↵. Then you can click any drawing's button to display that drawing.

If you're using the default task bar setting, switch from drawing to drawing in one of the following ways:

 • Click the Quick View Drawings button on the status bar to display previews of all the open drawings, as shown in Figure 2.4. Above the drawings, you see a second level, showing model space and the layouts (which I cover in Chapter 17) contained in the drawing. Click the drawing, or layout, that you want to display. The small toolbar below the drawings lets you pin them (so they remain displayed), start a new drawing, open an existing drawing, and close the Quick View display.

 • Click the Application Button and click the Open Documents button at the top. Then choose from the files listed on the right.

FIGURE 2.4

The Quick View feature lets you see other open drawings and switch among them.

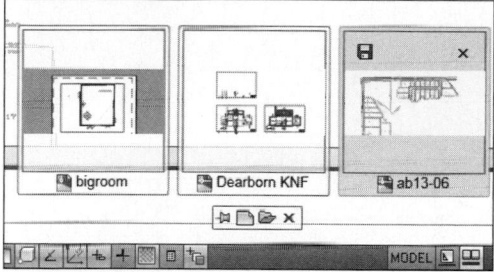

On the DVD

The drawing used in the following exercise on opening a drawing, abqs-01.dwg, is in the Results folder of the AutoCAD 2011 and AutoCAD LT 2011 Bible DVD. ∎

STEPS: Opening a Drawing

1. If AutoCAD or AutoCAD LT is not open, start the program.

2. Click Open on the Quick Access Toolbar.
3. In the Select File dialog box, choose the drive for your DVD in the Look In drop-down list.
4. In the main box, double-click the Results folder.
5. In the main box, click abqs-01.dwg.
6. Click Open. The drawing opens.
7. Click the Close (X) button in the upper-right corner of the drawing window to close the drawing.

Saving a Drawing under a New Name

Whether you want to use an existing drawing as a prototype or simply make a copy of a drawing, you need to save the drawing under a new name. First open the drawing and then choose Save As from the Quick Access Toolbar or Application Button ⇨ Save As.

In the Save Drawing As dialog box, type a new name in the File Name text box. Then click Save. You may also want to change the location of the new drawing by changing the folder in the Save In drop-down list box.

Summary

In this chapter, you explored the various ways of opening a drawing. You learned about:

- Starting a new drawing based on a template
- Customizing a template
- Creating your own templates
- Starting a new drawing with no template
- Opening an existing drawing and switching among open drawings
- Saving a drawing under a new name

In the next chapter, you read about using commands.

Using Commands

AutoCAD and AutoCAD LT have been around for a long time. As a result, the way you give the program commands — called the *user interface* — is somewhat unique. You can give the same command in several ways. In this chapter, you read about the various possibilities and start to get acquainted with all of them.

Commands are important. In a word processing program, you can simply start typing, and in a spreadsheet program, you can begin by entering data; but in most cases, nothing happens in AutoCAD or AutoCAD LT until you give it a command.

The AutoCAD and AutoCAD LT Interface

Many new commands have been added to AutoCAD and AutoCAD LT over the years. Often, older commands that were no longer necessary were kept to maintain compatibility with earlier releases. A number of these older commands, as well as certain rarely used commands, are not found in the interface. Other than this idiosyncrasy, the interface is similar to those of other Windows programs. Specifically, the Ribbon is similar to the latest version of Microsoft Office.

You use the user interface to execute commands and to specify settings and values. The user interface consists of the default Ribbon, the Quick Access Toolbar, the optional drop-down list bar, shortcut (right-click, or contextual) menus, the optional toolbars, palettes, the dynamic input tooltip, dialog boxes, and the command line. For executing commands, all the aspects of the user interface except dialog boxes work in conjunction with the command line. Looking at the command line whenever you execute a command is important, because that command appears on the command line, and a prompt or list of options may appear as well. If you have Dynamic Input on, the tooltip also displays the prompt. (Click the Dynamic Input button on the status bar to turn it on — and off.) See the section, "Responding to commands," later in this chapter for more information on what to do next.

IN THIS CHAPTER

Using the Ribbon, menus, dialog boxes, toolbars, and palettes

Working with Dynamic Input and the command line

Repeating, canceling, undoing, and redoing commands

Executing a command within another command

Using the Help system

Using the Ribbon

AutoCAD 2011 and AutoCAD LT 2011 use a Ribbon, which is a horizontal, tabbed area at the top of the screen. The Ribbon contains buttons like a toolbar, but is wider. You can drag it to the left or right side of your screen to make it vertical. You can customize the Ribbon, as I explain in Chapter 33. The Ribbon is the user interface in the default workspace, 2D Drafting & Annotation. It's also the user interface for the 3D Basics and 3D Modeling workspaces that come with AutoCAD (but not with AutoCAD LT).

New Feature

The 3D Basics workspace is a simplified version of the 3D Modeling workspace. It puts more emphasis on 3D solid modeling than on surface and mesh modeling. ■

The Home tab contains many of the commands that you use most often. The Ribbon is divided into control panels (panels, for short). Each panel contains a related group of commands. Other features of the Ribbon are:

- **More Commands arrows.** Many of the panels have a down arrow to the right of the panel name that you can click to display more buttons for commands that you don't use as often.
- **Dialog box launchers.** Some panels have an arrow at the right end of the panel, which opens a related dialog box or palette. This arrow is called a *dialog box launcher*.
- **Contextual tabs.** When you select certain types of objects, *contextual* tabs appear. For example, if you attach an image into a drawing and select the image, the Image tab appears.

Note

This book provides instructions for executing a command by using the default workspace. For information on changing the workspace, see Appendix A. For information on customizing the user interface, see Chapter 33. ■

To execute a command, click the tab that you need, and click the command's button. If the button doesn't have a label, hover the mouse cursor over the button to read its tooltip and a brief description of the button's command. If you continue to hover a little longer, the description expands, explaining the command in more detail. Some items on the Ribbon are drop-down lists from which you choose an option.

Note

The Ribbon and Quick Access Toolbar support KeyTips. KeyTips allow you to access commands and controls with a keyboard combination. To display KeyTips, press the Alt key. KeyTips are not available when you display the menu bar. The menu bar is covered in the following section. ■

 The Ribbon has several states that you can choose from to balance between convenience and space. The button to the right of the rightmost tab lets you toggle between the full Ribbon and three states. Choose one the following states from the button's drop-down list, and then click the full button to return to the full Ribbon.

- **Minimize to Tabs.** Displays one row of the tab names only.
- **Minimize to Panel Titles.** Displays the tab names and the panel names for the current tab.
- **Minimize to Panel Buttons.** Displays the current tab and buttons for each of the panels.

To move the Ribbon to the left or right of your screen in a vertical configuration, right-click any blank space on the tab bar at the top of the Ribbon, and choose Undock. The Ribbon undocks and then functions like a palette, which I cover later in this chapter. You can dock it on the left or right and auto-hide it. Right-click the gray, vertical title bar for more options.

The Application menu is under the Application button at the upper-left corner of the screen. The menu contains file-related commands, such as saving, exporting, and printing (plotting).

Using menus

In the default workspace (2D Drafting & Annotation), the drop-down menus are hidden. You can display the menus by changing the MENUBAR system variable to 1: type **menubar** ↵ on the command line, then type **1** ↵. (I discuss system variables in Chapter 5.) This method lets you use the Ribbon and the menu together. To use a menu, choose the menu title and then the item that you want from the menu list that drops down.

Note

In early releases, AutoCAD provided a menu on the right side of the screen, called the screen menu. Few people still use it these days. AutoCAD's current default is to not show the screen menu, so I don't cover it in this book. To display it, choose Application Button⇨Options. Click the Display tab. In the Window Elements section, choose Display Screen Menu. Click OK. AutoCAD LT doesn't offer a screen menu. ∎

Using shortcut menus

Shortcut menus appear when you right-click your mouse. The purpose of shortcut menus is to speed up your work; they can be faster than using the command line because you don't have to take your eyes off the screen. The shortcut menus try to anticipate the most common tasks you might want to complete. As a result, the menu that appears when you right-click depends on the situation:

- If you have neither started a command nor selected any objects, you get the default menu when you right-click in the drawing area. Here you can cut, copy, paste, undo, pan, zoom, and so on.
- If you've selected any objects, you see the edit-mode menu, which lists the most common editing commands. Selecting one or more objects of the same or of different types affects the commands that are available.
- If you've started a command, the command-mode menu opens, letting you choose an option for that command. I explain this in more detail later in this chapter.
- Other menus include the toolbar list you get when you right-click a toolbar and the command-line history you see when you right-click the command line and choose Recent Commands.

Tip

In early releases, right-clicking was equivalent to pressing Enter. You can customize how right-clicking works — and that includes changing it back to the way it worked in earlier releases. Choose Application Button⇨Options and choose the User Preferences tab. Then click the Right-click Customization button. For more information, see Appendix A.

When you set right-click customization, you can turn on time-sensitive right-clicking. Time-sensitive right-clicking is a great feature that gives you the best of two worlds — the right mouse button can be used both as an equivalent to pressing Enter and as a way to open the shortcut menus. When you turn on time-sensitive right-clicking, a quick right-click is equivalent to pressing Enter and will repeat the last command or end any commands that require Enter to end. A longer right-click (hold your finger on the mouse button slightly longer) opens the shortcut menu. You can specify the length of time required for the longer right-click, which is 250 milliseconds by default. ∎

Using dialog boxes

Dialog boxes offer the user a simple way to control AutoCAD or AutoCAD LT without memorizing a lot of technical commands and option names. They guide you through a task by clearly laying out all the choices. If you're familiar with any other Windows program, you're familiar with dialog boxes. Dialog boxes provide contextual help in the form of a tooltip that provides information on an option or control. To use contextual tooltips, position the cursor over a control.

Tip

You can enter mathematical expressions for values in dialog box text boxes; start an expression with an equal sign (=). For example, in the Angle box of the Hatch and Gradient dialog box, you can enter =20+10. Press Alt+Enter to complete the process. You can also enter mathematical expressions in palette text boxes. ■

When you've finished using a dialog box, click OK to accept any settings you specified, or click Cancel to discard any changes. In some cases, you can click Apply to save the changes made without closing the dialog box.

Using the Quick Access Toolbar

The Quick Access Toolbar provides a quick way to execute a command with one click of the mouse. If you're not sure what a toolbar button does, hover the cursor over a button and read the tooltip. The Quick Access Toolbar contains a few often-used commands, starting with QNEW, OPEN, QSAVE, SAVEAS, UNDO, REDO, and PLOT. In Chapter 29, I explain how to customize the tools that are on this toolbar.

When you click a toolbar button, in order to complete the command, you usually need to look at the Dynamic Input tooltip or the command line to follow the prompts there. I explain the command line and Dynamic Input later in this chapter.

Using palettes

A palette is a window that you can dock or float (like a toolbar). Palettes combine related functions in one place. AutoCAD and AutoCAD LT have several palettes that are covered throughout this book. To see palettes only when you need them, you can auto-hide them. Right-click the palette's title bar and choose Auto-hide from the shortcut menu. To dock a palette, choose Allow Docking from the same shortcut menu. You can dock and auto-hide a palette: Right-click the palette's title bar and choose Anchor Right or Anchor Left. The palette collapses to a thin vertical strip and opens only when you hover the mouse cursor over it. You can also anchor more than one palette on a side. They fit together on the right or left side and unroll to their full length when you hover the cursor over them.

Tool palettes

 Tool palettes are another way to give AutoCAD and AutoCAD LT commands. To open the Tool Palettes window, shown in Figure 3.1, choose View tab ⇨ Palettes panel ⇨ Tool Palettes. The palettes are actually a collection of tabs that are used to organize tools with similar functionality. Because of the number of tabs, some of the tabs are bunched up at the bottom. To choose these tabs, right-click those bottom tabs and choose a tab from the list that appears. The AutoCAD LT Tool Palettes window contains fewer tabs, and some of the tabs are slightly different.

FIGURE 3.1

The Tool Palettes window, as shown in AutoCAD.

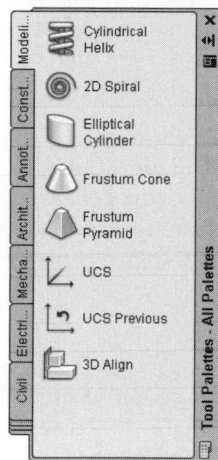

Each of the items on a tool palette is a tool. The tools on the Command Tool Samples tab contain commands that you can use. For example, you can draw a line by clicking the Line tool. The effect is the same as choosing Home tab ⇨ Draw panel ⇨ Line. The first two tools have *flyouts*, which are like toolbar flyouts. Click the small arrow and the flyout appears, containing other command buttons. Click the command button that you want in order to start that command.

Cross-Reference

You can use tool palettes to insert objects, fill in closed areas, and add other content. For more information, see Chapter 26. I also explain how to customize tool palettes in Chapter 29. For example, you can put custom commands on a tool palette. ∎

The Command Line and Dynamic Input

You can execute a command by typing it directly on the command line, directly to the right of the Command: prompt. The command line is a place to enter commands as well as coordinates and values, as shown in Figure 3.2.

FIGURE 3.2

The command line.

The command line is actually a window that you can move like a palette. By default, it is docked at the bottom of the application window. The window usually shows three lines of text, the Command: prompt, where you type, and two lines of text from the previous command. You can drag the top edge of the window to display more than three lines. Commands that you choose from the Ribbon, a toolbar button, a menu, or a tool palette are all echoed on the command line.

Note

By default, AutoCAD and AutoCAD LT display the command line. You can hide the command-line window by using the COMMANDLINEHIDE command, and display it with the COMMANDLINE command, or press Ctrl+9, which toggles the Command window on and off. Another option for the command line is to undock the Command window, right-click the window's title bar on the left, and choose Auto-hide. The Command window collapses to its title bar until you place the cursor over it. ■

Using Dynamic Input

You can use the Dynamic Input feature to execute commands that you type. Dynamic Input displays whatever you type in a tooltip box near the cursor. Dynamic Input also displays prompts at the cursor, so that you don't have to look down at the command line. Note that Dynamic Input does not completely replace the command line; in some situations the command line displays necessary prompts that the Dynamic Input tooltip omits. For more information about Dynamic Input settings, see Chapter 4.

 You can turn Dynamic Input on and off by using the Dynamic Input button on the status bar. When Dynamic Input is on, a tooltip box echoes what you type, displays prompts, and then displays your responses at the cursor as you type, as shown in Figure 3.3. This input is echoed on the command line after you press Enter. When Dynamic Input is off, commands and other input that you type appear on the command line only.

FIGURE 3.3

The Dynamic Input tooltip prompts you for input and then displays your input as you type.

Understanding command names

All commands have a special one-word command name. This may or may not be the same as the wording that appears on the toolbar's tooltip or on the menu. However, you can be sure of one thing: Every command can be executed by typing its name on the command line or in the Dynamic Input tooltip. Fast typists often prefer to type the command because they find it faster than searching for a command on the Ribbon, a menu, a toolbar, or a palette. Most users use a combination of the command line and other user interface options.

Some of the commands are easy to type, such as LINE or ARC. Others are long and harder to remember, such as HATCHEDIT, DDPTYPE, or EXTERNALREFERENCES. Command names such as these can quickly drive you to use one of the user interface elements.

Cross-Reference

If you like typing commands, you can create short versions of the command names, called aliases. Many are already included with AutoCAD and AutoCAD LT. Aliases are covered in Chapter 29. ■

You can edit what you have typed on the command line. If you type a long command or a difficult coordinate, and make a mistake, you can backspace up to the mistake and retype the last part correctly. Table 3.1 shows how to use the keyboard edit keys to edit the command line.

Tip

When you start to type a command, and you aren't sure of the exact spelling, you can start typing what you know and then press the Tab key to cycle through all the possibilities in the Dynamic Input tooltip or on the command line. Press Enter when you see the command that you want. This AutoComplete feature works for system variables (which I cover in Chapter 5) and command aliases as well. For example, several commands start with "COPY". You can type copy and then repeatedly press Tab to see these commands. ■

TABLE 3.1

Command-Line Editing Keys

Key	Function
Backspace	Backspaces through the text on the command line, erasing each letter as it backspaces.
Left arrow	Moves backward through the text of the command, without erasing.
Right arrow	Moves forward through the text of the command, without erasing.
Home	Moves the command-line cursor to the beginning of the text.
End	Moves the command-line cursor to the end of the text.
Insert	Toggles between Insert/Overwrite modes. Insert mode inserts text. Overwrite mode types over existing text. Note that there is no visual confirmation of which mode you are in.
Delete	Deletes the character to the right of the cursor on the command line.
Ctrl+V	Pastes text from the Windows Clipboard.

You can scroll through and reuse previous command-line entries. To repeat the last line you entered, press the up arrow. Press Enter to execute it. To see more of the command-line entries, press F2 on your keyboard to open the Text Window. Scroll until you find the entry you want, highlight it, and then right-click and choose Paste To CmdLine from the shortcut menu. You now see the highlighted text on the current command line. You can copy selected text from the command-line history or the entire history to the Clipboard. You can also choose Recent Commands from the Text Window's shortcut menu and choose one of the commands from the submenu that appears.

Tip

Switching from the mouse to the keyboard and back is time-consuming. In general, if you're picking points by using the mouse (covered in Chapter 4), using the Ribbon and other graphic user interfaces to give commands is faster. If you're typing coordinates as you did in Chapter 1, your hands are already at the keyboard, so typing commands at the keyboard is easier. ■

Responding to commands

When you execute a command by any method, you usually need to respond to the command. AutoCAD displays a prompt that tells you what you need to do next.

The format for command prompts on the command line is as follows:

```
current instruction or [options] <current value>:
```

The current instruction explains what you need to do. For example, if you choose an editing command, the prompt usually instructs you to "Select objects." The text in the square brackets lists the various options available for the command. The angled brackets tell you the current value or default option for the command, if any.

In the Dynamic Input tooltip, you first see the following:

```
current instruction or ↓
```

If the current instruction is to specify a point, you also see the cursor's X and Y coordinates. Figure 3.4 shows a prompt for the CIRCLE command. After specifying the center of the circle, this command has a current instruction to specify the radius, an option to specify the diameter, and a current value of 1.0000, the radius of the previously drawn circle.

FIGURE 3.4

To see the options and a current value (if any) in the Dynamic Input tooltip, press the down arrow on your keyboard.

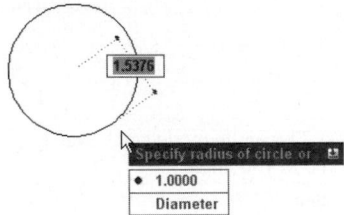

Note

Throughout this book, I show the prompt as it appears on the command line, because this prompt includes the options. If you are looking at the Dynamic Input tooltip, press the down arrow to display the options at the tooltip or right-click to display the shortcut menu. ■

When you see a prompt, the possible types of responses are as follows:

- **Specify a point.** You can pick a point by clicking with the mouse. You can also enter an X,Y coordinate or displacement — whatever you type appears both in the Dynamic Input tooltip and on the command line. Chapter 4 explains how to specify points.
- **Enter a value or text.** You type the value or the text and press Enter. If Dynamic Input is on, you see your input as you type in the tooltip but you don't see the value on the command line until you press Enter. If Dynamic Input is off, you see your input as you type on the command line.
- **Select an object.** Most editing commands require that you select one or more objects. You can click an object to select it. I explain all the other methods to select objects in Chapters 9 and 10.

- **Choose an option.** Many commands have options that you need to choose before continuing to use the command. To choose an option by using the command line, do one of the following:

  - Type the one or two letters that are capitalized in the option name — usually (but not always) the first letter(s) of the option. You can type the letter(s) in lowercase. Press Enter.
  - Press Enter to choose a default option or current value.
  - Right-click in the drawing area and choose one of the options from the shortcut menu. This works best for options that won't need any numerical input on the command line.

  To choose an option by using the Dynamic Input tooltip, press the down arrow on your keyboard to display the options. If there is a default value, you see a mark next to it. Then click one of the options.

At this point, additional options and prompts may appear; you respond in the same way that I have just described, depending on the type of information that the command needs.

In the following exercise, you practice using command options and picking points on the screen with the mouse.

STEPS: Using Command Options

1. Open a new drawing by using the `acad.dwt` or `acadlt.dwt` template. Make sure that the 2D Drafting & Annotation workspace is chosen from the Workspace Switching drop-down list to the right of the Application button. Close any palettes that may be open.

2. Choose Home tab ⇨ Draw panel ⇨ Polyline. (A polyline can contain both line and arc segments. I discuss polylines in Chapter 16.)

3. Look at the command line and the Dynamic Input tooltip. (If you don't see the Dynamic Input tooltip near the cursor, click the Dynamic Input button on the status bar.) You see the following prompt:

   ```
   Specify start point:
   ```

   You also see the current coordinate location of the cursor in the Dynamic Input tooltip. Move the mouse cursor anywhere in the middle of the screen, and click to specify the start point. This is called *picking a point.*

4. Now you see the following prompts, the first on the command line and the second in the Dynamic Input tooltip:

   ```
   Specify next point or [Arc/Halfwidth/Length/Undo/Width]:
   Specify next point or ↓
   ```

   Suppose that you want to specify the width of the polyline. Because specifying the next point is the main instruction, right-click to display the shortcut menu and choose Width, which is one of the options. The program responds with the `Specify starting width:` prompt. Follow the prompts:

   ```
   Specify starting width <0.0000>: .5 ↵
   Specify ending width <0.5000>: .25 ↵
   ```

5. The prompt to specify the next point returns. Move the mouse so that your cursor is away from the first point that you picked and pick another point. You now see the same prompt repeated.

6. This time, you want to change the width. To specify the width this time, type **w** ↵. Follow the prompts:

   ```
   Specify starting width <0.2500>: ↵ to accept the default value.
   Specify ending width <0.2500>: ↵ to accept the default value again.
   ```

7. Move your mouse so that the new segment is at a different angle than the first one. Pick any point on the screen. The same prompt appears again.

8. Press the down arrow to display the Dynamic Input shortcut menu. Choose Close from the menu. AutoCAD closes the polyline so that you now have a triangle, and ends the command.

   Do not save this drawing.

Note

You may have noticed an underscore (_) before commands. This mark allows translation to foreign languages and can be ignored. ■

Command Techniques

To make working with commands easier, AutoCAD and AutoCAD LT offer shortcuts for repeating and canceling commands as well as sophisticated undo and redo options. You can also use certain commands in the middle of another command.

You can have more than one command active concurrently, one in each open drawing. You can switch from one drawing to another without interrupting your commands. For example, if you're in the middle of drawing a circle in one drawing, you can open a new drawing and start another command to get some information you need for the circle. Then you can return to the first drawing and complete the circle.

Repeating commands

The most common way to repeat a command you have just used is to press Enter. The most recent command appears again.

Tip

You can also press the Spacebar at the Command: prompt to repeat a command you just used. This technique works well if you want to keep one hand on the mouse and use the other hand to press the Spacebar. ■

If you know in advance that you'll be using a command several times, you can use another technique — type **multiple** ↵. At the Enter command name to repeat: prompt, type the command name on the command line. The command automatically reappears on the command line. For example, you could type **multiple** and then **arc** if you knew you were going to draw several arcs in a row. To stop repeating the command, press Esc.

Tip

If you create a Ribbon or toolbar button that executes a customized set of actions (as I explain in Chapters 29 and 33), right-click and choose the top option of the shortcut menu to repeat the action of the custom button. You cannot press Enter to get this effect. ■

Using recent input

You may need to use the same input again and again. For example, you may want to draw several circles with the same radius. You can use the recent input list to choose a recently used radius instead of typing it again. You can access recent points, values (such as distances and angles), and text strings.

When you see a prompt for input, right-click and choose Recent Input from the shortcut menu. (In a few instances, no shortcut menu is available, so you can't use this feature.) You can then choose one of the recent input items from the list. You can also press the up or down arrows to cycle through the recent input in the Dynamic Input tooltip.

The Recent Input feature displays items that are appropriate for the current prompt. For example, if the prompt asks for a radius, you don't see angles or X,Y coordinates; you see only lengths.

Canceling commands

Sometimes you start a command and then realize you don't need it. In this situation, you can cancel the command and then choose a different command. Press the Esc key to cancel a command that you've already started. The Command: prompt reappears.

In the following exercise, you practice the techniques for repeating and canceling commands, as well as using recent input.

STEPS: Repeating and Canceling Commands

1. Start a new drawing by using the acad.dwt or acadlt.dwt template. Make sure that the 2D Drafting & Annotation workspace is chosen from the Workspace Switching drop-down list to the right of the Application button. Close any palettes that may be open.

2. Choose Home tab ⇨ Draw panel ⇨ Circle.

3. At the Specify center point for circle or [3P/2P/Ttr (tan tan radius)]: prompt, pick a center point anywhere near the center of the screen.

4. At the Specify radius of circle or [Diameter]: prompt, type **2** ↵. The circle appears in the drawing area.

5. Press Enter. The CIRCLE command's first prompt appears again.

6. Follow these prompts:

    Specify center point for circle or [3P/2P/Ttr (tan tan radius)]:
    Right-click and choose 2P from the shortcut menu.
    Specify first end point of circle's diameter: *Pick any point on the screen.*
    Specify second end point of circle's diameter: *Press Esc.*

    The prompts disappear.

7. Press the Spacebar. Looking at the Dynamic Input tooltip, you see the Specify center point for circle or ↓: prompt. Pick any point on the screen.

8. At the Specify radius of circle or ↓: prompt, press Enter to create another circle with a radius of 2.

9. Press Enter to start the CIRCLE command again. At the first prompt, right-click and choose Recent Input. Choose the top item, which is the center of the last circle you drew.

10. At the prompt to specify a radius, pick any point to create a concentric circle.

    Do not save this drawing.

Undoing a command

Most Windows applications offer Undo and Redo commands. AutoCAD and AutoCAD LT are no different. AutoCAD and AutoCAD LT remember every command you execute, starting from the time you open a drawing. You can therefore undo every action and return your drawing to its condition when you opened it.

There are a few obvious exceptions. For example, if you print a drawing, you can't unprint it, and you can't unsave a drawing, either. Similarly, you can't undo commands that provide you with information, such as the coordinates of a point.

Note

Some commands have their own undo options. I explain these undo options when I discuss these commands throughout the book. ∎

 Each time you click Undo on the Quick Access Toolbar, you undo one command. You can click the Undo button's drop-down list and choose an earlier command to undo that command and all later commands. If you continue back to the first command of the session, you undo all the commands and get the message:

```
Everything has been undone
```

When you start the UNDO command, which you enter on the command line, you see the following options:

```
Enter the number of operations to undo or [Auto/Control/BEgin/End/
    Mark/Back] <1>:
```

Enter the number of operations to undo is the default instruction. If you type a number, such as **3**, you undo your last three commands. This action is equivalent to clicking the Undo button three times. Here are the other options:

- **Auto.** Applies to a menu item that executes more than one command at a time. When Auto is On (the default), the entire menu item is undone in one step. When Auto is Off, UNDO undoes each step one at a time.

- **Control.** Offers five suboptions. All, the default, gives you the full UNDO capability. None disables the UNDO command. The One suboption enables you to undo only one step at a time, effectively turning the UNDO command into the U command. The Combine suboption groups consecutive pan and zoom operations into a single operation. The Layer suboption groups multiple operations from the Layer Properties Manager palette into a single operation.

- **Begin.** Works with the End option. This starts a group at the current point of the list of commands. Then when you use the End option, UNDO undoes all the commands in the group. The U command also undoes everything within a group.

- **End.** Marks the end of all commands in the group created by using the Begin option.

- **Mark.** Works with the Back option. It is somewhat similar to the Begin option, but you can place several marks as you work.

- **Back.** When you use this option, AutoCAD or AutoCAD LT undoes only to the most recent Mark point. The next Back option you use undoes to the Mark point before that.

As you undo commands, the command line lists the commands that are being undone. Sometimes, you see the word *Group,* which means that a group of commands is being undone. However, sometimes the word *Group* is used even for a single command. This use of the word *Group* is not significant and can be ignored.

Tip

You can tell AutoCAD or AutoCAD LT to combine consecutive zooms and pans when you undo commands to help you quickly get back to your previous situation. Choose Application Button ⇨ Options and click the User Preferences tab. Then check the **Combine Zoom and Pan Commands** check box in the Undo/Redo section. As mentioned earlier, you can also use the Combine suboption of the UNDO command's Control option. ■

Using the Back option when no mark has been created undoes everything you have done in a drawing session! Luckily, you get the following warning message:

```
This will undo everything. OK? <Y>
```

Type **n** ↵ if you do not want to undo everything.

Redoing a command

If you undo a command, you might realize that you want to undo the undo. This is called redoing a command. Don't confuse redoing a command with repeating a command. Redoing only applies when you have just undone a command.

 The REDO command on the Quick Access Toolbar redoes the effect of the previous UNDO command. You can redo multiple UNDO commands.

Note

The MREDO command lets you undo multiple UNDO commands at one time. You can enter it on the command line. ■

In the following exercise, you practice using the UNDO and REDO commands.

STEPS: Undoing and Redoing Commands

1. Start a new drawing by using acad.dwt or acadlt.dwt as the template. Make sure that the 2D Drafting & Annotation workspace is chosen from the Workspace Switching drop-down list to the right of the Application button.
2. Choose Home tab ⇨ Draw panel ⇨ Line.
3. Follow the prompts to draw one line, and press Enter to end the command.
4. Choose Home tab ⇨ Draw panel ⇨ Arc.
5. Using the default options, pick any three points to draw an arc.
6. Choose Home tab ⇨ Draw panel ⇨ Circle.
7. Pick one point to be the center of the circle and another nearby point to specify the radius. Your drawing now contains a line, an arc, and a circle, and looks something like Figure 3.5. Of course, your objects will look different because you picked different points.

 8. Click the Undo button on the Quick Access Toolbar; the circle disappears.

9. Click the Undo button on the Quick Access Toolbar; the arc disappears. Click the Undo button again; the line disappears.

10. Click the drop-down arrow to the right of the Redo button on the Quick Access Toolbar, and select Circle. All three objects reappear because they were undone by the previous UNDO commands.

   Do not save this drawing. If you are continuing, keep the drawing on the screen for the next exercise.

FIGURE 3.5

Your drawing should contain a line, an arc, and a circle.

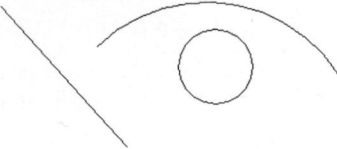

Cross-Reference

The OOPS command restores the most recently erased object or set of objects, even if you have used other commands in the meantime. See Chapter 18 for further information. ■

Using one command within another command

Certain commands can be used within another command. These are called *transparent commands*. After a transparent command is completed, the original command continues its regular operation. Many transparent commands help you display the drawing differently so that you can complete the original command easily. Other transparent commands change settings. In fact, almost any command that doesn't select objects, create new objects, cause regeneration, or end the drawing session can be used transparently.

When you start transparent commands from the Ribbon or menus, they are automatically transparent. If you want to type a transparent command on the command line or in the Dynamic Input tooltip, you need to type an apostrophe (') before the command name. Experiment using transparent commands, and you'll soon find them indispensable.

Of Mice and Pucks

For the sake of simplicity, this book assumes that you're using a mouse, but some people use a digitizing tablet and a *puck* (or a stylus). A typical digitizing tablet and puck are shown in Figure 3.6. A puck often has more buttons than a mouse and also has crosshairs on a transparent area that you can use for accurately picking points from a paper drawing.

A digitizing tablet is generally configured to include an area that represents the screen you draw on as well as a customizable command area that you use for commands. This command area of the tablet functions as another menu. Usually, you would customize the tablet to suit individual needs, as explained in Chapter 33.

FIGURE 3.6

A digitizer and puck.

In the center, the puck functions like a mouse to draw, as well as to access menus and dialog box options. You can use the tablet for a process called *digitizing*, which means transferring data from paper into AutoCAD or AutoCAD LT. This transference is often done by putting a paper document directly on the tablet and using the entire tablet as a drawing area. Because the puck has crosshairs on a transparent surface, you can pick points on the drawing, which then become endpoints of lines, for example. Chapter 16 has an exercise on digitizing.

Getting Help

AutoCAD and AutoCAD LT have so many commands with so many options that every user needs help at some time. AutoCAD and AutoCAD LT come with a very complete Help system.

Cross-Reference
See Appendix B for help that is available on the Internet and other resources for AutoCAD and AutoCAD LT. ■

Getting help on a command
The easiest way to get help on a command is to start the command and press F1. The Help screen for that command opens. Figure 3.7 shows the screen that opens when you type **zoom** ↵ and then press F1.

New Feature

The Help system is now browser-based. To specify your browser, click Application button ⇨ Options and click the System tab. In the Help section, you can choose the Default System Browser option. You can also opt to use online Help from the Autodesk Web site. ■

FIGURE 3.7

The Help screen for the ZOOM command.

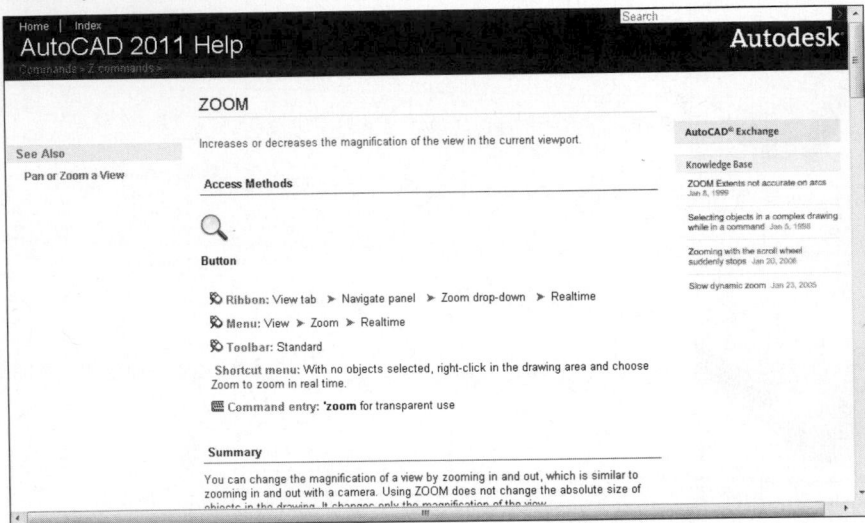

Finding help with Quick start links

Quick start links are hyperlinks that you find at selected locations to help you understand a feature or concept. For example, if you choose Plot from the Output tab, the Plot dialog box opens with a link, `Learn about Plotting`, to give you more help on plotting. If the feature is new, the link goes to the New Features Workshop, which I cover later in this chapter.

Using the main Help system

When you have a question, try the Help system. AutoCAD and AutoCAD LT come with the most complete Help documentation I have ever seen in a program. Pressing F1 (with no command active) or clicking the question mark at the right end of the title bar opens the main Help window in your browser, as shown in Figure 3.8. Wherever you are in the Help system, you can click the Home icon at the upper-left corner to return to the main Help page.

FIGURE 3.8

The main Help page in AutoCAD.

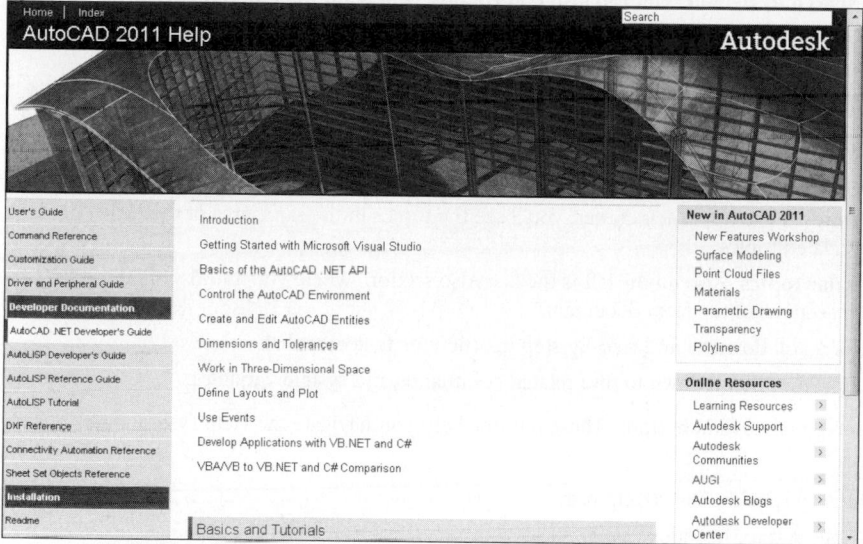

The Help content

Click the User's Guide item to display help organized by topic. It's like the table of contents of a book. The User's Guide is AutoCAD's "how to" manual. Click a topic to open that topic and see subtopics. Click a subtopic to display its Help content.

Click the Command Reference item to get help on commands and system variables, listed alphabetically.

Other Help content contains information on customization, drivers and peripherals, programming (Developer Documentation), and installation.

The Index

The index is an alphabetical listing of topics. Click the Index link at the upper-left corner of any Help page. Type the word or words for which you want help in the Search for Keyword text box, or scroll through the topics. When you've found the topic you want, click it. The topic may open in another tab or a new window of your browser.

The Search feature

The Search feature enables you to enter keywords. Type keywords or a phrase in the text box and click the Search button, or just press Enter. You can refine your results by choosing one of the guides on the left. For example, you can click User's Guide to see results only from the User's Guide. Choose a topic to display it.

Tip

After using Search, you arrive at the Search page. Click Advanced Search Options to control which sections (books) of Help you want to search by default. You can also control how you want the entered keywords used to generate the search results. For example, you can choose to find whole words only. ■

Working with Help pages

When you get to the Help page of the topic you want, several features can help you make the best use of the screen:

- **Nearby topic.** At the upper-left corner, you'll see the topics in the same area of the Help "book." These are related topics.
- **Other similar topics.** Also on the left is the See Also section, where you'll find similar topics from other sections of the Help document.
- **Procedure.** Scroll down to find step-by-step instructions to accomplish a task.
- **Quick Reference.** Scroll down to find related commands and system variables.

At the top of each screen are several buttons. These buttons help you navigate the Help system quickly and easily:

- **Home.** Takes you to the main Help page.
- **Index.** Brings you to the index.
- **Search box.** Gives you access to the Search feature.
- **Breadcrumbs.** Shows you the structure of the current Help "book," letting you click back to more general topics.

Using the InfoCenter

The InfoCenter is a simple way to access Help, the Communication Center, and Favorite resources. This tool is located in the upper-right corner of the AutoCAD or AutoCAD LT window, as shown in Figure 3.9.

FIGURE 3.9

The InfoCenter gives you easy access to Help, the Communication Center, and your Favorite resources.

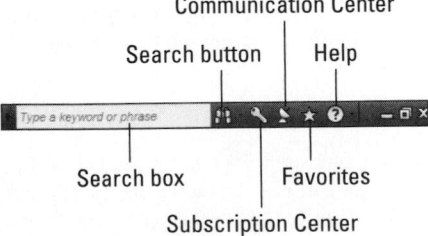

Search Help

The Search field enables you to enter a search term and get results from the Help files and the New Features Workshop. Enter one or more terms and press Enter. The results drop down, and you can choose the item you want in order to open it in the Help window.

Tip

You can add your own resources to search through those, as well. Click the down arrow to the right of the Search button and click Add Search Location to browse to files on your computer or network. You can add resources from the following file types: TXT, DOC, DOCX, CHM, HTML, HTM, PDF, and XML. This is a great place to reference your CAD Standards Manual and/or those of your clients. From the same down arrow, you can choose Search Settings to specify which of the standard resources you want to search, depending on your needs. ■

The Subscription Center

Click the Subscription Center button to access services available to subscription customers.

The Communication Center

The Communication Center tool in the InfoCenter shows Live Updates (software updates), subscription announcements and lessons (for subscription members), articles, and tips. It also displays RSS feeds of the knowledge base, blogs, and the discussion group. You can customize the settings. For more information, see Chapter 26.

Favorites

These are quick links to items that you have tagged as useful. You can tag these items from your Search results or in the Communication Center drop-down list. When you hover over an item, a white star appears on the right. Click the star to turn it yellow and add it to the Favorites list.

In this exercise, you practice using the Help system.

STEPS: Using AutoCAD Help

1. If AutoCAD or AutoCAD LT is not open, start the program with the `acad.dwt` or `acadlt.dwt` template. If the program is already open, you can do this exercise with any drawing on the screen. Make sure that the 2D Drafting & Annotation workspace is chosen from the Workspace Switching drop-down list to the right of the Application button or on the right side of the status bar. Close any palettes that may be open.

2. Choose Home tab ⇨ Draw panel ⇨ Circle. At the prompt, press F1 on the keyboard. The Circle Help screen opens in your browser.

Note

You may have to click a message to allow your browser to display the content. Also, if you're not using Internet Explorer, you may not get Help specific to a circle, but you may see the main Help page instead. In that case, click Command Reference ⇨ C Commands ⇨ Circle. I got the Circle page with the Firefox browser. ■

3. Under the List of Prompts heading, click 2P (meaning two points), which appears underlined. The 2P description appears. Read the description of the 2P option.

4. Close your browser or the browser tab and return to the AutoCAD or AutoCAD LT window. Press Esc to cancel the CIRCLE command.

5. Click the Help (question mark) button on the right side of the title bar.

6. In the Search box, type **shortcut menus** ↵. Click User's Guide.

7. Click Other Tool Locations. On the resulting page, click Shortcut Menus. Read the text on the topic.

8. Scroll down to the Procedure heading. Click the To Display a Shortcut Menu link and read the text.

9. Return to the AutoCAD window. In the InfoCenter's Search text box, type **transparent commands** ↵.

10. From the list that drops down, click the `Enter Commands on the Command Line` item.

11. In your Web browser, scroll down until you see the `Interrupt a Command with Another Command or System Variable` section and read the text.

12. In the upper-left corner, click Home. From the Home page, click Command Reference, then click Commands.

13. Click C Commands, and then click CIRCLE. You see the Circle Help page again. You can find help on any command from the Command Reference. Close or minimize the Web browser.

Summary

In this chapter, you read all you need to know about how to use AutoCAD and AutoCAD LT commands. Specifically, you read about:

- Using the Ribbon
- Using menus and shortcut menus
- Using dialog boxes
- Working with toolbars
- Using tool palettes
- Understanding command names
- Using and editing the command line
- Using the Dynamic Input tooltip to enter and respond to commands
- Responding to command options and using the command line and shortcut menus
- Repeating and canceling commands
- Undoing and redoing commands
- Using transparent commands
- Using a puck and digitizing tablet to enter commands
- Getting help

In the next chapter, I explain how to specify coordinates, an essential skill before you start to draw.

Specifying Coordinates

Specifying points in a drawing is one of the most fundamental tasks you do in AutoCAD and AutoCAD LT. Unless you know how to specify a point, you can't draw anything real, whether a house or a gasket. Most objects you draw have a specific size, and you need to specify that information. You draw lines, arcs, and circles by specifying the coordinates of points on the screen. As with most tasks, AutoCAD and AutoCAD LT offer many ways to accomplish this.

Understanding the X,Y Coordinate System

AutoCAD and AutoCAD LT work the same way as the graphs with X and Y axes that you plotted in high school. Look at the User Coordinate System (UCS) icon shown in Figure 4.1.

Cross-Reference

The UCS icon can take on different appearances. See Chapter 8 for details. For information on the UCS icon in 3D drawing and 3D coordinates, see Chapter 21. ∎

The X arrow points along the X axis in the positive direction. This means that as you go in the direction of the arrow, the X coordinates increase. The Y arrow points along the Y axis in the positive direction. Using this system, every 2D point on the screen can be specified by using X and Y coordinates. This is called a *Cartesian* coordinate system. The universal convention is to place the X coordinate first, and then a comma (but no space), and then the Y coordinate. By default, the intersection of the X,Y axes is 0,0. Use negative numbers for points to the left of the X axis or below the Y axis.

IN THIS CHAPTER

Working with absolute, relative, and polar coordinates

Using direct distance entry, orthogonal mode, and polar tracking

Using snap settings

Working with object snaps

Locating points

FIGURE 4.1

The UCS icon shows the direction of the X and Y axes. If you're in a 3D display, you also see the Z axis.

Drawing units

When you draw in AutoCAD or AutoCAD LT, you draw in undefined units. A line from point 3,0 to point 6,0 is three units long. While you're drawing, these units can be anything — a millimeter, a centimeter, a meter, an inch, a foot, or a mile. In reality, you should know exactly what the units represent. After all, you don't want your 36-foot-wide house to end up 36 inches wide!

When you set up a drawing, you specify how units are displayed — for example, whether partial units show as decimal points or fractions. (I cover units in Chapter 5.) However, you don't actually specify what the units represent until you print or plot your drawing — covered in Chapter 17.

To ensure accuracy, you should draw full size. If you're drawing a plan for a factory that will be 120 feet long, for example, you create lines with those measurements. On the screen, you can zoom in to see small details or zoom out to see the whole factory, so that you have no reason not to use the actual line lengths. It's only when you need to print those 120-foot-long lines on a real sheet of paper that you have to specify how to plot out your drawing at a reduced scale.

Users are typically familiar only with the type of notation used in their own field of specialty, whether scientific, architectural, engineering, or whatever. However, you should be at least somewhat familiar with all the major forms of measurement notation.

Note

If you are using engineering or architectural units, AutoCAD and AutoCAD LT display parts of inches (fractions) differently than the format you must use to type them in. You must type in coordinates without any spaces because in AutoCAD a space is equivalent to pressing Enter, and that ends your input. Use a hyphen between whole and partial inches — for example, 3'2-1/2". (You can omit the " after the number because inches are assumed in engineering and architectural units if no symbol follows a number.) However, this appears on the status bar as 3'-2 1/2". This can be confusing because the hyphen is in a different place, and you see a space between the whole and partial inches. ■

Typing Coordinates

One basic way to specify the location of an object is to type its coordinates by using the keyboard. You can enter several types of coordinates. Use the type of coordinates that suit your specific situation.

Tip

If you need to enter a coordinate that you've typed recently, use the Recent Input feature. Right-click and choose Recent Input from the shortcut menu. Then choose the coordinate that you want from the list that appears. ■

Using the Dynamic Input tooltip to enter coordinates

Dynamic Input enables you to enter text input near the cursor. In Chapter 3, I explain how to use the Dynamic Input tooltip for commands and command options. Here I explain how to use it to enter coordinates.

 The Dynamic Input button on the status bar turns Dynamic Input on and off. Because you can look at the tooltip near the cursor when you enter text, you can keep your attention on the drawing area, instead of looking down at the command line. Dynamic Input applies to commands that you type, responses to prompts, and coordinates.

Typing coordinates in the Dynamic Input tooltip

You can type 2D coordinates in the Dynamic Input tooltip in the same way that you type them on the command line — in the format **x,y**. You can press Tab between the X and Y coordinates instead of typing a comma, but typing the comma is probably easier and therefore more accurate.

When you draw a line, after you specify the first point, you see only one tooltip box because AutoCAD assumes that you want to enter only the distance, using the current angle of the temporary line shown on the screen. However, as soon as you type a comma or press the Tab key, a second box appears so that you can enter the Y coordinate, as shown in Figure 4.2. The same situation applies when you want to move or copy an object and want to specify an X,Y displacement.

In Figure 4.2, note the lock next to the X coordinate. Before you type any part of the coordinate, both the X and Y values vary as you move the mouse. When you enter a value for the X coordinate, you fix this value, as the lock indicates. However, the Y coordinate is still unlocked until you type a value.

FIGURE 4.2

As you enter an X,Y coordinate, two boxes appear, one for each part of the coordinate.

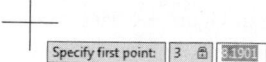

Specifying Dynamic Input settings

You can specify how Dynamic Input works for coordinates that you type. Changing the settings gives you very different results when you type coordinates. To specify settings for the Dynamic Input feature, right-click the Dynamic Input button on the status bar and choose Settings to display the Dynamic Input tab of the Drafting Settings dialog box, as shown in Figure 4.3.

FIGURE 4.3

Use the Dynamic Input tab of the Drafting Settings dialog box to specify how your Dynamic Input works when you type coordinates.

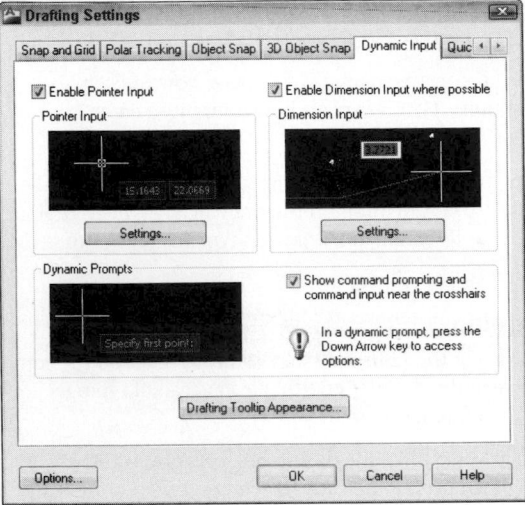

Pointer Input section

The Enable Pointer Input check box is selected by default, which means that the Dynamic Input tooltip includes an input box where you can type coordinates at the start of any command. If you uncheck this check box, you see these first coordinates only on the command line as you enter them. However, whether the check box is checked or not, as long as the Dynamic Input button is selected on the status bar, you see the input box for subsequent coordinates in a command. For example, if you are drawing a line, and the Enable Pointer Input check box is not checked, you don't see coordinates that you type for the start point in the Dynamic Input tooltip, but for the next point, you see the input box and coordinates that you type appear in that box.

Click the Settings button to open the Pointer Input Settings dialog box, as shown in Figure 4.4. Here you can make the following choices:

- **Default format for second or next points.** You can choose to default to polar or Cartesian format. The default is polar format, which shows distances. I explain polar format in the "Polar coordinates" section, later in this chapter. You can also choose between relative and absolute coordinates. The default is relative coordinates, which indicate a distance and direction from a previously specified point. I explain both absolute and relative formats in the next few sections of this chapter.

- **Tooltip visibility.** You can specify that you see the tooltip only when you start typing a point in response to a prompt, automatically at a prompt for a point (the default), or always.

The Pointer Input Settings dialog box sets important options for Dynamic Input.

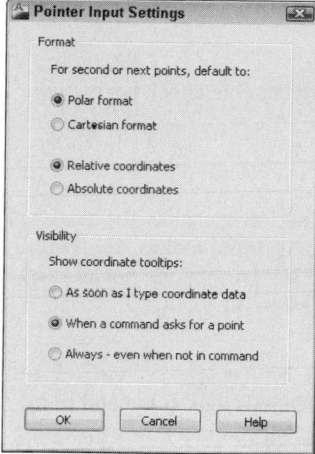

Caution

The settings in this dialog box are very important for determining how all of your coordinate entries work when Dynamic Entry is turned on. If you are upgrading from an earlier release of AutoCAD, you may be used to the entry of X,Y coordinates denoting absolute, not relative, coordinates. However, with Dynamic Input turned on, the default is relative coordinates. This is a great default and will speed up your coordinate entry, but can be very confusing if you are unaware of this setting or where to change it. ■

Dimension Input section

The Enable Dimension Input Where Possible check box is selected by default. This section has nothing to do with dimensions! Instead, it refers to distances or lengths as well as angles, as opposed to points or coordinates. With this check box selected, after you indicate a first point, such as the start of a line or the center of a circle, you see a dimension tooltip that shows the length of the line segment or radius of the circle, as shown in Figure 4.5. You specify the length by typing in this tooltip. If you uncheck the check box, you don't see this dimension tooltip.

The so-called dimension input tooltip shows distances and angles.

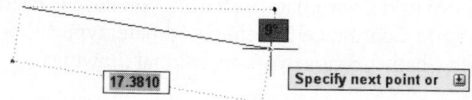

Click the Settings button in this section of the dialog box to open the Dimension Input Settings dialog box. Here you can change settings relating to dimension input during grip editing. I discuss grip editing in Chapter 10.

Note

If you uncheck both the Enable Pointer Input and the Enable Dimension Input Where Possible check boxes, you turn off Dynamic Input. ■

Dynamic prompts section

The Show Command Prompting and Command Input Near the Crosshairs check box enables the display of command prompts and your input in response to these prompts in the Dynamic Input tooltip. This part of Dynamic Input is supposed to take the place of the command line. However, the prompts are not an exact echo of what you see on the command line, and certain prompts do not appear in the tooltip.

Note

If you like Dynamic Input, try turning off the command line by using the COMMANDLINEHIDE command or by pressing Ctrl+9. You can get the command-line window back with the COMMANDLINE command or by pressing Ctrl+9 again. You can also undock the Command Line window, right-click its title bar, and choose Auto-hide. Then the Command Line window collapses to just its title bar; when you place the cursor over it, it automatically expands again. ■

Click the Drafting Tooltip Appearance button to open the Tooltip Appearance dialog box. Here you can change the color of the tooltip, change its size and transparency, and apply the settings to all drafting tooltips in AutoCAD.

Overriding Dynamic Input settings

The default Dynamic Input settings ensure that your input in the tooltip is always interpreted as polar, relative coordinates. However, you may want to override this setting for an individual coordinate. You can override this setting by using a symbol before your X coordinate as you type it. AutoCAD provides three overrides that you can use:

- **Absolute.** To override the default setting of relative coordinates and enter an absolute coordinate, type #. For example, you could type **#0,0** to specify the 0,0 coordinate. See the next section of this chapter, "Absolute Cartesian coordinates," for more information on absolute coordinates.
- **Relative.** If you have set your Dynamic Input for absolute coordinates, you can enter **@** to override the setting and type a relative coordinate. For example, you could type **@3,4**. See the "Relative Cartesian coordinates" and "Polar coordinates" sections for a detailed explanation of relative coordinates.
- **World.** Normally, coordinates that you type are interpreted in the current User Coordinate System. The default coordinate system is called the World Coordinate System. If you have created a custom coordinate system but want to enter a World Coordinate System coordinate, type * before the X coordinate. For more information, see Chapter 8 (for two-dimensional drawings) and Chapter 21 (for three-dimensional drawings).

Tip

To temporarily turn off Dynamic Input, press and hold the F12 key. You might do this while you are picking points if you find that the tooltip obscures objects that you need to see. As soon as you release the F12 key, Dynamic Input returns. ■

Absolute Cartesian coordinates

When you type a line and enter the actual coordinates, such as a line from point 3,2 to 6,9, you are using absolute Cartesian coordinates. Absolute coordinates are measured from 0,0.

If you have Dynamic Input on with the default setting of relative units, you must enter the # symbol before entering the X portion of an absolute Cartesian coordinate when specifying the second or next point, as explained in the previous section. In this exercise, you practice entering absolute Cartesian coordinates.

STEPS: Entering Absolute Cartesian Coordinates

1. Start a new drawing by using the `acad.dwt` or `acadlt.dwt` template. Close any palettes that may be open.

2. If you have Dynamic Input on, right-click the Dynamic Input button on the status bar and choose Settings. In the Pointer Input section, click the Settings button. In the Pointer Input Settings dialog box, click the Absolute Coordinates option (unless this option is already selected). Click OK twice to return to your drawing.

3. Choose Home tab ⇨ Draw panel ⇨ Line. Follow these prompts:

```
Specify first point: -10,-5 ↵
Specify next point or [Undo]: 21,-5 ↵
Specify next point or [Undo]: 21,49 ↵
Specify next point or [Close/Undo]: -10,49 ↵
Specify next point or [Close/Undo]: c ↵ (to close the rectangle)
```

   Most of the lines are off the screen. By default, a new drawing starts with 0,0 at the lower-left corner of your screen; therefore, negative coordinates do not show.

4. Choose View tab ⇨ Navigate panel ⇨ Zoom drop-down list ⇨ Out. If you still can't see the entire rectangle, repeat the zoom out process until you can see it.

Note

If the prompt responds with `Invalid Point` or `Point or option keyword required`, you have entered a coordinate incorrectly. Try typing the coordinate again. Also, don't forget that you can undo a command if you make a mistake. (See Chapter 3 for details.) ■

5. Start the LINE command again and follow these prompts:

```
Specify first point: -8,-2 ↵
Specify next point or [Undo]: 19,-2 ↵
Specify next point or [Undo]: 19,21.5 ↵
Specify next point or [Close/Undo]: -8,21.5 ↵
Specify next point or [Close/Undo]: c ↵
```

6. Once more, start the LINE command and follow these prompts:

```
Specify first point: -8,22.5 ↵
Specify next point or [Undo]: 19,22.5 ↵
Specify next point or [Undo]: 19,46 ↵
Specify next point or [Close/Undo]: -8,46 ↵
Specify next point or [Close/Undo]: c ↵
```

7. If you changed the Dynamic Input settings in Step 1, you should change them back. Right-click the Dynamic Input button on the status bar and choose Settings. In the Pointer Input section, click the Settings button. In the Pointer Input Settings dialog box, click the Relative Coordinates option. Click OK twice to return to your drawing.

8. Save this drawing in your `AutoCAD Bible` folder as `ab04-01.dwg`.

You can now see that you've drawn a simple window, as shown in Figure 4.6.

A window drawn with absolute coordinates.

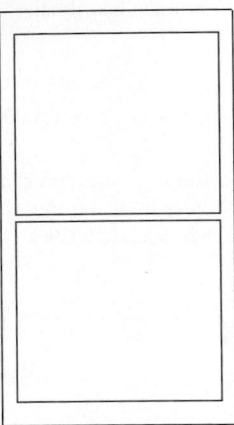

Two questions may have occurred to you during this exercise. First, isn't there a better way of entering absolute coordinates? Typing them in is slow and prone to error. Second, how do you know the absolute coordinates for what you're drawing? Read on for the answers.

Relative Cartesian coordinates

In practice, you usually don't know the absolute coordinates of the points you need to specify in order to draw an object. Whether you're drawing an architectural layout, a physical object (as in mechanical drawing), or an electrical schematic, you don't have X,Y coordinates from which you can work. However, you often do have the measurements of what you're drawing. Usually, you start from any suitable point and work from there. In this situation, you know only the length of the lines you're drawing (if you're drawing lines). Real life doesn't have a 0,0 point. Relative coordinates were developed for these situations.

Relative coordinates specify the X and Y distance from a previous point. They are called *relative coordinates* because they have meaning relative only to a point previously specified. Suppose that you need to draw a window. You can start the window from any point. From there, you have the measurements you need.

If you have Dynamic Input on — set to the default option of relative units — X,Y coordinates are automatically relative. If you have Dynamic Input off or have set Dynamic Input to absolute coordinates, as described earlier in this chapter, you specify that the coordinates are relative by using the @ symbol. For example, if you start a line by picking any point with the mouse, and you know it should be two units long, you can specify the next point as @2,0. The result is a line starting with the first point you picked and ending two units along the X axis, as shown in Figure 4.7. The line is horizontal because the Y coordinate is 0. In a relative coordinate, this means that the Y distance does not change.

FIGURE 4.7

A line whose start point could be anywhere and whose endpoint is specified with the relative point @2,0 is a horizontal line two units long.

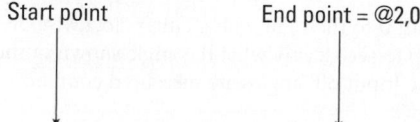

Relative Cartesian coordinates are often used for lines drawn at 90-degree angles (that is, they are either horizontal or vertical). These are called *orthogonal lines.* However, when you create a diagonal line from point 3,3 to point @2,5, the length of the line is not immediately obvious.

When you specify a positive number, such as the 2 in @2,0, the direction is positive. If you want to draw a line in the negative direction of an axis, type a minus sign before the number. Figure 4.8 shows how to draw lines in four directions, using relative coordinates.

FIGURE 4.8

Drawing lines in the four orthogonal directions with relative coordinates. The arrow on each line shows the direction of the line.

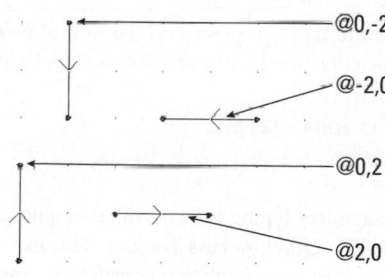

Polar coordinates

Another common situation is to know the distance and angle of a point from either 0,0 or a previous point. In this case, you can use *polar coordinates,* which can be either absolute or relative. Most commonly, you use relative polar coordinates.

Polar coordinates take the form distance<angle. (To type the angle symbol, use the less-than symbol on your keyboard.) If you have Dynamic Input on, set to the default options of relative coordinates, polar coordinates are automatically relative. If you have Dynamic Input off or have set Dynamic Input to absolute

coordinates, as described earlier in this chapter, you need to add the @ sign before a relative polar coordinate. If you also have the default option of polar format selected, you first see coordinates in polar format. Enter the distance, press the Tab key, and then enter the angle. You can also type the angle (<) symbol instead of using the Tab key. To switch to Cartesian format, just type a comma between the X and Y coordinates.

With Dynamic Input on, angles are measured from 0 to 180, with 0 to the right, going either clockwise or counterclockwise. Watch the dotted lines near the angle's tooltip to see exactly what the angle shown in the tooltip is measuring. You can use negative angles. With Dynamic Input off, angles are measured counter-clockwise, with 0 to the right, ranging from 0 to 360.

In the following series of steps, you draw part of a portico, the decorative molding above a door or window. You'll use architectural units. In this case, only inches are used, which don't need to be specified. You can specify feet by using an apostrophe (also called a *prime*) after any number.

When typing architectural units, partial inches are indicated by fractions in the form a/b. You need to sepa-rate the fraction from the whole inches by a hyphen. This can be a little confusing because the hyphen is also used for negative numbers. For example, to draw a horizontal line of 5¼ inches in the negative direc-tion of the X axis, you would type **-5-1/4,0**. (The 0 indicates no change in the Y axis because it is a horizon-tal line.)

On the DVD

The drawing used in this exercise on using relative and polar coordinates, ab04-a.dwg, is in the Drawings folder on the DVD. ∎

STEPS: Using Relative and Polar Coordinates

1. Open ab04-a.dwg from the DVD. Close any palettes that may be open.

2. As you move your mouse around, notice that the coordinates displayed on the status bar are in architectural units (that is, in feet and inches). If the coordinates are grayed out, click them to turn them on.

3. Save the drawing in your AutoCAD Bible folder as ab04-02.dwg.

Note

The next steps involve some complex typing. If you get an error message, try typing the coordinate again. If you realize you made a mistake after ending the command, click Undo on the Quick Access Toolbar. This exercise assumes that you are using the default Dynamic Input settings of polar format and relative coordinates and that Dynamic Input is on. See the "Using the Dynamic Input tooltip to enter coordinates" section earlier in this chap-ter for details. ∎

4. Choose Home tab ⇨ Draw panel ⇨ Line to start the LINE command. Follow these prompts:
   ```
   Specify first point: Pick any point at the lower-left corner of your
      screen.
   Specify next point or [Undo]: 0,-3/4 ↵
   Specify next point or [Undo]: 75-1/4,0 ↵
   Specify next point or [Close/Undo]: 0,3/4 ↵
   Specify next point or [Close/Undo]: c ↵
   ```

5. Start the LINE command again. Follow the prompts:

Specify first point: ⏎. *This starts the line at the last endpoint you specified.*
Specify next point or [Undo]: **4-3/4,0** ⏎
Specify next point or [Undo]: **43<40** ⏎
Specify next point or [Close/Undo]: **43<-40** ⏎
Specify next point or [Close/Undo]: **-2-1/4,0** ⏎
Specify next point or [Close/Undo]: **39-7/8<140** ⏎
Specify next point or [Close/Undo]: **39-7/8<-140** ⏎
Specify next point or [Close/Undo]: ⏎ *to end the command.*

Note

In this exercise, you draw a line on top of a line, which is not good drawing practice. Later in this chapter and in upcoming chapters, you learn techniques to avoid this. ■

6. Save your drawing. You have created a portion of a portico, which goes over a window of a house, as shown in Figure 4.9.

FIGURE 4.9

Part of a portico over a window, drawn by using relative Cartesian and polar coordinates in architectural notation.

Tip

You can type @ ⏎ at the first prompt of any drawing command to indicate the most recent coordinate specified. ■

Notice that using relative coordinates, both Cartesian and polar, is much more realistic than using absolute coordinates. However, typing in coordinates is still awkward. Typing in coordinates is often the only way to get exactly what you want. Nevertheless, several other techniques for specifying coordinates are easier in many circumstances. I discuss these techniques in the next few sections.

Direct distance entry

One shortcut for entering coordinates is direct distance entry. After you specify the start point of a line, at the Specify next point or [Undo]: prompt, simply move the mouse cursor in the direction you want the line to go and type in the line's length. It works best in orthogonal mode or with polar tracking (discussed in the following section), which makes specifying the exact angle easy.

Note

You can use direct distance entry for any command that requires you to specify a distance and a direction, including both drawing and editing commands. ■

Orthogonal mode

Lines drawn at 0, 90, 180, and 270 degrees are orthogonal lines. When in orthogonal mode — *ortho* for short — you can only draw orthogonal lines with the mouse. Ortho Mode also affects editing. For example, with Ortho Mode on, you can move objects only vertically or horizontally. Combined with snap and grid, Ortho Mode makes drawing easier and more efficient. Ortho Mode is also great for direct distance entry.

 Click Ortho Mode on the status bar to toggle Ortho Mode on and off, or press F8. You cannot have polar tracking on at the same time that Ortho Mode is on. Polar tracking is discussed next.

Note

Orthogonal mode only affects points picked directly on the screen by using your mouse. Any relative or absolute coordinates that you type in the Dynamic Input tooltip or on the command line override orthogonal mode. For example, if you use a polar coordinate of 5<45 in the Dynamic Input tooltip, you'll get a line at an angle of 45 degrees, even when Ortho Mode is on. ■

Polar tracking

Polar tracking guides you, using a tooltip and vector line, when you want to draw (or edit) at an angle other than the four orthogonal angles, as shown in Figure 4.10. You can use polar tracking for orthogonal angles as well. If you have Dynamic Input on, just look for the word "Polar" to distinguish between the Dynamic Input and the polar tooltips.

FIGURE 4.10

When polar tracking is on, a tooltip appears when you move the cursor close to one of the polar angles. Here you see a tooltip indicating an angle of 45 degrees.

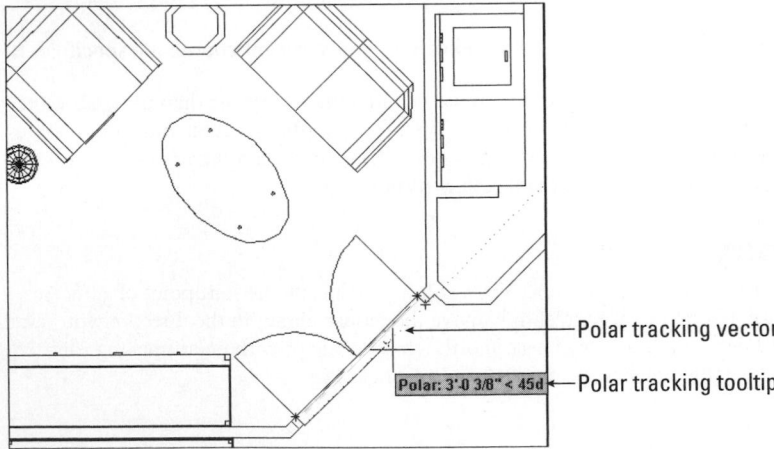

Polar tracking vector
Polar tracking tooltip

Polar tracking makes it easy to use direct distance entry to specify distances for many angles. To use polar tracking, you first set the angles that you want to use.

Setting polar tracking angles

 To set the angles, right-click the Polar Tracking button on the status bar and choose Settings. The Polar Tracking tab of the Drafting Settings dialog box is displayed, which you can see in Figure 4.11.

FIGURE 4.11

The Polar Tracking tab of the Drafting Settings dialog box.

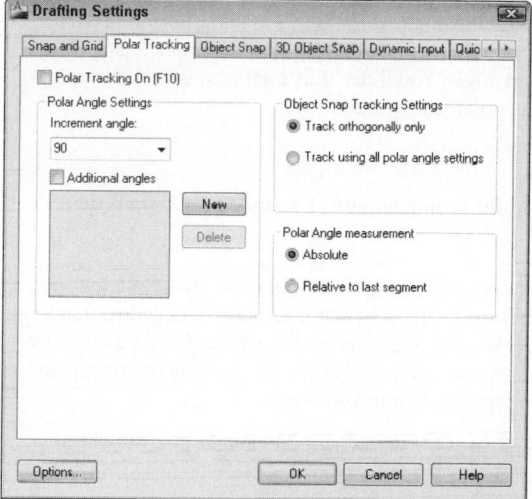

To set polar tracking, you can define two types of angles:

- **Increment angle.** To set the increment angle, click the Increment Angle drop-down arrow, where you can pick from angles that range from every 90 degrees to every 5 degrees. You can also type your own incremental angle in the text box. Polar tracking will then apply to that angle and its multiples.

- **Additional angles.** If you think that you'll need other angles, check Additional Angles, click New, and then type in an angle. You can add up to ten angles. Note that additional angles are not incremental angles — if you type 35, only 35 degrees will be marked, not 70 degrees or other multiples of 35. To delete an additional angle, select it and click Delete.

 On the right side of the dialog box, you can choose how polar tracking works with object snap tracking (covered later in this chapter). You can set object snap tracking to use all the polar angle settings or limit it to orthogonal angles only. You can also set whether polar angles are measured absolutely (relative to 0 degrees) or relative to the segment drawn most recently. By default, absolute angles are used. To turn on polar tracking, check the Polar Tracking On check box in the dialog box. If you are not in the dialog box, press F10 or click the Polar Tracking button on the status bar.

To customize how polar tracking works, click Options in the Drafting Settings dialog box to open the Options dialog box with the Drafting tab on top. The following settings in the AutoTracking Settings section apply to polar tracking:

- **Display polar tracking vector** turns on and off the polar tracking vector, which is the faint dotted line that extends to the end of the screen.
- **Display AutoTrack tooltip** turns on and off the tooltip that tells you the distance and angle.

Using polar tracking

To use polar tracking, you need to move the cursor slowly through the angles to allow time for the calculation and display of the vector and tooltip. Suppose that you're drawing a line. Specify the start point. To specify the second point, move the cursor in the approximate angle of the line you want to draw. When you see the polar tracking vector and tooltip, leave the mouse where it is and type the length of the line. Then press Enter to create the line with the proper length and angle. You'll find this method easier than typing polar coordinates for lines with angles specified in your polar tracking settings.

Tip

Turn on NumLock on your keyboard and use the numerical pad for typing lengths. Use the Enter key on the numerical pad as well. ■

You can specify a polar angle for just one command. If you're drawing a line, after specifying the first point, for example, type the angle preceded by the angle symbol (<). The next segment is then locked to that angle while you type its length. A polar angle specified in this way is called a *polar override angle* because it overrides the current polar angles in effect. Of course, a polar override is not faster than simply typing a polar coordinate, but it does let you see the angle of the line segment before you type its length.

In the following exercise, you practice using direct distance entry with Ortho Mode and polar tracking.

On the DVD

The drawing (ab04-b.dwg) used in the following exercise on using direct distance entry with Ortho Mode and polar tracking is in the Drawings folder on the DVD. ■

STEPS: Using Direct Distance Entry with Ortho Mode and Polar Tracking

1. Open ab04-b.dwg from the DVD. Close any palettes that may be open.

2. Right-click the Polar Tracking button on the status bar, and choose 45 to set a 45° polar tracking angle.

3. Save the drawing in your AutoCAD Bible folder as ab04-03.dwg. If Ortho Mode is not on, click the Ortho Mode button on the status bar.

4. Choose Home tab ⇨ Draw panel ⇨ Line to start the LINE command and, at the Specify first point: prompt, type **2,2** ↵.

5. Move the mouse horizontally to the right and then type **.5** ↵.

6. Move the mouse up vertically (in the 90-degree direction) and then type **.5** ↵.

7. Move the mouse horizontally to the right and then type **2** ↵. Your drawing should look like Figure 4.12.

FIGURE 4.12

Drawing with direct distance entry enables you to specify coordinates by typing in a length after you move the pointer in the desired direction.

8. Move the mouse up in the 90-degree direction and then type **.5** ↵.

9. Move the mouse to the left in the 180-degree direction and then type **2** ↵.

10. Move the mouse up in the 90-degree direction and then type **.5** ↵.

11. Move the mouse to the left in the 180-degree direction and then type **.5** ↵.

12. Type **c** ↵ to close the figure. Press Enter again to end the command.

 13. Click Polar Tracking on the status bar. The Ortho Mode button becomes deselected.

14. Start the LINE command again. Press Enter to start the new line from the most recent point. At the Specify next point or [Undo]: prompt, move the cursor diagonally up and to the left so the line is approximately in the 135-degree direction. When you see the tooltip confirming the angle, release the mouse button and type **.7071** ↵.

15. Move the cursor up until you see the polar tracking tooltip confirming a 90-degree angle. Type **.5** ↵.

16. Move the cursor diagonally in the 45-degree direction until you see the tooltip. Type **.7071** ↵. Press Enter again to end the LINE command.

17. Save your drawing. It should look like Figure 4.13.

FIGURE 4.13

The completed drawing of a bolt.

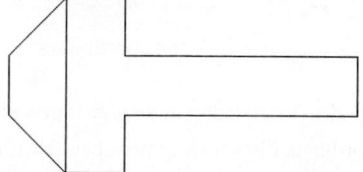

Displaying Coordinates

As you work, you can refer to the coordinate display on the status bar. This display helps you know where your cursor and objects are when you draw and is also helpful when editing, by informing you how far and in what direction you are moving or copying objects.

Note

You can set the Dynamic Input tooltip to show coordinates all the time, even when you're not in a command. See the "Specifying Dynamic Input settings" section, earlier in this chapter. ■

AutoCAD and AutoCAD LT have three coordinate display modes:

- **Dynamic absolute coordinates (absolute).** Absolute coordinates that change as you move the mouse, as shown in Figure 4.14 on the left.

- **Static absolute coordinates (off).** Absolute coordinates that change only when you specify a point, as shown in Figure 4.14 in the middle. The coordinate display is dimmed.

- **Dynamic polar coordinates (relative).** Polar coordinates that change continuously as you move the mouse, as shown in Figure 4.14 on the right. They appear after you've already specified a point and are ready to specify the next point, as when you're in the process of drawing a line.

FIGURE 4.14

Dynamic absolute coordinates, static absolute coordinates, and dynamic polar coordinates.

| 0.7409, 2.1450 , 0.0000 | 0.3485, 3.0654 , 0.0000 | 1.4580< 29 , 0.0000 |

Dynamic absolute coordinates.   Static absolute coordinates.   Dynamic polar coodinates.

To change the coordinate display, click the coordinates area on the status bar. For purposes of this chapter, I ignore the Z coordinate that follows the X and Y coordinates (in AutoCAD only). In two-dimensional drawings, the Z coordinate is always zero.

In the following exercise, you practice using the coordinate display options. You can do this exercise with any new or existing drawing open on the screen. If you have Dynamic Input on, compare the display in the Dynamic Input tooltip and the display on the status bar.

STEPS: Using Coordinate Display Options

1. Look at the coordinate display on the status bar. It should be shown in black. If the coordinates are shown in gray, click the coordinates.

2. Move the mouse around in a few directions. Notice how the coordinates constantly change with the mouse movement.

3. Right-click the coordinates and choose Off. The coordinate display is grayed out.

4. Move the mouse around again. The coordinate display does not change with the movement of the mouse.

5. Choose Home tab ⇨ Draw panel ⇨ Line to start the LINE command and pick any point on the screen.

6. Watch the coordinate display as you pick any point at the `Specify next point or [Undo]:` prompt.

7. Pick several other points and watch as the coordinate display changes only when you pick a point. This is the static coordinate display.

8. Click the coordinates again without ending the LINE command.

9. Move the mouse to another point that you would like to pick, but watch the coordinate display before you pick the point. This time, the length and angle of the new line segment are shown. These are dynamic polar coordinates.

10. Pick a few more points, watching the polar coordinates.

11. Right-click the coordinates and choose Absolute to return to dynamic absolute coordinates.

12. Press Enter to end the LINE command. Do not save your drawing.

Picking Coordinates on the Screen

The easiest and quickest way to specify coordinates is to pick them directly on the screen with the mouse. Several techniques are available to help you do so accurately.

You can adjust the size of the crosshairs that cross the cursor. By default, they are 5 percent of screen size. To change the crosshair size, choose Application Button ⇨ Options, and click the Display tab. In the Crosshair Size text box, type a new percentage or drag the bar to increase or decrease the percentage. Click OK.

Using Snap settings

The SNAP command is often an alternative to tedious entry of coordinates. This command restricts the cursor to an incremental distance that you choose, such as 0.5 units. You can set the snap spacing to anything you want. For example, if all your measurements are rounded off to the nearest 0.25 units, you can set your snap to 0.25.

The snap technique is not very useful when you need to draw to three or more decimal places of accuracy. And when you're zoomed out in a large drawing, the snap points may be so close together that you cannot easily find the one you want. But in the right situation, snap is one of the quickest, most accurate drawing techniques available. AutoCAD and AutoCAD LT provide two types of snap settings, Grid Snap and PolarSnap.

Snapping to a grid

When you snap to a grid, the mouse cursor can move only to the Grid Snap points.

 To set the snap spacing, right-click the Snap Mode button on the status bar and choose Settings. The Drafting Settings dialog box opens, as shown in Figure 4.15. In the Snap X Spacing text box of the Snap Spacing section, type the spacing you want between snap points. Make sure that Grid Snap and Rectangular Snap are checked in the Snap Type section of the dialog box. Click OK.

Cross-Reference

In Chapter 8, I discuss rotating the angle of the snap and grid. Chapter 8 also discusses Isometric snap, used for isometric drawing. ∎

Usually you want the X spacing (going across) to be the same as the Y spacing (going up and down). By default, the Equal X and Y Spacing check box is selected, so you need to specify only the X spacing; the Y spacing changes automatically to equal the X spacing. X and Y spacing will be different only if you type a different number in the Snap Y Spacing text box.

FIGURE 4.15

The Snap and Grid tab of the Drafting Settings dialog box. (The AutoCAD LT dialog box is slightly different.)

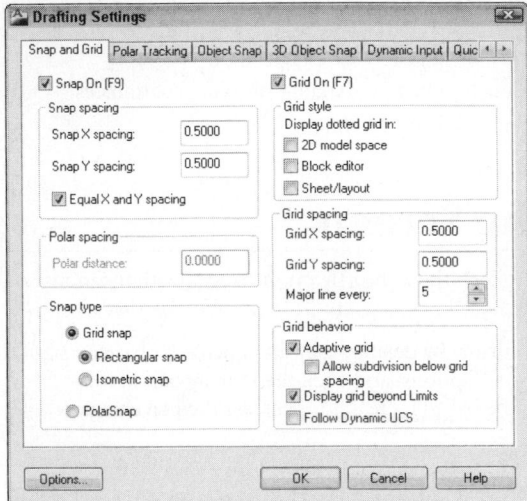

 You can also turn snap on in this dialog box by clicking the Snap On check box. However, the most common way to turn snap on, after you've set the spacing, is to click the Snap Mode button on the status bar (or press the F9 key). Click it again to turn snap off.

Snapping at polar angles

After you set polar tracking settings, discussed earlier in this chapter in the "Polar tracking" section, you can snap to increments along the polar angles you have set. When PolarSnap is on, the polar tooltip only shows distances in increments of the snap setting. When you see the distance you want, just click. PolarSnap makes it easy to draw accurately without having to type coordinates.

To use PolarSnap, follow these steps:

1. Right-click the Snap Mode button on the status bar and click Settings to open the Drafting Settings dialog box with the Snap and Grid tab displayed.
2. Check PolarSnap in the Snap Type section of the dialog box (refer to Figure 4.15).
3. Type a distance in the Polar Distance text box.
4. Click OK to close the dialog box.
5. Click Snap Mode on the status bar.

Note that PolarSnap and Grid Snap are mutually exclusive. If PolarSnap is on, the cursor will not snap to the grid. Used with polar tracking, PolarSnap is a powerful tool. Remember that you can polar track along orthogonal as well as other angles.

Tip

You can choose either PolarSnap or Grid Snap (switch between them) by right-clicking Snap Mode on the status bar. A shortcut menu lets you choose the type of snap you want, or turn both off. ■

Viewing with the grid

Sometimes you may find it helpful to see a grid to help get your bearings while you draw, as shown in Figure 4.16. To toggle the grid, click Grid Display on the status bar or press the F7 key. Notice how you can quickly judge the approximate width of a windowpane, knowing that the grid lines are half a foot apart. If you turn on snap, the grid helps you visualize the snap points. However, the grid lines do not have to be set to the same spacing as the snap points.

New Feature

The grid is on by default. It displays light lines every .5 units and heavier lines every five grid lines (every 2.5 units). ■

FIGURE 4.16

A portion of a drawing with the grid turned on and set to 6 inches.

Thanks to Henry Dearborn, AIA, Fairfield, Iowa, for this drawing.

Some users find the grid annoying, but when you first start to use AutoCAD or AutoCAD LT, you may find it helpful. Even accomplished users can take advantage of the grid, especially when starting a new drawing.

Tip

If you're working with a small snap spacing and the grid is too dense, set the grid to two or more times the spacing of the snap. ■

To set the grid size, right-click the Grid Display button on the status bar and choose Settings to open the Drafting Settings dialog box (refer to Figure 4.15). In the Grid X Spacing text box of the Grid Spacing section, type the spacing you want between grid points. Click OK.

As with the snap feature, you usually want the X spacing (going across) to be the same as the Y spacing (going up and down). You only need to specify the X spacing; the Y spacing automatically changes to be the same, as long as the Equal X and Y Spacing check box is selected in the Drafting Settings dialog box. X and Y spacing will only be different if you type a different number in the Grid Y Spacing text box.

New Feature

You can choose to display the grid as dots instead of the default lines. In the Grid Style section of the Snap and Grid tab of the Drafting Settings dialog box, check the contexts in which you want to display dots. ■

You can turn on the grid in this dialog box by clicking the Grid On check box, but it's easier to click Grid Display on the status bar (or press F7).

In the following exercise, you practice using PolarSnap and Grid Snap points as well as the grid.

On the DVD

The drawing used in the following exercise on using snap points and the grid, ab04-b.dwg, **is in the** Drawings **folder on the DVD. ■**

STEPS: Using Snap Points and the Grid

1. Open ab04-b.dwg from the DVD. Close any palettes that may be open.

2. Save the drawing in your AutoCAD Bible folder as ab04-04.dwg.

 3. Right-click the Snap Mode button on the status bar and choose Settings. The Drafting Settings dialog box opens with the Snap and Grid tab displayed. In the Snap Type section, make sure that Grid Snap and Rectangular Snap are selected.

4. In the Snap Spacing section, the Snap X Spacing should be 0.5.

5. In the Grid Spacing section, the Equal X and Y Spacing check box should be selected. The Grid X Spacing should be 0.5. Click OK.

6. On the status bar, click Snap Mode, Grid Display, and Ortho Mode. The grid appears. Make sure that the Object Snap and Object Snap Tracking buttons on the status bar are off.

7. Choose View tab ⇨ Navigate panel ⇨ Zoom drop-down list ⇨ All.

8. Move the mouse around and watch the coordinates on the status bar. (Right-click the coordinate and choose Absolute if they are in static mode.) They show halves of units because you have set the snap to 0.5.

9. Choose Home tab ⇨ Draw panel ⇨ Line to start the LINE command. At the Specify first point: prompt, click when the coordinates on the status bar show 2.0000,2.0000. (AutoCAD users can ignore the third Z coordinate, which is always 0.0000 in 2D drawings.) If you have Dynamic Input on, you'll find the coordinates in the Dynamic Input tooltip easier to read.

10. Move the mouse around and watch the coordinates. If you don't see polar coordinates (for example, 3.0000<0), right-click the coordinates and choose Relative.

11. Move the mouse to the right until the coordinates read 8.5000<0 and click. You have drawn a horizontal line with a length of 8.5 units.

12. Right-click and choose Enter to end the LINE command.

13. Move the mouse cursor away from the end of the new line and back to it again, and the absolute coordinates appear. They should be 10.5000,2.0000.

14. Right-click and choose Repeat LINE to start the LINE command again. Use the coordinate display to start the line at 1.5000,1.5000. (For the rest of this exercise, ignore the Dynamic Input tooltip.) Continue to pick points (rather than type them) and draw the following line segments, as shown in the coordinate display:

    ```
    0.5000<0
    3.0000<90
    0.5000<180
    3.0000<270
    ```

15. End the LINE command.

16. Start the LINE command and pick points, drawing the following line segments (as shown in the coordinate display) starting from 10.5000,1.50. Then end the LINE command:

    ```
    0.5000<0
    3.0000<90
    0.5000<180
    3.0000<270
    ```

17. Starting from 2.0000,4.0000 draw an 8.5-unit line at 0 degrees. End the LINE command.

18. Start the LINE command again. At the first prompt, pick 11.0000,2.0000. Right-click the Snap Mode button on the status bar and choose Settings. In the Snap Type section, choose PolarSnap. (This is equivalent to choosing the PolarSnap On feature on the Snap Mode button's shortcut menu.) In the Polar Spacing section, change the Polar Distance to 0.5. Choose the Polar Tracking tab and set the Increment Angle to 45 degrees. Click OK. Click Polar Tracking on the status bar.

19. Move the cursor in a 45-degree direction from 11.0000,2.0000 until you see the tooltip. Move along the polar tracking vector until the tooltip says 3.5000 < 45° and click. End the LINE command.

20. Right-click the Snap Mode button and choose Grid Snap On. Start the LINE command and, at the Specify first point: prompt, choose 11.0000,4.0000.

21. Right-click the Snap Mode button and choose PolarSnap On. Move the cursor in a 45-degree direction until the tooltip says 3.5000 < 45° and click. End the LINE command.

22. Save your drawing. Your drawing should look like Figure 4.17.

FIGURE 4.17

The completed pipe section.

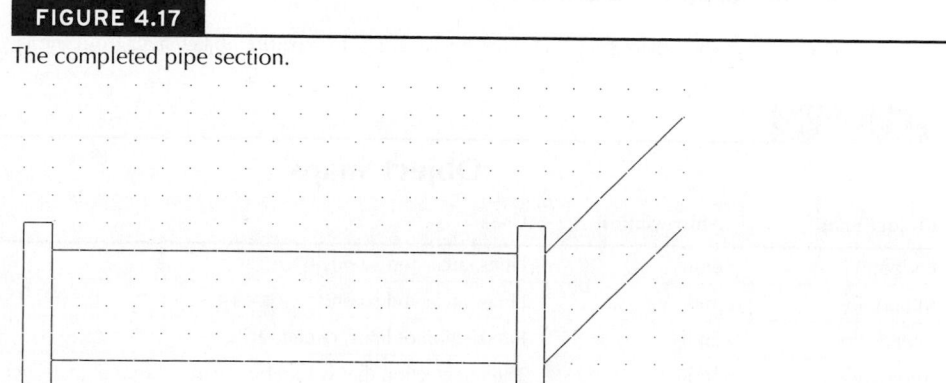

As you no doubt experienced, this is a much easier way to draw compared to typing in coordinates. Note that drawing with Snap on works better when you're drawing small objects. However, even when drawing an office building, you spend a great deal of time working on small details that may be easier to draw with Snap on.

Using Object snaps

Often you need to draw relative to an existing object. For example, you may need to start a line from the endpoint or midpoint of an existing line. *Object snaps* (OSNAPS for short) enable you to precisely specify a point by snapping to a geometrically defined coordinate on an existing object. Object Snaps provide a very precise and efficient way to draw.

Here are three ways to specify an object snap:

- Right-click, choose Snap Overrides from the shortcut menu, and then choose the object snap that you want from the menu.
- Access the Object Snap shortcut menu by holding down the Shift key and right-clicking. Choose the object snap that you want from the shortcut menu.
- Type the object snap's abbreviation on the command line.

Cross-Reference

On multi-button mice, you can customize one of the buttons to show the Object Snap shortcut menu. Displaying the Object Snap shortcut menu with the click of a mouse button is very convenient. I discuss customizing the mouse in Chapter 33. ■

When you specify an object snap, a prompt for that object snap appears on the command line. For example, if you choose a midpoint object snap, you see mid of on the command line. Unfortunately, the Dynamic Input tooltip does not show this prompt.

Tip

When you use Dynamic Input and object snaps together, the tooltip alternates between showing the Dynamic Input tooltip and the object snap tooltip, or displays them as separate tooltips. To keep all the tooltips together, set the TOOLTIPMERGE system variable to 1. ■

Table 4.1 lists the object snaps. Use the abbreviation to type the object snap from the keyboard.

TABLE 4.1

Object Snaps

Object Snap	Abbreviation	Uses
Endpoint	end	Lines, arcs, and so on.
Midpoint	mid	Lines, arcs, and so on.
Intersection	int	Intersection of lines, circles, arcs.
Apparent Intersection*	app	The intersection that would be created if two objects were extended until they met.

Object Snap	Abbreviation	Uses
Extension	ext	Extends lines, arcs, and so on past their endpoints but in the same direction. After choosing this object snap, pause over the endpoint of a line or arc until you see a small plus sign. As you move the mouse cursor along the extension path, a temporary extension path appears so that you can draw to or from points on the extension path.
Center	cen	Circles, arcs, ellipses.
Quadrant	qua	Nearest quadrant (0-, 90-, 180-, or 270-degree point) of a circle, arc, or ellipse.
Perpendicular	per	Arc, circles, ellipses, lines, multilines, polylines, rays, splines, or construction lines. The Deferred Perpendicular mode lets you draw a line perpendicular *from* one of these objects. Start the LINE command and choose the Perpendicular object snap. Click the object that you want to draw perpendicular from and then move the cursor away from that object. You see the Deferred Perpendicular tooltip and a temporary perpendicular line that follows your cursor along the original object. You can then complete the perpendicular line.
Parallel	par	Continues a line, polyline, and so on so that it's parallel to an existing line or other straight-line segment. After you choose this object snap, pause over the line you want to draw parallel to until you see a small parallel line symbol. As you move the mouse cursor parallel to the object, a temporary parallel path appears to help you create the parallel segment.
Tangent	tan	Starts or continues a line from or to a point tangent with an arc, circle, or ellipse.
Node	nod	Point objects (discussed in Chapter 7) and origin point (defpoint) on dimensions (covered in Chapter 14).
Insertion	ins	Insertion point of text (see Chapter 13) or a block (see Chapter 18).
Nearest	nea	Nearest point on any object.
None	non	Turns off any object snap modes.

* Apparent Intersection also applies to 3D objects that appear to intersect because of the angle of view.

When you draw a line, you think of it as having a starting point and an ending point. After the line is drawn, however, both of these points are considered endpoints in terms of object snaps. When picking the endpoint of a line for the endpoint object snap, pick a point on the line closer to the endpoint that you want. The same applies to arcs. Although the arc prompts read Start point and End, both are considered endpoints for purposes of object snaps.

AutoSnap is a feature that helps you work with object snaps. When you move the cursor near the geometric point you have specified, such as an endpoint, you are notified in three ways:

- **Marker.** An object snap shape appears. Each object snap has a differently shaped marker.
- **AutoSnap tooltip.** A label displays the name of the object snap.
- **Magnet.** A pull gently moves the cursor toward the geometric point.

Figure 4.18 shows an endpoint marker and AutoSnap tooltip.

FIGURE 4.18

AutoSnap shows you the endpoint of the line.

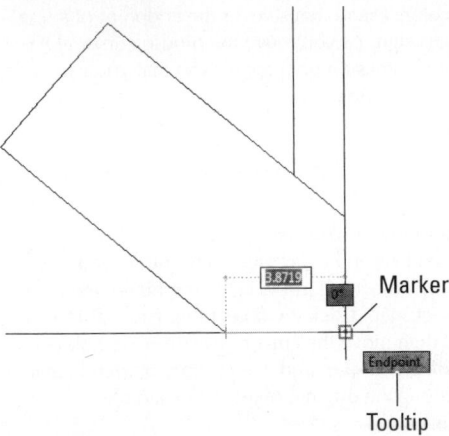

Marker

Tooltip

You can customize the AutoSnap feature to suit your needs or make it go away completely if you want. Choose Application Button ⇨ Options, and click the Drafting tab. Here you can individually turn on and off the marker, the AutoSnap tooltip, and the magnet. You can also change the marker size and color. For more information, see Appendix A.

In the following exercise, you practice using object snaps.

STEPS: Using Object Snaps

1. Start a new drawing by using the `acad.dwt` or `acadlt.dwt` template. Close any palettes that may be open.

2. Save the drawing in your `AutoCAD Bible` folder as `ab04-05.dwg`.

3. Click Ortho Mode on the status bar to turn on Ortho Mode. If the Object Snap button on the status bar is on, click it to turn off running object snaps (covered in the next section).

4. Choose Home tab ⇨ Draw panel ⇨ Line to start the LINE command. Follow the prompts:

    ```
    Specify first point: 2,7 ↵. Move the cursor downward.
    Specify next point or [Undo]: 4 ↵. Move the cursor to the right.
    Specify next point or [Undo]: 4 ↵. Move the cursor up.
    Specify next point or [Close/Undo]: 4 ↵
    Specify next point or [Close/Undo]: Press Enter to end the command.
    ```

    Your drawing should look like Figure 4.19. The circled numbers are reference points for this exercise.

FIGURE 4.19

These three lines are the start of a mounting bracket.

5. Choose Home tab ⇨ Draw panel ⇨ Arc. Follow these prompts:

   Specify start point of arc or [Center]: *Right-click. From the shortcut menu, choose Snap Overrides⇨Endpoint.*
   _endp of *Move the cursor to* ❶ *in Figure 4.19. When you see the endpoint marker and AutoSnap tooltip, click.*
   Specify second point of arc or [Center/End]: *Right-click and choose Center.*
   Specify center point of arc: *Press Shift and right-click. Choose Midpoint from the shortcut menu.*
   _mid of *Move the cursor to* ❷ *and pick.*
   Specify end point of arc or [Angle/chord Length]: **end** ⏎. *Move the cursor to* ❸ *and pick.*

6. Choose Home tab ⇨ Draw panel ⇨ Circle. Follow the prompts:

   Specify center point for circle or [3P/2P/Ttr (tan tan radius)]: *Choose Center from the Object Snap shortcut menu.*
   cen of *Move the cursor over the arc until you see the Center marker and tooltip, and then click.*
   Specify radius of circle or [Diameter]: **.75** ⏎

7. Start the LINE command and use any method you want to draw a line from the endpoint at ❸ to the endpoint at ❹. End the LINE command.

Note

When you press Shift and right-click to get the Object Snap menu, the mouse pointer must be in the drawing area. If the mouse pointer is on the Ribbon or command line area, press the Esc key, or hold down the Shift key and right-click again in the drawing area. ∎

8. Save your drawing. It should look like Figure 4.20.

The start of a drawing of a mounting bracket (including a construction line that would later be erased). It was created by using the endpoint, midpoint, and center object snaps.

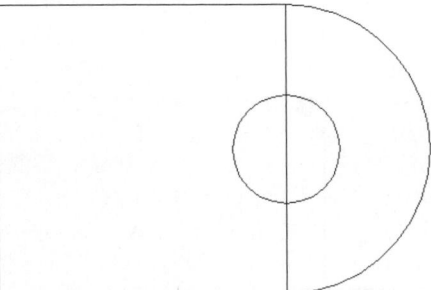

Running object snaps and Object Snap mode

The Endpoint object snap is probably the most commonly used of all the object snaps. It would be nice to have a method of using object snaps that you use often without resorting to a menu, toolbar, or keyboard entry. The solution is to set a *running object snap*, which keeps one or more object snaps on until you turn them off.

Tip

Many users like to work with three or four running object snaps on at once, such as Endpoint, Midpoint, Center, and Intersection. If you can't find the object snap you want because you have several object snaps near each other, press the Tab key to cycle through the object snaps, one by one, until you find the one that you want. ■

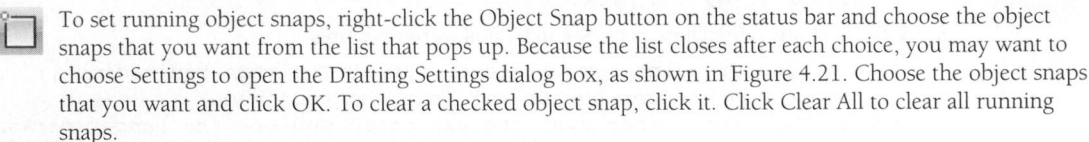

To set running object snaps, right-click the Object Snap button on the status bar and choose the object snaps that you want from the list that pops up. Because the list closes after each choice, you may want to choose Settings to open the Drafting Settings dialog box, as shown in Figure 4.21. Choose the object snaps that you want and click OK. To clear a checked object snap, click it. Click Clear All to clear all running snaps.

You use the Object Snap button on the status bar to turn on your running object snaps. If you want to turn them off temporarily, just click the Object Snap button or press F3. This capability to toggle running object snaps on and off makes it easy to work with running object snaps on almost all the time, because you can turn them off at the click of a button.

FIGURE 4.21

Use the Object Snap tab of the Drafting Settings dialog box to set running object snaps.

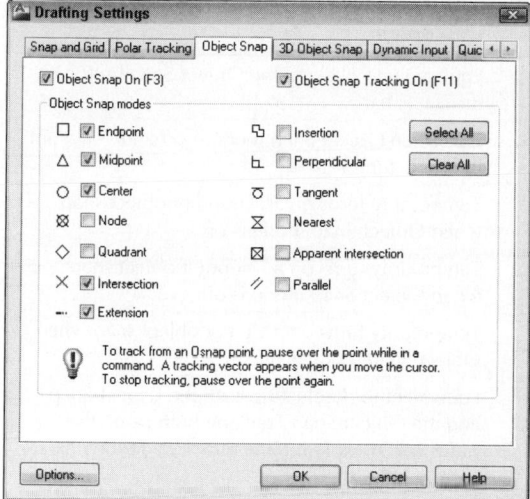

Overriding Coordinate Settings

Sometimes you're in the middle of a command and want to turn off an object snap just for a second. You're trying to pick a point and that pesky object snap marker keeps appearing just when you don't want it. Or you may want to turn Snap mode on or off for part of a command. Temporary overrides exist for this purpose. There are two kinds of temporary overrides:

- **Toggles.** You press a key or combination of keys. The setting switches on or off. You then press the same keyboard shortcut to reverse the setting. For example, if you have Ortho Mode on, you can press F8 to turn it off. To turn Ortho Mode back on, press F8 again.

- **Temporary overrides.** You press and hold a key or key combination. The setting switches on or off only while you're holding down the keyboard shortcut. The setting reverts to its original setting when you release the key or key combination. For example, if you have Ortho Mode on, you can press Shift to temporarily turn it off. As soon as you release the Shift key, Ortho Mode comes back on.

Table 4.2 lists these overrides. Note that each setting has two shortcuts, one for your left hand and one for your right hand. Use whichever one you like. You can customize the keys for these overrides. (For more information, see Chapter 33.)

TABLE 4.2

Coordinate Setting Overrides

Setting	Toggle	Temporary Override	Description
Toggle Object Snap mode	F3	Shift+A; Shift+'	Equivalent to clicking the Object Snap button on the status bar.
Turn on Object Snap mode		Shift+S; Shift+;	Use when Object Snap mode is off and you want to briefly turn it on.
Endpoint object snap		Shift+E; Shift+P	Temporarily turns on an Endpoint object snap when Object Snap mode is off.
Midpoint object snap		Shift+V; Shift+M	Temporarily turns on a Midpoint object snap when Object Snap mode is off.
Center object snap		Shift+C; Shift+,	Temporarily turns on a Center object snap when Object Snap mode is off.
Turn off Object Snap and Object Snap Tracking modes		Shift+D; Shift+L	Equivalent to deselecting both the Object Snap and the Object Snap Tracking buttons on the status bar. (I explain object tracking in the next section.)
Ortho Mode	F8	Shift	Equivalent to clicking the Ortho Mode button on the status bar.
Snap mode	F9		Equivalent to clicking the Snap Mode button on the status bar.
Polar mode	F10	Shift+X; Shift+.	Equivalent to clicking the Polar Mode button on the status bar.
Object Snap Tracking mode	F11	Shift+Q; Shift+]	Equivalent to clicking the Object Snap Tracking button on the status bar (I explain this in the next section).
Dynamic UCS mode	F6	Shift+Z, Shift+/	Equivalent to clicking the Allow/Disallow Dynamic UCS button on the status bar.
Dynamic Input	F12		Equivalent to clicking the Dynamic Input button on the status bar.

Tip

To customize the hold-down time for temporary overrides, go to the Windows Control Panel (Start ⇨ Control Panel) and double-click the Keyboard item. In the Character Repeat section, adjust the Repeat Rate control. ■

In the following exercise, you practice using running object snaps with Object Snap mode.

STEPS: Using Running Object Snaps with Object Snap Mode

1. Start a new drawing by using the `acad.dwt` or `acadlt.dwt` template. Close any palettes that may be open.
2. Save the file in your `AutoCAD Bible` folder as `ab04-06.dwg`.
3. Right-click the Object Snap button on the status bar and choose Settings. Choose Endpoint. Uncheck all other object snaps and click OK.

4. Choose Home tab ⇨ Draw panel ⇨ Line to start the LINE command. At the prompt, enter **2,2** ↵ to start the line at coordinate 2,2.

5. Turn on Ortho Mode by clicking the Ortho Mode button on the status bar. If Object Snap mode is not on, click it on the status bar.

6. Move the mouse in the 0-degree direction and type **6** ↵.

7. Move the mouse up in the 90-degree direction, type **3** ↵, and end the LINE command.

8. Start the ARC command. At the `Specify start point of arc or [Center]:` prompt, pick the endpoint at ❶, as shown in Figure 4.22. (Look for the marker and AutoSnap tooltip.) This is the right endpoint of the horizontal line that you just drew.

FIGURE 4.22

Drawing a steam boiler with an endpoint running object snap.

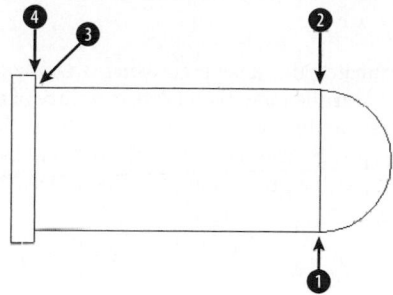

9. At the `Specify second point of arc or [Center/End]:` prompt, right-click (or press the down arrow if Dynamic Input is on) and choose End. Pick the endpoint at ❷, as shown in Figure 4.22.

10. At the `Specify center point of arc or [Angle/Direction/Radius]:` prompt, right-click (or press the down arrow if Dynamic Input is on) and choose Angle, and then type **180** ↵.

11. Start the LINE command and at the `Specify first point:` prompt, pick the endpoint at ❷, as shown in Figure 4.22.

12. Move the mouse to the left in the 180-degree direction, type **6** ↵, and end the LINE command.

13. Right-click the Snap Mode button on the status bar and choose Settings. Make sure that the Equal X and Y Spacing check box is selected. Click Grid Snap in the Snap Type section. Set the Snap X Spacing to 0.25. Check the Snap On check box. Click OK.

Note

If the boiler is too small, choose View tab ⇨ Navigate panel ⇨ Zoom drop-down list ⇨ All. ∎

14. Start the LINE command. At the `Specify first point:` prompt, place the cursor 0.25 units above ❸, as shown in Figure 4.22 (at 2,5.25). If you see the endpoint marker for the nearby line, press F3 to turn off the running Object Snap temporarily. Pick point 2,5.25.

15. At the `Specify next point or [Undo]:` prompt, pick point 2,1.75. (If necessary, right-click the coordinates and choose Absolute to get absolute coordinates.)

16. If Dynamic Input is not on, click the Dynamic Input button on the status bar. Follow the prompts:

```
Specify next point or [Undo]: Pick .5<180. (This means that you see a
    length tooltip of .5 and an angle tooltip of 180°.)
Specify next point or [Close/Undo]: Pick 3.5<90.
Specify next point or [Close/Undo]: (If you turned off Object Snap
    mode in Step 13, press F3 to turn it on again.) Pick the endpoint
    at ❹ in Figure 4.22.
Specify next point or [Close/Undo]: ↵
```

17. Save your drawing.

Note

Even if you have running object snaps, if you specify an object snap during a command, it overrides the running object snap. For example, having a running endpoint object snap does not mean that you can't use a midpoint object snap for any specific drawing command. ■

By default, if you type absolute or relative coordinates, they take precedence over any running object snaps. This lets you leave running object snaps on but override them with keyboard entry of typed coordinates whenever you want. In general, the default gives you the most control and flexibility. However, you can change this default to give running object snaps precedence. To change the default, choose Application Button ⇨ Options, click the User Preferences tab, and use the Priority for Coordinate Data Entry section of the dialog box.

Locating Points

Sometimes you need to locate a point that is not on an existing object. For example, you may need a point a certain distance and angle from an existing object. This section explains three techniques that enable you to locate points that are not on objects — object snap tracking, point filters, and the From feature.

Object snap tracking

The purpose of object snap tracking is to let you specify a point based on the object snaps of existing objects. Temporary tracking lines are drawn from points you specify, and guide you so that you can easily specify the point that you want. Use the Object Snap Tracking button on the status bar to turn object snap tracking on and off. Object snap tracking can easily handle all the following tasks and many more:

- You're drawing a line and have specified the start point. You want the endpoint to be exactly vertical to the endpoint of an existing line.

- You're drawing a circle inside a rectangle (which could be a hole inside a sheet-metal plate). You want the center of the circle to be exactly centered inside the rectangle, at the intersection of the midpoints of the rectangle's two sides.

- You want to start a line at the point where two existing lines would intersect if they were extended.

To start using object snap tracking, at least one object snap must be active. Turn on a running object snap, as explained in the previous sections. Then click the Object Snap Tracking button on the status bar.

With object snap tracking on, follow these steps:

1. Start a command that requires you to specify a point.

2. Place the cursor briefly over an object snap, such as the endpoint of a line, to temporarily *acquire* it. You can acquire more than one point. These acquired points are used to calculate the tracking paths. You see a small plus sign (+) over the object snap as confirmation, as shown in Figure 4.23.

FIGURE 4.23

When you pause over an object snap and then move the cursor slightly, you see a plus sign (+) at the acquired point to show that the point has been acquired and that you can now use it for object snap tracking.

Acquired point

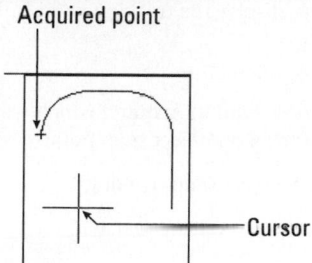

Cursor

3. Move the cursor away from the object snap toward your desired point. You see the temporary alignment paths as you move the cursor over available drawing paths, as shown in Figure 4.24. If Ortho Mode is on, you see only horizontal and vertical paths. If Polar mode is on, you see polar paths based on the polar angle settings, as explained earlier in this chapter.

FIGURE 4.24

With the endpoint object snap active and Ortho Mode on, AutoCAD displays temporary alignment paths based on the acquired point.

Acquired endpoint of existing arc

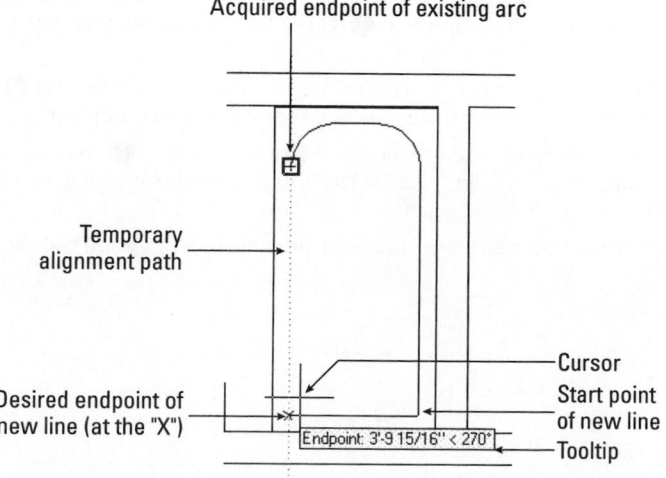

Temporary alignment path

Desired endpoint of new line (at the "X")

Endpoint: 3'-9 15/16" < 270°

Cursor

Start point of new line

Tooltip

4. When you see a tooltip and a small x, click it. You can now continue or complete the command, using this point.

After you acquire a point, you can clear it in any one of three ways:

- Move the cursor back over the point's plus sign.
- Click the Object Snap Tracking button on the status bar to turn it off.
- Start any new command.

You can customize the following features of object snap tracking on the Drafting tab of the Options dialog box (choose Application Button ⇨ Options):

- Uncheck Display Polar Tracking Vector to eliminate the tracking paths.
- Uncheck Display Full-Screen Tracking Vector to display the tracking paths only from the cursor to the object snap point.
- Uncheck Display AutoTrack Tooltip to eliminate the tooltips.
- In the Alignment Point Acquisition section, choose Shift to Acquire, which will require you to press Shift to acquire a point when the cursor is over an object snap point.

In the following exercise, you practice locating points with object snap tracking.

On the DVD

The drawing used in the following exercise on locating points with object snap tracking, ab04-c.dwg, **is in the** Drawings **folder on the DVD.** ■

STEPS: Locating Points with Object Snap Tracking

1. Open ab04-c.dwg from the DVD. Close any palettes that may be open.

2. Save the drawing as ab04-07.dwg in your AutoCAD Bible folder. This drawing is a section of a simple plan layout of an apartment. Set Endpoint and Midpoint running object snaps only. Make sure that Object Snap mode and Object Snap Tracking are on and that Polar Tracking and Ortho Mode are off.

3. Choose Home tab ⇨ Draw panel ⇨ Line to start the LINE command. At the Specify first point: prompt, pick the endpoint at ❶, as shown in Figure 4.25. Be sure to pick the endpoint itself, in order to acquire it.

4. At the Specify next point or [Undo]: prompt, pass the cursor over ❷. Move the cursor down a little, and you see the small plus sign showing that this endpoint has been acquired.

5. Move the cursor down until it is to the left of ❶ and vertical to ❷. When you see the tooltip (reading Endpoint: < 270°, Endpoint: < 180°) and the small x marking the intersection of the two points, click to end the line segment.

6. At the Specify next point or [Undo]: prompt, click at ❷ and end the LINE command.

FIGURE 4.25

The tub, door, and sink to be completed in this plan layout.

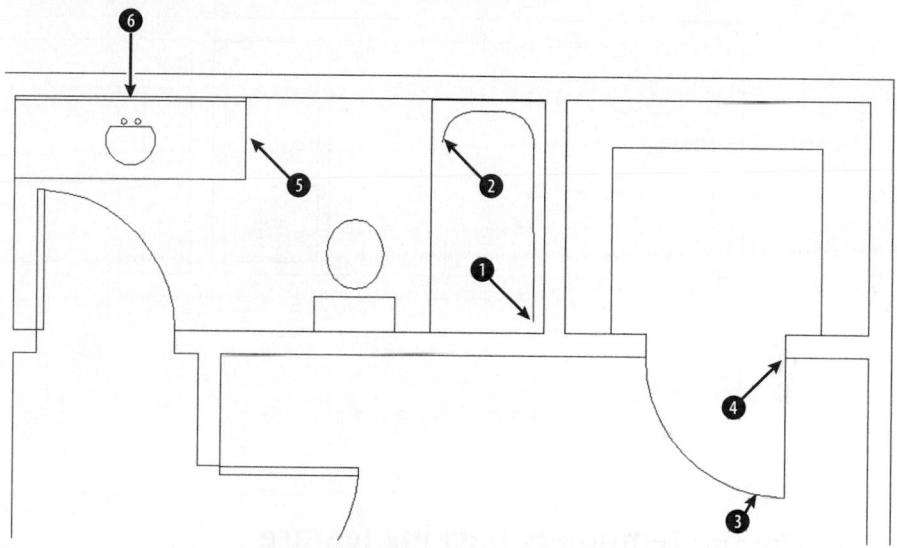

7. Start the LINE command again. At the `Specify first point:` prompt, pick the endpoint of the arc at ❸, as shown in Figure 4.25. If you're not sure that you found the right endpoint, press Tab until the arc is highlighted. Make sure that you've acquired the endpoint by clicking the endpoint itself or passing the crosshairs over it.

8. At the `Specify next point or [Undo]:` prompt, pass the cursor over ❹ until you see the small plus sign. Move the cursor slightly to the left until you see the tooltip (reading Endpoint: < 90°, Endpoint: < 180°) and click.

9. At the `Specify next point or [Undo]:` prompt, pick the endpoint at ❹ and end the LINE command.

10. Choose Home tab ⇨ Draw panel ⇨ Circle to start the CIRCLE command. At the `Specify center point for circle or [3P/2P/Ttr (tan tan radius)]:` prompt, pass the cursor over ❺ and then over ❻ to acquire both midpoints.

11. Move the cursor to the middle of the sink, where lines from both midpoints would intersect until you see the tooltip (reading Midpoint: < 270°, Midpoint: < 180°) and click.

12. At the `Specify radius of circle or [Diameter]:` prompt, type 7.5 ↵ to complete the sink.

13. Save your drawing. It should look like Figure 4.26.

FIGURE 4.26

The completed drawing.

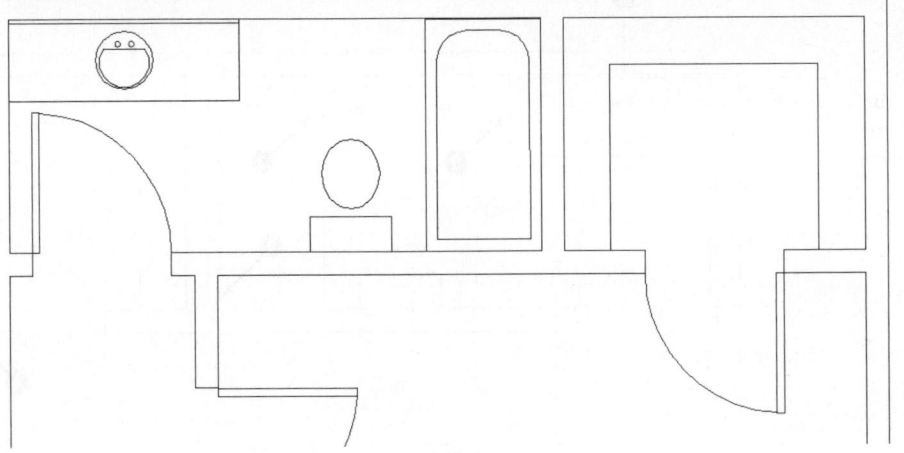

Using the temporary tracking feature

The temporary tracking feature is similar to object snap tracking, but limits you to horizontal and vertical directions. Follow these steps:

1. Start a command.

2. At a prompt to specify a point, enter **tracking** ↵ (or **tk** ↵) at the command prompt.

3. At the First tracking point: prompt, specify a point (usually using object snaps) that is horizontal or vertical to the final point that you want to specify.

4. Immediately move the cursor horizontally or vertically toward the final point that you want to specify. You see a rubber-band line.

5. At the Next point: prompt, move the cursor from the rubber-band line to specify a second point that is also vertical or horizontal to the final point.

6. Press Enter to end tracking and continue the command.

The cursor moves to the intersection of the vertical and horizontal rubber-band lines. You can now continue your command.

Point filters

Point filters enable you to specify a coordinate by using the X coordinate of one existing object snap and the Y coordinate of another. You construct an X,Y coordinate based on coordinates of existing objects. If this sounds complicated, it is. Object snap tracking should mostly eliminate the need to go back to the old point filter way of doing things. (Point filters have been around for a long time.)

Here's how to use point filters:

1. Start a command to draw an object.

2. To specify a coordinate, enter **.x** or **.y** ↵ on the command line. You can also find point filters on the Object Snap shortcut menu (Shift+right-click).

3. The prompt requests a point. Generally, you specify the point by using an object snap.

4. The prompt requests the other coordinate value, which you generally provide by using an object snap. (If you're working in 2D, ignore the request for a Z coordinate.)

5. Continue your command.

Tip

You don't need to use existing coordinates for both the X and Y portions of the coordinate. For example, you can construct an X,Y coordinate by using the Y coordinate of an existing line and picking the X coordinate anywhere on the screen. ■

From feature

The From feature enables you to create a new object starting at a known distance and direction from an existing object. It's like creating one or more invisible lines between the existing object and the new object, helping you to start the new object in the proper place. Use the From feature when the point you need to specify is a known X,Y distance from an object snap but not on any object snap itself. Here's how to use the From feature:

1. Start a command to draw an object, such as LINE.

2. Press Shift+right-click, and choose From on the shortcut menu. You can also enter **from** ↵ on the command line or in the Dynamic Input tooltip.

3. The prompt requests a base point, which you usually provide by using an object snap, such as an endpoint.

4. The prompt requests an Offset, which you provide by using relative or polar coordinates. You can type coordinates or look at the coordinates in the Dynamic Input tooltip or on the status bar and click when you see what you want.

Note

When you specify the offset for the From feature, you need to use the @ symbol to indicate relative coordinates, even if Dynamic Input is set to the default of relative coordinates. The Dynamic Input relative coordinate's setting only applies to the second coordinate that you enter. For example, if you are drawing a line, the first coordinate you enter is considered absolute, and subsequent coordinates are considered relative. ■

5. Continue the command you started (in Step 1).

In the following exercise, you practice using the From feature.

On the DVD

The drawing used in the following exercise on using the From feature, ab04-06.dwg, is in the Results folder on the DVD. ■

STEPS: Using the From Feature

1. Open ab04-06.dwg, which you created in an earlier exercise. If you did not do the previous exercise, open the drawing from the Results folder of the DVD. Close any palettes that may be open. Make sure Ortho Mode is on and Snap mode is off. Object Snap should be on. Set a running object snap for Endpoint.

2. Save the drawing as ab04-08.dwg in your AutoCAD Bible folder.

3. Choose Home tab ⇨ Draw panel ⇨ Line to start the LINE command.

4. From the Object Snap shortcut menu, choose From.

5. The prompt asks you for a base point. Pick the endpoint at ❶, as shown in Figure 4.27.

Using the From feature to complete the steam boiler.

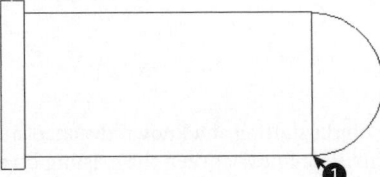

6. At the <Offset>: prompt, type @–1,0.5 ↵.

7. You are now ready to continue the line at the Specify next point or [Undo]: prompt. Press F3 to turn off Object Snap mode. Move the cursor in the 90-degree direction and type 2 ↵.

8. Move the mouse in the 180-degree direction and type 1 ↵.

9. Move the mouse in the 270-degree direction and type 2 ↵.

10. Right-click and choose Close from the shortcut menu to close the rectangle and end the LINE command.

11. Save your drawing. It should look like Figure 4.28.

The completed steam boiler.

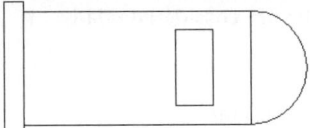

Summary

This chapter covers a great deal about specifying coordinates. These skills form the basis for all your future work with AutoCAD and AutoCAD LT. You read about:

- The X,Y coordinate system
- Using Dynamic Input
- Using absolute Cartesian coordinates
- When and how to use relative Cartesian coordinates
- Absolute and relative polar coordinates
- Direct distance entry
- The orthogonal (Ortho) mode
- Using polar tracking
- Controlling the display of coordinates on the status bar
- Grid and PolarSnap settings
- Using the visible grid
- Using object snaps to specify geometric points on objects
- Running object snaps and turning Object Snap mode on and off
- Temporarily overriding coordinate settings
- Using object snap tracking to locate points
- Using point filters to locate points
- The From feature for locating points not on an object

The next chapter introduces you to the basics of setting up a drawing.

Setting Up a Drawing

O ften, the first step after you start a new drawing is to set its size and unit type. These and other setup options are discussed in this chapter. The entire process of setting up a drawing is essential for ensuring accurate results. You can save most of these settings in a template to avoid having to re-create them each time you start a new drawing.

IN THIS CHAPTER

Determining the unit type

Setting the drawing size

Working with drawing scales

Adding a titleblock

Understanding system variables

Automating setup

Choosing Unit Types

One of the first tasks in setting up a drawing is to choose the unit type. Units define how objects are measured. You can save the unit type in a template.

Note

The Initial Setup dialog box allows you to specify your industry and a template. These can affect your units. For example, if you choose the Architecture option on Page 1 and a template suitable for your industry on the last page, whenever you start a new drawing, your units will be architectural. You can change these settings at any time by choosing Application Button ➪ Options and clicking the User Preferences tab. Then click the Initial Setup button to open the dialog box. ■

The coordinates that you use in AutoCAD or AutoCAD LT are measured in units that can represent any real-world measurement, such as inches or millimeters. A surveyor or city planner might even use miles or kilometers as the base unit. However, different disciplines have customs that express units differently, and you should use the unit type appropriate for the type of drawing you're creating. This ensures that everyone involved understands the drawing. AutoCAD and AutoCAD LT offer five types of units, as shown in Table 5.1. The sample measurement column shows how a line 32.5 units long would be displayed in the various unit types.

TABLE 5.1

Unit Types

Unit Type	Sample Measurement	Description
Decimal	32.50	Number of units, partial units in decimals
Engineering	2'–8.50"	Feet and inches, partial inches in decimals
Architectural	2'–8 1/2"	Feet and inches, partial inches in fractions
Fractional	32 1/2	Number of units, partial units in fractions
Scientific	3.25E+01	Base number + exponent

Notice how the engineering and architectural units translate a line of 32.5 units into feet and inches. Engineering and architectural units assume a unit of 1 inch, unlike the other unit types, which can represent any measurement.

The unit type affects how coordinates are shown on the status bar and how information about objects is listed. You generally input coordinates by using the type of units you've chosen, although in some cases you can input coordinates in another unit type.

Note
If you're using engineering or architectural units, AutoCAD and AutoCAD LT display partial inches differently than the format you must use to type them in. You must type coordinates without any spaces, because a space is equivalent to pressing Enter, and that ends your input. Use a hyphen between whole and partial inches, for example, 3'2-1/2". (You can omit the " after the inches because inches are assumed in engineering and architectural units if no symbol follows a number.) However, this appears on the status line as 3'-2 1/2". This can be confusing because the hyphen is in a different place, and you see a space between the whole and partial inches. ■

Setting the drawing units
When you know the units you want to use, you set them in the Drawing Units dialog box. To set the units, choose Application Button ➪ Drawing Utilities ➪ Units, to open the Drawing Units dialog box, as shown in Figure 5.1. The left side of the Drawing Units dialog box enables you to choose which unit type you want to use. In the Precision box in the Length section, click the arrow and a list of precision options drops down. Click the one you want.

Caution
AutoCAD and AutoCAD LT round off measurements to the nearest precision value you choose. Say that you choose a precision of two decimal places, using decimal units. You want to draw a line so that it is 3.25 units long, but when you type the coordinate, by accident you press the 4 key at the end, resulting in a line 3.254 units long. This line is displayed as 3.25 units long, making it difficult for you to spot the error. Therefore, setting a higher precision than you need to show is a good idea. ■

Setting the angle type
As with units, your choice of angle type depends on your profession and work environment. Decimal Degrees is the default. Table 5.2 lists the types of angles.

FIGURE 5.1

The Drawing Units dialog box.

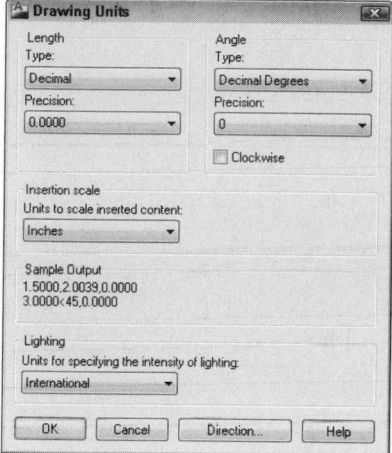

TABLE 5.2

Angle Types

Angle Type Name	Sample Measurement	Description
Decimal Degrees	32.5	Degrees, partial degrees in decimals
Deg/Min/Sec	32°30'0"	Degrees, minutes, and seconds
Grads (gradians)	36.1111g	Gradians
Radians	0.5672r	Radians
Surveyor	N 57d30' E	Surveyor (directional) units

Note

A minute is ¹⁄₆₀ degree and a second is ¹⁄₆₀ minute. Gradians and radians are simply alternate ways of measuring angles. A gradian is a metric measurement equal to ¹⁄₁₀₀ of a right angle. Radians measure an angle by placing a length, equal to the radius, along the circle's circumference. Radians range from 0 to $2 \times \Pi$ rather than from 0 to 360 as degrees do. A radian is approximately 57.30 degrees. Surveyor units measure angles in directions, starting with north or south and adding an angle in degrees/minutes/seconds format that shows how far the angle is from north or south and in which direction (east or west). ■

To set the angle type, choose the option you want from the Type drop-down list of the Angle section of the Drawing Units dialog box (shown in Figure 5.1).

Cross-Reference

Changing these angle settings does not automatically change the way your dimension annotations appear. Use the Dimension Style Manager, which is discussed in Chapter 15, to change dimensions. ■

Setting the angle measure and direction

By convention, degrees increase in a counterclockwise direction, and you measure angles so that 0 degrees starts to the right, also called the East direction. To change the angle direction, click Clockwise in the Drawing Units dialog box. To change the direction of 0 degrees, click Direction to open the Direction Control dialog box, as shown in Figure 5.2.

FIGURE 5.2

The Direction Control dialog box.

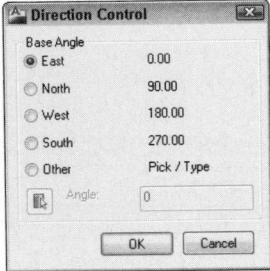

Here you can choose to have 0 degrees start in a direction other than East. You can also choose Other and type any other angle or click the Pick an Angle button to pick two points on your screen that specify an angle. Click OK to close the Direction Control dialog box. Click OK to close the Drawing Units dialog box.

Note

Changing the angle direction affects what happens when you input angles and what you see in the coordinate display. It does not change the absolute coordinates, which are set according to the User Coordinate System (UCS). Chapter 8 covers using and customizing UCSs. ∎

If you are using Dynamic Input, the angle that you see in the Dynamic Input tooltip never goes above 180°. This angle in the tooltip represents the angle to your current point and goes from 0° to 180° in both the clockwise and counterclockwise directions.

Cross-Reference

At the bottom of the Drawing Units dialog box, you can choose units for lighting. See my discussion of lighting in Chapter 25 for more information. ∎

STEPS: Setting Drawing Units

1. Begin a new drawing by using the acad.dwt or acadlt.dwt template. Close any palettes that may be open. If Dynamic Input isn't on, click the Dynamic Input button on the status bar. This exercise assumes that you have input of coordinates set to relative coordinates, the default setting. (For more information, see Chapter 4.)

2. Save the drawing as ab05-01.dwg in your AutoCAD Bible folder.

3. Choose Application Button ➪ Drawing Utilities ➪ Units, to open the Drawing Units dialog box.

4. In the Length section, choose Architectural.

5. Click the arrow to the right of the Precision drop-down list in the Length section. Choose 0'-0 1/8".

6. In the Angle section, choose Deg/Min/Sec.

7. In the Precision box, choose 0d00'.

8. In the Units to Scale Inserted Content drop-down list, set the units to Inches.

9. Click OK.

10. Choose Home tab ⇨ Draw panel ⇨ Line to start the LINE command. Follow the prompts:

```
Specify first point: 2,2 ↵
Specify next point or [Undo]: 1'<0 ↵
Specify next point or [Undo]: 6-3/4<153 ↵
Specify next point or [Close/Undo]: Right-click and choose Close.
```

11. Choose View tab ⇨ Navigate panel ⇨ Zoom drop-down list ⇨ All to zoom to the entire drawing. Save your drawing. If you're continuing through the chapter, keep it open.

Note

You would not actually use Deg/Min/Sec for angles in an architectural drawing, but the exercise gives you the opportunity to set the angular units. ■

Drawing Limits

You can specify the area of your drawing, also called the *limits*. The drawing limits are the outer edges of the drawing, specified in X,Y units. You need to set only the width and length of the drawing. Together, these two measurements create an invisible bounding rectangle for your drawing.

Almost universally, the lower-left limit is 0,0, which is the default. Therefore, the upper-right corner really defines the drawing size. Remember that you typically draw at life size (full scale). Therefore, the size of your drawing should be equal to the size of the outer extents of what you're drawing, plus a margin for a titleblock (if you plan to add one), annotation, and dimensioning. If you want to show more than one view of an object, as is common in both architectural and mechanical drawings, you need to take this into account.

To decide on the upper-right corner limits (the width and length) for your drawing, you need to consider what the drawing units mean for you. Generally, the smallest commonly used unit is used, often inches or millimeters. Therefore, if you're drawing a plan view of a house that is approximately 40 feet across (in the X direction) by 30 feet deep (in the Y direction), this translates to a top-right corner of 480,360. Adding room for a titleblock brings you to about 500,380.

Cross-Reference

In Chapter 17, I explain how you can put the titleblock on a layout. A layout simulates the sheet of paper that you will use to plot the drawing. If you use a layout, you don't need to leave room for the titleblock when you set the limits. ■

The limits define an artificial and invisible boundary to your drawing. However, you can draw outside the limits. The limits affect the size of the grid, when displayed. (See Chapter 4 for a discussion of the grid.) The ZOOM command with the All option also uses the limits, but only if no objects are outside the limits. (See Chapter 8 for a discussion of the ZOOM command.)

To set the drawing limits, type **limits** ↵ on the command line, to start the LIMITS command. Press Enter to accept the lower-left corner default of 0,0 that appears on the command line. Then type the upper-right corner coordinate that you want and press Enter.

Understanding Scales

You need to consider the fact that your drawing will most likely be plotted onto a standard paper (sheet) size. The standard orientation for drafting (and the default for most plotters) is *landscape* orientation, meaning that as you look at the drawing, the paper is wider than it is tall. Figure 5.3 shows an example. To scale a drawing onto a piece of paper in a pleasing manner requires a rectangular shape that somewhat resembles the proportions of standard paper sizes.

FIGURE 5.3

Drawings are usually oriented horizontally, as in this example.

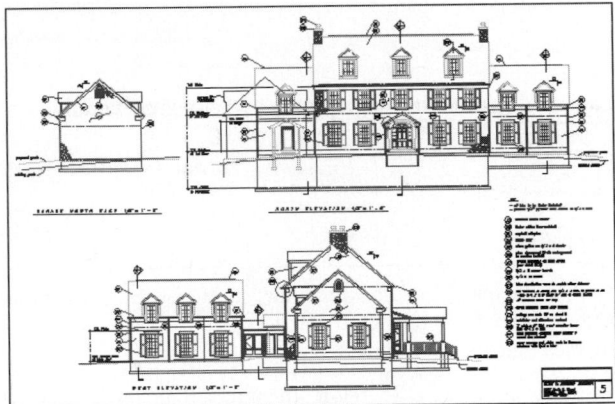

Thanks to Henry Dearborn, AIA, Fairfield, Iowa, for this drawing, which I have altered slightly.

In addition, although you specify the scale at plotting time, it helps to be aware at the outset of the scale you'll use when plotting your drawing. One important reason for establishing the scale at the beginning is to ensure that text, whether annotations or dimensions, is readable in its final plotted form. Applying a scale ensures that text remains a reasonable size even as the rest of the drawing is scaled up or down. Scale also affects linetypes that contain dots or dashes.

Some drawings are not scaled. Examples are electrical or electronic schematics, piping diagrams, and railroad schematics. These drawings are representations of electrical or electronic connections but do not resemble the actual physical object that will eventually be created from the drawing. These drawings can be any size as long as they are clear and organized.

Cross-Reference

You can lay out various views of your drawing on an imaginary piece of paper, a paper space layout, to prepare it for plotting. You can annotate on the layout to avoid having to scale these components. See Chapter 17 for more information on layouts and plotting. ■

When determining your scale to fit a drawing on a sheet of paper, be aware that a plotter cannot print on the entire sheet. A certain amount of the margin around the edge is not available for drawing. The plotter's manual can let you know the width of this unprintable margin. On average, you can assume a half-inch margin on each side; thus you should subtract 1 inch from both the length and width sheet measurements to determine the actual drawing space. Table 5.3 shows standard U.S. sheet sizes.

TABLE 5.3

Standard Paper Sheet Sizes in the United States (in inches)

Size	Width	Height	Size	Width	Height
A	11	8½	D	34	22
B	17	11	E	44	34
C	22	17			

Table 5.4 lists standard metric sheet sizes.

TABLE 5.4

Standard Metric Paper Sheet Sizes (in millimeters)

Size	Width	Height	Size	Width	Height
A4	297	210	A1	841	594
A3	420	297	A0	1,189	841
A2	594	420			

Working with scale formats

A scale is often indicated in the format *plotted size=actual size* or *plotted size:actual size*. Because you draw at actual size, the actual size is also the drawing size. For example, a scale of ¼"=1' means that ¼ inch on the drawing, when plotted out on a sheet of paper, represents 1 foot in actual life — and in the drawing. This is a typical architectural scale. A windowpane 1 foot wide would appear ¼-inch wide on paper.

From the scale, you can calculate the scale *factor*. You use the factor when you set the size for text (see Chapter 13) or for dimensions (see Chapter 15). To do this, the left side of the scale equation must equal 1, and the two numbers must be in the same measurement (for example, both in inches). This requires some simple math. For ¼"=1', you would calculate as follows:

¼"=1'

1"=4'   Both sides of the equation multiplied by 4

1"=48"   4' converted to 48"

Therefore, the scale factor is 48. This means that the paper plot is ¹⁄₄₈ of real size.

In mechanical drawing, you might draw a metal joint that is actually 4 inches long. To fit it on an 8½-x-11-inch sheet of paper, you could use a 2"=1" scale, which means that 2" on the paper drawing equals 1" in actual life and the drawing. Calculate the scale factor:

2"=1"

1"=½"

The scale factor is ½. This means that the paper plot is twice the real size.

Most professions use certain standard scales. Therefore, you do not usually have a choice to pick any scale you want, such as 1":27'. Instead, the conventions of your profession, client, or office dictate a choice of only a few scales. Some typical architectural scale factors are:

- 192: 1/16" = 1'
- 96: 1/8" = 1'
- 48: 1/4" = 1'
- 24: 1/2" = 1'
- 12: 1" = 1'

Civil engineering scales are somewhat different and range to larger sizes — a bridge is bigger than a house. Some typical scale factors are 120 (1" =10') and 240 (1" =20').

Metric scales can be used for any purpose. Example scale factors are 10000 (1mm = 10 meters), 5000 (1mm = 5 meters), 1000 (1 mm = 1 meter), or 100 (1cm = 1 meter).

Using annotative scales

You can assign an *annotative property* to certain objects so that they automatically resize to the proper scale when you lay out the drawing for plotting. The following types of objects can be annotative:

- Text (see Chapter 13)
- Dimensions and leaders (see Chapters 14 and 15)
- Hatches (see Chapter 16)
- Blocks and attributes (see Chapter 18)

You would especially use annotative scaling when you need to display your drawing at more than one scale. For example, you might display the entire drawing at one scale and a detail at another scale. (See Chapters 13, 14, 15, 16, 17, and 18 for more detailed information on annotative styles and objects.)

Using annotative objects avoids the necessity to manually figure out how large these objects need to be; when you scale them, they will be the proper size. For example, if your drawing scale will be 1:48, and you want your text to be ¼" high, then you would need to multiply the desired height of the text (¼") by the scale factor to get a text height of 12. However, by setting the annotative scale for the text to 1/4" = 1'-0", you can simply set the height of the text to ¼" and not worry about the calculations.

The procedure for creating annotative objects differs somewhat for each type of object, but the overall process is the same:

1. If necessary, create an annotative style and make it current. Annotative text, dimensions, and multileaders require an annotative style.

2. Decide on the scales that you will use for each object. For example, you might have two text objects each at a different scale, or one text object that you need to display at two different scales.

 3. If you want each text object to have a different scale, turn off the ANNOAUTOSCALE system variable. This system variable, when on, automatically adds scales to annotative objects as you add annotative scales; the result is that each object has more than one scale. To turn ANNOAUTOSCALE off, click the icon on the right side of the status bar to the right of the Annotation Scale pop-up list. When on, there's a yellow lightning bolt; when off, the lightning bolt is gray.

4. Set the annotation scale for the first object. To do so, click the Annotation Scale button at the right side of the status bar to display the scale list and choose the scale you want. For example, choose 1/4" = 1'-0" if you plan to display the text at the 1/4" = 1'-0" scale.

5. Create the object.

6. When you're ready to plot, you can set the desired annotative scale, and plot. You can also create viewports and set their scale. See Chapter 17 for details and an exercise using annotative objects.

If you want one object to have more than one scale, you can add an annotative scale to it. Follow these steps:

1. Select the object and right-click in the drawing area.

2. Choose Annotative Object Scale ➪ Add/Delete Scales to open the Annotation Object Scale dialog box, as shown in Figure 5.4.

The Annotation Object Scale dialog box enables you to add an annotation scale to an annotation object.

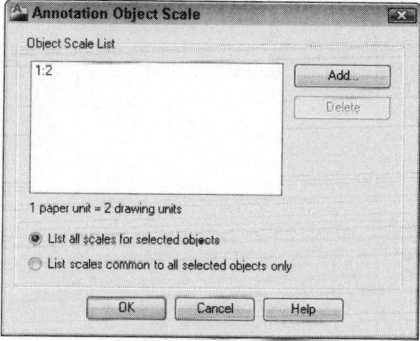

3. Click Add to display the Add Scales to Object dialog box, where you can choose one or more scales.

4. Click OK twice to close both dialog boxes.

You can also open the dialog box by displaying the Properties palette, clicking the Annotative Scale item, and clicking the Ellipsis button that appears.

 For each scale that you assign to an object, AutoCAD or AutoCAD LT automatically creates a representation of that object in an appropriate size. Therefore, you may have a text object shown at three sizes. At any time, you can view any single scale for an annotative object, or view all its scales. If you don't see all scales of an annotative object, click the Annotation Visibility button on the right side of the status bar. This button controls the ANNOALLVISIBLE system variable. By default, it is on, displaying all scales. When you turn it off, you see only the text for the current annotative scale. To immediately plot, you would turn off this system variable so that you plot only the text for the current annotative scale.

Customizing the scale list

You generally choose a scale during the process of laying out a drawing. AutoCAD and AutoCAD LT have a list of scales from which you can choose. You can find this list in several places (which I discuss throughout the book):

- On the Annotation Scale list on the status bar, as mentioned earlier
- In the Add Scales to Object dialog box, also mentioned earlier
- In the VP Scale list of the status bar, when you select a viewport (see Chapter 17)
- In the Plot Scale section of the Page Setup dialog box (see Chapter 17)
- In the Plot Scale section of the Plot dialog box (see Chapter 17)
- In the Standard scale item of the Properties palette when a viewport is selected (see Chapter 17)
- In the Sheet Set Manager (AutoCAD only), when placing a view on a layout (see Chapter 26)

You might use unusual scales in your office or want a list that includes only the scales that you use. You can customize the scale list for this purpose. To customize the scale list, choose Annotate tab ➪ Annotation Scaling panel ➪ Scale List. The Edit Drawing Scales dialog box opens, as shown in Figure 5.5.

FIGURE 5.5

Use the Edit Drawing Scales dialog box to create your own custom scales.

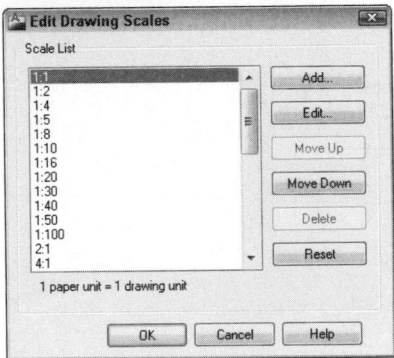

To add a new scale, click Add. In the Add Scale dialog box, name the scale. The name is what will show on the list. Then define the scale by completing the Paper Units and Drawing Units text boxes. For example, to add a 1:12 scale, you would name the scale 1:12, set the Paper Units to 1 and the Drawing Units to 12.

To delete scales that you don't use, select the scale and click Delete. You can also edit existing scales (select the scale and click Edit), move them up or down in the order of the list, and reset the list (click Reset) to its original status. Click OK when you're done.

New Feature

AutoCAD 2011 stores a default scale list in the Windows registry. You can customize this list by going to Application Button ➪ Options, choosing the User Preferences tab, and clicking the Default Scale List button. This list will appear in all drawings. However, you can still use the Edit Drawing Scales dialog box (see Figure 5.5) to edit the scale list within any drawing file, so this list can vary with the drawing. To reset a scale list in a drawing to match the scale list in the Windows registry, click the Reset button in the Edit Drawing Scales dialog box. ■

Deciding on a scale and sheet size

As soon as you know the size of your drawing and the scale appropriate for your situation, you need to consider the sheet size of the paper on which you want to plot. Again, you often find that certain factors limit your choices. Your plotter or printer may be limited to certain sheet sizes. The conventions used in your discipline or working environment also affect your decision. You may be working on a series of drawings that are all to be plotted on the same size sheet of paper.

As an example, the architectural drawing in Figure 5.3 is 175 feet wide by 120 feet high. The two most typical scales for a drawing of a house are ¼"=1' and ⅛"=1'. On a small plotter, you might have a choice of sheet sizes A, B, or C. The following steps show the calculations you need to do in order to decide on a scale, obtain the scale factor, and determine the appropriate sheet size.

In this exercise, you practice determining the scale and sheet size. You need only a sheet of paper and a pencil. Use Figure 5.3 as a reference.

STEPS: Determining the Scale and Sheet Size

1. To calculate the plotted size of the drawing at ¼"=1', you can start with the width, which is 175'. Take one-quarter of 175 to get the width of the drawing in inches, which is 43¾".

2. Take one quarter of the height, 120', to get the height of the drawing in inches, which is 30".

3. A C-size sheet (see Table 5-3) is 22"×17", which is too small for a 43¾"×30" drawing.

4. Recalculate the drawing at ⅛"=1'. Take one-eighth of 175 to get 21⅞. Take one-eighth of 120 to get 15".

5. The actual drawing space (minus the margins the printer requires) on a C-size sheet is about 21"×16". The height of the drawing at this scale is adequate, but the width is ⅞" too long. Therefore, the best option is to simply make the drawing ⅞" narrower because the drawing has some extra room. This lets you fit the drawing on a C-size sheet.

6. To calculate the scale factor of a ⅛"=1' scale, multiply 1' by 8 to get 8' and convert it to inches, which is 96 (8×12).

Rearranging the views, dimensions, and text on a drawing to fit a standard scale factor and sheet size is a typical task. There is no actual setup step for setting the drawing scale, but you use it when you insert text or dimensions and when you plot the drawing.

Creating a Titleblock

A *titleblock* is a rectangle that includes spaces for the drawing title, company name, drafter name, and so on. It generally comes with a border that bounds your drawing. Many drawings require titleblocks. You can insert an existing titleblock in two ways:

- When creating a new drawing, choose Application Button ➪ New to open the Select Template dialog box. Choose one of the templates that include a titleblock, either one that comes with AutoCAD or a custom template that you created. For example, `Tutorial-iArch.dwt` includes a titleblock and border that fit on a D-size sheet. The titleblock and border appear on a layout tab. (Chapter 17 covers layouts.)

- After you open a drawing, you can insert a drawing of a titleblock into it. Choose Home tab ➪ Block panel ➪ Insert. (Chapter 18 covers blocks.) In the Insert dialog box, type the name of the drawing or block, or click Browse to find it. To insert the file or block at 0,0 with no scaling or rotation, uncheck all the Specify On-Screen check boxes. Check Explode if you expect to edit text included as part of the titleblock. Click OK.

To find the location of the templates, choose Application Button ⇨ Options, and click the Files tab. Double-click Template Settings and then double-click Drawing Template File Location. You see the path to the location displayed. (The path is very long!) This folder may be hidden in Windows Explorer. For instructions on displaying hidden folders, go to Windows Help and type **hidden folders** in the search box.

Cross-Reference

As explained in Chapter 2, you can create your own titleblock, make a template from it, and then start a drawing based on that template. ∎

Specifying Common Setup Options

A few other items are generally set up in advance and are included in a template. Other chapters of this book cover the following:

- **Layers** (covered in Chapter 11) enable you to organize your drawing into meaningful groups. In an architectural drawing, for example, you might create layers for walls, doors, and electrical fixtures.
- **Text styles** (covered in Chapter 13) enable you to format the font and other text characteristics.
- **Table styles** (covered in Chapter 13) format tables.
- **Multileader styles** (covered in Chapter 14) create styles for multileaders.
- **Dimension styles** (covered in Chapter 15) format the dimensions that measure your objects.

System variables

When you change AutoCAD or AutoCAD LT settings, such as the unit type, angle type, drawing limits, blip marks, snap mode (on or off), grid mode, or ortho mode, you are actually changing *system variables*. These are settings that are stored in each drawing or in the Windows registry (which stores settings that apply to all drawings). Usually, you don't need to pay any direct attention to them, but they're the nuts and bolts behind the dialog boxes that you use to change the settings. When you start customizing AutoCAD, you need to learn about them because programming code and script files (macros) cannot access dialog boxes. Also, a few system variables are accessible only by typing them on the command line. Some system variables store information about a drawing or its environment, such as the drawing name and path. These are *read-only*, meaning that you cannot change them. They are often used in AutoLISP programs (AutoCAD only).

Information about each system variable, where it is stored, its default, and whether it is read-only is in the Help system. Press F1 (with no command active) and click Command Reference on the Home page. Then click System Variables. In the Options dialog box (Application Button ⇨ Options), system variables that are stored in a drawing have a drawing file icon next to them. You can type system variables on the command line, just like regular commands. The Express Tools (AutoCAD only) contain an editor (choose Express Tools tab ⇨ Tools panel ⇨ System Variable Editor [the SYSVDLG command]) that enables you to view and edit system variable values in a dialog box; the command also provides helpful supporting information.

If you know that you'll be using snap, grid, and ortho modes (covered in Chapter 4) a lot in certain drawings, and you know the suitable settings for snap and grid, you can set these and save them in a template because these settings are saved with the drawing. In other cases, you might want to leave them off and turn them on only when you need them.

Many settings, such as running object snaps, the type of snap (grid or polar), and the polar distance, are saved in the Windows registry, not in your drawing. As a result, when you open AutoCAD or AutoCAD LT, they're automatically set to the same setting that you had when you last closed the program, regardless of the setting in the drawing. Therefore, you cannot save these settings in a template.

On the DVD

The drawing used in the following exercise on setting drawing aids and creating a template, ab05-01.dwg, is in the Results folder on the DVD. ■

STEPS: Setting Drawing Aids and Creating a Template

1. If you did the exercise on setting drawing units, use that drawing; otherwise, open ab05-01. dwg from the Results folder of the DVD.

2. Save the drawing as ab05-02.dwg in your AutoCAD Bible folder.

3. Right-click the Snap Mode button on the status bar, and choose Settings.

4. On the Snap and Grid tab, the snap spacing is set to ½". In the Grid Spacing section, change the X and Y spacing to 1". Make sure that the Snap Type is set to Grid Snap and Rectangular Snap. Click OK.

5. Click Snap Mode and Grid Display on the status bar to turn them on. Make sure that Object Snap Mode is turned off.

6. Choose Application Button ➪ Drawing Utilities ➪ Units. Change the Angle Type back to Decimal Degrees (if necessary). Click OK.

7. Using the coordinate display as your guide, start the LINE command and draw line segments from 2.5, 1.5 to .5<270 to 11<0 to .5<90. End the LINE command.

8. Restart the LINE command. Again use the coordinate display to draw line segments from 2,2 to .5<270 to 12<0 to .5<90. End the LINE command.

9. Save your drawing. It should look like Figure 5.6. Notice how the grid and snap settings facilitate the drawing process.

The architectural units create a different drawing experience than decimal units would. Setting up a drawing creates a drawing environment suited to your work needs.

10. Choose Application Button ➪ Save As. In the Save Drawing As dialog box, click the Files of Type drop-down list and choose AutoCAD Drawing Template (*.dwt) or AutoCAD LT Drawing Template (*.dwt). Notice that you're automatically in the Template folder.

11. In the File Name text box, change the name to archroof.dwt. Click Save.

12. In the Template Options dialog box, type **Arch units, 16,10 limits, snap & grid** and click OK. The Measurement drop-down list should be set to English.

FIGURE 5.6

The final architectural drawing.

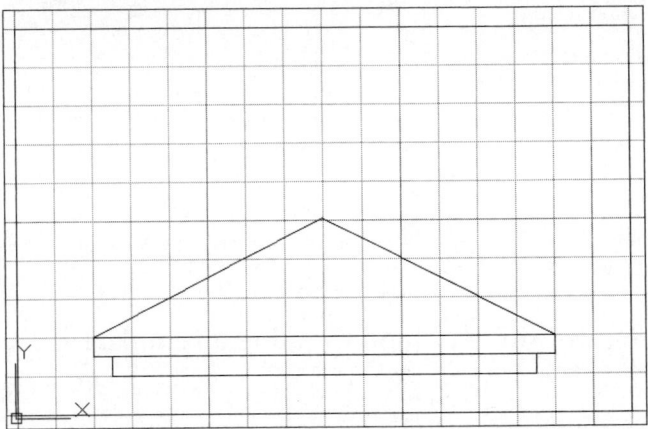

13. Choose Application Button ⇨ New. Choose the `archroof` template and click Open. A new drawing is created based on the template.

14. Move the cursor around and look at the coordinate display to confirm that the grid is set to 1", although the snap is set to ½".

    Do not save this new drawing.

Customizing with the MVSETUP Command and Setup Wizards

The MVSETUP command is used in two different ways: to set up a drawing and to create viewports for paper space layouts (covered in Chapter 17). This command does not exist in AutoCAD LT.

MVSETUP provides a command-line routine to walk you through some of the basic setup functions discussed in this chapter. You can use MVSETUP when you start to customize AutoCAD to set up a drawing from a script file or AutoLISP program (topics covered in Parts VI and VII of this book). To use MVSETUP, type **mvsetup** ⏎ on the command line. AutoCAD responds with the following prompt:

```
Enable paper space? [No/Yes] <Y>:
```

Type **n** ⏎ to use MVSETUP without entering paper space.

The next prompt lets you enter the units type:

```
Enter units type [Scientific/Decimal/Engineering/Architectural/
    Metric]:
```

Choose the option you want. Then AutoCAD displays a list of scale factors appropriate to the units option you chose. (To see them all, you may have to press F2 to open the AutoCAD Text Window.) At the `Enter the scale factor:` prompt, type in a numeric scale factor.

Finally, AutoCAD prompts you to set the drawing limits with the following two prompts:

```
Enter the paper width:
Enter the paper height:
```

After each prompt, enter a number based on the size of the paper on which you plan to plot. AutoCAD draws a rectangle of the size that you indicated for the drawing limits.

Note

There are two wizards to help you set up a drawing. You need to activate the Startup dialog box to find them. To do so, enter startup ⏎ on the command line and then enter 1 ⏎. Then start a new drawing; the Startup dialog box appears. Click the Use a Wizard button. You can choose Quick Setup for fewer options or Advanced Setup for more options. Click OK and follow the prompts of the wizard. ■

Summary

This chapter explained setting up a drawing so that it behaves the way you want it to. You read about:

- Setting the unit type
- Setting the angle type, measurement, and direction
- Drawing limits
- Using scales and calculating a scale factor
- Setting drawing aids and creating a template that includes the settings that you want
- Using MVSETUP (AutoCAD only) or the setup wizards to set up your drawing

This chapter ends Part I, "AutoCAD and AutoCAD LT Basics." Now that you know the basics, you can go on to Part II, "Drawing in Two Dimensions." The next chapter covers drawing simple lines, polygons, rectangles, and infinite construction lines.

Part II

Drawing in Two Dimensions

Now that you have the basics under your belt, it's time to draw! This part contains all the basic information you need for two-dimensional drawing and design in AutoCAD and AutoCAD LT — which is quite a lot of content!

Part II starts with a discussion on drawing simple lines and curves. Then I explain how you can control the display of your drawings. Chapters 9 and 10 cover all the ways to edit an existing drawing. Chapter 11 is about organizing your drawing with layers. You can also find chapters on creating text, drawing dimensions, and creating dimension styles. Separate chapters cover how you can obtain information from your drawing and how to draw complex objects. Part II winds down with a chapter on plotting and printing.

Drawing Simple Lines

ines are the most commonly drawn object in 2D AutoCAD drawings — you'll use the LINE command a lot! Straight edges just happen to be very common in the real world. Related commands for drawing rectangles, polygons, and construction lines are also important, so you should have all these commands in your arsenal. This chapter explains how to draw all these types of objects.

Using the LINE Command

The LINE command draws straight line segments. Part I includes several exercises in which you draw lines. However, the LINE command has several options, and you can still learn a few tricks of the trade by focusing on the LINE command itself.

To draw a line, choose Home tab ⇨ Draw panel ⇨ Line. At the `Specify first point:` prompt, specify any point. Continue to specify points until you're finished. Press Enter to end the command. You can also right-click and choose Enter from the shortcut menu. The LINE command assumes that you will continue to use it over and over. For this reason, the command continues to prompt you until you press Enter.

If you continue to draw line segments, the subsequent prompts are different. Here's how to use them:

- The command displays the `Specify next point or [Undo]:` prompt for the next two segments. Right-click (or press the down-arrow key if you have Dynamic Input turned on) and choose Undo (or type **u** ↵) to undo only the last line segment that you created — without exiting the LINE command.

- After creating at least two line segments, the command displays the `Specify next point or [Close/Undo]:` prompt. Right-click (or press the down-arrow key if you have Dynamic Input on) and choose Close (or type **c** ↵) to automatically draw a line from the endpoint of the last segment to the original start point, thereby creating a closed figure. You can continue to use the Undo option as well.

If you previously drew a line, press Enter at the `Specify first point:` prompt to start the line at the endpoint of the last line. If you most recently drew an arc, press Enter to start the line at the endpoint of the arc and draw it tangent to the arc.

STEPS: Using the LINE Command

1. Start a new drawing by using the `acad.dwt` or `acadlt.dwt` template.

Note

This exercise assumes that you have Dynamic Input on (click the Dynamic Input button on the status bar to turn it on, if necessary) and that you are using the default settings of polar format and relative coordinates. Make sure that the 2D Drafting & Annotation workspace is chosen from the Workspace drop-down list on the Quick Access Toolbar. Close any palettes that may be open. ■

2. Save the drawing in your `AutoCAD Bible` folder as `ab06-01.dwg`.

3. Choose Home tab ➪ Draw panel ➪ Line to start the LINE command. At the `Specify first point:` prompt, choose any point in the center of your drawing.

4. Click the Ortho Mode button on the status bar.

5. Move the cursor to the right in the 0-degree direction and type **.4667** ↵.

6. Type **.7341<129** ↵. (Instead of typing the < symbol, you can press the Tab button to move to the Dynamic Input angle tooltip.)

7. Move the cursor to the right in the 0-degree direction and type **.4668** ↵.

8. Assume that this was a mistake. Type **u** ↵.

9. The `Specify next point or [Close/Undo]:` prompt reappears. With the cursor still in the 0-degree direction, type **.4667** ↵.

10. Type **c** ↵ to close the figure. This ends the LINE command.

11. Start the LINE command again.

12. At the `Specify first point:` prompt, press Enter. The line starts at the previous endpoint.

13. Type **.8071<270** ↵ and press Enter to end the LINE command.

14. Save your drawing. It should look like Figure 6.1.

FIGURE 6.1

The completed gate valve symbol.

Cross-Reference

Other aspects of lines are covered elsewhere in this book. Chapter 11 explains how to draw dashed and dotted lines. Chapter 16 explains how to create polylines, which combine line segments and arcs into one object. Chapter 16 also covers multilines and dlines — sets of parallel lines that you draw all at once. Chapter 21 discusses how to draw 3D lines and polylines. ■

Drawing Rectangles

The RECTANG command draws rectangles. Rectangles are used in all disciplines. The RECTANG command has a number of options that specify how the rectangle appears and how you define the rectangle's dimensions.

 To draw a rectangle, choose Home tab ⇨ Draw panel ⇨ Rectangle. The first prompt is as follows:

```
Specify first corner point or [Chamfer/Elevation/Fillet/Thickness/
    Width]:
```

Select one of the options. If you don't want to use any of the options, just specify one corner of the rectangle, using any method of specifying a coordinate.

Cross-Reference

You can chamfer and fillet the corners as you create the rectangle. (Chapter 10 covers chamfering and filleting.) You can specify a width for the rectangle's line (see Chapter 16). You can also create a 3D box by using the elevation and thickness options (see Chapter 21). The RECTANG command creates a polyline, meaning that all four sides of the rectangle are one object, rather than four separate line objects. Chapter 16 covers polylines. ■

If you use one of the options, the first prompt returns so that you can specify the first corner point or use another option. After you specify the first point, you see the `Specify other corner point or [Area/ Dimensions/Rotation]:` prompt.

To immediately create the rectangle, specify the corner diagonally opposite the first corner that you specified. You can use any method of specifying coordinates. For example, if you know that the rectangle should be 6 inches wide and 3 inches high, you can specify the second point as 6,3. (If Dynamic Input is turned off or set to absolute coordinates, add the @ symbol before the X,Y coordinates.) You can also use one of the options below:

- **Area.** If you know the area of the rectangle, and only its length or width, then use this option. First you enter the area. Then you specify either the length or the width, and AutoCAD calculates the side that you didn't specify, based on the area you entered.

- **Dimensions.** If you know the length and width of the rectangle, then use this option (although it may be simpler to specify the opposite corner, as I described earlier). You are prompted for the length and width. You then need to move the mouse to specify if you want the second corner to be above and to the right, or in any other direction from the first corner. When you see the rectangle you want, click it.

- **Rotation.** If you want to rotate the rectangle as you create it, then simply enter a rotation angle and pick the opposite corner. Alternatively, instead of entering a rotation angle, you can pick two points to specify a rotation angle and then pick the opposite corner. This last option is great if you want to align the rectangle with an existing object.

Drawing Polygons

 The POLYGON command enables you to draw multisided, closed figures with equal side lengths. You can draw polygons that have from 3 to 1,024 sides. To draw a polygon, choose Home tab ⇨ Draw panel (expanded) ⇨ Polygon. The POLYGON command creates a polyline, meaning that the entire polygon is one object, rather than a series of line segments.

First specify the number of sides. Then choose one of three methods of defining the polygon, as described in Table 6.1.

TABLE 6.1

POLYGON Command Options

Option	Description
Edge	Right-click and choose the Edge option. Specify the two endpoints of any edge of the polygon to complete the polygon.
Inscribed in circle	After specifying the center, right-click and choose Inscribed in Circle. Then specify the radius from the center to a vertex (point). This defines the polygon with reference to an imaginary circle whose circumference touches all the vertices of the polygon.
Circumscribed about circle	After specifying the center, right-click and choose Circumscribed about Circle. Then specify the radius from the center to the midpoint of a side. This defines the polygon with reference to an imaginary circle whose circumference touches all the midpoints of the polygon's sides.

If you type a number for the radius, then the bottom edge of the polygon is horizontal. However, if you pick a point for the radius with your mouse, you can specify the orientation of the polygon. As you rotate the mouse cursor around the center, you see the polygon rotate. Click when you like what you see.

Cross-Reference

When you type a number for the radius, the bottom edge aligns with the snap rotation angle, which is usually 0. Chapter 8 explains how to change this angle. ■

In the exercise that follows, I indicate inches with a double prime (") and feet with a single prime ('). You may find this notation clearer when a measurement has both feet and inches, but you do not actually need to type the double prime for inches. When you have a measurement that is only in inches, it saves time to leave out the double prime.

On the DVD

The drawing used in this exercise on drawing rectangles and polygons, ab06-a.dwg, is in the Drawings folder on the DVD. ■

STEPS: Drawing Rectangles and Polygons

1. Open ab06-a.dwg from the DVD.

2. Save the drawing in your AutoCAD Bible folder as ab06-02.dwg. Verify that snap and grid are on, set at 1". Object Snap should be off.

Note

This exercise assumes that you have Dynamic Input on (click the Dynamic Input button on the status bar to turn it on, if necessary), that you use the default settings for the polar format and relative coordinates, and that you are in the default 2D Drafting & Annotation workspace (if necessary, click the Workspace drop-down list on the Quick Access Toolbar and select it). ■

3. Choose Home tab ➪ Draw panel ➪ Rectangle.

4. At the Specify first corner point or [Chamfer/Elevation/Fillet/Thickness/Width]: prompt, move the cursor to 0'-1",0'-1" and click. At the Specify other corner point or [Area/Dimensions/Rotation]: prompt, type **2'1",1'9"** ↵.

5. Start the RECTANG command again. At the Specify first corner point or [Chamfer/Elevation/Fillet/Thickness/Width]: prompt, Shift+right-click and choose the From object snap. Pick the bottom-left corner of the rectangle. At the <Offset>: prompt, type **@2,2** ↵ to start the second rectangle 2 inches up and 2 inches to the right of the first rectangle.

6. At the Specify other corner point or [Area/Dimensions/Rotation]: prompt, type **1'9",1'3"** ↵.

7. Right-click and choose Repeat RECTANG. At the prompt, find 0'8",1'7" (on a snap point) and click. At the Specify other corner point or [Area/Dimensions/Rotation]: prompt, type **11,2** ↵. (You don't need to type the double-prime for inches.)

8. Again, start the RECTANG command. At the prompt, find 1'1",1'8" and click. At the Specify other corner point or [Area/Dimensions/Rotation]: prompt, type **1,-5** ↵.

9. Choose Home tab ➪ Draw panel (expanded) ➪ Polygon. At the Enter number of sides <4>: prompt, type **5** ↵. At the Specify center of polygon or [Edge]: prompt, type **10,1'8** ↵ to indicate the center.

10. At the Enter an option [Inscribed in circle/Circumscribed about circle] <I>: prompt, press Enter to accept the default. This means that you indicate the radius from the center to the vertices. (If your prompt shows <C> as the default, type **i** ↵.)

11. At the Specify radius of circle: prompt, type **1/2** ↵. AutoCAD or AutoCAD LT draws the pentagon.

12. Repeat Steps 9 through 11, using a center of 1'5",1'8".

13. Start the POLYGON command again. At the Enter number of sides <5>: prompt, type **3** ↵.

14. At the Specify center of polygon or [Edge]: prompt, right-click and choose the Edge option.

15. At the Specify first endpoint of edge: prompt, choose the top-left corner of the faucet rectangle (1'1",1'8"), which is on a snap point.

16. At the Specify second endpoint of edge: prompt, choose the top-right corner of the faucet rectangle to complete the triangle.

17. Turn off the grid to get a better look at the drawing. You have completed the sink, which should look like Figure 6.2. Save your drawing.

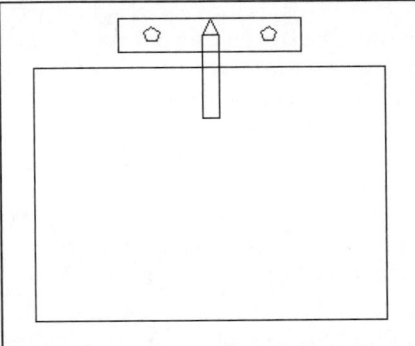

FIGURE 6.2

The completed sink, drawn with rectangles and polygons.

Thanks to Bill Wynn of New Windsor, Maryland, for this drawing, which he created in his AutoCAD class as part of a plan drawing of an entire house.

Creating Construction Lines

Sometimes you want to create a line that is used solely for the purpose of reference. A construction line is a temporary or reference line used to help you draw or to show a relationship between objects. For example, you might want to do the following:

- Draw two lines from the midpoints of two perpendicular lines so that you can use their intersection as the center for a circle.

- Draw a line from one object to another to visually indicate the relationship between the two objects.

- Show the relationship between equivalent parts of a model shown in front and right-side views.

- Draw a line through the center of an object shown in cross-section so that you can show dimensions from the centerline to the edge of the object.

You could use regular lines for these purposes. However, construction lines (also known as xlines) are unique in that they extend infinitely in both directions. This makes them especially useful for seeing the relationships among various objects in your drawing.

Of course, construction lines are not actually infinite. However, they extend to the edge of the drawing area on your screen, and if you zoom out to see more of your drawing, they expand so that they always extend to the edge of the screen. The object snap tracking feature (covered in Chapter 4) sometimes eliminates the need for construction lines; nevertheless, sometimes you can work more easily having a line visible for several commands and then erasing it.

If you zoom to show the extents of your drawing, AutoCAD or AutoCAD LT ignores the xlines and shows you just the extents of the regular objects in your drawing. Chapter 8 covers the ZOOM command.

The XLINE command offers several ways to create construction lines. Start the command by choosing Home tab ⇨ Draw panel (expanded) ⇨ Construction Line. You see the following prompt:

```
Specify a point or [Hor/Ver/Ang/Bisect/Offset]:
```

Table 6.2 lists the possible options. AutoCAD or AutoCAD LT continues to prompt you for more points so that you can continue to draw construction lines — much like the LINE command. Press Enter to end the command.

TABLE 6.2

XLINE Command Options

Option	Description
Specify a point	This option enables you to define the construction line with two points. At the first prompt, specify a point. At the Specify through point: prompt, specify another point. The first point becomes the base point for subsequent construction lines that you can draw by specifying other through points.
Hor	To draw a construction line parallel to the X axis, type **h** ↵ to specify the Horizontal option. The command responds with the Specify through point: prompt. Specify one point. This is useful for drawing a series of horizontal construction lines.
Ver	To draw a construction line parallel to the Y axis, type **v** ↵ to specify the Vertical option. The command responds with the Specify through point: prompt. Specify one point.
Ang	Type **a** ↵ (for Angle). The command responds with the Enter angle of xline (0) or [Reference]: prompt. If you enter an angle, the command asks for a through point. You can also type **r** ↵ and select a line as a reference, and then provide an angle and a through point. AutoCAD or AutoCAD LT then calculates the angle of the construction line from the angle of the reference line. This is useful for drawing a series of construction lines at a specified angle.
Bisect	To draw a construction line that bisects an angle (divides the angle in half), type **b** ↵. The command responds with the Specify angle vertex point: prompt. Choose any point that you want the construction line to pass through. Then at the Specify angle start point: prompt, choose a point that defines the base of the angle. At the Specify angle end point: prompt, choose a point that defines the end of the angle.
Offset	To draw a construction line parallel to a line, type **o** ↵. You can specify the offset distance by typing in the number or using the Through option to pick a point through which the construction line should pass. Either way, the next step is to select a line. If you specified an offset distance, the command displays the Specify side to offset: prompt. Respond by picking a point on the side of the selected line on which you want the construction line to appear.

Creating Rays

Rays are similar to construction lines, except that they start at a specific point and extend to infinity in one direction only. If you need a line to extend in only one direction, using a ray may be less confusing.

Note

You can use most object snaps with construction lines and rays. (You can't use an endpoint for construction lines or a midpoint for rays.) You can edit construction lines and rays like any other object. ∎

 To draw a ray, choose Home tab ⇨ Draw panel (expanded) ⇨ Ray. At the Specify start point: prompt, specify the start point for the ray. At the Specify through point: prompt, specify another point. AutoCAD or AutoCAD LT continues to ask for through points. Press Enter to end the command.

On the DVD

The drawing used in this exercise on drawing construction lines and rays, ab06-b.dwg, is in the Drawings folder on the DVD. ■

STEPS: Drawing Construction Lines and Rays

1. Open ab06-b.dwg from the DVD.

2. Save the drawing as ab06-03.dwg in your AutoCAD Bible folder.

 3. Choose Home tab ⇨ Draw panel (expanded) ⇨ Construction Line.

4. At the Specify a point or [Hor/Ver/Ang/Bisect/Offset]: prompt, choose point ❶, as shown in Figure 6.3.

5. At the Specify through point: prompt, choose point ❷, as shown in Figure 6.3.

FIGURE 6.3

A pipe with cross-section.

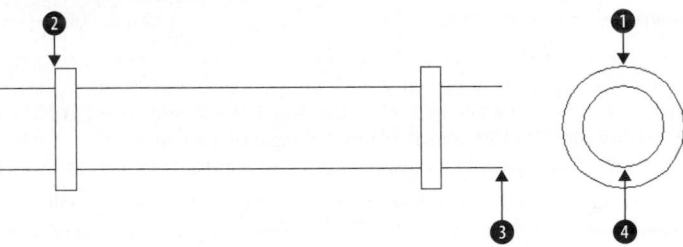

---

6. Press Enter to end the command. Notice that the drawing has been set up so that the construction line is drawn in green and with a noncontinuous linetype. This is to distinguish it from the main drawing. (See Chapter 11 for details on how to set up a drawing in this way.)

 7. Choose Home tab ⇨ Draw panel (expanded) ⇨ Ray.

8. At the Specify start point: prompt, choose point ❸, as shown in Figure 6.3.

9. At the Specify through point: prompt, choose point ❹, as shown in Figure 6.3. Press Enter to end the command.

10. Save your drawing.

Summary

This chapter covered the ins and outs of lines. You read about:

- Using the LINE command
- Drawing rectangles
- Drawing polygons
- Creating construction lines, including xlines that extend infinitely in both directions and rays that extend infinitely in one direction

The next chapter explains how to draw curves and point objects. Curves include circles, arcs, ellipses, and donuts.

Drawing Curves and Points

A utoCAD and AutoCAD LT offer a number of ways to create curved objects. You can draw circles, arcs, ellipses, and donuts (also spelled as doughnuts). In this chapter, I also cover point objects, which are neither curves nor lines but don't deserve their own chapter.

Cross-Reference
Several complex objects — such as polylines, splines, regions, and boundaries — involve curves. These are covered in Chapter 16. ∎

Drawing Circles

Circles are common objects in drawings. In mechanical drawings, they often represent holes or wheels. In architectural drawings, they may be used for doorknobs, trash baskets, or trees. In electrical and piping schematics, they are used for various kinds of symbols.

Understanding the circle options

The CIRCLE command provides six ways to draw a circle. To draw a circle, choose Home tab ⇨ Draw panel ⇨ Circle, and follow the prompts. You can just click the Circle button and follow the options on the command line, or access the options by clicking the button's down arrow. Table 7.1 describes how to use these options. You can access the options directly by clicking the down arrow next to the Circle button on the Ribbon.

TABLE 7.1

Six Ways to Draw a Circle

Option	Description
Center, Radius	This option is the default. Specify the center and then the radius. You can type the radius as a distance, or pick a point where you want the circumference to be.
Center, Diameter	Specify the center. Choose the `Diameter` option and type the length of the diameter, or pick a point to specify the diameter.
2P (2 Points)	Choose the `2p` option. Specify one point on the circumference, and then an opposite point on the circumference. These two points define the diameter of the circle.
3P (3 Points)	Choose the `3p` option. Specify three points on the circumference.
Tan, tan, radius (Tangent, Tangent, Radius)	Choose the `Ttr` option. The CIRCLE command prompts `Specify point on object for first tangent of circle:` and provides an aperture to let you pick a point. Then the command prompts `Specify point on object for second tangent of circle:` and you pick a second point. These points can be any points on the object(s) to which you want your circle to be tangent. Finally, type a radius.
Tan, tan, tan (Tangent, Tangent, Tangent)	This option is available only from the Circle's drop-down menu on the Ribbon. You are prompted for three points, and AutoCAD automatically applies the Tangent object snap to each point.

Tip

You can also create a circle tangent to other objects by using the two-point (2P) method or three-point (3P) method, picking those points with the Tangent object snap. ■

Drawing circles

Drawing circles is fairly straightforward. Often, you can use object snaps to define part of the circle. In the following exercise, you practice using the most common methods of creating a circle.

On the DVD

The drawing used in the following exercise on drawing circles, ab07-a.dwg, is in the Drawings folder on the DVD. ■

STEPS: Drawing Circles

1. Open ab07-a.dwg from the DVD.

2. Save the file as ab07-01.dwg in your AutoCAD Bible folder. This is a drawing of an air compressor from which all the circles have been removed. Make sure that Object Snap is turned on. Set a running object snap for Endpoint only. You should be in the default 2D Drafting & Annotation workspace (if necessary, choose it from the Workspace drop-down list on the Quick Access Toolbar).

 3. Choose Home tab ⇨ Draw panel ⇨ Circle drop-down list ⇨ 2-Point. At the `Specify first endpoint of circle's diameter:` prompt, pick the endpoint at ❶, as shown in Figure 7.1. At the `Specify second endpoint of circle's diameter:` prompt, pick the endpoint at ❷.

FIGURE 7.1

The air compressor without its circles.

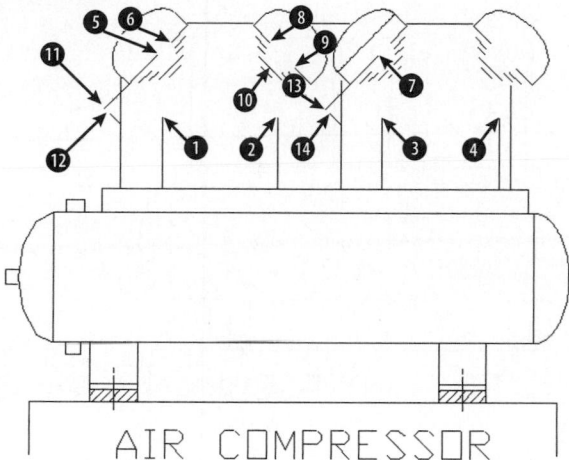

4. Repeat the CIRCLE command by right-clicking and choosing Repeat CIRCLE. Right-click and choose 2P from the shortcut menu. Pick the endpoints at ❸ and ❹, as shown in Figure 7.1.

5. Repeat the CIRCLE command by pressing Enter. At the `Specify center point for circle or [3P/2P/Ttr (tan tan radius)]:` prompt, pick the endpoint at ❺. At the `Specify radius of circle or [Diameter]:` prompt, pick the endpoint at ❻.

6. Repeat the CIRCLE command. At the `Specify center point for circle or [3P/2P/Ttr (tan tan radius)]:` prompt, pick the endpoint at ❼. At the `Specify radius of circle or [Diameter]:` prompt, right-click and choose Diameter; and then type .25 ↵.

7. Repeat the CIRCLE command by right-clicking and choosing Repeat CIRCLE. At the `Specify center point for circle or [3P/2P/Ttr (tan tan radius)]:` prompt, right-click and choose 3P. At the `Specify first point on circle:` prompt, pick the endpoint at ❽, as shown in Figure 7.1. At the `Specify second point on circle:` prompt, pick the endpoint at ❾. At the `Specify third point on circle:` prompt, choose the Midpoint object snap and pick the midpoint at ❿.

8. For the last circle on the right, choose any method that you want to use to draw a circle. The circle should be the same size and placement as the second circle from the left.

9. Repeat the CIRCLE command. At the `Specify center point for circle or [3P/2P/Ttr (tan tan radius)]:` prompt, choose the Center object snap and pick ❼. At the `Specify radius of circle or [Diameter]:` prompt, type .05 ↵.

10. Repeat Step 9 to create a circle inside the circle whose center is at ❺ and whose radius is 0.05.

11. Repeat the CIRCLE command. At the `Specify center point for circle or [3P/2P/Ttr (tan tan radius)]:` prompt, pick the endpoint at ⓫. At the `Specify radius of circle or [Diameter]:` prompt, pick the endpoint at ⓬.

12. Repeat Step 11, choosing the endpoint at ⓭ for the center of the circle and the endpoint at ⓮ for its radius, as shown in Figure 7.1.

13. Save your drawing. It should look like Figure 7.2.

FIGURE 7.2

The completed air compressor.

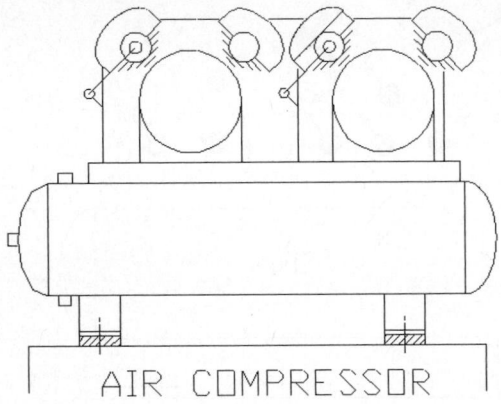

Thanks to the U.S. Army Corps of Engineers at Vicksburg, Mississippi, for this drawing. They maintain a Web site of drawings at `http://cadlib.wes.army.mil`.

Cross-Reference

It may have occurred to you that this task would have been easier if you could simply have copied one circle to another location instead of creating each circle from scratch. I cover copying in Chapter 9. ■

Drawing Arcs

An arc is a portion of a circle. Therefore, to define an arc, you have to define not only a circle — for example, by specifying a center and a radius — but also the start and endpoints of the arc. The ARC command offers several methods for defining an arc. The method you pick depends on the information that you have about the arc that you want to draw.

Cross-Reference

You can close an arc to create a circle by using the JOIN command. You can also use the BREAK command to create an arc from a circle. For more information, see Chapter 10. ■

Understanding arc options

After you understand the parts of an arc, you can choose the options that suit your needs. Figure 7.3 shows the parts of an arc that you can use to draw an arc.

FIGURE 7.3

The parts of an arc.

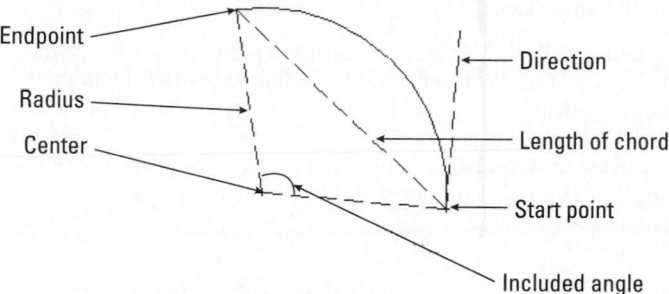

Endpoint — Direction

Radius — Length of chord

Center — Start point

Included angle

Figure 7.4 shows the flow of the arc options. When you start the ARC command, you have two options, Start Point and Center. Depending on how you start, more options become available.

You can also press Enter at the first arc prompt to draw a second arc starting from the endpoint of the most recently drawn arc, line, polyline, or other object. The new arc continues in the same direction as the end of the first object. The only other prompt is the endpoint.

FIGURE 7.4

The ARC command options.

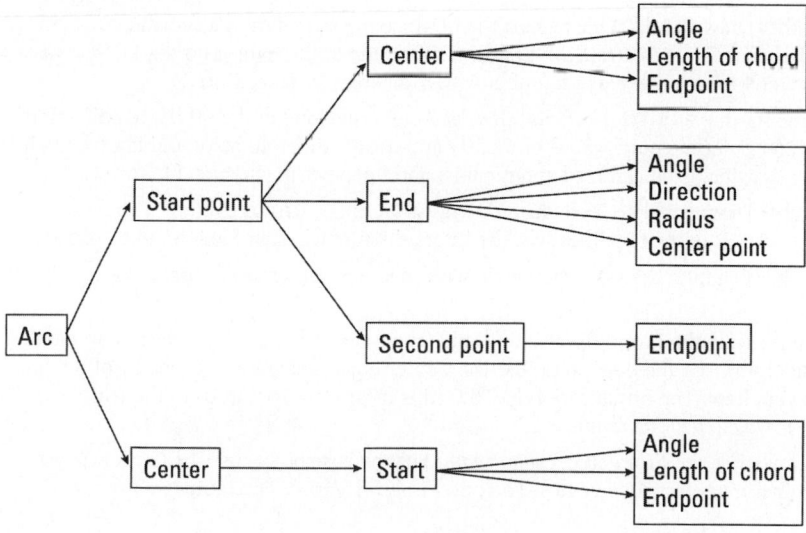

Drawing arcs

To draw an arc, choose Home tab ⇨ Draw panel ⇨ Arc, and follow the prompts. You can just click the Arc button and follow the options on the command line, or access the options by clicking the button's down arrow. Object snaps are often helpful when drawing arcs.

When drawing an arc by using the Start, End, and Radius options, the three specifications actually define two possible arcs, one minor and one major. The ARC command draws the minor arc by default, in the counterclockwise direction. (A minor arc is less than half a circle.) If you enter a negative number for the radius, the command draws the major arc. The options requiring an angle also define two possible arcs, one drawn counterclockwise and one drawn clockwise. AutoCAD and AutoCAD LT draw the counterclockwise arc by default. If you type a negative number for the angle, the arc is drawn clockwise.

On the DVD

The drawing used in the following exercise on drawing arcs, ab07-b.dwg, is in the Drawings folder on the DVD. ∎

STEPS: Drawing Arcs

1. Open ab07-b.dwg from the DVD.

2. Save the file as ab07-02.dwg in your AutoCAD Bible folder. Ortho mode is on, and units are set to Fractional. Right-click the Object Snap button on the status bar and set running object snaps for Intersection, Center, and Endpoint. Make sure that Object Snap is on. You should be in the default 2D Drafting & Annotation workspace (if necessary, choose it from the Workspace drop-down list on the Quick Access Toolbar). In this exercise, you draw part of the sealing plate shown in Figure 7.5 from scratch; therefore, the drawing is blank.

3. Choose Home tab ⇨ Draw panel ⇨ Line to start the LINE command. Start at a coordinate of 2,3 and use Direct Distance Entry to create a 7-unit horizontal line to the right. End the LINE command. (See Chapter 4 for a full explanation of how to use Direct Distance Entry.)

4. Draw another line starting at 5-1/2,1-5/8 and draw it 2-3/4 units long in the 90-degree direction. These two lines are centerlines and would ordinarily appear in a different color and linetype than the object you're drawing. (You can read about colors and linetypes in Chapter 11.)

5. Choose Home tab ⇨ Draw panel ⇨ Circle drop-down list ⇨ Center, Radius to draw a circle with its center at the intersection of the two lines (use the Intersection object snap) and a radius of 11/16.

6. Use the Center object snap to draw another circle with the same center as the first circle and a radius of 1.

7. Draw a third circle, using the From object snap (Shift+right-click to open the Object Snap menu, and then choose From). For the base point, use the Center object snap and pick either of the first two circles that you drew. The offset is @-1-15/16,0 (this means 1-15/16 units to the left of the center of the first two circles). Its radius is ⅜.

8. Draw a fourth circle. Use the From object snap again. For the base point, use the Center object snap and pick either of the first two circles. The offset is @1-15/16,0. The radius is ⅜.

FIGURE 7.5

The dimensioned sealing plate for a valve.

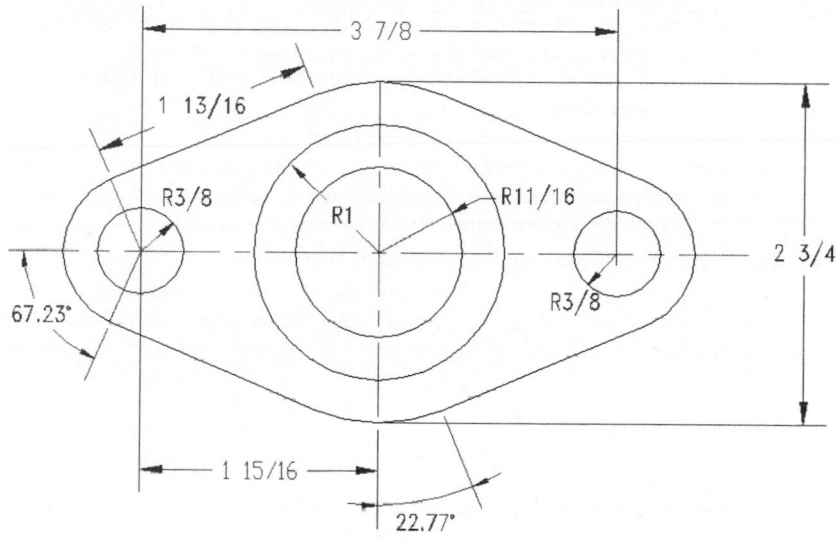

Thanks to Jerry Bottenfield of Clow Valve Company in Oskaloosa, Iowa, for this drawing.

9. Choose Home tab ⇨ Draw panel ⇨ Arc drop-down list ⇨ 3-Point. Follow the prompts:

   ```
   Specify start point of arc or [Center]: Choose the From object snap.
   Base point: Use the Center object snap to pick the center of the
        leftmost circle.
   <Offset>: @-5/8,0 ↵
   Specify second point of arc or [Center/End]: Right-click and choose
        Center. Use the Center object snap to pick the center of the
        leftmost circle.
   Specify endpoint of arc or [Angle/chord Length]: Right-click and
        choose Angle.
   Specify included angle: 67.23 ↵
   ```

10. Start the LINE command. At the Specify first point: prompt, press Enter to continue the line in the same direction as the end of the arc. At the Length of line: prompt, type **1-13/16** ↵. End the LINE command.

11. Start the ARC command again. Follow the prompts:

    ```
    Specify start point of arc or [Center]: Use the Endpoint object snap
         to pick the end of the line that you just drew.
    Specify second point of arc or [Center/End]: Right-click and choose
         Center. Use the Center object snap and pick any point on one of
         the large central circles.
    Specify endpoint of arc or [Angle/chord Length]: Use Endpoint object
         snap to pick the lower end of the vertical construction line.
    ```

12. Repeat the ARC command. Follow the prompts:

    ```
    Specify start point of arc or [Center]: Right-click and choose
        Center. Use the Center object snap and pick any point on one of
        the large central circles.
    Specify start point of arc: Use the Endpoint object snap to pick the
        endpoint of the arc that you just completed.
    Specify endpoint of arc or [Angle/chord Length]: Right-click and
        choose Angle.
    Specify included angle: 22.77 ↵
    ```

13. Start the LINE command. At the Specify first point: prompt, press Enter to continue the line in the same direction as the end of the arc. At the Length of line: prompt, type **1-13/16** ↵. End the LINE command.

14. Start the ARC command. Follow the prompts:

    ```
    Specify start point of arc or [Center]: Use the Endpoint object snap
        to pick the endpoint of the line that you just drew.
    Specify second point of arc or [Center/End]: Right-click and choose
        End.
    Specify endpoint of arc: Choose the From object snap.
    _from Base point: Use the Center object snap to pick the center of
        the rightmost circle.
    <Offset>: @5/8,0 ↵
    Specify center point of arc or [Angle/Direction/Radius]: r ↵
    Specify radius of arc: 5/8 ↵
    ```

15. Save your drawing. Your drawing should look like Figure 7.6. You can complete this drawing in Chapter 10 by creating a mirror image.

FIGURE 7.6

The partially completed sealing plate, created by using lines, circles, and arcs.

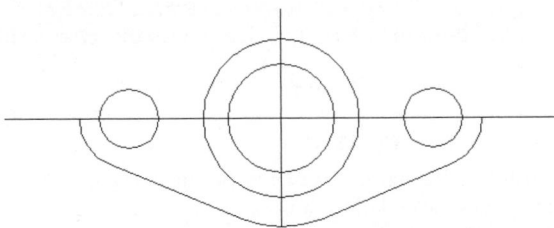

Creating Ellipses and Elliptical Arcs

You can create ellipses (ovals) as well as elliptical arcs, which are partial ellipses. Like a circle, an ellipse has a center. The difference, of course, is that an ellipse has a longer radius along its major axis and a shorter radius along its minor axis.

Understanding ellipse options

You can draw an ellipse by defining the center first. Another option is to define the axis endpoints first. If you want to draw an elliptical arc, you must specify the start and end angles.

Creating ellipses

The default option is to specify endpoints 1 and 2 of the first axis. Then you specify the second distance of the axis, which is the distance from the first axis line to the circumference along the second axis.

Instead of specifying a second axis distance, you can choose the Rotation option. The Rotation option defines the minor axis by specifying an angle from 0 degrees to 90 degrees, which is the ratio of the major axis to the minor axis. (Actually, the command only accepts up to 89.4 degrees.) When the angle is 0, you get a circle. As the angle increases, the ellipse gets flatter and flatter until you reach 89.4 degrees. A 45-degree angle results in a minor axis whose length is the square root of the major-axis length.

Instead of specifying endpoints, you can use the Center option to specify the center of the ellipse. Then specify the endpoint of the first axis, which can be either the major or the minor axis. Finally, specify the other axis distance, which is the radius from the center to the circumference along the second axis. Again, instead of specifying the second axis distance, you can define the ellipse by using the Rotation option.

Creating elliptical arcs

To draw an elliptical arc, use the Arc option of the ELLIPSE command. The first prompts are the same as for an ellipse. Then the command continues with the `Specify start angle or [Parameter]:` prompt, offering the following options:

- **Start angle.** This option is the default. Specify the start angle, which the command redefines to start along the major axis. The command responds with the `Specify end angle or [Parameter/Included angle]:` prompt.
- **End angle.** Specify the end angle to complete the ellipse arc.
- **Included angle.** After specifying the start angle, you can complete the arc by specifying the included angle from the start point to the endpoint, going counterclockwise.
- **Parameter.** Choose this option to define the arc portion by the ellipse's area rather than by its included angle (which defines the arc portion by its circumference). The command responds with the `Specify start parameter or [Angle]:` and `Specify end parameter or [Angle/Included angle]:` prompts. By typing in angles, you define the percent of the full ellipse's area that you want to include. (For example, starting at 15 degrees and ending at 105 degrees includes 90 degrees and therefore draws one quarter of an ellipse.) The options in brackets let you return to regular angle specification.

Drawing ellipses

 To draw an ellipse, choose Home tab ➪ Draw panel ➪ Ellipse, and follow the prompts. You can just click the Ellipse button and follow the options on the command line, or access the options by clicking the button's down arrow. In addition to the information that the command explicitly requests in the prompts, you need to know the angle of the first axis that you define. Not all ellipses are horizontal or vertical. You control the orientation when you stipulate the second point of the first axis. The second axis is automatically perpendicular to the first axis.

To draw an elliptical arc, choose Elliptical Arc from the Ellipse button's drop-down list or use the Arc option of the ELLIPSE command. When you draw an elliptical arc, the command introduces a helpful but sometimes confusing feature: While you're defining the arc angles, the command redefines 0 degrees along the major axis. This helps you to define the included angle in an orientation that relates to the ellipse, rather than the usual orientation where 0 degrees is to the right.

In this exercise, you practice drawing ellipses and elliptical arcs.

On the DVD

The drawing used in the following exercise on drawing ellipses and elliptical arcs, ab07-c.dwg, **is in the** Drawings **folder on the DVD.** ∎

STEPS: Drawing Ellipses and Elliptical Arcs

1. Open ab07-c.dwg from the DVD.

2. Save the file as ab07-03.dwg in your AutoCAD Bible folder. The drawing shows an empty conference room. Snap is on, and set to 6". Ortho mode and Object Snap should be on, with a running object snap set for Endpoint only. You should be in the default 2D Drafting & Annotation workspace (if necessary, choose it from the Workspace drop-down list on the Quick Access Toolbar).

3. Choose Home tab ⇨ Draw panel ⇨ Ellipse drop-down list ⇨ Center. At the Specify center of ellipse: prompt, choose 8',10', which is a snap point. At the Specify endpoint of axis: prompt, move the cursor to the right until the coordinates read 3'<0 and click. (If necessary, right-click the coordinates on the status bar and choose Relative, or look at the Dynamic Input tooltips.) At the Specify distance to other axis or [Rotation]: prompt, move the cursor up until the coordinates read 6'6"<90 and click. This completes the conference table.

4. Repeat the ELLIPSE command. Follow the prompts:

   ```
   Specify axis endpoint of ellipse or [Arc/Center]: Right-click and
       choose Arc (or choose Home tab⇨Draw panel⇨Ellipse drop-down
       list⇨Elliptical Arc).
   Specify axis endpoint of elliptical arc or [Center]: Right-click and
       choose Center.
   Specify center of elliptical arc: Pick 8',3', a snap point.
   Specify endpoint of axis: Move the cursor to the right until the
       coordinates read 1'<0 and pick. (You can also look at the Dynamic
       Input tooltips.)
   Specify distance to other axis or [Rotation]: Move the cursor up
       until the coordinates read 6"<90 and pick.
   Specify start angle or [Parameter]: 162 ↵
   Specify end angle or [Parameter/Included angle]: 18 ↵
   ```

5. Turn off Ortho mode. Start the LINE command. At the Specify first point: prompt, use the Endpoint running object snap and pick the right side of the elliptical arc. At the Specify next point or [Undo]: prompt, right-click the coordinates and choose Absolute (if necessary), and press and hold Shift+A to temporarily override Object Snap mode while you pick the snap point 8'6",3'. End the LINE command.

6. Start the LINE command. At the Specify first point: prompt, use the Endpoint object snap to pick the left side of the ellipse arc. At the Specify next point or [Undo]: prompt, press and hold Shift+A while you pick the snap point 7'6",3'. End the LINE command.

7. Start the ELLIPSE command. Follow the prompts:

```
Specify axis endpoint of ellipse or [Arc/Center]: Right-click and
     choose Arc.
Specify axis endpoint of elliptical arc or [Center]: Use the Endpoint
     object snap to pick the free endpoint of the line on the right.
Specify other endpoint of axis: Use the Endpoint object snap to pick
     the free endpoint of the line on the left.
Specify distance to other axis or [Rotation]: 3<90 ↵ (If you don't
     have Dynamic Input on and set to the default of relative
     coordinates, then type @ before the distance.)
Specify start angle or [Parameter]: Use the Endpoint object snap to
     pick the free endpoint of the line on the right.
Specify end angle or [Parameter/Included angle]: Use Endpoint object
     snap to pick the free endpoint of the line on the left.
```

8. Choose Home tab ⇨ Draw panel ⇨ Ellipse drop-down list ⇨ Axis, End. At the `Specify axis endpoint of ellipse or [Arc/Center]`: prompt, pick point 2',18', a snap point. At the `Specify other endpoint of axis`: prompt, pick point 2',16', also a snap point. (The coordinates on the status bar display this point in absolute coordinate mode. The Dynamic Input tooltips show 2' and 90°.) At the `Specify distance to other axis or [Rotation]`: prompt, move the cursor to the right until the coordinates read 6"<0. (Right-click the coordinates and choose Relative, if necessary.) This is also a snap point. Click the mouse button to complete the small side table.

9. Save your drawing. It should look like Figure 7.7.

FIGURE 7.7

The conference room with a conference table, a chair, and a side table.

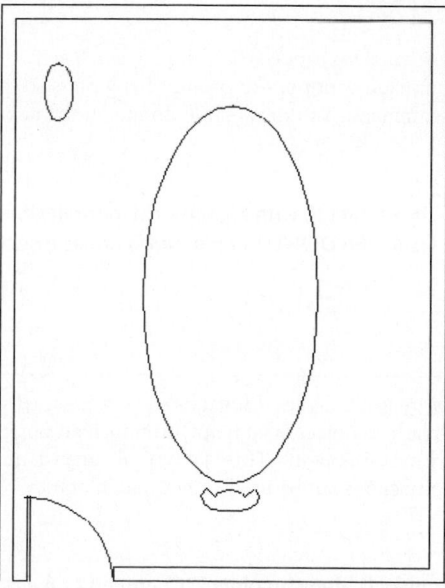

Making Donuts

A donut is a wide polyline that looks like two concentric circles, with the area between the circles filled in. You define a diameter for the inner and outer circles. Donuts are often used in electrical drawings to create symbols. If the inner circle's radius is zero, you create a filled-in circle.

The setting of the FILL command determines whether the donut is filled. Type **fill** ↵ and type **on** ↵ or **off** ↵. FILL is on by default. Turning FILL off displays a radial pattern of lines, rather than a solid fill. Type **regen** ↵ to update existing donuts to the new FILL setting.

Understanding DONUT options

The DONUT command has the following prompts:

- `Specify inside diameter of donut <0.5000>`. Type the diameter of the inside circle or pick two points to specify the inside diameter. The number in brackets is the last inside diameter that you defined, or 0.5 if you haven't previously used the DONUT command in this drawing session.

- `Specify outside diameter of donut <1.0000>`. Type the diameter of the outside circle or pick two points to specify the outside diameter. The outside diameter must be larger than the inside diameter. The number in brackets is the last outside diameter that you defined, or 1.0 if you haven't previously used the DONUT command in this drawing session.

- `Specify second point`. If you define the inside or outside diameter by picking a point, the command asks for a second point. Use this technique if you're using object snaps to define the diameters.

- `Specify center of donut or <exit>`. Specify the center of the donut. Pressing Enter ends the command.

Drawing donuts

 To draw a donut, choose Home tab ⇨ Draw panel (expanded) ⇨ Donut. Then specify the inner and outer diameters and the center. The DONUT command continues to prompt for centers so that you can place additional donuts. Press Enter to end the command. You draw some donuts in the next exercise.

Note
You can use the hatch feature to fill in any object with a solid fill, with a great deal more flexibility in the shape of your objects. (Chapter 16 discusses hatching.) As a result, the DONUT command is not as essential as it once was. ∎

Placing Points

A point simply marks a coordinate. Points are generally used for reference. It is sometimes helpful to mark a point that you will use later as a guide to place an object or to help you return an object to its original position. When it's no longer needed, you may erase the point. This is a typical construction method. In some cases, the From object snap or object snap tracking can be used rather than a point.

Cross-Reference
The DIVIDE and MEASURE commands place point objects along an object. Chapter 12 covers these commands. ∎

Changing the point style

Because points can be hard to see, and because various disciplines have different conventions for drawing point objects, AutoCAD and AutoCAD LT provide 20 types of point styles that you can use in your drawing. Before you draw a point, you should set the point style. You can save this setting in your template.

Choose Home tab ⇨ Utilities panel (expanded) ⇨ Point Style (the DDPTYPE command) to open the Point Style dialog box, as shown in Figure 7.8. To set the point style, click the box showing the style that you want. Then set the point size, which has the following options. When you are done, click OK to close the dialog box.

FIGURE 7.8

The Point Style dialog box.

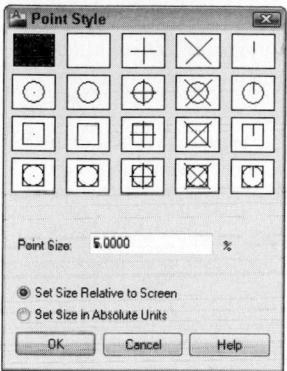

- **Set Size Relative to Screen.** Use this option if you want the point to always appear the same size, no matter how much you zoom in and out — for example, when you're using the point as a reference. The size is set as a percentage of the screen. This option is the default, with the size set to 5 percent of the screen.

- **Set Size in Absolute Units.** Use this option if you want the point to have a real size, just like any other object. The size is set in units. Use this option when you want the point to stay the same size relative to other objects in your drawing.

Creating points

After you determine the point style, you're ready to create points. Choose Home tab ⇨ Draw panel (expanded) ⇨ Point drop-down list ⇨ Multiple Points. At the Specify a point: prompt, specify the point that you want, either by picking a point on the screen or by typing coordinates. (You can specify a Z coordinate to create a point in 3D space. For more information, see Chapter 21.) You can use object snaps to specify the point. When you choose the POINT command from the Draw panel, the command automatically repeats the prompt so that you can continue to specify points. To end the command, press Esc. When you type **point** ↵ on the command line, the command ends after you specify one point.

If BLIPMODE is on and you're using the first point style — a small dot — you cannot see the point until you use the REDRAW command to remove the blips. After you create a point, use the Node object snap to snap to the point.

Tip

If you're using the points for temporary reference, instead of erasing them, you can set the point style to the second style in the Point Style dialog box (no dot) before plotting. As a result, the points do not appear on your plot. You can also put your points on a layer with a Not Plottable property. (See Chapter 11 for more on layers.) ∎

On the DVD

The drawing used in the following exercise on drawing donuts and points, ab07-d.dwg, is in the Drawings folder on the DVD. ∎

STEPS: Drawing Donuts and Points

1. Open ab07-d.dwg from the DVD.

2. Save the file as ab07-04.dwg in your AutoCAD Bible folder. The drawing contains a rectangle and connecting wires for an electrical switch. Make sure that Object Snap is on. Set running object snaps for Endpoint, Center, Node, and Quadrant. This exercise assumes that you have Dynamic Input on, with the default setting of relative coordinates.

3. Choose Home Tab ⇨ Utilities panel (expanded) ⇨ Point Style. The Point Style dialog box opens. Choose the third point type, which is the plus sign. The Set Size Relative to Screen check box should be selected. The Point Size should be 5.0000%. Click OK.

4. Choose Home tab ⇨ Draw panel ⇨ Point drop-down list ⇨ Multiple Points. Follow the prompts:

   ```
   Specify a point: Use the From object snap. (Shift+right-click to open
       the Object Snap shortcut menu.)
   Base point: Use the Endpoint object snap to pick the top-left corner
       of the rectangle.
   <Offset>: @.08,-.09 ↵
   Specify a point: Press Esc to complete the command.
   ```

5. Choose Home tab ⇨ Draw panel (expanded) ⇨ Donut. Follow these prompts:

   ```
   Specify inside diameter of donut <0.5000>: .04 ↵
   Specify outside diameter of donut <1.0000>: .06 ↵
   Specify center of donut or <exit>: Use the Node object snap to pick
       the point that you drew.
   Specify center of donut or <exit>: @.19,0 ↵
   Specify center of donut or <exit>: ↵
   ```

6. Start the POINT command again. Follow the prompts:

   ```
   Specify a point: Press Shift+right-click and choose Mid Between 2
       Points from the shortcut menu.
   First point of mid: Use the Center object snap to pick the center of
       the right-hand donut. (You may have to press Tab until you get the
       Center object snap, and not a Quadrant object snap.)
   Second point of mid: Press Shift+right-click and choose Perpendicular
       from the shortcut menu. Press and hold Shift to temporarily turn
       on Ortho mode and pick the lower horizontal line of the rectangle.
       Release the Shift key.

   Specify a point: Press Esc.
   ```

7. Choose Home tab ⇨ Draw panel ⇨ Line to start the LINE command. Follow the prompts:

    ```
    Specify first point: Use the Quadrant object snap to pick the right
        (0 degrees) quadrant of the left donut. If you don't see the
        Quadrant SnapTip, press Tab until it appears.
    Specify next point or [Undo]: Use the Node object snap to pick the
        point that you just drew. End the LINE command.
    ```

8. Save your drawing. It should look like Figure 7.9.

FIGURE 7.9
_____

The completed electrical switch. The points show as plus signs.

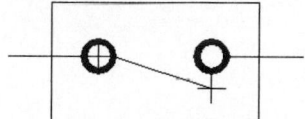

Summary

In this chapter, you learned how to draw curved objects and points in AutoCAD and AutoCAD LT. You discovered:

- All the ways to draw circles
- How to define and draw an arc
- How to define an ellipse and an elliptical arc
- How to draw a donut
- How to set the point style and draw points

In the next chapter, you learn how to display your drawing for the greatest ease and comfort.

Viewing Your Drawing

O ften you may wish that you could zoom in to see a particular part of a drawing more closely or move the display in a certain direction to reveal an area that is hidden. You may also want to save a view so that you can return to it at some other time. In this chapter, you read about controlling the display of your drawing to meet all your drawing needs and increase your productivity. This chapter covers viewing a 2D drawing.

Note

This entire chapter assumes that you're using the 2D Drafting & Annotation workspace and (for AutoCAD) the 2D Wireframe visual style. To check, choose 2D Drafting & Annotation workspace from the Workspace Switching list on the Quick Access Toolbar or on the status bar. To set the visual style to 2D Wireframe, type vscurrent ↵ at the command line, and then choose the 2D Wireframe option. Visual styles are mostly used for 3D drawings. I cover viewing 3D drawings in Chapter 22. ■

IN THIS CHAPTER
Panning and zooming
Using the SteeringWheel
Working with views
Creating tiled viewports
Rotating the snap angle
Creating User Coordinate Systems
Drawing isometrically

Regenerating and Redrawing the Display

AutoCAD and AutoCAD LT are *vector programs,* which means that they store information about objects in your drawing in terms of coordinates and equations. To display your drawing on your computer screen, the programs convert the vector information to pixels. Occasionally, you may need to re-display the objects on your screen. One way is to recalculate the entire drawing, in a process called regenerating (the REGEN command). Another way is to quickly access a virtual screen from your computer's memory; this is called *redrawing* (the REDRAW command). Keep in mind that redrawing is quicker than regenerating.

When should you use the REDRAW and REGEN commands?

- Use the REDRAW command to remove blips or to quickly refresh the screen. (In AutoCAD only, the REDRAWALL command redraws the display in all viewports. Viewports are covered later in this chapter.) To redraw the screen, type **redraw** ↲ at the command line.

- Use the REGEN command whenever you want to recalculate and redisplay the entire drawing. In common usage, the word *regen* refers to the REGEN command as well as regenerate or regeneration. To regenerate the entire drawing, type **regen** ↲ at the command line. (The REGENALL command regenerates all viewports.)

Panning

Often you cannot see the entire drawing on your screen. You therefore need a way to see the parts of your drawing that are not currently visible.

To pan means to move the display without changing the magnification. The word *pan* refers to the expression of panning a camera across a scene or view. You pan to view a different part of your drawing.

Using the PAN command

The PAN command moves the display in the direction and distance that you indicate without changing the magnification. *Real-time* panning moves the drawing as you move the cursor.

 To pan the drawing, click and hold down the mouse wheel. Alternatively, click the Pan button on the vertical Navigation bar. The cursor changes to a hand. With the cursor anywhere in your drawing, click and drag in the direction that you want the objects to go. You can pan transparently, while you're in the middle of another command.

New Feature

The Navigation bar is new for AutoCAD 2011. This vertical bar sits on the right side of the drawing window (by default) and contains tools for panning, zooming, and 3D navigation (3D Orbit), as well as the Steering Wheel and the Show Motion feature. The Navigation bar is transparent until you hover the mouse cursor over it. You can turn the Navigation bar on and off with the NAVBAR command, or choose View tab ⇨ Windows panel ⇨ User Interface drop-down list ⇨ Navigation Bar. ■

Tip

You can pan past the edge of the screen (actually the viewport). This means that when the cursor reaches the edge of the screen, you can continue moving your mouse in the same direction to continue the pan. ■

If you use the Pan button on the Navigation bar, then to leave Pan mode, press Esc or Enter, or start any command by using the Ribbon, a menu, or a toolbar. You can also right-click to open the shortcut menu and choose Exit or one of the other display options. If you pan by using the mouse wheel, you don't need to press Esc or Enter to leave Pan mode.

Using the scroll bars

You can use the scroll bars to pan vertically and horizontally as you would with any Windows program. However, you can't easily predict just how much the drawing view will move. Therefore, the scroll bars are less useful than the PAN command.

Note

You can turn the display of the scroll bars on and off. Choose Application Button ⇨ Options to open the Options dialog box. On the Display tab, check or uncheck the Display Scroll Bars in Drawing Window check box. ■

Using the ZOOM Command

The ZOOM command enables you to zoom in and out of your drawing, like the zoom lens of a camera. When you zoom in, everything is magnified so that you can see it more easily, but you see less of the entire drawing. When you zoom out, objects look smaller, but you can see more of the drawing. The ZOOM command has several options that make it easy to see just what you need at an appropriate size.

Cross-Reference

Zooming does not affect the actual size of objects. Chapter 9 covers changing the actual size of objects, known as scaling. ■

 You can zoom by rotating the mouse wheel forward to zoom in and backward to zoom out. There is no Zoom cursor, and you don't need to press Esc or Enter to leave Zoom mode. Alternatively, you can click the Zoom button's down arrow on the Navigation bar and then choose Zoom Realtime from the drop-down list. The cursor changes to a magnifying glass with a plus sign on one side and a minus sign on the other side. To zoom in, click and drag up in the direction of the plus sign. To zoom out, click and drag down in the direction of the minus sign. Press Esc or Enter to leave Zoom mode.

Tip

You can zoom past the edge of the screen (actually the viewport). As you move the mouse up or down to zoom, when you reach the edge of the viewport, continue to move the mouse in the same direction to continue the zoom in or out. To control how much you zoom for each incremental movement of the wheel, change the ZOOMFACTOR system variable. ■

Understanding ZOOM options

The ZOOM command has many options that let you fine-tune the process. Start the command by choosing one of the options on the Zoom drop-down list of the Navigation bar, or go to View tab ⇨ Navigate panel and choose one of the options on the Zoom drop-down list there. Table 8.1 outlines the Zoom options.

TABLE 8.1

Zoom Options

Button	Option	Description
	Extents	Zooms to the outer extents of the drawing. You can also double-click the wheel of your mouse.
	Window	Lets you define a rectangular window as the boundaries of the new display. Use the Window option to zoom in on any area already displayed in your drawing. When you use Zoom Window, the command displays everything in the window that you specify but reshapes the display to fit your screen. As a result, you may see objects that were outside the specified window. You can move the mouse past the drawing area to define the window past the edge of the screen — the display moves to allow you to pick a corner. You don't need to specify this option separately, because the command initially prompts you to specify the first corner of a window. When you do so, you're prompted for the opposite corner.
	Previous	Redisplays the most recent display of your drawing. This option has its own button on the status bar.
	Realtime	Displays the Zoom cursor and lets you drag up to zoom in and down to zoom out. Press Esc or Enter to exit Realtime Zoom mode.
	All	Zooms the display to the greater of the drawing extents or the drawing limits.
	Dynamic	Enables you to zoom and pan in one operation. This option is covered in the following section.
	Scale	Lets you enter a number to scale the display relative to the drawing limits (a kind of absolute scaling). Enter a number followed by **x** to scale the display relative to the current view (relative scaling). Enter a number followed by **xp** to scale the display relative to paper space units (discussed in Chapter 17). A number less than 1 (such as 0.5) reduces the size of the objects on the screen (by half when you use 0.5). A number greater than 1 (such as 2) increases the size of the objects on the screen (to twice the size when you use 2).
	Center	Lets you specify a new center for the display, and then a new magnification/height. The current magnification/height is shown in brackets for your reference. Type a smaller number to increase the magnification, making the objects larger. Type a larger value to decrease the magnification, making the objects smaller.
	Object	Lets you zoom in to selected objects.
	In	Uses the Scale option with a value of 2x. See the Scale option. It's only available from the Ribbon drop-down list.
	Out	Uses the Scale option with a value of 0.5x. See the Scale option. It's only available from the Ribbon drop-down list.

When you use one of the Zoom options, you see the objects in your drawing become larger or smaller in a smooth transition. The smooth transition helps you to orient yourself to the new display. To turn off this feature, use the VTOPTIONS command. In the View Transitions dialog box that opens, uncheck the Enable Animation for Pan & Zoom check box.

Note

When you undo consecutive ZOOM or PAN commands, they count as one operation. Because people often use several ZOOM or PAN operations together, combining them helps you to get back to your previous state more quickly. To disable this feature, choose Application Button ⇨ Options. On the User Preferences tab, uncheck the Combine Zoom and Pan Commands check box in the Undo/Redo section. ∎

Using ZOOM Dynamic

The Dynamic option of ZOOM enables you to pan and zoom in one operation. When you start ZOOM Dynamic, you see the virtual screen area of the drawing in a blue, dashed rectangle; this view box represents the drawing extents or limits, whichever is greater. Your current view is bounded in a green, dashed rectangle. Your mouse cursor changes, based on the two modes of ZOOM Dynamic. Each time you click the left mouse button, you switch modes. Here's how the two modes work:

- **Pan mode.** The view box contains an X and can move freely around any displayed area of the drawing.

- **Zoom mode.** The view box contains an arrow. The left side of the box is fixed at the point where you changed to Zoom mode. As you move the cursor, the box expands or shrinks, letting you zoom to any magnification.

When the view box displays the view that you want, click the right mouse button and choose Enter (or press Enter). The command pans and zooms to show that view. Figure 8.1 shows the screen during a ZOOM Dynamic operation.

FIGURE 8.1

Using ZOOM Dynamic.

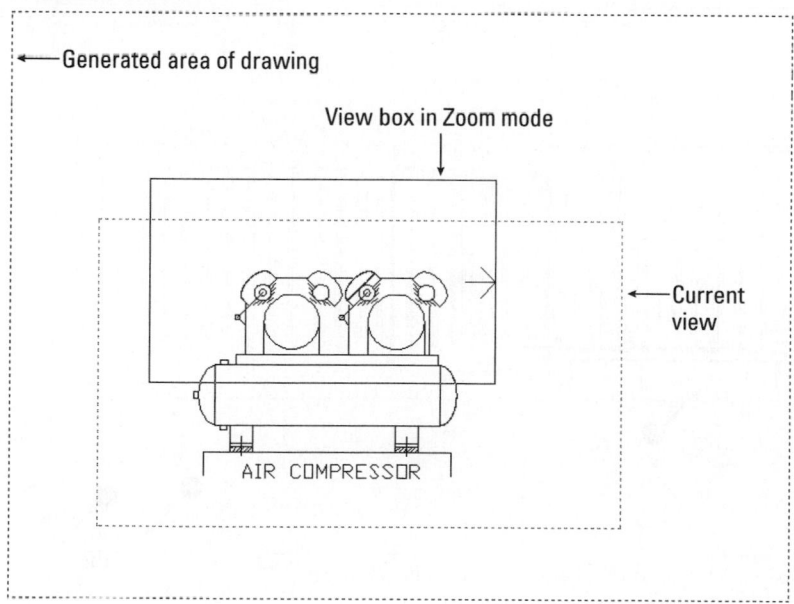

143

On the DVD

The drawing used in the following exercise on panning and zooming, `ab08-a.dwg`, is in the `Drawings` folder on the DVD. ∎

STEPS: Panning and Zooming

1. Open `ab08-a.dwg` from the DVD. This is a drawing of a warehouse, as shown in Figure 8.2.

 2. To read the text in the lower-right corner, choose Zoom Window from the Zoom drop-down list on the Navigation bar.

3. At the Specify corner of window, enter a scale factor (nX or nXP), or [All/Center/Dynamic/Extents/Previous/Scale/Window/Object] <real time>: prompt, pick ❶, as shown in Figure 8.2. At the Specify opposite corner: prompt, pick ❷. AutoCAD or AutoCAD LT zooms in to display the window that you specified.

 4. Choose View tab ⇨ Navigate panel ⇨ Zoom drop-down list ⇨ All.

 5. Choose View tab ⇨ Views panel ⇨ Previous View. You return to the previous display.

 6. If you have a mouse with a wheel, double-click the wheel. Otherwise, choose Zoom Extents from the Zoom drop-down list on the Navigation bar. The drawing fills the screen. In this drawing, the drawing extents are similar to the drawing limits, so that you see little difference between using Zoom All and Zoom Extents.

FIGURE 8.2

A drawing of a large warehouse, with shelving and conveyor belts.

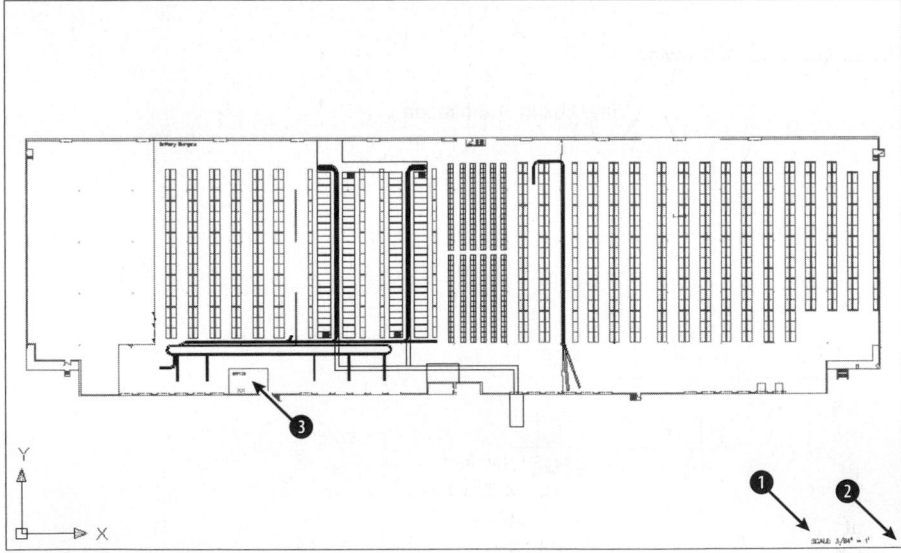

Thanks to Bryan Kelly of ATI Corporation, Fairfield, Iowa, for this drawing.

7. Choose Navigation bar ⇨ Zoom drop-down list ⇨ Zoom Center. At the `Specify center point:` prompt, pick ❸, as shown in Figure 8.2. At the `Enter magnification or height <5315.176>:` prompt, type **500** ↵. You zoom in on the office.

 8. Choose Zoom Realtime from the same Zoom drop-down list. Place the cursor at the top of the drawing, then click and drag to the bottom of the screen. The display zooms out about 200 percent.

 9. Choose Zoom Scale from the Navigation bar's Zoom drop-down list. Type **2x** ↵. The display zooms in, doubling the scale of the view and returning you approximately to the previous view of the office.

 10. Press and hold your mouse's wheel and move the mouse to the left, horizontally, until the office is on the left side of the screen. Or, choose Pan from the Navigation bar, drag to the left with the mouse's pick button, and then press Enter to exit Pan Realtime mode.

 11. Choose Zoom Dynamic from the Navigation bar's Zoom drop-down list. You now see the entire drawing. The current view is shown with a green dashed line. The mouse cursor is a box with an X in it. You are now in Pan mode. To zoom in on the right side of the warehouse, move the Pan box to the lower-right corner of the warehouse and click with the pick (left) button.

12. You are now in Zoom mode. The Zoom box contains an arrow. Move the mouse to the left to shrink the Zoom box. Notice that the Zoom box is fixed at its left side. When the Zoom box is about half of its original size, left-click again.

13. You are back in Pan mode again. Move the Pan box to the bottom-right corner of the warehouse. Right-click and choose Enter to zoom in on this new view. Your display should look approximately like Figure 8.3.

FIGURE 8.3

The new view of the drawing after using Zoom Dynamic.

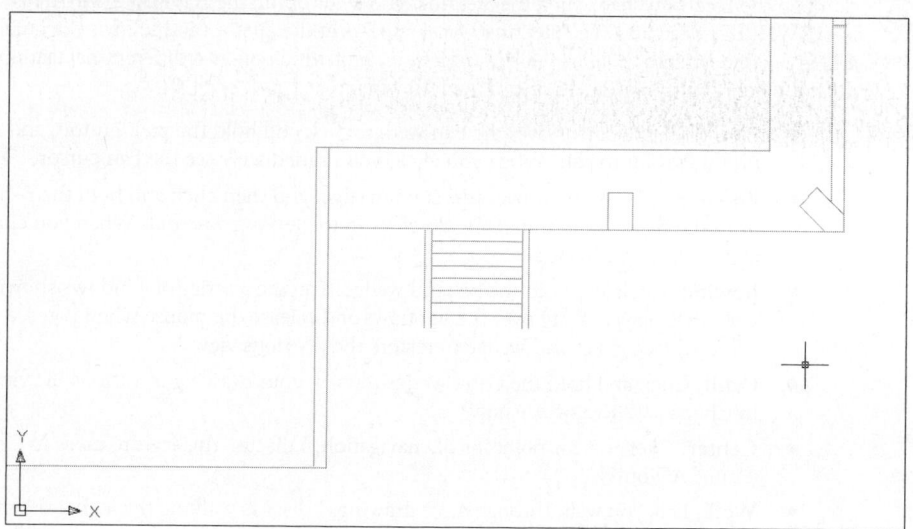

14. Choose Extents from the Navigation bar's Zoom drop-down list. Do not save your drawing. If you're continuing to the next exercise, leave the drawing open.

Using the SteeringWheel

The SteeringWheel is a navigation device that allows you to zoom and pan from a single interface. It also lets you rewind through previous displays. This wheel is an all-in-one navigation tool for both 2D and 3D use. For more information on 3D navigation, see Chapter 22. In AutoCAD LT, the wheel offers only 2D navigation tools. Figure 8.4 shows the default SteeringWheel in AutoCAD.

FIGURE 8.4

The SteeringWheel is a quick navigation device that hovers at the cursor.

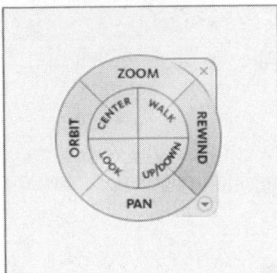 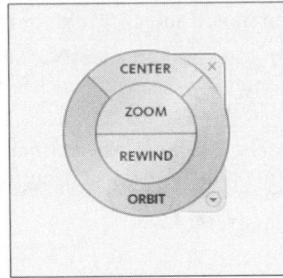 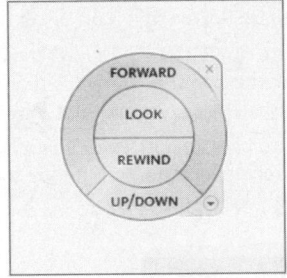

  To open the SteeringWheel, click the SteeringWheel button on the Navigation bar. This starts the NAVSWHEEL command. The SteeringWheel appears at the cursor (and follows the cursor as you move it) and is divided up into sections (called *wedges*), each of which offers a different navigational aid. To use the default wheel configuration, do one of the following:

- **Pan.** Place the cursor over the Pan wedge, click and hold the pick button, and drag in the direction you want to pan. When you click, you immediately see the Pan cursor.
- **Zoom.** Place the cursor over the Zoom wedge, and then click and hold the pick button. Drag up or to the right to zoom in. Drag down or to the left to zoom out. When you click, you immediately see the Zoom cursor.
- **Rewind.** Click and hold the Rewind wedge. You see a series of windows showing each view that you've displayed. Drag over the windows and release the mouse when you see the view that you want. Click the Rewind wedge to restore the previous view.
- **Orbit.** Click and hold the Orbit wedge to view your drawing in various 3D views. I discuss Orbit in Chapter 22 (AutoCAD only).
- **Center.** Click a pivot point for 3D navigation. I discuss this feature more in Chapter 22 (AutoCAD only).
- **Walk.** Lets you walk through a 3D drawing. I discuss walking through a drawing in Chapter 22 (AutoCAD only).
- **Look.** Swivels the 3D view. I discuss this further in Chapter 22 (AutoCAD only).
- **Up/Down.** Moves the view along the Y axis, like going up or down in an elevator. I discuss this further in Chapter 22 (AutoCAD only).

To exit, Press Esc or Enter or click the wheel's X button. To configure the wheel, right-click and choose SteeringWheel Settings. In the SteeringWheel Settings dialog box, you can configure both 2D and 3D features. For example, you can change the wheel's size and opacity, and display a mini wheel, which is a smaller version of the SteeringWheel. You can also quickly choose one of the configurations from the shortcut menu. The SteeringWheel Settings dialog box and option are in AutoCAD only.

Creating Named Views

After you've done a lot of panning and zooming in a drawing, you may find that you return to the same part of your drawing again and again, especially if the drawing undergoes a lot of changes. In a large drawing, it can take some time to display the part of the drawing that you want. You can speed up the process by saving views.

A view is simply a display of a drawing on your screen. A view can show any part of your drawing at any magnification. After you have the display that you want, you give the view a name and then save it. AutoCAD or AutoCAD LT then lets you retrieve that view at any time, without zooming or panning.

Saving a view

First display the view that you want to save on the screen. Then choose View tab ⇨ Views panel ⇨ Named Views to start the VIEW command and open the View Manager, as shown in Figure 8.5.

FIGURE 8.5

The View Manager dialog box.

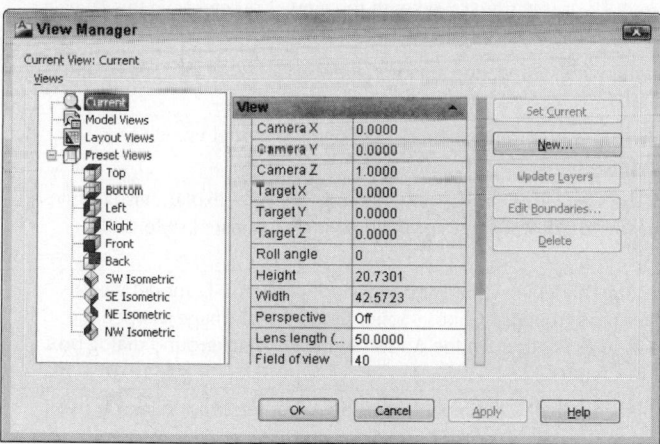

The Views pane lists the following types of views:

- **Current.** The current display.
- **Model views.** All named views, including cameras, in model space. *Model space* is where you draw. I cover the concept of model space in Chapter 17. Cameras are a way to define 3D views (they are not available in AutoCAD LT); I explain cameras in Chapter 22.

- **Layout views.** All named views created in a layout (paper space). A layout is a mechanism for laying out your drawing in preparation for plotting or printing. I explain layouts in Chapter 17.
- **Preset views.** Preset views that come with AutoCAD and AutoCAD LT. These are the same views that you see by choosing View tab ⇨ Views panel ⇨ Views drop-down list.

When you choose a view in the Views panel, you see its properties in the central panel of the View Manager dialog box. The available properties depend on the type of view. You can use the properties panel to change most of a view's properties; however, some are for information only and are not editable. Some of the properties only apply to 3D views, and some are not available in AutoCAD LT. Table 8.2 lists the properties that may appear in the View Manager.

TABLE 8.2

View Properties

Property	Description
Name	Named Views, Cameras, and Layout Views
Category	The category that you specify when you create a new named view. A category is optional and applies only to model and layout views. If you specify a category, it appears on the Sheet Views tab of the Sheet Set Manager (covered in Chapter 26).
Viewport Association	Specifies whether the view is associated with a viewport on a sheet in a sheet set. This applies only to layout views.
UCS	The name of the User Coordinate System (UCS) saved with the view. When you create a named view, you can save a UCS with that view. I cover UCSs later in this chapter.
Layer snapshot	Specifies whether the current layer states are saved with the view. You can save this *layer snapshot* with a model or layout view. I cover layer states in Chapter 11.
Location	Specifies the layout tab name when you define a named view on a layout tab. See Chapter 17 for a discussion of layout tabs.
Annotation Scale	Stores the annotation scale that was current when you defined the model view. See Chapter 17 for more on annotation scales.
Visual style	Specifies a visual style for the view. This applies only to model views. I explain visual styles in Chapter 22; they apply mostly to 3D drawings. For 2D drawings, the visual style is 2D Wireframe.
Background	Specifies a background for the model view. Backgrounds apply only to 3D model views (AutoCAD LT does not offer backgrounds). Choose Solid, Gradient, or Image to open the Background dialog box or Sun & Sky to open the Adjust Sun & Sky Background dialog box. I cover backgrounds more in Chapter 22.
Live section	Specifies a live section object applied to the model view. See Chapter 24 for more on live sections.
View type	Displays the type of *shot*, used for animation and playbacks. I discuss creating animated presentations (the ShowMotion feature) later in this chapter.
Transition type	Displays the type of transition between views, when shown as an animated presentation (the ShowMotion feature).
Transition duration	Displays the length of the transition between shots.
Playback duration	Displays the length of the display of the shot, when played back as an animated presentation.

Property	Description
Camera X	Displays the X coordinate of the view's camera. This is for information only and does not apply to layout views.
Camera Y	Displays the Y coordinate of the view's camera. This is for information only and does not apply to layout views.
Camera Z	Displays the Z coordinate of the view's camera. This is for information only and does not apply to layout views.
Target X	Displays the X coordinate of the view's target. This is for information only and does not apply to layout views.
Target Y	Displays the Y coordinate of the view's target. This is for information only and does not apply to layout views.
Target Z	Displays the Z coordinate of the view's target. This is for information only and does not apply to layout views.
Roll angle	Specifies the angle that the view is tilted around the line of site. This is for information only and does not apply to layout views.
Height	Specifies the height of the view. This is for information only and does not apply to camera views.
Width	Specifies the width of the view. This is for information only and does not apply to camera views.
Perspective	Specifies whether a view is a perspective view. This applies to model views. I discuss perspective views in Chapter 22.
Lens length (mm)	Specifies the lens length in millimeters. This applies to perspective views only. The LENSLENGTH system variable controls the default value for this setting. Changing this value also changes the Field of View setting, which is another way of expressing this setting.
Field of view	Specifies the field of view of a perspective view. Changing this value also changes the Lens Length setting. This does not apply to layout views.
Front plane	Specifies the offset for the front clipping plane if you enabled front clipping. I cover clipping in Chapter 22; it applies to 3D views only.
Back plane	Specifies the offset for the back clipping plane if you enabled back clipping.
Clipping	Turns clipping on or off.

To create a new named view, click New to open the New View / Shot Properties (or New View in AutoCAD LT) dialog box, as shown in Figure 8.6. Type a name for your view in the View Name text box. To specify a view, you use the View Properties tab in AutoCAD.

View names can be up to 255 characters and can include spaces. As explained in Table 8.2, you can save a category, a layer snapshot, a User Coordinate System, a live section, and a visual style with a view. Select the Current Display option button to use the current display as the view. Otherwise, click the Define View Window button, and specify a window around the view that you want. Press Enter to return to the New View / Shot Properties (New View in AutoCAD LT) dialog box.

Click OK to return to the View Manager dialog box, where you see your new view listed. Click New again to define another new view or click OK to return to your drawing.

FIGURE 8.6

The New View / Shot Properties dialog box, with the View Properties tab active.

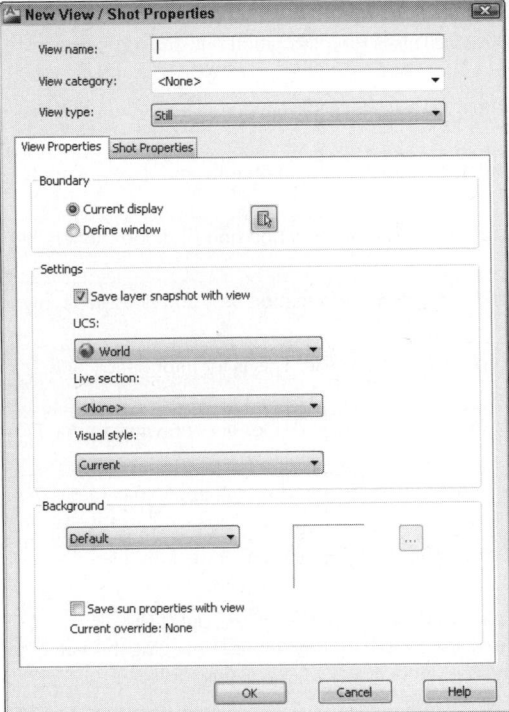

Tip

In a very large drawing, you might create views as soon as you create the titleblock — for example, one for each quadrant of the drawing and another for the titleblock lettering. This helps you move quickly from one section of the drawing to another. As you determine the need for more specific views, you can add them. ∎

Displaying a view

You can easily display any view that you have saved. The easiest way is to go to View tab ➪ Views panel, and click the Views drop-down list, where you can find the named views that you created. Alternatively, choose View tab ➪ Views panel ➪ Named Views, choose your named view, click Set Current, and click OK.

Managing named views

You can use the View Manager to manage named views. You can also find these features by right-clicking inside the View Manager.

- To delete a view, choose the view that you want to delete and click the Delete button or press the Delete key on your keyboard.
- To rename a view, select it, type a new name in the Properties pane (next to the Name property), and press Enter.

- To change the layer states that you saved with the view, change the states of any layers before opening the dialog box. Then open the View Manager dialog box, choose a named view, and click Update Layers. The view now uses the current layer states. (I explain layers in Chapter 11.)

- To edit the boundaries of a view, choose the Edit Boundaries button. You are now back in your drawing and the current view boundaries are shown in black or white (depending on the color of your background). At the prompts, specify the two opposite corners that you want to serves as boundaries for the view and press Enter.

Creating animated presentations from named views

You can create a presentation that displays one named view after another, as a way to show the drawing, perhaps to a client or colleague. In essence, you create a slide show from named views in your drawing. Each view can have a transition, as well as timing for the transition and the display of the view itself; together, these properties are called a shot. A looping feature lets you create an ongoing display of views. This feature, called ShowMotion, is not available in AutoCAD LT. You define the shot on the Shot Properties tab of the New View / Shot Properties dialog box, as shown in Figure 8.7.

FIGURE 8.7

Use the Shot Properties tab of the New View / Shot Properties dialog box to create and configure a presentation of your drawing.

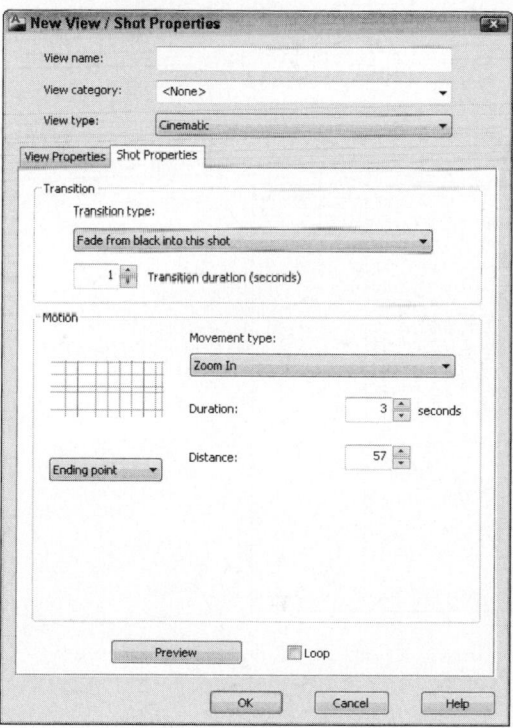

To configure the shot, first choose one of the view types:

- **Cinematic.** Allows you to choose a movement for the view. Most of the options are appropriate for 3D drawings only. The options are Zoom In, Zoom Out, Track Left, Track Right, Crank Up, Crank Down, Look, and Orbit. Each movement has its own settings. Try them out and click the Preview button to see what they look like.

- **Still.** Displays a still view. You can specify the duration of the view.

- **Recorded Walk.** Lets you record a walk-through of a 3D model. I discuss this feature in Chapter 22.

Next, choose a transition from the Transition Type drop-down list. Then enter a duration for the transition in the Transition Duration text box. Finally, change the options under the Motion section as desired based on the transition type selected. Click OK when you're done.

Tip

The Fade from Black into This Shot option looks best with a black background. The Fade from White into This Shot option looks best with a white background. See Appendix A for instructions on changing the background color of the drawing area. ■

 To play the show or use other related features, click ShowMotion on the Navigation bar to start the NAVSMOTION command. At first, you see one window, displaying the drawing, along with some navigation tools. However, if you move the cursor over that window, thumbnails of all the views appear, as shown in Figure 8.8.

FIGURE 8.8

The ShowMotion feature creates a slide show from named views.

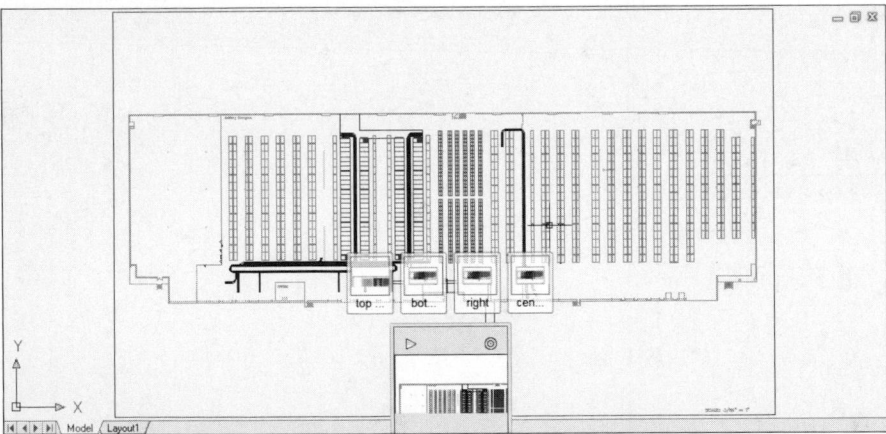

Use the navigation tools to do the following:

- Click any view to display that view.

- Click the Pin button to pin the ShowMotion box, so that it doesn't disappear when you click elsewhere in the drawing area.

- Click the Play All button to play the slide show. Click in the drawing area to hide the ShowMotion window (if it isn't pinned) so that it doesn't obscure the show.

- Click the Stop button to stop the slide show.

- Click the Turn On Looping button to repeat the playback over and over.

- Click the New Shot button to open the New View / Shot Properties dialog box, with the Shot Properties tab on top so that you can create a new view and define its shot properties.

To edit the properties of a shot, right-click the thumbnail of an individual shot and choose Properties, or use the EDITSHOT command and enter the name of the shot. The View / Shot Properties dialog box opens, where you can change the settings of the shot.

On the DVD

The drawing used in the following exercise on working with views, ab08-a.dwg, is in the Drawings folder on the DVD. ∎

STEPS: Working with Views

1. Open ab08-a.dwg from the DVD if it is not already open from the previous exercise.
2. Save the file as ab08-01.dwg in your AutoCAD Bible folder.
3. Choose View tab ⇨ Views panel ⇨ Named Views to open the View Manager.
4. Click New to open the New View / Shot Properties (New View in AutoCAD LT) dialog box, with the View Properties tab on top if you are using AutoCAD.
5. In the View Name text box, type **top left**.
6. Click the Define View Window button to return to your drawing temporarily.
7. At the Specify first corner: prompt, pick the top-left corner of the drawing. At the Specify opposite corner: prompt, pick somewhere around the center of the warehouse. Press Enter to return to the New View / Shot Properties (New View in AutoCAD LT) dialog box.
8. If you are using AutoCAD LT, go to the next step. Click the Shot Properties tab. Check that the View type is set to Still. Change the Transition Duration to 0.5 seconds. In the Motion section, change the Duration to 1 second.
9. Click OK once.
10. Click New again. Type **bottom left** in the text box of the New View / Shot Properties (or New View in AutoCAD LT) dialog box.
11. Click the Define View Window button. At the Specify first corner: prompt, pick the bottom-left corner of the drawing. At the Specify Opposite corner: prompt, again pick around the center of the warehouse. Press Enter.
12. If you are using AutoCAD LT, go to the next step. Click the Shot Properties tab. Again, change the Transition Duration to 0.5 seconds. In the Motion section, change the Duration to 1 second, as you did previously.
13. Click OK. The View Manager dialog box should list both of your views. Click OK to close the View Manager.
14. Choose View tab ⇨ Views panel ⇨ Named Views. If necessary, expand the Model Views item, and choose bottom left. Click Set Current, and then click OK. AutoCAD or AutoCAD LT displays the view.

15. If you are using AutoCAD LT, go to the next step. Click ShowMotion on the Navigation bar. Click the Play button. The ShowMotion feature displays the two views, one after the other, using the transition and timing that you specified.

16. Save your drawing. The views that you created are now part of the drawing database.

Using named views to manage a drawing

Using named views provides three additional advantages:

- You can use named views when you open a drawing so that one of its views is immediately displayed.
- You can open only the part of a drawing contained in a view.
- You can turn a named view into a floating viewport for plotting purposes (AutoCAD only).

I explain these techniques in the next three sections.

A drawing with a view

After you've saved views, you can use them to open a drawing so that a view is immediately displayed. Click Open on the Quick Access Toolbar. In the Select File dialog box, choose the file that you want to open and check the Select Initial View check box. Then click Open. In the Select Initial View dialog box, choose the view that you want to display, and click OK.

Partially opening a drawing

You may have a very large drawing that is slow and cumbersome to work with when it is completely loaded. For example, if you have a surveyor's drawing of an entire county, but you need to work only with one plat, you can open a named view containing only that plat. This feature is not available in AutoCAD LT.

To partially open a drawing from within AutoCAD, follow these steps:

1. Click Open on the Quick Access Toolbar to open the Select File dialog box.

2. Choose a drawing and then click the Open button's drop-down list. Choose Partial Open to open the Partial Open dialog box, as shown in Figure 8.9.

3. Choose a view from the list of named views.

4. Check the check box of one or more layers. To include all the layers, click Load All. If you don't include at least one layer, no objects are loaded. (Chapter 11 covers layers.) Click Open.

After you've partially opened a drawing, you can load more of the drawing. Enter **partialload** ↵ on the command line. This command is functional only if the current drawing has been partially opened. AutoCAD opens the Partial Load dialog box. You can change the view. To display the entire drawing (from whatever is loaded), choose the default view, *Extents*. Check the layers that you want to include or click Load All. Click OK to load the newly specified view and layers.

Using named views with sheet sets

You can combine layouts from more than one drawing into a sheet set. (AutoCAD LT doesn't include this feature.) Sheet sets are a powerful way to organize many layouts. I cover them in detail in Chapter 26. However, at this point you should know that named views have a value beyond helping you display an area of your drawing. They can become your final layout for plotting.

Suppose that you're drawing a mechanical model with a top view, a side view, and a section view. In the final plot, you want to display these three views on one sheet of paper. Without sheet sets, you would create three floating viewports and individually pan and zoom to get the three views. (For more information on floating viewports, see the "Floating viewports" sidebar in this chapter, as well as Chapter 17.) Using the sheet-set feature as you work, you can create named views of the three parts of the drawing. Then you can use those same views to create the floating viewports for plotting.

FIGURE 8.9

Use the Partial Open dialog box to open only the part of a drawing contained in a named view.

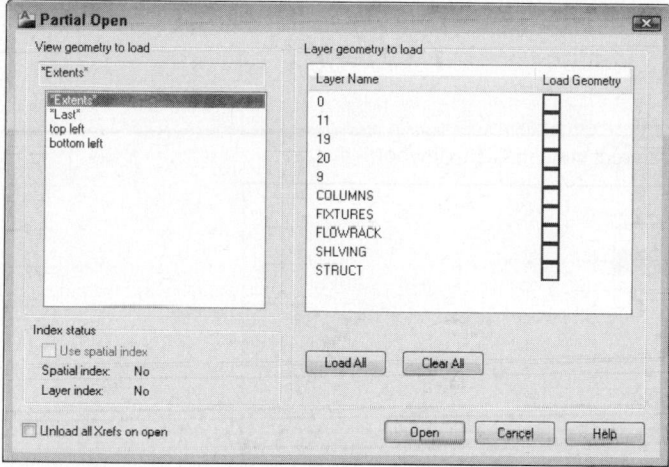

Working with Tiled Viewports

Tiled viewports enable you to divide up the screen into rectangular bounding boxes. You can then show different views of your drawing in each viewport — at one time. The purpose of tiled viewports is to help you draw. For example:

- You can see the whole drawing in one viewport and a zoomed-in portion of that drawing in another viewport.
- You can see widely separated views of a large drawing at one time.

Cross-Reference
There are two types of viewports — tiled and floating. For more information on floating viewports, see the "Floating viewports" sidebar in this chapter. For a detailed discussion, turn to Chapter 17. ∎

Actually, you're already using a tiled viewport because the regular single view of your drawing that you've been working with represents the default of a one-tile viewport. Tiled viewports have the following characteristics:

- No matter how many viewports you have, they always collectively take up the entire screen. They are not separate entities but a way of dividing the screen.
- Only one viewport can be active at a time. The active viewport has a bold border.
- The crosshairs appear only in the active viewport.
- The UCS (User Coordinate System) icon (if set to On) appears in each viewport.

- Any change that you make to your drawing in one viewport automatically appears in every other viewport (or in viewports that show the part of the drawing where you made the change).
- You can create up to 64 viewports — but you'll never want to create that many!
- You can begin a command in one viewport and finish it in another. For example, you can start a line in one viewport, switch to a second viewport, and end the line there.
- You can save and restore viewport configurations.

Figure 8.10 shows a drawing divided into three tiled viewports. Each viewport shows a different view of the same drawing.

FIGURE 8.10

A drawing showing three tiled viewports with a different view in each viewport.

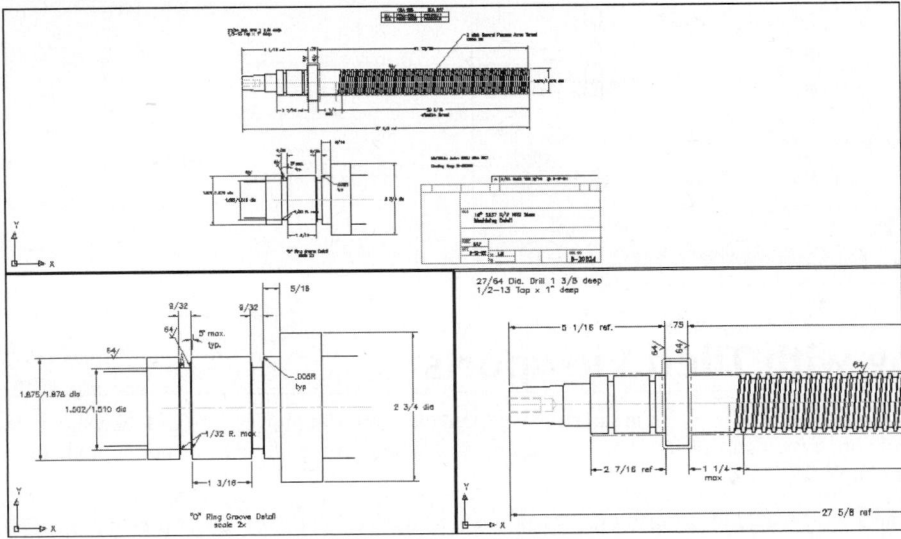

Thanks to Jerry Bottenfield of Clow Valve Company, Oskaloosa, Iowa, for this drawing.

Configuring tiled viewports

Creating tiled viewports involves deciding how you want to divide up the screen. A set of tiled viewports is called a *configuration*. A few simple configurations come with AutoCAD and AutoCAD LT, but you can create your own by further dividing up any of the viewports. You can also join two adjacent viewports. Finally, you can always return to the default of one viewport.

Creating tiled viewports

To add viewports, choose View tab ➪ Viewports panel ➪ New. The Viewports dialog box opens with the New Viewports tab on top, as shown in Figure 8.11. You choose the configuration that you want here. You see a preview of the configuration.

If you have named views in your drawing, you can specify a view for each viewport to display. Click a viewport in the Preview pane and choose a named view from the Change View To drop-down list at the bottom of the dialog box. You can also choose a visual style from the Visual Style drop-down list if you are using AutoCAD. If your drawing is in 3D, you can choose 3D from the Setup drop-down list, and AutoCAD creates standard orthogonal views in the viewports. When you've specified your viewport configuration, click OK to return to your drawing.

The Viewports dialog box is usually the best place to start creating viewports. However, if the standard configurations do not meet your needs, you can use one of them as a starting point and then use the other options.

The Viewports dialog box makes it easy to choose a configuration.

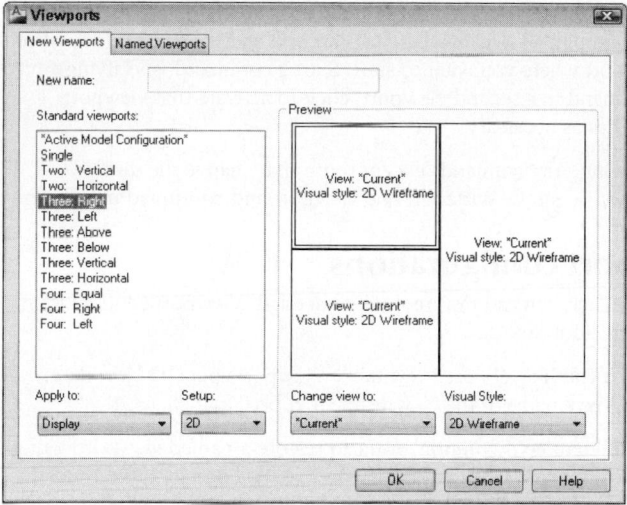

Notice the Apply To drop-down list at the bottom-left corner of the Viewports dialog box in Figure 8.11. By default, the tiled viewport configurations apply to the entire display, meaning that they replace your current configuration. You can also choose to apply the configuration to the viewport that is currently displayed in the drawing area. The active viewport has a bold border and crosshairs. To make a viewport active, click anywhere inside that viewport. Then choose View tab ➪ Viewports panel ➪ New, choose Current Viewport from the Apply To drop-down list, and choose the configuration that you want for that viewport.

Let's say that you have four equal viewports, and the top-left viewport is active. If you choose the Four: Equal configuration from the Viewports dialog box while the top-left viewport is active and apply it to the current viewport, the top-left viewport is divided into four viewports. Now you have seven viewports in the drawing.

Removing tiled viewports

One way to remove a tiled viewport is to join it to another viewport. To join one viewport to another, choose View tab ➪ Viewports panel ➪ Join Viewports. At the `Select dominant viewport <current viewport>:` prompt, click the viewport that you want to retain or press Enter if you want to retain the current viewport. At the `Select viewport to join:` prompt, click the adjacent viewport that you want to join into the dominant viewport. When the two viewports merge, you lose the display in the second viewport. Together, the adjacent viewports must form a rectangle.

The only other way to remove all tiled viewports in one step is to return to the single viewport configuration. Choose View tab ➪ Viewports panel ➪ Viewport Configurations drop-down list ➪ Single. The display in the current viewport remains.

Using tiled viewports

After you've created the viewport configuration that you want, the first step is to create the views that you need in each viewport. Just click in a viewport, and zoom and pan until you have the view that you want.

Tip

Many users choose one viewport to display the entire drawing and the other viewports to display zoomed-in views of smaller sections. ■

One of the great advantages of viewports is that you can draw from one viewport to another. In a large drawing, you may need to draw a line from one end of the drawing to another, but when you display the entire drawing, you can't see the detail well enough to specify where to start and end the line. To draw from one viewport to another, just click the viewport where you want to start. Start a command, specifying any necessary coordinates. To continue the command in a second viewport, click to activate that viewport. Continue the command, specifying coordinates as necessary.

You can also use viewports to edit your drawing. All commands except those that change the display — such as zooming, panning, and creating views — can be started in one viewport and continued in another.

Saving and restoring viewport configurations

You can save a tiled viewport configuration. Then you can restore it when needed. Viewport configuration names can be up to 255 characters and can include spaces.

After you create a viewport configuration that you like, choose View tab ➪ Viewports panel ➪ New if you aren't already in the Viewports dialog box. Type a name in the New Name text box, and click OK.

After returning to one viewport or using a different configuration, you can restore a named viewport configuration. Choose View tab ➪ Viewports panel ➪ Named to open the Viewports dialog box with the Named Viewports tab on top. Choose the viewport that you want to restore from the list, and click OK.

Floating viewports

AutoCAD and AutoCAD LT have two types of viewports: *tiled viewports,* which are discussed here, and *floating viewports,* which I cover in Chapter 17. These two types of viewports have many similarities, but they have different purposes. Whereas the purpose of tiled viewports is to help you draw and edit your drawing, you use floating viewports to lay out your drawing for plotting.

Floating viewports create layouts, which enable you to treat your screen like a sheet of paper. You create floating viewports and perhaps a titleblock on this electronic sheet of paper. You can create one or more layouts. Each floating viewport can show a different view of your drawing — just like tiled viewports. But floating viewports then let you plot all those views on one sheet of paper. You can't do that with tiled viewports, which are just devices to let you temporarily display your drawing in a way that helps you draw and edit. However, you can also draw and edit by using floating viewports.

Tiled viewports are covered here because they are appropriate for learning how to draw and edit your drawing. Floating viewports are covered in Chapter 17 because you use them to lay out your drawing for plotting.

On the DVD

The drawing used in the following exercise on creating, naming, and restoring tiled viewport configurations, ab08-b.dwg, is in the Drawings folder on the DVD. ■

STEPS: Creating, Naming, and Restoring Tiled Viewport Configurations

1. Open ab08-b.dwg from the DVD.

2. Save the file as ab08-02.dwg in your AutoCAD Bible folder.

3. Choose View tab ⇨ Viewports panel ⇨ New to open the Viewports dialog box.

4. In the listing at the left of the dialog box, choose Three: Above. Click OK. You see three tiled viewports.

5. Click the bottom-right viewport. Choose View tab ⇨ Navigate panel ⇨ Zoom drop-down list ⇨ Window and choose a window around the left portion of the threaded model (the upper part of the drawing).

6. Click the bottom-left viewport. Again choose Window from the Zoom drop-down list and choose a window around the bottom-left portion of the drawing (not including the titleblock).

7. Click the top viewport. Choose View tab ⇨ Navigate panel ⇨ Zoom drop-down list ⇨ Extents. Figure 8.12 shows the results.

8. Choose View tab ⇨ Viewports panel ⇨ New. In the New Name text box, type **3 view O Ring** and click OK.

9. With the top viewport still active, choose View tab ⇨ Viewports panel ⇨ Viewport Configurations drop-down list ⇨ Single to display the view shown in the last active viewport.

10. Choose View tab ⇨ Viewports panel ⇨ Named.

FIGURE 8.12

The three tiled viewports now display three different views.

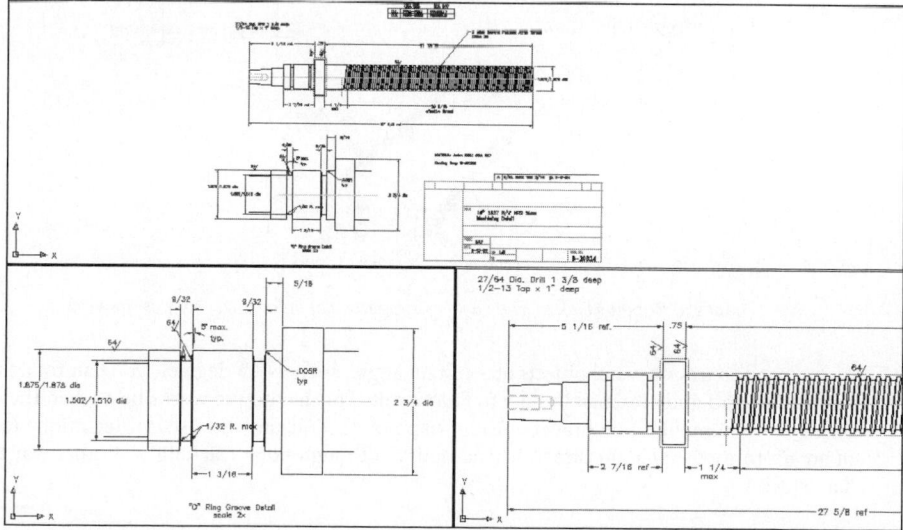

11. Choose 3 view O Ring and click OK to restore the viewport configuration, including the views in each viewport.

12. Save your drawing.

Using Snap Rotation

Not all 2D drawings are vertical and horizontal. In some drawings, significant portions of your objects need to be at nonorthogonal angles. One example is an auxiliary view to show the "true size" of an inclined surface. Sometimes it helps to rotate the crosshairs to match the major angles of the drawing.

Consider Figure 8.13. A great deal of this drawing is at an angle. You could handle this in five ways:

- Draw as normal, specifying the necessary angles.
- Rotate the snap, which also rotates the grid and crosshairs.
- Use the ViewCube to rotate the drawing.
- Create a new User Coordinate System (UCS). (Creating a new UCS is covered later in this chapter.)
- Draw the entire model vertically and rotate it afterward.

FIGURE 8.13

In 2D drawings such as this, you should consider various options, such as rotating the snap or creating a new UCS.

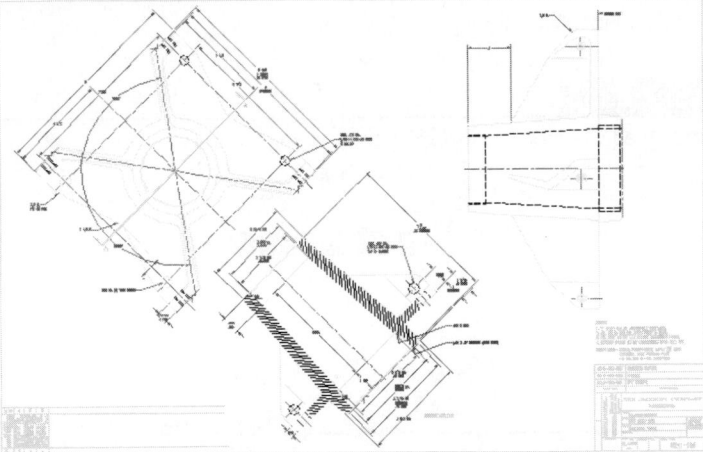

Thanks to Robert Mack of The Dexter Company, Fairfield, Iowa, for this drawing.

If you need to draw several objects at a certain angle, such as 45 degrees, you can rotate the snap to that angle. The grid and crosshairs rotate to follow suit. This technique works best when the decimal point accuracy required lets you draw by using snap points. You can also use this technique to guide the cursor at an appropriate angle for direct distance entry, although polar tracking is another way to accomplish the same task.

To change the snap rotation angle, you use the SNAPANG system variable. Enter **snapang** ↵ on the command line. At the `Enter new value for SNAPANG <0>:` prompt, enter an angle. For example, if you enter **45** ↵, the crosshairs, snap, and grid rotate 45 degrees.

Note that you can also set an X base and a Y base. This simply ensures that the grid goes through a point of your choice, which is very important if you're using Snap mode to draw. If you're just starting to draw an object, use the 0,0 base and draw to the existing snap points. However, if you have an existing object and need to add to it, changing the base can be very helpful. Setting X and Y bases does not change the coordinates, which are tied to the UCS. (The UCS is discussed in the next section.) To set the base, use the SNAPBASE system variable on the command line and specify a coordinate for the base. You can use an object snap.

Cross-Reference

You can use the ID command to get the coordinates of a point. Then use these coordinates as the X and Y bases. Chapter 12 covers the ID command. ■

After setting the snap angle, you may want to turn the grid on to help you get your bearings. The crosshairs and grid now reflect the new snap angle. Figure 8.14 shows the same drawing with a snap angle of 45 degrees. Notice how the crosshairs now match the angle of the drawing. The crosshairs have been set to 100 percent of screen size, which is useful when rotating the snap angle. (To reset the crosshairs size, choose Application Button ➪ Options and use the Crosshair Size section of the Display tab.)

FIGURE 8.14

The snap angle in this drawing has been changed to 45 degrees. Note that the grid follows the snap.

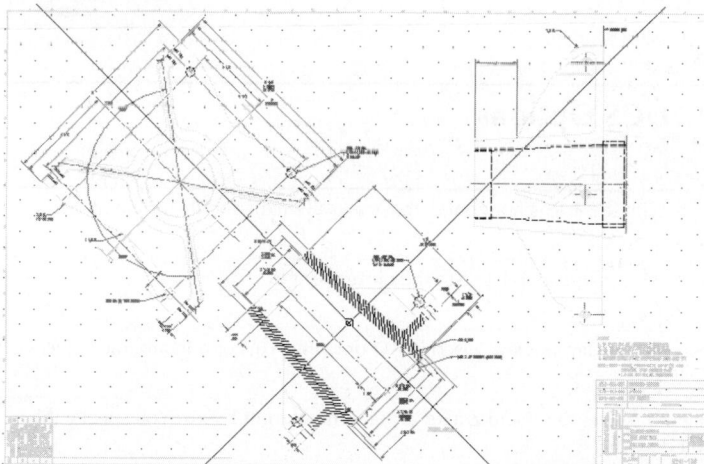

New Feature

You can use the ViewCube to rotate the drawing, along with the UCS icon and the grid. I cover the ViewCube in Chapter 22, because it's most often used in 3D drawings. When you place the cursor outside the edge of the ViewCube, you see a circle that you can drag clockwise or counterclockwise to rotate the drawing. ■

Understanding User Coordinate Systems

You can create a new User Coordinate System (UCS) rather than rotate the snap angle. The results are similar, except that when you create a UCS, you also affect the X,Y coordinates. The UCS is much more flexible when you start drawing in three dimensions.

By default, a drawing is set up by using a World Coordinate System. This sets the origin of the X,Y points at 0,0 and the angles using the familiar East (right-facing) equals 0 degrees system. Figure 8.15 shows the UCS icon in its default display in a 2D environment. The X axis is red and the Y axis is green.

FIGURE 8.15

The UCS icon in its default display.

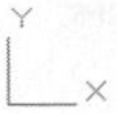

You can easily create your own UCS and even save it for future use in the drawing. To define a UCS in a 2D drawing, you indicate the angle of the X and Y axes and an origin point. The origin point then becomes the new 0,0 coordinate. You have several options for specifying the UCS.

Understanding UCS options

Understanding the UCS options will help you create a new UCS more easily, based on the information that you have available. To create a UCS, choose View tab ⇨ Coordinates panel and click one of the options, as listed in Table 8.3.

TABLE 8.3

UCS Options

Button	Option	Meaning
	World	Specifies the default UCS, with the X axis horizontal, the Y axis vertical, and the origin at the initial 0,0 location.
	Origin	Specifies a new 0,0 point of your choice, relative to the current origin.
	View	Aligns the X and Y axes with the current view. Used in 3D drawing. This option arbitrarily sets the origin.
	X	Keeps the current origin and rotates the Y and Z axes around the current X axis. You specify the angle. This is used in 3D drawing.
	Y	Keeps the current origin and rotates the X and Z axes around the current Y axis. You specify the angle. This is used in 3D drawing.
	Z	Keeps the current origin and rotates the X and Y axes around the current Z axis. You specify the angle. This option can be used in 2D drawing.
	Object	Enables you to align the UCS with an object. In general, this option uses the most obvious object snap as the origin and aligns the X axis with the object. For example, when you choose a line, the endpoint nearest your pick point becomes the origin and the X axis aligns with the angle of the line. When you choose a circle, the X axis points toward the point that you pick on the circumference.

Button	Option	Meaning
	Z-Axis Vector	Specifies which way the Z axis points. This option is not used in 2D drawing.
	Face	Aligns the UCS with the face of a 3D solid.
	3 Point	Enables you to specify three points. The first point is the origin, the second point indicates the positive direction of the X axis, and the third point indicates the positive direction of the Y axis.

Saving and restoring a custom UCS

After you create a UCS, you can save it so that you can easily switch back and forth between the World Coordinate System and your UCS. To save a UCS, follow these steps:

1. Specify the UCS as described in the previous section.

2. Choose View tab⇨Coordinates panel⇨UCS, Named UCS to open the UCS dialog box, as shown in Figure 8.16. If your current UCS is not named, it is listed as Unnamed and highlighted. Previously named UCSs are also listed. You can also use this dialog box to return to the previous UCS or the World Coordinate System (WCS).

3. Click Unnamed. Type a name for the UCS and press Enter. The name can be up to 255 characters and can include spaces.

4. Click OK.

To restore a saved UCS, return to the same dialog box, choose the UCS that you want to use, and click Set Current. To delete a saved UCS, select it in the UCS dialog box and press the Del key. You can also select a UCS, right-click, and choose one of the options from the shortcut menu. When you're done, click OK to close the dialog box.

FIGURE 8.16

Use the UCS dialog box to save and restore a UCS.

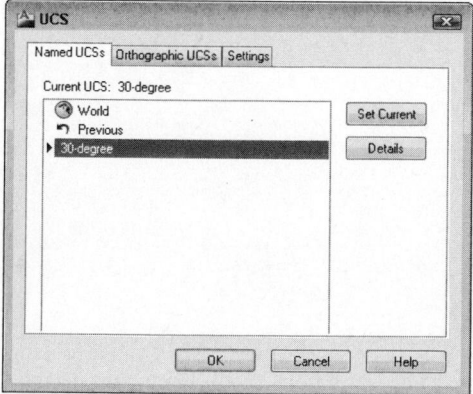

Controlling the UCS icon

When you start a new drawing, the UCS icon is at the bottom left of your drawing at 0,0. By default, the icon remains at 0,0 even if you pan around the drawing. The icon may, therefore, end up in the middle of your drawing. If 0,0 is off the screen, then the icon reverts to the bottom left of your drawing.

You can turn off the UCS icon completely. If you aren't working with customized UCSs, you often have no reason to see the UCS in a 2D drawing. If you want the UCS icon on, you can also display it only at the bottom left of your drawing. This keeps the icon out of the way so that it does not obstruct your drawing.

If you create a new UCS, keeping the UCS icon at the 0,0 point (the origin) of your new UCS helps you to get your bearings. A plus sign appears in the icon to indicate the origin. However, if the origin is out of the current display or so close to the edge that the icon won't fit, the UCS icon appears at the lower-left corner of your drawing anyway.

To control the UCS icon, choose View tab ➪ Coordinates panel, and click the dialog box launcher arrow to the right of the panel name to open the UCS dialog box. Click the Settings tab, where you can control the UCS icon with the following items:

- **On.** Toggles the display of the UCS icon on and off. You can also turn the display on and off by choosing View tab ➪ Coordinates panel ➪ Display UCS Icon.
- **Display at UCS Origin Point.** Toggles the placement of the UCS icon at the origin on and off.
- **Apply to All Active Viewports.** Applies the preceding two settings to all viewports, rather than to just the current viewport.

 You can customize the look of the UCS icon. To do this, choose View tab ➪ Coordinates panel ➪ UCS Icon, Properties to open the UCS Icon dialog box, as shown in Figure 8.17. As you make changes, you can see the result in the preview box.

FIGURE 8.17

Use the UCS Icon dialog box to customize the look of the UCS icon.

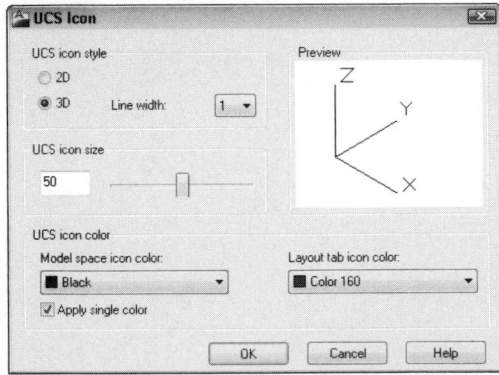

Choose between 2D and 3D styles. The 3D style shows the Z axis, but you won't see it when you're looking at your model from the top (called *Plan view*). You can choose a line width from 1 to 3, 1 being the default.

You can change the size of the icon. Just drag the slider up and down to get the result you like. Finally, you can change the color of the icon, both in model space and in paper space layouts. (I cover paper space layouts in Chapter 17.) Click OK to close the dialog box.

Using a custom UCS

In this exercise, you practice drawing with a custom UCS to create the basic framework for the drawing shown previously in Figures 8.13 and 8.14, a bearing housing for a commercial dryer.

On the DVD

The drawing used in the following exercise on drawing with a custom UCS, ab08-c.dwg, is in the Drawings **folder on the DVD.** ■

STEPS: Drawing with a Custom UCS

1. Open ab08-c.dwg from the DVD. This exercise assumes that you have Dynamic Input on, with the default relative coordinates setting.

2. Save the file as ab08-03.dwg in your AutoCAD Bible folder. Ortho Mode and Object Snap should be on. Set a running object snap for Endpoints only.

3. Choose View tab ⇨ Coordinates panel ⇨ Z. Because no objects exist in the drawing, you cannot easily use the 3 Point or Object options that might otherwise be useful.

4. At the Specify rotation angle about Z axis <90>: prompt, type **45** ↵. The UCS icon and crosshairs are displayed at a 45-degree angle.

5. Choose Home tab ⇨ Draw panel ⇨ Line. At the prompt, pick a point in the middle of your screen. At the Specify next point or [Undo]: prompt, type **1.25<90** ↵. End the LINE command.

6. Choose Home tab ⇨ Draw panel ⇨ Rectangle. Choose the From object snap. At the Base point: prompt, use the Endpoint object snap to pick the endpoint of the line that you just drew. At the <Offset>: prompt, type **@.875,0** ↵. At the Specify other corner point or [Dimensions]: prompt, type **@-5.5,1.5** ↵. The command creates the rectangle at the proper angle.

7. Start the LINE command again. Follow the prompts:

   Specify first point: *Choose the From object snap.*
   Base point: *Use the Endpoint object snap to pick point* ❶ *in Figure 8.19.*
   <Offset>: *Type* **@-.875,0** ↵
   Specify next point or [Undo]: *Move the cursor in the 90° direction (which looks like the 135° direction because of the rotated UCS).* **.625** ↵
   Specify next point or [Undo]: *Move the cursor in the 180° direction.* **3.75** ↵
   Specify next point or [Close/Undo]: *Move the cursor in the 270° direction.* **.625** ↵
   Specify next point or [Close/Undo]: ↵

8. Start the LINE command again.

   Turn on Object Snap Tracking on the status bar and follow the prompts:

   Specify first point: *Pass the cursor over* ❷ *and then over* ❸ *in Figure 8.18 to acquire these points. Move the cursor to* ❹ *at the intersection of the two temporary tracking lines and click.*
   Specify next point or [Undo]: *Move the cursor in the 270° direction relative to the UCS.* **1.25** ↵.

   Specify next point or [Undo]: ↵

FIGURE 8.18

Using a customized UCS to start to draw a detail for a drill.

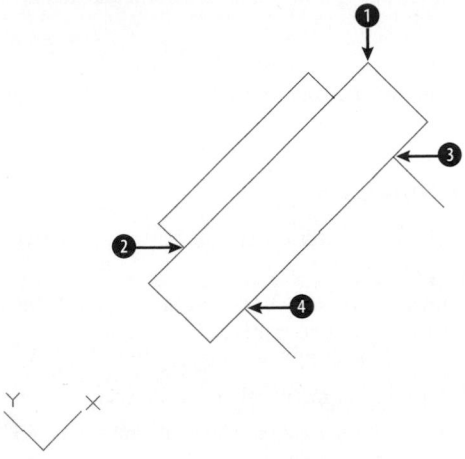

9. Because you would normally continue working on this drawing, you should save the UCS. Choose View tab ⇨ Coordinates panel ⇨ UCS, Named UCS. In the UCS dialog box, on the Named UCSs tab click Unnamed. Type **Rotated 45** and press Enter.

10. Still in the dialog box, choose World, click Set Current, and click OK to return to your drawing. The UCS icon and crosshairs return to their familiar angle.

11. To return to the Rotated 45 UCS, again open the UCS dialog box with the Named UCSs tab on top. Choose Rotated 45 and click Set Current. Click OK to restore the Rotated 45 UCS.

12. Save your drawing.

Tip

After creating a new, rotated UCS such as the one in the previous exercise, type plan (to start the PLAN command) and use the Current UCS option to remove the rotation. Now you aren't working at an angle in your UCS. To return to the World UCS, type plan again and choose the World option to return to your drawing's previous state. ■

Creating Isometric Drawings

An *isometric* drawing is a 2D drawing made to look like a 3D drawing. Every child learns how to draw a box that looks three dimensional. By drawing parallelograms instead of squares, the drawing gives the impression of being in three dimensions. AutoCAD and AutoCAD LT enable you to do the same thing. However, most people use true 3D tools these days. For more information, see Part IV of this book.

Understanding isometric planes

The ISOPLANE (short for isometric plane) command rotates the crosshairs to the special angles required for isometric drawing. You then toggle the ISOPLANE setting from left to right to top, to draw on each of the three "planes." As you do so, the angles of the crosshairs, snap, and grid change to the appropriate angles.

These angles are 30 degrees for the X axis, 90 degrees for the Z axis, and 150 degrees for the Y axis. As you toggle among the planes, you see the crosshairs take on various configurations of these angles. Figure 8.19 shows the standard isometric cube. You can see three sides — left, right, and top. In the figure, the crosshairs are set to the right isometric plane.

Isometric drawing is not often used for precise drawing because specifying the exact points that you need can be difficult. Also, true 3D drawing has mostly supplanted isometric drawing. Isometric drawings are sometimes still used for piping work as well as for illustrations.

Tip

Use snap points and object snaps as much as possible in an isometric drawing. Also, you can enlarge crosshairs to better visualize the isometric planes. (Choose Application Button ⇨ Options and click the Display tab. Set the Crosshair Size value to 100.) The grid is also a helpful aid. ■

FIGURE 8.19

The Isometric cube.

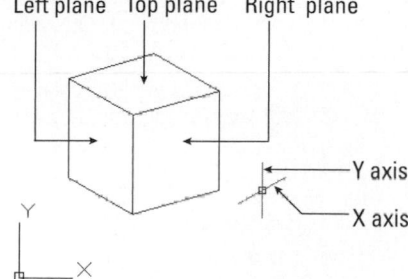

Left plane   Top plane   Right plane

Y axis
X axis

Drawing in Isometric mode

To start Isometric mode, right-click the Snap button on the status bar and choose Settings to open the Drafting Settings dialog box. On the Snap and Grid tab, in the Snap Type section, choose Grid Snap (if it is not already selected), and then Isometric Snap to enter Isometric mode. While you're there, turn on Snap and Grid if you want them on. Click OK. After you're in Isometric mode, press F5 to toggle from plane to plane.

Drawing lines in Isometric mode is fairly straightforward if the lines are parallel to one of the isometric plane angles. Circles and arcs in Isometric mode must be drawn as ellipses and elliptical arcs. When you're in Isometric mode, the ELLIPSE command has an Isocircle option.

Tip

Polar coordinate display is very helpful while drawing isometrically. The coordinates are easier to understand than the unusual absolute snap point coordinates created by ISOPLANE. ■

Summary

In this chapter, you read how to control the display of your drawing. You learned about:

- The PAN and ZOOM commands, including real-time pan and zoom and the many ZOOM options
- Using the SteeringWheel
- Saving several views of your drawing so that you can retrieve them quickly
- Creating animated presentations of your drawing
- Creating tiled viewports for drawing and editing, as well as naming and displaying useful viewport configurations
- Rotating the snap and grid
- Creating a User Coordinate System, saving a UCS, and then setting it as current
- Setting the snap style to isometric to create isometric drawings

In the next chapter, you discover how to start editing your drawings.

Editing Your Drawing with Basic Tools

No drawing project is ever completed without changes. You make changes in a drawing for many reasons. Some editing processes are simply part of the drawing process, such as copying an object rather than drawing it a second time from scratch. Other types of editing involve making changes to many objects at once, such as moving an entire section of a drawing to make room for additional objects. You often also need to erase, move, rotate, and resize objects.

Editing a Drawing

Making changes to a drawing is called *editing*. In order to edit an object, you need to select it. AutoCAD and AutoCAD LT offer numerous techniques for selecting objects. In this chapter, I cover basic editing commands as well as most of the ways to select objects. The rest of the 2D editing commands, as well as additional selection and editing methods — grips, the Properties palette, selection filters, and groups — are covered in the next chapter.

Most of the editing commands are on the Home tab in the Modify panel. In most cases, you can do either one of the following:

- Start the command first and then select the objects to which the command applies.
- Select the objects first and then start the command.

The question of which comes first, the command or the object, is fully covered later in this chapter.

Note

Although you can use the editing tools that I describe in this chapter in a 3D environment, this chapter assumes that you are working in a 2D environment. (AutoCAD LT doesn't offer a 3D environment.) To make sure that you're in a 2D environment, set the workspace to AutoCAD Classic or 2D Drafting & Annotation (choose it from the Workspace Switching list on the Quick Access Toolbar or the status bar) and set the visual style to 2D Wireframe (use the 2D Wireframe option of the `vscurrent` command). If you still see the Z axis on the UCS icon, choose View tab ⇨ Views panel ⇨ 3D Navigation drop-down list ⇨ Top. Another method is to set the workspace to 2D Drafting & Annotation, and then start a new drawing based on the default `acad.dwt` template. ■

Understanding object-selection basics

When you start to edit drawings, it is important to first learn how to select objects. The simplest selection technique is to place the *pickbox* — the box at the intersection of the crosshairs — over the object and click with the pick button on the mouse. This is known as *picking* an object. By default, when you select an object, the Quick Properties panel appears. I discuss this panel in Chapters 10 and 12.

When you pass the cursor over an object before choosing any editing command, the object becomes thicker and dashed. This *rollover highlighting* helps you to know which object you will select when you click. This feature is helpful in a busy drawing with many objects close together or overlapping. I explain how to fine-tune the effect in the next chapter. You also see a rollover tooltip that displays some basic properties of the object.

If you start an editing command before selecting an object, the command responds with the `Select objects:` prompt. When you then pick an object to select it, AutoCAD or AutoCAD LT highlights it, usually by making the object dashed, as shown on the left side of Figure 9.1.

The command continues to provide `Select objects:` prompts so that you can select other objects. Continue to select objects until you have selected all the objects that you want to edit. Then press Enter to end the `Select objects:` prompt.

When you select an object before choosing an editing command, the lines of the selected object become dashed and you also see one or more small boxes, called *grips,* as shown on the right side of Figure 9.1 for a line. Chapter 10 covers grips. In the next few exercises, you use this picking technique to select objects. Other selection methods are covered later in this chapter.

FIGURE 9.1

On the left, the selected line is dashed. On the right, the selected line also displays grips.

Erasing objects

The ERASE command is very simple — it has no options. To erase an object, select the object and choose Home tab ⇨ Modify panel ⇨ Erase, or press Del on the keyboard. Alternatively, choose Erase and then select the object.

Cross-Reference

The PURGE command erases two kinds of undesirable objects that sometimes mistakenly exist in a drawing — zero-length lines and empty text objects. I cover the PURGE command more in Chapter 11. ∎

On the DVD

The drawing used in the following exercise on picking and erasing objects, `ab09-a.dwg`, **is in the** `Drawings` **folder on the DVD.** ∎

STEPS: Picking and Erasing Objects

1. Open `ab09-a.dwg` from the DVD.

2. Save the file as `ab09-01.dwg` in your `AutoCAD Bible` folder. This drawing is a schematic of a gas extraction well, as shown in Figure 9.2.

3. To erase the line at point ❶ of Figure 9.2, move the mouse until the pickbox at the intersection of the crosshairs is anywhere over the line. The line thickens and is dashed. Click the line. Now the line is dashed and displays grips.

FIGURE 9.2

The gas extraction well schematic.

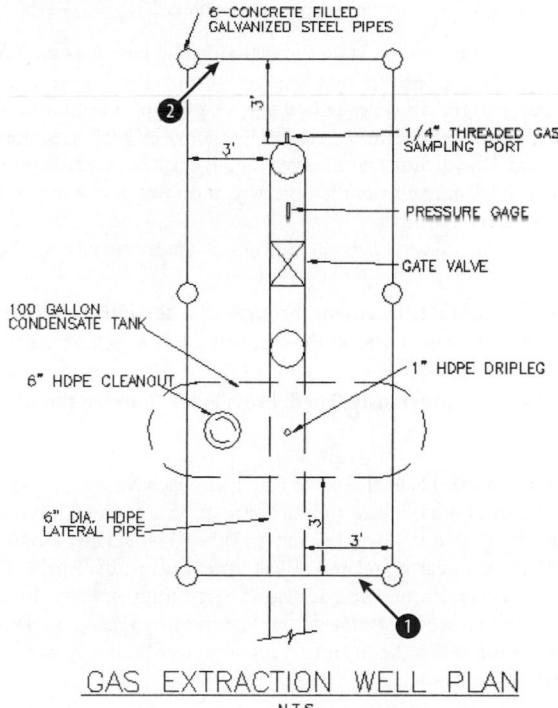

Thanks to the Army Corps of Engineers for this drawing.

4. Choose Home tab ⇨ Modify panel ⇨ Erase. The line is erased.

5. Right-click and choose Repeat ERASE.

6. At the Select objects: prompt, pick the line at point ❷, as shown in Figure 9.2.

7. The command responds with 1 found and repeats the Select objects: prompt. Right-click to end the Select objects: prompt. The line is erased.

8. Save your drawing.

Cross-Reference
The OOPS command restores the most recently erased object and is covered in Chapter 18. ∎

Moving objects

Use the MOVE command to move objects in your drawing. You need to specify the distance and direction that you want the object to move.

To move an object, select it and choose Home tab ⇨ Modify panel ⇨ Move. Alternatively, choose Move and then select the object. When you start the MOVE command and then select an object, the command responds with the following prompt:

```
Specify base point or [displacement] <Displacement>:
```

You now have two ways of specifying how to move the object or objects:

- **Displacement method.** At the prompt, state the entire displacement as an X,Y coordinate such as 2,3 or a polar coordinate such as 2<60. The command responds with the Specify second point or <use first point as displacement>: prompt. Because you've already specified all the necessary information, press Enter. AutoCAD or AutoCAD LT uses the first point you indicated as the displacement (the default) and moves the object. (Because the word *displacement* already implies the relative distance from the object, you do not use @, even if you have Dynamic Input on and set to Absolute coordinates.)

Tip
The MOVE command remembers the most recent displacement throughout a session. To move an object the same displacement as you just moved another object, press Enter at the Specify base point or [Displacement] <Displacement>: prompt. At the Specify displacement <2.0000, 3.0000, 0.0000>: prompt, you see in angled brackets the last displacement that you previously typed. Press Enter to move the object using this displacement. ∎

- **Base point/second point method.** At the Specify base point or [Displacement] <Displacement>: prompt, pick a base point. This can be anywhere in your drawing but is usually on or near the object that you want to move. When you specify a base point, choose an object snap on the object or a nearby, related object for exact results. At the Specify second point or <use first point as displacement>: prompt, specify the distance and angle of movement either by picking a second point on the screen or by typing a relative coordinate. (If you have Dynamic Input on, set to the default of relative coordinates, you don't need to add the @ symbol before the coordinates.)

The displacement method requires less input and is simpler when you know the exact displacement so that you can type it in. The only disadvantage is that, as soon as you type in the displacement, you sometimes see a confusing temporary drag line and copy of your object or objects. Ignore this display and press Enter.

Your object or objects move as you specified. The base point/second point method works best when you want to move an object relative to another object on the screen.

You can use PolarSnap with the base point/second point method to move an object. Turn on PolarSnap and, if necessary, use the Drafting Settings dialog box to set the increment. If the polar distance is 0, you can set it to a new value. AutoCAD and AutoCAD LT use the Snap X spacing value that you specified in the Drafting Settings dialog box. At the first prompt, pick a point such as an object snap on the object. At the second prompt, drag the object in the desired direction. Use the tooltip to guide you and then click.

You can use drag-and-drop to move objects if you aren't too particular about where they end up. Here's how it works:

1. Pick an object.
2. Continue to pick as many objects as you want to move. They all show grips.
3. Pick any of the objects, but not on a grip. Keep the mouse button pressed until the cursor changes to an arrow with a small rectangle.
4. Drag the object(s) to any other location in your drawing.

For a little more control over the placement of your objects, you can use the Windows Clipboard. Pick the object(s) that you want to move. Right-click and choose Cut from the shortcut menu. Right-click a second time and choose Paste. At the prompt for an insertion point, you can pick with an object snap or by typing coordinates. However, you can't control the base point (which is 0,0) as you can with the MOVE command, because it's always the lower-left corner of the object or of a bounding box around the object.

On the DVD
The drawing used in the following exercise on moving objects, ab09-b.dwg, is in the Drawings folder on the DVD. ∎

STEPS: Moving Objects

1. Open ab09-b.dwg from the DVD.
2. Save the file as ab09-02.dwg in your AutoCAD Bible folder. This drawing shows the plan of a bathroom. Each object is a *block*, a set of objects that you can select as one object. (Chapter 18 covers blocks.) Make sure that Object Snap mode is turned on. Set a running object snap for Intersection only.

3. Pick anywhere on the tub to select it. Notice the rollover highlighting before you click, and the grip and dashed lines that appear after you click. Choose Home tab ➪ Modify panel ➪ Move. Follow the prompts:

   ```
   Specify base point or [Displacement] <Displacement>: Move the cursor
       to the Intersection at ❶ in Figure 9.3 and click.
   Specify second point of displacement or <use first point as
       displacement>: Move the cursor to the Intersection at ❷ in Figure
       9.3 and click.
   ```

   The tub moves to the bottom-right corner of the bathroom.

4. Choose Move again. Follow the prompts:

   ```
   Select objects: Pick the sink.
   Select objects: ↵
   Specify base point or [Displacement] <Displacement>: 4'<0 ↵
   Specify second point of displacement or <use first point as
       displacement>: ↵
   ```

   The sink moves 4 feet to the right.

FIGURE 9.3

The bathroom plan.

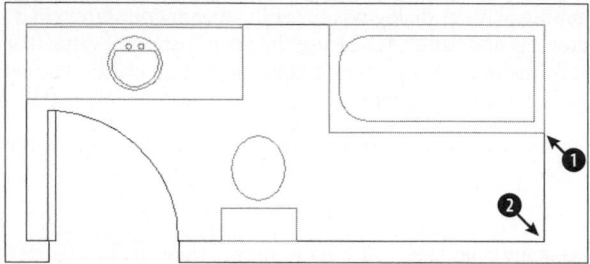

Thanks to Bill Wynn of New Windsor, Maryland, for this drawing.

5. Click Snap Mode on the status bar to turn it on. Now, right-click Snap Mode. Choose PolarSnap On (unless it is already on, in which case it is unavailable). Click Polar Tracking on the status bar.

6. Pick the toilet and choose Move again. At the `Specify base point or [Displacement]` `<Displacement>:` prompt, pick the intersection at the bottom-left corner of the toilet tank. At the `Specify second point or <use first point as displacement>:` prompt, move the toilet to the left until you see `0'-6"<180°` on the tooltip, and click. The toilet moves 6 inches to the left. (If you can't get a 180° tooltip, check your polar angle settings.)

7. Save your drawing.

Copying objects

Copying is very similar to moving. In fact, the only difference is that AutoCAD or AutoCAD LT does not remove the object from its original spot, so you end up with two objects rather than one.

 To copy an object, select it and choose Home tab ⇨ Modify panel ⇨ Copy. Alternatively, choose Copy and then select the object. When you start the COPY command and have selected an object, the command responds with the following prompt:

```
Specify base point or [Displacement/mOde] <Displacement>:
```

You now have two ways of specifying where to copy the object or objects:

● **Displacement method.** At the `Specify base point or [Displacement/mOde]` `<Displacement>:` prompt, state the entire displacement as an X,Y coordinate such as 2,3 or a polar coordinate such as 2<60. The command responds with the `Specify second point or <use first point as displacement>:` prompt. Because you've already specified all the necessary information, press Enter. The command uses the first point that you indicated as the displacement (the default), copies the object, and ends the command. (Because the word *displacement* already implies the relative distance from the object, you do not use @, even if you have Dynamic Input on and set to Absolute coordinates.)

Tip

The COPY command remembers the most recent displacement throughout a session. To copy an object the same displacement as you just copied any object, press Enter at the `Specify base point or [Displacement/mOde] <Displacement>:` **prompt. At the** `Specify displacement <2.0000, 3.0000, 0.0000>:` **prompt, you see in angled brackets the last displacement that you previously typed. Press Enter to copy the object using this displacement.** ■

- **Base point/second point method.** At the `Specify base point or [Displacement/mOde]` `<Displacement>:` prompt, pick a base point. This can be anywhere in your drawing. At the `Specify second point or <use first point as displacement>:` prompt, specify the distance and angle of movement either by picking a second point on the screen or by typing in a relative coordinate. (If you have Dynamic Input on and set to the default of relative coordinates, you don't need to add the @ symbol before the coordinates.)

If you use the base point/second point method, the COPY command continues to prompt you for additional copies. However, scripts and other routines use the earlier functioning, in which the command ends after creating one copy. After you make one copy, you see the `Specify second point or [Exit/Undo] <Exit>:` prompt. Press Enter to use the Exit option and end the command.

Note

The COPYMODE system variable lets you specify if you want the COPY command to repeat or not. By default, as I just described, COPY repeats. Set the system variable's value to 1 to end the COPY command after one copy. You can also change how the COPY command works as you use it, with the Mode option. Choose either the Single or Multiple (the default) suboption. ■

If you've created more than one copy, the Undo option enables you to undo the last copy that you created. You can then continue to make more copies or end the command.

You can use PolarSnap to copy objects in the same way that you use it to move objects. For details, see the previous section. You can also use drag-and-drop to copy objects. Follow the steps in the previous section on moving objects, but press and hold the Ctrl key as you drag the object. Notice the plus sign in the cursor's rectangle. As also described in the previous section, you can use the Clipboard to copy and paste objects from one location in a drawing to another.

New Feature

The Add Selected feature (the ADDSELECTED command) lets you create a new object that has the same properties as an existing object. For example, you can create a new line that has the same color as an existing line. To use the Add Selected feature, select an existing object that has the properties you want, right-click in the drawing area, and choose Add Selected. Follow the prompts to create a new object. ■

On the DVD

The drawing used in the following exercise on copying objects, `ab09-c.dwg`, is in the `Drawings` folder on the DVD. ■

STEPS: Copying Objects

1. Open `ab09-c.dwg` from the DVD.
2. Save the file as `ab09-03.dwg` in your `AutoCAD Bible` folder. This drawing shows part of an electrical schematic. Make sure that Object Snap is turned on. Set a running object snap for Endpoint only.
3. Use ZOOM Window to zoom into the area of the drawing marked ❶, as shown in Figure 9.4. This shows a 24-volt transformer.

FIGURE 9.4

The electrical schematic.

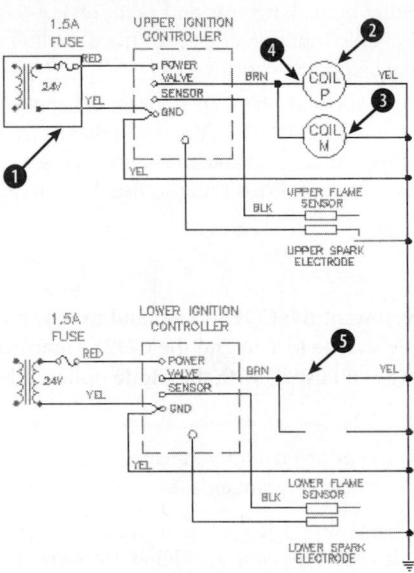

Thanks to Robert Mack of the Dexter Company, Fairfield, Iowa, for this drawing.

4. Note that three of the arcs that make up the right side of the transformer are missing. Pick the arc at ❶, as shown in Figure 9.5. Choose Home tab ⇨ Modify panel ⇨ Copy. Follow the prompts:

   ```
   Specify base point or [Displacement/mOde] <Displacement>: Pick the
       endpoint at the top of the arc at ❷ (see Figure 9.5).
   Specify second point or <use first point as displacement>: Pick the
       endpoint at the bottom of the first arc at ❸.
   Specify second point or [Exit/Undo] <Exit>: Pick the endpoint at the
       bottom of the second arc at ❹.
   Specify second point or [Exit/Undo] <Exit>: Pick the endpoint at the
       bottom of the third arc at ❺.
   Specify second point or [Exit/Undo] <Exit>: ↵
   ```

5. Use ZOOM Previous to return to your previous view.

6. Pick the circle at ❷, as shown in Figure 9.4 (which shows the entire schematic section). Note the grips. You also want to select the text inside the circles, but it's hard to see because of the grips. Press Esc to remove the grips.

7. Choose Copy again. Now select the circle at ❷, shown in Figure 9.4, again. This time no grips obscure the text. Separately pick both lines of text inside the circle.

8. Continuing to select objects to copy, select the circle at ❸, as shown in Figure 9.4. Also select the two lines of text inside the circle. Right-click to end the `Select objects:` prompt.

FIGURE 9.5

Close-up of the transformer.

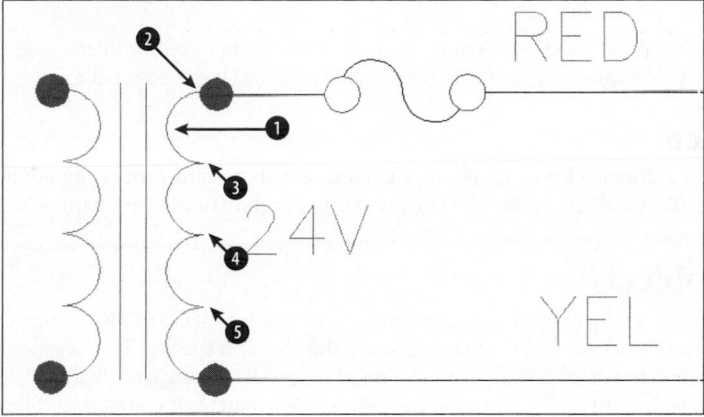

9. At the `Specify base point or [Displacement/mOde] <Displacement>:` prompt, pick the endpoint at ➍, as shown in Figure 9.4. At the `Specify second point or <use first point as displacement>:` prompt, pick the endpoint at ➎, as shown in Figure 9.4. Press Enter to end the COPY command. This action copies the two circles with the text.

10. Save your drawing.

Copying and moving objects from one drawing to another

If you use other Windows programs, you often cut, copy, and paste objects. In AutoCAD and AutoCAD LT, these commands are called CUTCLIP, COPYCLIP, and PASTECLIP. (The CLIP refers to the Windows Clipboard.) Although the MOVE and COPY commands provide more accuracy within one drawing, you can use the Clipboard to move and copy objects from one drawing to another.

You can copy objects from one drawing to another by using the drag-and-drop technique. The easiest way is to open both drawings and then choose View tab ➪ Windows panel ➪ Tile Vertically. Select the object(s) that you want to copy, point to one of them, and drag them to the second drawing. However, you don't have much control over the exact placement of the new objects. From drawing to drawing, AutoCAD or AutoCAD LT copies the objects instead of moving them.

For more control over the placement of your objects, use the Windows Clipboard. A special feature, Copy with Base Point, gives you control over the placement of your objects. Follow these steps:

1. Pick the object(s) that you want to copy.
2. Right-click and choose Clipboard ➪ Copy with Base Point from the shortcut menu.
3. At the `Specify base point:` prompt, specify a base point. An object snap is a good idea here. This action copies the object(s) to the Clipboard, including the base point.
4. Switch to the second drawing.
5. Right-click in the drawing area and choose Clipboard ➪ Paste. At the prompt for an insertion point, specify the insertion point by picking, using an object snap, or typing coordinates. This action pastes the object.

To copy the object(s) to the same coordinates as the original drawing, in Step 5 choose Clipboard⇨Paste to Original Coordinates from the shortcut menu. AutoCAD or AutoCAD LT pastes the object(s) in the second drawing, matching the coordinates. Depending on your drawing, you may need to ZOOM and PAN to see the copy.

You cannot specify a base point for moving (cutting) an object, but you can specify the insertion point when you paste it. The lower-left extent of the selected object(s) is the base point.

Cross-Reference

You can drag objects from a drawing into another application, such as a word-processing document. For more information on working with AutoCAD or AutoCAD LT and other applications, see Chapter 27. ■

Rotating objects

If your design changes or you drew at an incorrect angle, you may need to rotate one or more objects. You can easily rotate an object or objects around a base point that you specify. The base point is usually an object snap point on the object. To indicate the rotation, specify an angle of rotation. As explained in Chapter 5, by default, zero degrees is to the right, and degrees increase counterclockwise. (To change the default, choose Application Button⇨Drawing Utilities⇨Units.) By specifying a negative angle, you can rotate objects clockwise.

 To rotate an object, choose Home tab⇨Modify panel⇨Rotate. Alternatively, select an object and then choose Rotate. At the `Specify base point:` prompt, indicate the point around which you want to rotate. At the `Specify rotation angle or [Copy/Reference]:` prompt, type an angle at the command line.

Tip

Use the Copy option to create a copy of the original object. After you use this option, the same prompt returns so that you can specify a rotation angle. You end up with two objects, one at the original rotation angle and one at the new rotation angle. ■

The most recent rotation angle that you specify becomes the default for other rotations during the same session. For example, if you rotate an object 330°, the next time you rotate an object, the prompt appears as `Specify rotation angle or [Copy/Reference] <330>:`. Press Enter to rotate the object using the default rotation.

The purpose of the Reference option is to let you specify an absolute rotation angle for an object. For example, let's say you want to rotate a line, whose angle you don't know, to 45°. At the `Specify the reference angle <0>:` prompt, you type in an angle or specify an angle by picking two points. These can be object snap points on the object that specify the object's current angle; in the example, you would use the endpoints of the line. At the `Specify the new angle or [Points] <0>:` prompt, type or pick a new angle or specify two points to determine the new angle. You can also pick an object snap on another object in the drawing to indicate this new angle. In the example, you would enter **45** to rotate the line to 45°. You can use the Reference option to align the object with the X or Y axis or with another object in your drawing.

On the DVD

The drawing used in the following exercise on rotating objects, `ab07-03.dwg`, is in the `Results` folder on the DVD. ■

STEPS: Rotating Objects

1. Open ab07-03.dwg from the Results folder of the DVD. If you did the exercise on ellipses in Chapter 7, you can open this drawing from your AutoCAD Bible folder.

2. Save the file as ab09-04.dwg in your AutoCAD Bible folder. This drawing shows a conference room, as shown in Figure 9.6.

3. Set Center, Quadrant, and Perpendicular running object snaps. Object Snap mode should be on. Polar Tracking should be off.

4. Pick the small elliptical table at the top-left corner of the conference room. Choose Home tab ⇨ Modify panel ⇨ Rotate.

FIGURE 9.6

The conference room.

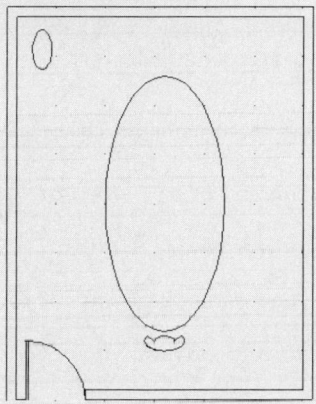

5. At the Specify base point: prompt, pick the top quadrant of the ellipse. At the Specify rotation angle or [Copy/Reference]: prompt, type **90** ↵. This action rotates the small table 90 degrees around the base point.

6. Click Snap Mode on the status bar to turn off snap.

7. To make a copy of the chair and rotate it at the same time, start the ROTATE command. At the Select objects: prompt, pick the arc that makes the back of the chair at the bottom of the drawing. The command responds 1 found. Continue to pick the two lines that make the armrests and the arc that makes the front of the chair, making sure, each time, that you see the response 1 found, for a total of 4. Press Enter to end the Select objects: prompt.

8. To copy and rotate the selected chair, follow the prompts:

```
Specify base point: Use the Center object snap to select the center
    of the large table.
Specify rotation angle or [Copy/Reference] <90>: Right-click and
    choose Copy.
Specify rotation angle or [Copy/Reference] <90>: 180 ↵
```

9. Start the COPY command and select the four objects in the new chair. Press Enter to end object selection. Follow the prompts:

   ```
   Specify base point or [Displacement/mOde] <Displacement>: Use the
       Center object snap to select the center of the arc that makes up
       the back of the chair.
   Specify second point of displacement or <use first point as
       displacement>: Pick a point about a third of the way around the
       right side of the conference table.
   Specify second point or [Exit/Undo] <Exit>: Pick a point about
       halfway around the right side of the conference table.
   Specify second point or [Exit/Undo] <Exit>: Pick a point about two-
       thirds of the way around the right side of the conference table.
   Specify second point or [Exit/Undo] <Exit>: ↵
   ```

10. Start the ROTATE command and select the four objects in the first of the three chairs (the top one) that you just created. Right-click to end object selection. At the `Specify base point:` prompt, pick the Center object snap of either arc of the chair. At the `Specify rotation angle or [Copy/Reference]:` prompt, move the cursor around, watch the image of the chair rotate, and click when the chair faces the angle of the table.

11. Repeat Step 10 for the second chair.

12. Start the ROTATE command and select the four objects in the last chair that you created by using the COPY command. Follow the prompts:

    ```
    Specify base point: Choose the Center object snap of either of the
        chair arcs.
    Specify rotation angle or [Copy/Reference]: Right-click and choose
        Reference from the shortcut menu.
    Specify the reference angle <0>: Use the Quadrant object snap to pick
        the back arc of the chair.
    Specify second point: Use the Quadrant object snap to pick the front
        arc of the chair.
    Specify the new angle or [Points] <0>: Use the Perpendicular object
        snap to choose the conference table next to the chair.
    ```

13. Save your drawing.

Scaling objects

Scaling, or resizing, objects is another common editing task in AutoCAD or AutoCAD LT. As with rotating objects, you specify a base point, usually an object snap on the object. The base point is the one point on the object that does not move or change as you scale the object. The most common way to resize an object is to specify a scale factor. The current object has a scale factor of 1. Therefore, to increase the size of the object, type in a number greater than 1. For example, a scale factor of 2 doubles the size of the object. To decrease the size of the object, type in a number less than 1. A scale factor of 0.25 creates an object one quarter of its previous size. The most recent scale factor that you specify becomes the default for other scaling operations during the same session.

Use the Copy option to create a copy of the original object. After you use this option, the same prompt returns so that you can specify a scale factor. You end up with two objects, one at the original scale and one at the new scale.

As with the ROTATE command, you can scale by using the Reference option to specify an absolute length. You specify the reference length, usually the current length of the object, by typing it in or using object snaps on the object. At the `Specify new length or [Points] <0'-1">` prompt, you can type a new length or pick two points. You can use the Points option to match the size of another existing object.

To scale an object, choose Home tab ➪ Modify panel ➪ Scale, and select the object. Alternatively, you can select the object and choose Scale.

On the DVD

The drawing used in the following exercise on scaling objects, `ab09-d.dwg`**, is in the** `Drawings` **folder on the DVD.** ■

STEPS: Scaling Objects

1. Open `ab09-d.dwg` from the DVD.
2. Save the file as `ab09-05.dwg` in your `AutoCAD Bible` folder. This drawing, shown in Figure 9.7, shows part of a valve that is manufactured in several sizes. In this exercise, you scale both views to represent a different-sized valve piece. Ensure that Object Snap is on. Set running object snaps for Quadrant and Endpoint.

FIGURE 9.7

The valve piece in two views.

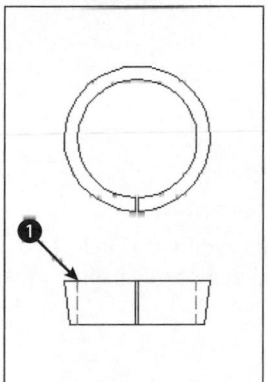

Thanks to Jerry Bottenfield of Clow Valve Company, Oskaloosa, Iowa, for this drawing.

3. Choose Home tab ➪ Modify panel ➪ Scale. At the `Select objects:` prompt, pick both circles in the top view (they're actually arcs because they're broken at the bottom) and the two short lines at the bottom of the circles. Press Enter to end object selection. Follow the prompts:

```
Specify base point: Use the Quadrant object snap to pick the left
    quadrant of the inner circle.
Specify scale factor or [Copy/Reference] <1.000>: Right-click and
    choose Reference.
Specify reference length <1.000>: Use the Quadrant object snap to
    pick the left quadrant of the inner circle again.
Specify second point: Use the Quadrant object snap to pick the right
    quadrant of the inner circle.
Specify new length or [Points] <1.000>: 1 ↵
```

Because the distance between the two quadrants that you chose is 2.5 units, the SCALE command scales the objects to 40 percent (1 divided by 2.5).

4. Right-click and choose Repeat SCALE. Select all eight lines in the bottom view, including the green dashed lines. Be sure that you see 1 found each time. If necessary, use ZOOM Window to zoom in. Right-click to end object selection after you finish selecting the lines. Follow the prompts:

```
Specify base point: Use the Endpoint object snap at point ❶ in
    Figure 9.8.
Specify scale factor or [Copy/Reference] <0.400>: .4 ↵
```

5. Save your drawing. It should look like Figure 9.8.

FIGURE 9.8
_____

The valve piece has now been scaled down.

Using the CHANGE command

The CHANGE command changes the endpoint of a line and the radius of a circle. Note that you can also use grips and the Properties palette, both of which are covered in the next chapter, to change line endpoints and circle radii (among other object properties).

Note

You can use the CHANGE command to change text (which I cover in Chapter 13), the text and text properties of block attributes (not yet contained in a block), as well as the location and rotation of blocks (Chapter 18), but other newer commands do those jobs better. The Properties option of this command can change many object properties, but it's generally easier to use the Properties palette. However, these features of the CHANGE command can be useful when writing scripts or AutoLISP code, covered in Parts VI and VII of this book. ■

New Feature

The Properties option of the CHANGE command has a new suboption, Transparency, which allows you to change an object's transparency value. I cover transparency in Chapter 11. ■

To change an object, select it and type **change** ↵ on the command line. Alternatively, you can type **change** ↵ on the command line and select the object.

Caution

The CHANGE command works differently, depending on whether you select lines or circles. For this reason, it can give unexpected results if you choose lines and circles at the same time. ∎

Changing lines

If you select one line, the CHANGE command changes the endpoint closest to where you picked the line. The command prompts you for a change point. When you pick the point, the command brings the endpoint of the line to that change point, as shown in Figure 9.9. You can use an object snap to specify the change point. If Ortho Mode is on, the line becomes orthogonal, bringing the endpoint of the line as close as possible to the change point that you specify, as shown in Figure 9.9.

FIGURE 9.9

Using the CHANGE command on one line.

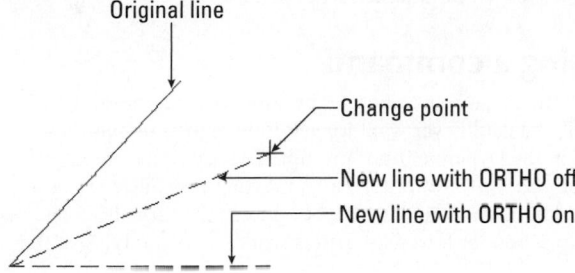

If you select more than one line, CHANGE works differently: It moves the nearest endpoints of all the lines to the change point so that all the lines meet at one point, as shown in Figure 9.10.

FIGURE 9.10

Using the CHANGE command on several lines. The original lines are shown as continuous. The new lines, after using the CHANGE command, are dashed.

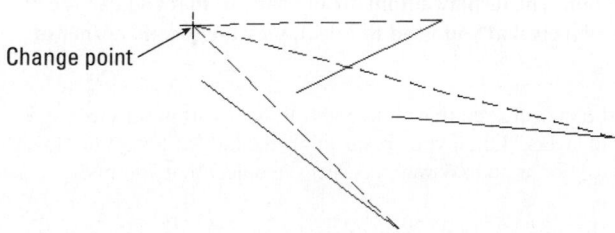

Changing circles

Changing the radius of a circle has the same result as scaling it. When you select a circle, the command prompts you for a change point. AutoCAD or AutoCAD LT resizes the circle so that it passes through the new point. You can also press Enter. You then get a prompt to enter a new radius.

If you select more than one circle, the command moves from circle to circle, letting you specify a new radius for each, one at a time. You can tell which circle is current because of its drag image, which lets you drag the size of the circle.

Selecting Objects

If you've been following through this chapter's exercises, you've probably thought it tedious to pick several objects one at a time. Imagine trying to individually pick every object in a drawing just to move all the objects one-half unit to the left! Of course, there is a better way. In fact, AutoCAD and AutoCAD LT offer many ways of selecting objects. Selected objects are called the *selection set* of objects.

Selecting objects after choosing a command

When you choose an editing command, you see the Select objects: prompt. This prompt has 18 options (16 if you are using AutoCAD LT) — all you could ever want for selecting objects — but these options are not shown on the command line or in the Dynamic Input prompt. To specify an option, type the option abbreviation. Because the Select objects: prompt repeats until you press Enter, you can combine options to select objects for any command. In the following list of options, the capitalized letters of the option are the abbreviation that you type (uppercase or lowercase letters work when you type) at the Select objects: prompt.

- **Window.** The Window option lets you pick two diagonal corners that define a window. All objects entirely within the window are selected. Figure 9.11 shows the process of picking the window on the left and the result on the right — to indicate that the selected objects are highlighted, they display dashed rather than continuous lines. As you move your mouse to specify the second diagonal corner, a blue transparent rectangle appears to help you preview which objects will be selected.

Tip

You can drag past the edge of the screen (actually the viewport) to specify a window. Hold down the mouse button and continue to move the mouse in the same direction. The display automatically pans so that you can see objects that were off the screen. When you see all the objects that you need to select, pick the second corner of the window. ∎

- **Last.** The Last option selects the last object created that is on a visible layer within the current view. (See Chapter 11 for more about layers.) Often you create an object and then want to move or copy it. In this situation, the Last option is an easy way to select the object that you just created.

- **Crossing.** Crossing enables you to pick two diagonal corners that define a window. All objects entirely or partly within the window are selected. As you move your mouse to specify the second diagonal corner, a green transparent rectangle appears to help you preview which objects will be selected. Figure 9.12 shows the process of picking the window on the left and the result on the right — the selected objects are highlighted.

FIGURE 9.11

Selecting objects with a window. The window selects only objects that lie entirely within the window.

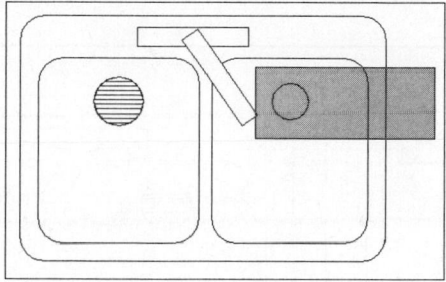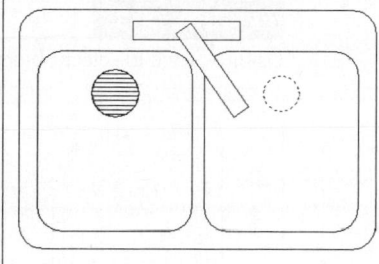

Tip

You can drag past the edge of the screen (actually the viewport) to specify a crossing window. Hold down the mouse button and continue to move the mouse in the same direction. The display automatically pans so that you can see objects that were off the screen. After you see all the objects that you need to select, pick the second corner of the crossing window. ■

FIGURE 9.12

Selecting objects with a crossing window. The crossing window selects any objects that lie within or partly within the window.

Crossing window   Selected objects

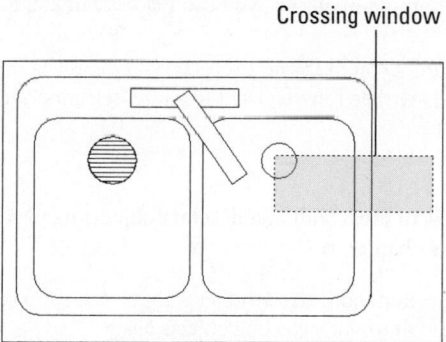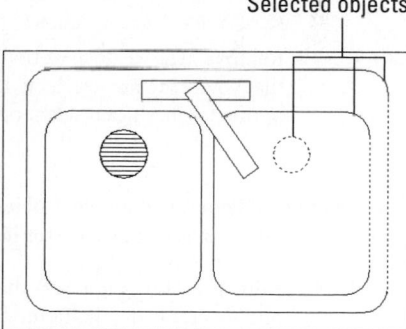

- **BOX.** The BOX option is a combination of the Window and Crossing options. If you pick the two window corners from left to right, the selection functions as if you used the Window option. If you pick the two points from right to left, the selection functions as if you used the Crossing option. By default, you can select objects this way without specifying the BOX option. See the description of implied windowing later in this chapter.

- **ALL.** The ALL option selects all objects on thawed and unlocked layers in the drawing. (I discuss layers in Chapter 11.) Use the ALL option when you want to select everything, including objects that you can't currently see on the screen.

- **Fence.** The Fence option enables you to specify a series of temporary lines to select any object crossing the lines. Figure 9.13 shows the process of defining a selection fence on the left and the result on the right — the selected objects are highlighted.

FIGURE 9.13

Using a fence to select objects.

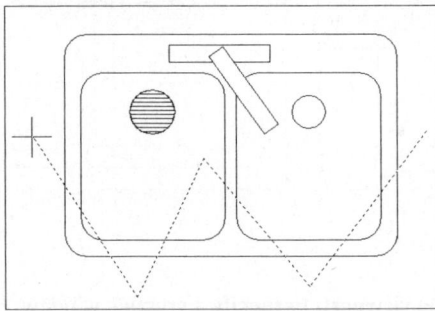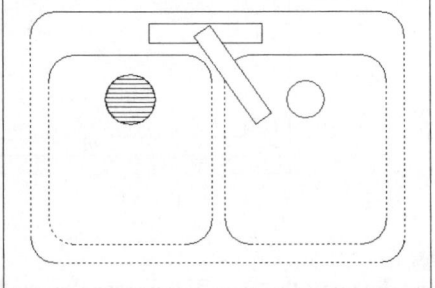

- **WPolygon.** The Window Polygon option (WPolygon) is like the Window option, except that you create a polygon rather than a rectangular window. This option selects all objects that lie entirely within the polygon.
- **CPolygon.** The Crossing Polygon option (CPolygon) is like the Crossing option, except that you create a polygon rather than a rectangular window. This option selects all objects that lie entirely or partly within the window.
- **Group.** The Group option selects a named group of objects. (Chapter 10 covers groups.) If you need to work regularly with a certain set of objects, you can place them in a group and then easily select them with one click.
- **Remove.** The Remove option enables you to deselect objects. After you use this option, all objects that you select are deselected and are therefore removed from the selection set. Use the Add option to once again select objects.

Tip

An alternative to using Remove to deselect objects is to press Shift and deselect objects by picking or implied windowing. Implied windowing is discussed later in this chapter. ■

- **Add.** The Add option sets the selection mode to add objects to the selection set. Use the Add option after using the Remove option to start selecting objects again.
- **Multiple.** The Multiple option turns off highlighting as you select objects. However, you cannot preview which objects are in the selection set.
- **Previous.** The Previous option automatically selects all objects that you selected for the previous command. Objects selected and edited by using grips are not remembered for this option. (The next chapter covers grips.)
- **Undo.** The Undo option deselects the object(s) selected at the last Select objects: prompt. (If you removed objects from the selection set at the last Select objects: prompt, Undo reselects them.)

- **AUto.** The AUto option combines picking with the BOX option. By default, you can select objects this way without specifying this option. See the description of implied windowing later in this chapter.

- **SIngle.** When you specify this option, you get another `Select objects:` prompt. You select objects by using any option, and then AutoCAD immediately ends the selection process. You don't have to press Enter.

- **SUbobject.** The SUbobject option is used only for 3D solids and allows you to select vertices, edges, and faces. For more information, see Chapter 24. (AutoCAD only)

- **Object.** This option ends the selection of subobjects so that you can select other objects. (AutoCAD only)

Cycling through objects

If you have many objects close together in a drawing, it can be hard to select the object or point that you want. You could always zoom in, but another trick is to use *selection cycling*.

New Feature

AutoCAD 2011 and AutoCAD LT 2011 introduce an improved object selection cycling feature, making it easier to select the object you want. ∎

When you hover the crosshairs over two or more overlapping objects, an icon with two overlapping rectangles appears near the crosshairs. When you click on a point where objects overlap, the Selection dialog box appears, listing the objects, so that you can easily select the one you want. Hover over an object's listing in the dialog box to see the corresponding object highlight in the drawing. To select an object, click its item in the dialog box. Continue selecting other objects or use an editing command to work with the selected object.

 Click the Selection Cycling button on the status bar to turn on or off the display of the Selection dialog box. Right-click the Selection Cycling button and choose Settings to control the display of the Selection dialog box.

Tip

At the `Select objects:` prompt, place the cursor over the area where more than one object overlaps. Then hold down the Shift key and press the Spacebar. One object is highlighted. If it is not the one you want, with the Shift key still down, press the Spacebar again to cycle through the objects. When the object that you want is highlighted, pick the object. You can continue to select other objects or end object selection by pressing Enter. ∎

Selecting objects before choosing a command

If you select objects before choosing a command, your options are more limited than if you choose a command first. Nevertheless, you have enough flexibility for most situations. The reason for the limitation is that the `Command:` prompt is active, and anything that you might type at the keyboard to indicate a selection option could be confused with a command. You can pick the object to highlight it, use implied windowing, or use the SELECT command on the command line to select objects in advance.

Tip

To select all objects, choose Home tab ⇨ Utilities panel ⇨ Select All, or press Ctrl+A. Choosing Select All or pressing Ctrl+A cancels the current command, so you need to use these options before you start a command. ∎

The purpose of the SELECT command is simply to select objects. This command then saves these objects for use with the Previous selection option. Choose an editing command and type **p** ↵ at the `Select objects:` prompt to select the objects that you selected with the SELECT command.

New Feature

The SELECTSIMILAR command allows you to select objects in a drawing that are similar to a selected object or objects. Select one or more objects, then right-click and choose Select Similar from the shortcut menu. The objects remain selected when you then choose an editing command, so you can immediately apply that command to the selected objects. Use the Settings option to control which object properties AutoCAD uses to compare the selected objects with others that are in the drawing. I cover object properties in Chapter 11. ■

Implied windowing

Implied windowing is equivalent to the Auto selection option discussed earlier in this chapter. By default, implied windowing is always active. As a result, implied windowing is useful for selecting objects before or after choosing a command. By carefully choosing which way you create a selection window, you determine how you select objects:

- **From left to right.** If the first window corner is to the left of the second one, you create a regular selection window. The window selects all objects entirely within the window.

- **From right to left.** If the first window corner is to the right of the second one, you create a crossing window. The crossing window selects all objects that lie entirely or partially within the window.

On the DVD

The drawing used in the following exercise on selecting objects, ab09-e.dwg, is in the `Drawings` folder on the DVD. ■

STEPS: Selecting Objects

1. Open ab09-e.dwg from the DVD, as shown in Figure 9.14.

2. Save the file as ab09-06.dwg in your `AutoCAD Bible` folder. Make sure that Object Snap mode is on. Set running object snaps for Endpoint and Perpendicular.

3. Draw a line from ❶ to ❷, as shown in Figure 9.14. You will use this later to illustrate the Last selection option.

4. Type **select** ↵.

5. To select the six-burner stovetop, pick a point near ❸, being careful that the pickbox at the intersection of the crosshairs doesn't touch any object. Transparently zoom in and back out, if necessary. Then move the mouse to ❹, again making sure not to pick on any object, and pick again. The objects that you have chosen appear dashed to indicate that they have been selected.

6. To select the last object that was created — the line drawn in Step 1 — type **l** ↵. It now appears dashed.

7. Turn off Object Snap mode. To select the interior lines on the kitchen's island by using a fence, type **f** ↵. Then pick points ❺, ❻, and ❼. Press Enter to end the fence.

8. Type **r** ↵ at the `Select objects:` prompt (the prompt changes to `Remove objects:`) and pick the line at ❽ to remove the external island line picked in Step 7. At this point, all the selected items should be dashed, as shown in Figure 9.15.

FIGURE 9.14

A kitchen floor plan.

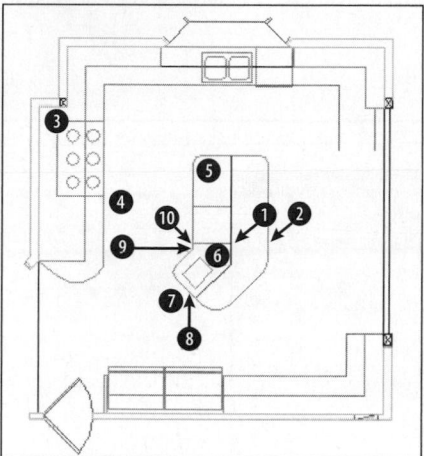

FIGURE 9.15

Kitchen floor plan with all selected items shown with dashed lines.

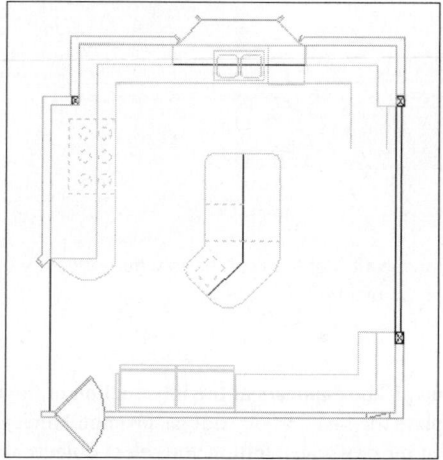

9. Press Enter to complete the command.

10. Turn on Object Snap mode. Start the MOVE command. At the Specify base point or [Displacement] <Displacement>: prompt, pick the endpoint at **9**, as shown in Figure 9.14. At the Specify second point or <use first point as displacement>: prompt, pick the endpoint at **10**. All the objects move.

11. Save your drawing.

Customizing the selection process

You can customize the way that you select objects. To do so, choose Application Button ⇨ Options to open the Options dialog box and click the Selection tab, as shown in Figure 9.16. The next few sections describe the settings on the left side of this tab.

The Selection tab of the Options dialog box.

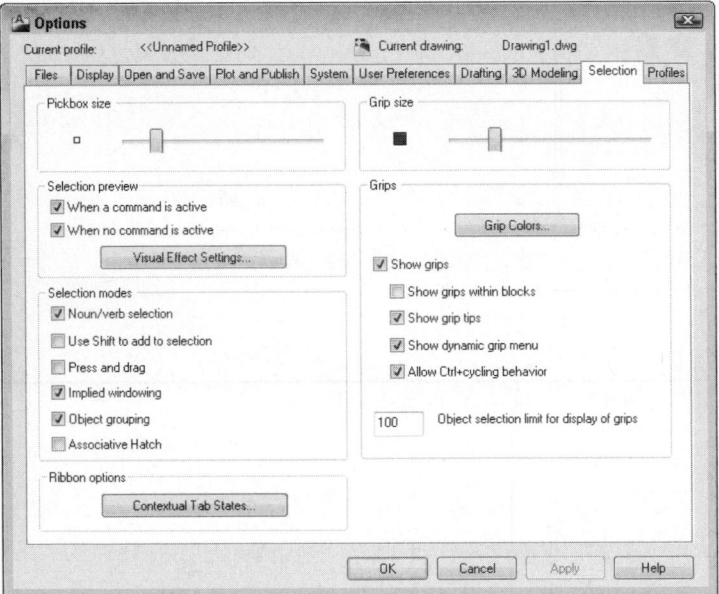

Pickbox Size

The pickbox is the box that you see at the intersection of the crosshairs when selecting (or picking) objects. The Pickbox Size area lets you set the size of the pickbox.

Note

If Noun/verb Selection is off and grips are disabled, no pickbox appears at the intersection of the crosshairs until you start an editing command and the command line displays the `Select objects:` prompt. However, if either Noun/ verb Selection or grips are on, the pickbox is always at the crosshairs, letting you select objects at any time. ■

Selection Preview

The Selection Preview option applies to rollover highlighting and the transparent selection rectangle. You can specify whether you want these effects to appear only if a command is active or even when no command is active (when you are selecting objects before choosing a command).

Click the Visual Effect Settings button to open the Visual Effect Settings dialog box, where you can specify the following settings:

- **Rollover highlighting.** In the Selection Preview Effect section, you can control the highlighting of faces (of 3D objects) and lines. Highlighting makes lines thicker, dashed, or both. The default is to show both. Click the Advanced Options button to exclude certain types of objects from the rollover highlighting effect.
- **Selection effect.** In the Area Selection Effect section, you can turn the effect off, change the colors for the window, crossing rectangles, and polygons, and change the opacity percentage.

Noun/verb selection

As you already know, the editing process consists of two parts: using a command, such as COPY or MOVE, and selecting objects. In AutoCAD/AutoCAD LT lingo, *noun* means an object in your drawing. *Verb* refers to a command because a command acts on an object. This option lets you decide whether you want to be able to select objects before starting a command.

In Windows programs, you typically select objects before starting a command. For example, if you're using Microsoft Word and want to erase a sentence, you select the sentence first, and then press Del.

By default, Noun/verb selection is active. With this option enabled, you can select objects first, without giving up the ability to choose commands first. This gives you maximum flexibility. Most commands let you choose an object first, but a few don't because they require a specific order for selecting objects. For those commands, the selected object is ignored and you just follow the prompts.

The advantage of selecting objects first is that, when you switch between Windows programs, you don't have to change habitual ways of selecting objects. The disadvantage of selecting objects first is that some AutoCAD and AutoCAD LT commands don't let you select objects first, which can be confusing. Also, when you select objects first, grips appear — sometimes obscuring the objects that you need to select.

Use Shift to Add to Selection

The Use Shift to Add to Selection option is not checked by default. In AutoCAD and AutoCAD LT, you often select more than one object at a time for editing. As a result, when you select a second object, the first object stays selected. If you check the Use Shift to Add to Selection option, then after selecting one object, you must hold down Shift to select any additional objects.

Press and Drag

One of the ways to select objects is to create a window that includes a number of objects. If the Press and Drag option is checked, you need to pick at one corner of the window and, without releasing the pick button, drag the cursor to the diagonally opposite corner. This type of action is typical of Windows programs. By default, this option is off, which means that to create a window, you pick at one corner of the window, release the mouse button, and pick again at the diagonally opposite corner. This setting does not affect the ZOOM Window operation, which always requires two separate picks, one for each corner.

Implied windowing

Implied windowing means that if you pick any point not on an object, AutoCAD or AutoCAD LT assumes that you want to create a selection window. By default, this option is on. You can then pick the opposite corner to select objects. If you pick the corners from left to right, you get a standard selection window. If you pick the corners from right to left, you get a crossing window.

This option applies only when you start a command and see the Select objects: prompt. If you turn this option off, you can still enter the Window or Crossing selection options manually (by typing **c** ↵ or **w** ↵). When selecting objects before starting the command, implied windowing is always on.

Object grouping

Groups are sets of objects that you name. Creating groups of objects is discussed in the next chapter. If object grouping is on (the default) when you select one object in a group, all the objects in the group are automatically selected.

Associative Hatch

The Associative Hatch option selects boundary objects when you select a hatch within the boundary. This option is off by default. Checking this option is equivalent to setting the PICKSTYLE system variable to 2. Chapter 16 covers hatches.

Cross-Reference

The Ribbon Options section of the Selection tab lets you customize when certain Ribbon tabs appear, based on the type of object selected or the active command. I cover this topic in Chapter 33. ■

Summary

All drawings need to be edited, either as part of the drawing process or to make corrections. In this chapter, you read about:

- Erasing objects
- Moving objects
- Copying objects
- Rotating objects
- Scaling objects
- Using the CHANGE command on lines and circles
- The many ways of selecting objects
- Customizing the object-selection features

The next chapter covers the more advanced editing commands and options.

Editing Your Drawing with Advanced Tools

This chapter completes the discussion, started in the preceding chapter, of geometric editing commands — covering the more complex commands you can use to refine the details of your drawing. These commands enable you to copy, move, resize, break, and cover objects, as well as construct corners and constrain objects using parameters. I also discuss grips, which make it easy to move, copy, mirror, rotate, scale, and stretch objects, and I explain how to use the Quick Properties panel and the Properties palette to edit objects. I end the chapter with a discussion of three ways to control the selection of objects — groups, filters, and the Quick Select feature.

Note

Although you can use the editing tools that I describe in this chapter in a 3D environment, this chapter assumes that you are working in a 2D environment, using the default 2D Drafting & Annotation workspace. (AutoCAD LT doesn't offer a 3D environment.) To make sure that you're in a 2D environment, set the workspace to 2D Drafting & Annotation (from the Workspace Switching list on the Quick Access toolbar or the status bar) and set the visual style to 2D Wireframe (type vscurrent and choose the 2D Wireframe option). If you still see the Z axis on the UCS icon, choose View tab ➪ Views panel ➪ 3D Navigation drop-down list ➪ Top. Another method is to set the workspace to 2D Drafting & Annotation, and then start a new drawing based on the default acad.dwt or acadlt.dwt template. ∎

Copying and Moving Objects

Three commands enable you to copy objects in very specific ways. MIRROR creates a mirror image. ARRAY copies objects in a rectangular or circular pattern. OFFSET creates parallel objects. Although these commands make copies of objects, they produce a result that would be difficult or impossible to produce simply by using the COPY command. The ALIGN and 3DALIGN commands move objects by aligning them with other objects in the drawing.

Mirroring objects

Many drawings have symmetrical elements. Often, especially in mechanical drawings, you can create one half or one quarter of a model and complete it simply by mirroring what you have drawn.

 To mirror, select an object or objects and then choose Home tab ➪ Modify panel ➪ Mirror. Alternatively, start the MIRROR command first and then select an object or objects.

The command prompts you for the first and second points of the mirror line. This is an imaginary line across which the command creates the mirrored object. The length of the line is irrelevant — only its start point and direction are important.

Tip

Most mirror lines are orthogonal. Therefore, after you specify the first mirror point, you can turn on Ortho Mode and move the mouse in the direction of the second point. You can then quickly pick the second point. Polar tracking can also easily guide you to specify an orthogonal mirror line. ■

The command then asks if you want to erase the source objects. The source objects are the objects you have selected to mirror. If you want to keep them, type **n** ↵ or press Enter. You keep the source objects when you're building a symmetrical model and want the mirror image to be added to the original object(s). Type **y** ↵ when you want to edit an object (change its orientation) so that only the mirror image is retained in the drawing.

On the DVD

The drawing used in the following exercise on mirroring objects, ab07-02.dwg, is in the Results folder on the DVD. ■

STEPS: Mirroring Objects

1. Open ab07-02.dwg from the Results folder of the DVD. If you completed the exercise on arcs in Chapter 7, you can open this drawing from your AutoCAD Bible folder.

2. Save the file as ab10-01.dwg in your AutoCAD Bible folder. Make sure Object Snap mode is on. Set a running object snap for Intersection only.

3. Choose Home tab ➪ Modify panel ➪ Erase. At the Select objects: prompt, pick the line and two arcs to the bottom right of the two centerlines, and then press Enter. The resulting model should look like Figure 10.1.

 4. Choose Home tab ➪ Modify panel ➪ Mirror. At the Select objects: prompt, pick the remaining exterior line and two arcs, and press Enter.

5. At the Specify first point of mirror line: prompt, pick intersection ❶, as shown in Figure 10.1. At the Specify second point of mirror line: prompt, pick intersection ❷.

6. The command prompts Erase source objects? [Yes/No] <N>: Press Enter to accept the default, No.

7. Start the MIRROR command again. At the Select objects: prompt, type **p** ↵ to pick the original lines. Then pick the new exterior line and two arcs, and press Enter.

FIGURE 10.1

A partially completed mounting plate.

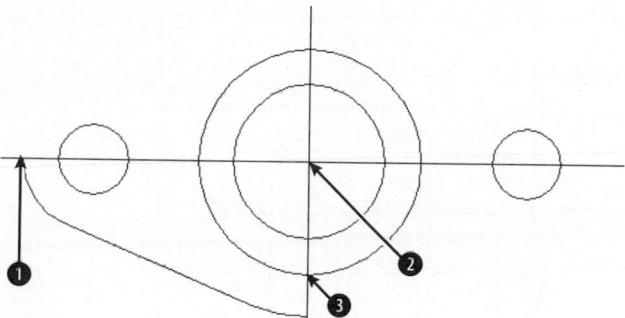

8. At the `Specify first point of mirror line:` prompt, pick intersection ❷. At the `Specify second point of mirror line:` prompt, pick intersection ❸. Press Enter again at the `Erase source objects? [Yes/No] <N>:` prompt.

9. The command completes the mounting plate. Save your drawing. It should look like Figure 10.2.

FIGURE 10.2

The completed mounting plate.

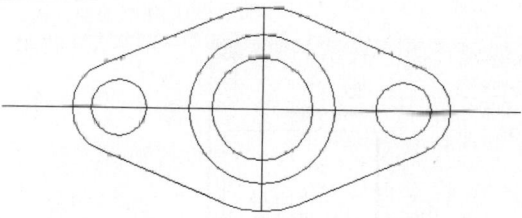

Using the ARRAY command

The ARRAY command creates a rectangular or polar (circular) pattern by copying the object(s) you select as many times as you specify. The ARRAY command is a powerful drawing tool. It can quickly create large numbers of objects, thus saving a huge amount of time and effort.

Rectangular arrays

A rectangular array creates a grid of rows and columns of one or more objects. Figure 10.3 shows an example of a rectangular array. To create a rectangular array, follow these steps:

FIGURE 10.3

The garage door was drawn with one panel, as shown on the left side. A rectangular array created the rest of the door panels, as shown on the right.

Thanks to Henry Dearborn, AIA, Fairfield, Iowa, for this drawing.

1. Choose Home tab ⇨ Modify panel ⇨ Array. You can choose the objects first if you want. The Array dialog box opens, as shown in Figure 10.4.

FIGURE 10.4

The Array dialog box.

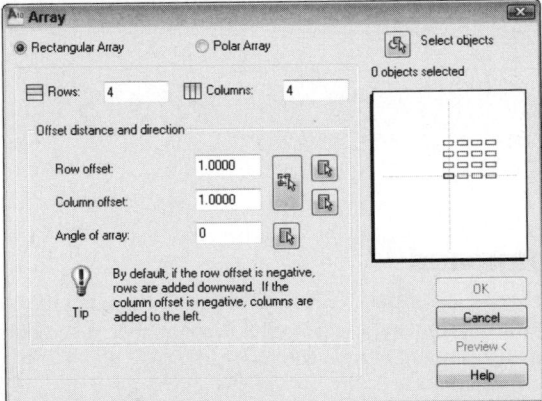

2. Click Rectangular Array at the upper-left corner of the dialog box (if it is not already selected).

3. If you've already selected one or more objects, the dialog box indicates the number of selected objects. If you haven't selected any object, click Select Objects to return to your drawing and select objects. Press Enter to end object selection and return to the dialog box.

4. In the Rows and Columns text boxes, type the total number of rows and columns that you want.

5. Type the distance you want between the rows in the Row Offset text box, and type the distance you want between the columns in the Column Offset text box. If you want to specify the offsets by picking points on your screen, click the Pick button next to the Row Offset or Column Offset text box, or use the longer Pick button spanning both text boxes to pick diagonal points and specify both offsets at once.

6. If you want to change the angle of the array, type an angle in the Angle of Array text box. The preview panel displays the results of this value. To specify the angle by picking, click the Pick Angle of Array button.

7. To preview the array, click Preview. Click anywhere (pick) or press Esc to return to the Array dialog box if you want to make changes; otherwise, right-click to accept the array and end the command. If you change the snap angle or the UCS (as explained in Chapter 8), AutoCAD and AutoCAD LT create the rectangular array at the angle of the snap or UCS.

Polar (circular) arrays

A polar array creates copies of one or more objects arrayed in a circle around a center point. An example of a polar array is shown in Figure 10.5.

FIGURE 10.5

The pulley was drawn with one spoke, as shown on the left. A polar array created the additional spokes.

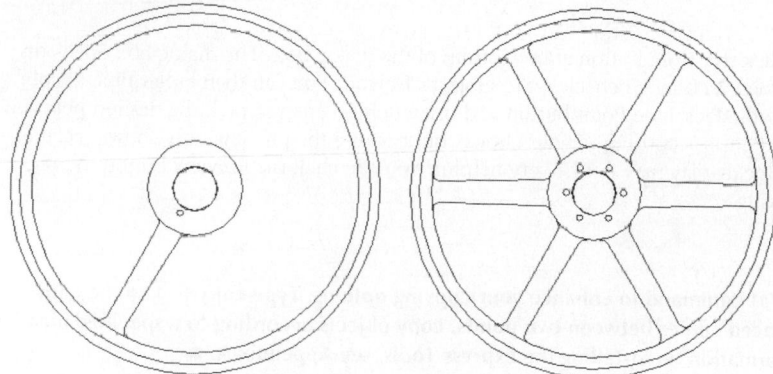

Thanks to Robert Mack of the Dexter Company, Fairfield, Iowa, for this drawing.

To create a polar array, follow these steps:

1. Choose Home tab ⇨ Modify panel ⇨ Array, and select the object or objects. You can choose the objects first if you want. The Array dialog box opens.

2. Click Polar Array at the top of the dialog box (if it is not already selected).

3. If you've already selected one or more objects, the dialog box indicates the number of selected objects. If you haven't selected any objects, click Select Objects to return to your drawing and select objects. Press Enter to end object selection and return to the dialog box.

4. Specify the center point by typing X and Y coordinates, or click the Pick Center Point button. If you selected an object first, check that the center point displayed is what you want.

5. Select the two items that you want to specify from the Method drop-down list. You can choose any two from the three choices:

   • **Total Number of Items.** Sets the total number of items in the resulting array, including the one that you are arraying.

   • **Angle to Fill.** Sets the number of degrees that the polar array covers. For example, to array around half of a circle, specify 180°.

   • **Angle Between Items.** Specifies the number of degrees between each item in the polar array.

6. Complete the values of the two items that you specified. You can click the buttons to pick the angle to fill or the angle between items on the screen.

7. Check the Rotate Items as Copied check box to rotate the objects that you are arraying. Uncheck the box to leave them unrotated.

8. Click Preview to preview the array. Click anywhere (pick) or press Esc to return to the Array dialog box if you want to make changes; otherwise, right-click to accept the array and end the command.

You can specify which point on the last object selected that AutoCAD or AutoCAD LT uses to array the objects. The command makes a calculation of the distance from the center point of the array to a base point on the last object selected. Otherwise, the command uses a default point based on the type of object selected. Table 10.1 lists the default base points. If you are arraying more than one object, you may not obtain the result you want without specifying the base point. Even for one object, you may want to change the base point that is used.

To specify the base point, click the More button at the bottom of the dialog box. The dialog box opens up to display the Object Base Point section. Uncheck Set to Object's Default. You can then either type in coordinates or, more likely, click the Pick Base Point button and use an object snap to pick the desired point on an object. The preview box adjusts according to your choice, but because the preview only shows rectangles in the place of your object, the display may not be very helpful. You can click the Preview button to preview the result in your drawing.

AutoCAD Only

You can use the Express Tools COPYM command to enhance your copying options. Type copym ↵ on the command line. You can create evenly spaced copies between two points, copy objects according to a specified measurement, and create arrays. For information on installing the Express Tools, see Appendix A. ■

TABLE 10.1

Object Base Points for Arrays

Type of Object	Default Base Point
Arc, circle, or ellipse	Center point
Polygon or rectangle	First corner
Line, polyline (2D or 3D), ray, spline, or donut	Starting point
Text (single-line or paragraph), block	Insertion point
Construction line (xline)	Midpoint
Region	Grip point

On the DVD

The drawing used in the following exercise on arraying objects, ab10-a.dwg, is in the Drawings folder on the DVD. ■

STEPS: Arraying Objects

1. Open ab10-a.dwg from the DVD.

2. Save the file as ab10-02.dwg in your AutoCAD Bible folder. It looks like Figure 10.6. Object Snap mode should be on. Set Center and Intersection running object snaps.

FIGURE 10.6

A partially completed mounting bracket.

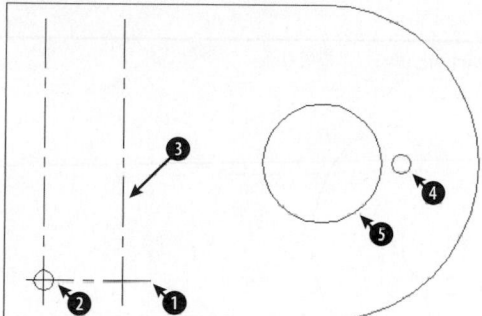

---

3. Choose Home tab ➪ Modify panel ➪ Array. The Array dialog box opens.

4. Click the Select Objects button of the Array dialog box. In the drawing, pick the horizontal centerline ❶, shown in Figure 10.6, and then press Enter. You return to the dialog box.

5. Make sure that Rectangular Array is selected at the top of the dialog box.

6. In the Rows text box, type **4**. In the Columns text box, type **1**.

7. In the Row Offset text box, type **1**. (You don't need to specify the column offset because you are creating only one column.)

8. Click Preview. You should see a total of four horizontal lines, as shown in Figure 10.7. Right-click to accept the array. (If you don't see the four lines, click anywhere in the drawing area and recheck the settings in the Array dialog box.)

9. To add the holes to the pattern, again start the ARRAY command.

10. Click the Select Objects button in the Array dialog box. In the drawing, pick circle ❷, shown in Figure 10.6, and then press Enter.

11. Back in the Array dialog box, type **4** in the Rows text box and type **2** in the Columns text box.

12. Click the Pick Both Offsets button. In the drawing, pick the center of circle ❷ (or the intersection of the centerlines at the center of circle ❷) and the intersection of centerlines near ❸, as shown in Figure 10.6. (If necessary, press Tab until you see the object snap that you want.)

13. Click Preview to preview the array. If the circles look like Figure 10.7, right-click. Otherwise, click in the drawing area or press Esc and check your settings. After you're done, the command arrays the holes to fit the centerlines.

14. To create a six-hole bolt circle, pick hole ❹, as shown in Figure 10.6.

15. Start the ARRAY command again.

16. In the Array dialog box, choose Polar Array.

17. Next to the Center Point text boxes, click the Pick Center Point button. In the drawing, pick the center of the large circle at ❺, as shown in Figure 10.6.

18. Make sure that the Method reads "Total number of items & Angle to fill." In the Total Number of Items text box, type **6**. In the Angle to Fill text box, type **360**.

19. Click Preview to see the array. It should look like Figure 10.7. If it does, right-click. Otherwise, click in the drawing area or press Esc and recheck the settings in the Array dialog box. AutoCAD or AutoCAD LT completes the mounting bracket.

20. Save your drawing. It should look like Figure 10.7.

FIGURE 10.7

The completed mounting bracket.

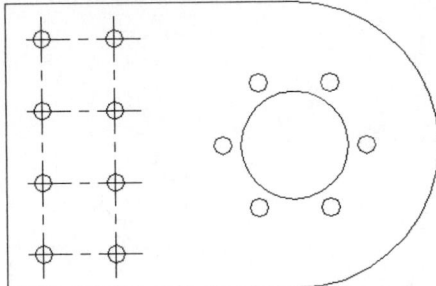

Offsetting objects

The OFFSET command creates lines or curves parallel to one existing object. The beauty of this command is apparent when you start to create complex objects, such as polylines, which are covered in Chapter 16. Polygons and rectangles are *polylines,* which means that all the line segments are one object. For example, using OFFSET, you can create concentric polygons in one step. Figure 10.8 shows two concentric polygons. The outside polygon was created with the POLYGON command, and the inside polygon was created by using OFFSET.

 To offset an object, choose Home tab ⇨ Modify panel ⇨ Offset.

The command responds with the following list of settings and prompt:

```
Current settings: Erase source=No Layer=Source OFFSETGAPTYPE=0
Specify offset distance or [Through/Erase/Layer] <Through>:
```

The settings show how the OFFSET command's options will function. Set the Erase option to Yes to erase the selected object and leave only the offset. Use the Layer option to specify if you want the new object to be on the same layer as the source object or on the current layer.

Note

The OFFSETGAPTYPE system variable determines what the command does to close gaps when you offset closed polylines. By default (a value of 0), AutoCAD extends the polyline segments. A value of 1 fills the gaps with arcs, and a value of 2 fills the gaps with chamfered corners. (I cover chamfers later in this chapter.) ∎

FIGURE 10.8

Use OFFSET to create concentric polygons.

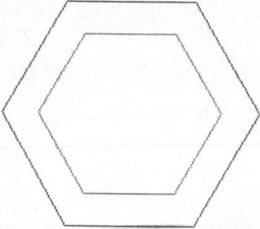

The OFFSET command offers two ways to specify the offset:

- If you type an offset distance, the command responds with the Select object to offset or [Exit/Undo] <Exit>: prompt. You can select one object. Then the Specify point on side to offset or [Exit/Multiple/Undo] <Exit>: prompt appears. Pick a point to indicate on which side of the object you want to create the offset copy. The command creates the offset and continues to show the Select object to offset or [Exit/Undo] <Exit>: prompt so that you can offset other objects by using the same offset distance. Press Enter to exit the command.

- If you want to indicate a *through point* (a point that the offset passes through, such as an object snap on another object), type **t** ↵ or right-click and choose Through from the shortcut menu. The command displays the Select object to offset or [Exit/Undo] <Exit>: prompt. Pick one object. At the Specify through point or [Exit/Multiple/Undo] <Exit>: prompt, pick a point through which you want the offset to go to create the offset.

Use the Undo option if you don't like the result of the offset. After you offset an object, the prompt repeats so that you can offset additional objects. Press Enter to end the command.

On the DVD

The drawing used in the following exercise on using the OFFSET command, ab10-b.dwg, is in the Drawings folder on the DVD. ■

STEPS: Using the OFFSET Command

1. Open ab10-b.dwg from the DVD.
2. Save the file as ab10-03.dwg in your AutoCAD Bible folder. It looks like Figure 10.9. Set a running object snap for Center, and turn on Object Snap mode.

 3. Choose Home tab ⇨ Modify panel ⇨ Offset. Follow the prompts:

```
Specify offset distance or [Through/Erase/Layer] <Through>: ↵ or
    specify the Through option if it does not appear as the default.
Select object to offset or [Exit/Undo] <Exit>: Pick ❶ in Figure 10.9.
Specify through point or [Exit/Multiple/Undo] <Exit>: Pick the center
    of ❷.
    Select object to offset or [Exit/Undo] <Exit>: ↵
```

This action copies the centerline through the upper circles.

FIGURE 10.9

A tension arm for a commercial dryer.

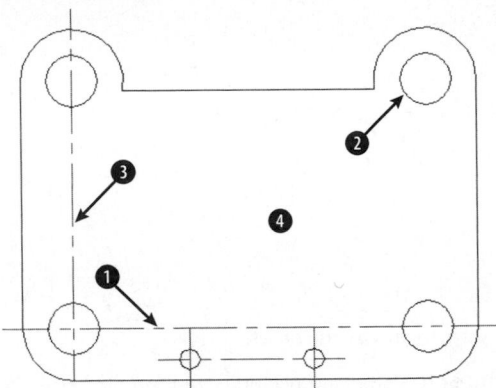

Thanks to Robert Mack of the Dexter Company, Fairfield, IA for this drawing.

4. Repeat the OFFSET command. At the `Specify offset distance or [Through/Erase/Layer] <Through>:` prompt, type **4-19/64** ↵. Pick the centerline ❸ at the `Select object to offset or [Exit/Undo] <Exit>:` prompt, and then click near ❹ at the `Specify point on side to offset or [Exit/Multiple/Undo] <Exit>:` prompt. Press Enter to end the command. The vertical centerline appears 4-19/64 units to the right of the original.

5. Save your drawing. It should look like Figure 10.10.

FIGURE 10.10

The completed tension arm.

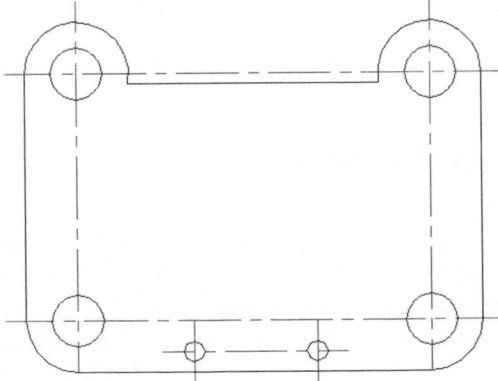

Aligning objects

The ALIGN and 3DALIGN commands let you move and rotate an object or objects in one procedure. They are useful in both 2D and 3D environments. By specifying where selected points on an object move, you can align the object with other objects in your drawing, as shown in Figure 10.11. You can align in two ways:

- **ALIGN command.** This command prompts you by point. You specify the first source point (on the object you're aligning), and then the first destination point (where that source point will end up). Then you specify the second set of source and destination points. For 3D, you go on to a third set. Finally, you can scale the selected object to match the destination points.

- **3DALIGN command.** This command prompts you by object. You specify two or three points on the source object, and then the points at the destination location. As you specify destination points, you see the object move and align in real time. You cannot scale the object. See Chapter 24 for an exercise that uses the 3DALIGN command in 3D editing.

AutoCAD Only

AutoCAD LT doesn't include the 3DALIGN command. ■

Aligning requires several steps. Even so, it can save you time when you need to move and rotate at the same time, especially if you don't know the rotation angle that you need.

FIGURE 10.11

Aligning a door with a wall.

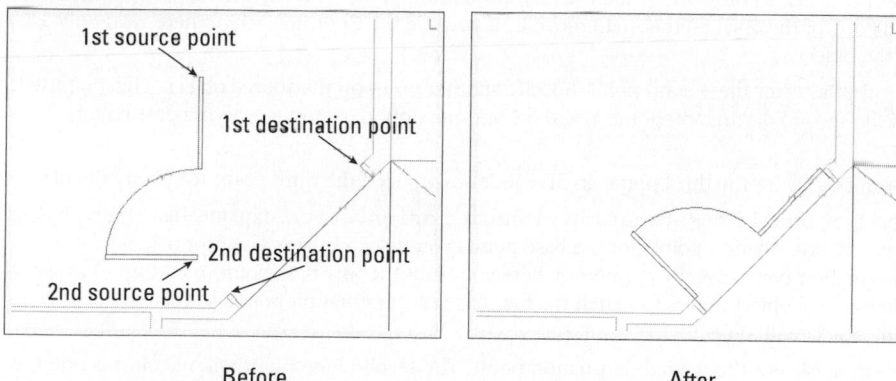

Before   After

Using the ALIGN command

 If you prefer to think, "This point will go here and that point will go there," use the ALIGN command. You can also scale the object that you're aligning. Choose Home tab ⇨ Modify panel (expanded) ⇨ Align and select an object or objects. You can also select the object or objects first. Then follow these steps:

1. The prompt asks for the first source point. Specify a point, usually an object snap on the object that you want to move.

2. The prompt asks for the first destination point. Specify the point where you want the first source point to end up.

3. The prompt asks for the second source point. If you press Enter, AutoCAD simply moves the selected objects. To continue to align, specify another point, usually another object snap on the object that you want to move.

4. The prompt asks for the second destination point. Specify the point where you want the second source point to end up.

5. The prompt asks for the third source point. You use this for 3D alignment, to specify how you want to rotate the object in the third dimension. For 2D alignment, press Enter to continue the command.

6. The prompt displays the `Scale objects based on alignment points? [Yes/No] <N>:` prompt. If the distances between the source and destination points are not the same, type **y** if you want to scale the original object so that the source and destination points match exactly.

Using the 3DALIGN command

 If you like to think, "These are the points on the source object that I want to align and then these are the destination points that I want to align them to," and if you don't need to scale your object, use the 3DALIGN command. To align an object by using the 3DALIGN command, enter **3dalign** ↵ on the command line, and select an object or objects. You can also select the object or objects first. (In the 3D Modeling workspace in AutoCAD, you can choose Home tab ⇨ Modify panel ⇨ 3D Align.)

Then follow these steps:

1. The message, `Specify source plane and orientation`, explains that you now need to specify the source points, which define the plane and orientation of the source object. The first prompt asks for the base point. Specify a point, usually an object snap on the object that you want to move. This point will match the first destination point. You can use the Copy option to make a copy of the object rather than move it. If you use the Continue option here, you only move the object.

2. The prompt asks for the second point. Specify another point on the source object. This point will match the second destination point. Use the Continue option to start specifying destination points.

3. The prompt asks for the third point. In 3D models, you need the third point to specify the plane.

4. The message, `Specify destination plane and orientation`, explains that you now need to specify the destination points for the base points you just specified: The prompt asks for the first destination point. Specify the point where you want the first base point to end up. As soon as you do this, the object moves to match the first base and destination points so that you can see how the object will look.

5. The prompt asks for the second destination point. The second base point will match this point. If you press Enter at this point, the command aligns the object with the X axis of the current UCS.

6. The prompt asks for the third destination point. You use this for 3D alignment, to specify how you want to rotate the object in the third dimension. For 2D alignment, you can place the cursor on either side of the aligning line you specified, to mirror the object in either direction. When you see the direction that you want, press Enter to end the command and align the object.

The following exercise uses the ALIGN command to align objects.

On the DVD

The drawing used in the following exercise on aligning objects in two dimensions, ab10-c.dwg, is in the Drawings folder on the DVD. ∎

STEPS: Aligning Objects in Two Dimensions

1. Open ab10-c.dwg from the DVD.
2. Save the file as ab10-04.dwg in your AutoCAD Bible folder. It looks like Figure 10.12. Set a running object snap for Endpoint.

A base assembly for a commercial washing machine.

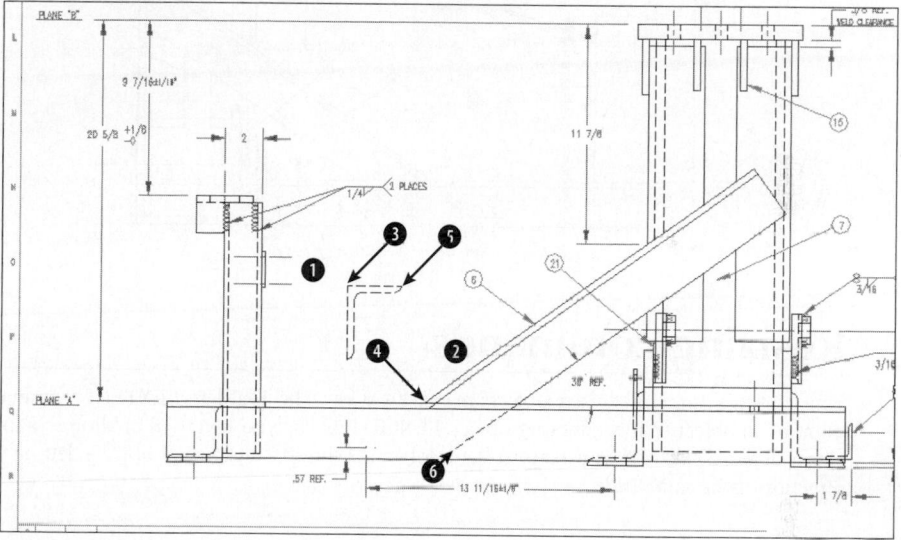

Thanks to Robert Mack of the Dexter Company, Fairfield, Iowa, for this drawing.

3. Home tab ⇨ Modify panel (expanded) ⇨ Align, and follow the prompts:

   Select objects: *Select the horizontal angle by using a window, picking near ❶ and then ❷. Press Enter to end object selection. This angle needs to be aligned with the long, diagonal support angle.*
   Specify first source point: *Pick the endpoint at ❸ in Figure 10.12.*
   Specify first destination point: *Pick the endpoint at ❹.*
   Specify second source point: ↵
   Pick the endpoint at ❺.
   Specify second destination point: *Pick the endpoint at ❻.*
   Specify third source point or <continue>: ↵
   Scale objects based on alignment points? [Yes/No] <N>: ↵ *to accept the default No answer.*

4. Save your drawing. It should look like Figure 10.13.

FIGURE 10.13

The washing machine base.

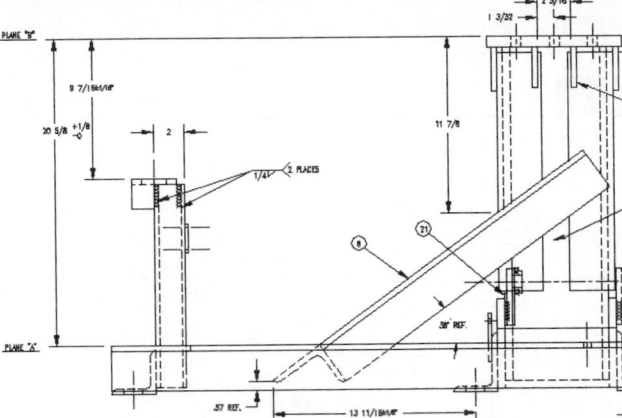

Resizing commands

Four editing commands resize objects in specific ways. The TRIM and EXTEND commands change the end-point of an object to meet another object. LENGTHEN lets you lengthen or shorten a line, polyline, arc, or elliptical arc. STRETCH is used to stretch (longer or shorter) a group of objects, letting you change their direction at the same time.

Trimming objects

As you edit a drawing, you may find that lines or arcs that once perfectly met other objects now hang over. To trim an object, you must first specify the *cutting edge,* which defines the point at which to cut the object you want to trim. You define the cutting edge by selecting an object. You can select several cutting edges and several objects to trim at one time, as shown in Figure 10.14. When you select an object to trim, you must pick the object on the side that you want trimmed (not on the side that you want to remain). A common use for the TRIM command is to create intersections of walls in architectural floor plans.

Tip
While using the TRIM command, you can switch to extending objects by pressing the Shift key as you select objects to trim. ■

The object you want to trim does not have to actually intersect the cutting edge. You can trim an object to a cutting edge that would intersect the object if extended. This is called *trimming to an implied intersection,* an example of which is shown in Figure 10.15.

You can trim arcs, circles, ellipses, elliptical arcs, hatches, lines, polylines, xlines, rays, and splines. You can use 2D helixes, polylines, arcs, circles, ellipses, elliptical arcs, lines, rays, regions, splines, text, or xlines as cutting edges. An object can be used as both a cutting edge and an object to be trimmed in the same trimming process. You can also trim to objects within blocks. (Chapter 18 covers blocks.)

FIGURE 10.14

Trimming two objects by using two cutting edges.

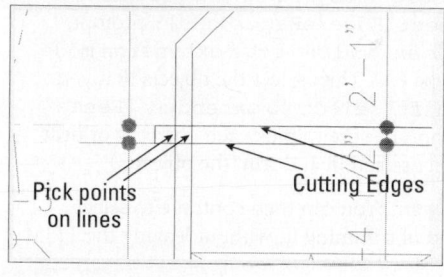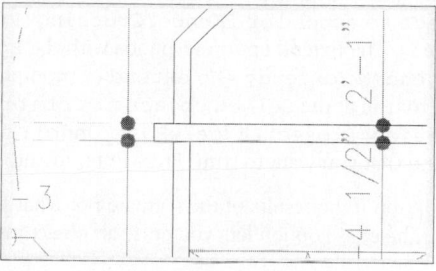

Before trimming   After trimming

FIGURE 10.15

Trimming two arcs to an implied intersection.

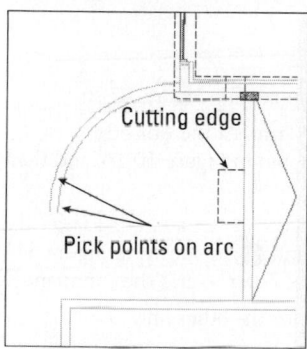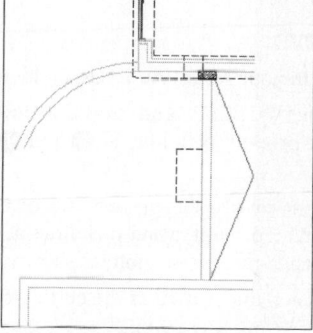

Before trimming   After trimming

 To trim an object, choose Home tab ⇨ Modify panel ⇨ Trim/Extend drop-down menu ⇨ Trim. The command displays the Current settings: Projection=UCS, Edge=None Select cutting edges . . . Select objects or <select all>: prompt. The prompt lets you know the values of the two system variables that affect trimming. The Projection setting is used only for 3D models and can trim based on either the current UCS or the current view. The Edge setting is used for implied intersections. When Edge is set to Extend, the command trims to the implied intersection of the cutting edge and the object to be trimmed. At this prompt, pick the object(s) that you want to use as a cutting edge or press Enter to select all objects as edges. Press Enter to end object selection.

You can trim to an actual or an *implied* intersection (an intersection that would exist if objects were extended):

- If you want to trim to an actual intersection, at the Select object to trim or shift-select to extend or [Fence/Crossing/Project/Edge/eRase/Undo]: prompt, select the objects that you want to trim. You can use the Fence option to draw lines that crisscross the objects that you want to trim. Use the Crossing option to select the objects with a crossing window. Be sure to pick each object between the cutting edge and the end you want to trim off. Press Enter to end object selection. This action trims the object(s).

- If you want to trim to an implied intersection, at the `Select object to trim or shift-select to extend or [Fence/Crossing/Project/Edge/eRase/Undo]:` prompt, type **e** ↵. The Extend option responds with the `Enter an implied edge extension mode [Extend/No extend] <No extend>:` prompt. Type **e** ↵. Then select the objects that you want to trim at the `Select object to trim or shift-select to extend or [Fence/Crossing/Project/Edge/eRase/Undo]:` prompt. Be sure to pick each object at or near the end that you want to trim. Press Enter to end object selection and trim the object(s).

Use the Undo option if the results of the trim are not what you want. You can then continue to select objects to trim. The eRase option lets you erase an object instead of trimming it, without leaving the TRIM command.

On the DVD

The drawing used in the following exercise on trimming objects, ab10-d.dwg, is in the Drawings folder on the DVD. ∎

STEPS: Trimming Objects

1. Open ab10-d.dwg from the DVD.
2. Save the file as ab10-05.dwg in your AutoCAD Bible folder. It looks like Figure 10.16.

3. Choose Home tab ⇨ Modify panel ⇨ Trim/Extend drop-down list ⇨ Trim. At the `Select objects or <select all>:` prompt, pick lines at ❶ and ❷, shown in Figure 10.16, and then press Enter.
4. At the `Select object to trim or shift-select to extend or [Fence/Crossing/Project/Edge/eRase/Undo]:` prompt, again pick lines at ❶ and ❷, as shown in Figure 10.16. Be sure to pick them outside the intersection, as shown. Press Enter to end the command.

   The command trims the lines. Each line is used as the cutting edge for the other line.
5. Again start the TRIM command. At the `Select objects or <select all>:` prompt, pick the line at ❸, shown in Figure 10.16, and press Enter.
6. At the `Select object to trim or shift-select to extend or [Fence/Crossing/Project/Edge/eRase/Undo]:` prompt, right-click and choose Edge. Then right-click and choose Extend at the `Enter an implied edge extension mode [Extend/No extend] <Extend>:` prompt.
7. Pick the line at ❹, shown in Figure 10.16, to trim the line. Press Enter to end the command.
8. Start the TRIM command again. At the `Select objects or <select all>:` prompt, pick ❺ and press Enter. At the `Select object to trim or shift-select to extend or [Fence/Crossing/Project/Edge/eRase/Undo]:` prompt, pick the lines at ❻ and ❼. Press Enter to end the command.
9. Save your drawing. It should look like Figure 10.17.

FIGURE 10.16

A schematic of an air compressor.

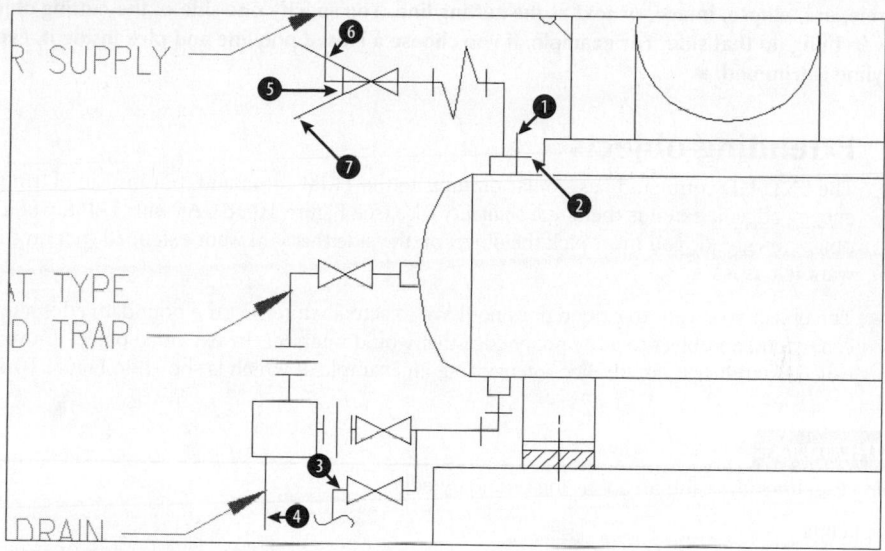

FIGURE 10.17

The completed clamp in two views.

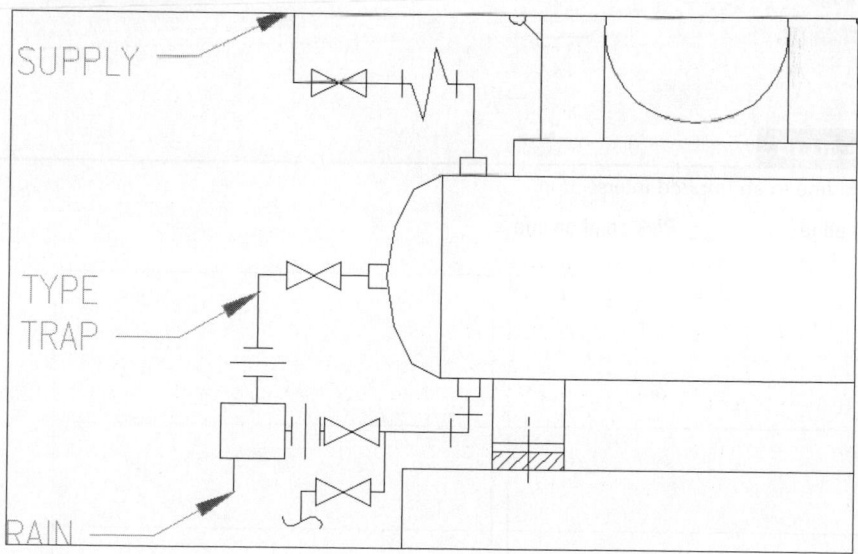

AutoCAD Only

Express Tools contains a command, EXTRIM, which is available on the command line. EXTRIM can use a polyline, line, circle, arc, ellipse, image, or text as the cutting line. You specify one side of the cutting object, and EXTRIM trims everything on that side. For example, if you choose a closed polyline and pick inside it, every object inside the polyline is trimmed. ■

Extending objects

The EXTEND command has similar prompts to the TRIM command, but instead of trimming objects to a cutting edge, it extends them to a *boundary edge* (see Figure 10.18). As with TRIM, when you select an object to extend, you must pick the object on the side that you want extended (not on the side that you want left as is).

The object you want to extend does not have to actually intersect the boundary edge after its extension. You can extend an object to a boundary edge that would intersect the extended object if it were longer. This is called extending to an implied intersection, an example of which is shown in Figure 10.19.

FIGURE 10.18

Extending two lines by using an arc as the boundary edge.

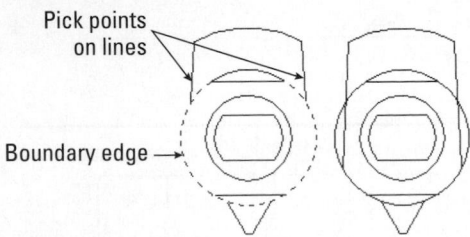

FIGURE 10.19

Extending a line to an implied intersection.

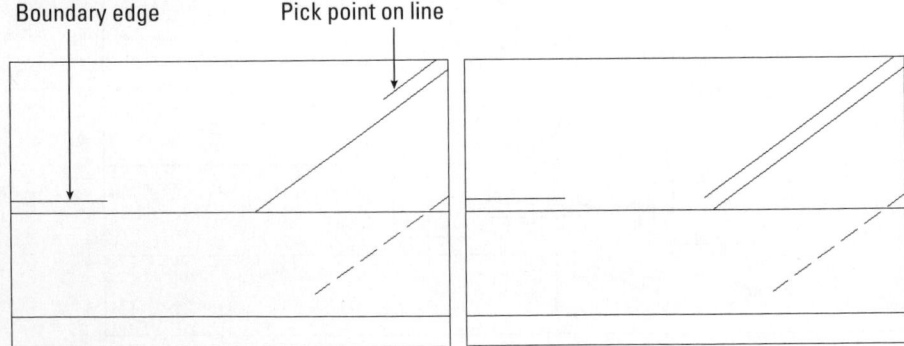

You can extend arcs, elliptical arcs, lines, open polylines, and rays. You can use 2D helixes, polylines, arcs, circles, ellipses, elliptical arcs, lines, rays, regions, splines, text, or xlines as boundary edges. An object can be used as both a boundary edge and an object to be extended in the same extending process.

Tip

While using the EXTEND command, you can switch to trimming objects by pressing the Shift key as you select objects to trim. ■

 To extend an object, choose Home tab ⇨ Modify panel ⇨ Trim/Extend drop-down list ⇨ Extend. The command displays the Current settings: Projection=UCS, Edge=Extend Select boundary edges ... Select objects or <select all>: prompt. The prompt lets you know the values of the two settings that affect how the object is extended. Projection is used only for 3D models and can extend based on either the current UCS or the current view. Edge is used for implied intersections. When Edge is set to Extend, the command extends to the implied intersection of the boundary edge and the object to be extended. At this prompt, pick the object(s) that you want to use as the boundary edge(s) or press Enter to select all objects. Press Enter to end object selection. You can extend to an actual or implied intersection:

- If the extension will result in an actual intersection, at the Select object to extend or shift-select to trim or [Fence/Crossing/Project/Edge/Undo]: prompt, select objects to extend. You can use the Fence option to draw lines that crisscross the objects you want to extend. Use the Crossing option to select the objects with a crossing window. Be sure to pick each object at the end that you want to extend. Press Enter to end object selection and extend the object(s).

- If you want to extend to an implied intersection, at the prompt, right-click and choose Edge. The option responds with the Enter an implied edge extension mode [Extend/No extend] <Extend>: prompt. Right-click and choose Extend. Then select the objects that you want to extend at the Select object to extend or shift-select to trim or [Fence/Crossing/Project/Edge/Undo]: prompt. Be sure to pick each object at the end that you want to extend. Press Enter to end object selection and extend the object(s).

Use the Undo option if the results of the extension are not what you want. You can then continue to select objects to extend. You can use the Fence object selection method to select objects to extend the side of the object that the fence line crosses.

On the DVD

The drawing used in the following exercise on extending objects, ab10-e.dwg, is in the Drawings folder on the DVD. ■

STEPS: Extending Objects

1. Open ab10-e.dwg from the DVD.
2. Save the file as ab10-06.dwg in your AutoCAD Bible folder. It looks like Figure 10.20.
3. Choose Home tab ⇨ Modify panel ⇨ Trim/Extend drop-down list ⇨ Extend. At the Select objects or <select all>: prompt, pick the line at ❶, shown in Figure 10.20, and then press Enter.

FIGURE 10.20

FIGURE 10.20

An electrical schematic.

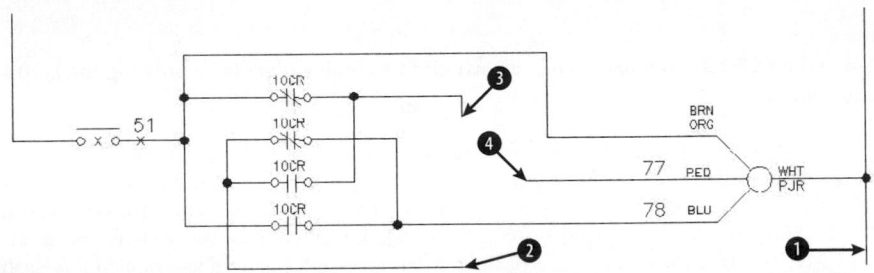

4. At the Select object to extend or shift-select to trim or [Fence/Crossing/Project/Edge/Undo]: prompt, pick the line at ❷, as shown in Figure 10.20. Press Enter to finish selecting objects. The command extends the line.

5. Repeat the EXTEND command. At the Select objects or <select all>: prompt, pick the lines at ❸ and ❹, shown in Figure 10.20, and then press Enter.

6. At the Select object to extend or shift-select to trim or [Fence/Crossing/Project/Edge/Undo]: prompt, right-click and choose Edge. Right-click and choose Extend at the Enter an implied edge extension mode [Extend/No extend] <No extend>: prompt.

7. Pick lines ❸ and ❹, shown in Figure 10.20, again at the points shown. The lines extend to meet. Press Enter to end the command.

8. Save your drawing. It should look like Figure 10.21.

FIGURE 10.21

The completed electrical schematic.

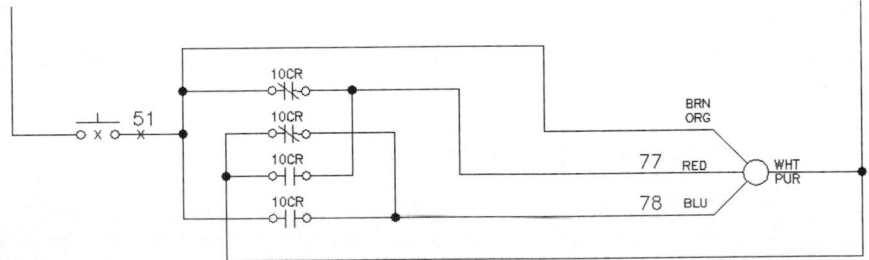

Lengthening objects

The LENGTHEN command both lengthens and shortens. It works on open objects, such as lines, arcs, and polylines, and also increases or decreases the included angle of arcs. AutoCAD and AutoCAD LT offer several ways of defining the new length or included angle. Use LENGTHEN if you want to lengthen or shorten an object when there is no available intersecting edge or boundary to use with TRIM or EXTEND.

In the LENGTHEN command, the length of an arc is measured along its circumference. Don't confuse this with the Length of Chord option of the ARC command, which refers to the length of a line stretched from one endpoint of the arc to the other endpoint.

 To lengthen (or shorten) an object, choose Home tab ⇨ Modify panel (expanded) ⇨ Lengthen. You cannot select objects before the LENGTHEN command. The command responds with the `Select an object or [DElta/Percent/Total/DYnamic]:` prompt. Choose one of the following options:

- **Select object.** This is the default. However, its purpose is to display the current measurements of the object. This can help you to decide how to define the final length or angle of the object. The current length is displayed at the command line, and the previous prompt is repeated.

- **DElta.** Right-click and choose DElta. *Delta* means the change, or difference, between the current and new length or included angle. The option responds with the `Enter delta length or [Angle] <0.0000>.` prompt. If you want to change an included angle, right-click and choose Angle. Then type the change in the included angle. Otherwise, simply type the change in the length of the object. A positive number increases the length or included angle. A negative number decreases the length or included angle.

- **Percent.** Right-click and choose Percent. At the `Enter percentage length <100.0000>:` prompt, type in what percent of the original object you want the final object to be. Amounts over 100 lengthen the object. Amounts under 100 shorten the object. You cannot change an included angle by using this option.

- **Total.** Right-click and choose Total. At the `Specify total length or [Angle] <1.0000>:` prompt, you can either choose the Angle suboption, as described for the DElta option, or use the default total-length option. Either way, you enter the total angle or length you want.

- **DYnamic.** Right-click and choose DYnamic. This option lets you drag the endpoint of the object closest to where you picked it. You can use an object snap to specify the new endpoint.

After you've used an option to specify the length you want, you see the `Select an object to change or [Undo]:` prompt. Here you select the object you want to change. Be sure to pick the endpoint of the object for which you want to make the change.

The same prompt continues so that you can pick other objects by using the same length specifications. Choose Undo to undo the last change. Press Enter to end the command.

On the DVD

The drawing used in the following exercise on lengthening and shortening objects, `ab10-f.dwg`, is in the `Drawings` folder on the DVD. ∎

STEPS: Lengthening and Shortening Objects

1. Open `ab10-f.dwg` from the DVD.
2. Save the file as `ab10-07.dwg` in your `AutoCAD Bible` folder. It is a capacitor symbol from an electrical schematic, as shown in Figure 10.22.

FIGURE 10.22

A poorly drawn capacitor symbol.

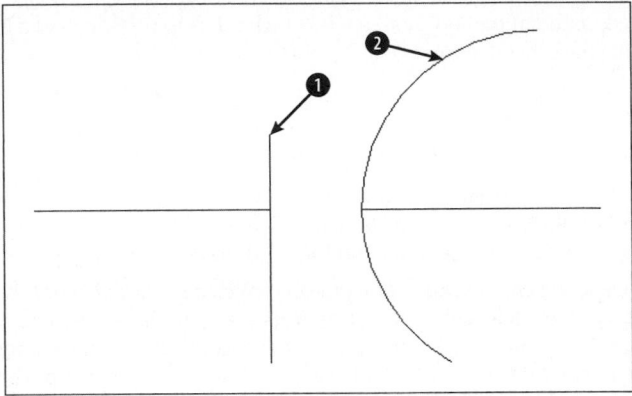

3. Choose Home tab ⇨ Modify panel (expanded) ⇨ Lengthen, and follow the prompts:

```
Select an object or [DElta/Percent/Total/DYnamic]: Pick the line at
    ❶ in Figure 10.22.
Current length: 0.200
Select an object or [DElta/Percent/Total/DYnamic]: Right-click and
    choose DElta.
Enter delta length or [Angle] <0.000>: .07 ↵
Select an object to change or [Undo]: Pick the line at ❶ in Figure
    10.22.
Select an object to change or [Undo]: ↵
```

This action lengthens the line.

4. Start the LENGTHEN command again and follow the prompts:

```
Select an object or [DElta/Percent/Total/DYnamic]: Pick the arc at ❷
    in Figure 10.22.
Current length: 0.407, included angle: 150
Select an object or [DElta/Percent/Total/DYnamic]: Right-click and
    choose Total.
Specify total length or [Angle] <1.000)>: Right-click and choose
    Angle.
Specify total angle <57>: 120 ↵
Select an object to change or [Undo]: Pick the arc at ❷ in Figure
    10.22.
Select an object to change or [Undo]: ↵
```

This action shortens the arc.

Save your drawing. It should look like Figure 10.23.

The completed capacitor symbol.

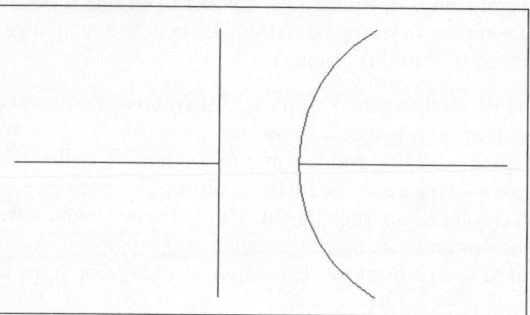

Stretching objects

The STRETCH command is generally used to stretch groups of objects. For example, you can use this command to enlarge a room in a floor plan. You can also shrink objects. You can change not only the length of the objects but the angle as well. You use a crossing window to choose the objects to be stretched. All objects that cross the boundaries of the crossing window are stretched. All objects that lie entirely within the crossing window are merely moved. Successful stretching involves precise placement of the crossing window. Figure 10.24 shows the process of stretching a garage. Note that the walls that cross the boundaries of the crossing window are stretched. However, the dormer that is entirely within the crossing window is just moved. This maintains the integrity of the model.

Stretching a garage.

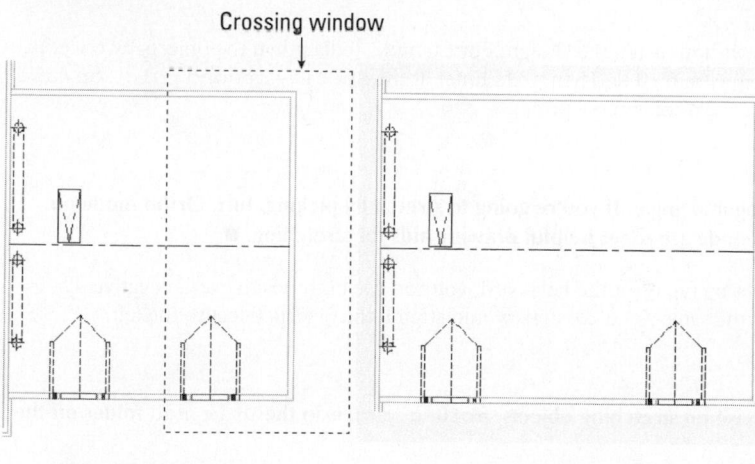

Crossing window

Before stretching

After stretching

You cannot stretch circles, text, or blocks. You can stretch arcs, although the results may not be what you expect.

The real power of the STRETCH command is in stretching a number of objects at once. However, you can also stretch one line. The results are similar to using the CHANGE command to change the endpoint of a line or to editing with grips (discussed later in this chapter).

 To stretch objects, choose Home tab ➪ Modify panel ➪ Stretch. The command responds with the `Select objects to stretch by crossing-window or crossing-polygon . . .` instruction and then the `Select objects:` prompt. Create the crossing window and select the objects that you want to stretch. (You can also use a crossing polygon — type **cp** at the `Select objects:` prompt.) After completing the crossing window, check to see which objects are highlighted. This helps you avoid unwanted results. You can use the object selection Remove option (type **r** ↵ at the Command prompt) to remove objects by picking the objects that you don't want to stretch or move. Then use the Add option (type **a** ↵) to continue selecting objects if necessary.

The STRETCH command remembers the most recent displacement throughout a session. To stretch an object by the same displacement that you most recently used, press Enter at the `Specify base point or [Displacement] <Displacement>:` prompt. At the `Specify displacement <0.0000, 0.0000, 0.0000>:` prompt, you see in angled brackets the last displacement that you used. Press Enter to stretch the object using this displacement.

Tip

You can use multiple crossing windows to select the objects that you want to stretch. You can also pick to select objects, although these objects are simply moved. ■

When you've finished selecting objects, you see the `Specify base point <Displacement>:` prompt. This step is just like moving objects, and you can respond in two ways:

- Pick a base point. At the `Specify second point or <use first point as displacement>:` prompt, pick a second point. Object snap and PolarSnap are helpful for picking these points.
- Type a displacement without using the @ sign. For example, to lengthen the objects by 6 feet in the 0-degree direction, type **6'<0** ↵. Then press Enter at the `Specify second point or <use first point as displacement>:` prompt.

Tip

Usually, you want to stretch at an orthogonal angle. If you're going to stretch by picking, turn Ortho mode on. Object snaps, polar tracking, and Snap mode are other helpful drawing aids for stretching. ■

When specifying a displacement by typing at the keyboard, you can use both positive and negative distances. For example, 6'<180 is the same as –6'<0. Both would stretch the objects 6 feet to the left.

On the DVD

The drawing used in the following exercise on stretching objects, `ab10-g.dwg`, is in the `Drawings` folder on the DVD. ■

STEPS: Stretching Objects

1. Open ab10-g.dwg from your DVD.

2. Save the file as ab10-08.dwg in your AutoCAD Bible folder. This drawing is the plan view of a garage, as shown in Figure 10.25. Turn on polar tracking by clicking Polar Tracking on the status bar. Click Snap Mode on the status bar and then right-click the Snap Mode button to make sure that PolarSnap is on (the PolarSnap item will be unavailable if it is already on); otherwise, choose PolarSnap. Turn on Object Snap mode and set a running object snap to Endpoint.

 3. Choose Home tab ➪ Modify panel ➪ Stretch. At the Select objects: prompt, pick ❶, as shown in Figure 10.25. At the Specify opposite corner: prompt, pick ❷. The prompt notifies you that it found 32 objects. Press Enter to end object selection.

FIGURE 10.25

A plan view of a garage.

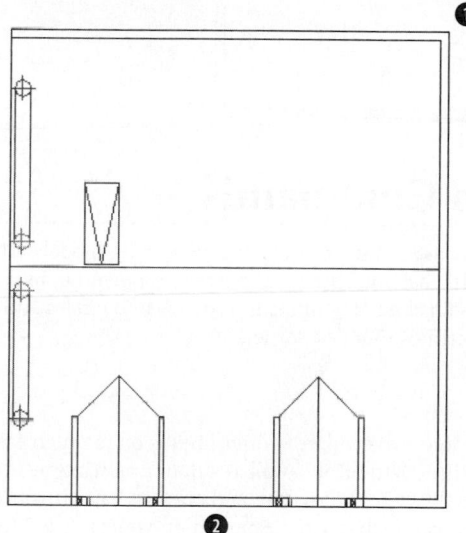

4. At the Specify base point or [Displacement] <Displacement>: prompt, pick the endpoint at the bottom-right corner of the garage. At the Specify second point or <use first point as displacement>: prompt, move the cursor to the right until you see the polar tracking tooltip. Click when the tooltip says 6'-0"<0. (If you can't find it, type 6',0 ↵. If you're not using Dynamic Input or have Dynamic Input set to absolute coordinates, add the @ symbol first.) This action stretches the garage by 6 feet.

5. Save your drawing. It should look like Figure 10.26.

FIGURE 10.26

The longer garage.

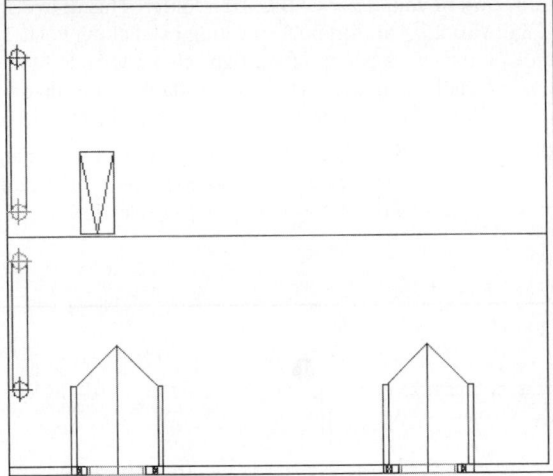

Using Construction Commands

Four additional commands are commonly used in the process of constructing models. The BREAK command removes sections of objects at points that you specify. The JOIN command joins co-linear lines, polylines, arcs, elliptical arcs, or splines, and can close arcs and elliptical arcs into circles and ellipses. CHAMFER creates corners, and FILLET creates rounded corners.

Breaking objects

Drawing a long line and then breaking it into two or more shorter lines is often much easier than drawing two separate lines. A common use for BREAK is to break a wall at a door or a window in an architectural floor plan. You specify two points on the object, and the command erases whatever is between those two points. Typically, you use object snaps to specify the points. Sometimes, you can use TRIM to break an object, but if you have no convenient cutting edge, you may find BREAK more efficient.

You can break lines, polylines, splines, xlines, rays, helixes, circles, arcs, elliptical arcs, and ellipses. To break a line, choose Home tab ⇨ Modify panel (expanded) ⇨ Break. You cannot select the object first. The command responds with the Select object: prompt. (Notice that you can only select one object to break.) At this prompt, you have two choices:

- Select the object at one of the break points that you want to create. You then see the Specify second break point or [First point]: prompt. Because you have already specified the first point, you can now specify the second point. The command breaks the object between the two points.

- Select the object by using any method of object selection. You then see the Specify second break point or [First point]: prompt. Right-click and choose First point. At the Specify first break point: prompt, pick the first break point. At the Specify second break point: prompt, pick the second break point. The command breaks the object between the two points.

Tip

Sometimes you may want to break an object into two pieces at a point, without erasing any part of the object. Choose Home tab ⇨ Modify panel (expanded) ⇨ Break at Point to help you easily break an object at a point. After selecting the object, pick where you want to break the object at the `Specify first break point:` prompt. The two new objects look the same as before on the screen — until you select one of the objects. AutoCAD and AutoCAD LT use @ to signify the last point entered; thus, the first and second break points are the same. ■

You can use BREAK to shorten an object. Pick one point on the object where you want the new endpoint to be. Pick the other point past its current endpoint to cut off the object at the point you picked on the object.

On the DVD

Pend inserts a pipe break symbol in a line. Look for it in `Software\Chapter 10\Pend`. ■

Joining objects

The opposite of breaking objects is joining them. The JOIN command lets you join lines, polylines, arcs, elliptical arcs, and splines. The objects must be along the same linear, circular, or elliptical path. The objects can overlap, have a gap between them, or touch end to end.

To join objects, choose Home tab ⇨ Modify panel (expanded) ⇨ Join. Follow these prompts:

```
Select source object: Select the first object that you want to join.
Select lines to join to source: Select the second object. (AutoCAD
    knows which type of object you've selected for the first prompt
    and inserts it into the second prompt.) You can continue to select
    other objects. Press Enter to end selection.
```

AutoCAD joins the objects.

A nice touch is the ability to close arcs (to circles) and elliptical arcs (to ellipses). If your first object is either type of arc, you see the `Select arcs to join to source or [cLose]:` prompt. Use the cLose option to close the arc.

Tip

You can reverse the direction of lines, polylines, splines (see Chapter 16), and helixes (see Chapter 21) with the REVERSE command. The direction of these objects influences how noncontinuous linetype patterns (covered in Chapter 11) flow, such as from left to right, or from right to left. Choose Home tab ⇨ Modify panel (expanded) ⇨ Reverse. ■

On the DVD

The drawing used in the following exercise on breaking and joining objects, `ab10-h.dwg`, is in the `Drawings` folder on the DVD. ■

STEPS: Breaking and Joining Objects

1. Open `ab10-h.dwg` from your DVD.
2. Save the file as `ab10-09.dwg` in your `AutoCAD Bible` folder. This is a site plan, as shown in Figure 10.27. Turn on Object Snap mode and set running object snaps for Endpoint and Intersection.

FIGURE 10.27

A site plan.

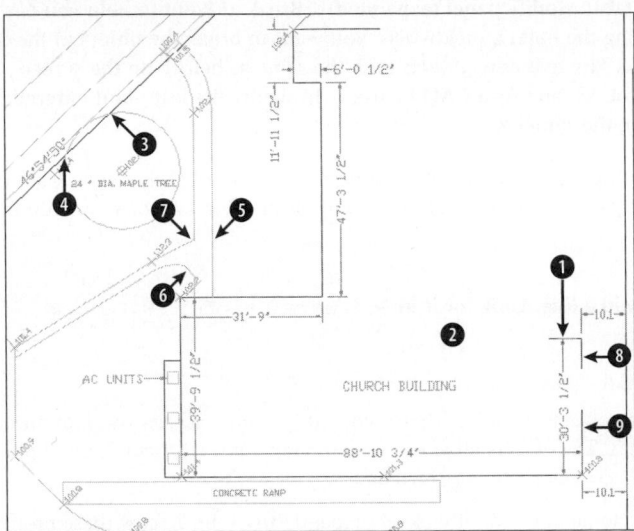

3. Choose Home tab ⇨ Modify panel (expanded) ⇨ Break. At the Select object: prompt, pick the line at **1**. At the Specify second break point or [First point]: prompt, pick **2**. This action shortens the line.

4. Repeat the BREAK command. At the Select object: prompt, pick the circle (it's a maple tree) anywhere along its circumference. At the Specify second break point or [First point]: prompt, right-click and choose First point. At the Specify first break point: prompt, pick the intersection at **3**. At the Specify second break point: prompt, pick the intersection at **4** to break the circle.

Note

AutoCAD and AutoCAD LT break circles counterclockwise. If you had picked **4**, and then **3**, only the smaller arc would have remained. ■

5. Let's say that you decide this is a mistake. Choose Home tab ⇨ Modify panel (expanded) ⇨ Join. At the Select source object: prompt, select the circle (tree) that you just broke into an arc. At the Select arcs to join to source or [cLose]: prompt, right-click and choose cLose. The arc becomes a full circle again.

6. To break the line at **5**, click the Object Snap Tracking button on the status bar. Start the BREAK command again. Follow the prompts:

```
Select object: Pick the line at 5.
Specify second break point or [First point]: Right-click and choose
    First point.
Specify first break point: Move the cursor to 6 to acquire it as a
    tracking point. Then move the cursor to the right onto the line
    you are breaking. When you see the Endpoint: Intersection tooltip,
    click. (You have no visual confirmation yet that you picked the
    right point.)
```

> Specify second break point: Move the cursor to **7** to acquire it as a tracking point. Then move the cursor onto the line you are breaking. At the Endpoint: 4'-2 3/4"<0.0000 tooltip, click.

7. Start the JOIN command. At the Select source object: prompt, select the line at **8**. At the Select lines to join to source: prompt, select the line at **9**. Press Enter to end the selection and join the lines into one.

8. Save your drawing. It should look like Figure 10.28.

FIGURE 10.28

The edited site plan.

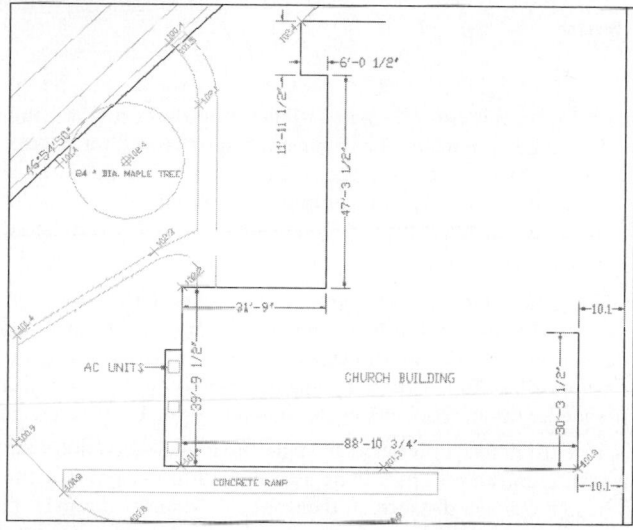

AutoCAD Only

The Express Tools contain a command, BREAKLINE, to create a break symbol. Choose Express Tools ⇨ Draw panel ⇨ Break-line Symbol. Another Express Tools command, OVERKILL, deletes objects that are on top of other objects. ∎

Creating chamfered corners

The CHAMFER command creates corners from two nonparallel lines. You can also chamfer xlines, rays, and polylines. You can simply extend the lines to meet at an intersection (a square corner), or create a beveled edge. If you create a beveled edge, you define the edge by either two distances or one distance and an angle relative to the first line that you're chamfering. Figure 10.29 shows the elements of a chamfered corner.

Chamfering is a two-step process. First you define how you want to chamfer the corner, specifying either two distances from the corner or a distance and an angle. Then you select the two lines that you want to chamfer.

FIGURE 10.29

A chamfered corner.

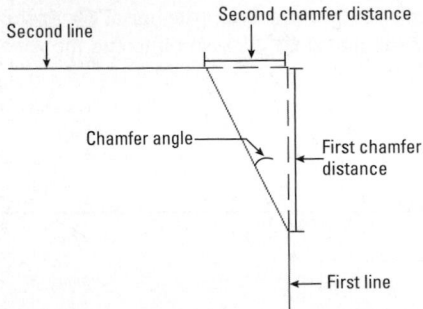

 To chamfer, choose Home tab ➪ Modify panel ➪ Chamfer/Fillet drop-down list ➪ Chamfer. You cannot select objects before the CHAMFER command. The command responds with the (TRIM mode) Current chamfer Dist1 = 0.0000, Dist2 = 0.0000 Select first line or [Undo/Polyline/ Distance/Angle/Trim/mEthod/Multiple]: prompt. The command starts by listing the current settings. (The CHAMFER command remembers the last-used chamfer data.) You can define two distances from a corner or one distance and an angle:

- To define two distances from the corner, right-click and choose Distance. At the Specify first chamfer distance <0.0000>: prompt, type the first chamfer distance or press Enter to accept the default (which is the last distance that you defined). At the Specify second chamfer distance <0.0000>: prompt, type the second distance. The default for this is always the first chamfer distance because equal chamfer distances are so common.

- To define a distance (from the corner) and an angle, right-click and choose Angle. At the Specify chamfer length on the first line <1.0000>: prompt, enter a distance. This is the same as the first chamfer distance. At the Specify chamfer angle from the first line <0.0000>: prompt, type the angle between the first line and the chamfer line.

Now that you have specified the settings that you want, you're ready to chamfer. Your distances or distance and angle are displayed as you just specified them. The command repeats the Select first line or [Undo/Polyline/Distance/Angle/Trim/mEthod/Multiple]: prompt. Select the first line. If you aren't creating a chamfer with equal distances, the order in which you select the lines is important. The command trims the first line selected by the first distance, and the second line selected based on either the second distance or the angle. At the Select second line or shift-select to apply corner: prompt, select the second line to chamfer the lines.

If the lines already intersect, the command trims them to create a corner. The pick points on intersecting lines should be on the part of the lines that you want to keep, not on the part of the lines that you want to trim off.

Tip

To quickly create a square corner if you have non-zero settings, press Shift as you select the second line. Of course, you can still set each distance to zero. ■

Cross-Reference

Choose the Polyline option to chamfer an entire polyline at once. Chapter 16 covers polylines, and Chapter 24 discusses chamfering 3D models. ∎

By default, CHAMFER trims the original lines that it chamfers. If you want to keep the full original lines when you add the chamfer line, choose the Trim option and choose No Trim. Use the Multiple option to continue the prompts and chamfer several corners in one command. The Undo option lets you undo your last chamfer and try again.

On the DVD

The drawing used in the following exercise on chamfering lines, ab10-i.dwg, is in the Drawings folder on the DVD. ∎

STEPS: Chamfering Lines

1. Open ab10-i.dwg from your DVD.

2. Save the file as ab10-10.dwg in your AutoCAD Bible folder. This drawing is a very small section of a "porcupine" mixer, as shown in Figure 10.30.

FIGURE 10.30

A mechanical drawing showing a small section of a "porcupine" mixer.

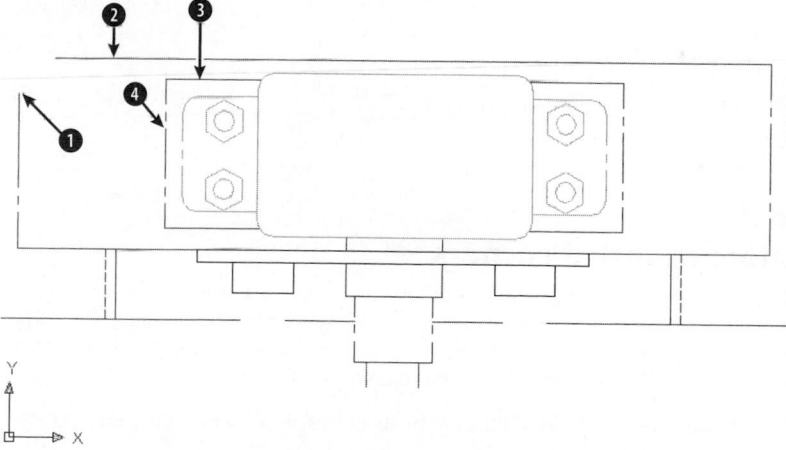

3. Choose Home tab ➪ Modify panel ➪ Chamfer/Fillet drop-down list ➪ Chamfer. CHAMFER states the current mode and distances. At the Select first line or [Undo/Polyline/ Distance/Angle/Trim/mEthod/Multiple]: prompt, pick ❶, as shown in Figure 10.30. At the Select second line: prompt, pick ❷. (If the current distances are not zero, press Shift as you pick ❷.) The command chamfers the two lines to make a corner. (If this doesn't work, you may have the Trim option set to No Trim. Change the setting to Trim and try again.)

4. Repeat the CHAMFER command. Follow the prompts:

```
Select first line or [Undo/Polyline/Distance/Angle/Trim/mEthod/
    Multiple]: Right-click and choose Angle.
Specify chamfer length on the first line <1>: 9/16 ↵
Specify chamfer angle from the first line <0>: 45 ↵
```

5. At the Select first line or [Undo/Polyline/Distance/Angle/Trim/mEthod/
   Multiple]: prompt, pick ❸, as shown in Figure 10.30. At the Select second line:
   prompt, pick ❹. The command chamfers the two lines, as shown in Figure 10.31.

6. Save your drawing.

FIGURE 10.31

The edited drawing after using the CHAMFER command.

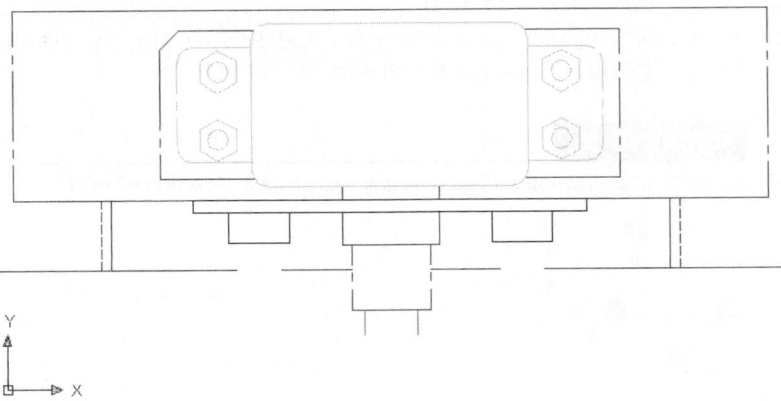

Creating rounded corners

The FILLET command creates rounded corners, replacing part of two lines with an arc. Fillets are often used in mechanical drawings. In certain cases, you can use FILLET instead of the ARC command to create arcs. As with CHAMFER, you can fillet lines, xlines, rays, and polylines — they can even be parallel. You can also fillet circles, arcs, elliptical arcs, and ellipses.

The FILLET command defines the fillet arc by its radius, as shown in Figure 10.32.

Like chamfering, filleting is a two-step process. First you define the radius of the fillet arc. Then you select the two lines that you want to fillet. You cannot select objects before the FILLET command.

FIGURE 10.32

A fillet between two lines.

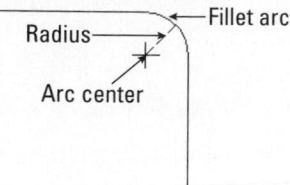

To fillet, follow these steps:

1. Choose Home tab ⇨ Modify panel ⇨ Chamfer/Fillet drop-down list ⇨ Fillet. The command responds with the Current settings: Mode = TRIM, Radius = 0.0000 Select first object or [Undo/Polyline/Radius/Trim/Multiple]: prompt.

2. Right-click and choose Radius.

3. At the Specify fillet radius <0.0000>: prompt, type the radius you want. The default is either 0.0000 or the last radius that you specified.

4. The command repeats the Select first object or [Undo/Polyline/Radius/Trim/Multiple]: prompt. Select the first object that you want to fillet.

5. At the Select second object or shift-select to apply corner: prompt, select the second object that you want to fillet. This action creates the fillet.

By default, FILLET trims the original lines that it fillets, but the FILLET command recalls the last setting you used. If you want to keep the full original lines when you create a fillet, right-click and choose the Trim option, and then choose No Trim.

Cross-Reference

Choose the Polyline option to fillet an entire polyline at once. Chapter 16 covers polylines, and Chapter 24 discusses filleting 3D models. ∎

Filleting with a zero radius gives the same results as chamfering with distances set to zero. (See the previous section on chamfering.) If your existing settings are non-zero, you can press Shift as you select the second object to create a square corner.

The order in which you select the two objects to be filleted is not important. However, *where* you pick the objects is quite important. If two objects intersect, the command keeps the objects on the same side of the intersection as your pick point and fillets them. Those parts of the objects on the far side of the intersection are erased.

When you fillet arcs and lines, if more than one fillet is possible, FILLET connects the endpoints closest to your pick points. Filleting circles and lines can produce unexpected results. Sometimes you need to experiment to find the proper pick points.

Tip

Use the Multiple option to continue the prompts and fillet several corners in one command. ∎

On the DVD

The drawing used in the following exercise on filleting objects, ab10-i.dwg, is in the Drawings folder on the DVD. ∎

STEPS: Filleting Objects

1. Open ab10-i.dwg from your DVD.

2. Save the file as ab10-11.dwg in your AutoCAD Bible folder. This is the same drawing used in the previous exercise. It is shown in Figure 10.33.

A mechanical drawing showing a small section of a "porcupine" mixer.

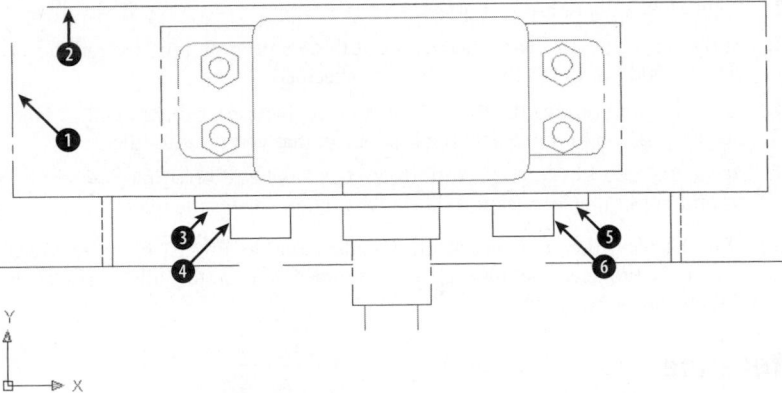

3. Choose Home tab ⇨ Modify panel ⇨ Chamfer/Fillet drop-down list ⇨ Fillet. At the `Select first object or [Undo/Polyline/Radius/Trim/Multiple]:` prompt, right-click and choose Radius. At the `Specify fillet radius <1/2>:` prompt, type **5/8** ↵.

4. At the `Select first object or [Undo/Polyline/Radius/Trim/Multiple]:` prompt, pick the line at ➊, as shown in Figure 10.33. At the `Select second object or shift-select to apply corner:` prompt, pick the line at ➋ to fillet the two lines.

5. Repeat the FILLET command. At the `Select first object or [Undo/Polyline/Radius/Trim/ Multiple]:` prompt, right-click and choose Radius. At the `Enter fillet radius <5/8>:` prompt, type **1/4** ↵.

6. At the `Select first object or [Undo/Polyline/Radius/Trim/Multiple]:` prompt, right-click and choose Multiple. Pick the line at ➌, as shown in Figure 10.33. At the `Select second object or shift-select to apply corner:` prompt, pick the line at ➍ to fillet the two lines. The prompts continue. This time pick at ➎ and ➏.

7. If you want, you can connect the two loose lines that the fillets created and create some more fillets in the drawing.

8. Save your drawing. It should look like Figure 10.34.

FIGURE 10.34

FIGURE 10.34

The filleted drawing.

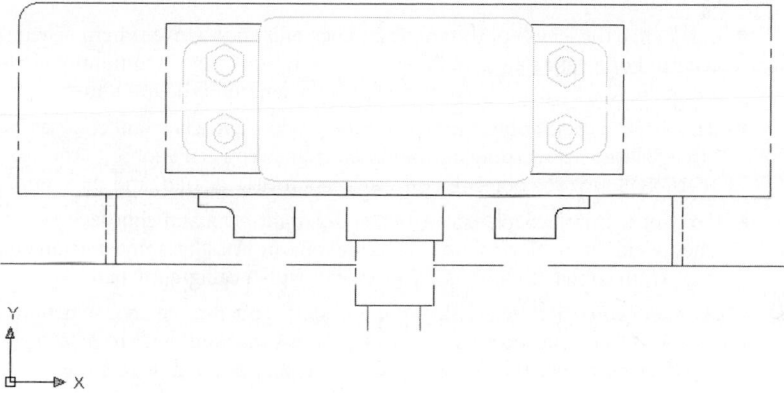

Creating a Revision Cloud

You may need to mark areas of your drawings that contain revisions in order to draw attention to these revisions. A common method is to draw a *revision cloud* around the revised objects. Figure 10.35 shows a drawing with a revision cloud, which is a series of arcs that indicate that an area of the drawing has been revised.

FIGURE 10.35

The revision cloud shows where the drawing has been modified.

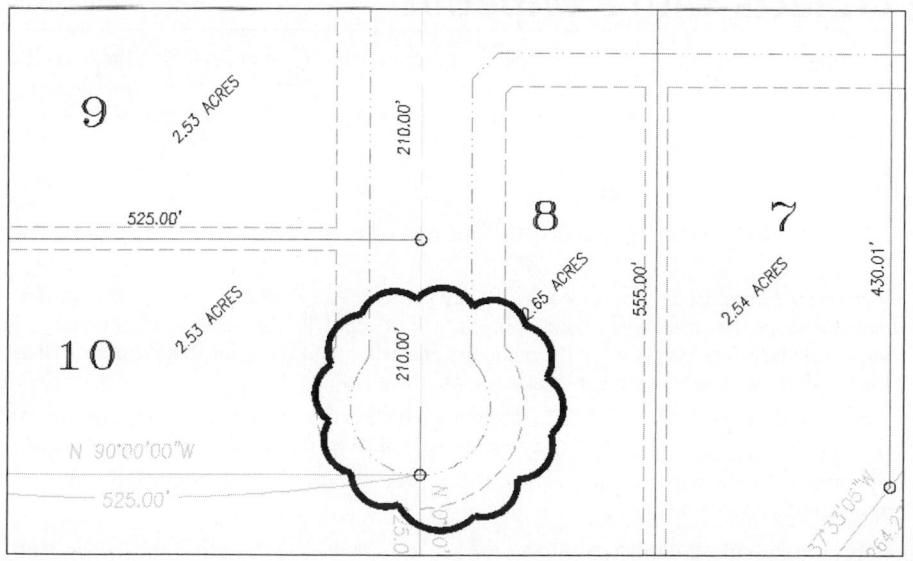

To create a revision cloud, follow these steps:

1. Choose Home tab ➪ Draw panel (expanded) ➪ Revision Cloud.

2. At the Specify start point or [Arc length/Object/Style] <Object>: prompt, you can choose from three options:
   - To change the length of the arc, right-click and choose Arc Length. Then specify a new arc length. For a variable, hand-drawn look, you can specify a minimum arc length and a maximum arc length that is up to three times the length of the minimum.
   - To change a closed object into a revision cloud, right-click and choose Object. Then pick a circle, ellipse, closed polyline, or closed spline. You can choose to reverse the direction of the revision cloud. The object is converted to a revision cloud, and the command ends.
   - To choose from two available cloud styles, right-click and choose Style. At the next prompt, choose either the Normal or Calligraphy option. A calligraphy revision cloud has a variable line width so that it looks as if you drew it with a calligraphy pen.

3. Click where you want the revision cloud to start. You also see an instruction, Guide cross-hairs along cloud path . . ., which means that you don't have to pick to create the arcs. You just have to move the crosshairs along the path of the desired cloud.

4. Move the crosshairs counterclockwise to create a circular or elliptical shape. When you approach the start point, the command ends automatically. (You can end the cloud at any time by pressing Enter.)

Note

If you want, you can pick each arc endpoint to control the size of the arcs. However, if you move the crosshairs farther than the arc length, an arc is created automatically. REVCLOUD multiplies the arc length by the Overall Scale factor (see Chapter 15) to adjust for different scale factors. ■

Hiding Objects with a Wipeout

A *wipeout* covers existing objects in order to clear space for some annotation or to indicate that the covered objects will be changed and should therefore be ignored. A wipeout is a polygonal area with a background that matches the background of the drawing area. The WIPEOUT command creates a polygon of the same color as the background of your drawing area.

To create a wipeout, follow these steps:

1. Choose Home tab ➪ Draw panel (expanded) ➪ Wipeout.

2. At the Specify first point or [Frames/Polyline] <Polyline>: prompt, specify the first point of a shape that will cover existing objects. To use a polyline as the shape, right-click and choose Polyline. (The polyline can't contain any arcs when you use it for this purpose.) Then select the polyline and choose whether or not to erase the polyline.

3. At the Specify next point or [Undo]: prompt, if you specified a point, specify the next point.

4. At the Specify next point or [Close/Undo]: prompt, specify another point or use the Close option to close the wipeout shape. You can also press Enter to end the command and use the shape that you specified.

By default, the wipeout has a frame around it, using the current layer's color. You can hide the frames of all wipeouts by starting the WIPEOUT command, choosing the Frames option, and then choosing Off.

Cross-Reference

You can create a background mask especially for text. This mask covers a rectangle around your text so that you can read the text more easily. For more information, see Chapter 13. ∎

Constraining Objects with Parameters

You can control objects by specifying parameters that constrain their relationships with other objects or their measurements. For example, you can constrain one line to be always perpendicular to another line, or you can constrain the diameter of a circle to a specific value. Using parameters adds intelligence to your drawing and helps to ensure accuracy of the entire drawing when you modify objects. Parameters can also save a huge amount of time that you would otherwise need to spend editing objects, because when you change one object, other objects automatically adjust to comply with their constraints.

Parametric constraints are not available in AutoCAD LT. The feature includes two types of constraints: geometric and dimensional. Figure 10.36 shows a model with several concentric geometric constraints and a diameter dimensional constraint.

FIGURE 10.36

You can control object properties and relationships by applying geometric and dimensional constraints.

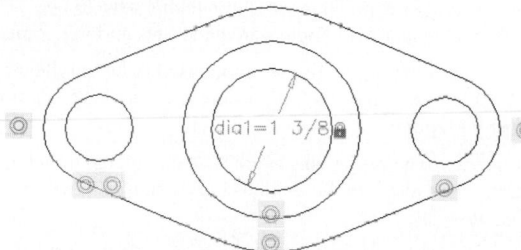

Using geometric constraints

Geometric constraints apply to the geometric properties of objects. The basic principle is that the first object that you specify is the base object, and the second object that you specify moves or adjusts in accordance with the constraint. For example, if you have two lines at different angles and use the parallel constraint, the second line will rotate to become parallel with the base object. In most cases, you can specify a specific point on an object to manage the constraint.

To specify a geometric constraint for one or more objects, display the Parametric tab and use the Geometric panel. Table 10.2 lists the available geometric parameters, the command names, and their functions.

New Feature

The commands listed in Table 10.2 are new for AutoCAD 2011. Previously, these constraints were options of the GEOMCONSTRAINT command; you can still access them that way. ∎

TABLE 10.2

Geometric Parameters

Geometric Parameter	Command Name	Function
Coincident	GCCOINCIDENT	Constrains a geometric point on one object to be at a point on another object. The objects can be a line, polyline, circle, arc, ellipse, or spline. The first object can be a point object. Valid geometric points are endpoints, midpoints, and centers (for arcs).
Collinear	GCCOLLINEAR	Constrains a second object to lie along the same path as the first. Valid objects are lines, polylines, ellipses, and elliptical arcs. For ellipses, you can choose which axis to make collinear.
Concentric	GCCONCENTRIC	Constrains a second arc, circle, or ellipse to have the same center as a first one.
Fix	GCFIX	Locks an object in place. You can lock lines (by endpoint or midpoint), polylines (by endpoint or midpoint, and by center of arc segments), arcs (by center, endpoint, or midpoint), circles (by center), ellipses (by center and by endpoint or midpoint for elliptical arcs), and splines (by endpoint).
Parallel	GCPARALLEL	Constrains a second line, polyline, ellipse (either axis), or multiline to be parallel to the first. Valid points are endpoints and midpoints.
Perpendicular	GCPERPENDICULAR	Constrains a second line, polyline, or ellipse (either axis) to be perpendicular to the first. Valid points are endpoints and midpoints.
Horizontal	GCHORIZONTAL	Constrains a line, polyline, or ellipse (either axis) to be parallel to the X axis. You can also use the 2 Points option to make two points on an object horizontal.
Vertical	GCVERTICAL	Constrains a line, polyline, or ellipse (either axis) to be parallel to the Y axis. You can also use the 2 Points option to make two points on an object vertical.
Tangent	GCTANGENT	Constrains curves to be tangent to other curves or lines. You can specify a line (endpoints or midpoints), polyline (endpoints, midpoints, or center-of-arc segments), and endpoints, midpoints, or centers of an arc, circle, or ellipse. Objects don't need to touch to be tangent.
Smooth	GCSMOOTH	Creates a continuous curvature between two splines (or a spline and a line, arc, or polyline). This process makes endpoints of the two curves coincident.
Symmetric	GCSYMMETRIC	Constrains a point on a second object to be the same angle and distance from a symmetry line as a point on the first object. You can choose the endpoints and midpoints of lines, polylines, and arcs. You can choose centers of arcs, circles, ellipses, and polyline arc segments.
Equal	GCEQUAL	Resizes lines and polyline segments to have equal length, as well as resizing arcs and circles to have equal radius. You can specify endpoints and midpoints of lines, polylines, and arcs, as well as the center of arcs, circles, and polyline arc segments.

Note

Not every combination of parameters is possible. For example, a line can't have both horizontal and vertical parameters. When you try to apply a parameter that is impossible due to previous constraints, you get a message saying that applying the constraint would overconstrain the geometry. ■

By default, you see small, semitransparent icons for each geometric parameter. You can turn the display of these icons on and off, or turn them on for specific objects. Choose Parametric tab ⇨ Geometric panel and use the Show/Hide, Show All, and Hide All buttons. When you choose the Show/Hide button, select the objects for which you want to see the icons. Then choose the option to show or hide the icon. For further control, click the dialog box launcher on the Geometric panel and use the Geometric tab of the Constraint Settings dialog box. Here you can uncheck icons for specific parameters that you don't want to see.

If you pass your cursor over an icon, you see the name of the constraint. Also, the objects that it affects appear dashed.

Auto-constraining objects

 AutoCAD can automatically apply constraints to objects to keep them the way they are. For example, if you draw two horizontal, parallel lines, AutoCAD applies the horizontal and parallel constraints automatically. To apply auto-constraints, choose Parametric tab ⇨ Geometric panel ⇨ Auto Constrain and then select the objects that you want to constrain.

The Auto Constrain feature adds nine of the possible parameters, omitting Fix, Smooth, and Symmetric. You can specify which parametric constraints to apply and in which order. To do so, click the dialog box launcher arrow on the Geometric panel's title bar to open the Constraint Settings dialog box, and then click the AutoConstrain tab. The settings are self-explanatory.

New Feature

 A new button on the status bar, Infer Constraints, lets you automatically add geometric constraints as you work. This button is a toggle, so you can turn off the feature if you want. ■

You can add constraints as you work by turning on the Infer Constraints feature. Click the Infer Constraints button on the status bar. The Infer Constraints feature uses Endpoint, Midpoint, Center, Node, and Insertion object snaps to calculate the constraints, as you draw or edit. For example:

- If you draw a circle and then draw a line that starts at the center of the circle, AutoCAD adds a coincident constraint linking the line's endpoint to the circle's center. If you move the circle, the line moves with the circle.

- If you move multiline text (which I cover in Chapter 13) so that its Insertion object snap is on the endpoint of a line, AutoCAD adds a coincident constraint, so that if you move the line, the text moves with the line.

The Infer Constraints feature also creates constraints as follows:

- AutoCAD applies perpendicular, tangent, and parallel constraints when you use the corresponding object snaps. When you use the Perpendicular or Tangent object snaps, AutoCAD also applies a coincident constraint at the point where the two objects meet.

- When you draw vertical or horizontal lines or polylines (which I cover in Chapter 16), AutoCAD applies the corresponding vertical or horizontal constraints.

- When you draw a rectangle, AutoCAD applies parallel constraints to each pair of parallel sides and a perpendicular constraint to one corner. As a result, you can easily stretch a corner of the rectangle to resize it without losing the rectangular shape.

- When you create a fillet (covered earlier in this chapter), AutoCAD applies coincident and tangent constraints between the new arc and its surrounding lines.

- When you create a chamfer (covered earlier in this chapter), AutoCAD applies coincident constraints between the new line and its surrounding lines.

- If you use the Nearest object snap when drawing or editing an object, you automatically create a coincident constraint between an object snap on one object and any location on the other object. For example, if you use the Nearest object snap to place the endpoint of a line on a side of a rectangle, you can move the line's endpoint only along that side and its extension (where the line would be if you extended it). If you move the rectangle, AutoCAD continues to constrain the line's endpoint along the side (or extension of the side) of the rectangle.

Tip
You can temporarily relax a constraint by pressing the Ctrl key while you grip-edit constrained objects. (I cover grip-editing at the end of this chapter.) Select the object, and click a grip to highlight it. Then press and release the Ctrl button. You can now stretch or move the object. ∎

Using dimensional constraints

For more precision, you can apply dimensional constraints, which apply a constraint based on a number or an equation. For example, you can specify a 4-unit distance between two lines. You can specify the dimensional constraint from scratch, or convert an existing dimension. After you create a dimensional constraint, you can change the constraint's value to modify the affected objects. Dimensional constraints show a lock next to their icon to distinguish them from geometrical constraints.

Cross-Reference
Dimensional constraints have many similarities to dimensions. I cover dimensions in Chapters 14 and 15. You may want to turn your constrained objects into blocks so that you can use them again. Also, constrained objects can act like dynamic blocks. Certain features of constraints (parametric constraints) apply only to dynamic blocks. For more information on blocks and dynamic blocks, see Chapter 18. ∎

To apply a dimensional constraint, choose the Parametric tab ⇨ Dimensional panel, and then choose one of the options. For each of the options, follow the prompts to specify the objects or points that you want to use. Table 10.3 lists the constraints and their function.

New Feature
The commands in Table 10.3 are new for AutoCAD 2011. Previously, they were available as options of the DIMCONSTRAINT command; you can still access them that way. ∎

You can convert a dimension to a dimensional constraint. Choose Parametric tab ⇨ Dimensional panel ⇨ Convert.

TABLE 10.3

Dimensional Parameters

Dimensional Parameter	Command Name	Function
Linear	DCLINEAR	Constrains the distance between two points. The points can be at any angle from each other, but the constraint measures only the vertical or horizontal distance. You can use the same types of points as for geometrical constraints. Specify the first and second constraint points. When you choose a line or arc, the constraint applies to the endpoints of the object (constraining the object's length), or you can use the Object option to apply a linear constraint to lines, polyline segments, or arcs. Specify the dimension line location and press Enter to end the command.
Vertical	DCVERTICAL	Constrains the distance between two points that are parallel to the Y axis. Otherwise, this constraint works just like the linear one.
Horizontal	DCHORIZONTAL	Constrains the distance between two points that are parallel to the X axis. Otherwise, this constraint works just like the linear one.
Aligned	DCALIGNED	Constrains the distance between two points that are not at orthogonal angles from each other.
Angular	DCANGULAR	Constrains the angle between lines, polyline segments, and arc endpoints (using the arc center as the angle vertex). Specify the first and second lines or the arc. You can use the 3 Points option to specify individual points. Specify the dimension line location and press Enter to end the command.
Radial	DCRADIUS	Constrains the radius of a circle, arc, or arc segment of a polyline. Specify the circle, arc, or arc segment of a polyline, and then specify the location for the dimension line. Press Enter to end the command.
Diameter	DCDIAMETER	Constrains the diameter of a circle, arc, or arc segment of a polyline. Specify the circle, arc, or arc segment of a polyline, and then specify the location for the dimension line. Press Enter to end the command.

The Form option of the DIMCONSTRAINT command lets you choose one of two forms (or formats) to apply to subsequent dimensional constraints that you create:

- **Dynamic.** Dynamic constraints, the default, don't change size as you zoom in or out, and they have a predefined style, including a gray color. You can show or hide dynamic constraints by choosing Parametric tab ⇨ Dimensional panel, and using the Show/Hide, Show All, or Hide All buttons. Importantly, dynamic constraints don't plot.

- **Annotational.** Annotational constraints look like regular dimensions, and you can format how they appear. They use the current layer properties. (I cover layers in Chapter 11.) They plot, and so you can use annotational constraints both to constrain objects and in the place of dimensions.

Note
By default, AutoCAD displays hidden dynamic constraints for selected objects. If you never want to display hidden dynamic constraints, on the Parametric tab, in the Dimensional panel, click the dialog box launcher arrow on the panel's title bar. The Constraint Settings dialog box opens with the Dimensional tab on top. Uncheck the Show Hidden Dynamic Constraints for Selected Objects check box. In the same place, you can control whether the dynamic constraint displays its name, value, or name and expression. When you're done, click OK. ■

To change the form of an existing dimensional constraint, select the constraint, display the Properties palette (Ctrl+1), and use the Constraint Form drop-down list.

AutoCAD doesn't let you *over-constrain* geometry. That means that you can't add more constraints than necessary. If you try to add another constraint, AutoCAD opens a message telling you that applying the constraint would over-constrain the geometry. In this situation, you can back out and add a different constraint, or you can create a *reference* dimension. A reference dimension is just for show; it doesn't actually constrain objects. You might use a reference dimension to show relationships that other constraints create, or to add a second label in a different location. You can change the reference property of a constraint in the Properties palette. AutoCAD displays reference constraints in parentheses.

Working with the Parameters Manager

AutoCAD gives each dimensional constraint a name and you can create expressions that reference another dimensional constraint. In this way, you can create relationships between objects. For example, the radius of a circle can be one-half the distance between two lines. The result is that modifying one object then updates related objects; in the example, changing the distance between the lines would change the radius of the circle. The result is a powerful way to control the geometry of your drawing.

You edit and manage dimensional constraints in the Parameters Manager palette, as shown in Figure 10.37. The Parameters Manager palette lists existing dimensional parameters. You can modify these parameters and create user parameters. The Name column lists the name of each parameter. AutoCAD assigns a default name when you create a dimensional parameter, but you can change the name. Click a name to highlight it, enter a new name, and press Enter. Names cannot start with a number, contain spaces, or be more than 256 characters.

FIGURE 10.37

The Parameters Manager palette lets you modify dimensional parameters and create user parameters.

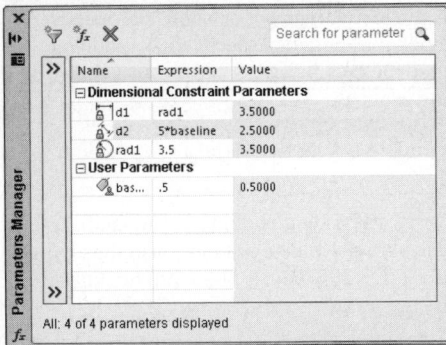

To change a value, you use the Expression column, not the Value column. For example, if you have a dimensional parameter that specifies a distance of 3.0 units and you want to change that value to 4.0 units, click the number in the Expression column so that it's selected, enter a new value, and press Enter. The objects adjust in accordance with the new constraint.

You can enter expressions in the Expression column. For example, if you want the diameter of a circle to be two times the length of a line, and the parameter for the line is named length, you can enter **length*2** for the circle's parameter. Then when you change the line parameter's value, which changes the length of the line, the circle's diameter automatically adjusts accordingly. In this way, you maintain the required relationships among objects.

You can also create user parameters. A user parameter can be a value or expression that you want to use as a basis for another parameter. It can be a number or equation.

Tip

To edit a dimensional constraint, select the constraint, right-click, and choose Edit Constraint. You can then change the equation or value in-place, without using the Parameters Manager. To add trigonometric and other functions to an expression, click the expression, right-click, and choose Expressions. Then choose the function you want. ■

New Feature

Click the double arrows in the bar at the left side of the Parameters Manager palette to open the new Filters pane. You can create groups of parameters by clicking the Creates a New Parameter Group button. Then name the new filter. Click the default All Used in Expressions filter, select the constraints you want to put in the group, and drag them to the new filter on the left. You can then click that new filter to display only parameters in the group. To remove a parameter from a group, right-click it, and choose Delete. In addition, you can use the new search box at the upper-right corner of the Parameters Manager palette to search for parameters by name. ■

On the DVD

The drawing used in the following exercise on using parametric constraints to constrain objects, ab10-j.dwg, is in the Drawings folder on the DVD. ■

STEPS: Using Parametric Constraints to Constrain Objects

1. Open ab10-j.dwg from your DVD.

2. Save the file as ab10-12.dwg in your AutoCAD Bible folder. This drawing is blank. Set a running object snap for Endpoint and Center. You want to be able to scale the plate, shown in Figure 10.38, without changing the size of the circle, which represents a hole for a fixed-width axle. You also want to constrain the relationships between the objects.

3. Check that the Infer Constraints button on the status bar is active. (It should appear blue, not gray.) Also check that Polar Tracking is on.

4. To draw the model shown in Figure 10.38, go to Home tab⇨Draw panel⇨Line and follow the prompts:

```
Specify first point: Pick a point slightly to the right and above the
    middle of the drawing area.
Specify next point or [Undo]: Move the cursor to the left, using
    polar tracking to keep the line horizontal. 4 ↵.
Specify next point or [Undo]: Move the cursor down, using polar
    tracking to keep the line vertical. 4 ↵.
Specify next point or [Close/Undo]: Move the cursor to the right,
    using polar tracking to keep the line horizontal. 4 ↵.
Specify next point or [Close/Undo]: ↵.
```

FIGURE 10.38

This plate consists of three lines, a circle, and an arc.

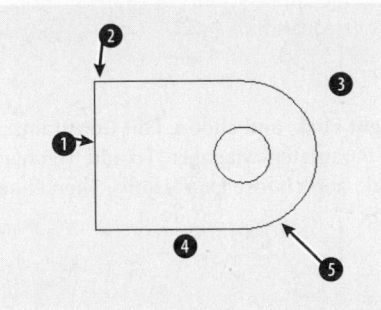

 5. Start the ARC command. Press Enter to start the arc at the endpoint of the last line you drew. At the prompt for the end point of the arc, use the Endpoint object snap to specify the start point of the first line you drew. You should already see some of the geometric parameters in your drawing.

6. Start the CIRCLE command. Follow these prompts:

```
Specify center point for circle or [3P/2P/Ttr (tan tan radius)]: Use
    the Center object snap to specify the center of the arc.
Specify radius of circle or [Diameter]: .75 ↵
```

7. You should now see one horizontal constraint, two perpendicular constraints, and four coincident constraints. To let AutoCAD do most of the work, choose Parametric tab ⇨ Geometric panel ⇨ AutoConstrain. At the `Select objects or [Settings]:` prompt, select all of the objects that you drew and press Enter to end selection. Notice that this action adds tangent and coincident constraints.

8. To constrain the three lines to be of equal length, you only need to constrain two of the three lines. (If you try all three, you over-constrain the geometry.) Click the Equal button in the Geometric panel. At the `Select first object or [Multiple]:` prompt, select the vertical line at ❶ and the horizontal line at ❷. You now see Equal Sign icons next to the two lines.

9. You want to be able to scale this plate, but you want to make sure that the circle's diameter doesn't change. In the Dimensional panel, click the Diameter button. At the `Select arc or circle:` prompt, select the circle. At the `Specify dimension line location:` prompt, pick a location. Then press Enter to end the command.

10. Choose Home tab ⇨ Modify panel ⇨ Scale. At the `Select objects:` prompt, click above and to the left of the plate and then click below and to the right, selecting all of the objects. Press Enter to end selection. At the `Specify base point:` prompt, pick the lower-left corner of the plate. At the `Specify scale factor....:` prompt, enter **2** ↵. The plate scales to twice its original size, but the circle's diameter remains unchanged.

11. Click the Parametric tab again. In the Manage panel, click Parameters Manager. Click the `dia1` item to select the row, again to select just the name, and type **hole** ↵, to rename the parameter. Click the item in the Expression column and enter **2** ↵ to change the diameter. The circle's diameter changes accordingly.

12. To prepare for the stretching action in the next step, you need some room above and below the model in the drawing area. If necessary, click the Pan button on the status bar and drag downward a little. Press Esc to end Pan mode.

13. Click the Home tab. In the Modify panel, click Stretch. At the `Select objects:` prompt, pick at ❸ and then at ❹. Press Enter to end selection. At the `Specify base point or [displacement] <Displacement>:` prompt, pick the endpoint near ❺. At the next prompt, pick a point to the right of ❺. You'll see that the constraints fix the plate so that as you stretch, the three lines always remain the same length and the circle remains the same diameter.

14. Save your drawing.

Double-Clicking to Edit Objects

You can double-click objects to edit them. What happens after you double-click depends on the type of object. In most cases, double-clicking an object just opens the Properties palette where you can change the object's properties. For more information about using the Quick Properties palette and Properties palette, see the section, "Editing with the Quick Properties Palette and the Properties Palette," later in this chapter.

When you double-click certain types of objects in a drawing, you see a dialog box that is specific to these objects, or a related editing command starts:

- **Attribute definition.** Opens the Edit Attribute Definition dialog box (the DDEDIT command). See Chapter 18 for more information.

- **Attribute within a block.** Opens the Enhanced Attribute Editor dialog box (the EATTEDIT command). See Chapter 18 for more information.

- **Block.** Opens the Edit Block Definition dialog box. You can choose the block from a list and click OK to enter the Block Editor. See Chapter 18 for more information.

- **Image.** Opens the IMAGEADJUST command. See Chapter 27 for more information.

- **Livesection.** Starts the LIVESECTION command. See Chapter 24 for more information.

- **Mline.** Opens the Multilines Edit Tools dialog box (the MLEDIT command). Mlines are not available in AutoCAD LT, which has a similar feature, called Dlines. See Chapter 16 for more information.

- **Mtext or leader text.** Opens the In-Place Text Editor (the MTEDIT command). See Chapter 13 for more information.

- **Polyline.** Starts the PEDIT command.

- **Spline.** Starts the SPLINEDIT command.

- **Text (TEXT commands).** Opens the In-Place Text Editor (the DDEDIT command). See Chapter 13 for more information.

- **Xref.** Opens the Reference Edit dialog box (the REFEDIT command). See Chapter 19 for more information.

Cross-Reference

You can customize what happens when you double-click an object. For example, you could choose to display the Properties palette rather than the Reference Edit dialog box when you double-click an xref. See Chapter 33 for details. ■

The DBLCLKEDIT system variable specifies whether double-clicking activates the default editing command or dialog box. To turn off double-clicking to edit objects, choose Application Button ➪ Options and click the User Preferences tab. In the Windows Standard Behavior section of the dialog box, uncheck the Double Click Editing check box.

Grips

Grips offer a way to edit objects without choosing commands. By using grips, you can quickly stretch, move, rotate, scale, copy, and mirror objects.

When you select an object without first choosing a command, the object appears highlighted with *grips* — small boxes at preset object snap points. (If you don't see grips, they may be turned off. See the "Customizing grips" section later in this chapter to find out how to turn them back on.) You can continue to select more objects in this way.

You then click to activate a grip and use the grip to manipulate the object. When the grip is activated, it turns red (by default). An activated grip is also called a *hot grip,* as shown in Figure 10.39. In some cases, you activate more than one grip at a time. To activate more than one grip, hold down Shift and then click the grips. If you activate a grip in error, click it again to deactivate it. Grips are so called because you can "hold on to" the object by dragging the grips with the mouse.

After you activate a grip, right-click with the mouse to open the Grip shortcut menu, which lists all the grip options. You can also press the Spacebar or Enter to cycle through five possible commands on the command line.

Cross-Reference

Polylines include secondary grips, which allow additional editing options. I discuss polylines and how to edit them in Chapter 16. ∎

FIGURE 10.39

Moving a line. Grips appear at preset object snaps. You use the hot grip to manipulate an object.

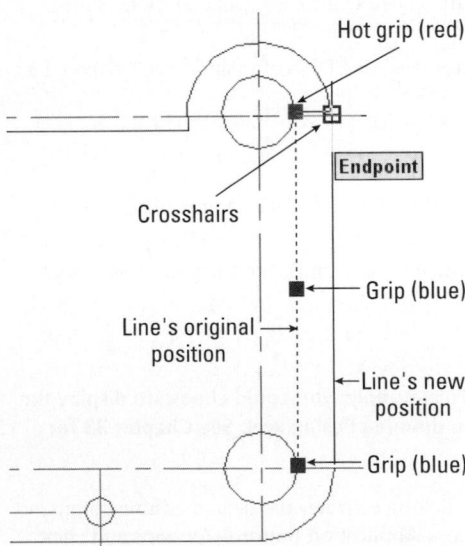

As long as you're familiar with the STRETCH, MOVE, COPY, ROTATE, SCALE, and MIRROR commands, you can easily learn how to accomplish the same edits by using grips because the prompts are similar. After you complete the edit, the object remains highlighted and the grips remain so that you can further edit the object. If you want to edit another object, press Esc once to remove the grips. Then select another object or objects or choose another command.

Note

If you use Dynamic Input, you can customize how many and which tooltips appear when you grip edit. Right-click the Dynamic Input button on the status bar and choose Settings to open the Drafting Settings dialog box with the Dynamic Input tab on top (I explain this dialog box in Chapter 4). Click the Settings button in the Dimension Input section to open the Dimension Input Settings dialog box. The settings here apply to grip editing. By default, the Show Two Dimension Input Fields at a Time option is selected. Although this setting usually works well, you can go down to one input field or specify additional fields. When you select multiple grips to edit an object, no Dynamic Input field appears. ■

Stretching with grips

Stretching with grips involves understanding how the grip points relate to the object. For example, you cannot stretch a line from its midpoint — if you think about it, there's no way to define in which direction to stretch the line. Also, you cannot stretch a circle, you can only scale it. Aside from these types of limitations, anything goes.

Stretching one line

You can stretch one line. The result is similar to using the CHANGE command to change a line's endpoint. To stretch a line, select it, and click the grip at the endpoint that you want to stretch. You see the Specify stretch point or [Base point/Copy/Undo/eXit]: prompt on the command line.

STRETCH is the first grip-editing command on the command line. Simply specify the new endpoint for the line, using any method of specifying a coordinate, to stretch the line. The other options work as follows:

- Base point lets you define a base point — other than the activated grip — and a second point. Right-click to open the Grip shortcut menu and choose Base Point. The option displays the Specify base point: prompt. Define a base point. Again you see the original Specify stretch point or [Base point/Copy/Undo/eXit]: prompt. Define the second stretch point to stretch the line.

- Copy puts you in Multiple mode. Right-click to open the Grip shortcut menu and choose Copy. Again you see the original Specify stretch point or [Base point/Copy/Undo/eXit]: prompt. Specify a new point to keep the original line, and create a new line stretched to the new point. You can continue to create new stretched lines.

- Undo undoes the last edit. Right-click to open the Grip shortcut menu and choose Undo.

- eXit returns you to the Command prompt. Right-click to open the Grip shortcut menu and choose Exit. Esc also returns you to the Command prompt.

Stretching multiple lines

Stretching more than one line at a time is similar to the most common use of the STRETCH command. However, it can also be somewhat confusing.

As explained earlier in this chapter, when you use the STRETCH command, objects that cross the crossing window are stretched, while objects entirely within the crossing window are moved. When you stretch multiple lines, you should activate endpoint grips to stretch lines, and activate midpoint grips to move lines. Picking all those grips accurately can be difficult and time-consuming. Also, small objects that are close together create a lot of overlapping grips that are hard to select. For this reason, stretching multiple lines works best with simple models.

To stretch multiple lines, follow these steps:

1. Choose the objects that you want to stretch. The objects are highlighted and display grips. You can use any method of choosing objects — you are not limited to crossing windows.

2. Hold down Shift and pick each grip that you want to stretch. If there are internal objects that you want to move with the stretch, select their grips, too; these include the midpoints of the lines and arcs, and the centers of the circles.

3. Release Shift and pick a grip to use as a base point. You see the `Specify stretch point or [Base point/Copy/Undo/eXit]:` prompt.

4. Specify a new stretch point. You can also use any of the other options.

At the end of this section on grips, you have the opportunity to try them out in an exercise.

Moving with grips

It's easy to move objects with grips. First, choose all the objects that you want to move. Then click any grip to activate it. This becomes the base point. Right-click to open the Grip shortcut menu and choose Move or press the Spacebar once. At the `Specify move point or [Base point/Copy/Undo/eXit]:` prompt, use any method to specify the second point. The selected objects move. The other options work as follows:

- Base point lets you define a base point other than the activated grip. Right-click to open the Grip shortcut menu and choose Base Point. You see the `Specify base point:` prompt. Define a base point. The original `Specify move point or [Base point/Copy/Undo/eXit]:` prompt returns. Define the second move point to move the objects.

- Copy puts you in Multiple mode and lets you copy objects. Right-click to open the Grip shortcut menu and choose Copy (or type c ↵). You see the original `Specify move point or [Base point/Copy/Undo/eXit]:` prompt. Specify a new point to keep the original object and create a new object where you specify. You can continue to create new objects.

- Undo undoes the last edit. Right-click to open the Grip shortcut menu and choose Undo.

- eXit returns you to the Command prompt. You can also press Esc.

Rotating with grips

Rotating with grips is very similar to using the ROTATE command. First, choose all the objects that you want to rotate. Then click any grip to activate it. This becomes the base point. Right-click to open the Grip shortcut menu and choose Rotate. At the `Specify rotation angle or [Base point/Copy/Undo/Reference/eXit]:` prompt, type in a rotation angle or pick a point to rotate the objects. The other options work as follows:

- Base point lets you define a base point other than the activated grip. Right-click to open the Grip shortcut menu and choose Base Point. You see the `Specify base point:` prompt. Define a base point. The original `Specify rotation angle or [Base point/Copy/Undo/Reference/eXit]:` prompt returns. Specify the rotation angle to rotate the objects.

- Copy puts you in Multiple mode and lets you copy objects. Right-click to open the Grip shortcut menu and choose Copy. Again, you see the original `Specify rotation angle or [Base point/Copy/Undo/Reference/eXit]:` prompt. Specify a rotation angle to keep the original object and create a new rotated object where you specified. You can continue to create new objects.

- Undo undoes the last edit. Right-click to open the Grip shortcut menu and choose Undo.

- Reference lets you specify both a reference angle and a new angle. Right-click to open the Grip shortcut menu and choose Reference. You see the `Specify a Reference angle <0>:` prompt. Type an angle or pick two points to specify an angle. The `Specify new angle or [Base point/Copy/Undo/Reference/eXit]:` prompt appears. Type an angle or pick a point. This works like the Reference option for the ROTATE command. (See Chapter 9.)

- eXit returns you to the Command prompt. Right-click to open the Grip shortcut menu and choose Exit. Esc also returns you to the Command prompt.

Scaling with grips

Scaling with grips is very similar to using the SCALE command. First, choose all the objects that you want to scale. Then click any grip to activate it. This becomes the base point. Right-click to open the Grip shortcut menu and choose Scale. At the `Specify scale factor or [Base point/Copy/Undo/Reference/eXit]:` prompt, type a scale factor to scale the objects. The other options work as follows:

- Base point lets you define a base point other than the activated grip. Right-click to open the Grip shortcut menu and choose Base Point. You see the `Specify base point:` prompt. Define a base point. The original `Specify scale factor or [Base point/Copy/Undo/Reference/eXit]:` prompt appears. Define the scale factor to scale the objects.

- Copy puts you in Multiple mode and lets you copy objects. Right-click to open the Grip shortcut menu and choose Copy. You see the original `Specify scale factor or [Base point/Copy/Undo/Reference/eXit]:` prompt. Specify a scale factor to keep the original object and create a new scaled object. You can continue to create new scaled objects.

- Undo undoes the last edit. Right-click to open the Grip shortcut menu and choose Undo.

- Reference lets you specify a reference length and a new scale. Right-click to open the Grip shortcut menu and choose Reference. You see the `Specify reference length <1.0000>:` prompt. Type a length or pick two points to specify a length. You see the `Specify new length or [Base point/Copy/Undo/Reference/eXit]:` prompt. Type a length or pick a point. This works like the Reference option for the SCALE command. (See Chapter 9.)

- eXit returns you to the Command prompt. You can also press Esc.

Mirroring with grips

Mirroring with grips is similar to using the MIRROR command. First, choose all the objects that you want to mirror. Then click any grip to activate it. This becomes the first point of the mirror line. Right-click to open the Grip shortcut menu. Choose Mirror. At the `Specify second point or [Base point/Copy/Undo/eXit]:` prompt, specify the second point of the mirror line to mirror the objects.

Caution

By default, AutoCAD and AutoCAD LT erase the original objects. To keep the original objects, you must use the Copy option. This feature is the opposite of the MIRROR command, where the default is to keep the original objects. ∎

The other options work as follows:

- Base point lets you define a base point other than the activated grip, as well as a second point. Right-click to open the Grip shortcut menu and choose Base Point. You see the `Specify base point:` prompt. Define a base point — that is, the first point of the mirror line. The original `Specify second point or [Base point/Copy/Undo/eXit]:` prompt appears. Define the second point of the mirror line to mirror the objects.

- Copy puts you in Multiple mode and lets you keep the original objects. Right-click to open the Grip shortcut menu and choose Copy. You see the original `Specify second point or [Base point/Copy /Undo/eXit]:` prompt. Specify the second point to keep the original objects and create new mirrored objects. You can continue to create new mirrored objects.

- Undo undoes the last edit. Right-click to open the Grip shortcut menu and choose Undo.

- eXit returns you to the Command prompt. You can also press Esc.

On the DVD

The drawing used in the following exercise on editing with grips, ab10-k.dwg, is in the Drawings folder on the DVD. ■

STEPS: Editing with Grips

1. Open ab10-k.dwg from the DVD.

2. Save the file as ab10-13.dwg in your AutoCAD Bible folder. This is a small section of a drive block, seen from above, as shown in Figure 10.40. Make sure that Ortho mode and Object Snap mode are on.

3. Use a selection window to select the entire model. Now hold down Shift and place a selection window around the small circles and rectangle at the center of the model to deselect them.

4. Pick the grip at ❶, shown in Figure 10.40, to activate it. You see the `Specify stretch point or [Base point/Copy/Undo/eXit]:` prompt.

5. Right-click and choose Mirror from the shortcut menu. You see the `Specify second point or [Base point/Copy/Undo/eXit]:` prompt.

6. Right-click and choose Copy so that the original objects that you mirror are not deleted.

7. At the `Specify second point or [Base point/Copy/Undo/eXit]:` prompt, move the cursor to the right. You can see the mirror image of the model. Pick any point to the right (in the 0-degree direction) of the activated grip.

8. Right-click and choose Exit to return to the command line. Press Esc to deselect all of the objects.

9. Zoom out a little so that you can see the entire model. Use a large selection window to select all the objects, including the small rectangle and circles in the middle. Everything should be highlighted and display grips.

10. Pick the grip at ❷, shown in Figure 10.40, to activate it. Right-click and choose Rotate from the shortcut menu. At the `Specify rotation angle or [Base point/Copy/Undo/Reference/eXit]:` prompt, type **90** ↵. This action rotates the model.

11. Pick the bottom-right grip to activate it. Right-click and choose Scale from the shortcut menu. At the `Specify scale factor or [Base point/Copy/Undo/Reference/eXit]:` prompt, type **.5** ↵. This action scales the model.

FIGURE 10.40

This small section of a drive block, seen from above, can be edited with grips.

12. Pick the grip at the midpoint of the bottom line. Press the Spacebar once to activate the Move option. At the `Specify move point or [Base point/Copy/Undo/eXit]:` prompt, type **0,–3** ↵. The model should look like Figure 10.41.

FIGURE 10.41

The drive block section, after several grip edits, looks a little like a cookie jar.

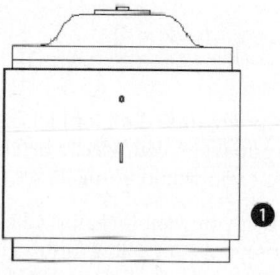

13. Press Esc to remove all grips. Define a crossing window by picking first at ❶, and then at ❷ (see Figure 10.41).

14. Hold down Shift and pick all the grips along the bottom three lines. Release Shift and pick the grip at the middle of the bottom line. At the `Specify stretch point or [Base point/ Copy/Undo/eXit]:` prompt, type **0,1** ↵ to shrink the model.

    If the stretch does not come out right (it might be hard to see and activate all the grips), choose Undo from the Standard toolbar to undo the stretch and try again.

15. Save your drawing.

Customizing grips

You can turn grips on and off and customize their size and color. Choose Application Button ➪ Options and click the Selection tab to open the dialog box shown in Figure 10.42.

FIGURE 10.42

Use the Selection tab of the Options dialog box to customize grips.

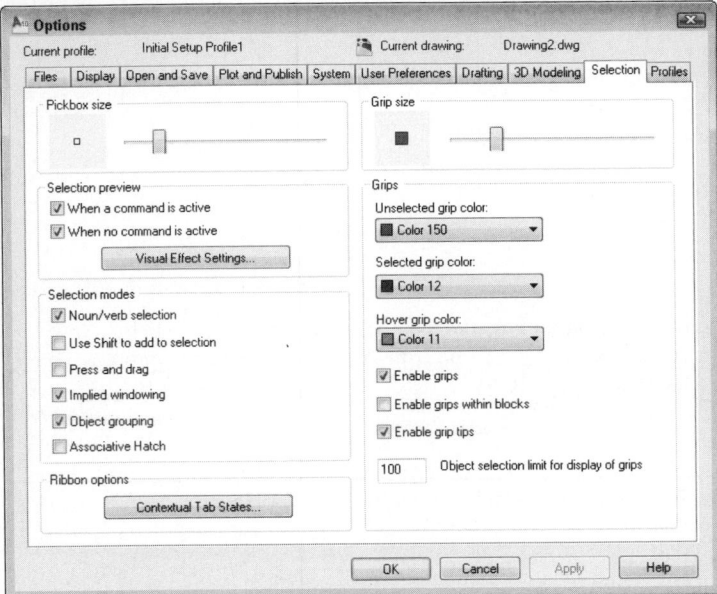

By default, grips are enabled. Also by default, grips are turned off for blocks. (Chapter 18 covers blocks.) When grips are off for blocks, you see only one grip when you select a block; this is its insertion point. When grips for blocks are on, you see all the grips you would normally see for objects.

In the Grips section, you can choose the colors that you want for grips. Click the Grip Colors button to open the Grip Colors dialog box. There you can separate set colors for unselected and selected grips, the color that appears when you hover your cursor over a grip, and the color of the grip's contour (outline).

The Grip Size section lets you drag the slider bar to set the size of the grips. Click OK after you have made the desired changes.

Editing with the Quick Properties Palette and the Properties Palette

The Quick Properties palette and Properties palette are windows that show the properties of a selected object and allow you to change those properties by entering or choosing new values. The Quick Properties palette is small and is useful for simple, quick changes; it is also highly customizable. The Properties palette offers more options for each object.

Using the Quick Properties palette

By default, when you select an object, the Quick Properties palette appears, displaying some basic properties of the object, such as its layer, color, and linetype. Other properties that appear depend on the type of object. For example, you see the length of a line, as shown in Figure 10.43. To change an object's properties, enter or choose a new value in the Quick Properties palette. If you select more than one object, you see properties that apply to all the selected objects.

FIGURE 10.43

The Quick Properties palette shows you an object's properties in a small space and allows you to change those properties.

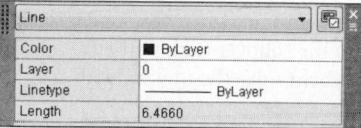

You can configure the Quick Properties palette in several ways:

- **Customize.** Click the Customize button at the upper-right corner of the palette to open the Customize User Interface dialog box, where you can define which objects open the palette and which properties appear. For more information, see Chapter 33.

- **Settings.** Click the Options button beneath the palette's Close button at the upper-right corner, and choose Settings to open the Quick Properties tab of the Drafting Settings dialog box, shown in Figure 10.44, where you can control the functioning of the panel in one location. You can also set the default height of the palette to display more or fewer properties.

FIGURE 10.44

You can configure the Quick Properties palette from the Drafting Settings dialog box.

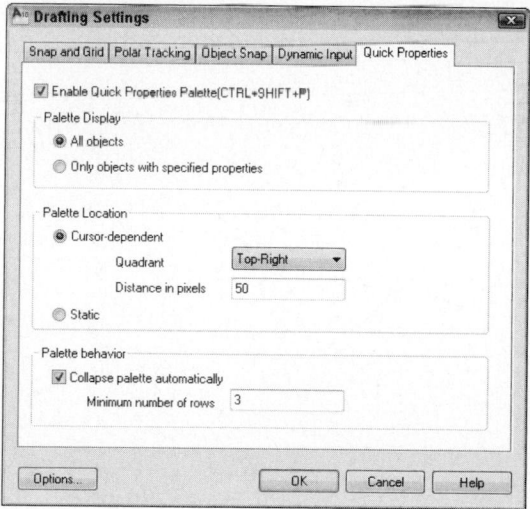

- **Location Mode.** Click the Options button beneath the palette's Close button at the upper-right corner, and choose Location Mode ⇨ Cursor or Static. By default, the palette displays at the cursor. Choose Static to display the palette in the drawing area, wherever you drag it. These options control the QPLOCATION system variable.

- **Auto-Collapse.** By default, the palette is small and you usually need to expand it to see all the properties. You can uncheck this option to display the palette big enough to show all the properties.

Tip
Click the Quick Properties button on the status bar to turn the Quick Properties palette on and off. ■

The rollover tooltip is a smaller version of the Quick Properties palette that appears when you hover your cursor over an object, without selecting it. You can't change properties in the rollover tooltip; they're just for your information. You can customize which properties appear, and synchronize the tooltip, with the Quick Properties palette; see Chapter 33 for more information.

Using the Properties palette

The Properties palette displays an extended list of the properties of selected objects. You can also use the Properties palette to change the properties of objects.

 To open the Properties palette, click View tab ⇨ Palettes panel ⇨ Properties, or press Ctrl+1. The Properties palette, shown in Figure 10.45, opens on your screen.

FIGURE 10.45

Use the Properties palette to edit objects and their properties.

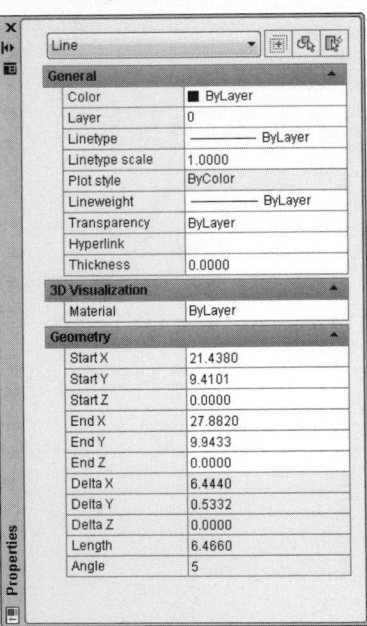

The auto-hide feature of the Properties palette makes it easy to work with the palette open all the time. Whenever the cursor moves off the palette, it collapses to just display the title bar. To auto-hide the palette, right-click the title bar and choose Auto-hide. You can also dock it; choose Anchor Left or Anchor Right from the title bar's shortcut menu. The Allow Docking item should also be checked; if it isn't, choose it from the same shortcut menu.

Tip

The Properties palette has its own undo function. Right-click the palette (but not on the item that you changed) in the Properties palette and choose Undo. Multiple levels of undo are available. For more information about palettes, see Chapter 26. ■

You can use the Properties palette to directly edit objects and to edit other object properties as well:

- You can change the layer, color, linetype, linetype scale, lineweight, and transparency of objects (see Chapter 11).
- You can edit text and text properties (see Chapter 13).
- You can edit plot styles (see Chapter 17).
- You can edit blocks (see Chapter 18).
- You can edit hyperlinks (see Chapter 28).

To change values in the Properties palette, do one of the following:

- Click a value, select the text, type a new value, and press Enter.
- Click a value, click the down arrow to the right of the value, and choose from the drop-down list.

- Click a value, click the Pick a Point button, and specify a new point by picking on the screen.

The information that you see in the Properties palette depends on the object selected. If you select more than one object, the palette shows properties that are common to those objects.

The Properties palette has three buttons in its upper-right corner: the Toggle Value of PICKADD Sysvar button, the Select Objects button, and the Quick Select button.

The Toggle Value of PICKADD Sysvar button turns PICKADD on and off. PICKADD changes how you select more than one object. When it's on (set to 1), which is the default, you can continue to select objects and they're added to the selection set. When it's off (set to 0), you need to press Shift to add objects to the selection set; otherwise, selecting an object deselects previously selected objects. Here's how to change the PICKADD variable:

- When you see the 1, PICKADD is off. Click the button to turn PICKADD on.

- When you see the plus, PICKADD is on. Click the button to turn PICKADD off.

The Select Objects button enables you to select objects for editing in the Properties palette. After you select the objects you want, you can change their properties. If you're going to pick objects or use implied windowing, the Select Objects button offers no advantage. You can just select the objects and apply changes in the Properties palette. However, if you want to use a fence or polygon method of selection, the Select Objects button is helpful. Follow these steps:

1. Click the Select Objects button.
2. On the command line, type the selection method that you want (such as **f** for fence) as you would if a command were active or you had started the SELECT command.
3. Select the objects that you want.

4. Press Enter to end object selection.

5. Use the Properties palette to make the desired changes. (You can also start an editing command to use with the selected objects.)

 The Quick Select button opens the Quick Select dialog box, which is covered in the next section. Click the Properties palette's close box to close the window. I cover the Properties palette further in the next chapter and in later chapters as appropriate.

Selection Filters

Sometimes you need a more powerful way to select objects. For example, you may want to:

- Select all the lines in your drawing to change their color.
- Check the arc radii of all your fillets.
- Find short line segments that should be erased.

Using Quick Select to select objects

As its name suggests, Quick Select is a quick, flexible, and simple way to create object selection filters. Use the FILTER command, which is covered in the following sections, to create more-complex filters or when you want to save filtering criteria for future use.

Start Quick Select in one of these ways:

- Choose Home tab ⇨ Utilities panel ⇨ Quick Select.
- With no command active, right-click in the drawing area and choose Quick Select.
- Click the Quick Select button in the Properties palette.
- Type **qselect** ↵ on the command line.

The Quick Select dialog box opens, as shown in Figure 10.46.

To create a filter, start at the top of the dialog box and work your way down. Here's how it works:

- **Apply to.** By default, the filter applies to the entire drawing, but you can use the Select Objects button to return to your drawing and select objects. The rest of the filter will then apply only to selected objects, which is called Current Selection in the drop-down list. If you use this feature at all, you would usually use a window to select an area of your drawing. (The Select Objects button is unavailable if Append to Current Selection Set is checked at the bottom of the dialog box.)

- **Object type.** By default, the filter lists Multiple as the object type. Click the drop-down list to choose from the object types available in your drawing (or in your selection set if you created one), such as line, circle, ellipse, polyline, and so on. You can choose only one type of object. To create a filter that includes more than one type of object (but not all types), use the FILTER command, which I describe in the next section.

- **Properties.** Here you choose the properties that you want to filter. (Most of these properties are covered in the next chapter.) The drop-down list includes all properties in the drawing's database; these properties depend on the object type you chose. You can choose only one property. The values in the next two sections depend on your choice in the Properties section. If you want to create a filter that specifies criteria for more than one property, use the FILTER command.

- **Operator.** After you've chosen a property, you can set it equal to or not equal to a certain value. You can set certain properties as greater than or less than a value. You can use wild card matching characters (such as * and ?) for editable text. Choose the desired operator from the drop-down list. You can also select all objects that fit the previous criteria.

- **Value.** Here you finally choose the value for your property. For example, you can set the color equal (or not equal) to green or the linetype equal to DASHED. Choose the desired value from the drop-down list or enter a value in the text box.

Tip

You can choose Block Reference as the object type, Name as the property, and the name of a block as the Value to select all instances of that block. I cover blocks in Chapter 18. ∎

- **How to apply.** As soon as you create a filter, you can use it to create a selection set. To do this, check Include In New Selection Set. To use Quick Select to select everything except objects that meet your selection criteria, choose Exclude from New Selection Set.

- **Append to current selection set.** Check this box to add objects that meet your criteria to an existing selection set.

Click OK to select the objects that meet your criteria, and close the dialog box. You can start a command and use the selection set. If the command must be started before selecting objects, you can use the Previous option (type **p** ↵) at the Select objects: prompt to select the objects that you selected by using Quick Select.

AutoCAD Only

The Express Tools include an additional command that lets you create filtered selection sets. Type getsel ↵ on the command line to create a selection of objects of the layer and object type that you select. ∎

FIGURE 10.46

Use the Quick Select dialog box to quickly create a selection set of objects based on specified criteria.

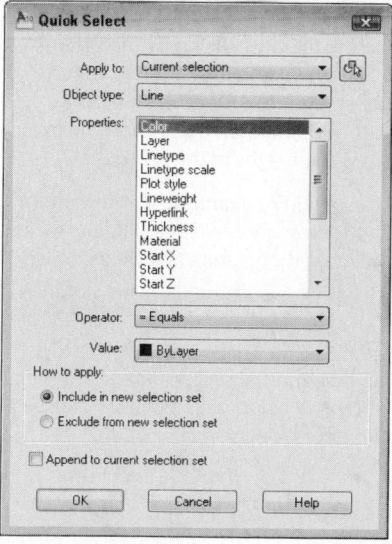

Using the FILTER command

The advantage of using the FILTER command over Quick Select is that you can create more-complex filters and save them.

To create a filter, type **filter** ↵ on the command line to open the Object Selection Filters dialog box, as shown in Figure 10.47. If you've already chosen a command, type '**filter** ↵ at the Select objects: prompt to create the selection filter transparently. The box at the top of the dialog box lists the filters that you specified.

Note
The selection filter finds only colors and linetypes of objects that have been specifically set as such, rather than as part of a layer definition. Chapter 11 covers layers, colors, and linetypes. ■

Creating a single filter

Use the Select Filter section of the dialog box to specify a filter. The drop-down list lists all the possible filters. Click the arrow to display the drop-down list. You can choose from several types of items:

- Objects
- Object properties such as color or layer
- Object snaps such as arc center or circle radius
- Logical operators such as AND, OR, and NOT (these logical operators combine filter specifications in various ways)

The first step is to choose a filter. For example, to create a filter that chooses all lines, choose Line from the drop-down list. If the item chosen does not need any further clarification, click Add to List. The filter appears in the box at the top of the dialog box. This filter would appear as Object = Line.

Many filters require a value. You can enter a value in two ways:

- If you choose an object that can be listed, the Select button becomes active. Click it and choose the value that you want. For example, if you choose Color or Layer, you can choose from a list of colors or layers.
- If you choose an object that can have any value, the boxes below the drop-down list become active. They are labeled X, Y, and Z, but this is misleading. These boxes are used for X, Y, and Z coordinates only when you choose a filter requiring coordinates, such as Viewport Center. In most cases, you use the X text box to give the filter a value. In this situation, the Y and Z boxes are not used. For example, if you choose Text Height, you type the height in the X box.

Keep in mind that you don't always want to specify that a filter *equals* a value. For example, if you want to create a filter that selects all circles with a radius less than 0.75, then when you choose Circle Radius, the X box becomes active. Click the arrow to display the drop-down list of relational operators and then choose one. Table 10.4 lists the relational operators.

Adding a second filter

To add a second filter, you first decide on the relationship between the first and the second filters and then assign a logical operator. Logical operators always come in pairs — when you begin one operator, you must also end it. The logical operators are at the end of the drop-down list of filter objects.

TABLE 10.4

Relational Operators in the Object Selection Filters Dialog Box

Operator	Definition
=	Equal to
!=	Not equal to
<	Less than
<=	Less than or equal to
>	Greater than
>=	Greater than or equal to
*	Equal to any value

Note

When two or more filters are listed without logical operators, the filter calculates them as if they were grouped with the AND operator. This means that the filter selects only objects that meet all the criteria specified. ∎

Table 10.5 explains the four logical operators, which are called *grouping operators* because they group filter specifications together. The Example column explains the results of two filter specifications: Color = 1-Red and Object = Circle.

TABLE 10.5

Logical (Or Grouping) Operators Used for Selection Filters

Operator	Explanation	Example
AND	Finds objects that meet all criteria.	Finds red circles.
OR	Finds objects that meet any of the criteria.	Finds all red objects and all circles.
XOR	Finds objects that meet one criterion or the other but not both. Requires two criteria between Begin XOR and End XOR.	Finds red objects that are not circles and circles that are not red.
NOT	Excludes objects that meet the criteria. May have only one criterion between Begin NOT and End NOT.	If the NOT operator groups the Object = Circle filter, then it finds all red objects that are not circles.

Click Substitute and choose a saved filter to insert a saved filter into the filter you're currently defining. To add filters based on existing objects, choose Add Selected Object. This action adds all the properties of the object to the filter definition, which is often more than you want.

Figure 10.47 shows a filter that selects all lines and all polylines. The XOR operator finds objects that meet one criterion or the other but not both. Obviously, no object can be both a line and a polyline. This is a good example of a filter that you cannot create by using Quick Select.

FIGURE 10.47

A filter that selects all lines and all polylines.

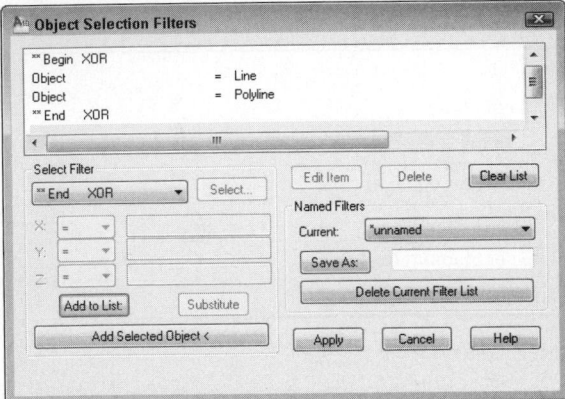

Naming and editing filters

After you've completed the filter, you should save it. Even if you don't think you'll use it again, you may make an editing error in the drawing while using it and have to go back to it. To save a filter, type a name in the Save As text box and click Save As.

You edit a listed filter by using three buttons:

- **Edit Item.** Choose the line containing the item and click this button to edit the item. The object name now appears in the drop-down list, and you can specify new values for it.
- **Delete.** Choose Delete to delete a chosen item in a filter.
- **Clear List.** Choose Clear List to clear all the items in a filter and start over.

To choose a named filter to edit, choose it from the Current drop-down list.

Using filters

You can use filters in two ways. Most often, you choose a command first and then realize that you need a filter to select the objects. In this situation, follow these prompts:

```
Select objects: 'filter ↵
Define the filter in the Object Selection Filters dialog box. Click
    Apply.
Applying filter to selection.
Select objects: Type all ↵ or use a large selection window to select
    all the objects that you want to consider in the filter.
x found
Select objects: ↵
Exiting filtered selection. x found
Select objects: ↵
```

The command's usual prompts then continue.

Alternatively, you can start the FILTER command and define the filter. Click Apply. At the `Select objects:` prompt, type **all** or use a selection window. Press Enter to end object selection. Then start the editing command and use the Previous selection option to select the filtered objects.

On the DVD

The drawing used in the following exercise on using selection filters, `ab10-1.dwg`, **is in the** `Drawings` **folder on the DVD.** ∎

STEPS: Using Selection Filters

1. Open `ab10-1.dwg` from the DVD.

2. Save the file as `ab10-14.dwg` in your `AutoCAD Bible` folder. Notice that two lines of text appearing in the middle of the drawing, plus the text at the bottom of the drawing, are black/white rather than blue like all the other text. You want to check the color of all the text and correct it if necessary.

3. Right-click the drawing area and choose Quick Select. In the Quick Select dialog box, click the Object Type drop-down list and scroll down until you see Text. Choose it.

4. In the Properties section, Color should be selected. If not, select it. In the Operator section, choose <> Not Equal. In the Value section, choose ByLayer. Include In New Selection Set should be chosen. Append to Current Selection Set should not be checked. Click OK to select three items of black/white text.

5. Press Esc to deselect the objects and remove the grips. Now you'll try the same thing, using the FILTER command, but adding a level of complexity.

6. Type **filter** ↵. The Object Selection Filters dialog box opens.

7. In the Select Filter drop-down list, choose Text. Click Add to List. At the top, the filter reads `Object = Text`.

8. From the Select Filter drop-down list, choose `**Begin AND` (this is toward the bottom of the list) and click Add to List.

9. From the Select Filter drop-down list, choose Color. In the drop-down list next to X:, choose `! =` (not equal). Then choose Select. In the Select Color dialog box, click ByLayer. Click OK. In the Object Selection Filters dialog box, choose Add to List. The ByLayer color number displays as 256. (Layers and colors are covered in the next chapter.)

10. You may want to select only the smaller text, and not the heading at the bottom of the drawing, where you know that the larger text's height is greater than .1 and the smaller text's height is smaller than .1. From the Select Filter drop-down list, choose Text Height. From the X: drop-down list, choose < (less than). In the text box to the right of X:, type **.1**. Choose Add to List.

11. From the Select Filter drop-down list, choose `**End AND` and click Add to List.

12. In the Save As text box, type **bad text**. Click Save As. The Object Selection Filters dialog box should look like the following:

```
Object = Text
**Begin AND
Color !=256 - ByLayer
Text Height < 0.100000
**End AND
```

13. Click Apply.

14. At the Select objects: prompt, type **all** ↵. The prompt tells you that two were found. Press Enter until you see the Command prompt.

15. In the Properties panel of the Home tab, choose ByLayer from the Color drop-down list. The two text objects change to the BYLAYER layer, where they change to a blue color like all the other text.

16. Save your drawing.

Groups

Groups let you save a selection set of objects so that you can easily select them whenever you need to edit them. If you have a certain set of objects that you need to edit as a group, and a busy drawing that makes their selection time-consuming, then groups are for you. After you set up the group, you can pick any object in the group to automatically select all the objects in the group. An object can belong to more than one group.

Note
Although both AutoCAD and AutoCAD LT include the group feature, the dialog box for creating and managing groups is different for AutoCAD and AutoCAD LT. Over the next few sections, be sure to note which program I'm discussing. ■

Creating and modifying groups in AutoCAD

To create or modify a group, type **group** ↵ on the command line to open the Object Grouping dialog box, as shown in Figure 10.48.

FIGURE 10.48

The Object Grouping dialog box.

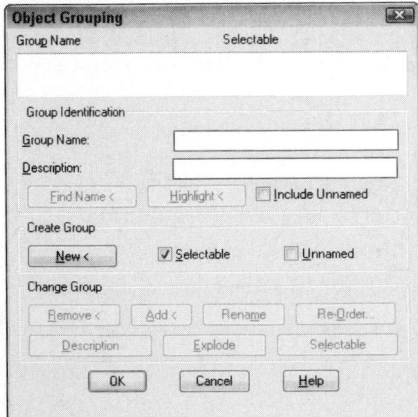

Creating a new group

To create a new group in AutoCAD, follow these steps:

1. Type a name in the Group Name text box. You can use a maximum of 31 characters with no spaces. You can use the hyphen (-) and underscore (_) anywhere in the name.

2. If you want, you can type a description of up to 448 characters. The description can include spaces.

3. Click New. AutoCAD returns you to your drawing with the Select objects: prompt. Select the objects that you want to be in the group. Press Enter to end object selection. AutoCAD returns you to the dialog box.

4. Click OK.

The Group Identification section of the Object Grouping dialog box also has a Find Name button. Use this feature to find the name of the group to which an object belongs. AutoCAD lets you select an object and then lists the group's name or names.

The Highlight button highlights a group. First choose a group from the list in the Object Grouping dialog box. Click Highlight and AutoCAD returns to your drawing and highlights all the objects in your group. Click Continue to return to the dialog box. Use this feature when you aren't sure which group you want to work with.

Changing a group

To change a group in AutoCAD, click any existing group in the Group Name list at the top of the dialog box. The buttons in the Change Group section all become active. You can then do the following:

- **Remove.** AutoCAD switches to the drawing area with the Select objects to remove from group . . . : prompt. Select objects to remove and press Enter to end object removal. AutoCAD returns you to the dialog box. Click OK.

- **Add.** AutoCAD switches to the drawing area with the Select objects to add to group . . . : prompt. Select objects to add and press Enter to end object selection. AutoCAD returns you to the dialog box. Click OK.

- **Rename.** Choose the group that you want to rename. Change the name in the Group Name text box. Click Rename. The name changes in the Group Name list at the top of the dialog box. Click OK.

- **Re-Order.** Each object in the group has a number, starting with zero. In rare cases, if you are running a program that processes the members of a group, the order may be important. Choose a group. Click Re-Order. In the Order Group dialog box, to reverse the order of all the objects, click Reverse Order. Otherwise, click Highlight. AutoCAD opens a small Object Grouping message box with Next and Previous buttons. At the bottom-right corner, the box displays Object: 0, and one of the objects in the group is highlighted. Click Next to move from object to object. You'll probably need to write down the number of each object. Click OK to return to the Order Group dialog box. Complete the following text boxes:

  - **Remove from position.** This text box is the position number of the object that you want to move.

  - **Enter new position number for the object.** This text box is the new position number that you want for the object.

  - **Number of objects.** This text box is the object number or range of numbers that you want to reorder.

- **Description.** Updates a description for the group. Type a new description in the Group Identification section of the dialog box. Then click Description.

- **Explode.** Removes the group entirely. All the objects remain in your drawing, but they are no longer grouped.

- **Selectable.** Toggles the selectability of the group. If a group is selectable, then selecting one object of the group selects the entire group. If a group is not selectable, then selecting one object of the group does not select the entire group. This option lets you temporarily work with one object in the group without having to explode the group. You can also press Ctrl+Shift+A to toggle the selectability of the group.

Creating and modifying groups in AutoCAD LT

To create or modify a group in AutoCAD LT, type **group** ↵ on the command line to open the Group Manager window, as shown in Figure 10.49. You can dock this window by dragging it to the top or bottom of the drawing area.

Use the Group Manager window to create and manage groups in AutoCAD LT.

Creating a new group

To create a new group in AutoCAD LT, follow these steps.

1. With the Group Manager open, select the objects that you want to include in the group. (An object can belong to more than one group.)

2. Click the Create Group button. An empty box appears under the Group column of the Group Manager.

3. Type a name for your group and press Enter. You can use a maximum of 31 characters with no spaces. You can use the hyphen (-) and underscore (_) anywhere in the name.

4. If you want, click in the Description column and add a description for your group.

A light bulb appears in the Selectable column to indicate that the group is selectable (that is, functioning as a group). To close the Group Manager, click its Close button at the upper-right corner of the window. You can now use your group.

Changing a group in AutoCAD LT

Use the Group Manager toolbar to manage your groups. To work with your groups, click any existing group. You can then do the following:

- **Ungroup.** Deletes the group. All the group's objects become individual objects again.

- **Add to Group.** Select an object or objects not in the group and click this button to add the selected object or objects to the group.

- **Remove from Group.** To remove an object from a group, click the Selectable icon. You can now choose individual objects in the group without selecting the entire group. Click in your drawing and pick the object that you want to remove. Then click the Remove from Group button.

- **Details.** Opens a window with more information about the group and its objects.

- **Select Group.** To select the group from the Group Manager, select the group name and click the Select Group button.

- **Deselect Group.** Deselects the group.

To toggle a group from selectable to not selectable, click the group's icon in the Selectable column. When a group is not selectable, you can individually select its objects.

Using groups

Using a group is very simple. If a group is selectable, just pick any object in the group to select all the objects in the group. You can then edit the objects in the group as a whole. If you need to temporarily edit one object in a group, then turn off the group's selectability, as described in the previous sections.

You can change the selectable status of all groups in your drawing by choosing Application Button ➪ Options, and clicking the Selection tab. Deselect Object Grouping in the Selection Modes section to disable object grouping entirely.

Summary

This chapter covered all the more advanced editing commands. You read about:

- Mirroring objects
- Creating rectangular and polar arrays
- Creating an offset of an object
- Aligning objects
- Trimming and extending objects
- Stretching objects
- Lengthening (and shortening) objects
- Breaking and joining objects
- Creating chamfered corners and fillets for square, beveled, and rounded corners
- Drawing revision clouds and using wipeouts
- Constraining objects with geometric and dimensional parameters
- Using grips to stretch, move, mirror, rotate, and scale objects
- Double-clicking objects to edit them
- Using the Quick Properties panel and the Properties palette to see the properties of objects and edit them
- Creating filtered sets of selected objects with the Quick Select feature and the FILTER command
- Creating and using named groups of objects

In the next chapter, I cover layers, colors, linetypes, and lineweights.

Organizing Drawings with Layers and Object Properties

U ntil you learn about layers, you draw everything in black or white. Drawing everything in one color is not a very good way to draw — besides, it's boring! If everything is the same color, it's hard to distinguish the various elements of a drawing. If you've followed the exercises throughout this book, you've opened some drawings from the DVD that used various colors and linetypes (such as dashed lines). For example, in some of the architectural drawings, you may have noticed that the walls are a different color than the fixtures in the kitchen. When you create text and dimensions, covered in Chapters 13, 14, and 15, you almost always use a color that stands out from the main model that you're drawing. You can also create objects with varying line widths, called *lineweights*. Finally, you can set the transparency of objects. This use of color, linetype, lineweight, and transparency helps to organize your drawings, making them easier to understand.

Most often, you assign color, linetype, lineweight, and transparency to a layer. A layer is simply an organizational tool that lets you organize the display of objects in your drawing. Every object must be on a layer, and every layer must have a color, a linetype, a lineweight, and a transparency value. You define layers to meet your drawing needs. Layers, colors, linetypes, lineweights, and transparency are called *object properties*. You can easily change any object's properties. This chapter explains how to create and change these object properties to organize your drawing.

IN THIS CHAPTER

Organizing your drawing

Working with layers

Changing object color, linetype, lineweight, and transparency

Working with linetype scales

Importing layers and linetypes from other drawings

Matching properties

Working with Layers

Layers offer powerful features that enable you to distinguish all the various elements of your drawing. In an architectural drawing, for example, you'll commonly create layers for walls, doors, windows, plumbing, electrical fixtures, structural elements, notes (text), dimensions, and so on. Mechanical drawings might use center, hidden, hatch, object, and titleblock layers. Each discipline has its own conventions, and where you work you might have specific conventions that you must follow.

Creating layers is an important part of setting up a drawing, in addition to the setup features covered in Chapter 5. You should create and save layers in your templates so that they're available to you when you start to draw. Layers give you many ways to organize your drawing. For example, you can:

- Assign different colors, linetypes, lineweights, and transparency to layers.
- Assign the various colors to different pens in a pen plotter, resulting in a paper drawing with varying colors or line widths.
- Control the visibility of layers. Making a layer invisible lets you focus on just the objects that you need to draw or edit.
- Control which objects are plotted.
- Lock a layer so that objects on that layer cannot be edited.

Cross-Reference

You can also assign a plot style to a layer. A plot style is a group of settings that affects how your drawing is plotted. Chapter 17 covers plot styles. ■

Understanding layers

Besides having a color, linetype, lineweight, and transparency value, every layer must have a name. All drawings come with a default layer, called layer 0 (zero). Its color is black/white (depending on the background color of the drawing area), its linetype is Continuous, its lineweight is Default (0.010 inch or 0.25 mm), and its transparency is 0 (opaque). Most of the exercises in this book up to this point have used layer 0. To create a new layer, you must give it a name, a color, a linetype, a lineweight, and a transparency value. You can then start drawing on that layer.

Layers have four *states*. These states control visibility, regeneration, editability, and plottability of layers:

- **On/Off.** On layers (the default) are visible. Off layers are invisible and are regenerated with the drawing. Off layers are not plotted.
- **Thawed/Frozen.** Thawed layers (the default) are visible. Frozen layers are invisible and are *not* regenerated with the drawing. However, when you thaw a frozen layer, the drawing regenerates. If you have floating viewports (covered in Chapter 17), you can also freeze a layer just in the current viewport, or only for new viewports that you create. You can also create a layer that is frozen in all viewports. Frozen layers are not plotted.
- **Unlocked/Locked.** Unlocked layers (the default) are visible and editable. Locked layers are visible but cannot be edited.
- **Plottable/Not Plottable.** Plottable layers are plotted. Not plottable layers are not plotted. This setting affects only layers that are on or thawed, because off and frozen layers are not plotted anyway.

Creating new layers

 To create a new layer, choose Home tab ⇨ Layers panel ⇨ Layer Properties. The Layer Properties Manager palette opens, as shown in Figure 11.1. This palette lists all current layers and their properties. You can also create new layers and modify existing ones. The left panel allows you to filter the list of layers. For more information on layer filtering, see the section, "Filtering the layer list," later in this chapter.

Note

The Layer Properties Manager is a palette that you can auto-hide and dock. Changes that you make to layer properties and states in the palette apply immediately in your drawing. ■

FIGURE 11.1

The Layer Properties Manager is the place to manage all your layers.

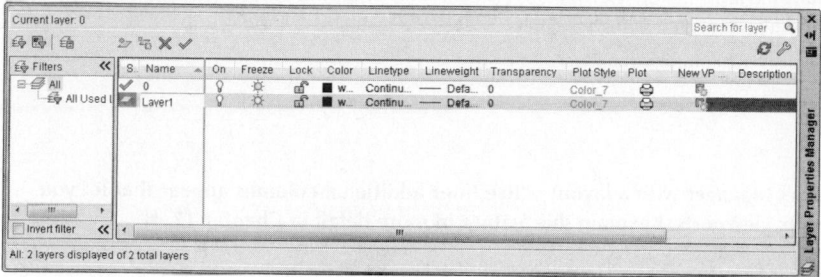

Table 11.1 explains the columns in the palette. For a description of the icons in most of the columns, see Table 11.2, later in this chapter.

TABLE 11.1

Columns in the Layer Properties Manager

Column Name	Description
Status	The status of each layer. A darker layer icon is used, and a lighter icon is unused. The current layer shows a checkmark.
Name	The name of the layer. To change the layer, click once to display a border and click again to type a new name.
On	The current on/off state of a layer. Click to turn the layer on or off.
Freeze	The current freeze/thaw state of a layer. Click to freeze or thaw a layer.
Lock	The current locked/unlocked state of a layer. Click to lock or unlock a layer.
Color	The current color of the layer. Click to change the color.
Linetype	The current linetype of the layer. Click to change the linetype.
Lineweight	The current lineweight of the layer. Click to choose a new lineweight.
Transparency	The current transparency (from 0 to 90) of the layer. Click to choose or enter a new value.
Plot Style	The current plot style of the layer. Click to select a new plot style. (Chapter 17 covers plot styles.)
Plot	The current plottable/not plottable state of the layer. Click to make the layer plottable or not plottable.

continued

TABLE 11.1	(continued)
Column Name	Description
Current VP Freeze	The freeze/thaw state of the layer in the current floating viewport. Click to freeze or thaw the layer in active floating viewports. This column is displayed only if you have floating viewports and a layout tab is active. (Chapter 17 covers floating viewports.)
New VP Freeze	The current freeze/thaw state of the layer in new floating viewports that you create. Click to freeze or thaw the layer in new viewports. This column is displayed only if you have floating viewports and a layout tab is active. (Chapter 17 covers floating viewports.)
Description	A place to enter a description of a layer.

Note

When you open the Layer Properties Manager with a layout active, four additional columns appear that let you override layer properties for specific viewports. I explain this feature in more detail in Chapter 17. ■

To adjust the display in the Layer Properties Manager, you can do the following:

- Display or hide the Filters pane by clicking the double-arrow icon at the top of that pane.
- Change the width of any column in the Layer Properties Manager by placing the cursor over the line dividing two column headings and dragging.
- Double-click the line dividing two columns to minimize/maximize the column width.
- Click any column head to sort the layers by that column. Click again to sort in the opposite order.
- Right-click any heading and display a shortcut menu where you can choose which columns you want to see.
- Drag any column to any location to specify the order of the columns.
- Right-click any heading and choose Freeze or Unfreeze Column (depending on the current status). Freezing a column forces it to the left of a gray, vertical line and holds it visible, even if you scroll to the right.
- Resize the entire dialog box by dragging on any side.

Naming the layer

 Click the New Layer icon in the Layer Properties Manager. A new layer appears, named Layer1. The name is highlighted so that you can immediately type in a new name for the layer. Press Enter after you type the name.

Note

Next to the New Layer button is the New Layer VP Frozen in All Viewports button for creating a layer that is frozen in all viewports. I discuss freezing layers in viewports in Chapter 17. ■

Tip

If you want a new layer to have the same color and/or linetype as an existing layer, choose that existing layer and click New. The new layer inherits the properties of the selected layer. You can then make any changes that you want. ■

Layer names can be up to 255 characters long and may include spaces. Layer names retain the uppercase/lowercase characters that you type. Layer names may not include the following symbols: < > / \ " ; ? * | , = `.

Assigning a color

To change the default color, move the cursor to the color box in the same row as the new layer. Click to open the Select Color dialog box, shown in Figure 11.2, with the Index Color tab displayed.

FIGURE 11.2

The Select Color dialog box.

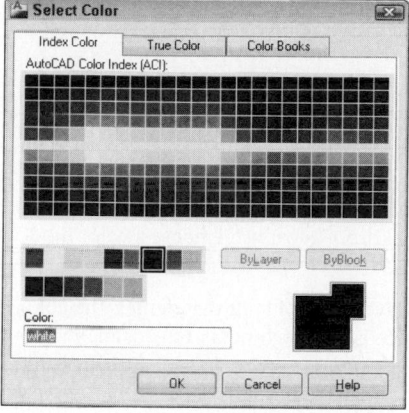

Click the color that you want. At the bottom of the dialog box, the color's name or number appears along with a sample of the color. Click OK to close the dialog box and return to the Layer Properties Manager.

Note that the Index Color tab offers you a choice of standard colors, gray shades, and a fuller palette of colors. The standard colors are the original colors that AutoCAD (and then AutoCAD LT) offered, and they're the ones often used, even today. These colors have both a name and a number, whereas other colors have only a number (an *index*). The standard colors are red (1), yellow (2), green (3), cyan (4), blue (5), magenta (6), and white (7). For more color choices, click the True Color tab, as shown in Figure 11.3.

Note

You can choose any color you want for the background color of a drawing, but commonly it is a black, white, or off-white screen. The default screen is almost black and the default color for 7 is black, but the color is called white. When you work on a black screen, objects using the color of 7 appear white (or else they would be invisible) and vice versa. To change the screen color, choose Application Button ⇨ Options and click the Display tab. Then click the Colors button under the Window Elements section. For a 2D drawing, choose 2D Model Space from the Context list box and choose Uniform Background from the Interface Element list box. Then use the Color drop-down list to specify a color. ■

FIGURE 11.3

The True Color tab of the Select Color dialog box offers a more precise way to define color.

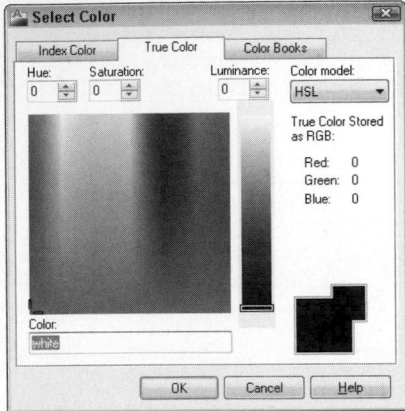

To define a color, first choose the color model from the Color Model drop-down list. Choose a color model based on familiarity or existing specifications. You have two choices:

- **HSL (Hue, Saturation, Luminance).** Hue is the actual wavelength of light that defines the color. Saturation is the purity or intensity of the color. Luminance is the brightness of the color.
- **RGB (Red, Green, Blue).** Defines a color according to the intensity of red, green, and blue in the color.

If you choose the HSL color model, specify the color as follows:

1. Specify the hue by dragging the crosshairs horizontally across the colors, or type a value from 0° to 360° in the Hue text box.
2. Specify the saturation by dragging the crosshairs vertically over the colors, or type a value from 0% to 100% in the Saturation text box.
3. Specify the luminance by dragging the bar on the color slider, or type a value from 0% to 100% in the Luminance text box.

Note

When you define a color by using the HSL color model, you also see the RGB values displayed in the Select Color dialog box. ■

If you choose the RGB color model, specify the red color by dragging the color bar, or type a value from 1 to 255 in the Red text box. Do the same for the green and blue color values.

You can also choose a color by using the Color Books tab, as shown in Figure 11.4.

The Color Books tab displays colors in *color books.* Color books are files that define colors. AutoCAD includes several Pantone color books. Pantone is a commonly used system of matching colors that is often used for printing on paper and fabric.

The Color Books tab of the Select Color dialog box.

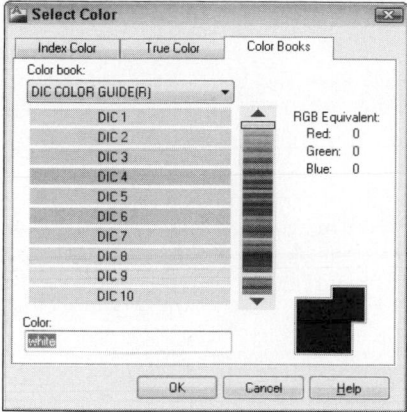

To use a color from a color book, follow these steps:

1. On the Color Books tab of the Select Color dialog box, choose a color book from the Color Book drop-down list.

2. Drag the color slider or use the up and down arrows to choose a "page" of the color book. On the left, you see the colors for that page. A page can hold up to ten colors.

3. Choose one of the colors on the left side of the dialog box.

4. Click OK.

Assigning a linetype

The default linetype is a continuous line, but you can use many other linetypes. These linetypes are repeating patterns of dashes and/or dots and spaces, although they can also include text and shapes. Linetypes are covered more fully later in this chapter.

To change the default linetype, move the cursor to the linetype in the new layer's row. Click to open the Select Linetype dialog box, as shown in Figure 11.5.

If the linetype that you want appears on the list, click the linetype and choose OK to close the dialog box. If the linetype does not appear, you need to load the linetype. Click Load to open the Load or Reload Linetypes dialog box, as shown in Figure 11.6.

Linetypes are stored in text (ASCII) files with the filename extension LIN. The standard linetypes are in `acad.lin` in AutoCAD and in `acadlt.lin` in AutoCAD LT. You can create your own linetypes and store them in these files. You can also store them in another file that you create with the extension `.lin`. Click File at the top of the dialog box if you want to load a linetype from a file that you created. Choose the linetype file that you want to load and click Open.

FIGURE 11.5

The Select Linetype dialog box as it appears before you have loaded any linetypes.

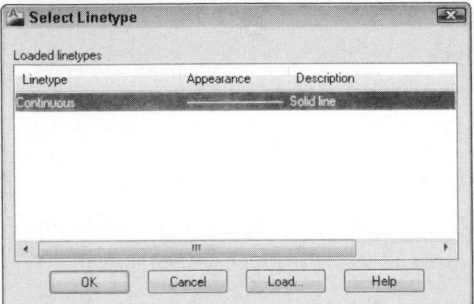

FIGURE 11.6

The Load or Reload Linetypes dialog box.

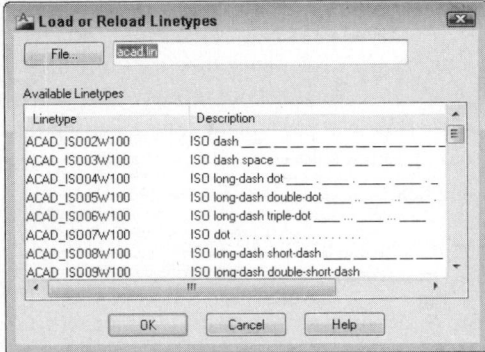

Cross-Reference

See Chapter 31 for a full discussion of how to create custom linetypes. ■

Choose the linetype to load and click OK. You return to the Select Linetype dialog box. The loaded linetype now appears on the list. Choose it and click OK. You're now back in the Layer Properties Manager dialog box and the layer now uses that linetype.

Assigning a lineweight

A lineweight assigns a width to a line. When you give a layer a lineweight, every object on that layer has the same lineweight. A lineweight can help to distinguish various elements of your drawing, both on-screen and on paper. For example, you could use a thicker lineweight to indicate planned construction changes, for dimension lines, or to represent the true width of an object. The Show/Hide Lineweight button on the status bar toggles the display of lineweights on and off. By default, lineweight display is off.

To set a lineweight for a layer, click the Lineweight column of that layer to open the Lineweight dialog box, as shown in Figure 11.7. Choose a lineweight and click OK.

FIGURE 11.7

When you click the Lineweight column of the Layer Properties Manager, the Lineweight dialog box opens so that you can choose a lineweight.

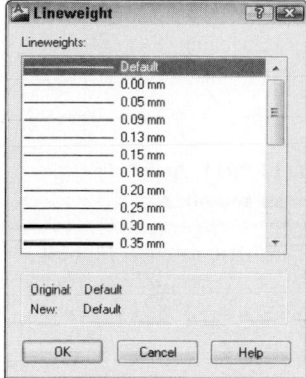

Lineweights have the following features:

- The default lineweight value for layers and objects is called DEFAULT, which has a value of 0.010 inch or 0.25 mm.

- On the Model tab, where you draw, lineweights are displayed in relation to pixels, the unit of measurement for computer screens. A lineweight of 0 is displayed with a width of 1 pixel. Wider lineweights are calculated proportionally to the actual width of the lineweight. The lineweight display on the Model tab does not change as you zoom in or out.

- On Layout tabs, lineweights are displayed in real-world units as they will be plotted. Lineweights act like other objects in your drawing and look bigger or smaller as you zoom in and out.

- By default, lineweights are measured in millimeters. You can format lineweights by choosing Home tab ➪ Properties panel ➪ Lineweight drop-down list ➪ Lineweight Settings. The Lineweight Settings dialog box opens, as shown in Figure 11.8. Choose a default lineweight from the Default drop-down list. The Adjust Display Scale slider determines how lineweights are displayed on the Model tab. Adjust this setting if you use several closely related lineweights but can't distinguish them on your screen. The Display Lineweight check box turns the display of lineweights on and off, which is the same as clicking the Show/Hide Lineweight button on the status bar.

FIGURE 11.8

The Lineweight Settings dialog box lets you format how lineweights are measured and displayed.

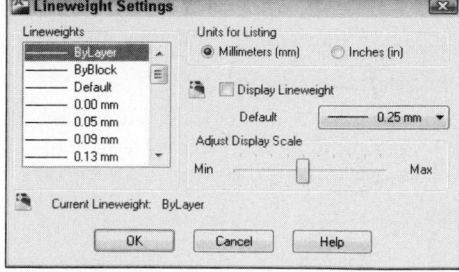

If you don't want to use lineweights, you can just ignore them and display every object by using the default lineweight.

Assigning a transparency value

A transparent object lets you see other objects behind it. Actually, you can make objects only partially transparent, because a completely transparent object would be invisible. You can set transparency from 0 (completely opaque) to 90.

New Feature

Transparency for layers and objects is new for AutoCAD 2011 and AutoCAD LT 2011. A new Transparency button on the status bar turns the display of transparency on and off. ■

When you specify transparency for a layer, every object on that layer has the same transparency. In most cases, you'll use transparency for solid hatch fills, which are covered in Chapter 16. Generally, you won't notice transparency for the outlines that define most objects, such as lines, circles, and rectangles, unless you use a very thick lineweight.

To set a transparency value for a layer, click the Transparency column of that layer to open the Layer Transparency dialog box. Then either choose a default value from the drop-down list or enter a new value. You can specify a value from 0 to 90. Click OK. If you want objects to be opaque, you can ignore the transparency value. After you've set your new layer's color, linetype, lineweight, and transparency in the Layer Properties Manager, you're ready to use the layer.

Note

Many people have CAD standards that restrict which layers should be in a drawing. You can specify that you want to receive a notification whenever a new layer is added to a drawing. Then you can decide if the layer meets your CAD standards. For more information, see Chapter 26, where I cover CAD standards. ■

On the DVD

The drawing used in the following exercise on creating layers, `ab11-a.dwg`, is in the `Drawings` folder on the DVD. ■

STEPS: Creating a New Layer

1. Open `ab11-a.dwg` from the DVD.
2. Save the file as `ab11-01.dwg` in your `AutoCAD Bible` folder.

3. Choose Home tab ➪ Layers panel ➪ Layer Properties to open the Layer Properties Manager.

4. Click the New Layer icon. A new layer named `Layer1` appears, highlighted. Type **Walls** ↵ as the name for the new layer.
5. Click the color square in the Color column to open the Select Color dialog box. Choose the blue square from the Standard Colors and click OK.
6. Choose the New Layer icon again to create another new layer. Type **Hidden** ↵.
7. Click the color square in the Color column to open the Select Color dialog box.
8. In the Select Color dialog box, click the True Color tab. From the Color Model drop-down list, choose RGB. In the Color text box, type **141,218,189.** (In some instances, you may have to re-choose RGB from the Color Model drop-down list to make the Color text box active.) Press Tab. You should see a teal (blue-green) color. Click OK.

9. In the main layer listing, click Continuous in the same row as the Hidden layer to open the Select Linetype dialog box. Click Load to open the Load or Reload Linetypes dialog box. Scroll down until you see the HIDDEN linetype. Choose it and click OK. In the Select Linetype dialog box, choose HIDDEN and click OK.

10. Click the Description column for the Hidden layer. (If you can't see this column, which is usually the rightmost column, drag the edge of the palette that is opposite the title bar to widen the palette. Click again so that a text cursor appears. Type **teal, hidden lines** ↵.

11. Select the Walls layer by clicking its name. Choose the New Layer icon again to create another new layer with the same properties as the Walls layer. Type **Fill** ↵.

12. Click the color square in the Color column to open the Select Color dialog box. Choose the green square from the Standard Colors and click OK.

13. Click in the Transparency column of the Fill layer's row to open the Layer Transparency dialog box. Choose 40 from the drop-down list. Click OK.

14. Close or auto-hide the palette.

15. Choose Home tab ➪ Layers panel and click the Layer drop-down list to see the three layers that you just created listed. Click again to close the drop-down list.

16. Save your drawing.

On the DVD

Layerhtm displays a copy of the Layer Properties Manager dialog box in your browser so that you can print it. Look in `\Software\Chapter11\layerhtm.zip.` ■

Using layers

To use a layer that you have just created, click the Set Current icon in the Layer Properties Manager or double-click the layer's name. Objects that you create now are drawn on that layer and display with the layer's color, linetype, and lineweight. (The lineweight shows only if the Show/Hide Lineweight button on the status bar is on.)

After you have the layers you need, you need to switch from layer to layer as you draw. To do so, choose Home tab ➪ Layers panel ➪ Layer drop-down list, as shown in Figure 11.9.

The Layer drop-down list.

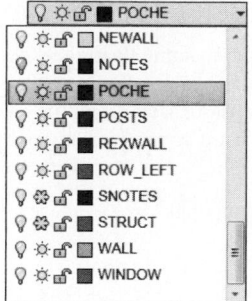

The Layer drop-down list has three display modes:

- If no object is selected, it displays the current layer.
- If one or more objects are selected, it displays the layer of the selected object(s).
- When objects on varying layers are selected, the Layer drop-down list goes blank, indicating that more than one layer is included in the selection.

To check the current layer, make sure that no object is selected. If necessary, press Esc to deselect any objects.

To open the Layer drop-down list, click its down arrow. You see a list of all of your layers, including their states and colors. When you pass the mouse over the items, a tooltip tells you what they mean. The Layer drop-down list has three functions:

- It switches the current layer so that you can draw on a new layer.
- It changes the certain states of any specific layer on the list.
- It changes the layer of a selected object.

Switching the current layer

To switch the current layer, make sure that no object is currently selected, click the Layer drop-down list arrow, and click the name of the layer that you want to be current. Be careful to click only the name — otherwise, you may change the layer's state. After you click a new layer name, the drop-down list automatically closes.

 Choose Home tab ⇨ Layers panel ⇨ Previous to undo changes that you made to layer settings. It's like an UNDO command for the Layer Properties Manager.

Changing a layer's state

After you create a layer, you can manage that layer — and all the objects on that layer — by changing its states. You can change some layer states through the Layer drop-down list; others must be changed in the Layer Properties Manager. Each layer state has different properties and uses:

- **On/Off.** Turn layers off when seeing objects on those layers interferes with the drawing process. For example, if you want to edit only objects on your Object layer, but objects on other layers are nearby, you can turn off the other layers and easily select the objects on the Object layer with a window. Then turn the other layers back on. The on/off state is available on the Layer drop-down list.
- **Thaw/Freeze.** You can freeze layers for reasons similar to those that lead you to turn off layers. In general, freeze layers when you want to work without those layers for a longer period of time. The thawed/frozen state is available on the Layer drop-down list.
- **Thaw/Freeze in Current Viewport.** You may want to freeze or thaw layers in some floating viewports but not in others. (I cover floating viewports in Chapter 17.) For example, if you want to display dimensions in one viewport but not in others, freeze your dimensions layer in all the viewports except one. You can change this state on the Layer drop-down list if you're working on a layout. You can also click the Current Viewport Freeze icon in the Layer Properties Manager.

- **Thaw/Freeze in New Viewports.** You can also freeze or thaw layers in future viewports that you create. For example, after you display dimensions or text in one viewport, you may want to make sure that they won't appear in any new viewports that you create. This state is available in the New Viewport Freeze column of the Layer Properties Manager.

New Feature

Three new commands help you hide and display objects, although not by layer: The ISOLATEOBJECTS command hides all objects except those that you select. After selecting objects, right-click in the drawing area and choose Isolate ⇨ Isolate Objects. The HIDEOBJECTS command hides selected objects. Select the objects, right-click in the drawing area, and choose Isolate ⇨ Hide Objects. The UNISOLATEOBJECTS command undoes either of the previous commands, displaying objects that those commands hid. ■

Note

When you make several layer property changes in a row and then undo them, AutoCAD and AutoCAD LT count these changes as one change. Therefore, Undo brings you back to the state before the first change. You can change this behavior by choosing Application Button ⇨ Options, clicking the User Preferences tab, and unchecking the Combine Layer Property Change check box in the Undo/Redo section. ■

- **Unlock/Lock.** Lock a layer when you want to ensure that objects on that layer are not changed. You can still use objects on locked layers for reference (for example, you can use their object snaps). Click the Lock/Unlock icon on the Layer drop-down list.

Note

When you select an object on a locked layer, it doesn't display grips, because you can't edit it. ■

- **Plot/No Plot.** Make a layer not plottable when you want to create reference text or revision marks on your drawing but don't want to plot them. You may also have a drawing that contains both actual and planned structures; this feature enables you to plot showing only the actual structures. Being able to change a layer's plottable state makes it possible for you to create variations on your drawing, perhaps for different users, such as electricians, plumbers, and roofers. The plot/no plot state is available in the Plot column of the Layer Properties Manager.

Tip

Both the off and frozen states make layers invisible. The purpose of the frozen/thawed layer states is to reduce regeneration time — this is the main difference between On/Off and Thawed/Frozen layer visibility options. However, today's computers are faster, and recent releases of the software have reduced the need for regeneration. Because thawing a layer causes a regeneration, whereas turning a layer back on only causes a redraw, you actually save a regeneration by using On/Off rather than Thawed/Frozen. ■

Click any of the state icons to toggle a layer's state. For example, if you want to freeze a layer, click its sun icon; it switches to a snowflake icon. Table 11.2 shows the icons for each state.

TABLE 11.2

Layer State Icons

State	Icon	State	Icon
On		Off	
Thawed (in all viewports)		Frozen (in all viewports)	
Thawed (in new viewports)		Frozen (in new viewports)	
Unlocked		Locked	
Plottable		Not plottable	

When you change a layer's state from the Ribbon, the drop-down list stays open so that you can change the state of more than one layer at a time. Click the top of the list to close it.

Caution

Be careful when editing a drawing with frozen or off layers — it's easy to forget about them. For example, you could move a whole section of your drawing and inadvertently leave the frozen objects in that section behind. ■

Saving layer states

Often you work with sets of layer states. For example, you may lock certain layers during part of the editing process to avoid changing objects on those layers. You may also set some layers as not plottable just before final plotting, but want them plotted for a draft plot. You may also want to temporarily change the properties of certain layers — color, linetype, lineweight, transparency, and plot style — and then change them back.

You could spend a lot of time adjusting all these layer states and properties. Instead, you can save and restore sets of layer states — the properties and states of all the layers in a drawing. You can save layer states to automate the process of restoring layer states and properties by saving the set of all layer states and properties. After you save this set, you can restore it at any time. The term *layer states* includes the set of all layer states as well as their properties (such as color and linetype).

You can also export layer state settings to a file. You can then use the layer-state settings in another drawing with the same or similar layers.

To save a layer state, follow these steps:

1. Set all the layer states and properties the way you want them. Usually, you've already done this and should save the state before making changes that you plan to reverse later on.

2. Choose Home tab ⇨ Layers panel ⇨ Layer States drop-down list ⇨ Manage Layer States to open the Layer States Manager dialog box, as shown in Figure 11.10. Alternatively, you can click the Layer States Manager icon in the Layer Properties Manager.

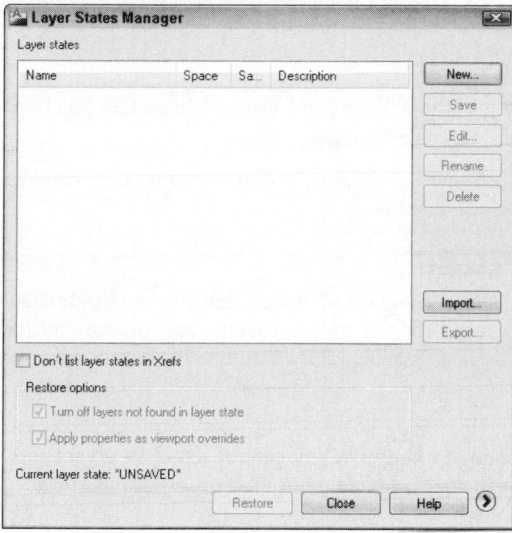

FIGURE 11.10

The Layer States Manager dialog box.

3. Click New and type a name for your layer state in the New Layer State Name text box of the New Layer State to Save dialog box. If you want, type a description. Click OK.

4. Back in the Layer States Manager, choose the layer states and properties that you want to save in the Layer Properties to Restore section. (If you don't see this section, click the More Restore Options right-arrow button at the lower-right corner of the dialog box.)

Caution

States and properties that you do not save are not affected later when you restore the layer state. For example, if you save only the on/off state and then change both a layer's on/off state and its color, when you restore the layer state, only the on/off state is returned to its original setting; the layer retains its new color. ■

5. If you want your drawing to look exactly as it did when you saved the layer state (in terms of layers), check the Turn Off Layers Not Found in Layer State check box. Any new layers that you create after saving the layer state are then turned off when you restore your layer state.

6. Click Close.

The Layer States Manager enables you to manage layer states in the following ways:

- **Restore.** Click the Restore button to restore a saved layer state.
- **Delete.** Click the Delete button to delete a layer state.
- **Import.** Click Import to import a layer state that has been previously exported as an .las file. Importing a layer state gives you access to layer states that others have saved. Click Import to open the Import Layer State dialog box.

Note

You can also import a layer state from a DWG (drawing), DWT (template), or DWS (standards) file. (Standards files are covered in Chapter 26.) In the Import Layer States dialog box, choose the type of file you want from the Files of Type drop-down list. Also, the Layer States Manager includes layer states from xrefs. (See Chapter 19 for information about xrefs.) ∎

- **Export.** Click Export to export the settings of a layer state in an LAS file. Exporting a layer state gives others access to your layer-state settings.

To rename a layer state, click its name, type a new name, and press Enter. After you finish using the Layer States Manager, click Close to close the dialog box.

Changing an existing object's layer

Sometimes you need to change the layer of an object or objects that you've already drawn. You can do this easily by selecting one or more objects and clicking the layer name that you want for the object in the Layer drop-down list of the Layers panel on the Home tab. The list automatically closes.

Note

If you turn off Noun/Verb selection, as I explain in Chapter 9, you cannot select an object and change its layer from the Layer drop-down list. Instead, you can change the layer in the Properties palette. ∎

You can also change an object's layer in the Quick Properties palette or the Properties palette. The Quick Properties palette opens automatically (by default) when you select an object. To use the Properties palette, choose View tab ➪ Palettes panel ➪ Properties or press Ctrl+1. Use the Properties palette if you want to change more than one property of an object at one time.

Caution

It's easy to inadvertently change an object's layer. Make sure that objects are not selected (press Esc) if you're about to use the Layer drop-down list just to change the current layer. ∎

Making an object's layer current

 If you're adding an object, you usually want to draw on the same layer as an existing object. You could select the object to see what layer it's on, press Esc to deselect the object, and then choose that layer from the Layer drop-down list to make it current. However, this process is easier with the Make Object's Layer Current button. Choose Home tab ➪ Layers panel ➪ Make Object's Layer Current, select an object, and click the button. That object's layer is now current.

Using special layer tools

A set of layer tools that were once in the Express Tools collection are very helpful for working with layers. Table 11.3 lists the Layer tools and what they do.

TABLE 11.3

Layer Tools

Layer Tool Name	Menu	Description
LAYWALK	Home tab ⇨ Layers panel (expanded) ⇨ Layer Walk	A full-featured command that helps you to see which objects are on which layers. Using the dialog box and the shortcut menu, you can list the number of objects on each layer, count the total number of layers, save layer states, and purge unused layers.
LAYMCH	Home tab ⇨ Layers panel ⇨ Match	Changes the layer of selected objects to match that of another selected object.
LAYCUR	Home tab ⇨ Layers panel (expanded) ⇨ Change to Current Layer	Changes the selected object's layer to the current layer.
COPYTOLAYER	Home tab ⇨ Layers panel (expanded) ⇨ Copy Objects to New Layer	Copies objects while changing the copy to the layer that you specify.
LAYISO	Home tab ⇨ Layers panel ⇨ Isolate	Turns off all layers except the layer of an object that you select, to isolate a specific layer. You can lock and fade layers. (I explain this command further after this table.)
LAYUNISO	Home tab ⇨ Layers panel ⇨ Unisolate	Restores the state of layers that existed before you used LAYISO. (I explain this command further after this table.)
LAYVPI	Home tab ⇨ Layers panel (expanded) ⇨ Isolate to Current Viewport	Freezes all layers except the layer of an object that you select in all viewports except the current one, isolating the selected layer in the current viewport. (See Chapter 17 for information on viewports.)
LAYOFF	Home tab ⇨ Layers panel ⇨ Off	Turns the layer of the selected object(s) off.
LAYON	Home tab ⇨ Layers panel (expanded) ⇨ Turn All Layers On	Turns all layers on.
LAYFRZ	Home tab ⇨ Layers panel ⇨ Freeze	Freezes the layer of the selected object(s).
LAYTHW	Home tab ⇨ Layers panel (expanded) ⇨ Thaw All Layers	Thaws all layers.
LAYLCK	Home tab ⇨ Layers panel (expanded) ⇨ Lock	Locks the layer of the selected object(s).
LAYULK	Home tab ⇨ Layers panel (expanded) ⇨ Unlock	Unlocks all layers.
LAYMRG	Home tab ⇨ Layers panel (expanded) ⇨ Merge	Changes the layer of all objects on the first layer selected to the second layer selected. The first layer is purged.
LAYDEL	Home tab ⇨ Layers panel (expanded) ⇨ Delete	Deletes objects from the specified layer and purges that layer.

The LAYISO command can lock layers (other than the one you're isolating) and fade those layers instead of turning them off. The default is to lock layers and fade them by 50 percent. You can change the default by using the Settings option. For example, you can choose to turn off the layers or change the fade percentage. Use the LAYUNISO command to unisolate layers. Choose Home tab ⇨ Layers panel (expanded). Then drag the Locked Layer Fading slider to the left or right to decrease or increase fading. You can also specify Layer Isolate controls in the Layer Settings dialog box, which I discuss in the next section of this chapter.

On the DVD

The drawing used in the following exercise on working with layers, ab11-b.dwg, is in the Drawings folder on the DVD. ■

STEPS: Working with Layers

1. Open ab11-b.dwg from the DVD.

2. Save the file as ab11-02.dwg in your AutoCAD Bible folder. This drawing is shown in Figure 11.11. The current layer is 0. Make sure that Object Snap is on. Set running object snaps for Endpoint and Quadrant. Turn Infer Constraints off.

FIGURE 11.11

This gas extraction well plan drawing needs to be completed.

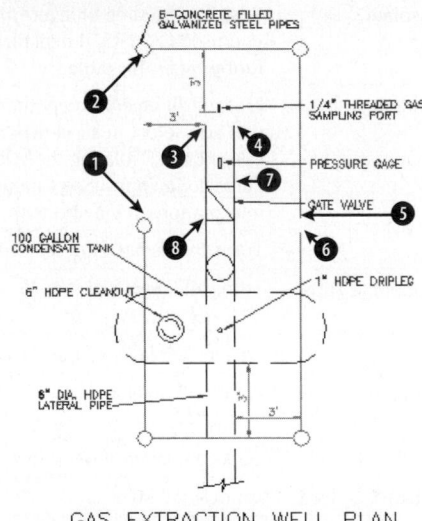

Thanks to the Army Corps of Engineers for this drawing.

3. From Home tab ⇨ Layers panel, click the Layer drop-down list and click Pipes to change the current layer to Pipes.

4. Start the LINE command. Draw a line from ❶ to ❷, shown in Figure 11.11, using the Quadrant running object snap.

5. Click the Layer drop-down list and click Object to change the current layer to Object.

6. Click the Layer drop-down list and click the On/Off icon of the Dim layer. Click again at the top of the list to close it.

7. Start the CIRCLE command. Right-click and choose 2p to use the two-point option. Draw a circle from the endpoint of ❸ to ❹, shown in Figure 11.11, using the Endpoint running object snap.

8. Without changing the layer, start the CIRCLE command and again use the 2p option. Draw a circle between the endpoints at ❺ and ❻.

9. The last circle was drawn on the wrong layer. To change its layer, select the circle. Then click the Layer drop-down list and choose Pipes. Press Esc to remove the grips and see the result. The circle is now on the Pipes layer. Notice that the current layer is still Object in the Layer display.

10. Pick any red object (the Pipes layer). Choose Home tab ⇨ Layers panel ⇨ Make Object's Layer Current. The Pipes layer is now the current layer. Draw a line from the right quadrant of the circle at ❶ to the left quadrant of the circle at ❺ and ❻, as shown in Figure 11.11.

11. You want to draw a line on the Object layer. This is the previous layer that you used. Choose Home tab ⇨ Layers panel ⇨ Previous. The Object layer is now the current layer.

12. Draw a line from the endpoint at ❼ to the endpoint at ❽.

13. Pick any text to see what layer it is on. The Layer drop-down list changes to show the Text layer. Choose Home tab ⇨ Layers panel ⇨ Match. Now choose the words gas extraction well plan at the bottom of the drawing. The text gas extraction well plan is now on the Text layer.

14. Save your drawing. It should look like Figure 11.12.

FIGURE 11.12

The completed drawing.

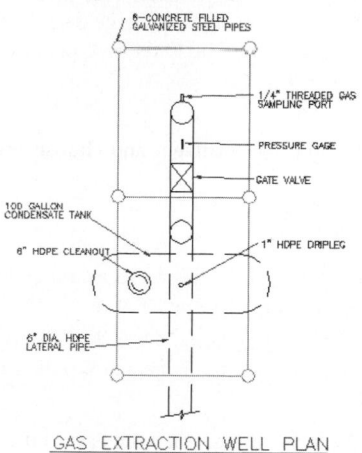

Modifying layers

Sometimes you need to change the layers that you display in the Layer Properties Manager to facilitate working with only certain layers. You may also need to change the properties of a layer, such as its color or linetype. Changing a layer's properties is a powerful tool because every object on that layer is automatically regenerated with the new properties. Other layer housekeeping tasks are renaming and deleting layers. You use the Layer Properties Manager for these functions.

Managing columns

If you have many layers in a drawing, sorting can help you find the layers on which you need to work. You can sort the layer listing in a drawing by any column, by clicking once on the column title. Click again to see the list in reverse order. Long layer names display a tooltip with the entire layer name.

Note

If sorting by layer name does not appear to be working, increase the value for the MAXSORT system variable, which determines the maximum number of symbols that AutoCAD or AutoCAD LT sorts. Type maxsort ↵ on the command line and enter a larger number. Press Enter. ■

You can change the order of the columns by dragging them. For example, you may want to place the Color column next to the Name column. You can also choose which columns appear in the Layer Properties Manager. Right-click any column name and uncheck any column that you don't want to see. This choice remains until you change it. If you want to see a column again, right-click a column name again and check that column. As mentioned earlier in this chapter, you can freeze certain columns so that they always appear to the left, even if you scroll to the right. Right-click a column name and choose Freeze Column.

Filtering the layer list

Some complex drawings may have dozens of layers, and you may have a hard time finding the layer that you want in the Layer Properties Manager. You can filter the layer list so that you only see the layers that you want. This makes it easy to change a group of layers at once. The Filter Tree panel on the left side of the Layer Properties Manager contains one filter, All Used Layers, as well as the default that displays all layers. To display only used layers, click the All Used Layers filter in the Filter Tree panel.

Note

If you don't see the Filter Tree panel, right-click in the Layer Properties Manager and choose Show Filter Tree or click the double arrow on the left side of the palette. ■

You can create your own filters. There are two types of filters:

- **Properties filter.** Defines a filter by the properties of the layer. For example, you can create a filter that displays only green layers or layers that start with the letter *A*.
- **Group filter.** Defines a filter by selecting layers that go into a filter. A group filter offers complete flexibility to filter layers. For example, you might want to create a group filter that contains all your text, annotation, and dimension layers.

 To create a properties filter, click the New Property Filter button to open the Layer Filter Properties dialog box, as shown in Figure 11.13. Notice that the Filter Definition pane at the top has the same columns as the Layer Properties Manager.

FIGURE 11.13

The Layer Filter Properties dialog box.

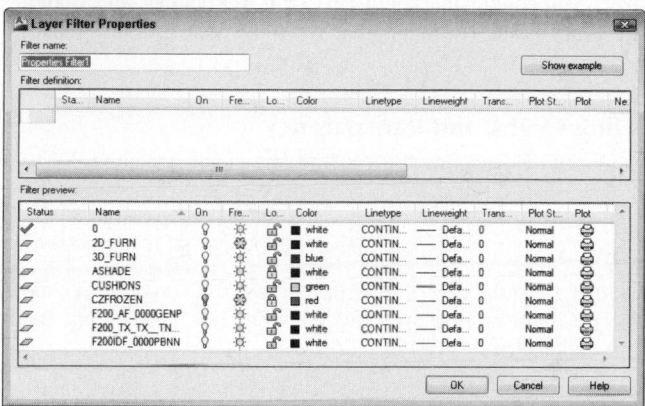

Name the filter in the Filter name text box. To choose a property, you use the Filter Definition pane. Click in the first row of that property's column. Then do one of the following:

- If a drop-down arrow appears, click the arrow and choose one of the options from the drop-down list. (To remove a property, choose the blank line at the top of the drop-down list.)

- If an ellipsis button appears, click the button and choose a property from the dialog box that opens. For example, you can choose a layer color from the Select Color dialog box. (To remove a property, select the text, press Del, and click anywhere outside the column.)

- To specify a filter for a named property, such as the name or linetype of a layer, you can use wild-cards. The two most common wildcard characters are * (asterisk), which replaces any number of characters, and ?, which replaces any single character. For example, you could set the layer name filter to h* and the color to magenta. The resulting filter would include only magenta layers whose names start with the letter *H*.

As you work, the Filter Preview pane shows the results of your filter. When you're done, click OK. The Layer Properties Manager now shows only the layers that match your filter specifications.

 To create a group filter, open the Layer Properties Manager and click the New Group Filter button. Enter a name for the filter in place of the default name that appears. In the Filter Tree panel, choose a filter that displays the layers you need, such as All. Then simply drag the layers that you want onto the group filter's name.

Tip

To add layers by selecting objects that are on the layers you want, right-click the filter and choose Select Layers ⇨ Add. You return to your drawing where you can select objects. Press Enter to end object selection. ∎

 To display all layers except the ones specified by any filter, click Invert Filter. If you want to filter the Layer listing in the same way, click the Settings button. In the Layer Settings dialog box that opens, check Apply Layer Filter to Layer Toolbar. This dialog box also lets you specify settings for the Layer Isolate feature (locking and fading). (I discuss the New Layer Notification section in Chapter 26.) Click OK.

Tip

When you work with a large number of layers, think carefully about how you name them. Naming layers in groups is common. For example, if you have several text layers, you could name them Text Title, Text Notes, and Text Schedule. A systematic layer-naming scheme makes it easy to filter the layers that you need, which in turn makes it easy to make changes to groups of layers. ■

Changing a layer's color, linetype, lineweight, and transparency

You can modify the color of a layer. To do so, open the Layer Properties Manager, and choose the color swatch of the layer that you want to modify. The Select Color dialog box opens. Choose a color and click OK. For more information about choosing colors, see the section, "Assigning a color," earlier in this chapter.

To change a layer's linetype, click the layer's linetype in the Layer Properties Manager. If you need to choose a linetype that is not on the list, click the linetype of the layer to open the Select Linetype dialog box. There you can either choose a loaded linetype or load a linetype if necessary.

To change a layer's lineweight, click the layer's lineweight. Choose a new lineweight from the Lineweight dialog box.

To change a layer's transparency, click the layer's transparency value. Choose or enter a new value in the Layer Transparency dialog box. Click OK.

Tip

You can modify more than one layer at a time. In the Layer Properties Manager, right-click and choose Select All to choose all the layers. Choose Clear All to deselect all the layers. You can choose a range of layers by clicking the first layer in the range, pressing Shift, and clicking the last layer in the range. Finally, you can choose individual layers by pressing Ctrl for each additional layer. Changes that you make to color, linetype, lineweight, or transparency affect all the selected layers. ■

Cross-Reference

When you're ready to lay out a drawing for plotting, you generally work on a layout and create floating viewports. You can change the properties of a layer in a viewport. For example, you might want a layer to appear in a different color when you display it in a small detail view from the color that you want in a larger context. For more information, see Chapter 17 where I cover overriding layer properties for layouts and viewports. ■

Renaming layers

Thinking out your layer-naming scheme in advance is best. Many disciplines and organizations have layer-naming standards. However, sometimes you simply need to rename a layer.

To rename a layer, open the Layer Properties Manager. Click the name of the layer, and then click a second time. A border appears, and the name is highlighted. Type the new name and press Enter. Alternatively, you can right-click the layer name and choose Rename Layer from the shortcut menu or just press F2.

Note

You cannot rename layer 0. Layer 0 is the default layer and always remains the same. You can set CAD standards that allow you to check for nonstandard layer names. For more information, see Chapter 26. ■

Deleting layers

 To delete a layer, open the Layer Properties Manager. Click the name of the layer and click the Delete Layer button.

Note

You cannot delete the current layer or any layer that has objects on it. (Where would those objects go?) You also cannot delete layer 0, which is the default layer. Finally, you cannot delete layers from external references (covered in Chapter 19). However, the LAYDEL command deletes all objects on a layer and purges the layer. ■

Purging layers and linetypes

Layer and linetype definitions add to the size of your drawing because they're kept in the drawing's database. Therefore, eliminating layers and linetypes that you aren't using is worthwhile. You can delete them, but sometimes it's hard to know which layers contain no objects. The PURGE command lets you delete many types of unused definitions, including layers and linetypes.

 To purge layers and linetypes, choose Application Button ➪ Drawing Utilities ➪ Purge. The Purge dialog box opens, as shown in Figure 11.14.

FIGURE 11.14

The Purge dialog box.

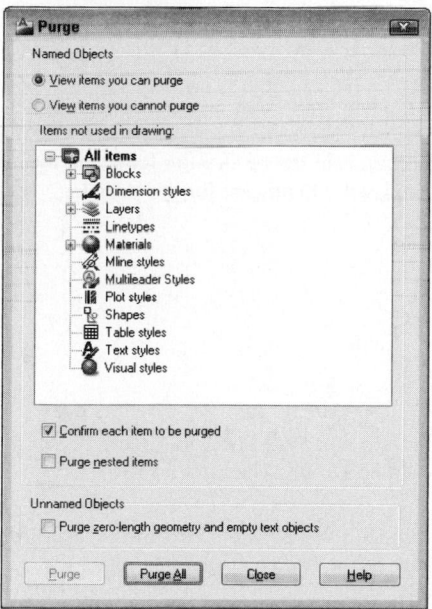

Note

The Incremental Save Percentage option may prevent a purge during a drawing session from removing all unreferenced layers or linetypes from the drawing. To avoid this, you can either set incremental save to zero, or save the drawing and re-open it and then immediately use the PURGE command. To set this option, choose Application Button ⇨ Options ⇨ Open and Save tab. ∎

At the top of the dialog box, you can choose to view objects that you can purge or objects that you cannot purge. Why would you want to view objects that you cannot purge? Sometimes it's hard to figure out why you can't purge a certain object, and the dialog box has a handy feature that lets you select an object and view possible reasons why it cannot be purged.

To start purging, choose View Items You Can Purge. A plus sign (+) next to each type of object indicates that it contains purgeable objects. Click the plus sign to display the specific items.

To purge an individual item, select it and click Purge. Check the Confirm Each Item to Be Purged option if you want to see a dialog box asking you to confirm each purge. Click Purge All to purge all possible items. Check the Purge Nested Items option to purge items within other named objects. Usually, these are layers, linetypes, and so on inside blocks.

Tip

You can select more than one item at a time to purge. To select an additional item, press Ctrl as you click. To select a contiguous group of items, click the first item in the group, press and hold Shift, and then select the last item in the group. ∎

After you're done purging, click Close to close the Purge dialog box.

On the DVD

The drawing used in the following exercise on modifying layers, ab11-c.dwg, is in the Drawings folder on the DVD. (Thanks to Michael J. Lemmons of Winston Products Company in Louisville, Kentucky, for this drawing.) ∎

STEPS: Modifying Layers

1. Open ab11-c.dwg from the DVD.

2. Save the file as ab11-03.dwg in your AutoCAD Bible folder.

 3. Choose Home tab ⇨ Layers panel ⇨ Layer Properties.

 4. Click the New Property Filter button. In the Filter Name text box, type **M layers**. In the Name column, type **m*** to list all layers starting with the letter M. Click OK. The layer list now shows only those layers.

5. In the Layer Properties Manager, click the top layer. Press Shift and click the next-to-last layer. All the layers except for Mydims are selected. Click anywhere in the Linetype column to open the Select Linetype dialog box and choose Dashed. Click OK. Notice that all the selected layers now have a dashed linetype. Close or collapse the Layer Properties Manager. You can now see that the layers that you selected have the dashed linetype.

6. Open or expand the Layer Properties Manager. Choose Mydims. Click it a second time so that the name of the layer is highlighted. Type **Titles** ↵ to change the name of the layer. Close or collapse the Layer Properties Manager.

7. Start the ERASE command and pick anywhere on the titleblock (it is all one object) and the three labels FRONT, TOP, and RIGHT SIDE. Press Enter to end the command.

8. Again display the Layer Properties Manager. In the Filter Tree panel, click All to display all the layers.

9. Click the Settings. In the Layer Settings dialog box, check the Indicate Layers in Use check box at the bottom of the dialog box. Click the OK button.

10. Scroll down the list of layers and choose Titles. Click Refresh. You can see that its Status icon is off, indicating that the layer contains no objects. Click the Delete button.

11. Save your drawing.

Changing Object Color, Linetype, Lineweight, and Transparency

The properties of layers — color, linetype, lineweight, and transparency — can also apply directly to objects. You can assign a color, linetype, and lineweight to an object. You can also set a current color, linetype, and lineweight so that all the future objects that you draw have those properties, regardless of the properties assigned to their layer. In most cases, you should avoid assigning properties directly to objects because you lose the organizational value of layers. When you create a layer, and assign it a color, linetype, lineweight, and transparency, those properties of the object are *ByLayer*. This means that the object picks up those properties from the properties of its layer.

Cross-Reference
You can also assign plot styles to objects. See Chapter 17 for more information. When you create a block with objects whose properties are ByBlock and you insert the block, it takes on the current color (or the color of the current layer). (For more information about blocks and layers, see Chapter 18.) ■

Because it's so helpful to organize object properties by layer, you can use the SETBYLAYER command to return objects' properties to ByLayer. Choose Home tab ➪ Modify panel (expanded) ➪ Set to ByLayer. At the Select objects or [Settings]: prompt, select objects. At the Change ByBlock to ByLayer? [Yes/No] <Yes>: prompt, choose Yes if you want to change the properties of objects in blocks to ByLayer. At the Include blocks? [Yes/No] <Yes>: prompt, choose Yes if you want to include blocks that are in the selection set. (Chapter 18 covers blocks.) All objects that you selected become ByLayer and therefore pick up the properties of their layer (unless you chose objects that were set to ByBlock and chose No at the first prompt).

If you choose the Settings option at the first prompt, the SetByLayer Settings dialog box opens, where you can choose which properties you want to set to ByLayer. For example, if you had an object whose color was set to green and whose linetype was set to Dashed, you could uncheck the Linetype check box to change the color to ByLayer, but leave the linetype set to Dashed.

Changing an object's color

You can control an object's color by using the Color drop-down list, which you can find by choosing Home tab ➪ Properties panel. You can also change an object's color by using the Quick Properties palette that opens when you select an object, or in the Properties palette. For more information about choosing colors, see the section, "Assigning a color," earlier in this chapter. As with the Layer drop-down list, the Color drop-down list shows the color of any selected object. When you create a layer, assign it a color, and draw with that layer, the color is displayed as ByLayer.

The ByBlock color creates objects by using color 7 (white or black, depending on the screen color), but if the objects are placed in a block, the block takes on the current color when inserted. (For information about blocks, see Chapter 18.)

The best practice for organizing a drawing is to assign colors by layer. It can be confusing if related elements, such as centerlines in a mechanical drawing, appear in different colors. Also, if you see another line with the same color and linetype as most centerlines, you may assume that it's a centerline in the wrong place. It is standard practice to organize colors by layer.

Colors have a special significance because when you plot, you can assign colors to pens — although you can also use plot styles (see Chapter 17). If you use a color-based system, color is the basis that you use for plotting with various width pens or colors. You may want to temporarily change the color of an object to emphasize it in a plot or for some other reason. However, you should generally refrain from directly changing the color of objects.

If you need to change the color of an object, here are two ways to do it:

- To change just an object's color, select the object. Click the Color drop-down list by choosing Home tab ⇨ Properties panel, or the Quick Properties palette, and then choose the color that you want.

- If you want to change other properties at the same time, select the object and open the Properties palette (press Ctrl+1). There you can change all the properties of the object. To change the color, choose Color and click the drop-down arrow that appears. Choose the color that you want.

You can always change an object's color back to ByLayer, using the same technique, or by using the SETBYLAYER command, described in the preceding section.

Changing the current color

When you change the current color, all future objects are drawn using that color, regardless of their layer. In general, you should do this only when you have a special need for two objects to be on one layer but have different colors. An example might be text in a titleblock. You might want the text to have the same layer so that you can freeze it and thaw it (or turn it on and off) easily without having to remember that the text and titleblock are on two separate layers. If you also want part of the text to have a different color, change the current color before typing in that part of the text. Remember to change the current color back to ByLayer before drawing anything else.

To change the current color, make sure that no object is selected. Then click the Color drop-down list on the Properties panel on the Home tab. You can also open the Properties palette and choose the color that you want. To use a color not on the list, choose Select Color to open the Select Color dialog box. (See the section "Assigning a color" earlier in this chapter for more information on assigning colors.) To change the current color back to ByLayer, use the same techniques and choose ByLayer or use the SETBYLAYER command. You have an opportunity to do an exercise on changing colors after the "Changing the current lineweight" section.

Changing an object's linetype

Linetypes work according to the same principles as colors. You can change the linetype of an existing object or objects. You can control an object's linetype by using the Linetype drop-down list in the Properties panel of the Home tab, or in the Quick Properties palette. The Linetype drop-down list shows the linetype of any selected object. When you create a layer, assign it a linetype, and draw with that layer, the linetype is displayed as ByLayer.

The ByLayer linetype simply means that the linetype of the object is taken from the linetype of the object's layer.

The best way to organize a drawing is to assign linetypes by layer. It can be confusing if similar elements, such as plat borders in a surveyor's drawing, appear in different linetypes. Also, if you see another line with the same color and linetype as most plat borders, you may assume that it's a plat border in the wrong place.

If you need to change the linetype of an object, you have two options:

- To change an object's linetype, select the object. Click the Linetype drop-down list in the Properties panel of the Home tab, or in the Quick Properties palette, and then choose the linetype that you want.
- Select the object and open the Properties palette. Click the Linetype item, and then click the drop-down arrow that appears. Choose from one of the linetypes.

You can always change an object's linetype back to ByLayer, using the same methods or with the SETBYLAYER command, discussed earlier in this chapter.

As discussed in the "Assigning a linetype" section earlier in this chapter, you need to load a linetype before you can use it for the first time. To load a linetype, choose Home tab ⇨ Properties panel ⇨ Linetype drop-down list. Choose Other to open the Linetype Manager. Choose Load to open the Load or Reload Linetypes dialog box, choose the linetype file (if not the default), and choose the linetype that you want to load. Click OK. Choose the linetype again in the Linetype Manager and click OK to return to your drawing.

To filter the list of linetypes, choose from the Linetype Filters drop-down list box in the Linetype Manager.

Changing the current linetype

You can also change the current linetype. When you change the current linetype, all future objects that you draw have that linetype and are not drawn according to their layer's assigned linetype. In general, you should do this only when you have a special need for two objects to be on one layer but have different linetypes. An example might be a table containing notes in one corner of a drawing. You might want the lines that make up the table to have the same layer so that you can freeze it and thaw it (or turn it on and off) easily without having to remember that the table is on two separate layers. If you also want some of the lines to have a different linetype, change the current linetype before adding those lines. Remember to change the current linetype back to ByLayer before drawing anything else.

To change the current linetype, click the Linetype drop-down list and choose the linetype that you want, first making sure that no objects are currently selected. You can also use the Properties palette. To change the current linetype back to ByLayer, choose ByLayer for the linetype or use the SETBYLAYER command, discussed earlier in this chapter.

Changing an object's lineweight

Lineweights let you represent objects with varying line widths. The widths can represent the width of a pen in a pen plotter that will be used to plot that object. Lineweights can also be used as an organizational tool, to distinguish certain types of objects just as colors and linetypes do. Finally, you can use lineweights to represent the actual properties of objects, such as the width of wires in an electrical schematic.

Lineweights work according to the same principles as colors and linetypes. You can control an object's lineweight by using the Lineweight drop-down list in the Properties panel of the Home tab. The Lineweight drop-down list shows the lineweight of any selected object. When you create a layer, assign it a lineweight, and draw with that layer, the lineweight is displayed as ByLayer.

As with colors and linetypes, the best way to organize a drawing is to assign lineweights by layer. If you need to change the lineweight of an object, do one of the following:

- Select the object. Click the Lineweight drop-down list in the Properties panel of the Home tab and choose the lineweight that you want.

- Select the object and open the Properties palette. To change an object's lineweight, click Lineweight, and then click the drop-down arrow that appears. Choose from one of the lineweights.

Changing the current lineweight

You can also change the current lineweight. When you change the current lineweight, all future objects that you draw have that lineweight and are not drawn according to their layer's assigned lineweight.

To change the current lineweight, click the Lineweight drop-down list and choose the lineweight that you want, first making sure that no objects are currently selected. You can also use the Properties palette. To change the current lineweight back to ByLayer, choose ByLayer as the lineweight or use the SETBYLAYER command, discussed earlier in this chapter.

Changing an object's transparency

Transparency lets you see multiple layers of objects. Most often, you would use transparency for filling closed areas, such as the inside of a circle or rectangle. (You create fills using the HATCH command; I cover hatches in Chapter 16.) You may want to allow an image or text to show through an object that is on top.

Transparency works according to the same principles as colors and linetypes. You can control an object's transparency by using the Transparency slider in the Properties panel of the Home tab. The Transparency slider shows the transparency value of any selected object. When you create a layer, assign it a transparency value, and draw with that layer, the transparency is displayed as ByLayer.

As with colors and linetypes, the best way to organize a drawing is to assign transparency by layer. However, you may want to make an object transparent temporarily so that you can see objects behind it. If you need to change the transparency of an object, do one of the following:

- Select the object. Click the Transparency slider in the Properties panel of the Home tab, and drag it to the transparency value that you want.

- Select the object and open the Properties palette. Click Transparency, and then type the transparency value (from 0 to 90) that you want.

Changing the current transparency

You can also change the current transparency. When you change the current transparency, all future objects that you draw have that transparency and are not drawn according to their layer's assigned transparency.

To change the current transparency, click the Transparency slider and drag it to display the value that you want, first making sure that no objects are currently selected. You can also use the Properties palette. To change the current transparency back to ByLayer, choose ByLayer as the transparency or use the SETBYLAYER command, discussed earlier in this chapter.

On the DVD

The drawing used in the following exercise on changing colors, linetypes, and lineweights, ab11-d.dwg, **is in the** Drawings **folder on the DVD.** ∎

STEPS: Changing Colors, Linetypes, Lineweights, and Transparency

1. Open ab11-d.dwg from the DVD.

2. Save the file as ab11-04.dwg in your AutoCAD Bible folder. This is an elevation view of a lavatory cabinet, as shown in Figure 11.15. Turn Selection Cycling on (if it isn't already on) by clicking the Selection Cycling button on the status bar.

FIGURE 11.15

A lavatory cabinet.

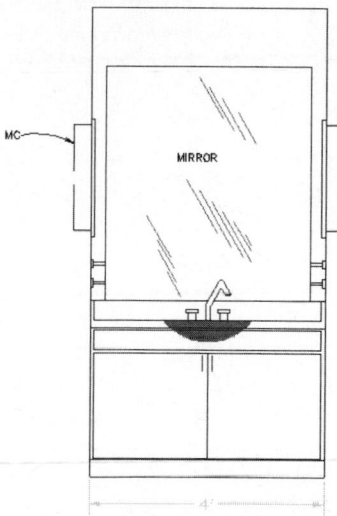

Thanks to the Army Corps of Engineers for this drawing.

3. Pick one of the reflection lines in the mirror. Notice that the color is red but the layer's color, as shown in the Layer drop-down list, is Magenta. Select all the reflection lines. Choose Home tab ⇨ Properties panel, click the Color drop-down list, and choose ByLayer from the top of the list. Press Esc to remove the grips.

4. Select the green dimension at the bottom of the cabinet. (The dimension is all one object.) To make it more visible, click the Color drop-down list and choose Red. Press Esc to see the result.

5. Pick the lines at ❶ and ❷, as shown in Figure 11.15. On the Home tab in the Properties panel, click the Linetype drop-down list and choose the Hidden linetype. Press Esc so that the hidden lines are no longer selected.

6. Select the dashed arc that represents the bottom curvature of the sink. In the Selection pane that opens, click Arc. In the Properties panel, click the Lineweight drop-down list and choose 0.30 mm. Press Esc. Click the Show/Hide Lineweight button on the status bar to turn on the display of lineweights and see the result.

7. Select the sink's fill. Click the Home tab. In the Properties panel, drag the Transparency slider to about 50. Press Esc to deselect the fill. The arc at the edge of the sink is now much more visible.

8. In the Properties panel, click the Color drop-down list box and choose Cyan to make it the current color.

9. Start the RECTANG command. Draw a rectangle inside the left cabinet. The exact size and placement are not important. Use the COPY command to copy the rectangle to the right cabinet. To copy, use an intersection object snap at point ❸ as the base point and ❹ as the second point of displacement. The rectangles are drawn in cyan.

10. Save your drawing. It should look like Figure 11.16.

FIGURE 11.16

The finished cabinet.

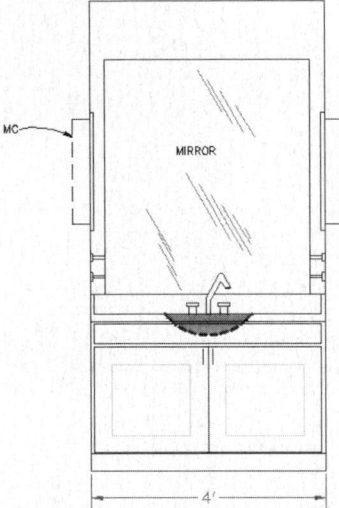

Working with Linetype Scales

A noncontinuous linetype is a repeating pattern of dots, dashes, and spaces. Linetypes can also include repeating text or shapes. You may find that the linetype patterns in your drawing are too long or short for clarity. The linetype scale may even be so big or so small that the line looks continuous. How often the pattern is repeated is affected by three factors:

- The linetype definition
- The global linetype scale
- The individual object's linetype scale

Changing linetype spacing by using a different linetype

One choice is to change the linetype. A number of linetypes come in short, medium, and long variations, such as Dashedx2, Dashed, and Dashed2, as shown in Figure 11.17.

AutoCAD's `acad.lin` and AutoCAD LT's `acadlt.lin` contain a number of ISO linetypes that meet the specifications of the International Standards Organization. Your organization or field of specialty may require the use of these linetypes. The ISO linetype pattern definitions are much longer than the other linetype definitions. You may need to make adjustments to the linetype scale as a result.

FIGURE 11.17

A number of the standard linetypes come in three variations, such as Dashedx2, Dashed, and Dashed2.

— — — — —◄——— Dashedx2
– – – – – – – – –◄——— Dashed
- - - - - - - - - - - - - - - -◄——— Dashed2

Changing linetype spacing by changing the global linetype scale

Another choice is to change the global linetype scale, which affects all noncontinuous linetypes in your drawing. AutoCAD and AutoCAD LT multiply the linetype definition by the global linetype scale to calculate the length of each repetition of the linetype:

- Linetype scales larger than 1 result in longer sections — and fewer repetitions of the linetype definition per unit.
- Linetype scales smaller than 1 result in shorter sections — and more repetitions of the linetype definition per unit.

Cross-Reference

You can also change the scale of a linetype that appears in a viewport on a layout. For more information, see Chapter 17. ■

When you change the linetype scale, the drawing regenerates to change all the linetypes. Figure 11.18 shows three versions of a drawing with linetypes at linetype scales of 0.5, 1, and 2. As you can see, a scale of 2 is too large and a scale of 0.5 is too small. A scale of 1 is just right. (Goldilocks would have been happy with it.)

FIGURE 11.18

Three versions of a drawing, using linetype scales of 0.5, 1, and 2.

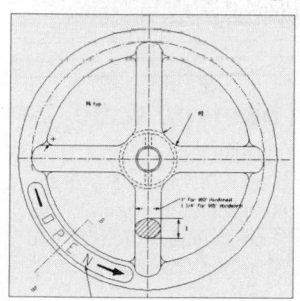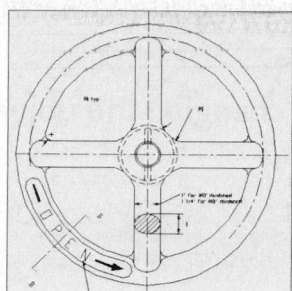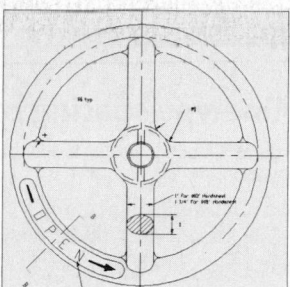

For purposes of drawing, you simply want to make sure that you can distinguish the linetype both when you can see the entire drawing on the screen and when you zoom in close. The main reason to scale linetypes is for plotting. A linetype scale that works for a drawing of a house on-screen may appear continuous when you plot it at a scale factor of 1 = 96.

If you want the linetype to appear exactly according to its definition, use the scale factor for the linetype scale. Chapter 5 covers scale factors. If the scale factor doesn't give you the results that you want, try a linetype scale of one quarter to one half of the scale factor — in the 1 = 96 example, you might use a linetype scale of 24 or 48.

To change the linetype scale, choose Home tab ⇨ Properties panel ⇨ Linetype drop-down list ⇨ Other (the LINETYPE command) to open the Linetype Manager, as shown in Figure 11.19. Click Show Details if the lower portion of the dialog box is not displayed.

FIGURE 11.19

The Linetype Manager dialog box.

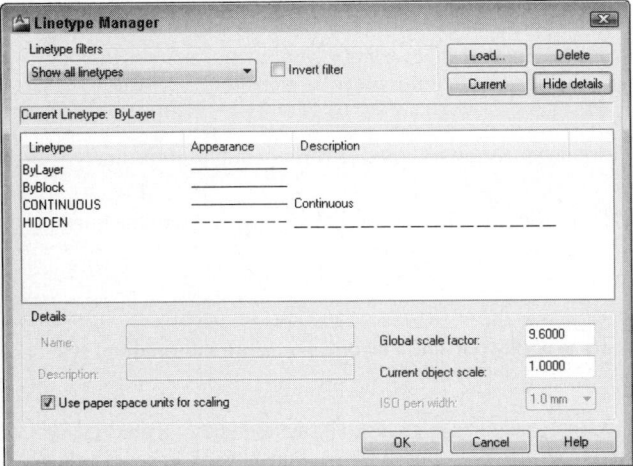

In the Global Scale Factor text box, type the scale factor that you want. Click OK. The drawing regenerates, changing the scale of every noncontinuous linetype in the drawing.

Tip

The global linetype scale is held in the LTSCALE system variable. You can change the linetype scale by typing ltscale ↵ at the command line and typing a scale. ∎

Changing linetype spacing by changing the object linetype scale

On occasion, you may want the linetype spacing to be different for one object — or a small group of objects — only. Perhaps the object is too small to show the linetype pattern or you want to set it off visually. The *current object linetype scale* works like setting a current color or linetype — all objects drawn after you set the object linetype scale are drawn with the new linetype scale. In most cases, you want to make sure that you change the current object linetype scale back to its default of 1 after using it for that one object or group of objects.

Changing the current object linetype scale

To change the linetype scale, choose Home tab ⇨ Properties panel ⇨ Linetype drop-down list ⇨ Other to open the Linetype Manager. Click Show Details if the lower portion of the dialog box is not displayed. In the Current Object Scale text box, type the scale factor that you want. Click OK. Now all objects that you draw use the current object linetype scale. When you're done drawing objects at that linetype scale, remember to change the linetype scale back to 1.

The current object linetype scale is held in the CELTSCALE system variable. You can also change the current object linetype scale by typing **celtscale** at the command line and typing in a scale.

If you have also set the global linetype scale to a value other than 1, AutoCAD and AutoCAD LT multiply the two linetype scales to calculate the final result. For example, if you have a global linetype scale of 12 and a current object linetype scale of 0.5, objects you draw will have a resulting linetype scale of 6.

Changing an existing object's linetype scale

You will often draw an object without setting a special object linetype scale and then decide that you want to change its linetype scale. To change an object's linetype scale, select the object and open the Properties palette. Click Linetype Scale and then type the new linetype scale. This linetype scale affects only the selected object. It does not affect the global linetype scale.

On the DVD

The drawing used in the following exercise on changing linetype scales, ab11-e.dwg, is in the Drawings folder on the DVD. ■

STEPS: Changing Linetype Scales

1. Open ab11-e.dwg from the DVD.

2. Save the file as ab11-05.dwg in your AutoCAD Bible folder. This drawing is of a bushing, as shown in Figure 11.20. Notice that the linetype doesn't show clearly on the short line at ❶ and in the small circle at ❷.

> **FIGURE 11.20**
>
> This drawing of a bushing has two noncontinuous linetypes.

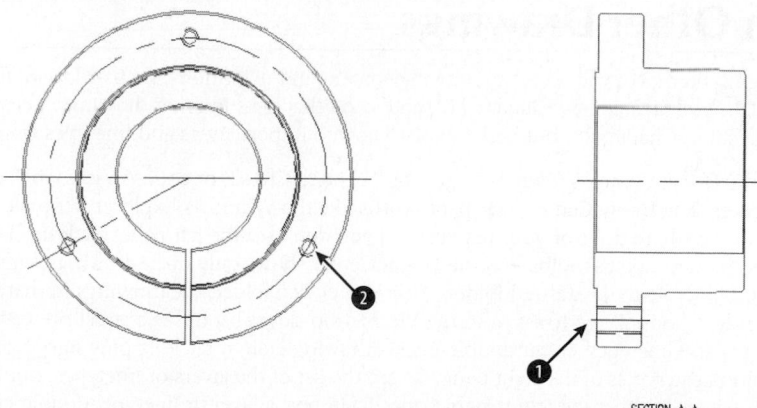

SECTION A–A

Thanks to Robert Mack of the Dexter Company, Fairfield, Iowa, for this drawing.

3. Choose Home tab ⇨ Properties panel ⇨ Linetype drop-down list ⇨ Other. Click Show Details to open the Details section of the Linetype Manager, if necessary. Change the Global scale factor to 0.5. Click OK. The drawing regenerates. Note that the circles are better, but the short line at ❶ still looks like a continuous line.

4. Choose the line at ❶. Choose View tab ⇨ Palettes panel ⇨ Properties to open the Properties palette (if it isn't already open). Click Linetype scale and change it to 0.5. Press Enter. Press Esc to remove the grips and see the result. Notice the difference in the line, which now has a linetype scale of 0.5 (global) times 0.5 (object) = 0.25.

5. Save your drawing. It should look like Figure 11.21.

FIGURE 11.21

The drawing's noncontinuous lines are now more appropriate.

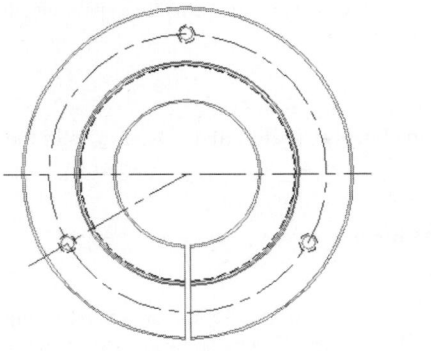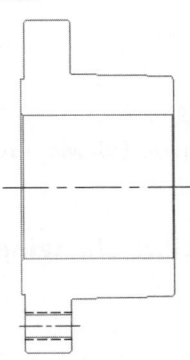

SECTION A–A

Importing Layers and Linetypes from Other Drawings

The DesignCenter gives you access to drawing content and definitions, such as layers, linetypes, blocks (see Chapter 18), plot layouts (see Chapter 17), and so on that exist in other drawings. I cover the DesignCenter in more detail in Chapter 26, but here I explain how to import layers and linetypes from another drawing.

 To open the DesignCenter, shown in Figure 11.22, press Ctrl+2, or choose View tab ⇨ Palettes panel ⇨ DesignCenter. The DesignCenter's left pane works like the Windows Explorer left pane, letting you navigate throughout your hard drive or your network. (If you don't see the left pane, click the Tree View Toggle button on the DesignCenter's toolbar.) If the DesignCenter shows only open drawings, click Desktop on the toolbar and navigate to the desired folder. After you click a folder, the drawings in that folder are listed on the right side. Choose Large Icons from the Views drop-down list to see a small preview of each item. To access layers and linetypes, either double-click a drawing icon or click its plus sign. Now you see the various definition categories in the right pane. To see the list of the layers or linetypes, double-click the layers or linetypes icon in either the left or right pane. To import a layer or linetype, double-click the layer or linetype's icon to bring the layer or linetype definition into your drawing. Click the Layer or Linetype drop-down list to check it out. Click the DesignCenter's Close button to close the DesignCenter.

FIGURE 11.22

The DesignCenter lets you locate definitions that are contained in other drawings and import them into your current drawing.

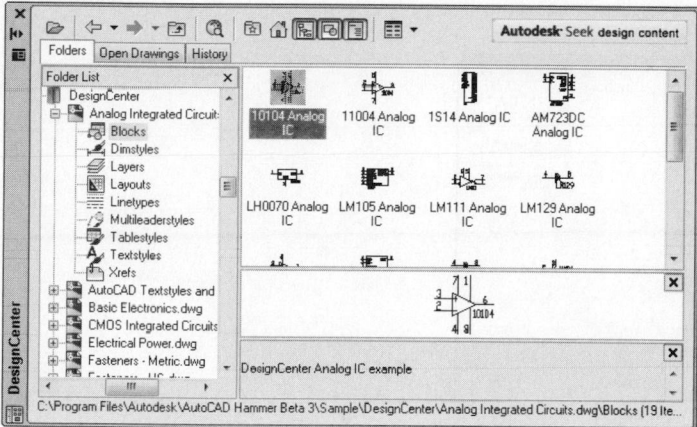

Cross-Reference

AutoCAD enables you to translate layers. For example, you can specify that all objects on layer dashed be changed to the layer hidden. Use this feature to maintain layer standards that you have set up. Chapter 26 fully covers layer translating. This feature is not available in AutoCAD LT. ■

Matching Properties

You may be familiar with the Format Painter button available in many Windows applications. AutoCAD and AutoCAD LT offer something similar that at the same time enables you to specify which properties you want to match. AutoCAD calls this process *matching properties*.

An object can have so many properties that this can be a useful tool. To match properties, you need two objects, a source object and a destination object (or objects). Follow these steps to match properties:

1. Choose Home tab ⇨ Clipboard panel ⇨ Match Properties. You see a Format Painter cursor with a pickbox. On the command line, you see the Select source object: prompt.

2. Choose the object whose properties you want to match (the source object).

Tip

You can choose the source object first and then start the command. ■

3. Then you see the Select destination object(s) or [Settings]: prompt. If you want to match all the object's properties, select the object(s) that you want to receive the matching properties, that is, the destination object(s).

4. If you want to match only some of the object's properties, right-click and choose Settings to open the Property Settings dialog box, as shown in Figure 11.23. Uncheck all the properties that you don't want to match and click OK. The previous prompt returns. Select the object(s) that you want to receive the matching properties, that is, the destination objects(s).

5. Press Enter to end object selection and match the properties.

FIGURE 11.23

The Property Settings dialog box.

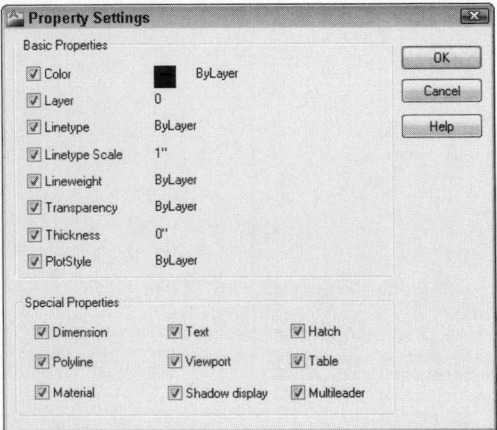

Summary

In this chapter, you read all about layers, colors, linetypes, and lineweights. You learned about:

- Using layers to help you organize your drawings by assigning the same properties to related objects
- Creating a layer by giving it a name, color, linetype, lineweight, and transparency in the Layer Properties Manager
- Changing the layer of existing objects
- Setting layer states — On/Off, Thawed/Frozen, Unlocked/Locked, and Plottable/Not Plottable
- Changing the properties of existing layers
- Saving sets of layer states and properties and later restoring them
- Filtering the layer listing
- Purging unused layers and linetypes
- Altering the color, linetype, lineweight, and transparency of any object
- Globally changing the linetype scale, changing the current linetype scale, and changing the object linetype scale of existing objects
- Using the DesignCenter to import layers and linetypes from other drawings
- Utilizing the Match Properties feature to copy properties from one object to one or more destination objects

The next chapter explains how to get detailed information from your drawing.

Obtaining Information from Your Drawing

Y our drawing is intelligent in many ways. For example, several commands can give you the details of each object. In addition, you can view listings that provide information about your drawing as a whole. You can also list system variables, which I've mentioned previously in this book, along with their current settings.

You can perform calculations on objects that may assist you in certain drawing tasks. For example, you can divide an object into any number of segments by placing point objects along the object, or you can place point objects at a specified distance along the object. You can use AutoCAD's calculator, which not only does regular numerical calculations but also works with coordinates and geometric points on objects. This chapter shows you how to discover the hidden data in your drawing.

Drawing-Level Information

Some information applies to the drawing as a whole or even to your computer system as a whole, rather than to individual objects. This information can be important when there is a problem or when you simply need to find the status of system variables.

Listing the status of your drawing

The STATUS command is available only in AutoCAD and provides a standard list of information that can be very helpful. The most common use for STATUS is to troubleshoot problems. You can send the listing to a colleague in another office who needs to work on the same drawing. Your colleague can then work more easily by using the same settings that you have used. Enter **status** ↵ on the command line. Figure 12.1 shows a sample status listing.

FIGURE 12.1

A sample listing from the STATUS command.

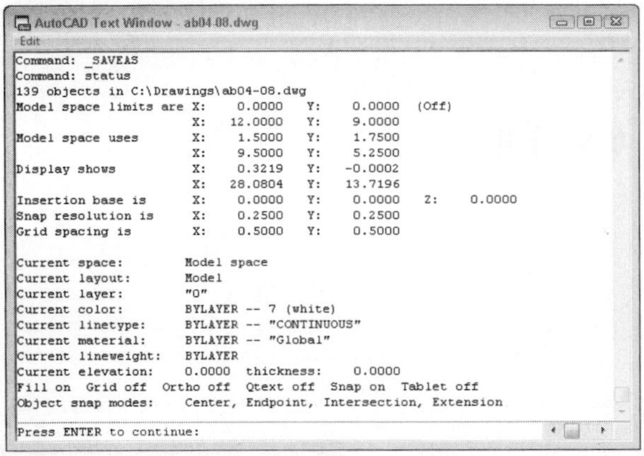

```
AutoCAD Text Window - ab04-08.dwg

Edit
Command: _SAVEAS
Command: status
139 objects in C:\Drawings\ab04-08.dwg
Model space limits are X:    0.0000   Y:    0.0000   (Off)
                       X:   12.0000   Y:    9.0000
Model space uses       X:    1.5000   Y:    1.7500
                       X:    9.5000   Y:    5.2500
Display shows          X:    0.3219   Y:   -0.0002
                       X:   28.0804   Y:   13.7196
Insertion base is      X:    0.0000   Y:    0.0000   Z:    0.0000
Snap resolution is     X:    0.2500   Y:    0.2500
Grid spacing is        X:    0.5000   Y:    0.5000

Current space:         Model space
Current layout:        Model
Current layer:         "0"
Current color:         BYLAYER -- 7 (white)
Current linetype:      BYLAYER -- "CONTINUOUS"
Current material:      BYLAYER -- "Global"
Current lineweight:    BYLAYER
Current elevation:     0.0000   thickness:    0.0000
Fill on  Grid off  Ortho off  Qtext off  Snap on  Tablet off
Object snap modes:     Center, Endpoint, Intersection, Extension

Press ENTER to continue:
```

The command lists the number of objects in your drawing, followed by the limits and extents of the drawing, and the extents of the current display on your screen. Other items are the snap and grid spacing as well as the current layer, color, linetype, and lineweight.

Obviously, much of this information is available without using the STATUS command. The easiest items to find are the current layer, color, linetype, and lineweight, which are visible in the Layers and Properties panels on the Home tab of the Ribbon. However, you would have to use a number of commands to obtain other information such as the snap and grid spacing and the drawing limits. STATUS puts it all together in one listing.

Listing system variables

The SETVAR command provides a listing of all the system variables and their settings. It may be quicker to view system-variable settings by using the SETVAR command than by typing each individual system variable on the command line. For more information about how AutoCAD and AutoCAD LT store settings in system variables, see Chapter 5.

Too many system variables exist to show the entire listing here, but a few can convey the wealth of information that is available, as shown in Figure 12.2.

Note

Read-only system variables are for information only and cannot be changed. An example is LOGINNAME (AutoCAD only), which shows the name of the current user who is registered on the system. Other system variables can be changed. ■

Although some system variables allow a variety of values, many are either on or off. In general, a setting of 1 means on and 0 means off.

You can set most system variables in a dialog box. For example, in Chapter 11 you set the LTSCALE system variable in the Linetype Manager. However, some system variables are available only by typing them on the command line.

FIGURE 12.2

A partial SETVAR listing.

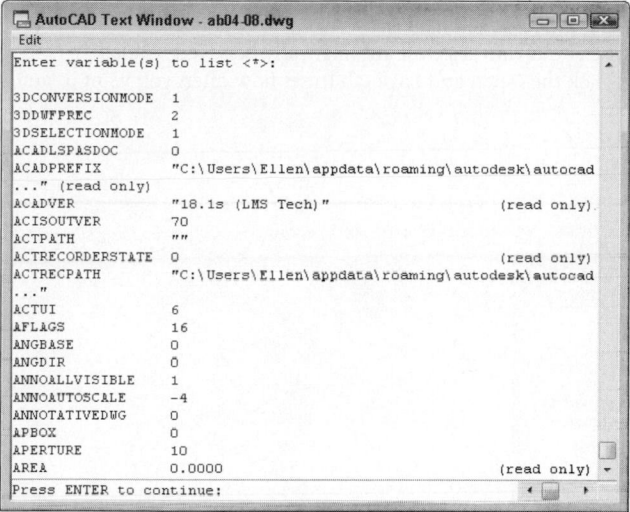

You can use SETVAR to set system variables that are not read-only, as well as to list them. To list the system variables, enter **setvar** ↵ on the command line. At the Enter variable name or [?]: prompt, type ? ↵. At the Enter variable(s) to list <*>: prompt, press Enter to list all the system variables, or type the name of a variable. (You can use the * and ? wildcards in the name.) The command either lists all the system variables or just the variable you typed.

If you type a variable, the command prompts you for a new value so that you can change it. For example, if you type **celtscale** ↵, you see the Enter new value for CELTSCALE <1.0000>: prompt. You can then change the system variable by typing in a new value. You can also press Enter to accept the current setting.

Tracking drawing time

You can track the time you spend working on a drawing. This feature is most often used for billing time to clients, or when your boss wants to see how much you're accomplishing.

Cross-Reference

Chapter 17 covers the PLOTSTAMP command, which can optionally make a log file of plotting activity. Chapter 26 explains how to keep a log file of your overall drawing activity. ∎

 To use the TIME command, enter **time** ↵ on the command line. A typical listing is shown in Figure 12.3.

The following explains the listing that you see when using the TIME command:

- **Current time.** The current date and time. The time is displayed to the nearest millisecond.
- **Created.** The date and time when the drawing was created.
- **Last updated.** The date and time of the last save of the drawing.

- **Total editing time.** Accumulates the time spent in the drawing from session to session, not including plotting time or time that you worked on the drawing and quit without saving your changes.

- **Elapsed timer.** Also accumulates time spent in the drawing, although you can turn this feature on and off and reset it.

- **Next automatic save in.** Shows when your drawing will automatically be saved. Choose Application Button ⇨ Options and click the Open and Save tab to set how often you want to automatically save your drawing.

FIGURE 12.3

A typical TIME listing.

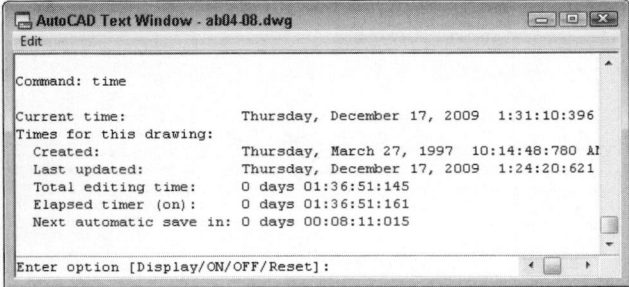

You can think of total editing time as your car's odometer, and elapsed time as a timer that is similar to a trip meter that some cars have to enable you to time a specific trip.

At the end of the listing, you see the `Enter option [Display/ON/OFF/Reset]:` prompt. The Display option re-displays the listing with updated times. ON and OFF turn the elapsed time on and off. The Reset option resets the elapsed time to zero.

AutoCAD Only

The Express Tools contain a tool called EDITTIME (enter edittime ↵ on the command line) that tracks active editing time. ∎

On the DVD

The drawing used in the following exercise on obtaining drawing information, `ab12-a.dwg`, is in the `Drawings` folder on the DVD. ∎

STEPS: Obtaining Drawing Information

1. Open `ab12-a.dwg` from the DVD.

2. If you are using AutoCAD LT, skip to Step 3. Type **status** ↵ on the command line. Look at the listing to see how many objects it contains. Check the limits of the drawing. Look at the grid spacing. Read through any other items that interest you.

3. Type **setvar** ↵ on the command line if you are using AutoCAD LT. At the `Enter variable name or [?]:` prompt, type ? ↵. At the `Enter variable(s) to list <*>:` prompt, press Enter to accept the default. Look for the BLIPMODE setting. Check the location of the drawing (DWGPREFIX). Look for the global linetype scale (LTSCALE). Press Enter until you see the `Command:` prompt again.

4. Press Enter to start the SETVAR command again. At the `Enter variable name or [?]:` prompt, type **ltscale** ⏎. Type **50** ⏎ to change the linetype scale. Type **regen** ⏎. The noncontinuous linetypes should now show up more clearly.

5. Type **time** ⏎ on the command line. Check the current time against your watch. The command takes the time from your computer's clock. Look at the total editing time to see the total time during which you have worked on the drawing. Press Enter to end the command.

6. Do not save this drawing. Leave the drawing open if you're going on to the next exercise.

Object-Level Information

Several commands and features exist solely to provide information about the objects in your drawing.

Listing objects

The LIST command displays information about selected objects. The information displayed depends on the object. For example, the LIST command gives you the radius of a circle and the length of a line.

 To list an object, choose Home tab ⇨ Properties panel ⇨ List, or type **list** ⏎ on the command line. Figure 12.4 shows a typical listing for a line.

FIGURE 12.4

A typical listing for a horizontal line.

```
Command: list
1 found

           LINE       Layer: "0"
                     Space: Model space
           Handle = 180
     from point, X=  10.7672  Y=   9.3826  Z=   0.0000
       to point, X=  23.0172  Y=   9.3826  Z=   0.0000
  Length =  12.2500,   Angle in XY Plane =      0
            Delta X =  12.2500, Delta Y =    0.0000, Delta Z =   0
```

Table 12.1 explains the information that you see when you list an object.

TABLE 12.1

LIST Command Information

Data	Comments
Layer	Lists the object's layer. If any of the properties, such as the color, linetype, lineweight, or transparency, are not ByLayer or ByBlock, then AutoCAD lists these as well.
Space	Tells you whether the object is in model space or paper space. (Chapter 17 covers paper space.)
Handle	Every object in your drawing has a handle. Your drawing's internal database uses handles to keep track of objects.
From point	Because the example in Figure 12.4 lists a line, it shows the start point.
To point	The endpoint of the line.

continued

TABLE 12.1 *(continued)*	
Data	**Comments**
Length	The line's length.
Angle in XY Plane	The line's angle. This line is horizontal, and so its angle is zero.
Delta X	The change in the X coordinate from the start point to the endpoint.
Delta Y	The change in the Y coordinate from the start point to the endpoint.
Delta Z	The change in the Z coordinate from the start point to the endpoint.

The Layer drop-down list in the Layers panel and drop-down lists in the Properties panel make it easy to tell an object's layer, color, linetype, lineweight, and transparency. Later in this chapter, I explain how you can use the Properties palette and Quick Properties panel to see most of the same information, plus other information; you can also use them to change the information.

Finding coordinates

 You can find the coordinate of any point. Choose Home tab ⇨ Utilities panel (expanded) ⇨ ID Point. The ID command prompts you for a point. You can use any means of specifying a point, although object snaps or snap mode are useful. Here is a typical listing:

```
X = 61' -5 1/8" Y = 32' -4 5/8" Z = 0' -0"
```

Caution

If you're working in 3D, be aware that if you check the Replace Z Value with Current Elevation check box on the Drafting tab of the Options dialog box, you may get inaccurate results when you pick points for the ID and DIST commands. For more information on this option, see Chapter 21, where I discuss 3D coordinates. ■

Measuring objects

The MEASUREGEOM command measures distance, radius, angle, area, and volume. You can use this information to check dimensions (covered in Chapter 14) or to make calculations that you need for drawing. To start the MEASUREGEOM command, choose Home tab ⇨ Utilities panel ⇨ Measuregeom drop-down list. Then choose the option that you want. Note that the last-used option displays on top and you have to click the drop-down list to access the other options.

Note

MEASUREGEOM takes the place of the AREA, DIST, and MASSPROP commands of releases before AutoCAD 2010, and adds ways to easily measure radii and angles. ■

Here's how to use the options:

 • **Distance.** Specify two points. The result shows you the distance, angle in the XY plane, angle from the XY plane (for 3D models), and the delta (change) of X, Y, and Z coordinates.

 • **Radius.** Select an arc or circle. The result shows you the radius and diameter.

- **Angle.** Select an arc, circle, or line, or press Enter to specify the vertex of the angle. If you select an arc, the result immediately shows you its included angle. If you select a circle, do so by specifying the first point of the desired angle, and then specify the second angle endpoint. If you select a line, then select a second line.

- **Area.** Specify the first corner point and then subsequent points, in a roundabout manner (not diagonally opposing corners) and press Enter to get the total. Or, use the Object suboption to select an object. You can also use the Add Area suboption to keep a running total, and the Subtract Area suboptions to remove areas, until you get just the combination of areas that you want. The Arc suboption lets you find the area of an arc, assuming that the two endpoints are joined by a line. In addition to the area, the Area option returns the perimeter for closed areas, the length for open areas, and the circumference for circles. You can't calculate the area of an arc.

- **Volume.** Specify the first corner point and then subsequent points, in a roundabout manner (not diagonally opposing corners), all on the XY plane, and press Enter to get the total. Then enter a height. Or, use the Object suboption to select an object. (You can select a 2D object and specify a height.) You can also use the Add Volume suboption to keep a running total, and the Subtract Volume suboptions to remove volumes, until you get just the combination of volumes that you want.

You can use any means of specifying the necessary points, but remember that object snaps or snap mode are useful for accuracy. Here is a typical display for a vertical line:

```
Distance = 5.7500,   Angle in XY Plane = 0,   Angle from XY Plane = 0
Delta X = 5.7500,   Delta Y = 0.0000,   Delta Z = 0.0000
```

After using an option, type **x ↵** to end the command, or choose another option.

Note

The precision set in the Drawing Units dialog box (Application Button ⇨ Drawing Utilities ⇨ Units) affects the results of the LIST and MEASUREGEOM commands. See Chapter 5 for more information on the Drawing Units dialog box. ■

You can also use the BOUNDARY command to create one polyline or region from a complex area. (Chapter 16 covers boundaries and polylines.) You can then use the MEASUREGEOM's Area option and its Object suboption instead of picking points.

On the DVD

The drawing used in the following exercise on using the MEASUREGEOM command, ab12-a.dwg, is in the Drawings folder on the DVD. ■

STEPS: Measuring Geometry

1. Open ab12-a.dwg from the DVD if it isn't already open from the previous exercise.

2. On the Navigation bar, click the Zoom button's drop-down list and choose Zoom Window. Define a window to zoom in on the parcels of land labeled D and E, as shown in Figure 12.5. Object Snap should be on with a running object snap for Endpoint.

3. Choose Home tab ⇨ Properties panel ⇨ List. At the Select objects: prompt, pick ❶, shown in Figure 12.5. Press Enter to end object selection. Note the surveyor's units.

FIGURE 12.5

The MEASUREGEOM command can calculate properties of the objects that make up the land parcels.

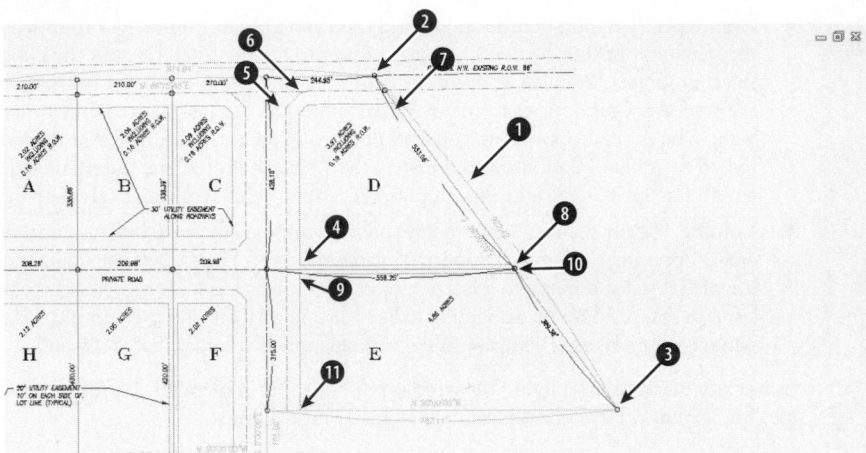

Thanks to Bill Maidment of Caltech, Inc., Fairfield, Iowa, for this drawing.

4. Choose Home tab ⇨ Utilities panel ⇨ MEASUREGEOM drop-down list ⇨ Distance. At the `Specify first point:` prompt, choose the endpoint at ❷, shown in Figure 12.5, using the Endpoint running object snap. At the `Specify second point:` prompt, choose the endpoint at ❸. Type **x** ↵ to end the command. Here's the result:

```
Distance = 922.42,  Angle in XY Plane = S 36d0'0" E,  Angle from XY
   Plane = E
Delta X = 542.18,  Delta Y = -746.25,  Delta Z = 0.00
```

5. Choose Home tab ⇨ Utilities panel (expanded) ⇨ ID Point. At the `Specify point:` prompt, pick the endpoint at ❹. Here is the result:

```
X = 6065.67      Y = 3775.58      Z = 0.00
```

6. Choose Home tab ⇨ Utilities panel ⇨ MEASUREGEOM drop-down list ⇨ Area. At the `Specify first corner point or [Object/Add area/Subtract area/eXit] <Object>:` prompt, right-click and choose Add Area to start Add mode. At the `Specify first corner point or [Object/Subtract area/eXit]:` prompt, pick ❹, by using the Endpoint running object snap. At the `(ADD mode) Specify next point or [Arc/Length/Undo]:` prompt, continue to pick ❺, ❻, ❼, and ❽. Press Enter. The command line lists the area and perimeter. (Your figures may be different if you picked different points.)

```
Area = 123575.16, Perimeter = 1480.17
Total area = 123575.16
```

7. At the `Specify first corner point or [Object/Subtract area/eXit]:` prompt, pick ❾. At the `(ADD mode) Specify next point or [Arc/Length/Undo]:` prompt, pick ❿, ❸, and ⓫. Press Enter to complete the point selection. The command line reports the area and perimeter of the second area and adds the two areas together to give you the total area. Type **x** ↵ twice to end the command.

```
Area = 183399.88, Perimeter = 1884.62
Total area = 306975.04
```

8. Do not save the drawing. Keep it open if you're continuing to the next exercise.

Note

The MASSPROP command is mostly used for 3D drawings, but it can also be used on regions, which are 2D solid surfaces, such as a shape cut from sheet metal. This command provides area and perimeter but also other engineering calculations, such as centroids, moments of inertia, the product of inertia, and so on. Chapter 24 covers this command further. ■

Getting information from the Properties palette

You can also obtain information about an object by selecting it and opening the Properties palette. Choose Home tab ➪ Properties panel and click the dialog box launcher on the panel's title, or press Ctrl+1. In Chapter 11, I discuss using this Properties palette to change layer, color, linetype, and lineweight properties. As you can see in Figure 12.6, the palette also lists the line's start and endpoints; delta (change) in X, Y, and Z; length; and angle — much like the LIST command. However, you can change the start and endpoints directly in the palette.

FIGURE 12.6

The Properties palette lists information about a selected object.

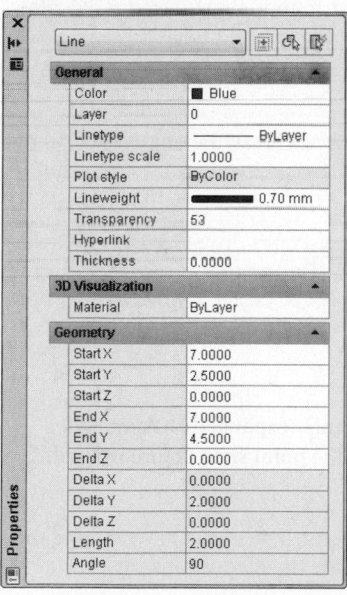

Getting information from the Quick Properties panel

The Quick Properties panel appears by default whenever you select an object, and it contains a smaller set of information about the object than the Properties palette. Like the Properties palette, you can change the properties. Figure 12.7 shows the Quick Properties panel for a line.

FIGURE 12.7

The Quick Properties panel pops up when you select an object and displays editable properties for that object.

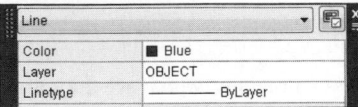

Click the Quick Properties button on the status bar to turn off the Quick Properties panel. You can customize what properties appear on the Quick Properties panel. For more information, see Chapter 29.

On the DVD

The DVD contains three routines that provide information about your objects. Linesum **provides the total length of selected lines.** Arcsum **adds the lengths of selected arcs.** Polydis **provides the length of a selected polyline. Look in the** Software\Chapter 12 **folder.** ■

Dividing and Spacing Commands

The DIVIDE command divides an object into equally spaced sections. The MEASURE command divides an object into sections of a specified length. These commands are useful in many fields. For example, you may need to space bolt holes evenly around the edge of a bushing, or place fence studs along the edge of a plot every 5 feet.

Dividing objects

The DIVIDE command divides an object into equal sections. DIVIDE does not break the object — it simply places point objects along the selected object. You can use the Node object snap if you want to draw from those points.

 To divide an object, choose Home tab ⇨ Draw panel (expanded) ⇨ Multiple Points drop-down list ⇨ Divide. Select the object that you want to divide. The command responds with the Enter the number of segments or [Block]: prompt. Enter the number of segments that you want to create. AutoCAD places the point objects and ends the command.

Note

Remember that you can set the point display by choosing Home tab ⇨ Utilities panel (expanded) ⇨ Point Style. An easy-to-see point style is especially useful for the DIVIDE command. Specify the point style before using the command. ■

For example, to create eight segments, you need to place seven point objects. If you have in your mind the number of point objects that you want, simply add one when specifying the number of segments.

You can use the Block option to place a block of your choice along the object rather than a point object. The block must exist in your drawing. (Chapter 18 covers blocks.) If you choose the Block option (right-click and choose Block), the option responds with the Enter name of block to insert: prompt. Type the name of the block. The prompt asks, Align block with object? [Yes/No] <Y>. Answer Y or N, depending on whether you want to align the block with the angle of the object.

Figure 12.8 shows an electrical schematic. Here you want to divide a line so that you can evenly space wires entering the ignition module. Four wires need to come in so that the line is divided into five segments by an easy-to-see point object.

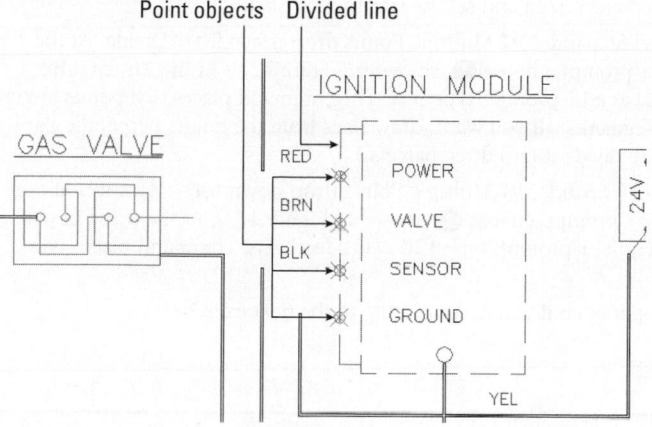

FIGURE 12.8

Dividing a line into five segments by using point objects.

Thanks to Robert Mack of the Dexter Company, Fairfield, Iowa, for this drawing.

You can practice using the DIVIDE command after the next section.

Measuring objects

The MEASURE command is similar to the DIVIDE command, except that you specify the distance between point objects rather than the total number of segments. The command starts measuring from the endpoint closest to where you pick the object. MEASURE does not break the object — it simply places point objects along the object. You can use the Node object snap if you want to draw from those points.

 To measure an object, choose Home tab ⇨ Draw panel (expanded) ⇨ Multiple Points drop-down list ⇨ Measure. Select the object that you want to measure. The command responds with the `Specify length of segment or [Block]:` prompt. Type the segment length where you want to place the point objects and end the command.

Remember that you can set the point display by choosing Home tab ⇨ Utilities panel (expanded) ⇨ Point Style. An easy-to-see point style is especially useful for the MEASURE command. Specify the point style *before* using the command.

As with the DIVIDE command, you can place a block along the object by using the Block option, as long as the block exists in your drawing. The option prompts you for the name of the block and lets you choose whether you want to align the block with the object. The prompt asks for the segment length, and you type in the lengths between the points, as described earlier.

On the DVD

The drawing in the following exercise on using the DIVIDE and MEASURE commands, `ab12-a.dwg`, is in the Drawings folder on the DVD. ∎

STEPS: Using the DIVIDE and MEASURE Commands

1. Open `ab12-a.dwg` from the DVD if it isn't already open from the previous exercise.

2. If you didn't do the previous exercise, on the Navigation bar, click the Zoom button's drop-down list and choose Zoom Window. Specify a window to zoom in to the parcels labeled D and E, as shown in Figure 12.9.

3. Choose Home tab ➪ Utilities panel (expanded) ➪ Point Style and choose the fourth style in the first row. Choose Set Size Relative to Screen and set the size to 5%. Click OK.

4. Choose Home tab ➪ Draw panel (expanded) ➪ Multiple Points drop-down list ➪ Divide. At the `Select object to divide:` prompt, choose ❶, shown in Figure 12.9. At the `Enter the number of segments or [Block]:` prompt, type **3 ↵**. The command places two points along the line, dividing it into three segments. (If you want, draw lines from the points perpendicular to the opposite side of the parcel to divide it into three parcels.)

5. Choose Home tab ➪ Draw panel (expanded) ➪ Multiple Points drop-down list ➪ Measure. At the `Select object to measure:` prompt, choose ❷, shown in Figure 12.9. At the `Specify length of segment or [Block]:` prompt, type **120 ↵** (10 feet). The command places two points along the line.

6. Do not save your drawing. Keep it open if you're continuing to the next exercise.

FIGURE 12.9

The site plan zoomed in to parcels D and E.

AutoCAD's Calculator

To start the calculator, choose Home tab ➪ Utilities panel ➪ Quick Calculator or press Ctrl+8 to start the QUICKCALC command. The calculator opens as a palette. Use the palette for stand-alone calculations, as you would use a physical hand-held calculator. To start the calculator within a command, type **'quickcalc** or **'qc ↵** on the command line. When you start the calculator transparently, it appears as a window, rather than as a palette, as shown in Figure 12.10. Note that if you have the palette version of QuickCalc open when you use QuickCalc transparently, the palette temporarily closes until you finish the calculation. In other words, you can only use one format of QuickCalc at a time.

Note

The CAL command, which is the command-line calculator available in earlier releases of AutoCAD only, still exists. In fact, it's available in AutoCAD LT as well. ■

FIGURE 12.10

The graphical calculator looks similar to a hand-held calculator.

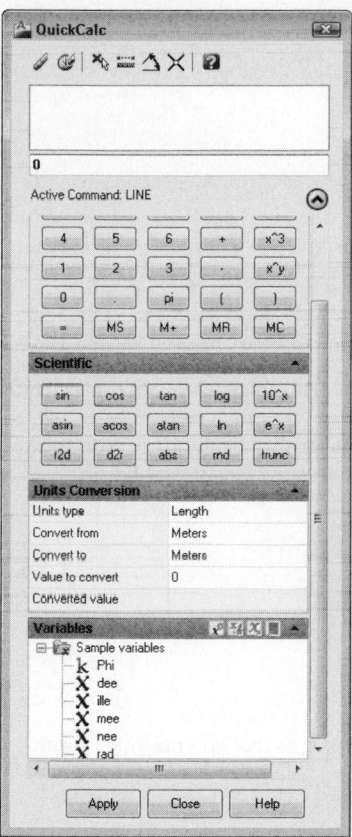

Tip

Press the Num Lock key on your keyboard and use your numerical pad to enter numbers into the calculator. ■

The History area stores previous calculations. You can reuse History area data by double-clicking the expression or the result that you want. This places the data in the input area. First be sure to clear the input area of current data, if you don't want to keep it.

Calculating numbers

Calculating numbers is straightforward and uses standard rules of precedence. For example, if you type **3*(2+3)/5-1** ↵, the calculator displays the answer, 2. Because the 2+3 sum is in parentheses, it is calculated first so that the expression multiplies 3 by 5 (which is 15), divides it by 5 (which is 3), and subtracts 1 (which is 2). After any calculation, you can either press Enter or click QuickCalc's = button.

Let's say that you want to draw a horizontal line. You know it has to be the total of two other lines whose length you know. Follow these steps:

1. Start the LINE command.

    ```
    Specify first point: Pick the start point for the line.
    Specify next point or [Undo]: Type 'quickcalc ↵ (The QuickCalc window
        opens.)
    ```

2. Press the Num Lock key.

3. In the Input area of the QuickCalc window, delete the 0.

4. Type **3.953+6.8725** ↵.

5. Click the Apply button at the bottom of the calculator. The QuickCalc window disappears and the sum appears on the command line.

6. Move the cursor to the right so that you can use Direct Distance Entry to draw at a zero-degree angle.

7. Press Enter to draw the line segment.

8. Continue the LINE command or press Enter to end the command.

You can use feet and inches as well. Use the format 6'5" or 6'-5". Don't put any spaces between the feet and inches. With the calculator, all inches must be marked with a double prime ("), unlike regular AutoCAD command-line usage. Note that your drawing must use architectural units for this technique to work properly. (For more information on using feet and inches, see the sidebar "Subtracting feet and inches in QuickCalc.")

The QuickCalc toolbar has several buttons that are shortcuts for often-used tasks:

*   Get Coordinates
*   Distance Between Two Points
*   Angle of Line Defined by Two Points
*   Intersection of Two Lines Defined by Four Points

In each case, you are returned to the drawing area to specify the point or points that you need. For example, to draw a line the same length as another line, follow these steps:

1. Start the line.

2. Start QuickCalc transparently.

3. Click the Distance Between Two Points button on the QuickCalc toolbar.

4. You then return to your drawing where you can specify two points by using any method, such as object snaps.

5. Back in QuickCalc, you see the distance in the Input area. Click Apply to paste this number into the command line.

6. Move the cursor in the direction that you want to draw, and press Enter to draw the line.

Subtracting feet and inches in QuickCalc

If you type the expression **3'2-1/2"**, AutoCAD converts it to 3'-2-1/2", adding a hyphen between the feet and inches.

However, if 3'2" is the same as 3'–2", then how do you subtract 2" from 3'?

The solution is to put parentheses around the 3 feet so that AutoCAD doesn't assume that the next expression is part of the same feet-inches expression, as shown here:

```
(3')-2"
```

The result is 2'-10". In this expression, AutoCAD subtracts 2" from 36" (3 feet).

Using coordinates

You can use coordinates in QuickCalc expressions. Coordinates are enclosed in square brackets. For example, if you want to draw a line that is equal to the length of two other objects in your drawing that you happen to know are 3.953 and 6.8725 units long, and you want the line to be at a 20-degree angle, then you can follow these steps:

1. Start the LINE command.
2. At the `Specify first point:` prompt, specify your first point.
3. At the `Specify next point or [Undo]:` prompt, type **'quickcalc**.
4. In the calculator input box, type **[@(3.953+6.8725)<20]** ↵. Note that the calculator converts your expression to absolute coordinates.
5. Click the Apply button at the bottom of the calculator. AutoCAD draws the line segment.

Using object snaps

To draw a line to the center of the triangle, follow these steps:

1. Start the LINE command.
2. At the `Specify first point:` prompt, pick any start point.
3. At the `Specify next point or [Undo]:` prompt, type **'quickcalc** ↵.
4. In the QuickCalc input box, type **(end+end+end)/3** ↵. The QuickCalc window disappears, and you see a pickbox.
5. Pick the three corners of the triangle in succession. The QuickCalc window reappears with a coordinate in the Input box.
6. Click Apply to draw the line.

You can use QuickCalc as a substitute for the From object snap. For example, at the `Specify first point:` prompt, you can start QuickCalc transparently and type **mid+[3,–2.5]** ↵ in the Input box. AutoCAD prompts you for the object for which you want the midpoint. Click Apply to start the line (3,–2.5) units from there.

Using the scientific calculator

QuickCalc has its own scientific calculator, which you can use to calculate advanced formulas. Table 12.2 lists these functions.

TABLE 12.2

CAL Mathematical Functions

Function	What It Does
sin(angle)	Calculates the sine of the angle
Cos(angle)	Calculates the cosine of the angle
Tan(angle)	Calculates the tangent of the angle
asin(real)	Calculates the arc sine of the real number
acos(real)	Calculates the arc cosine of the real number
atan(real)	Calculates the arc tangent of the real number
ln(real)	Calculates the natural log of the real number
Log(real)	Calculates the base-10 log of the real number
Exp(real)	Calculates the natural exponent of the real number
Exp10(real)	Calculates the base-10 exponent of the real number
Abs(real)	Calculates the absolute value of the real number (the number not including its + or – sign); this function is also used to calculate lengths
Rnd(real)	Rounds the number to its nearest integer
trunc(real)	Truncates any decimal value leaving only the integer
r2d(angle)	Converts radian angles to degrees
d2r(angle)	Converts degree angles to radians

Converting units

You can use the Units Conversion section of QuickCalc to convert units of length, area, volume, and angular measurements. For example, you can convert acres to square feet or meters to inches. Follow these steps:

1. If necessary, click the down arrow to expand the Units Conversion section of QuickCalc.
2. From the Units Type drop-down list, choose the type of units that you want to convert.
3. From the Convert From drop-down list, choose the unit with which you want to start.
4. From the Convert To drop-down list, choose the unit to which you want to convert.
5. In the Value to Convert text box, type the value that you want to convert, and press Enter.

 6. To use this value on the command line, click the value that you entered, and then click the Return Conversion to Calculator Input Area button. Then click the Paste Value to Command Line button on the calculator's toolbar.

Working with QuickCalc variables

QuickCalc comes with some variables that you can use as part of calculated expressions. These include functions and one constant — the so-called Golden Ratio or Golden Number, Phi. Table 12.3 lists the functions and what they do.

TABLE 12.3

Special CAL Functions

Function Name	Full Function	What It Does
Rad		Gets the radius of the selected object.
Dee	dist(end,end)	Calculates the distance between two points; you can also use the Distance Between Two Points button on the QuickCalc toolbar.
Ille	ill(end,end,end,end)	Calculates the intersection of two lines based on their four endpoints; you can also use the Intersection of Two Lines Defined by Four Points button on the QuickCalc toolbar.
mee	(end+end)/2	Calculates the midpoint between two endpoints.
Nee	nor(end,end)	Calculates a one-unit vector in the XY plane that is normal (perpendicular) to two endpoints.
Vee	vec(end,end)	Calculates a vector from two endpoints.
Vee1	vec1(end,end)	Calculates a one-unit vector from two endpoints.

To use these functions, follow these steps:

1. Start a command.
2. At the prompt where you need the function, type '**quickcalc**. The QuickCalc window opens.
3. From the Variables list, double-click the function that you want to place in the Input box of the QuickCalc window.
4. Press Enter. You return to your drawing and see a pickbox cursor.
5. Pick the required points, most commonly by object snaps. The QuickCalc window returns, and you see an absolute coordinate in the Input box.
6. Click the Apply button.
7. Continue the command.

Note

A vector is a direction that is expressed as delta X, delta Y, delta Z. For example, using the vee function on a horizontal line that is 4 units long results in a vector direction of 4,0,0. ■

Tip

When you click a function, you see a tooltip giving you the full format of the function. The full formats are in the Full Function column of Table 12.3. You can create your own functions. For example, to find the midpoint between two nodes (rather than two endpoints), you would use (nod+nod)/2. You can save your functions by clicking the New Variable button at the top of the Variables section. The Variable Definition dialog box opens, where you can define and save the variable. ■

Using QuickCalc in the Properties palette

QuickCalc is also available in the Properties palette, where you can use it to calculate values that represent properties of objects, such as the X coordinate of the start point of a line. You can even use QuickCalc like the CHANGE command to specify a new start point for a line, using the Get Coordinate button.

To change an object's property in the Properties palette, follow these steps:

1. Select the object.

2. Display the Properties palette. (Press Ctrl+1 or choose Home tab ⇨ Properties panel and click the panel's dialog box launcher.)

3. Click any value in a white text box. (Gray boxes are not editable.)

4. Click the QuickCalc icon to the right of the value. QuickCalc opens with the current value in the Input box.

5. Delete the value and enter any mathematical expression.

6. Click Apply to change the object. The new value also appears in the Properties palette.

Tip

For simple calculations, you don't need to use QuickCalc. When set to 1 (the default), the CALCINPUT system variable allows you to type expressions into any text box that can take a value, including the Properties palette. Start the expression with the equal sign (=) and press Alt+Enter on your keyboard at the end of the expression. For example, you could enter =1/16+1/8 to change the thickness of an object. You can even enter =sqrt(8) to obtain the square root of 8, or enter =2^3 to obtain the cube of 2! Don't forget to press Alt+Enter after you enter the expression. ■

On the DVD

The drawing used in the following exercise on using the QuickCalc command, ab12-a.dwg, is in the Drawings folder on the DVD. ■

STEPS: Using the QUICKCALC Command

1. Open ab12-a.dwg from the DVD if you don't have it open from the previous exercise.

2. Save the drawing as ab12-01.dwg in your AutoCAD Bible folder.

3. If you did not do the previous exercise, on the Navigation bar, click the Zoom button's drop-down list and choose Zoom Window. Specify a window to zoom in on the parcels labeled D and E, as shown in Figure 12.11.

4. In the exercise on calculating area earlier in this chapter, you calculated a total area of 306975.04, in square inches. To calculate this area in square feet, type **quickcalc** ↵. In the Units Conversion section, choose Area from the Units Type drop-down list. In the Convert From drop-down list, choose Square Inches. In the Convert To drop-down list, choose Square Feet. In the Value to Convert text box, type **306975.04** ↵. AutoCAD calculates 2131.77111.

 5. In the exercise on the DIVIDE command earlier in this chapter, you divided a line into three segments by placing two points on the line. To calculate the length of those segments, open QuickCalc. From the Variables section, choose the dee function and click the Return Variable to Input Area button. You see the expression dist(end,end) in the Input area. Click at the end of the expression and type /3 ↵. In your drawing, the command line prompts you for the two endpoints. Pick the two ends of the line at ④ in Figure 12.11. QuickCalc calculates 262.37.

6. Close the QuickCalc palette.

7. You may want to draw a line starting from the intersection of two intersecting lines, going from corner to diagonally opposite corner and ending perpendicular to the top line of the land parcel. To do this, start the LINE command. At the Specify first point: prompt, type 'quickcalc ↵.

FIGURE 12.11

Parcels D and E in the civil engineering drawing.

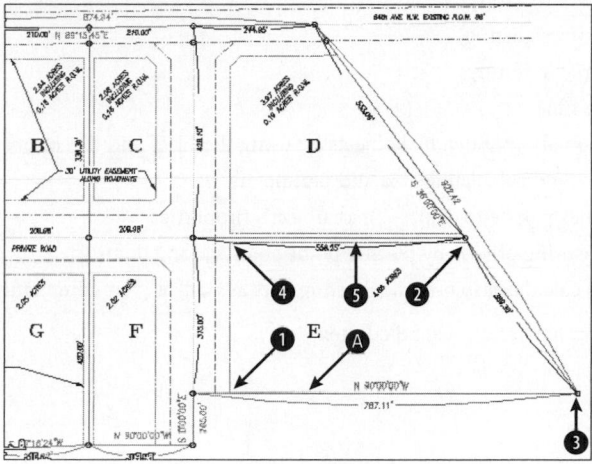

8. Click the Intersection of Two Lines Defined by Four Points button. Pick the endpoints shown in Figure 12.11 at ❶ and ❷ to define the first line, and then at ❸ and ❹ to define the second line. Click the Apply button. AutoCAD starts the line at the intersection of the two lines. At the `Specify next point or [Undo]:` prompt, choose the Perpendicular object snap and pick ❺. End the LINE command. Figure 12.12 shows the result.

9. Save your drawing.

FIGURE 12.12

You can use the QUICKCALC command to calculate the intersection of two lines without drawing the lines.

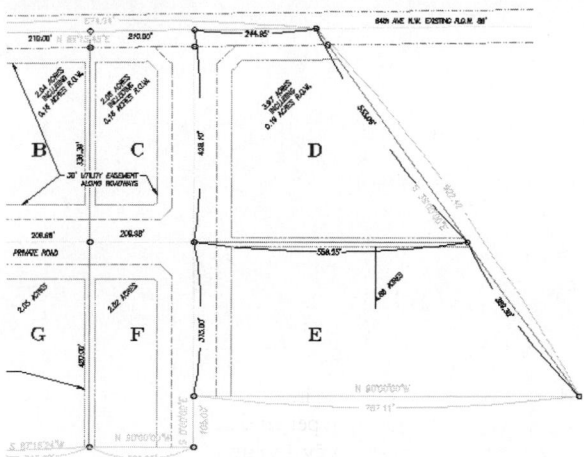

Summary

A great deal of information is available to you in each drawing. In this chapter you read about:

- Getting a general status listing
- Listing system variable settings
- Tracking drawing time
- Getting information about individual objects by using the LIST and ID commands
- Measuring objects, and calculating area and perimeters
- Using the Properties palette to display all an object's properties
- Dividing and measuring objects by placing point objects along them
- Using AutoCAD's calculator to use calculated results as part of your command input

In the next chapter, I explain how to create and edit text.

Creating Text

Every drawing includes text that labels or explains the objects in the drawing; this text is often called *annotation*. In each release, the capabilities of the text feature have improved so that you can now easily format and edit text to provide a professional appearance to your drawing. A wide range of font, alignment, and spacing options is available. You can also import text from a word processor. This chapter tells you all that you need to know about creating text in AutoCAD and AutoCAD LT.

Creating Single-Line Text

A great deal of text in a drawing consists of short labels or comments. Use single-line text when you want each line of text to be a separate object or when you're creating a small amount of text. Single-line text has fewer options than the multiline text that I explain later in this chapter, but it's easy to create and accurately place in a drawing.

It is very easy to create a single line of text by using the defaults, such as font and height. Choose Annotate tab ⇨ Text panel ⇨ Text drop-down list ⇨ Single Line. This starts the TEXT command.

Follow the prompts:

```
Current text style:  "Standard"  Text height:
   0.2000  Annotative:  No
Specify start point of text or [Justify/Style]:
   Pick a start point for the text.
Specify height <0.2000>: Type a height and press
   Enter, or just press Enter to accept the
   default.
Specify rotation angle of text <0>: Type a rotation
   angle and press Enter, or just press Enter to
   accept the default.
```

IN THIS CHAPTER

Creating and editing single-line text

Understanding text styles

Working with multiline (paragraph) text, including annotative text

Creating tables

Linking to data and extracting object data

Automating with fields

Managing text to improve performance

Using the FIND command

Checking spelling

> *You see a cursor at the insertion point. Type one line of text. Press*
> *Enter. You can continue to type more lines of text.*
> *Press Enter at a blank line to end the command. You can also click*
> *another location on the screen to start a new text object.*

Note

You cannot use the Return (usually the right) button of the mouse or the Spacebar to end the command. You can type -text on the command line to use the original TEXT behavior, which ends the command after one line of text. There is also a command called DTEXT which functions just like the TEXT command in recent releases of AutoCAD, but in earlier releases functioned differently. The 'D' in DTEXT stands for dynamic text, which allowed you to see the text in the drawing as you typed it. When working with script files, menus, or AutoLISP files; you must use the TEXT command (rather than the DTEXT command) for script files, menus, or AutoLISP routines. (See Parts VI and VII of this book for more information.) ■

The next section covers the Justify option. The Style option and the Annotative property are discussed later in this chapter.

One advantage of TEXT is that each line of text is a separate object, making it easy to move or copy individual lines of text. Unfortunately, you cannot control the spacing between the lines.

On the DVD

It (for the TEXT command) and Idt (for DTEXT) allow you to specify the spacing between lines of text as you create them. Look in \Software\Chapter 13\It. Txtstack, in \Software\Chapter 13\txtstack, adjusts spacing between lines of single-line text. You can use txt2mtxt to convert single-line text to multiline text. Look in \Software\Chapter 13\txt2mtxt. These programs work only in AutoCAD. (Thanks to Leonid Nemirovsky, http://home.pacifier.com/~nemi, for creating It.lsp and Idt.lsp at my request.) ■

TEXT remembers the location of the previous line of text even if you've used other commands in the meantime. To continue text below the last line of text that you have created, press Enter at the Specify start point of text or [Justify/Style]: prompt.

Justifying single-line text

When you pick a start point for text, the relationship between the start point and the actual letters is determined by the justification. The start point is also called the *insertion point*. When you want to refer to text by using object snaps, you use the Insertion object snap. If you select text without first choosing a command, grips appear at the insertion point as well as at the bottom-left corner.

By default, text is left-justified; therefore, there is no left justification option. To change the text's justification, right-click and choose Justify at the Specify start point of text or [Justify/Style]: prompt. The command responds with this bewildering prompt:

```
Enter an option [Align/Fit/Center/Middle/Right/TL/TC/TR/ML/MC/MR/BL/
    BC/BR]:
```

Align and Fit offer two ways to fit text into a specified space. Both respond with the same two prompts:

```
Specify first endpoint of text baseline:
Specify second endpoint of text baseline:
```

Specify the beginning and the end of the text line. Align then prompts you for the text and squeezes or stretches the text to fit within the text line. The height of the text changes accordingly, to maintain the proportions of the font.

Fit adds the `Specify height <0.2000>:` prompt. Type the height that you want and then type the text. Fit also squeezes or stretches the text to fit within the text line, but maintains the text height that you specified, distorting the font letters to fit the space. Figure 13.1 shows an example of normal, aligned, and fitted single-line text.

FIGURE 13.1

Normal (left-justified), aligned, and fitted text.

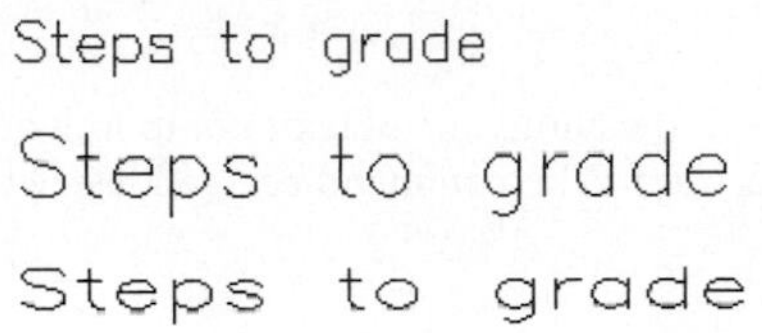

Steps to grade

Steps to grade

Steps to grade

Here is an explanation of the other justification options:

- **Center.** Text is centered around the insertion point. The insertion point is on the baseline.
- **Right.** Text is right-justified from the insertion point. The insertion point is on the baseline.
- **Middle.** Text is centered both vertically and horizontally. The vertical center point is measured from the bottom of the lowest to the top of the tallest possible letter.
- **TL, TC, TR (top-left, top-center, top-right).** The insertion point is at the top of the highest possible letter, and the text is left-, center-, or right-justified, respectively.
- **ML, MC, MR (middle-left, middle-center, middle-right).** Text is centered vertically. The vertical center point is measured from the bottom of the lowest to the top of the tallest possible letter. Text is left-, center-, or right-justified, respectively.
- **BL, BC, BR (bottom-left, bottom-center, bottom-right).** The insertion point is below the lowest descending letter. Text is left-, center-, or right-justified, respectively.

Tip

If you know the option abbreviation of the justification that you want, you can use it at the `Specify start point of text or [Justify/Style]:` **prompt.** ∎

Setting the height

Setting the height of text is fairly straightforward. The default is 0.2 units. The main point to consider is the scale factor. If you're drawing a house and plan to plot it at 1" = 8' (1 = 96), you need to figure out how big to make the text so that you can still read it when it is scaled down.

For example, if you want the text to be 0.2 units high and your scale factor is 96, your text needs to be 19.2 inches high (0.2 × 96). On the other hand, if you're drawing a very small object, such as a computer chip, and your scale is 0.10, then your text needs to be 0.02 inches high.

AutoCAD and AutoCAD LT calculate text height in units. Most word processors calculate text height in points. A point is $1/72$ of an inch. Therefore, 12-point text, a standard for most business letters, is about 0.17 inches high. The default of 0.2 units, if you're using inches as your unit, is just over 14 points.

You can create *annotative* single-line text, using an annotative text style. This feature automatically scales text according to your scale. For more information, see the section "Understanding Text Styles" later in this chapter. To make existing single-line text annotative, select the text and change the Annotative property in the Properties palette from No to Yes. For more information about changing the scale of text, see the section "Editing single-line text" later in this chapter.

Setting the rotation angle

The final prompt in TEXT is the rotation angle. This angle applies to the entire line of text, not to individual characters. (You can specify slanted text, called *obliqued text*, using the STYLE command covered later in this chapter.) Figure 13.2 shows text rotated to 315 degrees.

FIGURE 13.2

Text rotated to 315 degrees.

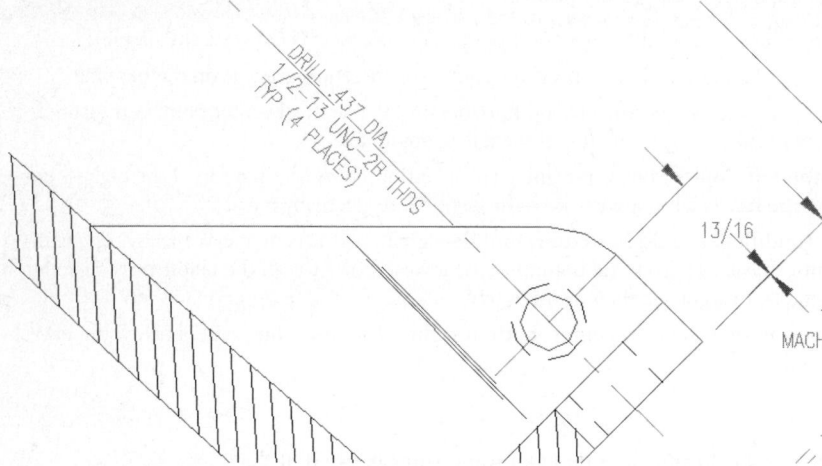

Adding special characters and formatting

To create special characters and formats for single-line text, you have to use codes. These codes are shown in Table 13.1.

Figure 13.3 displays text using some of these codes, along with the entries that created them.

TABLE 13.1

Special Character Codes for Text Fonts

Code	Results
%%o	Toggles the overscore mode on/off
%%u	Toggles the underscore mode on/off
%%d	Draws a degree symbol (°)
%%p	Draws a plus/minus tolerance symbol (±)
%%c	Draws a circle-diameter dimensioning symbol (Æ)

FIGURE 13.3

Using special characters and formatting with text fonts.

<u>35.3</u> not 35.8	%%u35.3%%u not **35.8**
Ø1.5	%%c1.5
±.002	%%p.002

On the DVD

The drawing used in the following exercise on creating text with TEXT, ab13-a.dwg, is in the Drawings folder on the DVD. ■

STEPS: Creating Text with TEXT

1. Open ab13-a.dwg from your DVD.

2. Save the file as ab13-01.dwg in your AutoCAD Bible folder. This is a master-bathroom plan drawing, as shown in Figure 13.4. Make sure that Object Snap is on. Set running object snaps for Endpoint, Midpoint, and Intersection.

 3. Choose Annotate tab ➪ Text panel ➪ Text drop-down list ➪ Single Line. Follow the prompts:

```
Current text style: "ROMANS" Text height: 0'-4 1/2" Annotative:  No
Specify start point of text or [Justify/Style]: Right-click and
    choose Justify.
Enter an option [Align/Fit/Center/Middle/Right/TL/TC/TR/ML/MC/MR/BL/
    BC/BR]: Right-click and choose BC.
Specify bottom-center point of text: Use the Midpoint running object
    snap to pick ❶ in Figure 13.4.
Specify rotation angle of text <0>: Pick the endpoint at ❷.
Enter text: 2-0 ↵
Enter text: ↵
```

The master bathroom.

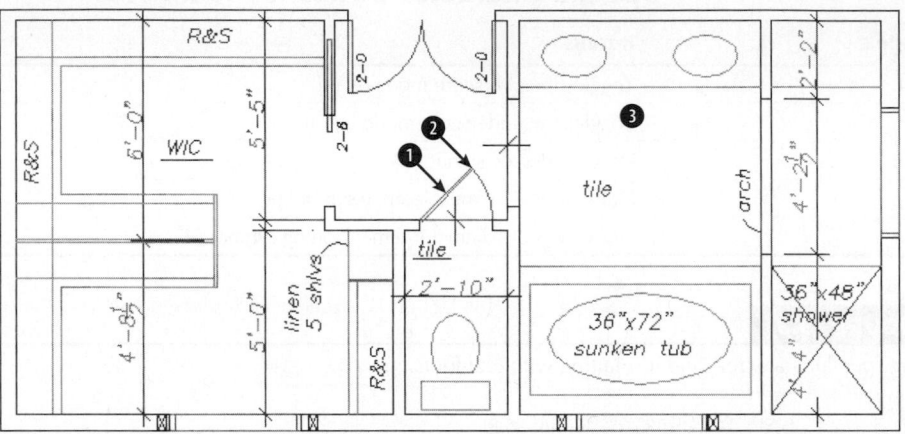

4. Start the TEXT command again. Follow the prompts:

```
Specify start point of text or [Justify/Style]: Right-click and
    choose Justify.
Enter an option [Align/Fit/Center/Middle/Right/TL/TC/TR/ML/MC/MR/BL/
    BC/BR]: Right-click and choose Middle.
Specify middle point of text: Pick ❸ in Figure 13.4. (This point
    doesn't have to be exact.)
Specify rotation angle of text <45>: 0 ↵
Enter text: %%UMASTER BATH ↵
Enter text: ↵
```

Save your drawing. It should look like Figure 13.5.

The master-bathroom plan drawing with added single-line text.

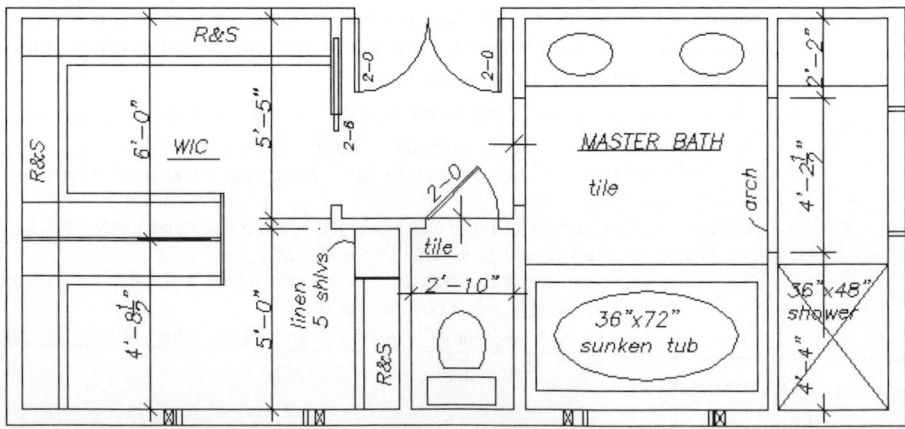

Editing single-line text

As with any drawing object, the need often arises to edit your text. The most common way to edit single-line text is to use the DDEDIT command. Double-click the text to start the command. Remember that each line of text created with TEXT is a separate object.

The text appears in a border with your text highlighted in an edit box, as shown in Figure 13.6. You can start typing to completely replace the text or click where you want to change part of the text and use standard Windows techniques to edit the text. Press Enter or click anywhere outside the border. DDEDIT prompts you to select another annotation object. Press Enter to end the command.

FIGURE 13.6

Editing single-line text in the drawing.

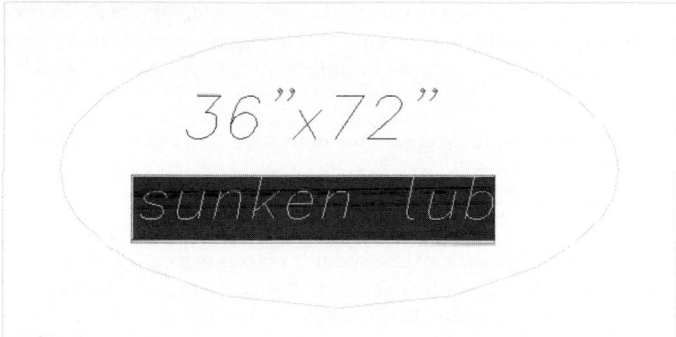

Tip

If you find other nearby or overlapping objects to be distracting, right-click and choose Editor Settings⇨Opaque Background to create an opaque background inside the editing border while you edit. Alternatively, you can right-click, choose Editor Settings⇨Text Highlight Color, and specify any color you want in the Select Color dialog box. ■

You can also change text by using the Quick Properties palette. Select any text and click in the Contents item of the Quick Properties palette to edit the text. To use the Properties palette, select any text object and open the Properties palette (Ctrl+1). Here you can edit the text content as well as every other conceivable property, including layer, linetype, lineweight, color, insertion point, justification, rotation angle, and others that I cover in the section on text styles.

Scaling text

If you want to scale text and use the SCALE command, the text may move, depending on the base point you use. Instead, you can use the SCALETEXT command to change the scale of selected text without moving the text insertion point. This command works with either one text object or several at once. All the text objects stay in their original location.

To use SCALETEXT, follow these steps:

1. Choose Annotate tab ⇨ Text panel (expanded) ⇨ Scale.
2. Select the text objects that you want to scale.

3. At the `Enter a base point option for scaling [Existing/Left/Center/Middle/Right/TL/TC/TR/ML/MC/MR/BL/BC/BR] <Existing>:` prompt, press Enter to use the existing insertion point of the selected text, or choose a new base point. (Your last choice for this prompt becomes the new default, so if you used another option, type **e** ↵.) These options are the same as the Justify options described earlier in this chapter.

4. At the `Specify new model height or [Paper height/Match object/Scale factor] <3/32>:` prompt, right-click and choose Scale Factor to specify a scale factor, just as you would for the SCALE command (see Chapter 9). You can also type a new height or use the Match Object option to match the height of the selected text objects to another existing text object. The prompt asks you to select an object with the desired height. For annotative text only, you can specify a paper height, which means the height you want the text to appear when plotted.

5. If you have chosen the Scale Factor option, then type the factor that you want at the `Specify scale factor or [Reference] <2>:` prompt.

6. If you want to specify the scale factor with reference to existing text or a value, use the Reference option. At the `Specify reference length <1>:` prompt, type a length or specify two points that measure the reference length. At the `Specify new length:` prompt, type a value or pick two points to indicate the new length.

If you want to scale text to automatically fit a drawing scale, you can use annotative text. For more information, see the upcoming section "Understanding Text Styles."

Justifying text

The JUSTIFYTEXT command lets you change the justification of selected text objects without moving the text. To use JUSTIFYTEXT, choose Annotate tab ➪ Text panel (expanded) ➪ Justify. Then select the text objects that you want to modify. At the `Enter a justification option [Left/Align/Fit/Center/Middle/Right/TL/TC/TR/ML/MC/MR/BL/BC/BR] <Left>:` prompt, right-click and choose the justification that you want.

On the DVD

The drawing used in the following exercise on editing text, `ab13-b.dwg`, is in the `Drawings` folder on the DVD. ■

STEPS: Editing Text

1. Open `ab13-b.dwg` from your DVD.

2. Save the file as `ab13-02.dwg` in your `AutoCAD Bible` folder. This is an air and vacuum release valve, as shown in Figure 13.7.

3. Double-click the text `1/2" PIPING`. A highlighted border appears around the text. Select only the text 1/2 and type **3/8**. Press Enter or click anywhere outside the text border. The DDEDIT prompt continues to prompt you to select another annotation object. Press Enter to end the command.

4. Display the Properties palette (Ctrl+1). Click Quick Select in the Properties palette. In the Quick Select dialog box, choose Text from the Object Type drop-down list. In the Operator drop-down list, choose Select All. Click OK to select all the text objects in the drawing.

5. In the Properties palette, choose Layer. From the Layer drop-down list, choose TEXT. Choose Color. From the Color drop-down list, choose ByLayer. All text is now on the TEXT layer using the ByLayer color. Press Esc to remove the grips and see the result.

6. Select the text at the bottom of the drawing that reads N.T.S. From the grips you can tell that it has a middle-left justification. Choose Annotate tab ➪ Text panel (expanded) ➪ Justify, or type **justifytext** ↵ on the command line. At the prompt, type **bc** ↵.

FIGURE 13.7

An air and vacuum release valve.

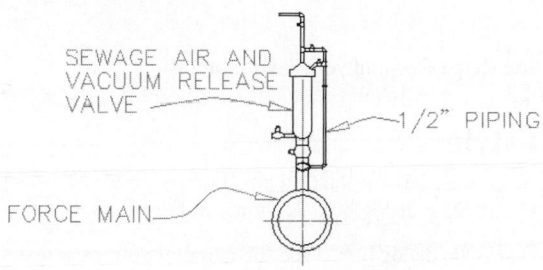

Thanks to the Army Corps of Engineers for this drawing.

The command ends. You can select the text again to see that the insertion point grip is now at the bottom center of the text.

7. Choose Annotate tab ⇨ Text panel (expanded) ⇨ Scale, or type **scaletext** ↵ on the command line. Follow the prompts:

```
Select objects: Select the two lines of text at the bottom of the
    drawing.
Select objects: ↵
Enter a base point option for scaling
[Existing/Left/Center/Middle/Right/TL/TC/TR/ML/MC/MR/BL/BC/BR] <BC>:
    Type e ↵ to use the existing base point.
Specify new model height or [Paper height/Match object/Scale factor]
    <1/8">: Right-click and choose Scale factor.
Specify scale factor or [Reference] <2">: Type 1.5 ↵
```

8. You can click the Properties palette's Close button to close it. Save your drawing.

Understanding Text Styles

You may not always want to use the default font. You can create text styles that give you full creative control over the font, font style (bold, italic, or both), character width, obliquing angle, and text height. You can even design backward, upside-down, and vertical text. (Vertical text is like the text that you occasionally see on the spine of a book. It goes down rather than to the right.)

Each text style

- Has a name and several properties
- Is saved with the drawing
- Can be made current when you want to use it
- Can be renamed and deleted

Creating text styles is part of the typical drawing setup procedure. You should include text styles in your drawing templates. AutoCAD and AutoCAD LT come with two types of fonts: the original .shx fonts, which are created by using *shape* files; and TrueType fonts, which are used by most Windows applications.

Cross-Reference

See Chapter 32 for instructions on creating shape files and your own fonts. ■

Creating a new text style

 To create a new text style, choose Home tab ⇨ Annotation panel (expanded) ⇨ Text Style. This starts the STYLE command and opens the Text Style dialog box, as shown in Figure 13.8.

Choose New to open the New Text Style dialog box. Type the name of your new text style and click OK. Text style names can be up to 255 characters and can include spaces. You return to the Text Style dialog box where you can define the new text style.

At the top left of the Text Style dialog box is a list of currently defined styles in the drawing. At the lower-left corner is a preview of the style that is selected in the Styles list.

FIGURE 13.8

The Text Style dialog box.

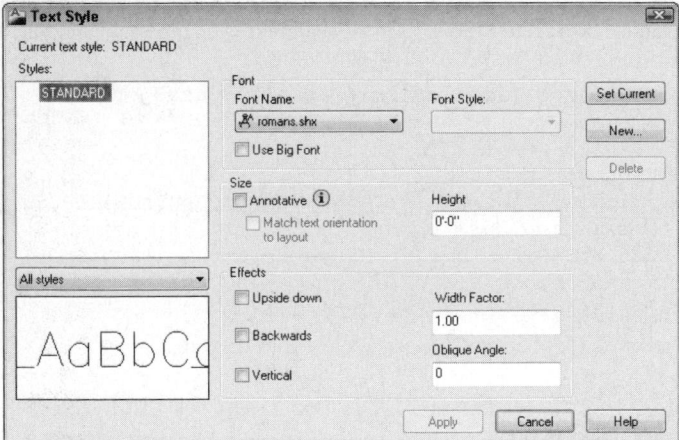

Font

In the Font section of the Text Style dialog box, you specify the font name and font style. Click the Font Name drop-down list arrow to see the list of fonts. Fonts with the double-T icon are TrueType fonts. The other fonts are defined in a shape file that has the SHP filename extension. They are compiled into a file with the SHX filename extension for faster access. For more information on working with fonts, see Chapter 32.

Click a font to choose it and see a preview in the Preview pane at the lower-left corner of the dialog box. If the font that you've chosen supports different styles, such as bold or italic, you can choose one of them in the Font Style drop-down list. None of the AutoCAD or AutoCAD LT fonts supports font styles, but many of the TrueType fonts do.

Note

AutoCAD supports fonts with many characters (called big fonts), such as Japanese and Chinese. To use these fonts, check the Use Big Font check box. The Font Style drop-down list changes to become the Big Font drop-down list, where you can choose from a list of big fonts. ■

Size

The Size section of the dialog box lets you specify the height of the text. There are two types of height:

- **Height in the drawing.** If you are going to use the text style in the main drawing area (model space, where you draw and edit), use the Height text box to enter the height of the text. Remember to take into account the scale factor, if necessary.

- **Height in a viewport.** If you are going to use the text style for text that you will display in a scaled viewport on a layout, check the Annotative check box. Then use the Paper Text Height text box to enter the height of the text. You don't need to adjust for the scale factor when you enter a height, because annotative objects facilitate that process for you. I cover layouts and using annotative objects in Chapter 17.

Note

If you check the Annotative check box, you can also check the Match Text Orientation to Layout check box. If you rotate the viewport by using the MVSETUP command, with the Align ⇨ Rotate view options, the text remains horizontal and does not rotate. ■

In both types of height, you can leave the height at zero if you want to be able to vary the text height within that one style. If the height is zero, the TEXT command prompts you for a height when you use these commands to place text.

Caution

If you create a text style using a height other than zero and then use that text style when you define a dimension style, the text style height overrides the text height that you specify in the dimension style. See Chapter 15 for more information on dimension styles. ■

Effects

In the Effects section, you specify the orientation, width factor, and oblique angle of the text style. The default width factor of characters is set to 1. You can specify a smaller number to compress text and a larger number to expand it, as shown in Figure 13.9.

FIGURE 13.9

Text using different width factors.

Width = 1.5 Bearing Housing
Width = .8 Bearing Housing

The term *oblique angle* refers to the angle of the individual letters. It is generally used to create an effect, such as italic text. You don't need to use an oblique angle if you're using a TrueType font that supports italic text.

The angle definition used to define oblique text is different from the angle definition used for other objects. Up and down text, which is normal text, has a zero oblique angle. A positive angle slants the text to the right; this is typical for italic text. A negative angle slants the text to the left. Figure 13.10 shows text with a positive and negative oblique angle.

FIGURE 13.10

Text using different oblique angles.

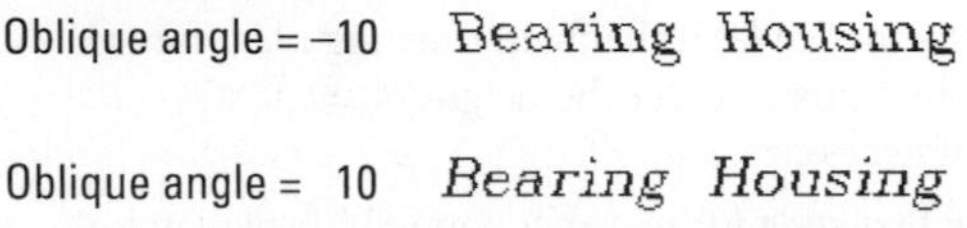

Oblique angle = –10   Bearing Housing

Oblique angle = 10   *Bearing Housing*

You can create text that is backward (like a mirror image) or upside down. Some fonts also let you create vertical text. Figure 13.11 shows an example of each kind of text. Check the appropriate check box to create the effect that you want.

FIGURE 13.11

Upside-down, backward, and vertical text.

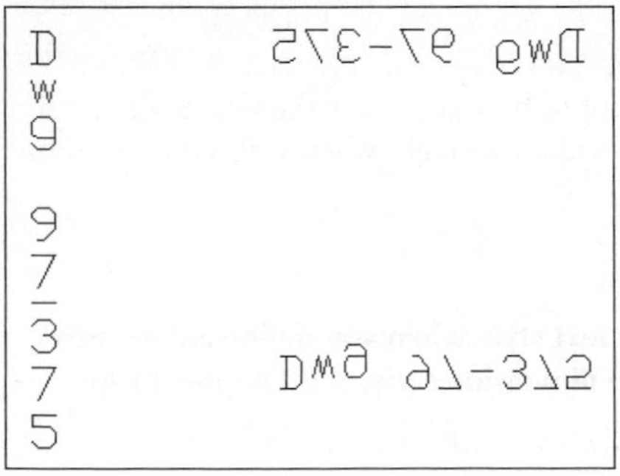

After you finish defining your text style, click Apply to make it current. Click Close to return to your drawing.

Renaming and deleting text styles

You can rename and delete text styles easily. To rename a text style, start the STYLE command to open the Text Style dialog box. Select the text style, click the text style's name again, enter a new name, and press Enter.

To delete a text style, choose it from the Styles list box of the Text Style dialog box and click Delete. A message box asks you to confirm the deletion. Click OK to delete the text style. You cannot delete a text style that is being used.

On the DVD

The drawing used in the following exercise on creating text styles, ab13-b.dwg, is in the Drawings folder on the DVD. ∎

STEPS: Creating Text Styles

1. Open ab13-b.dwg from your DVD.

2. Save the file as ab13-03.dwg in your AutoCAD Bible folder.

 3. Choose Home tab ⇨ Annotation panel (expanded) ⇨ Text Style to open the Text Style dialog box. Click New. In the New Text Style dialog box, type **Notes** and click OK.

4. From the Font Name drop-down list, choose romans.shx. In the Height text box, enter a height of **1/16"**. In the Width Factor text box, enter a width factor of **.95**. In the Oblique Angle text box, type **10**. Click Apply to make the new style current. Click Close.

5. Start the TEXT command. At the Specify start point of text or [Justify/Style]: prompt, pick a start point at the lower-left corner of the drawing. At the Specify rotation angle of text <0>: prompt, press Enter. At the prompt, type **Note: Not drawn to scale.** ↵. Press Enter again to end the command.

6. Save your drawing. It should look like Figure 13.12. If you're going on to the next exercise, keep this drawing open.

FIGURE 13.12

The addition of text using a new text style.

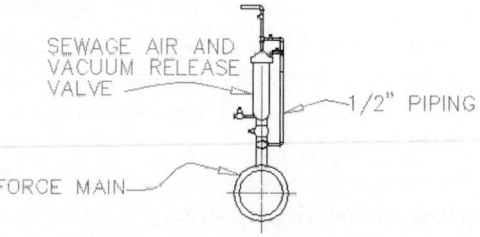

Modifying a text style

To change a style, choose Home tab ⇨ Annotation panel (expanded) ⇨ Text Style. From the Styles list box in the Text Style dialog box, choose the text style that you want to change. Make changes in the same way that you did when creating the style. Choose Apply and then Close. The drawing regenerates, and the text that uses the style that you changed is modified accordingly. This is a powerful way to control the look of text in your drawing.

Note

Unfortunately, only changes to the font and text style affect current text. Other changes, such as width factor, oblique angle, orientation, and height, are ignored. However, new text takes on these other changes. ■

Making a style current or changing a text object's style

You can choose the current style when you use one of the text commands. If you use TEXT, the command displays the `Specify start point of text or [Justify/Style]:` prompt. Right-click and choose Style. (The prompt also displays the current style, height, and annotative setting.) If you know the name of the style that you want to use, type it and press Enter. The `Specify start point of text or [Justify/Style]:` prompt repeats. You can choose the Justify option or pick a start point to continue the command.

If you use MTEXT, the In-Place Text Editor opens, as explained in the next section. Choose the text style that you want from the Style drop-down list.

An easy way to make a style current or to change the text style of existing text is to choose Home tab ⇨ Annotation panel (expanded) ⇨ Text Style drop-down list or Annotate tab ⇨ Text panel ⇨ Text Style drop-down list. To make a style current, choose the style from the Text Style drop-down list with no text selected. To change the text style of existing text, select the text and choose a new style from the list. You can also change the style of selected text in the Quick Properties palette or the Properties palette.

Importing a text style

As explained in Chapter 11, you can use the DesignCenter to import features from other drawings. To import a text style, follow these steps:

1. Open the DesignCenter (Ctrl+2).
2. In the left pane, navigate to the drawing that has the text style that you want.
3. Double-click the drawing icon or click its plus sign.
4. To see the list of the text styles, double-click the text style's icon in either the left or right pane.
5. Double-click the text style's icon in the right pane to import it into your drawing.

On the DVD

The drawing used in the following exercise on modifying text styles, `ab13-03.dwg`, is in the `Results` folder on the DVD. ■

STEPS: Modifying Text Styles

1. If you have `ab13-03.dwg` open from the previous exercise, continue to use it for this exercise. Otherwise, open `ab13-03.dwg` from the `Results` folder of your DVD.
2. Save the file as `ab13-04.dwg` in your `AutoCAD Bible` folder.
3. The note at the bottom-left corner of the drawing uses the Notes text style. Choose Home tab ⇨ Annotation panel (expanded) ⇨ Text Style. In the Text Style dialog box, make sure that the Notes style name is listed, and then choose `italic.shx` from the Font Name drop-down list. Choose Apply and then Close.
4. The drawing regenerates, and the font of the text changes.
5. Save your drawing.

Creating Multiline Text

Single-line text is awkward when you want to type quite a bit of text. The main disadvantage is that single-line text does not wrap text to the next line to keep a neat right margin. Multiline text solves this problem and also offers many more formatting options compared to single-line text. The entire paragraph of multi-line text is one object. Don't confuse multiline text, which is also called *paragraph text,* with *multilines* (which I cover in Chapter 16).

Using the In-Place Text Editor

To create paragraph text, choose Home tab ⇨ Annotation panel ⇨ Text drop-down list ⇨ Multiline Text. This starts the MTEXT command. The prompt tells you the current style, text height, and whether or not the style is annotative. For example:

```
Current text style: "ROMANS" Text height: 4 1/2" Annotative: No
```

The command continues with the `Specify first corner:` prompt. Specify one corner of a bounding box to indicate where to place the text. At the `Specify opposite corner or [Height/Justify/Line spacing/Rotation/Style/Width/Columns]:` prompt, specify the diagonally opposite corner of the bounding box. The Text Editor tab appears on the Ribbon. You can choose one of the other prompt options to specify the text properties before you type the text. Some of these options are also available in the In-Place Text Editor, which opens after you specify the bounding box. Figure 13.13 shows the Text Editor tab and the In-Place Text Editor.

Note

You can use the MTEXTTOOLBAR system variable to display the Text Formatting toolbar. Change its value to 1 to display the Text Formatting toolbar rather than the Ribbon tab. ■

Tip

When you specify the corners of the Mtext bounding box, you see sample text at the cursor to give you an idea of the actual current height of the text. You can change the sample text with the MTJIGSTRING system variable. ■

FIGURE 13.13

The Text Editor tab and the In-Place Text Editor.

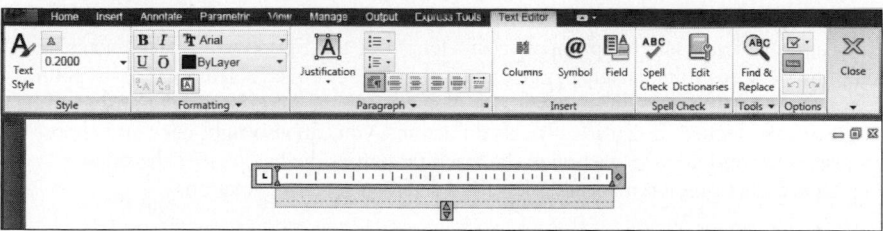

Type your text in the bounding box. The In-Place Text Editor wraps the text to the next line when the text meets the right side of the bounding box that you specified. Although you've created a bounding box with four sides, only the *paragraph width* (that is, the left and right margins) limits the text. If you type too much text for the bounding box, the bounding box expands vertically. To format selected or new text, use the buttons on the panels of the Text Editor tab of the Ribbon. In the Style panel, you can do the following:

- **Style.** Choose any text style by clicking the Text Style button and choosing from the thumbnail images.

• **Annotative.** Click to turn the annotative feature on or off.

- **Text Height.** Choose a height from the drop-down list or type a new height in the Text Height box.

In the Formatting panel, you can do the following:

- **Bold.** If Bold style is supported for the font, select text and click the Bold button.
- **Italic.** If Italic style is supported for the font, select text and click the Italic button.
- **Underline.** Select text and click the Underline button.
- **Overline.** To overscore selected text, click the Overline button.
- **Font.** Choose any font from the Font drop-down list.
- **Color.** Choose ByLayer or any color from the Color drop-down list. To choose from additional colors, choose Select Color to open the Select Color dialog box. (See Chapter 11 for details on using this dialog box.)
- **Make Uppercase.** Click to make selected text all uppercase.
- **Make Lowercase.** Click to make selected text all lowercase.
- **Background Mask.** Opens the Background Mask dialog box. This feature creates a background around your text that covers other objects so that you can easily read the text. Check the Use Background Mask check box. Specify a border offset factor to create a margin around the text. A margin setting of 1 does not create any margin. Then check the Use Drawing Background Color check box to use the color of your drawing screen, or choose another color from the drop-down list. Click OK.
- **Oblique Angle (in the expanded Formatting panel).** Enter a number that represents an angle from upright to specify the angle for the selected characters. For example, you can use the oblique angle to create italicized text. A negative value angles text to the left.
- **Tracking (in the expanded Formatting panel).** Enter a number in the text box to specify the spacing between letters of selected text. The number works like a scale factor.
- **Width Factor (in the expanded Formatting panel).** Enter a number in the text box to specify the width of selected letters. The number works like a scale factor.
- **Stack (in the expanded Formatting panel).** Toggles stacking and unstacking fractions. (This option only appears if you select appropriate characters.) Use this option to stack characters if they are not numerals or immediately before or after the three AutoStack symbols (slash, pound sign, and carat). Select the text, and choose Stack. You can use the same process to unstack text that you previously stacked. If you select stacked fractions, you can also right-click and choose Stack Properties to configure the fraction in the Stack Properties dialog box. See the sidebar, "Creating stacked fractions automatically," for more details on creating fractions.

Tip

To create an exponent (or superscript), type a number and then a carat, as in 2^. Select the number and the carat, and then choose Stack. To create a subscript, type a carat, and then the number, as in ^2, and then stack it. ■

In the Paragraph panel, you can control formatting that applies to an entire paragraph, as follows:

- **Justification.** Choose a justification from the Justification drop-down list. The justifications are discussed in the "Justifying single-line text" section earlier in this chapter.
- **Bullets and Numbering.** Displays a submenu that lets you manage bullets and numbering:
  - **Off.** Removes bullets and numbering from the selected text.
  - **Numbered.** Creates a numbered list.

- **Lettered.** Lets you create lettered lists. You can choose uppercase or lowercase letters.
- **Bulleted.** Creates a bulleted list.
- **Start.** Restarts numbering (or lettering) from the beginning.
- **Continue.** Continues numbering (or lettering) from the last list.
- **Allow Auto-list.** Automatically starts a numbered list if you type **1.**, a lettered list if you type **A.**, or a bulleted list if you type a dash (-) or an asterisk (*).
- **Use Tab Delimiter Only.** Creates a list only if you use a tab after some text, and not when you use a space. On by default.
- **Allow Bullets and Lists.** Turns on the feature that automatically numbers (or letters) items that are in a list. For example, if you delete an item, the rest of the items are automatically adjusted.

- **Line Spacing.** Set line spacing in multiples of single-line spacing. You can choose More to open the Paragraph dialog box, discussed later in this list.
- **Default.** Sets the default alignment, usually left-justified.
- **Left.** Left-justifies text and sets the insertion point to the left of the text.
- **Center.** Centers text and sets the insertion point to the center of the text.
- **Right.** Right-justifies text and sets the insertion point to the right of the text.
- **Justify.** Aligns both the left and right margins on the text.
- **Distribute.** Spreads out the text to meet the left and right margins.
- **Paragraph.** Click the dialog box launcher arrow at the right side of the panel's title bar to open the Paragraph dialog box, shown in Figure 13.14, where you can specify the following settings:

FIGURE 13.14

The Paragraph dialog box offers one place where you can specify many settings relating to paragraphs.

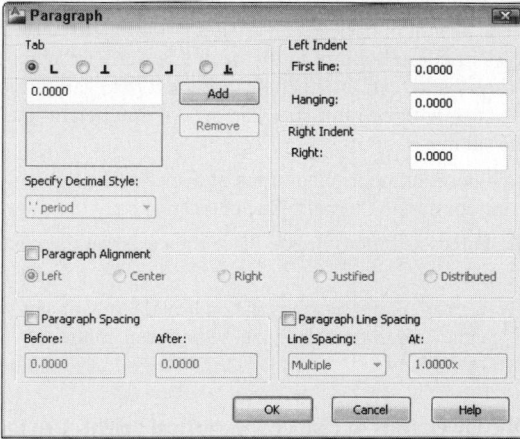

- **Tabs.** You can choose left, center, right, and decimal tabs, as well as their position. Click Add to add the tab. A decimal tab centers text around a decimal point. (If you choose a decimal tab, you can choose a decimal style from the Specify Decimal Style drop-down list — period, comma, or space.)

- **Paragraph Alignment.** Check the Paragraph Alignment check box and choose Left, Center, Right, Justified, or Distributed. These buttons are also on the Paragraph panel.

- **Paragraph Spacing.** Sets spacing between paragraphs. You can set spacing both before and after, but if you set both, the two values are added.

- **Left Indent.** Sets the left margin for the first line of a paragraph and the rest of the paragraph. Use this indentation for creating bulleted and numbered lists. To indent an entire paragraph, use both first-line and paragraph indentation. You can also use the two left triangle indent markers on the Text Editor ruler.

- **Right Indent.** Sets the right margin for the paragraph. You can also use the right triangle indent marker on the Text Editor ruler.

- **Paragraph Line Spacing.** You can set the spacing of lines of text within a paragraph. For example, from the Line Spacing drop-down list, you can choose Multiple to Single or Double-space lines. Choose Exactly to specify the distance between lines in units — great for inserting text into titleblocks. Choose At Least to set a minimum spacing ¾ this is good for situations when you have text or symbols of varying heights and want to leave room for the larger items. For simple formatting, you can use the Line Spacing button in the Paragraph panel.

- **Combine Paragraphs** (on the expanded Paragraph panel). Combines separate paragraphs into one. Select the paragraphs that you want to combine before applying the command.

Tip

To set indentation and tabs on the In-Place Text Editor's ruler, drag the first-line indent marker (the top triangle at the left of the ruler) or the paragraph indent marker (the bottom triangle) to the left or right. To set a tab, click on the ruler where you want the tab. To delete a tab, drag a tab marker off the ruler. Note that the bullets and numbering feature makes these settings less important than previously. ■

The Insert panel enables you to do the following:

- **Columns.** Create multiple-column text. You have the following options:

  - **No Columns.** Creates one column of text.

  - **Dynamic Columns.** The default option, which creates columns based on the amount of text. Text automatically flows from one column to the next. The vertical height of the bounding box does not change as you add text; if you enter more text than can fit in the box, another column automatically starts, with no limit. You can set column height to automatic or manual (the default), using the submenu.

  - **Static Columns.** Creates a set number of columns of a specified height and width. Text automatically flows from one column to the next, but you can specify the number of columns.

  - **Insert Column Break.** Forces a column break. Place the cursor at the desired location and press Alt+Enter.

  - **Column Settings.** Opens the Column Settings dialog box. Here you can specify the type of columns, their width, height, and gutter (the spacing between columns).

Tip

You can grip-edit column text. Use one of the lower grips to change the vertical height. Use the right-facing arrow to change the column width. ■

- **Symbol.** Insert the degree, plus/minus, or diameter symbol, a non-breaking space, and a number of other symbols. You can also choose Other to open the Windows Character Map to select any of the available symbols. Click a symbol, and then click Select. Click Copy and then click the Close button to close the Windows Character Map. In the In-Place Text Editor, press Ctrl+V to paste the symbol.

- **Field.** Insert a field into the text. For more information, see the section "Inserting Fields" later in this chapter.

In the Spell Check panel, you can do the following:

- **Spelling Check.** Find misspelled words in the selected Mtext object. Be sure to place the cursor at the beginning of the text. Misspelled words are underlined with a dashed red line. You can then right-click to choose from suggested words. At the end of this chapter, I explain how to check the spelling of an entire drawing.
- **Edit Dictionaries.** You can edit the dictionaries that AutoCAD and AutoCAD LT use to check spelling. I discuss this process at the end of this chapter.
- **Check Spelling Settings.** Click the dialog box launcher arrow at the right side of the panel's title bar to open the Check Spelling Settings dialog box, where you can specify which types of words to exclude from spell checking.

In the Tools panel, you have the option to do the following:

- **Find and Replace.** Open the Find and Replace dialog box so that you can find or replace specified text. If you want the search to match the case of the specified text, choose Match Case. If you want to restrict the search to whole words that match the specified text, choose Find Whole Words Only. If you only want to find text, ignore the Replace text box. To both find and replace text, enter text in both boxes. Make sure that the cursor is at the beginning of the text if you want to search the entire Mtext object. At the end of this chapter, I explain how to find and replace text in an entire drawing.

Tip

You can check the Use Wildcards check box and use wildcards, such as * (any number of characters) and ? (any single character) to search for text. You can check the Match Diacritics check box to match words with diacritical marks. Finally, you can check the Match Half/Full Width Forms check box to refine searching for text in East Asian languages. ■

- **Import Text** (on the expanded Tools panel). Opens the Select File dialog box, which lets you choose a text (TXT) or Rich Text Format (RTF) file to import. (Rich Text Format preserves formatting from application to application, while text-only documents do not retain formatting.) Find the file, choose it, and click Open to place the text in the In-Place Text Editor. The maximum file size is 256K. I cover other techniques for importing text later in this chapter.
- **AutoCAPS** (on the expanded Tools panel). Automatically changes newly typed and imported text to uppercase, even if the Caps Lock key is not on. (And it's a cute pun on AutoCAD.)

On the Options panel, you can find the following:

- **Character Set** (on the More drop-down list). Lets you choose the language that you want to work with, so that you have the characters that you need for that language.
- **Remove Formatting** (on the More drop-down list). Removes character formatting, such as bold and italic, paragraph formatting (such as indenting), or all formatting.
- **Editor Settings** (on the More drop-down list). Opens a submenu that lets you toggle the display of the Text Formatting toolbar and control if the editor uses WYSIWYG (what you see is what you get). You can also create a temporary opaque background for the In-Place Text Editor that may

help you to edit text more easily if the text overlaps other objects. This background disappears when you close the editor. Finally, you can choose the color of the highlight when you select text.

- **Ruler.** Turn the ruler on and off.
- **Undo.** Undo the last Mtext edit.
- **Redo.** Redo the last undo operation.

In the Close panel, click Close Text Editor to close the editor. You can also close the editor by clicking anywhere outside the editor or by pressing Ctrl+Enter.

Right-click in the editor to display the shortcut menu. The shortcut menu contains many of the options that are on the Ribbon. Here I discuss the options that are not available on the Ribbon.

- **Select All.** Selects all the text in the current Mtext object.
- **Cut.** Places selected text in the Windows Clipboard and removes it from the editor.
- **Copy.** Places selected text in the Windows Clipboard without removing it from the editor.
- **Paste.** Places text from the Windows Clipboard.
- **Paste Special.** Opens a submenu where you can paste without character formatting, paragraph formatting, or any formatting at all.

The TEXTTOFRONT command moves all text in your drawing to the front (top) of the drawing order. For the background mask to work, your text needs to be on top, so that you can use this command when you are creating text with background masks. The display order of objects is controlled by the DRAWORDER command, which I discuss in Chapter 27.

You can snap to the corners of the Mtext bounding box by using the node object snap. (See Chapter 4 for an explanation of object snaps.) To turn this feature off, change the OSNAPNODELEGACY system variable to 1.

Creating stacked fractions automatically

You can create automatic stacked fractions and tolerances as you type by using a system similar to those described earlier for creating special characters with TEXT.

You can also type unstacked fractions (as in 1/2); select the fraction text and choose Stack from the expanded Formatting panel. To create stacked fractions as you type, open the In-Place Text Editor and follow these steps:

1. Type the numerator, which is the character that you want on top.
2. Type the character that defines the fraction format that you want (see the example):

   - Type a slash (/) to create a fraction separated by a horizontal line.
   - Type a pound symbol (#) to create a fraction separated by a diagonal line.
   - Type a carat (^) to create a tolerance stack, which is like a fraction separated by a horizontal line, except that there is no horizontal line.

3. Type the denominator.
4. Type a space (or other nonnumeric character). The AutoStack Properties dialog box opens.

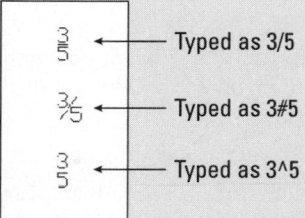

Typed as 3/5

Typed as 3#5

Typed as 3^5

5. Choose the option you want to create the stacked fraction:

- Uncheck Enable AutoStacking to disable the automatic stacked fraction feature.
- Uncheck Remove Leading Blank if you want to retain a space between whole numbers and fractions.
- Choose whether you want the slash to result in a fraction with a horizontal line or a fraction with a slash. This choice does not affect how the pound sign and carat work. If you want the slash to result in a fraction with a slash (which would seem to make more sense), then you do not have an automatic way to create a fraction with a horizontal line.
- Check Don't Show This Dialog Again; Always Use These Settings to stop the dialog box from opening when you create automatic stacked fractions.
- Click OK to create the stacked fraction, or Cancel to leave the numbers as you typed them.

AutoStack works only with numerals immediately before and after the slash, pound sign, and carat. You can also set the properties of individual stacked fractions. Select and right-click the fraction in the In-Place Text Editor and choose Stack Properties from the shortcut menu. In the Stack Properties dialog box, you can change the following properties:

- **Text.** Edit the upper and lower text.
- **Style.** Change the fraction style. (Refer to the example under Step 2 for the three possible styles.)
- **Position.** Position the fraction so that the top, center, or bottom is aligned with other text.
- **Text Size.** Change the size of the numbers that make up the fraction. Fraction numbers are usually smaller than regular numbers.

Specifying and changing line spacing

You can specify the spacing between lines in multiline text before you open the Multiline Text Editor. (You can also use the Paragraph dialog box when you're in the editor, as described previously.) Line spacing is useful for fitting text into a schedule or table in your drawing. Of course, you can also use the table feature, which I discuss in the "Creating Tables" section later in this chapter. To set line spacing to an exact unit distance, follow these steps:

1. Start the Mtext command.
2. At the `Specify first corner:` prompt, pick the first corner of your Mtext box.
3. At the `Specify opposite corner or [Height/Justify/Line spacing/Rotation/ Style/Width/Columns]:` prompt, choose the Line Spacing option.

4. At the `Enter line spacing type [At least/Exactly] <Exactly>:` prompt, choose Exactly.

5. At the `Enter line spacing factor or distance <1x>:` prompt, type a number, such as **1x** for specifying a one-unit space between lines of text. (If you type **1x**, you get single-line spacing, which varies according to the size of the text.)

6. Continue with the command.

This setting persists for future Mtext objects. To change existing line spacing, select (but do not double-click) the multiline text object. Open the Properties palette and set one or more of the following:

- **Line space factor.** Specifies line spacing as a multiple of lines. Single-line spacing is 1.0000, and double-line spacing is 2.0000.

- **Line space distance.** Specifies line spacing in units. Use this measurement (along with a line space style of Exactly) to fit text into an existing table or schedule.

- **Line space style.** Choose At Least (the default) to adjust line spacing based on the height of the largest character in the line of text. Choose Exactly to specify line spacing that is the same, regardless of differences in character height.

Specifying width and rotation

To change the width of an Mtext object, you can use its right triangular grip. Select the Mtext object and drag the grip to the desired location.

You can use the Properties palette to change the width and height. You can specify the exact width when creating the Mtext object by using the Width option after you specify the first corner of the Mtext bounding box. Otherwise, you generally specify the width by picking the two corners of the Mtext bounding box.

Tip
When the In-Place Text Editor is open, you can change the width of the Mtext object by dragging on the right edge of the ruler. ■

To rotate an existing Mtext object, use the Properties palette's Rotation item, or use the top-left square grip, as follows:

1. Select the Mtext object.

2. Click the grip to make it "hot."

3. Right-click and choose Rotate.

4. At the `Specify rotation angle or [Base point/Copy/Undo/Reference/eXit]:` prompt, pick a new location for the grip or type a rotation angle.

You can also specify the rotation while creating the Mtext object. Use the Rotation option that appears on the command line after you specify the first corner.

Creating text for different scales

You may plan to display certain sections of your drawing at more than one scale. For example, you may want to show the entire model at a 1:4 scale, but a detail of the model at a 1:1 scale. If you have some text next to the model and want that text to appear at both scales, you have a problem ¾ how do you get the text to appear the same size in both places? Without addressing this problem, your text will be either too big or too small at one of the scales. Another situation may be that you want one text object to appear at one scale, but another to appear at a different scale.

You create displays of various scales by using floating viewports on a layout. I cover viewports and layouts in Chapter 17, and you'll find further coverage of this topic there. However, if you know the scales you want to use, you can plan for this situation while you're in the drawing and editing stage by using *annotative* text.

Annotative objects create representations at various scales that you can automatically display at those scales when you lay out your drawing for plotting. The following objects can be annotative: text, dimensions, geometric tolerances, multileaders, blocks, and attributes. Text styles, dimension styles, and multileader styles can also be annotative; if you create an object using an annotative style, then the object is annotative. See the chapters that cover each of these objects for more information on their annotative property.

Previously, to create text that appeared in viewports of different scales, you needed to create a separate layer for each scale. You could then put the text on different layers and turn off the layers that you didn't want in each viewport. You might also have created separate text styles for each text object. This was a complicated and time-demanding task. Annotative text can eliminate the need for separate layers and text styles when you need to display text at more than one scale.

To create annotative text, follow these steps:

1. Create an annotative text style and make it current. To create an annotative text style, see the "Understanding Text Styles" section earlier in this chapter. AutoCAD also comes with a text style named `Annotative` that you can use.

2. Decide on the scales that you will use for each text object. For example, you might have two text objects each at a different scale, or one text object that you need to display at two different scales.

 3. If you want each text object to have a different scale, turn off the ANNOAUTOSCALE system variable. When this system variable is on, it automatically adds scales to annotative objects as you add annotative scales; the result is that each object has more than one scale. To turn ANNOAUTOSCALE off, click the icon on the right side of the status bar to the right of the Annotation Scale list. The tooltip reads "Automatically Add Scales to Annotative Objects When the Annotation Scale Changes." When on, there's a yellow lightning bolt; when off, the lightning bolt is gray.

4. Set the annotation scale for the first text object. To do so, click the Annotation Scale button at the right side of the status bar to display the scale list and choose the scale you want. For example, choose 1:4 if you plan to display the text in a viewport at the 1:4 scale. (The first time you add an annotative object to a drawing, a dialog box may open automatically, asking you for the scale.)

Cross-Reference

In Chapter 5, I explain scales in general and how to edit the scale list. ∎

5. Start the TEXT or MTEXT command and enter the text.

6. Repeat Steps 4 and 5 for each separate scale and text item.

7. When you're ready to plot, you can set the desired annotative scale, and plot. You can also create viewports and set their scale. See Chapter 17 for details and an exercise using annotative objects.

If you want one text object to have more than one scale, you can add an annotative scale to it. Follow these steps:

1. Select the text.

2. Choose Annotate tab ⇨ Annotation Scaling panel ⇨ Add/Delete Scales to open the Annotation Object Scale dialog box, as shown in Figure 13.15. You can also display the Properties palette, click the Annotative Scale item, and click the Ellipsis button that appears.

3. Click Add to display the Add Scales to Object dialog box, where you can choose one or more scales.

4. Click OK twice to close both dialog boxes.

You can add or delete scales for annotative objects in the Annotation Object Scale dialog box.

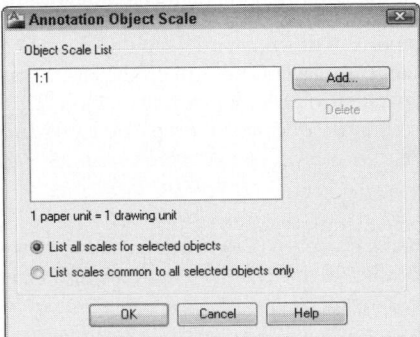

 At any time, you can view the text for any single scale, or view the text for all scales. (This applies to all types of annotative objects, not just text.) Remember that you may have one or more scales for any one text item. If you don't see all the scales of an annotative object, click the Annotation Visibility button on the right side of the status bar. This button controls the ANNOALLVISIBLE system variable. By default, it is on, displaying all scales. When you turn it off, you see only the text for the current annotative scale. To immediately plot, you would turn off this system variable so that you plot only the text for the current annotative scale.

If you want to change a text object that is not annotative to one that is annotative, you can use the Properties palette. Follow these steps:

1. Select the text.

2. Display the Properties palette.

3. In the Properties palette, select the Annotative property and choose Yes from the drop-down list. The Annotative Scale property is displayed in the Properties palette when the Annotative property is set to Yes.

4. Select the Annotative Scale property and click the Ellipsis button that is displayed to open the Annotation Object Scale dialog box, shown in Figure 13.15.

5. Click Add to display the Add Scales to Object dialog box, where you can choose one or more scales.

6. Click OK twice to close both dialog boxes.

Editing paragraph text

To edit paragraph text, double-click the text to start the In-Place Text Editor.

Make your changes in the editor. The techniques are similar to those in any word processor. You can:

● Select text and press the Delete key to delete the text, or type to replace the selected text.

- Click to move the insertion point to where you want to insert text and start typing. (To type over text, press Insert to enter overtype mode.)
- Use the Ribbon or shortcut menu (right-click) to change formatting.

To change characters, you must first highlight the characters. This lets you make height or font changes to individual words or even letters. When changing properties that affect the entire paragraph, such as justification, you do not first highlight the characters.

If you right-click in the In-Place Text Editor with the cursor on a field, you have options to edit the field, update it, or convert it to regular text. For more information about fields, see the section "Inserting Fields" later in this chapter.

On the DVD

Mmt combines two Mtext objects into one Mtext paragraph. Look in \Software\Chapter13\Mmt on the DVD. Txtexprt exports text to a text file. It's in \Software\Chapter13\txtexprt. These features work with AutoCAD only. ■

Importing text

As mentioned earlier, you can import text by using the In-Place Text Editor. You can also import text in three other ways:

- You can use drag-and-drop to insert text from a .txt file into a drawing. Open Windows Explorer and locate the file. Position the Explorer window so that you can see the filename and your drawing at the same time. Click the file and drag it to your drawing. The new text becomes multiline text in the drawing.
- You can copy text from another file to the Windows Clipboard. Open the other file, select the text, and copy the text to the Windows Clipboard. Return to your drawing by clicking the AutoCAD or AutoCAD LT button on the Windows task bar. Choose Home tab⇨Clipboard panel⇨Paste drop-down list⇨Paste (or press Ctrl+V). If you double-click this text, the original application opens.
- If you have the In-Place Text Editor open, you can paste the text directly into the editor. Right-click in the editor and choose Paste (or press Ctrl+V). You can then format the text.

Cross-Reference

For more information on importing text, see Chapter 27. ■

On the DVD

The files used in the following exercise on creating multiline text, ab13-c.dwg and ab13-c.txt, are in the Drawings folder on the DVD. ■

STEPS: Creating Multiline Text

1. Open ab13-c.dwg from your DVD.
2. Save the file as ab13-05.dwg in your AutoCAD Bible folder. This is a plat drawing, as shown in Figure 13.16.

FIGURE 13.16

The plat drawing.

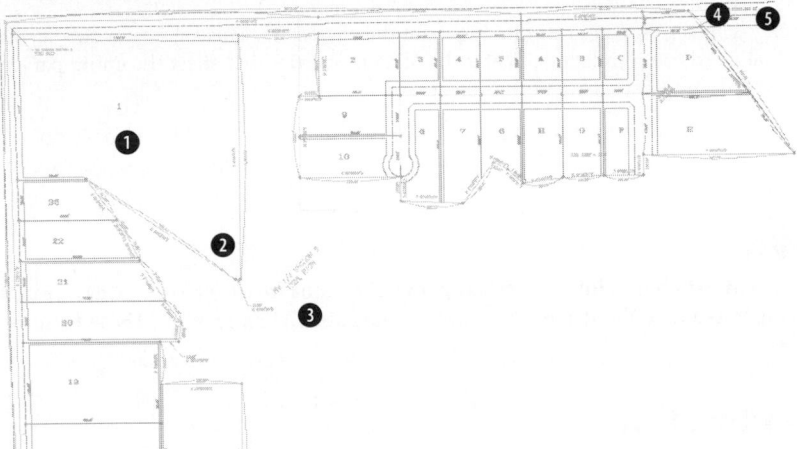

Thanks to Bill Maidment of Cantech, Inc., Fairfield, Iowa, for this drawing.

3. Choose Home tab ⇨ Annotation panel ⇨ Text drop-down list ⇨ Multiline Text. At the prompts, pick points ❶ and ❷, shown in Figure 13.16. The Text Editor tab is displayed. In the Text Height box in the Style panel, type a height of **12.5** and press Enter. In the main editing box, type the following:

   Containing 108.33 acres including 5.97 acres existing R.O.W. and 4.56 acres proposed R.O.W.

4. Highlight the text 108.33 and click Underline in the Formatting panel. In the Paragraph panel, choose Justification ⇨ Middle Left. Click outside the text editor to place the text.

5. Open Windows Explorer (right-click Start and choose Explorer or Open Windows Explorer). Find `ab13-c.txt` on your DVD. Move the Windows Explorer window so that you can see both `ab13-c.txt` and your drawing screen. Drag `ab13-c.txt` from the Windows Explorer window to ❸, shown in Figure 13.16, and release the mouse button. If necessary, pick a grip, press the Spacebar once to choose the Move option, and click at the proper location.

6. Select the text and open the Properties palette (Ctrl+1). Next to the Defined Width item, type 500 ↵. Next to the Defined Height item, type **12.5** ↵.

7. Zoom in on the new text. This text was originally single-line text in an older drawing. You can see why you wouldn't want to retype it!

8. Choose View tab ⇨ Zoom drop-down list ⇨ Previous to return to your original view. Repeat this process, this time choosing the Window option to zoom in to the area bounded by ❹ and ❺. Set the current layer to 0, which is a gray color.

9. Above the text about the proposed R.O.W. (right of way) is a yellow centerline. You want to place text on that line. Choose Home tab ⇨ Annotation panel ⇨ Text drop-down list ⇨ Multiline Text.

10. At the prompt, pick ❹ and ❺, centering the bounding box around the yellow centerline. In the Text Height box of the Style panel, change the text to 12.5. The text style should be ROMANS. Type the following text:

    64TH AVE N.W. EXISTING R.O.W. 66' – CURRENT

11. Press the Spacebar to add a space after CURRENT. From the Insert panel, choose Symbol ⇨ Center Line to add the centerline symbol to the end of the text.

12. To add a background mask so that the yellow centerline doesn't make the text hard to read, choose Background Mask from the Formatting panel. In the Background Mask dialog box, select the Use Background Mask check box. Choose Red as the background color and click OK. Click anywhere outside the In-Place Text Editor to place the text. You can see that it uses the centerline symbol and has a red background that hides the yellow centerline behind the text.

13. Start the MTEXT command. At the prompts, define a border somewhere in the middle of the drawing. The width should be equal to about three of the plats that you see at the top. Type **Plat Acreage** ↵.

14. Type **1.**, press Tab, and type **22.93** ↵. Be sure to insert a tab after the period. AutoCAD or AutoCAD LT automatically creates a numbered list when you use this format. You should now see the number two with a period after it (2.).

15. Finish the rest of the numbered list as follows:

    2. 2.85 ↵
    3. 1.51 ↵
    4. 1.38

16. Click anywhere outside the In-Place Text Editor area to end the MTEXT command.

17. Zoom to the Previous display to return to your original view. Save your drawing.

Creating Tables

Tables, which are often called schedules, are very common in drawings. You can save your formatting in table styles for consistency among drawings. You should save table styles in your templates.

Inserting a table

 To insert a table, choose Home tab ⇨ Annotation panel ⇨ Table, to start the TABLE command. The Insert Table dialog box opens, as shown in Figure 13.17.

On the left side of the Insert Table dialog box, you see a preview of how the table will look. By default, you see either the Standard table style or the last table style that you used. Choose the table style that you want from the Table Style name drop-down list. In the next section, I explain how to define a table style.

In the Insert Options section, you can choose from three options for getting data into the table:

- **Start from empty table.** Use this option when you want to manually enter the data.

- **From a data link.** This option creates a table from Microsoft Excel spreadsheet data or a comma-delimited (CSV) file. When you choose this option, most of the rest of the Insert Table dialog box is unavailable.

- **From object data in the drawing (Data Extraction).** This option creates a table from properties of existing objects in the drawing (AutoCAD only).

FIGURE 13.17

Use the Insert Table dialog box to create a table in your drawing.

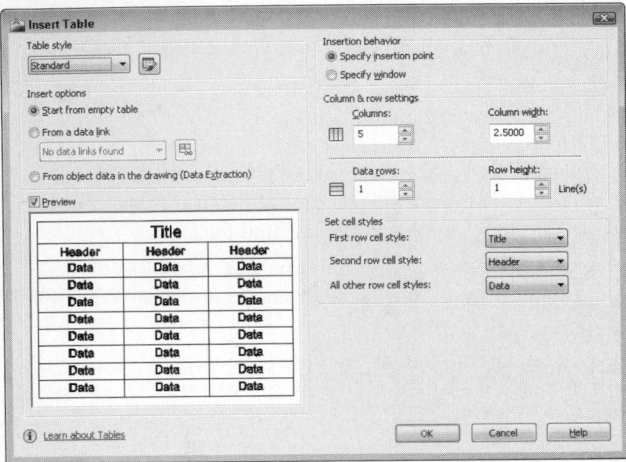

If you choose to start from an empty table, you can choose from one of the following options in the Insertion Behavior section of the dialog box:

- **Specify insertion point.** You place the table in your drawing by specifying an insertion point (the default). You use the Column & Row Settings section to specify the number of columns and their width, as well as the number of rows and their height (in terms of lines of text).

- **Specify window.** You pick a point at the upper-left and then lower-right corner of the table. You use the Column & Row Settings section to specify the number of columns and the line height of the rows. As you move the mouse to the right, the columns widen, and as you move the mouse downward, additional rows are added. Click when you see the size that you want.

In the Set Cell Styles section, you specify which cell styles go where. See the next section for an explanation of cell styles. By default, the First Row Cell Style uses the Title cell style, the Second Row Cell Style uses the Header cell style, and All Other Row Cell Styles use the Data cell style. If you create your own cell styles, you can choose them from the drop-down lists here.

If the table style shown is what you want, click OK. Then specify an insertion point or window to place the table.

Cross-Reference

You can also add a table to a tool palette and insert a table from the tool palette. For more information on tool palettes, see Chapter 26. ■

Specifying a table style

You have a great deal of control over how your table looks. You can make it plain or fancy. To design your table, you create a table style by choosing Home tab ⇨ Annotation panel (expanded) ⇨ Table Style to open the Table Style dialog box, as shown in Figure 13.18. Alternatively, you can click the Launch the Table Style Dialog button in the Table Style section of the Insert Table dialog box.

FIGURE 13.18

The Table Style dialog box gives you the tools to create tables with style.

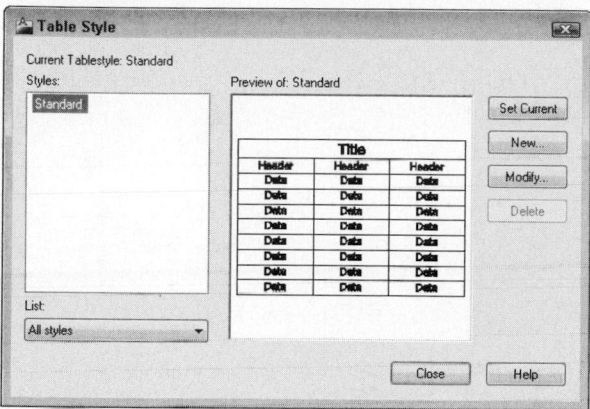

On the left side of the Table Style dialog box is a list of styles. From the List drop-down list at the bottom, you can choose to display all styles or only styles that are in use in your drawing. To make a table style current, choose the style that you want and click Set Current.

Tip

An easier way to make a table style current is to choose the table style from the Table Style drop-down list in the Annotation panel (expanded) of the Home tab or the Tables panel on the Annotate tab. Choose your table style before you start to create a table. You can also import table styles from the DesignCenter. (For more information on the DesignCenter, see Chapter 26.) ∎

To create a new style, click the New button. In the Create New Table Style dialog box, enter a Name in the New Style Name text box. From the Start With drop-down list, choose an existing table style as a basis for your new style. The new table style inherits the properties of this existing style so that you have to specify only the differences that you want. Then click Continue to open the New Table Style dialog box, as shown in Figure 13.19.

Note

You can select an existing table in the drawing as a starting point. In the Starting Table section, click the button to select a table in your drawing. ∎

As you define your new table style, the preview panel shows you the results. You use the Cell Styles drop-down list to format data in the cells of the table, column headers, and the table's main title. Each category is one of the preexisting *cell styles* ¾ data, header, and title ¾ but you can create your own.

You use the three tabs to define general, text, and border formatting for each cell style. In this way, you format the entire table. The three cell styles are very similar, but have slightly different defaults. For example, the Title cell style has centered text and a larger height than the headers and data cells.

 To create a cell style as you work, first click the Create a New Cell Style button in the Cell Styles section of the dialog box. In the Create New Cell Style dialog box, enter a name and choose an existing cell style to start from. Click Continue. You return to the New Table Style dialog box, where you can now specify formatting.

FIGURE 13.19

The New Table Style dialog box is the place to define a new table style.

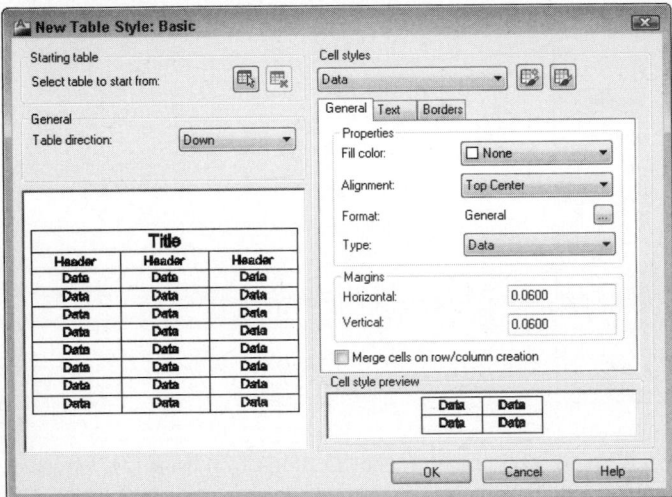

 At any time, you can manage cell styles by clicking the Manage Cell Styles Dialog button. In the Manage Cell Styles dialog box, you can rename and delete existing cell styles.

General properties

The General tab lets you define the following properties:

- **Fill color.** Click the Fill Color drop-down list to choose a color, or choose Select Color to open the Select Color dialog box. The default is None, which shows the background color of your drawing area.

- **Alignment.** Use the Alignment drop-down list to specify the text alignment within each cell. For example, you might want to use Middle Center for the title and column headings, and Middle Left for the data cells.

- **Format.** Click the Ellipsis button to open the Table Cell Format dialog box, where you can specify the data format. The default is general, which is good for text, but you can also format data for angles, currency, dates, decimal numbers, percentages, points, text, and whole numbers. Click the Additional Format button to open the Additional Format dialog box, where you can add a prefix or suffix, specify the number separator, and format zero suppression.

- **Type.** Choose Data or Label. Use a label cell for a header or title. If you break a table into sections, then you can repeat label cells for each section. It's common to repeat headers when breaking a table.

- **Margins.** The cell margins are the space between the text and the cell borders. The horizontal margins affect the left and right sides of the text, while the vertical margins affect the top and bottom of the text. Enter a value in the Horizontal and Vertical text boxes.

Check the Merge Cells on Row/Column Creation check box for titles that you want to span across an entire table.

Text properties

The Text tab lets you specify properties for cells. You can choose a text style from the Text Style drop-down list or click the Ellipsis button to open the Text Style dialog box. (See the "Understanding Text Styles" section earlier in this chapter.)

You can also specify the text height (if the text style has a height of 0), a text color, and a text angle. The default text color is ByBlock, which means that the text color is the same as the actual table ¾ which is a block. (I explain blocks and the ByBlock attribute in Chapter 18.) You can also choose ByLayer, which gives the text the properties of the current layer.

Border properties

Use the Borders tab to specify the properties of the lines around the cells. Choose one of the border buttons to specify which borders you want to see. For example, for the data cells, if you choose Outside Borders, the data area of the table will not have any grid lines between the data cells, only around the outside of the cells.

Caution

If you inadvertently create a table style with only outside borders, you may not notice the absence of borders in your drawing, where grid lines show between the cells so that you can more easily fill in the table. Choose Preview on the Plot panel of the Output tab on the Ribbon to see the final result more accurately. ■

Choose a border lineweight from the Lineweight drop-down list. For example, you may want a slightly thicker lineweight for the title cell. If you don't want to use continuous lines, then choose a linetype from the Linetype drop-down list. Then choose a color from the Color drop-down list. If you leave the ByBlock defaults, the lineweight, linetype, and color will match the layer of the table. Check Double Line to show two lines instead of one along the edge of the border for a cell. You control the spacing between the double lines with the value in the Spacing box.

Completing the table style

Repeat the process of specifying general, text, and border properties for each of the three cell styles or your own styles. You access the styles from the Cell Styles drop-down list.

If you're creating your own cell styles, you specify which cell style goes where when you insert the table. (See Figure 13.17 earlier in this chapter.) Remember that you choose a cell style for the first row (usually the title), second row (usually the headers), and for all other rows (usually the data cells). Therefore, you would usually create three cell styles, one for each of these categories.

When you're done, click OK to return to the Table Style dialog box. Click Close. If you opened the Table Style dialog box from the Insert Table dialog box, then you're back in the Insert Table dialog box. If you opened the Table Style dialog box separately, open the Insert Table dialog box as described earlier in this chapter and choose the table style you want from the Table Style drop-down list. Either way, specify any other settings you want and insert the table.

Adding data to a table

You can add data to a table from three sources:

- You can enter data by typing it.
- You can link to external data — a Microsoft Office Excel worksheet or comma-delimited (CVS) file.
- You can extract data from existing objects in the drawing (AutoCAD only).

You choose which method you want to use in the Insert Options section of the Insert Table dialog box. I discuss the first two methods in the next two sections.

AutoCAD Only

AutoCAD LT includes the ability to create a table from external data, but not from object data. ∎

Entering data into a table

After you've placed a table, you can then enter data into the table. The cursor is automatically placed in the first cell, and you can just start typing. Press Tab to move to the next cell or press an arrow key to move to an adjacent cell. Continue in this way until you have completed the table. Figure 13.20 shows an example of a table.

FIGURE 13.20

A nicely styled schedule of parts.

Parts Schedule		
Tag	Part No.	Description
11	9075-052-002	Collar-Shaft
17	9029-072-001	Bracket-Tube Assembly
19	9081-114-001	Channel Motor Mtg. Rod

Tip

You can create a complete table on the fly by importing data from Microsoft Excel. Select the data in Excel and copy it to the Windows Clipboard. In AutoCAD, choose Home tab ⇨ Clipboard panel ⇨ Paste drop-down list ⇨ Paste Special. In the Paste Special dialog box, choose AutoCAD Entities and click OK. At the prompt, pick an insertion point. ∎

You can insert a field into any cell in a table. Select a blank cell, right-click, and choose Insert ⇨ Field. For more about fields, see the "Inserting Fields" section, later in this chapter. You can also insert blocks into a table. (I explain blocks in Chapter 18.) To do so, select a blank cell, right-click, and choose Insert ⇨ Block.

You can create tables that function like a spreadsheet. To enter a formula into a cell, follow these steps:

1. Select the cell.
2. Right-click and choose Insert ⇨ Formula.
3. Choose one of the suboptions.

   - **Sum.** Adds rows or columns. At the Select first corner of table cell range: prompt, pick inside the first cell. At the Select second corner of table cell range: prompt, pick inside the last cell. You see the formula listed in the cell, for example, =Sum(C3:C5).
   - **Average.** Averages rows or columns. At the Select first corner of table cell range: prompt, pick inside the first cell. At the Select second corner of table cell range: prompt, pick inside the last cell. You see the formula listed in the cell, for example, =Average(C3:C5).

- **Count.** Counts the number of cells in a row or column. At the `Select first corner of table cell range:` prompt, pick inside the first cell. At the `Select second corner of table cell range:` prompt, pick inside the last cell. You see the formula listed in the cell, for example, =Count(C3:C5).

- **Cell.** Displays the value of another cell. At the `Select table cell:` prompt, select the cell that you want to display. You see the formula listed in the cell, for example, =C3.

- **Equation.** Lets you write your own equation. You just see an equal sign (=) in the cell. Enter the equation, for example =a3+b4.

Note

To create equations, you use the same conventions as for spreadsheets. For example, you use an asterisk (*) for multiplication, a slash (/) for division, a caret (^) for powers, and `sqrt` for a square root. ∎

You also see row headings (1, 2, 3, and so on) and column headings (A, B, C, and so on), so that you can easily determine any cell's address.

4. Press Enter to place the value of the formula.

Tip

You can auto-fill data like you can in Excel. This makes it easy to copy data along a row or column and to automatically create incremental data, such as consecutive numbers. To auto-fill cell data, click in a cell that you've already filled with a value. Click and drag the cyan (turquoise) diamond to the desired cell and click. To auto-fill incremental data, such as consecutive numbers, drag across two cells that already have incremental data. For example, if you typed 1 and 2, drag across those cells. Then click and drag the cyan diamond to the desired cell and click. Before the final click, a tooltip shows you what results to expect. ∎

Linking to external data

You can create a table that links to external data that was created in Microsoft Excel or that is in comma-delimited (CSV) format. The link maintains its connection, so that if you change the spreadsheet, the table in your drawing also changes. You also have the option to change the external data from within AutoCAD.

Cross-Reference

In Chapter 20, I cover the external database connectivity feature. While this feature also allows you to connect to Microsoft Access databases and other types of databases, it's more complicated to use. ∎

To create a linked table, you first need an Excel or CSV file. Make sure that you know the file's name and location. Then choose Home tab ⇨ Annotation panel ⇨ Table. From the Insert Options section of the Insert Table dialog box, choose From a Data Link. For the rest of the dialog box, see the section "Creating Tables" earlier in this chapter.

 To connect to a link you've already created, choose it from the drop-down list. To create a new link to a spreadsheet, click the Launch the Data Link Manager Dialog button to open the Select a Data Link dialog box. Choose Create a New Excel Data Link. In the Enter Data Link Name dialog box, enter a meaningful name and click OK.

The New Excel Data Link dialog box opens. Click the Ellipsis button at the right to choose an Excel file. When you click Open, you return to the New Excel Data Link dialog box. Select the Preview check box to list your data link, as shown on the left in Figure 13.21.

FIGURE 13.21

You can create a table that links to Excel data.

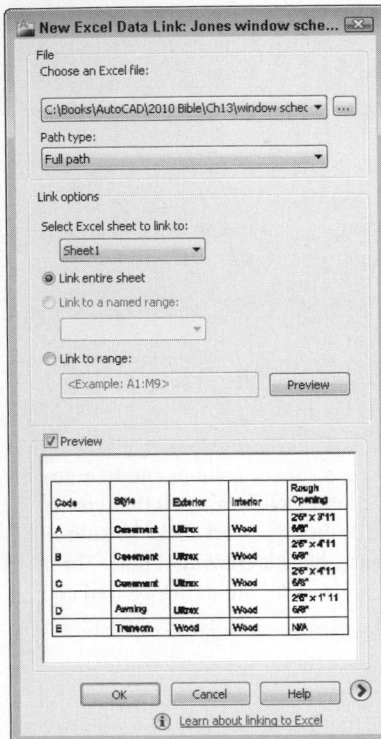

Code	Style	Exterior	Interior	Rough Opening
A	Casement	Ultrex	Wood	2'5" x 3'11 5/8"
B	Casement	Ultrex	Wood	2'5" x 4'11 5/8"
C	Casement	Ultrex	Wood	2'5" x 4'11 5/8"
D	Awning	Ultrex	Wood	2'5" x 1'-11 5/8"
E	Transom	Wood	Wood	N/A

In the Link Options section, you can choose which sheet you want to use, and you can link to a named range (you can name ranges of cells in Excel) or you can specify a range, such as A1:H20. Click OK to return to the Select a Data Link dialog box, where your data link is now listed and highlighted. Click OK to return to the Insert Table dialog box. You should see your table in the Preview box.

Note

You can click the More Options arrow at the lower-right corner of the New/Modify Excel Data Link dialog box to convert cell data to text, to turn off the ability to save changes that you make in AutoCAD back to the source spreadsheet, and to control cell formatting. You can choose whether or not to use Excel formatting and keep the table updated to the formatting in the Excel file. ∎

Click OK one more time and specify an insertion point to insert the table into your drawing. You may have to resize the table to avoid unwanted word wrapping in the cells. (See the upcoming section, "Modifying a table," for instructions.) Figure 13.21 shows the result on the right.

When you create a linked table, it's locked to prevent changes; this makes sense, because the content should come from the Excel spreadsheet. However, you can unlock it and make changes; you can save these changes back to the spreadsheet to keep the two data sources the same. To unlock data (both content and formatting), select one or more cells, right-click, and choose Locking⇨Unlocked. After changing the data, right-click and then choose Data Links⇨Upload User Changes to Source File.

Extracting data from drawing objects

You can create a table that contains information about the objects in your drawing. For example, you might want to display the number of window blocks and their location. If a circle represents trees and bushes in a landscaping plan, you could list the number of circles and their layer; perhaps you have a tree and a bush layer. You can extract data from all objects, not just blocks. For information about extracting data from blocks using attributes, see Chapter 18. You cannot extract data from drawing objects in AutoCAD LT.

To create a table from object data, choose Home tab⇨Annotation panel⇨Table. In the Insert Table dialog box (see Figure 13.17 earlier in this chapter), choose From Object Data in the Drawing (Data Extraction) in the Insert Options section and click OK. Page 1 of the Data Extraction Wizard opens, as shown in Figure 13.22.

FIGURE 13.22

The Data Extraction Wizard guides you through the process of creating a table from object data.

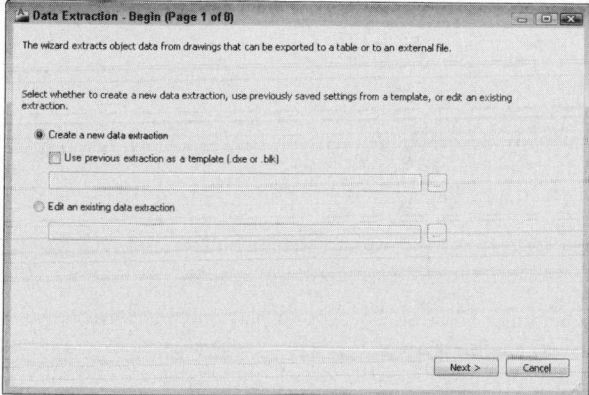

Choose to create a new extraction or edit an existing one. If you want to create a new extraction, you can use one of two types of files as a template to use settings you've specified previously:

- **DXE.** When you create a data extraction table, AutoCAD creates a DXE file that contains settings for the extraction.
- **BLK.** When you extract attribute information from blocks, you can save a BLK file, which is a template that defines the settings for the extraction.

The following explains how to create a new data extraction without a template. Choose Create a New Data Extraction and click Next. The Save Data Extraction As dialog box opens, so you can save a DXE file; this is the file that you can use in the future as a template. Choose a name and location and click Save.

On the Define Data Source (Page 2 of 8) page of the wizard, you define which objects you want to include and where they come from. You can use a Sheet Set, which is a collection of drawings (covered in Chapter 26) or choose any drawings that you want. The Drawing Files and Folders box lists the drawings and their locations. If you want to use objects from other drawings, click Add Drawings. To add all the drawings in a folder, click Add Folder.

If you choose multiple drawings, you create a table from all the objects in those drawings. If you want to select specific objects, you can do so only in the current drawing. In that case, choose the Select Objects in the Current Drawing option. The following assumes that you are selecting objects in the current drawing.

Click the Settings button to open the Data Extraction - Additional Settings dialog box, shown in Figure 13.23, where you define which types of objects you want to include. These settings are particularly important if you are extracting data from entire drawings (rather than selecting objects) and you have blocks or xrefs in those drawings. (I cover blocks in Chapter 18 and xrefs in Chapter 19.) Choose whether you want to extract data from blocks and xrefs and whether to include xrefs in the block count. You can also choose whether to include objects only in model space or all objects in the drawing, meaning also objects in layouts. (See Chapter 17 for coverage of layouts.)

FIGURE 13.23

You can specify what kinds of objects you want to include in your data extraction.

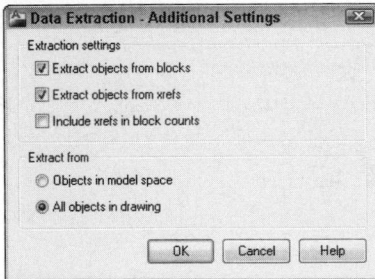

 You're now ready to select objects. Click the Select Objects in the Current Drawing button. You return to your drawing, where you select objects. End selection to return to the wizard. Click Next.

The Select Objects page shows the objects you've selected. You can choose to display only blocks or only non-blocks, instead of the default, which is to display all object types. If you're interested in blocks, you can choose to include only blocks with attributes. Finally, you can choose to display objects that are currently in use because some blocks may be defined but not inserted into the drawing. (See Chapter 18 for information about attributes.) Then click Next.

On the Select Properties page, you specify which properties of the objects you want to include. The properties come in 10 categories:

- **3D Visualization.** Includes materials assigned to objects. (See Chapter 22.)
- **Attribute.** Includes blocks and dynamic blocks with attributes. (See Chapter 18.)
- **Drawing.** File-related information including the author, date created, dated accessed, location, name, size, total editing time, and so on.
- **Dynamic blocks.** Properties of dynamic blocks. (See Chapter 18.)
- **General.** Includes color, layer, linetype, linetype scale, plot style, thickness, and hyperlink.
- **Geometry.** Depending on the type of object, can include area; center; circumference; diameter; length; radius; start angle; total angle; delta (change) in X, Y, and Z; start of X, Y, and Z coordinates; and so on.
- **Misc.** Includes closed (or open).

- **Pattern.** Includes hatch pattern properties, which I cover in Chapter 16.
- **Table.** Includes table properties.
- **Text.** Includes single or multiline text properties.

For each category, you can choose which property you want to include by checking the check boxes. As you can see, your choices depend on why you're extracting the data. In some cases, you may want drawing information for archiving purposes; in other cases, you may be interested only in geometry data. When you're done, click Next.

On the Refine Data page, you can reorder and sort columns, filter the results, combine identical rows, specify if you want a count or a name column, add formulas, and include external data. Click on a column and right-click for numerous options, including the ability to rename and hide columns. Click on any column to sort by that column, and click again to reverse the sorting order. Right-click and choose Filter Options to open the Filter dialog box, which is similar to the Quick Select feature (described in Chapter 10), but has fewer options.

Tip

When extracting data, you can add formulas such as totals to a column. Right-click the column and choose Insert Totals Footer. You can choose Sum, Max, Min, or Average. You can also create a new column from data in other columns. Right-click any column and choose Insert Formula Column. Use the Insert Formula Column dialog box to specify the formula. Click OK. ■

Click the Full Preview button to see what the table will look like in a new window; then click the window's Close button to return to the wizard and click Next.

On the Choose Output page, you can choose to create a table and insert it into a drawing, output the data to an external file (XLS, CSV, MDB, or TXT), or both. If you choose to create an external file, click the Ellipsis button to browse to a location and give the file a name. Then click Next.

If you chose to create a table, you now choose a table style or manually set up the table. Then click Next. The Finish page explains that you need to specify an insertion point for the table and that the external file you requested (if any) will be created when you click the Finish button. Click the Finish button and you're done.

Modifying a table

You may need to change the data in a table, or you may want to change the way the table looks. Either way, you can modify a table easily. However, you need to know some of the techniques involved, because tables in AutoCAD and AutoCAD LT are a little different from tables in your word processor.

Changing the text

Changing the text of a table is like changing any multiline text. Double-click the text inside a table, being careful not to double-click the grid lines. The In-Place Text Editor opens. You can use any of the techniques for editing text that I discuss in the "Editing paragraph text" section earlier in this chapter. You can change the properties of the text so that they don't match the table style. For example, you can change the height or font of the text.

Changing table properties

You can also change properties of the table itself. Open the Properties palette (Ctrl+1) and select the table. Here, you can modify any conceivable table property, including its layer, its color, the number of rows or columns, or any of its style properties. If you want to revert to old-fashioned lines, you can explode the table. Of course, you can no longer edit the table as a table anymore; you just have lines and text.

To select the entire table, click any gridline of the table. You see grips at the corners of the table and at several other cell junctions. To understand editing tables with grips, imagine that the left side of the table is the stable side, while the right side of the table is the flexible side. The top-left grip is the base point for the entire table. You can do the following edits with grips:

- **Upper-left grip.** Moves the entire table.
- **Upper-right grip.** Stretches the table horizontally. As you change the width of the table, the columns also stretch proportionally.
- **Lower-left grip.** Stretches the table vertically. As you change the height of the table, the rows also stretch proportionally.
- **Lower-right grip.** Stretches the table both vertically and horizontally. The columns and rows adjust proportionally.
- **Top-of-column grip.** Adjusts the width of the column to the left or right of the grip. The entire table adjusts accordingly. If you press Ctrl while moving a column grip, the adjacent columns adjust, but the width of the table remains unchanged.
- **Bottom-center grip.** Adjusts the table break height. Drag the grip up or down to adjust the height at which the table breaks into additional tables. See "Breaking a table into sections" for more information.

If you select the table and right-click, then you can use the shortcut menu to make additional changes to the table. For example, you can size columns or rows equally or remove property overrides. If you make a change to a cell, such as the cell's alignment or color, you can use the Remove All Property Overrides item on the shortcut menu to change the cell's properties back to match the rest of the table.

Changing cell properties

To select a cell, click inside that cell. You can also click a column or row header, or drag across several cells to select them. The Table Cell tab appears on the Ribbon. (If you're using the AutoCAD Classic workspace, you'll see a Table toolbar.)

In the Rows panel, the following items are available:

- **Insert Above.** Inserts a row above the selected cell or row.
- **Insert Below.** Inserts a row below the selected cell or row.
- **Delete Row(s).** Deletes the selected row or the row of the selected cell.

In the Columns panel, the following items are available:

- **Insert Left.** Inserts a column to the left of the selected cell or row.
- **Insert Right.** Inserts a column to the right of the selected cell or row.
- **Delete Column(s).** Deletes the selected column or the column of the selected cell.

In the Merge panel, you have the following options:

- **Merge Cells.** Merges selected cells. You need to select multiple cells. (See techniques for doing so after this list.) The suboptions let you merge by row or by column. By merging cells, you can create complex table structures.
- **Unmerge Cells.** Unmerges selected cells that you previously merged.

In the Cell Styles panels, the following options are available:

- **Match Cell.** Matches cell properties. At the `Select destination cell:` prompt on the command line, pick another cell that you want to have the same properties. The prompt repeats until you press Enter.
- **Cell Alignment.** Changes the alignment of the text in the cell, using the standard text-alignment options available for multiline text.
- **Cell Styles.** Enables you to choose a cell style for the selected cell from the drop-down list. You can also choose to create a new cell style or manage existing cell styles.
- **Background Fill.** Sets a background color for the selected cell.
- **Edit Borders.** Opens the Cell Border Properties dialog box, where you can specify border properties for that individual cell.

The Cell Format panel has two options:

- **Locking.** Locks or unlocks the format and/or the data of the selection. Text from external links or data extraction is locked by default.
- **Data Format.** Allows you to choose a format from a drop-down list. Choose Custom Table Cell Format to open the Table Cell Format dialog box, where you can change the data type and format.

The Insert panel has the following options:

- **Block.** Opens the Insert a Block in a Table Cell dialog box, where you can select the block that you want to insert, specify the block's alignment in the cell, and set its scale and rotation angle. If you select the AutoFit check box, the block is automatically scaled to fit the table cell.
- **Field.** Lets you insert or edit a field. I discuss fields in the next section of this chapter.
- **Formula.** Lets you insert a formula, as explained in the "Entering data into a table" section earlier in this chapter.
- **Manage Cell Contents.** Applies when you have more than one block in a cell. The Manage Cell Content dialog box opens, where you can change the order of the blocks and change the way they're laid out.

In the Data panel, the following options are available:

- **Link Cell.** Enables you to link the selected cell to an Excel spreadsheet. For more information, see the section "Linking to external data" earlier in this chapter.
- **Download from Source.** Updates links, if available, from an external spreadsheet, in case that spreadsheet has changed.

You can access some additional options by right-clicking with a cell or cells selected:

- **Remove All Property Overrides.** Removes any formatting that you applied to the selected cell.
- **Edit Text.** Opens the In-Place Text Editor so that you can edit text.
- **Delete All Contents.** Deletes any text or block in the current cell.
- **Columns ⇨ Size Equally.** Makes two or more columns that you select equally wide.
- **Rows ⇨ Size Equally.** Makes all your rows an equal height.
- **Properties.** Opens the Properties palette so that you can change the cell's properties.
- **Quick Properties.** Opens the Quick Properties palette so that you can change the cell's properties.

When you edit a table, column and row headers appear so that you can easily refer to cells in your formulas. You can change the background color of these headers to make the text clearer. Select a table, right-click, and choose Table Indicator Color. You can then choose a color in the Select Color dialog box.

You can select multiple cells and apply changes to those cells. To select multiple cells, use one of the following techniques:

- Click a row or column header to select an entire row or column.
- Click inside one cell and drag over the other cells that you want to select. Release the mouse button at the last cell.
- Click inside one cell, hold down Shift, and click inside the last cell that you want to select.

Tip

To enter the same text in multiple cells, select the cells. Then open the Properties palette and enter the text in the Contents item. The text appears in all the selected cells. ■

You can export a table to comma-delimited (.csv) format. You can then open the table data with a database or spreadsheet program. To export a table, follow these steps:

1. Select the table.
2. Right-click and choose Export.
3. In the Export Data dialog box, choose a name and location for the file.
4. Click Save.

Breaking a table into sections

Sometimes you need to fit a table into a tight space; to do so, you might want to break up the table into two or more sections.

Breaking a table is easy, but you can also access a number of settings to fine-tune how it works. To break a table, click it once to select it. Then drag the cyan down arrow, located at the bottom of the table, upward to the point where you want the table to break (see Figure 13.24), and click.

FIGURE 13.24

You can break a table by dragging upward on the Table Breaking arrow.

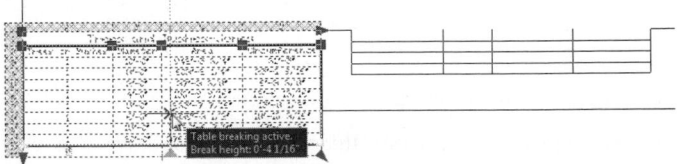

To adjust breaking settings, open the Properties palette. In the Table Breaks section, you can set the direction of subsequent sections, repeat top labels, and repeat bottom labels. You can also manually set the position of sections, individually set the height of subsequent sections (otherwise, they're the same size as the first section), and set the spacing between the sections. In this example, I chose to repeat top labels; you can see the result in Figure 13.25.

FIGURE 13.25

After breaking, the table appears in two sections with top labels on each section.

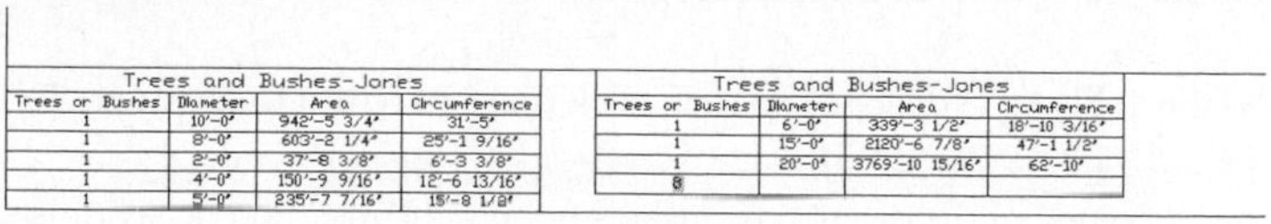

Trees and Bushes-Jones			
Trees or Bushes	Diameter	Area	Circumference
1	10'-0"	942'-5 3/4"	31'-5"
1	8'-0"	603'-2 1/4"	25'-1 9/16"
1	2'-0"	37'-8 3/8"	6'-3 3/8"
1	4'-0"	150'-9 9/16"	12'-6 13/16"
1	5'-0"	235'-7 7/16"	15'-8 1/8"

Trees and Bushes-Jones			
Trees or Bushes	Diameter	Area	Circumference
1	6'-0"	339'-3 1/2"	18'-10 3/16"
1	15'-0"	2120'-6 7/8"	47'-1 1/2"
1	20'-0"	3769'-10 15/16"	62'-10"
8			

Tip

To disable table breaks, change the Enabled property of a table in the Properties palette to No. ■

On the DVD

The drawing used in the following exercise on creating tables, `ab13-c.dwg`, is in the `Drawing` folder on the DVD. ■

STEPS: Creating Tables

1. Open `ab13-c.dwg` from the DVD. This is the same drawing used in the previous exercise.
2. Save the file as `ab13-06.dwg` in your `AutoCAD Bible` folder.
3. Choose Home tab ➪ Annotation panel ➪ Table. You'll create a table showing some of the plat numbers and their acreage.
4. In the Insert Table dialog box, click the Launch the Table Style Dialog button to the right of the Table Style Name drop-down list.
5. In the Table Style dialog box, click New. In the Create New Table Style dialog box, enter **Acreage Schedule** in the New Style Name text box. The Start With text box should read `Standard`. Click Continue. The New Table Style dialog box opens.
6. Make sure that the Data cell style appears in the Cell Styles drop-down list. To the right, click the Create a New Cell Style button, so that you can save the formatting that you will specify. In the Create New Cell Style dialog box, enter **Plat Data** and click Continue.
7. On the General tab, you want to set the numbers in the table to be right-aligned, so choose Middle Right from the Alignment drop-down list. In the Cell Margins section, change both the Horizontal and Vertical text box values to **5**.
8. Click the Text tab. From the Text Style drop-down list, choose `ROMANS`. In the Text Height text box, enter **12.5**.
9. To format the column headers, choose Header from the Cell Style drop-down list. Again, click the Create a New Cell Style button, name the cell style **Plat Header**, and click Continue. On the General tab, leave the alignment as Middle Center, but change the cell margins to **5**. On the Text tab, again set the Text Style to `ROMANS` and the Text Height to **12.5**.
10. Choose Title from the Cell Style drop-down list. Create a new cell style named **Plat Title**. Make the following changes:
    - **General tab.** Change the cell margins to **5**. From the Fill Color drop-down list, choose `Blue`.
    - **Text tab.** Choose `ROMANT` (for a different look). Change the Text Height to **13.5** to make the title text bigger than the rest of the table text. Click the Text Color drop-down list and choose

Select Color. From the Select Color dialog box, choose the light gray color (254) on the Index Color tab. Click OK to return to the New Table Style dialog box.

- **Borders tab.** From the Color drop-down list, choose Blue to match the fill. Click the All Borders button.

11. Click OK to return to the Table Style dialog box. Then click Close to return to the Insert Table dialog box.

12. In the Insertion Behavior section of the dialog box, make sure that the insertion behavior is set to `Specify insertion point`. In the Columns & Row Settings section, set the number of columns to 2 and the column width to 100. Set the number of data rows to 5. The row height should be 1 (which means one row high).

13. In the Set Cell Styles section, set the First Row Cell Style to Plat Titles, set Second Row Cell Style to Plat Header, and set All Other Row Cell Styles to Plat Data. Then click OK.

14. In your drawing, pick an insertion point anywhere in the lower-right area of the drawing. The In-Place Text Editor opens. Because you need to zoom in first, click anywhere outside the editor and do a Zoom Window around the table. Then double-click the table to open the In-Place Text Editor again, with the cursor in the title cell.

Tip

To zoom in without exiting the In-Place Text Editor, you can use the wheel of your mouse (if you have one). I explain how to zoom with the mouse wheel in Chapter 8. ∎

15. Complete the data for the four plats, shown in Figure 13.26, pressing Tab to go from cell to cell.

16. Type **Total** in the last row. Text Editor tab ⇨ Paragraph panel ⇨ Justification drop-down list ⇨ Middle Left.

17. Click anywhere outside the In-Place Text Editor and then click the lower-right cell to select it. Right-click the cell and choose Insert ⇨ Formula ⇨ Sum from the shortcut menu.

18. At the `Select first corner of table cell range:` prompt, click anywhere inside cell B3. At the `Select second corner of table cell range:` prompt, click anywhere inside cell B6. Press Enter. Your table should look like Figure 13.26.

19. Save your drawing.

FIGURE 13.26

The plat acreage table.

Plat Acreage	
Plat	Acreage
1	22.93
2	2.85
3	1.51
4	1.38
Total	28.67

Inserting Fields

Most drawings contain information about the drawing, such as the last date it was revised, the person who saved the drawing, or the sheet number in a sheet set. Draft plots often contain additional information, such as the time and drawing name. You may also want to insert information about drawing objects, such as the area or circumference of a circle. Fields store information and allow you to insert it into a drawing. You can also place fields in block attributes, which I discuss in Chapter 18. When your drawing changes, you can update the fields to keep them current. You can insert fields anywhere that you might normally use text. As you start using fields, you'll think of many uses for them. You can format the text of a field in the same way that you format any multiline text.

On the DVD

Sfld creates custom fields. Look in `\Software\Chapter 13\sfld.` ∎

Creating fields

To create a new field as a multiline text object, you can use two methods:

- Choose Insert tab ➪ Data panel ➪ Field (the FIELD command).
- Open the In-Place Text Editor or any other text box where you can enter text, right-click in the editor or text box, and choose Insert Field from the shortcut menu.

Whichever method you use, the Field dialog box opens, as shown in Figure 13.27.

FIGURE 13.27

Use the Field dialog box to choose, format, and insert a field into your drawing.

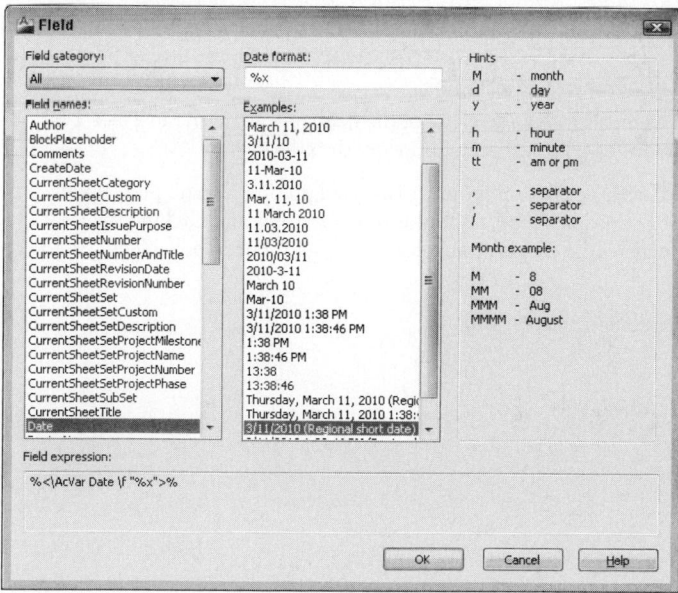

The Field dialog box offers a huge variety of fields. To give you an idea of the possibilities, here are the available categories of fields:

- **Date & Time.** Offers various formats for inserting dates and times.
- **Document.** Relates to data that you complete in the Properties dialog box. (Choose Application Button ⇨ Drawing Utilities ⇨ Drawing Properties.) I cover the Properties dialog box in Chapter 26.
- **Linked.** Creates a field from a hyperlink.
- **Objects.** Offers properties relating to block attributes, formulas in tables, named objects (such as named views, layers, blocks, and so on), and objects (any drawing object that you select).
- **Other.** Displays values of AutoLISP variables (AutoCAD Only) and system variables.
- **Plot.** Displays plot-related information such as scale, sheet size, and orientation.
- **SheetSet.** Displays values relating to sheet sets. (Sheet sets are available only in AutoCAD; I cover them in Chapter 26.)

Note that there are two date-related fields. The CreateDate field creates a date based on the current date. This field does not change if you open the drawing on a future date. For example, you can use this field to show the last time a drawing was updated. The Date field always shows the current date.

To insert a field, follow these steps:

1. Choose a field category from the Field Category drop-down list. You can use the All category to display all the fields. The other categories help you to filter the fields.
2. From the Field Names list, choose the field that you want to use.
3. Depending on the field that you choose, you can usually select a format or example for the field. For example, you can choose a date format (such as m/d/yyyy) or a text format (such as title case).
4. Click OK.
   - If you opened the Field dialog box by choosing Insert tab ⇨ Data panel ⇨ Field, the FIELD command starts, and you see the Specify start point or [Height/Justify]: prompt. Pick a start point or use one of the options.
   - If you started the MTEXT command first, the value of the field appears in the In-Place Text Editor. Click outside the editor to place the text, and close the editor.

By default, fields appear in your drawing with a gray background. This background doesn't plot. If you want, you can remove the background by choosing Application Button ⇨ Options, and clicking the User Preferences tab. In the Fields section, uncheck the Display Background of Fields check box. Click OK to close the Options dialog box.

Figure 13.28 shows an example of a titleblock that uses fields.

FIGURE 13.28

Filling in a titleblock is easier when you use fields.

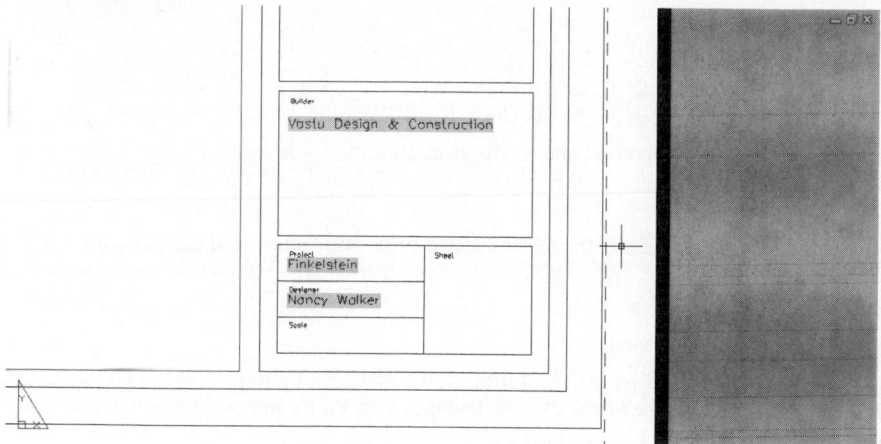

Editing and updating fields

To edit a field, double-click the field's text to open the In-Place Text Editor. Select the text, right-click, and choose Edit field. The Field dialog box opens. You edit a field in the same way that you define the field originally. When you're done, click OK. The field is reevaluated immediately. Close the In-Place Text Editor to place the edited field.

By default, a field is evaluated and updated, if necessary, whenever you open, save, plot, eTransmit, or regenerate a drawing. (See Chapter 28 for information on eTransmitting a drawing.) You can change when AutoCAD updates a field by choosing Application Button ⇨ Options, and clicking the User Preferences tab. In the Fields section, click Field Update Settings. Check or uncheck the items that you want, and then click Apply & Close. Click OK to close the Options dialog box.

You can manually update a field if you want. For example, you may have an object field that displays the radius of a circle. If you resize the circle, you probably want to update the field.

To update a field, double-click the field to open the In-Place Text Editor. Select the text, right-click, and choose Update Field. Close the In-Place Text Editor to return to your drawing. Another method is to select the field and choose Insert tab ⇨ Data panel ⇨ Update Fields (the UPDATEFIELD command). You can press Ctrl+A to select all the objects in your drawing.

You can convert a field to text. Open the In-Place Text Editor. Select the text in the field, right-click, and choose Convert Field to Text.

What happens to fields when you save a 2005 or later drawing to an earlier release of AutoCAD? The fields display as their last value in the newer drawing but are not updated.

On the DVD

The drawing used in the following exercise on using fields, `ab13-d.dwg`, is in the `Drawing` folder on the DVD. ∎

STEPS: Using Fields

1. Open `ab13-d.dwg` from your DVD. Save the file as `ab13-07.dwg` in your `AutoCAD Bible` folder. This drawing is zoomed in on the titleblock.

2. To set some of the drawing properties, choose Application Button ➪ Drawing Utilities ➪ Drawing Properties. On the Summary tab, type the following in the Title field: **6" thru 12" 2727 EPV Valves**.

3. On the Custom tab, click Add. Enter the following two fields and values, and click OK after each:

   ```
   Drafter      Enter your initials
   Dwg No       SK-1972
   ```

4. Click OK to return to your drawing.

5. Choose Home tab ➪ Annotation panel ➪ Text drop-down list ➪ Multiline Text. Pick two boundary points within the Title box of the titleblock. The In-Place Text Editor opens. Right-click and choose Insert Field to open the Field dialog box.

6. From the Field Category drop-down list, choose Document. From the Field Names list, choose Title. From the Format list, choose Title Case. Click OK. Click anywhere outside the In-Place Text Editor to place the field.

7. Again start the MTEXT command. Pick two boundary points within the Dwg No box of the titleblock. In the In-Place Text Editor, right-click and choose Insert Field to open the Field dialog box.

8. From the Field Names list, choose Dwg No. Click OK. Click anywhere outside the In-Place Text Editor to place the field.

9. Choose Insert tab ➪ Data panel ➪ Field. From the Field Category drop-down list, choose Date & Time. From the Field Names list, choose CreateDate. From the Format list, choose M/d/yy (fourth from the top). Click OK.

10. Pick a point within the Date box of the titleblock.

11. If necessary, move the text so that it fits better in the titleblock. Save your drawing. The titleblock should look like Figure 13.29.

FIGURE 13.29

The titleblock after adding some fields.

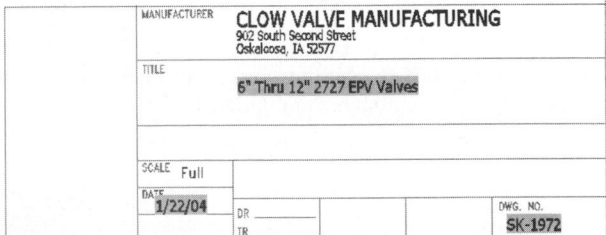

Managing Text

Text is a complex object type that increases your drawing size and adds redraw and regeneration time. TrueType fonts can have an impact on how long it takes to open and save a file. The techniques described in this section help you to manage text and improve performance while editing your drawing.

Using Quicktext

The QTEXT command replaces all text with rectangles that approximate the placement of the original text. All text objects, including dimensions, attributes, and tolerances, are affected. To use QTEXT, type **qtext** ↵ on the command line. Type **on** ↵ to display the rectangles; type **off** ↵ to return to regular text. Then type **regen** ↵ at the command line. Quicktext takes effect only after a regeneration; it does not apply to OLE objects that you have pasted into a drawing from the Windows Clipboard (see Chapter 27).

Using AutoCAD and AutoCAD LT fonts

AutoCAD and AutoCAD LT fonts are simpler than TrueType fonts, and offer a range of complexity. The simplest font is txt.shx. You can easily define a text style by using an AutoCAD or AutoCAD LT font and then change the font to something nicer just before plotting. Be aware that the text may take up more or less space than before.

When your drawing cannot find the specified font, it uses an alternate font. This may happen if you receive a drawing from someone else that uses a custom or third-party font that you don't have. You can specify the alternate font by choosing Application Menu ⇨ Options, and clicking the plus sign next to Text Editor, Dictionary, and Font File Names on the Files tab. Choose Alternate Font File to specify the alternate font, which is simplex.shx by default.

You can further control the fonts used in your drawing by customizing the Font Mapping File, acad.fmp (or acadlt.fmp). The format is current_font; font_to_substitute. (You need to use the actual filenames of the fonts.) To substitute a simpler font for the Arial Black font, you can add the following line:

```
Ariblk.ttf;simplex.shx
```

To find the Windows TrueType fonts, look in the Fonts subfolder of your Windows folder.

Note

To find acad.fmp **(or** acadlt.fmp**), choose Application Button ⇨ Options, and click the File tab. Double-click Text Editor, Dictionary, and Font File Names. Double-click Font Mapping File. Click the path list to view the location of** acad.fmp **(or** acadlt.fmp**). AutoCAD and AutoCAD LT only read the font-mapping file when you open a new drawing, so any changes that you make are effective only after you start a new drawing. ■**

Turning off text layers

Turning off (or freezing) text layers can reduce regeneration time dramatically; this is a good reason to give text its own layer. Don't forget to turn off dimension text, as well. Dimensions (see Chapter 14) are usually placed on a separate layer.

Using MIRRTEXT

When you mirror sections of your drawing that include text, you usually don't want any backward text (unless you're Alice going through the looking glass). The MIRRTEXT system variable controls whether text is mirrored or retains its normal orientation. The default value for MIRRTEXT is off, so mirrored text is not backward. The text is copied to the mirrored location, but reads from left to right (if that's the direction of the language that you're using).

If you do want to mirror the text, type **mirrtext** ↵. At the Enter new value for MIRRTEXT <0>: prompt, type **1** ↵ to turn MIRRTEXT on. This system variable is saved with the drawing, so you may still need to change it when you open older drawings.

AutoCAD Only

Express Tools has a number of text routines that you may find very helpful. Table 13.2 lists these tools. ∎

TABLE 13.2

Express Tools for Text

Command	Ribbon Location	Description
RTEXT	Express Tools tab ⇨ Text panel (expanded) ⇨ Remote Text	Displays text from an outside file. You can specify the text style, height, and rotation. Use RTEDIT on the command line to edit remote text.
TEXTFIT	Express Tools tab ⇨ Text panel ⇨ Modify Text drop-down list ⇨ Fit	Stretches or shrinks Text objects (but not Mtext) to fit between two points.
TEXTMASK	Express Tools tab ⇨ Text panel (expanded) ⇨ Text Mask	Creates a wipeout, 3D face, or 2D solid object behind the text, with a little extra space around the text. You can use this to make text on top of a hatch more legible.
TEXTUNMASK	Express Tools tab ⇨ Text panel (expanded) ⇨ Text Unmask	Removes a text mask.
TXTEXP	Express Tools tab ⇨ Text panel ⇨ Modify Text drop-down list ⇨ Explode	Transforms Text or Mtext into geometrical shapes.
TXT2MTXT	Express Tools tab ⇨ Text panel ⇨ Convert to Mtext	Converts Text objects to Mtext objects.
ARCTEXT	Express Tools tab ⇨ Text panel ⇨ Arc Aligned	Aligns text along an arc.
TORIENT	Express Tools tab ⇨ Text panel ⇨ Modify Text drop-down list ⇨ Rotate	Rotates multiple text, Mtext, and attribute definitions to a specified angle without moving them, or aligns them so that they're horizontal or right-side up for easy reading.
TCIRCLE	Express Tools tab ⇨ Text panel ⇨ Enclose in Object	Encloses selected Text or Mtext inside a circle, a *slot* (a rectangle, but with arcs at each end), or a rectangle.
TCOUNT	Express Tools tab ⇨ Text panel ⇨ Auto Number	Numbers lines of text by adding a prefix or suffix, or by overwriting the text.
TCASE	Express Tools tab ⇨ Text panel ⇨ Modify Text drop-down list ⇨ Change Case	Offers the following ways to change the case of text: uppercase, lowercase, sentence case, title case, and toggle case.

Finding Text in Your Drawing

 In a large, complex drawing with a lot of text, you may have difficulty finding specific text that you need to edit. The FIND command lets you find and replace text anywhere in your drawing — not only single-line text and multiline text but also text in tables, block attributes, dimensions, hyperlink descriptions, and hyperlinks. To use the FIND command, choose Annotate tab ➪ Text panel ➪ Find Text, enter the text you want to find in the Ribbon's text box, and click the Find Text button. The Find and Replace dialog box opens, as shown in Figure 13.30.

FIGURE 13.30

The Find and Replace dialog box finds text anywhere in your drawing.

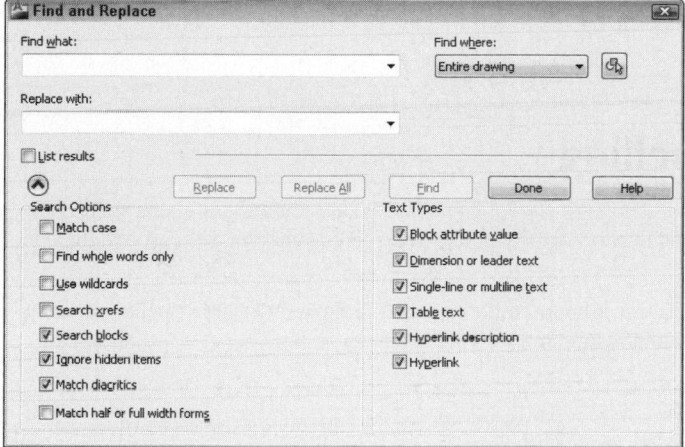

Here's how to use the Find and Replace dialog box:

1. If the text you want to find isn't in the Find What text box, enter it now. Use the drop-down list to choose recently used text strings.

Tip

When finding text, you can use wildcard characters such as * (for any number of characters), ? (for any single character), and # (for any numeric character) in the Find Text String text box. ■

2. If you want to replace the text that you find with new text, type it in the Replace With text box. This box also includes a drop-down list of recently used text strings.

3. If you want to limit or expand the scope of your search, use the Find Where drop-down list. If you selected objects before starting the FIND command, this drop-down list displays Selected Objects. You can choose Entire Drawing from this list. You can also click the Select Objects button to return to your drawing and select objects. The FIND command then limits its search to selected objects. Choose Current Space/Layout to look for the text string only on the Model or layout tab that is current.

4. Click the More Options down arrow to expand the dialog box and specify the type of text that FIND will search in the Text Types list. By default, it searches all types of text, including attributes (Chapter 18), dimensions (Chapter 14), tables, and hyperlinks (Chapter 28). The command can find text in fields, as well.

5. In the Search Options list, you can also choose the Match Case and Find Whole Words Only options. You can also choose to use wildcards, search xrefs and blocks, ignore hidden items, match diacritics (such as accent marks), and match half/full width forms (for East Asian languages).

Note

Hidden items are text on frozen or off layers, text in block attributes using invisible mode, and text in dynamic block visibility states. ∎

6. Click Find or Find Next to find the next instance of the text string. The drawing zooms in to the text and moves the dialog box so that it doesn't cover up the text.

7. Click Replace to replace the text string with the replacement text. Click Replace All to replace all instances of the text string with the replacement text.

8. Check the List Results check box to list the results that have been found.

9. After you're finished, click Done to close the dialog box.

Checking Your Spelling

If you take pride in the accuracy of your drawings, you might as well make sure that the text is spelled correctly. You can use the SPELL command to check your spelling. The spelling checker acts just like the one in your word processor.

If you want, you can select some objects first. Choose Annotate tab ➪ Text panel ➪ Check Spelling to open the Check Spelling dialog box, as shown in Figure 13.31.

FIGURE 13.31

The Check Spelling dialog box.

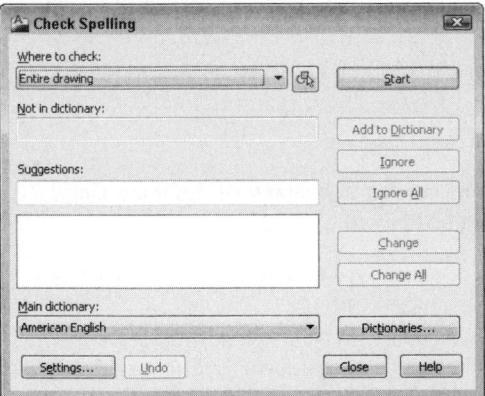

From the Where to Check drop-down list, choose Entire Drawing, Current Space/Layout, or Selected Objects. (I cover layouts in Chapter 17.) Click the Settings button to open the Check Spelling Settings dialog box, where you can choose if you want to include dimension text (see Chapter 14), block attributes (see Chapter 18), or external references (see Chapter 19). You can also ignore capitalized words (proper names), words that include numbers, uppercase words, words with mixed cases, such as EllenFinkelstein.com, and words containing punctuation. Click OK when you're done.

In the Check Spelling dialog box, click Start. When the first misspelled word appears in the Not in Dictionary text box, you have the following options:

- **Add to Dictionary.** Choose Add to Dictionary to add the word to the dictionary. The word will not appear again as misspelled.
- **Ignore.** Choose Ignore to ignore the current instance of this word only.
- **Ignore All.** Choose Ignore All to ignore all instances of this word.
- **Change.** Select the suggested word that you want, and choose Change to change the current instance of the word to the suggested word that you selected.
- **Change All.** Select the suggested word that you want, and choose Change All to change all instances of the word to the suggested word that you selected.

Notice that the drawing zooms in and highlights each word. The command automatically moves from word to word until you see the message `Spelling Check Complete`. Click OK and click Close to close the Check Spelling dialog box.

When you edit text, the Text Editor tab appears, which contains a Spell Check panel. Click the dialog box launcher arrow at the right end of the panel's title bar to open the Check Spelling Settings dialog box, where you can specify which type of text you want to include in spell checks and set options for ignoring certain types of text, such as capitalized words. You can change the main and custom spelling dictionaries. To change the main dictionary, choose one from the Main Dictionary drop-down list; these are dictionaries in different languages. Choose Dictionaries from the Check Spelling dialog box to open the Dictionaries dialog box, as shown in Figure 13.32.

FIGURE 13.32

The Dictionaries dialog box.

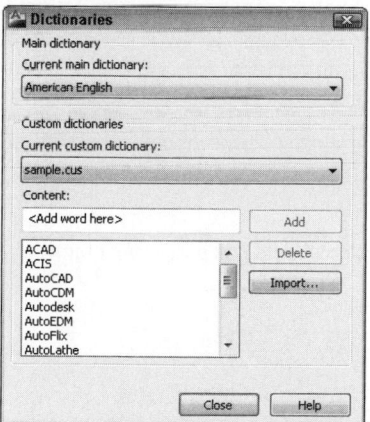

The custom dictionary is the dictionary that you add to when you click Add in the Dictionaries dialog box. It is a simple text file that includes words that you have added during spelling checks, as well as a list of drawing-related words that come with the file. You can add words to the custom dictionary by typing them in the Content text box and clicking Add.

Tip

Another way to edit the custom dictionary is to open the file directly with a text editor. The custom dictionary is called `sample.cus`. **To find** `sample.cus`, **choose Application Button ⇨ Options, and click the File tab. Double-click Text Editor, Dictionary, and Font File Names. Then double-click Custom Dictionary File. Click the path list to view the location of** `sample.cus`. ■

You can use a different custom dictionary. For example, it can be useful to use the same dictionary in your drawing as you use in your word processor. Here's how to use the Microsoft Word dictionary:

1. Find Word's custom dictionary. If necessary, choose Start ⇨ Find (or Search) and use the Windows Find dialog box to find the file or click Start and type the file name in the Search text box. Search for `custom.dic`. You can open this file with Notepad and edit it directly.

2. As explained in the previous Tip, find the location of `sample.cus`. Use Windows Explorer to copy `custom.dic` to that folder. You can hold down Ctrl as you drag it from one folder to another or use the right mouse button to click the file, choose Copy, and then paste it in its new location.

3. Click `custom.dic` to highlight it. Click it again and change its filename extension to `.cus`. Press Enter. Windows asks you whether you are sure you want to do this. Click Yes.

4. Click Dictionaries in the Check Spelling dialog box to open the Dictionaries dialog box. From the Current Custom Dictionary drop-down list, choose Manage Custom Dictionaries, and click Add. Find the file, and click Open.

5. Click Close three times to return to your drawing.

Summary

In this chapter, you learned how to create, edit, and manage text. You read about:

- Using TEXT to create single-line text
- Editing single-line text
- Creating text styles to control the formatting of your text, including creating annotative text styles
- Utilizing MTEXT for creating and editing paragraph text, including using the In-Place Text Editor
- Importing text
- Creating tables to clearly display data, including linking to external data and extracting object data
- Using fields to automate the insertion of text
- Managing text for the fastest display
- Finding and replacing text
- Checking spelling in your drawing and editing the spelling dictionaries

In the next chapter, you read about how to create dimensions.

Drawing Dimensions

Dimensions are an important part of most drawings. Dimensions indicate the measurement of the models that you've created and are used in the manufacturing process. The dimensions in AutoCAD and AutoCAD LT offer a great deal of flexibility. In this chapter, I cover the process of drawing dimensions. In the next chapter, I explain how to customize the format of your dimensions by using dimension styles. (Even though you should create a dimension style before you dimension, you need to understand dimensions before you can create a style; therefore, I cover dimensions first.)

Working with Dimensions

You usually add dimensions after you complete all or most of a drawing. When you dimension a drawing all at once, you can create a unified, organized look for your dimensions. Before you can dimension a drawing, you need to understand the elements of a dimension and how to prepare for dimensioning.

Cross-Reference

In Chapter 17, I explain how to dimension a drawing on a paper space layout and also how to work with *annotative* dimensions that automatically scale according to the scale of the drawing. In Chapter 15, I explain how to create a dimension style, including one that is annotative. ∎

The elements of a dimension

A dimension is a complex object, containing many parts. Figure 14.1 shows a typical linear dimension using the default dimension style. Mechanical drawings use dimensions that look like this.

FIGURE 14.1

The parts of a dimension.

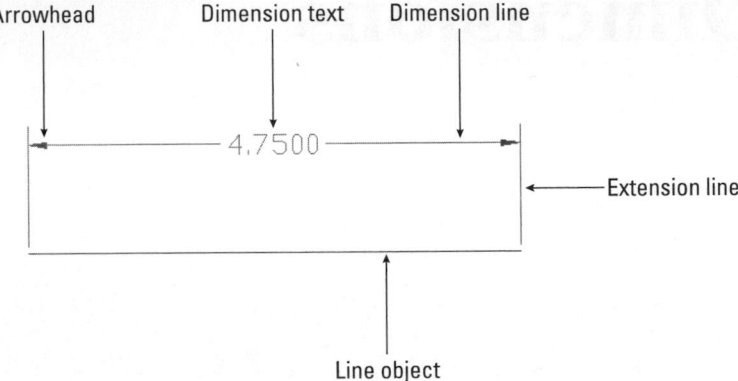

The parts of a dimension are:

- **Extension lines.** These extend from the dimensioned object to the dimension line and arrowheads. A small gap usually separates the dimensioned object and the start of the extension lines. Extension lines visually clarify the extents of the object being dimensioned.

Note
Relative to dimensions, the word extension (or extend) is used in two other ways besides referring to extension lines. First, the extension line itself usually extends from the object being dimensioned past the dimension line. You can specify the amount of this extension. Second, in architectural dimensions, the dimension line extends past the extension lines. You can specify this extension as well. ■

- **Dimension text.** This tells you the actual measurement of the dimensioned object. You can format this text in decimals, fractions, scientific units, and so on.
- **Dimension line.** This extends between the extension lines.
- **Arrowheads.** These mark the intersection of the dimension line and the extension lines. They can take several forms, such as tick marks, open arrows, or dots.

Dimensions have two important characteristics:

- **Dimensions are blocks.** Blocks are groups of objects that you can manipulate as one object. As a result, if you pick a dimension, all parts of the dimension are selected. Blocks are fully covered in Chapter 18.
- **Dimensions are associative.** This means that an association connects the dimension and the object it dimensions. If you change the size of the object, the dimension automatically adjusts appropriately.

You can format all parts of a dimension individually. You generally format a dimension by creating a *dimension style,* which is a named set of formats for dimensions — just as a text style is a named set of formats for text. (Dimension styles are the topic of the next chapter.)

Cross-Reference

You can constrain the dimensions of objects using dimensional constraints, which I cover in Chapter 10.

Preparing to dimension

Dimensioning requires some preparation to get the result that you want. Before starting to create dimensions, you should prepare as follows:

1. Create a layer for your dimensions. It's important that dimensions be easily distinguishable from the rest of your drawing. The color is usually a contrast to that of your models. For example, if your models are black (and you're working on a white screen), you might want your dimensions to be green, magenta, or cyan.

Tip

If you often turn layers on and off (or freeze and thaw them), you may want to create a separate dimension layer for each layer of drawing data. For example, if you dimension an electrical layer that you turn off regularly, you can have a special Dim-elec dimension layer that you can turn off with the electrical layer. ■

Note

If you're dimensioning an existing drawing that was created in a pre-2002 version of AutoCAD or AutoCAD LT, turn on associative dimensioning with the DIMASSOC system variable. Type dimassoc ⏎ on the command line and type 2 ⏎ at the prompt. (You can also choose Application Button⇨Options, click the User Preferences tab, and check the check box in the Associative Dimensioning section of the dialog box. Then click OK.)■

2. Create a text style for your dimensions. If you want your dimensions to be annotative, make sure that the text style is annotative. For more information on text styles, see Chapter 13.

Tip

Set the height of the text style to zero. You can then set the text height when you create the dimension style. If you do specify a fixed height in your text style, that height overrides any height that you specify in the dimension style. ■

3. Right-click the Object Snap button on the status bar and set all the running object snaps that you want. Endpoint and Intersection are a necessity. Add Center and Quadrant if you need to dimension arcs and circles. Click the Object Snap button on the status bar to turn it on.

4. Create a dimension style. If you want your dimensions to be annotative, make sure that the dimension style is annotative. The next chapter covers dimension styles. Annotative dimensions are valuable when you will be displaying your model at more than one scale, in separate viewports.

5. Save your dimension layer, dimension text style, and dimension style in your drawing templates.

6. If you want your dimensions to be annotative, change to the desired annotation scale, using the Annotation Scale list on the status bar. (You can add or delete annotation scales later if you need to.)

The Annotation panel on the Home tab offers most of the dimensioning commands. You can find the complete set on the Annotate tab in the Dimensions panel.

Drawing Linear Dimensions

Just as the most common objects are lines, the most common dimensions are linear dimensions. Use linear dimensions for lines, or a straight segment of a polyline. You can also use a linear dimension for arcs and circles — you get the linear length of the arc (not its perimeter length) and the diameter of the circle.

Specifying the dimensioned object

To dimension a line, choose Home tab ⇨ Annotation panel ⇨ Dimension drop-down list ⇨ Linear or Annotate tab ⇨ Dimensions panel ⇨ Dimension drop-down list ⇨ Linear. The DIMLINEAR command responds with the `Specify first extension line origin or <select object>:` prompt. You can now proceed as follows:

- If you're dimensioning more than one object, such as the distance from the endpoint of one line to the endpoint of another line, pick the first extension line origin. At the `Specify second extension line origin:` prompt, pick the second extension line origin. The two points on the objects that you pick define the length of the dimension.

- If you're dimensioning one object, press Enter at the `Specify first extension line origin or <select object>:` prompt. The `Select object to dimension:` prompt appears. Pick the object.

Caution

Always use the Select Object option if possible, for the most reliable results. Proper association of dimensions with their objects depends on the points that you specify. If you can't select an object and the point you need to specify is an intersection, don't click on the intersection. Instead, click on the object that you want to measure near the intersection and let the object snap specify the intersection for you. If you're not using the Select Object option, always use an object snap for accuracy. ■

At the `Specify dimension line location or [Mtext/Text/Angle/Horizontal/Vertical/ Rotated]:` prompt, pick a point for the location of the dimension line. As you move the mouse, you can see the results on your screen, as shown in Figure 14.2. If you want an exact location, you can type in a relative coordinate, such as `@0,.5` to specify that the dimension line should be 0.5 units from the object. Snap mode may also work well for you, depending on the drawing environment.

Object snap tracking makes it a snap to pick points for dimensioning. For example, if you're dimensioning a house, your first extension line origin may be the outside corner of the house, but the second extension line origin may be an inner wall. At the `Specify first extension line origin or <select object>:` prompt, move the cursor over the inner wall endpoint to acquire it. Move the cursor back to the line you're dimensioning and click when you see the tooltip showing the snap point you chose. The dimension goes just where you need it.

On the DVD

The drawing used in the following exercise on drawing linear dimensions, `ab14-a.dwg`, **is in the** `Drawings` **folder on the DVD.** ■

FIGURE 14.2

Picking a dimension line location for a linear dimension.

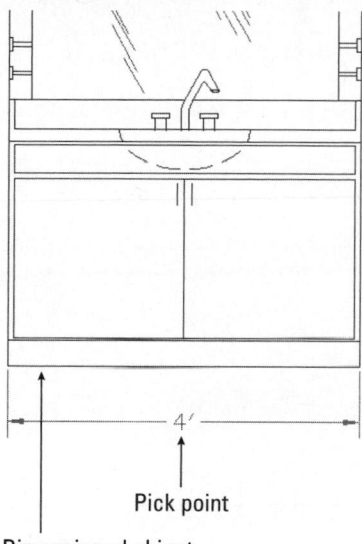

Pick point

Dimensioned object

STEPS: Drawing Linear Dimensions

1. Open ab14-a.dwg from your DVD.

2. Save the file as ab14-01.dwg in your AutoCAD Bible folder. This is a plan of a bedroom, as shown in Figure 14.3. Ortho mode and Object Snap should be on. Set a running object snap for Endpoint only. Object Snap Tracking should be off. The current layer should be set to Dim.

3. Choose Home tab ⇨ Annotation panel ⇨ Dimension drop-down list ⇨ Linear. Because you are dimensioning the vertical length of the room, you really want the dimension to be attached to the bottom and top horizontal lines, so that if you move those lines to make the room longer or shorter, the dimension changes. At the Specify first extension line origin or <select object>: prompt, pick **1**, shown in Figure 14.3, close enough to the corner to get the endpoint object snap marker. At the Specify second extension line origin: prompt, pick **2** in the same way. At the Specify dimension line location or [Mtext/Text/Angle/Horizontal/Vertical/Rotated]: prompt, move the cursor to the right until you have sufficient space for the dimension text and click.

4. Repeat the DIMLINEAR command. At the Specify first extension line origin or <select object>: prompt, press Enter. At the Select object to dimension: prompt, pick **3** (the window), shown in Figure 14.3. At the Specify dimension line location or [Mtext/Text/Angle/Horizontal/Vertical/ Rotated]: prompt, move the cursor down until you have sufficient space for the dimension text and click.

5. Save your drawing. It should look like Figure 14.4.

FIGURE 14.3

A bedroom plan.

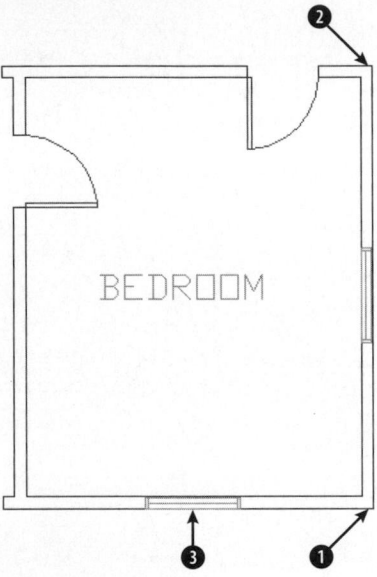

FIGURE 14.4

The bedroom with two linear dimensions.

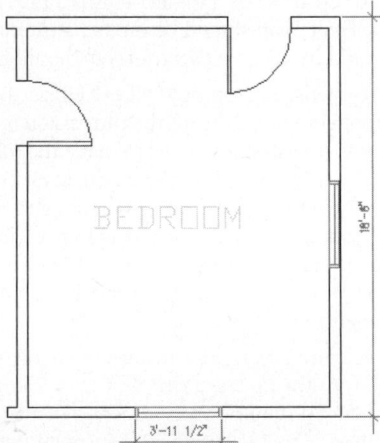

Using dimension options

You can also use one of the options offered at the command prompt to further control the final dimension. Dimension options control the text and the angle of the dimension.

MText

The Mtext option lets you replace the calculated dimension text or add a prefix or suffix to it. When you right-click and choose Mtext at the `Specify dimension line location or [Mtext/Text/Angle/ Horizontal/Vertical/Rotated]:` prompt, the In-Place Text Editor opens. The Text Editor tab appears on the Ribbon and the dimension text is highlighted in your drawing. (If you are using the AutoCAD Classic or AutoCAD LT Classic workspace, you'll see the Text Formatting toolbar.)

The best use of the Mtext option is to add some text before or after the measurement, such as **TYP** (typical, used when one dimension applies to several objects) or **subject to final approval.** To add text before the measurement, simply start typing. To add text after the measurement, press the End or right arrow key and then type. To replace the existing text, click the text to select it and enter the replacement text. Then click outside of the In-Place Text Editor to close it.

Note

Typing your own dimension text is most commonly used where a dimension represents several sizes and refers to a size chart elsewhere in the drawing. For example, the text "Dim A" might be used for this purpose. If you replace the existing text, you can obtain the original text again by editing the dimension (double-click the dimension) and clear the Text Override item in the Properties palette. ∎

If the measurement text itself does not appear the way you want it, you should change the annotation specifications in the dimension style. You can also specify a prefix or suffix (such as *mm*) for all dimensions, as I explain in the next chapter. When you delete the text and type your own dimension text, you lose the ability of the dimension's measurement to automatically adjust to any change in the object's size.

Tip

To add text below the dimension line, enter \X after the dimension text. Any text after the \X goes below the dimension line. The "X" must be uppercase. ∎

Text

The Text option also lets you change dimension text but does not open the In-Place Text Editor. Instead, you can quickly retype the entire dimension text as you want it on the command line.

Angle

The angle of the text (horizontal, vertical, or aligned) is specified in your dimension style. However, you can use this option to change the angle of the dimension text for a particular circumstance. Right-click and choose Angle to get the `Specify angle of dimension text:` prompt. Type in an angle or pick two points to align the text with an existing object.

Horizontal/Vertical

The DIMLINEAR command assumes that you want a horizontal dimension if you select a horizontal object or two definition points running horizontally — ditto for a vertical dimension. Also, if you want to draw a vertical dimension of an object at an angle, you can specify this by simply moving the mouse cursor horizontally when specifying the dimension line location, as shown in Figure 14.5. If for some reason you need to force either a horizontal or vertical dimension, you can use the vertical or horizontal options.

FIGURE 14.5

By dragging the mouse cursor to the right after specifying the two endpoints, you can create a vertical dimension for this angled line. The vertical dimension measures the change in the Y coordinates of the line, not the length of the line.

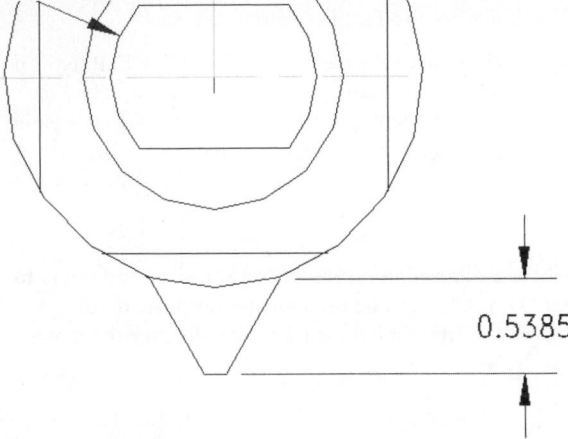

Rotated

Use a rotated linear dimension when the length that you want to dimension is not parallel to the extension line origins. Just as the vertical dimension in Figure 14.5 does not measure the length of the line to which its extension lines extend, a rotated linear dimension does not measure a specific object, but the distance of an imaginary line parallel to the dimension line. Rotated dimensions are not very common, but when you need them, they're the only way to get the dimension measurement that you need.

To use a rotated dimension, start a linear dimension, pick the two extension line origins, and choose the Rotated option. At the Specify angle of dimension line <0>: prompt, type the angle (or pick two points) to draw the dimension.

Figure 14.6 shows a hexagonal steppingstone with a rotated linear angle. The extension lines of the dimension extend to a line at 104.5 degrees, but in this case you want to measure a length at an angle of 135 degrees. Note that the dimension really measures an imaginary line parallel to the dimension line, shown in the figure as a dashed line, rather than the side of the hexagon.

FIGURE 14.6

Drawing a rotated linear dimension for a hexagonal steppingstone.

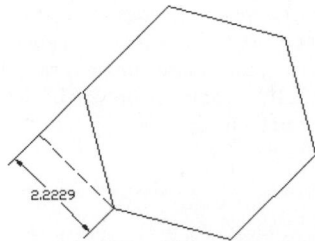

Creating jogged dimension lines

A jog line is a zigzag used to indicate that the displayed measurement doesn't match the length of an object. For example, you might shorten an object to display it within a certain area, but manually override the dimension text to show the proper length. In this case, the jog line indicates that the visual length of the line is not to scale (NTS).

 First you create a linear or aligned dimension. (You may have modified the measurement text, as explained previously in this chapter in the discussion of the Mtext option.) Then you add the jog line, using the DIMJOGLINE command. Choose Annotate tab ⇨ Dimension panel ⇨ Dimension, Dimjogline. At the Select dimension to add jog or [Remove]: prompt, select a dimension. At the Specify jog location (or press ENTER): prompt, press Enter to place the jog line midway between the dimension text and the first extension line, as shown in Figure 14.7. Alternatively, you can pick a location for the jog line.

You can move the jog line by stretching its grip. Select the dimension, select the jog line's grip, and move it to another location.

You can add a jog line to a dimension to indicate that the displayed measurement is different from the length of the dimensioned object.

24' NTS

Drawing Aligned Dimensions

When you want to dimension a linear object that is not orthogonal, use an aligned dimension. The dimension lines of an aligned dimension are always parallel to the object, unlike rotated dimensions. An aligned dimension measures the actual length of the object, not a vertical or horizontal distance that you dimension with a linear dimension. Therefore, your choice of linear, linear rotated, or aligned dimension depends on the distance that you want to measure. Figure 14.8 shows several aligned dimensions.

Specifying the dimensioned object

To create an aligned dimension, choose Home tab ⇨ Annotation panel ⇨ Dimension drop-down list ⇨ Aligned or Annotate tab ⇨ Dimensions panel ⇨ Dimension drop-down list ⇨ Aligned. This starts the DIMALIGNED command. The command responds with the Specify first extension line origin or <select object>: prompt. As with linear dimensions, you can now either pick two extension line origins or press Enter to select an object.

You then see the Specify dimension line location or [Mtext/Text/Angle]: prompt. Pick a point for the location of the dimension line. If you want an exact location, you can type in a relative coordinate, such as @2<45.

FIGURE 14.8

Three aligned dimensions.

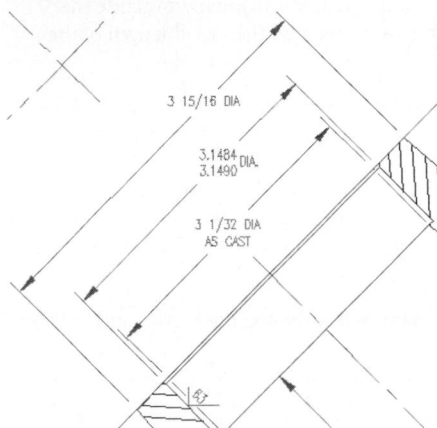

3 15/16 DIA

3.1484
3.1490 DIA.

3 1/32 DIA
AS CAST

Using the options

After you've chosen what you want to dimension, you have three options: Mtext, Text, and Angle. The previous section discusses these options in detail.

On the DVD

The drawing used in the following exercise on drawing aligned dimensions, ab14-b.dwg, **is in the** Drawings **folder on the DVD.** ∎

STEPS: Drawing Aligned Dimensions

1. Open ab14-b.dwg from your DVD.

2. Save the file as ab14-02.dwg in your AutoCAD Bible folder. This is part of a floor plan of a house, as shown in Figure 14.9. Object Snap should be on. Set running object snaps to Endpoint and Intersection.

3. Choose Home tab ⇨ Annotation panel ⇨ Dimension drop-down list ⇨ Aligned. Follow the prompts:

   ```
   Specify first extension line origin or <select object>: Choose ❶ in
       Figure 14.9.
   Specify second extension line origin: Choose ❷ in Figure 14.9.
   Specify dimension line location or
   [Mtext/Text/Angle]: Right-click and choose Mtext. In the In-Place
       Text Editor, press the End key on the keyboard and type a space,
       then type Typ. Click outside of the In-Place Text Editor.
   Specify dimension line location or
   [Mtext/Text/Angle]: Pick a location for the dimension line.
   ```

4. Save your drawing. It should look like Figure 14.10.

FIGURE 14.9

A section of a floor plan of a house.

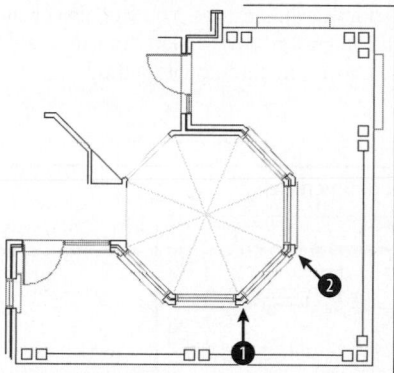

FIGURE 14.10

The house plan with an aligned dimension.

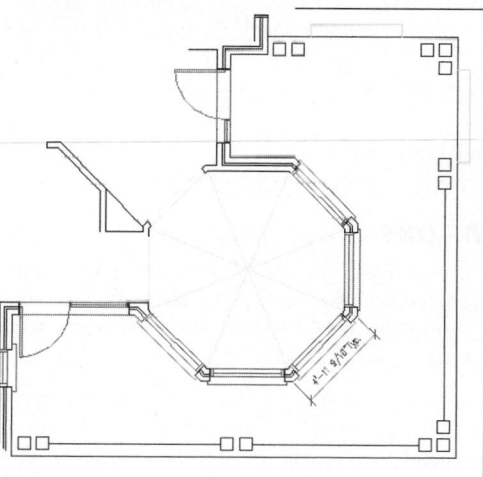

Creating Baseline and Continued Dimensions

Often, you want to create a whole series of attached, connected dimensions. You can accomplish this in two ways:

- *Baseline* dimensions are a series of dimensions that all start from one point. The first extension line is the same for all the dimensions. The second dimension includes the first dimension plus an additional distance, and so on.

- *Continued* dimensions are a series of dimensions that are all attached. The second dimension starts where the first dimension ends, and so on. Each dimension measures a different object or distance.

Figure 14.11 shows both baseline and continued linear dimensions. You can also create baseline and continued angular and ordinate dimensions. Quick Dimension, covered later in this chapter, can quickly create baseline and continued linear dimensions. Here I cover the traditional method.

FIGURE 14.11

A floor plan of a house using both baseline and continued dimensions.

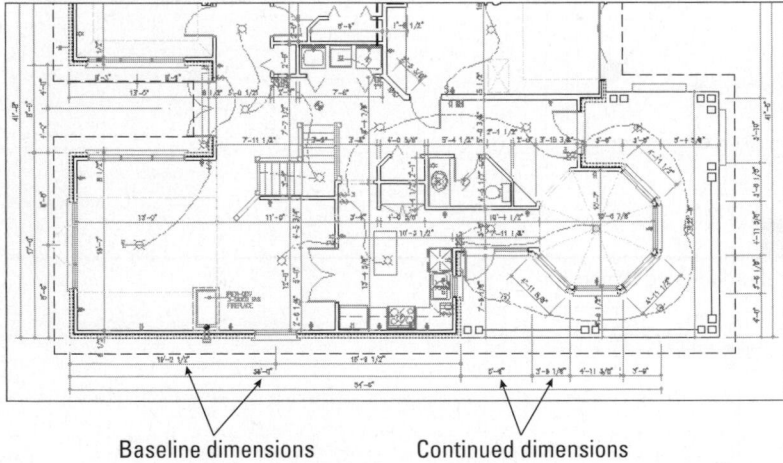

Baseline dimensions   Continued dimensions

Drawing baseline dimensions

To draw a baseline dimension, first create one linear, angular, or ordinate dimension in the regular way. (Angular and ordinate dimensions are covered later in this chapter.) Then choose Annotate tab ⇨ Dimensions panel ⇨ Continue/Baseline drop-down list ⇨ Baseline. The command responds with the `Specify a second extension line origin or [Undo/Select] <Select>:` prompt.

If the previous dimension was a linear, angular, or ordinate dimension, the command uses the second extension line as the base for the new baseline dimension. Specify a new second extension line origin, and the command creates the baseline dimension with the same first extension origin as the original dimension and the new second extension origin that you just specified.

If you don't want to work with the previous dimension in the drawing, press Enter. The command responds with the `Select base dimension:` prompt. Be careful to pick the dimension closer to the side you want to use as the baseline. The command then prompts you to specify a second extension line origin.

The command continues to prompt you for second extension line origins so that you can quickly create a chain of baseline dimensions. At each prompt, you can right-click and choose Undo to undo the previous dimension. You can also press Enter at any time and select a different dimension from which to work. Press Esc to end the command (or press Enter twice).

Drawing continued dimensions

Continued dimensions work similarly to baseline dimensions. To continue a dimension, first create one linear, angular, or ordinate dimension in the regular way. Then choose Annotate tab ⇨ Dimensions panel ⇨ Continue/Baseline drop-down list ⇨ Continue. The command responds with the `Specify a second extension line origin or [Undo/ Select] <Select>:` prompt.

If the previous dimension was a linear, angular, or ordinate dimension, the command uses the second extension line as the beginning of the new continued dimension. Specify a new second extension line origin to create the continued dimension.

If you don't want to continue from the previous dimension in the drawing, press Enter. The command responds with the `Select continued dimension:` prompt. Be careful to pick the dimension closer to the side from which you want to continue. You then get a prompt to specify a second extension line origin.

The command continues to prompt you for second extension line origins so that you can quickly create a chain of continued dimensions. At each prompt, you can right-click and choose Undo to undo the previous dimension. You can also press Enter at any time and select a different dimension from which to work. Press Esc to end the command (or press Enter twice).

On the DVD

The drawing used in the following exercise on drawing baseline and continued dimensions, ab14-b.dwg, **is in the** Drawings **folder on the DVD.** ■

STEPS: Drawing Baseline and Continued Dimensions

1. Open ab14-b.dwg from your DVD.

2. Save the file as ab14-03.dwg in your AutoCAD Bible folder. This is the same drawing used in the previous two exercises, as shown in Figure 14.12. Object Snap should be on with running object snaps for Endpoint and Intersection.

3. Turn on Ortho mode and Object Snap Tracking on the status bar.

4. Choose Annotate tab ⇨ Dimensions panel ⇨ Dimension drop-down list ⇨ Linear. Follow the prompts:

   ```
   Specify first extension line origin or <select object>: Pick the
       endpoint at ❶ in Figure 14.12.
   Specify second extension line origin: Pass the cursor over ❸ to
       acquire it for object snap tracking. Move the cursor to the right
       so that it's vertically under ❶, and click when you see the
       1'-6"<0° tooltip.
   Specify dimension line location or [Mtext/Text/Angle/Horizontal/
       Vertical/Rotated]: Pick a dimension line location to the right of
       the model.
   ```

5. Choose Annotate tab ⇨ Dimensions panel ⇨ Continue/ Baseline drop-down list ⇨ Continue.

   At the `Specify a second extension line origin or [Undo/Select] <Select>:` prompt, move the cursor over the endpoint or intersection at ❹ to acquire it for object snap tracking. Move the cursor to the right, vertically below ❶, and click when you see the tooltip.

This action places the continued dimension. Notice that the dimension uses a leader to place the text because there is not enough room between the extension lines. (If the leader is placed to the left, select it and pick the grip on the text. Pick a point to the right of the model and click to move the leader to the right.)

A house plan with an octagonal ceiling.

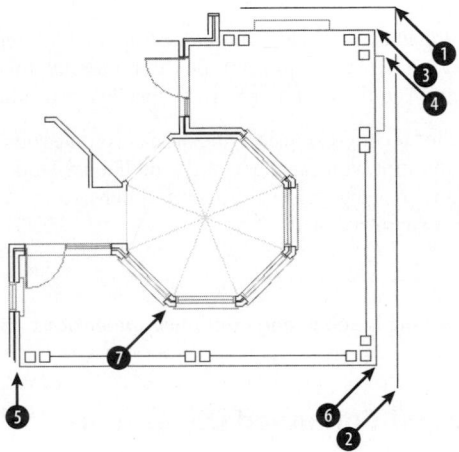

6. The command repeats the Specify a second extension line origin or [Undo/
   Select] <Select>: prompt. Pick the endpoint at **2**, shown in Figure 14.12, to place the
   dimension. Press Enter twice to end the command.

7. Repeat the DIMLINEAR command. Follow the prompts:

   Specify first extension line origin or <select object>: *Choose the*
      endpoint at **5** *in Figure 14.12.*

   Follow these prompts:

   Specify second extension line origin: *Move the cursor over* **7** *to*
      acquire it. Move the cursor down so that it's horizontal to **5**.
      When you see the 4'0"<270° tooltip, click.
   Specify dimension line location or [Mtext/Text/Angle/Horizontal/
      Vertical/Rotated]: *Pick a dimension line location fairly close to*
      the line you dimensioned, leaving just enough room for the
      dimension text.

8. Choose Annotate tab ⇨ Dimensions panel ⇨ Continue/ Baseline drop-down list ⇨ Baseline. At the
   Specify a second extension line origin or [Undo/Select] <Select>: prompt,
   pick the endpoint or intersection at **6**, shown in Figure 14.12. Press Enter twice to end the
   command.

9. Save your drawing. It should look like Figure 14.13.

The floor plan with baseline and continued dimensions.

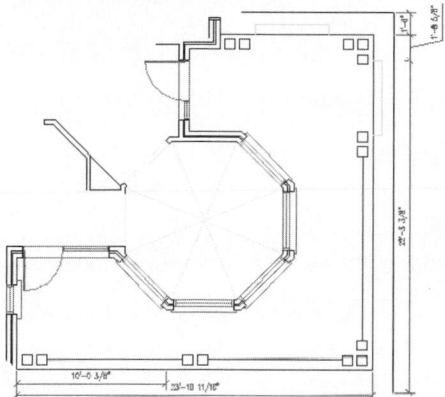

Dimensioning Arcs and Circles

When you dimension an arc or a circle, you measure its radius or diameter. It's also common to mark arc and circle centers to clarify what you're measuring. Arc and circle dimensions are most commonly used in mechanical drawings.

Marking arc and circle centers

Circle and arc centers are often marked in mechanical drawings because the center is an important aspect of a circle or arc but is not obvious without a mark. You set the size and type of mark when you create a dimension style, as explained in the next chapter. You can use a center mark (a small cross) or centerlines, as shown in Figure 14.14.

 Choose Annotation tab ➪ Dimensions panel (expanded) ➪ Center Mark to start the DIMCENTER command. At the Select arc or circle: prompt, pick the arc or circle you want to mark. The command draws the mark or lines.

Dimensioning arc lengths

 To dimension the length of an arc, choose Home tab ➪ Annotation panel ➪ Dimension drop-down list ➪ Arc Length or Annotate tab ➪ Dimensions panel ➪ Dimension drop-down list ➪ Arc Length. This starts the DIMARC command. You can dimension the length of an arc or an arc segment in a polyline. At the Select arc or polyline arc segment: prompt, select an arc. At the Specify arc length dimension location, or [Mtext/Text/Angle/Partial/Leader]: prompt, pick where you want the dimension line (which is an arc) to appear. The command automatically adds an arc symbol before the measurement. You can specify the arc symbol above the measurement or choose to display no symbol — you set this in your dimension style. Figure 14.15 shows an example of an arc length dimension.

FIGURE 14.14

Circles — one with a center mark and the other with centerlines.

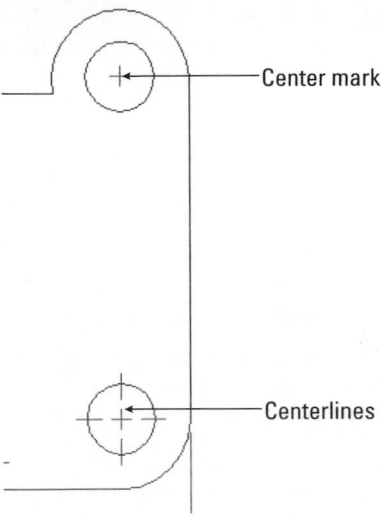

Center mark

Centerlines

You can also choose the Mtext, Text, or Angle option, as described in the section "Drawing Linear Dimensions." The Partial option lets you dimension part of an arc. At the prompts, you specify where you want to start and end the dimension. The Leader option inserts an arrow pointing to the arc.

Creating radial dimensions

To dimension the radius of a circle or arc, choose Home tab ➪ Annotation panel ➪ Dimension drop-down list ➪ Radius or Annotate tab ➪ Dimensions panel ➪ Dimension drop-down list ➪ Radius. The command responds with the `Select arc or circle:` prompt. Select an arc or circle. At the `Specify dimension line location or [Mtext/Text/Angle]:` prompt, pick where you want the dimension line to appear. The command automatically adds an R before the measurement to indicate the radius, as shown in Figure 14.15.

FIGURE 14.15

The circle's radius dimension uses a leader (a line and arrow pointing to the object) because the circle is too small to place the dimension inside it. The arc displays an arc length dimension.

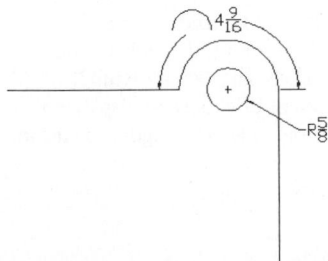

You can also choose the Mtext, Text, or Angle option, as described in the "Drawing Linear Dimensions" section earlier in this chapter.

A radius dimension usually passes through the center of the arc or circle. If you are dimensioning a large arc or circle, you may find that you can't see the center at the same time as you see the circumference without zooming out too far. In this instance, you can use the jogged radial dimension, which lets you specify an arbitrary center for the arc or circle. Choose Home tab ➪ Annotation panel ➪ Dimension drop-down list ➪ Jogged or Annotate tab ➪ Dimensions panel ➪ Dimension drop-down list ➪ Jogged.

You can create an extension arc (similar to an extension line) for a radius dimension that extends beyond the end of an arc. This allows you to place the dimension anywhere in the circle of which the arc is a part. When you specify the location of the dimension, just move the cursor past the arc's endpoint and continue around to the desired point.

Creating diameter dimensions

To dimension the diameter of an arc or circle, choose Home tab ➪ Annotation panel ➪ Dimension drop-down list ➪ Diameter or Annotate tab ➪ Dimensions panel ➪ Dimension drop-down list ➪ Diameter. The command responds with the `Select arc or circle:` prompt. Select an arc or circle. At the `Specify dimension line location or [Mtext/Text/Angle]:` prompt, pick where you want the dimension line to appear. The command automatically adds the diameter symbol before the measurement to indicate the dimension. You can create an extension arc (similar to an extension line) for a diameter dimension that extends beyond the end of an arc, in the same way I described just previously for a radius dimension.

You can also choose the Mtext, Text, or Angle option, as described in the section "Drawing Linear Dimensions."

Dimensioning Angles

You have several options for dimensioning angles. You may want to dimension the angular relationship between two lines, but the lines may intersect at their midpoints or may not intersect at all. Therefore, you need to be able to specify the vertex of the angle you want to dimension. Figure 14.16 shows an angular dimension with the points used to define it.

To create an angular dimension, choose Home tab ➪ Annotation panel ➪ Dimension drop-down list ➪ Angular or Annotate tab ➪ Dimensions panel ➪ Dimension drop-down list ➪ Angular. This starts the DIMANGULAR command. The command displays the `Select arc, circle, line, or <specify vertex>:` prompt, and responds differently, depending on what you select:

- If you press Enter, the command asks for the angle vertex, the first angle endpoint, and the second angle endpoint. These three points define the angle.

- If you select an arc, the command dimensions the entire arc, using the arc's center as the angle vertex.

- If you select a circle, the command uses the pick point as the first angle endpoint and the circle's center as the angle vertex. You then see the `Specify second angle endpoint:` prompt. Pick a point on the circle.

- If you select a line, the command asks for a second line. The command measures the angle between the two lines. If the lines don't intersect, the command uses their implied intersection as the angle vertex.

FIGURE 14.16

An angular dimension.

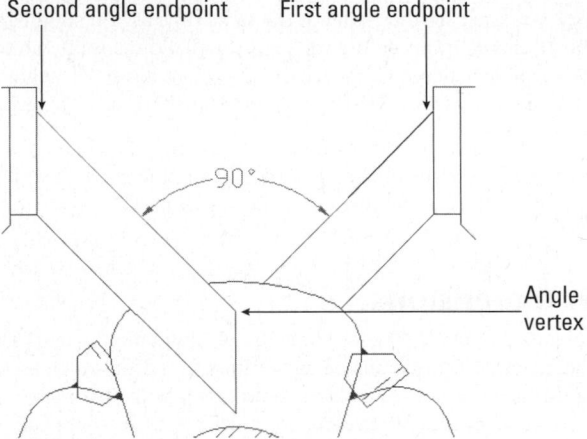

Thanks to Mary Redfern of the Bethlehem Corporation, Easton, Pennsylvania, for this drawing.

After you define the angle, the command responds with the `Specify dimension arc line location or [Mtext/Text/Angle/Quadrant]:` prompt. Pick a point for the dimension arc line — which is the same thing as a dimension line, except that the command uses an arc for angular dimensions.

The Quadrant option lets you lock the location of the dimension line to a specified quadrant of the circle in which the angle lies. For example, you can fix the dimension line outside two lines forming an angle while placing the text within those two lines. After choosing the Quadrant option, at the `Specify quadrant:` prompt, click where you want the dimension line to appear. You can then specify any location for the text of the dimension line. You can also choose the Mtext, Text, or Angle option, as covered in the section "Drawing Linear Dimensions."

Dimensioning minor, major, and supplemental angles —

When two lines meet at an angle, they create two angles, the *minor angle* and the *major angle*. The angle that is less than 180 degrees is the minor angle. The major angle is always more than 180 degrees. You can also measure the *supplemental angle*, which is the difference between 180 degrees and the minor angle. These angles are shown here.

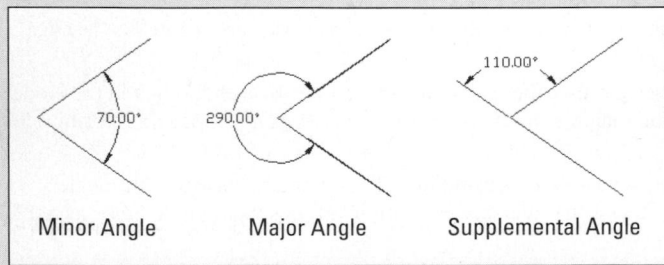

Here's how you create each type of dimension. Start the DIMANGULAR command. The command responds with the `Select arc, circle, line, or <specify vertex>:` prompt.

To dimension the minor angle, select both lines. Then at the `Specify dimension arc line location or [Mtext/Text/Angle/Quadrant]:` prompt, place the dimension arc line inside the angle, as shown in the figure. (You can also press Enter, specify the angle vertex and the two lines, and place the dimension arc line inside the angle.)

To dimension the major angle, press Enter. Do not select the lines. At the prompts, specify the angle vertex and the two lines. At the `Specify dimension arc line location or [Mtext/Text/Angle/Quadrant]:` prompt, place the dimension arc line outside the angle, as shown in the figure.

To dimension the supplemental angle, select both lines. At the `Specify dimension arc line location or [Mtext/Text/Angle/Quadrant]:` prompt, place the dimension arc line outside the angle, as shown in the figure.

As you can see, how you specify the angle and where you place the dimension arc line determine which angle you measure.

In the following exercise, you practice drawing radial, diameter, and angular dimensions.

On the DVD

The drawing used in the following exercise on drawing radial, diameter, and angular dimensions, `ab14-c.dwg`, is in the `Drawings` folder on the DVD. ■

STEPS: Drawing Radial, Diameter, and Angular Dimensions

1. Open `ab14-c.dwg` from your DVD.

2. Save the file as `ab14-04.dwg` in your `AutoCAD Bible` folder. This is a view of a bearing housing for an industrial washing machine, as shown in Figure 14.17. Object Snap mode should be on. Set running object snaps to Endpoint, Intersection, and Center.

3. Choose Annotate tab ⇨ Dimensions panel (expanded) ⇨ Center Mark. At the `Select arc or circle:` prompt, pick one of the four small circles at the corners of the model. Repeat the command for the other three circles.

4. Choose Annotate tab ⇨ Dimensions panel ⇨ Dimension drop-down list ⇨ Diameter. At the `Select arc or circle:` prompt, choose the outer of the two circles at ❶, shown in Figure 14.17. At the `Specify dimension line location or [Mtext/Text/Angle]:` prompt, pick a location for the dimension line.

5. Choose Annotate tab ⇨ Dimensions panel ⇨ Dimension drop-down list ⇨ Radius. At the `Select arc or circle:` prompt, choose ❷, shown in Figure 14.17. At the `Specify dimension line location or [Mtext/Text/Angle]:` prompt, pick a location for the dimension line to the left of the arc. To move the text outside the figure, select it, right-click, and choose Dim Text Position ⇨ Move with Leader. Then specify a location to the right of the arc.

FIGURE 14.17

A bearing housing for an industrial washing machine.

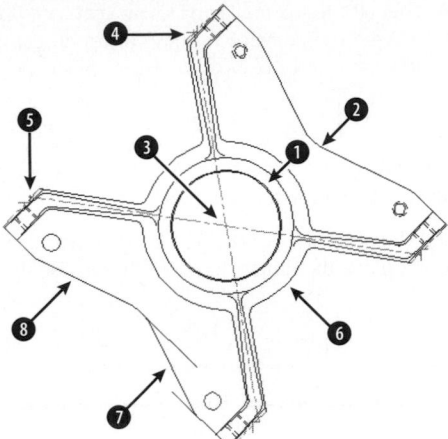

Thanks to Robert Mack of the Dexter Company, Fairfield, Iowa, for this drawing.

 6. Choose Annotate tab ➪ Dimensions panel ➪ Dimension drop-down list ➪ Angular. Follow the prompts:

```
Select arc, circle, line, or <specify vertex>: ↵
Specify angle vertex: Pick ❸ in Figure 14.17.
Specify first angle endpoint: Pick the endpoint at ❹. (Press Tab if
   necessary until you see the endpoint tooltip.)
Specify second angle endpoint: Pick the endpoint at ❺.
Specify dimension arc line location or [Mtext/Text/Angle/Quadrant]:
   Choose a location for the dimension line.
```

7. Repeat the DIMANGULAR command. At the Select arc, circle, line, or <specify vertex>: prompt, pick the arc at ❻. At the Specify dimension arc line location or [Mtext/Text/Angle/Quadrant]: prompt, pick a location for the dimension line.

 8. Choose Annotate tab ➪ Dimensions panel ➪ Dimension drop-down list ➪ Arc Length. At the Select arc or polyline arc segment: prompt, again pick the arc at ❻. At the Specify arc length dimension location, or [Mtext/Text/Angle/Partial]: prompt, pick a location for the dimension line farther out than the previous dimension that you drew.

9. Start the DIMANGULAR command. At the Select arc, circle, line, or <specify vertex>: prompt, pick ❼, shown in Figure 14.17. At the Select second line: prompt, pick ❽. At the Specify dimension arc line location [Mtext/Text/Angle/Quadrant]: prompt, pick a location for the dimension line to the left of the model.

10. Save your drawing. It should look like Figure 14.18.

FIGURE 14.18

The bearing housing with center marks, radial and diameter dimensions, arc length, and angular dimensions.

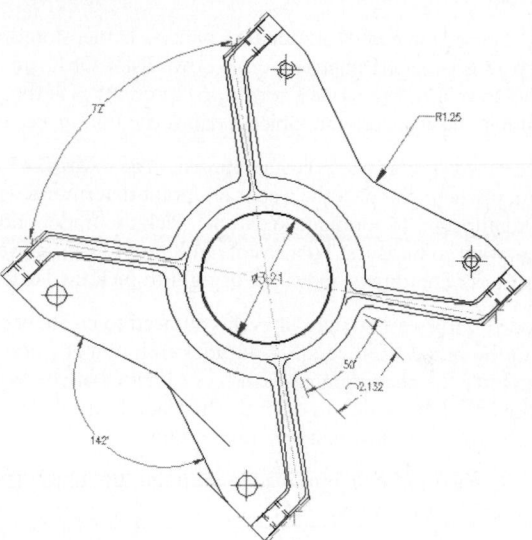

Creating Ordinate Dimensions

Ordinate dimensions are used in mechanical drawing. They dimension an object by labeling X or Y coordinates based on a 0,0 coordinate placed somewhere on the model. Figure 14.19 shows a drawing with some ordinate dimensions.

FIGURE 14.19

Ordinate dimensions in a mechanical drawing of a tension arm for a commercial dryer.

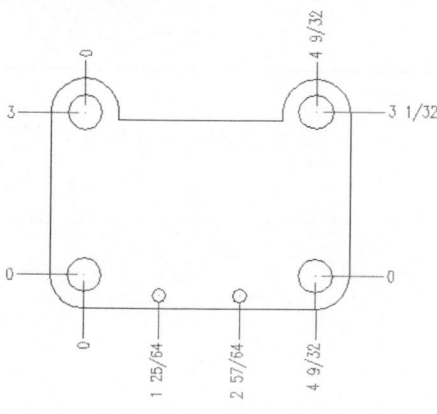

To place the 0,0 coordinate on the model, choose View tab ⇨ Coordinates panel ⇨ Origin. At the prompt, pick a point on the model, using object snaps for an exact measurement. If you want to check the UCS, choose View tab ⇨ Coordinates panel ⇨ UCS Icon drop-down list ⇨ Display UCS Icon. As long as there is room, the UCS icon moves to the new 0,0 coordinate.

To create an ordinate dimension, choose Home tab ⇨ Annotation panel ⇨ Dimension drop-down list ⇨ Ordinate or Annotate tab ⇨ Dimensions panel ⇨ Dimension drop-down list ⇨ Ordinate. This starts the DIMORDINATE command. At the `Specify feature location:` prompt, pick the part of the model that you want to dimension. Running object snaps with Object Snap turned on makes this an easy task.

At the `Specify leader endpoint or [Xdatum/Ydatum/Mtext/Text/Angle]:` prompt, pick the endpoint for the leader. The location where you pick the leader endpoint determines which coordinate to dimension — the X coordinate (Xdatum) or Y coordinate (Ydatum). Pick the leader endpoint perpendicular from the coordinate's axis that you want to measure. To measure an X coordinate, move up or down from the feature you selected. To measure a Y coordinate, move left or right to pick the leader endpoint.

Usually you work with Ortho mode on to create straight lines. If you need to create bent lines to avoid previously drawn dimensions, turn Ortho mode off. If you pick a leader endpoint at a nonorthogonal angle from the feature, you may need to force the measurement of the coordinate that you want by using either the Xdatum or Ydatum option. Use the Mtext option to open the In-Place Text Editor and edit the dimension text. Use the Text option to change all the text on the command line.

To perfectly line up the dimensions, when specifying the leader endpoint, use object tracking to track the endpoint of the previous leader. You can also turn on SNAP.

On the DVD

The drawing used in the following exercise on drawing ordinate dimensions, ab14-d.dwg, is in the Drawings folder on the DVD. ■

STEPS: Drawing Ordinate Dimensions

1. Open ab14-d.dwg from your DVD.
2. Save the file as ab14-05.dwg in your AutoCAD Bible folder. This drawing shows a simple sheet-metal template, as shown in Figure 14.20. Snap should be on and a snap distance of 0.25 units set. Right-click the Snap Mode button on the status bar and make sure that Grid Snap is on.

FIGURE 14.20

A sheet-metal template.

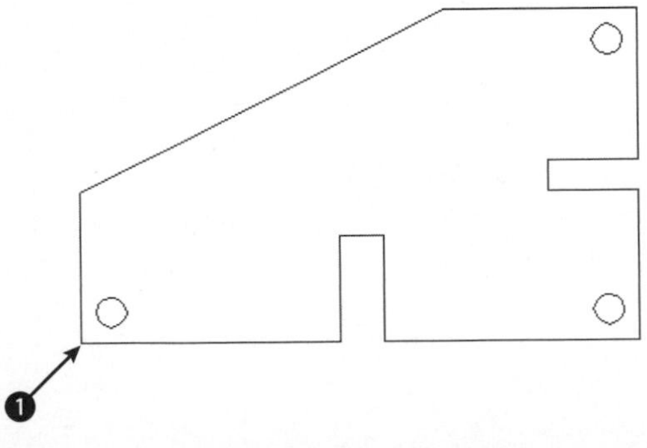

3. Choose View tab ➪ Coordinates panel ➪ Origin. At the `Specify new origin point <0,0,0>:` prompt, pick ❶, shown in Figure 14.20.

4. Choose Home tab ➪ Annotation panel ➪ Dimension drop-down list ➪ Ordinate. At the `Specify feature location:` prompt, choose ❶, shown in Figure 14.20. At the `Specify leader endpoint or [Xdatum/Ydatum/Mtext/Text/Angle]:` prompt, pick a point 0.5 units to the left of ❶, as shown in Figure 14.21. (Because Snap is on, this is easy. If necessary, click the coordinates at the lower-left corner of the screen until you get polar coordinates to display in the lower-left area of the drawing screen.)

FIGURE 14.21

The dimensioned template.

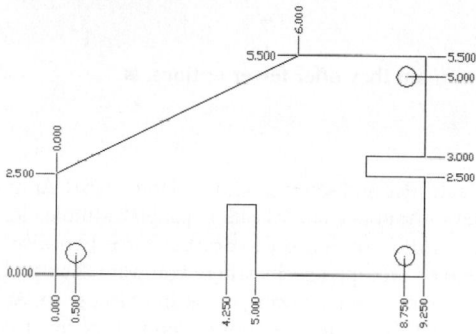

5. Repeat the DIMORDINATE command. At the `Specify feature location:` prompt, choose ❶, shown in Figure 14.20. At the `Specify leader endpoint or [Xdatum/Ydatum/Mtext/Text/Angle]:` prompt, pick a point 0.5 units below ❶.

6. Continue to dimension the drawing, using Figure 14.21 as a guide.

Tip

Type multiple ↵ dimordinate ↵ to automatically repeat the command. Press Esc when you no longer need the command. ∎

7. Save your drawing.

Drawing Leaders

Leaders are lines pointing to objects. At the end of a leader, you place any text that you want. Use leaders to label objects or provide explanatory text. Leaders do not calculate dimension text, but if you use an object snap to place the arrow point, they follow along if you move the object. Figure 14.22 shows two leaders.

Multileaders are leaders that support multiple lines. You format a multileader by configuring multileader styles. Multileader styles can be annotative, which allows them to scale automatically to the current annotative/viewport scale.

FIGURE 14.22

Use leaders to point to objects and add explanatory text.

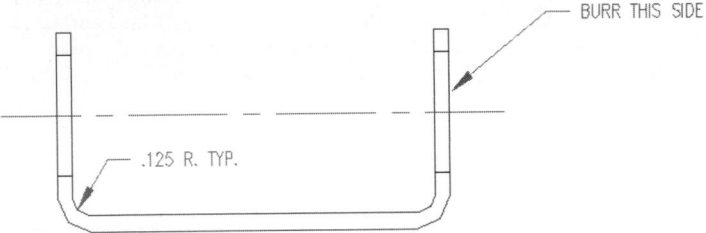

Note

Earlier QLEADER and LEADER commands still exist, but they offer fewer options. ■

Creating a multileader

To create a multileader by using the default style and settings, choose Home tab ⇨ Annotation panel ⇨ Multileader drop-down list ⇨ Multileader or Annotate tab ⇨ Leaders panel ⇨ Multileader. This starts the MLEADER command. At the `Specify leader arrowhead location or [leader Landing first/Content first/Options] <Options>:` prompt, specify where you want the tip of the arrow (the *head* of the leader) to go. If you want a precise point, you may want to use an object snap. At the `Specify leader landing location:` prompt, specify where you want the end of the line to go. This line will be next to the text or block.

The In-Place Text Editor opens, where you can enter the text for the leader. (See Chapter 13 for a discussion of the text editor.) You can use the editor to format the text at this time. For example, you can choose an existing text style, a font, or a font size. Close the editor to place the leader. Notice that the command adds a short horizontal *landing line* that connects a diagonal arrow to the text.

When you start the MLEADER command, you have the following options at the first prompt:

- **leader Landing first.** Lets you first specify the point where the line meets the text. If you choose this option, AutoCAD continues to prompt you for the leader landing first.
- **Content first.** Lets you specify a location for the text label, and then enter the text.
- **Options.** Displays the following suboptions:
  - **Leader type.** Offers you options relating to the leader. You can use the Type suboption to choose a straight line (the default), a spline, or no line at all. Choose the Landing suboption to choose whether or not you want a landing, and if so, its length.
  - **leader lAnding.** Lets you choose whether you want a landing (Yes) or not (No).
  - **Content type.** Lets you choose whether you want the leader to end with Mtext (the default), a block, or nothing. If you choose the Block suboption, you enter the name of the block. (Blocks are covered in Chapter 18.)
  - **Maxpoints.** Lets you specify the maximum number of points of the line. A three-point line will have three vertices.

- **First angle.** Lets you enter an angle to constrain the first angle after the arrowhead segment. For example, you could constrain the angle to 90°.
- **Second angle.** If you specified more than two points, you can constrain a second angle.
- **eXit options.** Exits the Options prompts and returns you to the main prompts for the MLEADER command.

Editing multileaders

To add or remove a leader, you use the MLEADEREDIT command. Go to Home tab ➪ Annotation panel ➪ Multileader drop-down list ➪ Add Leader or Annotate tab ➪ Leaders panel, choose Add Leader to add a leader, select the multileader, and specify the endpoint of the new arrowhead(s). Choose Remove Leader to remove a leader on a multileader that has more than one; select the multileader, specify which leader line to remove, and press Enter to end the command.

Tip

You can press the Ctrl key and pick a segment of a multileader, to select just that segment. You can then change the properties of that segment in the Properties palette (Ctrl+1). ■

Creating a multileader style

Although you have a lot of settings available when you create a multileader, you can best define its look by using a multileader style. Because you save a style, you can easily use it again and again.

To create a multileader style, choose Home tab ➪ Annotation panel (expanded) ➪ Multileader Style, or Annotate tab ➪ Leaders panel and click the dialog box launcher arrow on the panel title, to open the Multileader Style Manager, as shown in Figure 14.23.

FIGURE 14.23

The Multileader Style Manager.

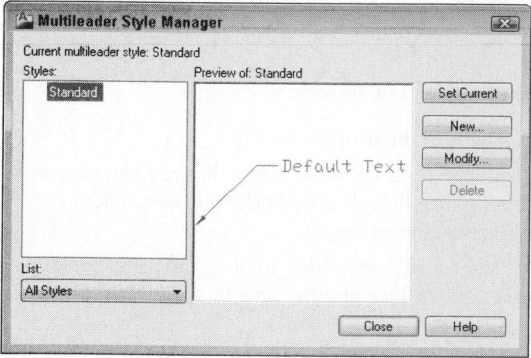

To create a new style, click the New button to open the Create New Multileader Style dialog box. Here you name your style and choose an existing style as a basis for the style. You can also specify that the style should be annotative by checking the Annotative check box. Note that if you want the multileaders to be annotative, then any blocks and text styles that they use need to be annotative, as well.

391

Cross-Reference

Annotative objects scale automatically to the current annotative/viewport scale when you plot them. For more information, see Chapter 17. For information about annotative text styles, see Chapter 13. I cover blocks in Chapter 18. ■

When you've named your style, click Continue to open the Modify Multileader Style dialog box, shown in Figure 14.24 with the Leader Format tab displayed. If you choose an existing multileader style from the Multileader Style Manager and click Modify, you get to this same dialog box.

Define a multileader style in the Modify Multileader Style dialog box.

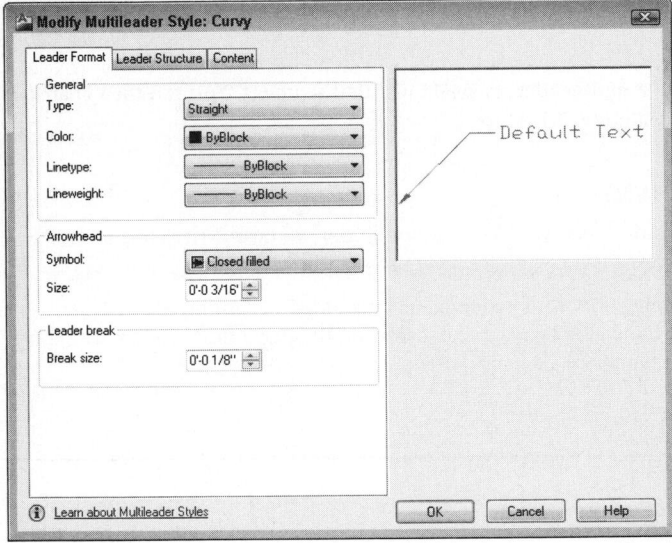

On the Leader Format tab, you can format the line and the arrow as follows:

- **Type.** Choose Straight, Spline (curved), or None from the drop-down list.
- **Color.** Choose a color from the drop-down list. These are the same colors that you can choose for any object. For more information, see Chapter 11. The default is ByBlock, which means that the leader takes on the color of the current layer (or the current color).
- **Linetype.** Choose a linetype from the drop-down list. Choose Other to open the Select Linetype dialog box, where you can choose a loaded linetype, or load another linetype. (I explain linetypes in Chapter 11.)
- **Lineweight.** Choose a lineweight from the drop-down list. (Chapter 11 discusses lineweights.)
- **Symbol.** In the Arrowhead section, you can choose the type of arrow you want to use from the drop-down list.
- **Size.** Enter an arrowhead size, or use the up and down arrows to change the current size.
- **Break size.** Enter a value for a break to use with the DIMBREAK command. (I explain the DIMBREAK command later in this chapter.)

On the Leader Structure tab, shown in Figure 14.25, you specify some more detailed information about the leader's line:

- **Maximum Leader Points.** By default, a leader line has two points. You can allow for more vertices by adding points.

- **First Segment Angle.** You can constrain the angle of the first segment, which is horizontal by default. Choose from 15° increments up to 90°.

- **Second Segment Angle.** You can constrain the angle of the second segment, which is horizontal by default. Choose from 15° increments up to 90°.

- **Automatically Include Landing.** In the Landing Settings section, you can decide whether you want a horizontal landing (the short line next to the text). Uncheck the check box if you don't want one.

- **Set Landing Distance.** To specify the length of the landing line, check this check box and enter a value in units.

- **Annotative.** In the Scale section, check this check box to make the multileaders annotative, as explained earlier in this section. If the multileaders are not annotative, you can automatically scale them to the scale of the viewport or specify a scale for all multileaders.

FIGURE 14.25

The Leader Structure tab of the Modify Multileader Style dialog box lets you specify detailed information about the leader line.

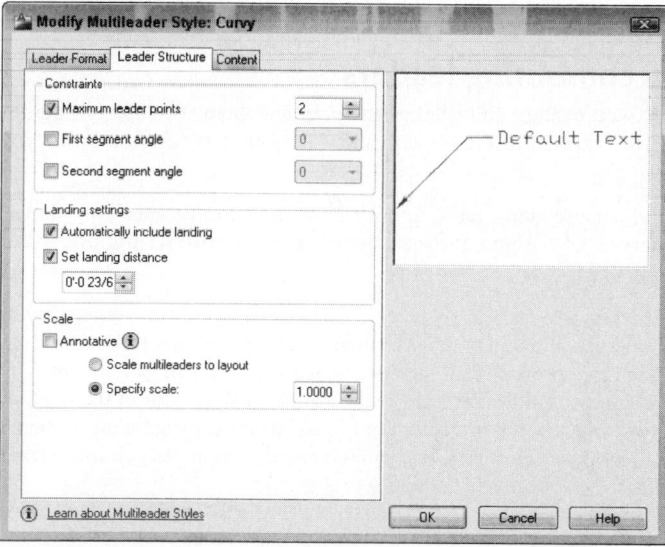

The Content tab offers settings related to text and the label part of the leader. First, you specify the Multileader Type, which can be Mtext, a block, or nothing at the end of a leader.

- **Mtext.** If you choose Mtext (multiline text), you specify default text content (if any), the text style, text angle, and text color. You specify the text height (which is the paper height if the style is annotative). You can force the text to be left-justified in all situations. Check the Frame Text check box to put a box around the text. Finally, you specify how the landing line attaches to the text and the gap between the landing line and the text.

Note

You can click the Ellipsis button next to the Text Style item to open the Text Style dialog box, where you can create a new text style or modify an existing one. You can specify a vertical attachment (from the top or bottom of the leader text) as well as a horizontal attachment (from the side of the leader text). ■

- **Block.** If you choose a block, you either specify one of several standard blocks or your own block (User Block). The standard blocks are detail callout, slot, circle, box, hexagon, and triangle. The blocks contain attributes (discussed in Chapter 18) that allow you to add a number (or a letter) inside each shape. For example, you might label various parts of the drawing A, B, and C. Usually, you would then have some annotation elsewhere to provide further information about these objects. You also choose how the landing line attaches to the block and the block's color.

Tip

You can scale the block. Enter a scale in the Scale text box. You see the result immediately in the preview pane. ■

Throughout this process, the preview window displays a representation of how the multileader will look. Note, however, that several features depend on how you insert the leader. For example, you don't see any difference in the preview when you constrain the leader line's angles. When you're done, click OK and then Close to return to your drawing.

Your multileader style is now current, and you can use it to draw multileaders. To change a current style, choose it from the Multileader Style drop-down list in the Leaders panel of the Annotate tab. You can also find it by choosing Home tab ⇨ Annotation panel (expanded) ⇨ Multileader Style. To change the style of an existing multileader, select it and choose the desired style.

Aligning and combining leaders

Two commands allow you to align multileaders and combine them. You align leaders to make them look more orderly, using the MLEADERALIGN command. There are several options that you can use, depending on the desired result.

 To start the command, choose Home tab ⇨ Annotation panel ⇨ Multileader drop-down list ⇨ Align or Annotate tab ⇨ Leaders panel ⇨ Align. At the `Select multileaders:` prompt, select the multileaders that you want to align.

At the `Select multileader to align to or [Options]:` prompt, you specify the multileader that you want to act as a basis for the others. The command then aligns the other multileaders with this one. At the `Specify direction:` prompt, you can specify a direction for the alignment. This default use of the command does not align the multileader lines or the arrows, just the end of the landing line nearest the Mtext or block. In most cases, you'll probably want to use a vertical alignment; in this case, the ends of the landing lines align, all in a row. However, you can use any direction. As you move the cursor, you see a preview of the results. When you like what you see, click.

Tip

When you select multileaders for the MLEADERALIGN command, you can include other objects, and the command filters them out. This makes it easy to use a window to select a number of multileaders that are interspersed among other objects. ■

Instead of selecting the multileader to align to, you can select the Options option and choose one of the following suboptions:

- **Distribute.** Lets you specify the two points between which the landing lines of all the selected multileaders fit, evenly spaced. For example, you can evenly space four multileaders between two points in this way. After you use this option, the command continues to default to this mode so that you can distribute other sets of multileaders. Use Options to switch to another mode.

- **Make leader segments parallel.** Makes the leader lines parallel, without changing their end-points. Select the multileader that you want to align the others to. After you use this option, the command continues to default to this mode. Use Options to switch to another mode.

- **Specify spacing.** You specify a spacing, in units, between each of the multileaders. Then you specify which multileader to align the others to and the direction; all of them line up (according to the ends of their landing lines), spaced according to the spacing you specified. After you use this option, the command continues to default to this mode. Use Options to switch to another mode.

- **Use current spacing.** Uses the current spacing between the ends of the landing lines. This is the default mode; as described previously, you specify which multileader to align the others to and the direction.

The MLEADERCOLLECT command works only with multileaders that use blocks as their content. The purpose of this command is to group separate leaders into one leader with all the blocks connected. For example, if you are using multileaders to point out objects that need additional annotation, multiple comments might apply to one object. You would then need a multileader that ended with more than one letter or number. Figure 14.26 shows three individual multileaders before and after being collected, using a vertical arrangement.

You can collect several multileaders that end in blocks into one multileader.

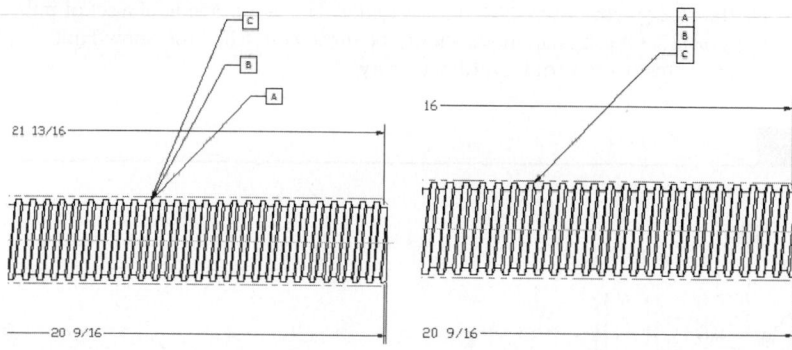

 To collect a multileader, remember that you need a style that uses blocks rather than Mtext. To collect them, choose Home tab ➪ Annotation panel ➪ Multileader drop-down list ➪ Collect or Annotate tab ➪ Leaders panel ➪ Collect. At the Select multileaders: prompt, select the multileaders in the order you want them to appear. This is important, because the command groups them according to how you select them.

However, the command also uses the last multileader you choose for its final location (assuming they point to different locations). For example, if you first choose a block labeled 1 and then choose a block labeled 2, the final multileader will point to the location of label 2. If necessary, you can easily move the multileader by using its grips.

At the Select multileaders: prompt, choose the multileaders, taking into account the final order and location you want, as I just described. At the Specify collected multileader location or

[Vertical/Horizontal/Wrap] <Horizontal>: prompt, specify where the blocks will now appear. You can see a preview as you move the cursor. You can also choose one of the following options:

- **Vertical.** Places the blocks in a vertical line.
- **Horizontal.** Places the blocks in a horizontal line.
- **Wrap.** Lets you specify either a width or a number of blocks. After that, the blocks wrap to the next line.

After you choose an option, the previous prompt repeats. Specify a location for the collected multileader.

AutoCAD Only

The Express Tools include the **QLDETACHSET** command, which detaches a leader's annotation from the leader line, to create two separate objects. Choose Express Tools tab ⇨ Dimension panel ⇨ Annotation Attachment drop-down list ⇨ Detach Leaders from Annotation. **QLATTACH** attaches leaders and MText objects. Choose Express Tools tab ⇨ Dimension panel ⇨ Annotation Attachment drop-down list ⇨ Attach Leader to Annotation. These tools work with leaders that you create with the **QLEADER** command; they don't apply to the new multileaders. ■

On the DVD

The drawing used in the following exercise on drawing multileaders, `ab14-e.dwg`, is in the `Drawings` folder on the DVD. ■

STEPS: Drawing Multileaders

1. Open `ab14-e.dwg` from your DVD.
2. Save the file as `ab14-06.dwg` in your `AutoCAD Bible` folder. This is a drawing of a set of pulleys, as shown in Figure 14.27. Object Snap mode should be turned off. Click the Show/Hide Lineweight button on the status bar to turn it on (if necessary).

A set of pulleys.

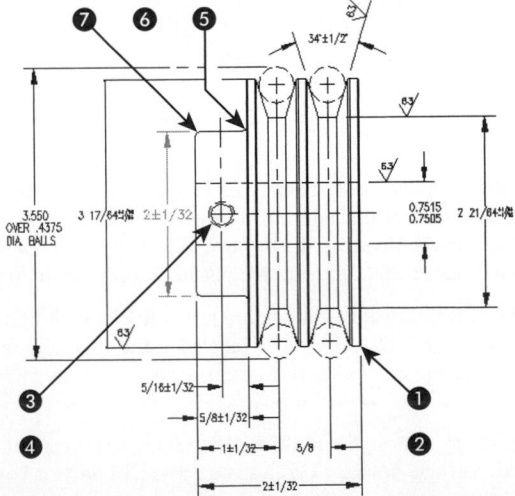

3. Choose Annotate tab ⇨ Leaders panel and click the dialog box launcher arrow on the right side of the panel title, to open the Multileader Style Manager. Click New, enter **Bold** in the New Style Name text box, make sure that the Annotative check box is checked, and click Continue. You'll create a multileader style that stands out by its color and width.

4. On the Leader Format tab, choose Green from the Color drop-down list. Choose 0.40 mm from the Lineweight drop-down list.

5. On the Leader Structure tab, check the Set Landing Distance check box (if necessary) and change the value to **1/2**.

6. On the Content tab, change the Text Style to DIMTXT. Check the Frame Text check box. Click OK to return to the Multileader Style Manager. The Bold style should be selected. Click Close to return to your drawing. You should see the Bold style displayed in the Multileader Style drop-down list of the Multileaders panel on the Annotate tab.

7. Choose Annotate tab ⇨ Leaders panel ⇨ Multileader. The Select Annotation Scale dialog box may open to remind you to set the annotation scale. Leave the default of 1:1 and click OK.

    Follow the prompts:

    ```
    Specify leader arrowhead location or [leader Landing first/Content
        first/Options] <Options>: Pick ❶ in Figure 14.27 (near but not on
        the drawing object).
    Specify leader landing location: Pick ❷.
    The In-Place Text Editor opens. Enter BREAK EDGES ↵. Enter TYP (8)
        PLACES. Click anywhere outside the editor.
    ```

8. Repeat the MULTILEADER command. Pick points ❸ and then ❹, shown in Figure 14.27. This time, type **DRILL 'F' HOLE**. Again, click anywhere outside the editor to place the multileader.

9. Repeat the MULTILEADER command. Pick points ❺ and ❻. The text should be **1/16 R**. If the AutoStack Properties dialog box appears after you type the fraction, uncheck the Enable AutoStacking check box and click OK. Click outside the editor to place the multileader.

10. To add a leader to the last multileader, choose Annotate tab ⇨ Leaders panel ⇨ Add Leader. Select the last leader that you drew. Specify ❼ and then press Enter.

11. Save your drawing. It should look like Figure 14.28.

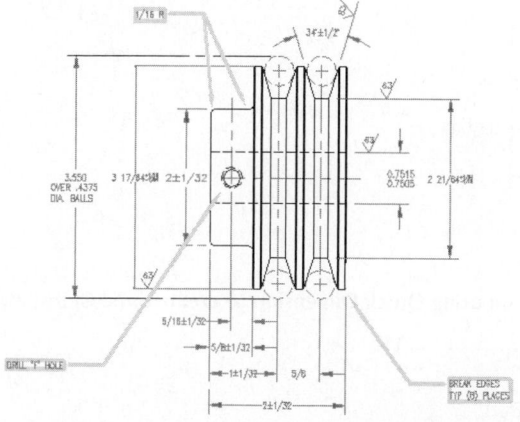

FIGURE 14.28

The pulleys with three multileaders.

Using Quick Dimension

Quick Dimension enables you to dimension several objects at one time. You can use Quick Dimension for baseline, continued, and ordinate dimensions. You can also dimension multiple circles and arcs. Later in this chapter, I explain how you can use Quick Dimension to edit dimensions as well. Although Quick Dimension may seem like the answer to all your dimension-related prayers, you can't use it in every case. However, it works well in "mass-production" situations. Dimensions created with the QDIM command are fully associative, so that any changes that you make to objects automatically update their associated dimensions.

New Feature

The Quick Dimension feature is now available in AutoCAD LT. ■

Here's how it works, in three easy steps:

1. Choose Annotate tab ⇨ Dimensions panel ⇨ Quick Dimension.
2. At the `Select geometry to dimension:` prompt, select all the objects that you want to dimension. You can't use object snaps; you need to select objects. If you select an object in error, type **r** ↵ and then pick the object again to remove it. Then type **a** ↵ to start adding objects again.
3. At the `Specify dimension line position, or [Continuous/Staggered/ Baseline/ Ordinate/Radius/Diameter/datumPoint/Edit/seTtings] <Continuous>:` prompt, right-click and choose the type of dimension that you want to create. Figure 14.29 shows a set of continuous dimensions. The Datum Point option sets a new base point for baseline and ordinate dimensions. You can press Enter to use the type of dimension that you just used previously because that shows as the default. The command immediately creates the dimensions for you.

FIGURE 14.29

A set of continuous dimensions created with Quick Dimension.

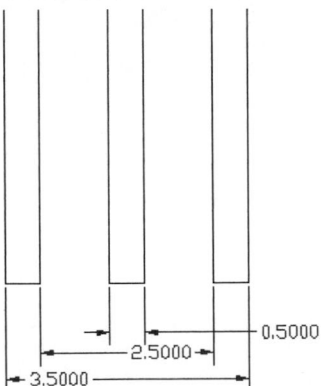

On the DVD

The drawing used in the following exercise on using Quick Dimension to create dimensions, ab14-f.dwg, is in the Drawings folder on the DVD. ■

STEPS: Using Quick Dimension to Create Dimensions

1. Open `ab14-f.dwg` from your DVD.

2. Save the file as `ab14-07.dwg` in your `AutoCAD Bible` folder. This is the same drawing that you used in the previous exercise, except that some of the dimensions have been removed (see Figure 14.30). Object Snap mode should be turned off.

FIGURE 14.30

You can use Quick Dimension to dimension the circles and create continuous dimensions.

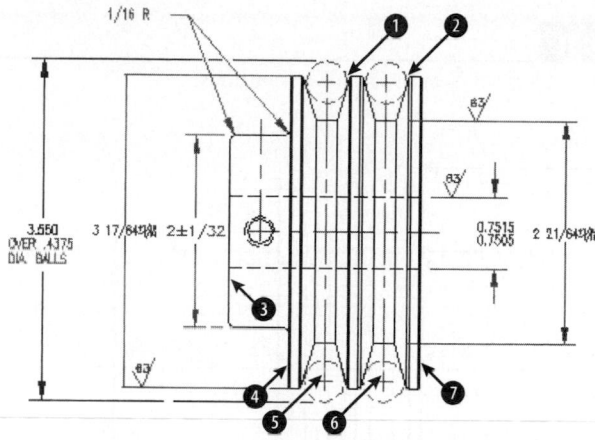

3. Choose Annotate tab ⇨ Dimensions panel ⇨ Quick Dimension. Follow the prompts:

```
Select geometry to dimension: Pick the circle at ❶ in Figure 14.30.
Select geometry to dimension: Pick the circle at ❷.
Select geometry to dimension: ↵
Specify dimension line position, or
[Continuous/Staggered/Baseline/Ordinate/Radius/Diameter/datum Point/
    Edit/seTtings]
<Staggered>: Right-click and choose Radius.
Specify dimension line position, or
[Continuous/Staggered/Baseline/Ordinate/Radius/Diameter/datum Point/
    Edit/seTtings]
<Radius>: Pick a point on the left circle at about 80 degrees from
    the right quadrant.
```

Quick Dimension places the radius dimensions.

4. Repeat the QDIM command. Follow the prompts:

```
Select geometry to dimension: Pick the line at ❸ in Figure 14.30.
Select geometry to dimension: Pick the line at ❹.
Select geometry to dimension: Pick the vertical centerline at ❺.
Select geometry to dimension: Pick the vertical centerline at ❻.
Select geometry to dimension: Pick the line at ❼.
Select geometry to dimension: ↵
```

```
Specify dimension line position, or
[Continuous/Staggered/Baseline/Ordinate/Radius/Diameter/datumPoint/
    Edit/seTtings]
<Staggered>: Right-click and choose Baseline.
Specify dimension line position, or
[Continuous/Staggered/Baseline/Ordinate/Radius/Diameter/datumPoint/
    Edit/seTtings]
<Baseline>: Pick a point below the model.
```

Quick Dimension places the baseline dimensions.

5. Save your drawing. It should look approximately like Figure 14.31.

FIGURE 14.31

The model with added radius and baseline dimensions.

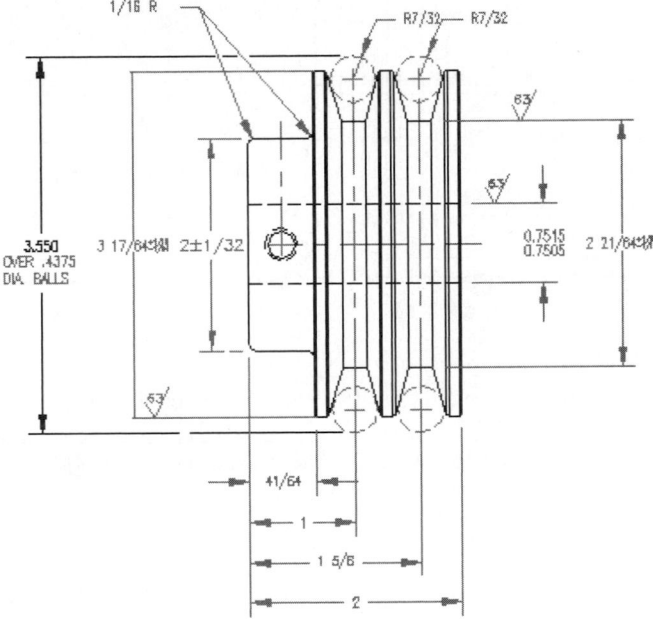

Creating Inspection Dimensions

Inspection dimensions specify how often you want the manufacturer of a part to check its measurements, and sometimes to what tolerance. For example, you may want 50 percent of the parts to be checked and require that they be accurate to within $\frac{1}{16}$ of an inch. Inspection dimensions allow you to add a label and inspection percentage to an existing dimension. Figure 14.32 shows an inspection dimension, using a rounded frame. You create inspection dimensions by selecting an existing dimension.

FIGURE 14.32

An inspection dimension adds a label and an inspection percentage to a dimension for the purpose of quality control.

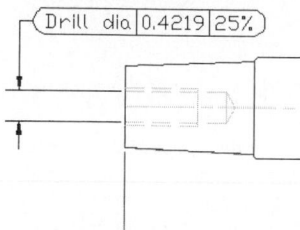

 To create an inspection dimension, first select an existing dimension. Then choose Annotate tab ⇨ Dimensions panel ⇨ Inspect to start the DIMINSPECT command and open the Inspection Dimension dialog box, as shown in Figure 14.33.

FIGURE 14.33

Use the Inspection Dimension dialog box to format inspection dimensions.

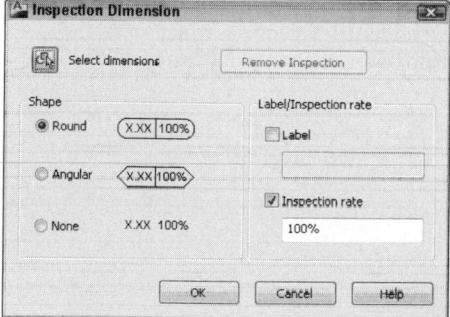

If you haven't already selected a dimension, you can click the Select Dimensions button and do so at this point. In the Shape section, choose the Round, Angular, or None option. In the Label/Inspection Rate section, check the Label check box if you want to add a text label. Then enter the text of the label. The Inspection Rate check box is checked by default. Enter an inspection rate and click OK.

To change the values of an inspection dimension, select it and use the Misc section of the Properties palette.

Creating Geometric Tolerances

You can use the TOLERANCE command to create geometric tolerances. (For another way to specify tolerances, see Chapter 15.) This command creates feature control frames, which define tolerances. This method of denoting tolerances conforms to international standards such as ISO (International Standards Organization), ANSI (American National Standards Institute), or JIS (Japanese Industrial Standards). Figure 14.34 shows a drawing that uses tolerance feature-control frames.

FIGURE 14.34

An example of tolerance feature-control frames.

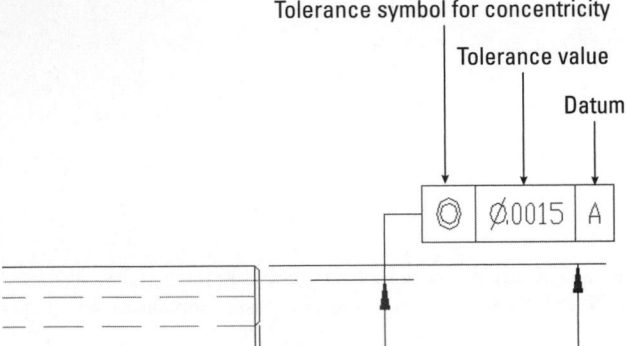

Thanks to Jerry Butterfield of Clow Value Company, Oskaloosa, Iowa, for this drawing.

Starting the tolerance frame

Creating a tolerance frame is a step-by-step process that depends on what information you want to include. To start the frame, choose Annotate tab ➪ Dimensions panel (expanded) ➪ Tolerance, which starts the TOLERANCE command and opens the Geometric Tolerance dialog box, as shown in Figure 14.35.

FIGURE 14.35

The Geometric Tolerance dialog box.

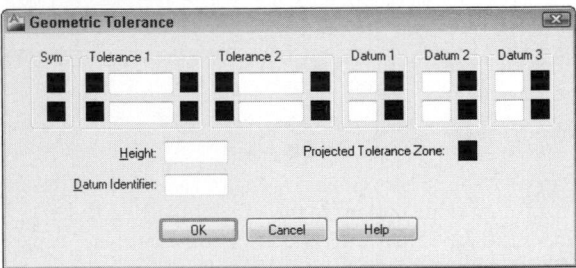

Use this dialog box to build the frame. The frame enables you to create two rows of two tolerances and three datum references (for up to three dimensions), as well as a projected tolerance zone value and a symbol and datum identifier. You'll rarely, if ever, use all the features in the frame.

Follow these steps to build the frame:

1. Click the first Sym box to open the Symbol dialog box, as shown in Figure 14.36.
2. Choose the symbol for the geometric characteristic that you are tolerancing. (Table 14.1 explains these symbols.) If you don't need a symbol, click the blank box. The Symbol dialog box disappears.
3. To insert a diameter symbol before the first tolerance, click the black Dia box to the left of the text box in the Tolerance 1 section.

FIGURE 14.36

Use the Symbol dialog box to choose the symbol for the type of geometry for which you want to specify tolerance.

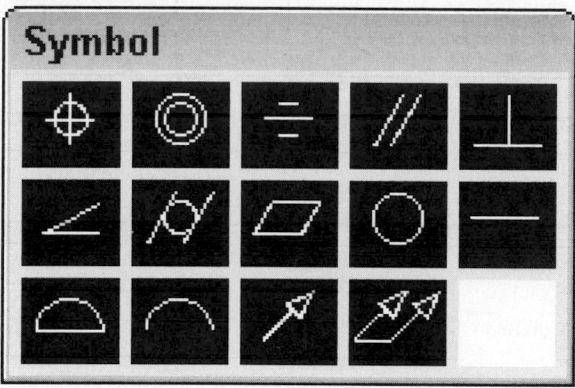

4. Type the tolerance value in the Value box.

5. If you want to specify a material condition, click the black MC box to the right of the text box. The Material Condition dialog box opens, as shown in Figure 14.37. Choose the symbol that you want. The dialog box disappears.

FIGURE 14.37

The Material Condition dialog box.

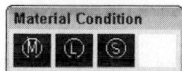

6. If desired, complete a second tolerance.

7. If desired, type a datum in the Datum box of the Datum 1 section, usually A.

8. If desired, add a material condition, using the same method described in Step 5.

9. If desired, type in datum references in the Datum 2 and Datum 3 sections, usually B and C with material conditions.

10. If you need to specify a projected tolerance zone for a perpendicular part, type a value in the Height box. Then click the Projected Tolerance Zone box to insert the Projected Tolerance Zone symbol.

11. Finally, if you want to specify a datum identifier, type the identifier letter in the Datum Identifier box.

12. Click OK to return to your drawing.

If you choose a material condition symbol and then change your mind, click the MC box again and choose the blank square to delete your symbol.

TABLE 14.1

Tolerance Symbols

Symbol	Name	Symbol	Name
⊕	Position	▱	Flatness
◎	Concentricity	○	Circularity
☰	Symmetry	—	Straightness
//	Parallelism	⌓	Surface profile
⊥	Perpendicularity	⌒	Line profile
∠	Angularity	↗	Circular runout
⌭	Cylindricity	⌰	Total runout

Inserting the tolerance frame

After you complete the frame, you're returned to your drawing with the `Enter tolerance location:` prompt on the command line. Specify any point to insert the frame.

Tip
You can create a matching Datum reference to place on your model by creating a tolerance frame with no symbol and only the Datum letter. ■

Editing a tolerance frame

To edit a geometric tolerance, select it and open the Properties palette. To change the text, click the Text Override item and then click the Ellipsis button at the right. The Geometric Tolerance dialog box opens, and you can make any changes that you need. Click OK to return to your drawing.

On the DVD
The drawing used in the following exercise on creating geometric tolerances, `ab14-g.dwg`, is in the `Drawings` folder on the DVD. ■

STEPS: Creating Geometric Tolerances

1. Open `ab14-g.dwg` from your DVD.
2. Save the file as `ab14-08.dwg` in your `AutoCAD Bible` folder. This drawing of a gear operator is shown in Figure 14.38. The Dim layer is current.

FIGURE 14.38

A mechanical drawing using geometric tolerances.

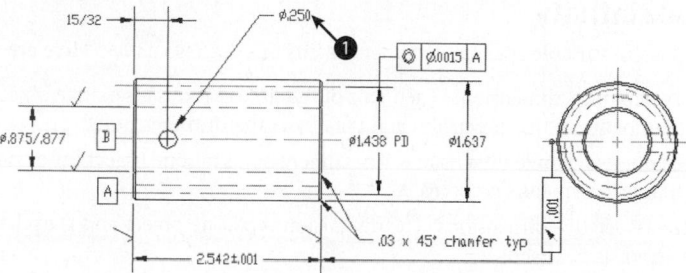

3. Choose Annotate tab ⇨ Dimensions panel (expanded) ⇨ Tolerance. In the Geometric Tolerance dialog box, click the top-left box, labeled Sym.

4. The Symbol dialog box opens. Choose the top-left symbol (for position).

5. In the Tolerance 1 section of the Geometric Tolerance dialog box, click the next black box, which is the Dia box, to insert the diameter symbol. In the Value box, type **.004**. Click the next black box, which is the MC box. In the Material Condition dialog box, choose the first image tile (for Maximum material condition).

6. In the Datum 1 section, type **B** in the Datum box. Click OK.

7. At the `Enter tolerance location:` prompt, pick ❶, shown in Figure 14.38, to place the geometric tolerance.

8. Save your drawing. It should look like Figure 14.39.

FIGURE 14.39

The drawing with the added geometric tolerance frame.

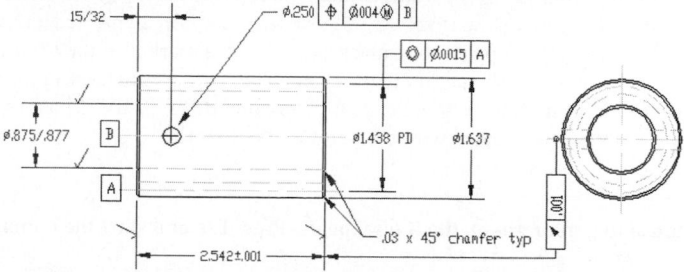

Editing Dimensions

Dimensions have many properties — text size, arrowhead size, text placement, and so on. You change most of these properties by changing the dimension style — either globally changing all dimensions using that style, or overriding a dimension style setting for a particular dimension. The next chapter covers dimension styles, but here I cover several other ways to edit dimensions.

Editing associativity

The DIMASSOC system variable specifies whether dimensions are associative. Here are the settings:

- **0** creates exploded dimensions. Each part of the dimension is a separate object, and there is no association between the dimension and the object that it dimensions.

- **1** creates nonassociative dimensions. The dimension is all one object but is not updated if the object that it dimensions is changed.

- **2** creates associative dimensions. The dimension is all one object and is updated if the object that it dimensions is changed.

Caution

By default, new drawings created in AutoCAD 2011 and AutoCAD LT 2011 are associative. However, drawings created in releases prior to 2002 or if you use an old drawing template are not associative. If you open pre-2002 release drawings and save them as 2011 drawings, you should change the DIMASSOC system variable's value to 2. ■

DIMREASSOCIATE

Use the DIMREASSOCIATE command to associate dimensions with their objects. You need to use this command when you open drawings that were dimensioned without the DIMASSOC system variable being set to 2 (typically, drawings created in releases prior to AutoCAD 2002.) You might also need to use this command when dimensions become disassociated from their objects, perhaps through some editing process, or to reassociate dimensions after you've disassociated them for some reason.

To use DIMREASSOCIATE, follow these steps:

1. Choose Annotate tab ⇨ Dimensions panel (expanded) ⇨ Reassociate.
2. At the `Select objects:` prompt, select the dimensions that you want to associate. Press Enter to end object selection.

   You see a prompt that varies according to the type of dimension you've selected. For example, for linear dimensions, you see the `Specify first extension line origin or [Select object] <next>:` prompt. At the same time, you see a marker in the form of an X that corresponds to the prompt, as shown in Figure 14.40. The marker indicates an *association point* (a point that connects an object and all or part of its dimension). If the X has a box around it, the dimension is already associated with the point marked by the X.

Note

If you use the wheel of a mouse to pan or zoom, the X disappears. Press Esc and start the command again or type 'redraw ↵. ■

3. Use an object snap to specify the location of the X (whether the same location as shown or a different location) or use the Select Object option to select an object (right-click and choose Select Object). To skip to the next prompt without associating the dimension to the marked point, press Enter.

FIGURE 14.40

When you associate a dimension with an object, an association point appears on the object.

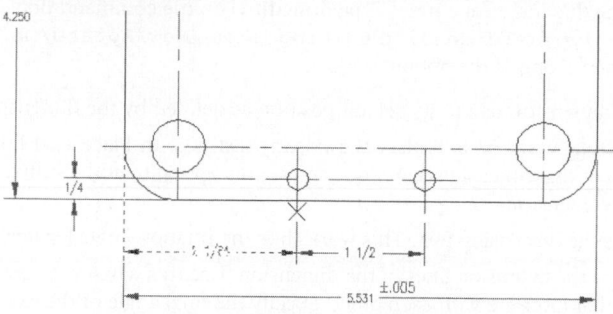

4. Continue to respond to the prompts in turn. The command prompts you through all the dimensions you selected.

Caution

When specifying object snaps, be careful that you choose the point you want. For example, if you use an endpoint object snap where two lines meet, you cannot be sure of which line's endpoint you've chosen. When you move or stretch the line that you expect to be associated with the dimension, you may find that the dimension doesn't budge. That's because it's actually associated with a different line. Selecting the object itself is often a better solution, because the dimension is associated with the object. ∎

DIMDISASSOCIATE

Occasionally, you may want to edit a dimension in such a way that you need to remove its associativity. Perhaps you need to squeeze it into a tight corner. For these times, use the DIMDISASSOCIATE command by typing it on the command line. At the prompt, select the dimensions that you want to disassociate from their objects.

Note

You cannot disassociate dimensions that are on locked layers. Unlock the layer first and then disassociate the dimension. ∎

DIMREGEN

The DIMREGEN command updates the locations of all associative dimensions. This command, which you type on the command line, is needed only if:

- You pan or zoom with a wheel mouse in a paper space layout while model space is active.
- You open a drawing containing dimensioned objects that have been edited with a previous release of AutoCAD or AutoCAD LT.
- You open a drawing containing external references that are dimensioned in the current drawing, and dimensioned objects in the external reference have been changed.

Using the DIMEDIT command

The DIMEDIT command offers four ways to edit dimensions. The advantage of this command is that you can change more than one dimension at a time. Type **dimedit** ↵ on the command line. The command responds with the `Enter type of dimension editing [Home/New/Rotate/Oblique] <Home>:` prompt. Right-click to choose one of the options:

- **Home.** Moves dimension text to its default position as defined by the dimension style.
- **New.** Lets you type new text to replace the existing text. The In-Place Text Editor opens, showing zeros to represent the dimension text. You can use this option to add a suffix, such as TYP (typical), to several dimensions.
- **Rotate.** Rotates the dimension text. This works like the rotation angle for text.
- **Oblique.** Angles the extension lines of the dimension. Use this when you have several dimensions close together that interfere with each other. Specify the final angle of the extension lines, *not* the rotation from the current angle.

Note

The Annotate tab ➪ Dimensions panel (expanded) ➪ Oblique item executes the DIMEDIT command with the Oblique option. ∎

As soon as you choose an option, DIMEDIT prompts you to select objects. You can select as many dimensions as you want. You have the opportunity to use the DIMEDIT command in an exercise after the next section.

Using the DIMTEDIT command

The DIMTEDIT command repositions dimension text. To start the command, choose Annotate tab ➪ Dimensions panel (expanded) and choose one of the options described in the following list. Although its name gives the impression that you can edit the text content, you can only change its position. Also, you can edit only one dimension at a time. The command responds with the `Select dimension:` prompt. Select a dimension.

At the `Specify new location for dimension text or [Left/Right/Center/Home/Angle]:` prompt, you can use the cursor to pick a text location. You can also right-click and choose one of the options:

- **Left Justify.** Left-justifies the text of linear, radial, or diameter dimensions.
- **Center Justify.** Centers the text of linear, radial, or diameter dimensions.
- **Right Justify.** Right-justifies the text of linear, radial, or diameter dimensions.
- **Restore Default Text Position (Home).** Returns dimension text to its default position and angle.
- **Text Angle.** Rotates dimension text. This option is equivalent to the Rotate option of the DIMEDIT command.

On the DVD

The drawing used in the following exercise on using DIMEDIT and DIMTEDIT to edit dimensions, `ab14-h.dwg`, is in the `Drawings` folder on the DVD. ∎

STEPS: Using DIMEDIT and DIMTEDIT to Edit Dimensions

1. Open ab14-h.dwg from your DVD.

2. Save the file as ab14-09.dwg in your AutoCAD Bible folder. This is a civil engineering drawing whose dimensions need some editing (see Figure 14.41).

3. The dimension at ❶ in Figure 14.41 is not in the proper units because the text was entered explicitly as 14.41 units. To correct this error, enter **dimedit** ↵ on the command line. At the Enter type of dimension editing [Home/New/Rotate/Oblique] <Home>: prompt, right-click and choose New. The In-Place Text Editor opens, showing zeros. Because you want the original text, click outside of the In-Place Text Editor. At the Select objects: prompt, pick ❶. Press Enter to end object selection. (You could correct several dimensions this way.) This action corrects the dimension, automatically creating the text in the current units.

4. The dimension text at ❷ in Figure 14.41 is too close to the dimension line of the vertical dimension that crosses it. Choose Annotate tab ➪ Dimensions panel (expanded) ➪ Right Justify. At the Select dimension: prompt, pick ❷. This action moves the text to the right.

5. Save your drawing.

FIGURE 14.41

A dimensioned civil engineering drawing.

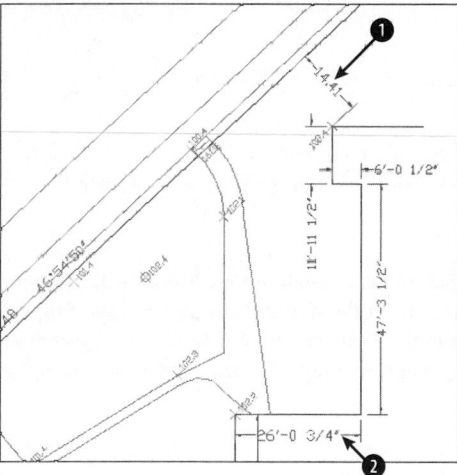

AutoCAD Only

The Express Tools command, DIMREASSOC, does the same thing that you accomplished in Step 3 of this exercise — restoring the default measurement value to modified dimension text. Choose Express Tools tab ➪ Dimension panel ➪ Reset Dim Text Value. ∎

Flipping dimension arrows

Sometimes you might want to place an arrow outside the extension line, but facing inward. For example, you might do this in a tight space. Figure 14.42 shows a dimension with a flipped arrow.

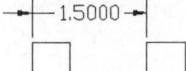

FIGURE 14.42

You can flip an arrow so that it displays outside the extension line, pointing inward.

To flip an arrow, pick a dimension nearest the arrow that you want to flip. Then right-click and choose Flip Arrow from the shortcut menu. Repeat the process to unflip the arrow.

Editing dimension text

You can edit dimension text as you would any other multiline text object. Enter **ddedit** ↵ on the command line. At the Select an annotation object or [Undo]: prompt, choose the dimension. The In-Place Text Editor opens. Using the In-Place Text Editor for dimension text has already been covered in this chapter under the Mtext option of the dimensioning commands.

Using the Properties palette to edit dimensions

You can edit dimensions by using the Properties palette just as you can edit the properties of any other object. Select any dimension and open the Properties palette. You see the properties of the dimensions that you can edit. You can also edit dimensions in the Quick Properties palette; however, fewer properties are available.

Many of these settings make more sense after you learn about dimension styles, which are covered in the next chapter. For example, the listings for Primary Units, Alternate Units, Fit, Lines & Arrows, Text, and so on duplicate the tabs in the New Dimension Style and Modify Dimension Style dialog boxes. You can change the color, layer, lineweight, and linetype. To override the automatic dimension text, enter the text in the Text Override field of the Text section of the Properties palette or the Quick Properties palette.

Tip

You can create a background mask like the one that you can create for multiline text. (For more information, see Chapter 13.) If dimension text covers other objects, select the dimension and open the Properties palette (Ctrl+1). Choose a color from the Fill Color drop-down list in the Text section. For the background mask to work, the dimension needs to be on top of any other objects that it overlaps. To bring a dimension to the top, use the TEXTTOFRONT command. ■

Note

You can convert a dimension to a dimensional constraint. For the complete discussion of constraints, see Chapter 10. Enter dimconstraint ↵ on the command line and select the dimension to convert. ■

Changing annotative scales

Dimension and multileader styles can be annotative, meaning that they can automatically change scale based on the scale of a viewport on a layout. (I discuss viewports and layouts in Chapter 17.) I've mentioned in this chapter how to make a dimension and multileader style annotative.

You can change the annotative scales of any dimension or multileader that uses an annotative style by using the OBJECTSCALE command. Follow these steps:

1. Select the dimension or multileader. (You can select more than one.)

2. Open the Properties palette. In the Misc section, click the Annotative Scale item to display the Ellipsis button.

3. Click the Ellipsis button to open the Annotation Object Scale dialog box.

   - To add an annotation scale, click the Add button. Choose a scale from the Add Scales to Object dialog box and click OK.

   - To delete an annotation scale, select it and click the Delete button.

4. Click OK.

Tip

You can also select one or more annotative objects, right-click in the drawing area, and choose Annotative Object Scale. ∎

Spacing dimensions equally apart

Sometimes, after you've created a number of linear or angular dimensions, you realize that they would look neater if they were equally spaced apart from each other. Rather than re-create or move them, you can use the DIMSPACE command to space existing dimensions. You can let the command determine the spacing automatically, or you can specify a spacing.

In order for this command to work, the dimensions must meet the following conditions:

- They must be linear or angular dimensions.

- They must be in a group of the same kind of dimension. For example, you might have all linear dimensions. If one is rotated, they must all be rotated; if one is aligned, they must all be aligned.

- The dimensions must be parallel (for linear) or concentric (for angular).

- The dimensions must share an extension line.

 To space dimensions, choose Annotate tab ⇨ Dimensions panel ⇨ Adjust Space. At the `Select base dimension:` prompt, select a dimension close to which you want to place the other dimensions. At the `Select dimensions to space:` prompt, select the rest of the dimensions that you want to space.

At the `Enter value or [Auto] <Auto>:` prompt, enter a spacing or use the Auto option to let the command figure out the spacing itself. You can use a value of 0 to align the dimensions along the same horizontal or vertical line.

Breaking dimensions

It's not good form for dimensions to cross other dimensions or objects. Many disciplines break a dimension or extension line where it crosses an object with a small space. This gives the appearance that the object is in front of the dimension. You can break dimensions or multileaders by using the DIMBREAK command.

The great feature of DIMBREAK is that if you move the object to another location where it still crosses the dimension, the break moves accordingly.

 To break a dimension or multileader, choose Annotate tab ⇨ Dimensions panel ⇨ Break. At the `Select a dimension to add/remove break or [Multiple]:` prompt, select the dimension you want to break. At the `Select object to break dimension or [Auto/Manual/Remove] <Auto>:` prompt, select the object that crosses the dimension. The `Select object to break dimension:` prompt repeats so that you can select another object that crosses the dimension, if any. Otherwise, press Enter to end the command.

You can use the Manual option to specify two points on the dimension line or extension line. In this way, you can set the size of the break yourself. However, if you use the Manual option, the break does not update if you move the crossing object.

Use the Multiple option at the first prompt to create breaks in more than one dimension at a time. You then select the dimensions. At the `Select object to break dimensions or [Auto/Remove] <Auto>:` prompt, choose the Auto option so that you can break all the dimensions.

If you want to remove an existing break, use the Remove option.

You can set a break size when you create a dimension or multileader style. For dimensions, use the Break Size text box on the Symbols and Arrows tab of the Modify Dimension Style dialog box. For Multileaders, use the Break Size text box on the Leader Format tab of the Modify Multileader Style dialog box.

Using Quick Dimension to edit dimensions

You can also use Quick Dimension to edit dimensions, whether created with QDIM or some other dimensioning command. When you select the geometry and dimensions you want to edit, you see an X at each eligible edit point, as shown in Figure 14.43.

FIGURE 14.43

When you edit with QDIM, you see an X at eligible edit points.

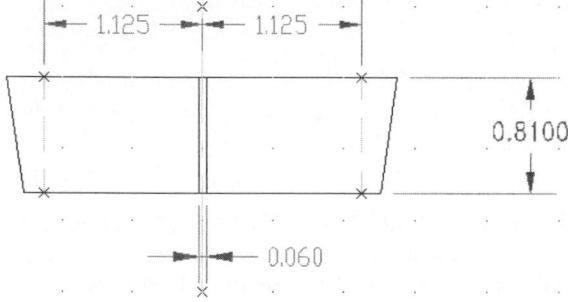

Here's what you can do with QDIM:

- You can join two dimensions by removing the edit points between them.
- You can split a dimension into two dimensions by adding edit points within the existing dimension.
- You can move the dimension line.
- You can change the type of dimension.

Caution

Editing with QDIM works best when the geometry is simple. Unless you can select only the geometry and dimensions that you want to work with, you'll end up changing dimensions that you don't want to edit. ■

To edit dimensions with QDIM, follow these steps:

1. Choose Annotate tab ➪ Dimensions panel ➪ Quick Dimension.

2. At the `Select geometry to dimension:` prompt, select the geometry and the dimensions that you want to edit.

3. At the `Specify dimension line position, or [Continuous/Staggered/ Baseline/ Ordinate/Radius/Diameter/datumPoint/Edit/seTtings] <Continuous>:` prompt, right-click and choose Edit. You see a cross at each eligible edit point.

4. At the `Indicate dimension point to remove, or [Add/eXit] <eXit>:` prompt, you can:
   - Select the points of the dimensions you want to remove. If you see two possible edit points in line with each other that could be creating the dimension you want to remove, select both of them.
   - Right-click and choose Add. Use object snaps to add one or more points.
   - Right-click and choose Exit to continue with the command.

5. At the `Specify dimension line position, or [Continuous/Staggered/ Baseline/ Ordinate/Radius/Diameter/datumPoint/Edit/seTtings] <Continuous>:` prompt, right-click and choose an option if you want to change the type of dimension.

6. The prompt repeats. Pick a location for the new set of dimensions.

7. Press Enter to end the command and update the dimensions.

Using grips to edit dimensions

Grips are ideal for moving dimension lines and text. The grips at the dimension line endpoints and the text insertion point are quite useful for making adjustments in dimensions. (I discuss grip editing in Chapter 10.)

To move a dimension line closer or farther from the dimensioned object, pick the dimension to display the grips. Pick one of the grips at the endpoints of the dimension line to highlight it. The `Specify stretch point or [Base point/Copy/ Undo/eXit]:` prompt appears. Drag the dimension line to the desired location. Press Esc to remove the grips.

To move dimension text, pick the dimension to display the grips. Pick the grip on the dimension text to highlight it. Drag the dimension text to its desired location.

Tip
For best results, turn Ortho mode on while trying to drag the dimension line or the dimension text. Polar tracking also works well. ■

You can also grip-edit multileaders in the same way. These also have two triangular grips that you can use to change the length of the landing line.

Editing objects and dimensions together

Because dimensions are associative, when you edit objects, the dimensions automatically adjust to the new object measurements. Stretching the object with the STRETCH command or grips is usually the best way to accomplish this. The object and the dimension adjust at the same time.

On the DVD
The drawing in the following exercise on using DDEDIT, QDIM, grips, and STRETCH to edit dimensions, `ab14-i. dwg`, **is in the** `Drawings` **folder on the DVD.** ■

STEPS: Using DDEDIT, QDIM, Grips, and STRETCH to Edit Dimensions

1. Open `ab14-i.dwg` from your DVD.

2. Save the file as `ab14-10.dwg` in your `AutoCAD Bible` folder. This is a cross-section of a valve part, as shown in Figure 14.44.

FIGURE 14.44

A dimensioned cross-section of a valve part.

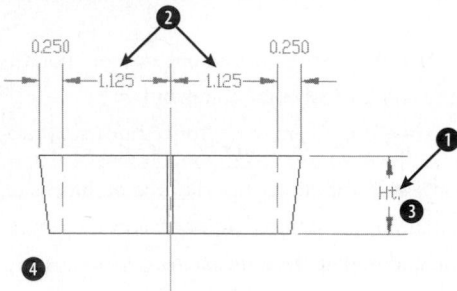

---

3. To replace the dimension marked Ht., type **ddedit** ↵ on the command line. At the `Select an annotation object or [Undo]:` prompt, choose the dimension at ❶, shown in Figure 14.44. The In-Place Text Editor opens with the text displayed. Select the current text and type **<>**. Click outside the editor. The command automatically creates the original measured dimension. Press Enter to end the command.

4. Select the two dimensions marked ❷, shown in Figure 14.44. Also select the cyan centerline and the two green hidden lines. Choose Annotate tab ⇨ Dimensions panel ⇨ Quick Dimension. At the first prompt, right-click and choose Edit. At the `Indicate dimension point to remove, or [Add/eXit] <eXit>:` prompt, choose the two edit points (each marked with an X) on the cyan centerline. Right-click and choose eXit. At the `Specify dimension line position, or [Continuous/Staggered/Baseline/Ordinate/Radius/Diameter/datumPoint/Edit/seTtings] <Continuous>:` prompt, place the dimension line where it was previously. (You can use the outside arrows as a guide.)

5. Pick the dimension at ❶. Press Shift and click the grip on the text and one of the dimension's grips to activate them. Click either of the grips and drag slightly to the left to place the dimension and its text closer to the object that you are dimensioning.

6. Choose Home tab ⇨ Modify panel ⇨ Stretch. Follow the prompts:

```
Select objects: Pick at ❸.
Specify opposite corner: Pick at ❹.
9 found
Select objects: ↵
Specify base point or [Displacement] <Displacement>: 0,-.25 ↵
Specify second point or <use first point as displacement>: ↵
```

The valve part stretches, and the dimension that measures its height changes accordingly.

7. Save your drawing. It should look like Figure 14.45.

FIGURE 14.45

The edited valve part.

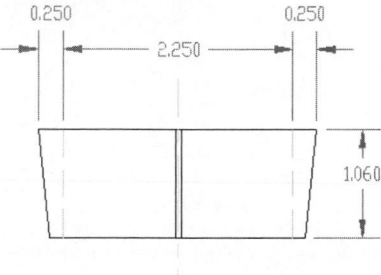

Summary

The dimension features in AutoCAD and AutoCAD LT enable you to dimension almost anything. In this chapter, you read about:

- Creating linear, radial, dimension, angular, and ordinate dimensions
- Formatting and creating multileaders
- Dimensioning with the Quick Dimension feature
- Creating inspection dimensions
- Creating tolerances
- Editing dimensions

In the next chapter, I continue the subject of dimensions by explaining how to gain total control with dimension styles.

Creating Dimension Styles

I n Chapter 14, you drew many dimensions using the default dimension style. However, you can create your own dimension styles to control the way dimensions appear. Once you're familiar with dimensions, you can learn how to customize them to suit your needs.

Understanding Dimension Styles

You should create your dimension styles before dimensioning. Some drawings have several dimension styles, although a drawing can look confusing if it has too many dimension styles. In general, you create a dimension style, save it in your template drawings, and (you hope) rarely have to deal with it again, except to override a setting for a unique situation.

The various disciplines each have their own standards and customs regarding dimensions. Dimension styles are flexible enough to accommodate any type of dimensioning practice.

 To create a dimension style, choose Annotate tab ⇨ Dimensions panel, and click the dialog box launcher arrow at the right end of the panel title bar to open the Dimension Style Manager, as shown in Figure 15.1. The current dimension style is shown as Standard, which is the default dimension style.

The Dimension Style Manager is the master control room for managing dimensions. Here you create new dimension styles and modify existing ones.

The preset Standard dimension style is most appropriate for mechanical drafting. Whichever type of drafting you do, you'll probably need to make some changes to the default dimension style or create a new dimension style. A preview of the current dimension style is shown at the right side of the dialog box.

FIGURE 15.1

The Dimension Style Manager.

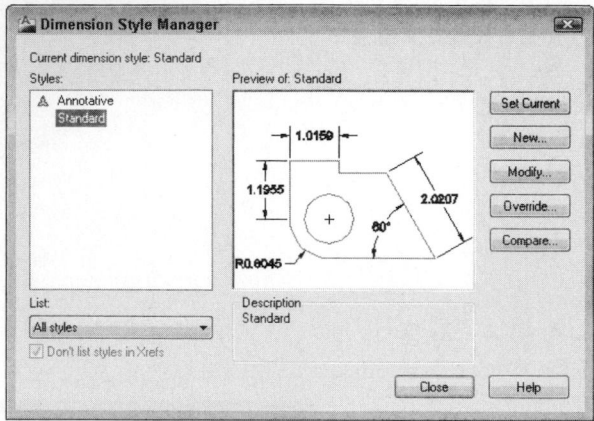

To create a new style, click New to open the Create New Dimension Style dialog box, as shown in Figure 15.2. Type a new name in the New Style Name text box. In the Start With drop-down list, choose which existing dimension style you want to use as a basis for the new dimension style. If you have more than one to choose from, choose the style that most resembles the new style you want to create.

FIGURE 15.2

The Create New Dimension Style dialog box.

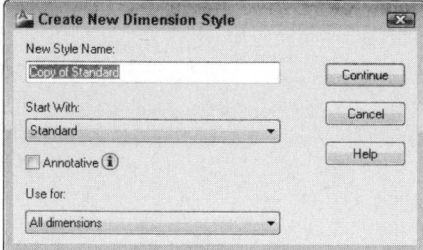

If you want dimensions that use this dimension style to be annotative, check the Annotative check box. Annotative dimensions are valuable when you will be displaying your model at more than one scale, in separate viewports.

Note

Annotative objects automatically scale according to the scale of model space or a viewport on a layout. You use a layout to lay out a drawing for plotting, and viewports display various views of the drawing. Each viewport can have a different scale, and annotative objects automatically adjust in size accordingly. I discuss annotative objects more in Chapter 17. ∎

The Use For drop-down list lets you decide whether you want to use the dimension style for all dimensions or only for a specific type of dimension; you can choose from Linear, Angular, Radius, Diameter, Ordinate, or Leaders and Tolerances. Usually, you create a dimension style for all dimension types. Later in this chapter, I explain how to create variants of dimension styles for specific types of dimensions. When you're done, click Continue.

You can also use the Dimension Style Manager to rename an existing dimension style. Click its name to select it. Click it a second time to see an edit box. Type the new name and press Enter.

Defining a New Dimension Style

Dimension styles have many components, and so the process of defining a dimension style is complex. Your task is organized for you by the tabs of the dialog box.

When you click Continue in the Create New Dimension Style dialog box, the New Dimension Style dialog box opens, as shown in Figure 15.3.

FIGURE 15.3

The New Dimension Style dialog box with the Lines tab displayed.

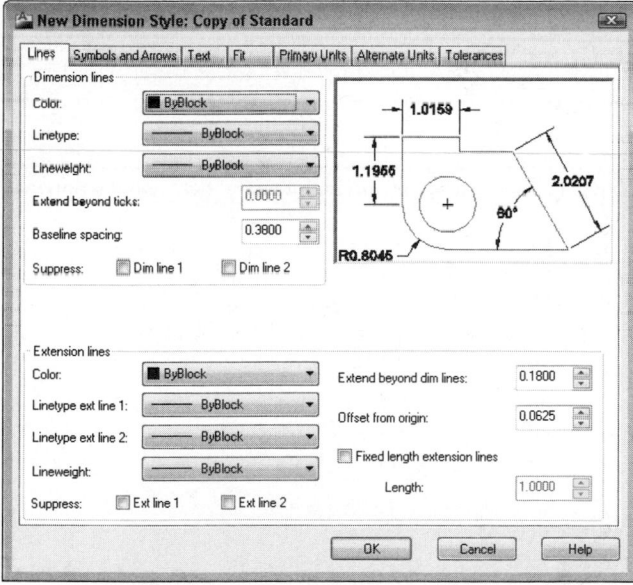

Managing dimension lines

An important part of defining a dimension style is specifying how the dimension lines and extension lines look, which you do on the Lines tab of the New Dimension Style dialog box. In Chapter 14, I illustrate the parts of a dimension. Refer to Figure 14.1, if necessary.

Dimension lines

To set the color of the dimension line so that it differs from that of the rest of the dimension, click the Color drop-down list and choose a color. Choose Select Color to open the Select Color dialog box if you want to use a nonstandard color. Remember, a dimension is a block — that is, it is one object. The default color is ByBlock so that dimensions take on the color of the current layer or color setting. In general, you should have a separate layer for dimensions so that the entire dimension is the color set for that layer. Use this setting only if you want the dimension lines to be a different color from your dimension layer color. The arrowheads do not have a separate color setting and always follow the dimension-line setting.

Cross-Reference

See Chapter 11 for a discussion of how to use the Select Color dialog box. See Chapter 18 for coverage of blocks. ■

To specify a linetype for a dimension, choose one from the Linetype drop-down list. If the linetype that you want isn't on the list, then you need to load it. To do this, choose Other to open the Select Linetype dialog box. (For more information on loading linetypes, see Chapter 11.) The default lineweight is ByBlock, which means that it takes on the lineweight of the current layer. To set a lineweight for the dimension line, click the Lineweight drop-down list and choose a lineweight. In general, you want your objects to stand out, so dimensions should have a lineweight the same as, or narrower than, the objects that you're dimensioning.

The Extend Beyond Ticks text box determines how far the dimension lines extend past the extension lines. When you have arrowheads at the ends of the dimension lines, the Extension option is unavailable. However, if you choose Architectural Tick, Oblique, Dot Small, Integral, or None in the Arrowheads section of the dialog box, the Extend Beyond Ticks option becomes available. This type of extension is typical for architectural drafting. Figure 15.4 shows a dimension with an architectural tick and a 0.1-unit extension.

FIGURE 15.4

A typical architectural dimension showing the text above one dimension line, an architectural tick, and the dimension line extending slightly beyond the extension lines.

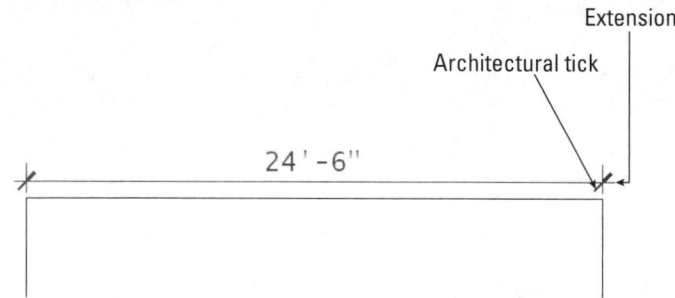

The Baseline spacing text box determines the distance between successive dimension lines when you create baseline dimensions with the DIMBASELINE command. This specification creates evenly spaced dimension lines. (In Chapter 14, I discuss the DIMSPACE command, which lets you evenly space any linear or angular dimensions.)

In some dimension styles, the dimension text splits the dimension line into two parts, as shown in Figure 15.5. This creates two dimension lines. You can suppress — that is, turn off — the first or second dimension line (or both dimension lines) by checking the appropriate box (or boxes). The first line is nearest where you specified the first extension-line origin. (If you selected an object instead of specifying two extension-line origins, you may not be able to predict which dimension line is the first and which is the second. Experiment.) You would usually suppress dimension lines when they interfere with other dimensions or with objects in your drawing. (The DIMBREAK command, which I cover in Chapter 14, breaks dimensions where they cross objects. You may be able to break a dimension instead of suppressing one of the dimension lines.)

FIGURE 15.5

A typical mechanical dimension with text splitting two dimension lines.

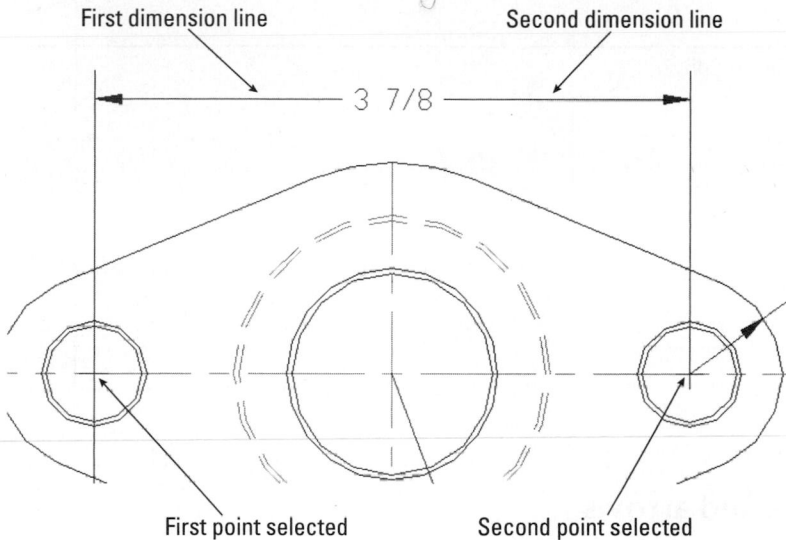

Extension lines

As with dimension lines, you can pick a color for the extension lines that differs from that of the rest of the dimension. Click the Color drop-down list and choose a color. Choose Select Color to open the Select Color dialog box if you want a nonstandard color. The default color is ByBlock so that extensions take on the color of the current layer or color setting.

You can choose a separate linetype for each extension line. Choose the linetype that you want from the drop-down lists. If the linetype that you want isn't listed, click Other to open the Select Linetype dialog box, where you can load the linetype that you need.

Extension lines typically extend slightly past the dimension line, as you can see in some of the figures in this chapter. Use the Extend Beyond Dim Lines text box to specify this extension distance.

Extension lines don't usually touch the object that they dimension to make it easier to distinguish the dimension from the object. Use the Offset from Origin text box to define the distance from the specified points on the object to the extension lines.

Extension lines usually vary in length throughout a drawing, depending on the shape of the objects that you're dimensioning. However, sometimes you may want the extension lines to all be the same length, even if they don't reach near their objects. This method avoids dimension lines crossing each other when you're dimensioning a complex shape.

To specify fixed-length extension lines, check the Fixed Length Extension Lines check box and specify the length in the Length text box.

You can suppress the first or second extension line (or both lines) so that either or both are not visible. To do this, check the appropriate box (or boxes). Figure 15.6 shows a dimension with the first extension line suppressed.

FIGURE 15.6

A dimension with the first extension line suppressed.

Defining symbols and arrows

The Symbols and Arrows tab organizes your settings related to arrowheads and certain dimension-related symbols, as shown in Figure 15.7. For example, you can define center marks and arc length symbols on this tab.

Defining arrowheads

The Arrowheads section controls the arrowheads at the ends of dimension lines. You don't actually have to use arrowheads, as you saw in Figure 15.4. You can also set the first and second arrowheads individually. However, if you change the first arrowhead, the second one follows suit, assuming that you want both ends of the dimension to look the same. To specify two different arrowheads, choose an arrowhead in the first drop-down list and then in the second drop-down list.

You can create and use your own arrowhead:

1. In any drawing, create the arrowhead that you want with a unit size of 1.
2. Make a block out of it. For an arrow-shaped block, pick the point of the arrow for the insertion point and create it pointing to the right. You may have to experiment with the right insertion point. Save the block. (See Chapter 18 for instructions on creating blocks. You can't use annotative blocks as arrowheads.)

3. In the first and second drop-down lists, choose User Arrow. The Select Custom Arrow Block dialog box opens, displaying the blocks available in the drawing.

4. Choose the block that you want from the drop-down list.

5. Click OK.

Figure 15.8 shows a dimension with a user arrow.

FIGURE 15.7

The Symbols and Arrows tab lets you define arrowheads and fine-tune dimension symbols.

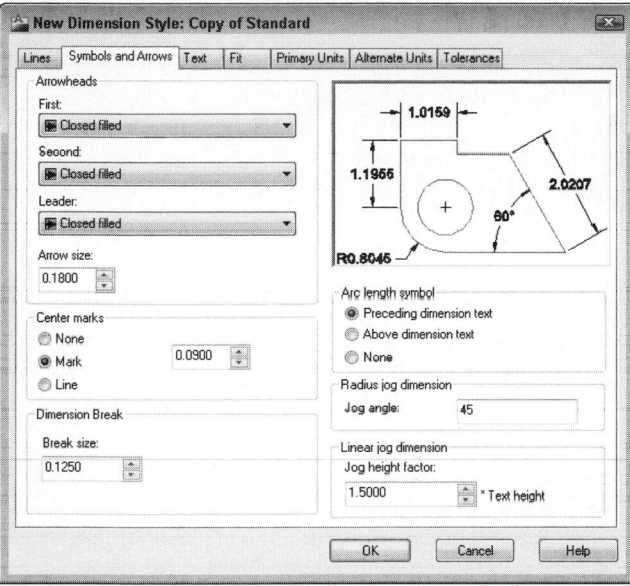

FIGURE 15.8

A dimension with a user arrow.

$7' - 7\frac{3}{4}''$

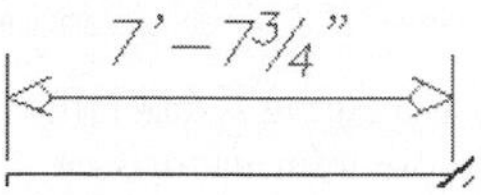

Tip

You can set a different arrow for leaders. Choose the arrow that you want from the Leader drop-down list. ■

Set the size of the arrowhead in the Arrow Size text box. As explained later in this chapter in the discussion of scale, you should use the final size that you want to see when the drawing is plotted on paper.

Defining symbols

The Center Marks section of the Symbols and Arrows tab in the New Dimension Style dialog box specifies how you want to mark the centers of arcs and circles when you choose Annotate tab ⇨ Dimensions panel (expanded) ⇨ Center Mark (the DIMCENTER command). In the Center Marks section, choose Mark to create a small cross, Line to create a cross plus four lines that cross, or None. Figure 15.9 shows a circle with centerlines and an arc with a center mark.

Specify the size of the center mark or centerline in the text box to the right of the Center Marks section. For center marks, the size is the distance from the intersection of the two lines to their endpoints. If you use centerlines, the size also determines the distance from the circle quadrants to the end of the centerlines.

A circle with a centerline and an arc with a center mark.

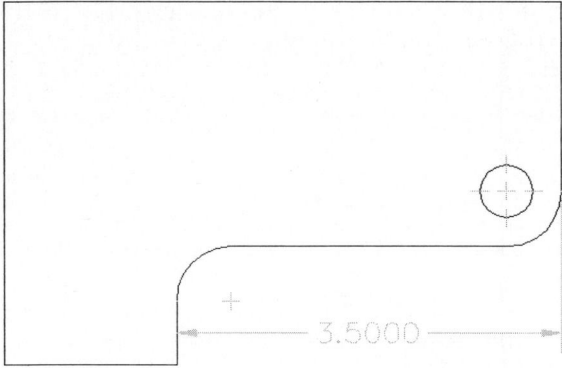

In the Dimension Break section, specify the break size. A dimension break is a gap in the dimension where it crosses an object. I discuss dimension breaks (the DIMBREAK command) in Chapter 14.

The Arc Length Symbol section is for specifying the location of the symbol used when you dimension arc lengths. By default, the symbol goes before the dimension value, but you can choose to put it on top or omit it completely.

The Radius Jog Dimension section lets you specify the angle used when you create a jogged dimension for circles or arcs with large radii. A jogged dimension is a small dimension that doesn't reach to the center of the circle or arc. For more information on jogged dimensions, see Chapter 14.

In the Linear Jog Dimension section, specify a jog height factor for linear jogs. A jog is a zigzag symbol that indicates that the object is not drawn to scale, usually due to space limitations. For more information, see Chapter 14. You specify the size in relation to the text height for the dimension. The default is 1.5 times the text height. I discuss dimension text height in the next section.

Because the Standard dimension style is closest to mechanical drafting standards, in the following exercise you start to create an architectural dimension style, using the Standard style as a base. This requires you to make a maximum number of changes, thereby letting you become as familiar as possible with the dimension style settings. Here you practice controlling dimension lines and arrows.

On the DVD

The drawing used in the following exercise on controlling dimension lines and arrows, ab15-a.dwg, is in the Drawings folder on the DVD. ∎

STEPS: Controlling Dimension Lines and Arrows

1. Open ab15-a.dwg from your DVD.

2. Save the file as ab15-01.dwg in your AutoCAD Bible folder. This drawing is an elevation of a garage, as shown in Figure 15.10. Ortho Mode and Object Snap should be on. Set running object snaps for Endpoint and Intersection. The Dim layer is current.

3. To see what the Standard dimension style looks like, choose Annotate tab ⇨ Dimensions panel ⇨ Dimension drop-down list ⇨ Linear. At the Specify first extension line origin or <select object>: prompt, pick ❶, shown in Figure 15.10. At the Specify second extension line origin: prompt, pick ❷. At the Specify dimension line location or [Mtext/Text/Angle/Horizontal/Vertical/Rotated]: prompt, pick a location for the dimension line below the line that you dimensioned. The arrows and text are so small that you can't even see them.

4. Choose View tab ⇨ Navigate panel ⇨ Zoom drop-down list ⇨ Zoom Window and specify a window near ❶ and the left end of the dimension. Press Enter to repeat the ZOOM command, and then enter **p** ↵ to perform a Zoom Previous. Zoom in on the center of the dimension to see the text. Do a Zoom Previous again. As you can see, this dimension needs some modification.

5. Choose Annotate tab ⇨ Dimensions panel, and click the dialog box launcher arrow on the right side of the panel title bar. The current dimension style should be Standard. Click New. In the New Style Name text box, type **Arch 48** and click Continue.

6. Click the Symbols and Arrows tab if it isn't on top. In the Arrowheads section, choose Oblique from the first drop-down list. The size should be 3/16".

7. Click the Lines tab. In the Dimension Lines section, type **3/32** in the Extend Beyond Ticks text box. (Because of the units precision setting — which you set with the UNITS command — this value is rounded off to 1/8" in the display, although the value is still 3/32.) Click OK to return to the Dimension Style Manager.

8. In the Dimension Style Manager, notice that the arrows have been changed to ticks in the preview. Click Close.

9. Select the dimension that you created in Step 3. Choose Annotate tab ⇨ Dimensions panel ⇨ Dimension Style drop-down list, and choose Arch 48. Press Esc. The dimension now has the geometry settings that you just made. To check it out, do a Zoom Window to the left end of the dimension. You can see that the oblique mark has replaced the arrow. Do a Zoom Previous.

10. Save your drawing. Keep this drawing open if you're continuing on to the next exercise.

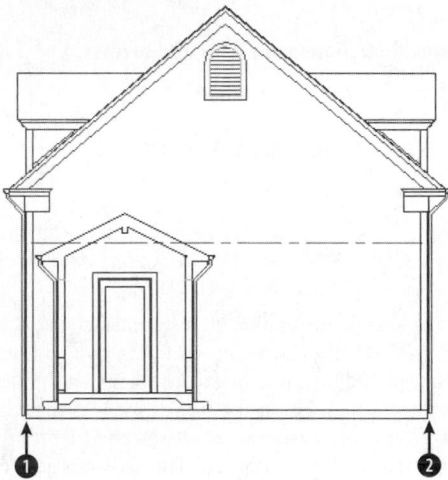

FIGURE 15.10

The garage elevation.

GARAGE SOUTH ELEV 1/4" = 1'-0"

Managing dimension text

You can format the text of the dimension for readability and to match other text in your drawing. In the New Dimension Style dialog box, the Text tab, shown in Figure 15.11, controls text appearance, placement, and alignment.

Text appearance

You have full control over dimension text appearance, as you do over any other text in your drawing. To specify a text style for your dimension text, choose a text style from the Text style drop-down list. You may want to create a special text style, such as Dim Text, for dimension text, to give you the flexibility to alter dimension text without changing other text in your drawing. Create the dimension text style before creating your dimension style. If you want the dimension to be annotative, its text style should also be annotative.

Cross-Reference

See Chapter 13 for a discussion of text styles. ∎

Choose a color from the Text Color drop-down list. You can pick a color for the dimension text that differs from that of the rest of the dimension. The default color is ByBlock so that dimensions take on the color of the current layer or color setting. Use this setting only if you want the dimension text to be a different color from your dimension layer color. To choose a nonstandard color, choose Select Color from the drop-down list to open the Select Color dialog box.

You can create a block of color around the dimension text so that if other objects are behind the dimension, you can still read the dimension text clearly. To add a color, choose one from the Fill Color drop-down list.

FIGURE 15.11

The Text tab of the New Dimension Style dialog box.

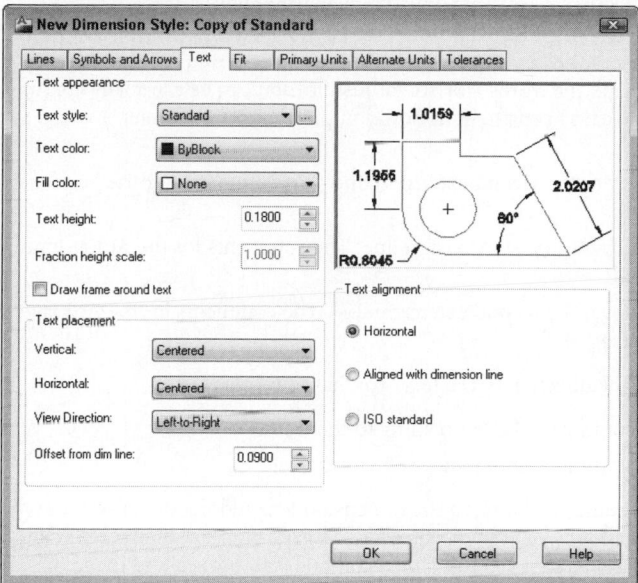

Choose the height for your dimension text. When you set the text style height to zero, you can set the height in the New Dimension Style dialog box. Otherwise, the text style height takes over. It's much easier to make all your dimension style adjustments in one place than to make changes in the text style as well.

If your unit type uses fractions, use the fraction height scale to set a ratio of fraction text to whole text. This option is available only if your units specify the use of fractions. You may want the fractions to be smaller than whole numbers. A scale of 0.5 makes the fractions half the size of whole numbers; the resulting overall fraction is slightly higher than the whole numbers of the dimension text.

Some dimension styles require a border around the dimension text. If you want to include a rectangular border, check the Draw Frame Around Text check box.

Text placement

The Vertical drop-down list affects how text is justified relative to the dimension line. As you make changes, be sure to look at the preview to see whether the results are what you want. You have the following options:

- **Centered.** Centers the text in the dimension line, breaking the dimension line into two. This is typical for mechanical drafting. You can see an example in Figure 15.5.
- **Above.** Places text above the dimension line. This is typical for architectural drafting. You can see an example in Figure 15.4.
- **Outside.** Places the text on the side of the dimension line that is farthest from the object that you're dimensioning.
- **JIS.** Places text in conformation to the Japanese Industrial Standards rules, which vary the placement according to the angle of the dimension line.
- **Below.** Places text below the dimension line.

The Horizontal drop-down list affects the placement of dimension text between the extension lines. Here again, you have a handy visual confirmation of your choice. You have the following choices:

- **Centered.** This is the default. It centers text between the two extension lines.
- **At Ext Line 1.** Places the text next to the first extension line. The first extension line is always the first point that you specified at the `Specify first extension line origin or <select object>:` prompt. The picture and the words Horizontal Justification can be especially confusing for vertical dimensions. If you aren't consistent in how you pick your dimensions, you can get some strange results.
- **At Ext Line 2.** Places the text next to the second extension line. The comments for the previous option apply to this option as well.
- **Over Ext Line 1.** Places the text over the first extension line. The comments for the At Ext Line 1 option apply to this option as well.
- **Over Ext Line 2.** Places the text over the second extension line. The comments for the At Ext Line 1 option apply to this option as well.

The View Direction drop-down list affects the direction of the text. You have two choices:

- **Left-to-Right.** Displays the text starting on the left reading to the right.
- **Right-to-Left.** Displays the text starting on the right reading to the left.

Use the Offset from Dim Line text box to set the gap between the dimension text and the dimension line. This sets the DIMGAP system variable. If the dimension line is broken, the gap is the space between each side of the dimension text and the two dimension lines. If the dimension line is unbroken and the text is above the line, the gap is the space between the bottom of the text and the dimension line. The gap also controls the space between the box created for Basic tolerance dimensions and the text inside them. Basic tolerances are discussed in the "Formatting tolerances" section later in this chapter.

Tip

When trying to fit dimension text, lines, and arrows into a narrow space, AutoCAD and AutoCAD LT also use the gap (the DIMGAP value) to calculate the minimum space required on either side of the dimension text. Therefore, reducing the gap can help fit more of the dimension elements between the extension lines. ■

Text alignment

Different disciplines have different standards for aligning dimension text. The Text Alignment section of the Text tab affects how the text is aligned relative to the dimension line, as follows:

- **Horizontal.** Keeps text between the extension lines horizontal, regardless of the angle of the dimension line (typical of mechanical drawings).
- **Aligned with Dimension Line.** Keeps text at the same angle as the dimension line (typical of architectural drawings).
- **ISO Standard.** Uses the ISO standard, which aligns text with the dimension line when text is inside the extension lines, but aligns text horizontally when text is outside the extension lines (because of a tight fit).

On the DVD

The drawing used in the following exercise on defining dimension text, `ab15-01.dwg`, is in the `Results` folder on the DVD. ■

STEPS: Defining Dimension Text

1. If `ab15-01.dwg` is open from the previous exercise, use it for this exercise as well. Otherwise, open `ab15-01.dwg` from the `Results` folder of the DVD. Ortho Mode and Object Snap should be on. Set running object snaps for Endpoint and Intersection. The Dim layer is current.

2. Save the file as `ab15-02.dwg` in your `AutoCAD Bible` folder.

3. Choose Annotate tab ⇨ Dimensions panel, and click the dialog box launcher arrow on the right side of the panel title bar. The Arch 48 dimension style should be current. Choose Modify to continue working on the Arch 48 dimension style. Click the Text tab.

4. In the Text Appearance section, choose ROMANS as the text style.

5. In the Text Placement section, choose Above from the Vertical drop-down list.

6. In the Text Alignment section, choose Aligned with Dimension Line. Although mechanical dimensions usually require horizontal text, architectural dimensions require that the text be aligned with the dimension line.

7. Click OK and then click Close to update the dimension to include the changes. The text is still too tiny to see clearly.

8. Save your drawing. Keep this drawing open if you're continuing on to the next exercise.

Fitting dimensions into tight spaces

When there is not enough room to place the arrowheads, dimension line, and text between the extension lines, some elements of the dimension need to go outside the extension lines. The Fit tab, shown in Figure 15.12, lets you specify how you want to handle this situation.

FIGURE 15.12

The Fit tab of the New Dimension Style dialog box.

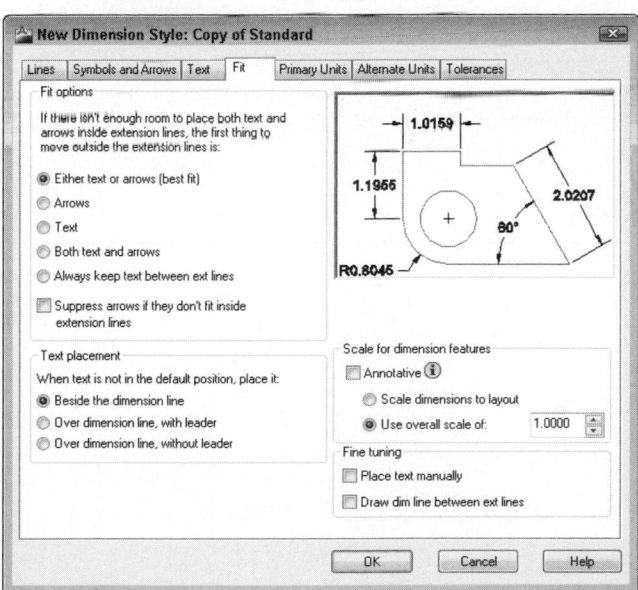

Fit Options

The Fit Options section determines which elements are moved outside the extension lines — text, arrows, or both — when they can't fit inside the extension lines. These are among the hardest of the dimension styles options to understand, yet they can greatly affect how your dimensions appear.

Caution

The Fit options specify what goes outside the extension lines. For example, choose the Arrows option to place the arrows outside the extension lines if there is not enough room for them. Be careful, or you'll get a result that is the opposite of what you intended. ■

Here are your choices:

- **Either Text or Arrows (Best Fit).** Puts whatever fits inside the extension lines. The arrowheads might fit inside and the text might not, or the other way around. If there isn't enough room for either text or arrows, then they both go outside the extension lines. Figure 15.13 shows a dimension using this option.

FIGURE 15.13

A narrow dimension using the Either Text or Arrows (Best Fit) option.

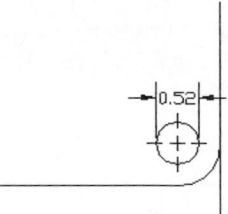

- **Arrows.** If there is not enough room for both the text and the arrows between the extension lines, the arrows go outside and the text goes between the arrows. Figure 15.14 shows a dimension using this option. The results of this option happen to look the same as Figure 15.13, but a different setting produced them.

FIGURE 15.14

A narrow dimension using the Arrows option.

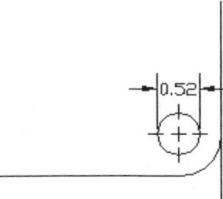

- **Text.** If there isn't enough room for the text and the arrows between the extension lines, the text goes outside and the arrows go between them. Figure 15.15 shows a dimension using this option.

FIGURE 15.15

A narrow dimension using the Text option.

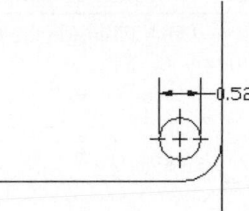

- **Both Text and Arrows.** Keeps the text and arrows together — between the extension lines if there is enough room, and outside the extension lines if there is not. Figure 15.16 shows a dimension using this option.

FIGURE 15.16

A narrow dimension using the Both Text and Arrows option.

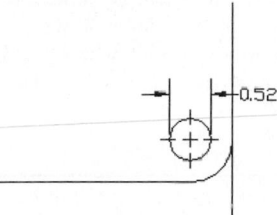

- **Always Keep Text between Ext Lines.** As it says, this option always keeps the text between the extension lines, even if they don't fit. Figure 15.17 shows a dimension using this option.

FIGURE 15.17

A narrow dimension using the Always Keep Text between Ext Lines option.

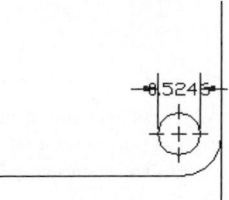

- **Suppress Arrows If They Don't Fit Inside the Extension Lines.** Use this check box to suppress the display of arrows completely if they don't fit inside the extension lines (instead of putting them outside). This option is used together with one of the previous options. Figure 15.18 shows a dimension using this option with the Either Text or Arrows (Best Fit) option.

FIGURE 15.18

A narrow dimension using the Suppress Arrows If They Don't Fit Inside the Extension Lines option along with the Either Text or Arrows (Best Fit) option.

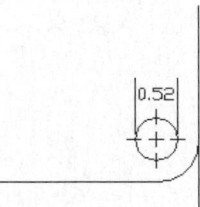

Text Placement

The Text Placement section determines where you want the dimension text when it isn't in its default position, due to a tight fit. Your options are:

- **Beside the Dimension Line.** Places the dimension text next to the dimension line, but outside the extension lines. Figure 15.19 shows a dimension using this option, as well as the same dimension edited to move the text off the model. You can move the text anywhere to the left or the right of the dimension line, but not above or below it. Editing dimensions is covered later in this chapter.

FIGURE 15.19

Dimension text is placed beside the dimension line when it doesn't fit inside the extension lines. You can move the text from side to side. On the right, the text has been moved to the right slightly so that it doesn't cross the model.

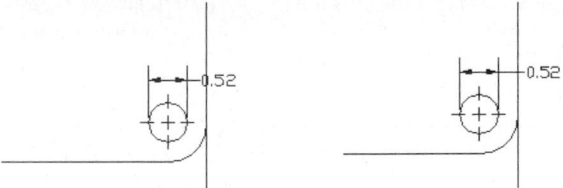

- **Over Dimension Line, with Leader.** Places the dimension text over the dimension line and between the extension lines with a leader from the dimension line to the text. You can move the text anywhere to suit your needs and dimensioning conventions, as shown in Figure 15.20.

FIGURE 15.20

Dimension text is placed over the dimension line with a leader. On the right, the text has been moved to the right of the model.

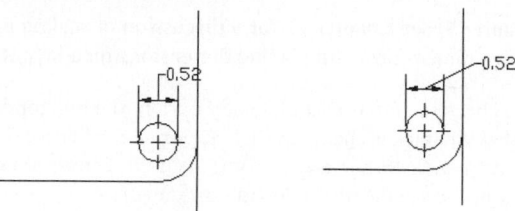

- **Over Dimension Line, without Leader.** Places the dimension text over the dimension line and between the extension lines with no leader, as shown in Figure 15.21. You can move the text anywhere.

FIGURE 15.21

Dimension text is placed over the dimension line without a leader.

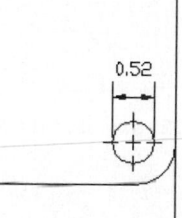

Scale for Dimension Features

The Scale for Dimension Features section lets you specify the scale factor. The reason you need to specify a scale factor is because you may have to scale the drawing when you plot it. The scale factor adjusts the size of dimension text (unless a nonzero text style height controls the text), arrowheads, spacing, and so on. It has no effect on the content of dimension text — that is, it does not affect actual measurements. So many size options are possible in a dimension style that you could spend all day trying to multiply each size option by the scale. Then if you have to change the scale of the drawing, you would need to recalculate all the size specifications. Setting the Overall Scale factor tells AutoCAD or AutoCAD LT to automatically multiply every size specification by the scale factor.

To scale dimensions according to the scale of the layout, check the Scale Dimensions to Layout option. You would use this feature if you plan to use more than one viewport, each with a different scale factor. If not, you can choose an overall scale, which would be the scale factor that you plan to use; check the Use Overall Scale Of option and enter a scale.

The annotative feature, which is available for text, hatches, blocks, and dimensions, replaces the previous dimension scaling. Therefore, when you check the Annotative check box, the two options become unavailable.

Cross-Reference
Scale factors are discussed in detail in Chapter 5. See Chapter 17 for a discussion of scaling dimensions in a paper space layout (including the use of annotative dimensions) and placing dimensions on a layout. ■

In the Fine Tuning section, if you check the Place Text Manually option, the horizontal text placement settings are ignored, and the point that you pick at the `Specify dimension line location or [Mtext/ Text/Angle/Horizontal/Vertical/ Rotated]:` prompt is used. Before you click, as you move the cursor along the dimension line, you can see the text following the cursor.

Check the Draw Dim Line Between Ext Lines option to force a dimension line between the extension lines, even when there isn't room for text or arrows, as shown in Figure 15.22.

FIGURE 15.22

A dimension with a forced dimension line.

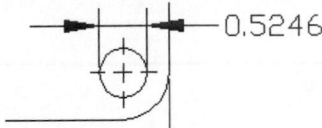

On the DVD
The drawing used in the following exercise on setting dimension fit, ab15-02.dwg, is in the Results folder on the DVD. ■

STEPS: Setting Dimension Fit

1. If ab15-02.dwg is open from the previous exercise, use it for this exercise as well. Otherwise, open ab15-02.dwg from the Results folder of the DVD. Ortho Mode and Object Snap should be on. Set running object snaps for Endpoint and Intersection. The Dim layer is current.

2. Save the file as ab15-03.dwg in your AutoCAD Bible folder.

3. Choose Annotate tab ⇨ Dimensions panel, and click the dialog box launcher arrow on the right side of the panel title bar. Make sure that the Arch 48 dimension style is current. Choose Modify to continue working on the Arch 48 dimension style.

4. On the Fit tab, in the Text Placement section, choose Over Dimension Line, with Leader.

5. In the Fine Tuning section, check Draw Dim Line Between Ext Lines. Architectural dimensions customarily place a line between the extension lines, even if the text cannot fit.

6. Because the drawing's scale is ¼"=1', or 1:48, type **48** in the Use Overall Scale Of text box.

7. Click OK. Click Close to return to your drawing.

8. Save your drawing. You can finally see the dimension! It should look like Figure 15.23. Keep this drawing open if you're continuing on to the next exercise.

FIGURE 15.23

As a result of changing the overall scale, you can finally see the dimension.

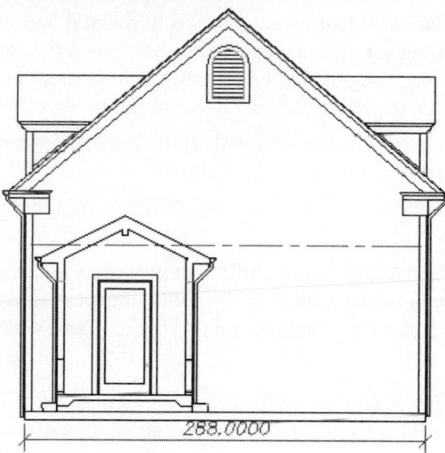

GARAGE SOUTH ELEV 1/4" = 1'–0"

Defining primary units

The primary units define the type of units used to display the dimension in your drawing. You need to set primary units separately from the units for the drawing, which affect coordinate display but not dimensions.

Click the Primary Units tab, shown in Figure 15.24, to set the format and precision for linear and angular dimensions. You should already be familiar with setting units, which I discuss in Chapter 5. You must set your units for dimensions separately.

Linear Dimensions

To get the look and accuracy that you want, you should specify the format and precision of your linear dimensions. The New Dimensions Style dialog box provides settings for linear dimensions. You have the following options:

- Choose a format from the Unit Format drop-down list. You have the same choices as in the Drawing Units dialog box: Scientific, Decimal, Engineering, Architectural, and Fractional, as well as an additional option, Windows Desktop.

Note

To see the current Windows Desktop units setting, choose Start ⇨ Control Panel ⇨ Regional Settings (or Regional Options, Regional and Language Options, or Clock, Language, and Region ⇨ Regional and Language Options or Regional and Language, depending on your operating system). Click the Numbers tab. (You might have to click the Customize This Format button on the Formats tab first.) The Windows Desktop setting does not give you complete control over units. However, if you need consistency with another Windows application, you might find this setting useful. ■

- Choose a precision (the number of decimal points or the fraction denominator) from the Precision drop-down list.

- Choose a fraction format from the Fraction Format drop-down list. This option is available only if the format that you chose uses fractions. Horizontal places a horizontal line between stacked numerators and denominators. Diagonal uses a diagonal slash between the stacked numerator and denominator. Not Stacked uses a diagonal line between the numerator and denominator, which are not stacked. You can see the effect of each choice in the preview box.

- Choose a decimal separator. This option is available only if the format that you chose uses decimals. You can choose from a period, a comma, and a space.

- Use the Round Off text box to round off linear dimension distances. For example, you can round to the nearest 0.1 unit or ½ inch.

- Use the Prefix and Suffix boxes to add a prefix or suffix that you want to place before or after every dimension. For example, you might want to add a suffix of mm after every dimension if you're measuring in millimeters and giving the drawing to a client who usually sees dimensions in inches.

You can use the Scale Factor text box to set a scaling factor for linear dimensions, including radial and diameter dimensions, and ordinal dimensions. This factor changes the actual measurement text. For example, if you draw a line 2.5 units long and you specify a linear scale of 0.5, the object is dimensioned as 1.25 units. You could set this scale to 25.4 to use metric measurements on a drawing that you have created with U.S. measurements. This can occur if you're sending the same drawing to certain clients in the United States and other clients elsewhere in the world. You can also use this scale in conjunction with alternate units, as explained in the next section.

FIGURE 15.24

The Primary Units tab of the New Dimension Style dialog box.

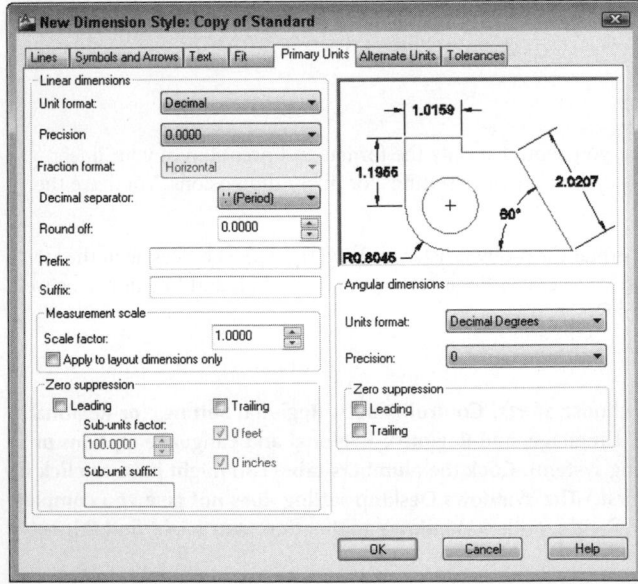

Check the Apply to Layout Dimensions Only option to apply the linear scaling factor only to layout (paper space) dimensions.

In the Zero Suppression section, choose whether you want to suppress leading and trailing zeros. If you suppress leading zeros, a number such as 0.375 appears as .375. If you suppress trailing zeros, a number such as 3.7500 appears as 3.75.

If you suppress leading zeros, you can choose to display a measurement of less than one unit in a *subunit*, which is an alternative, smaller unit. You can use subunits with decimal units only. For example, if your units represent feet, instead of displaying a dimension value as 0.25 feet, you may want to display the measurement as 3".

To do so, first check the Leading check box, to suppress leading zeros. Then specify the Sub-Units Factor value to set the number of subunits per unit. In the previous example, you would set the Sub-Units Factor to 12, because there are 12 inches in a foot. (If your units represent meters, you could set the Sub-Units Factor to 100 to show units of less than one in centimeters.)

Use the Sub-Units Suffix text box to specify a suffix for the dimension text. In the example you would set this value to ", to represent inches. AutoCAD multiples the actual value (.25) by the subunit factor (12), adds the suffix, and displays the results (3"). (If your units represent meters and you want to show centimeters for subunits, set the suffix to cm.)

For architectural units, you can choose to suppress 0 feet and 0 inches. If you suppress 0 feet, a number such as 0'-8" becomes 8". If you suppress 0 inches, a number such as 6'-0" becomes 6'.

Angular Dimensions

To get the look and accuracy that you need for angular dimensions, you should also set their format and precision. The Angular Dimensions section of the Primary Units tab lets you format angular measurements. You have the following options:

- Choose from Decimal Degrees, Degrees Minutes Seconds, Gradians, and Radians.
- Choose a precision from the Precision drop-down list.

In the Zero Suppression section, choose whether you want to suppress leading and trailing zeros for angular dimensions. For example, an angle of 37.0° would appear as 37° with the trailing zero suppressed.

Defining alternate units

If you want, you can show an alternate set of units in your dimensions. The most common use of this feature is to show millimeters and inches together. Alternate units appear in square brackets. To show alternate units, click the Alternate Units tab of the New Dimension Style dialog box, as shown in Figure 15.25. Check the Display Alternate Units check box.

As you can see, this dialog box is very similar to the Primary Units tab, discussed in the previous section. Notice the default scale of 25.40 in the Multiplier for Alt Units text box. There are 25.4 millimeters to an inch. If your primary units are millimeters, you can set the linear scale to 0.03937, which is the number of inches to a millimeter. Of course, if your units are not inches but meters, miles, or something else, you need to make the appropriate calculations.

Figure 15.26 shows two dimensions with alternate units.

The Alternate Units tab of the New Dimension Style dialog box.

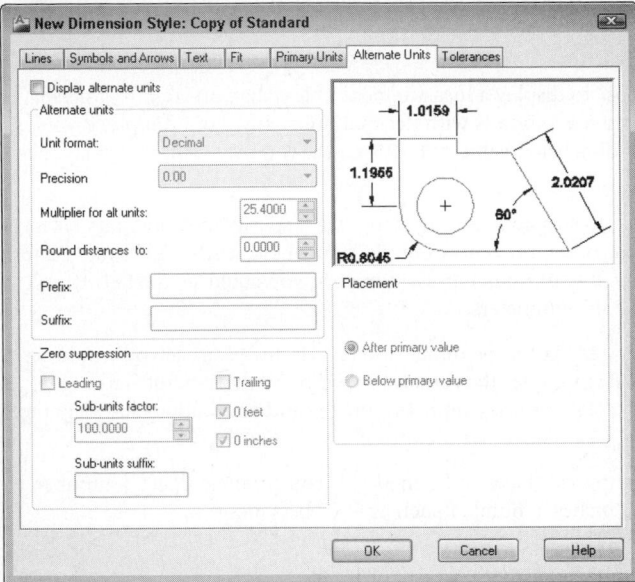

Dimensions showing both U.S. and metric measurements.

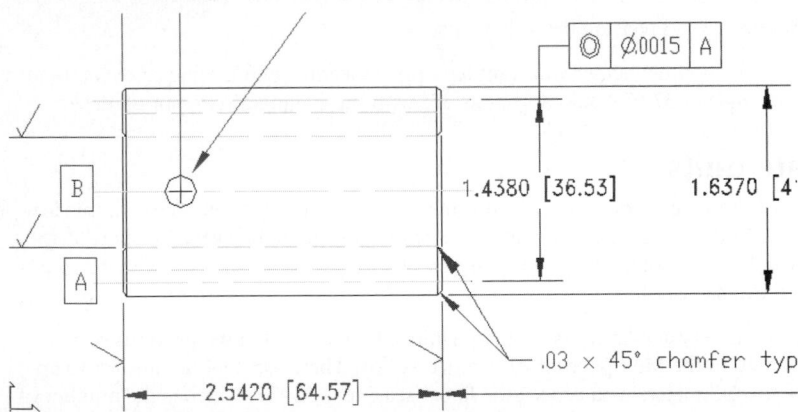

Thanks to Jerry Bottenfield of Clow Valve Company, Oskaloosa, Iowa, for this drawing.

In the Placement section, choose one of the options to place alternate units after or below the primary units.

On the DVD

The drawing used in the following exercise on defining primary units, ab15-03.dwg, is in the Results folder on the DVD. ∎

STEPS: Defining Primary Units

1. If ab15-03.dwg is open from the previous exercise, use it for this exercise as well. Otherwise, open ab15-03.dwg from the Results folder of the DVD. Ortho Mode and Object Snap should be on. Set running object snaps for Endpoint and Intersection. The Dim layer is current.

2. Save the file as ab15-04.dwg in your AutoCAD Bible folder.

3. Choose Annotate tab ⇨ Dimensions panel, and click the dialog box launcher arrow on the right side of the panel title bar. The Arch 48 dimension style should be current. Choose Modify to continue working on this dimension style. Click the Primary Units tab.

4. In the Unit Format drop-down list, choose Architectural.

5. In the Precision drop-down list, change the precision to 0'-0 1/8".

6. In the Fraction format drop-down list, choose Diagonal.

7. In the Zero Suppression section, uncheck the 0 Inches check box because architectural dimensions sometimes show 0 inches.

8. Click the Text tab. In the Fraction Height Scale text box, type **.75**.

9. Click OK. In the Dimension Style Manager, click Close to return to your drawing. The dimension is automatically updated and now looks appropriate for an architectural drawing.

10. To see how the stacked fractions appear, create a linear dimension from ❶ to ❷, as shown in Figure 15.27. If necessary, zoom in to see the dimension text clearly.

11. Return to the previous view if you zoomed in. Save your drawing. It should look like Figure 15.27.

FIGURE 15.27

The dimension style is now complete.

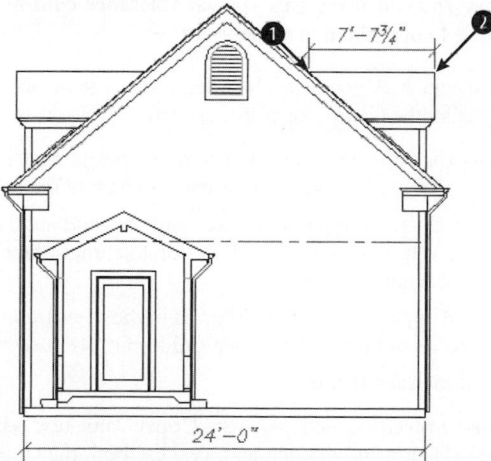

Formatting tolerances

Tolerances are used in mechanical drafting to specify how much deviation is allowed from the exact measurement when the model is manufactured. Format the tolerance notation on the Tolerances tab of the New Dimension Style dialog box. The Tolerances tab is shown in Figure 15.28.

FIGURE 15.28

The Tolerances tab of the New Dimension Style dialog box.

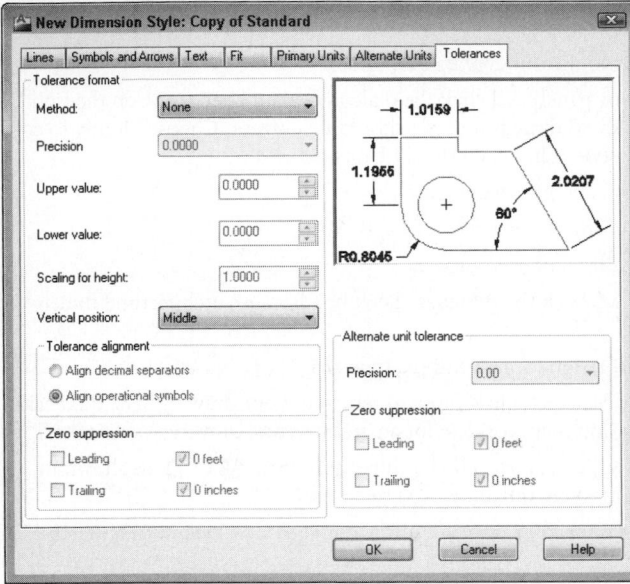

Cross-Reference

The Tolerances tab formats regular dimensions. You can also create special Tolerance control frames, which have the same purpose, but are separate object types. I cover them in Chapter 14. ■

Use the Tolerance Format section to specify how you want the tolerances to be displayed. You can choose one of four tolerance methods from the Method drop-down list, as shown in Figure 15.29:

- **Symmetrical** tolerances have the same upper and lower amounts and are shown with a plus/minus sign. The Upper Value text box is active so that you can type in the tolerance amount.

- **Deviation** tolerances can have different upper and lower amounts and are therefore shown after separate plus and minus signs. When you choose a deviation tolerance, the Upper Value and Lower Value text boxes become active.

- **Limits** dimensions include the upper and lower tolerances in the measurement. Use the Upper Value and Lower Value text boxes to type in the upper and lower tolerance amounts.

- **Basic** dimensions place the dimension in a box.

In the Precision drop-down list, choose a precision value. Use the Upper Value text box to set the tolerance value for symmetrical tolerances. For deviation and limits tolerances, use both the Upper Value and Lower Value text boxes.

The Scaling for Height text box lets you scale the height of the tolerance relative to the dimension text height. Using smaller text for the tolerances is common. A value of 1 creates tolerance text that is equal to the dimension text height. A setting of 0.5 creates tolerance text that is half the size of regular dimension text.

FIGURE 15.29

Four types of tolerances.

Symmetrical

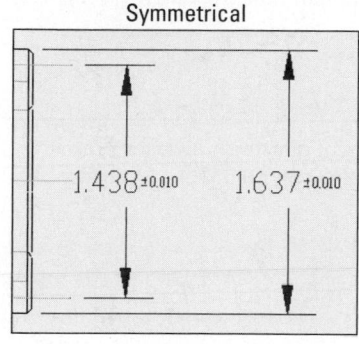

Deviation

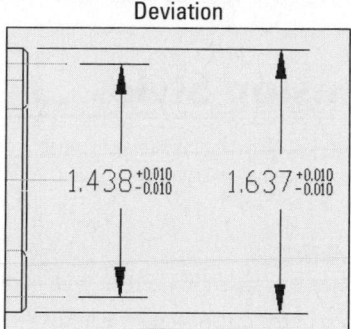

Limits

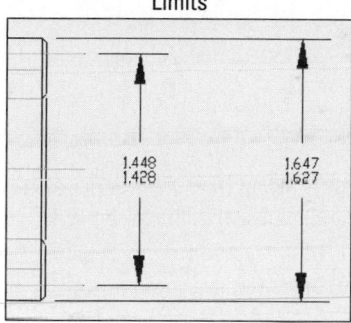

Basic

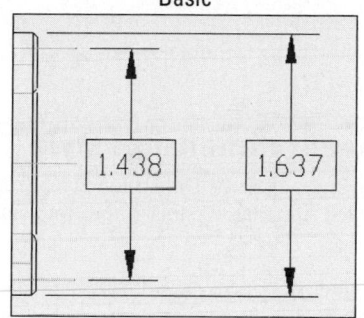

Use the Vertical Position drop-down list to determine how the tolerances are aligned with the main dimension text. This setting has the greatest effect on Deviation tolerances that display two lines of text for the one dimension text line. You have the following choices:

- **Bottom.** Aligns the tolerance text with the bottom of the dimension text.
- **Middle.** Aligns the tolerance text with the middle of the dimension text.
- **Top.** Aligns the tolerance text with the top of the dimension text.

Note

The Vertical position setting also applies to stacked fractions, determining how the fractions are justified with the whole-number dimensions. ∎

If you choose a Limits or Deviation tolerance, you can specify the alignment of stacked upper and lower tolerance values. You can align the values by the decimal separators (such as a decimal point) or by the operational symbols (such as the plus-minus symbol).

Use the Zero Suppression section to suppress leading or trailing zeros, or feet and inches. See the preceding explanation of the Primary Units tab for more information.

If you've turned on alternate units, you can separately set the precision and zero suppression for alternate unit tolerances in the Precision text box.

Click OK, and then click Close to return to your drawing. You're ready to start dimensioning!

Changing Dimension Styles

You may need to edit dimension styles. Whether you want to use a different dimension style for a certain object or change the properties of a dimension style, you have the flexibility you need. You can change dimensions in the following ways:

- Choose a new dimension style.
- Create a variant of a dimension style for a certain type of dimension.
- Modify the characteristics of the dimension style in use.
- Override the dimension style with different dimension options for one dimension that you want to be an exception.

Chapter 14 covers some dimension editing techniques. This section explains how to make changes related to dimension styles.

Choosing a new current dimension style

To start using another dimension style, click the Dimension Style drop-down list in the Dimensions panel of the Annotate tab or the expanded Annotation panel of the Home tab, and choose the dimension style that you want to use.

Existing dimensions remain unchanged, but any new dimensions that you add from this point forward will use the new current dimension style.

Creating a variant of a dimension style

Create a variant of a dimension style for a specific type of dimension, such as a leader or angular dimension. You might have an architectural dimension style with ticks (rather than arrows) at the end of the dimension lines, but you might want angular dimensions to have open arrows. Here are the steps to do this:

1. Choose Annotate tab ⇨ Dimensions panel, and click the dialog box launcher arrow on the right side of the panel title bar.
2. Click New.
3. From the Use For drop-down list, choose the type of dimension that you want to use with the new variant.
4. Click Continue.
5. Make the changes that you want, using the techniques described earlier in this chapter.
6. Click OK to return to the Dimension Style Manager. Here you see the variant listed under its base (parent) dimension style.
7. Click Close.

Dimensions of the type that you specified now take on the characteristics of the variant. For example, angular dimensions would have an open arrow.

Modifying a dimension to use a new dimension style

You can change the dimension style used by an existing dimension. Select the dimension and then choose a new dimension style from the Dimension Style drop-down list in the Dimensions panel of the Annotate tab or the expanded Annotation panel of the Home tab.

Another method of changing a dimension's style is to open the Properties palette (press Ctrl+1) and select one or more dimensions. In the Properties palette, click the Dim style item in the Misc section and choose a new dimension style from the drop-down list. You can also change the dimension style of a selected dimension in the Quick Properties palette.

Tip

Select any dimension to open the Quick Properties palette, where you can change some of the properties of that dimension. ■

Modifying dimension styles

You can easily change a dimension style. The advantage of changing a dimension style is that all dimensions using that style are automatically updated. To change a style:

1. Choose Annotate tab ➪ Dimensions panel, and click the dialog box launcher arrow on the right side of the panel title bar.
2. Choose the dimension style that you want to change from the list of styles.
3. Choose Modify.
4. AutoCAD opens the Modify Dimension Style dialog box, which is exactly the same as the New Dimension Style dialog box. Use the settings on all the tabs and make the changes that you want. Click OK to close these dialog boxes and return to the Dimension Styles Manager.
5. Click Close.

All dimensions automatically change to reflect the changed dimension style.

Tip

You can create a new dimension style from an existing dimension on the fly by using the Properties palette. Select a dimension and open the Properties palette. Click the arrow next to the type of change that you want to make, and make the change. After you're done, right-click in the drawing area and choose Dim Style ➪ Save as New Style. The New Dimension Style dialog box opens so that you can give the dimension style a name. Click OK. ■

Overriding a dimension style

Sometimes you want to make an exception to a style for one dimension — for example, when suppressing an extension line in a tight space. It isn't often worthwhile to create a new dimension style for such a situation. To override a dimension style, simply change the properties of the dimension by using the Properties palette.

You can also create an override to the current dimension style. The override is like a subset of the dimension style. After you create the override, all new dimensions that you create using the dimension style include the override changes. To revert back to the original dimension style, you must delete the override. You also have the option to incorporate the override into the dimension style or save it as a new style.

To create a dimension style override, follow these steps:

1. Choose Annotate tab ⇨ Dimensions panel, and click the dialog box launcher arrow on the right side of the panel title bar.

2. Choose the dimension style for which you want to create an override (if it isn't already selected).

3. In the Dimension Style Manager, click Override.

4. The Override Current Style dialog box opens, which is just like the New (or Modify) Dimension Style dialog box. Make the changes that you want by using any of the tabs. Click OK.

5. In the Dimension Style Manager, you see the style override listed beneath the dimension style that you selected. Click Close.

New dimensions that you create using the dimension style that you selected now include the override properties.

To stop using the override, open the Dimension Style Manager, right-click the style override to open the shortcut menu, and do one of the following:

• Choose Delete to delete the override.

• Choose Save to Current Style to incorporate the override properties into the current dimension style.

• Choose Rename to create a new dimension style from the override. You see a selection box around the name. Type a new dimension style name and press Enter. This action removes the override and replaces it with the new dimension style.

Removing the override doesn't change dimensions that you've already created with the override.

Tip

To quickly override a dimension's style, select a dimension. Then right-click and choose one of four options. Dim Text Position offers four suboptions to control the position of the dimension's text. Precision lets you quickly choose from 0 to 6 decimal places. The Dim Style option creates a new style from the selected dimension. Finally, the Flip Arrow option flips the selected arrow to the outside of the extension lines. ■

Updating dimensions

 The Dimensions panel of the Annotate tab includes an Update button. This command updates selected dimensions so that they use the current dimension style, including any overrides that you may have just made. Use this command when you realize that you want to include some existing dimensions in the overrides that you've made.

Comparing dimension styles

You can compare a dimension style with the current dimension style. To do this, follow these steps:

1. Choose Annotate tab ⇨ Dimensions panel, click the dialog box launcher arrow on the right side of the panel title bar, and choose Compare. The Compare Dimension Styles dialog box opens, as shown in Figure 15.30.

2. In the Compare and With drop-down lists, choose the two dimension styles that you want to compare. The resulting list shows the differences by system variable.

3. Click Close twice to return to your drawing.

FIGURE 15.30

The Compare Dimension Styles dialog box enables you to compare the properties of two dimension styles.

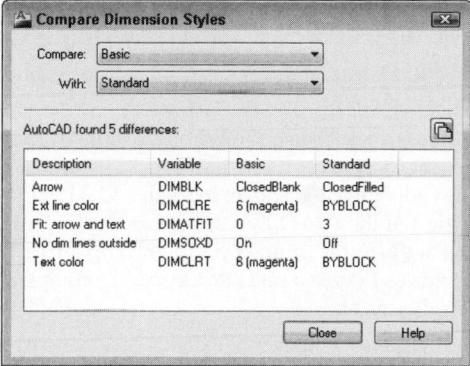

Tip

Click the Copy button at the right side of the Compare Dimension Styles dialog box to copy the comparison to the Clipboard. You can then paste it into another document, for example, an e-mail message to a client. ∎

Copying dimension styles from other drawings

With proper planning, dimension styles make dimensioning much easier and produce more-uniform results. Although you can save dimension styles in your templates, you may sometimes need to work with someone else's drawing or an old drawing that doesn't contain the dimension styles that you need. As explained in Chapters 11 and 13, you can use the DesignCenter to import features from other drawings. To import a dimension style, follow these steps:

1. Choose View tab ⇨ Palettes panel ⇨ DesignCenter (or press Ctrl+2) to open the DesignCenter.
2. In the left pane, navigate to the drawing that has the dimension style that you want.
3. Double-click the drawing icon or click its plus sign.
4. To see the list of the dimension styles, double-click the dimension style's icon in either the left or right pane.
5. Double-click the dimension style's icon to import it into your drawing.

AutoCAD Only

The Express Tools offer two commands, DIMIM and DIMEX, which enable you to save (export) and retrieve (import) dimension styles. Type these commands on the command line. For information on installing Express Tools, see Appendix A. ∎

On the DVD

The drawing used in the following exercise on changing dimension styles, ab15-b.dwg, is in the Drawings folder on the DVD. ∎

STEPS: Changing Dimension Styles

1. Open `ab15-b.dwg` from your DVD.

2. Save the file as `ab15-05.dwg` in your `AutoCAD Bible` folder. This is a tension arm for a commercial dryer, as shown in Figure 15.31. Ortho Mode and Object Snap should be on. Set running object snaps for Endpoint, Intersection, and Center. The Dim layer is current.

3. The current dimension style is CIR. Choose Annotate tab ⇨ Dimensions panel ⇨ Dimension Style to open the drop-down list, and choose LIN.

4. Choose Annotate tab ⇨ Dimensions panel ⇨ Dimension drop-down list ⇨ Linear to start the DIMLINEAR command. At the `Specify first extension line origin or <select object>:` prompt, choose the endpoint at ❶, shown in Figure 15.31. (If necessary, press Tab until you see the endpoint tooltip.) At the `Specify second extension line origin:` prompt, choose the intersection at ❷. At the `Specify dimension line location or [Mtext/Text/Angle/Horizontal/Vertical/Rotated]:` prompt, choose an appropriate location above the bottom-most dimension.

5. Choose Annotate tab ⇨ Dimensions panel, and click the dialog box launcher arrow on the right side of the panel title bar. Choose Override and click the Tolerances tab. Change the Tolerance Method to None. Click the Lines tab. In the Extension Lines section, check the Suppress: Ext Line 1 option to suppress the first extension line. Click OK. In the Dimension Style Manager, click Close.

6. Start the DIMLINEAR command again. At the `Specify first extension line origin or <select object>:` prompt, choose the intersection at ❷, shown in Figure 15.31. At the `Specify second extension line origin:` prompt, choose the intersection at ❸. At the `Specify dimension line location or [Mtext/Text/Angle/Horizontal/Vertical/Rotated]:` prompt, pick the endpoint object snap at the right side of the previous dimension's dimension line in order to align the two dimensions.

7. The first dimension (the one you created in Step 4) needs to be updated to remove the tolerance. Choose Annotate tab ⇨ Dimensions panel ⇨ Update. At the `Select objects:` prompt, choose the first dimension. Right-click to end object selection and update the dimension.

8. To list the overrides, choose Annotate tab ⇨ Dimensions panel, and click the dialog box launcher arrow on the right side of the panel title bar. Choose Compare. In the Compare Dimension Styles dialog box, `<style overrides>` should be displayed in the Compare drop-down list, and LIN should be displayed in the With drop-down list. You see a list of the overrides, which are the only differences between the two. Click Close.

9. To remove the overrides (no tolerance and the first extension line suppressed), right-click `<style overrides>` in the Dimension Style Manager and choose Delete. You get the message, `Are you sure you want to delete "<style overrides>"?` Click Yes. Click Close to return to the drawing.

10. Start the DIMLINEAR command again. At the `Specify first extension line origin or <select object>:` prompt, choose the intersection at ❹, shown in Figure 15.31. At the `Specify second extension line origin:` prompt, choose the intersection at ❺. At the `Specify dimension line location or [Mtext/Text/Angle/Horizontal/Vertical/Rotated]:` prompt, pick an appropriate location to the right of the model.

FIGURE 15.31

The tension arm needs some additional dimensions.

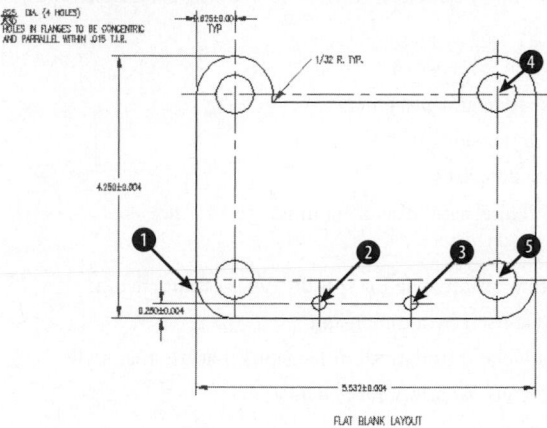

11. To compare the CIR and LIN dimension styles, open the Dimension Style Manager again. Choose Compare. LIN should appear in the Compare drop-down list. Choose CIR from the With drop-down list. The result is a list of the differences. Click Close twice to return to your drawing.

12. Save your drawing. It should look like Figure 15.32.

FIGURE 15.32

The dimensions have been added.

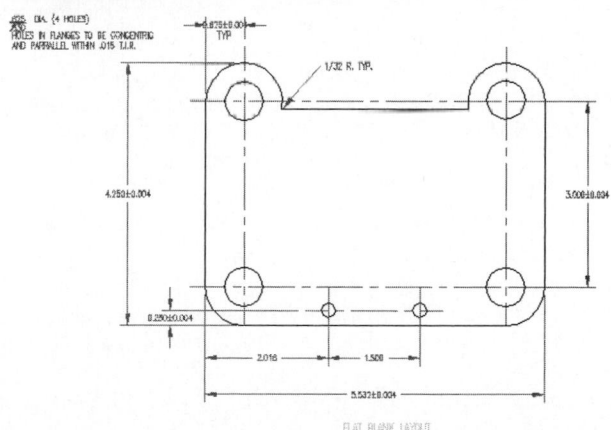

Summary

In this chapter, you gained a thorough understanding of how to use dimension styles to organize your dimensions. You read how to:

- Define a dimension's lines and arrows
- Define dimension text style and placement
- Create an annotative dimension style
- Fit dimensions into small spaces
- Define the primary and alternate measuring units
- Format tolerances
- Create a variant of a dimension style for specific types of dimensions
- Change dimension style used by a dimension
- Modify a dimension style and update all dimensions that use that style
- Override a dimension style for temporary changes
- Update existing dimensions
- Compare dimension styles
- Copy dimension styles from other drawings, using the DesignCenter

In the next chapter, you learn how to draw complex objects.

Drawing Complex Objects

AutoCAD and AutoCAD LT offer a number of complex objects that can help you create accurate, professional drawings. Polylines are single objects that can combine line segments and arcs. Splines are mathematically controlled curves that are based on points that you specify. Regions and boundaries create complex shapes from existing objects. Hatches create various types of fills inside closed objects. Multilines (in AutoCAD) and dlines (in AutoCAD LT) are sets of parallel lines. Sketching is a way to create freehand drawings. Digitizing with a tablet is a process that is used to transfer an existing paper drawing into your drawing. In this chapter, I introduce you to these complex objects and explain how to use them.

Creating and Editing Polylines

Polylines are single objects that combine line segments and arcs. In certain situations, being able to edit an entire set of lines and arcs as one object is useful. Polylines can have a width, which can vary from the start point to the endpoint of each segment. Polylines ensure that all the vertices of a series of lines and arcs actually touch. They're also useful for 3D drawing. In short, polylines are a neat, clean way to draw.

The RECTANG and POLYGON commands create polylines. Figure 16.1 shows a few examples of polylines.

IN THIS CHAPTER

Creating and editing polylines

Drawing and editing splines

Creating regions and boundaries

Using hatches to fill closed areas

Creating and editing multilines and dlines

Using the SKETCH command

Digitizing drawings with the TABLET command

FIGURE 16.1

Four examples of polylines.

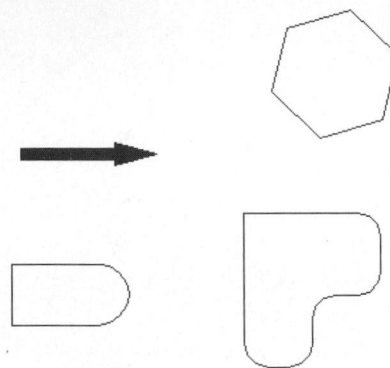

Using the PLINE command

To draw a polyline, choose Home tab ⇨ Draw panel ⇨ Polyline. This starts the PLINE command. The command responds with the `Specify start point:` prompt. Specify the start point. The main PLINE prompt is `Specify next point or [Arc/Close/Halfwidth/Length/Undo/Width]:`, which offers the following options:

- **Arc.** Draws arcs. This option opens up a set of arc suboptions, which are explained after this list.
- **Close.** Closes a polyline by drawing a line from the endpoint of the last line segment to the start point of the polyline. This option appears only after you've picked a second point.
- **Halfwidth.** Defines half of the width of the polyline — the distance from the center of the polyline to its edge. The option asks you for the starting halfwidth and the ending halfwidth, enabling you to create polylines that are tapered.
- **Length.** Specifies the length of the next line segment. The option draws the line segment in the same direction as the last line segment or tangent to the last arc.
- **Undo.** Undoes the last line segment.
- **Width.** Defines the width of the polyline. The option asks you for the starting width and the ending width.
- **Specify next point.** Enables you to create a line segment. This is the default option.

Like the LINE command, PLINE continues to prompt you for more points, repeating the entire prompt each time. When you're done, press Enter to end the command.

If you choose Arc, you see the `Specify endpoint of arc or [Angle/CEnter/CLose/Direction/Halfwidth/Line/Radius/Second pt/ Undo/Width]:` prompt. Most of the options are similar to the ARC command options. For details, see Chapter 7. The arc options are as follows:

- **Angle.** Specifies the included angle.
- **CEnter.** Specifies the arc's center.

- **CLose.** Closes the polyline by drawing an arc from the endpoint of the last arc to the start point of the polyline.

- **Direction.** Specifies the direction of the arc from the start point.

- **Halfwidth.** Defines half of the width of the polyline — the distance from the center of the polyline to its edge. The option asks you for the starting halfwidth and the ending halfwidth.

- **Line.** Returns you to the main polyline prompt so that you can draw line segments.

- **Radius.** Specifies the arc's radius.

- **Second pt.** Specifies the second point of the arc.

- **Undo.** Undoes the last arc.

- **Width.** Defines the width of the polyline. The option asks you for the starting width and the ending width.

- **Specify endpoint of arc.** Specifies the endpoint of the arc. This is the default. This option creates an arc tangent to the previous arc (continuing in the same direction).

PLINE continues to display the arc submenu until you use the Line suboption or end the command by pressing Enter.

On the DVD

The drawing used in the following exercise on drawing polylines, ab16-a.dwg, is in the Drawings folder on the DVD. ∎

STEPS: Drawing Polylines

1. Open ab16-a.dwg from your DVD.

2. Save the file as ab16-01.dwg in your AutoCAD Bible folder. It shows a small section of a drive block, as shown in Figure 16.2. In this exercise, you complete part of the drawing. Ortho Mode and Object Snap should be on. Set running object snaps to Endpoint, Midpoint, and Intersection. Layer 3 is current. This exercise assumes that you have Dynamic Input (the Dynamic Input button on the status bar) on, set to the default of relative coordinates.

Generating linetypes on polylines

When you create a polyline with a noncontinuous linetype, you may find that the linetype doesn't appear properly along the polyline. One reason is that the segments of the polyline may be too short to fit the entire linetype definition — in this case the polyline appears continuous. You can choose to generate the linetype continuously along the polyline, instead of starting the linetype definition anew at each vertex. This results in a more normal-looking linetype along the polyline. To do this, you need to turn on the PLINEGEN system variable. To turn on PLINEGEN, type **plinegen** ↵ and then **1** ↵.

As explained in the section "Editing polylines with the PEDIT command" later in the chapter, you can also modify the display of linetypes for existing polylines.

FIGURE 16.2

A small section of a drive block.

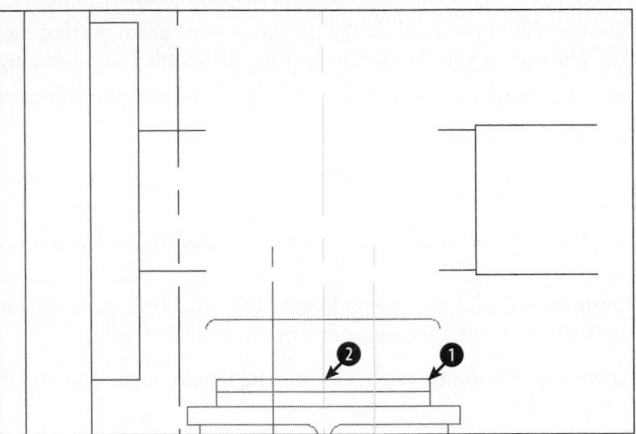

Thanks to Mary Redfern of the Bethlehem Corporation, Easton, Pennsylvania, for this drawing.

 3. Choose Home tab ⇨ Draw panel ⇨ Polyline. Follow the prompts:

```
Specify start point: Press Shift+right-click and choose the From
    object snap.
Base point: Choose ❶ in Figure 16.2.
<Offset>: @-1/2,0 ↵
Specify next point or [Arc/Halfwidth/Length/Undo/Width]: Move the
    cursor in the 90-degree direction and type 3/32 ↵.
```

4. Type **a** ↵ to continue with an arc. At the Specify endpoint of arc or [Angle/CEnter/ CLose/Direction/Halfwidth/Line/Radius/Second pt/Undo/Width]: prompt, type **3/16,3/16** ↵.

5. Type **l** ↵ to continue with a linear segment. At the Specify next point or [Arc/Close/ Halfwidth/Length/Undo/Width]: prompt, move the cursor in the 0-degree direction and type **11/32** ↵.

6. Type **a** ↵ to continue with an arc. At the prompt, type **3/16,3/16** ↵.

7. Type **l** ↵ to continue with a linear segment. At the prompt, move the cursor in the 90-degree direction and type **6-3/32** ↵.

8. Type **a** ↵ to continue with an arc. At the prompt, type **-5/16,5/16** ↵.

9. To create the last arc, type **r** ↵. Follow the prompts:

```
Specify radius of arc: 5-5/8 ↵
Specify endpoint of arc or [Angle]: Choose the From object snap.
Base point: Choose point ❷ in Figure 16.2.
<Offset>: @0,7-1/4 ↵
```

10. Press Enter to exit the PLINE command.

11. Save your drawing. It should look like Figure 16.3.

FIGURE 16.3

The completed polyline.

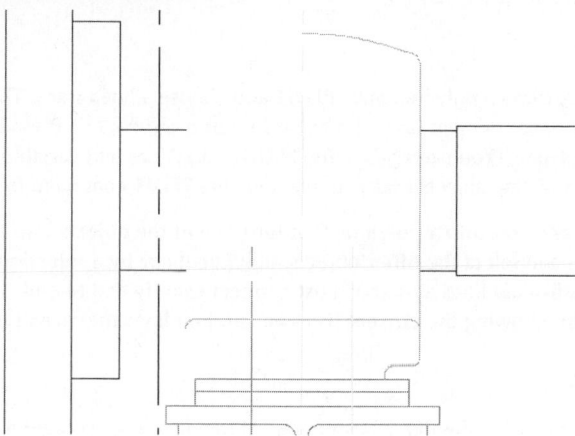

On the DVD

Ar1 creates a label of the area of an enclosed polyline. Look in `\Software\Chapter 16\ar1`. **Note that you can also create a similar label by using the area field. I cover fields in Chapter 13.** ∎

Editing polylines with the PEDIT command

Because polylines can be quite complex, there is a special command, PEDIT, to edit them. To edit a polyline, choose Home tab ⇨ Modify panel (expanded) ⇨ Edit Polyline. The command responds with the `Select polyline or [Multiple]:` prompt. When you select a polyline, you see the `Enter an option [Close/Join/Width/Edit vertex/Fit/Spline/Decurve/Ltype gen/Reverse/ Undo]:` prompt. The options are:

- **Close.** Closes an open polyline. If necessary, it adds a segment to connect the endpoint to the start point. If the polyline is already closed, this prompt becomes Open. Open creates a break between the first and last segments of the polyline.

- **Join.** Joins touching lines, arcs, or other polylines to the polyline. The polyline must be open and the other objects need to touch the beginning or end of the polyline.

- **Width.** Enables you to specify one width for the entire polyline.

- **Edit Vertex.** Provides a set of suboptions for editing vertices. These suboptions are explained after this list.

- **Fit.** Turns the polyline into a curve that passes through the vertices.

- **Spline.** Creates a curve by using the vertices as control points. The curve does not usually pass through the vertices. This is not the mathematically exact spline that the SPLINE command produces (covered later in this chapter).

- **Decurve.** Returns a Fit or Spline curve to its original vertices.

- **Ltype gen.** Turns on continuous linetype generation for the selected polyline.

- **Reverse.** Reverses the direction of the polyline so that the starting point becomes the end point, providing more control of the display of special linetypes.
- **Undo.** Undoes the most recent edit.

Tip

You can change any line, spline, or arc into a polyline. Start PEDIT and choose a line or arc. The command responds: `Object selected is not a polyline. Do you want to turn it into one? <Y>`. **Press Enter to accept the default and turn the object into a polyline. (You can change the PEDITACCEPT system variable to 1 to suppress this prompt and automatically turn non-polyline objects that you select for the PEDIT command to polylines.)**

To turn a series of connected lines and arcs into a polyline, first turn one of the objects into a polyline as I just explained. Then use the Join option and select the other objects individually or by a selection window. In order to create a polyline in this way, the individual lines and arcs must connect exactly end to end. However, if you use the Multiple option, which I explain following the current list, you can join lines that aren't exactly touching. ■

Tip

You can convert a spline to a polyline, using the PEDIT command. When doing so, you get a prompt to enter a precision value between 0 and 99. A higher number provides a more accurate conversion. You can also change the system variable PLINECONVERTMODE to 0 to convert polylines to linear segments, or leave it at 1 (the default) to use arcs. If you want to keep the original spline along with the new polyline, change the system variable DELOBJ to 0 (off) before making the conversion. ■

When you choose the Edit Vertex option, you see a new set of suboptions with the `Enter a vertex editing option [Next/Previous/Break/Insert/Move/Regen/Straighten/Tangent/ Width/eXit] <N>:` prompt. You see an X at one of the vertices. This is the current vertex, which you can edit. The suboptions are as follows:

- **Next.** Moves you to the next vertex so that you can edit it.
- **Previous.** Moves you to the previous vertex.
- **Break.** Breaks the polyline. You can choose the Go suboption to break the polyline into two (although you can't see the break). You can move to another vertex by using the Next or Previous suboptions and then choosing Go. This option breaks the polyline between the original vertex and the vertex to which you moved. Use the eXit suboption to return to the previous prompt. (You can also use the BREAK command.)
- **Insert.** Inserts another vertex. At the prompt, specify its location.
- **Move.** Moves the vertex. At the prompt, specify its location.
- **Regen.** Regenerates the polyline.
- **Straighten.** Deletes vertices. This works like the Break option with the same Next, Previous, Go, and eXit suboptions. As soon as you move to a new vertex, the option draws a straight line between it and the original vertex. If you don't move to a new vertex, this option affects only an arc by changing it to a straight line segment.
- **Tangent.** Specifies a direction from the vertex. The command uses this information if you choose the Fit option.
- **Width.** Enables you to specify starting and ending widths of the segment, starting with the current vertex.
- **eXit.** Exits this group of suboptions.

Caution

You can make many changes during the PEDIT session. If you return to the command line and use the U or UNDO command, the entire session is undone. If you want to undo only part of the session, use the Undo option of the PEDIT command. ■

To edit multiple polylines at one time, follow these steps:

1. Start the PEDIT command.

2. Choose the Multiple option (type **m** ↵ or right-click and choose Multiple from the shortcut menu) at the first prompt.

3. At the `Select objects:` prompt, select the polylines.

4. You then see the `Enter an option [Close/Open/Join/Width/Fit/Spline/Decurve/Ltype gen/Reverse/Undo]:` prompt.

5. Choose the option that you want. For example, you can change the width of all the selected polylines or apply the Spline option to them.

You can also join two polylines that aren't touching, if you use the Multiple option first. Select the polylines and then choose the Join option. You then need to specify two suboptions:

- **Fuzz distance.** The maximum distance that the endpoints of the polylines can be from each other. In other words, in order for the join to work, the fuzz distance must be greater than the distance of the endpoints. If you want to join the endpoints regardless, type in a large number.

- **Jointype.** The method of joining polylines. You can use the Extend method, which extends (or trims) the segments to the nearest endpoints, or the Add method, which adds a straight segment between the two nearest endpoints. You can choose the Both suboption, which tries to extend or trim; if it can't, it adds a segment.

Grip editing polylines

You can also edit polylines with grips. Grips make it easy to move vertices, for example. For more information on grip editing, see Chapter 10.

New Feature

Polylines have new secondary grips at the midpoint of each line or arc segment. You can use the secondary grips to stretch, add a vertex, or convert a line segment to an arc (and vice versa). You can also remove a vertex. The primary grips at segment endpoints also have these same new options. ■

Tip

When you click a primary or secondary grip, you can press the Ctrl key repeatedly to cycle among the options. ■

To grip edit a polyline, select the polyline to display its primary and secondary grips. Hover the cursor over a grip to see the options, and then choose an option, as follows:

- **Stretch/Stretch Vertex.** Specify the new location for the grip.

- **Add Vertex.** Specify the location for the new vertex. You can add a vertex to both line and arc segments.

- **Convert to Arc/Line.** If the segment is a line, specify the midpoint of the arc. If the segment is an arc, it converts automatically to a line.

- **Remove Vertex.** At a vertex (but not at a secondary grip), choose this option to remove the vertex.

Tip

You can press the Ctrl key and click any segment of a polyline to select just that segment. Because polylines are one object, you cannot make many kinds of edits. For example, you can't change the layer of a segment. However, you can rotate or stretch a segment, resulting in a corresponding change in a nearby vertex. ■

Editing polylines with the Properties palette or Quick Properties palette

You can edit selected polylines in the Properties palette. You can choose a vertex by clicking Vertex in the Geometry section of the palette, and use the left and right arrows to move to another vertex. An X appears on the polyline to let you know which vertex you've chosen. You can then edit the vertex's coordinates by typing them in, or by clicking the Pick a Point button that appears and then picking a point in the drawing. You can change the start and ending widths and specify a global width for the entire polyline.

You can close and open a polyline in the Misc section. You can also turn on continuous linetype generation for the selected polyline by choosing Linetype generation and then choosing Enabled from the drop-down list that appears. Of course, you can also change the layer, color, linetype, lineweight, and linetype scale.

 You can "paint" polyline properties from one polyline to another, using the MATCHPROP command. Select a polyline, choose Home tab ⇨ Clipboard panel ⇨ Match Properties, and then select the polyline that you want to edit. You can use the Settings option to refine the process.

On the DVD

The drawing used in the following exercise on editing polylines, `ab16-b.dwg`, is in the `Drawings` folder on the DVD. ■

STEPS: Editing Polylines

1. Open `ab16-b.dwg` from your DVD.

2. Save the file as `ab16-02.dwg` in your `AutoCAD Bible` folder. This is a topographical drawing, as shown in Figure 16.4. The contours are polylines.

 3. Choose Home tab ⇨ Modify panel (expanded) ⇨ Edit Polyline to start the PEDIT command. Select the polyline at ❶, shown in Figure 16.4.

4. At the `Enter an option [Close/Join/Width/Edit vertex/Fit/Spline/Decurve/ Ltype gen/Reverse/Undo]:` prompt, right-click and choose Width. At the `Specify new width for all segments:` prompt, type **.5** ↵.

5. Type **e** ↵ to choose the Edit vertex option. At the `Enter a vertex editing option [Next/ Previous/Break/Insert/Move/Regen/Straighten/Tangent/Width/eXit] <N>:` prompt, type **n** ↵ several times until the X mark is at ❶, shown in Figure 16.4. (There are many vertices, so it's not important that you find the exact one.)

6. Type **m** ↵ to move the vertex. At the `Specify new location for marked vertex:` prompt, pick a point slightly above the existing vertex. Then type **x** ↵ to exit the Edit vertex submenu.

7. At the main PEDIT prompt, type **s** ↵. PEDIT smoothes out the polyline.

8. Press Enter to exit the PEDIT command.

9. Choose the polyline at ❷. Hover over the vertex at that point to see the options. (There are several vertices there; you can choose any one.) Choose Remove Vertex.

FIGURE 16.4

The topographical drawing's contours are polylines.

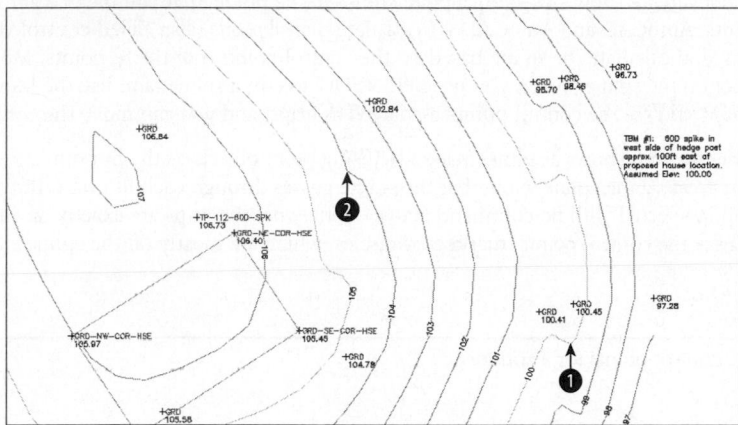

Thanks to Henry Dearborn, AIA, of Fairfield, Iowa, for this drawing.

10. Hover over the next vertex in the area and again remove the vertex. Continue until you have straightened out the jog in the polyline.

11. Save your drawing.

Drawing and Editing Splines

The SPLINE command draws a *NURBS*, which stands for nonuniform rational B-spline. A *spline* is a smooth curve that is defined by a series of points. The SPLINE command provides a more precise representation of a spline than the Spline option of the PLINE command. By default, the curve passes through each point that you specify. Figure 16.5 shows a beanbag chair created with two splines.

FIGURE 16.5

A beanbag chair created with two splines.

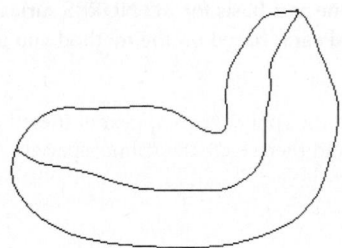

Understanding splines

By default, when you pick points to create the spline, AutoCAD stores these points as *fit points* (or data points). If the *tolerance* (how closely the spline comes to the points that you pick) is zero, the curve lies on these fit points. AutoCAD and AutoCAD LT calculate *control points* (also called control vertices) based on the fit points, and calculate the spline based on the control points, not the fit points. Most of the control points are not on the spline. When you use SPLINEDIT to edit a spline, and use the Move vertex option described later, you see the control points displayed as grips, and you can move the control points.

The top of Figure 16.6 shows a spline created by using point objects as the fit points; these are the points I picked when creating the spline. Note that the spline passes through each fit point. In the middle, you see the same spline selected with no command active. Notice that the grips are exactly on the fit points. At the bottom, you see the control points, marked by circles, which are mostly off the spline.

FIGURE 16.6

Viewing fit points and control points for a spline.

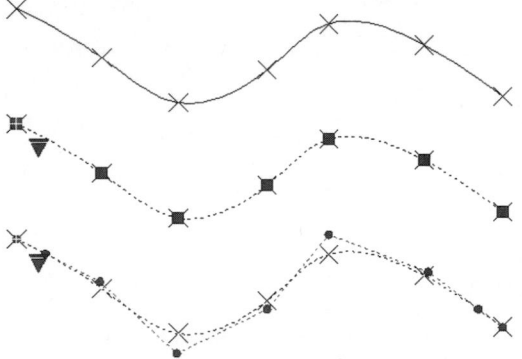

Because the spline is calculated based on the control points, the fit points are not necessary to generate the spline. In fact, if you move or edit a control point, only the control points are needed to generate the spline, and the fit point information is discarded so that you can no longer edit it.

New Feature

You can create splines using two methods: Fit Points and Control Points (or control vertices). The default option is to use fit points. Using control points is valuable when you are drawing a spline as a basis for 3D NURBS surfaces. (See Chapter 23 for more information.) The prompts for the SPLINE command vary, based on the method you use. You can also control the method with the SPLMETHOD system variable. ∎

When you create a spline using the default Fit method and then select the spline, grips appear at these fit points. When you create a spline using the Control Vertices method and then select the spline, special round grips appear at the control vertices.

New Feature

When you select a spline, you see a drop-down arrow that lets you choose to display fit points or control vertices. You can show the control vertices with the CVSHOW command even without selecting the spline. Use the CVHIDE command to hide them. CVSHOW and CVHIDE are in AutoCAD only. ∎

Creating splines

To create a spline, choose Home tab ⇨ Draw panel (expanded) ⇨ Spline. The command responds with the `Specify first point or [Method/Knots/Object]:` prompt.

Here are the options:

- **Method:** Lets you choose between Fit and CV (control vertices).

- **Knots:** Lets you choose the knot parameterization. The Knots option applies only to the Fit method. Knots control the shape of the spline as it passes through a fit point. The Chord suboption (the default) numbers edit points with decimal values representing their location on the curve. The Square Root suboption numbers edit points based on the square root of the chord length between consecutive knots. The Uniform suboption numbers edit points with consecutive integers.

- **Degree:** Lets you choose the number of directions allowed between the points you specify to define a spline. The Degree option applies only to the CV (control vertices) method. As you specify points for a spline, you define the spans of the spline. The value entered minus 1 determines the number of control points for each span. For example, a degree of 2 results in 1 control vertex between the points that define a span.

- **Object:** Converts a polyline that you've created with PEDIT's Spline option into a true spline. (It doesn't look any different, but its internal definition changes.)

When you choose a method and knot parameterization, you see the current settings displayed on the command line.

Drawing a spline with the Fit method

To start drawing the spline using the Fit (default) method, choose Home tab ⇨ Draw panel (expanded) ⇨ Spline. If the current method is CV, use the Method option to choose the Fit method. At the `Specify first point or [Method/Knots/Object]:` prompt, specify the first point for the spline.

When you choose a point using the Fit method, the command displays the `Enter next point or [start Tangency/toLerance]:` prompt so that you can pick a second point. After the second point, you see the `Enter next point or [end Tangency/toLerance/Undo/Close]:` prompt. Specify the next point or use the options as follows:

- **start Tangency.** Lets you specify the direction of the start of the spline. You specify a point to indicate the direction from the start point.

- **end Tangency.** Lets you specify the direction of the end of the spline. You specify a point to indicate the direction from the last point to the end.

- **toLerance.** Specifies how closely the spline comes to the points that you pick. The default, 0, creates a spline that passes through each point. If you want the curve to have a latitude of 0.5 units from the points, set the tolerance to 0.5.

- **Undo.** Undoes that last segment of the spline that you specified.

- **Close.** Closes the spline by connecting the last point with the first point in a continuous (tangent) curve. The prompt asks for a tangent direction. You can specify a direction by picking a point (watch the spline image change as you move the cursor) or pressing Enter to accept the default tangent direction.

When you are finished specifying fit points, press Enter to end the command.

Drawing a spline with the Control Vertices method

To start drawing the spline using the CV (control vertices) method, choose Home tab ⇨ Draw panel (expanded) ⇨ Spline. If the current method is Fit, use the Method option to choose the CV method. You see the `Specify first point or [Method/Degree/Object]:` prompt. The Object option is the same as for the Fit method.

The Degree option sets the maximum number of directions you see if you draw a line between each control vertex:

- A degree 1 spline has at least two control vertices, and is always a straight line.
- A degree 2 spline has at least three control vertices, becoming a parabola.
- A degree 3 spline (the default) has at least four control vertices, making an "S" shape.

Specify the first point of the splines. At the `Enter next point or [Close/Undo]:` prompt, enter subsequent points. The Close and Undo options are the same as for the Fit method. When you are finished specifying control vertices, press Enter to end the command. Remember that the spline will not be on the control vertices.

On the DVD

The drawing used in the following exercise on drawing splines, ab16-c.dwg, is in the Drawings folder on the DVD. ∎

STEPS: Drawing Splines

1. Open ab16-c.dwg from your DVD.
2. Save the file as ab16-03.dwg in your AutoCAD Bible folder. This is a topographical site map, as shown in Figure 16.7. Object Snap should be on. Set a running object snap for Insertion.

3. Use a Zoom Window to zoom in on the area near the start of the north edge of the drive. Choose Home tab ⇨ Draw panel (expanded) ⇨ Spline.

FIGURE 16.7

A topographical site map. You can complete the gravel road based on the surveyor's data.

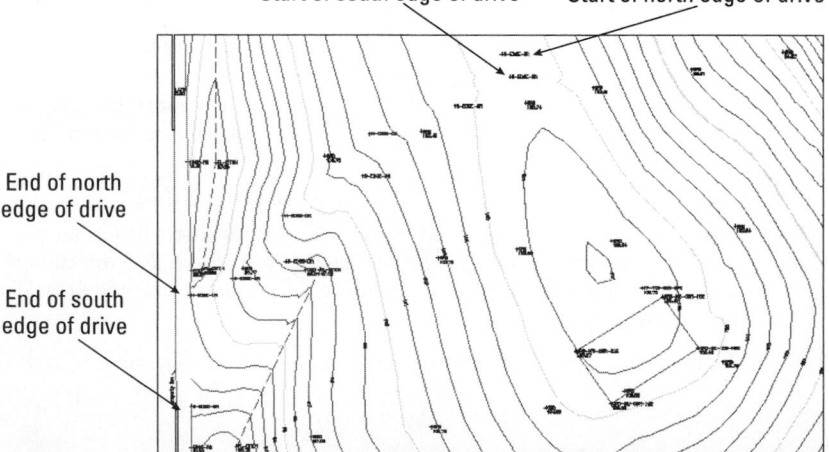

Start of south edge of drive   Start of north edge of drive

End of north edge of drive

End of south edge of drive

4. Check on the command line that the current setting shows Method=Fit and Knots=Chord. If not, use the Method and Knots options to change the current setting.

5. At the `Specify first point or [Method/Knots/Object]:` prompt, use the Insertion object snap to pick the cross at the start of the north edge of the drive, as shown in Figure 16.7. Continue to pick the crosses marked N-EDGE-DR. Choose Pan from the status bar to do a real-time pan when you reach the edge of the display. Press Esc. Continue picking points until you get to the end of the north edge of the drive, as shown in Figure 16.7. Press Enter to end point selection.

6. Start the SPLINE command again and pick points for the south edge of the drive, from the start of the south edge of the drive to the end, as shown in Figure 16.7. Pan as necessary. Again, press Enter to accept the default directions for the start and end tangents.

7. Select the last spline you drew. Click the down arrow near the beginning of the spline and choose Show Control Vertices to see the location of the control vertices. Deselect the spline.

8. If you want, Zoom Previous several times until you see the original view of the drawing. Save your drawing.

On the DVD

GeomCurves.lsp **is a routine that creates various kinds of geometrical curves, such as spirals and parabolas. You can find it in the** \Software\Chapter 16\GeomCurves **folder.** ∎

Editing splines

Like polylines, splines have their own editing command. To edit a spline, choose Home tab ⇨ Modify panel (expanded) ⇨ Edit Spline to start the SPLINEDIT command. After you select the spline, the command responds with the `Enter an option [Close/Join/Fit data/Edit vertex/convert to Polyline/Reverse/Undo/eXit]:` prompt. Here's how to use these options:

- **Close/Open.** If the spline is open, this option closes it by adding a continuous (tangent) curve from the last point to the start point. If the spline is closed, this option appears as Open. If the spline was originally closed, the Open option removes the connection between the last and first points, although the spline looks the same. If the spline was originally open and you closed it, when you use the Open option, this option erases the curve that it added when you closed it.

- **Join.** Joins selected splines, lines, and arcs to the current spline. These other objects must create a continuous object.

- **Fit Data.** Fit data means the points that you specified (if you used the Fit method of creating the spline), their tolerance, and the tangents (which specify the beginning and ending directions). This option has its own list of suboptions:
  - **Add.** Adds fit data points to the curve. The prompt asks you to select a point and then automatically selects the next point as well, shown with highlighted grips. At the prompt for a new point, which must be between the two highlighted points, the spline reshapes accordingly. Press Enter to exit the submenu.
  - **Open/Close.** Opens or closes the spline by using the fit points.
  - **Delete.** Deletes a selected fit point. Press Enter to exit the submenu.
  - **Move.** Moves a fit point. You can use the Next or Previous suboptions or the Select Point option to select the point that you want to move. Selected points appear as highlighted grips. You get a prompt for the new fit point location. You can also use grips to edit fit points. Use the eXit suboption to exit the submenu.
  - **Purge.** Deletes fit point information. Only the control vertices remain.

461

- **Tangents.** Enables you to specify start and end tangents of open splines, or one tangent for closed splines. If you don't use this option, a default tangent is calculated.
- **toLerance.** Enables you to specify the tolerance, which determines how closely the spline comes to the fit points. A 0 tolerance puts the spline on the fit points.
- **eXit.** Exits the suboption menu.
- **Edit Vertex.** Displays the control vertices as round grips. This option has its own suboptions:
  - **Add.** Specify a point on the spline to add a vertex. Press Enter to exit the suboption menu.
  - **Delete.** Specify a control vertex to delete. Press Enter to exit the suboption menu.
  - **Elevate order.** Adds evenly spaced control vertices along the spline, in addition to the existing control vertices. You can specify up to 26 control vertices.
  - **add Kink.** Specify a point on the spline. This option adds a number of control vertices equal to the degree of the spline, which is three by default. You can then move one of these vertices to create a sharp angle (the kink) in the spline. Press Enter to exit the suboption menu.
  - **Move.** Use the Next or Previous suboptions to specify which vertex you want to move, or use the Select point suboption to pick the vertex. Then specify the new location. Use the eXit suboption to exit the suboption menu.
  - **Weight.** Use the Next or Previous suboptions to specify which vertex you want to move, or use the Select point suboption to pick the vertex. Enter a new weight. A higher weight pulls the spline closer to the selected vertex. Use the eXit suboption to exit the suboption menu.
  - **eXit.** Exits the suboption menu.
- **convert to Polyline.** Changes the spline to a polyline. The prompt asks you to specify a conversion precision. Enter a value between 0 and 99. A higher value results in a more accurate polyline, but adds many more grips.
- **Reverse.** Reverses the direction of the spline so that the start point becomes the endpoint, and vice versa.
- **Undo.** Undoes the most recent edit operation.
- **eXit.** Exits the SPLINEDIT command.

Note

When you use the PEDIT command's Spline option on a polyline, the result is a splined polyline. The SPLINEDIT command automatically converts splined polylines to splines, even if you just select the splined polyline and exit the SPLINEDIT command. ■

You can edit a spline in the Properties palette or the Quick Properties palette. It works similarly to editing a polyline. The Properties palette displays the fit points or the control points so that you can change them.

Creating Regions

Regions are two-dimensional surfaces. They look like closed polylines, but your drawing can calculate more information from regions than from polylines, such as the centroid, moments of inertia, and other properties relating to mass. You can also create complex shapes by combining, subtracting, and intersecting regions. The REGION command is helpful as a preparation for 3D drawing.

You create a region from closed polylines, closed splines, circles, ellipses, and combinations of lines, arcs, and elliptical arcs that create a closed shape. The shape cannot intersect itself like a figure-8.

Figure 16.8 shows a complex region above. Although it looks like a circle with seven circles inside it, it's actually a circular surface with seven holes in it. When you select it, you can see that it's one object. The real proof is when you try to extrude it to create a 3D object out of it. You can then view it at an angle, hide background lines, and clearly see the holes, as shown below.

 To create a region, choose Home tab ⇨ Draw panel (expanded) ⇨ Region. The prompt asks you to select objects. Select all the objects and press Enter to end object selection. If all the objects create a closed, nonintersecting shape, the prompt tells you:

```
1 loop extracted.
1 Region created.
```

FIGURE 16.8

A region can be used to create a complex 3D object.

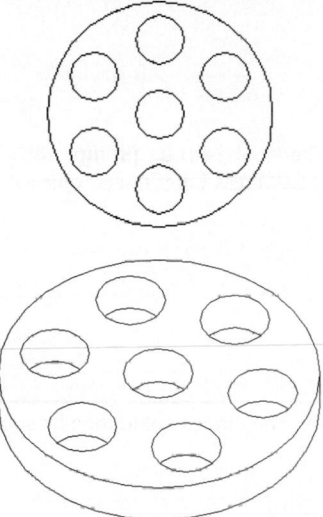

The original objects are deleted. If your objects aren't perfectly end-to-end, the prompt merely states:

```
0 loops extracted.
0 Regions created.
```

Tip

If you want to keep the original objects when converting closed shapes to a region, change the DELOBJ system variable to 0 (off) before you use the REGION command. The DELOBJ system variable determines whether objects that are used to create other objects are deleted. ■

The BOUNDARY command (see the next section) offers a way to create regions in situations where objects are not neatly drawn end to end.

If you had a hatch inside the objects, you lose hatch associativity. You can rehatch the region if you want.

Note

The XEDGES command extracts the edges of a region. For example, if you create a closed polyline of line and arc segments and make a region out of it, you can then use the XEDGES command to change the region to individual lines and arcs. (The EXPLODE command would have the same effect.) I discuss the XEDGES command more in Chapter 24, because it can also extract edges from solids. ∎

You can combine, subtract, and intersect regions to create complex objects. The three commands to accomplish these functions are UNION, SUBTRACT, and INTERSECT. These commands are discussed in Chapter 24 because they're most common in 3D modeling.

On the DVD

The drawing used in the following exercise on creating regions, ab16-d.dwg, is in the Drawings folder on the DVD. ∎

STEPS: Creating Regions

1. Open ab16-d.dwg from your DVD.

2. Save the file as ab16-04.dwg in your AutoCAD Bible folder.

 3. Choose Home tab ⇨ Draw panel (expanded) ⇨ Region. At the Select objects: prompt, use a selection window to select the entire model, as shown in Figure 16.9. Press Enter to end object selection. The prompt responds with this message:

```
7 loops extracted.
7 Regions created.
```

4. Save your drawing.

FIGURE 16.9

The outer profile and the six circles can all be turned into regions. The circles could then be subtracted from the outer profile to create a surface with six holes.

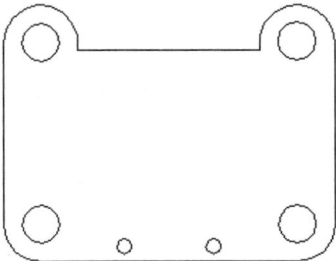

Creating Boundaries

 The BOUNDARY command creates either polylines or regions from an enclosed area. This command has the capability of analyzing an area and ignoring intersecting lines that give the REGION command so much trouble. However, no spaces are allowed between objects. (Chapter 12 explains how to use the BOUNDARY command to calculate the area of a closed space.) Use the BOUNDARY command whenever you need to create a closed complex area. To create a boundary, choose Home tab ⇨ Draw panel (expanded) ⇨ Boundary to open the Boundary Creation dialog box, as shown in Figure 16.10.

FIGURE 16.10

Boundary Creation dialog box.

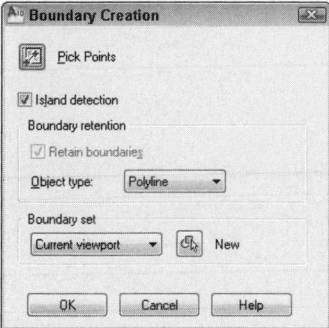

Follow these steps:

1. If you want the command to detect internal closed areas, leave the Island Detection check box checked. Otherwise, uncheck this check box.

2. The Object Type drop-down list determines the type of object that BOUNDARY creates. Choose either Region or Polyline.

3. Choose the boundary set, which is the area to include in the analysis for the boundary. Usually, you can accept the default of Current viewport. However, if you have a very complex drawing, choose New to temporarily return to your drawing. Specify a window around the area that you want for the boundary set. The command then returns you to the dialog box.

4. To specify the enclosed area for the boundary, choose Pick Points. You return to your drawing with the `Pick internal point:` prompt.

5. Pick any point inside the closed area that you want for your boundary. The command analyzes the area that you picked.

6. You then get a prompt for another internal point. If you want to create other boundaries, continue to pick internal points. Press Enter to end point selection.

When BOUNDARY creates a region or polyline, the original objects remain. You end up with a region or polyline on top of your original objects.

On the DVD

The drawing used in the following exercise on creating boundaries, `ab16-e.dwg`, **is in the** `Drawings` **folder on the DVD.** ∎

STEPS: Creating Boundaries

1. Open `ab16-e.dwg` from your DVD.

2. Save the file as `ab16-05.dwg` in your `AutoCAD Bible` folder. This is a bushing, as shown in Figure 16.11.

FIGURE 16.11

A bushing.

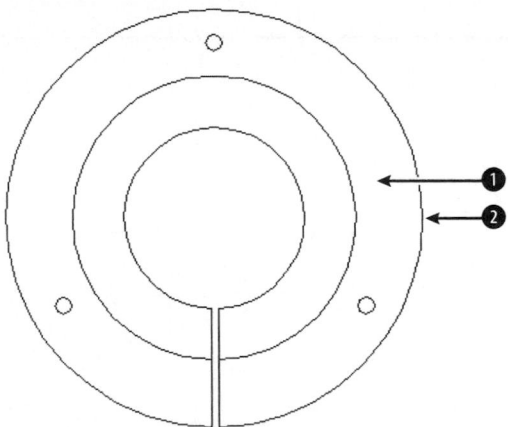

3. Choose Home tab ⇨ Draw panel (expanded) ⇨ Boundary. In the Boundary Creation dialog box, choose Region as the Object type.

4. Choose Pick Points.

5. At the Pick internal point: prompt, choose ❶, shown in Figure 16.11.

6. Press Enter to end internal point selection. The prompt responds:

```
4 loops extracted.
4 Regions created.
BOUNDARY created 4 regions
```

7. To see the new region, start the MOVE command. At the Select objects: prompt, pick ❷. Move the region to the right; the exact distance is not important. You see both the new region and the original objects.

8. Save your drawing.

Creating Hatches

Hatches are repeating patterns of lines that fill in an area. Most types of drafting make use of hatching. In architectural drafting, hatched areas are used to indicate materials, such as insulation or grass. In mechanical drafting, hatching often indicates hidden areas or certain materials. AutoCAD and AutoCAD LT provide a large number of hatch patterns. You can create solid fills in the same way that you create hatch patterns.

Cross-Reference

Chapter 31 explains how to create your own hatch patterns. ■

Figure 16.12 shows a drawing with a simple hatch pattern. Here the cross-section shows solid metal that is hatched to distinguish it from the holes.

FIGURE 16.12

Hatch patterns help you to distinguish different materials or textures.

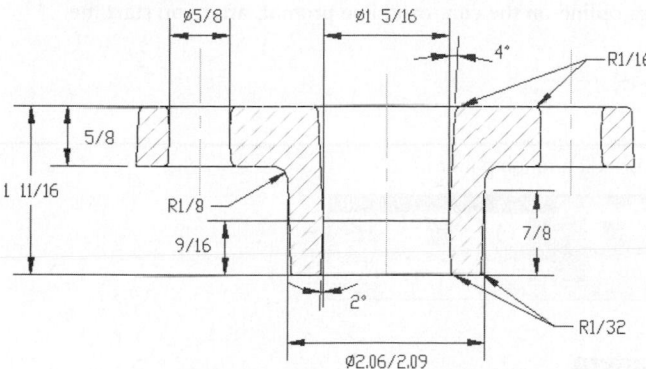

Thanks to Jerry Bottenfield of Clow Valve Company, Oskaloosa, Iowa, for this drawing.

Understanding hatch patterns

Hatch patterns have three characteristics that are similar to dimensions:

- **They are blocks.** This means that all the lines that fill in an area are one object. Blocks are covered in Chapter 18.

- **They are associative.** If you edit the object that is hatched, the hatch automatically adjusts to fit the new shape of the object.

- **They can be annotative.** If you activate the annotative property of the hatch, the hatch can automatically adjust its display scale in a viewport. (See Chapter 17 for a discussion of annotative objects and viewports.)

You can specify exactly which area you want to hatch in several ways. Often, the key to successful hatching lies in how you construct the area that you want to hatch. For example, you can use the BOUNDARY and REGION commands covered in previous sections of this chapter to create complex closed areas that you can hatch.

AutoCAD stores hatch pattern definitions in the `acad.pat` and `acadiso.pat` files. AutoCAD LT uses the `acadlt.pat` and `acadltiso.pat` files. If you create your own hatch patterns, you can put them in another file with the PAT filename extension.

Tip

Create a separate layer for hatch patterns. You may want to turn off or freeze your hatch layer to reduce visual clutter or assist in selecting objects. The hatch layer is typically a different color from the layer of the model that you're hatching. ■

Defining a hatch

To hatch an area, choose Home tab ⇨ Draw panel ⇨ Hatch. This starts the HATCH command. The Hatch Creation tab appears, as shown in Figure 16.13.

New Feature

The Hatch Creation tab is new for AutoCAD and AutoCAD LT 2011. You now create and edit hatches on the Ribbon. The old dialog box is available by clicking the dialog box launcher arrow at the right of the Options panel on the Hatch Creation tab or by using the seTtings option on the command line prompt, after you start the HATCH command. ■

FIGURE 16.13

The Hatch Creation tab appears when you create or edit a hatch pattern.

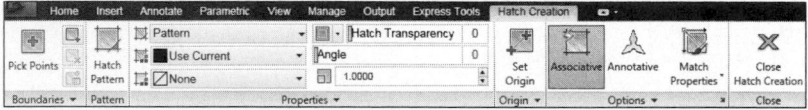

Specifying the hatch type and pattern

In the Properties panel of the Hatch Creation tab, click the Hatch Type drop-down list, and choose one of these four options:

- **Solid.** Lets you fill an enclosed area with a solid fill (rather than a hatch pattern).
- **Gradient.** Lets you fill an enclosed area with a gradient. I cover gradients later in this chapter.
- **Pattern.** Lets you choose any of the standard hatch patterns that come with AutoCAD and AutoCAD LT.
- **User defined.** Lets you define your own hatch pattern by specifying the angle and spacing, using the current linetype.

To specify a hatch pattern, click the Hatch Pattern button in the Pattern panel. A gallery of hatch patterns opens, as shown in Figure 16.14. Scroll down to see all of the patterns. Click an image tile to choose a hatch pattern or choose the Solid tile to choose a solid fill.

FIGURE 16.14

The Hatch Pattern gallery.

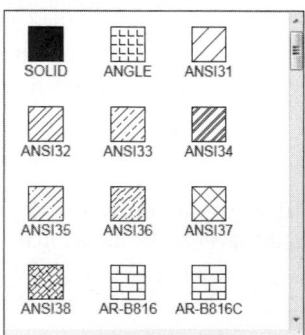

On the DVD

Mhatch **is a program that creates solid fills for a selection of closed objects. Look in** \Software\Chapter 16\ mhatch. **It works with AutoCAD only.** ■

Cross-Reference

You can drag hatches from your drawing to the Tools Palette window to create hatch tools that you can then drag into your drawing. See Chapter 26 for a description of the Tools Palette window.

I explain how to create custom hatch patterns in Chapter 31. To access custom hatch patterns, choose them from the bottom of the Hatch Pattern gallery; they appear there if they are in the support file search path. To add a folder to the support file search path, start the OPTIONS command, click the Files tab, expand the Support File Search Path item, click Add, and then click Browse. ■

Setting the hatch angle and scale

Use the Angle text box or slider in the Properties panel of the Hatch Creation tab to rotate the angle of the hatch pattern. Watch out here, as many of the patterns are already defined at an angle. The hatch pattern in Figure 16.15 uses a 0-degree angle because the hatch pattern that was used (ANSI31) is defined as diagonal lines.

 The Scale determines the scale of the hatch pattern. You can type a scale in the Hatch Pattern Scale text box in the Properties panel, or use the up or down arrows. A scale of 1 (the default) creates the hatch as defined. A scale of 0.5 shrinks it by one-half. Figure 16.15 shows two hatch patterns using the ANSI31 pattern. The left one uses a scale of 1, and the right one uses a scale of 0.5.

FIGURE 16.15

You can scale the hatch pattern to suit your needs.

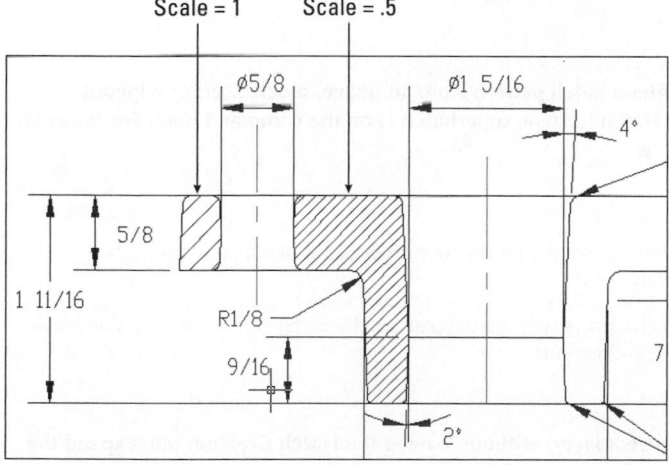

If you choose User Defined from the Hatch Type drop-down list, you can create a hatch that uses the current linetype, based on the spacing and angle that you specify. To create cross-hatching, click the Double button on the expanded Properties panel. The Hatch Pattern Scale area becomes the Hatch Spacing text box, where you can define the spacing between the lines. Figure 16.16 shows a user-defined double hatch with an angle of 45 degrees and 0.1-unit spacing.

FIGURE 16.16

A user-defined hatch.

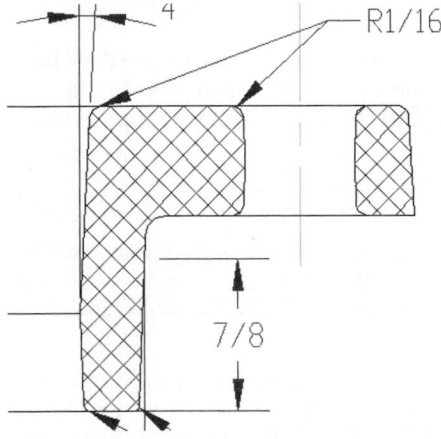

The ISO Pen Width drop-down list in the expanded Properties panel is available only for ISO predefined hatch patterns. (They all have ISO in their name.) This feature adjusts the scale of the pattern according to the pen width that you specify. When you choose a pen width from the drop-down list, the scale shown in the Hatch Pattern Scale text box automatically changes to equal the pen width. Note that you still have to separately set the width of your plotter pens when you plot your drawing.

AutoCAD Only

The Express Tools SUPERHATCH command creates a hatch pattern from an image, block, xref, or wipeout. Choose Express Tools tab ⇨ Draw panel ⇨ Super Hatch (or type superhatch ↵ on the command line). For information on installing Express Tools, see Appendix A. ■

Setting hatch properties

Besides the pattern, angles, and scale, you can set the following properties of hatch patterns in the Properties panel of the Hatch Creation tab:

- **Hatch color.** By default, a hatch's properties are determined by its layer, but you can choose a color from the Hatch Color drop-down list.

New Feature

You can set the hatch's layer (and change the current layer) without leaving the Hatch Creation tab. Expand the Properties panel, and choose a layer from the Hatch Layer Override drop-down list. ■

- **Background color.** By default, a hatch has no background color, so you see the drawing area color between the lines. You can specify a background color from the Background Color drop-down list.

New Feature

Background color is a new feature for AutoCAD 2011 and AutoCAD LT 2011. You see the background color between the hatch pattern's lines. The background color doesn't have a layer. Although you would usually set the background color on the Ribbon, you can also use the HPBACKGROUNDCOLOR command; this command's setting lasts through the drawing session, unless you change it. ∎

- **Hatch Transparency.** You can make the hatch partially transparent. You would be most likely to use transparency for solid fills or gradients (rather than line patterns). You can set the transparency by layer, block, or individually for the hatch object. To set the transparency by layer or block, use the Transparency Value drop-down list to the left of the Hatch Transparency slider. To set the transparency for the object, choose Transparency Value from the drop-down list and use the Hatch Transparency slider or text box. The highest value is 90, which makes the hatch 90-percent transparent.

New Feature

Transparency for hatches is new for AutoCAD 2011 and AutoCAD LT 2011. For more about transparency of layers and objects, see Chapter 11. ∎

Setting the hatch origin

The Origin panel lets you determine where the hatch pattern starts. By default, the pattern starts at the origin of the drawing, which is generally 0,0. As a result, the hatch in your object may start somewhere in the middle. This effect is very visible with certain hatch patterns, such as bricks. In Figure 16.17, you see two rectangles. The one on the left uses the default origin; the one on the right uses the lower-left corner of the rectangle as the origin.

FIGURE 16.17

You can specify where the hatch pattern starts.

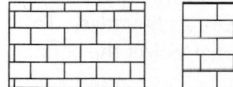

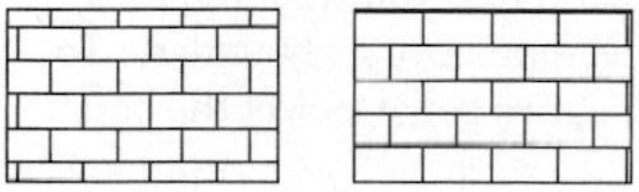

To specify the hatch origin, use the options in the Origin panel of the Hatch Creation tab. Click the Set Origin button to specify any point in your drawing. However, if you want the origin to be one of the corners or the center of the hatched boundary area, you need to expand the Origin panel and choose one of the options.

If you always want to use the same hatch origin (such as the lower-left corner of the boundary), expand the Origin panel and click the Store as Default Origin button.

Determining the hatch boundary

Hatching an entire object is the simplest way to place a hatch. However, the area that you want to hatch is often fairly complex, and the program needs to do some calculations to determine the area.

You can specify the hatch boundary in two ways: you can pick points inside an area (an internal point) and let the command try to find an enclosed boundary, or you can select objects. By default, the HATCH command prompts you to pick an internal point.

When you start the HATCH command, you see the `Pick internal point or [Select objects/seTtings]:` prompt. When you have specified the hatch pattern's properties, click the internal point that you want to specify.

New Feature

When you hover the cursor over an internal point, you see a preview of the hatch. If you don't like what you see, change the hatch's properties and try again. ■

When you click inside a closed area, you see the following on the command line:

```
Pick internal point or [Select objects/remove Boundaries]: Selecting
    everything...
Selecting everything visible...
Analyzing the selected data...
Analyzing internal islands...
Pick internal point or [Select objects/seTtings]:
```

The command is determining the *boundary set,* which is simply everything visible on the screen. You can continue to pick internal points to hatch adjoining areas. Each boundary is helpfully highlighted. Press Enter to place the hatch.

 If you want to hatch an entire object, choose Select Boundary Objects in the Boundaries panel of the Hatch Creation tab or use the command's `Select objects` option. Select the object or objects, and press Enter to end object selection and place the hatch.

Note

You can hatch outside the display on the screen. The hatch pattern extends to include the entire object or boundary that you specified. ■

 Sometimes, you need more control over the boundary and you also need to remove a boundary that you've selected, without starting from scratch. For example, if you have an inner island that you want to hatch, then by default, the hatch excludes the island. One way to hatch the island is to remove its boundary. To remove a boundary, click the Remove Boundary Objects button in the Boundaries panel. Select the boundaries that you want to remove.

When you pick points to determine the hatch boundary, the hatching process uses the same mechanism as the BOUNDARY command to temporarily create a boundary for hatching. To draw the boundary as a polyline or region, choose Retain Boundaries-Polyline or Retain Boundaries-Region from the Retain Boundary Objects drop-down list of the expanded Boundaries panel. Otherwise, placing the hatch discards the boundary. For more information, see the discussion of the BOUNDARY command earlier in this chapter.

When you hatch an unclosed area, sometimes picking points is more successful; other times, selecting objects works best, so try both options. You can sometimes hatch areas that are not completely closed by using the Gap Tolerance feature. In the expanded Options panel, use the Gap Tolerance text box or slider to specify a value greater than the size of the gap. You can use values from 0 to 5,000. In order to hatch an unclosed area in this way, you need to pick internal points rather than choose objects. Note that the hatch is not associative, which means that if you modify your almost-closed area, you need to rehatch. Using this feature sets subsequent hatches as nonassociative, so be sure to reclick the Associative button in the Options panel.

You may see the Hatch – Boundary Definition Error message, telling you that a closed boundary cannot be determined. Sometimes, you need to modify your objects before you can hatch.

Note

When you attempt to create a hatch boundary and are unsuccessful, the command sometimes attempts to show you where gaps are. Red circles appear around the endpoints of the boundary openings. Cancel the command and edit your objects accordingly, and then try again. ■

Note

To display hatches, either solid fill or lines, the FILLMODE system variable must be on, which it is by default. To turn FILLMODE off, type fillmode ↲ and 0 ↲. You must regenerate the drawing to see the effect. ■

The Hatch Creation tab has several other options:

- Click the Associative button in the Options panel to deselect it if you want to create a hatch that is not associated with its object. By default, hatches are associative.

- Click Annotative in the Options panel if you want to create a hatch with the ability to automatically resize its appearance according to viewport scale. (See Chapter 5 for information on using annotative scales, and see Chapter 17 for an exercise on using annotative objects.)

- Check Create Separate Hatches in the expanded Options panel if you are selecting several separate enclosed areas and want each area to be a separate hatch object. Otherwise, you create one hatch object that hatches these separated areas.

- Choose a draw order for hatches from the Draw Order drop-down list on the expanded Options panel. By default, hatches display behind their boundaries, so when you pick a boundary, you select the boundary, not the hatch.

New Feature

The new HATCHTOBACK command sends hatches beneath all other objects. ■

- Choose Match Properties in the Options panel to use the hatch type, pattern, angle, scale, and/or spacing of an existing hatch. You then select a hatch pattern. You can fine-tune this process by specifying the hatch's origin. From the Match Properties drop-down list, choose Use Current Origin to use the current origin setting, or choose Use Source Hatch Origin to use the setting of the source hatch.

Managing Islands

Islands are areas that are entirely enclosed inside a hatch boundary. Islands can make hatching more difficult because you may or may not want to hatch the inside of the island.

Note

Text is counted as an island, enabling you to hatch areas that contain text without hatching over the words. ■

How you specify the boundary can affect the results you get:

- **Picking internal points.** When you pick points, you don't need to select the islands. Hatching detects islands by default. As soon as you pick points, the Remove Boundary Objects button in the Boundaries panel of the Hatch Creation tab becomes available. You can select the islands to remove them from consideration if you want to hatch them. For example, if you remove all the islands shown in Figure 16.18, the result is the same as using the Ignore style, where everything inside the outside boundary is hatched.

- **Selecting objects.** When you select objects, you must also select the islands. If you select the entire area by window, you automatically include the internal islands. If you need to pick individual objects, you must pick the islands individually. If you later erase an island, you don't lose hatch associativity, and the hatch regenerates so that it covers the entire outer boundary.

The resulting hatch depends on the island detection setting. To specify island detection, in the expanded Options tab of the Hatch Creation tab, click the Island Detection drop-down menu and choose one of the options:

- **Normal Island Detection.** Hatches alternate areas so that the outer area is hatched, the next inner island is not hatched, the next inner island is hatched, and so on.
- **Outer Island Detection.** Hatches only the outer area and does not hatch any inner islands.
- **Ignore Island Detection.** Ignores islands and hatches everything from the outside in.
- **No Island Detection.** Uses legacy island behavior.

Figure 16.18 shows three copies of a nut hatched in the three styles. To hatch this model, I selected the entire model, except for the spout at the bottom, with a window.

FIGURE 16.18

Hatching islands using three of the boundary styles.

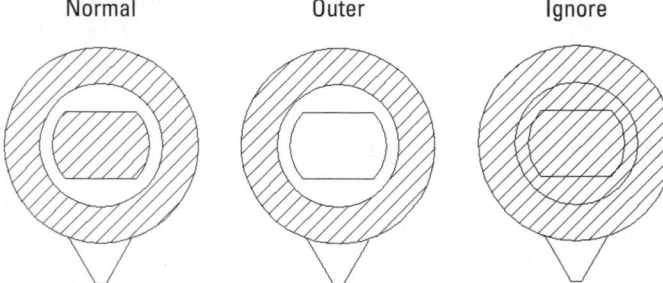

Normal   Outer   Ignore

Dragging and dropping hatch patterns

After you have spent the time creating a hatch, especially a custom hatch (as I describe in Chapter 31), you may want to use that hatch in other drawings. You can open a PAT (hatch pattern) file from the DesignCenter, preview its hatch patterns, and drag any hatch pattern into any closed object in your current drawing. Here's how to drag a hatch pattern from the DesignCenter:

1. Choose View tab ⇨ Palettes panel ⇨ Design Center (or press Ctrl+2) to open the DesignCenter.
2. Use the Tree view to navigate to the folder that contains your `acad.pat`, `acadlt.pat`, or other `.pat` file. If necessary, click the Desktop button and navigate from there.

Note
To find the location of your `.pat` files, choose Application Button ⇨ Options and click the File tab. Double-click the Support File Search Path option. One of the paths listed contains your hatch files. ∎

3. Double-click the folder and select a hatch pattern (`.pat`) file. A preview of all the hatch patterns appears in the right pane.

4. From the right pane of the DesignCenter, drag the hatch pattern that you want into a closed object in your drawing (or an unclosed object with the gap tolerance value greater than the gap). If you need more options, right-click the pattern as you drag, then choose BHATCH from the shortcut menu to display the Hatch Creation tab, and then specify the hatch parameters in the usual way.

You can drag a hatch pattern to a tool palette to create a hatch with the properties of the hatch in your drawing. Then you can drag that hatch tool from the palette into any closed area in your drawing. The hatch automatically fills the area with the same properties. For more on tool palettes, see Chapter 26.

Creating gradient fills

Gradients are fills that gradually change from one color to another. You can use gradients to create presentation-quality illustrations without rendering. Because gradient fills can be partially transparent, you can use them where you need to see objects underneath.

To create a gradient:

1. Choose Home tab ⇨ Draw panel (expanded) ⇨ Gradient to display the Hatch Creation tab, with the Hatch Type drop-down list set to Gradient, as shown in Figure 16.19. (You can also choose Hatch from the Draw panel and choose Gradient from the Hatch Type drop-down list.)

FIGURE 16.19

Use the Hatch Creation tab to create gradient fills of closed objects.

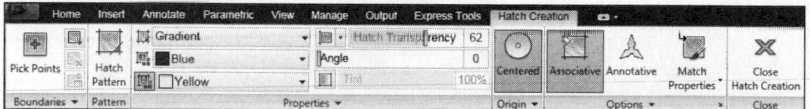

2. Specify the boundary as described in the "Determining the hatch boundary" section earlier in this chapter.

3. Choose whether you want a two-color gradient by selecting or deselecting the Gradient Colors button, to the left of the Gradient Color 2 drop-down list.

- If you deselect the Gradient Colors button, click the Gradient Color 1 drop-down list to choose a color from the list, or choose Select Colors to open the Select Color dialog box, where you can choose the color you want. (For instructions on using this dialog box, see Chapter 11.) Click OK to close the dialog box.

Note

You can click the Gradient Tint and Shades button, and specify a tint percentage for a one-color gradient. A tint is the color mixed with white. A low tint percentage creates a gradient with the Gradient Color 1 and black (or a dark shade of the color). A high tint percentage creates a gradient with the Gradient Color 1 and white (or a light tint of the color). ∎

- If you select the Gradient Colors button, you can specify a color from both the Gradient Color 1 and the Gradient Color 2 drop-down lists, as just described.

4. From the Hatch Pattern drop-down list in the Pattern panel, choose one of the nine gradient styles: linear, cylinder, inverted cylinder, sphere, inverted sphere, hemisphere, inverted hemisphere, curved, and inverted curved.

5. If you want the gradient to be symmetrical, click the Centered button in the Origin panel. To create a gradient that isn't symmetrical, deselect the Centered button. When you deselect the Centered button, the gradient focus moves up and to the left. (You can change this location by changing the angle, as explained in the next step.)

6. Use the Angle slider or text box in the Properties panel to choose an angle. If your gradient is centered, the gradient rotates around its center and remains symmetrical. If your gradient is not centered, the gradient rotates around the edges. If you have already specified an internal point, you can see the change as you drag the slider.

7. Press Enter to finalize the gradient.

See Figure 16.20 for an example of some gradient fills. You could turn off the boundary's layer for a more realistic look.

FIGURE 16.20

The gradient on the left gives the illusion of light shining from the left. On the right, you see a sophisticated use of gradients to create a presentation-quality drawing.

Thanks to James Wedding for permission to use the drawing on the right from Jones & Boyd, Inc.

Editing hatches

To edit a hatch pattern, including a solid or gradient fill, choose Home tab ⇨ Modify panel (expanded) ⇨ Edit Hatch and select a hatch object to display the Hatch Edit dialog box. An easier way is to just select a hatch object. The Hatch Editor Ribbon appears. The Hatch Editor tab is the same as the Hatch Creation tab, except that not all the options are available. You can use this tab to change any of the hatch properties.

Because hatches are associative (unless you explode them or choose to create them as nonassociative), when you edit their boundaries, they adjust to fit the new boundary. However, if the new boundary is no longer closed, the hatch may lose its associativity, and you see the Hatch boundary associativity removed warning message.

Tip

If a hatch has lost its associativity to a boundary, you can still alter its shape by using its grips to edit the hatch. Select the nonassociative hatch, select the grip, and drag. ■

By default, object snaps don't work with hatch lines. This prevents you from accidentally drawing to a hatch line instead of a nearby object. If you want to snap to hatch lines, choose Application Button ⇨ Options, click the Drafting tab, and uncheck the Ignore Hatch Objects check box. Click OK to return to your drawing.

Tip

You can obtain the area of a hatch in the Properties palette. Select a hatch and open the Properties palette. Look for the Area item in the Geometry section.

 You can re-create the boundary of any hatch as a polyline or region. Select the hatch and choose Recreate Boundary in the Boundaries panel of the Hatch Editor tab. You can use this feature to create a boundary for a hatch if you have deleted it. ■

You can also edit a gradient in the Properties palette; use the items in the Pattern section. You can change the colors, angle, type, and whether it is centered.

New Feature

The center grip of a hatch is now circular; you can use it to stretch or move the hatch. If you hover the cursor over the center grip, you see options to change the origin point, hatch angle, and hatch scale. Secondary grips between the corner grips are also new. (See the discussion on editing polylines earlier in this chapter for more information.) You can easily move vertices (with the Stretch option), add and remove vertices, and convert a straight edge to an arc. ■

You can trim hatches. Choose any object that crosses the hatch as the cutting edge and then select the hatch (on the side that you want to trim) as the object to trim. Chapter 10 covers trimming objects.

New Feature

The MIRRHATCH system variable determines what happens when you mirror hatches. If you set MIRRHATCH to 0 (the default), mirroring a hatch maintains the original angle; the lines of the hatch pattern don't change. If you set it to 1, mirroring a hatch mirrors the angle as well so that the lines look like a true mirror image. Compare this system variable to MIRRTEXT (which determines what happens when you mirror text). I cover MIRRTEXT in Chapter 13. ■

On the DVD

The drawing used in the following exercise on creating and editing hatches, ab16-f.dwg, is in the Drawings folder on the DVD. ■

STEPS: Creating and Editing Hatches

1. Open ab16-f.dwg from your DVD.
2. Save the file as ab16-06.dwg in your AutoCAD Bible folder.
3. Choose Home tab ⇨ Draw panel ⇨ Hatch. Click Hatch Pattern in the Pattern panel of the Hatch Creation tab that appears, and choose ANSI35 from the Pattern drop-down list.
4. Hover in the enclosed area ❶, as shown in Figure 16.21. You see a preview of the hatch. Click inside ❶ and ❷. Press Enter to create the hatch and end the HATCH command.

FIGURE 16.21

The result after placing the two hatch patterns and the solid fills.

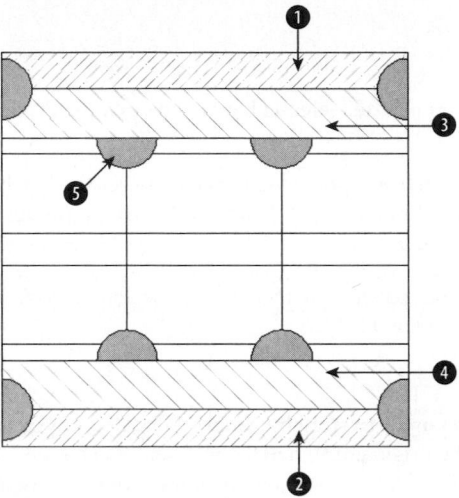

5. Start the HATCH command again. From the Hatch Type drop-down list in the Properties panel, choose User defined. In the Angle text box, type **135** ↵. In the Hatch Spacing text box, type **0.25** ↵.

6. In your drawing, pick points ❸ and ❹, shown in Figure 16.21. Press Enter to create the hatch.

7. Start the HATCH command again. From the Hatch Pattern drop-down list, choose Solid. Click inside all the semi-circle arcs and press Enter.

8. Click the circumference of the arc at ❺, making sure that you select the arc. Pick the bottom square grip to make it hot, and drag downward slightly. At the `Specify stretch point or [Base Point/Copy/Undo/eXit]:` prompt, type **.1** ↵ to make the arc larger. Press Esc to remove the grips. The solid fills expand to fill the larger area. Click Undo on the Quick Access Toolbar to return the arc to its original size.

9. Click the hatch at ❸ . Notice that this action selects the hatching in both areas (❸ and ❹) because they were created with one command. In the Properties panel of the Hatch Editor tab that opens, change the angle to 90 and the spacing to 0.15. Click OK.

10. Save your drawing.

Using the SOLID command

The SOLID command creates solidly filled 2D areas. (It is not directly related to 3D solids.) In general, the HATCH command is much more flexible. Although the SOLID command is a 2D command, it's sometimes used in 3D drawing. When you create a 2D solid and give it thickness, it creates surfaces with tops and bottoms. I cover using thickness in Chapter 21.

SOLID creates straight-edged shapes. If FILLMODE is on, AutoCAD or AutoCAD LT fills in the shape with a solid fill. (That's why it's called SOLID.)

To draw a solid, type **solid** ↵. The command prompts you for first, second, third, and fourth points. You must specify these points in zigzag order (defining triangular shapes), not around the perimeter of the shape. After the fourth point, the command continues to prompt you for third and fourth points, which you can use to create new adjacent solids. Press Enter to end the command.

Creating and Editing Multilines

Multilines are sets of parallel lines that you draw with one command. You can specify how far apart they are, and each line can have its own color and linetype. Multilines are common in architectural plans where you need to draw an inner and outer wall. (I cover a 3D version, polysolids, in Chapter 24.) To draw a multi-line, you first define, save, and load a multiline style. Then you can use the multiline style to draw multi-lines. There is a separate command for editing multilines. Figure 16.22 shows a floor plan for an apartment drawn using multilines.

AutoCAD Only

AutoCAD LT doesn't have the Multiline feature but has a similar feature called dlines. I cover dlines in the section, "Creating Dlines in AutoCAD LT." ■

FIGURE 16.22

This floor plan of an apartment uses multilines.

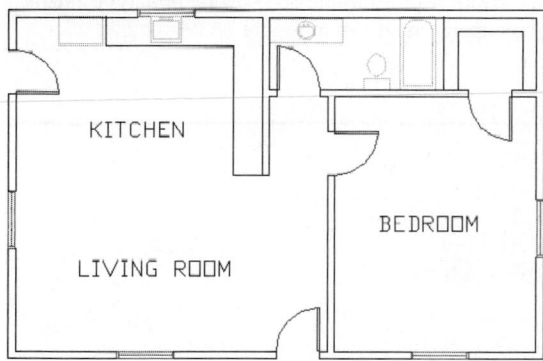

KITCHEN

LIVING ROOM

BEDROOM

Thanks to Bill Wynn of New Windsor, Maryland, for this drawing.

Creating a multiline style

The first step in drawing multilines is to design the multiline style. To create a multiline style, type **mlstyle** ↵ at the command line to open the Multiline Style dialog box, as shown in Figure 16.23.

Like text styles and dimension styles, multiline styles group a set of properties under one name. The default multiline style, called Standard, defines two lines, one unit apart. Multiline styles have two parts: element properties and multiline properties. The element properties define each individual line element. The multi-line properties define properties that apply to the multiline as a whole.

FIGURE 16.23

The Multiline Style dialog box.

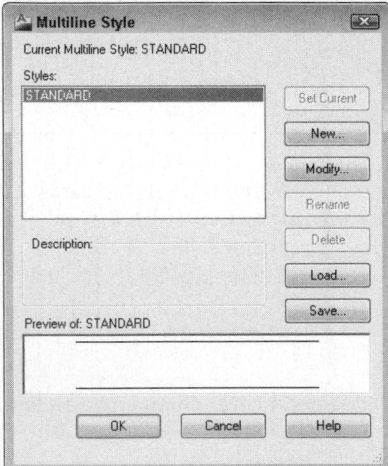

Defining multiline style properties

To start defining the multiline style, click New. In the Create New Multiline Style dialog box, type a name and click Continue. The New Multiline Style dialog box opens, as shown in Figure 16.24.

FIGURE 16.24

The New Multiline Style dialog box.

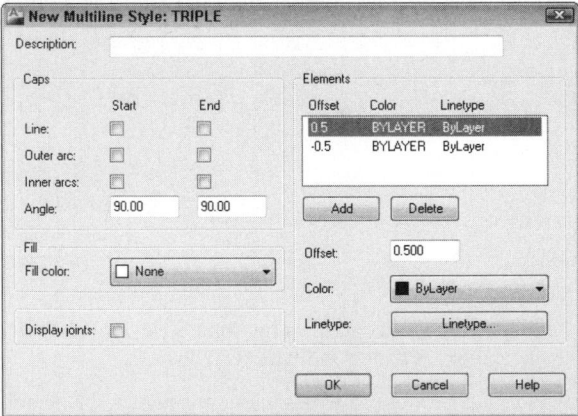

The Elements section lists the current elements of the multiline. Elements are the lines that make up the multiline. The offset defines the distance of the line from the start point when you start to draw. An offset of zero places the line on the start point. As you can see, the Standard multiline style has two elements, each 0.5 units from the start point. Figure 16.25 shows the Standard multiline style as it appears in relation to the start point that you pick.

FIGURE 16.25

The Standard multiline style places two lines on either side of the start point.

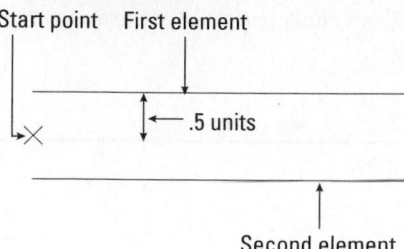

Note

You can change the relationship of the start point and the element lines with the Justification option, as explained later in the "Drawing multilines" section. ∎

To define the element lines of a multiline style, follow these steps:

1. In the Elements section, highlight the first element. Even if you typed a new name for the multiline style, the elements listed are the same as the current multiline style.

Tip

When creating a new multiline style, first set as current the multiline style that is the most similar to the one that you want to create. ∎

2. In the Offset box, type the offset value that you want. The offset should be zero if you want the line to appear on your pick points, a positive number (in units) if you want the line to appear above your pick points, and a negative number (in units) if you want the line to appear below your pick points. (This assumes the default of zero justification, explained later in this chapter.)

Tip

When defining the multiline style elements, think of the multiline as being drawn horizontally to the right to help you visualize what above and below mean. ∎

3. Choose Color to choose a color for the line element.
4. Choose Linetype to choose a linetype for the line element.
5. Choose Add to add a new element, or choose Delete to delete a listed element.
6. To define the next element, select the second element in the Elements box and repeat Steps 2 through 5. Continue to define elements until you're done.
7. If you want, enter a description for the multiline style in the Description text box.
8. Click OK to return to the Multiline Style dialog box.

Note

A multiline style can have up to 16 elements. All 16 elements must be on the same layer, but you can vary the linetypes and colors. ∎

Use the left side of the New Multiline Style dialog box to set the overall properties of the multiline. Caps cross the ends of multilines to close them. You can choose line or arc caps. Figure 16.26 shows the effects of all the possible choices in this box. You can also choose a color to add a solid fill to the multiline. To display a line at the junction of each line segment, check the Display Joints check box. After you make your choices, click OK to return to the Multiline Style dialog box.

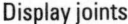

FIGURE 16.26

The results of choosing the various options in the New Multiline Style dialog box.

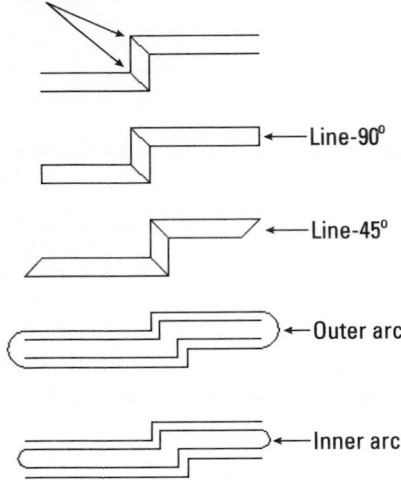

Saving a new multiline style

Before you can use the multiline style, you must save it. AutoCAD saves multiline styles in a file with the MLN filename extension. After you click Save, the Save Multiline Style dialog box opens.

In general, you can save your multiline styles in the default file, which is `acad.mln`. Click Save to return to the Multiline Style dialog box.

Loading a multiline style

As with linetypes, you must load multiline styles before you can use them. Choose Load to open the Load Multiline Styles dialog box. Choose the style that you created from the list and click OK. You return to the Multiline Styles dialog box. You're now ready to use the multiline style. Click OK to return to your drawing.

You can also use the Multiline Style dialog box to rename multiline styles and make another multiline style current.

On the DVD

The drawing used in the following exercise on creating a multiline style, `ab16-g.dwg`, is in the `Drawings` folder on the DVD. ∎

STEPS: Creating a Multiline Style

1. Open ab16-g.dwg from your DVD.

2. Save the file as ab16-07.dwg in your AutoCAD Bible folder. This is a site plan, as shown in Figure 16.27.

FIGURE 16.27

The parallel lines at the bottom of the site plan can be drawn by using a multiline.

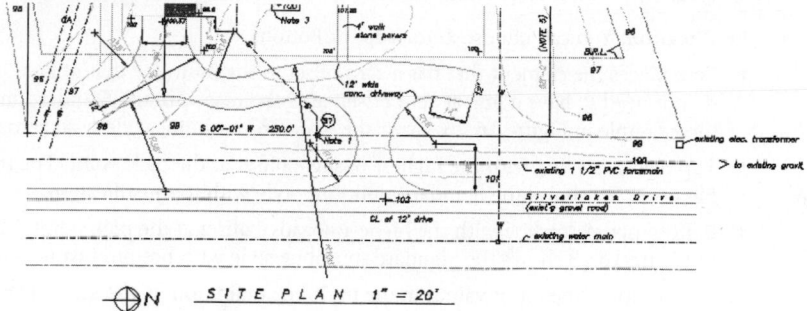

3. Type **mlstyle** ↵ on the command line to open the Multiline Style dialog box. Click New. In the text box, type **siteplan**. Choose Continue.

4. In the Elements section of the dialog box, the top element should be highlighted. Change the offset to 0, the color to black (it may list as white), and the linetype to DASHDOT.

5. Highlight the second element. Change the offset to –132 (11' × 12"), the color to magenta, and the linetype to continuous.

6. Click Add. Change the offset to –180 (15' × 12"), the color to red, and the linetype to center.

7. Click Add. Change the offset to –228 (19' × 12"), the color to magenta, and the linetype to continuous.

8. Click Add. Change the offset to –360 (30' × 12"), the color to black, and the linetype to dashdot.

9. Click Add. Change the offset to –480 (40' × 12"), the color to red, and the linetype to center.

10. Click OK. In the Multiline Style dialog box, click Save.

Caution

If you are using someone else's computer, check with the owner before saving the linestyle to acad.mln. You can't do any damage, but the owner may not want to have your multiline style there. You can change the name in the File Name text box to something else, such as my_mls.mln. ∎

11. In the Save Multiline Style dialog box, you should see acad.mln in the File Name text box. You can also type a new MLN filename. Choose Save.

12. With the new multiline style selected, choose Set Current, and click OK to return to your drawing.

13. Save your drawing. If you're continuing on to the next exercise, keep the drawing open.

Drawing multilines

Defining a multiline style is the hard part. As soon as the style is defined, saved, loaded, and made current, you can draw with it. You may find that you need some practice to get the hang of it because you're drawing more than one line at once. To draw a multiline, type **mline** ↵ on the command line to start the MLINE command. The command responds with the `Specify start point or [Justification/Scale/ STyle]:` prompt. The prompt also displays the current justification, scale, and style. The default is to pick a point. From there you get the `Specify next point:` prompt. After the first segment, you get the `Specify next point or [Undo]:` prompt, and after the second segment, the `Specify next point or [Close/Undo]:` prompt. Here is how to use the options:

- **Justification.** You can choose Zero, Top, or Bottom.
  - Zero places the element that has a zero offset in the multiline definition at the pick point. You do not need to have a line at zero offset, as is the case with the Standard multiline style. The top example in Figure 16.28 shows the Standard multiline style with zero justification.
  - Top places the line with the highest positive offset at the pick point. The middle example in Figure 16.28 shows the Standard multiline style with top justification.
  - Bottom places the line with the highest negative offset at he pick point. The bottom example in Figure 16.28 shows the Standard multiline style with bottom justification.
- **Scale.** Multiplies the offset values in the multiline definition by the scale. The Standard multiline style places two lines 1 unit apart. A scale of 6 would place them 6 units apart.
- **Style.** Enables you to specify the current multiline style. Type **?** ↵ to get a list of the available multiline styles.

As you draw a multiline, whenever you create a corner by changing direction, the command creates a clean corner.

FIGURE 16.28

Drawing a multiline using the Standard multiline style in zero, top, and bottom justification.

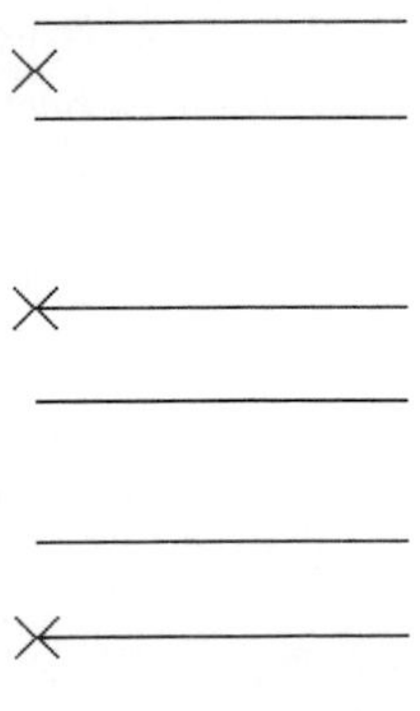

STEPS: Drawing Multilines

1. Continue from the previous exercise. (If you didn't do the previous exercise, you should do it to create the multiline style.) Set a running object snap for Intersection. Turn on Ortho Mode.

2. Type **mline** ↵ on the command line. The prompt displays the following message:

   `Current settings: Justification = Top, Scale = 1.00, Style = SITEPLAN`

3. At the `Specify start point or [Justification/Scale/STyle]:` prompt, press Shift+right-click and choose the From object snap. At the `Base point:` prompt, choose ❶, shown in Figure 16.29. (If necessary, press Tab until you get the Intersection object snap.) At the `<Offset>:` prompt, type **@0,–10'** ↵.

4. At the `Specify next point:` prompt, move the cursor to the right and type **255'** ↵. If you want, you can experiment by drawing other line segments. Press Enter to end the command. The drawing should look like Figure 16.29.

5. Save your drawing.

FIGURE 16.29

The completed multiline.

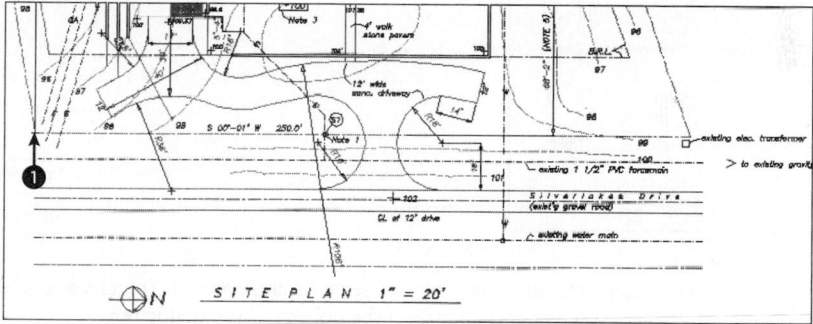

Editing multilines

No matter how many segments it contains, the entire multiline is one object. Many editing commands simply do not work with multilines. Table 16.1 shows the editing commands and whether they work with multilines.

TABLE 16.1

Using Editing Commands with Multilines

Command	Usable with Multilines	Command	Usable with Multilines
ARRAY	Yes	LENGTHEN	No
BREAK	No	MIRROR	Yes
CHAMFER	No	MOVE	Yes
COPY	Yes	ROTATE	Yes
EXPLODE	Yes	SCALE	Yes
EXTEND	Yes	STRETCH	Yes
FILLET	No	TRIM	Yes

You can use grips to stretch, move, copy, mirror, and rotate multilines.

To edit multilines, you use the MLEDIT command. To start MLEDIT, type **mledit** ↵ on the command line and select the multiline to open the Multilines Edit Tools dialog box, as shown in Figure 16.30.

The Multilines Edit Tools dialog box.

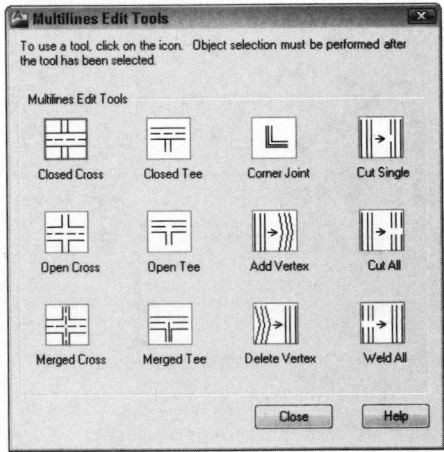

This dialog box enables you to edit multiline intersections and corners. You can also add or delete a vertex. Click one of the images, and its name appears at the bottom of the dialog box.

The first column manages crossing intersections. To edit a crossing intersection, choose one of the tiles in the first column and click OK. The command prompts you to pick a first multiline and then a second multiline. MLEDIT always cuts the first multiline that you pick. The second one may be cut if it is called for by the edit type.

Note

Although the command prompts you to pick two multilines, they can actually be two parts of the same multiline. ∎

The second column manages T-shaped intersections. To edit a crossing intersection, choose one of the tiles in the second column and click OK. The command prompts you to pick a first multiline and then a second multiline. MLEDIT always cuts the first multiline that you pick. The second one may be cut if called for by the edit type and depending on the shape of the multiline.

The third column manages corners and vertices. The top tile creates a corner. The second tile adds a vertex, and the third deletes a vertex. Choose the edit that you want and click OK. The command prompts you to select a multiline. Be careful — you must pick the point where you want to add or delete the vertex. To see the current vertices, pick the multiline with no command active to see the grips.

The last column of the dialog box makes cuts through multilines and welds them back together again. Here's how to use these options:

- Use the top tile to make a cut through one element of a multiline.
- Use the middle tile to cut through all the elements of a multiline.
- In both cases, you get a prompt to select a multiline and then a second point. Be careful — the point that you use to select the multiline is the first point of the cut. For a single cut, the pick point of the multiline also determines which element the command cuts.
- Use the bottom tile to remove the cuts. Removing cuts is called *welding*.

For all these editing tools, you get prompts for further edits. Press Enter to end selection.

You can also move vertices by using grips with the Stretch option.

Note

An old command, TRACE, draws lines with width. Usually you can use polylines or multilines instead to create the same effect. ■

Multiline styles are stored with the drawing, so you can update and view them even if the multiline style file containing the multiline definition is not available.

Creating Dlines in AutoCAD LT

Dlines are the AutoCAD LT equivalent of multilines. AutoCAD does not include dlines. Dlines (double lines) create line segments and arcs that are individual objects. The double lines and arcs have nicely finished corners and ends. You can specify the width between the lines, offset the lines from your pick points, and cap the lines with a simple square cap.

To create a dline, type **dline** ↵ on the command line. The first prompt, `Specify start point or [Break/Caps/Dragline/Snap/Width]:`, gives you the following options:

- **Break.** Breaks the dline when it crosses other double lines, single lines, or arcs.
- **Caps.** Places a square cap at the start or end of the double line or at both the start and end. Otherwise, use the None suboption.
- **Dragline.** Offsets the double line from your pick points. A positive value for this option offsets to the right, and a negative value offsets to the left of your pick points. By default, the double line is centered on either side of your pick points. You can also choose to use the Left or Right suboptions to align the left or right line with your pick points.
- **Snap.** Ends a double line whenever you use an object snap.
- **Width.** Specifies the distance between the double lines.

After you specify the first point, the prompt expands to give you three more options:

- **Arc.** Creates double arcs. (You can't easily do this in AutoCAD!) You have suboptions that are similar to the ARC command options, including a Line option to return to drawing line segments.
- **CLose.** Draws a double line from the last point back to the first point.
- **Undo.** Undoes the last line segment or arc.

Because dlines are individual lines and arcs, there are no special editing tools and they are easy to edit.

Using the SKETCH Command

The SKETCH command enables you to draw freehand. Freehand drawing is useful for contour lines in architectural or civil engineering drawings, for illustrative effects, and for when you're feeling artistic. Although you may get best results if you have a digitizer and a stylus pen, you can sketch with a mouse or puck as well. Figure 16.31 shows some contour lines created with SKETCH.

FIGURE 16.31

Contour lines drawn with SKETCH.

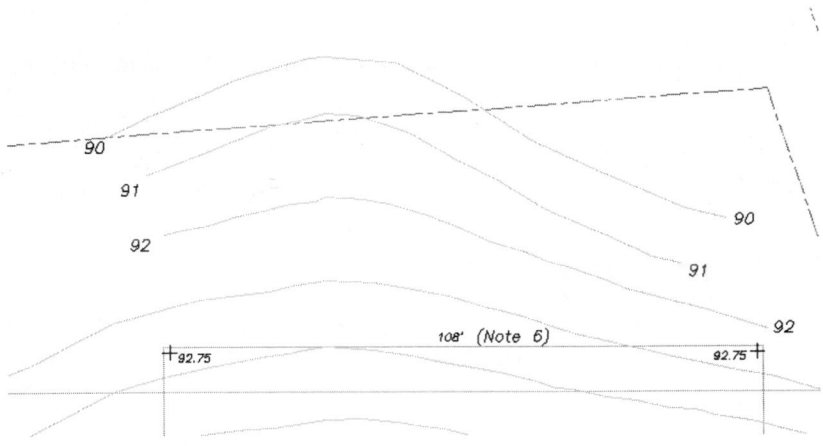

SKETCH can create lines, polylines, or splines. Start the SKETCH command by typing **sketch** ↵.

New Feature

The ability to create splines with the SKETCH command is new for AutoCAD 2011 and AutoCAD LT 2011. Previously, you could only create lines or polylines. ■

You see the following on the command line.

```
Type = Lines Increment = 0.1000 Tolerance = 0.5000:
Specify sketch or [Type/Increment/toLerance]:
```

Use the Type option to choose to draw lines, a polyline, or a spline. The Increment option defines the length of the line or polyline segment that you want to create. The Tolerance option only applies to splines and specifies how closely the curve fits to the sketch that you draw.

Note

If the increment is too big, small movements do not create a segment at all, and the sketch line appears jagged instead of smooth. However, you need to take into account the scale of your drawing and your zoom factor. You should also turn off Ortho Mode and Snap Mode if they're on. ■

To sketch, click and drag with your mouse. Sketching is like drawing. By releasing the mouse button, you can end one sketch and then start another in a new location. Press Enter to end the command.

On the DVD

The drawing used in the following exercise on sketching, ab16-h.dwg, is in the Drawings folder on the DVD. ■

STEPS: Sketching

1. Open ab16-h.dwg from your DVD.

2. Save the file as ab16-08.dwg in your AutoCAD Bible folder. It shows the front elevation of a house. You'll add the sketched path and contours, as shown in Figure 16.32.

3. Type **sketch** ↵. At the Specify sketch or [Type/Increment/toLerance]: prompt, type **t** ↵ and then type **p** ↵ to draw polylines.

4. Type **i** ↵ and then type **1** ↵ to set the increment to 1".

5. Move the cursor to ❶, shown in Figure 16.32. Click and hold the pick button, and draw the first line of the path. Release the pick button to end the sketch segment.

6. Use the same technique to draw the other lines in Figure 16.32.

7. After you're done, press Enter to end the SKETCH command.

8. Save your drawing.

FIGURE 16.32

A sketched path and contours.

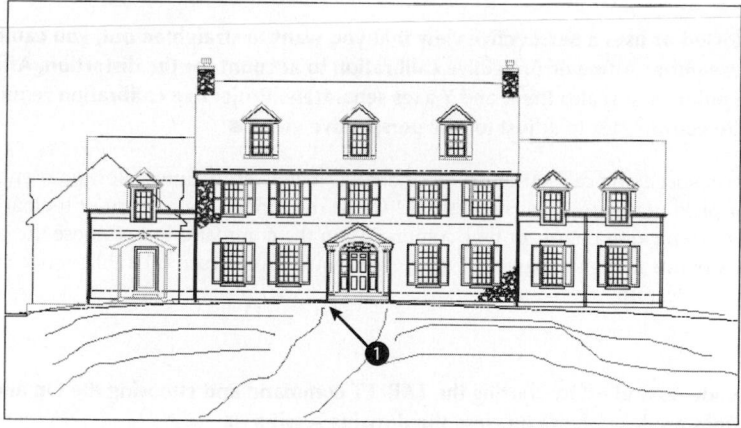

Digitizing Drawings with the TABLET Command

In Chapter 3, I explained that you can use a digitizer to execute commands. One important use for a digitizer is to copy paper drawings into your drawing. Many companies have used this technique to copy old drawings that were drafted by hand so that they could be edited electronically. Digitizing can also be used to copy artwork and logos into a drawing.

To digitize a paper drawing, you use a special digitizing mode that turns the entire digitizer into a drawing tablet. To start the TABLET command, type **tablet** ↵ on the command line and choose one of the options.

If you've been using the digitizer to execute commands, you need to reconfigure it to eliminate the command areas and enlarge the drawing area. Use the Configure option of the TABLET command and reconfigure the digitizer for 0 tablet menus. Respecify the screen pointing area so that the fixed screen pointing area covers the entire digitizing area.

Attach the paper drawing securely to the digitizer so that it won't move as you work.

To set up the digitizing mode, start the TABLET command and choose the Calibrate option. The option prompts you to pick two points on the paper drawing and specify which coordinates they represent. To do this, you need to mark two points on the paper drawing; take out a ruler and measure their distance. If the drawing has a titleblock, two corners of the titleblock are distinctive points to mark and measure. If the drawing is drawn to a scale — and it probably is — the coordinates you type should be the distance in real life, not the measurement. In other words, if the two horizontal points are 1 inch apart and 1 inch represents 48 inches (a scale of 1 = 48), you could enter 0,0 for the first point and 48,0 for the second point. However, it is usually useful to choose points over a wider area of your drawing. You can calibrate more than two points if you want.

Note

If your drawing is distorted or uses a perspective view that you want to straighten out, you can calibrate additional points and choose either Affine or Projective calibration to account for the distortion. Affine calibration requires at least three points and scales the X and Y axes separately. Projective calibration requires at least four points and stretches the coordinates to adjust for the perspective view. ■

After you finish specifying calibration points and coordinates, press Enter. Now your entire tablet can be used only for picking points. You can press F12 to use the Ribbon (or a menu or toolbar) and press F12 again to return to picking points, or type commands on the command line. Choose the command that you need and pick points along the paper drawing. After you're done, turn off Tablet mode and do any necessary editing and cleanup.

Note

You can turn Tablet mode on and off by starting the TABLET command and choosing the On and Off options. Tablet calibration settings are lost when you close the drawing session. ■

In this exercise, you practice digitizing drawings. If you have a digitizer, try this exercise. Otherwise, skip it.

STEPS: Digitizing Drawings

1. Start a new drawing using `acad.dwt` or `acadlt.dwt` as your template.
2. Save the file as `ab16-09.dwg` in your `AutoCAD Bible` folder. This is a sheet-metal template, as shown in Figure 16.33.
3. Make a photocopy of Figure 16.33 and tape it to the active area of your digitizer.
4. Type **tablet** ↵ on the command line and choose the Calibrate (CAL) option. Follow the prompts:

```
Digitize point #1: Pick ❶ in Figure 16.33.
Enter coordinates for point #1: 0,0 ↵
Digitize point #2: Pick ❷.
Enter coordinates for point #2: 7,5 ↵
Digitize point #3 (or RETURN to end): ↵
```

5. Type **tablet** ↵ and **on** ↵.
6. Type **line** ↵.
7. In Figure 16.33, pick ❸ with the digitizer, then ❹, and then each line endpoint in turn, counterclockwise around the figure.
8. After you reach ❺, do not digitize point ❶ again. Instead, type **c** ↵ to close the figure exactly.
9. Type **tablet** ↵. Type **off** ↵ to return the digitizer to Screen Pointing mode.
10. Save your drawing.

FIGURE 16.33

An unfolded sheet-metal template.

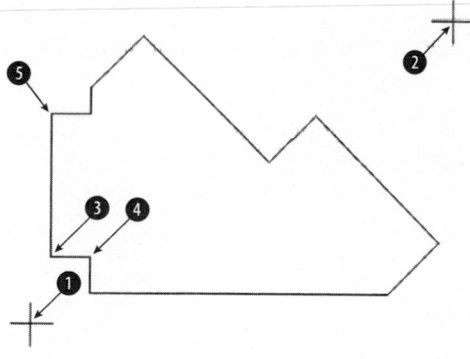

Summary

Several types of complex objects add greatly to the capabilities of AutoCAD and AutoCAD LT. In this chapter, you read about:

- Using polylines to combine lines, segments, and arcs of any width into one object
- Utilizing splines to draw mathematically calculated curves, fit to points that you specify
- Using regions, which are two-dimensional surfaces
- Creating regions or polylines from complex areas by using the BOUNDARY command
- Filling in an area with lines, a solid fill, or a gradient with the hatch feature
- Drawing complex parallel lines at one time with multilines (AutoCAD only), and drawing double lines with AutoCAD LT
- Drawing freehand with the SKETCH command
- Using a digitizer in Tablet mode, when you need to copy a paper drawing into AutoCAD or AutoCAD LT

In the next chapter, I explain how to layout and plot a drawing.

Plotting and Printing Your Drawing

M ost drawing jobs are not complete until you see the final result on paper. Traditionally, drawings are plotted on a plotter. However, you can also print a drawing on a regular computer printer. Many printers and plotters can handle a wide range of drawing sizes and paper types. In this chapter, I explain the process of preparing a drawing for plotting, including laying it out in paper space, more properly known as a *layout*. Finally, I cover the actual process of creating a plot.

Preparing a Drawing for Plotting or Printing

When you complete your drawing, you often have some details to finish. If you didn't start with a titleblock, you may need to insert one. Even if you have a title-block, you may need to complete some of its annotation, such as the date that you completed the drawing. If the drawing has layers that you don't want to appear on paper, you should set their layer state to Frozen, Off, or Not Plottable.

Many architectural and mechanical drawings show several views of the model. Now is the time to check that the views are pleasingly laid out, with enough space between them for dimensions and annotation. Later in this chapter, I explain how to create viewports that lay out the drawing in various views.

Doing a draft plot

You may want to do a draft plot, either to check the drawing itself or to be sure that it will print out properly. Although you can preview the plot, sometimes the results are not what you want, and it pays to test the plot on inexpensive paper before plotting on expensive vellum. Draft plots for checking purposes can often be done on a printer. Some companies have wide-format inkjet printers that accept 17 × 22-inch paper and are used exclusively for check plots. Even if the final plot will be all in black, a color printer is a good choice for draft plots because you can easily check the layer scheme.

Plotting a drawing from model space

Model space refers to the mode in which you work when you draw and edit your model. Throughout this book, the discussions and exercises have assumed that you were in model space. After you've prepared your drawing for plotting, as just discussed, you can plot your drawing. See the discussion on plotting later in this chapter.

Cross-Reference

You can also plot entire sheet sets. For more information, see Chapter 26. The PUBLISH command, which I cover in Chapter 28, lets you plot multiple drawings. You can output your drawing to STL format, which supports 3D printing. See Chapter 22. ∎

Creating a Layout in Paper Space

Paper space is a tool for laying out a drawing. It's analogous to creating a sheet of paper at the size on which you'll plot, and placing views on the paper. You place the views by means of *floating viewports*. Floating viewports on a paper space layout are windows into model space, through which you see your drawing.

If you're using several views of your model, you should consider creating a paper space layout. Although paper space was designed for the needs of 3D drawings, it's often used for 2D layout as well. If you want to show views of your model at different scales, paper space is indispensable. If you use a titleblock, paper space is a good choice, because the size of the titleblock needs to be appropriate for the sheet of paper on which you will plot.

A layout provides a visual environment that lets you know what your plot will look like. By creating more than one layout for a drawing, you can create more than one plot for a single drawing. For example, you can create layouts at different scales for different sheet sizes, layouts with different layer states for contractors who need to see varying aspects of a drawing, or layouts that show different sets of views of the drawing.

Entering paper space

You draw in model space. You use a paper space layout to lay out a drawing. When you're in paper space, you can view your drawing only through floating viewports.

 You can easily switch from model space to paper space and back again. If you see the Model and Layout buttons on the status bar, click them to switch. When the Model button is selected, you know that you're in model space.

By default, you see tabs for model space and each of the layouts, as shown in Figure 17.1. If you don't, right-click either the Model or Layout button on the status bar, and choose Display Layout and Model Tabs. If you don't see the Model tab, right-click any layout tab and choose Activate Model Tab. To enter a paper space layout, click a layout tab. If you don't have tabs, simply click the Layout button on the status bar. By default, you see one floating viewport through which you can view your model. An example is shown in Figure 17.1. The paper space icon and the active layout tab confirm that you're looking at a paper space layout.

Tip

When you hover the mouse cursor over an inactive tab, you see a preview of that tab. ∎

FIGURE 17.1

When you display a layout, the layout is automatically created, with one floating viewport through which you can see your entire drawing.

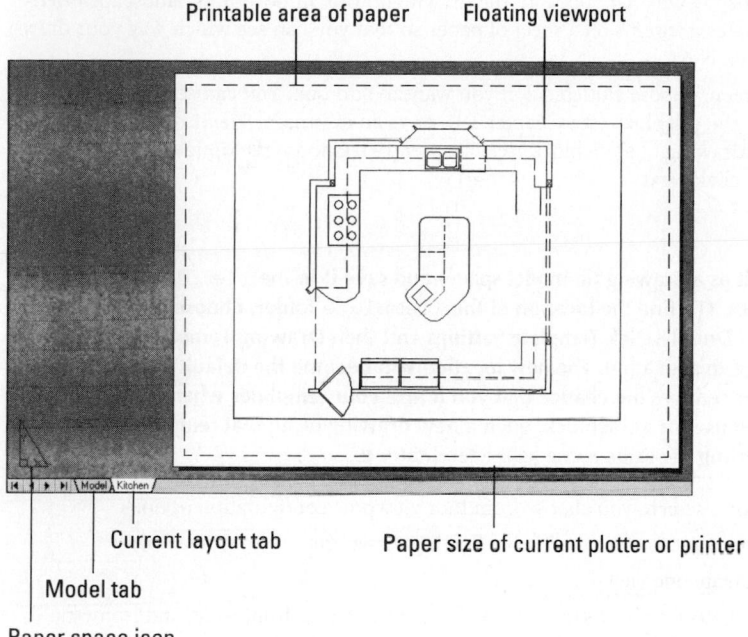

Printable area of paper Floating viewport

Current layout tab Paper size of current plotter or printer

Model tab

Paper space icon

 To switch back to model space, click the Model tab or button. Quick View Layouts help you switch between layouts when you have more than one. Click the Quick View Layouts button on the status bar to display a preview of the existing layouts, plus model space. Click the one you want to display. The previews disappear when you click in the drawing area. A small toolbar under the previews lets you pin the preview (so it doesn't disappear), create a new layout tab, publish the layout, or close the preview display. (I cover the PUBLISH command in Chapter 28.) You can also plot or publish by clicking the appropriate icon at the upper-left and upper-right corners of the preview, respectively.

Using the Layout Wizard

The Layout Wizard guides you through the process of laying out a drawing in paper space. Although you'll eventually want to lay out your drawings on your own, the Layout Wizard is one way to get started using a paper space layout.

To use the Layout Wizard, follow these steps:

1. Enter **layoutwizard** ↵ on the command line. You see the Begin screen, where you name the layout. This name will appear on the Quick View Layouts previews or on the layout tab at the bottom of the drawing window.

2. Type a name for the layout and click Next.

3. The second screen asks you to choose a configured plotter. This list also includes printers. For more information on configuring a plotter or printer, see Appendix A. Click Next after you're done.

4. On the third screen, specify a paper size and drawing units, and then click Next.

5. On the next screen, specify whether you want the drawing to plot in portrait or landscape orientation. The wizard rotates a letter *A* on a sheet of paper so that you can see which way your drawing will plot. Then click Next.

6. On the Title Block screen, choose a titleblock if you want to add one. You can add it as a block, which actually inserts the titleblock (see Chapter 18), or as an *external reference*, or *xref*, which references an outside drawing of a titleblock (see Chapter 19). Choose the option you prefer in the Type section, and click Next.

Note

To add your own titleblock, first create it as a drawing (in model space) and save it in the \Template folder, or create your own folder for your templates. (To find the location of the \Template folder, choose Application Button ⇨ Options, and click the Files tab. Double-click Template Settings and then Drawing Template File Location. To use your own folder, change this location. The new location will become the default location for all of your templates. Using your own folder reduces the chance that you'll lose your templates when you reinstall or upgrade.) If you have a template that you use for a titleblock, open a new drawing using that template and save it as a drawing in the \Template folder, using the same name as the template. ■

7. On the Define Viewports screen, you choose from four viewport configuration options:
   - Choose None if you want to create your own floating viewports.
   - Choose Single to create one viewport.
   - Choose Std. 3D Engineering Views to create a 2 × 2 array of top, front, side, and isometric views.
   - Choose Array to specify how many views you want, in rows and columns.

   You can also set the viewport scale. If you want to set the scale of each viewport individually, leave the default Scaled to Fit option for now. Then click Next.

Cross-Reference

For more information on scales, see Chapter 5. ■

8. On the Pick Location screen, the wizard prompts you to pick two corners to define the size of the viewport configuration that you chose. If you chose more than one viewport, these two corners define the extents of all the viewports combined, not the extents of the individual viewports. Click Next.

9. On the last screen, click Finish to close the wizard and return to your drawing.

Figure 17.2 shows the result of completing the wizard with a 2 × 1 array of viewports. Usually, you still need to pan the model and change the scale to get the view that you want in each viewport. I discuss that process later in this chapter.

Laying out a drawing in paper space on your own

The Layout Wizard is a good way to learn, but soon you'll want to create layouts on your own. The Layout Wizard creates only the floating viewports, leaving the scaling, panning, and other tasks up to you.

FIGURE 17.2

After completing the Layout Wizard, you now see your model in the viewport(s) that you created.

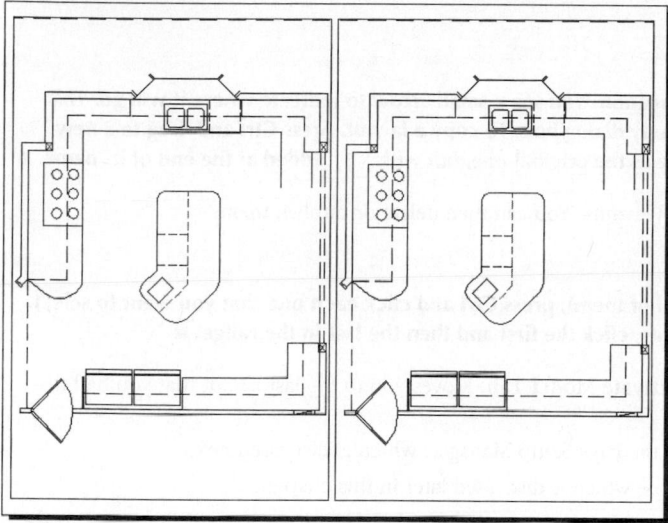

Managing layouts

You can have up to 256 layouts, including the Model tab for model space. If the tabs are not displayed, click the Quick View Layouts button on the status bar. Right-click a layout tab or preview, and choose from the following options on the shortcut menu:

- **New layout.** Creates a new layout.
- **From template.** Opens the Select File dialog box in which you can choose a .dwg, .dxf, or .dwt file. Click Open. You can then choose the layout or layouts that you want from the Insert Layout(s) dialog box. When you import a template, you import everything that exists on the paper space layout, including viewports, any existing text, the titleblock, and so on. (You can then get rid of anything you don't want, if necessary.)

Cross-Reference

If you import a layout from a drawing, any layers, linetypes, and such also come along for the ride. Use the PURGE command to get rid of anything that is not being used. See Chapter 11 for information on purging. You can also import a layout by using the DesignCenter. See Chapter 26 for details. ∎

- **Delete.** Deletes the selected layout. A warning dialog box appears. Click OK to delete the layout.
- **Rename.** Allows you to edit the name of a layout in-place on the tab or preview. Press Enter after you are done entering a new layout name.

Tip

You can also rename a layout tab by double-clicking it. Then just type the new layout name and press Enter. ∎

- **Move or Copy.** Opens the Move or Copy dialog box. To change the order of a layout, you choose the layout that you want the selected layout to be to the left of. You can also choose to move it to the end. Click Create a copy to copy the selected layout. (You can then rename it.) Click OK after you're done.

Tip

You can move a layout by dragging it to a new location. You see a small arrow to indicate where it will go. This method is much easier than using the Move or Copy dialog box. To copy a layout, press Ctrl and drag to a new location. The new layout takes on the same name as the original one, but with (2) added at the end of its name. ■

- **Select All Layouts.** Selects all layouts. You can then delete or publish them.

Tip

To select multiple layouts (but not necessarily all of them), press Ctrl and click each one that you want to select. By pressing Shift, you can select a range of layouts; click the first and then the last in the range. ■

- **Activate Previous Layout/Activate Model Tab.** Moves you to the last layout that you had displayed or to the Model tab.
- **Page Setup Manager.** Opens the Page Setup Manager, which is discussed next.
- **Plot.** Opens the Plot dialog box, which is discussed later in this chapter.
- **Publish Selected Layouts.** If two or more layouts are selected, you can use this item to start the PUBLISH command with the selected layouts in the list of sheets to publish. For more information on the PUBLISH command, see Chapter 28.
- **Import Layout as Sheet.** Imports the layout to a sheet in a sheet set. (See Chapter 26 for information on sheet sets.)
- **Export Layout to Model.** Saves the contents of the layout to a new drawing.
- **Hide Layout and Model Tabs.** Hides the layout tabs.

Tip

To move through the layouts (Model and all the layout tabs) from left to right, press Ctrl+Page Down. To move from right to left, press Ctrl+Page Up. ■

Note

If you choose not to display the model space and layout tabs, or use Quick Views Layout, you can use the LAYOUT, PLOT, and PUBLISH commands to accomplish many of the tasks available from the right-click menu. ■

Using the Page Setup Manager

When you click a new (unused) layout tab, or choose it from the layout button (or a preview from Quick View Layouts) on the status bar, by default you see one floating viewport. However, you can create and save page setups that store many of the settings that were explained previously in the discussion of the Layout Wizard. The value in saving page setups is that the settings are attached to the layout. If you have more than one layout, each with its own page setup, then you can quickly switch the page settings as you move from layout to layout. After you have page setups, you can manage them in the Page Setup Manager, as shown in Figure 17.3.

 To display the Page Setup Manager, right-click the active layout tab and choose Page Setup Manager. Alternatively, choose Output tab ⇨ Plot panel ⇨ Page Setup Manager.

FIGURE 17.3

The Page Setup Manager helps you to control your page setups.

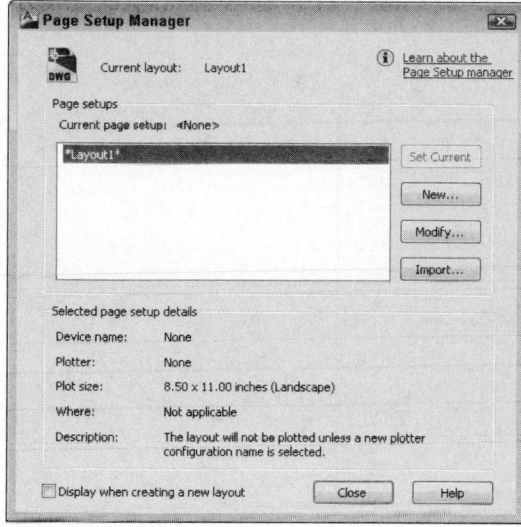

Note

When you check the Display When Creating a New Layout check box (at the bottom of the Page Setup Manager dialog box), the Page Setup Manager automatically appears each time you display a layout for the first time. If it does not appear, to make it display each time, right-click the current paper space layout tab (or a layout from Quick View Layouts) and choose Page Setup Manager; then check the check box. You can also specify whether you want the Page Setup Manager to appear when you click a new layout by choosing Application Button ⇨ Options and clicking the Display tab. Check or uncheck the Show Page Setup Manager for New Layouts check box. ∎

The Page Setup Manager lists your layouts and page setups. You can create a new page setup, modify an existing setup, or set a page setup current for the active layout. Click the Import button to import a page setup from another drawing.

To create a new page setup, click New. In the New Page Setup dialog box, enter a name for the page setup. Choose an existing page setup to start from so that you don't have to change all the settings, and click OK. The Page Setup dialog box appears, as shown in Figure 17.4.

Here's how to use the Page Setup dialog box:

- **Printer/Plotter.** Choose a printer or plotter from the drop-down list. For more information, see "Specifying plot settings" later in this chapter.
- **Paper size.** Choose a paper size from the drop-down list.
- **Plot area.** By default, the plot is set to the layout. However, you can choose to plot the current display, the drawing extents, a named view, or a window that you specify; the options that are available depend on whether you're on the Model tab or a layout tab.
- **Plot offset.** You can move the plot from the lower-left corner. Specify the X and Y offset in inches. If you aren't plotting the layout, but rather some smaller area, you can check the Center the Plot check box to center the plot on the paper.

FIGURE 17.4

The Page Setup dialog box.

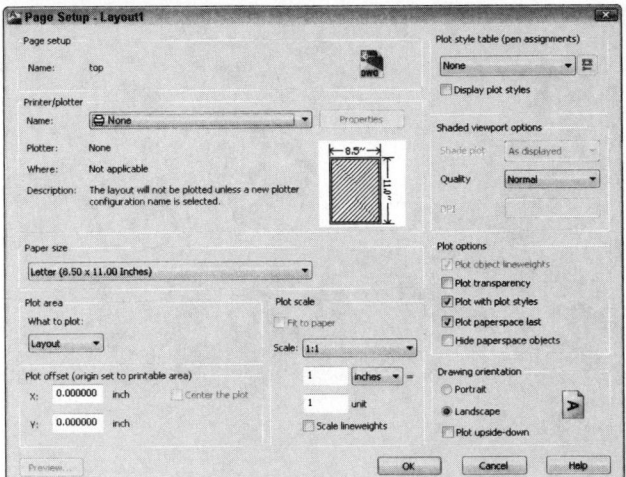

- **Plot scale.** Set the scale from the drop-down list. You can also type a scale in the text boxes. Because you scale your model in your floating viewports, you usually don't have to scale the layout as well. Therefore, you typically plot a layout in paper space at 1:1. If you're using lineweights and want to scale them, check the Scale Lineweights check box.

- **Plot style table.** Choose a plot style table if you want to use one. For more information, see the section "Working with Plot Styles" later in this chapter.

- **Shaded viewport options.** Use this feature to determine the display of the Model tab. (To set the display of a viewport on a layout, select the viewport and make the changes in the Properties palette.) With the Model tab displayed, choose one of the Shade Plot display options: As Displayed, Legacy Wireframe, Legacy Hidden, Conceptual, Hidden, Realistic, Shaded with Edges, Shades of Gray, Sketchy, Wireframe, X-Ray, Rendered, Draft, Low, Medium, High, or Presentation. (I cover these options in the "Setting hidden and shaded views for viewports" section later in this chapter.) You can also choose a quality (resolution) — Draft, Preview, Normal, Presentation, Maximum, or Custom. If you choose the Custom quality, you can specify the dots per inch (dpi). (AutoCAD only.)

- **Plot options.** Clear the Plot Object Lineweights check box if you used lineweights but don't want the lineweights to be plotted. Check the Plot Transparency check box if you want to plot transparent objects as they appear in the drawing area. Clear the Plot with Plot Styles check box if you assigned plot styles to layers or objects but don't want to plot them. (Plot styles are discussed later in this chapter.) Clear the Plot Paperspace Last check box in order to plot objects drawn on the paper space layout first. Check the Hide Paperspace Objects check box to hide lines of 3D objects that you created *in paper space*. (Later in this chapter, I explain how to hide lines of 3D objects that were created in model space, a more common situation.)

New Feature

Transparency is a new feature. Plotting with transparency may take more time. See Chapter 11 for more on transparency. ■

- **Drawing orientation.** Choose portrait or landscape. You can also choose to plot upside down. Use these settings to rotate a drawing when you plot it.

When you've completed your settings in the dialog box, click OK to return to the Page Setup Manager. You can see the new page setup in the list. To make the page setup active, click Set Current. Then click Close to return to your drawing.

Note
You can import settings saved in PCP or PC2 files from earlier releases of AutoCAD or AutoCAD LT. PCP and PC2 files contain plot settings that are similar to those that you set in the Page Setup dialog box. Click the layout that you want to use and enter pcinwizard on the command line. In the Import PCP or PC2 Settings Wizard, follow the instructions to import the PCP or PC2 file. ∎

Preparing layers

If necessary, create the layers that you need. If you want to insert a titleblock, create a separate layer for it. The actual viewports should also be on their own layer, because it's common to freeze that layer or set it to non-plottable, so that the borders don't show. Even if you want to plot the viewports, making them a different color from your model helps you to easily distinguish them.

Inserting a titleblock

Insert the titleblock. You can have a file that contains just the titleblock. You can also use a block or external reference. Putting the titleblock on your layout is common because it defines the edges of your paper and is not a real-life object. These qualities make it appropriate for paper space.

Creating floating viewports

Remember that you need a floating viewport to see your model on a paper space layout. The default is one floating viewport. Floating viewports have properties that are important to understand when you're creating layouts in paper space:

- Unlike tiled viewports (which I cover in Chapter 8), floating viewports are actual objects that you can erase, move, and stretch. They can — and should — be on separate layers, so that you can control the visibility of the viewport borders when desired. They don't need to take up the entire screen. You can change their size and location freely.

- In paper space, the crosshairs are not limited to one floating viewport.

- You can separately set the visibility of the UCS icon in each floating viewport.

- You can create as many viewports as you want, but don't go overboard!

- After you create floating viewports, you can switch to model space and work on your models while still on the layout. To do so, double-click inside a viewport. You do this mostly to adjust the view of the model in the viewport. In model space, floating viewports are similar to tiled viewports in that only one can be active at a time.

Whatever you draw in paper space does not affect your models; it exists only in paper space and disappears when you click the Model tab or button.

Because viewports are created on the current layer, you need to make the desired layer current. If the default viewport appears and you don't want it, select and delete it. Then to create floating viewports, choose View tab ⇨ Viewports panel while on a layout. Choose from the following items:

- **Named.** If you've saved a tiled viewport configuration, choose this option to open the Viewports dialog box. On the Named Viewports tab, choose the configuration from the list and click OK. In other words, you can use a tiled viewport configuration for floating viewports. See Chapter 8 for a full discussion of saving viewport configurations.

- **New.** Choose this item to open the Viewports dialog box, as shown in Figure 17.5. Choose one of the standard configurations, which you can see in the Preview box. Click OK to create the viewports.

Tip

If you have saved named views, you can immediately display them in a viewport. Click one of the viewports in the Preview pane and choose the named view from the Change View To drop-down list. At the same time, you can specify a visual style for each viewport. (I cover visual styles in Chapter 22; visual styles are available in AutoCAD only.) You can do this for each viewport that you create. ■

FIGURE 17.5

Use the Viewports dialog box to choose one of the standard configurations of floating viewports.

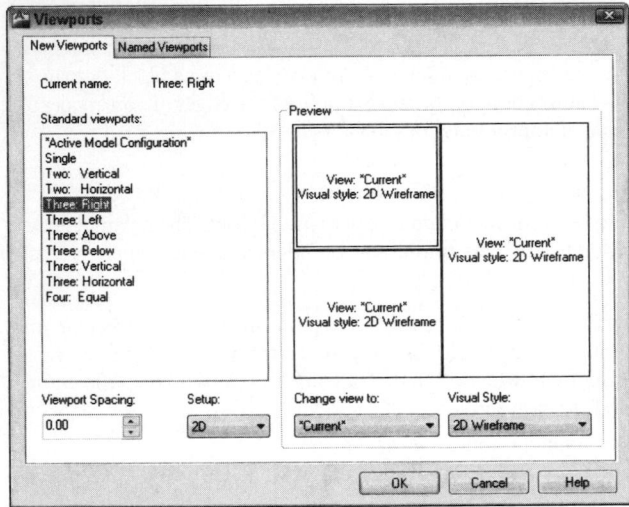

You can also create a polygonal viewport. Follow these steps:

1. Choose View tab ➪ Viewports panel ➪ -VPORTS drop-down list ➪ Create Polygonal.
2. At the `Specify start point:` prompt, pick a point.
3. At the `Specify next point or [Arc/Length/Undo]:` prompt, continue to specify points or right-click to choose one of the options. If you choose the Arc option, you see suboptions that are just like those you see when drawing an arc in a polyline.
4. Press Enter to use the Close option (which appears after you've specified two or more points) to complete the viewport.

You can create a viewport by converting an existing closed object, such as an ellipse. Choose View tab ⇨ Viewports panel ⇨ -VPORTS drop-down list ⇨ Create from Object. Then select the object.

As soon as you create a viewport, you see your drawing in the new viewport.

Note
The VPROTATEASSOC system variable controls the rotation of a view within a floating viewport. The default setting, 1, rotates the view when you rotate the viewport object. When you set this system variable to 0, the view within the viewport does not rotate when you rotate the viewport. ■

Returning to model space while on a layout

After creating viewports, the next step is to set the view in each viewport. To do this, you need to return to model space, while still on the layout, and make a viewport active. The active viewport shows a dark border. You can do this in two ways:

- Double-click inside the viewport that you want to become active.
- If you have layout tabs displayed, click PAPER on the status bar. (The button then says MODEL.) Then click the viewport that you want to become active.

To help you work more easily in a viewport, you can maximize the viewport temporarily without leaving the layout. Just double-click the selected viewport's border. Another way to maximize a viewport is to right-click with the viewport border selected and choose Maximize Viewport. The viewport takes up the entire screen, and you see a red border around the edge. You can draw, edit, zoom, or pan in the view as you normally would in model space; however, zooming and panning have no effect on the viewport's view or scale. When you've finished making the desired changes, right-click and choose Minimize Viewport. The commands that maximize and minimize a viewport are VPMAX and VPMIN. While you're in a layout, you can use the following buttons on the status bar:

 - Maximize Viewport: Maximizes the viewport to take up the entire screen

 - Minimize Viewport: Returns the viewport to its original size

 - Maximize Next Viewport: Switches to the next viewport, still maximized

 - Maximize Previous Viewport: Switches to the previous viewport, still maximized

Tip
To cycle from viewport to viewport while in model space, press Ctrl+R. (This technique doesn't work if the viewport is maximized.) ■

Setting viewport scale

You'll probably want to set the zoom for each viewport to exact scale. Each viewport can have its own scale, and you can set the zoom in three ways:

- If you're still in paper space, select the viewport on its border. Open the Properties palette. Choose Standard Scale and choose one of the standard scales from the drop-down list that appears.

- If you select the viewport, or double-click inside it to enter model space, the Viewport Scale pop-up list appears on the status bar, where you can choose a scale.

- From model space, choose Zoom Scale from the Zoom drop-down list on the Navigation bar or choose View tab ⇨ Navigate panel ⇨ Zoom drop-down list ⇨ Scale. You need to use the inverse of the scale factor with the xp option of the ZOOM command. If you have an architectural drawing at a scale of 1:48, type **1/48xp** ↵. (The abbreviation *xp* stands for "times paper space.")

After you scale each viewport, you need to go back and pan until you see what you want in the viewport. If necessary, you can also change the size of the viewport itself.

Locking the viewport

If you remain in model space with a viewport active, and then zoom in or out, you change the displayed scale of the model. After you set the scale, you should lock it to avoid this problem. To lock a viewport, select the viewport's border (while in paper space) and display the Properties palette. Choose Display Locked and then choose Yes from the drop-down list. (You can also select the viewport, right-click, and choose Display Locked ⇨ Yes.) Now, when you zoom in and out, only paper space objects will be affected.

Tip

You can lock and unlock any selected viewport on the status bar by using the lock icon to the left of the VP Scale pop-up list, or in the Quick Properties palette. ∎

Setting viewport size, placement, and display

To adjust the viewports themselves, return to paper space by clicking MODEL on the status bar or by double-clicking anywhere outside a viewport (but in the drawing area). You cannot access your models anymore, but you can now move and resize the viewports if necessary. You can use grips to stretch and move them, or use the STRETCH and MOVE commands.

The VPCLIP command enables you to redefine the boundary of an existing viewport. You can delete the boundary of a clipped viewport and change it to a rectangular viewport or create a polygonal boundary just as you do when creating a polygonal viewport.

 To redefine the boundary of a viewport, you must be in paper space. Choose View tab ⇨ Viewports panel ⇨ Clip to start the VPCLIP command. Select a clipped viewport boundary from paper space. At the `Select clipping object or [Polygonal/Delete] <Polygonal>:` prompt, you can select an object to use for the new boundary or press Enter to see the same prompts that you see when you create a polygonal viewport. Right-click and choose Delete to delete the boundary of a clipped viewport (one created by choosing an object or using the Polygonal option).

You can also turn viewports on and off. When a viewport is off, it doesn't display your model. Do this when the regeneration process becomes slow as a result of a large number of viewports or a complex drawing. To turn off a viewport, select it (in paper space); then right-click and choose Display Viewport Objects ⇨ No.

Controlling scale for noncontinuous linetypes

The PSLTSCALE system variable controls linetype scaling in paper space viewports. By default, it is set to 1 so that the paper space scale controls the scale of any noncontinuous linetypes. This lets you have viewports of differing scales while displaying linetypes identically. When you set PSLTSCALE to 0, linetype scales are based on the drawing units where the object was created (in either model space or paper space). Linetypes are still scaled by the LTSCALE factor. When you either change PSLTSCALE or change the zoom scale in a viewport with PSLTSCALE set to 1, you need to do a regen to update the linetype scales in each viewport.

Setting layer visibility and properties within a viewport

If you want, you can individually set layer visibility in floating viewports. For example, you might have some text or dimensions that appear in more than one floating viewport, but you may not want to show them more than once. Or perhaps you don't want a hatch to appear in one of the viewports. You must be in model space, so double-click in any viewport. To freeze a layer in an active viewport, click the Layer drop-down list in the Home tab ⇨ Layers panel. Find the layer that you want to freeze in that viewport and click the icon in the Freeze or Thaw in Current Viewport column. Click the top of the drop-down list to close it. That layer disappears in the active viewport.

You can also freeze/thaw layers in new viewports; these are viewports that you haven't yet created. Choose Home tab ⇨ Layers panel ⇨ Layer Properties to open the Layer Properties Manager. Click the icon for the layer that you want in the New VP Freeze column, and auto-hide or close the palette.

Cross-Reference
Remember that layers have a plottable/not plottable state. Therefore, you can set certain layers to not plottable if you don't want them to appear on the plot. For more information, see Chapter 11. ■

You can change the properties of a layer ¾ color, linetype, lineweight, transparency, and plot style ¾ by viewport. For example, you could make a layer that is green in model space display as blue in one of the viewports. This feature is called *layer overrides*.

To set layer properties for individual viewports, follow these steps:

1. Display a layout and double-click the desired viewport to enter model space from that layout.

2. Open the Layer Properties Manager. You now see five new columns ¾ VP Color, VP Linetype, VP Lineweight, VP Transparency, and VP Plot Style ¾ as shown in Figure 17.6.

FIGURE 17.6

When you open the Layer Properties Manager from model space on a layout, you see columns that let you override layer properties for the current viewport.

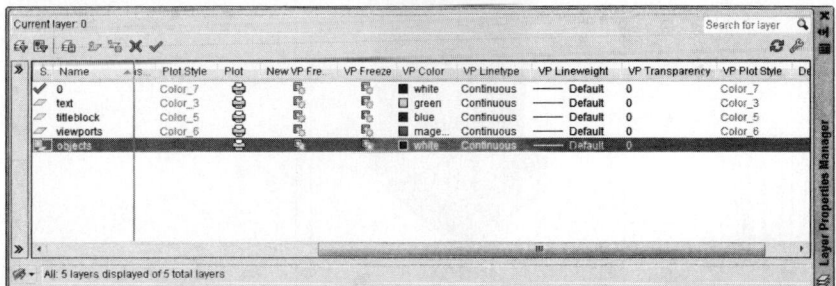

---

3. To override the properties of a layer for that viewport, you use the same method as for any other property. (See Chapter 11 for a full explanation of the Layer Properties Manager and layers.) For example, to override the color, click the layer's item in the VP Color column to open the Select Color dialog box, where you can choose a new color.

When you create a layer override, the Layer Properties Manager displays a light blue block in the column for the layer's name, the column for the property you overrode, and the VP column for that property. You see the same block for that layer in the Layer drop-down list in the Layers panel on the Home tab.

The block only appears when the affected viewport is current. A new layer filter, Viewport Overrides, appears in the Layer Filter list, which displays only layers that have viewport overrides.

You can remove overrides in several ways, depending on whether you want to remove all of a layer's overrides and whether you want to remove overrides in all viewports (as opposed to the current one). To remove an override, open the Layer Properties Manager and do one of the following:

- To remove one property override (such as Color) for a layer, right-click the Color column for the layer containing the override and choose Remove Viewport Overrides For⇨Color⇨In Current Viewport Only or In All Viewports.

- To remove all property overrides for a layer (or all selected layers), right-click the layer and choose Remove Viewport Overrides For⇨Selected Layers⇨In Current Viewport Only or In All Viewports.

- To remove all property overrides, right-click any layer and choose Remove Viewport Overrides For⇨All Layers⇨In Current Viewport Only or In All Viewports.

Setting hidden and shaded views for viewports

If you have a 3D drawing, you may want to hide back lines for objects in a viewport when you plot (similar to using the Hidden visual style on the Model tab). This procedure lets you hide lines in one viewport but not in others. You don't see the result until you plot or display a plot preview. You can also specify shading and rendered views for each viewport, from both model space and paper space layouts, as shown in Figure 17.7.

FIGURE 17.7

In this drawing, one viewport displays a wireframe, one a hidden view, and one a rendered view.

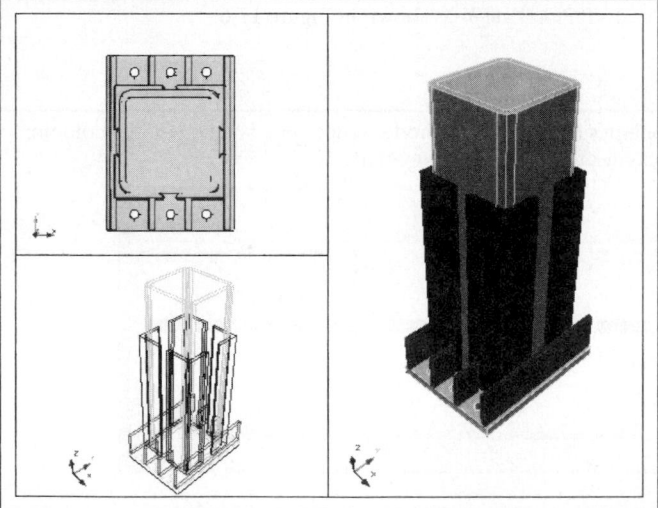

To choose the type of shaded view, select any viewport in paper space. Right-click, and choose Shade Plot. Then choose one of the following options:

- **As Displayed.** Plots the objects as they're currently displayed.
- **Wireframe.** Plots the objects in 2D wireframe display.
- **Hidden.** Plots the objects with back lines removed.

- **Conceptual.** Shades the model with flat colors on its faces (AutoCAD only).

- **Realistic.** Shades the model with a special color palette and gradients (AutoCAD only).

- **Shaded.** Displays surfaces with smooth shading in their assigned color (AutoCAD only).

- **Shaded with Edges.** Displays surfaces with smooth shading in their assigned color with visible edges (AutoCAD only).

- **Shades of Gray.** Shades the model using grayscale colors (AutoCAD only).

- **Sketchy.** Shades the model with black and white colors, but gives a hand-sketched look to the edges (AutoCAD only).

- **Wireframe.** Plots the objects in 3D wireframe display (AutoCAD only).

- **X-Ray.** Displays objects with transparency (AutoCAD only).

- **Rendered.** Plots objects using the default rendering settings. (See Chapter 25 for information on rendering. This option is not available in AutoCAD LT.) Express Tools (in AutoCAD only) include several commands for working with layouts:

  - The ALIGNSPACE command (choose Express Tools tab ⇨ Layout panel ⇨ Align Space) aligns objects in different viewports.

  - The VPSYNC command (choose Express Tools tab ⇨ Layout panel ⇨ Synchronize Viewports) changes the pan and zoom of a second viewport to match that of the first ("master") viewport that you select, so that the view of the objects is consistent (synchronized) from viewport to viewport.

  - The VPSCALE command (choose Express Tools tab ⇨ Layout panel (expanded) ⇨ List Viewport Scale) displays the scale from paper space to model space of the selected viewport.

  - The LAYOUTMERGE command (choose Express Tools tab ⇨ Layout panel ⇨ Merge Layout) moves all objects on one or more layouts that you specify to a single layout.

Annotating a layout

Before plotting, you may want to add notes, dimensions, and other annotations. You also need to pay attention to the scale of certain items in your viewports to make sure that they appear properly. For example, if you have one viewport at 1:1 and another at 1:4 and you show dimensions in both viewports, the dimensions will appear at different sizes in each viewport. This makes legibility difficult. Other items that may need adjustment are text, hatches, blocks, and linetypes.

You can annotate a drawing in two different ways:

- You can use *annotative objects,* which store representations at various scales and display them according to the scale of a specific viewport. They automate the process of scaling certain types of objects in viewports at various scales. You can create annotation objects for text, Mtext, dimensions, tolerances, leaders, multileaders, hatches, blocks, and block attributes. You create these objects in model space. For example, you can display objects at 1:1 in one viewport and 1:4 in another viewport, but the text will be the same size in each viewport. You can control the display of more types of objects in this way, but the process is somewhat more complex.

Cross-Reference

I discuss how to create annotative objects in the following chapters: text and Mtext in Chapter 13; dimensions, tolerances, multileaders, and leaders in Chapters 14 and 15; hatches in Chapter 16; and blocks and attributes in Chapter 18. ■

- You can annotate in paper space, in which case you create the annotations at their desired plotting size, without scaling them. This method is fairly easy, but it doesn't allow control over drawing objects such as blocks, attributes, and hatches.

Before these methods were available, for each object, you needed to create a separate layer for each scale, calculate the appropriate size for each object, and freeze layers in the viewports where you didn't want certain objects to appear. For example, if you wanted one text object to appear at 1:1 in one viewport and another text object to appear at 1:4 in another viewport, you created them at the appropriate size on different layers. Then you froze one layer in one viewport and the other layer in the other viewport. As you can imagine, this was a complicated process.

Using annotation objects on a layout

The purpose of using annotation objects is to automate the process of scaling these objects when you display them at different scales in different viewports. To use this feature, each of the objects needs to be annotative; you add this property when you create the object or its style (such as a text style).

Follow these steps to create and use annotation objects:

1. For the following objects, first create an annotative style:

   - **Mtext.** Use the default Annotative text style or create an annotative text style by checking the Annotative check box in the Text Style dialog box. At the same time, you use the Paper Text Height text box to set the final height you want for your text when you plot it on paper. See Chapter 13 for details.

   - **Dimensions.** Use the default Annotative dimension style or create an annotative dimension style by checking the Annotative check box in the Create New Dimension Style dialog box or on the Fit tab of the New (or Modify) Dimension Style dialog box. See Chapter 15 for details. Note that you need an annotative text style for the text in your annotative dimensions.

   - **Multileaders.** Use the default Annotative multileader style or create an annotative multileader style by checking the Annotative check box in the Create New Multileader Style dialog box or on the Leader Structure tab of the Modify Multileader Style dialog box. See Chapter 14 for details. Note that you need an annotative text style for the text in your multileaders.

Note

You can also create annotative leaders by using the QLEADER command. You don't create a special style for the leader, but you need to use an annotative text style for its text. You also need an annotative text style for block attributes (covered in Chapter 18). ■

2. Decide which objects you will display at which scales. If you don't know this when you draw your objects, you can add scales to them later. Remember that you might have objects that you want to appear at one scale, but not at another scale; however, you might have objects that you want to appear at more than one scale. Of course, you can change the scales of your objects later. A good way to help you figure out the scales that you need is to set up your viewports before you finish drawing, including their scales.

Note

When you turn the ANNOAUTOSCALE system variable on, it automatically adds scales to annotative objects as you add annotative scales. If you have an object that you want to have only one scale, then turn off this system variable. It's off by default. Use the icon on the right side of the status bar to the right of the Annotation Visibility button to toggle ANNOAUTOSCALE on and off. When on, there's a yellow lightning bolt; when off, the lightning bolt is gray. In general, leave ANNOAUTOSCALE off unless you want to update all the annotative objects in your drawing to a new annotative scale. ■

3. You need to assign an annotation scale to all objects that you want to be annotative. You can do so as you draw, or afterwards. To set the annotation scale as you draw, click the Annotation Scale button at the right side of the status bar to display the scale list and choose the scale you want. For example, choose 1:4 if you plan to display the object in a viewport at the 1:4 scale.

Cross-Reference

In Chapter 5, I explain scales in general and how to edit the scale list. It's easier to work with the scale list when it doesn't include scales that you don't use. You can also change the order of the list to place scales that you use most often at the top. ■

4. Create the object. The Select Annotation Scale dialog box opens the first time that you create an annotation object in your session, and requests that you choose an annotation scale. You can do so from the drop-down list in that dialog box. If you've already set the scale, just click OK. Remember that you can add and change annotation scales at any time.

5. Add other annotation scale to existing objects. You can do this in two ways:
   - If ANNOAUTOSCALE is on, to add another annotation scale to existing objects, you just choose another annotation scale by clicking the Annotation Scale button on the status bar.

   - If ANNOAUTOSCALE is off, you need to add annotation scales manually. Use this method if you don't want all objects to have every annotation scale that you'll be using. Select the object, right-click it, and choose Annotative Object Scale ⇨ Add/Delete Scales to open the Annotation Object Scale dialog box, as shown in Figure 17.8. You can also open the dialog box by choosing Annotate tab ⇨ Annotation Scaling panel ⇨ Add/Delete Scales, or by displaying the Properties palette, clicking the Annotative Scale item, and clicking the Ellipsis button that appears.

Note

When you hover the cursor over an annotation object, you see a special annotation icon near the cursor, which lets you know that the object is annotative. If an object has two or more annotation scales, you see a double annotation icon. ■

6. If you're manually adding an annotation scale, click the Add button. In the Add Scales to Object dialog box, choose the scale or scales that you want, and click OK twice to return to your drawing.

FIGURE 17.8

Use the Annotation Object Scale dialog box to add or delete annotation scales for selected objects.

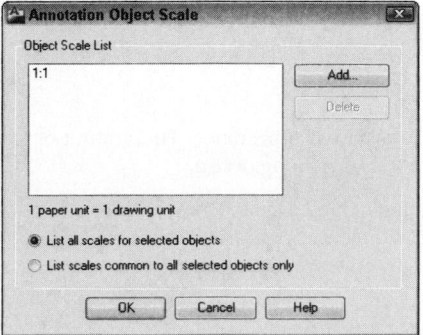

Note

The ANNOALLVISIBLE system variable determines whether you see all the scales for an object (On) or only the current scale (Off). Use the Annotation Visibility button on the status bar to the right of the Annotation Scale pop-up list. On the Model tab, turn this variable on to check that objects have the multiple annotation scales that you want them to have. On a layout, you usually want to keep this variable off, because seeing multiple scales is confusing.

The SELECTIONANNODISPLAY system variable specifies whether you see alternative sizes of an annotative object when you select it. The size of the object for the current annotative scale shows whether or not the object is selected, but when you select the object, you see all sizes if this system variable is set to 1, the default. However, objects at sizes for noncurrent scales are dimmed. ■

7. Switch to a layout and create the viewports that you need at the scales that you have chosen. Pan to get the display you want. Then lock the display, as explained earlier in this chapter.

Your annotation objects now automatically scale to match the scale of their viewport. If you don't get the results you want, you can check that the viewport scale and the annotative scale match by selecting a viewport and looking on the right side of the status bar. If they don't match, change the annotative scale from the pop-up list; your objects should now scale properly.

Tip

To synchronize the viewport and annotative scales, click the Annotation Scale Is Not Equal to Viewport Scale button to the right of the annotative scale list on the status bar. ■

Adding text and dimensions in paper space

Annotation that applies to the entire drawing, such as titleblock text, can be, and often is, created on the paper space layout. You can change to a text layer and use the TEXT or MTEXT command, as usual.

Sometimes you create an object in model space — perhaps some text or a logo — and want to move it to paper space, or vice versa. For example, you may want to move a text label that you inserted in model space into your titleblock, which you inserted in paper space. The CHSPACE command makes it easy to move objects from one space to the other, without worrying about scale differences.

To move an object in either direction, follow these steps:

1. Display a layout.
2. Switch to the space where the object that you want to move resides. For example, if you want to move text from model space to paper space, double-click inside the viewport containing the text to switch to model space.
3. Choose Home tab ⇨ Modify panel (expanded) ⇨ Change Space.
4. Select the object that you want to move.
5. Make the desired viewport active and press Enter.

The command scales objects to maintain the same visual appearance. The amount of scaling depends on the scaling of the viewport. If the viewport scale is 1:1, no scaling occurs.

In Chapters 14 and 15, I discussed dimensioning in model space, but you can dimension in paper space, as well. The Trans-Spatial Dimensioning feature automatically adjusts dimensions for the scale of the viewport. These paper space dimensions are fully associative. Dimensioning in paper space has several advantages:

- You don't have to worry about the size of the individual dimension components themselves, such as the text and the arrows. If you plot from paper space, you plot at 1:1 scale.

- If you don't need to scale other objects (such as hatches and blocks), dimensioning in paper space is probably simpler than using the annotative feature.

- You can place the dimensions outside the border of the floating viewport, which may make it easier to fit the dimensions. (On the other hand, you may find it harder to fit the dimensions if you have other viewports on the layout.)

- You can easily dimension just one view of the model.

Tip

If you create dimensions in a viewport in paper space and then zoom or pan in that viewport, the objects and the dimension get out of sync. Use the DIMREGEN command on the command line to reset the dimension to match its object. ∎

You still need to scale the size of the dimension to your viewport scale, including the text, arrows, and so on, as follows:

1. Open the Dimension Style Manager.
2. Choose the dimension style that you want to use and click Modify.
3. On the Fit tab, choose Scale Dimensions to Layout.
4. Click OK and then click Close.

When you follow this procedure, all the dimensions using the dimension style that you chose appear the same size on your final plot.

Note

Drawings created in earlier releases (before AutoCAD 2002 and AutoCAD LT 2002) do not automatically have the new associative dimensions. If necessary, change the DIMASSOC system variable's value to 2. Also, you usually need to use the DIMREASSOCIATE command to associate existing dimensions to their objects. See Chapter 14 for more information on associative dimensions. ∎

Export a layout to model space of a new drawing

You can create a new drawing by exporting a layout tab. All visible layout tab objects appear in model space in the new drawing. Right-click a layout tab (or preview in Quick View Layouts) and choose Export Layout to Model (the EXPORTLAYOUT command) to open the Export Layout to Model Space Drawing dialog box. The command creates a default filename based on the current drawing and layout names. You can change the name and location. Click Save. You can then choose to open the new drawing immediately.

Saving a layout template

After you do all the work to create a layout, you can save it as a template so that you can use it in other drawings. (The template includes all objects on the layout.) Here's how:

1. Type **layout** ↵ on the command line.
2. At the prompt, right-click and choose SAveas.

3. At the `Enter layout to save to template <Layout2>:` prompt, press Enter to save the current layout, the name of which appears in brackets, or type the name of another layout.

4. The Create Drawing File dialog box opens, with the `Template` folder active. The Files of Type drop-down list shows AutoCAD (LT) Drawing Template File (`*.dwt`). Type a name for the drawing template and click Save.

To use the template to add a new layout in any drawing, right-click a layout tab (or preview in Quick View Layouts) and choose From Template, as explained earlier in this chapter.

On the DVD
The drawings used in the following exercise on laying out a drawing in paper space, `ab17-a.dwg` **and** `ab-17-a-blk.dwg`, **are in the** `Drawings` **folder on the DVD.** ■

STEPS: Laying Out a Drawing in Paper Space

1. Open `ab17-a.dwg` from your DVD.

2. Save the file as `ab17-01.dwg` in your `AutoCAD Bible` folder. This file already has a text style, dimension style, and multileader style that are annotative. If you do not have tabs displayed at the bottom of the drawing area, right-click the Model button on the status bar and choose Display Layout and Model Tabs.

3. Click the Layout1 tab. Right-click the tab and choose Page Setup Manager.

4. Click New. In the New Page Setup Name text box, type **PrinterDraft**. Click OK. The Page Setup dialog box opens.

5. In the Paper Size section, the paper size should be set to Letter (8.50 × 11 inches). (This enables you to plot to a printer if you don't have a plotter available.) In the Shaded Viewport Options section, choose Draft from the Quality drop-down list. Choose your printer from the Name drop-down list of the Printer/Plotter section. Click OK to return to the Page Setup Manager.

6. The `PrinterDraft` page setup should be highlighted. Click Set Current. Click Close.

7. Double-click the Layout1 tab. Type **2-view** ↵.

8. From Home tab ⇨ Layers panel, click the Layer drop-down list arrow. Choose the `TB` layer to make it current.

9. Choose Insert tab ⇨ Block panel ⇨ Insert to open the Insert dialog box. Click Browse. Choose `ab17-a-blk.dwg` from the DVD and click Open.

10. Uncheck any checked Specify On-Screen check boxes. Click OK to insert the titleblock, as shown in Figure 17.9.

11. On the Home tab, choose the `Np` layer from the Layer drop-down list to make it current.

12. Choose View tab ⇨ Viewports panel ⇨ New. In the Viewports dialog box, choose Single, and click OK. At the first prompt, choose ❶, shown in Figure 17.9. At the second prompt, choose ❷.

13. Right-click and choose Repeat VPORTS. Again, choose Single and click OK. At the prompt, choose ❸. At the next prompt, choose ❹. You now see the drawing in the two viewports.

 14. Check that the ANNOAUTOSCALE button on the status bar is off. (Its tooltip reads `Automatically add scales to annotative objects when the annotation scale changes`. When the button is selected, it has a tiny yellow annotative icon.)

FIGURE 17.9

The titleblock inserted into paper space.

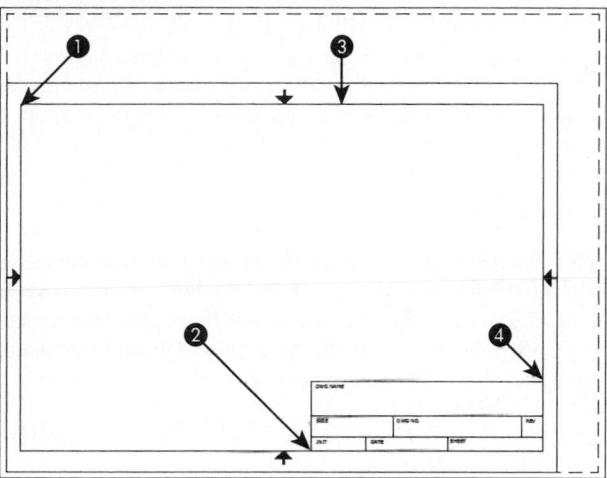

15. Click the border of the left viewport. Press Ctrl+1 to open the Properties palette, if it isn't already open. Choose Standard Scale from the Properties palette. Click the Standard Scale drop-down arrow and choose 1:2 from the scale list. Again in the Properties palette, click the Annotation Scale item and choose 1:2. Press Esc to deselect the left viewport.

16. Select the right viewport and set its standard scale to 1:1. Deselect the right viewport.

17. Double-click inside each viewport in turn to switch to model space, and pan until you see the view shown in Figure 17.10. It doesn't have to match exactly. Notice that the dimension text objects don't display in the left (1:2) viewport, because they only have a 1:1 scale assigned to them.

18. Click the Model tab. Change the current layer to HATCH. Choose Home tab ⇨ Draw panel ⇨ Hatch. You'll leave the defaults of the ANSI31 pattern, 1.0000 Scale, and 0 Angle. Choose Hatch Creation tab ⇨ Options panel ⇨ Annotative. At the `Pick internal point or [Select objects/seTtings]:` prompt, click inside the ellipse at the lower section of the handwheel. Press Enter to end the HATCH command.

Note

If you pass the cursor over the hatch, you see the annotative icon. When you move the cursor over the dimensions and the multileader, you see that they are also annotative. This is because they were created using annotative styles. ∎

19. Using the Annotation Scale pop-up list on the status bar, change the current scale to 1:2. You need to add this scale to the annotative objects. Select all the dimensions, except the two diameter dimensions in the lower-right quadrant of the handwheel (which read ∅ 1 and ∅ 7/8) and the multileader in the upper-right quadrant of the wheel (that contains the text R3/8). Also select the

multileader below the handwheel and the hatch that you just drew. Choose Annotate tab ⇨ Annotation Scaling panel ⇨ Add Current Scale. Notice that the size of the dimensions changes.

20. On the status bar, change the annotation scale back to 1:1. The dimensions, multileaders, and hatch return to their original sizes.

21. Switch to the 2-view tab. You should see that the text of the dimensions in both viewports is the same size, as is the hatch pattern. Note that the diameter dimensions in the lower-right quadrant that don't have a 1:2 annotation scale don't appear in the left-hand viewport, which has a 1:2 annotation scale. Similarly, the multileader in the upper-right quadrant (with the text R3/8) also appears only in the right-hand 1:1 viewport because it has a 1:1 annotation scale only.

Note

If you don't see these results, first select each viewport in turn, making sure that both the viewport scale and the annotation scale are the same (look in the Properties palette), and that the left viewport is set to 1:2 and the right viewport is set to 1:1. Also, return to model space, select the dimensions that appear incorrect, right-click them, and choose Annotative Object Scale ⇨ Add/Delete Scales. In the Annotation Object Scale dialog box, make sure that the scales are correct; if not, add or delete a scale as necessary. ∎

22. Double-click the right-hand viewport to enter model space from the layout with that viewport current. You'll create a layer override for the hatch. Display the Layer Properties Manager. In the VP Color column, click the HATCH row, which reads cyan. In the Select Color dialog box that opens, choose the Red swatch. The hatch now displays as red in the right viewport.

23. Double-click inside the left viewport. Go to Home tab ⇨ Layers panel ⇨ Layer drop-down list and click the icon in the third column (Freeze or Thaw in Current Viewport) next to the HATCH layer to freeze that layer in the viewport.

24. From the same Layer drop-down list, click the name of the Dim layer to make it current. Go to Annotate tab ⇨ Dimensions panel ⇨ Dimension Style drop-down list and choose STYLE1. This dimension style is set to be scaled to paper space.

25. Double-click outside a viewport, but in the drawing area, to enter paper space. Go to Annotate tab ⇨ Dimensions panel ⇨ Dimensions drop-down list and choose Linear. In the left viewport, use the Quadrant object snap to create a dimension from the top quadrant to the bottom quadrant of the ellipse below the center of the handwheel. Place the dimension to the left of the ellipse. The ellipse is correctly dimensioned at ¾ unit, although it is zoomed in to a 1:2 scale. (It's too small, however.) Because you wouldn't dimension using annotative dimensions in paper space, erase the new dimension that you just created; it was just an exercise to show how dimensioning in paper space works.

26. Go to Home tab ⇨ Layers panel ⇨ Layer drop-down list and change the current layer to TEXT. Click the Layer drop-down arrow again. Click the icon in the second column (Freeze or Thaw in ALL Viewports) next to the NP layer to freeze the layer containing the viewport borders. Click the top of the drop-down list to close it.

27. Choose Annotate tab ⇨ Text panel ⇨ Text drop-down list ⇨ Single Line. Complete the text in the titleblock at the default height, as shown in Figure 17.10. (You'll probably find this easier if you turn Object Snap off on the status bar.)

28. Save your drawing.

FIGURE 17.10

The completed drawing layout is now ready for plotting.

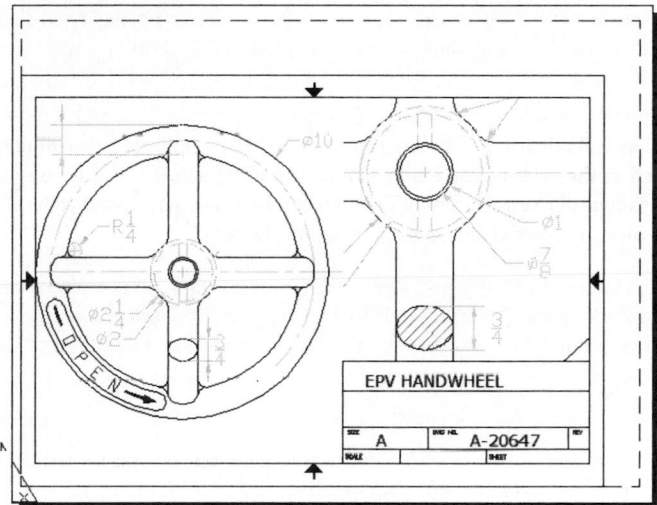

Working with Plot Styles

A *plot style* is an object property, like color, linetype, lineweight, transparency, or layer. Just as you can assign a color to an object and also to a layer, you can assign a plot style to an object and also to a layer. Because a plot style determines how an object is plotted, its function is to override the object's original properties. However, a plot style is more complex than a color or a linetype because it contains a set of properties, such as color-related properties, linetype, lineweight, and line styles. The use of plot styles is completely optional. Without plot styles, objects are simply plotted according to their properties.

You can use plot styles to create several types of plots for one drawing or layout. Plot styles also enable you to use some of the printer-like capabilities of plotters, such as screening and dithering.

Plot styles are stored in plot-style tables, which are files that you can create and edit. You generally follow these steps to use plot styles in your plots:

1. Create a plot-style table.
2. Attach a plot-style table to a layout.
3. Set the plot-style property for a layer or object.
4. Plot.

Setting the plot-style mode

Plot styles come in two types, color-dependent and named. Before you work with plot styles, you need to choose which type you want to use:

- **Color-dependent plot styles,** the default, are saved in color-dependent plot-style tables, which are files with a file extension of .ctb. You assign plotting properties based on object color.

The disadvantage of color-dependent plot styles is that you can't assign different properties to two objects that have the same color.

- **Named plot styles** are saved in named plot-style tables, which are files with a file extension of .stb. Named plot styles let you assign plotting properties to objects regardless of their color. Therefore, two objects of the same color can be plotted differently.

Note

Dimensions and tables don't take full advantage of named plot styles. They support color-dependent plot styles only for their components, such as the arrows and extension lines of dimensions. Also, if you use visual styles in 3D drawings (any visual style except 2D Wireframe), plot styles are ignored. The visual style takes precedence in determining how the drawing plots. I cover visual styles in Chapter 22. ∎

After you decide which type of plot style you want to use, you set the mode by choosing Application Button ⇨ Options and clicking the Plot and Publish tab. Click the Plot Style Table Settings button. In the Plot Style Table Settings dialog box, choose either Use Color Dependent Plot Styles *or* Use Named Plot Styles.

In the same location, you can set the following:

- Default plot-style table (the default is acad.stb or acadlt.stb for named and acad.ctb or acadlt.ctb for color-dependent plot styles).
- Default plot style for layer 0 (the default is Normal for named plot styles and ByColor for color-dependent plot styles).
- Default plot style for objects (the default is ByLayer for named plot styles and ByColor for color-dependent plot styles).

The default plot style for objects is the current plot style for new objects, and is similar in concept to the current color or layer for new objects. After you're done, click OK.

It is important to understand that changing the plot-style mode does not affect the current drawing. To use the new setting, you must either open a new drawing or open a drawing from a previous release that has not been saved in an AutoCAD 2000/AutoCAD LT 2000 or later format. Moreover, any template that you use to open a new drawing must be set to use named plot styles. AutoCAD and AutoCAD LT come with a template called acad -Named Plot Styles.dwt (acadlt -Named Plot Styles.dwt) that you can use, or you can create your own template. Several other templates have the words "Named Plot Styles" in their title, indicating that they include the setting for named plot styles.

Caution

If you have color-dependent plot styles for existing pre–AutoCAD 2000/AutoCAD LT 2000 drawings (and want to keep them that way) but decide to use named plot styles for new drawings, you need to avoid opening any of the existing drawings while you're in named plot-style mode. If you do, they'll be changed to named plot-style mode. Remember that pre–Release 2000 drawings don't have any plot styles — plot settings had to be according to color. You might consider setting the mode to color-dependent plot styles, creating a script file to open and save all your existing drawings as AutoCAD 2011 or AutoCAD LT 2011 drawings, and only then change the mode to named plot styles. Chapter 30 explains how to create script files. ∎

You can convert color-dependent plot-style tables to named plot-style tables by using the CONVERTCTB command. You can then use the CONVERTPSTYLES command to convert the drawing so that it uses named plot styles. You can also use the CONVERTPSTYLES command to convert a drawing from using named plot styles to using color-dependent plot styles.

Creating a plot-style table

Each named plot-style table comes with a default plot style called Normal. By default, the plot style for each layer in a named plot style drawing is Normal. Figure 17.11 shows the Normal plot style, shown in a plot-style table with a Style1 that you can use to create a new plot style. The Normal plot style is grayed out because you cannot change it.

The Table View tab lists your plot styles side by side. Each plot style includes settings for the various categories that are available in a plot style.

Plot-style tables are stored in the `Plot Styles` folder. The default plot-style tables are `acad.stb` or `acadlt.stb` (named plot style) and `acad.ctb` or `acadlt.ctb` (color-dependent plot style).

Note

To find the location of the `Plot Styles` **folder, choose Application Button ➪ Options and click the Files tab. Double-click Printer Support File Path and then double-click Plot Style Table Search Path.** ■

You can import plot configuration files (PCP and PC2 files) or the Release 14 configuration file (`acadr14. cfg`) to create plot-style tables or create plot-style tables from scratch.

FIGURE 17.11

The Normal plot style is the default plot style for layers.

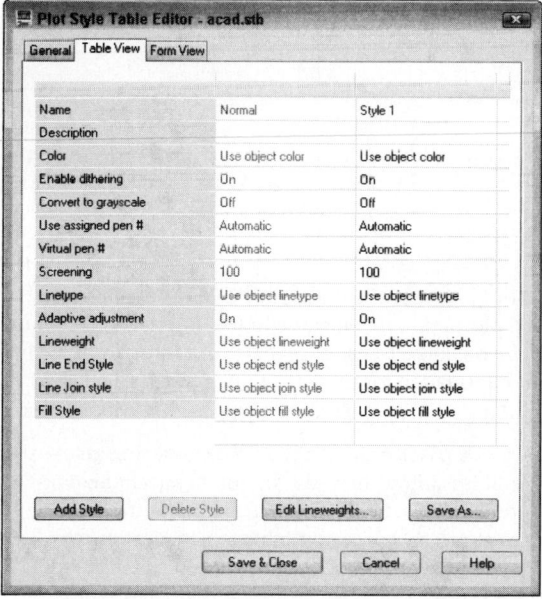

Creating a named plot-style table

To use plot styles, you can add a plot style to an existing plot-style table or create a new plot-style table. Each plot-style table is a separate file. To create a named plot-style table, use the Add Plot Style Table

Wizard. You can access this wizard by choosing Application Button ⇨ Print ⇨ Manage Plot Styles to open the \Plot Styles folder. (You may have to click the down arrow at the bottom of the Print menu to see this item.) Then double-click the Add-A-Plot Style Table Wizard icon. From this folder you can also access existing plot-style tables for editing.

To use the wizard, follow these steps:

1. The wizard opens with an explanation of plot-style tables. Choose Next.

2. On the Begin screen, shown in Figure 17.12, choose the source that you want to use for the plot-style table. You can start from scratch or use an existing plot-style table. Choose Use My R14 Plotter Configuration (CFG) to use the pen assignments from the acadr14.cfg file. If you have a PCP (Release 12/13) or PC2 (Release 14) configuration file, you can use it to import the settings from that file into the plot-style table. Then click Next.

FIGURE 17.12

Choose the source that you want to use for the new plot-style table.

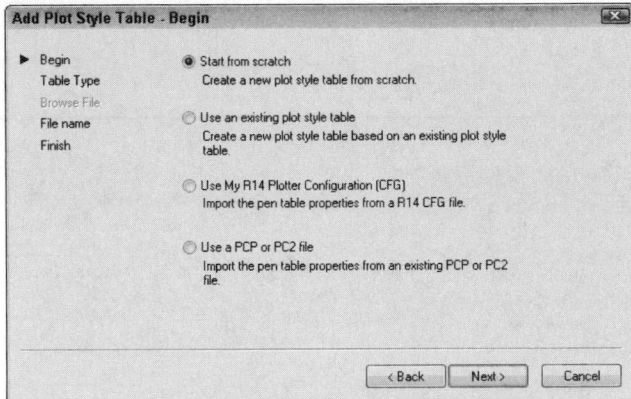

3. If you chose to start from scratch or to use R14 Plotter Configuration or PCP/PC2 files, choose whether you want color-dependent or named plot styles. If you chose to use an existing file as a basis for the plot-style table, choose the file. If you chose to use a CFG file, you must also specify the plotter, because the CFG file can contain information for more than one plotter. Click Next.

4. On the File Name screen, type a name for the plot-style table file. Click Next.

5. On the Finish screen, an option labeled Use this plot style table for new and pre-AutoCAD 2011 drawings may be available. If it is, then check this option to attach the plot-style table to all new drawings by default. You don't have to use the plot styles, but they will be available. Clear the option if you don't want to attach this plot-style table to new drawings by default. You can also click Plot Style Table Editor to edit plot styles immediately. You can edit plot styles at any time, as explained next. Click Finish.

Creating a color-dependent plot-style table

Prior to AutoCAD and AutoCAD LT 2000, plotting was integrally related to object color. For example, you assigned pens in a pen plotter according to color. If you want to continue to create settings based on color, you can create a color-dependent plot-style table. To do this, follow the same steps for creating a named plot-style table. On the Pick Plot Style Table screen, choose Color-Dependent Plot Style Table and click Next. The rest of the steps are the same.

The result is a CTB file with 255 styles, one for each color. You cannot add, delete, or rename these styles, but you can edit their properties. For example, you can specify that objects on color 1 should be plotted with no lineweight or a specific linetype. However, be aware that color-dependent plot styles result in slower display regeneration.

In this chapter, I focus on named plot styles. However, creating color-dependent plot styles is very similar.

Editing a plot-style table

After you create a plot-style table, you can edit it by adding, naming, and deleting its plot styles (for named plot-style tables only) and, of course, creating the settings that you want for the plot styles. To open the Plot Style Table Editor, do one of the following:

A. Choose Plot Style Table Editor from the Finish screen of the Add Plot Style Table Wizard.

B. Choose Application Button ⇨ Print ⇨ Manage Plot Styles (scroll down if necessary to see this item) and double-click any existing CTB or STB file.

C. From the Page Setup dialog box (discussed earlier in this chapter) or the Plot dialog box (discussed later in this chapter), choose the named plot-style table that you want to edit from the Plot Style Table drop-down list, and click Edit.

D. From the Select Plot Style dialog box (accessed from the Layer Properties Manager after you click the Plot Style column), choose Editor.

The Plot Style Table Editor's Table View tab was shown in Figure 17.11. The Form View tab is shown in Figure 17.13. You can edit styles by using either view tab. The Form View tab focuses on one style at a time and provides better visual confirmation of some of the choices. The Table View tab lets you compare your style to existing styles as you work.

A new Plot Style Table includes one default style, Normal. To add a style, click Add Style. Then click the style name and type a more descriptive name for the style.

Caution

You can't rename a plot style that is currently assigned to an object or layer, so it's best to name it when you create it. You can't change the names of styles in a color-dependent plot-style table. ■

Each plot style has a description area that you can use to provide a more detailed description of the plot style. For example, you could summarize a plot style as "color black & no lineweight."

FIGURE 17.13

The Form View tab of the Plot Style Table Editor.

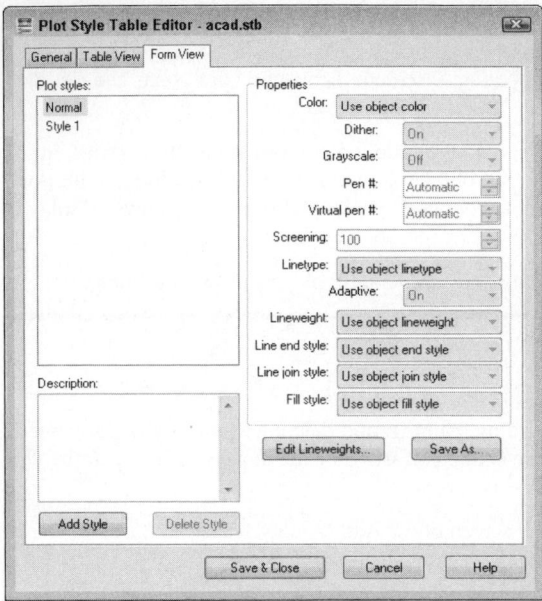

Now go through each of the properties and make any changes that you want. In Table view, you need to click the property in the Plot Styles column for a drop-down list to appear. The properties are as follows:

- **Color.** You can specify a color other than the default, which is Object Color. For example, you might want to create a plot style that plots everything in black. Choose Select Color and define a color in the Select Color dialog box. (See Chapter 11 for an explanation of this dialog box.)

- **Dither.** Dithering uses dot patterns to approximate a greater range of colors. Not all plotters support dithering. Dithering can make thin lines and dim colors look unclear.

- **Grayscale.** Converts objects to grayscale, if supported by the plotter. You could use grayscale to de-emphasize certain layers or to print a draft plot on a black-and-white laser printer.

- **Pen # and Virtual Pen #.** These settings apply to pen plotters (a Virtual Pen # applies to non-pen plotters that simulate pen plotters) and specify the pen for the object that is assigned the plot style.

- **Screening.** Specifies the amount of ink used for a color. The range is from 0 (no ink; that is, white) to 100 (full intensity of the color). Some plotters, such as pen plotters, do not support screening. You could use a 50 percent screen to de-emphasize certain layers, such as those containing proposed changes, or to save ink.

- **Linetype.** You can specify a linetype other than the default, Object Linetype, to override the object's linetype when you plot. For example, you might want to have the option to plot certain objects that are not yet approved in a dashed or dotted linetype.

- **Adaptive.** Choose On to adapt the scale of a linetype to complete the linetype pattern on the object. Choose Off if maintaining the proper linetype scale is essential.

- **Lineweight.** You can specify a lineweight other than the default, Object Lineweight.

- **Line End Style.** When you use lineweights, you need to specify how you want to end lines. You can choose from Butt, Square, Round, and Diamond. The default is Object End Style.
- **Line Join Style.** Specifies how objects with lineweights are joined. The choices are Miter, Bevel, Round, and Diamond. The default is Object Join Style.
- **Fill Style.** You can choose from Solid, Checkerboard, Crosshatch, Diamonds, Horizontal Bars, Slant Left, Slant Right, Square Dots, and Vertical Bar. The default is Object Fill Style.

To delete a style, select it and click Delete Style. In Table view, click a style's gray column head to select it. After you're done, click the Save & Close button.

Attaching a plot-style table to a layout

As soon as you have your plot-style table and the plot styles that you want, you can start using the plot styles. The first step is to attach the table to a layout (including model space). Remember that you can attach different plot-style tables to different layouts (or the Model tab).

To attach a plot-style table to a layout or the Model tab, display the tabs if necessary (right-click the Model or Layout button on the status bar and choose Display Model and Layout tabs), and follow these steps:

1. Choose the layout or Model tab.
2. Right-click the tab and choose Page Setup Manager.
3. Choose a page setup and click Modify (or click New and create a new one).
4. In the Plot Style Table section of the Page Setup dialog box, choose a plot-style table from the Plot Style Table drop-down list.
5. If you're on the Model tab, choose Yes or No to the question asking whether you want to apply the plot-style table to the Model tab only or to all layouts. If you're on a layout tab, check the Display Plot Styles check box to see the result of the plot styles in your drawing.
6. Click OK. Then click Close to return to your drawing.

To see the result, you still need to attach a plot style to a layer or object, as I explain in the next section.

Setting the plot-style property for a layer or object

To use a plot style, you need to assign it to a layer or an object. The plot style is only applied if the plot style is first defined in the plot-style table that you've assigned to a layout (or Model tab).

To set the plot style for a layer, follow these steps:

1. Display the layout tab that you want to use, and open the Layer Properties Manager.
2. Choose the layer whose plot style you want to change, and click the Plot Style column to open the Select Plot Style dialog box.
3. Choose the plot-style table from the Active Plot Style Table list at the bottom of the dialog box.
4. Choose a plot style from the Plot Styles list.
5. Click OK to return to your drawing. If you are using the Layer Properties Manager dialog box, click OK again.

If you checked Display Plot Styles in the Page Setup dialog box, as explained in the preceding section, you should see the result of the plot style. If not, type **regenall** ↵.

To set the plot style for an object, select the object and display the Properties palette (Ctrl+1). Choose the Plot Style item, and choose a plot style from the drop-down list. You can attach a plot style to a viewport (which is an object), but the plot style doesn't affect the objects in the viewport.

You can view the effects of plot styles in two ways:

- To display plot styles in your drawing all the time, display the layout for which you want to view the plot style. Right-click the layout's tab and choose Page Setup Manager. Then select the page setup associated with the layout and click Modify. In the Page Setup dialog box, check Display Plot Styles in the Plot Style Table section. Click OK and then click Close to return to the drawing window. (You may have to use REGENALL to see the result.)

- You can also see the effects of plot styles in a preview of your plot. Choose Plot from the Quick Access toolbar and click Preview.

On the DVD

The drawing used in the following exercise on creating and applying a plot style, ab17-b.dwg, is in the Drawings folder on the DVD. ■

STEPS: Creating and Applying a Plot Style

1. With any drawing open, choose Application Button ⇨ Options and click the Plot and Publish tab. Now click the Plot Style Table Settings button and take note of the current setting under Default Plot Style Behavior for New Drawings. Remember this setting so that you can set it back to its original setting at the end of the exercise.

2. Click Use Named Plot Styles (unless that is the current setting) and click OK twice.

3. Open ab17-b.dwg from your DVD.

4. Save the file as ab17-02.dwg in your AutoCAD Bible folder.

5. Choose Application Button ⇨ Print ⇨ Manage Plot Styles to open the Plot Styles window. Double-click the Add-A-Plot Style Table Wizard item. Click Next.

6. In the Begin screen, choose Start from Scratch and click Next. In the next screen, choose Named Plot Style Table (it's probably already selected) and click Next. In the File Name screen, type **ab17-02** and click Next.

7. In the Finish screen, click Finish. (Don't check Use for New and Pre-AutoCAD 2011 Drawings, because this is just an exercise.)

8. Return to the Plot Styles folder window, which should still be open on the Windows task bar. (If not, choose Application Button ⇨ Print ⇨ Manage Plot Styles.) You could have opened the new plot-style table from the wizard, but this is how you usually do it when you haven't just finished creating a table. Double-click ab17-02.stb.

9. In the Description box of the General tab, type **AutoCAD Bible Plot Style Table**.

10. Click the Table View tab. Click the Add Style button. Click the name Style1. Type **Black Color** and press Enter.

11. Click the Color row under the Black Color column, and choose Black from the drop-down list. Click Save & Close. Close the Plot Styles folder window.

12. If you don't have Model and layout tabs displayed, right-click the Model or Layout button on the status bar and choose Display Layout and Model Tabs. Select Layout1, right-click it, and then choose Page Setup Manager from the shortcut menu.

13. In the Page Setup Manager, choose New. In the New Page Setup dialog box, enter **AB 2011** and click OK.

14. In the Page Setup dialog box, make sure that your printer or plotter is listed in the Printer/Plotter section. Then choose ab17-02.stb from the Plot Style Table drop-down list. Check the Display Plot Styles check box and click OK. Select AB 2011 and click Set Current. Click Close. This assigns the plot-style table to Layout1.

15. Choose Home tab ⇨ Layers panel ⇨ Layer Properties. In the Layer Properties Manager, choose A-DETL-PATT (the layer with the magenta color). Click that layer's Plot Style column to open the Select Plot Style dialog box. Choose Black Color and click OK. The Plot Style for the A-DETL-PATT layer now shows as Black Color. Click OK if you are using the Layer Properties Manager dialog box and not the palette.

16. Type **regenall** ⏎. The objects on A-DETL-PATT (the diagonal marks on the mirror) now show as black, and will plot as black.

17. Click PAPER on the status bar to switch to model space.

18. Select the bottom horizontal line of the sink cabinet.

19. Open the Properties palette (Ctrl+1). In the Properties palette, click Plot Style. From the drop-down list to the right, choose Black Color.

20. Press Esc so that the object is no longer highlighted. The line appears as black.

21. Choose Application Button ⇨ Options. On the Plot and Publish tab, click the Plot Style Table Settings button and change the Default Plot Style Behavior for New Drawings setting to what it was at the beginning of this exercise.

22. Save your drawing.

On the DVD

The plot style that you created, ab17-02.stb, is in the Results folder on the DVD. ∎

Plotting a Drawing

After you lay out your drawing, you're ready to plot it. Plotting outputs your drawing onto paper (or perhaps vellum or some other medium). The first step is to check the plotter or printer. It should be on, connected to your computer, and have the appropriate paper in it.

Cross-Reference

For more information on configuring plotters, see Appendix A. For information on plotting drawing sets, see Chapter 26. I cover plotting electronically to a DWF file in Chapter 28. ∎

 To start plotting, choose Output tab ⇨ Plot panel ⇨ Plot to open the Plot dialog box, as shown in Figure 17.14. As you can see, this dialog box is almost identical to the Page Setup dialog box.

Note

You can hide the right side of the Plot dialog box if you don't need the features there. Click the arrow at the lower-right corner of the dialog box. Click the same arrow to expand the dialog box, if necessary. ∎

FIGURE 17.14

The Plot dialog box.

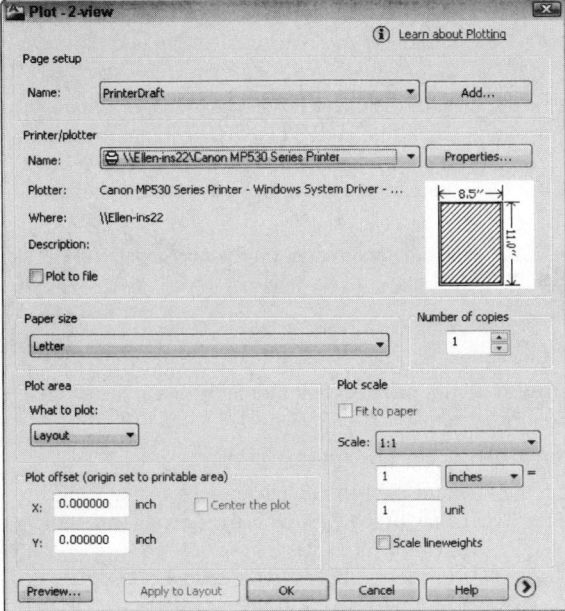

If you set the layout settings in the Page Setup dialog box as current, those settings were saved with the tab that was current at the time. You can usually just click OK in the Plot dialog box and plot immediately. Plot settings are saved in your drawing.

Specifying plot settings

If you saved a page setup, you can choose it from the drop-down list in the Page Setup section of the dialog box. See the discussion of the Page Setup dialog box earlier in this chapter for details.

To select a plotter or printer, choose from the drop-down list in the Printer/Plotter section of the dialog box. A plotter must be either a Windows system printer or a configured plotter. To add a system printer in Windows, choose Start ⇨ Printers and Faxes (or Start ⇨ Control Panel ⇨ Hardware and Sound ⇨ Printers). Click or double-click Add a Printer. (The exact instructions vary with your version of Windows.) To add a configured plotter, which has a driver specifically to optimize the functioning of that plotter, use the Add Plotter Wizard. Choose Output tab ⇨ Plot panel ⇨ Plotter Manager. Then double-click the Add-a-Plotter Wizard item.

Tip

To avoid inadvertently plotting to a Windows system printer when you should be plotting to a plotter, you can hide the display of Windows system printers in the Plot and Page Setup dialog boxes. Because these printers won't appear on the list of plotters, you can't plot to them. To hide system printers, choose Application Button ⇨ Options and click the Plot and Publish tab. In the General Plot Options section of the dialog box, check Hide System Printers and click OK. ∎

To choose how many copies you want to plot, change the number in the Number of Copies text box.

Check the Plot to File check box to create a plot file rather than a paper plot. When you click OK, the Browse for Plot File dialog box opens so that you can choose a name and location. Click Save.

If you want to use a plot-style table, check that it appears in the Plot Style Table drop-down list, which is in the extended portion of the dialog box, on the right. Also make sure that the Plot with Plot Styles check box is checked in the Plot Options section. In the same extended area, you can set shading options. I discuss these options in Chapter 22, because they are generally used for 3D drawings. From the Quality drop-down list, you can choose a plot quality, such as Draft, Normal, or Presentation. You can set the orientation (Portrait or Landscape) in the Drawing Orientation section.

You can merge overlapping objects so that the same area is not printed more than once. To set the Merge Overlapping property:

1. Click Properties in the Printer/Plotter section of the Plot dialog box.

2. In the Plotter Configuration Editor that opens, display the Device and Document Settings tab. Click the plus sign (+) next to Graphics. If you see Merge Control in the Graphics list that opens, you can use this feature on your printer or plotter. (For more information about the Plotter Configuration Editor, see the sidebar "Configuring your plotter.")

3. Click Merge Control. In the Merge Control area that is displayed, choose either Lines Overwrite or Lines Merge, and click OK.

4. You then have the choice of applying the change to the current plot only or making the change permanent by editing the PC3 file that contains the parameters for your plotter or printer. Choose one of the options and click OK.

Previewing your plot

You should preview your drawing before you plot. Click the Preview button in the Plot dialog box to see exactly how your drawing will plot. You can also choose Output tab ⇨ Plot panel ⇨ Preview. Right-click to open the shortcut menu that lets you plot, zoom, pan, or exit the preview.

I cover previewing a plot last because it should be the last step before you actually plot. However, it can also be the first step to help you to determine the settings that you need.

Creating a plot stamp

The PLOTSTAMP command places text in a specified corner of the plot, such as the drawing name, layout name, date and time, and so on. To create a plot stamp, enter **-plotstamp** on the command line. Use the options to specify what you want to appear, and use the On and Off options to turn the stamp on and off. You can enter **plotstamp** to set the plotstamp in a dialog box, which is easier; however, you should then look at the Plot Options section of the extended Plot dialog box to make sure that the plot stamp is on ¾ the Plot Stamp On check box should be checked. Click the Advanced button in the Plot Stamp dialog box to specify the location, offset, and text properties of the plot stamp. (You can use fields to add information about the drawing; for more information, see Chapter 13.)

On the DVD

Stmplot **stamps a drawing with its name and location, your name, the date, and the time, and starts the PLOT command. Look in** \Software\Chap17\Stmplot **(AutoCAD only).** ∎

Configuring your plotter

Most printers and plotters have settings that you can control from within AutoCAD or AutoCAD LT. You can also control how information about the drawing is sent to the printer or plotter. Configuring a plotter usually provides you with more options than if you choose the default Windows system printer settings. The settings that configure how your printer or plotter functions are in the Plotter Configuration Editor, as shown here.

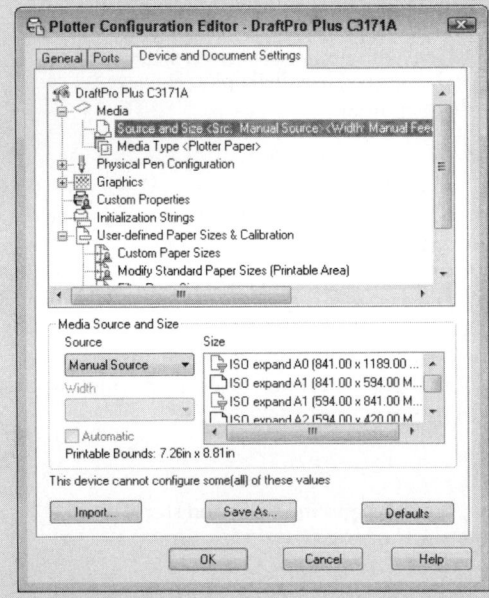 To configure your plotter, choose Output tab⇨Plot panel⇨Plotter Manager to open the Plotters folder. Plotter configuration settings are stored in PC3 files. Double-click the PC3 file icon for the plotter that you want to configure to open the Plotter Configuration Editor. (You can also open the Plotter Configuration Editor from the Plot dialog box by clicking Properties in the Printer/Plotter section.) Click the Device and Document Settings tab. The top section lists the possible types of settings. To open a list with a plus sign to its left, click the plus sign; suboptions appear. As you click each item on the top, the appropriate settings appear in the lower section. To specify settings for raster and vector graphics, choose Graphics. Choose Custom Paper Sizes to add custom sheet sizes; these will then appear in the Page Setup and Plot dialog boxes so that you can choose them when you plot. In each case, the Editor walks you through the choices that you need to make to configure your plotter. See Appendix A for further information.

You can filter out unused paper sizes by using the Plotter Configuration Editor. However, at the end of the process, you can opt to apply the change only to the current plot. Follow these steps:

1. On the Device and Document Settings tab, choose Filter Paper Sizes.

2. In the list of paper sizes, uncheck any sizes that you don't want to display, and click OK.

3. In the Changes to a Printer Configuration File dialog box, choose to apply the changes only to the current plot or to the file. When you apply the changes to the file, they are permanent until you edit the printer configuration file again.

4. Click OK.

Creating the plot

To start the plotting process, simply click OK in the Plot dialog box.

You can plot *in the background,* and continue to work while your drawing is plotting. By default, background plotting is off. To turn it on, choose Application Button⇨Options and click the Plot and Publish tab. In the Background Processing Options section, check the Plotting check box. If you're plotting in the background, you can place your cursor over the plotter icon in the status tray to view information about the status of the plot.

When the plot is finished, a notification bubble appears at the lower-right corner of your screen, as shown in Figure 17.15. You can click the link to view the Plot and Publish Details.

FIGURE 17.15

This bubble appears when your plot is done.

If you view the Plot and Publish Details, you see a report like the one shown in Figure 17.16. You can see details for all plots that you did in the current session of AutoCAD or AutoCAD LT.

FIGURE 17.16

The Plot and Publish Details report tells you what happened when you plotted your drawings.

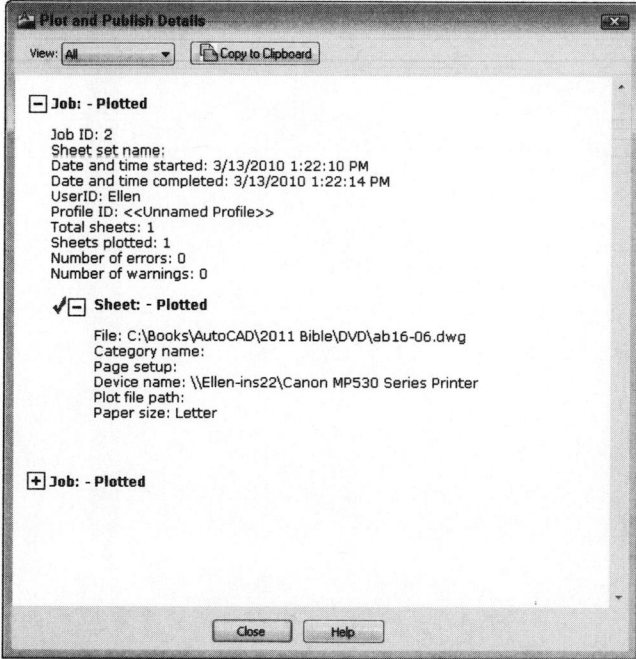

If you need to plot large numbers of drawings or multiple layouts, use the PUBLISH command, which I cover in Chapter 28.

Summary

In this chapter, you learned how to lay out and plot a drawing. You discovered how to:

- Lay out a drawing in model space
- Use a paper space layout
- Create layouts, using the Layout Wizard and using the commands individually
- Use annotative objects in a viewport
- Add text and dimensions in paper space
- Use the Page Setup dialog box to specify layout settings
- Create plot-style tables and apply plot styles
- Plot a drawing

This chapter ends Part II, "Drawing in Two Dimensions." Part III, "Working with Data," explains how to integrate your drawing with data about your objects. The next chapter covers blocks and attributes.

Part III

Working with Data

Part III covers the various ways that you work with data in your drawings. This part brings you to a new level of sophistication in terms of automation and interfacing with other drawings and data. Chapter 18 covers blocks and attributes, which enable you to work repetitively with objects and text. You can build intelligent, flexible blocks using the Dynamic Blocks feature. You can use attribute text to accurately place text and to create a simple database of information related to your objects. Chapter 19 explains how to refer to other drawings with external references, also called *xrefs*. Chapter 20 describes how to connect sophisticated external databases to objects in your drawings.

Working with Blocks and Attributes

As you draw, you'll find that you often need to place the same group of objects several times in a drawing. An architect needs to place windows and doors many times in a plan layout of a house. An electrical engineer places electrical symbols in a drawing again and again. A mechanical model may include nuts, bolts, and surface finish symbols many times in a drawing. *Blocks* are groups of objects that you save and name so that you can insert them in your drawing whenever you need them. A block is one object, regardless of the number of individual objects that were used to create it. If necessary, you can *explode* a block to obtain the original individual objects. Many disciplines use *parts libraries* that may consist of thousands of items. You use the block feature to save and insert these parts.

A great advantage of blocks is that by changing the block definition, you can update all the instances of that block in that drawing. Blocks also reduce the size of the drawing file. A drawing stores the definition of a block only once, along with a simple reference to the block each time it's inserted.

Dynamic blocks are blocks that contain parameters for insertion and editing. You can create a dynamic block that takes the place of numerous similar regular blocks by giving it the flexibility to take on various sizes, rotations, visibility variations, and more. Dynamic blocks support parametric constraints, which give them more intelligence.

You can attach *attributes* to blocks. Attributes are labels that are associated with blocks. Attributes have two main uses: to label objects and to create a simple database. You can use fields in your attributes to automate the generation of text. (Chapter 13 explains all about fields.)

This chapter explains how to make the most of blocks and attributes.

Combining Objects into Blocks

Any object or set of objects can be saved as a block. Creating a block is easy, but a little planning makes using it much simpler. Before you create a block, you need to understand how blocks are inserted and how you want to use the specific block that you're creating.

Understanding base points and insertion points

Figure 18.1 shows the legend for a plat drawing. Each legend symbol is a block that is then inserted in the drawing as needed. A symbol has been selected, and you can see that it has one grip at the *base point*. The base point is the point that you use to insert the block. Every block must have a base point. When you insert the block, the base point is placed at the coordinate that you specify for inserting the block — the *insertion point*. All the objects of the block are then inserted in their proper place relative to that insertion point.

FIGURE 18.1

Each legend symbol is a block. Every block has a base point.

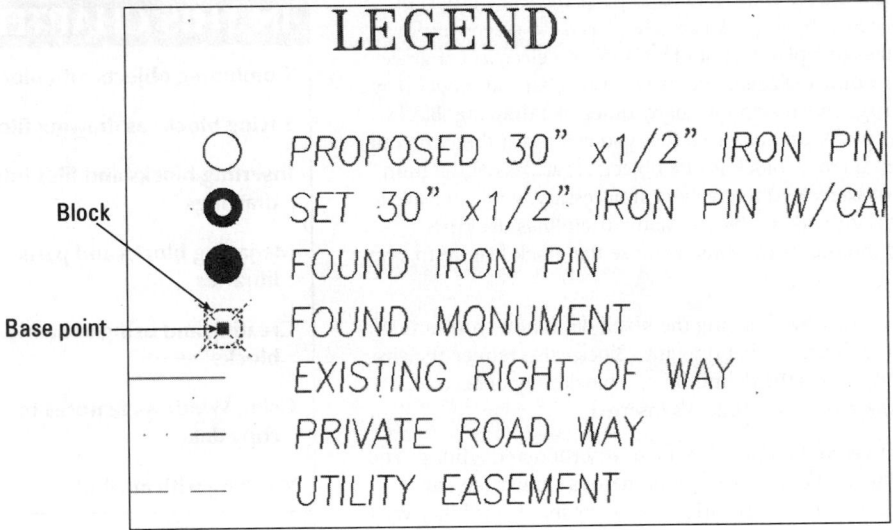

The base point does not have to be on the object, but it should be in a location that makes it easy to insert the block. Figure 18.2 shows a different sort of block, a title border/block. In this case, the base point is usually inserted at 0,0 of the drawing. By placing the base point at the lower-left corner of the border, you can easily place this block in any drawing. The base point is similar in concept to the justification point on text objects.

FIGURE 18.2

This titleblock is a block. Its base point is at the lower-left corner.

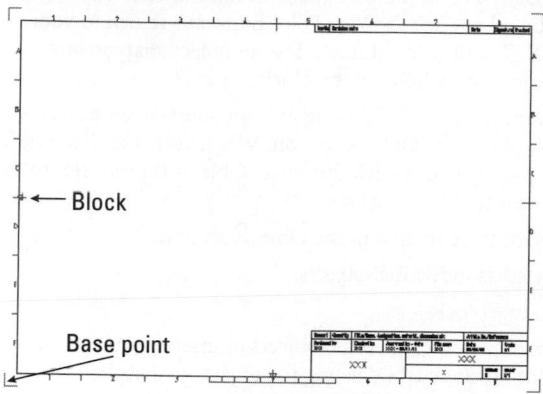

Creating a block

To create a block, first create the objects just as you want to save them. You may include other blocks as objects in your block. (A block within a block is called a *nested block.*)

After you've created the objects for your block, follow these steps:

1. Choose Home tab ⇨ Block panel ⇨ Create to start the BLOCK command and open the Block Definition dialog box, as shown in Figure 18.3. The dialog box guides you through the process of defining a block.

FIGURE 18.3

The Block Definition dialog box.

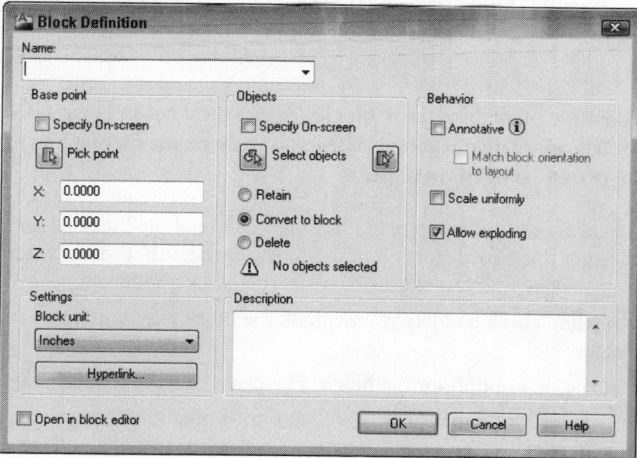

2. In the Name text box, type a name for the block. The name can be up to 255 characters, and spaces are allowed.

3. If you want to specify a base point in the dialog box, in the Base Point section, uncheck the Specify On-Screen check box. Then you can either click the Pick Point button to return to your drawing and specify a base point, or enter X, Y, and Z coordinates. Use an object snap on any of the objects in the block to place the base point somewhere on the block.

4. You can select objects for a block before starting the BLOCK command. If you have not done so, you can check the Specify On-Screen check box in the Objects section. When you click OK, you will get a prompt to select objects. Alternatively, you can click the Select Objects button, return to your drawing to select objects, and then return to the dialog box.

5. Choose how you want the objects of the block to be treated in the Objects section:

   - **Retain.** Keeps the objects that you selected as individual objects.
   - **Convert to Block.** Converts the objects to a block.
   - **Delete.** Deletes the objects. Use this option if you created the objects to insert them elsewhere and do not need the original objects. One advantage of deleting the objects is that their disappearance confirms that you selected the right objects.

6. Choose the insert units that you want to use when defining your block in the Settings section. (You can choose anything from microns to parsecs!) Let's say you work in kilometers and save a block with an insert unit of kilometers. When you insert a block, it will be measured in kilometers, rather than millimeters or inches. If the units aren't important to you, you can specify the units as Unitless. In the same section, you can click the Hyperlink button to add a hyperlink to the block.

7. If you want the block to be annotative, check the Annotative check box in the Behavior section of the dialog box. You can set up annotative objects to scale automatically to the scale of a viewport. When you make a block annotative, you can also check the Match Block Orientation to Layout check box to match the block's orientation to that of the paper space layout (portrait or landscape). You set a layout's orientation in the Page Setup or Plot dialog box.

Cross-Reference
For more information on using annotative objects, see Chapter 17. I cover hyperlinks in Chapter 28. ■

Caution
You cannot put annotative blocks inside other annotative blocks. Also, you shouldn't manually scale (as with the SCALE command) blocks that contain annotative objects. When you scale an annotative block, the resulting scale includes your scale as well as the current annotation scale. ■

8. Check the Scale Uniformly check box to force any scaling of the block to scale at equal X and Y factors. This feature prevents distortion of the block. By default, this option is not checked. However, it's not available if you choose to make the block annotative.

9. The Allow Exploding check box lets you explode the block after you insert it. This option is checked by default.

10. If you want, enter a description for the block. The description is used by the DesignCenter.

11. Check the Open in Block Editor check box if you know that you want to create a dynamic block. (I explain dynamic blocks later in this chapter.) Then when you click OK to close the dialog box, the Block Editor immediately opens.

Caution

For precision, you should always use an object snap when defining the base point. If the base point that you need to use is not on any object, you can use the From object snap, object snap tracking, or some other means of specifying a precise coordinate. ∎

    12. Click OK to return to your drawing.

The definition of the block is now stored in the drawing, ready for you to insert as many times as needed. If you selected Delete, your objects disappeared. You can retrieve them by using the one command with a sense of humor: OOPS. The OOPS command restores the last object or set of objects that you erased. This command works whether you used the ERASE command or created a block, and even if you used some other command in the meantime. By contrast, UNDO undoes commands only in the order that you executed them.

Tip

If you create a number of block definitions that you don't end up using in the drawing, use the PURGE command to delete them. This reduces the size of the drawing file. ∎

On the DVD

The drawing that you need for the following exercise on creating a block, ab18-a.dwg, is in the Drawings folder on the DVD. ∎

STEPS: Creating a Block

1. Open ab18-a.dwg from the DVD.
2. Save the file as ab18-01.dwg in your AutoCAD Bible folder. This is a small portion of an electrical schematic drawing, as shown in Figure 18.4. Object Snap should be on. Set running object snaps for Endpoint, Quadrant, and Intersection.

FIGURE 18.4

A portion of an electrical schematic.

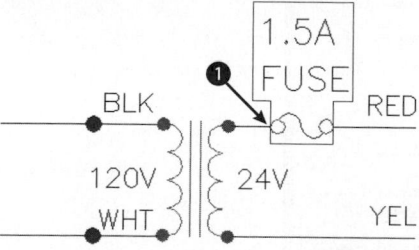

3. To make a block of the 1.5-amp fuse, choose Home tab ⇨ Block panel ⇨ Create.

4. In the Name text box of the Block Definition dialog box, type **1-5 amp fuse**.
5. In the Base Point and Objects sections, check the Specify On-screen check box.

6. In the dialog box's Objects section, choose Delete. The Insert Units should be Unitless. Leave the Description blank. The Open in Block Editor check box should not be checked.

7. Click OK.

8. In the drawing, at the `Specify insertion base point:` prompt, use the Quadrant object snap to pick ❶, shown in Figure 18.4.

9. At the `Select objects:` prompt, select the boxed objects shown in Figure 18.4 (the two lines of text, the two circles, and the two arcs). Press Enter to end selection.

10. To check that the block has been created, choose Home tab ➪ Block panel ➪ Create. Click the Name drop-down arrow to see your block. Click Cancel.

11. Save your drawing.

Saving blocks as files

You can use the DesignCenter (as explained later in this chapter) to insert blocks from any drawing. Nevertheless, many users organize their blocks in their own files so that they can be easily stored and located. Parts and symbols libraries are made up of many individual drawing files, one for each part or symbol. These libraries are a powerful aid to drawing more efficiently.

To save a block as a file, follow these steps:

1. Type **wblock** ↵ to open the Write Block dialog box, as shown in Figure 18.5. (WBLOCK stands for write block. Writing to a file is another expression for saving to a file.)

FIGURE 18.5

Use the Write Block dialog box to save a block as a separate drawing file.

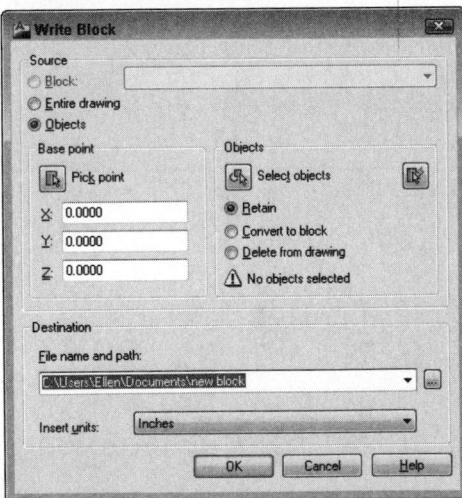

2. In the Source section, choose how you want to create the drawing file:
   - **Block.** Use this option when you've already created the block and now want to save it as a drawing file. Choose the block from the drop-down list.

- **Entire drawing.** Use this option to make a copy of your drawing.
- **Objects.** Use this option to start defining the block in the same way that you define a block within a drawing, as described in the preceding section of this chapter. The Base Point and Objects sections become available.

3. Choose the location (drive and folder) for the file in the File Name and Path text box. If you're creating the file from objects, insert a name for the file in place of the default New Block at the end of the path.

4. In the Insert Units drop-down list, choose the units that you want for your block, or choose Unitless for no units.

5. Click OK to create the drawing file.

When you save a drawing that you plan to insert as a block, use the BASE command (Home tab ➪ Block panel (expanded) ➪ Set Base Point) to create the insertion point. By default, the base point is 0,0,0. By setting the base point to another point in the drawing, such as an object snap on one of the objects, you can more easily control the insertion of that drawing.

Tip

If you want a drawing to act like an annotative block when you insert it, set its ANNOTATIVEDWG system variable to 1. ■

Replacing an existing file

If you make a mistake when selecting objects to write to a file with WBLOCK, or you want to change the objects in the file, you can replace the file. Start WBLOCK and type the name of the block file that you want to change. Be sure to choose the same file location. When you click OK, a message asks whether you want to replace the existing file. Click Replace the Existing `filename.dwg`.

On the DVD

The drawing that you need for the following exercise on saving a block to a file, ab18-b.dwg, is in the Drawings folder on the DVD. ■

STEPS: Saving a Block to a File

1. Open `ab18-b.dwg` from the DVD.

2. Save the file as `ab18-02.dwg` in your `AutoCAD Bible` folder. This is a large titleblock, as shown in Figure 18.6. Object Snap should be on. Set a running object snap for Endpoint.

3. Type **wblock** ↵. In the Source section of the Write Block dialog box, choose Entire Drawing. Set the File Name and Path box to `AutoCAD Bible\tb-f` by typing the path and the filename. (Alternatively, click the Ellipsis [...] button and navigate to your `AutoCAD Bible` folder. In the File Name text box, type **tb-f**. Click Save.) Click OK.

4. Press Enter to repeat the WBLOCK command.

5. In the Source section of the dialog box, choose Objects. In the Objects section, click Select Objects.

6. Use Zoom Window to zoom in on the text at the bottom-right corner of the titleblock. At the `Select objects:` prompt, select all the 90°-rotated text at ❶, shown in Figure 18.6. Press Enter to end selection.

FIGURE 18.6

A titleblock can be saved as a file and inserted into any other drawing.

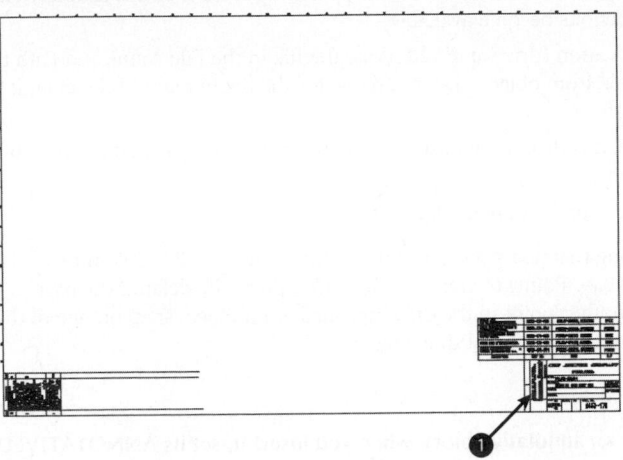

7. In the Base Point section, click Pick Point. Use the Endpoint object snap to pick the bottom-left corner of the box containing the text that you selected. Using this base point lets you easily place the text in the box at any time.

8. In the Objects section, choose Delete from Drawing.

9. In the File Name and Path text box, type **notes-tol** after the path, which should already be set to your AutoCAD Bible folder. Click OK to save the block as a file.

10. Type **oops** ↵ to bring back the text.

11. Choose View tab ➪ Navigate panel ➪ Zoom drop-down list ➪ Extents, and save your drawing.

Inserting Blocks and Files into Drawings

The process for inserting blocks and separate files is the same. After you choose the location, you can change the size and rotation of the block. This capability is ideal for parts libraries. You can create parts at the size of 1 unit and then scale or rotate them as needed. Figure 18.7 shows a window block inserted at various scales and rotation angles. (You could also create one dynamic block with the capability of inserting it at various scales and rotation angles. I cover dynamic blocks later in this chapter.)

Using the Insert dialog box

To insert a block or file, follow these steps:

1. Choose Home tab ➪ Block panel ➪ Insert to start the INSERT command. The Insert dialog box opens, as shown in Figure 18.8.

Note

If the block is annotative, you see an annotative icon next to the block's preview. ■

FIGURE 18.7

A block of a window inserted at various rotation angles and scales.

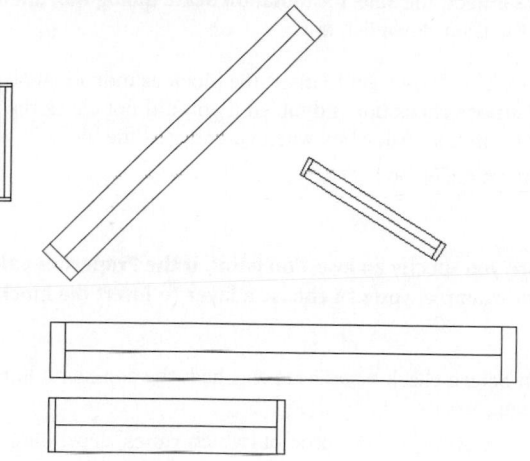

FIGURE 18.8

The Insert dialog box.

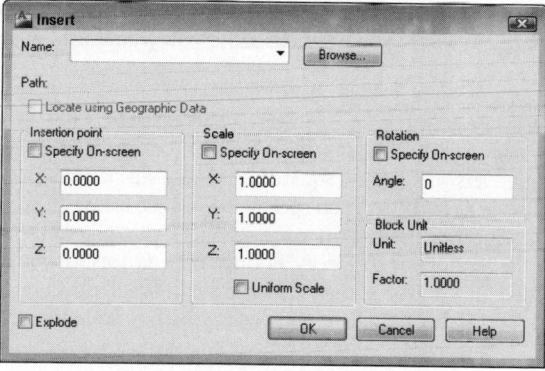

2. You can insert a block or a file as follows:

   • To insert a block from within your drawing, click the Name drop-down list and choose one of the existing blocks.

   • To insert a file, click Browse. The Select Drawing File dialog box opens. Locate the file's drive and folder, and then choose the file. A preview appears to the right. Click Open. The Insert dialog box displays the path of the file.

3. Uncheck Specify On-screen in the Insertion Point, Scale, and Rotation sections if you want to specify the insertion point, scale, and rotation angle in the dialog box. Then provide the requested information in the dialog box.

Note

The Uniform Scale check box forces scaling to be the same for the X and Y directions. The first time in each session that you insert or create an annotative object, the Select Annotation Scale dialog box opens, where you can choose the desired annotation scale from the drop-down list. ■

4. Check the Explode check box if you want to insert the block as individual objects rather than as one block object. The Explode check box is disabled if you did not check the Allow Exploding check box in the Block Definition dialog box when you created the block.

5. Click OK to close the Insert dialog box.

Tip

While you're dragging the block and before you specify an insertion point, if the Properties palette is open, you can change the properties of the block. For example, you can choose a layer to insert the block on a layer other than the current layer. ■

6. If any of the Specify On-Screen check boxes were checked, the command line prompts you for the necessary information:

- At the `Specify insertion point:` prompt (which varies, depending on whether or not you checked the Explode check box in Step 4), specify the insertion point. You see the block with its base point at the cursor, so you can judge how it looks.

Tip

A Basepoint option appears with the `Specify insertion point:` **prompt. When you use this option, you can move the insertion base point of the block to anywhere you want. Usually, you would use an object snap to specify a different point on the block.** ■

- At the `Enter X scale factor, specify opposite corner, or [Corner/XYZ] <1>:` prompt, press Enter to accept the default scale factor of 1, or type another scale. The Specify Opposite Corner option lets you define a square box whose side defines the scale factor. A side of 1 unit results in a scale factor of 1. If you specify the X scale factor, the command line prompts you for the Y scale factor. The default is the same scale as X, but you can specify a different one. For 3D models, use the XYZ option to specify all three scale factors. (If you checked Explode, the prompt is slightly different, and you specify the scale factor for all directions at once. If the Uniform Scale check box is checked, the prompt asks you for a scale factor.)

- At the `Specify rotation angle <0>:` prompt, type in a rotation angle. You can also pick a point to use the angle from the insertion point to the point that you picked as the rotation angle. This technique is useful for aligning a block with an existing object.

After you provide all the necessary information, the command inserts the block or file. A negative scale factor for any of the axes creates a mirror image of the block or file. When you specify a negative X scale axis, the block is mirrored around the Y axis. When you specify a negative Y scale axis, the block is mirrored around the X axis. Figure 18.9 shows a door block inserted with positive and negative scale factors. The rotation angle of all the blocks is 0 degrees. By combining negative and positive scale factors with rotation angles, you can get any door configuration that you want. Dynamic blocks also offer a way to insert blocks at various scales and rotation angles.

When you insert a drawing file, paper space objects are not included in the block definition created in your drawing. To insert paper space objects in another drawing, open the original drawing and define the objects as a block. Then use the DesignCenter to insert that block into any other drawing.

FIGURE 18.9

A door block inserted at various positive and negative scale factors, creating mirror images in different directions.

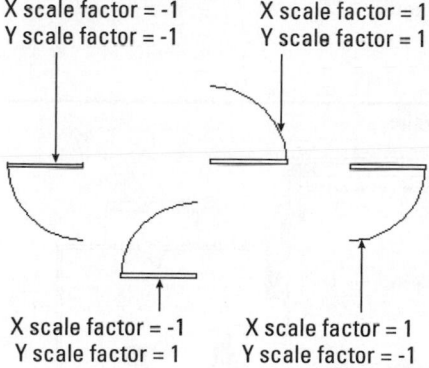

X scale factor = -1
Y scale factor = -1

X scale factor = 1
Y scale factor = 1

X scale factor = -1
Y scale factor = 1

X scale factor = 1
Y scale factor = -1

Using the DesignCenter

 When you want to insert a block from another drawing, use the DesignCenter. The DesignCenter is the tool to use if you have a block library containing multiple blocks within one drawing. Choose View tab ➪ Palettes panel ➪ DesignCenter or press Ctrl+2. In the left pane, navigate to the drawing that contains the block that you want. Double-click the drawing and choose Blocks from the list that appears. In the right pane, you see a list of the blocks in that drawing. Click Preview to see a preview of each block that you select. Click Description to see a description of the block. (The description only appears if you saved one when creating the block.) You can insert the block in two ways:

- Double-click the block's icon to open the Insert dialog box so that you can specify exactly how you want to insert the block, just as I described earlier for blocks within a drawing.

- Drag the block's icon onto the drawing area to insert the block at the point where you release the mouse button, using the default scale and rotation.

You can use the DesignCenter to insert entire drawings. In the left pane, navigate to the folder containing the drawing. The drawings are then listed in the right pane. Choose a drawing and drag it onto the drawing area. On the command line, you'll see the -INSERT command, the command-line version of INSERT.

Cross-Reference

The DesignCenter is covered in more detail in Chapter 26. You can also insert blocks from a tool palette. Many people use tool palettes, also covered in Chapter 26, as the primary way to insert blocks from a block library. You can quickly create a tool palette containing all the blocks in a folder. ■

On the DVD

The drawings that you need for the following exercise on inserting blocks, ab14-b.dwg and ab18-c.dwg, are in the Drawings folder on the DVD. ■

STEPS: Inserting Blocks

1. Open ab18-c.dwg from the DVD.

2. Save the file as ab18-03.dwg in your AutoCAD Bible folder. This is the floor plan of the first floor of a house, as shown in Figure 18.10. Many of the doors and a toilet need to be inserted. Object Snap should be on. Set running object snaps for Endpoint and Midpoint. The current layer is Door.

3. Use Zoom Window to zoom in on the left wing of the house.

The floor plan of the house needs some doors and a toilet.

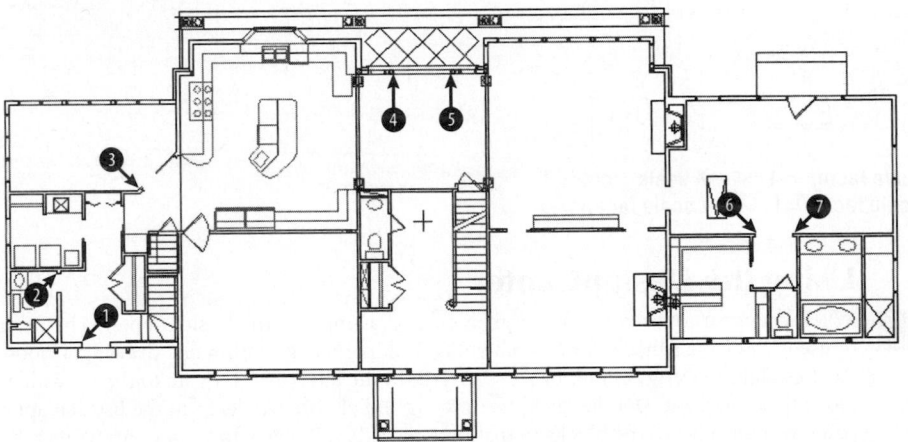

 4. Choose Home tab ⇨ Block panel ⇨ Insert to start the INSERT command. In the Name drop-down list of the Insert dialog box, choose DOOR (if it isn't already selected). Check all three Specify On-screen check boxes. Make sure that the Uniform Scale check box is not checked. Click OK to close the Insert dialog box.

Tip

If you make a mistake while inserting a door, press Esc if you're in the middle of the prompts. If you've completed the command, click Undo on the Quick Access Toolbar or erase the door and start over. ■

5. As you move the cursor, you can see the dragged image of a door. This image shows you the block at an X and Y scale of 1, and a 0-degree rotation angle. Follow the prompts:

```
Specify insertion point or [Basepoint/Scale/X/Y/Z/Rotate]: Use the
    Endpoint object snap to pick ❶ in Figure 18.10.
Enter X scale factor, specify opposite corner, or [Corner/XYZ] <1>:
    -1 ↵
Enter Y scale factor <use X scale factor>: 1 ↵
Specify rotation angle <0>: 270 ↵ (You could also specify -90
    degrees.)
```

6. Repeat the INSERT command. The Insert dialog box already shows the DOOR block. Click OK. Follow the prompts. You'll probably want to zoom into the area of ❷, shown in Figure 18.10. (To do so, choose View tab ⇨ Navigate panel ⇨ Zoom drop-down list ⇨ Window.)

```
Specify insertion point or [Basepoint/Scale/X/Y/Z/Rotate]: Pick ❷ in
    Figure 18.10.
Enter X scale factor, specify opposite corner, or [Corner/XYZ] <1>:
    2/3 ↵
Enter Y scale factor <use X scale factor>: ↵
Specify rotation angle <0>: 180 ↵
```

7. If you zoomed in for the previous step, return to the previous view by using Zoom Previous (View tab ⇨ Navigate panel ⇨ Zoom drop-down list ⇨ Previous). Zoom in to the area around ❸, shown in Figure 18.10. Choose Home tab ⇨ Block panel ⇨ Insert. Click OK. Follow the prompts:

```
Specify insertion point or [Basepoint/Scale/X/Y/Z/Rotate]: Pick ❸ in
    Figure 18.10.
Enter X scale factor or specify opposite corner, or [Corner/XYZ] <1>:
    -3/4 ↵
Enter Y scale factor <use X scale factor>: 3/4 ↵
Specify rotation angle <0>: 315 ↵
```

8. Zoom in to the area around ❹ and ❺, shown in Figure 18.10. Repeat the INSERT command. Click OK. Follow the prompts:

```
Specify insertion point or [Basepoint/Scale/X/Y/Z/Rotate]: Pick ❹ in
    Figure 18.10.
Enter X scale factor, specify opposite corner, or [Corner/XYZ] <1>: 1 ↵
Enter Y scale factor <use X scale factor>: ↵
Specify rotation angle <0>: 270 ↵
```

9. Repeat the INSERT command and click OK. Follow the prompts:

```
Specify insertion point or [Basepoint/Scale/X/Y/Z/Rotate]: Pick ❺ in
    Figure 18.10.
Enter X scale factor, specify opposite corner, or [Corner/XYZ] <1>: -1 ↵
Enter Y scale factor <use X scale factor>: 1 ↵
Specify rotation angle <0>: 90 ↵
```

10. Zoom in on the area around ❻ and ❼, shown in Figure 18.10. Start the INSERT command and click OK. Follow the prompts:

```
Specify insertion point or [Basepoint/Scale/X/Y/Z/Rotate]: Pick ❻ in
    Figure 18.10.
Enter X scale factor, specify opposite corner, or [Corner/XYZ] <1>:
    -2/3 ↵
Enter Y scale factor <use X scale factor>: 2/3 ↵
Specify rotation angle: 270 ↵
```

11. Repeat the INSERT command and click OK. Follow the prompts:

```
Specify insertion point or [Basepoint/Scale/X/Y/Z/Rotate]: Pick ❼ in
    Figure 18.10.
Enter X scale factor, specify opposite corner, or [Corner/XYZ] <1>:
    2/3 ↵
Enter Y scale factor <use X scale factor>: ↵
Specify rotation angle: 90 ↵
```

12. Beneath the doors that you just inserted is a water closet with a toilet. Pan down to it by choosing View tab ➪ Navigate ➪ Pan and dragging. Erase the toilet, which is a block. Change the current layer to FIXTURE.

13. Choose View tab ➪ Palettes panel ➪ DesignCenter or press Ctrl+2. (If you don't see the two panes, click Tree View Toggle on the DesignCenter toolbar.) In the left pane, navigate to your DVD drive. (You may need to use the horizontal scroll bar if the left side of the list of drives and folders is not in view.) Double-click the DVD drive. Double-click Drawings and then finally double-click ab14-b.dwg. Click Blocks from the list of named objects below ab14-b.dwg. On the right, you see the blocks in the drawing.

14. Double-click TOILET2. You see a preview at the bottom of the DesignCenter. (If you don't, click Preview on the DesignCenter toolbar.) The Insert dialog box opens. Because you can see the preview, you know the rotation angle is correct; you can assume that the scale is correct because toilets are generally about the same size. The Insertion Point Specify On-Screen check box should be checked. The other Specify On-Screen check boxes should be unchecked. Click OK.

15. Drag the toilet into the water closet and use a Midpoint object snap to place it at the middle of the bottom wall of the water closet. If you want, close the DesignCenter by clicking its Close button.

16. Do a Zoom Extents and save your drawing.

The MINSERT command (AutoCAD only) lets you insert blocks (but not annotative blocks) in a rectangular array. Type **minsert** ↵. MINSERT prompts you for an insertion point, scale factors, and rotation angle using the same prompts as the INSERT command, but without the dialog box. It then starts the same prompts as the Rectangular option of the ARRAY command, asking for the number of rows and columns and the distance between them. The value of MINSERT is that it reduces the size of your drawing because the array is one block object. The disadvantage is that you can't edit the individual blocks in the array or the array as a whole in any way. If you need to edit them, erase the entire array of blocks, redefine the single block, if necessary, and start over, this time using INSERT and ARRAY separately. You cannot explode a minserted block.

Managing Blocks

Several factors require care when working with blocks. Large libraries of blocks need to be well managed so that you can find the block that you need quickly. You also need to consider the issue of which layers you use when you define your blocks so that you get the desired results when you insert them.

Tip
You can use the QSELECT command to select all instances of a block from a drop-down list. Choose Block Reference as the object type and Name as the property. From the Value drop-down list, choose the block that you want. ■

Working with layers

You may want a block to take on the current layer when inserted, or to retain its original layer. You can manage block layers, along with their other properties, to obtain the desired result. A block can be defined in four ways to determine which layer, color, linetype, transparency, and lineweight properties it will use when you insert it, as shown in Table 18.1.

As Table 18.1 makes clear, two of the methods (setting the objects to ByBlock and creating them on layer 0) create chameleon blocks that take on the properties of the current layer. Use the other two methods when you want the block to retain its properties, regardless of the current layer.

Creating blocks on layer 0 is the simplest method. If you want the blocks to have a specific color and linetype, create a layer for them and switch to that layer before inserting the blocks. You can also change the layer of a block, after it's inserted, in the same way that you change the layer of any object.

Properties of Block Component Objects and Insertion Results

Properties of Component Objects	Insertion Results
On any layer (except layer 0), with color, linetype, transparency, and lineweight set to ByLayer	The block keeps properties of that layer. If you insert a block into another drawing without that layer, the drawing creates the layer. If you insert the block into another drawing with that layer, but the layer has a different color and linetype properties, the block takes on properties of the layer that are different from those that you created it on. If you insert the block on a different layer, the block keeps the properties of the layer on which it was created, but the Properties palette reports the block as being on the layer on which it was inserted, because it reports the layer of the insertion point, not the block objects.
On any layer (including layer 0), with color, linetype, transparency, and lineweight set explicitly	The block keeps the color, linetype, transparency, and lineweight with properties that were explicitly set. If you insert the block into another drawing, the drawing creates the layer on which original objects were made.
On any layer (except layer 0), with color, linetype, transparency, and lineweight set to ByBlock	The block takes on the color of the current color setting. (If the current color is set to ByLayer, the block will take on the current layer's color.) If you insert the block into another drawing, the drawing creates the layer on which original objects were made. *Note:* If the color, linetype, transparency, and lineweight are ByBlock when you create objects for a block, the objects are always shown with black/white color, a continuous linetype, no transparency, and the default lineweight.
On layer 0 (with color, linetype, transparency, and lineweight set to ByBlock or ByLayer)	The block takes on the layer and properties of the current layer on which it's inserted. If you insert the block into another drawing, no layers are created.

On the DVD

The drawing that you need for the following exercise on working with blocks and layers, ab18-d.dwg, **is in the** Drawings **folder on the DVD.** ∎

STEPS: Working with Blocks and Layers

1. Open ab18-d.dwg from the DVD.
2. Save the file as ab18-04.dwg in your AutoCAD Bible folder. This is a portion of an electrical schematic, as shown in Figure 18.11. Object Snap should be on. Set running object snaps for Endpoint, Midpoint, Quadrant, and Intersection.
3. Choose Home tab ⇨ Block panel ⇨ Create. In the Name text box of the Block Definition dialog box, type **hl switch**. Make sure that the Specify On-screen check boxes in both the Base Point and Objects sections are checked. Choose Retain in the Objects section. Click OK.

FIGURE 18.11

The electrical schematic has several symbols that would be useful as blocks.

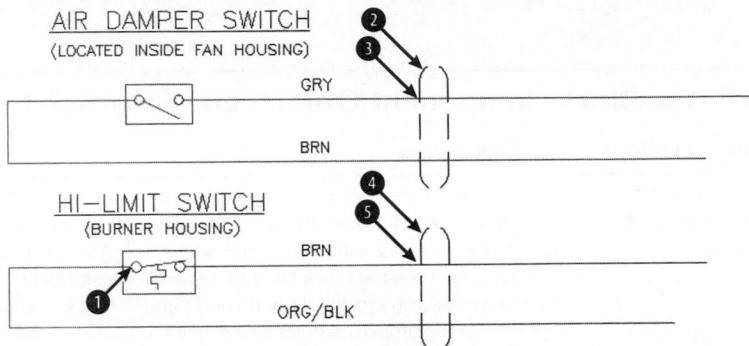

4. Use the Quadrant object snap to pick the left quadrant of the left circle in the switch, at ❶ in Figure 18.11. Use a selection window to select the entire hi-limit switch box (not including the text labels). Right-click to end selection. The objects in this block were created on the Object layer, which is red with a continuous linetype. The color, linetype, transparency, and lineweight are set to ByLayer.

5. Use a selection window to select the air damper switch. (The objects are currently on the Object layer, which is red with a continuous linetype.) Choose Home tab ⇨ Properties panel and select ByBlock from the Color drop-down list. Do the same with the Linetype and the Lineweight drop-down lists. The switch turns black (or white if you're using a black screen). The objects are still selected.

6. Choose Home tab ⇨ Block panel ⇨ Create. In the Name text box, type **ad switch**. The dialog box says 4 objects selected. Check the Specify On-screen check box in the Base Point section. Uncheck the Specify On-screen check box in the Objects section (because the objects are already selected). Check the Retain check box. Click OK. Use the Quadrant object snap to pick the left quadrant of the left circle in the switch.

7. Use a selection window to select the top conduit symbol at ❷, shown in Figure 18.11 (it consists of four objects). (It is currently on the Conduit layer, which is black and has a linetype of Hidden2.) Use the Color drop-down list to set the color to Green. Use the Linetype drop-down list to set the linetype to Hidden2. Choose Home tab ⇨ Block panel ⇨ Create. In the Name text box, type **top conduit**. The dialog box tells you that four objects are selected. The Specify On-screen check box in the Base Point section should be checked. Click OK. Use the Intersection object snap to pick ❸. The conduit appears green with the Hidden2 linetype.

8. Use a selection window to select the bottom conduit at ❹. (It is currently on the Conduit layer, which is black and has a linetype of Hidden2.) Use the Layer drop-down list to set the layer to 0. Repeat the BLOCK command. In the block Name text box, type **bot conduit**. The dialog box tells you that four objects are selected. Click OK. Use the Intersection object snap to pick ❺. The conduit appears black with a continuous linetype.

9. Save your drawing. Choose Application Button ⇨ New. In the Select Template dialog box, click the down arrow next to the Open button. Choose one of the Open with No Template options. A new drawing opens with only one layer, layer 0. (You can choose Home tab ⇨ Layers panel ⇨ Layer drop-down list to check.)

10. Choose View tab ⇨ Palettes panel ⇨ DesignCenter. In the left pane, locate your AutoCAD Bible folder and then locate ab18-04.dwg. (You can also click the Open Drawings tab and find ab18-04.dwg there.) Double-click the drawing, and then click Blocks. In the right pane, double-click h1 switch. In the Insert dialog box, check Specify On-screen for Insertion Point and Scale. Click OK. Follow the prompts to insert the file anywhere in the drawing, using a scale factor of 3. The block, whose objects were created on the Object layer, retained its original color (red), linetype, transparency, and lineweight but is listed as being on layer 0. Select the block and look at the Layer drop-down list to verify this.

11. Check the Layer drop-down list. A new layer, Object, is the layer that the original objects were on.

12. In the right pane of the DesignCenter, double-click top conduit. In the Insert dialog box, click OK. Follow the prompts to insert the file anywhere in the drawing, using a scale factor of 3. Again, the object retains its explicitly set properties of green color and Hidden2 linetype but is listed as being on layer 0. Click the Layer drop-down list to see that the Conduit layer has been added to the drawing.

13. Click Home tab ⇨ Properties panel ⇨ Color, and choose Cyan from the Color drop-down list to make it the current color.

14. In the DesignCenter's right pane, double-click ad switch. In the Insert dialog box, click OK. Follow the prompts to insert the file anywhere in the drawing, using a scale factor of 3. The block (whose objects were created on the Object layer and whose properties were set to ByBlock) takes on the current color of Cyan and is listed on layer 0.

15. Choose Home tab ⇨ Layers panel ⇨ Layer Properties, and click New Layer in the Layer Properties Manager. Name the new layer **Green** and set its color to Green. Click Set Current to make it the current layer. Close or hide the Layer Properties Manager.

16. In the DesignCenter, double-click bot conduit. In the Insert dialog box, click OK. Follow the prompts to insert the file anywhere in the drawing, using a scale factor of **3**. The block, whose original objects were on layer 0, has the properties of layer Green and is listed on layer Green.

17. Click the DesignCenter's Close button to close the DesignCenter. Don't save this new drawing.

Exploding blocks

 You can explode blocks into their original objects. You may need to do this to edit a block. If you want, you can then redefine the block, as explained earlier in this chapter. To explode a block, choose Home tab ⇨ Modify panel ⇨ Explode. (You can select objects before or after choosing the EXPLODE command.) You can also explode polylines, dimensions, leaders, multileaders, hatches, regions, multilines, and certain 3D objects (bodies, 3D meshes, 3D solids, various types of surfaces, polyface meshes, and polygon meshes) into simpler types of objects. (Drawing in 3D is covered in Part IV.) Exploding a block with nested blocks explodes only the top-level block. You need to use the EXPLODE command again to explode the next level of blocks.

When you explode blocks that were created on layer 0 or with BYBLOCK objects, the objects return to their original status and appear black/white with a continuous linetype and default lineweight again. If you insert a block with different X and Y scales, the command does its best to create objects based on their new shapes. For example, if you have a block that includes a circle and insert it with an X scale of 1 and a Y scale of 2, you see an ellipse. Therefore, when you explode the block, you get an ellipse from what used to be a circle.

Note

When you explode an annotative block, you get the components of the current scale presentation only. The components are not annotative. ■

Using the XPLODE command

The XPLODE command is a version of the EXPLODE command that you can use to control the final layer, color, and linetype of the objects. If you select more than one object, you can set the properties for all the objects that you select at once (that is, *globally*) or for each object individually.

To xplode an object, type **xplode** ↵. (XPLODE is an AutoLISP program in AutoCAD and is built into AutoCAD LT.) At the `Select objects:` prompt, select one or more blocks. If you select more than one object, XPLODE displays the `XPlode Individually/<Globally>:` prompt. Type **i** ↵ to get prompts for each block individually. Press Enter to accept the Globally default option. If you choose the Individually option, XPLODE highlights each block in turn so that you know which block you're working on as you respond to prompts.

At the `Enter an option [All/Color/LAyer/LType/LWeight/Inherit from parent block/ Explode] <Explode>:` prompt, choose whether you want to specify color, layer, linetype, lineweight, or all four. The Inherit from Parent Block option works only for blocks created on layer 0 whose color and linetype were also set to ByBlock. These ByBlock objects then retain their color and linetype after you explode them.

Xplode cannot explode blocks whose X and Y scale factors have unequal absolute values. That means an X scale of 1 and a Y scale of –1 is okay, but not an X scale of 2 and a Y scale of –3.

On the DVD

The drawing that you need for the following exercise on exploding and xploding blocks, ab18-e.dwg, **is in the** Drawings **folder on the DVD.** ■

STEPS: Exploding and Xploding Blocks

1. Open ab18-e.dwg from the DVD.
2. Save the file as ab18-05.dwg in your AutoCAD Bible folder. This is the same electrical schematic used in the previous exercise, except that the objects are now blocks that have been inserted (see Figure 18.12). Object Snap should be on. Set running object snaps for Endpoint, Midpoint, Quadrant, and Intersection. The current layer is Object.

FIGURE 18.12

The electrical schematic has several blocks that have been inserted.

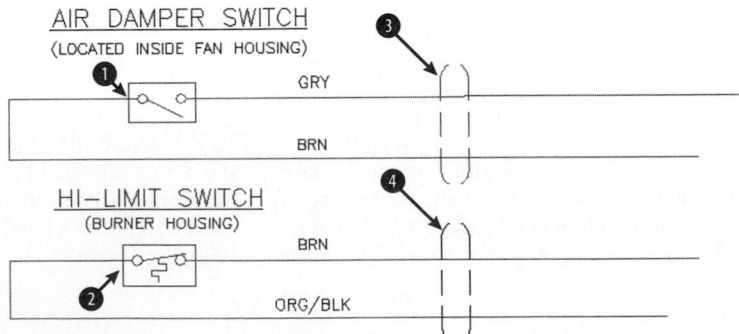

3. Choose Home tab ⇨ Modify panel ⇨ Explode. At the `Select objects:` prompt, choose the air damper switch at ❶, shown in Figure 18.12. Press Enter to end selection. The switch turns black or white (the opposite of your screen color) because it was created from objects whose color and linetype were set to ByBlock.

4. Choose Undo from the Quick Access Toolbar.

5. Type **xplode** ↵. At the `Select objects:` prompt, choose the air damper switch again. Press Enter to end selection. At the `Enter an option [All/Color/LAyer/LType/LWeight/Inherit from parent block/Explode] <Explode>:` prompt, right-click and choose LAyer. At the `Enter new layer name for exploded objects <OBJECT>:` prompt, press Enter to accept the default of OBJECT, the current layer. The command line informs you that `Object exploded onto layer OBJECT`.

6. Choose the `hi-limit` switch at ❷. Choose Home tab ⇨ Modify panel ⇨ Explode. The command explodes the block onto the Object layer because these objects were created on that layer with their color and linetype set to ByLayer.

7. Type **xplode** ↵. The top conduit was created from objects set explicitly to green color and Hidden2 linetype. The bottom conduit was created from objects set to layer 0. Follow the prompts:

```
Select objects: Choose the conduits at ❸ and ❹. End selection.
2 objects found.
Xplode Individually/<Globally>: ↵ to accept the default.
Enter an option [All/Color/LAyer/LType/LWeight/Inherit from parent
    block/Explode] <Explode>: Right-click and choose All.
New Color [Truecolor/Colorbook] <BYLAYER>: ↵
Enter new linetype name for exploded objects <BYLAYER>: ↵
Enter new lineweight < >: ↵
Enter new layer name for exploded objects <OBJECT>: conduit ↵
Objects exploded with color of BYLAYER, linetype of BYLAYER, and
    layer conduit.
```

8. Save your drawing.

Redefining a block

If you make a mistake, or if you want to change the block in some way, you can redefine it. If you just created the block, use UNDO and make any necessary changes. If you created the block earlier, follow these steps:

1. Insert the block and explode it. (Exploding is covered earlier in this chapter.)

2. Make the desired changes and repeat the process of defining the block, using the same name for the block.

Caution

When you specify the name of the block, you should type it, rather than choose it from the Name drop-down list. Choosing the name from the list replaces selected objects that you want to be in the new version of the block with the objects from the previous block definition, and sets the insertion point to 0,0. ■

3. Click Redefine (or Redefine Block) when the message asks whether you want to redefine the block.

Redefining a block that has been inserted in your drawing updates all the blocks in that drawing. This is a powerful technique to control your drawing. If you have repetitive symbols in your drawing, it's worthwhile to make blocks out of them just so that you can make this type of global change if necessary.

Editing blocks

Blocks can be complex objects. You may need to add, remove, or change a component of a block. You can also update or substitute blocks. Here are a few additional points that can help you to work with blocks.

Using the Block Editor to edit blocks

If you double-click a block, you open the Edit Block Definition dialog box. (You can also choose Home tab ⇨ Block panel ⇨ Edit, which executes the BEDIT command.) Choose the block from the Block to Create or Edit list and click OK. The Block Editor opens. I explain the Block Editor in detail later in this chapter in connection with dynamic blocks. However, you can use the Block Editor to edit all blocks, not just dynamic ones. Make the changes you want.

 When you're done, choose Block Editor tab ⇨ Open/Save panel ⇨ Save Block and click the Close Block Editor button in the Close panel.

Cross-Reference
You can also use in-place editing to edit blocks. I cover in-place editing in Chapter 19. ■

Editing blocks with grips

To a certain extent, you can use grip editing with blocks. By default, when you select a block, only one grip — at the base point — is displayed. However, you can show the grips of all the objects. Choose Application Button ⇨ Options. On the Selection tab, choose Enable Grips within Blocks and click OK.

As a general rule, you don't want to enable grips for blocks when working with complex blocks. However, you can turn them on to use grips to mirror, rotate, move, or scale the block if you want to use the grip of a component object as a base point for the edit.

Updating blocks

As I mentioned earlier in the chapter, when you redefine a block, all instances of that block are automatically updated. However, if you inserted a file to use as a block in a drawing and then changed that file, your current drawing has no way of knowing of the change in that drawing file. (Instead, use an external reference to solve this problem. See Chapter 19 for more on external references.)

To update a block that came from inserting an entire file, you can reinsert the file. Follow these steps:

1. Choose Home tab ⇨ Block panel ⇨ Insert.
2. Click Browse.
3. Choose the file that you've changed, and click Open. (You must locate the actual file rather than choose the block of the same name that already exists in the drawing.)
4. A message asks whether you want to redefine the block because that block already exists in the drawing. Choose Redefine Block.
5. Press Esc to avoid actually inserting a new copy of the block.

The drawing updates all the instances of the block with the new file. You can also use the DesignCenter to insert and update blocks.

Tip

You can update a block definition in your current drawing to match a block on a tool palette by right-clicking the block tool on the tool palette and clicking Redefine. All instances of the block are redefined to match the tool on the tool palette. (The block on the tool palette must be in the current drawing, not an external drawing.) ■

Substituting blocks

You can substitute a different file as the basis for blocks in your drawing. There are three reasons for doing this:

- If you have many instances of complex blocks, you may find that regen times are slow. You can create a simple block, WBLOCK it, and substitute it for the original blocks until plotting time.
- You can create more than one version of a drawing — for example, an office layout with various kinds of desks. You can create the drawing with one type of desk, inserting files of the desks. Substitute a file of another type of desk, and you have a new office layout design.
- Another common reason to substitute blocks is when your company switches to a different standard for a part.

To substitute blocks, follow these steps:

1. Type **-insert** ⏎ on the command line.
2. Type *blockname=filename* where blockname is the name of the block and filename is the name of the file. (If the file is not in the support file search path, type the entire path.) Press Enter.

Note

To place a folder in the support file search path, choose Application Button ⇨ Options and click the Files tab. Double-click Support File Search Path. Click Add, and then type the path or browse to it. After you're done, click OK to close the Options dialog box. ■

3. A message tells you that the block with this name already exists, and asks whether you want to redefine it. Type **y** ⏎.
4. Press Esc to avoid actually inserting a new copy of the new file.

The file that you inserted replaces the current blocks.

AutoCAD Only

The Express Tools command BLOCKREPLACE (choose Express Tools tab ⇨ Blocks panel ⇨ Replace Block) is another way to substitute blocks. Another Express Tools command, NCOPY (choose Express Tools tab ⇨ Blocks panel [expanded] ⇨ Copy Nested Objects), copies objects nested inside blocks or xrefs. XLIST (choose Express Tools tab ⇨ Blocks panel ⇨ List Properties) lists properties of nested objects within blocks. SHP2BLK (choose Express Tools tab ⇨ Modify panel [expanded] ⇨ Convert Shape to Block) converts a shape definition to a block. (I cover shape definitions in Chapter 32.) ■

Usually when you insert a file into a drawing, the block name and filename are the same. Likewise, when you WBLOCK a block, you usually name the file with the name of the block. Be aware that when you use block substitution, you have a block in your drawing that is the same as a file of a different name. For example, if you have a block in your drawing called smalldesk and substitute a file called bigdesk, you now have a block called smalldesk that is actually the same as the file bigdesk. This can become confusing, so use block substitution with care.

On the DVD

Wb.zip **unzips to three programs that create a list of blocks in your drawing, and writes them to separate drawing files. Display the list of blocks and open selected drawings from the list; after you modify them, update those drawings as blocks in your current drawing. WBLOCKM also writes all the blocks in your drawing to a folder that you specify. Look in** \Software\Chapter 18\Wb. **These programs work with AutoCAD only.** MPE-arch **is a library of mechanical, plumbing, and electrical symbols for architectural drawings, mostly lights and outlets.** Mpe. dwg **contains all the symbols and can be used as a legend. Look in** \Software\Chapter 18\Mpe-arch. North **is a collection of North symbols for architectural drawings. Look in** \Software\Chapter 18\North. ■

Creating and Using Dynamic Blocks

You probably have multiple similar blocks that you store and use on a regular basis. Moreover, you might insert these blocks at various scales and rotation angles. For example, you could have several sizes of doors that you insert at various angles, sometimes right-opening and sometimes left-opening. Dynamic blocks are blocks that contain intelligence and flexibility so that you can insert them in many variations. Thus, they can significantly reduce the number of blocks in your block library.

Dynamic blocks support both geometric and block parametric constraints. You can convert dimensional parametric constraints to block parametric constraints by choosing Block Editor tab ⇨ Dimensional panel ⇨ Convert. I cover geometric and dimensional parametric constraints in Chapter 10.

Dynamic blocks let you specify the types and amounts of variations for each block. You create (author) dynamic blocks in the Block Editor. You can use one of two systems to accomplish your goal. Each system has its strengths; use the system that most easily gives you the results you need.

Tip

You can control many of the colors used in the Block Editor as well as other display features. Click the dialog box launcher arrow at the right end of the Block Editor's Manage panel to open the Block Editor Settings dialog box. To change the background color of the Block Editor, choose Application Button ⇨ Options and click the Display tab. Click the Colors button. From the Context list, choose Block Editor. Then choose Uniform Background from the Interface Element list, and choose a color from the Color drop-down list. Click Apply & Close, and then click OK. ■

Understanding action-based parameters

This section describes action-based parameters. Action-based parameters allow for complex systems of flexibility. For a block to be dynamic, it must include at least one *parameter*. A parameter usually has an associated *action*. (I cover parametric constraints, which are different, including geometric and dimensional constraints, in Chapter 10.)

Parameters define the special properties of the dynamic block, including locations, distances, and angles. Parameters can also constrain the values within which the parameter can function. An action specifies how a block uses its associated parameter to change in some way.

For example, you may want to move one component of a block independently of the block, such as the chair in a block containing a desk and a chair. To accomplish this, you add a point parameter that specifies a point on the chair. You then add a move action that allows you to move the chair from that point. Figure 18.13 shows a desk and a chair block that includes the following dynamic components:

- The desk has a distance parameter with a stretch action. Therefore, you can stretch the desk without affecting the chair. You would use this type of action if you have several sizes of desks that you need to include in your drawing.

- The chair contains a point parameter with a move action. As a result, you can move the chair independently of the rest of the block. If you stretch the desk, you might want to move the chair so that it remains centered in front of the desk, or you might simply want to move the chair farther away from the desk.

FIGURE 18.13

This dynamic block contains components that enable you to stretch the desk's length and move the chair.

Stretch action grip   This desk is being stretched

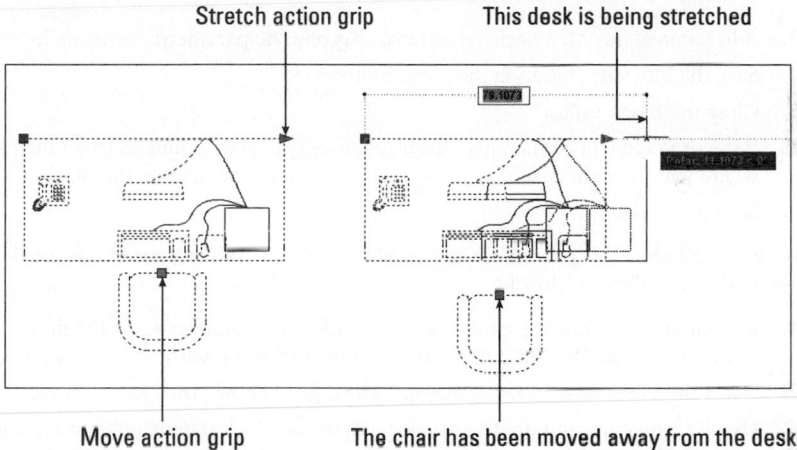

Move action grip   The chair has been moved away from the desk

If you open a dynamic block in a pre-2006 release of AutoCAD or AutoCAD LT, you see the last current view of the block. You cannot use the dynamic features of the block, but you can edit it as a regular block. The block is assigned a name, such as U2.

Understanding the work flow of dynamic blocks

Because defining a dynamic block takes some time — although simpler dynamic blocks are not very time-consuming to set up — the most common use for dynamic blocks is to create a block library. Normally, you define your dynamic blocks and save them for future use in your drawings. In other words, unless you need to insert a new block many times in several variations in a drawing, you won't create dynamic blocks for the current drawing on which you're working.

A block library can have two configurations:

- **One block per drawing.** You save each block in its own drawing. Use the BASE command to specify the origin of the drawing, which is usually on an object snap somewhere on the block. (I explain the BASE command in the "Saving blocks as files" section earlier in this chapter.) You use the INSERT command to insert the drawing, thereby inserting its block.

- **Many blocks per drawing.** You put a number of (usually) related blocks in a drawing. To insert the block, you use the DesignCenter to locate the drawing and find the individual block that you want. (See the section "Using the DesignCenter" earlier in the chapter for information on inserting blocks with the DesignCenter.)

The first part of the process of creating dynamic blocks is to define the block. I explain the details in the next few sections, but here I provide an overview of the workflow:

1. In your block library drawing or in a new drawing, create the block.
2. Choose Home tab ➪ Block panel ➪ Edit (the BEDIT command). In the Edit Block Definition dialog box, choose the block, and click OK to open the Block Editor. (You can also start the BEDIT command, name the block, and create the objects in the Block Editor.) Select <Current Drawing> to work with the objects in model space if the drawing is inserted as a block in a different drawing.
3. Add parameters and associated actions, or geometric parametric constraints.
4. Save the block definition in the Block Editor.
5. Close the Block Editor.
6. If the drawing will contain just this block, use the BASE command to set the drawing origin where you want the insertion point to be, usually somewhere on the block.
7. Save the drawing.

You may want to follow this process for any number of blocks. When your blocks are defined, do the following to insert your dynamic blocks:

1. In your current drawing, either use the INSERT command to insert the drawing containing the block, or use the DesignCenter to choose the block from within the drawing.
2. Select the block to see its special grips. These grips show you where you can modify the block.
3. Usually, you click and drag a grip. Some dynamic block parameters involve choosing a visibility or option from a drop-down list or table.

Defining a dynamic block with action-based parameters

 To define a dynamic block, first create the objects that you want for the block, or display an existing block. Then choose Home tab ➪ Block panel ➪ Edit to start the BEDIT command. In the Edit Block Definition dialog box, choose <Current Drawing> or the block's name and click OK. (You can also copy and paste individual objects from the drawing into the Block Editor to create a block from those objects.) The Block Editor opens, shown in Figure 18.14, and a new Block Editor tab appears on the Ribbon. At the same time, the Block Authoring Palettes window opens.

Before you start defining your block, you need to decide the types of variations that you want the block to have. You build flexibility into your blocks with a combination of parameters and actions. Table 18.2 lists the parameters, the actions that you can add to each parameter, and a description of the uses for the parameters and actions on the specified component of the dynamic block.

FIGURE 18.14

The Block Editor is a special window for authoring dynamic blocks.

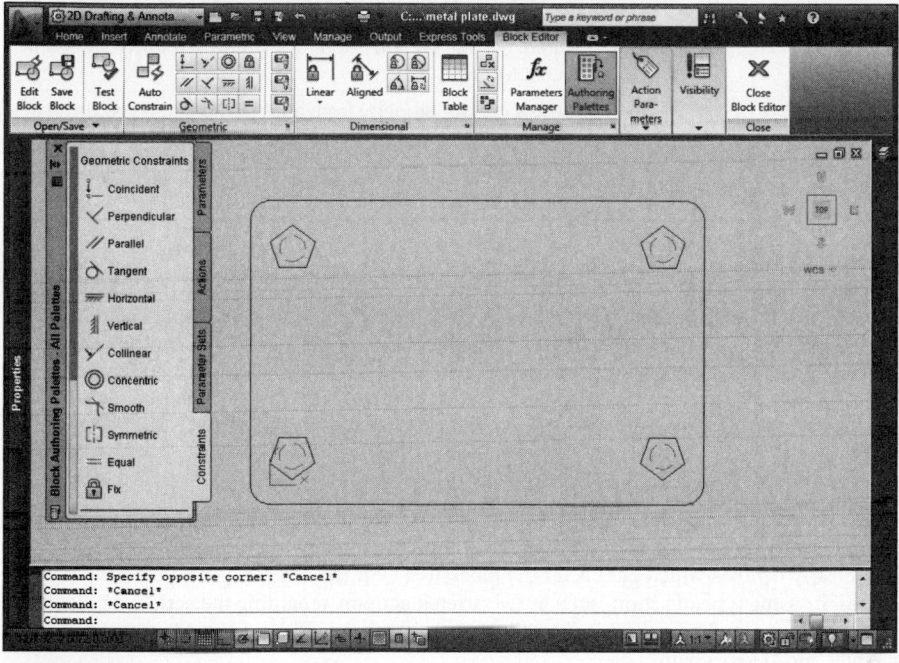

TABLE 18.2

Dynamic Block Parameters and Actions

Parameter	Available Actions	Uses
Point	Move, Stretch	Move or stretch from that point (X,Y coordinate).
Linear	Move, Scale, Stretch, Array	Move, scale, stretch, or array along the line between two points.
Polar	Move, Scale, Stretch, Polar Stretch, Array	Move, scale, stretch, stretch at an angle, or array along the line between two points and at the specified angle.
XY	Move, Scale, Stretch, Array	Move, scale, stretch, or array at the specified X and Y distance.
Rotation	Rotate	Rotate at the specified angle.
Alignment	None	Align the entire block with other objects. You can align perpendicular or tangent to other objects. No action is required.
Flip	Flip	Flip along a *reflection line*. Flipping is like mirroring without retaining the original objects.

continued

TABLE 18.2	*(continued)*	
Parameter	**Available Actions**	**Uses**
Visibility	None	Control the visibility of components in the block. No action is required. See the section "Adding visibility parameters" later in this chapter.
Lookup	Lookup	Choose a custom property from a list or table that you define. See the section "Adding lookup parameters and actions" later in this chapter.
Basepoint	None	Define a base point for the dynamic block.

Adding a parameter

To create a dynamic block, you start by adding a parameter. Click the parameter that you want from the Parameters tab of the Block Authoring Palettes window. Each parameter prompts you for the information it needs. For example, the linear parameter responds with the `Specify start point or [Name/Label/Chain/Description/Base/Palette/Value set]:` prompt. When you specify the start point, you get a prompt for the endpoint. The flip parameter prompts you for a reflection line, which is like a mirror line.

The options for each parameter are fairly similar. Here's how to use the options:

- **Name.** You can change the name of the parameter. The name appears in the Properties palette when you select the parameter. However, you may find it confusing to change the name, because the name clearly denotes which parameter the block uses. On the other hand, if you have more than one of the same type of action, such as two stretch actions, renaming the actions to identify what they apply to can eliminate confusion. For example, you could have two Move actions, "Move table" and "Move chair."

- **Label.** The label appears in the Properties palette, but also next to the block when you have the Block Editor open. Change the label to suit your needs. For example, the linear parameter uses a label of "Distance." You might want to change that to Length, Width, or even something more specific.

- **Chain.** Sometimes, you might want one action to cause more than one change in a block. To do this, you can chain parameters. As a result, activating one parameter's actions causes the secondary parameter's action to occur. The primary parameter must have an action whose selection set includes the secondary parameter in addition to any other objects it will act on. (If the action is a stretch action, the stretch frame also needs to include the secondary parameter.) You must then set the secondary parameter's Chain Actions property to Yes.

- **Description.** You can add a description to a parameter. This description displays in the Properties palette when you select the parameter in the Block Editor.

Note

If you add a description, it appears as a tooltip when you select the inserted dynamic block in your drawing and hover the cursor over the parameter's grip. You could use this feature to provide a brief description of the type of parameter or instructions on how to use it. ■

- **Base.** Creates a base point parameter, which sets a base point for the block.
- **Palette.** By default, displays parameter labels in the Properties palette when you select the block reference in a drawing. Change to No if you don't want to display the labels.

- **Value set.** You can constrain the available values for your block's size, either as increments (for example, from 3 feet to 7 feet in 6-inch increments) or by providing a list (for example, only 36", 40", and 42"). This option prompts you to choose either the increment or the list method, and then prompts you for values. You can also specify a value set later in the Properties palette.

When you are finished using the options or have specified the necessary coordinates (such as a start point and endpoint for a linear parameter), the `Specify label location:` prompt appears. Pick a point to place the label for the parameter.

An exclamation point now appears next to the parameter. This exclamation point alerts you that you have not yet added an action to the parameter. Most parameters require an action to function properly. Figure 18.15 shows a chair with a linear parameter.

FIGURE 18.15

This chair has a linear parameter, but no action.

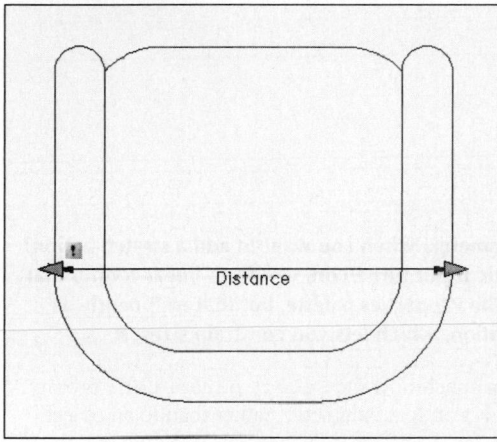

You can use the grips of the parameters as insertion points when you insert the dynamic block. During insertion, you press Ctrl to cycle among the grips if their Cycling property is set to Yes. To check, select a grip, open the Properties palette, and look for the Cycling property. You can specify the order of the cycling. Select a grip, right-click, and choose Insertion Cycling to open the Insertion Cycling Order dialog box, where you can turn cycling on or off for each grip and move the grips up and down in the order of the list.

Adding an action

When you have placed a parameter, you're ready to add an associated action. Table 18.2 lists which actions you can associate with your parameter. Click the Actions tab of the Block Authoring Palettes window, as shown in Figure 18.16.

Sometimes, the parameter that you want to use has more grips than you need. For example, if you use a linear parameter, you end up with two grips, one at each end of the length that you define. However, you might want to stretch only in one direction; in this case, you need to have only one grip. To remove the extra grip, select the parameter, right-click, and choose Grip Display ⇨ 1. The other possibility is to use a point parameter with a stretch action.

FIGURE 18.16

Use the Actions tab of the Block Authoring Palettes window to associate an action with a parameter.

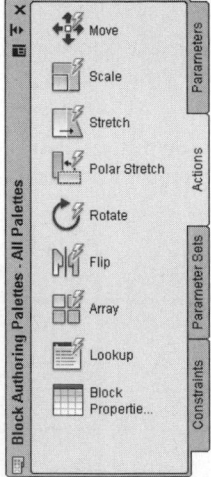

Tip

Why would you use the linear parameter (rather than a point parameter) when you want to add a stretch action? When you stretch the inserted dynamic block, if you have Dynamic Input turned on, you see a linear tooltip that allows you to enter a total length. You can set the total length in the Properties palette, but that isn't nearly as convenient. Also, a point parameter doesn't offer the Value Set option, which lets you constrain sizes. ∎

To add an action, choose an appropriate action for your parameter. At the `Select parameter:` prompt, select the parameter. Remember that you always apply an action to a parameter, rather than to an object. However, as part of the process, you specify a selection set for the action, which means selecting the object or objects. Note that you can add more than one action to a parameter.

Caution

Be sure to select the actual parameter, and not the object or the grip. An easy way to select the parameter is to click its label. ∎

The next prompts depend on the action that you choose and on the parameter to which you're attaching the action. Table 18.3 explains some of the prompt options that you find for commonly used actions.

Note

Defining the stretch frame for a stretch action is similar to specifying a crossing selection window in the STRETCH command, except that you can create the stretch frame from left to right. Objects within the frame are moved, and objects that cross the frame are stretched. However, you also select objects for a stretch action. If objects are in the stretch frame but not in the selection set, they are not stretched or moved. If objects are outside the frame, but are in the selection set, they are moved. After you select objects, you can select or deselect individual objects to add them to, or subtract them from, the selection set. ∎

TABLE 18.3

Action Prompt Options

Action	Parameter	Option Responses
Move	Point	Select the objects.
Move	Linear, polar, or XY	Because you have more than one point, you need to specify which point you want to associate with the action. You can choose the point by moving the cursor over it; a red circle appears over the active point. You can also use the sTart point/Second point options. You can press Enter to use the second point (the default), and then select the objects.
Scale	Linear, polar, or XY	You select the objects. You can also specify a dependent base (relative to the base point of the action's parameter) or an independent base point (which you specify). If you used an XY parameter, you can also specify whether the distance is the X distance, the Y distance, or the XY distance (the default).
Stretch	Point	Select the objects.
Stretch	Linear, polar, or XY	Because you have more than one point, you need to specify which point you want to associate with the action. You can choose the point by moving the cursor over it; a red circle appears over the active point. You can also use the sTart point/Second point options or press Enter to use the second point (the default), and then select the objects. Then you specify diagonal corners of a *stretch frame* that defines the area that is included in the stretch. (You can also use a Cpolygon.) Finally, you select objects. You can continue to add or remove objects, just as you do when stretching.
Polar stretch	Polar	Identical to the prompts for the Stretch parameter. In addition, you specify objects to rotate only (but not stretch).

When you complete your answers for the prompts, AutoCAD displays an icon for the action. As you add more parameters and actions to a block, you may sometimes need to know which parameter goes with which action. To find out, hover the cursor over an action's icon to highlight its parameter.

Caution

If the exclamation point doesn't disappear after you add an action, the action was not successfully added! Undo the last command (BACTIONTOOL) and try again. Usually the problem involves selecting the proper parts of the parameter and correctly selecting the applicable objects. Reducing the number of grips may also solve this problem. Select the parameter, right-click, and choose Grip Display. ■

You can modify the action to multiply the parameter value by a factor or change the parameter angle. To do so, select the action's icon and display the Properties palette (Ctrl+1). Then do one of the following:

- **Distance Multiplier.** Click next to the Distance Multiplier item in the Properties palette and enter another value to multiply the parameter by that factor. For example, you can multiply a stretch by a factor of .5. If you want to keep a circle centered inside a rectangle that you're moving or stretching, use a .5 multiplier so that the circle moves or stretches half of the distance of the rectangle, thereby remaining centered.

- **Angle Offset.** Click next to the Angle Offset item in the Properties palette and enter an angle to offset the parameter angle by that angle. For example, you can increase an angle by 90 degrees. This allows you to move the cursor to the right (0 degrees) and stretch an object in the 90-degree direction.

Adding visibility parameters

Visibility parameters enable you to turn the visibility of a block component on and off when you insert it. You can use visibility parameters either with other action-based parameters, or with geometric and dimension parametric constraints. You can define multiple named visibility states, thereby creating many variations of visibility or invisibility. Visibility parameters are a very powerful way to add flexibility to a block and to reduce the number of similar blocks that you store. You can add only one visibility parameter per block. You can use visibility parameters in two ways:

- **Make one component visible or invisible.** You can choose to display or not display one component. For example, if you have a telephone on a desk, you can display or not display the telephone.

- **Switch among multiple components.** You can include variations of a component, and cycle among them during insertion. For example, you can have three types of telephones (such as single-line, two-line, and multiple-line), all in the same location, with one on top of the other. When inserting the block, you can choose which telephone to display.

To add a visibility parameter, follow these steps:

1. Open the Block Editor in a drawing that contains the components that you need. If you want to switch among multiple components, place them on top of each other.

2. Choose Visibility from the Parameters tab of the Block Authoring Palettes window, and place it near the components. Before placing the parameter, you may want to use the Label option to change the label.

 3. Choose Block Editor tab ⇨ Visibility panel ⇨ Visibility States (or double-click the visibility parameter) to open the Visibility States dialog box, as shown in Figure 18.17.

FIGURE 18.17

Use the Visibility States dialog box to add and name visibility states.

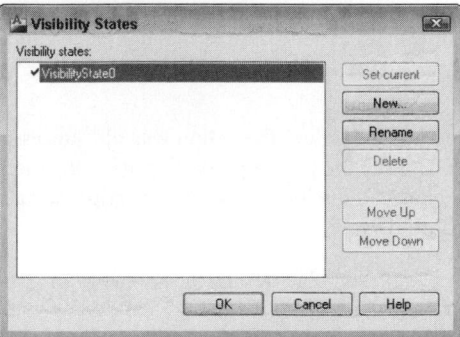

4. Click the default visibility state (VisibilityState0) to select it. Enter a new name for your first state and press Enter. The name should relate to what the state will display. In the telephone example, you might use `telephone` or `single-line` as the state.

5. Click New to open the New Visibility State dialog box, as shown in Figure 18.18.

FIGURE 18.18

The New Visibility State dialog box.

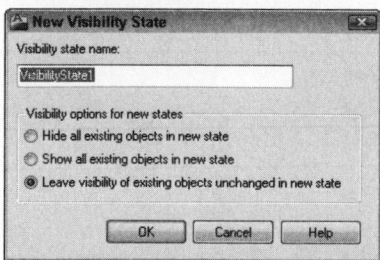

6. Enter a new visibility state name. In the telephone example, you might use no telephone or two-line. To leave the visibility of existing objects unchanged, use the default option, Leave Visibility of Existing Objects Unchanged in New State. If you want the new state to hide all objects, choose Hide All Existing Objects in New State. To display all objects, choose Show All Existing Objects in New State. Whichever option you choose, you can change the visibility of individual objects for each state afterwards. Click OK.

7. If you need more visibility states, repeat Steps 5 and 6 until you're done.

8. Click OK to close the Visibility States dialog box and return to the Block Editor.

 9. Choose the first state from the Visibility States drop-down list in the Block Editor tab's Visibility panel. For that state, select all the objects that you want to make invisible, if any. Then choose Block Editor tab ➪ Visibility panel ➪ Make Invisible.

 10. Repeat Step 9 for each state. If you chose to hide objects when you created the state, you may instead need to make certain objects visible by choosing Block Editor tab ➪ Visibility panel ➪ Make Visible.

Note

If you need to select an object that's invisible, choose Block Editor tab ➪ Visibility panel ➪ Visibility Mode. The object is displayed in a light gray color so that you can see and select it. ■

11. Check each visibility state by choosing each state in turn from the Visibility States drop-down list in the Visibility panel and making sure that each state displays what you want it to display.

When you insert the dynamic block and select it, you see a down arrow. Click the arrow to display the list of visibility states. Choose the state that you want.

Adding lookup parameters and actions

A lookup parameter/action combination creates a table that pairs labels with values. For example, you might have a desk that comes in three sizes. You can create this desk and use the Value Set option to create a list of three sizes: 4 feet, 5 feet, and 6 feet. You can then create labels that say 4' desk, 5' desk, and 6' desk. When you insert the desk, you can choose the label that you want from a drop-down list; the desk automatically stretches to the proper size. You don't need to use the Value Set option, because you specify values in the lookup table. Later in this chapter, I discuss Block Tables, which are another way to create a list of size variations. If you are using parametric constraints, you use a Block Table, rather than a lookup table.

Lookup tables are great when you want preset sizes for a block. When you insert the block, you don't even have to think about exact measurements; you just choose from a drop-down list, as shown in Figure 18.19.

FIGURE 18.19

You can specify a preset size by choosing from the drop-down list.

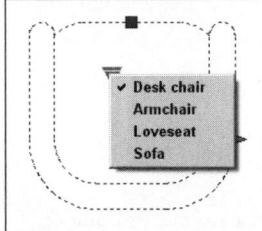

To create a lookup parameter and action, follow these steps:

1. In the Block Editor, add a parameter and action that you will use as the basis for the Lookup parameter and action. For example, add a linear parameter and a stretch action. If you add a value set (list or increment), the measurements will be available in advance when you create the lookup table.

2. From the Parameters tab of the Block Authoring Palettes window, add a Lookup parameter.

3. From the Actions tab, add a Lookup action. At the prompt, select the lookup parameter. The Property Lookup Table dialog box opens, as shown in Figure 18.20.

4. Click the Add Properties button, choose the parameter that you want to work with (for example, the linear parameter), and click OK. You return to the Property Lookup Table dialog box.

FIGURE 18.20

The Property Lookup Table dialog box enables you to associate values with labels.

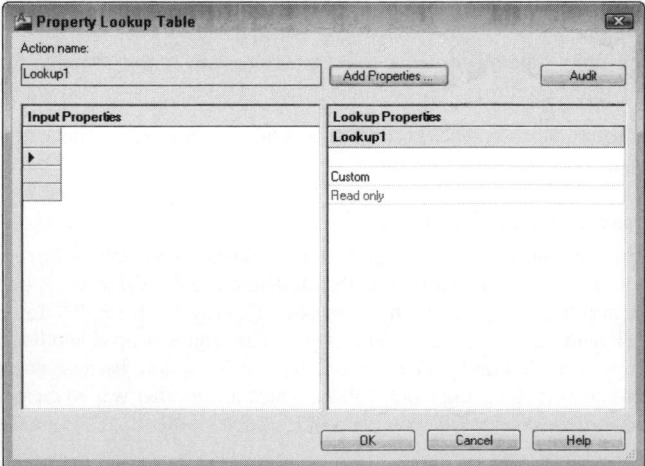

5. If you have values from a value set, you can see them by clicking the first row in the Input Properties side of the dialog box. A drop-down arrow appears. Choose the first value. If you don't have a value set, click the Add Properties button, choose the parameter you want, and click OK. Click on the Input Properties side, and choose a value from the drop-down list that appears. Click the same row on the Lookup Properties side of the dialog box and enter the label that corresponds with the value. Then click the next row, choose the next value, and enter the next label. Continue until you're done.

6. If the lower-right cell in the dialog box says Read Only, click it so that it changes to read Allow Reverse Lookup. (To do this, all the rows in the table must be unique.) You need to use this option in order to choose a value from a drop-down list of labels when you insert the block. Click OK.

7. Click Block Editor tab ➪ Close panel ➪ Close Block Editor.

Now each value in the lookup table is associated with the labels that you entered. When you insert the dynamic block and select it, click the down arrow and choose from the options that drop down.

Tip

To edit the lookup action, right-click it and choose Display Lookup Table to open the Property Lookup Table dialog box. There you can make your changes. ■

Using parameter sets

The Parameter Sets tab of the Block Authoring Palettes window contains a number of ready-made parameter-action combinations that you can use. These sets are great for quick creation of dynamic blocks that are not complex. Hover the cursor over any parameter set to see a tooltip explaining the set's functioning.

When you place a parameter set, you see an exclamation point, because you have not yet selected the objects for the action. Right-click the action icon and choose Action Selection Set ➪ New Selection Set to display prompts that allow you to select objects.

Tip

You can edit these parameter sets and create new ones. To create a new one, right-click the parameter set on the Parameter Sets tab and choose Copy. Then right-click the tab itself and choose Paste. To change a parameter set, right-click a parameter set and choose Properties. Then change the settings in the Tool Properties dialog box. To add an action, click the Actions item, and then click the Ellipsis button to open the Add Actions dialog box. ■

Using parametric constraints

Parametric constraints allow you to control the geometric and dimensional relationships among objects. I cover parametric constraints in full in Chapter 10. This discussion assumes that you have read that chapter.

AutoCAD Only

You can't create parametric constraints in AutoCAD LT, but if they are in a drawing that you open, you can use them. ■

Caution

Dynamic block parameters and actions, just previously described, and parametric constraints have some overlap in their capabilities. In most cases, you should use one or the other, but not both, for any dynamic block. Combining the parameters-actions feature with the parametric constraints feature can create undesirable results, because constraints may prevent an action from functioning the way you want it to, or may allow a valid yet unintended result. However, visibility, alignment, and base point parameters should not cause a problem when you use them along with parametric constraints because they don't change the geometry of the block itself. ■

 You can apply parametric constraints to your objects in the drawing window, before creating the block and entering the Block Editor. If you don't see your constraints in the Block Editor, click Block Editor tab ➪ Geometric panel ➪ Show All.

 It is important to constrain your objects as fully as possible, because the purpose of dynamic blocks is to allow for modification. Underconstrained blocks may break apart or act in other unpredictable ways. To start the process, choose Block Editor ➪ Geometric panel ➪ Auto Constrain. Then add other constraints that you think may be necessary. You can customize the auto-constraining process. Click the dialog box launcher arrow at the right end of the Geometric panel to open the Constraint Settings dialog box. For more information, see Chapter 10.

AutoCAD Only

To help create constraints, you can use click the Infer Constraints button on the status bar. For more information, see Chapter 10. ■

 To check the level of constraint on a block, choose Block Editor tab ➪ Manage panel ➪ Constraint Display Status. The objects in the block turn various colors, depending on their status. Click the button again to remove these colors. By default, the colors are as follows:

- **White.** Unconstrained
- **Blue.** Partially constrained
- **Magenta.** Fully constrained
- **Red.** Improperly constrained

To change the colors for each category, click the dialog box launcher arrow at the right end of the Manage panel to open the Block Editor Settings dialog box (the BSETTINGS command); this feature is hard to understand if the colors of your objects are the same as the default colors.

 You may find that you need to add a line or other object as a bridge between two objects, in order to set a desired distance, for example. This is called *construction geometry*. Normally, you would use a separate layer for construction geometry and then freeze or turn off that layer, or set it to Not Plottable. However, in the Block Editor, you can simply choose Block Editor tab ➪ Manage panel ➪ Construction Geometry and select the line or object. Press Enter to accept the default Convert option. That object then appears dashed, and does not plot.

Tip

You can add a Fix geometric constraint to fix the block's base point to a specific point. This ensures that the block changes relative to that fix point. Sometimes, this is all you need to add to the auto-constraining process to make a block fully constrained. ■

Add the geometric constraints you need from the Block Editor's Geometric panel (or the Constraints tab of the Block Authoring Palettes window), whether manually or by auto-constraining; then move on to dimensional constraints from the Dimensional panel. When you add dimensional constraints inside the Block Editor, you get a prompt for the number of grips. By including one or more grips, the dimensional constraint allows you to modify the block in your drawing, just like grips for actions (discussed earlier in this chapter). In this way, a linear constraint can replace a linear parameter/stretch action combination.

To restrict allowable values, you can add a value set to a dimensional constraint. (I cover value sets earlier in this chapter.) Select the constraint, display the Properties palette (Ctrl+1), and use the Value Set section.

Creating a Block Table

A Block Table allows you to specify defined sizes for dimensional constraints and select those sizes from a drop-down list when you modify the dynamic block. A Block Table is similar to a lookup table, covered earlier in this chapter, but has some differences. You cannot use a Block Table with action-based parameters; instead, use a lookup table.

A dynamic block can have only one Block Table. When you use the Block Table for one dimensional constraint, it functions like a lookup table, allowing you to choose a size from the drop-down list. However, the Block Table can include more than one dimensional constraint; in this case, you can create combinations of sizes. For example, you might allow a rectangle with two dimensional constraints to be 2 x 3, 3 x 4, or 4 x 5. In this situation, you could not choose 2 x 5 from the drop-down list, because that combination is not in the Block Table. However, you can allow other values, but they wouldn't be available from the drop-down list.

 To add a Block Table, first create the dimensional constraints that you need. Then choose Block Editor tab ⇨ Dimensional panel ⇨ Block Table. Follow the prompts:

```
Specify parameter location or [Palette]: Specify a location where the
     drop-down list will appear. Use the Palette option and choose Yes
     or No to specify whether you want to display the Block Table in
     the Properties palette.
Enter number of grips [0/1] <1>: Enter 1 ↵ to display a down-facing
     triangle, which will open the drop-down list of values. Enter 0 ↵
     to hide the drop-down list.
```

 The Block Properties Table dialog box opens. Click the Adds Properties which Appear as Columns in the Table button. The Add Parameter Properties dialog box opens, listing the dimensional parameters available in the dynamic block. Choose the ones that you want to include in the Block Table, and click OK to return to the Block Properties Table dialog box. The parameters you chose are now listed as columns in the Block Table.

Enter the desired values in the cells of the table. Remember that if you chose more than one constraint, the drop-down list will only allow the combinations that you enter. Figure 18.21 shows a table with two dimensional constraints (d1 and d2) applied to a rectangle, and three size options.

Note

If you created a value set for a dimensional constraint, you cannot enter values that are not specified in the value set. ∎

If the Block Properties Must Match a Row in the Table check box is checked, you can't modify the dynamic block to sizes not in the table. If you uncheck this check box, only sizes in the table will appear in the drop-down list, but you will be able to drag the block to sizes not listed.

FIGURE 18.21

This Block Table provides three sizes for a rectangle dynamic block.

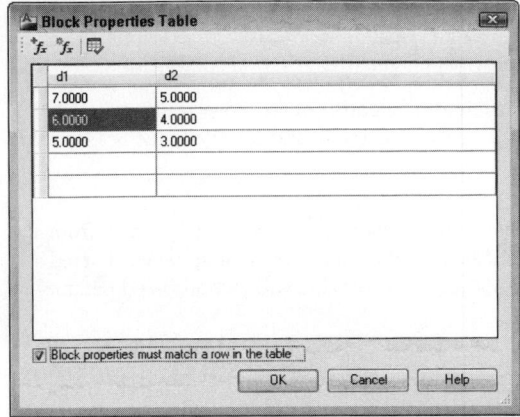

 When you're done entering values in the Block Table, click the Audit the Block Property Table for Errors button. The audit process finds cells that are missing values or empty rows for values in a value set that you created, for example. After fixing any errors, click OK. Click Block Editor tab ➪ Open/Save panel ➪ Save Block to save the block.

Saving and testing dynamic blocks

 When your dynamic block is done, choose Block Editor tab ➪ Open/Save panel ➪ Save Block.

Tip

To make a copy of the block, choose Block Editor tab ➪ Open/Save panel (expanded) ➪ Save Block As. You can then modify the new block to make a variation of the original block. You can use the Save Block As button to create a duplicate of any block, not just a dynamic one. ■

 Before continuing, you should test the block to make sure that it works the way you want it to. To test a block, choose Block Editor tab ➪ Open/Save panel ➪ Test Block.

A new Test Block Window opens. Select the block and try out its dynamic features. For more information about using a dynamic block, see the "Inserting and using dynamic blocks" section later in this chapter. When you are done, click the Close Test Block Window button on the Close panel to return to the regular Block Editor window.

To close the Block Editor, choose Block Editor tab ➪ Close panel ➪ Close Block Editor.

If you want to put the base point for the block somewhere on the block, use the BASE command. Then save your drawing.

Inserting and using dynamic blocks

You insert a dynamic block in the same way that you insert a regular block: by using the Insert dialog box or the DesignCenter. For more information, see "Inserting Blocks and Files into Drawings" earlier in this chapter.

During insertion, you can press Ctrl to cycle among the grips if their Cycling property is set to Yes. Each time you press Ctrl, the cursor moves to another grip on the block. Also, before you specify the insertion point, you can open the Properties palette and specify values, such as the distance value of a length parameter.

To use the dynamic features of the block, first select the block. You see turquoise dynamic block grips, depending on the type of action. You click and drag these grips in the same way that you do for regular grips; the difference is that the resulting modification is controlled by the parameters-actions or the parametric constraints that you defined. If you have created a value set, you see vertical lines at the available lengths, as shown to the right of the cursor in Figure 18.22. Lookup and visibility actions, as well as Block Tables, have a down arrow so that you can open a drop-down list and choose a lookup table, visibility state, or table row, respectively.

FIGURE 18.22

This block can be a chair, loveseat, or sofa. The faint vertical lines indicate the available lengths as you drag.

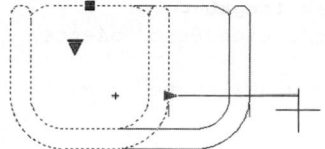

On the DVD

The drawing that you need for the following exercise on creating and inserting dynamic blocks using action-based parameters, ab18-f.dwg, is in the Drawings folder on the DVD. Following this exercise is one on creating and inserting dynamic blocks using parametric constraints and a Block Table. ∎

STEPS: Creating and Inserting Dynamic Blocks Using Action-Based Parameters

1. Open ab18-f.dwg from the DVD. This is a set of office furniture, as shown in Figure 18.23.

2. Save the drawing as ab18-06.dwg in your AutoCAD Bible folder. Set an Endpoint running object snap.

3. Hover the cursor over any part of the drawing. You can see that it is all one block, called DeskSet.

4. Double-click the block. In the Edit Block Definition dialog box, choose DeskSet and click OK. The Block Editor opens with the desk set (including a desk, armchair, computer, monitor, and phone) displayed. Inside the Block Editor, you work with the individual components of the DeskSet block. The Block Authoring Palettes window also opens.

5. You want to be able to move the armchair separately from the rest of the block. To add a point parameter to the chair, click the Parameters tab of the Block Authoring Palettes window and choose Point.

6. Follow these prompts:

```
Specify parameter location or [Name/Label/Chain/Description/Palette]:
     Right-click and choose Label.
Enter position property label <Position>: Chair Location ↵
```

```
Specify parameter location or [Name/Label/Chain/Description/Palette]:
   Pick the endpoint at the middle of the front of the chair.
Specify label location: Pick a location for the Chair Location label.
```

7. To add a Move action to the point parameter, click the Actions tab and choose Move. Follow the prompts:

```
Select parameter: Select the point parameter by clicking its label.
Specify selection set for action. Select objects: Select all the
   objects that make up the chair. (In this instance, it doesn't make
   any difference whether or not you include the actual parameter in
   the selection set.)
Select objects: ↵
```

8. To add a linear parameter to the desk, click the Parameters tab and choose Linear. Follow the prompts:

```
Specify start point or [Name/Label/Chain/Description/Base/Palette/
   Value set]: Right-click and choose Label.
Enter distance property label <Distance>: Desk length ↵
Specify start point or [Name/Label/Chain/Description/Base/Palette/
   Value set]: Right-click and choose Value Set.
Enter distance value set type [None/List/Increment] <None> : Right-
   click and choose Increment.
Enter distance increment: 6 ↵
Enter minimum distance: 48 ↵
Enter maximum distance: 72 ↵
Specify start point or [Name/Label/Chain/Description/Base/Palette/Value
   set]: Choose the endpoint at the upper-left corner of the desk.
Specify endpoint: Choose the endpoint at the upper-right corner of
   the desk.
Specify label location: Pick a location above the desk.
```

FIGURE 18.23

The office furniture is a block that can be more useful if it is dynamic.

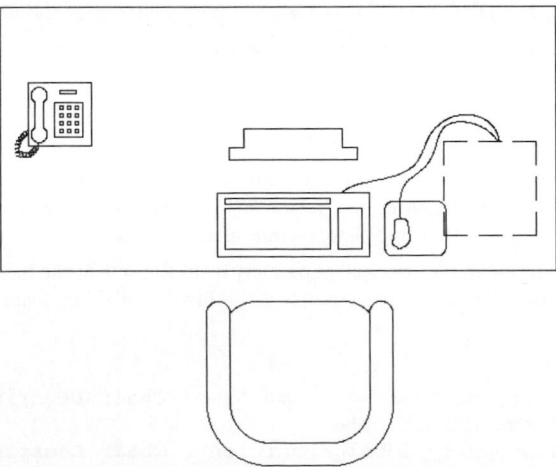

9. We only want the right grip for the linear parameter. This makes sure that the desk can only be stretched toward the right. Select the linear parameter. Right-click and choose Grip Display ⇨ 1. The left grip disappears.

10. Click the Actions tab and choose Stretch. Follow the prompts:

```
Select parameter: Select the linear parameter by clicking its label.
Specify parameter point to associate with action or enter [sTart
    point/Second point] <Start>: Pass the cursor over the right grip
    and click.
Specify first corner of stretch frame or [CPolygon]: Click at ❶ in
    Figure 18.24.
Specify opposite corner: Click at ❷.
Specify objects to stretch. Select objects: Click close to but not on
    top of ❷.
Specify opposite corner: Click close to but not on top of ❶. The
    command line should show 52 found.
Select objects: ↵
```

11. The block should look like Figure 18.24.

FIGURE 18.24

The DeskSet block after adding a move action to the armchair and a stretch action to the desk.

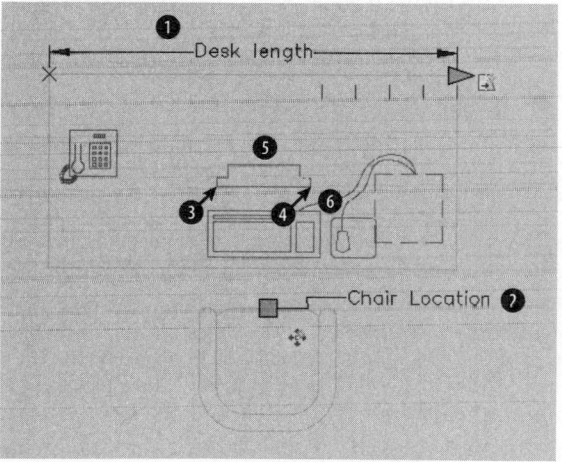

12. To allow for various sizes of monitors, click the Parameters tab and choose Linear. Right-click and choose the Label option. Type **Monitor width** ↵.

13. At the next two prompts, pick points ❸ and ❹, shown in Figure 18.24. Then place the parameter label above the monitor.

14. You can also create a value set in the Properties palette. Select the `Monitor width` parameter and open the Properties palette (Ctrl+1). In the Value Set section, choose List from the `Dist Type` drop-down list. Next to the `Dist Value List` item, click the Ellipsis (...) button to open the Add Distance Value dialog box. The current width is already there. In the Distances to Add text box, type **18-1/2** ↵. The value moves below to the list box and changes to 1'-6 ½". Again in the Distances to Add text box, type **20-1/2** ↵. Click OK to close the dialog box.

15. With the linear parameter still selected, in the Properties palette, change the value of the Number of Grips item (in the Misc section) to 1. Close or minimize the Properties palette.

16. Click the Actions tab in the Block Authoring Palettes window and choose Stretch. At the `Select parameter:` prompt, select the linear parameter that you just created. At the next prompt, click the right parameter point. To specify the stretch frame, pick ❺ and then ❻, shown in Figure 18.24. To select objects, pick near ❻ and then near ❺. Press Enter to end selection.

17. You want to create a lookup parameter for the monitor. On the Parameters tab, choose Lookup and pick a location on the monitor. On the Actions tab, choose Lookup. Select the lookup parameter. The Property Lookup Table dialog box opens.

18. Click the Add Properties button. In the Add Parameter Properties dialog box, choose the `Linear 1` parameter and click OK. Back in the Property Lookup Table dialog box, click the first row on the Input Properties side, below the Monitor width heading, and choose the first measurement from the drop-down list. In the same row on the Lookup Properties side, type **15" monitor**. (Note that monitors are measured diagonally, so the horizontal width of a 15" monitor is not 15".) In the second row on the Input Properties side, choose the second measurement and enter **17" monitor** on the right. In the third row on the left, choose the last measurement and enter **19" monitor** on the right.

19. Click the Read Only cell; it changes to read Allow Reverse Lookup. The Property Lookup Table dialog box should have the rows shown below. Click OK.

    ```
    1'-4 1/2"          15" monitor
    1'-6 1/2"          17" monitor
    1'-8 1/2"          19" monitor
    ```

20. Because some people may not have a land-line phone, we want to create a visibility parameter and action for the phone. On the Parameters tab, choose Visibility. Follow the prompts:

    ```
    Specify parameter location or [Name/Label/Description/Palette]:
        Right-click and choose Label.
    Enter visibility property label <Visibility>: Phone/No Phone ↵
    Specify parameter location or [Name/Label/Description/Palette]: Pick
        a location near the phone.
    ```

 21. Choose Block Editor tab ➪ Visibility panel ➪ Visibility States. The Visibility States dialog box opens. Click the VisibilityState0 item and type **Has phone** ↵. Click New. In the Visibility State Name text box of the New Visibility State dialog box, type **No phone** ↵. Click OK twice to return to the Block Editor.

22. From the Visibility States drop-down list, make sure that No Phone is displayed; if not, choose it. Choose Block Editor tab ➪ Visibility panel ➪ Make Invisible. At the `Select objects:` prompt, select all the objects of the phone and press Enter to end selection. To double-check the visibility states, choose the Has Phone state and make sure that the phone appears.

23. Your block should look like Figure 18.25. Choose Block Editor tab ➪ Open/Save panel ➪ Save Block. Then click Close Block Editor in the Close panel. Save your drawing.

FIGURE 18.25

The completed dynamic block in the Block Editor.

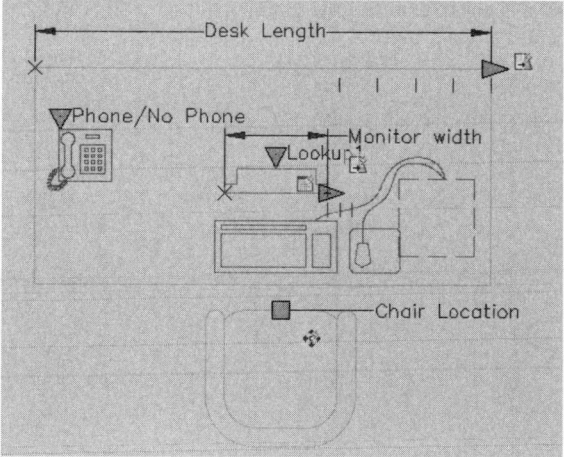

24. Open a new drawing based on the default template or any template that you usually use. Open the DesignCenter. In the Open Drawings pane, browse to, and double-click, ab18-06.dwg. Click Blocks. Drag the DeskSet block from the right side of the DesignCenter to your drawing. Close or minimize the DesignCenter.

Note

If you create a block inside a drawing and then make it dynamic, you need to use the DesignCenter to insert it. If you try to insert the entire drawing, you see only a regular block. However, if you don't create a block in the source drawing and create the dynamic block in the Block Editor without ever creating and naming a block, you can use the INSERT command to insert the entire drawing and use the dynamic features of the block. ■

25. Choose View tab ⇨ Navigation panel ⇨ Zoom drop-down list ⇨ Extents.

26. Select the DeskSet block. It should look like Figure 18.26.

27. Click the desk's stretch grip and stretch the desk one vertical line to the left to make it 6 inches shorter. The computer moves with the desk.

28. Click the armchair's move grip and move the chair to the left so that it is still centered in front of the computer.

29. Click the monitor's lookup grip and choose 19" monitor from the drop-down list. The monitor becomes wider.

30. Click the phone's visibility grip and choose No phone from the drop-down list. The phone disappears.

31. Continue to experiment with the grips to see all the possible variations. You do not need to save this drawing.

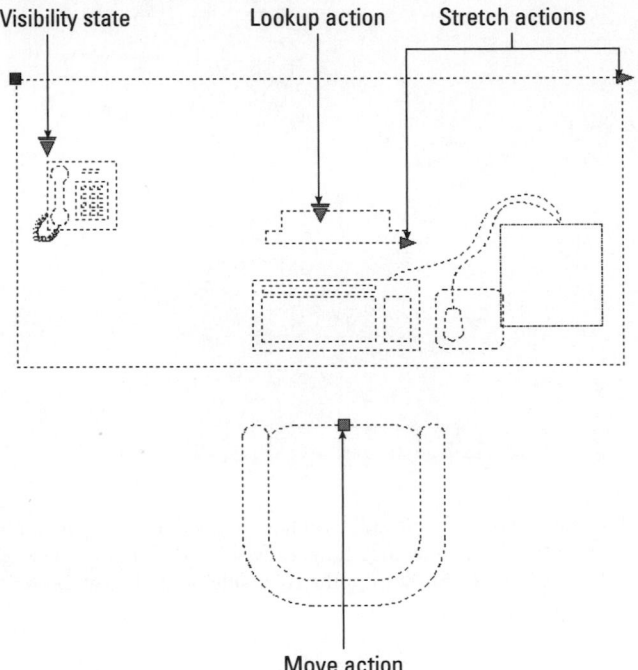

FIGURE 18.26

When you select a dynamic block, you see grips for its dynamic features.

Visibility state Lookup action Stretch actions

Move action

On the DVD

The drawing that you need for the following exercise on creating and inserting dynamic blocks using parametric constraints and a Block Table, ab18-g.dwg, is in the Drawings folder on the DVD. ■

STEPS: Creating and Inserting Dynamic Blocks Using Parametric Constraints and a Block Table

AutoCAD Only

This exercise does not apply to AutoCAD LT. ■

1. Open ab18-g.dwg from the DVD. This is a sheet metal plate, similar to the one used in the Chapter 10 exercise on parametric constraints, as shown in Figure 18.27.

2. Save it as ab18-07.dwg in your AutoCAD Bible folder. Set a running object snap for Endpoint.

3. The goal is to create a block that can be four sizes; however, the central hole's diameter should remain unchanged. To create the block, select all the objects, and choose Home tab ➪ Block panel ➪ Create.

FIGURE 18.27

A sheet-metal plate that comes in several sizes.

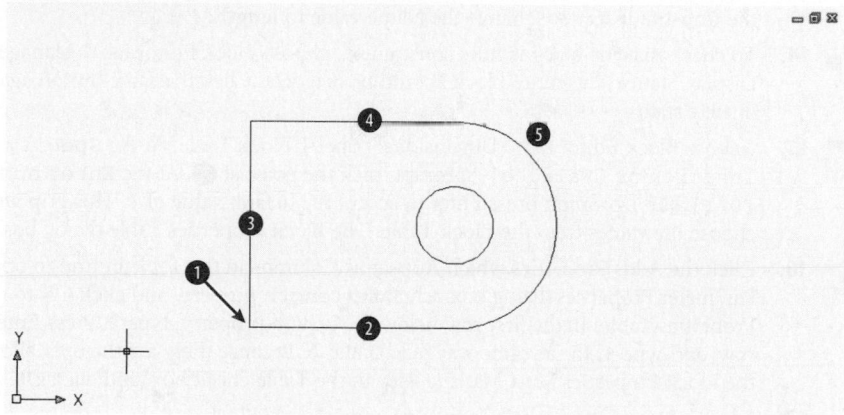

4. In the Block Definition dialog box, enter **ab18-g1** for the block name. In the Base Point section, the Specify On-Screen check box should be checked; the other Specify-On-Screen check box should not be checked. Check the Open in Block Editor check box and click OK.

5. At the `Specify insertion base point:` prompt, pick the endpoint at ❶ in Figure 18.27. The block opens in the Block Editor.

6. Choose Block Editor tab⇨Geometric panel⇨Auto Constrain. At the `Select objects or [Settings]:` prompt, type **all** ↵. Press Enter to end the command. AutoCAD adds a number of geometric constraints to the drawing — coincident, tangent, concentric, parallel, perpendicular, and horizontal.

7. As you stretch the block, the three straight sides need to remain equal. You only need to specify two of the sides. Choose Block Editor tab⇨Geometric panel⇨Equal. At the prompts, pick the bottom horizontal side at ❷ and the left vertical side at ❸.

8. As you stretch the block, you don't want the base point to move, so choose Block Editor tab⇨Geometric panel⇨Fix and choose the endpoint at ❶.

9. To keep the inner circle unchanged, add a diameter parameter. Choose Block Editor tab⇨Dimensional panel⇨Diameter. Follow the prompts:

    ```
    Select arc or circle: Pick the inner circle.
    Specify dimension line location: Pick a location to the left of the
        circle.
    Enter value or name and value, and press Enter
    ```

10. Select the diameter parameter. Right-click and choose Grip Display⇨0. (You enter 0 because you don't need to change the diameter.)

11. To add a linear dimensional constraint, choose Block Editor tab⇨Dimensional panel⇨Linear. Follow the prompts:

    ```
    Specify first constraint point or [Object] <Object>: ↵
    Select object: Pick the top horizontal line at ❹.
    Specify dimension line location: Pick a location above the line.
    Enter value or name and value, and press Enter
    ```

12. Select the diameter parameter. Right-click and choose Grip Display ⇨ 0. (You would need a grip if you wanted to drag the block, but you will use the Block Table feature instead.)

13. To change the name of the linear constraint, select it and open the Properties palette (Ctrl+1). In the Constraint section, change the Name value to **length**.

 14. To check that the block is fully constrained, choose Block Editor tab ⇨ Manage panel ⇨ Constraint Display Status. The entire block should be magenta. Click the same button again to turn off the display status.

 15. Choose Block Editor tab ⇨ Dimensional panel ⇨ Block Table. At the `Specify parameter location or [Palette]:` prompt, pick the point at ❺. At the `Enter number of grips [0/1] <1>:` prompt, press Enter to accept the default value of 1. This grip will allow you to choose the values from the Block Table. The Block Properties Table dialog box opens.

16. Click the Adds Properties which Appear as Columns in the Table button to open the Add Parameter Properties dialog box. Click the `length` property and click OK to return to the Block Properties Table. In the first row below the Length property, type **3**. Press Enter to go to the next row, and type **4**. In the same way, add **5** and **6**. Because these are the only allowable sizes, check the Block Properties Must Match a Row in the Table check box, and click OK.

17. Choose Block Editor tab ⇨ Open/Save panel ⇨ Save Block.

18. Choose Block Editor ⇨ Open/Save panel ⇨ Test Block. The Test Block Window opens. Select the block. Click the down arrow to reveal the length values you specified, as shown in Figure 18.28.

FIGURE 18.28

The metal plate has four sizes that you can choose from the Block Table's drop-down list.

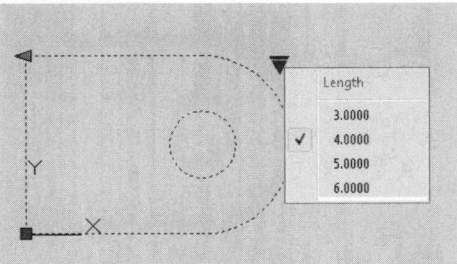

19. Choose the various sizes to see the result. The inner circle should remain concentric with the outer arc but should not change size. The three sides should always be the same length.

20. Click Close panel ⇨ Close Test Block Window to return to the Block Editor.

21. Click Block Editor tab ⇨ Close panel ⇨ Close Block Editor. At the message to save, choose the option to save. You return to your drawing. If you want, you can again test the block.

22. Save your drawing.

Using Windows Features to Copy Data

You can insert objects by copying them from other drawings and pasting them into your current drawing or using the drag-and-drop feature. You may be able to insert objects in this way without creating blocks.

Manipulating objects with the Windows Clipboard

You're probably familiar with cutting or copying data in other Windows applications and then pasting it, either within a file or from file to file. Table 18.4 compares copying, using blocks, and using the Clipboard with the CUTCLIP, COPYCLIP, and PASTECLIP commands.

TABLE 18.4

Comparison of Methods of Moving/Copying Objects

Method	Features
MOVE/COPY	Precise placement of objects; only works within a drawing.
BLOCK/WBLOCK/INSERT	Precise placement of objects; can scale and rotate; creates block definition; can insert many times, even after other commands; can insert files (other drawings) that you save permanently. With the DesignCenter or Tool Palettes window, you can insert blocks from other drawings.
CUTCLIP/COPYCLIP/PASTECLIP	No precise placement of objects (uses bottom-left corner of extents of object[s] that you copy); creates anonymous block in file with a name like A$CE314; can scale and rotate; can both move and copy objects; can insert (paste) many times; can copy from drawing to drawing or to other Windows applications.

In general, for one-time moving or copying with a drawing, you should use the MOVE or COPY command. If you want to copy an object several times over a period of time, use a BLOCK command. Use the Clipboard when you want to insert objects into another drawing one or more times without saving the objects. Also, the Clipboard is indispensable for copying objects to other applications.

 To place objects on the Clipboard, first select them. To move them, choose Home tab ➪ Clipboard panel ➪ Cut or press Ctrl+X. To copy them, choose Copy Clip in the same panel. You can paste objects that you've copied to the Clipboard into the same drawing as a block by using the PASTEBLOCK command; right-click and choose Clipboard ➪ Paste as Block. If you want to paste the objects in another drawing, open that drawing. Choose Paste in the Clipboard panel. The command line prompts you for an insertion point.

Cross-Reference
Chapter 27 covers moving and copying objects, images, and data to and from other applications. ■

Using drag-and-drop

The drag-and-drop feature in Windows enables you to drag another drawing file into your drawing. Your drawing then prompts you as it would if you inserted the file by using the -INSERT command. You need to open either My Computer or Windows Explorer. In the following steps, I use Windows Explorer.

To insert a drawing file by using drag-and-drop, follow these steps:

1. Open Windows Explorer. (Right-click the Start button and choose Explore.)
2. Navigate to the drawing file.
   - If the drawing window is visible, drag the drawing file into the AutoCAD or AutoCAD LT window.
   - If the drawing window is not visible, drag the drawing file onto the AutoCAD or AutoCAD LT button on the task bar, wait for your drawing to appear, and then drag the file into the drawing window.
3. Respond to the prompts of the -INSERT command on the command line.

When you drag the file into the drawing area, you see a plus sign at the cursor (or a rectangular cursor, depending on your operating system), indicating that you can drop the file.

To open a drawing file instead of inserting it, drag the file onto the application title bar at the very top of the application window, or simply double-click its icon in Windows Explorer. If you drag with the right-mouse button, when you release the mouse button in the drawing area, you have some additional options to create an external reference (Create Xref) or to create a hyperlink.

Tip

If you really don't know where the file is, or you're not even sure of its name, use the Windows Find feature. Choose Start ➪ Search ➪ For Files or Folders. (In Windows Vista and Windows 7, choose Start and type in the Start Search text box.) On the screen that appears, set the criteria for the file. For example, you could find all drawing names that start with the letter C by typing c*.dwg in the Named text box. From the resulting list, choose the drawing that you want, and drag it onto your drawing by using the same steps listed previously. ■

Drag-and-drop is easy to use. It's a helpful tool if you aren't sure where the file that you want is located because it's easier to navigate with Windows Explorer than from the Select Drawing File dialog box.

You can also drag an object from one drawing to another. First open both drawings. It helps to be able to see them both at once. Choose View tab ➪ Windows panel ➪ Tile Vertically to see them side by side. Select the object or objects that you want to copy. Now click the object or objects again, and hold down the mouse button until the cursor displays a small rectangle. Then drag the object(s) to the other drawing.

On the DVD

The drawings that you need for the following exercise on using the Windows Clipboard and drag-and-drop, ab18-h-1.dwg and ab18-h-2.dwg, are in the Drawings folder on the DVD. ■

STEPS: Using the Windows Clipboard and Drag-and-Drop

1. Open ab18-h-1.dwg from the DVD. This is a set of office furniture, as shown in Figure 18.29. Before proceeding, close any other drawings that you have open.

FIGURE 18.29

A set of office furniture.

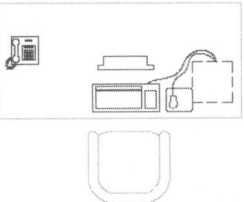

2. Pick the chair, which is a block, and choose Home tab ➪ Clipboard panel ➪ Copy Clip.
3. Choose Open from the Quick Access Toolbar. Open ab18-h-2.dwg from the DVD. This is the plan of an office building, as shown in Figure 18.30.
4. Save the drawing as ab18-08.dwg in your AutoCAD Bible folder.

5. Choose Paste from the Clipboard panel on the Home tab. At the Specify insertion point: prompt, pick ❶, shown in Figure 18.30. This action inserts the armchair in the lobby using the default scale and rotation.

6. Choose View tab ⇨ Windows panel ⇨ Tile Vertically. You can now see both drawings at once. Click in ab18-h-1.dwg to activate it. Select the chair. Click and hold the left-mouse button on the chair again until you see the small rectangle at the cursor. Drag the chair into ab18-08.dwg and place it next to the first chair.

7. Click the Close button of ab18-h-1.dwg. (You don't need to save any changes.) Click the Maximize button of ab18-08.dwg.

8. From the task bar menu, right-click Start, and choose Explore (or Open Windows Explorer). Locate ab18-h-1.dwg on the DVD. If necessary, resize the Exploring window so that you can see some of the drawing window.

9. Drag ab18-h-1.dwg from its listing in Windows Explorer onto the drawing area, and release the mouse button.

FIGURE 18.30

The office plan.

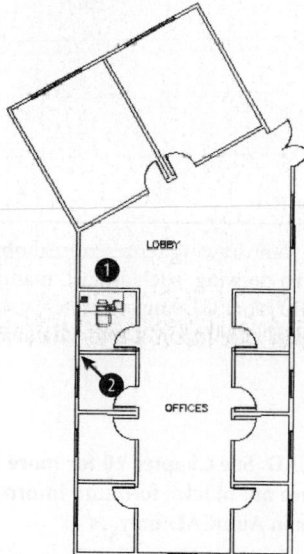

10. Use Zoom Window to zoom in to the area around ❷, shown in Figure 18.30. At the prompt, pick ❷.

11. Press Enter three times to accept the defaults and insert the entire drawing.

12. Choose View tab ⇨ Navigate panel ⇨ Zoom drop-down list ⇨ Previous. Save your drawing. It should look like Figure 18.31.

As you can see, copying to the Clipboard is ideal when you want to insert part of an existing drawing into another drawing. Drag-and-drop is also a simple way to insert one or more objects or an entire drawing.

FIGURE 18.31

The office plan with added chairs and office furniture.

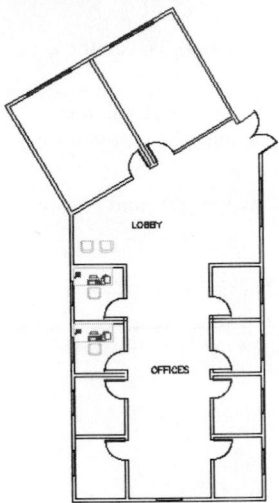

Working with Attributes

Your drawings do not exist in a vacuum. The objects in your drawing represent real objects. These objects have characteristics that you cannot visually represent in a drawing, such as cost, manufacturer, date purchased, and so on. *Attributes* are labels that are attached to blocks. Using attributes, you can attach labels with pertinent data to blocks. You can then extract the data and import it into a database program or spreadsheet, or redisplay the data in an AutoCAD table.

Cross-Reference

You can access and link to outside databases from within AutoCAD. See Chapter 20 for more information on external databases. You can also access data from objects that are not blocks; for more information, see the section on tables in Chapter 13. Both of these features are available in AutoCAD only. ■

You can also use attributes to place text relative to blocks. A common example is to use attributes for completing titleblock information, such as the drawing name, drawing number, date, scale, revision number, drafter, and so on. In this case, your plan is not to extract the data at all; you just use the attributes to help you precisely place the text in the titleblock. By inserting fields into these attributes, you can gain another benefit from attributes: automating the creation of titleblock text. For more information, see the discussion of fields in Chapter 13.

Attributes have several limitations. For example, they can only be attached to blocks (either regular or dynamic). However, you can create a dummy block that contains only attributes. The database features are also limited. Nevertheless, attributes are quite useful for simple database needs, as well as for placing text.

Defining an attribute creates a template into which you can place values when you insert the block. You define a tag that is equivalent to a field or category in a database. When you insert the block, you're prompted for the tag's value. For example, if your tag is COST, the value may be 865.79. This template is called an attribute definition.

Creating attribute definitions

The first procedure when working with attributes is to draw the individual objects that are to make up the block. If the block already exists, explode it, add the attributes, and then redefine the block.

The exception is when you want to create attributes without creating any other objects in the block. You might do this to extract attributes that apply to the drawing as a whole.

 After you have the objects, choose Home tab ⇨ Block panel (expanded) ⇨ Define Attributes to start the ATTDEF command. The Attribute Definition dialog box opens, as shown in Figure 18.32.

FIGURE 18.32

The Attribute Definition dialog box.

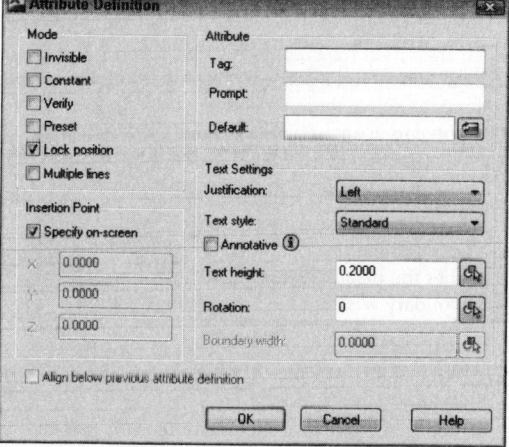

Mode section

The Mode section of the dialog box sets certain attribute properties, including visibility and default value. These properties are shown in Table 18.5.

Tip

Although by default, you see the simplified multiline text editor, you can use the full In-Place Text Editor to format multiple line attributes. Set the ATTIPE system variable to 1. However, if you need compatibility with earlier releases of AutoCAD or AutoCAD LT, you may need to return this system variable to its default value of 0. Otherwise, earlier releases may not display the attributes properly. ■

TABLE 18.5

Attribute Modes

Mode	Explanation
Invisible	The attribute values that you set are not displayed in the drawing. Use this mode for attributes that you want to extract into a database but do not want to see in the drawing. Examples would be model numbers, purchase dates, cost, and so on. Of course, if you're using attributes to place text in a drawing, then you want them to be visible.
Constant	Sets a constant value for an attribute. The attribute automatically takes the attribute value that you set (in the Attribute section of the dialog box), and you do not get a prompt for a value. You might use this for the first three digits of employees' telephone numbers that have the same first three digits. You cannot edit constant attribute values.
Verify	When you insert an attribute, a prompt appears, asking you to verify the value. Use this option if you have a preset default.
Preset	Automatically inserts a default value that you specify. For example, if the most common manufacturer of a chair is American Interiors, you can specify this as a preset value. As you insert the block, this default is inserted for you, and you have to type a value only if it differs from the default. (You need to insert the attribute with the ATTDIA system variable set to 1 to get a prompt allowing you to change the value. See the explanation of ATTDIA later in this chapter.)
Lock Position	Locks the position of the attribute relative to the block. When you insert a block with attributes, locked attributes do not have their own grip and you can't move them independently from the block. Unlocked attributes have their own grip that you can use to separately move the attribute. If you want to include an attribute in the selection set of an action in a dynamic block, you must lock that attribute. You can then move it by using the –ATTEDIT command on the command line.
Multiple Lines	Allows an attribute to contain multiple lines of text. An Ellipsis button appears to the right of the Default text box, which you click to open a simplified multiline text editor. A new MText tab appears on the Ribbon. The text that you enter becomes the default text, but you can change it when you insert the block. You can then specify a boundary width in the Text Settings section.

Attribute section

In the Attribute section of the dialog box, specify the tag, which is the name of the attribute. You use this tag when you extract the attributes. A tag is equivalent to a field in a database. For example, if you import the data into a spreadsheet, the tags would be the column heads. The tag name cannot include spaces or exclamation points (!), and it is converted to uppercase letters.

The prompt is simply a plain-English version of the tag. The prompt asks you for the value of the attribute. For example, if the tag is PUR_DATE, you could define the prompt as Date Purchased.

The default is used for setting a default value. You can use this if the value is usually the same. To insert a field, click the Insert Field button and choose a field from the Field dialog box, as I explain in Chapter 13. When you insert the block and are prompted for a value, you can either use the field value or you can change it.

If you checked the Multiple Lines check box, the Default text box is not available; instead, click the Ellipsis button that appears, and enter the default value in the simplified multiline text editor.

Tip

You can use the value to clarify a format that should be followed when entering information. For example, you could set the value of a date to dd/mm/yy so that users know how to format the date. ■

Text Settings section

Use the Text Settings section to format the text. Choose a justification and text style from the drop-down list boxes. When you set the height, be sure to take into account the scale factor if you're not using annotative attributes. You can also set a rotation angle for the text.

Check the Annotative check box to make the attribute annotative so that it will automatically scale to match the scale of the viewport. For more information on annotative objects, see Chapter 17. I discuss annotative text, which is similar, in Chapter 13.

If you checked the Multiple Lines check box, the Boundary Width text box is available so that you can specify the width of the text. However, you can also adjust the width by dragging the arrows on the ruler of the simplified multiline text editor.

Insertion Point section

In the Insertion Point section, check the Specify On-Screen check box to specify the insertion point in your drawing. Uncheck the same check box if you want to prespecify coordinates. If you're using the attributes to place text in a schedule or titleblock, then the placement is obviously very important. If you're inserting invisible attributes, simply place them near the block. If you're creating more than one attribute for a block, place the attribute so that there is room for the other attributes underneath. When you've completed the dialog box, click OK. If you chose to specify the insertion point in the drawing, specify the point to insert the attribute.

Caution

If you're creating an attribute for a table or an electrical symbol, for example, you don't want the insertion point to be 0,0. Instead, you want an insertion point near the block. If you uncheck the Specify On-Screen check box and click OK to close the dialog box, the default insertion point is at 0,0. If 0,0 isn't visible on the screen, then you don't see the attribute — it seems to disappear! You can choose Undo from the Quick Access Toolbar and create a new attribute in the right location, or move the attribute as explained in the section on editing attributes later in this chapter. ■

After you define one attribute, the Align Below Previous Attribute Definition check box is active. Select this option to line up succeeding attributes under the first one.

Now is the time to confirm that the attribute definitions are the way you want them. You can edit attribute definitions before they've been placed into a block in two ways:

- Open the Properties palette (press Ctrl+1), select one attribute definition, and edit all its properties, such as the tag, value, prompt, and modes. You can also change properties such as the layer, text style, and so on.
- Double-click the attribute text to start the DDEDIT command and change the tag, the prompt, and the default in the Edit Attribute Definition dialog box.

Tip

If you're creating many blocks with similar attributes, you can copy just the attributes, modify them as just described, place them near other objects, and then create the blocks. This way, you don't have to define all the attributes from scratch. ■

Creating the block

After you create the objects and their attribute definitions, you generally create a block. Choose Home tab ➪ Block panel ➪ Create, and select the objects and the attributes in the block.

Tip

If the order of the attribute prompts is important, don't use a window to select the attributes. Select them in the order in which you want the prompts to appear. You can then use a crossing or window box to select the rest of the objects to be included in the block. The order of the attribute prompts will be important if you're taking the data for the attributes from a listing, such as a spreadsheet that you've printed out. ∎

Name the block and define the block's insertion point as you would normally. Generally, you want to check Delete because you don't need the block without the attribute tags in your drawing. Remember that you can make the block annotative, if you want.

Don't forget to pay attention to the layer of the attributes, just as you would the layer of the block objects. The same layer rules apply to attributes as to blocks.

Note

If you want to insert the objects and the attributes as a file rather than as a block, you don't need to create a block at all. Create a drawing that contains just the objects and its attributes. Use the BASE command to change the base point of the drawing to the desired insertion point of the block. Then save the drawing. When you insert the drawing, you are prompted for the attributes, as usual. Use this technique for blocks and attributes that you use for more than one drawing, such as a titleblock. ∎

After you create the block, you cannot edit the attributes in the Properties palette. I cover other techniques for editing attributes later in this chapter.

On the DVD

The drawing that you need for the following exercise on creating attributes, ab18-i.dwg, is in the Drawings folder on the DVD. ∎

STEPS: Creating Attributes

1. Open ab18-i.dwg from the DVD. This is a plan of an office building zoomed in to one office. A file containing one set of office furniture has been inserted, as shown in Figure 18.33.

2. Save the drawing as ab18-09.dwg in your AutoCAD Bible folder.

3. Choose Home tab ➪ Modify panel ➪ Explode, select the furniture in the office, and press Enter. This block has nested blocks. Choose the chair and explode it again to get its component objects.

 4. Choose Home tab ➪ Block panel (expanded) ➪ Define Attributes. In the Attribute Definition dialog box, check Invisible in the Mode section.

5. In the Attribute section, enter the following:

   ```
   Tag: mfr
   Prompt: Manufacturer
   Default: American Office Furniture
   ```

6. Leave the Text Settings as they are. Make sure that the Specify On-Screen check box is checked and click OK. Pick point ❶, shown in Figure 18.33.

7. Repeat the ATTDEF command. Check the Align Below Previous Attribute Definition check box. Enter the following:

```
Tag: pur_date
Prompt: Date purchased
Default: 3/91
```

8. Click OK.

FIGURE 18.33

An office with a set of office furniture.

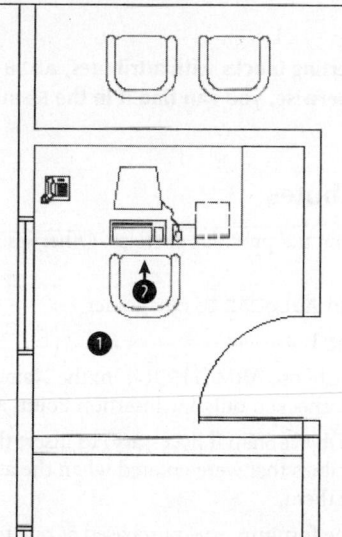

9. Choose Home tab ⇨ Block panel ⇨ Create. In the Name text box, type **armchair**. Click Select Objects. Select the entire chair, along with the two attributes. End selection. The dialog box shows that 18 objects are selected. Click Pick Point. Uncheck the Specify On-Screen button in the Base Point section first, if checked. Use the Endpoint object snap to choose ❷ as the base point. Check Delete. Uncheck the Open in Block Editor check box. Click OK.

10. A message asks whether you want to redefine the block because there is already a block definition with the same name in the drawing. Choose Redefine Block.

11. Save your drawing. If you're continuing on to the next exercise, leave the drawing open.

Note

Redefining a block updates only block geometry, not attributes. Therefore, if you add attribute definitions to a block, only new blocks that you'll insert include the attributes. Existing blocks don't gain these new attribute definitions. To update existing blocks with their current attribute definitions, use the ATTSYNC command. ∎

Inserting blocks with attributes

After you define a block with attributes, you insert it as you would any block. AutoCAD and AutoCAD LT automatically detect the existence of the attributes and prompt you for their values. After you enter the values, the block and its attributes appear in the drawing.

Note

You can insert attributes either in a dialog box or on the command line. By default, you insert them on the command line. To use a dialog box, set the ATTDIA system variable to 1. You would use the command line to automate the insertion of attributes by using an AutoLISP routine, menu item, or script file. When you use a dialog box, the Verify and Constant modes are not used. To skip all the prompts and automatically use default values that you have set, set the ATTREQ system variable to 0. ∎

On the DVD

The drawing that you need for the following exercise on inserting blocks with attributes, ab18-08.dwg, is in your AutoCAD Bible folder if you did the previous exercise. Otherwise, you can find it in the Results folder on the DVD. ∎

STEPS: Inserting Blocks with Attributes

1. Use ab18-09.dwg if you have it open from the previous exercise. Otherwise, open it from the Results folder of the DVD.

2. Save the drawing as ab18-10.dwg in your AutoCAD Bible folder.

3. Type **attdia** ↵. If it's currently set to 0, type **1** ↵.

4. Choose Home tab ⇨ Block panel ⇨ Insert. Choose ARMCHAIR from the Name drop-down list. Verify that the Specify On-screen option is checked only for Insertion Point, and click OK.

5. Pick a point in front of the desk (turn off Object Snap if necessary) to insert the armchair and open the Edit Attributes dialog box. The values that were entered when the attributes were defined are displayed, but you can change them.

6. The default values exist because most of the furniture was purchased at one time when the office was opened. However, let's assume that this chair was purchased later. Change the purchase date to 3/10. Click OK. Because the attributes are invisible, you see only the chair, but the values do exist in the drawing database.

7. Save the drawing.

Editing attributes

After you create the block, you can use the Block Attribute Manager. The Block Attribute Manager manages all properties of block attributes in one place. Use the Block Attribute Manager and its Edit Attribute dialog box to edit any aspect of block attributes.

Editing attribute properties with the BATTMAN command

After you insert a block and give values to its attributes, you can modify the following:

- Attribute prompt order
- Tag and prompt names

- Attribute visibility
- Text options (text style, justification, height, annotative, among others)
- Properties (layer, linetype, color, lineweight, and plot style)
- Attribute default value

After you make your changes, you can update all the blocks in your drawing to reflect the changes.

Choose Home tab ⇨ Block panel (expanded) ⇨ Manage Attributes to start the BATTMAN command and open the Block Attribute Manager, as shown in Figure 18.34.

FIGURE 18.34

The Block Attribute Manager.

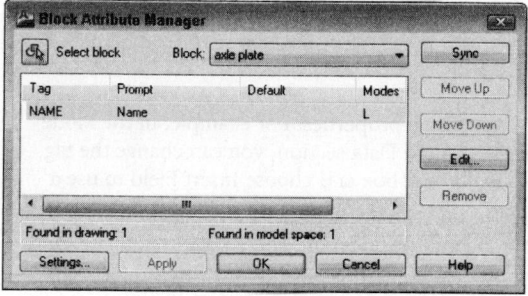

From the Block drop-down list in the Block Attribute Manager, choose the block whose attribute values you want to change. You can also click Select Block to select the block in your drawing. Use the Block Attribute Manager to:

- **Change the order of the attribute prompts when you insert a block with attributes.** Choose any attribute from the list in the Block Attribute Manager, and click Move Up or Move Down. Continue to use this procedure until you have the order that you want.
- **Delete an attribute.** Choose it and click Remove.
- **Change which attribute properties are listed in the Block Attribute Manager.** Click Settings. In the Block Attribute Settings dialog box, click all the properties that you want to see listed. For example, you can include columns for layer, style (text style), and color. Click OK.

Tip

When you add properties to the listing in the Block Attribute Manager, resize the dialog box so that you can see all the columns. ∎

- **Edit the attributes, including prompt, default, text display, and properties.** Click Edit to open the Edit Attribute dialog box, as shown in Figure 18.35.
- **Update all the blocks in your drawing to reflect the changes that you've made.** Click Sync. Usually you do this after using the Edit Attribute dialog box. Because changes such as attribute order and mode affect only new insertions of the block, this update brings existing blocks into concordance with new blocks.

FIGURE 18.35

The Edit Attribute dialog box.

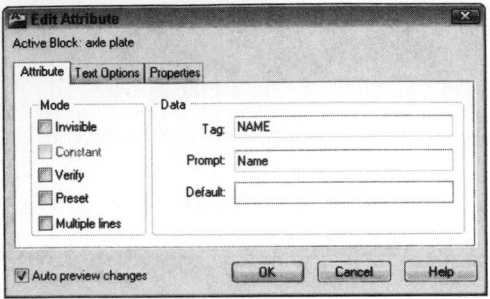

Use the Edit Attribute dialog box to edit all the properties of individual attributes. This dialog box has three tabs:

- **Attribute.** Allows you to change the mode and attribute properties. For example, in the Mode section, you can change the visibility of attributes. In the Data section, you can change the tag, prompt, and default. You can right-click the Default text box and choose Insert Field to use a field. (See Chapter 13 for a discussion of fields.)

- **Text Options.** Allows you to change text style, height, justification, and so on.

- **Properties.** Allows you to change attribute layer, color, linetype, and so on.

After you finish making changes, click OK in the Edit Attribute dialog box to return to the Block Attribute Manager. Click OK again to return to your drawing.

On the DVD

`Insrot` **is a program that inserts a block at a specified rotation but keeps the attributes horizontal. Look in** \
`Software\Chapter 18\Insrot.` `Attstrip` **removes all attributes from selected blocks. Look in** `\Software\`
`Chapter 18\attstrip.` ■

 You may need to change the values of an attribute. Perhaps you entered the wrong purchase date or a part number has changed. Choose Home tab ⇨ Block panel ⇨ Edit Attributes drop-down list ⇨ Single to start the EATTEDIT command, and select the block containing the attributes that you want to change. You see the Enhanced Attribute Editor, as shown in Figure 18.36.

As you can see, the Enhanced Attribute Editor is similar to the Edit Attribute dialog box. For example, it has the same three tabs. However, the Attribute tab enables you to change attribute values, something that you can't do in the Edit Attribute dialog box. To change an attribute's value, select it and type a new value in the Value text box. You can right-click the Value text box and choose Insert Field to use a field. (See Chapter 13 for more about fields.) The Text Options and Properties tabs of the Enhanced Attribute Editor are the same as in the Edit Attribute dialog box.

Caution

If you explode a block with attributes, you lose the attribute values. ■

The Enhanced Attribute Editor.

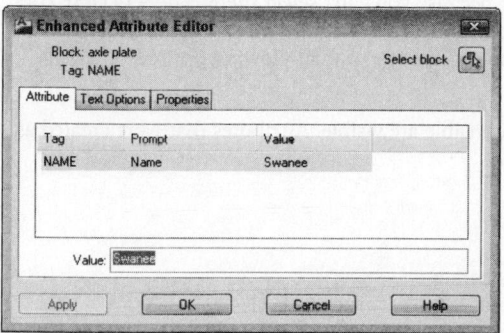

Editing attribute properties with the ATTEDIT command

You can also change attribute values by using the ATTEDIT command to open the Edit Attributes dialog box, as shown in Figure 18.37.

The Edit Attributes dialog box.

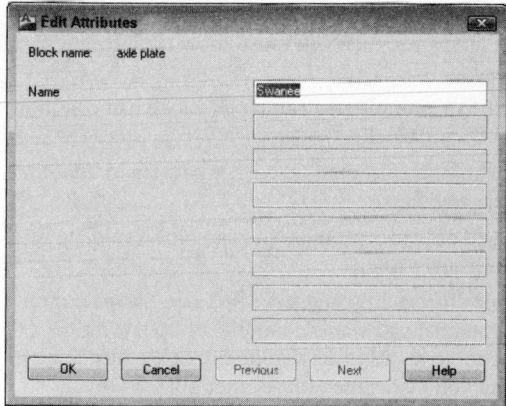

If a block has a number of attributes and you want to change them all in order, this dialog box makes it easy to go through all the attributes quickly. Press Tab to go to the next attribute.

One way to change attribute properties is to explode the block and double-click the attribute. This starts the DDEDIT command and opens the Edit Attribute Definition dialog box, where you can change the tag, prompt, and default value. You can then redefine the block. The preferred method though is to use the Block Attribute Manager, as explained in the previous section.

 To edit attributes on the command line, choose Home tab ⇨ Block panel ⇨ Edit Attributes drop-down list ⇨ Multiple, or type **-attedit**. At the Edit attributes one at a time? [Yes/No] <Y>: prompt, select the Yes option. This command then prompts you for changes in attribute values and properties, such as position, text style, color, and so on.

When you create invisible attributes, you can't edit them because you can't select them. The ATTDISP command controls attribute visibility globally, for all attributes in your drawing. Choose Home tab⇨ Block panel (expanded)⇨ Attribute Display drop-down list, and choose one of the following options. The currently active option is checked on the menu.

- **Retain Display.** Attributes that were created as visible are visible. Attributes that were created as invisible are invisible. This is the default option.
- **Display All.** All attributes are visible.
- **Hide All.** All attributes are invisible.

Changing the current option causes your drawing to regenerate.

Making global changes in attributes

You can use the -ATTEDIT command on the command line to make global changes. If you answer No to the Edit attributes one at a time? [Yes/No] <Y>: prompt, you can make global changes to attribute values. For example, you can change all instances of A- in your part numbers to B-. You can even change invisible attribute values.

To use -ATTEDIT to make global changes, follow these steps:

1. Choose Home tab⇨ Block panel⇨ Edit Attributes drop-down list⇨ Multiple.
2. At the Edit attributes one at a time? [Yes/No] <Y>: prompt, type n ↵.
3. At the Edit only attributes visible on screen? [Yes/No] <Y>: prompt, answer y or n ↵, as desired. If you answer **n** to edit invisible attributes, then you must know the attribute text string that you want to change because it is invisible.
4. At the Enter block name specification <*>: prompt, you can type a block name to limit the changes to one block, or press Enter to include any block.
5. At the Enter attribute tag specification <*>: prompt, you can type a tag to limit the changes to one tag type, or press Enter to include any tag.
6. At the Enter attribute value specification <*>: prompt, you can type a value to limit the changes to one value, or press Enter to include any value.
7. If you chose to edit only attributes that are visible on-screen, you see the Select Attributes: prompt. (If not, skip to Step 8.) Pick each attribute that you want to modify, or use a window. Press Enter to end selection. If you include other objects or blocks that do not fit the block name, attribute tag, or attribute value specifications that you made, then these other objects are not selected. The command line informs you of how many attributes were selected.
8. At the Enter string to change: prompt, type the text string (any consecutive text) that you want to change.
9. At the Enter new string: prompt, type the text string that will replace the old string.

If you chose to edit attributes that are not visible on the screen, the drawing regenerates, and the command line lists the changes that it made.

Redefining attributes

You can redefine a block with attributes to include different objects and attributes, using the ATTREDEF command. Redefining a block lets you add or delete attributes or redefine a block that contains attributes. Follow these steps:

AutoCAD Only

AutoCAD LT does not include this feature. Instead, explode the block and start from scratch. You can use the DDEDIT command to change attributes after you explode a block. ■

1. Explode one of the blocks with attributes. If there are nested blocks that you want to change, explode them, too.

2. If you want to add attributes, define and place them. Delete unwanted attributes. Make any other changes that you want to the objects.

3. Type **attredef** ↵.

4. At the Enter name of block you wish to redefine: prompt, type the name of the block.

5. At the Select objects for new Block...: prompt, select the objects and the attributes that you want to include. Do not include any existing attributes that you want to delete.

6. At the Specify insertion base point of new Block: prompt, pick the base point for the block.

Here's how your drawing handles the changes:

- If you created new attributes, the command places them for all existing blocks and gives them their default values.

- Any attributes that you did not change retain their old values for all existing blocks.

- Any attributes that you did not include in the new block definition are deleted from existing blocks.

On the DVD

The drawing that you need for the following exercise on editing attributes, ab18-j.dwg, is in the Drawings folder on the DVD. ■

STEPS: Editing Attributes

1. Open ab18-j.dwg from the DVD.

2. Save the file as ab18-11.dwg in your AutoCAD Bible folder. This is a portion of an office building plan layout, as shown in Figure 18.38.

3. Choose Home tab ⇨ Block panel ⇨ Edit Attributes drop-down list ⇨ Single. At the Select a block: prompt, pick the chair at ❶, shown in Figure 18.38. In the Value text box of the Enhanced Attribute Editor, change the date purchased to 4/10.

   Notice that the manufacturer is American Office Furniture. Because these attributes are invisible, you can't see the result in the drawing. Click OK.

4. To see the attributes, choose Home tab ⇨ Block panel (expanded) ⇨ Attribute Display drop-down list ⇨ Display All. You can now see the attributes for the chair, as well as nearby attributes for the desk. To turn off the attributes, repeat the process, this time choosing the Normal option.

5. Choose Home tab ⇨ Block panel ⇨ Edit Attributes drop-down list ⇨ Multiple. Follow the prompts:
```
Edit attributes one at a time? [Yes/No] <Y>: n ↵
Performing global editing of attribute values.
Edit only attributes visible on screen? [Yes/No] <Y>: n ↵
Drawing must be regenerated afterwards.
Enter block name specification <*>: armchair ↵
Enter attribute tag specification <*>: ↵
```

```
Enter attribute value specification <*>: ↵
6 attributes selected.
Enter string to change: American ↵
Enter new string: Acme ↵ (Press F2 to hide the text window if it is open.)
```

FIGURE 18.38

An office building plan layout.

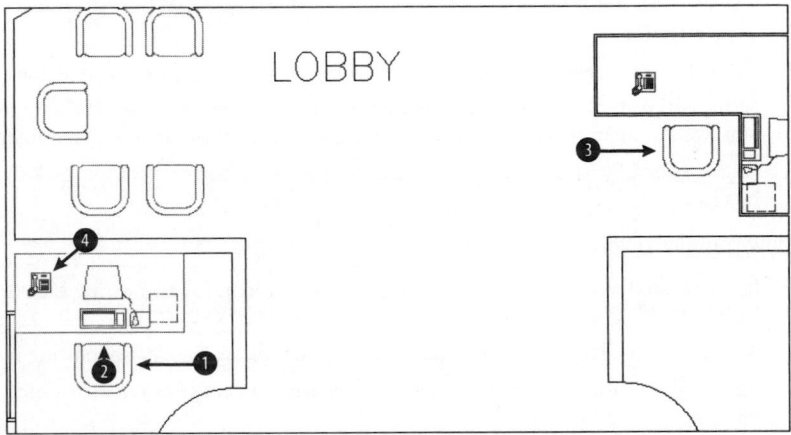

6. Choose Home tab ⇨ Modify panel ⇨ Explode and select the chair at ❶, shown in Figure 18.38.
Press Enter to end selection. The attributes reappear, but without their values. Choose Home tab ⇨ Block panel (expanded) ⇨ Define Attributes. Uncheck the Multiple Lines check box in the Mode section, if checked. Create an invisible attribute with a tag and prompt of Color, and a default value of Dusty Blue. Click OK and pick an insertion point underneath the other two attributes of the armchair. (You'll need to pan down a little. Exact placement is not important.)

7. To redefine the block, do one of the following:

   If you have AutoCAD: Type **attredef** ↵. Follow the prompts:

   ```
   Enter name of Block you wish to redefine: armchair ↵
   Select objects for new Block...Select objects: Use a window to select
       the chair and the three attributes. Press Enter to end selection.
   Specify insertion base point of new Block: Use an Endpoint object
       snap to pick the endpoint at ❷.
   ```

   If you have AutoCAD LT: Choose Home tab ⇨ Block panel ⇨ Create. In the Name text box, enter **armchair**. Click the Pick Point button and use an Endpoint object snap to pick the endpoint at ❷. Click the Select Objects button and select all the objects that make up the chair, and then the three attributes. Press Enter to end selection. In the Objects section, choose the Delete option. Click OK. Click Redefine Block to redefine the block.

   The armchair block disappears.

8. Choose Insert in the Block panel. In the Insert dialog box, choose **armchair** from the Name drop-down list. With Specify On-screen checked only for Insertion Point, click OK. Insert the chair at ❷. In the Edit Attributes dialog box, click OK to accept the values, or press Enter to accept the values on the command line.

9. **AutoCAD only:** To verify that your drawing has redefined the block elsewhere, choose Home tab ⇨ Block panel ⇨ Single. Select the block at ❸. Notice that the Color tag has been added with a value of Dusty Blue. Click OK to accept the values. (In AutoCAD LT, the new attribute appears only in the block that you redefined and in new blocks that you insert.)

10. Zoom in closely to the telephone at ❹, shown in Figure 18.38. The telephone has a visible attribute of the phone number. The number is so small that it cannot usually be seen, so it does not interfere with the drawing.

11. Choose Home tab ⇨ Block panel (expanded) ⇨ Manage Attributes. From the Block drop-down list, choose Phone. Click Edit. On the Attribute tab of the Edit Attribute dialog box, change the prompt to **Extension**. On the Text Options tab, choose Fit from the Justification drop-down list. On the Properties tab, choose Blue (if you're using a white background) or Cyan (if you're using a black background) from the Color drop-down list. Click OK twice to return to your drawing. The text of the phone extension is now blue and fills up the entire rectangle on the phone.

    The phone number is now blue (or cyan).

12. Choose View tab ⇨ Navigate panel ⇨ Zoom drop-down list ⇨ Previous. Save the drawing.

AutoCAD Only

The Express Tools command BURST (choose Express Tools tab ⇨ Blocks panel ⇨ Explode Attributes) converts attributes to text. Apply the ATTOUT and ATTIN commands (choose Express Tools tab ⇨ Blocks panel ⇨ Export Attribute, and Express Tools tab ⇨ Blocks panel ⇨ Import Attribute, respectively). Export Attribute Information and Import Attribute Information work together to enable you to edit attributes in another program. For example, ATTOUT creates a tab-delimited file that you can open in Notepad or Excel. When you use ATTIN, existing blocks are updated with the new attribute information. ■

Extracting a database from attributes

 After you insert all your blocks and attributes, you can extract the data by using the Data Extraction Wizard. To start the wizard, choose Insert tab ⇨ Linking & Extraction panel ⇨ Extract Data. For information on extracting data from objects that are not blocks, see my coverage of tables in Chapter 13.

AutoCAD Only

The Data Extraction Wizard exists only in AutoCAD. For AutoCAD LT, you need to use the method that I explain in the sidebar, "Creating a template file the old-fashioned way." ■

On the Begin screen of the wizard, choose one of two options:

- **Create a new data extraction.** You can start from scratch or use a DXE or BLK file, which are templates that you create in the Data Extraction Wizard of AutoCAD 2011 or previous releases. These extraction template files save the parameters of the data extraction, so that you don't have to create them all over again.

- **Edit an existing data extraction.** Choose this option if you previously extracted data and want to modify the results.

Note

Don't confuse the template file used for extracting attributes with the template file (with a filename extension of DWT) that you use as a basis for opening a drawing. Keep in mind that you can't use ASCII template files with the Data Extraction Wizard; you can only use .dxe or .blk templates. ■

In either case, click Next. The following instructions assume that you chose the first option.

AutoCAD saves the extraction parameters as a DXE file, and so the Save Data Extraction As dialog box opens, where you choose a location and name for the file.

 On the Define Data Source screen, choose from where you want to extract attributes. Most often, you want to select objects in the current drawing. In that case, click the Select Objects in the Current Drawing button to return to the drawing. However, you can choose other drawings (including the current drawing) or a drawing set. If you choose the current drawing and don't add any other drawings, you'll be able to extract from all objects in the drawing. On the next screen, you can individually choose which objects you want to include.

Click Settings to specify some block and block-count settings:

- **Extract Objects from Blocks.** Includes nested blocks.
- **Extract Objects from Xrefs.** Includes objects in external references (xrefs). See Chapter 19 for coverage of xrefs.
- **Include Xrefs in Block Counts.** When counting blocks, counts xrefs as blocks.

In the Extract From section, you can include all objects in a drawing or only objects in model space. Then click OK. Click Next to go to the next screen, Select Objects, as shown in Figure 18.39. Here you choose the objects with which you want to work. If you selected objects in the previous screen, you may have what you want here, but you may still find objects that you don't want to include.

FIGURE 18.39

The Select Objects screen of the Data Extraction Wizard.

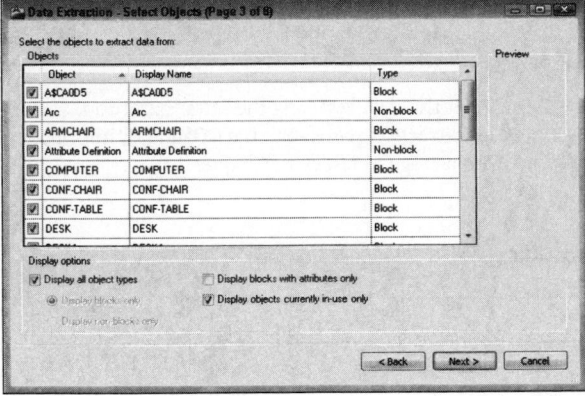

Note

You can extract data from any object in your drawing, but attributes apply only to blocks. ■

If you're only interested in blocks and attributes that you've created, uncheck the Display All Object Types check box and choose the Display Blocks Only option. By checking the Display Blocks with Attributes Only check box, you can remove other blocks from your drawing. Check the Display Objects Currently In-Use Only check box to remove objects such as blocks that are defined but not inserted into the drawing, or objects from other drawings that you don't want to include. Uncheck this check box if you need to extract objects across multiple drawings and need access to certain objects not in the current drawing.

When you're done, you should see listed only the types of objects that you need. Then individually check or uncheck the objects listed. For example, you may want to extract attributes from some blocks, but not from others. Then click Next.

On the Select Properties screen, shown in Figure 18.40, you choose which properties you want to extract. If you want to extract only attributes, uncheck all the other check boxes in the Category Filter section. (I discuss the other categories more in Chapter 13.) You should be left with just the attributes that you want to extract. Click Next.

FIGURE 18.40

The Select Properties screen of the Data Extraction Wizard.

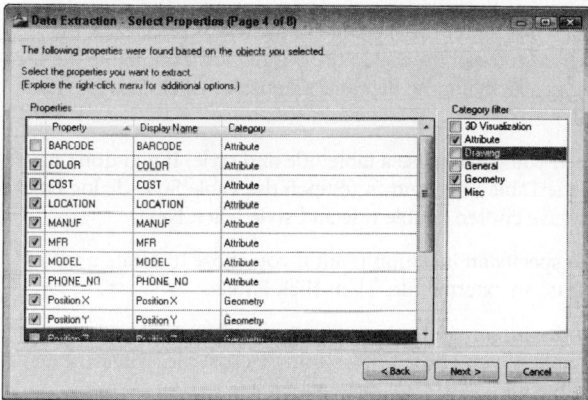

On the Refine Data screen, shown in Figure 18.41, you have three check boxes which allow you to combine (or not combine) identical rows, show (or not show) a column that counts the blocks, and show (or not show) a column that lists the name of the block. You can sort each column by clicking the column's heading. Finally, you can add a link to external data by clicking the Link External Data button. I cover this feature in Chapter 13.

FIGURE 18.41

The Refine Data screen of the Data Extraction Wizard.

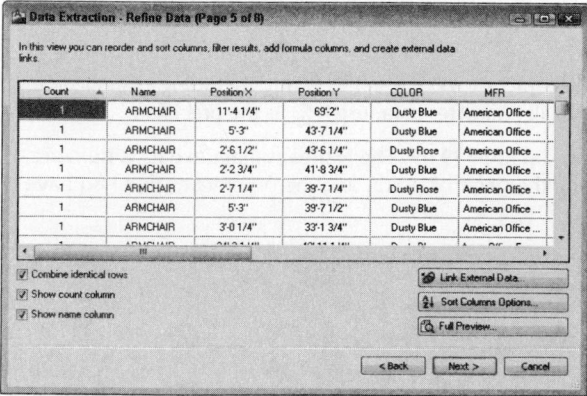

You can click Full Preview to preview the resulting data. Click the window's Close button to return to the wizard. Then click Next.

On the Choose Output screen, check the output that you want to create. You can output to an AutoCAD table, an external file, or both. You can create the following types of files:

- **CSV (Comma Delimited)** (*.csv). Lists its attribute values with a comma between each value. Most spreadsheets and databases can import this format.
- **Tab Delimited File** (*.txt). This is like a CSV file, except that there is a tab between each attribute value.
- **Microsoft Excel** (*.xls). Creates an Excel spreadsheet.
- **Microsoft Access Database** (*.mdb). Creates a Microsoft Office Access database file.

If you check the Output Data to External File check box, enter the filename in the text box, or click the Ellipsis button to open the Save As dialog box, where you can browse to the desired location, name the file, and choose the file type. You choose the file type by specifying the filename extension. Click Save. To continue, click Next.

If you chose to export to a table, on the next screen you can choose a table title and style. If you don't have a table style (except the default, Standard), click the Table Style button to open the Table Style dialog box. Click New to create a new table style. When you have chosen a table title and style, click Next.

The Finish screen just tells you that you'll need to specify an insertion point if you chose to create a table and that your file will be saved if you chose to create an external file. Then click Finish.

If you chose to create a table, you see the table at the cursor, and you see the `Specify insertion point:` prompt. Specify a location to place the table. If you chose to create an external file, you see a message on the command line providing the name of the file.

Creating a template file the old-fashioned way

With AutoCAD's Data Extraction Wizard, you don't need to create templates "by hand." You can still create templates on your own, but you must use the ATTEXT command to extract them. If you have AutoCAD LT, you must use the following method.

Create the template file in a text editor such as Windows Notepad. The template file contains two columns. The first is the name of the attribute tag. The second is a format code that specifies whether the data is a character or number, how many spaces to allow for the data, and the decimal precision to use. The format code uses the following syntax:

TWWWPPP

where T is the data type (either N for numeral or C for character), WWW is the width, including commas and decimal points, and PPP is the precision. For integers and all character data, use 000 as the precision.

For example, you would use N006002 for costs that range up to $999.99. The N means that the data is numeric, 006 means that you will have up to six spaces, including the decimal point, and the 002 means that you have precision to two decimal places.

In addition to information from your attributes, you can extract certain standard fields from the drawing's database. The table that follows lists these fields and their formatting.

The block number is a number given to the blocks that you select when extracting the data. The block handle is a unique alphanumeric code given to all objects in your drawing; to see a block's handle, use the LIST command and select the block. Handles are used for referring to objects when you write AutoLISP or other programming code. The extrusion data is used for 3D drawing. See Chapter 24 for an explanation of extrusion.

Field	Format	Explanation
BL: LEVEL	NWWW000	Block nesting level
BL: NAME	CWWW000	Block name
BL: X	NWWWPPP	X coordinate of block insertion point
BL: Y	NWWWPPP	Y coordinate of block insertion point
BL: Z	NWWWPPP	Z coordinate of block insertion point
BL: NUMBER	NWWW000	Block counter
BL: HANDLE	CWWW000	Block handle
BL: LAYER	CWWW000	Block insertion layer name
BL: ORIENT	NWWWPPP	Block rotation angle
BL: XSCALE	NWWWPPP	X scale factor
BL: YSCALE	NWWWPPP	Y scale factor
BL: ZSCALE	NWWWPPP	Z scale factor
BL: XEXTRUDE	NWWWPPP	X component of Block's extrusion direction
BL: YEXTRUDE	NWWWPPP	Y component of Block's extrusion direction
BL: ZEXTRUDE	NWWWPPP	Z component of Block's extrusion direction

Template files are quite finicky. Here are the rules that you should follow:

- You must include at least one attribute tag in your template.
- Each row must be unique — don't include the same attribute more than once.
- You must use only spaces to line up the two columns — no tabs! (Lining up the two columns just makes it easier to read.)
- End each line, including the last line, with a return.
- Don't put any extra spaces after any line or any extra returns after the last return that is after the last line of text.

Each row in the template file becomes a column in the resulting output file. If you choose space-delimited form for the output file, then spaces do not automatically appear between the columns; as a result, the output files are hard to read. You can place dummy rows in the template file for the purpose of creating spaces in the resulting columns. A typical dummy row looks like this:

```
DUMMY1      C002000
```

continued

continued

Because each row must be unique, if you need another dummy row, call it DUMMY2. This row creates a blank column of two spaces in the output file.

The figure shows a typical template file that tracks the company division, as well as the furniture's manufacturer, purchase date, cost, and color.

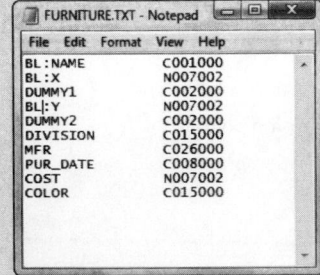

After you're done, save the file with a filename extension of .txt. To use the file, you must use the ATTEXT command, which opens the Attribute Extraction dialog box. In this dialog box, click Template File and choose the file that you created. Choose the file format that you want to create, and name the output file. Then click OK to extract the attributes.

Note

If you have AutoCAD LT, skip this exercise, and use the following exercise instead. ∎

On the DVD

The drawing that you need for the following exercise on extracting attribute data in AutoCAD, ab18-k.dwg, is in the Drawings folder on the DVD. ∎

STEPS: Extracting Attribute Data in AutoCAD

1. Open ab18-k.dwg from the DVD. This is the same office building plan used earlier in this chapter, as shown in Figure 18.42. Save the drawing as ab18-12.dwg in your AutoCAD Bible folder. Change the current layer to 0.

 2. Choose Insert tab ⇨ Linking & Extraction panel ⇨ Extract Data to open the Data Extraction Wizard.

3. The Create a New Data Extraction option should be selected on the Begin screen. Click Next.

4. The Save Data Extraction As dialog box opens. Navigate to your AutoCAD Bible folder. In the File Name text box, enter **ab18-12** and click Save.

5. On the Define Data Source screen, the Drawings/Sheet Set option should be selected. The Include Current Drawing check box should also be checked. Click Next.

The office building plan includes several blocks of armchairs with invisible attributes.

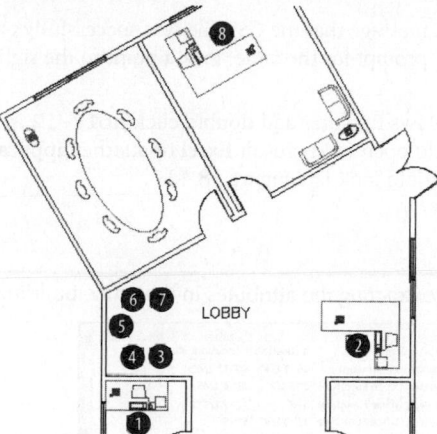

6. On the Select Objects screen, uncheck the Display All Object Types check box and check the Display Blocks Only option. Check the Display Blocks with Attributes Only check box. You should now see three objects listed, ARMCHAIR, DESK, and PHONE. Uncheck DESK and PHONE to extract the data for the armchair blocks only. Click Next.

7. On the Select Properties screen, uncheck 3D Visualization, Drawing, and General in the Category Filter pane. In the Properties pane, click the Category column to sort by category. Leave only the following properties checked:

   - **For the Attributes category.** COLOR, MFR, and PUR_DATE
   - **For the Geometry category.** Position X and Position Y
   - **For the Misc category.** Rotation

8. You can change the display name of the properties. Click in the appropriate row of the Display Name column twice to select the display name and make the following changes:

   - Change COLOR to Color
   - Change PUR_DATE to Purchase Date
   - Change MFR to Manufacturer
   - Change Position X to X Location
   - Change Position Y to Y Location

9. Click Next. (If you get a message about nonuniformly scaled blocks, click OK.)

10. On the Refine Data screen, you should see the data with each attribute in its own column. You can resize the window to see all the data. Click the Manufacturer column to sort the list by manufacturer. Note how the column names match the changes you made to the display names. Click Next.

11. In the Output Options section, check both check boxes to create both a table and an external file. Click the Ellipsis button next to the External File text box. In the Save As dialog box, navigate to your AutoCAD Bible folder. From the Files of Type drop-down list, choose *.csv. Leave the default name (ab18-12.csv) and click Save. (If you have Microsoft Excel or Access, you can choose the appropriate file type for one of those applications.) Click Next.

12. On the Table Style screen, type **Armchair Data** in the Enter a Title for Your Table text box. The table style should be set to Office. Click Next.
13. On the Finish screen, click Finish.
14. On the command line, you see a message that the CSV file was successfully created. You also see a `Specify insertion point:` prompt for the table. Pick a point to the right of the floor plan to insert the table.
15. To view the CSV file, open Windows Explorer and double-click `ab18-12.csv` in your `AutoCAD Bible` folder. It should open in Microsoft Excel or another application that opens CSV files on your system. The data should look like Figure 18.43.

FIGURE 18.43

The output file that results from extracting the attributes in the office building plan.

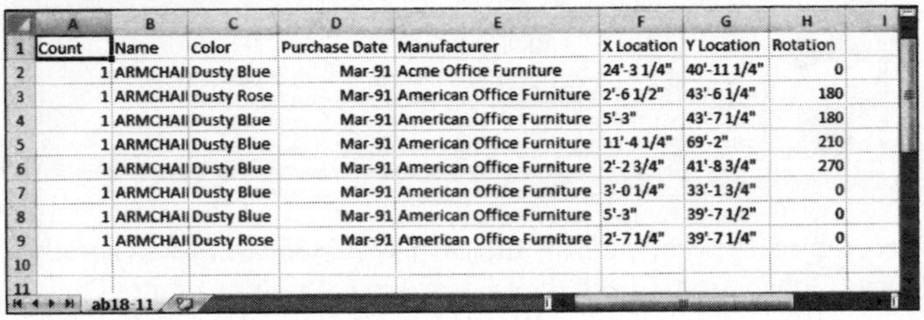

Count	Name	Color	Purchase Date	Manufacturer	X Location	Y Location	Rotation
1	ARMCHAII	Dusty Blue	Mar-91	Acme Office Furniture	24'-3 1/4"	40'-11 1/4"	0
1	ARMCHAII	Dusty Rose	Mar-91	American Office Furniture	2'-6 1/2"	43'-6 1/4"	180
1	ARMCHAII	Dusty Blue	Mar-91	American Office Furniture	5'-3"	43'-7 1/4"	180
1	ARMCHAII	Dusty Blue	Mar-91	American Office Furniture	11'-4 1/4"	69'-2"	210
1	ARMCHAII	Dusty Blue	Mar-91	American Office Furniture	2'-2 3/4"	41'-8 3/4"	270
1	ARMCHAII	Dusty Blue	Mar-91	American Office Furniture	3'-0 1/4"	33'-1 3/4"	0
1	ARMCHAII	Dusty Blue	Mar-91	American Office Furniture	5'-3"	39'-7 1/2"	0
1	ARMCHAII	Dusty Rose	Mar-91	American Office Furniture	2'-7 1/4"	39'-7 1/4"	0

16. Save your drawing.

Note

If you export attributes in tab-delimited (`.txt`) format, you can open the Multiline In-place Text Editor and click Import Text to import the output file into your drawing. You can also open the output file, copy it to the Clipboard, and paste it into your drawing. The Import Text method enables you to format the text as you would any multiline text, but may take some experimenting to align the columns. You cannot format the text that you import by using the Clipboard method, but it's nicely lined up in columns. Using the table option as you did in the exercise provides the best combination of formatting options. ■

On the DVD

The files that you need for the following exercise on extracting attribute data in AutoCAD LT, `ab18-k.dwg` and `ab18-k.txt`, are in the `Drawings` folder on the DVD. ■

STEPS: Extracting Attribute Data in AutoCAD LT

1. Open `ab18-k.dwg` from the DVD. This is the same office building plan used earlier in this chapter, as shown in Figure 18.42.
2. Type **attext** ↵ to open the Attribute Extraction dialog box.
3. Choose the Space Delimited File (SDF) option.
4. Choose Select Objects. Pick the five armchairs in the lobby and the three offices. Press Enter to end selection.

5. Choose Template File. In the Template File dialog box, navigate to and choose `ab18-k.txt` from the DVD. Click Open.

6. Choose Output File. In the Output File dialog box, choose your `AutoCAD Bible` folder and name the file `ab18-12.txt`. Click Save.

7. Click OK. The command line displays the message `8 records in extract file`.

8. To view the output file, if you are using Windows XP, choose Start ➪ Run from the Windows task bar. Type **Notepad** and click Run. If you are using Windows Vista or Windows 7, choose Start and type **Notepad** in the Start Search text box. Press Enter. In Notepad, choose File ➪ Open, and locate the `ab18-12.txt` file in your `AutoCAD Bible` folder. Click Open.

This exercise shows how to extract attributes using space-delimited format. This format is easier to import into AutoCAD by copying and pasting. However, comma-delimited format is easier to import into most spreadsheet programs.

Summary

In this chapter, I covered all the ways that you can use blocks and attributes in your drawings. You read about:

- Combining objects into blocks in your drawings so that you can edit them as a unit
- Inserting blocks at any scale and rotation
- Saving a block as a file
- Inserting blocks with the INSERT command
- Using the DesignCenter to import blocks from other drawings
- Creating dynamic blocks with action-based parameters and parametric constraints
- Using dynamic blocks
- Copying objects by using the Windows Clipboard and drag-and-drop
- Using attributes to place text and to create simple databases
- Defining attributes
- Inserting blocks with attributes and assigning values to the attributes
- Extracting attribute data in both AutoCAD and AutoCAD LT

In the next chapter, I explain how to insert references (xrefs) to other files in your drawings.

Referencing Other Drawings

S ometimes you need to refer to another drawing without inserting it. You may want to use part of another drawing as an example for your current drawing, or to see how the model in your drawing fits in with models in other drawings. You may want the flexibility of seeing the other drawing sometimes, but not seeing it at other times. Using an external reference is like laying one drawing on top of another and being able to see both at the same time. You can easily load and unload the other drawing.

Understanding External References

External references, commonly called *xrefs*, enable you to view any drawing as a reference while in your current drawing. The external drawing is not part of your current drawing. The current drawing keeps track of the location and name of an external reference so that you can always reference it easily. As with blocks, you can snap to objects in the external reference, thereby using it as a reference for the drawing process. You can also change the visibility settings of the xref's layers.

Xrefs have several advantages over blocks:

- **Xrefs keep your drawing smaller than blocks.** The externally referenced drawing doesn't become part of your drawing. Your drawing maintains only a reference (name and location) to the other drawing.

- **You always have the most updated version of the xref.** Each time that you open a drawing, a current copy of the xref loads. By contrast, you would need to reinsert a file inserted as a block to see the most updated version.

- **In a team project, several people can use the same drawing as an xref, each having access to the latest changes.**

- **Xrefs can be attached and detached easily for maximum flexibility, loaded and unloaded to display or hide them, or overlaid for temporary use.** If you're only using the xref for reference, you may detach it before plotting.

Attaching an external reference

The first step is to attach the external reference, which is just another drawing, to your current (host) drawing. You can underlay DWF and DWFx files, which are covered in Chapter 28, DGN, and PDF files. I explain underlays at the end of this chapter.

To attach an xref of an AutoCAD or AutoCAD LT drawing, follow these steps:

1. Choose Insert tab ➪ Reference panel ➪ Attach to start the ATTACH command. The Select Reference File dialog box opens.

2. Choose the file you want to attach and click Open. The Attach External Reference dialog box (shown in Figure 19.1) opens. This dialog box displays the file that you chose, along with its path (location).

FIGURE 19.1

The Attach External Reference dialog box.

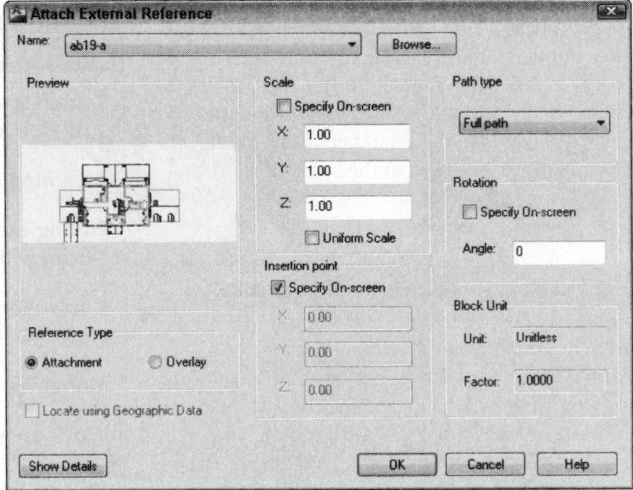

3. Choose the type of xref that you want in the Reference Type section:

   - **Attachment.** Use an attachment when you want to be sure that the xref will be displayed if someone else xrefs your current drawing. In other words, that person will see your current drawing, and your xref will be nested within it.

   - **Overlay.** Use an overlay when you're sharing drawings in a networked environment and you don't want to change your drawing by attaching an xref. If someone else attaches your drawing while you're working on it, the overlay is not displayed.

Note

The XREFTYPE system variable determines which of these two choices, Attachment or Overlay, is automatically chosen in the Reference Type section. The default value, 0, uses the Attachment option. ∎

4. Choose Locate using Geographic Data if the drawing you are attaching has a geographic location that you want to use. The check box is only enabled when the drawing has a geographic location. For more information on geographic location data, see Chapter 22.

5. From the Path Type drop-down list, choose the type of path that you want to use:

- **Full path.** Specifies the full path of the xref drawing, including the drive letter (such as c:).

- **Relative path.** Specifies only part of the xref drawing's path, and uses the current drive or folder. This option enables you to move a host drawing and its xrefs to a different drive that has the same folder structure.

- **No path.** Uses the current folder of the host drawing. This option enables you to use an xref when you move the drawing; for example, when you send it to someone else with a different folder structure. To make sure that the drawing can find the xref, ensure that it is in the project files search path or in the same folder as the host drawing.

6. Use the Scale, Insertion Point, and Rotation sections of the dialog box to specify the X, Y, and Z scale factors, the insertion point, and the rotation angle, either in the dialog box or on-screen. These prompts are the same ones that you use when inserting a block or file.

Note

A check box in the Scale section lets you specify a uniform scale, so the Y and Z values are always the same as the X value. The Block Unit section displays the units set for the referenced drawing. This is the same setting you use when you create a block and allows for the automatic scaling of the drawing. You can set this value with the INSUNITS system variable or by entering units ↵ on the command line to set it in the Units dialog box; you must do this when the drawing file is open for editing. ∎

7. Click OK to attach the xref.

If your current view does not show the entire xref, do a Zoom Extents (choose View tab ⇨ Navigate panel ⇨ Zoom drop-down list ⇨ Extents).

Cross-Reference

You can also attach an xref from a tool palette. For more information on tool palettes, see Chapter 26. ∎

After you have the xref in your drawing, you can start to work. The xref is like a block, although you cannot explode it. However, you can use object snaps on all the objects in an xref, just as you can with blocks. This enables you to use the xref as a basis for your own drawing.

Opening an xref

Sometimes you need to open the xref to work on it directly. For example, you may see an error that you want to correct. The XOPEN command opens xrefs. The easiest way to use XOPEN is to click the xref to select it in your drawing, right-click, and choose Open Xref. The xref opens in its own drawing window.

If you select an xref, then by default, the External Reference contextual tab appears, with tools that allow you to open and modify the selected xref.

Using the External References palette

To see what type of xrefs you have in your drawing, choose View tab ⇨ Palettes panel ⇨ External References Palette, or choose Insert tab ⇨ Reference panel and click the dialog box launcher at the right end of the panel's title bar.

New Feature

By default, selecting a reference in the External References palette highlights the attached external reference in the drawing. Similarly, selecting an external reference in a drawing highlights the reference in the External References palette. You can control this behavior with the ERHIGHLIGHT system variable. ∎

The external references are listed in the External References palette, as shown in Figure 19.2. This palette shows the following types of references:

- **Images.** Any type of bitmap (raster) image that you can import. (See Chapter 27 for more information.)
- **DWF underlays.** DWF and DWFx files that act like xrefs. I explain how to attach DWF files at the end of this chapter, and I cover creating DWF and DWFx files in Chapter 28.
- **DGN underlays.** DGN files (MicroStation drawings) that act like xrefs. I cover DGN files at the end of this chapter.
- **PDF underlays.** PDF files that act like underlays. I explain how to attach PDF files at the end of this chapter, and I cover creating PDF files in Chapter 28.

Along with the above-mentioned external reference types, the External References palette also displays data extraction tables and data links. For more information on data extraction and data links, see Chapter 13.

Note

The External References palette replaced the Xref Manager as of AutoCAD 2007 and AutoCAD LT 2007. You can open the earlier Xref Manager with the CLASSICXREF command. ∎

FIGURE 19.2

The External References palette displays a referenced drawing, raster images, PDF file, and data extraction table.

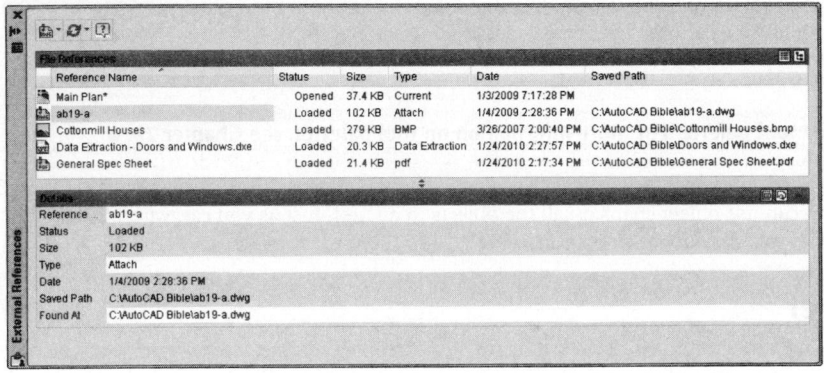

The palette lists all the referenced drawings and files. You can choose one of two views, using the buttons at the top-right corner of the palette:

- **List view** lists all the references along with their status, size, type, date and time saved, as well as the saved path, if any. Figure 19.2 shows the referenced files of Main Plan.dwg in list view.
- **Tree view** lists all the references in a graphical view that shows their relationships. This view is great for understanding nested xrefs.

Tip

You can change the width of the columns in List view by placing the cursor on a column dividing line until it changes to a two-headed arrow. Then drag in either direction. You can also double-click the dividing line between two columns to automatically resize the column to the left based on the widest value. ∎

When you click any xref, you see a preview tooltip that shows the reference and lists its details. You can control the preview format to display a preview thumbnail, file details, or a combination. Right-click in the palette, choose Tooltip Style, and choose one of the options.

If you move or delete a referenced item, the External References palette notes that the file is not found. To troubleshoot, it helps to know where it searches for xrefs. The External References palette searches for references according to a specific order:

- **Path specified.** Locates the specified path xref.
- **Current folder.** Locates the current folder of the host drawing.
- **Project path.** The path for external references. To check or change the project path, choose Application Button ⇨ Options and click the Files tab. Double-click Project Files Search Path. Click Add and then click Browse to navigate to a folder where you keep drawings that you may want to use as xrefs. (AutoCAD LT doesn't offer the Project Files Search Path.)
- **Support path.** The location for support files. To check or change the support path, choose Application Button ⇨ Options and then click the Files tab. Double-click Support File Search Path. Click Add and then click Browse to navigate to a folder.
- **Start-in folder.** To find the start-in folder, right-click your AutoCAD 2011 or AutoCAD LT 2011 desktop shortcut and choose Properties.

On the DVD

The drawings used in the following exercise on attaching xrefs, ab19-a.dwg and ab19-b.dwg, are in the Drawings folder on the DVD. ∎

STEPS: Attaching Xrefs

1. Open ab19-a.dwg from the DVD. This is the floor plan for a house.
2. Open Windows Explorer (right-click Start on the task bar and choose Explore). Copy ab19-b. dwg from the DVD to your AutoCAD Bible folder.

 3. In your drawing, choose Insert tab ⇨ Reference panel ⇨ Attach. In the Select Reference File dialog box, choose ab19-b.dwg. Click Open. You can choose Drawing (*.dwg) from the Files of Type drop-down list to filter the files displayed in the Select Reference File dialog box.

4. In the Attach External Reference dialog box, you see the filename displayed. Make sure that all Specify On-Screen check boxes are unchecked. Select Attachment from the Reference Type section, and click OK. You see ab19-b.dwg, which is a titleblock, in ab19-a.dwg.

5. Save the drawing as ab19-01.dwg in your AutoCAD Bible folder. Click the drawing's Close box to close the drawing.

6. Start a new drawing, using the acad.dwt or acadlt.dwt template. On the command line, type **units** ↵. In the Drawing Units dialog box, choose Architectural from the Type drop-down list under the Length section. In the Units to Scale Inserted Content drop-down list, choose Inches. Click OK. Save it as ab19-02.dwg in your AutoCAD Bible folder.

7. Again choose Insert tab ⇨ Reference panel ⇨ Attach. In the Select Reference File dialog box, choose ab19-01.dwg, which you just saved in your AutoCAD Bible folder. Click Open.

8. In the Attach External Reference dialog box, you see the filename displayed. Leave the defaults and click OK. Choose View tab ⇨ Navigate panel ⇨ Zoom drop-down list ⇨ Extents. You see ab19-01.dwg, which includes both the titleblock and the floor plan of the house in your new drawing. The titleblock drawing (ab19-b.dwg) is a nested xref in the floor plan (ab19-01.

dwg) xref. You see the following message (press F2 to open the AutoCAD Text Window so you can see the message that scrolls by):

```
Attach Xref "ab19-01": C:\AutoCAD Bible\ab19-01.dwg
"ab19-01" loaded.
Attach Xref "ab19-b": C:\AutoCAD Bible\ab19-b.dwg
"ab19-b" loaded.
```

9. To help you visualize the relationships among the three drawings, choose View tab ➪ Palettes panel ➪ External References Palette. The External References palette lists both drawings. Click Tree View at the top-right corner of the palette. You now see the two xrefs listed in a tree structure, showing their relationship more clearly. Close or auto-hide the palette.

10. Save your drawing. It should look like Figure 19.3.

FIGURE 19.3

The current drawing is blank but displays an xref of a house plan that has a nested xref of a titleblock. The grid was turned off in the figure for clarity.

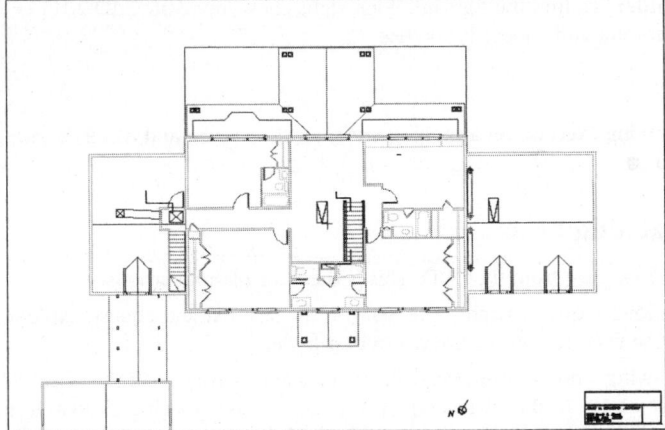

Editing an Xref within Your Drawing

While you're working in a drawing with an external reference, you may decide that the external reference needs some modification. The same may apply if you inserted a file as a block. You can make changes to the xref or block and save those changes back to the original drawing. You can even transfer objects from your drawing to the xref or block, and vice versa. This feature is called *in-place editing*.

Choosing the xref or block to edit

 To start the process of in-place editing, double-click the xref that you want to edit. The Reference Edit dialog box opens, as shown in Figure 19.4. You can also choose Insert tab ➪ Reference panel (expanded) ➪ Edit Reference, and then select the xref that you want to edit.

FIGURE 19.4

The Reference Edit dialog box enables you to choose which reference you want to edit, including nested references.

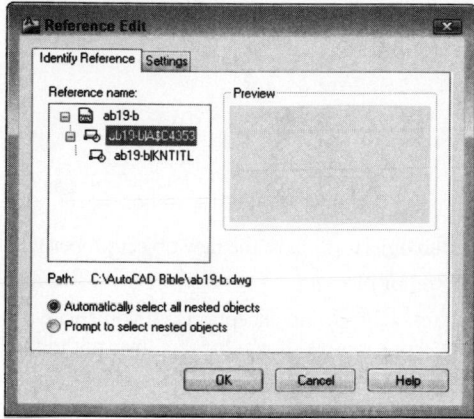

As you click each of the available references, its preview appears at the right. If the xref has nested objects, choose one of the following options (if it does not, then ignore this section of the dialog box):

- **Automatically select all nested objects.** Includes all nested objects in the editing process.

- **Prompt to select nested objects.** Prompts you to select which nested objects you want to edit.

For more control, click the Settings tab to set the following options:

- **Create unique layer, style, and block names.** Displays layer, style, and block names with a prefix of $#$, to help distinguish them from the named items in your main drawing.

- **Display attribute definitions for editing.** Enables you to edit attribute definitions of blocks with attributes. (See Chapter 18 for details on attributes.)

- **Lock objects not in working set.** Locks objects in the host drawing so that you can't accidentally modify them.

Click OK to close the Reference Edit dialog box.

Note

If the reference drawing is saved in an earlier format, you see a warning that if you save your changes back to the xref, that xref will be updated to the current file format for the release, which is the AutoCAD 2010 format. ∎

If you checked the Prompt to Select Nested Objects option, you see a prompt to select nested objects. Complete object selection to define the working set, that is, the objects that you can edit. Other objects are faded by 50 percent (this is the default, determined by the XFADECTL system variable).

The Edit Reference panel appears on the current tab, shown in Figure 19.5, and you see the message Use REFCLOSE or the Refedit toolbar to end reference editing session on the command line. You're now ready to edit the xref or block.

The Edit Reference panel on the Insert tab.

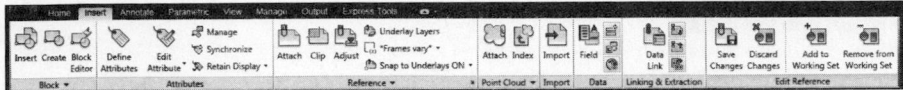

Editing the xref

There are several types of edits that you can make on the working set of objects from the xref or block:

- If you change an object's properties, such as its layer, the object will have the new object property.

- If you erase an object, the object is deleted from the xref or block.

- If you draw a new object, the object is added to the xref or block. An exception is if you create a new object by editing objects outside the working set. For example, if you break a line (not in the working set) into two lines, then nothing is added to the working set.

- You can transfer an object from the main drawing to the xref or block. Select an object and choose <current> tab ⇨ Edit Reference panel ⇨ Add to Working Set. Remember that the working set consists of objects from the xref or block, so if you add objects to the working set, they become part of the xref or block.

- You can transfer an object from the xref or block to the host drawing. Select an object and choose <current> tab ⇨ Edit Reference panel ⇨ Remove from Working Set. The working set consists of objects from the xref or block, so if you remove objects from the working set, they're no longer part of the xref or block; instead, they become part of your main drawing.

After you finish editing the working set, if you like what you did, choose <current> tab ⇨ Edit Reference panel ⇨ Save Changes. Otherwise, choose Discard Changes.

When you save changes to a block, block definitions are redefined and all instances of the block are regenerated according to the new definition. If you gave an xref object properties that don't exist in the xref, such as a layer, the new property is copied to the xref so that the object can keep that property.

On the DVD

The drawings used in the following exercise on editing an xref in place, ab19-a.dwg **and** ab19-b.dwg, **are in the** Drawings **folder on the DVD.** ■

STEPS: Editing an Xref in Place

1. Open ab19-a.dwg from the DVD. Save it as ab19-03.dwg in your AutoCAD Bible folder.

2. Open ab19-b.dwg from the DVD. Save it as ab19-04.dwg in your AutoCAD Bible folder. Click the Close box of ab19-04.dwg to close the drawing (but not the program), leaving ab19-03.dwg on your screen.

3. Choose Insert tab ⇨ Reference panel ⇨ Attach and choose ab19-04.dwg from the AutoCAD Bible folder. Click Open. From the Attach External Reference dialog box, uncheck all the Specify On-Screen check boxes and click OK to insert the xref.

4. Double-click the titleblock (ab19-04.dwg). The Reference Edit dialog box opens. Choose ab19-04. It is displayed in the preview box. Click OK. The Edit Reference panel appears, and you can now edit the xref. Your drawing should look like Figure 19.6.

FIGURE 19.6

The titleblock is an xref in the drawing of the floor plan.

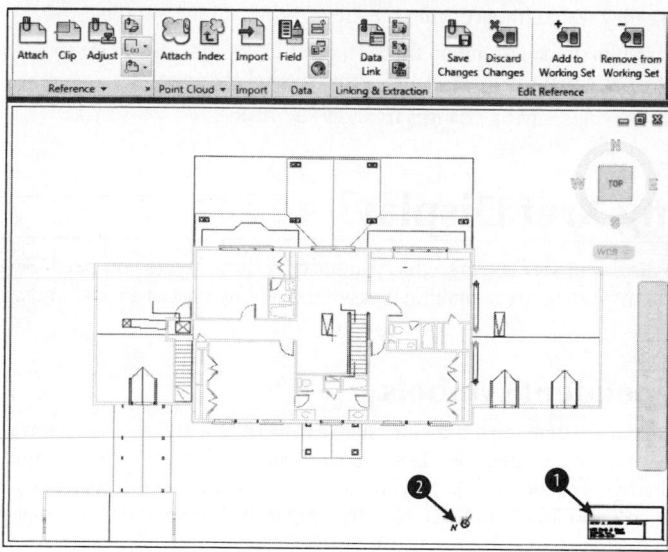

5. Select the titleblock (ab19-04.dwg) again and choose Home tab ⇨ Modify panel ⇨ Explode.

6. Choose Annotate tab ⇨ Text panel ⇨ Text drop-down list ⇨ Single Line. At the Specify start point of text or [Justify/Style]: prompt, pick ❶, shown in Figure 19.6. At the Specify height <0'-0 3/16">: prompt, type **10** ↵. Press Enter again for the rotation angle.

7. Type **Davis Floor Plan** and press Enter twice to end the command.

8. Choose the text (the name and address of the architect) at the bottom of the titleblock and change its color to red to make it stand out.

9. Select the letter N and arrow symbol at ❷, shown in Figure 19.6. To transfer these objects from the xref to the floor plan drawing, choose <current> tab ⇨ Edit Reference panel ⇨ Remove from Working Set.

10. To save the changes, choose <current> tab ⇨ Edit Reference panel ⇨ Save Changes. Click OK again at the dialog box that informs you that all reference edits will be saved. You see the following information on the command line:

```
The following symbols will be permanently bound to the current
    drawing:
Layers: $0$TITLEBLK
Text Styles: $0$ROMANS, $0$ROMAND
Blocks: $0$KNTITL

Enter option [Save/Discard reference changes] <Save>: _sav
Regenerating model.
11 objects added to ab19-04
1 object removed from ab19-04
1 xref instance updated
```

11. Choose View tab ⇨ Palettes panel ⇨ External References Palette. In the External References palette, right-click ab19-04 and choose Detach from the shortcut menu. (Detaching xrefs is covered later in this chapter.) You can now see that ab19-03.dwg includes the letter N and arrow symbol because they were removed from the xref.

12. To see the results of the editing on the xref, open ab19-04.dwg. You can see the changes in the titleblock text and that the letter N and arrow symbol are gone.

13. Close both drawings, saving changes to ab19-03.dwg.

Controlling Xref Display

You can control the display of xref layers so that you see only those layers you need. Several features let you control the process of displaying xrefs, making it easier to see only part of an xref and speeding up the display of very large xrefs.

Xrefs and dependent symbols

Dependent symbols are named items in a drawing, such as layers, text styles, dimension styles, and so on. When you attach an xref, these symbols are listed in your current drawing. For example, the Layer drop-down list displays the layers of the xref. Xref symbols have the format xref_name|symbol_name. This system distinguishes xref symbols from those of your current drawing and ensures that there are no duplicate symbols.

Xrefs and layers

You can turn on and off, or freeze and thaw, xref layers. You can also change an xref layer's properties in the Layer Properties Manager palette. By default, these changes are retained. However, you can set the VISRETAIN system variable to 0 to discard these changes. The next time you open the drawing or reload the xref, the original settings are restored.

Objects created on layer 0 do not take on the typical xref layer name format, but stay on layer 0. If objects in the xref are on layer 0 with the color and linetype set to ByLayer, they take on the color and linetype properties of the current layer in the current drawing. If color and linetype are set to ByBlock, then objects assume the current properties when the xref is attached. If you explicitly set color and linetype, then objects retain those settings.

The XBIND command

You can use the XBIND command to import only the symbols that you want from the external reference into the current drawing. This makes it easy to work with a consistent set of symbols in the current drawing and the xrefs. For example, you can choose to import the titleblk layer and the kntitl block. On the command line, type **xbind** ↵ to open the Xbind dialog box. The Xbind dialog box lists each xref in the drawing, along with its symbols in a Windows Explorer–like display, as shown in Figure 19.7.

Click the plus sign next to any symbol type to open a list of symbols. Click the one you want and choose Add to add it to the Definitions to Bind list. Click OK when you're done.

Later in this chapter, I explain how you can use the DesignCenter to move xrefs and other dependent symbols from one drawing to another.

FIGURE 19.7

Using the XBIND command to import symbols, such as layers, text styles, and so on.

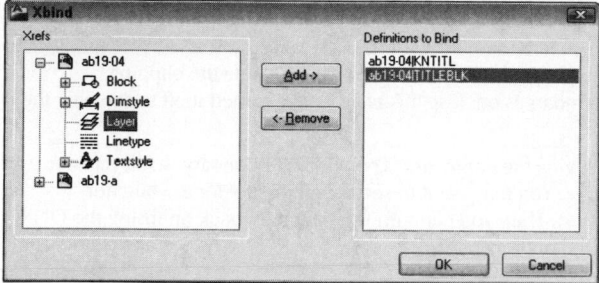

Circular references

If drawing *a* includes drawing *b* as an xref and drawing *b* includes drawing *a* as an xref, then you have a circular reference. Circular references can exist among three or more xrefs when you have nested xrefs. The program detects circular references and loads as much as it can. If you try to load an xref in such a situation, you see the following message:

```
Warning: Circular reference from XREF to current drawing.
Circular reference(s) have been found. Continue? <N> Type y to
    continue to load the xref.
Breaking circular reference from XREF to current drawing.
```

Clipping xrefs

You may want to see only part of an xref. This option is especially important when you're using very large xref drawings. The CLIP and XCLIP commands enable you to create a border in an xref, and hides any part of the xref outside the border.

 To clip an xref, choose Insert tab ➪ Reference panel ➪ Clip. At the prompt to select objects, pick the xref you want to clip. Note that any nested xrefs are clipped with the main xref that you select.

Table 19.1 explains the options of this command.

Tip
In addition to clipping xrefs, the CLIP and XCLIP commands can also clip blocks. ■

To see the clipping boundary (if you haven't used an existing polyline to define it), change the value of the XCLIPFRAME system variable to 1. When you do so, you can select the boundary and modify it by using its grips. You can also click the blue arrow to invert the clip.

You can use the FRAME system variable to override the setting of the XCLIPFRAME system variable and the frame settings for all raster images and underlays in a drawing. Setting FRAME to 3 allows you to control the frame display by object type (xref, raster image, and underlays) individually. The frame settings for underlays are covered later in this chapter.

Figure 19.8 shows an xref clipped with a polygonal boundary.

TABLE 19.1

XCLIP Options

Option	How to Use It
ON	Turns the clipping boundary on, displaying only the portion of the xref inside the clipping boundary. By default, the clipping boundary is on. Use this after you've turned it off to see only the clipped portion again.
OFF	Turns the clipping boundary off, displaying the entire xref. The clipping boundary is still retained. This is somewhat like turning off a layer. You may want to see the entire xref for a while (for example, while redefining the boundary). Then you can turn the boundary back on (using the ON option) when you need only the clipped portion again.
Clipdepth	This is used for 3D drawings only. After you set a clipping boundary, you can set front and back planes parallel to the boundary to display only the portion of the xref within that three-dimensional space. You create the front and back planes by specifying a distance from the clipping boundary. The Remove suboption removes the clipping planes.
Delete	Deletes the clipping boundary. The boundary is no longer retained in the drawing.
generate Polyline	Creates a polyline from the clipping boundary, using the current layer, color, and linetype. If you want to change the clipping boundary, you can edit the polyline by using PEDIT and redefine the boundary with the new polyline.
New boundary	This is the default option. Press Enter to see the suboptions, which follow.
Select polyline	Enables you to specify the clipping boundary by selecting an existing polyline. This option decurves fit-curved or arc portions of the polyline when creating the boundary.
Polygonal	Enables you to specify a polygonal area, such as a polyline with straight edges. This option creates a rubber-band line as you pick points, keeping the polygon closed. You can use this option to create an irregularly shaped area that includes only the portion of the xref that you want to see.
Rectangular	Enables you to pick two points on diagonally opposite corners of a rectangle, such as creating a selection window.
Invert clip	Enables you to hide any part of the xref inside the border. After choosing this suboption, choose one of the previous suboptions to define the clipping boundary.

FIGURE 19.8

An xref clipped with a polygonal boundary.

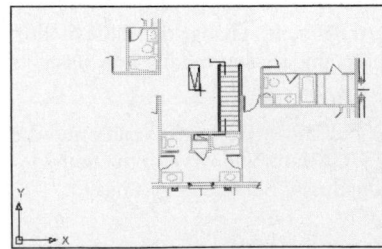

Speeding up the display of large xrefs

In order to reduce the time needed to display large xrefs, such as those used in GIS or 3D drawings, you can use *demand loading*. This feature enables you to load only the objects necessary to display the xref in your drawing. Demand loading works together with spatial and layer indexes.

- The spatial index is created when you save a drawing. This index is used when you have enabled demand loading and attach a clipped xref that was saved with a spatial index. The index determines how much of the xref needs to be read to display it.

- The layer index is also created when you save a drawing. This index is used when you've enabled demand loading and attach an xref that was saved with a layer index and has frozen or turned off layers. The index determines how much of the xref needs to be read to display it.

To make it perfectly clear, you need all the following in order to use demand loading:

- Demand loading must be enabled in the current drawing.
- The xref must have been saved with a spatial and/or layer index.
- The xref must either be clipped (for a spatial index) or have layers that are frozen or turned off (for a layer index).

Cross-Reference

Demand loading is similar to partial opening and loading of drawings, explained in Chapter 8. ∎

Demand loading

You can turn on demand loading in your current drawing. To turn on demand loading, choose Applications Button ⇨ Options, and then click the Open and Save tab. In the Demand Load Xrefs drop-down list, choose Enabled. Others on a networked system cannot then edit the original drawing while you're referencing it. To let others edit the original drawing, choose Enabled with Copy. This option uses a copy of the referenced drawing for your xref. Click OK. You can turn on demand loading just before you attach an xref; you don't need to keep demand loading on all the time.

Spatial indexes

You save a spatial index for a drawing that you expect to use as an xref. The saving process takes a little longer, but you save time at the other end when you load a clipped xref or clip an xref for the first time. To create a spatial index in AutoCAD, choose Application Button ⇨ Save As to open the Save Drawing As dialog box. From the Tools menu at the top right of the dialog box, choose Options to open the Saveas Options dialog box, shown in Figure 19.9, with the DWG Options tab on top.

From the Index Type drop-down list, choose Spatial or Layer & Spatial. Click OK. Then click Save in the Save Drawing As dialog box. In AutoCAD LT, use the INDEXCTL system variable on the command line and set its value to 2 for just a spatial index, or to 3 for both spatial and layer indexes.

Tip

If you want to create an index for an existing drawing, click OK once to return to the Save Drawing As dialog box. Click Cancel. In other words, you don't have to actually save the drawing to set up the index, which is controlled by the INDEXCTL system variable. ∎

FIGURE 19.9

The DWG Options tab of the Saveas Options dialog box enables you to save spatial and layer indexes.

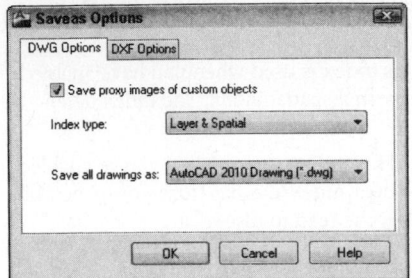

After you create a spatial index, each time you save the drawing, you see the following message:

```
Updating Indexes for block *MODEL_SPACE
```

To stop saving the index each time you save in AutoCAD, choose Application Button ⇨ Save As. Choose Tools ⇨ Options. In the Saveas Options dialog box, choose None from the Index Type drop-down list. Click OK and then click Cancel. In AutoCAD LT, change the value of the INDEXCTL system variable to 0.

Layer indexes

You save a layer index for a drawing that you expect to use as an xref to create an index of all the layers in the drawing. As with a spatial index, the saving process takes a little longer, but you save time at the other end when you load an xref with frozen or turned off layers. To create a layer index in AutoCAD, choose Application Button ⇨ Save As to open the Save Drawing As dialog box. From the Tools menu at the upper-right corner of the dialog box, choose Options to open the Saveas Options dialog box, as shown in Figure 19.9.

From the Index Type drop-down list, choose Layer or Layer & Spatial. Click OK, and then click Cancel. In AutoCAD LT, set the INDEXCTL system variable to 1 for just a layer index, or to 3 for both layer and spatial indexes.

After you create a layer index, each time you save the drawing, you see the following message:

```
Updating Indexes for block *MODEL_SPACE
```

To stop saving the index in AutoCAD, choose Application Button ⇨ Save As. Choose Tools ⇨ Options. In the Saveas Options dialog box, choose None from the Index Type drop-down list. Click OK once and then click Cancel. In AutoCAD LT, change the value of the INDEXCTL system variable to 0.

On the DVD

The drawings used in the following exercise on controlling xref display — ab19-a.dwg, ab19-b.dwg, ab19-01. dwg, **and** ab19-02.dwg — **are in the** Drawings **and** Results **folders on the DVD.** ∎

STEPS: Controlling Xref Display

1. Open ab19-01.dwg from your AutoCAD Bible folder if you did the first exercise in this chapter.

    If you didn't do the first exercise in this chapter, use Windows Explorer to find ab19-b.dwg in the Drawings folder on the DVD and ab19-01.dwg and ab19-02.dwg in the Results folder on the DVD. Copy all three files to your AutoCAD Bible folder. In Windows Explorer, right-click each file and choose Properties. Uncheck the Read-Only option (if checked) and click OK. Then open ab19-01.dwg from your AutoCAD Bible folder.

If you get a message that the drawing cannot find the xrefs and you are using AutoCAD, you can choose Application Button ⇨ Options and click Project Files Search Path on the Files tab. On the Files tab, click Add and add your AutoCAD Bible folder. Click Browse and choose the folder from the dialog box.

2. **To create layer and spatial indexes, do one of the following:**

    - **If you have AutoCAD.** Choose Application Button ⇨ Save As. In the Save Drawing As dialog box, choose Tools ⇨ Options. In the Index Type drop-down list of the Saveas Options dialog box, choose Layer & Spatial. Click OK. (It may already be set for these indexes.) Click Cancel.

    - **If you have AutoCAD LT.** On the command line, enter **indexctl** ⏎. Then enter **3** ⏎.

3. Choose Save from the Quick Access Toolbar. Note the message on the command line that the indexes are being updated.

4. Close ab19-01.dwg.

5. Open ab19-02.dwg from your AutoCAD Bible folder. This drawing has an attached xref of a house plan and a nested xref of a titleblock, as shown in Figure 19.10.

6. Save it as ab19-05.dwg in your AutoCAD Bible folder.

7. Choose Application Button ⇨ Options and click the Open and Save tab. In the Demand Load Xrefs drop-down list, choose Enabled. (It may already be set to Enabled.) Click OK.

8. Click the Layer drop-down list. Click the On/Off icon next to the Ab19-01|notes layer to turn the layer back on. Click the top of the drop-down list box to close it. The notes layer displays.

FIGURE 19.10

Picking a polygonal boundary to clip an xref.

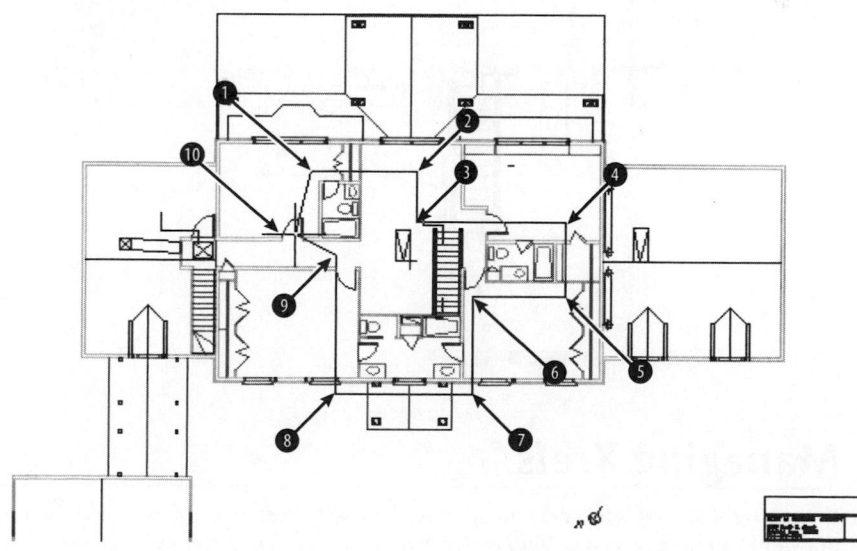

9. Choose Insert tab ⇨ Reference panel ⇨ Clip to start the CLIP command. Follow the prompts:

```
Select Object to clip: Pick anywhere on the xref in Figure 19.10.
Enter clipping option
[ON/OFF/Clipdepth/Delete/generate Polyline/New boundary] <New>: ↵
Outside mode - Objects outside boundary will be hidden.
Specify clipping boundary or select invert option:
[Select polyline/Polygonal/Rectangular/Invert clip] <Rectangular>:
   Right-click and choose Polygonal.
Specify first point: Pick ❶ in Figure 19.10. (It might help to turn
   off Object Snap if it is on.)
Specify next point or [Undo]: Pick ❷.
Specify next point or [Undo]: Pick ❸.
Specify next point or [Undo]: Pick ❹.
Specify next point or [Undo]: Pick ❺.
Specify next point or [Undo]: Pick ❻.
Specify next point or [Undo]: Pick ❼.
Specify next point or [Undo]: Pick ❽.
Specify next point or [Undo]: Pick ❾.
Specify next point or [Undo]: Pick ❿.
Specify next point or [Undo]: ↵
```

This action clips the xref.

10. Turn off the Ab19-01|notes layer again.

11. Save your drawing. It should look like Figure 19.11. Keep the drawing open if you're continuing on to the next exercise.

FIGURE 19.11

The clipped xref.

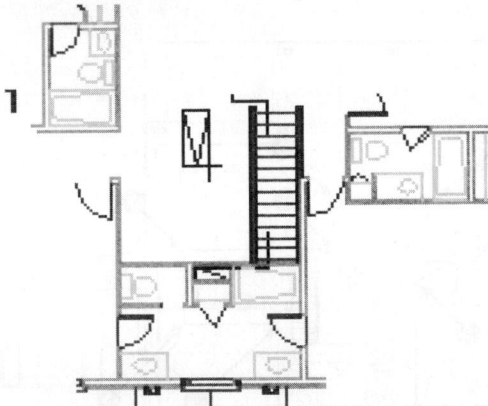

Managing Xrefs

If you have many xrefs in a drawing, you need a way to keep track of them and their relationships to your drawing. You have several techniques for managing xrefs. The External References palette, DesignCenter, and the xref notification feature are all tools to help you with this task.

Tip

Though it may be obvious, the first principle of managing xrefs is to keep them simple. Overly complex nested configurations are hard to manage, no matter what you do. ■

The External References palette is designed to let you manage xrefs (as well as DWF, DWFx, DGN, and PDF underlays, raster images, data extraction tables, and data links) from one place. I explain the features of the External References palette in Table 19.2. You access these features by right-clicking a reference and choosing from the shortcut menu.

TABLE 19.2

External References Palette Features

Feature	What It Does	
Attach	Opens the Attach External Reference dialog box so you can specify an xref to attach to your drawing, as explained earlier in this chapter.	
Detach	Detaches an xref or data extraction table. The xref is not displayed, and the xref definition is no longer saved in the drawing. The table object linked with the data extraction file is broken, and the table no longer updates automatically.	
Reload	Reloads the most recent version of the xref. Use this whenever the xref has changed during a session (because someone else on a networked system has edited the xref drawing) or after unloading an xref.	
Unload	Unloads the xref without detaching it. The xref is not displayed, but the xref definition is still saved in the drawing. You can then use Reload to display the xref again.	
Bind	Changes the xref to a block. Opens the Bind Xrefs dialog box, which enables you to choose to either bind or insert the xref.	
	Bind	When creating a block from the xref, this feature changes named layers, text styles, dimension styles, and so on (called *symbols*) from the format xref_name|symbol_name to drawing_name\$#\$symbol_name, where # is 0 if the same name does not exist in the current drawing or 1 if it already exists. In this way, no symbol names are duplicated. This method enables you to keep track of where the symbols came from.
	Insert	When creating a block from the xref, this feature removes the xref_name| portion of symbol names. For example, if a layer of that name already exists in your drawing, objects on that layer take on the properties of that layer, as defined in your drawing. The same applies to text styles, dimension styles, and so on. This method removes the complexity that arises with the xref naming of these symbols.
Open	Opens the selected xref in a new drawing window or the linked data source in its native program.	
Update Data Links	Refreshes the table in the drawing associated with the referenced data source.	
Update Data Extraction	Refreshes the table in the drawing using the criteria in the referenced data extraction file.	
Xref Found At	Specifies where the xref was actually found, which may be different from the saved path. You can then click Save Path to save the current path. If the location of an xref is changed and is not in the Support Files or Project Files search path, the status of the xref displays as Not Found. Use the Browse button to find and open the xref and click Save Path. Click OK to automatically reload the xref.	

Note

You cannot bind or detach nested xrefs without binding the parent xref. ∎

You can also click the Refresh button to refresh the selected reference, or use its down button to choose Reload All References.

AutoCAD Only

Express Tools offer two commands that can help you work with xrefs. Choose Express Tools tab ⇨ Blocks panel ⇨ List Properties to list the properties of xrefs and blocks, such as object type, layer, object, and linetype. Choose Express Tools tab ⇨ Blocks panel (expanded) ⇨ Convert Block to Xref to replace a block with an xref (that is, another drawing file). ∎

Xref notification

If an xref is moved or renamed while you have it displayed in an open drawing, you need to reload it. An xref can change if someone else on your network opens and edits it while you're using it. External Reference Notification offers instant notification if an xref changes.

 When you open a drawing with an xref, the status bar displays the Manage Xrefs icon in the tray area at the right. When an xref changes, a "balloon message" or window appears to notify you, including the name of the drawing and the person who changed it. Click the link to reload the xref (or xrefs). If you want to open the External References palette, perhaps to choose which xrefs you want to reload, click the Manage Xrefs icon on the status bar. The XREFNOTIFY system variable controls the use of the xref notification balloon.

DesignCenter

As explained in earlier chapters, you can use the DesignCenter to copy named objects, including xrefs, from one drawing to another. (I cover the DesignCenter in detail in Chapter 26.) To insert an xref from another drawing, press Ctrl+2. Navigate to the drawing and double-click it to open the list of named objects. Double-click Xrefs to see a list of xrefs in the right pane.

Double-click the xref that you want to insert. The Attach External Reference dialog box opens (refer to Figure 19.1) so that you can insert the xref. You can also right-click and choose Attach Xref, or right-click and drag a drawing from the DesignCenter into your drawing.

The xref log file

If you set the XREFCTL system variable to 1 (by default, it's set to 0), a copy of all xref activity for your current drawing is saved in an ASCII text file. You can read the log to troubleshoot problems that may occur. The log file goes in the same folder as your drawing and uses your drawing name with the `.xlg` filename extension. This file can become long. Therefore, once in a while, you should delete all or part of the file.

Cross-Reference

The Reference Manager is a stand-alone program that manages xrefs, images, fonts, and plot configurations, which are all outside files that are referenced in your drawing. See Chapter 26 for full coverage of the Reference Manager. The Reference Manager is only available if you have AutoCAD. ∎

On the DVD

The drawing used in the following exercise on managing xrefs, ab19-05.dwg, is in the Results folder on the DVD. ∎

STEPS: Managing Xrefs

1. Use ab19-05.dwg from your AutoCAD Bible folder if you did the previous exercise. Otherwise, open it from the Results folder of the DVD.

2. Save it as ab19-06.dwg in your AutoCAD Bible folder.

3. Choose Insert tab ➪ Reference panel ➪ Clip. At the Select Object to clip: prompt, pick the xref anywhere. At the Enter clipping option [ON/OFF/ Clipdepth/Delete/generate Polyline/New boundary] <New>: prompt, right-click and choose Delete to delete the clip and restore the entire view of both xrefs.

4. Choose View tab ➪ Palettes panel ➪ External References Palette. Click the Tree View button. Right-click ab19-b, the nested xref, and choose Unload.

5. Right-click ab19-b again. Choose Reload to reload the xref.

6. This time right-click ab19-01. Choose Bind. In the Bind Xrefs dialog box, choose Insert and click OK. This action inserts both xrefs (ab19-01 and ab19-b) as blocks. (Click the Layer drop-down list to see that there are no xref-type layer names.)

7. Save your drawing.

Working with DWF, DGN, and PDF Underlays

You can use DWF, DGN, and PDF files as *underlays*, which are similar to xrefs. A DWF file is an accurate, compressed vector image representation of a drawing, and I explain how to create DWF and DWFx files in Chapter 28. DGN files are drawings created with Bentley MicroStation®, another CAD program. You can produce PDF files by plotting or publishing a drawing, or by using an application such as Adobe Acrobat.

Underlays are different from xrefs in that you cannot bind them to a drawing file. The primary reasoning for this is that you use underlays as reference documents that you might not be able to obtain as a DWG file. Underlays also help to protect the original owner's investment and integrity in the design or information contained in the original document.

Attaching a DWF underlay

Attaching a DWF file is similar to attaching an xref or inserting a block. To attach a DWF file, follow these steps:

1. Choose Insert tab ➪ Reference panel ➪ Attach (the ATTACH command), or choose Attach DWF from the Attach File drop-down list of the External References palette (the DWFATTACH command).

2. In the Select Reference File dialog box, choose the DWF or DWFx file and click Open.

3. In the Attach DWF Underlay dialog box, choose a sheet from the DWF or DWFx file, if it contains more than one page. The Attach DWF Underlay dialog box is similar to the Attach External Reference dialog box shown in Figure 19.1.

4. From the Path Type drop-down list, choose the type of path you want to specify for the underlay. (See the "Attaching an external reference" section earlier in this chapter for more information.)

5. To specify the insertion point, scale, and rotation, uncheck the respective check boxes in the dialog box; otherwise, specify them on-screen.

6. Click OK to attach the DWF or DWFx file as a DWF underlay.

If your current view does not show the entire underlay, use ZOOM Extents to see it (choose View tab ⇨ Navigate panel ⇨ Zoom drop-down list ⇨ Extents).

Attaching a DGN underlay

To underlay a DGN file, choose Insert tab ⇨ Reference panel ⇨ Attach (the ATTACH command), or choose Attach DGN from the Attach File drop-down list of the External References palette (the DGNATTACH command). The Select Reference File dialog box opens; select a DGN file and click Open. The Attach DGN Underlay dialog box opens, which is similar to the Attach External Reference dialog box shown in Figure 19.1.

If the drawing has more than one model, choose the one you want to attach from the Select a Design Model from the DGN File list box. DGN files can have master units (Imperial or metric) and another set of units, called sub units. Choose which one you want to use. AutoCAD converts one unit (either master or sub) to one drawing unit. Click OK to attach the DGN underlay.

Attaching a PDF underlay

Attaching a PDF file is similar to attaching a DWF file. Choose Insert tab ⇨ Reference panel ⇨ Attach (the ATTACH command), or choose Attach PDF from the Attach File drop-down list of the External References palette (the PDFATTACH command). The Select Reference File dialog box opens; select a PDF file and click Open. The Attach PDF Underlay dialog box opens, which is similar to the Attach External Reference dialog box shown in Figure 19.1. If the PDF file contains more than one page, choose the one you want to attach from the Select One or More Pages from the PDF File list box. Click OK to attach the PDF underlay.

Modifying an underlay

After an underlay is created, you can control its display and how you can work with the underlay's geometry.

Adjusting the appearance of an underlay

You can change the appearance of an underlay to make it more or less prominent, by using the ADJUST command. This command has three options:

- **Fade.** Blends the underlay more or less with the background color. You can choose a value from 0 to 100, where 100 fades the underlay completely with the background. The default value is 0 for images and PDF underlays, and 25 for DWF and DGN underlays.

- **Contrast.** Increases or decreases the contrast of the colors. The values range from 0 to 100, where 100 changes the colors to their closest primary or secondary color. The default is 50 for images, 75 for DWF and DGN underlays, and 100 for PDF underlays.

- **Monochrome.** Displays the underlay as shades of gray. Choose Yes or No.

If you selected a single underlay, the default values for Fade, Contrast, and Monochrome are the current property settings of the selected underlay. If you select multiple underlays, the default values for Fade, Contrast, and Monochrome remain as they were set the last time the command was used.

Clipping an underlay

If the underlay is large, you may not want to view all of it in your drawing. You can clip an underlay in the same way that you clip an xref or block, by using the CLIP command. To access this command, choose Insert tab ⇨ Reference panel ⇨ Clip and then select the underlay to clip. The options are:

- **ON.** Turns on an existing clipping boundary. By default, a clipping boundary is on.

- **OFF.** Turns off an existing clipping boundary so that you can see the entire underlay.

- **Delete.** Deletes a clipping boundary.
- **New boundary.** Creates a new rectangular or polygonal clipping boundary.

Displaying the frame of an underlay

You can turn the display of the frame for an underlay on or off. This is very similar to the frame that is displayed after clipping an xref or block. If the underlay is not clipped, the frame shows the rectangular border of the entire underlay. If you clipped the underlay, the frame shows the clipping border.

To display the frames for all underlays in a drawing, use the FRAME system variable and set its value to 1 (displays the frame and plots it) or 2 (displays the frame, but doesn't plot it). To turn off the display of all frames, set the value to 0. Even with the frames turned off, you can select an underlay. To change the display of the frames for underlays, choose Insert tab⇨Reference panel⇨Frame Settings drop-down list.

When FRAME is set to 3, you can control the frame display for xrefs, underlays, and raster images in the drawing by using the appropriate system variable. Use the following system variables to control the display of the frames for underlays; except for value 3, they support the same values as FRAME:

- **DWFFRAME.** Controls the frame display for DWF underlays.
- **DGNFRAME.** Controls the frame display for DGN underlays.
- **IMAGEFRAME.** Controls the frame display for raster images.
- **PDFFRAME.** Controls the frame display for PDF underlays.
- **XCLIPFRAME.** Controls the frame display for xrefs.

Using object snaps with underlays

By default, you can use object snaps with underlays. If you need to use the object snaps of your underlay, this is the ideal setting. In PDF underlays, object snaps only work with vector-based objects; they do not work with raster-based (bitmap) objects.

However, if you don't want to use object snaps with underlays or you find yourself getting "caught" on an underlay's object snaps, you can turn object snaps off. To change the status of object snaps for underlays, choose Insert tab⇨Reference panel⇨Snap to Underlays Settings drop-down list, and choose Snap to Underlays On or Snap to Underlays Off (the UOSNAP system variable). Note that even with UOSNAP set to 0, you can snap to the insertion point of the underlay.

You can control the use of object snaps by underlay type, using the following system variables:

- **DWFOSNAP.** Controls the use of object snapping with DWF underlays.
- **DGNOSNAP.** Controls the use of object snapping with DGN underlays.
- **PDFOSNAP.** Controls the use of object snapping with PDF underlays.

Note

When you set one of the underlay-specific system variables that control object snap settings to a value that is not equal to the current value of UOSNAP, UOSNAP changes to a value of 2. This value honors the underlay-specific snap settings for underlays. ■

Control the layers of an underlay

You can control the layers that are displayed for an underlay if the attached file was published with layer information. When you publish a DWF or DWFx file, you use the Publish Options dialog box to set Layer information to Include. (See Chapter 28 for more information on DWF and DWFx files.) The layers in a

DGN underlay are based on the levels used in the original DGN file. PDF files can contain layer information if the application that created the PDF file saved the information during output.

Use the ULAYERS command to turn layers on or off for an underlay. To access this command, choose Insert tab ⇨ Reference panel ⇨ Underlay Layers or type **ulayers** ↵ on the command line. In the Underlay Layers dialog box, select an underlay from the Reference Name drop-down list. Click the light bulb icon next to the layers you want to turn on or off, and then click OK to apply the changes to the underlay.

Summary

In this chapter, I covered the techniques that you need to know to work with xrefs and underlays. You read about:

- Attaching and overlaying xrefs
- Opening an xref in its own window
- Editing xrefs and blocks from within the drawing in which they appear
- Clipping xrefs so that only the portion you need to see is displayed
- Setting spatial and layer indexes to speed up the display of large xrefs
- Deleting, unloading, and reloading xrefs
- Binding an xref to make it part of your drawing
- Working with DWF, DGN, and PDF underlays

In the next chapter, I cover database connectivity, which enables you to access outside databases.

Working with External Databases

The AutoCAD database connectivity feature enables you to communicate with an external database from within AutoCAD.

AutoCAD Only

AutoCAD LT does not include the database connectivity feature. This entire chapter applies to AutoCAD only. ■

Database connectivity is a powerful way to link drawing objects with data and is more flexible than using block attributes. With database connectivity, you can link data in an external database to any object in a drawing. In this chapter, I show you that database connectivity does not have to be as difficult as it often sounds.

Many AutoCAD users maintain databases separately from their drawings. You can work directly with your data by linking the rows of the database tables to objects in your drawings. The drawing objects thus become intelligent and carry these links with them in the drawing. You can also change data, such as a price or a part number, from within AutoCAD, and have that change automatically applied and available in all drawing objects that are linked to that database item. Finally, you can create labels in your drawing, based on the data in the database.

Cross-Reference

You can link to external Microsoft Excel spreadsheets and comma-delimited (CSV) files in a table. For more information, see Chapter 13. Using that feature, you can view the external data and change it (both in the table and in Excel). Your table always displays the current data in the spreadsheet. However, the external database access feature described in this chapter offers some additional capabilities, such as linking rows of data to objects in your drawing, creating labels, and creating SQL queries. ■

Understanding External Database Access

Many organizations maintain extensive databases of objects that are in their AutoCAD drawings. Manufacturers maintain databases of parts, offices maintain databases of furniture, and so on. You need to keep your drawings and the databases synchronized so that the information in the databases and in the drawings is always accurate and up to date.

The linking of databases and AutoCAD drawings is referred to as *external database access*. External database access enables you to:

- Create links between AutoCAD drawing objects and the external data.
- View data in external databases.
- Edit data in external databases.
- Display external database data in your drawing.

The database connectivity feature works with the following databases:

- Microsoft Access
- dBASE
- Microsoft Excel
- Oracle
- Paradox
- Microsoft Visual FoxPro
- SQL Server

After you configure a database, as explained later in this chapter, you can access the data in the database even if you don't have the database program that created the data.

A *database* is a set of related information, usually maintained by a database-management system (DBMS) — an application that manages databases. A database is stored in the form of a table that contains rows and columns. A row, also called a *record,* contains one element of data, such as the information for one desk. A column, also called a *field,* contains the attributes of the data, such as the price.

Table 20.1 shows the first three rows of the database used as an example in this chapter.

TABLE 20.1

A Simple Database Table

Part Number	Description	Dwg Size	Made/Purchased	Units
8665-023-012	Welding Wire — 0.030 StainlessB	B	P	FT
8665-023-013	Weld Rod — 0.045 Dia Stainless Steel	B	P	FT
8665-023-014	Welding — Rod 0.045 Dia S.S.	B	P	FT

A *relational database* is a type of database that contains a collection of tables. Each table represents a set of data for a defined use.

Structured Query Language (SQL — pronounced *sequel* or *S-Q-L*) was created to provide users with a database language that would be applicable across multiple platforms and database-management programs.

Some database systems use environments, catalogs, schemas, and tables to create a hierarchy of *database objects*. A database object is simply the term used to specify any of the following SQL objects: environment, catalog, schema, or table.

- The *environment* is the entire database system — the DBMS, the databases it can access, the users, and the programs that can access those databases.

- A *catalog* is a collection of schemas and has the same name as the folder where the database is located.

- A *schema* is a set of tables and other database components. It has the same name as the catalog subfolder where the database tables reside.

You don't need to work with these concepts if your database system does not require or specify it. AutoCAD can connect to an individual table or to a collection of tables stored in an environment, catalog, or schema.

Caution

The 64-bit release of AutoCAD does not support these drivers for connectivity to Microsoft Access and Excel databases. The solution is to use SQL Server instead of the OLE DB driver. For more information, view the Configure External Databases topic in the Driver and Peripheral Guide from the AutoCAD Help Home page. Microsoft has more information on the changes in its support for database access at `msdn.microsoft.com/library/default.asp?url=/library/en-us/mdacsdk/htm/mdac_deprecated_components.asp.` ∎

Preparing for Database Connectivity

Database connectivity involves several components that you need to prepare in advance. When they are in place, the connection should go smoothly. In this section, I explain the necessary preparation steps.

The basic steps for starting to work with database connectivity are as follows:

1. Make sure that you have the ODBC Data Source program from Microsoft.
2. Arrange your database tables into catalogs (folders) and schemas (subfolders) appropriate for your application, if necessary.
3. Configure the appropriate database driver by using Microsoft's ODBC (Open Database Connectivity) or OLE DB program.
4. Configure your data source from within AutoCAD.
5. Start the dbCONNECT command.
6. Establish a user access name and password, if required by the database system.
7. Connect to your data source.
8. Open the Data View window containing your data table.
9. Edit the data, if desired.
10. Link database rows to objects in your drawing.
11. Create labels based on the data in your drawing, if desired.

Organizing the database structure

To connect to a database, you need to know the type of database-management system that created the database and the structure of the database itself, along with the folders that contain that structure. In the following exercise, you create a simple structure for a Microsoft Access database table.

Note

In this chapter, you cannot do the later exercises without doing the earlier ones. The later exercises depend on the setup and configuration that you create in the earlier exercises. ∎

On the DVD

The file used in the following exercise on creating the structure for the database, ab20-prt.mdb, is in the Drawings folder on the DVD. ∎

STEPS: Creating the Structure for the Database

1. Right-click Start on the task bar. Choose Explore to open Windows Explorer.

2. If your AutoCAD Bible folder is not displayed in the Folders window, click the plus sign (+) next to the drive containing the AutoCAD Bible folder.

3. Click the AutoCAD Bible folder and choose File ➪ New ➪ Folder from the Explorer menu. (In Windows Vista, click Organize ➪ New Folder. In Windows 7, click New Folder.) A new folder appears in the right window, called New Folder. Type **Databases** ↵ to rename the folder.

4. If necessary, in the Folders window, click the plus sign to open the AutoCAD Bible folder. You should see the new Databases folder. (If not, press F5 to refresh the Explorer view.)

5. From the DVD, copy ab20-prt.mdb to the Databases folder that you just created. (Be sure to choose the ab20-prt.mdb file, not the ab20-prt.xls file.) The .mdb file is a database of parts. Figure 20.1 shows this database.

6. Because this file is coming from a DVD, you may need to change its read-only property. Still in Explorer, right-click ab20-prt.mdb and choose Properties from the menu. Uncheck Read-Only and click OK.

7. Click the Close button of Explorer to close it.

Note

If you have Microsoft Access 2007, you may want to open this database in Access and convert it to 2007 format. When you open the database, you'll automatically see a dialog box prompting you to convert the file. ∎

Configuring a data source

To start working with external databases, you must tell AutoCAD how to communicate with your database, called a *data source*. AutoCAD uses ODBC and OLE DB for this communication. AutoCAD provides a sample Microsoft Access file, called db_samples.mdb in AutoCAD's Sample\Database Connectivity folder, that you can work with to get started.

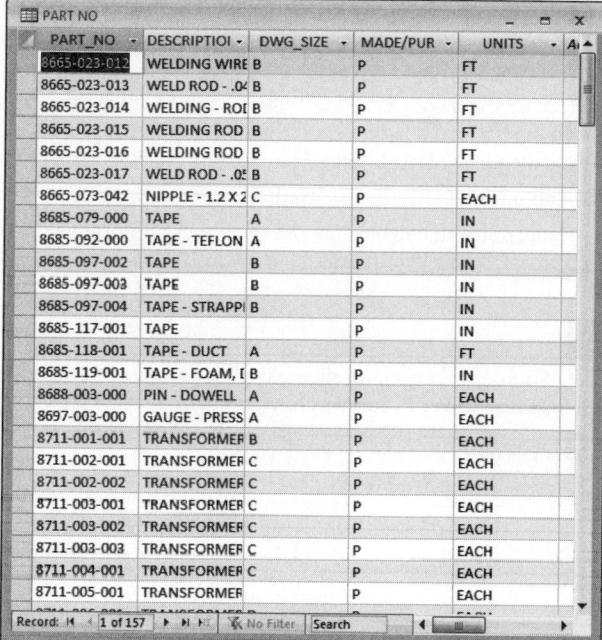

FIGURE 20.1

The Microsoft Access database.

Thanks to Gary Morris of the Dexter Company, Fairfield, Iowa, for this database.

First, you must install and configure the ODBC Data Source Administrator. To check if the ODBC Data Source Administrator is installed on your computer, open the Control Panel by choosing Start ➪ Settings ➪ Control Panel (or Start ➪ Control Panel), and look for one of the following items:

- Administrative Tools ➪ Data Sources (ODBC)
- ODBC Data Sources (32-bit) or Data Sources (ODBC)

Note

You might need to click Switch to Classic View (or Classic View) on the left side of the Control Panel window in order to see these in the Control Panel. ∎

To check if you have the required drivers installed, double-click the Data Sources (ODBC) item. You might need to click Continue. In the ODBC Data Source Administrator dialog box, you'll see a list of database application drivers. (A database driver contains information about how to connect to your database.) Check to see that your database application is listed. Click OK to close the dialog box.

In most cases, your operating system will include the ODBC Administrator. If you don't have the ODBC 32-bit Administrator, you need to install the Microsoft ODBC Driver Pack. The ODBC Driver Pack 3.0 (or later) is free from the Microsoft Web site at msdn2.microsoft.com/en-us/data/aa937730.aspx. The MDAC (Microsoft Data Access Components) 2.8 download should provide you with everything you need.

The instructions to set up the database vary according to the drivers that you use. The AutoCAD online help contains help on all supported databases. Look in Help (press F1) and click Driver and Peripheral Guide from the left side of the Home page; then click Configure External Databases under the Configure External Databases section. Click the Procedures link from the left and follow the procedure for your database.

To set up your database by using ODBC, follow these steps:

1. From the Windows task bar, choose Start ➪ Settings ➪ Control Panel (or Start ➪ Control Panel).
2. Double-click the Administrative Tools icon, and then double-click the Data Sources (ODBC) item. Windows opens the ODBC Data Source Administrator dialog box, as shown in Figure 20.2.
3. Click the User DSN tab if it isn't already displayed. Choose Add.
4. In the Create New Data Source dialog box, choose the driver appropriate for your database (for example, Microsoft Access Driver [*.mdb]) and click Finish.

FIGURE 20.2

Use the ODBC Data Source Administrator dialog box, accessed from the Windows Control Panel, to choose a database driver to connect to your database.

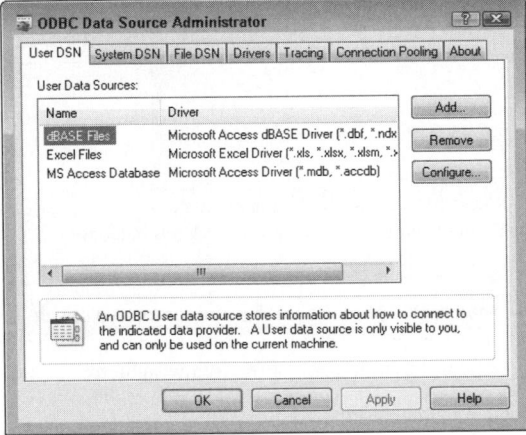

5. In the ODBC Setup dialog box, which is now titled with the name of the driver that you chose (for example, ODBC Microsoft Access Setup), type a name for your data source in the Data Source Name text box. You can also add a description. In general, this name refers to your database program, not the individual database file.
6. Click Select and navigate to the folder containing your database. Choose the database file and click OK.
7. Click OK again in the Setup dialog box.
8. In the ODBC Data Source Administrator dialog box, your data source is listed with its appropriate driver. Click OK. Close the Administrative Tools window and the Control Panel.

You're now ready to configure your database from within AutoCAD. Follow these steps:

1. At the command line, type **dbconnect** ↵ (or press Ctrl+6) to open the dbConnect Manager palette.

2. On the dbConnect Manager, right-click Data Sources and choose Configure Data Source from the shortcut menu. In the Configure a Data Source dialog box, type a name representing your database file. Click OK.

3. On the Provider tab of the Data Link Properties dialog box, choose Microsoft OLE DB Provider for ODBC drivers. Click Next.

4. From the Use Data Source Name drop-down list on the Connection tab, choose the name of the data source that you used in the ODBC Setup dialog box, as shown in Figure 20.3.

FIGURE 20.3

Use the Data Link Properties dialog box to configure your data source within AutoCAD.

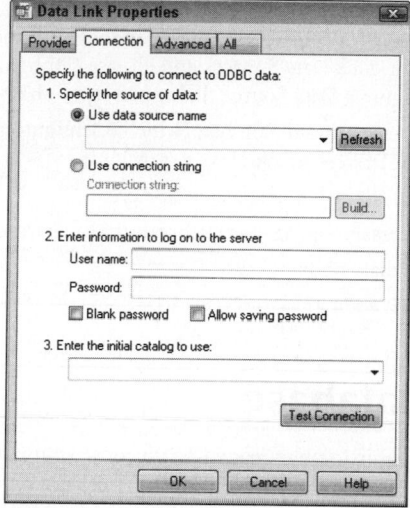

5. For server-based databases, enter the user name and password.

6. Click Test Connection. If you see a message saying Test Connection Succeeded, click OK. (If not, check your settings as well as the spelling and case of the name of the data source.)

7. Click OK in the Data Link Properties dialog box.

You're now ready to establish a connection between a database and an AutoCAD drawing.

On the DVD

The drawing used in the following exercise on configuring a Microsoft Access database, ab20-a.dwg, is in the Drawings folder on the DVD. This exercise requires that you have completed the steps in the previous exercises. ∎

STEPS: Configuring a Microsoft Access Database

1. From the task bar, choose Start ⇨ Settings ⇨ Control Panel (or Start ⇨ Control Panel). Double-click the Administrative Tools icon, and then double-click the Data Sources (ODBC) icon. (Your item may have a slightly different name.)

2. On the User DSN tab of the ODBC Data Source Administrator dialog box, choose Add.

3. In the Create New Data Source dialog box, choose Microsoft Access Driver (*.mdb), or Microsoft Access Driver (*.mdb, *.accdb) if you have Microsoft Access 2007. Choose Finish.

4. In the Data Source Name text box of the ODBC Microsoft Access Setup dialog box, type **ab20-Access**.

5. Click Select and navigate to your `AutoCAD Bible\Databases` folder (which you created in the previous exercise). Choose `ab20-prt.mdb` and click OK.

6. Click OK twice more to exit the ODBC Data Source Administrator.

7. Close the Administrative Tools and Control Panel windows.

8. Open AutoCAD. Open `ab20-a.dwg` from the DVD. Save it as `ab20-01.dwg` in your `AutoCAD Bible` folder.

9. At the command line, type **dbconnect** ↵ (or press Ctrl+6) to open the dbConnect Manager palette. On the dbConnect Manager, right-click Data Sources and choose Configure Data Source from the shortcut menu. In the Configure a Data Source dialog box, type **ab20-prt**. Click OK.

10. On the Provider tab of the Data Link Properties dialog box (which opens automatically), choose Microsoft OLE DB Provider for ODBC Drivers. Click Next.

11. From the Use Data Source Name drop-down list, choose ab20-Access.

12. Click Test Connection. If you see a message saying `Test Connection Succeeded`, click OK.

13. Click OK in the Data Link Properties dialog box.

14. Keep `ab20-01.dwg` open for the next exercise.

Connecting to Your Database

After you configure the database connectivity feature, you're ready to connect to your database. Here you actually start making connections between objects in your drawing and rows in your database.

Before connecting to your database, you should think about the relationship between the drawing and the database. For example, you should decide:

- If the data is to be in one database with many tables or in several separate databases
- Which data you want to link to which drawing objects
- If several drawing objects will be linked to one row or only one object will be linked to a row
- If you want a drawing object linked to more than one row
- Which column(s) will identify unique records

You're now ready to connect your database to your drawing.

Connecting a database to a drawing

You use the dbConnect Manager, shown in Figure 20.4, to perform all the connectivity functions. The dbConnect Manager has its own toolbar, which becomes active when you choose a connected data source. All configured data sources are listed.

You can dock and undock the dbConnect Manager like any palette. You can also resize it by dragging its right border left or right. After you open the dbConnect Manager, you see a list of open drawings and configured data sources.

FIGURE 20.4

The dbConnect Manager palette.

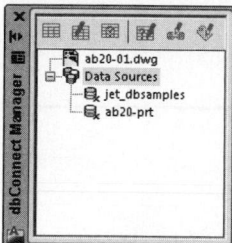

Follow these steps to connect an external database to a drawing:

1. Open the drawing that you want to connect with a database.
2. At the command line, type **dbconnect** ↵ (or press Ctrl+6) to open the dbConnect Manager palette.
3. Right-click the data source to which you want to connect. (The names listed come from the names that you entered when you configured the data source in AutoCAD.) Choose Connect.

AutoCAD lists the database tables associated with the data source. The entire database structure is now connected, and you can view and work with the database data within AutoCAD. In order to do the following exercise, you must have completed the previous two exercises.

STEPS: Connecting a Database to a Drawing

1. You should have ab20-01.dwg open from the previous exercise.
2. At the command line, type **dbconnect** ↵ (or press Ctrl+6) to open the dbConnect Manager palette.
3. Right-click ab20-prt and choose Connect. The dbConnect Manager lists the database table PART NO.
4. Save the drawing. Keep it open. Continue to the next exercise.

Opening a data table

After your database is connected, you choose the database table with which you want to work. If necessary, click the plus sign next to the desired database to see the actual database files that are available. The database file also displays a plus sign. If necessary, click it to display the database tables within the database file. (A database file can contain more than one table.)

You can view or edit a table in the Data View window:

- View the data when you have no need to edit it. To view your data, right-click the table that you want to view and choose View Table.
- Edit the data when you need to make changes to your database from within AutoCAD. To edit your data, right-click and choose Edit Table.

To view or edit a table, select the table. Choose View Table or Edit Table from the dbConnect Manager's toolbar. You can also right-click the table and choose View Table or Edit Table from the shortcut menu.

Figure 20.5 shows the Data View window when you choose Edit Table. (When you choose View Table, you see the same view but the data cells are gray.)

The Data View window presents your data in a grid, with each piece of data in a cell, like a spreadsheet. You can use the scroll bars to scroll through the data. To the left of the horizontal scroll bar, you can use the arrows to move from record to record. The far left and right arrows with a vertical bar move you to the first and last records, respectively.

The Data View window displays your data.

You can temporarily change the way the data is displayed. These changes are discarded after you close the Data View window; they don't affect the data file in your database. Here are your options:

- **Resize a column.** You may find that your data doesn't completely display in a column or that columns don't all appear in the window. Click the grid line to the right of any column header and drag it to the left or right. You can also resize the entire Data View window by dragging on its sides or bottom. Double-click between two columns to resize the column to the left based on its widest value.

- **Move a column.** You can change the order of the columns by moving a column to another location. Click the column's header to select the column. Then click and drag the column to the location you want. A black vertical line indicates where the column will land.

- **Hide a column.** You can hide a column with which you don't need to work. This is especially helpful if you have many columns and can't fit them easily on the screen. Click the column's header to select the column. Then right-click the column header and choose Hide. To re-display the column, right-click any column header and choose Unhide All.

- **Sort records.** You can sort records in ascending (low to high) or descending (high to low) order. Sorting helps you to more easily find the records that you want. Right-click any column header and choose Sort to open the Sort dialog box. In the Sort By drop-down list, choose the column that you want to sort by first. Then choose Ascending or Descending. This column may have duplicate records. If so, you may want to choose a secondary column for sorting in the Then By drop-down list. Choose Ascending or Descending for the secondary column. AutoCAD will then sort first by the first column and then by the second column. You can choose up to five columns to sort by.

- **Freeze one or more columns.** Freezing one or more contiguous columns moves them to the left column. Select the columns by clicking their column headers. (Press Ctrl to select additional columns. You can also select one column, press Shift, and select another column to select all the columns in between.) Then right-click a selected column and choose Freeze. To return the column to its original location, right-click and choose Unfreeze All.

- **Align text.** You can align text in a column or columns. By default, columns use the Standard alignment, which right-aligns numbers and left-aligns everything else. Select a column or columns by clicking the column header(s), right-click any column header, and choose Align. Then choose Standard, Left, Center, or Right.

- **Format text.** You can format the font, font style, font size, effects (strikethrough and underline), and color of the text in the Data View window. Note that, unlike the other changes previously listed, these changes continue to affect the formatting of the Data View window the next time you open a Data View window. Right-click the upper-left corner of the data grid and choose Format to open the Format dialog box. Choose the formatting that you want and then click OK.

Tip

To get the Data View window out of the way, you can dock it. Right-click in the Data View window's toolbar area and choose Allow Docking. Then drag the window to the right edge of your screen (assuming your dbConnect Manager is on the left side of your screen). ■

Although you can scroll through your data's records, if you have many records, this can be time-consuming. You can search for a particular record by specifying a desired value. Follow these steps:

1. Select any cell in the column that contains the record that you want to find. If you want to search the entire column, choose the first or last cell in the column.

2. In the Data View, right-click over a cell and choose Find to open the Find dialog box.

3. In the Find What text box, type a value (text, numbers, or a combination). Choose to search either Up (from the selected cell to the first record) or Down (from the selected cell to the last record). If desired, choose Match Case. Then click Find Next to find the next instance of the value. Continue to click Find Next to move to the next matching record.

Tip

If you want, you can copy your formatting, including sorting, to the Clipboard and paste it into your DBMS. To do this, select the records that you want to export. To export the entire database, click the grid header. Then right-click any cell and choose Copy. Open your DBMS and click Paste from the Standard toolbar. ■

In the following exercise, you practice using the Data View window.

STEPS: Working with the Data View Window

1. Ab20-01.dwg should still be open from the previous exercise. If there's a plus sign next to ab20-prt, click it to display the "PART NO" table.

2. Right-click the table icon and choose Edit Table. The Data View window opens.

3. Right-click the grid header (in the upper-left corner of the grid) and choose Format. In the Format dialog box, choose Arial as the font and 10 as the font size. Click OK.

4. The columns are too wide and you can't see all of them. Click the grid line to the right of the PART_NO column and drag it to the left so that the width of the column just fits the width of the part numbers. Do the same with the other columns. (You can also double-click the grid line between columns to automatically resize the column to the left to the widest value.) To access the right grid line of the last column (UNITS), expand the right side of the entire window. Then resize the UNITS column and shrink the Data View window to fit.

5. Right-click the PART_NO column's header and choose Align ➪ Right to right-align the first column.

6. To practice moving around the table, click the rightmost arrow at the bottom of the Data View window (to the left of the horizontal scroll bar) to move to the last record. Use the vertical scroll bar to scroll through the database and get an idea of its contents. Click any cell. Click a row header to select an entire row. Click a column header to select an entire column.

7. To sort the records by description and help you to find all the angles, right-click the DESCRIPTION column header and choose Sort. In the Sort dialog box, choose DESCRIPTION from the Sort By drop-down list, and then click Ascending (if it's not already selected). Because there are a number of duplicate records in the DESCRIPTION column, choose PART_NO in the Then By drop-down list, which should also be sorted in ascending order. Click OK. AutoCAD sorts the data by description, and then by part number.

8. Say that you want to find part number 9003-242-001. Right-click the top cell in the PART_NO column. Choose Find. In the Find dialog box, type **9003-242-001** and choose Down in the Direction section. Click Find Next. AutoCAD highlights the cell containing that part number.

9. Close the Find dialog box and save your drawing. Keep it open for the next exercise.

Editing data in the Data View window

After you open your data in Edit mode, you can easily edit the data. You can change the value of any record. You can add or delete records to reflect new or deleted objects in your drawing. Changing a record is as simple as selecting a cell and typing a new value.

To add a new record, right-click any record (row) header and choose Add New Record. AutoCAD opens up a space for a new record at the end of the list of records. Type the data for the new record, tabbing from column to column. (You can also use the right-arrow key to move to the next column.)

To delete a record, right-click the record header of the record that you want to delete, selecting the entire record. Choose Delete Record. You need to confirm the deletion in the dialog box that pops up.

Caution
You should not use the DBMS to edit a database separately while it is connected to AutoCAD. If you do edit the database table outside of AutoCAD during an AutoCAD connection, you may get system crashes or corrupted data. If you need to edit the database by using the DBMS, make sure that you disconnect the table first in the dbConnect Manager. ∎

AutoCAD doesn't save your changes until you commit them. To save your changes, right-click the *grid header* — the cell at the top-left corner of the Data View window — and choose Commit. To discard your changes, choose Restore, which restores the original values of the database when you opened the Data View window.

STEPS: Editing Data

1. With ab20-01.dwg and the Data View window still open from the preceding exercise, the part number that you found in the previous exercise (9003-242-001) should still be highlighted. If not, find it following the instructions in Step 8 of the preceding exercise.

2. Note that the MADE/PUR column indicates that this horizontal angle is purchased. Say that the company has decided to make this angle. Click the P in the MADE/PUR column of the 9003-242-001 record and type **M**.

3. To add a record, right-click any record (row) header and choose Add New Record. AutoCAD moves you to the end of the records with a space for a new record. Type the following, tabbing between each column:

```
8665-023-018    WELDING ROD - .05 DIA S.S.    B    P    FT
```

4. I don't recommend saving the changes to the database because you may want to do this exercise again in the future. Right-click the grid header (in the upper-left corner of the grid) and choose Restore. AutoCAD closes the Data View window.

5. Keep the drawing open for the next exercise.

Linking Data to Drawing Objects

The main purpose of using data connectivity is to link data to objects in your drawing. A row of data contains information about the real-life object that objects in your drawing represent. By connecting a row of data to an object or objects in your drawing, you can do the following:

- View information, such as price, source, next service date, and so on, about the real-life object while in your drawing.

- Update a drawing based on changes in the database, or vice versa, to keep your drawings and your database synchronized.

- Display a label containing data information next to a drawing object.

Creating a link template

When AutoCAD creates a link, it associates an object or objects with a row in your database. To do so, AutoCAD needs to know which field (column) to look in to identify the row. For example, let's say you want to link price information to some objects. However, several rows may contain the same price information. If you provide a field that contains no duplicate data, AutoCAD can always locate the required row. If AutoCAD finds two rows with the same data, it accesses the first row. It makes sense, therefore, to be careful to choose a column that contains no duplicate values. If your data doesn't contain such a column, most DBMSs can create an index field that ensures that each row is unique.

A *link template* identifies which fields are associated with a link between the data and a drawing object. A link template also identifies your database. After you create a link template, you can open your data directly from the template, which is listed in the dbConnect Manager.

If you want to associate data from more than one database table to a single object, you may need to create more than one link template for an object.

To create a link template, follow these steps:

1. On the dbConnect Manager, select a table, and click New Link Template on the dbConnect Manager's toolbar.

2. In the New Link Template Name text box of the New Link Template dialog box, shown in Figure 20.6, type a name for the link template. AutoCAD assigns an automatic name, using the name of the data source and _Link1, _Link2, and so on. You can use that name or type your own. If you have a previous link template that you want to use as a basis for the new template, choose it from the Start with Template drop-down list. Click Continue.

FIGURE 20.6

The New Link Template dialog box.

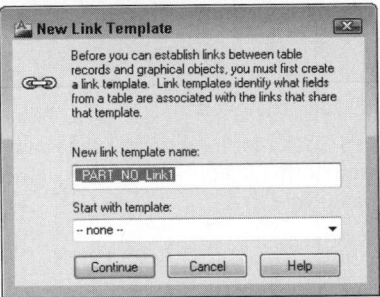

3. In the Link Template dialog box, check a key field. If the key field that you choose contains any duplicate rows, you should choose a second key field.

4. Click OK. AutoCAD creates the link template, which is added to the dbConnect Manager beneath the current drawing.

You're now ready to link data with drawing objects.

If the structure of your database changes dramatically, you may need to edit a link template. For example, a field that contained no duplicate entries might now contain some. Other changes requiring a change in the template would be a change in the name or length of a field. To edit a link template:

1. Connect to the desired database table.

2. On the dbConnect Manager, right-click over a link template and choose Edit. You can use the DBCEDITLT command to display the Select a Database Object dialog box. From the Select a Database Object dialog box, choose a link template and click Continue.

3. Check one (or more) of the key fields and click OK.

You can delete a link template by right-clicking over the link template and choosing Delete. You can also rename or duplicate a link template by right-clicking the link template and choosing Rename or Duplicate.

This exercise requires that you have completed the previous exercises in this chapter.

STEPS: Creating a Link Template

1. Continue with ab20-01.dwg from the previous exercise. On the dbConnect Manager, right-click "PART NO" and choose New Link Template.

2. In the New Link Template dialog box, use AutoCAD's suggested name, _PART_NO_Link1. Click Continue.

3. In the Link Template dialog box, check PART_NO. This column contains no duplicate rows.

4. Click OK to return to the drawing. You see the new link template with a chain-link icon in the dbConnect Manager just under the name of the open drawing.

5. Save your drawing. Leave it open to continue with the next exercise.

You're now ready to link drawing objects to your database.

Creating a link

You can link a drawing object to as many records in a database as you want, and you can link one database record to several drawing objects. For example, you may want to link a record containing part-number information to the part in the drawing. However, that part may be made up of a number of objects, such as lines, arcs, and circles. You can link the record to all those objects in your drawing that make up the part. On the other hand, if you have a database of office equipment, you may attach a row representing telephone numbers and telephones to an object in your drawing representing a phone. However, if someone has a two-line phone, you may need to attach two rows to that one telephone object in your drawing.

Here's how to create a link:

1. Open a Data View window that has a defined link template and choose a link template from the Select a Link Template drop-down list at the top of the window.

2. Select one or more records that you want to link to your drawing.

3. Click the down arrow next to Link and Label Settings on the Data View's toolbar, and choose Create Links.

 4. Click Link! on the Data View's toolbar.

5. AutoCAD returns you to your drawing. Select one or more objects and press Enter to end object selection.

AutoCAD provides a message on the command line, for example: 1 Record(s) linked with 1 Object(s). You now have a link between your data and your drawing.

Caution

If you create a link between a drawing object and a row and in a later session of AutoCAD edit that object without connecting to the database table, the link information may become corrupted. ■

You can delete a link by selecting a linked object and right-clicking in the drawing area. From the shortcut menu, choose Links ⇨ Delete Links.

Viewing linked objects and rows

After you create a link, you need to be able to see which rows are linked to which objects before you can make decisions regarding either the data or the drawing objects. You can view the link from either side. That is, you can select an object and see which row or rows it is linked to or you can select a row and have AutoCAD select the object or objects to which it's linked. In both cases, you need to have a Data View table displayed.

 ● To find out which row or rows an object is linked to, select one or more objects. Then click View Linked Records in Data View on the Data View's toolbar. AutoCAD displays (by default) or highlights the row or rows that are linked to the selection set of objects. Later in this section, I explain how to customize the display of a row or rows.

Note

To restore the full data in the Data View window, close the Data View window and then re-open it from the dbConnect Manager. ■

● To find out which object a row is linked to, select one or more records. Click View Linked Objects in Drawing on the Data View's toolbar. AutoCAD pans, zooms (or does both so that you can see the objects in the center of the screen), and selects them. If the drawing does not pan or zoom, don't worry as I explain how to customize the panning and zooming later in this section.

You'll find that the Data View window obscures your drawing. You can drag it to the bottom of your screen, resize it, or dock it.

Tip

When you use View Linked Objects, the selected objects form a selection set. You can then use the results with other commands that allow prior selection of objects. For commands that you must execute before selecting objects, type p ↵ at the `Select objects:` **prompt to use the Previous option and get the selection set. ■**

If you want to move from object to object or row to row to view your links one after another, try Auto-View. The AutoView feature automatically highlights either objects, when you choose a row in the Data View window, or rows, when you choose objects in your drawing. However, you can work from only one side of the equation — either rows or objects — at a time. Here's how it works:

 ● To automatically select linked objects when you select a row, click the AutoView Linked Objects in Drawing button in the Data View window. Then select a record (or records) by clicking the row header(s) in the Data View window. AutoCAD highlights the linked objects. You can continue to select different records to highlight their linked objects. Choose Auto-View Linked Objects (or click the button) again to turn off Auto-View.

 ● To automatically select linked rows when you select an object, click the AutoView Linked Records in Data View button in the Data View window. Then select an object (or objects). AutoCAD highlights the linked rows. You can continue to select different objects to highlight their linked rows. Click Auto-View Linked Records (or choose the menu item) again to turn off Auto-View.

When you're in Auto-View, you can't select records. If you click another record's row header to create a link, AutoCAD just tells you `0 Object(s) found matching 0 selected Record(s)`. Be sure to turn off Auto-View when you go on to another task.

 You can customize how AutoCAD displays linked rows and how AutoCAD pans (AutoPan) and zooms (AutoZoom) to display selected objects. Click Data View and Query Options from the Data View toolbar. In the Record Indication Settings section of the Data View and Query Options dialog box, choose either Show Only Indicated Records (the default) or Show All Records, Select Indicated Records. You can also choose the highlight color. To set AutoPan and AutoZoom, use the AutoPan and Zoom section of the same dialog box. Uncheck Automatically Pan Drawing and Automatically Zoom Drawing if you don't want this feature. When Automatically Zoom Drawing is checked, you can also choose a zoom percentage. You can choose from 20 to 90 percent. The default, 50 percent, means that the height (or width, if less) of the extents of the zoomed area is 50 percent of the drawing area. Click OK after you finish using the dialog box.

Editing links

After you create links in your drawing, you need to be careful how you edit your database from within AutoCAD. For example, you don't want to inadvertently delete a record that is linked to an object.

You may need to edit the key value assigned to a linked object. For example, your company may change the part-numbering scheme or you may have simply assigned the wrong part number to an object. The Link Manager enables you to edit key values for linked objects. Follow these steps:

1. Select a linked object in the drawing area and right-click. From the shortcut menu, choose Links⇨ Link Manager to open the Link Manager, as shown in Figure 20.7.
2. In the Link Manager, choose the Link Template that you want to work with from the drop-down list.

FIGURE 20.7

The Link Manager enables you to edit key value data for its linked object.

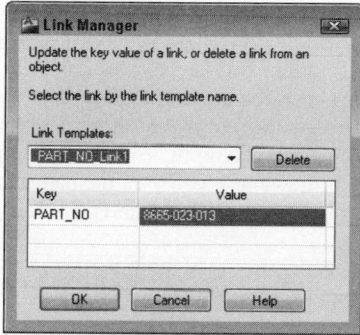

3. In the Value column, type a new value, such as a new part number.
4. Click OK.

AutoCAD updates the link.

You can also click the Delete button to delete the object's link.

Exporting link information

You can export a list of links and the handle of the associated links' objects. A *handle* is a unique name that AutoCAD gives to each object in the drawing. (To view an object's handle, at the command line, type **list** ↵.) You can export the reports in the same format as your database (called the *native format*) or in space- or comma-delimited formats. You might use these reports to keep track of how many objects are linked to a row because the exported information tells you how many instances a drawing contains of a record in a database. For example, if your database lists configurations of desktop computers and you've linked each person's computer to the appropriate row in the database, the list will let you know how many people have each configuration.

Follow these steps to export links:

1. Select a linked object, right-click in the drawing area, and choose Links⇨Export Links. You can use the DBCEXPORTLINKS command; at the Select objects: prompt, choose the objects whose links you want to export.

Tip

You can select the entire drawing (type all ↵ at the Select Objects: prompt), and AutoCAD finds just the linked objects. ■

2. In the Include Fields section of the Export Links dialog box, select the fields that you want to include.

3. In the Save In drop-down list, navigate to the folder where you want to save the file.

4. In the Save as Type drop-down list, choose one of the three options: comma-delimited format, space-delimited format, or native database format.

5. In the File Name text box, type a name for the file.

6. Click Save.

   AutoCAD creates the file.

You can use this file to create a schedule of objects with links — but it takes some work. The comma-delimited format seems to work better than the space-delimited format. You'll probably want to edit the file first to remove the object handles. You can open the Multiline In-Place Text Editor and click Import Text to import the output file into your drawing. You can also open the output file, copy it to the Clipboard, and paste it into your drawing. The Import Text method enables you to format the text as you would any multi-line text but takes some experimenting to set up in the proper columns. You can also import the file into a spreadsheet and format it before importing it into your drawing. If you used the native format, you can open it in your DBMS, format it, and import it into your drawing. (See Chapter 27 for more information on importing files.)

STEPS: Creating and Viewing Links

1. You should have ab20-01.dwg open from the previous exercise. The Data View window is open with the database visible. The _PART_NO_Link1 link template is current. You can see the entire drawing in Figure 20.8.

FIGURE 20.8

This drawing of a base assembly for a commercial washing machine has objects that can be linked to the database of parts.

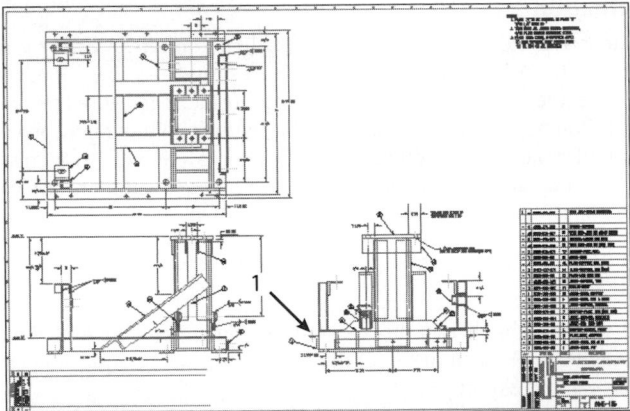

Thanks to Robert Mack of The Dexter Company, Fairfield, Iowa, for this drawing.

2. To locate the record that you need, in the Data View window click the leftmost arrow next to the horizontal scroll bar to move to the first record. Right-click in the PART_NO column of the Data View window and choose Find. In the Find dialog box, type **9003-242-001**. The direction should be down. Click Find Next. AutoCAD finds the record. Close the Find dialog box by clicking its Cancel button.

3. Click the row's header (the arrow to the left of the row) to select the entire row.

4. Click the down arrow next to Link and Label Settings on the Data View's toolbar and choose Create Links. The Create Links menu item may already be checked.

5. Click Link! on the Data View's toolbar.

6. AutoCAD returns you to your drawing. Use a Zoom window to zoom into the area marked ❶, shown in Figure 20.8.

7. Select all the objects that make up the angle bracket indicated by ❶, shown in Figure 20.8 (and which the drawing itself labels as 2), as shown in Figure 20.9. Include the two cyan hidden lines representing the hole, but not the yellow centerline. Don't select the vertical line on the right of the angle, which belongs to another part. Press Enter to end the selection. AutoCAD returns you to the Data View table and displays 1 Record(s) linked with 8 Object(s) on the command line.

8. The linked row is highlighted in yellow. Make sure that the arrow cursor in the row header points to the highlighted row. (AutoCAD moves it down one so that you can work on the next row.) To view the objects connected to the row, click View Linked Objects in Drawing from the Data View's toolbar. Drag the Data View window to the bottom of the screen so that you can see the drawing (or dock it). The objects that you selected in Step 7 are selected.

FIGURE 20.9

The horizontal angle.

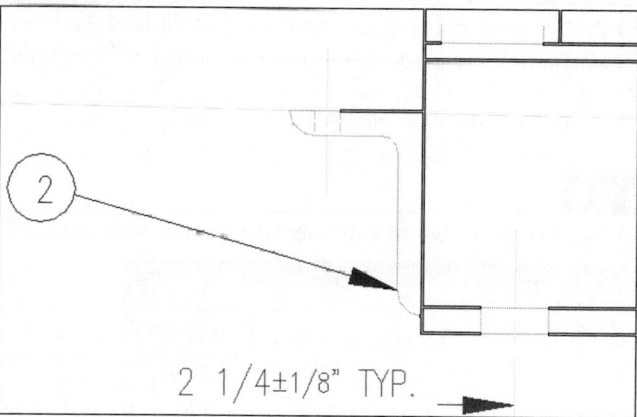

2 1/4±1/8" TYP.

9. In the drawing, press Esc to deselect the objects and remove the grips. To check the link, click any other row in the Data View window to move the cursor. (Try to position the Data View window so that you can see both the row you were working with and the objects you linked it to at the same time.) Click View Linked Records in Data View from the Data View's toolbar. At the Select objects: prompt, select one of the objects in the angle and press Enter. AutoCAD displays the correct row in the database.

10. Save your drawing and keep it open for the next exercise.

Creating Labels

A *label* is multiline text that appears in your drawing, displaying data from a row in your database. You can choose which fields from the row are displayed. There are two types of labels:

- **Attached labels** are attached to objects and are displayed with a leader pointing to the object. If you move the object, the label moves as well. Use an attached label when the row in the database applies to one or more specific objects in your drawing.

- **Freestanding labels** are independent of any object. You would use freestanding labels when your database applies to the drawing as a whole.

Creating label templates

Before creating a label, you need to create a label template. A label template specifies which fields will be included in the label, as well as text formatting. Here's how to create a label template:

1. On the dbConnect Manager, select a table or link template, and click New Label Template on the dbConnect Manager's toolbar.

2. In the New Label Template dialog box, type a template name in the New Label Template Name text box. AutoCAD suggests a default name. If you have an existing label template that you would like to use as a basis for the new label template, choose it from the Start with Template drop-down list. Click Continue.

3. AutoCAD opens the Label Template dialog box, shown in Figure 20.10, with the Label Fields tab displayed. Use the Character and Properties tabs to format the text.

4. On the Label Fields tab, choose a field that you want to appear on the label from the Field drop-down list. Then click Add. Continue to add fields as desired. You can add text to this field. For example, you could type **Part No:** before the PART_NO field.

FIGURE 20.10

Use the Label Template dialog box to format and define label templates.

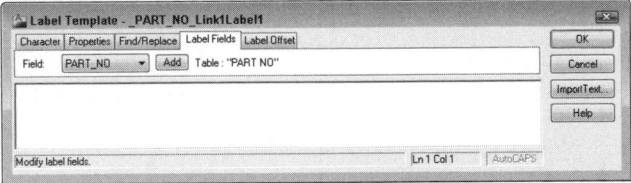

Note

If you add text before or after the field, don't forget to add a space between the text and the field so that the result is Part No: 9003-242-001 rather than Part No:9003-242-001, for example. ■

5. Click the Label Offset tab, as shown in Figure 20.11. This tab defines the placement of the label and the leader that connects the label with the object. In the Start drop-down list, choose a justification. This defines where on the object AutoCAD places the tip of the leader.

FIGURE 20.11

The Label Offset tab of the Label Template dialog box.

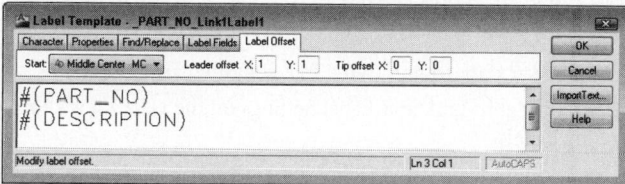

6. In the Leader Offset text boxes, type an X and Y offset (in units). This offset represents the X and Y distances between the point of the leader arrow and the insertion point of the text. (If this distance is too small to fit an arrow, the arrow is suppressed.)

7. In the Tip Offset text boxes, type an X and Y offset (in units). This offset represents the distance between the point of the leader arrow and the object to which it points. By default, this is set to 0,0 so that the point of the leader arrow touches its object.

8. Click OK to close the Label Template dialog box and place the label. For information on placing the label, see the sections "Creating attached labels" and "Creating freestanding labels."

After you create the label template, you can create attached and free-standing labels. The settings on the Label Offset tab apply only to attached labels.

You can edit a label template to change the included fields or the formatting. To edit a label template, right-click the label template on the dbConnect Manager and choose Edit. Use the Label Template dialog box to edit the label template by using the same steps that you used to create it. Click OK after you're done.

Creating attached labels

You create a link between a row and an object and an associated attached label at the same time. You need to have a table open and to have defined both a link and label template. If you have defined more than one link or label template, choose the desired template(s) from the drop-down list at the top of the Data View window. Follow these steps:

1. Select the record that you want to link by clicking its row header in the Data View window.

2. Click the down arrow next to Link and Label Settings on the Data View's toolbar, and choose Create Attached Labels. This puts you in Creating Attached Labels mode, which means that from now on any links that you create also create labels.

3. Click Create Attached Label on the Data View's toolbar.

4. At the Select objects: prompt, choose the object(s) that you want to attach to the label. End object selection.

5. AutoCAD automatically places the label based on the label template. If you selected more than one object, labels are placed on all the objects (which can get confusing).

Of course, you can then move the labels and leaders to a more suitable location.

If you've already created a link to an object, follow the same procedure. The link is re-created along with the attached label.

Creating freestanding labels

To create a free-standing label, you need to have a table open with at least a link and a label template. If you have more than one template defined, choose the one that you want to use in the drop-down list at the top of the Data View window. Follow these steps:

1. Select the record that you want to link to the free-standing label.
2. Click the down arrow next to Link and Label Settings on the Data View's toolbar, and choose Create Freestanding Labels.
3. Click Create Freestanding Label on the Data View's toolbar.
4. At the Specify point for label: prompt, pick a point in your drawing. AutoCAD places the free-standing label and displays this message on the command line: 1 Record(s) linked with 1 Label(s).

When you create a free-standing label, the row and the label are linked. If you select a row linked to a free-standing label and click View Linked Objects in Drawing on the Data View's toolbar, AutoCAD selects the label.

If the data in the database is changed from within the DBMS, the labels in your drawing may become outdated. To ensure that your labels are always accurate, you should periodically update them. To update labels, on the dbConnect Manager, right-click the current drawing file and choose Reload Labels (or right-click a label template and choose Reload).

STEPS: Creating a Label Template and a Label

1. Continue with ab20-01.dwg from the previous exercise. The Data View window should still be open. Press Esc to make sure that no objects are still selected.
2. On the dbConnect Manager, select a table or link template, and click New Label Template on the dbConnect Manager's toolbar.
3. In the New Label Template dialog box, click Continue to use the default name.
4. In the Label Template dialog box, click the Label Fields tab. Choose PART_NO from the Field drop-down list. Click Add.
5. Choose DESCRIPTION from the Field drop-down list and then click Add.
6. Click the Label Offset tab. In the Start drop-down list, choose Top Left. Set the Leader offset X and Y values to 2.
7. Click the Character tab. Select all the text and change the height to 5/16.
8. Click OK.
9. Click the down arrow next to Link and Label Settings on the Data View's toolbar, and choose Create Attached Labels.
10. Click Create Attached Label on the Data View's toolbar.
11. At the Select objects: prompt, choose the horizontal line marked at the top of the angle that you linked in the previous exercise. Press Enter to end object selection. AutoCAD automatically places the label.
12. The label covers existing objects. Pick the text of the label and then click its grip. Move the text to the left and pick a better location. The leader automatically changes direction and ends at the left side.
13. Save your drawing. Leave it open for the next exercise.

Querying with the Query Editor

You can use SQL (Structured Query Language) statements to gather more information about the elements in the drawing and database files. SQL is the language used by almost all database-management systems for refining the information that you get from a database.

AutoCAD uses the Query Editor to enable you to design queries. For example, you can do the following:

- Query the contents of a database to view a specified subset of the data.
- View a subset of records that falls into a certain range of values.
- Access all the tables in one data source with a series of SQL commands.

In addition, the Link Select dialog box enables you to create a selection set of objects by combining SQL queries and direct selection of objects in your drawing.

To open the Query Editor, follow these steps:

1. On the dbConnect Manager, select a table or link template and click New Query on the dbConnect Manager's toolbar.

2. In the New Query dialog box, type a name for the new query or accept the name that AutoCAD supplies. To base a query on an existing query, choose an existing query from the drop-down list. Click Continue.

AutoCAD opens the Query Editor, as shown in Figure 20.12. The Query Editor is designed to provide something for everyone — whether you're just starting out or you're an expert at SQL.

To restore the original view in the Data View window after a query, do one of the following:

- Close the Data View window and then re-open it from the dbConnect Manager.
- Click the Query Builder tab and right-click any used cell. Choose Clear Grid. Click Yes at the warning message. Then click Execute.

FIGURE 20.12

The Query Editor's four tabs enable you to build queries to refine how you view your database.

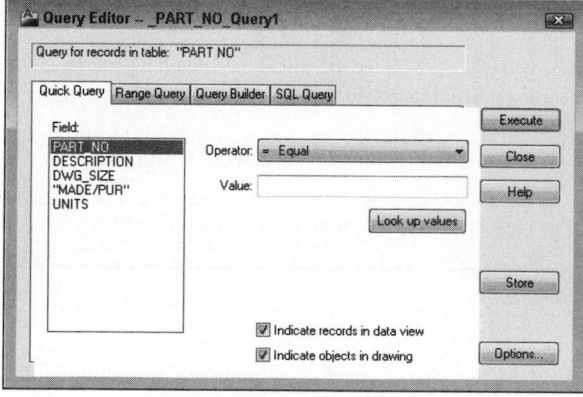

Using the Quick Query tab

Use the Quick Query tab to create simple queries based on one field, an operator, and a single value. For example, you can create a query that finds all records from the current table where the field DWG_SIZE equals E. You can also find all records where DWG_SIZE does not equal E.

From the Field box, choose a field. In the Operator drop-down list, choose an operator, such as equal (=) or greater than (>). In the Value box, type a value for the field. If you're not sure what values are available, click Look Up Values. (This can be slow in a large database or when you're working with a database across a busy network.)

Caution

Queries are case-sensitive. A value of "B" is not the same as "b." You need to be aware of the case used in your database. Some databases are all uppercase, making it easy to specify values. Just turn on Caps Lock and type away. ■

Choose Indicate Records in Data View and/or Indicate Objects in Drawing. By default, both are checked. To save the query for future use, click Store. Click Execute to see the results. To return to the Query Editor, choose Return to Query on the Data View window toolbar. Table 20.2 lists the available operators.

TABLE 20.2

Query Operators

Operator	Description
Equal (=)	Records that match the value exactly.
Not equal (<>)	All records except those that match the value exactly.
Greater than (>)	Records greater than the value. Includes text. For example, D is greater than B.
Less than (<)	Records less than the value.
Greater than or equal (>=)	Records that are greater than or match the value exactly.
Less than or equal (<=)	Records that are less than or match the value exactly.
Like	Records that contain the value. You must use the % wildcard (which is like the * wildcard used in Windows).
In	Records that match the values that you specify. You list the values, separated by a comma. For example, you could find records for which the field DWG_SIZE is B or D by typing **B,D** in the Value box.
Is null	Records that have no value. The Value box is unavailable. You can use this to find missing data.
Is not null	Records that have a value. You can use this to remove from view all records with missing data.

Using the Range Query tab

The Range Query tab finds records based on one field and a range of values. For example, you can find all records where the field DWG_SIZE ranges from B to D. The range can be either textual or numeric.

To construct a range query, choose a field from the Fields list. Then type the beginning value of the range in the From box and the ending value of the range in the Through box. In both cases, you can click Look Up Values to choose from a list of available values.

Click Store to save the query. Click Execute to execute the query.

Using the Query Builder tab

The Query Builder enables you to create multiple criteria. For example, you can create a query that finds records where the field DWG_SIZE ranges from B to D and the field PART_NO is greater than 9029-072-001. In order to build the criteria, you use Boolean operators and parenthetical grouping. This tab also enables you to specify which fields will appear in the Data View window and to sort the records. Using all these options offers a great deal of flexibility to create a complex query without knowing SQL. Here's how it works:

- And **operator.** Displays the records that meet both the criteria before and after the And operator.
- Or **operator.** Displays records that meet either of the criteria before and after the Or operator.
- **Parenthetical grouping.** Enables you to group sets of criteria. For example, you can group one set of two criteria that use an And operator and a second set of two criteria that use an And operator. Then you can put an Or operator between the two group's sets.

Building a query with multiple criteria

To create a query using multiple criteria, follow these steps:

1. On the first line, choose a field from the Field column. (When you click the first cell in the Field column, a drop-down arrow appears.)
2. Choose an operator from the Operator column.
3. Type a value in the Value cell. (An ellipsis button appears, and you can choose from all the values in the database.)
4. Click in the Logical cell to insert the And operator. Clicking again changes the operator to Or.
5. Move to the second line and create the next row of criteria. Continue until you've specified all the criteria that you want.
6. Add parenthetical grouping. Click to the left of the Field column of a row to insert a left parenthesis and between the Value and Logical columns to insert a right parenthesis. Continue to insert all the parentheses that you need. You can't insert parentheses until you have enough rows defined for a parenthesis to make sense.
7. Click Store to save the query. Click Execute to execute the Query.

Specifying fields and sorting

You can also limit which fields appear in the Data View window. First define the query in the top half of the tab. The query does not need to be complex. Then select the first field from the Fields in Table list. Click Add above the Show Fields list. Continue until you have all the fields that you want. To start from scratch, right-click in the Show Fields list and choose Clear All. To remove one field, right-click it and choose Clear Field Name.

To sort the data, choose the first field that you want to sort by from the Show Fields list. (You can only sort by fields that you're showing.) Click Add above the Sort By list. By default, AutoCAD sorts by ascending order. To sort by descending order, click the Ascending/Descending button. You can click it again to change the order back to ascending. You can also repeat the process for additional fields.

Click Store to save the query. Click Execute to execute the Query.

Using the SQL Query tab

Here's where the fun is. Try creating a query in one of the first three tabs and then click the SQL Query tab. Lo and behold, there is your query in SQL language. This is a great way to learn SQL.

The SQL Query tab is the only tab you can use to create a query to search more than one database table. Choose a table in the Table section and click Add. You can build the query by specifying fields, an operator, and values. As you work, you see the results in the top box, in SQL language.

The Check button enables you to check the SQL query before executing it. Click Store to save the query. Click Execute to execute the Query.

Although complete coverage of SQL syntax is beyond the scope of this book, you may find a few rules helpful:

- Text data must be enclosed in single quotation marks ('B').
- Column names are not case-sensitive, but column values are.
- There are certain SQL keywords that are used in the program. You cannot use these as table or column names. Examples include CHAR, GROUP, SQL, TABLE, USER, and CURRENT.
- In most standard SQL syntax, you need to end each statement with a semicolon (;). However, this is not necessary in AutoCAD.
- You cannot use AutoCAD or DOS wildcard characters such as ? or * in column values or names.
- To name more than one specification, separate each one with a comma.

The SELECT statement is probably the most common SQL statement. The SELECT statement can retrieve a subset of the rows in one or more tables, retrieve a subset of the columns in one or more tables, or link rows in two or more tables to retrieve common data to both tables.

The following shows the syntax of the SQL SELECT statement, including modifying statements that instruct the DBMS exactly which rows to select:

```
SELECT <select list>
FROM <table name> [{,<table name>}...]
[WHERE <search condition>]
[GROUP BY <column spec>[{,<column spec>}...]
[HAVING <search condition>]
[ORDER BY <sort spec> [{,<sort spec>}...]
```

In the preceding syntax, square brackets ([]) indicate optional elements, an ellipsis (...) indicates that the statement may be repeated, and curly brackets ({}) mean that the elements are listed in sequence.

Here is the meaning of the statement functions:

- The SELECT statement specifies the columns to retrieve.
- The FROM clause specifies the tables containing the specified columns.
- The WHERE clause specifies the rows that you want to retrieve in the tables.
- The GROUP BY clause divides a table into groups. Groups are designated by a column name or by the results of computed numeric data type columns.
- The ORDER BY clause sorts results into one or more columns in either ascending (ASC) or descending (DESC) order.

Creating selection sets with Link Select

Link Select enables you to create combined selection sets of objects. You can define the selection sets either by using the Query Editor or by selecting objects directly in your drawing, or you can use a combination of these two methods. You first define a selection set called A. Then you define a selection set called B. Then you combine the two selection sets by using logical operators.

You need to have your links already set up so that AutoCAD knows the relationship between your records and objects in the drawing.

As you work, the status area at the bottom of the dialog box displays the results of the running Link Select operation, both in terms of the number of linked objects and the number of records that currently meet your specifications.

Table 20.3 shows how the logical operators work.

TABLE 20.3

Logical Operators for Selection Sets in Link Select

Operator	Function
Union	Combines both selection sets
Subtract A-B	Subtracts the second selection set of objects from the first
Subtract B-A	Subtracts the first selection set of objects from the second
Intersect	Selects only objects that are contained in both selection sets

The Link Select dialog box contains its own version of the Query Editor so that you can build queries without leaving the dialog box.

To use Link Select, follow these steps:

1. On the dbConnect Manager, select a link template and right-click. Choose Link Select to open the Link Select dialog box, as shown in Figure 20.13.
2. At the top-center of the dialog box, choose either Use Query or Select in Drawing.
   - If you choose Use Query, use the Query tabs to specify a query.
   - If you choose Select in Drawing, click Select (the Execute button changes to the Select button) to return to your drawing and choose objects in the drawing at the `Select objects:` prompt. End object selection to return to the Link Select dialog box.
3. Click Execute to add the query or selection of objects in your drawing to the Link Select operation.
4. Create a second selection set by using the same process.
5. From the Do drop-down list, choose one of the logical operators. You now have one selection set from the combined selection sets that you specified.
6. If you want, you can now create an additional selection set and use an operator to combine it with the previous selection set created in Step 5.
7. Choose Finish to complete the process.

FIGURE 20.13

Use the Link Select dialog box to create combined selection sets of objects from queries and/or direct selection in your drawing.

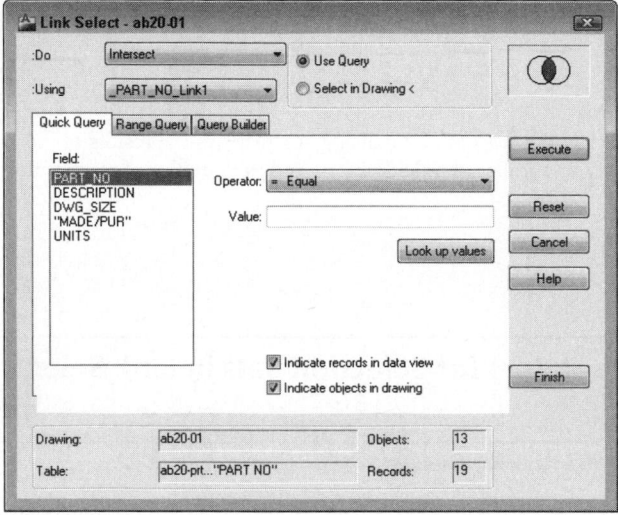

Working with Query Files

If you use queries a lot, you want to keep track of them. You can store, edit, rename, and delete queries. You can also import and export them for use by others. You do this by saving the information in a query file.

Storing queries

As I discussed previously, you can store a query by clicking Store on any tab. Stored queries are displayed under the drawing in the dbConnect Manager. To execute a stored query, on the dbConnect Manager, right-click over a stored query and choose Execute. It helps if the queries have names that relate meaningfully to the query.

You can edit stored queries by right-clicking over a stored query in the dbConnect Manager and choosing Edit. In the Query Editor, make the desired changes and choose Store.

To rename a query, click it in the dbConnect Manager. Click it again to display an edit box. You can now edit the query's name. Remember that you have to name the query upfront. If you're not sure what the query will consist of, use the default name, construct your query, and then rename it to something more meaningful afterward.

To delete a query, right-click over a stored query in the dbConnect Manager and choose Delete.

Importing and exporting queries

To export a query that has been saved (by clicking Store in the Query Editor), right-click the drawing that contains stored queries in the dbConnect Manager and choose Export Query Set. In the Export Query Set dialog box, navigate to the desired folder and choose a name. Click Save. Queries have a DBQ filename extension.

Note

To find the location of your queries, choose Application Button ⇨ Options and click the Files tab. Double-click Data Sources Location to see the path. ■

To import a query that has been exported and named, right-click over the drawing that you want to import queries into in the dbConnect Manager and choose Import Query Set. You need to know the name and location of the .dbq file. In the Import Query Set dialog box, locate the file and click Open. AutoCAD assigns default names to queries.

Summary

Using external databases to store data about drawing objects can reduce the size of drawings, simplify reporting, make data accessible to all users on a network, and enable you to edit a database from inside AutoCAD. In this chapter you read about:

- Configuring a data source
- Connecting a database table with your drawing
- Creating a link template
- Creating links between drawing objects and rows in the database
- Creating labels containing information from the database
- Defining SQL queries to select and sort the data that you view
- Selecting objects based on queries
- Storing and saving queries

This chapter ends Part III, "Working with Data." In Part IV, you start to draw in three dimensions. In the next chapter, I discuss how to specify 3D coordinates.

Part IV

Drawing in Three Dimensions

art IV introduces you to three-dimensional drawing. AutoCAD creates three types of 3D objects (also called *models*): wireframes, surfaces, and solids. Wireframes, as the name implies, look like models created with wire. They don't have real surfaces or solidity. However, they're useful for creating shapes that you can turn into surfaces or solids. Surfaces, unlike wireframes, can hide objects behind them. They're especially useful for creating unusually shaped objects. Solids are defined as the entire volume of space that they enclose. You can add and subtract solids from each other, creating realistic objects.

AutoCAD LT can create only wireframes and 2D objects with thickness, which is a kind of surface. Although AutoCAD LT's 3D capabilities are quite limited, you can still create simple 3D objects. Furthermore, AutoCAD LT can open and display a drawing that contains 3D objects created in AutoCAD.

In Chapter 21, I explain the basics of 3D drawing. This includes specifying 3D coordinates, using the User Coordinate System for 3D drawing, and creating objects with elevation and thickness. Chapter 22 explains the techniques for viewing, and navigating through, 3D objects. Chapter 23 covers surface models. Chapter 24 explains how to create true solids and covers editing in three dimensions. Chapter 25 explains how to create photorealistic views of your 3D drawings using the AutoCAD rendering feature.

Chapters 23 through 25 apply only to AutoCAD.

CHAPTER

21

Specifying 3D Coordinates

IN THIS CHAPTER

Understanding 3D drawings

Working with 3D coordinates

Using point filters, object snaps, grips, and point clouds in 3D

Using elevation and thickness

Creating a custom UCS for 3D drawings

The topics in the previous chapters have worked with two axes, X and Y. In this chapter, I add the Z axis. When you have a drawing with 3D objects, you can view it from any angle. The view that you've been using in 2D drawings is like looking at a house from the top, which you could call a plan view or a floor plan. From this view, even a 3D drawing looks two dimensional. But when you look at a 3D drawing from an angle, you can see that there's more to it than meets the eye. Figure 21.1 shows the plan view of an office building on the left. On the right, you see the same drawing viewed in a perspective view from the front.

Although this drawing is quite complex, you can easily get started by working on simpler models. Three-dimensional drawing is not as difficult as it seems at first. In this chapter, I start by explaining how to work with 3D coordinates. I also cover wireframe models and 3D surfaces created with thickness and elevation. These are essentially 2D objects placed in 3D space and are therefore a good place to start when learning about drawing in 3D. Most of the features that I cover in this chapter apply to AutoCAD LT as well as to AutoCAD.

Working in a 3D Environment

AutoCAD comes with two 3D workspaces and two templates that set you up to work easily in 3D. These are not available in AutoCAD LT. To use the workspaces, choose 3D Modeling or 3D Basics from the Workspace Switching lists on the Quick Access Toolbar or status bar. (I cover workspaces in detail in Appendix A.)

To use a 3D template, choose Application Button ➪ New. In the Select Template dialog box, choose `acad3D.dwt` (or `acadiso3D.dwt` for metric drawings) and click Open. The tool palettes open and the panels on the Ribbon tabs change as well. In Figure 21.2, you see the result, with some minor changes that I made to make some elements clearer.

FIGURE 21.2

An office building in plan view (on the left) and perspective view (on the right).

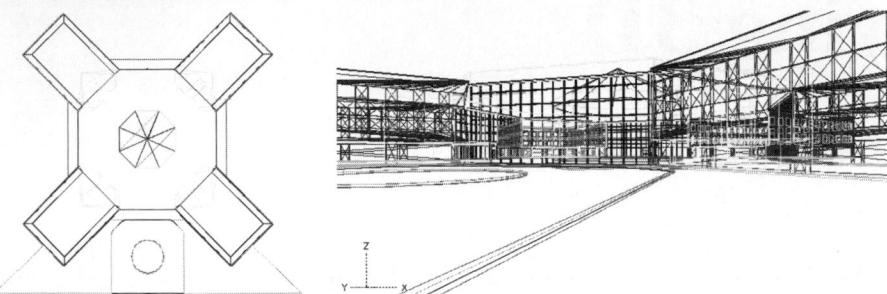

FIGURE 21.2

The acad3D.dwt template and the 3D Modeling workspace provide a suitable environment for working in 3D.

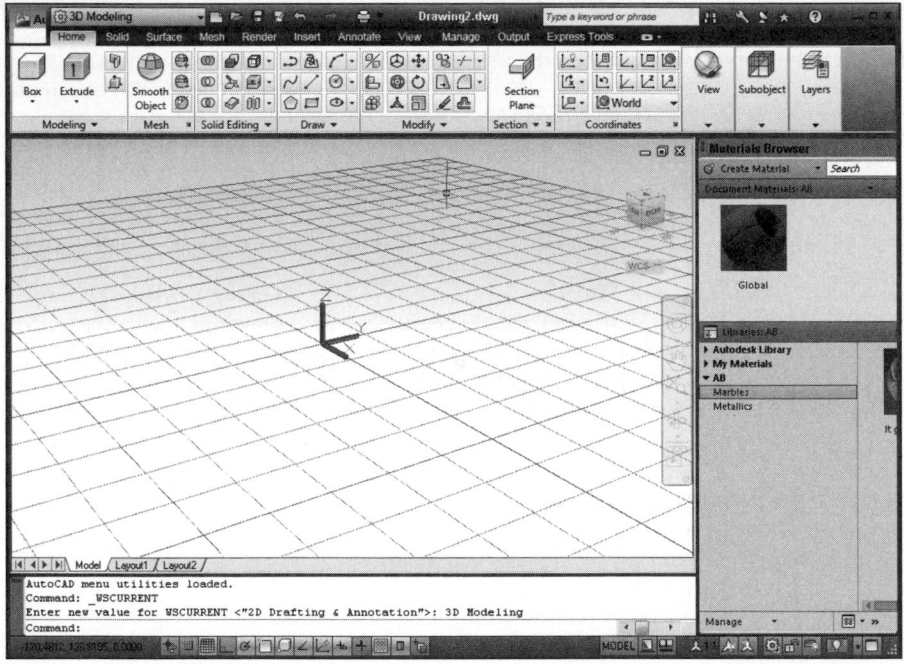

The grid is on, by default, to give you a sense of perspective and depth. The default viewpoint helps you see your 3D objects more clearly. You can change every aspect of what you see, including the colors, which palettes appear, and the viewpoint. Chapter 22 covers the ways to change the viewpoint and the visual style. Appendix A explains how to configure AutoCAD to look the way you want, including the colors of the grid and background.

New Feature

A new workspace, 3D Basics, offers a good option for simple 3D work. ■

Using 3D Coordinates

All the 2D methods of specifying coordinates have their 3D counterparts. Just as you can draw a line by specifying a start point of 3,4 and an endpoint of 5,7, you can draw a 3D line by specifying a start point of 3,4,2 and an endpoint of 5,7,6. Absolute coordinates are the same in 3D — you just add a Z coordinate. In the same way, you can specify relative coordinates. In 3D drawings, you can use two new types of coordinates that are 3D counterparts of polar coordinates, *cylindrical* and *spherical*.

Cross-Reference

Working with the User Coordinate System (UCS) is essential in 3D work. If you aren't familiar with the User Coordinate System, review the discussion in Chapter 8. ■

Most 2D commands accept 3D coordinates (a coordinate that includes a Z value) only on the first point. After that, you omit the Z coordinate because the Z value will be the same as that of the first point. For example, if you draw a rectangle, you can specify its first corner as 2,3,8 but the second corner must be specified without the Z value, as in 6,7. The Z value for the opposite corner is automatically 8.

The LINE command is an exception. It is a true 3D command, so you can specify X, Y, and Z values at all points.

Absolute and relative Cartesian coordinates in 3D

You don't use absolute coordinates more in 3D than you do in 2D — in fact, you may even use them less. But understanding absolute coordinates is important to understanding the Cartesian coordinate system that defines every point in your drawing. Figure 21.3 shows a wireframe model of a square and a triangle drawn with absolute coordinates, viewed from above (plan view) and from the southeast view (above, to the right, and in front). The rectangle is drawn in 2D — which means that the Z coordinates are all zero — as a reference point for visualizing the 3D points of the triangle.

You can use relative coordinates in the same way by including the change in coordinates. For example, to draw the line from (3,2,1) to (6,4,3), shown in Figure 21.3, you can start with the absolute coordinate (3,2,1) and then specify 3,2,2 because that's the difference between (3,2,1) and (6,4,3).

Cross-Reference

If you are using Dynamic Input with the default settings, specifying 3,2,2 as a second point is the same as specifying @3,2,2 with Dynamic Input off. For more information on Dynamic Input, see Chapter 4. ■

FIGURE 21.3

A rectangle and triangle viewed from plan view and southeast view.

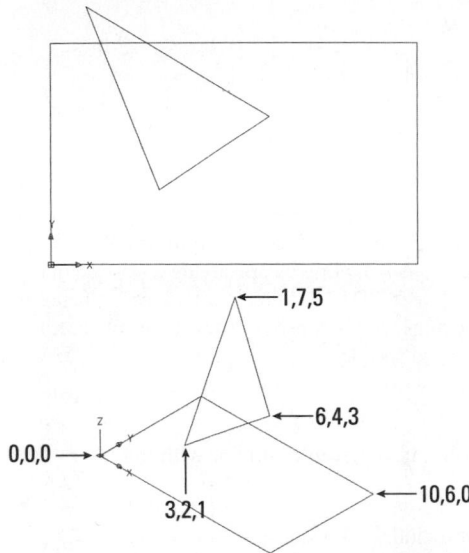

Cylindrical and spherical coordinates

Just as polar coordinates are often more useful than Cartesian coordinates in 2D, cylindrical and spherical coordinates can be more useful in 3D. Here's how they work.

Cylindrical coordinates have the format (@)distance<angle,distance:

- The first distance is the number of units in the XY plane from the origin (for absolute coordinates) or from your last point (for relative coordinates).
- The angle is the number of degrees from the X axis in the XY plane.
- The second distance is the number of units along the Z axis.

Cylindrical coordinates can be absolute or relative. You don't need to use the @ symbol for relative coordinates if Dynamic Input is on and set to the default option of relative coordinates. When you draw a line using cylindrical coordinates, neither distance that you specify is the length of the line. In essence, you're defining the lengths of two sides of a triangle to draw the hypotenuse. Figure 21.4 shows an example of a line drawn with cylindrical coordinates. The line was drawn from 0,0,0 to 5<30,3, which results in a line 5.8310 units long.

Note

You may find that cylindrical coordinates do not work very well with Dynamic Input turned on. In that case, click the Dynamic Input button on the status bar to turn off Dynamic Input. ∎

FIGURE 21.4

A line drawn using cylindrical coordinates.

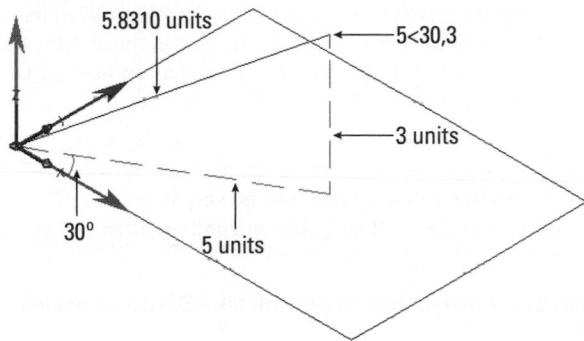

Spherical coordinates have the format distance<angle<angle:

- The distance is the total number of units from the origin (for absolute coordinates) or from your last point (for relative coordinates).
- The first angle is the number of degrees from the X axis in the XY plane.
- The second angle is the number of degrees from the XY plane in the Z direction.

Spherical coordinates can be absolute or relative. You don't need to use the @ symbol for relative coordinates if Dynamic Input is on and set to the default option of relative coordinates. When you draw a line using spherical coordinates, the distance is the actual length of the line. Figure 21.5 shows an example of a line drawn with spherical coordinates. The line was drawn from 0,0,0 to 5<15<30.

FIGURE 21.5

A line drawn using spherical coordinates.

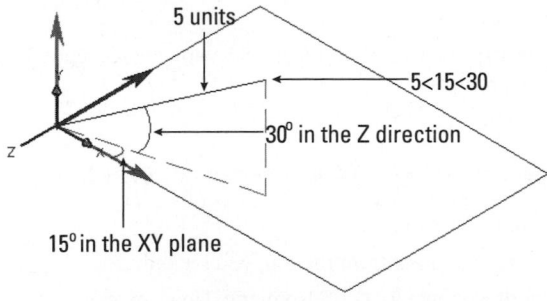

Using editing commands with 3D wireframes

Certain 2D editing commands work well in 3D. Others have special 3D versions. Because wireframes are simply 2D objects placed in 3D space, you can generally use the familiar editing commands. For example,

659

to move an object 3 units in the positive Z axis direction, start the MOVE command and type **0,0,3** at the `Specify base point or [Displacement] <Displacement>:` prompt and press Enter twice. You can also use the 3DMOVE command, which I cover in Chapter 24.

You need to be careful when selecting objects for editing. For example, if you draw two identically sized rectangles at different Z coordinates, when you look at them from plan view, you see only one rectangle. How do you know which rectangle you're selecting? By changing the angle from which you view your drawing (as I explain in the next chapter), you can see all the parts of the drawing and can select objects easily.

Cross-Reference

Multiple tiled viewports in which you view your drawing from different viewpoints can be very helpful in 3D drawing. For example, you can have a plan view in one viewport and a southeast view in another. Tiled viewports are covered in Chapter 8.

You can convert solids and certain surfaces to wireframes by extracting their edges with the XEDGES command (AutoCAD only). I cover this command in Chapter 23. ■

In the following exercise, you draw a simple wireframe piano bench and practice using 3D coordinates for both drawing and editing commands. You also view the drawing from two different angles.

On the DVD

The drawing used in the following exercise on using 3D coordinates, ab21-a.dwg, is in the Drawings folder on the DVD. ■

STEPS: Using 3D Coordinates

1. Open `ab21-a.dwg` from the DVD. This exercise assumes that you have Dynamic Input turned on, set to the default of relative coordinates. The drawing uses a 2D environment.

2. Save it as `ab21-01.dwg` in your `AutoCAD Bible` folder.

3. Choose Home tab ⇨ Draw panel ⇨ Rectangle. At the `Specify first corner point or [Chamfer/Elevation/Fillet/Thickness/Width]:` prompt, type **0,0,19** ↵. At the `Specify other corner point or [Area/Dimensions/Rotation]:` prompt, type **39,15** ↵. This creates a rectangle 39 units long by 15 units wide that is 19 units above the XY plane. Notice that you omit the Z coordinate for the second corner.

4. Choose Home tab ⇨ Modify panel ⇨ Copy to start the COPY command. To copy the rectangle 2 units above the original rectangle, follow the prompts:

   ```
   Select objects: Pick the rectangle.
   Select objects: ↵
   Specify base point or [Displacement/mOde] <Displacement>: 0,0,2 ↵
   Specify second point or <use first point as displacement>: ↵
   Specify second point or [Exit/Undo] <Exit>: ↵
   ```

   You now have two rectangles, but because you're looking from the top, you see only one.

5. Choose View tab ⇨ Views panel ⇨ 3D Views drop-down list ⇨ SE Isometric. Now you can see the two rectangles, as shown in Figure 21.6.

6. If Object Snap is not turned on, click the Object Snap button on the status bar. Set a running object snap for Endpoint.

FIGURE 21.6

The two rectangles, shown from Southeast Isometric view.

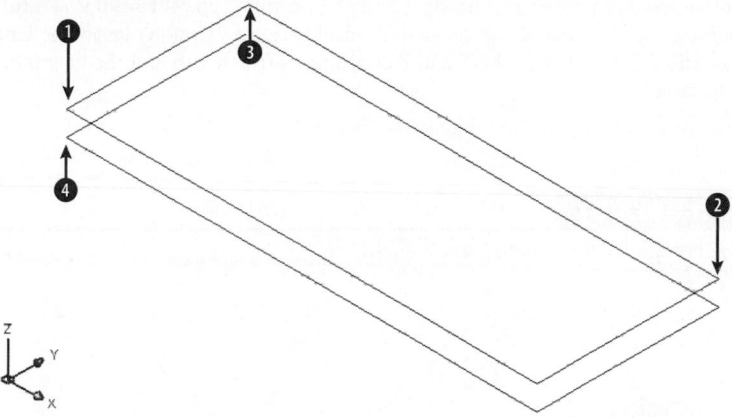

7. Start the LINE command. Follow the prompts:

   ```
   Specify first point: Pick the endpoint at ❶ in Figure 21.6.
   Specify next point or [Undo]: #0,0,0 ↵ (The # symbol forces an
     absolute coordinate.)
   Specify next point or [Undo]: 1,0,0 ↵
   Specify next point or [Close/Undo]: 0,0,21 ↵
   Specify next point or [Close/Undo]: ↵
   ```

8. Start the COPY command. At the Select objects: prompt, select the three lines that you just drew. End object selection. At the Specify base point or [Displacement/mOde] <Displacement>: prompt, type **38,0,0** ↵. At the Specify second point or <use first point as displacement>: prompt, press Enter to copy the three lines. Because the bench is 39 units long and the legs are 1 unit wide, copying the leg 38 units in the X direction places the copy in the right location.

9. Double-click your mouse wheel or choose View tab ⇨ Navigate panel ⇨ Zoom drop-down list ⇨ Extents so that you can see the entire drawing.

10. Repeat the COPY command. Use two separate crossing windows to select the first leg; then the second leg. Each window should select three objects. End object selection. At the Specify base point or [Displacement/mOde] <Displacement>: prompt, type **0,15,0** ↵ to copy the legs 15 units in the Y direction. Press Enter at the Specify second point or <use first point as displacement>: prompt to copy the legs to the back of the bench.

11. To draw an open cover for the piano bench, start the LINE command. Start it at the endpoint at ❷, shown in Figure 21.6. At the Specify next point or [Undo]: prompt, type **15<90<45** ↵. You know the length of the line because the cover is the same as the width of the piano bench. At the Specify next point or [Undo]: prompt, turn on Ortho Mode, move the cursor parallel to the length of the bench, and type **39**. At the Specify next point or [Close/Undo]: prompt, use the Endpoint object snap to pick ❸. End the LINE command. Zoom out and pan so that you can see the entire bench.

12. Turn Dynamic Input off by clicking the Dynamic Input button on the status bar. (Dynamic Input doesn't support cylindrical coordinates very well.) To draw some bracing inside the bench, start the LINE command again. At the Specify first point: prompt, choose the endpoint at ❹. At the Specify next point or [Undo]: prompt, type **@15<90,2** ↵. End the LINE command. Here, cylindrical coordinates are ideal because you don't know the length of the line but you know the change in the X and Z coordinates (the width and the height of the bench's body, respectively).

13. Save your drawing. It should look like Figure 21.7.

FIGURE 21.7

The completed wireframe piano bench.

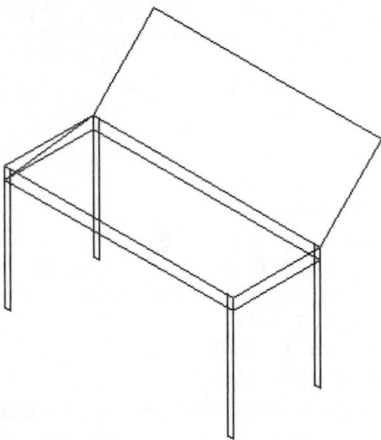

Using point filters, object snaps, object tracking, and grips in 3D

As mentioned earlier, it's often hard to tell which point you're picking in 3D. On a flat screen, you can be sure of only two dimensions. The other dimension is, so to speak, going in or out of the screen — it could be X, Y, or Z, depending on the angle that you're using to look at the drawing. That dimension is the one that's hard to pick on the screen. You use point filters, object snaps, object tracking, and grips to be sure that you have the right point in 3D drawings.

Point filters

In Chapter 4, I discuss point filters for 2D objects. They work the same way in 3D. You usually use point filters together with object snaps. For example, for the X coordinate, you might pick the endpoint of a line. Often point filters are the only way to define a 3D point that isn't on an existing object. The point filters for 3D drawings are .xy, .xz, and .yz. For example, if you want to pick a point 3 units in the Z direction from the endpoint of an existing line, you can use the .xy point filter to choose the endpoint of the line. The prompt then asks you for the Z coordinate, which you can specify as a number or by using an object snap. You can also use point filters to specify each coordinate (X, Y, and Z) separately.

Object snaps

Object snaps are essential for 3D work. Turn on Object Snap and set running object snaps. Object snaps ensure that you're specifying the point that you want. However, don't forget that in 3D drawings, you can have two lines, one on top of the other. Use a view that enables you to see the two lines separately so that you can pick the object snap that you want.

When you use an object snap in 3D, the Z value of the point comes from the Z value of the object. If you want to force a constant Z value, based on the current UCS or elevation, for a specific operation, temporarily change the OSNAPZ system variable to 1. (This system variable is not available in AutoCAD LT.) I discuss UCSs in 3D and elevation later in this chapter.

Tip

You can use point objects to help you draw in 3D. Set a visible point style (Home tab ⇨ Utilities panel [expanded] ⇨ Point Style [the DDPTYPE command]). Then place a point at a known coordinate. You can then use the Node object snap to access that point. ∎

New Feature

3D object snaps are special object snaps that apply only to 3D objects. They're not available in AutoCAD LT. ∎

Table 21.1 lists the 3D object snaps and their keyboard shortcuts.

TABLE 21.1

3D Object Snaps

3D Object Snap Name	Description	Keyboard Shortcut
Vertex	Snaps to the vertex of a 3D object	zver
Midpoint on Edge	Snaps to the midpoint of a solid or surface face edge	zmid
Center of Face	Snaps to the center of a solid or surface face	zcen
Knot	Snaps to a spline knot. (I cover splines in Chapter 16.)	zkno
Perpendicular	Snaps to a point that is perpendicular to a face	zper
Nearest to Face	Snaps to the nearest point on a solid or surface face	znea
None	Turns off all 3D object snaps	znon

The 3DOSMODE system variable turns 3D object snaps on and off. You can also click the 3D Object Snap button on the status bar to toggle it on and off. To choose a specific object snap, right-click the button and click the one you want to turn on or off. By default, the Vertex, Midpoint on Edge, and Center of Face object snaps are active.

Object tracking

You can use object tracking in 3D as well. For example, if you want to draw a line starting from the middle of a box, you can acquire the midpoints of two sides and start the line there. (I cover object tracking in Chapter 4.) Object tracking in 3D improves the ease with which you can find the exact 3D point that you need.

Grips

You can use grips to edit 3D objects. Again, it's important to choose a view that makes the editing easy. Grip-editing wireframes is somewhat different from grip-editing solids. Chapter 24 discusses 3D editing in AutoCAD in more detail.

Note

Grips are shown parallel to the plane of the current User Coordinate System. When you change your viewpoint, the grips change their shape slightly to look as if they are lying on the XY plane. ∎

On the DVD

The drawing used in the following exercise on using point filters and object snaps with 3D wireframe objects, ab21-b.dwg, is in the Drawings folder on the DVD. ∎

STEPS: Using Point Filters, Object Tracking, and Object Snaps with 3D Wireframe Objects

1. Open ab21-b.dwg from the DVD.

2. Save it as ab21-02.dwg in your AutoCAD Bible folder. Object Snap should be on. Set a running object snap for Endpoint and Midpoint. Make sure that Object Snap Tracking is on. This drawing uses a 3D environment, based on acad3D.dwt. This is the same piano bench drawn in the previous exercise, but without the cover. In this exercise, you use the bench to create a chair.

3. Choose Home tab ⇨ Modify panel ⇨ Stretch. Use a crossing window to select the right side of the bench. Eight objects should be selected. End object selection. At the Specify base point or [Displacement] <Displacement>: prompt, use the Endpoint object snap to pick **❶**, as shown in Figure 21.8. At the Specify second point: prompt, type **-15,0** ↵. (If you're not using Dynamic Input, type **@-15,0**.)

4. Pan the chair to the bottom of your screen and zoom out a little to leave room for the back of the chair, which you will draw next.

FIGURE 21.8

The piano bench after being shrunk with the STRETCH command.

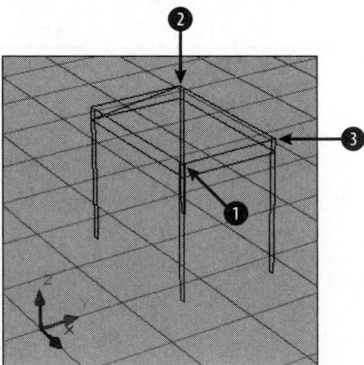

---

5. Start the LINE command. Follow the prompts:

```
Specify first point: Choose ❷ in Figure 21.8.
Specify next point or [Undo]: .xy ↵
of Pick ❷.
(need Z): 45 ↵
Specify next point or [Undo]: Pass the cursor over
the top endpoint of the line that you just drew, to acquire the
    point. Then pass the cursor over ❸ to acquire that point. Move
    the cursor to the approximate intersection of the two lines, until
    you see the Endpoint: -Z, Endpoint: Z tooltip, and click.
Specify next point or [Close/Undo]: Pick ❸.
Specify next point or [Close/Undo]: ↵
```

6. Repeat the LINE command. Draw a line from the midpoint of the left side of the back of the chair to the midpoint of the right side.

7. Choose Home tab ⇨ Modify panel ⇨ Fillet/Chamfer drop-down list ⇨ Fillet. At the `Select first object or [Undo/Polyline/Radius/Trim/Multiple]:` prompt, right-click and choose Radius. At the `Specify fillet radius <0.0000>:` prompt, type **1** ↵.

8. At the `Select first object or [Undo/Polyline/Radius/Trim/Multiple]:` prompt, pick ❶, as shown in Figure 21.9. At the `Select second object:` prompt, pick ❷.

9. Repeat the FILLET command and pick ❷ and ❸ for the two lines.

10. Save the drawing. It should look like Figure 21.9.

FIGURE 21.9

A wireframe model of a chair.

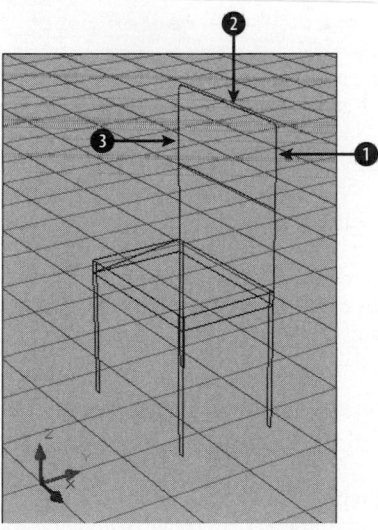

Creating 3D polylines

You've already created 3D lines by specifying 3D coordinates for the endpoints. One command that has a 3D counterpart is PLINE. The 3D command is 3DPOLY (Home tab ⇨ Draw panel ⇨ 3D Polyline in the 3D Modeling workspace or Home tab ⇨ Draw panel [expanded] ⇨ 3D Polyline in the 2D Drafting & Annotation workspace). The 3DPOLY command is like the PLINE command with a few differences:

- You cannot draw arcs.
- You cannot give the polyline a width.
- You cannot use a noncontinuous linetype.

The 3DPOLY command can accept all 3D coordinates. You can also edit it with the PEDIT command, although there are fewer options.

Tip

If you want to create curved shapes in 3D space, you can create 2D polylines with a width and then add a thickness and an elevation. Elevation and thickness are both explained in the next section. Other options are available if you want to create surfaces (Chapter 23) or solids (Chapter 24). ■

Creating helixes

You can create a wireframe helix, or spiral, by using the HELIX command. In the 3D Modeling or 2D Drafting & Annotation workspace, choose Home tab ⇨ Draw panel (expanded) ⇨ Helix. (It's not available in AutoCAD LT.) When you start the command, an initial message indicates the default number of turns and the direction of the twist (clockwise or counterclockwise).

Follow the prompts:

```
Specify center point of base: Specify the center point for the base
    at the bottom of the helix.
Specify base radius or [Diameter] <default>: Enter a radius (or
    diameter) using the option. The default is the last radius you
    used.
Specify top radius or [Diameter] <default>: Enter a radius for the
    top of the helix.
Specify helix height or [Axis endpoint/Turns/turn Height/tWist]
    <default>: Enter a height to use the default number of turns. You
    can also use the options to change the number of turns and the
    direction of the twist. You can specify the height by specifying
    an axis endpoint (the center of the top of the helix) or the turn
    height.
```

Figure 21.10 shows a helix with five turns. You can grip-edit the helix to increase its height.

Using point clouds

Point clouds are vast collections of 3D points that represent an object or landscape. They are usually created with a 3D scanner or some other type of equipment. AutoCAD can create 3D point clouds by indexing the raw point data from FLS, FWS, LAS, or XYB files. (Different types of equipment create different file types.) The result is an ISD or PCG file that AutoCAD can display.

FIGURE 21.10

A helix with a small base and a larger top looks like a whirlpool.

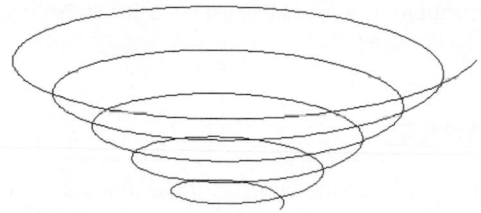

NOTE

Do not confuse the LAS files used for Layer States with the LAS files that can contain 3D point clouds. ■

New Feature

The ability to index and display point clouds is new for AutoCAD. This feature is not available in AutoCAD LT. ■

To index point cloud data, follow these steps:

1. Choose Insert tab ⇨ Point Cloud panel ⇨ Index (the POINTCLOUDINDEX command) to open the Select Data File dialog box.
2. Choose the FLS, FWS, LAS, or XYB file that you want to index, and click Open.
3. In the Create Indexed Point Cloud File dialog box, choose Autodesk Point Cloud (*.pcg) or Point Cloud (*.isd) from the Files of Type drop-down list.
4. Click Save.

You see a message on the command line that AutoCAD is indexing the file in the background. Indexing may take a while, depending on the size of the file. When complete, you see a balloon message, Point Cloud File Indexing Complete. The point cloud file is ready to be attached.

The next step is to attach the point cloud. Follow these steps:

1. Choose Insert tab ⇨ Point Cloud panel ⇨ Attach (the POINTCLOUDATTACH command) to open the Select Point Cloud File dialog box.
2. From the Files of Type drop-down list, choose the type of file you created and click Open.
3. In the Attach Point Cloud dialog box, you can choose to specify the insertion point, scale, and rotation in the dialog box or on-screen. If you check the Lock Point Cloud check box (the POINTCLOUDLOCK system variable), you will not be able to move or rotate the point cloud. Click OK.
4. At the Specify insertion point <0,0>: prompt, specify where you want to insert the point cloud or press Enter to accept the default coordinate.

Because point clouds are often very large, the POINTCLOUDDENSITY system variable controls the percentage of points displayed for all clouds in a drawing. The POINTCLOUDRTDENSITY system variable controls the percentage of points displaying during real-time zoom, pan, and other viewing operations. Finally, the POINTCLOUDAUTOUPDATE system variable determines whether AutoCAD dynamically updates a point cloud after you edit it or change the view. The reason for using this system variable is that the large number of points may make view changes slow.

Once you have the point cloud in your drawing, you may want to do a Zoom Extents to see the entire cloud. You can now use the points as a basis for your model. You can snap to any point using the Node object snap.

Using Elevation and Thickness

Wireframes have a number of limitations. In Figure 21.11, you can see the back leg through the seat of the chair. Also, creating the detail of a real chair would be tedious if you were to use individual lines or 3D polylines. Finally, wireframes don't have any surface or solid properties. You can't display them in any realistic fashion or calculate properties, such as area, mass, and so on.

Creating surfaces with thickness

You can create simple surfaces by adding thickness to 2D objects. When you add thickness to a 2D object, the object is pushed out into the third dimension. For example, a circle becomes a cylinder and a rectangle becomes a box. Remember that you won't see the thickness if you're looking at the object from the top. Figure 21.11 shows some objects created using thickness.

FIGURE 21.11

3D surfaces created by adding thickness to 2D objects.

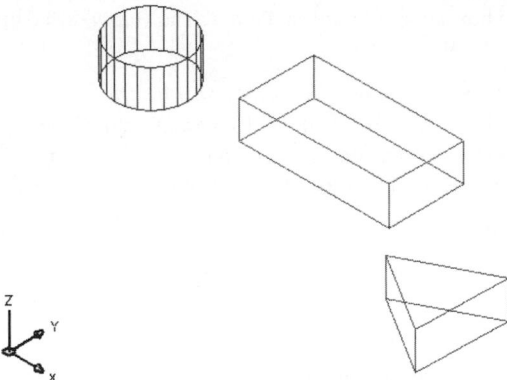

Surfaces created by adding thickness are sometimes called 2½D objects. Although they have three dimensions, the third dimension can only be a straight side perpendicular to the 2D object at the base.

The parallel lines on the cylinder are called *tessellation lines*. These lines help you to visualize curved surfaces. They aren't actually part of the cylinder; for example, you can't use object snaps on them.

To add thickness to an existing 2D object, display the Properties palette (Ctrl+1) and select the object. (You can also select the object first.) In the palette, click the Thickness property and change the value in the text box. Press Enter.

Note

You can use the CONVTOSURFACE command to convert open polyline figures with no width, lines, and arcs to surfaces — as long as they have a thickness. You can use the CONVTOSOLID command to convert three types of closed wireframe objects with thickness to solids — polylines with a uniform width, closed polyline figures with no width, and circles. I discuss surfaces in Chapter 23 and solids in Chapter 24. These commands are not available in AutoCAD LT. ■

You can also change the current thickness. The current thickness affects new objects as you draw them, but does not affect existing objects. There are two ways to change the current thickness:

- With no object selected, display the Properties palette (Ctrl+1). Click the Thickness property and type a value in the text box. Press Enter.
- Use the ELEV command (which can also change the current elevation, discussed in the "Adding elevation to objects" section) by typing it on the command line. The ELEV command prompts you for the current elevation and the current thickness. At the prompt for a thickness, type a number and press Enter.

In most cases, you use a positive number, which extrudes objects in the positive direction of the Z axis. However, you can use a negative number to extrude objects in the negative direction of the Z axis. As soon as you change the current thickness, all objects that you draw have that thickness.

Caution

Because it's easy to forget the current thickness, unless you're drawing a number of objects with the same thickness, it's usually safer to draw objects with no thickness and then change the thickness. If you do change the current thickness, don't forget to change it back to zero when you're finished creating the 3D objects. ■

Using the HIDE command

Because objects with thickness are surfaces, not wireframes, you can use the HIDE command to hide lines that would be hidden from view in real life. AutoCAD and AutoCAD LT calculate which lines are behind surfaces from the current viewpoint, and hide them. Figure 21.12 shows the same objects as Figure 21.11 after using the HIDE command. You may notice that the cylinder has a top, but the triangular prism and the box don't. For a further explanation, see the sidebar "Do objects with thickness have tops and bottoms?"

To return to the wireframe display, use the REGEN command. You use the HIDE command in AutoCAD LT or in a 2D environment in AutoCAD; in a 3D environment in AutoCAD, you use visual styles instead. I cover visual styles in Chapter 22.

Do objects with thickness have tops and bottoms?

If you look at Figure 21.12, you see that the cylinder has a top but the triangular prism and the box don't. AutoCAD creates top and bottom surfaces on some objects with thickness but not on others.

When you add a thickness to objects created with the SOLID command (a 2D command), circles, and wide polylines, they are surfaces with tops and bottoms.

However, if you draw a closed polyline, for example with the RECTANG or POLYGON command, and give it a thickness, there is no top or bottom surface. The same is true for a closed figure that you draw with the LINE command.

Therefore, if you want a top and bottom, use the SOLID command, draw a polyline with a width greater than zero, or draw a circle. (Hatching a closed figure with a solid fill does not have the same effect as the SOLID command.) These objects create opaque horizontal surfaces. You can see the difference when you use the HIDE command. Note that a circle doesn't display a top if you use the Hidden (or 3D Hidden in previous release) visual style. (See Chapter 22 for more on visual styles.)

FIGURE 21.12

3D surfaces after using the HIDE command.

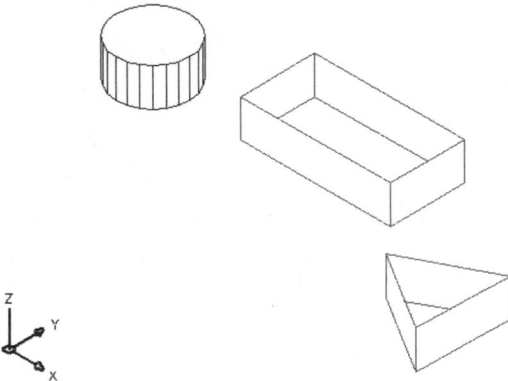

Controlling the display of hidden lines and objects

You can control the display of polylines at the face intersections of solid and surface objects, including surfaces that you create using thickness. In a 2D environment in AutoCAD, and in AutoCAD LT, you use the HLSETTINGS command to specify settings that affect the display of hidden lines. For example, instead of hiding back lines completely, you could display them as dashed lines or in a different color. In AutoCAD, this opens the Visual Styles Manager palette; in AutoCAD LT, this opens the Hidden Line Settings dialog box.

Several system variables affect the 3D display only when you use the HIDE command or the Hidden (or 3D Hidden) visual style. These system variables work on both solids and surfaces. Type **hlsettings** at the command prompt to open the Hidden Line Settings dialog box (AutoCAD LT) or Visual Styles Manager palette (AutoCAD), as shown in Figure 21.13. Note that I cover the Visual Styles Manager for other settings in Chapter 22.

FIGURE 21.13

The Hidden Line Settings dialog box and the Visual Styles Manager (shown here) allow you to control the display of back lines in AutoCAD LT and AutoCAD, respectively.

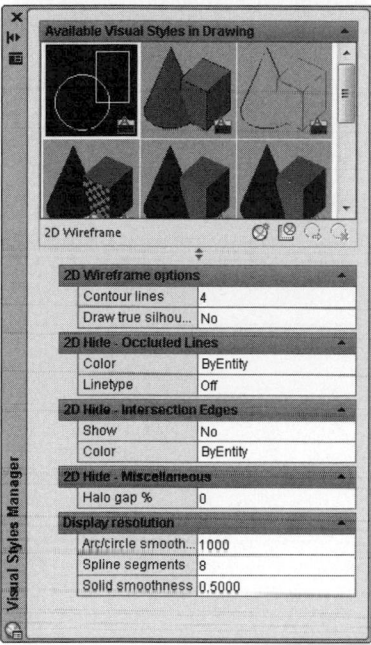

Here's how to use the Hidden Line Settings dialog box and the Visual Styles Manager palette to specify the display of hidden lines.

Use the 2D Hide - Occluded Lines section (Obscured Lines in AutoCAD LT) to choose a linetype and color for displaying hidden lines. When you choose a linetype, hidden lines are shown in the linetype that you choose. These linetypes are not affected as you zoom in or out. Choose from these linetypes:

- Off (fully hides back lines)
- Solid
- Dashed
- Dotted
- Short Dash
- Medium Dash
- Long Dash
- Double Short Dash
- Double Medium Dash
- Double Long Dash
- Medium Long Dash
- Sparse Dot

If you choose a linetype, then choose a color from the Color drop-down list. You can choose from one of the standard color index numbers (from 1 to 255). Use the 2D Hide - Intersection Edges section (Face Intersections in AutoCAD LT) to turn on the display of polylines at the intersections of 3D model faces. Then use the Color drop-down list to choose a color for the polylines.

Use the 2D Hide - Miscellaneous section (Halo Gap Percentage in AutoCAD LT) to create a gap that shortens lines at the point that they would be hidden by the HIDE command, in order to set off the lines from the unhidden portion of the model. By default, this percentage is set to 0, which creates no gap. Set the gap as a percentage of an inch. The gap doesn't change as you zoom in or out.

You can set the HIDEPRECISION system variable to 1 if you want a more exact calculation of the HIDE command results. The process takes longer but yields better results in a complex drawing with many surfaces and solids. In AutoCAD, enter **hideprecision** ↵ on the command line to set its value. The default is 0. In AutoCAD LT, you can choose the option in the Hidden Line Settings dialog box.

Use the HIDETEXT system variable to hide text behind other objects (a value of On, the default). When this system variable is set to Off, text will not hide other objects, or be hidden, unless it has a thickness. In AutoCAD LT, you can choose the Include Text in HIDE Operations option from the Hidden Line Settings dialog box.

Figure 21.14 shows a model using a halo gap value of 15; a green, dashed line to display hidden lines; and face intersections displayed in red.

FIGURE 21.14

This model uses HALOGAP, OBSCUREDLTYPE, and OBSCUREDCOLOR to display hidden lines.

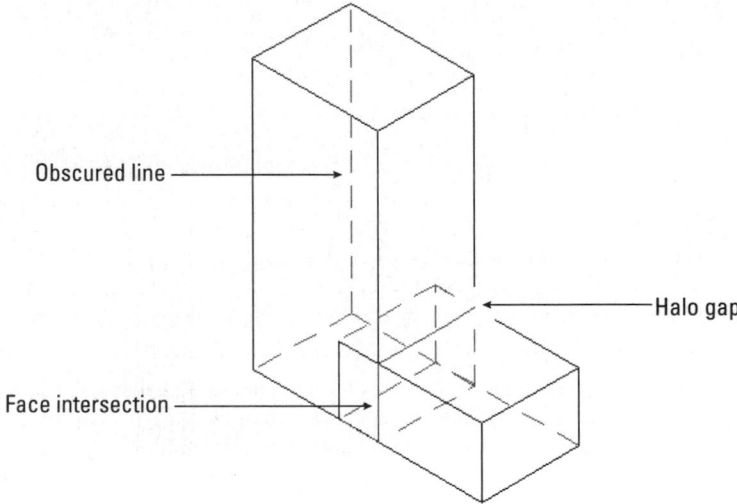

Note
The word wireframe is used in two ways. First, it means 3D objects that are created using only lines and 3D polylines. These objects have no surfaces or solidity. Second, it means surfaces and solids that are displayed as if they are created with lines and 3D polylines, such as the models in Figure 21.11. In this book, I usually distinguish between wireframes and wireframe display, or visual style. If the subject is surfaces and solids, the term wireframe generally means wireframe display. ∎

Adding elevation to objects

Until now, I've discussed 3D objects based on 2D objects that were on the XY plane. In other words, their Z coordinate was zero. Although you generally don't want objects to float in the air, you certainly may want to place one object on top of another. To do this, you need to start the object above the XY plane (you can also place objects below the XY plane) and give an object elevation, which is its Z coordinate.

To give elevation to an existing object, you can use several methods:

- Select the object and display the Properties palette (Ctrl+1). Click the Elevation property, type a new elevation in the text box, and press Enter.
- Move the object(s) with the MOVE command in the Z direction.
- Use the 3DMOVE command to move the object in the Z direction. I cover this command in Chapter 24, where I discuss editing in 3D.

For new objects, change the current elevation with the ELEV command as described earlier in this chapter in the discussion on thickness.

Note

For some objects, you can use the Properties palette (press Ctrl+1) to change the Z coordinate. This works for circles, lines, arcs, and ellipses but not for polylines. To elevate an entire line, you need to change the Z coordinate of both the start point and the endpoint. ∎

When you change the current elevation, all objects that you create are drawn on that elevation. Remember to change the elevation back to zero when you want to draw on the XY plane again.

Caution

If you specify an object snap of an object on a different elevation than your current elevation (with a different Z coordinate), AutoCAD and AutoCAD LT use the elevation of the object snap, not the current elevation. However, if you specify the first point of a 2D command, such as PLINE (to create a polyline), on the current elevation, you can use object snaps at a different elevation for subsequent points. Because the entire polyline must be on the same elevation, subsequent points follow the elevation of the first point. ∎

STEPS: Working with Elevation, Thickness, and the HIDE Command

1. Start a new drawing by using the acad.dwt or acadlt.dwt template. The Allow/Disallow Dynamic UCS button on the status bar should be off (if you have AutoCAD). This template uses a 2D environment.
2. Save it as ab21-03.dwg in your AutoCAD Bible folder.
3. Choose Home tab ⇨ Draw panel ⇨ Circle drop-down list ⇨ Center, Radius to start the CIRCLE command. Specify the center as 6,6 and the radius as 18.
4. Choose View tab ⇨ Views panel ⇨ 3D View drop-down list ⇨ SE Isometric to display a 3D view.
5. Select the circle. Display the Properties palette (Ctrl+1). Click the Thickness property. In the Thickness text box, type **3** ↵.
6. Type **elev** ↵. At the Specify new default elevation <0.0000>: prompt, type **3** ↵. Because you just changed the existing circle's thickness to 3, you set the elevation to 3 to place an object on top of the circle. At the Specify new default thickness <0.0000>: prompt, type **24** ↵.
7. Start the CIRCLE command again. Specify 6,6 as the center and set the radius to 3.
8. Zoom out and pan so that you can see the entire model.

9. Type **elev** ↵. At the Specify new default elevation <3.0000>: prompt, type **27**. At the Specify new default thickness <24.0000>: prompt, type **3** ↵. This places any new object on top of the two circles that you just drew.

10. Start the CIRCLE command. Specify the center as 6,6 and the radius as 18. Because you don't specify a Z coordinate, the current elevation is used. You can verify in the Dynamic Input tooltip that the Z coordinate is 27.

11. Type **hide** ↵. You can now see the cable spool clearly.

12. Save your drawing. It should look like Figure 21.15.

FIGURE 21.15

A cable spool created by drawing 2D circles with thickness and elevation.

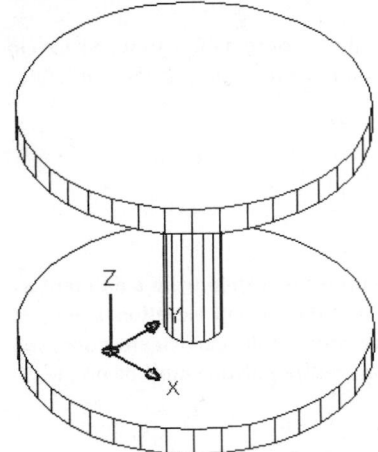

Working with the User Coordinate System

Except for certain true solids, much of 3D work starts with a 2D shape. However, the 2D drawing commands can be drawn only on, or parallel to, the XY plane. For example, the spool in Figure 21.15 consists of three circles, all parallel to the XY plane. How do you draw a circle, or any other 2D object for that matter, that is not parallel to the XY plane?

The answer is to change the User Coordinate System (UCS), thereby changing the definition of the XY plane. You can move the UCS to any location to define the XY plane in any way that you want. After you do so, you can draw a 2D object at any angle. This section offers a brief review of UCS features that are particularly useful for 3D drawing. (See Chapter 8 for complete coverage of the UCS feature.) Remember that you can save and name any UCS that you create by using the Named option of the UCS command.

Using the UCS icon

 Although you may have found the UCS icon an annoyance in 2D work, you should display it when working in 3D. Otherwise, it's easy to lose track of which direction is which. Remember that you can choose the Origin option, which displays the UCS icon, if possible, at the origin. Choose View tab ⇨ Coordinates panel ⇨ Origin.

Cross-Reference

You can customize the look of the UCS icon. The 3D style is helpful when you're working in 3D. See Chapter 8 for details on customizing the UCS icon display. ■

UCSs and viewpoints

A plan view of the World UCS (the default) is different from the plan view of a UCS that you've created by rotating the UCS around the X axis, for example. The UCS defines the orientation and origin of the X, Y, and Z axes. On the other hand, the viewpoint shows your drawing from different angles without changing the orientation or origin of the axes. Understanding the difference between the UCS and viewpoints is important. The next chapter is all about viewpoints.

The UCS is important because it enables you to draw and edit at unusual angles. However, after you have a suitable UCS, you need to look at the drawing from the best viewpoint, one that displays the objects clearly with as little overlapping as possible.

If you want to change your UCS when you change your viewpoint, you can use the UCSORTHO system variable. When this variable is on and you switch to an orthographic viewpoint (top, bottom, left, right, front, or back), the UCS changes to match the viewpoint.

When the UCSFOLLOW system variable is on (set to 1), it switches you to plan view whenever you change the UCS. This means that whenever you change the UCS, you start by looking at your model from the top. You can then change the viewpoint to anything that you want.

Note

In 3D work, you usually use a 3D UCS icon display. However, if you use the 2D display, and choose a viewpoint that looks straight across the XY plane, you see a broken pencil icon, indicating that you're looking at the XY plane edge on. ■

AutoCAD Only

Express Tools has a command, RTUCS, that enables you to rotate the UCS icon by dragging with the mouse. You can set an incremental angle for rotation and specify an active axis around which you rotate the UCS. Enter rtucs ↵ on the command line. ■

Using UCS options to change the UCS

To change the UCS, choose View tab ⇨ Coordinates panel, and choose one of the options. The following UCS options are useful for 3D drawing:

 • **Object.** You can align the UCS with any existing object. Because this option orients the UCS differently for different objects, this option can sometimes be confusing. However, to modify some objects, you must be on their XY plane — a good time to use the Object option. The overall principle is that the UCS's XY plane stays parallel to the previous UCS, except for 3Dface objects. Table 21.2 explains how the Object option aligns the UCS for various kinds of objects.

 • **Face.** The Face option aligns the UCS on a face of a solid object. At the `Select face of solid object:` prompt, click within the boundary of a face or on its edge to highlight the face, and align the X axis of the UCS with the closest edge of the first face that it finds. At the `Enter an option [Next/Xflip/Yflip] <accept>:` prompt, you can now refine the UCS. Right-click and choose Next to move the UCS to the adjacent face or the back face of the selected edge.

Right-click and choose Xflip to rotate the UCS 180 degrees around the X axis. Right-click and choose Yflip to rotate the UCS 180 degrees around the Y axis. When you have the UCS that you want, press Enter to accept the current location of the UCS.

- **View.** The View option aligns the X and Y axes with the current view. The current origin remains the same. The View option is often used for creating text that you want to appear flat from your viewpoint of a 3D view of the drawing.

- **Origin.** The Origin option creates a UCS parallel to the current UCS, but with a new origin that you specify. You can use the Origin option for working at a new elevation, instead of changing the current elevation.

- **Z Axis Vector.** The Z Axis Vector option enables you to define an origin and then a point on the positive side of the Z axis. You can keep the previous origin to twist the UCS around its origin.

- **3Point.** The first point that you specify is the origin, the second point indicates the positive direction of the X axis, and the third point indicates the positive direction of the Y axis.

- **X.** The X option maintains the current origin and rotates the Y and Z axes around the current X axis at the rotation angle that you specify. The most common rotation is 90 degrees or a multiple of 90 degrees, but you can specify any angle.

- **Y.** The Y option keeps the current origin and rotates the X and Z axes around the current Y axis. You specify the angle.

- **Z.** The Z option keeps the current origin and rotates the X and Y axes around the current Z axis. You specify the angle.

- **World.** The World option returns the UCS to the World Coordinate System.

- **Previous.** The Previous option switches to the previous UCS that you used.

TABLE 21.2	

UCS Orientation with the Object Option

Object	UCS Orientation
Line	The endpoint nearest your pick point is the origin. The line lies on the X axis.
2D Polyline	The endpoint of the polyline nearest your pick point is the origin. The first segment of the polyline lies on the X axis.
Dimension	Places the origin at the midpoint of the dimension text. The X axis is parallel to the X axis that you used when you created the dimension.
Text	Places the origin at the insertion point and aligns the X axis with the rotation angle of the text. The same applies to attributes.
Block	Places the origin at the insertion point and aligns the X axis with the rotation angle of the block.
Circle	The origin is at the circle's center. The X axis is aligned with your pick point.
Arc	The origin is at the arc's center. The X axis is aligned with the endpoint closest to your pick point.

Object	UCS Orientation
Point	The origin is at the point. The X axis may be difficult to determine in advance.
Solid	Uses the first point that you specified for the origin and the first and second points to align the X axis. AutoCAD LT doesn't offer solids, but you can open AutoCAD drawings containing solids.
3Dface	Uses the first point for the origin. The X axis is aligned with the first two points. The Y axis is aligned with the first and fourth points. The new UCS may not be parallel to the prior UCS. AutoCAD LT doesn't offer 3Dfaces, but you can open AutoCAD drawings containing 3Dfaces.

Changing the UCS dynamically

Creating a new UCS is great if you need to work in it for a while and if you want to save it for future use. However, sometimes you just want to draw one object on a certain plane of an existing solid object. For these times, you can use the dynamic UCS feature, which creates a UCS on the fly so that you can draw on any face of an object. You can also use the dynamic UCS feature to help you specify a regular UCS.

AutoCAD Only
AutoCAD LT does not have the dynamic UCS feature. ■

The dynamic UCS feature works only on solids (covered in Chapter 24). You turn this feature on and off by clicking the Allow/Disallow Dynamic UCS button on the status bar (or pressing F6). You can temporarily override the Dynamic UCS feature by pressing Shift+Z.

To create a temporary UCS, follow these steps:

1. Start a command. Some commands that work with the dynamic UCS feature are:
   - Commands that draw 2D geometry, text, a table, 3D solids, or a polysolid
   - The INSERT and XREF commands for inserting blocks or xrefs
   - Editing commands, such as the ROTATE, MIRROR, and ALIGN commands, and grip-editing
   - The UCS command
2. Pass the cursor over a face of a solid. A dashed border appears on the solid's face, as shown in Figure 21.16.
3. Continue the command. For example, if you're drawing a circle, specify the center point. The UCS icon appears near the cursor in its new direction so that you can see where the XY plane is. The temporary X axis is aligned with the edge of the face and always points to the right of your screen.

Note
If the grid is on, it flips to match the XY plane. This can be distracting, so you may want to turn it off. ■

4. Finish the command. The UCS automatically returns to its previous setting.

On the DVD
The drawing used in the following exercise on creating UCSs, `ab21-c.dwg`, is in the `Drawings` folder on the DVD. ■

FIGURE 21.16

When you pass the cursor over a face of a solid, the dashed border confirms the face, and you can temporarily draw on or edit that face.

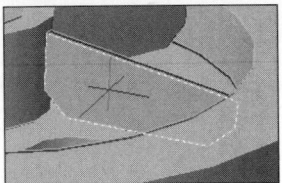

STEPS: Creating UCSs

1. Open `ab21-c.dwg` from the DVD.

2. Save it as `ab21-04.dwg` in your `AutoCAD Bible` folder. This drawing contains some center-lines based on measurements of a chair. Object Snap should be on. Set running object snaps for Endpoint, Midpoint, Center, and Quadrant. The UCS icon is set at the origin. This drawing starts in a 2D environment.

3. Choose Home tab ⇨ Draw panel ⇨ Circle drop-down list ⇨ Center, Radius. Use the From object snap to specify the center at an offset from ❶ (in Figure 21.17) of @2,0. Set the radius to 0.5.

FIGURE 21.17

These centerlines are the basis for drawing a chair.

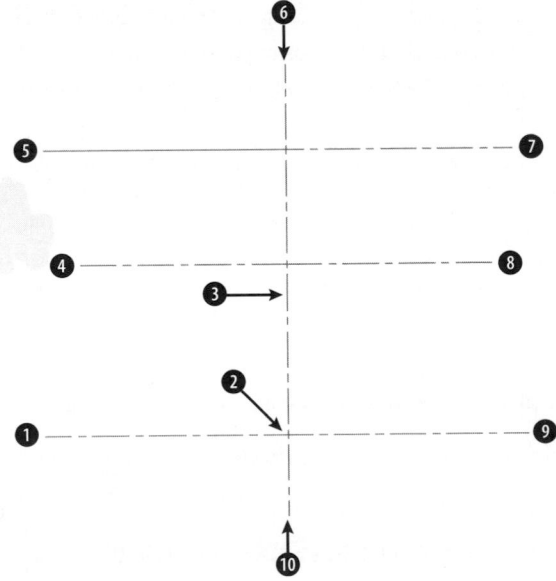

4. Display the Properties palette (Ctrl+1) and select the circle that you just drew. Change the thickness to 16. Press Enter. Close the Properties palette (or right-click its title bar and choose Auto-Hide).

5. Click Ortho Mode on the status bar to turn it on. Choose Home tab ⇨ Modify panel ⇨ Mirror. The circle should still be selected. (If it isn't, select it.) Specify the endpoint at ❷ for the first point of the mirror line. Specify any point vertical to ❷ for the second point of the mirror line. Choose not to delete the source object (the circle).

6. Repeat the MIRROR command. Select the two circles. Pick the midpoint of the line at ❸ for the first point of the mirror line. Pick any point horizontal to the first point for the second point of the mirror line. Press Enter. There are now four legs. Turn Ortho Mode off.

7. Type **elev** ↵. Change the elevation to 16 and the thickness to 1.

8. Choose View tab ⇨ Views panel ⇨ 3D Views drop-down list ⇨ SE Isometric. You can now see the four chair legs.

9. Choose Home tab ⇨ Draw panel ⇨ Polyline. At the `Specify start point:` prompt, choose the From object snap. Use the Center object snap of the top of the circle near ❶, shown in Figure 21.17, for the base point and an offset of @−2,0. (You may have to press the Tab key until you get the Center object snap.) Continue to pick points ❹ through ❿. Notice that the Endpoint object snap symbol appears at the height of the first point. Then right-click and choose Close to close the polyline.

10. Choose Home tab ⇨ Modify panel (expanded) ⇨ Edit Polyline (or type **pedit** ↵). Select the polyline. At the prompt, right-click and choose Fit to fit the polyline. Press Enter to end the command.

11. To see the result, type **hide** ↵. Remember that the polyline has no top or bottom surface. Imagine your model as a glass-bottomed chair. It should look like Figure 21.18.

FIGURE 21.18

Part of a 3D chair.

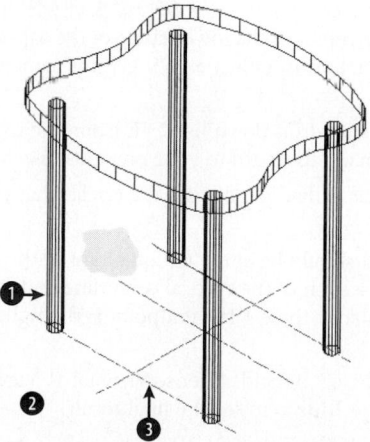

12. Choose Home tab ⇨ Properties panel ⇨ List. Select the front-left leg at ❶, shown in Figure 21.18. Press Enter. The center (of the circle at the bottom of the leg) is X = 3.5000, Y = −7.0000, Z = 0.0000.

13. To see the effect of a different UCS option, choose View tab ⇨ Coordinates panel ⇨ X. To rotate the UCS around the X axis, type **90** ↵. Again, choose Home tab ⇨ Properties panel ⇨ List and select the same leg of the chair. Now the center is X = 3.5000, Y = 0.0000, Z = 7.0000. Look at the UCS icon (which is at 0,0,0) and try to visualize why the coordinates are the way they are listed.

14. Because you know the center of the circle of the front leg, you can move the UCS there. Choose View tab ⇨ Coordinates panel ⇨ Origin. At the `Origin point <0,0,0>:` prompt, type **3.5,0,7** ↵. This places the X axis through the center of the circle.

15. Choose View tab ⇨ Coordinates panel ⇨ Define UCS drop-down list ⇨ View. The UCS is now parallel to your current view. Choose Home tab ⇨ Annotation panel ⇨ Multiline Text drop-down list ⇨ Single Line Text. Start the text at **2**, shown in Figure 21.18. Set the height to 1 and the rotation to 0. Type **A glass-bottomed chair**. Press Enter twice to end the command.

16. Choose View tab ⇨ Coordinates panel ⇨ Define UCS drop-down list ⇨ Object. Pick the line at **3**.

17. Choose View tab ⇨ Coordinates panel ⇨ Origin. Type **0,0,17** as the origin to place the UCS at the top of the seat.

18. Choose View tab ⇨ Coordinates panel ⇨ X. Type **−10** ↵ to rotate the UCS around the X axis by −10 degrees. This enables you to create the back of the chair at a 10-degree angle. Type **plan** ↵ and press Enter again to accept the default. It enables you to view your drawing from plan view (in this case, relative to the current UCS).

Tip

Although it's not necessary for this exercise, this would be a good UCS to save (choose View tab ⇨ Coordinates panel ⇨ UCS, Named UCS and rename the Unnamed current UCS to Chair Back). Now that you've gone through all these steps, it would be a shame to have to re-create the UCS again. ∎

19. With no objects selected, display the Properties palette (Ctrl+1). Set the thickness to 16. Close the Properties palette.

20. Start the CIRCLE command. Choose the center of the lower circle of the top-left leg (it's below the chair's seat) for the center. Accept the default radius of 0.5. Use the same technique to draw a circle at the corresponding right circle.

21. Choose View tab ⇨ Views panel ⇨ 3D Views drop-down list ⇨ SE Isometric to see the results. Use the Previous option of the ZOOM command to return to your previous display.

22. Change the thickness to −5. Type **hide** ↵ so that you can see the circles that you just created more clearly.

23. Start the ARC command. The start point should be at the left quadrant of the left circle that you just drew. The second point is the intersection of the vertical centerline and the top horizontal centerline. (There is an Endpoint object snap there.) The endpoint is the right quadrant of the right circle.

24. Choose View tab ⇨ Coordinates panel ⇨ UCS, World. Choose View tab ⇨ Views panel ⇨ 3D Views drop-down list ⇨ SE Isometric. Then type **hide** ↵ to see the final result.

25. Save your drawing. The chair should look like Figure 21.19.

FIGURE 21.19

The completed glass-bottomed chair.

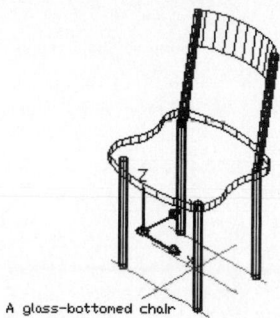

A glass-bottomed chair

Summary

This chapter introduced you to 3D drawing. You read about:

- Understanding all the types of 3D coordinates and how to use them
- Using editing commands in 3D
- Using point filters, object snaps, and grips in 3D drawings
- Utilizing elevation and thickness
- Understanding the HIDE command and the system variables that affect the hidden display
- Working with User Coordinate Systems in 3D

In the next chapter, I explain all the ways to view 3D drawings.

Viewing 3D Drawings

As soon as you start to work in three dimensions, you need to be able to see the drawing from different angles. By combining various User Coordinate Systems (UCSs) and different viewpoints, you can view and draw any object in 3D.

Unless otherwise stated, the features in this chapter apply to both AutoCAD and AutoCAD LT; however, note that many of the 3D features are for AutoCAD only. In AutoCAD, you'll find 3D viewing tools easier to find if you use the 3D Modeling workspace; this workspace is not available in AutoCAD LT. (To switch workspaces, choose from the Workspace drop-down list on the Quick Access Toolbar, or click the Workspace Switching button on the right side of the status bar.) Therefore, this chapter assumes that you're using the 3D Modeling work-space if you have AutoCAD.

Your basic point of reference is plan view in the World Coordinate System (WCS). This is the view that you use in 2D, so it's familiar. Plan view is the view from the top (although which side is the top is not always obvious). Figure 22.1 shows a plan view of a 3D model on the left. On the right, you see a 3D view of the same model, which lets you visualize the three dimensions much more clearly.

When working in 3D, you can use many of the familiar 2D techniques for view-ing your drawing:

- Use ZOOM Previous to display the previous viewpoint.
- Save views so that you can easily return to them.
- Use real-time zoom and pan as well as all the other zoom options.
- Create tiled viewports to display more than one view at a time.

IN THIS CHAPTER

Using the standard viewpoints

Using the DDVPOINT and VPOINT commands

Using the ViewCube

Creating a named view with a camera

Using 3D Orbit

Using ShowMotion to cycle through views

Walking through a model

Using the Wheel to navigate

Creating a perspective view with DVIEW

Working with visual styles

Laying out a 3D drawing

Printing in 3D

FIGURE 22.1

The left image is the plan view; the right image is a 3D view.

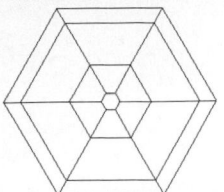
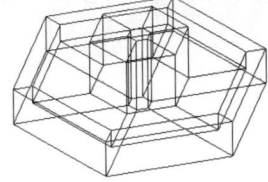

Cross-Reference

You can save drawings in the 3D DWF format (in AutoCAD only) for viewing on the Web or sending to people. For more information, see Chapter 28. ■

This chapter also explains how to save 3D views, create presentations from saved views, walk through a 3D model, create visual styles that control how your models look, lay out 3D drawings for plotting, and print in 3D.

Working with the Standard Viewpoints

AutoCAD and AutoCAD LT offer 10 standard viewpoints. These viewpoints are useful — and easy to use. They are relative only to the World Coordinate System (WCS), not the current User Coordinate System (UCS). Therefore, they're most useful when you're using the WCS.

To use a preset viewpoint, choose View tab ⇨ Views panel ⇨ Views (3D Navigation) drop-down list, and choose the viewpoint that you want from the list. Each of the preset viewpoints automatically does a Zoom Extents. In AutoCAD only, in the 3D Modeling workspace, you can also choose Home tab ⇨ View panel ⇨ Views (3D Navigation) drop-down list, and choose one of the viewpoints.

Using the VPOINT command

The VPOINT command was the original, command-line method of setting viewpoints. Now it's generally used for scripts and AutoLISP routines when you need a way to set a viewpoint from the command line. (AutoCAD LT does not support AutoLISP routines.)

The VPOINT command defines a viewpoint using X, Y, and Z vectors. The vectors for the standard viewpoints are based on a maximum of 1 unit. Imagine a model of the three axes floating out in space. You're a superhero and can fly around the model from any angle. When you're over the Z axis, you can define the Z vector from 0,0,0 to your position as 1. The other vectors are 0 (zero) because you're right over them, so that 0,0,1 defines the top, or plan, view. The next section shows the vector equivalents for the standard viewpoints, to give you a feel for the vector system. I explain the VPOINT command's compass and tripod later in this chapter.

Looking at a drawing from the standard viewpoints

Showing the viewpoints is easier than describing them. In Table 22.1, I show a simple 3D house from all ten standard viewpoints. Although the front of the house faces east, that is particular to this house. From your drawing's point of view, east is 0 degrees when looking from the top view, and 0 degrees faces to the right.

Note

A system variable, UCSORTHO, automatically changes the UCS to match the viewpoint when you switch to one of the orthographic (top, bottom, left, right, front, and back) viewpoints. In order to distinguish between the viewpoints and UCSs, I turned UCSORTHO off for the following section. ■

TABLE 22.1

Standard Viewpoints

Viewpoint	Description	Example
Top (see Note after table)	ma300 The top view is the plan view. You're looking at the model from a bird's-eye perspective, suspended over the model. VPOINT equivalent: 0,0,1.	
Bottom	ma301 The bottom view is the plan view for groundhogs. It's not very useful for buildings, but it may be useful for 3D mechanical drawings. Notice the direction of the UCS icon. If you're using the 2D UCS icon, you'll notice that the square is missing at the axis intersection, indicating that you're viewing from the negative Z direction, or from "underneath." VPOINT equivalent: 0,0,−1.	
Left	ma302 The left view shows you your model from the left side, of course. In architecture it would be one of the elevation views. Notice that the text appears backward. This is because the text was drawn from the right view. VPOINT equivalent: −1,0,0.	
Right	ma303 The right view shows you your model from the right side. Like the left view, the right view is an elevation view. Notice that the text now appears correctly because it was drawn from this view. VPOINT equivalent: 1,0,0.	
Front	ma304 The front view, another elevation view, shows your model from the front. The text, stating that the front faces the east, doesn't represent any rule in AutoCAD or AutoCAD LT. I simply use it to help you to see the differences in the sides of the house. VPOINT equivalent: 0,−1,0.	
Back	ma305 The back view, another elevation view, shows your model from the back. Here you see the text of the front of the house, shown backward. VPOINT equivalent: 0,1,0.	
Southwest	ma306 The SW (southwest) isometric view shows you your model from a diagonal viewpoint in all three dimensions. Notice how one corner of the house is closest to you (the corner between the left and front views), and how you're also looking at the house from a view halfway between a side view and the top view. The isometric views are excellent for viewing all the 3D objects in a drawing. As you can see, many more objects are visible than with the top view or any of the side views. VPOINT equivalent: −1,−1,1.	
Southeast	ma307 The SE (southeast) isometric view also shows your model from a diagonal viewpoint in all three dimensions. Here you're looking at the house at the corner between the right and front views, as well as halfway between a side view and the top view. You see the same objects as you do in SW isometric view. However, in a drawing not as symmetrical as the house, one view may bring certain objects to the front so that you can select them. VPOINT equivalent: 1,−1,1.	
Northeast	ma308 The NE (northeast) isometric view shows your model from the corner between the right and the back views, as well as halfway between a side view and the top view. VPOINT equivalent: 1,1,1.	
Northwest	ma309 The NW (northwest) isometric view shows your model from the corner between the left and the back views, as well as halfway between a side view and the top view. VPOINT equivalent: −1,1,1.	

685

Note

You can also access the top view by typing plan on the command line. Note that the PLAN command does not change the UCS, even though you choose to see the plan view of a different UCS. This actually makes it very flexible because you can see what your drawing looks like from a different UCS without actually changing the UCS. The PLAN command is explained later in this chapter. ∎

Note that the terms Northeast, Southwest, and so on are not related to any real directions. However, you can specify a North direction for your model. You would generally do this in an architectural or civil engineering drawing. To do so, choose Render tab ⇨ Sun & Location panel ⇨ Set Location (in AutoCAD only). If you are using AutoCAD LT, enter **geographiclocation** (the command name) on the command line.

You can then choose to specify the geographic information by importing a KML or KMZ file, by importing information from Google Earth, or by manually entering location values. KML and KMZ files are Google Earth file formats. For the Google Earth option to work, you need to install Google Earth (at http://earth.google.com). If you choose to enter location values, the Geographic Location dialog box opens. Here you can enter latitude and longitude measurements manually, or use a map. You specify which hemisphere (North/South and East/West) you're in. You can also set the time zone, North direction, and up direction (Z axis), and specify an elevation for a specific coordinate.

If you start the GEOGRAPHICLOCATION command in a drawing that already has a location, you get a choice to edit the current location, redefine it (start from scratch), or remove it.

Using DDVPOINT

If the standard views aren't sufficient for your needs, DDVPOINT can give you both flexibility and precision. To use this command, enter **ddvpoint** ↵ on the command line to open the Viewpoint Presets dialog box, as shown in Figure 22.2. This dialog box enables you to set the view to a great degree of accuracy.

The left side of the dialog box determines the angle from the X axis in the XY plane. These angles work as follows:

270	Front view
0	Right view
90	Back view
180	Left view

Other angles result in viewpoints between these views. For example, an angle of 315 degrees enables you to look at your drawing from a view between front and right. This is similar to the SE isometric view.

The right side of the dialog box determines the angle from the XY plane, in the Z direction. A 0-degree angle enables you to look at your drawing from the front, back, or one side (elevation views), depending on the setting on the left part of the dialog box. Often you want to look at your drawing from above. A 90-degree angle shows you the plan view. An angle between 0 and 90 gives you a slanted view from the top, such as for one of the isometric standard views. (The isometric views set the angle from the XY plane to 35.3 degrees.)

Tip

There's an art to using the two dials to set the view angle that you want. If you click the inside border of either one, close to the indicator needle, you set the angle based on exactly where you clicked. This results in uneven degrees, such as 47.6. However, if you click the outside border of either image, or the numbers themselves, the angle is rounded to the value in the segment. ∎

FIGURE 22.2

The Viewpoint Presets dialog box.

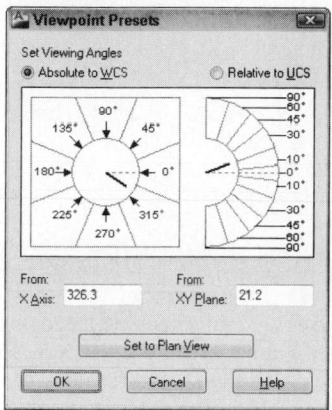

When you open the dialog box, the black needles indicate the angles for the current view. When you change the angles, the black (or white) needles move to the new angle, but the original needle remains to indicate the current angle. This enables you to constantly see the current angles for reference. Beneath the dials are text boxes that reflect your choices. You can simply type the angles that you want in the text boxes. A very handy Set to Plan View button is at the bottom of the dialog box. This enables you to quickly return to plan view when you become a little dizzy from flying around your model.

The default is to view the drawing based on the WCS. However, sometimes you need to see your drawing relative to a UCS that you've created. To do so, click Relative to UCS. Click OK after you finish making your changes.

Tip

Keep the number of UCSs to the minimum necessary and save them. When possible, use a new viewpoint instead of creating a new UCS. The Dynamic UCS feature (available in AutoCAD only) creates temporary UCSs; I discuss this feature in Chapter 21. ∎

Using the ViewCube to View Your Drawing

The ViewCube is a quick, visual way to switch your viewpoint. You can think of the preset viewpoints as sides, edges, or corners of a cube. The ViewCube is semitransparent until you hover the cursor over it. To display a viewpoint, click the side, edge, or corner that you want. You can also drag the ViewCube to interactively change your viewpoint. In this way, you can easily make small adjustments as you work. This is very similar to using 3D Orbit, which I discuss later in this chapter. Figure 22.3 shows the ViewCube.

AutoCAD Only

The ViewCube (NAVVCUBE command) is not available in AutoCAD LT. ∎

FIGURE 22.3

The ViewCube is an easy way to change the viewpoint of your 3D model.

The ViewCube has some additional features:

- **UCS menu.** Below the ViewCube is a list of saved and default UCSs. You can switch UCSs and create a new UCS.

- **Compass.** You see the four directions marked around the ViewCube. The directions are based on the settings for the GEOGRAPHICLOCATION command, discussed earlier in this chapter. You can click one of the directions, or the arrow next to it, to view the model from that direction.

- **Home.** Click the Home button at the top-left corner of the ViewCube area (only visible when you hover the cursor over it) to display the model at its default viewpoint, which is either the extents of the drawing (for preexisting models), or a top/left/front view. You can specify the definition of the Home view. To do so, set the view the way you want it, right-click the ViewCube, and choose Set Current View as Home.

You can right-click the ViewCube and choose the type of projection: parallel or perspective. I discuss these projections later in this chapter.

Choose View tab ➪ Windows panel ➪ User Interface drop-down list ➪ ViewCube (the NAVVCUBE command) to turn the display of the ViewCube on and off. To specify display settings, right-click the ViewCube and choose ViewCube Settings. When you choose the Settings option, the ViewCube Settings dialog box opens, where you can do the following:

- Specify in which corner of the screen the ViewCube appears
- Set the ViewCube size
- Set the ViewCube opacity when inactive
- Display or hide the UCS menu
- Snap to the closest view when dragging. If you want to make small adjustments by dragging, uncheck this check box.
- Zoom to extents after a view change
- Use view transitions when switching views to create a smooth, animated change
- Orient ViewCube to the current UCS
- Keep the scene upright. You can make sure that you can't turn the model upside-down.
- Show or hide the compass
- Restore default settings

Note

The ViewCube doesn't display in the 2D Wireframe visual style. If you don't see the ViewCube, change the visual style to Wireframe (or any other visual style other than 2D Wireframe). Choose Home tab ➪ View panel ➪ Visual Styles drop-down list ➪ Wireframe. ∎

Compare the ViewCube with the 3D Orbit feature, covered later in this chapter. Then you can choose the feature that will provide you with better control or quicker results.

Creating a Named View with a Camera

A camera is a way to define and save a 3D view. When you save a named view by using the VIEW command, you display the view that you want and then save it. When you use a camera, you define a location and a target to define the view. AutoCAD places a camera glyph (visual representation) in the drawing to represent the view. You can select the camera glyph and edit its properties by using its grips. You can also edit the camera's properties in the Properties palette. By default, the camera glyph does not plot. Cameras are listed in the View Manager dialog box, along with other named views.

AutoCAD Only

The CAMERA command is not available in AutoCAD LT. When you open an AutoCAD drawing containing a camera in AutoCAD LT, the camera glyph doesn't appear. ∎

Creating a camera

 To create a view with a camera, choose Render tab ⇨ Camera panel ⇨ Create Camera to start the CAMERA command. At the Specify camera location: prompt, specify a coordinate for the camera. You can place the coordinate on the XY plane and change the height later, using the Height option. At the Specify target location: prompt, specify the target, which is what the camera is looking at.

Note

The Camera panel is not displayed by default. To display it, right-click any area on the Render tab and choose Panels ⇨ Camera. ∎

The next prompt offers the following options:

- **?.** Displays the Enter camera name(s) to list <*>: prompt. Press Enter to list all current camera names and other named views in the drawing.
- **Name.** Lets you name the camera. If you don't use this option, the command assigns a default camera name, starting with Camera1 and so on.
- **LOcation.** Use this option to change the camera location.
- **Height.** Sets the camera height. You can use this to change the Z value of the camera after specifying its location on the XY plane.
- **Target.** Use this option to change the camera's target.
- **LEns.** Defines the field (width) of view in degrees, using a camera lens length in millimeters. Table 22.2 describes the relationship between lens length and field of view.
- **Clipping.** Creates front and back clipping planes for the view.
- **View.** You can use this option to make the camera's view current. Use the Yes suboption. This ends the command.
- **eXit.** Exits the command.

TABLE 22.2

Lens Length and Field-of-View Equivalents

Lens Length	Field of View (in Degrees)
15 mm	100
20 mm	84
24 mm	74
28 mm	65
35 mm	54
50 mm	40
85 mm	24
135 mm	15
200 mm	10

You can also create a camera from the tools palette. Display the Cameras tool palette tab. Choose one of the three cameras (Normal, Wide-angle, or Extreme Wide-angle) and drag it onto the drawing area. Release the mouse button. Then click to place the camera and click again to specify the target.

When you create the camera, you can set its view to current by using the View option. After you change the view, you can get back to the view by choosing it in the View Manager and setting it to current. You can also select the camera, right-click, and choose Set Camera View.

Editing a camera

When you edit a camera, the Camera Preview window opens to show you a preview of the camera's view, as shown in Figure 22.4. You can change the visual style within the Camera Preview window, using the Visual Style drop-down list. (This doesn't change the visual style in the main drawing area.)

FIGURE 22.4

The Camera Preview window shows you what the camera's view will look like.

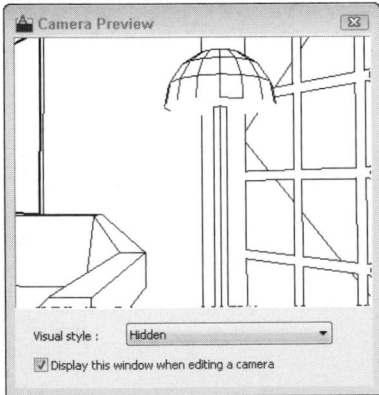

To edit a camera, select it and use its grips to change the camera location, target location, and lens length (field of view), as shown in Figure 22.5. Each grip has a tooltip to tell you its purpose. When you select a grip to make it hot, you can enter a new coordinate in the Dynamic Input tooltip. You can also edit the properties of a selected camera in the Properties palette.

FIGURE 22.5

Grip-editing a camera.

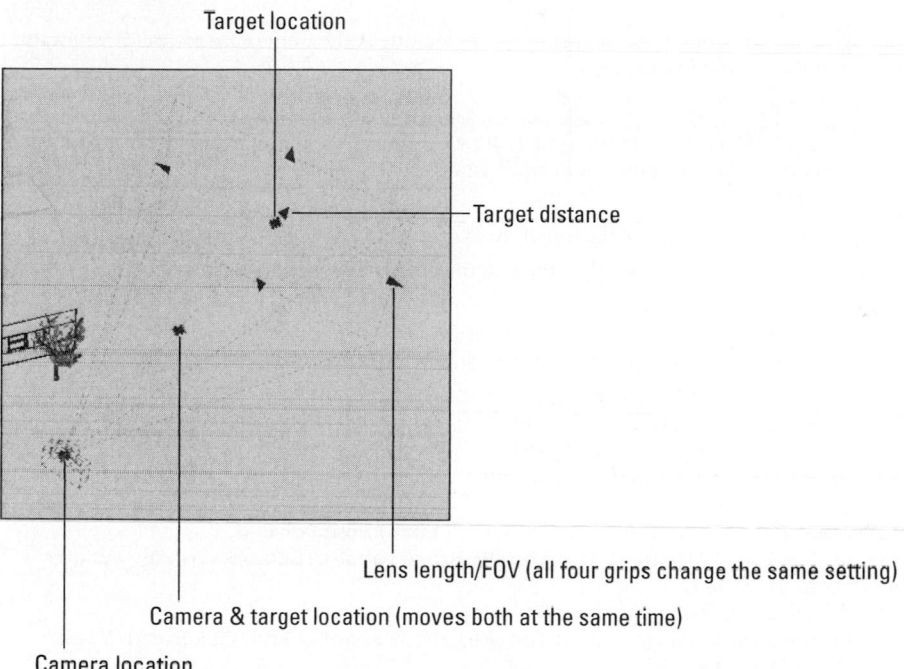

Target location

Target distance

Lens length/FOV (all four grips change the same setting)

Camera & target location (moves both at the same time)

Camera location

On the DVD

The drawing used in the following exercise on using standard viewpoints, CAMERA, the ViewCube, and DDVPOINT, ab22-a.dwg, is in the Drawings **folder on the DVD.** ■

STEPS: Using Standard Viewpoints, CAMERA, the ViewCube, and DDVPOINT

1. Open ab22-a.dwg from the DVD.
2. Save it as ab22-01.dwg in your AutoCAD Bible folder. It shows the same house used in Table 22.1, from the SE isometric view.
3. Type **ucsortho** ↵ 0 ↵ to turn off the UCSORTHO system variable. Turning off UCSORTHO prevents the UCS from changing whenever you switch to one of the six orthogonal viewpoints.
 4. Choose View tab ➪ Views panel ➪ Views (3D Navigation) drop-down list ➪ Top.

5. Choose View tab ⇨ Views panel ⇨ Views (3D Navigation) drop-down list ⇨ Bottom.

6. Choose View tab ⇨ Views panel ⇨ Views (3D Navigation) drop-down list ⇨ Front. You see the front of the house with the trees.

7. Choose Right from the same menu. You see the text `North side`.

8. Choose NW Isometric from the same menu. You're looking at the back of the house.

9. Choose SW Isometric from the same menu. You're looking at the front of the house. If you want, try the rest of the standard viewpoints.

10. Choose Top again.

11. If you have AutoCAD, click the bottom-right corner of the ViewCube's central square. Because this corner is between the South and East directions, as shown by the compass, you now see the SE Isometric view.

12. Click Top in the ViewCube to see the top of the house.

13. To see the front view of the house, click the S in the compass, or the arrow just above the S.

14. If you are using AutoCAD, choose Render tab ⇨ Camera panel ⇨ Create Camera. (If you are using AutoCAD LT, skip to the next step.) If you don't see the Camera panel, right-click any blank area on the Render tab and choose Panels ⇨ Camera. Follow the prompts:

```
Current camera settings: Height=0" Lens Length=50.0000 mm
Specify camera location: 27',-15' ↵
Specify target location: 15',20' ↵
Enter an option [?/Name/LOcation/Height/Target/LEns/Clipping/View/
   eXit]<eXit>: n ↵
Enter name for new camera <Camera1>: thruFrontDoor ↵
Enter an option [?/Name/LOcation/Height/Target/LEns/Clipping/View/
   eXit]<eXit>: h ↵
Specify camera height <14'>: 5' ↵
Enter an option [?/Name/LOcation/Height/Target/LEns/Clipping/View/
   eXit]<eXit>: le ↵
Specify lens length in mm <35.0000>: 28 ↵
Enter an option [?/Name/LOcation/Height/Target/LEns/Clipping/View/
   eXit]<eXit>: v ↵
Switch to camera view? [Yes/No] <No>: y ↵
```

15. Type **ddvpoint** ↵ on the command line to open the Viewpoint Presets dialog box. Set the left dial (angle from X axis) to 315 degrees by clicking the number 315. Set the right dial (angle from XY plane) to 60 degrees by clicking the second-from-the-top segment pointed to by the number 60. Click OK. You see a view somewhat like the SE isometric view, but from much higher up.

16. Repeat the DDVPOINT command. In the X Axis text box, type **240**. In the XY Plane text box, type **5**. Click OK. You view the house from slightly off the ground, much as you might see it if you were walking up to the house.

17. If you have AutoCAD, choose View tab ⇨ Visual Styles panel ⇨ Visual Styles drop-down list ⇨ Hidden. If you have AutoCAD LT, type **hide** ↵ on the command line. Notice that you can see the windows on the far side through the windows on your side of the house.

18. Choose View tab ⇨ Views panel ⇨ Named Views. Click the New button. In the New View/Shot Properties (or New View in AutoCAD LT) dialog box, type the name of the view, **walk up**. Click OK twice to return to your drawing. It should look like Figure 22.6.

19. If you're working on someone else's computer or want UCSORTHO on, type **ucsortho** ⏎ **1** ⏎ to turn it back on.

20. Save the drawing.

FIGURE 22.6

The final view of the house.

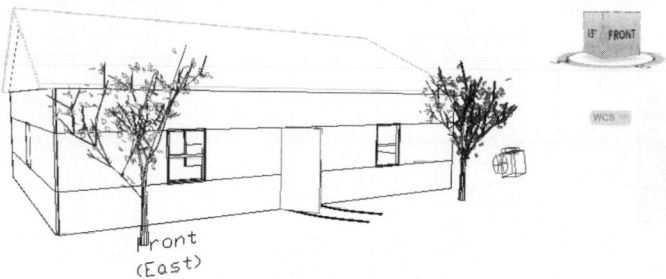

Note

In AutoCAD, when you save the view, by default you save it with the current visual style. Therefore, if you change the visual style and restore the view, the visual style changes back to the one you used when you saved the view. If you don't want to save the visual style, choose <None> from the Visual Style drop-down list in the New View/ Shot Properties dialog box. ■

Adding a Background to a Named View

When you save a named view in the View Manager, you can add a background. I discussed the View Manager in Chapter 8, but here I explain how to add a background. Backgrounds only apply to 3D views. They are not available in AutoCAD LT.

You can add a solid, gradient, or image background to a named view. Whenever you display that view, the background appears if the current visual style has backgrounds turned on (the VSBACKGROUNDS system variable). Backgrounds, especially image backgrounds, are usually used in the context of rendering, and I include an exercise on adding a background in Chapter 25.

To create a view with a background, choose View tab ⇨ Views panel ⇨ Views (3D Navigation) drop-down list ⇨ View Manager. In the View Manager, click the New button to define the new view. At the bottom of the New View/Shot Properties dialog box, choose Solid, Gradient, or Image from the drop-down list.

Note

You can specify lighting in real-world units. To turn on this feature, you set the LIGHTINGUNITS system variable to 1 or 2. By default, this feature is on (set to 2). When photometry is on, you have an additional background option, Sun & Sky. If you choose this option, the Adjust Sun & Sky Background dialog box opens. The settings in this dialog box are the same for creating sunlight when photometry is on. I explain this feature, called photometry, in Chapter 25 where I discuss lights. ■

The Background dialog box opens, shown in Figure 22.7, after choosing the Image option and clicking Browse to choose an image file.

Note

You can open the Background dialog box directly by using the BACKGROUND command. ■

The Background dialog box enables you to display a background while you work.

In the Background dialog box, you again have the opportunity to choose one of three options. To specify the background, choose one of the following:

- **Solid background.** Choose Solid (the default) from the Type drop-down list. Click the color swatch in the Color section. In the Select Color dialog box that opens, choose a color.

- **Gradient background.** Choose Gradient from the Type drop-down list. For a two-color gradient, uncheck the Three Color check box. Click in each color swatch to open the Select Color dialog box and choose a color. To rotate the gradient, enter a rotation angle in the Rotation text box or use the arrows to change the value.

- **Image background.** Choose Image from the Type drop-down list. Click the Browse button to choose an image file (in BMP, JPEG, TIF, PNG, TGA, GIF, or PCX format), and click Open. To adjust the position, scale, or offset of the image, click the Adjust Image button. In the Adjust Background Image dialog box, you can choose a position (Center, Stretch, or Tile) to specify how the image fits the viewport. You can also click the Offset or Scale option button and use the sliders to change the offset or scale of the image. Click OK when you're done. You can see an example of an image background near the end of Chapter 25.

When you specify the background, click OK to return to the View Manager, and click OK again to return to your drawing.

To edit a background, choose the view from the View Manager, click the Background Override item in the General category, click the down arrow, and choose Edit. You can also choose <None> to remove the image.

Note

The New View/Shot Properties dialog box lets you define shot properties. I discuss shot properties and the related ShowMotion feature later in this chapter. ■

Working with the Tripod and Compass

The VPOINT command offers another method of defining views, the tripod and compass. Note that this method is rarely used nowadays, because other viewing tools are more efficient. To start this command, enter **vpoint** ↵ on the command line. The tripod and compass appear, as shown in Figure 22.8 on the left.

If you type the VPOINT command, or press Enter to repeat the command, press Enter at the `Current view direction: VIEWDIR=-1.0000,-1.0000,1.0000 Specify a view point or [Rotate] <display compass and tripod>:` prompt to see the compass and tripod. (The numbers show the current viewpoint.)

Move the cursor about, and two things happen. The cursor moves within the compass, and the axes dynamically shift position.

Imagine that you take a tangerine and make a large, cross-shaped cut at the very bottom. Then you open out the bottom and remove the peel from the tangerine. Flatten the peel on the table. This is the concept of the compass, except that the outer edge is round. (The tangerine peel would have the shape of the cuts on its outer edge.) The very center of the compass — or the peel — is like the North Pole. When you're over the North Pole, you're looking straight down at your model — or the tangerine. This produces a plan view. The inner circle of the compass is where the middle of the tangerine was, at the equator. From the equator, you're looking sideways (from the front, back, or side) at your model. The outer circle of the compass represents the South Pole. From over the South Pole, you're looking at the bottom of your model — or the tangerine.

All of this determines your view relative to the XY plane:

- At the center of the compass, you're right on top, looking down. This is a plan view.
- At the inner circle, you're on the side, looking at the XY plane on its edge.
- At the outer circle, you're beneath the XY plane, looking up.

The cross that goes through the compass represents the X and Y axes. To summarize, going clockwise:

- The positive X axis gives you a right view.
- The negative Y axis is equivalent to a front view.
- The negative X axis gives you a left view.
- The positive Y axis gives you a back view.

When you have the cursor at the desired location, simply click. Your drawing displays the viewpoint that you specified.

Along with the tripod and compass, you see the current UCS icon based on the current UCS to help you find your bearings. Figure 22.8 shows, on the left, the cursor location that results in the viewpoint shown on the right. This is very close to the SE isometric view.

Displaying a Quick Plan View

The PLAN command is a quick way to return to plan view. Type **plan** ↵. This command has three options:

- **Current Ucs.** This is the default. You see the plan view of the current UCS.
- **Ucs.** The UCS option enables you to choose a named UCS. Type **?** ↵ to see a list of the named UCSs. Otherwise, type the name of a UCS.
- **World.** This option gives you the plan view of the WCS. If your current UCS is the WCS, there is no difference between this option and the Current UCS option.

FIGURE 22.8

The cursor location on the left results in the viewpoint shown on the right.

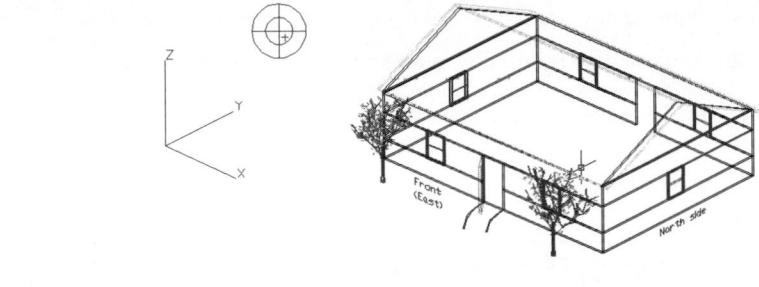

Figure 22.9 shows a sample UCS listing. The units are architectural.

FIGURE 22.9

A listing of saved UCSs.

```
Enter UCS name(s) to list <*>:

Current ucs name: *NO NAME*

Saved coordinate systems:

"EASTELEV"
      Origin = <0'-0",0'-0",0'-0">, X Axis = <0'-0",0'-0",0'-1">
      Y Axis = <0'-0",0'-1",0'-0">, Z Axis = <-0'-1",0'-0",0'-0">
"FRONTROOF"
      Origin = <0'-0",10'-0",0'-0">, X Axis = <0'-0",0'-0",0'-1">
      Y Axis = <0'-0 7/8",0'-0 7/16",0'-0">, Z Axis = <-0'-0 7/16",0'-0
7/8",0'-0">
"NORTHSIDE"
      Origin = <0'-0",0'-0",40'-0">, X Axis = <0'-1",0'-0",0'-0">
      Y Axis = <0'-0",0'-1",0'-0">, Z Axis = <0'-0",0'-0",0'-1">
```

AutoCAD Only

The Express Tools' extended PLAN command, EXPLAN, prompts you to select objects so that you can see the plan view zoomed in on those objects. Choose Express Tools tab ⇨ Tools panel (expanded) ⇨ Extended Plan. For information about installing Express Tools, see Appendix A. ∎

Returning to plan view when you change the UCS

If you like plan views, you'll love UCSFOLLOW. UCSFOLLOW is a system variable that returns you to plan view whenever you change the UCS. It's for those who like to find their bearings in plan view first, before going on to change the viewpoint in another UCS.

The default value is 0 (off), which means that your drawing does not return to plan view. In other words, your display remains unchanged when you change the UCS. Type **ucsfollow** and change the value to 1 to turn UCSFOLLOW on. From then on, your drawing automatically displays the plan view when you change the UCS.

Displaying Parallel and Perspective Projections

You may have noticed when you open AutoCAD with the default 3D environment that the grid lines look like they're receding into the distance. That's because AutoCAD is displaying a *perspective* view, which makes parallel lines converge as they get farther away. Because this is how parallel lines look in real life (try looking down a road into the distance), a perspective view looks more realistic than a parallel view that keeps lines parallel, regardless of their distance. However, when you zoom in, objects may appear distorted. Use a perspective view when you want to convey a realistic sense of depth. In general, perspective view is most useful in architectural settings. AutoCAD LT doesn't include perspective projections. The PERSPECTIVE system variable controls the current view. A value of 0 turns off perspective view; 1 turns it on.

Using 3D Orbit

The 3D Orbit feature is a fully interactive way to change your viewpoint in real-time. Using 3D Orbit is like orbiting the earth to view any continent or ocean below. When you enter 3D Orbit mode, you cannot use other commands. In this regard, 3D Orbit is like Realtime Pan and Realtime Zoom. Similarly, you can press Esc or Enter to exit 3D Orbit mode. You access the 3D Orbit options by right-clicking in the drawing area to display the 3D Orbit shortcut menu.

AutoCAD Only

3D Orbit is not available in AutoCAD LT. This entire section, including the exercise, is for AutoCAD only. ■

Use 3D Orbit for fine control over the viewpoint. To quickly change the viewpoint to one of the preset views, you can use the ViewCube, covered earlier in this chapter. (You can also drag the ViewCube, which then functions similarly to 3D Orbit.)

Starting 3D Orbit

To start the 3DORBIT command, choose View tab ➪ Navigate panel ➪ Orbit drop-down list ➪ Orbit. If another mode of 3D Orbit is active, right-click and choose Other Navigation Modes ➪ Constrained Orbit or type **1**. You enter 3D Orbit mode, and AutoCAD displays the 3D Orbit cursor, as shown in Figure 22.10. The term *constrained* means that the orbit is restricted to either the XY plane or the Z direction (but not both at once).

Tip

You can use 3D Orbit transparently, that is, in the middle of another command. Just press and hold Shift and your mouse's wheel (using it like a button), rotate your model as you want, and release the buttons. You then continue the command in progress. This way of using the 3DORBIT command without actually executing the command makes it very easy to navigate your model. You can also use 3D Orbit in the Block Editor when editing 3D blocks. ■

The 3D Orbit mode includes the ability to zoom and pan. Therefore, you can use this command for more than just orbiting.

Tip

For faster performance, select only the objects that you want to view with 3D Orbit before starting the command. Objects that you did not select disappear while you're in 3D Orbit mode. They reappear as soon as you leave 3D Orbit mode. ■

FIGURE 22.10

3D Orbit mode allows you to change the viewpoint of your drawing in real-time.

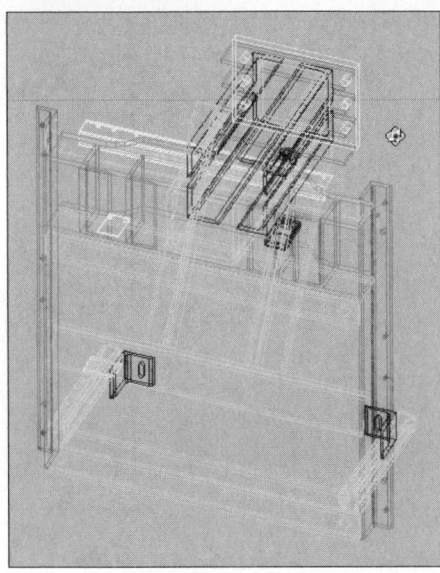

Navigating with 3D Orbit

The default 3D Orbit mode is Constrained Orbit. Drag to the left or right to rotate the model around on the XY plane, and drag up or down to rotate the model along the Z axis. You can't rotate the model upside down in Constrained Orbit mode. Drag diagonally to create isometric views.

 If you need more freedom, you can use Free Orbit mode. Choose View tab ⇨ Navigate panel ⇨ Orbit drop-down list ⇨ Free Orbit. If another mode of 3D Orbit is active, right-click and choose Other Navigation Modes ⇨ Free Orbit or type **2**. In Free Orbit mode, you have less control but more options.

Free Orbit mode displays an *arcball* and has four cursors that affect how your model rotates. Each cursor is location based. As you move your cursor to a new location, the cursor shape changes, and the type of rotation changes. The arcball is shown in Figure 22.11.

You use the arcball in the following ways:

 • **Rolling with the circular arrow cursor.** When you place your cursor outside the arcball, it takes the shape of a circular arrow. As you click and drag around the outside of the arcball, your model turns around an imaginary axis that extends from the center of the arcball outward and perpendicular to the screen — that is, pointing at you. This type of rotation is called a *roll*.

 • **Rotating freely with the sphere and lines cursor.** As soon as you move your cursor within the arcball, it takes the shape of a small sphere encircled by two lines. As you click and drag within the arcball, your model moves around the center of the arcball in the direction that you drag. Imagine that your model is encased in a transparent sphere, similar to a gerbil or hamster ball. As you drag the cursor, you're rotating the sphere around its center point. If you drag from one edge of the arcball to its opposite edge, you can release the mouse, move back to your starting point, and then click and drag again in the same direction. When you do this a few times, you rotate your model 360 degrees. You achieve the best results by dragging in a line in any direction, rather than 'round and 'round.

FIGURE 22.11

3D Orbit's Free mode uses an arcball.

Arcball

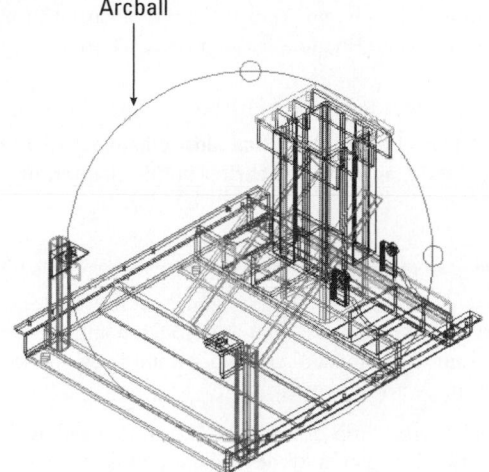

- **Rotating around the vertical axis with the horizontal ellipse cursor.** When you move your cursor over either the left or right quadrant circle on the arcball, it becomes a horizontal ellipse. As you click and drag from either quadrant, your model rotates around the arcball's vertical axis, which extends from the top quadrant to the bottom quadrant. Although your cursor enters the arcball, it retains its horizontal ellipse form until you release the mouse button. You can drag from one quadrant to its opposite quadrant, release the mouse button, move back to your starting point, and then click and drag again in the same direction. When you do this a few times, you rotate your model 360 degrees.

- **Rotating around the horizontal axis with the vertical ellipse cursor.** When you move your cursor over either the top or bottom quadrant circle on the arcball, it becomes a vertical ellipse. As you click and drag from either quadrant, your model rotates around the arcball's horizontal axis, which extends from the left quadrant to the right quadrant. You can drag from one quadrant to its opposite quadrant, release the mouse button, move back to your starting point, and then click and drag again in the same direction. When you do this a few times, you rotate your model 360 degrees.

Using the 3D Orbit visual aids

3D Orbit includes three visual aids that can help you find your bearings:

- **Compass.** Displays a sphere that is made up of three dashed lines labeled as the X, Y, and Z axes. The lines look like the threads of a baseball.
- **Grid.** Displays a grid of lines representing the XY plane. The Z coordinate of the grid is equal to the value of the ELEVATION system variable, which is set to 0 (zero) by default. You can specify the structure of the grid with the GRIDUNIT system variable. You can set this value by right-clicking the Grid Display button on the status bar and choosing Settings before you use this visual aid.
- **UCS icon.** Displays a shaded, three-dimensional 3D UCS icon. The X axis is red, the Y axis is green, and the Z axis is blue.

You would rarely want to use all three visual aids. The compass and grid can both interfere with viewing your model, so use them temporarily when needed.

To display the visual aids, right-click while in 3D Orbit mode and choose Visual Aids from the shortcut menu. Then choose the aid that you want from the submenu. To turn off the visual aids, follow the same procedure — the submenu items toggle the visual aids on and off when you click them.

Note
If you choose a visual style (other than the default 2D wireframe), the visual aids remain active after you exit 3D Orbit. You can switch to the 2D wireframe visual style, as explained earlier in this chapter, or you can re-enter 3D Orbit and turn off the visual aids. ■

Creating a continuous orbit

Absolutely the coolest feature of 3D Orbit — and one of the coolest features of AutoCAD as a whole — is continuous orbit. Continuous orbit enables you to choose a direction of rotation and then let go. 3D Orbit automatically continues the rotation in the same direction and continues it until you change or stop it. With continuous orbit, who needs screensavers? Here's how it works:

1. Choose View tab ⇨ Navigate panel ⇨ Orbit drop-down list ⇨ Continuous Orbit. If 3D Orbit mode is active, right-click and choose Other Navigation Modes ⇨ Continuous Orbit or type **3**.

2. Click and drag in the direction of rotation that you want to create. The faster you drag, the faster the resulting orbit.

3. Release your mouse button. Your model continues to rotate in the same direction. All you do is watch.

Continuous orbit is an ideal way to view your model. As your model rotates, you can pick out any errors and then stop continuous orbit to fix them. You can change the direction of your continuous orbit at any time by clicking and dragging in a new direction and then releasing the mouse button. To stop continuous orbit, choose any other 3D Orbit mode or click in the drawing window.

Resetting the view

You can end up with some strange views of your model when using 3D Orbit, so AutoCAD provides a way to reset your view to the view that was current when you first started 3D Orbit. With any 3D Orbit mode active, right-click and choose Reset View from the shortcut menu.

Refining your 3D Orbit view

3D Orbit offers many options for refining your view so that you see just the view that you want. You can pan and zoom, adjust the camera distance, create parallel and perspective views, set clipping planes, or display a preset view. You can also start Walk or Fly mode, as discussed later in this chapter.

Because you cannot use other commands while in 3D Orbit mode, you access most of these options by right-clicking in the drawing area to access the 3D Orbit shortcut menu.

Panning in 3D Orbit

To pan in 3D Orbit mode, right-click and choose Other Navigation Modes ⇨ Pan from the 3D Orbit shortcut menu or type **9**. You see the familiar hand cursor. Click and drag to pan, in the same way that you normally pan in real-time. To stop panning, right-click and choose another mode.

Zooming in 3D Orbit

To zoom in 3D Orbit, right-click and choose Other Navigation Modes ⇨ Zoom from the 3D Orbit shortcut menu or type **8**. You see the familiar magnifying glass cursor with a plus (+) and a minus (–) sign. Click and drag in the direction of the plus sign (toward the top of your screen) to zoom in; click and drag in the direction of the minus sign (toward the bottom of your screen) to zoom out, just as you do when you normally use zoom in real-time. To stop zooming, switch to any other mode.

Using Zoom options in 3D Orbit

To zoom to a window in 3D Orbit, right-click and choose Zoom Window from the shortcut menu. Your cursor displays a small rectangle. Click and drag, and then release the mouse button to define the two corners of the window.

To zoom to drawing extents in 3D Orbit, right-click and choose Zoom Extents. To return to the previous view, right-click and choose Zoom Previous.

Adjusting the camera distance

You can adjust the distance between the viewer, called the *camera,* and the target, which by default is set to the center of the 3D view (this view may be different from the center of your model). Changing this camera distance is equivalent to zooming in and out.

To adjust the camera distance in 3D Orbit, right-click and choose Other Navigation Modes ⇨ Adjust Distance from the shortcut menu or type **4**. The cursor changes to a horizontal line with a double-headed arrow pointing up and down. Click and drag toward the top of your screen to move the camera closer to your objects — similar to zooming in. Click and drag toward the bottom of your screen to move the camera away from your objects — similar to zooming out.

Controlling view properties

When you use 3D Orbit, the Properties palette displays special properties that relate to 3D Orbit features, as follows:

- **View Height** is a way to specify the distance of the imaginary camera. In other words, you can use this property to zoom in and out on your model. A larger number makes your model look smaller because the distance (or height) of the camera from the model increases.

- **View Width** is another way to zoom in and out. Here you specify the width of the view of the imaginary camera. A larger number makes your model look smaller because the view encompasses a larger area (and your model is a smaller part of that area).

- **Lens Length** and **Field of View** define the angle of the view. I discuss these concepts in the section "Creating a Named View with a Camera" earlier in this chapter.

To change one of these properties, click its row in the Properties palette. Type a new value and press Enter.

Creating parallel and perspective views

To create a perspective view in 3D Orbit, right-click and choose Perspective. To return to parallel view, choose Parallel. For more information on perspective views, see the section "Displaying Parallel and Perspective Projections" earlier in this chapter.

Using a preset view

After you use 3D Orbit a few times, your model may appear askew, with no indication of how to return it to a viewpoint that you can comprehend. You can switch to any of the preset views discussed at the beginning of this chapter. From 3D Orbit, right-click and choose Preset Views from the shortcut menu. Then choose one of the standard viewpoints on the submenu list.

On the DVD

The drawing used in the following exercise on working in 3D Orbit, ab22-b.dwg, is in the Drawings folder on the DVD. ■

STEPS: Working in 3D Orbit

1. Open ab22-b.dwg from the DVD. This is a 3D chair shown from a Northeast isometric view.
2. Choose View tab ⇨ Navigate panel ⇨ Orbit drop-down list ⇨ Orbit.
3. Place the mouse cursor to the right of the chair in the middle (vertically) of the screen. Drag to the left twice until the chair turns around completely and is back to approximately its original position.
4. Place the cursor below the chair and drag up until it stops. Drag down until the chair is in its original position. Place the cursor above the chair and drag down until it stops. Return the chair to its original position again.
5. Place the cursor above the chair until you are looking down at it — a Top view. The chair is still rotated. Drag from the left to the right until the chair's bottom is horizontal on the screen.
6. Right-click and choose Other Navigation Modes ⇨ Free Orbit. Place the cursor inside the arcball and drag in various directions to see that you now have more freedom to tumble the chair upside down.
7. Right-click and choose Zoom Previous to return to the Top view.
8. Type 1 to return to Constrained Orbit mode. The arcball disappears.
9. Right-click and choose Other Navigation Modes ⇨ Continuous Orbit. Click and drag with the cursor, making a small movement from right to left, and then release the mouse button. You may need to try this a couple of times to find a continuous orbit that you like. Try clicking and dragging in a different direction to change the direction of the continuous orbit, and then release the mouse button.
10. Type 1 to stop the continuous orbit.
11. Right-click and choose Reset View to re-display the chair exactly in its original view.
12. Type 9 (pan). Pan the chair to the right a little.
13. Right-click and choose Other Navigation Modes ⇨ Zoom. Drag upward to zoom the chair in slightly.
14. Right-click and choose Preset Views ⇨ NW Isometric.
15. Press Esc to exit 3D Orbit mode.

Don't save your drawing.

Using ShowMotion to Cycle Through Views

To show a drawing to others, or better visualize multiple angles of a model, you can create named views called *shots*, and then use the ShowMotion feature to display them one after another as a presentation. You can add motion and animation to your shots.

AutoCAD Only

The ShowMotion feature is not available in AutoCAD LT. ∎

Creating shots

 You start by creating the shots that you want. You may want to plan these in advance, by creating a storyboard to lay out the shots in the desired order. To create a shot, display the desired view, including the viewpoint, zoom, and visual style. (I discuss visual styles later in this chapter.) Then click the ShowMotion button on the Navigation bar to display the ShowMotion toolbar at the bottom of your screen. If you do not see the ShowMotion button on the Navigation bar, click the Customize button at the bottom or on the right side of the Navigation bar and choose ShowMotion.

From the ShowMotion toolbar, choose New Shot (the NEWSHOT command) to open the New View/Shot Properties dialog box, with the Shot Properties tab on top, as shown in Figure 22.12. Alternatively, you can choose View tab ⇨ Views panel ⇨ Named Views, click New, and click the Shot Properties tab.

In the View Name text box, enter a name for the shot. You can create view categories, which are groups of shots. Use categories to help you organize many shots into sections. To create a view category, enter a name in the View Category text box. After you create a view category, you can choose it for subsequent shots from the View Category drop-down list.

FIGURE 22.12

Use the Shot Properties tab of the New View/Shot Properties dialog box to specify the properties of a shot.

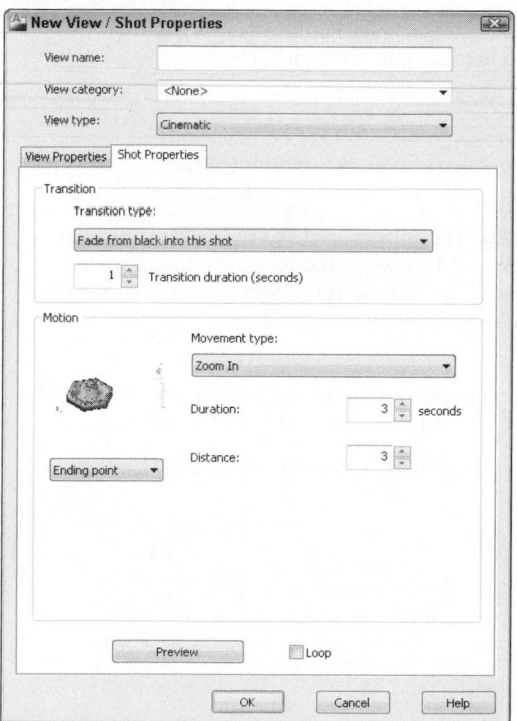

From the View Type drop-down list, you can create three types of shots:

- **Still.** A single camera position (For more information on cameras, see "Creating a Named View with a Camera" earlier in this chapter.)
- **Cinematic.** A single camera position, plus camera movement
- **Recorded Walk.** Animation along a path

In the Transition section, choose a transition type from the drop-down list. The transition occurs between the display of the previous shot and the current shot that you are defining. You have three choices:

- **Fade from black into this shot.** Creates a fade transition to the shot from a black screen. Use this option when you want the fade effect and have a black background.
- **Fade from white into this shot.** Creates a fade transition to the shot from a white screen. Use this option when you want the fade effect and have a white background.
- **Cut to shot.** Immediately switches to the new shot.

Then choose the duration of the transition in seconds by entering a value or clicking the up or down arrow.

The bottom part of the dialog box changes, depending on the view type. For a still shot, you simply choose the duration, in seconds. For a cinematic shot, you start by choosing one of eight movement types. For example, you can zoom in or out. For a recorded walk, you return to your drawing and drag in the direction of the walk. Release the mouse button to stop recording. (See the section "Walking through a Model" for another way to record a walk through your drawing.) You can preview the results by clicking the Preview button. You can also loop the entire presentation by clicking the Loop check box at the bottom. When you're done, click OK.

Continue to create new shots until you have the ones that you want. To modify any shot, right-click its thumbnail and choose Properties. Make your changes in the dialog box and click OK.

Displaying shots

To display the shots in order, use the NAVSMOTION command. Type **navsmotion** on the command line to display the ShowMotion toolbar at the bottom of your screen, as shown in Figure 22.13.

The ShowMotion feature displays two levels of thumbnails. The bottom level shows either the first of a set of shots or the first view in a view category. The upper level shows all the shots, organized by view categories, if any. As you pass your cursor over a thumbnail, it enlarges. When you hover the cursor over each thumbnail, two buttons appear — one to play or display the shot or view category, and the other to go to the beginning of that shot or view category.

The ShowMotion toolbar contains buttons that enable you to pin or unpin the ShowMotion interface, play the entire set of shots, stop the display, loop the display, create a new shot, and close the interface.

When you click the Play button on either a thumbnail or the toolbar, it becomes a Pause button that you can click to pause the display.

FIGURE 22.13

FIGURE 22.13

The ShowMotion toolbar lets you control your presentation.

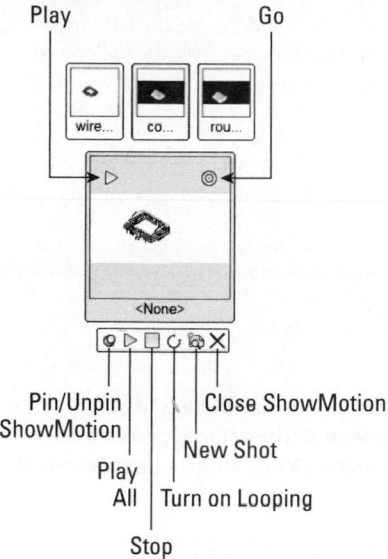

Play   Go

Pin/Unpin ShowMotion   Close ShowMotion

New Shot

Play All   Turn on Looping

Stop

Walking through a Model

To better see what a model looks like, and to show it to clients, you can "walk" through it. This feature is most useful for architectural models, because it simulates walking through a space, such as a building. Although Walk appears as a mode on the 3D Orbit shortcut menu, it has its own unique navigational system. Walking maintains your view parallel to the XY plane, but you can use the Fly mode to move away from the XY plane.

You can record your walk-through and save it as an animation file to play back later. In addition, you can create an object that functions as a motion guide, called a motion point or path. You can then record an animation file that uses the point or path to define the walk-through.

AutoCAD Only

AutoCAD LT doesn't include walk- or fly-throughs, nor does it include any way to create a movie file of your drawing navigation. ■

Navigating in Walk mode

To enter Walk mode, you need to display the Render tab's Animations panel. Right-click anywhere on the Render tab and choose Panels ⇨ Animations. Then choose Render tab ⇨ Animations panel ⇨ Walk and Fly drop-down list ⇨ Walk. Also from any 3D Orbit mode, right-click and choose Other Navigation Modes ⇨ Walk or type **6**. This executes the 3DWALK command.

You must be in perspective view to use Walk and Fly modes. If you aren't, a message asks you whether you want to toggle to a perspective view.

By default, you see a translucent balloon in the upper-right corner of the screen, providing the instruction to use the keyboard to navigate, and the mouse to look around and turn. (If you don't see the balloon, press the Tab key or right-click and choose Display Instruction Window.) Move the cursor over the balloon to make it opaque, and click its down arrow to expand the balloon and show navigation instructions, as follows:

- **Up arrow/W key.** Move forward
- **Down arrow/S key.** Move backward
- **Left arrow/A key.** Move left
- **Right arrow/D key.** Move right
- **Drag mouse.** Look around and turn
- **F key.** Toggle Fly mode (which lets you leave the XY plane)

Tip

Because walking through a model is sometimes a little cumbersome, depending on the capabilities of your graphics card and the complexity and size of your model, you should display your desired starting point before you enter 3DWALK. Also, switch to the visual style you want to use before entering Walk mode; otherwise, right-click and choose Visual Styles. ■

Because you turn by dragging with the mouse, you'll probably find it easiest to use the W, A, S, and D keys with your left hand (assuming you use your right hand for your mouse). This set of keys is used for navigating in computer games and provides an easy way to move in the four directions without looking at the keys.

When you start the 3DWALK command, the Position Locator window opens, and your cursor changes to a plus sign, as shown in Figure 22.14. The Position Locator window shows you your model from the top so you can gauge your position.

FIGURE 22.14

The Position Locator shows you a 2D map of your model.

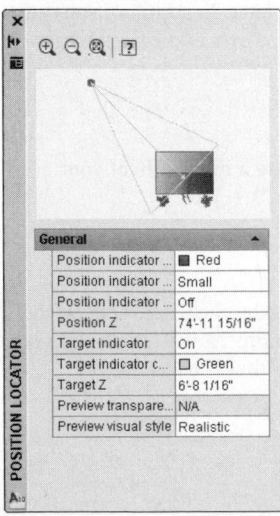

A helpful feature of the Position Locator is that you can drag the red dot that represents your position to move your current position. You can also drag the target indicator to change your view. In the General section of the Position Locator window, you can also specify the following settings:

- **Position indicator color.** Changes the color (which is red by default) to contrast better with your model.

- **Position indicator size.** Changes the indicator's size to small, medium, or large.

- **Position indicator blink.** Makes the indicator blink, if you want.

- **Position Z.** Sets the Z coordinate for the current position.

- **Target indicator.** Turns the target indicator on or off. Having it on is generally helpful because it explains what you are seeing in the main drawing area and you can drag it to change your view.

- **Target indicator color.** Changes the color (which is green by default) to contrast better with your model.

- **Target Z.** Sets the Z coordinate for the target.

- **Preview transparency.** Sets the transparency of the preview in the Position Locator window. For example, if you're in a house, shown in Figure 22.15, you want to be able to see through the roof. You can set a number from 0 to 95. Don't include the percent (%) symbol when you enter a new number.

- **Preview visual style.** Specifies a visual style for the preview.

When you're ready to walk, press the W or Up Arrow key. You can press the key repeatedly or hold it down, but if you hold it down for a while, you may need to wait for the display to catch up. As you walk, you can drag to the left or right to change your direction. You can also drag up or down. Whenever you need to get your bearing, just look over at the Position Locator window to see where you are as well as your view's target.

Note
The capabilities of your computer, including your graphics card, have a major effect on the performance when you walk through a model. AutoCAD needs to make many calculations each second to re-display your screen as you change position. ■

Specifying Walk mode settings

 You can specify several settings that affect how Walk mode works. While in Walk mode, right-click and choose Walk and Fly Settings. At other times, choose Render tab ⇨ Animations panel ⇨ Walk and Fly drop-down list ⇨ Walk and Fly Settings. The Walk and Fly Settings dialog box opens, as shown in Figure 22.15.

Note
The Animations panel is not displayed by default. To display it, right-click any blank area on the Render tab and choose Panels ⇨ Animation. ■

You can choose when the instruction window displays. After a while, you know the instructions, so you probably don't want the window to display each time you enter Walk or Fly mode. You can also choose whether or not to display the Position Locator window.

To change the size of your steps and how many steps you move per second, use the settings in the Current Drawing Settings section. If you set your steps too small, walking seems too slow, but if they're too big, you don't have as much control. Click OK when you're done changing the settings.

FIGURE 22.15

The Walk and Fly Settings dialog box allows you to fine-tune the Walk mode settings.

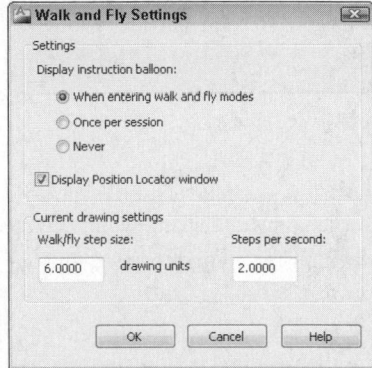

Flying through a model

Walking through a model keeps you parallel to the XY plane. However, sometimes you may want to look at the roof of a house or go up some stairs. Fly mode frees you to leave the XY plane.

 You can enter Fly mode by pressing the F key from Walk mode. From any 3D Orbit mode, right-click and choose Other Navigation Modes ⇨ Fly or type **7**. Otherwise, if the Render tab's Animations panel is not displayed, right-click anywhere on the Render tab and choose Panels ⇨ Animations. Then choose Render tab ⇨ Animations control panel ⇨ Walk and Fly drop-down list ⇨ Fly. This executes the 3DFLY command.

Note

You can use the Properties palette to switch between Walk and Fly modes, control the step size, and specify other settings that affect the display of the viewport. ∎

The controls are the same for Fly and Walk modes, except that when you drag the mouse forward in Fly mode, you go upward, away from the XY plane, and when you drag the mouse backward (toward you), you go downward. Figure 22.16 shows the process of "flying" up a flight of stairs.

Saving the walk as a movie file

You can record your walk- or fly-through as you go, and save the result as a movie (video) file. If you want, you can specify the movie settings before you start by entering 3D Orbit mode, right-clicking, and choosing Animation Settings. The Animation Settings dialog box opens, as shown in Figure 22.17.

In the Animation Settings dialog box, you can choose a visual style or presentation quality from the Visual Style drop-down list. Choose a resolution from the Resolution drop-down list. The Frame Rate (FPS) option determines the number of frames per second. Finally, choose one of the four available movie formats from the Format drop-down list: AVI, MOV, MPG, or WMV (the default). Note that the first three settings greatly affect the size of the resulting movie. When you're done, click OK.

Note

To save to the MOV format, you need to install Apple QuickTime Player. You need Microsoft® Windows Media Player® 9 or later installed to save to WMV format; if it isn't installed, AVI is the default format. ∎

FIGURE 22.16

You can use Fly mode to climb a flight of stairs.

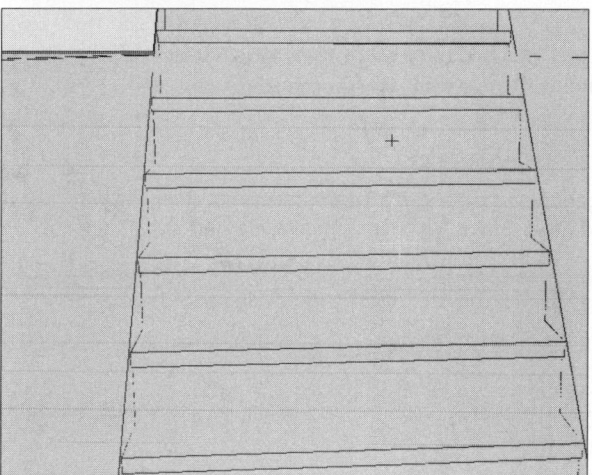

FIGURE 22.17

The Animation Settings dialog box specifies settings for a move that you record during Walk or Fly mode.

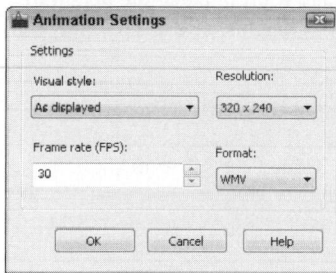

To start recording, if the Animations panel isn't displayed on the Render tab, right-click anywhere on the Render tab and choose Panels ⇨ Animations. Then click Render tab ⇨ Animations panel ⇨ Record Animation. Then start walking or flying, following the directions in the previous sections.

Tip
You can drag in the Position Locator while you're recording to move your current position, change your target position, or turn around. ∎

When you're done, click Render tab ⇨ Animations panel ⇨ Save Animation. In the same location are buttons to pause and play the recording. You can play the animation before you save it to make sure it's acceptable. The Animation Preview window opens and plays the animation. This playback is a preview and may not be as polished as the final version.

When you click the Save Animation button, the Save As dialog box opens, where you can save the movie. Navigate to the desired location, enter a name, and click Save. At this time, you can click the Animation

Settings button and change the animation settings. The Creating Video progress meter displays to show you the progress as the movie saves. When it's done, open the movie file and watch. Bring some popcorn!

Tip

If you don't like the result, press Esc to end the 3DWALK command, and choose View tab ⇨ Views panel ⇨ Previous View. Your display returns to the beginning of your walk, so you can start again. ■

Using a motion path to save a movie file

Using Walk and Fly modes can result in some jerkiness as you make little adjustments along the way. For a smoother ride, you can draw a motion path and save a movie file that automatically runs along the path.

You need to specify both the camera and its target. They can be either a point or a path (line, arc, elliptical arc, ellipse, circle, polyline, 3D polyline, spline, or helix), but they can't both be a point. For example:

- If the camera is a point and the target is a circle, the resulting movie is like standing in one place and turning around.

- If the camera is a circle and the target is a point, the result is like walking around a point (such as the center of a table) that you look at throughout.

The first step is to create one or two motion paths for the camera and/or the target. If you are using paths, a polyline is ideal if you want to add some turns, because you can only select one object for each motion path.

Tip

You may want to create a separate layer that you can later turn off. Also, you usually want to place the height of the motion paths at eye level. You can place the camera and target paths at different heights, or use a 3D polyline and vary the heights along the way. ■

 Then choose Render tab ⇨ Animations panel ⇨ Animation Motion Path to start the ANIPATH command and open the Motion Path Animation dialog box, as shown in Figure 22.18. (If the Animations panel isn't displayed on the Render tab, right-click anywhere on the Render tab and choose Panels ⇨ Animations.)

FIGURE 22.18

Specify the motion paths and movie settings before you create a motion path animation.

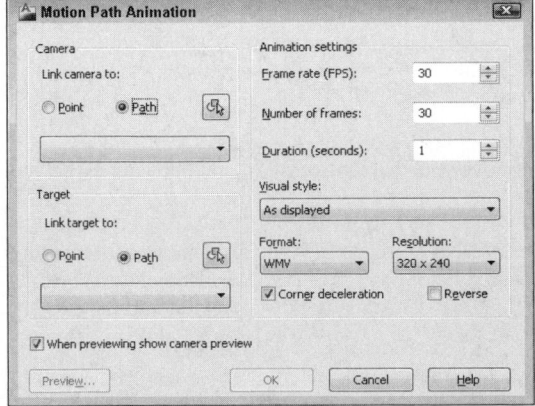

Follow these steps to set up the motion path animation:

1. In the Camera section, choose either Point or Path. Then click the Select Path or Pick Point button to select an object for a motion path or to specify a point. If you choose Path, name the path or accept the default name.

2. In the Target section, do the same. Remember that you can't choose a point for both the camera and the target.

3. In the Animation Settings section, set the frame rate in frames per second and set the number of frames. The Duration adjusts automatically, based on your choices.

4. Choose a visual style from the Visual Style drop-down list.

5. Choose a format and resolution. These settings are the same as for a walk-through animation, which I discussed in the previous section of this chapter.

6. By default, the movie slows down around corners. You can uncheck the Corner Deceleration check box if you want to. You can also check the Reverse check box to make the animation go backward.

7. Click the Preview button to preview the result. Remember that the preview may not be as good as the final movie. In my experience, the preview did not use the visual style I chose, but the final did. Close the Preview box.

8. Click OK.

9. In the Save As dialog box, navigate to the desired location. Enter a name and click Save. You can click the Animation Settings dialog box to change the settings before you save. The Creating Video progress meter shows your progress, and the Preview Animation window previews the animation.

On the DVD

The drawing used in the following exercise on using Walk mode and creating animations, ab22-c.dwg, is in the Drawings folder on the DVD. ■

STEPS: Using Walk Mode and Creating Animations

1. Open ab22-c.dwg from the DVD.

2. Save the drawing as ab22-02.dwg in your AutoCAD Bible folder. You're inside a 3D house, looking down a hallway, in the 3D Hidden visual style, as shown in Figure 22.19. Type **ucsortho** ↵ and set its value to 0.

3. If the Animations panel isn't displayed on the Render tab, right-click anywhere on the Render tab and choose Panels ⇨ Animations. Choose Render tab ⇨ Animations panel ⇨ Walk and Fly drop-down list ⇨ Walk and Fly Settings. In the Walk and Fly Settings dialog box, the Walk/fly Step Size should be set to 12 drawing units and the Steps per Second should be 2. Click OK.

4. Choose Render tab ⇨ Animations panel ⇨ Walk and Fly drop-down list ⇨ Walk. If the message appears asking you to toggle to perspective view, click Change. The Position Locator shows that you're in an open dining area, looking down a diagonal hallway. You want to go down that hallway, turn to the right, continue to the end of the hallway, and turn left into the master bedroom.

5. Press and hold the W key, or press the W key multiple times until the Position Locator indicates that you're in the narrow hallway. If necessary, let the screen re-display the model.

6. Continue to walk to the end of the diagonal segment of hallway, as shown in the Position Locator. If necessary, drag slightly to the left or right with your mouse to adjust your view. Don't mind that along the way you may be seeing through walls.

FIGURE 22.19

The start of a walk down a hall.

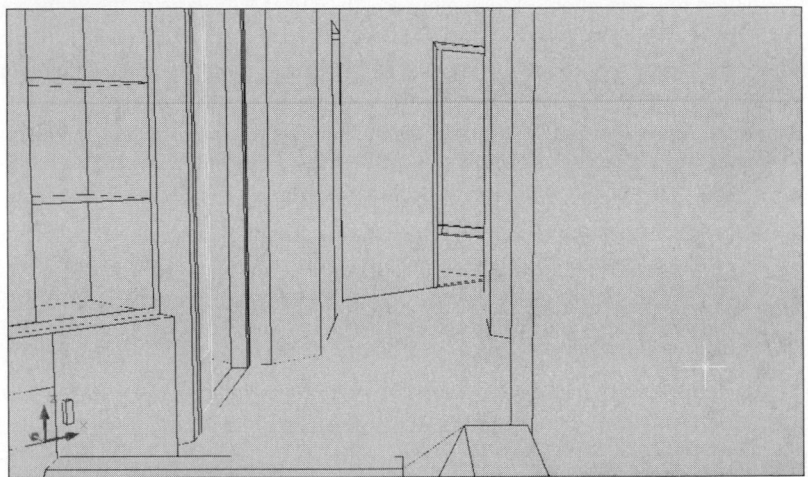

Thanks to Andrew Wilcox of Virtual Homes, Inc., Hammonds Plains, Nova Scotia, Canada, for this drawing.

7. With your mouse, drag to the right to turn to the right, until the Position Locator shows the center target line horizontal, facing right. You should be able to see the table inside the bedroom, through a partially open door. You might need to drag upward.

8. At this point, you'll record the rest of your walk as a video file. Right-click and choose Animation Settings. Change the Visual Style to Hidden and change the Frame Rate (FPS) to 15. Choose WMV or AVI as the format, depending on what you think you can play on your computer (probably either). Click OK.

9. Choose Render tab➪Animations panel➪Record Animation.

10. Continue to walk forward using the W key and dragging slightly to the left to keep the bed in the bedroom in the center of your view until your screen looks like Figure 22.20.

11. Click Render tab➪Animations panel➪Play Animation to see the preview. Close the preview window.

12. Choose Render tab➪Animations panel➪Save Animation. In the Save As dialog box, navigate to your AutoCAD Bible folder, name the file ab22-02a.wmv (or AVI, depending on the format you chose), and click Save. The Creating Video window shows the progress.

13. In Windows Explorer, double-click the file to open it and watch the animation.

14. Now you want to create an animation from a motion path. Type **plan** ↵ and then **w** ↵ to view the drawing from the top, using the default World UCS. Then change the visual style to 3D Wireframe by choosing Home tab➪View panel➪Visual Styles drop-down list➪Wireframe. Turn the Motion Path1 and Motion Path2 layers on. You should see two motion paths in the drawing, as shown in Figure 22.21.

15. Choose Render tab➪Animations panel➪Animation Motion Path. Set the Camera section to Path and click the Select Path button. Select Motion Path 1 and name it Motion Path 1 (see Figure 22.21). Set the Target section to Path and click the Select Path button. Select Motion Path 2 and name it Motion Path 2. Set the frame rate to 15 and the number of frames to 45, which makes a 3-second movie. Set the visual style to Hidden. Choose your preferred movie format and click OK. Save the movie as ab22-02b.wmv (or another format) in your AutoCAD Bible folder and click Save.

FIGURE 22.20

The master bedroom.

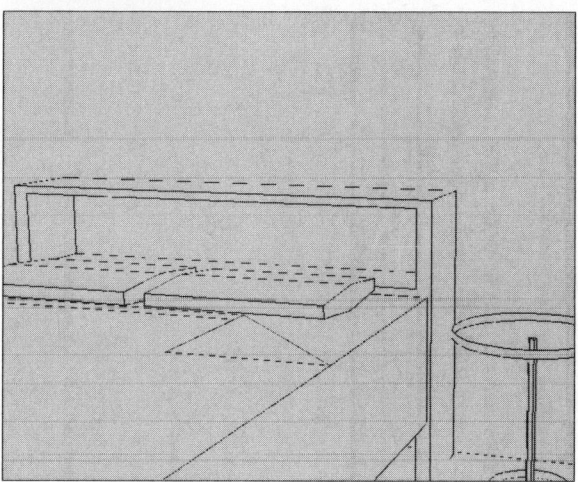

FIGURE 22.21

You can use these two motion paths to create a video file of a walk-through.

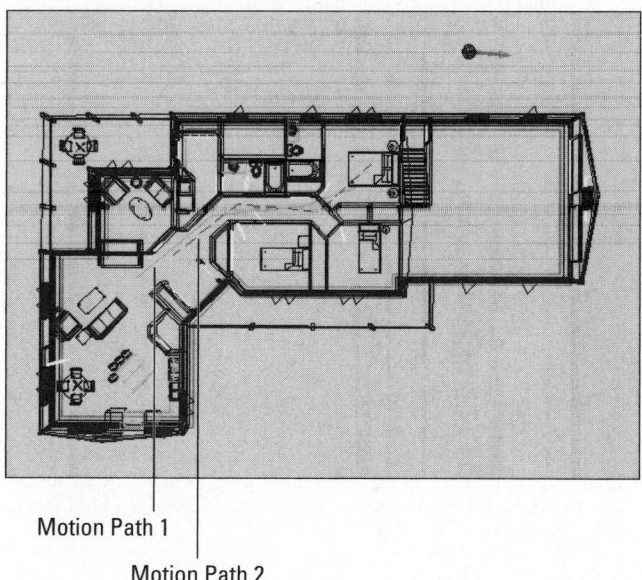

Motion Path 1

Motion Path 2

16. Double-click the movie file in Windows Explorer to view it.

17. Save your drawing.

On the DVD

You can find `ab22-02a.wmv` and `ab22-02b.wmv` in the `Results` folder of the DVD. ■

Navigating with the Wheel

The *SteeringWheel*, or *wheel* for short, is a navigation and viewing tool that combines several features in one place. The wheel appears at your cursor and comes in several variations, as shown in Figure 22.22.

FIGURE 22.22

The SteeringWheel has several variations, all of which help you navigate and view your drawing.

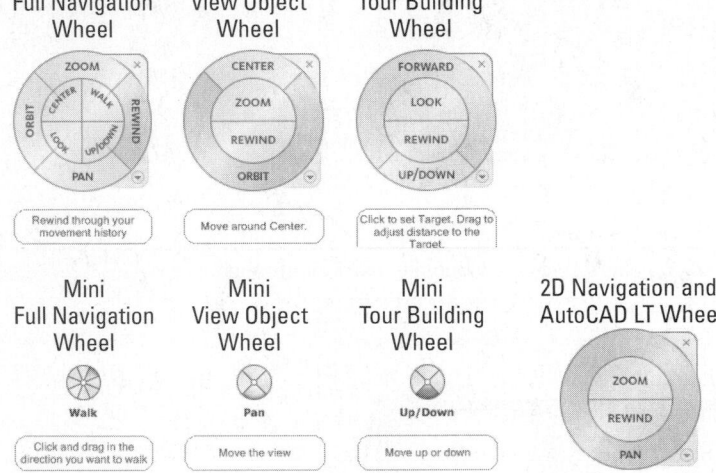

Note

The 2D Navigation and AutoCAD LT wheel doesn't offer any variations or settings. I cover the SteeringWheel for 2D navigation in Chapter 8. Here I explain the 3D navigation features, which are available in AutoCAD only. ■

 To display the wheel, choose View tab ⇨ Navigate panel ⇨ SteeringWheels (choose one from the drop-down list), or click the SteeringWheel button on the Navigation bar. If you are on a layout, or in AutoCAD LT, you see the 2D Navigation wheel.

To use any wheel, you place the cursor over the desired tool on the wheel, then click and drag. Each tool is in a section called a *wedge*. The default wheel in AutoCAD is shown at the top left in Figure 22.22 and includes the following tools:

- **Zoom.** Performs a real-time zoom.
- **Rewind.** Displays previous views in thumbnails. You can revert to any previous view by clicking its thumbnail.
- **Pan.** Pans the view.
- **Orbit.** Functions like the 3D Orbit feature, orbiting around a pivot point.

- **Center.** Defines the pivot point for orbiting. Press Ctrl as you zoom (or use the View Objects wheel) to provide a center point for zooming.
- **Walk.** Lets you walk through your drawing.
- **Look.** Swivels the view.
- **Up/Down.** Moves the view along the Z axis, like going up or down in an elevator. You drag along a Top-Bottom slider.

As you can see in Figure 22.22, the View Object and Tour Building wheels contain subsets of the tools in the default wheel. The mini wheels provide the same tools as their full counterparts, but they are smaller and don't contain the full labeling. All the wheels provide tooltips and brief instructional messages when you hover the cursor over a wedge.

To specify settings for the wheel (AutoCAD only), right-click it and choose SteeringWheel Settings to open the SteeringWheel Settings dialog box, where you can do the following:

- Set the wheel size and opacity.
- Specify if you want to see tooltips and messages.
- Specify if you want to see the wheel when you open AutoCAD.
- Specify settings for the Look, Orbit, Walk, Rewind, and Zoom tools.

When you're done with the wheel, press Esc or Enter. You can also click the wheel's X button (for the full-size version), or right-click and choose Close Wheel.

Using DVIEW to Create a Perspective View

The original command for defining views with perspective from any angle and distance was DVIEW. The newer 3D Orbit feature is easier to use than DVIEW, but you may still find DVIEW helpful for its precise ways of defining a view. DVIEW is also useful if you want to create 3D views by using AutoLISP. The DVIEW command is not available in AutoCAD LT.

Like 3D Orbit, DVIEW uses the metaphor of a camera. There is a camera point (where you are standing) and a target point (what you are looking at). By defining these two points, you can create either close-up or distance views, much as you would with the zoom or panoramic lens of a camera. The DVIEW command creates both parallel and perspective views.

Using DVIEW

To create a perspective view, type **dview** ↵ on the command line. At the `Select objects or <use DVIEWBLOCK>:` prompt, select the objects that you want to include in the process of defining the perspective view.

You should select as few objects as you need to visualize the final result if you have a complex drawing. If you want to select the entire drawing, type **all** ↵ even if the current view doesn't display the entire drawing.

Press Enter if you don't want to choose any objects. The command substitutes a block called `dviewblock`, which is a simple house. You can use the house to set your perspective view.

Tip
If you want, you can create your own block and name it `dviewblock`. **Create it with X, Y, and Z dimensions of 1 and save it in the support file search path. When you press Enter at the** `Select objects or <use DVIEWBLOCK>:` **prompt, the command looks for** `dviewblock` **and uses it to display the results of the perspective view settings.** ∎

715

Understanding the DVIEW options

When you start DVIEW, you see the following prompt:

```
Enter option
[CAmera/TArget/Distance/POints/PAn/Zoom/TWist/CLip/Hide/Off/Undo]:
```

Here's how to use the DVIEW options:

- **CAmera.** Specifies the angle of the camera, which represents where you're standing. You need to specify the angle from the X axis in the XY plane and the angle from in the XY plane. This is very similar to the way that you specify a view by using the DDVPOINT command, explained earlier in this chapter. At the `Specify camera location, or enter angle from XY plane, or [Toggle (angle in)] <35.2644>:` prompt, type in an angle from the XY plane, or move the cursor vertically to dynamically see the results. Keep in mind that moving the cursor horizontally changes the angle from the X axis in the XY plane. It can be confusing to change both angles at once, so you can limit the effect of your cursor movement to one angle with the Toggle suboption. At the `Specify camera location, or enter angle in XY plane from X axis, or [Toggle (angle from)] <66.12857>:` prompt, move the cursor horizontally to see your objects rotate around you at a constant altitude. Now, your cursor affects only the angle from the X axis. You can press Enter when you like what you see, or you can type in an angle.

- **TArget.** Works exactly like the Camera option, except that it defines the angles for the target of your viewpoint (what you would see through the camera lens). However, the angles are relative to the camera position. If you've already set the camera angles, then the target angles default to those angles that you create by drawing a straight line from the camera angle through 0,0,0. As with the Camera option, use the Toggle suboption to switch between the two angles that you need to specify.

- **Distance.** This option is very important because you use it to turn on Perspective mode. Before you use this option, the views that you see are parallel views. When you use the Distance option, you see a slider bar at the top of the screen. After you choose a distance, the Perspective mode icon replaces the UCS icon if your UCS display is set to 2D. At the `Specify new camera-target distance <3.0000>:` prompt, you can type a distance from the camera to the target or use the slider bar. Move the cursor to the right to zoom out. Moving the cursor to 4x is equivalent to using the ZOOM command and typing **4x** ↵. Move the cursor to the left of 1x to zoom in. The zoom factor is relative to the current display, so 1x leaves the zoom unchanged. You can also type a distance in drawing units.

- **POints.** Define the camera and target by specifying two points. The command line displays the `Specify target point <0.3776, -0.1618, 1.0088>:` prompt. The default target point, which is different for each drawing, is the center of the current view. You see a rubber-band line from the target point, which you can use to find your bearings when choosing a new target point. You can also type a coordinate. At the `Specify camera point <-1.5628, 0.9420, 2.2787>:` prompt, pick or type a point. You can use the rubber-band line stretching from the target so that you can visualize the camera and target points. Because it's difficult to know which 3D points you're picking, you should use an object snap or XYZ point filters to pick points.

Tip

Although it is common to choose a target point on one of the objects in your drawing, you often want the camera point to be off of the objects so that you're looking at the objects from a certain distance and angle. To pick the camera point, choose Home tab ⇨ Utilities panel (expanded) ⇨ Point Style or type ddptype ↵ on the command line (before starting DVIEW) and choose an easily visible point style. Decide which elevation you want, type elev ↵, and set a new elevation. From plan view, choose Home tab ⇨ Draw panel (expanded) ⇨ Point drop-down list ⇨ Multiple Points and pick a point. The point is created on the current elevation. Then use the Node object snap to snap to the point when specifying the camera point in the Points option. ∎

- **PAn.** At the `Specify displacement base point:` prompt, pick any point. At the `Specify second point:` prompt, pick the point to which you want the first point to pan. The model moves the distance and direction indicated by an imaginary line from the base point to the second point.

- **Zoom.** The Zoom option displays the same slider bar that you see with the Distance option, as I explained previously. If Perspective mode is not on, then you see the `Specify zoom scale factor <1>:` prompt, which works like the Distance option slider bar. If Perspective mode is on, then you see the `Specify lens length <50.000mm>:` prompt. A shorter lens length, such as 35mm, zooms you out, giving a wider viewing angle. A longer lens length, such as 70mm, zooms you in, giving a narrower viewing angle. Although the prompt shows a default in the form 50.000mm, you can only type in a number. Omit the mm.

- **TWist.** Turns your objects around in a circle parallel to the current view that you have defined. The default is 0 (zero) degrees, which is no twist. Assuming your current view looks at the objects right-side up, then 180 degrees turns the objects upside down, as if you had turned the camera in your hands upside down. You see a rubber-band line from the center of the view, which you can use to pick a twist point, or you can type in an angle.

- **CLip.** Enables you to create front and back planes that clip off the view. Objects in front of the front clipping plane or behind the back clipping plane are not displayed. You can use the front clipping plane to clip off a wall in front of the camera, thus letting you see through the wall to the objects beyond — a kind of CAD x-ray vision. Use the back clipping plane when you want to exclude objects in the distance from your perspective view. The clipping planes are always perpendicular to the line of sight, so you only need to set their distance from the target point. At the `Enter clipping option [Back/Front/Off] <Off>:` prompt, specify Back or Front to set the back or front clipping planes. Specify Off to turn off all previously defined clipping planes.

Note

When you use the Distance option to create a perspective view, the option automatically turns on a front clipping plane at the camera point. ■

- **Back suboption.** At the `Specify distance from target or [ON/OFF] <-5.5826>:` prompt, specify On or Off to turn the clipping plane on or off, or specify the distance as for the front clipping plane.

- **Front suboption.** At the `Specify distance from target or [set to Eye (camera) <556.78>:` prompt, specify Eye to set the clipping plane at the camera point. You can define the clipping plane by typing in a distance, or using the slider bar that appears at the top of your screen. As you move the cursor on the slider bar, stop to let the drawing redraw so that you can see the result.

- **Hide.** Performs a hide, just like the HIDE command, thus letting you clearly see the results of the view that you've created.

- **Off.** Turns off Perspective mode and returns you to a parallel view. Otherwise, when you leave DVIEW after going into Perspective mode, your drawing retains the perspective view until you change the view — for example, with VPOINT.

- **Undo.** Undoes the effect of the last DVIEW option. You can undo through all the changes that you have made in DVIEW.

Working with Visual Styles

Sometimes, you want to see the wireframes; other times, all the lines make visualizing your drawing difficult or you may want a more realistic look. Visual styles allow you to display your drawing in different ways, depending on your needs. Visual styles are very flexible, because you can create your own styles.

Note

Visual styles take the place of shading and the SHADEMODE command of earlier releases in AutoCAD. Visual styles are not available in AutoCAD LT. See the "Using the shading options in AutoCAD LT" section for more information about shading in AutoCAD LT. ■

New Feature

AutoCAD 2011 includes five new preset visual styles: Shaded, Shaded with Edges, Shades of Gray, Sketchy, and X-Ray. Previously, you had to create a custom visual style to get the same results. ■

Displaying visual styles in AutoCAD

To display a visual style in AutoCAD, choose Home tab ⇨ View panel ⇨ Visual Styles drop-down list. You have the following preset options:

- **2D Wireframe.** Displays objects in the familiar wireframe display, with no shading and the 2D UCS icon. It uses the 2D model space background (black by default) and offers only 2D options.
- **Conceptual.** Shades the objects, using the *Gooch* face style, which uses a gradation of cool and warm colors. The effect is somewhat cartoonlike, but can make details of your objects easier to see.
- **Hidden.** Hides the display of back edges and faces.
- **Realistic.** Shades the objects. This option displays materials that you have attached to the objects if materials are turned on. (You turn materials and textures on and off in the Materials panel of the Ribbon. I discuss materials in detail in Chapter 25.) If you are not working with materials, you'll get the clearest display with objects that are not black/white.
- **Shaded.** Shades objects, like the Realistic visual style, but shows only materials, not textures. This style doesn't show edges.
- **Shaded with Edges.** Like Shaded, but without edges.
- **Shades of Gray.** Shades objects with variations of gray.
- **Sketchy.** Adds a jitter edge. For an explanation, see the next section.
- **Wireframe.** A 3D version of 2D wireframe, with more options. Displays objects in wireframe, along with a shaded UCS icon. It uses the 3D parallel or perspective background, which by default is gray or shades of gray. (I explain these backgrounds later in this chapter.)
- **X-Ray.** Sets the opacity of faces to 50 percent.

Creating custom visual styles

 The full power of visual styles is apparent when you create your own. To create your own visual style, choose Home tab ⇨ View panel ⇨ Visual Styles drop-down list ⇨ Visual Styles Manager to open the Visual Styles Manager palette, as shown in Figure 22.23.

FIGURE 22.23

The Visual Styles Manager enables you to create and save custom visual styles.

Visual Style swatches

Create new visual

Apply selected Visual Style to Current Viewport

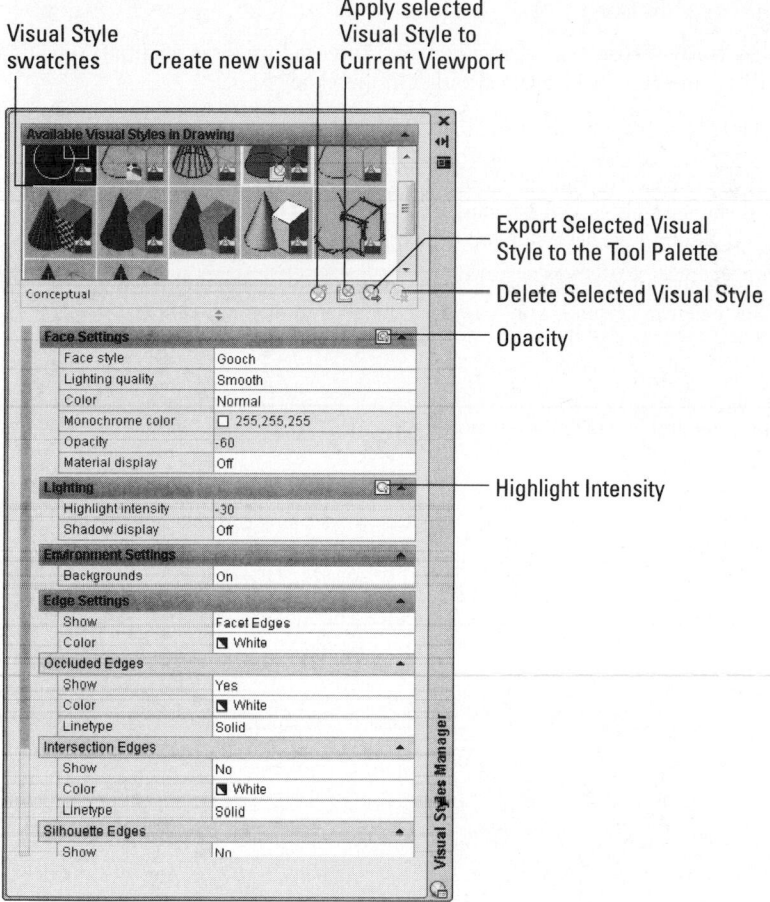

Export Selected Visual Style to the Tool Palette

Delete Selected Visual Style

Opacity

Highlight Intensity

To create a new visual style, click the Create New Visual Style button in the Visual Styles Manager to start from default settings. To use the settings of an existing style as a basis, select the visual style that most resembles the style that you want to create, right-click it, and choose Copy. Then right-click in the Visual Styles Manager and choose Paste. Then change the settings. The settings in the Visual Styles Manager fall into three groups: Face, Environment, and Edge.

Face settings determine how the faces of 3D objects look. You can set the following options:

- **Face Style.** You can set the face style to None (like 3D Wireframe or 3D Hidden), Gooch (used by Conceptual), or Realistic (used by Realistic).

- **Lighting Quality.** By default, the lighting is smoothed over curved objects. You can turn this off for a faceted look. The Smoothest option provides better results.

- **Highlight Intensity.** Controls the size of highlights created by lighting on objects without materials. The default is –30 and the value can range from –100 to 100. Larger numbers result in larger highlights. A negative number turns off highlights.
- **Opacity.** Sets the opacity of the faces.

Environment settings affect the display of shadows and backgrounds. You can turn these on or off. You add a background by using the VIEW command, as I explained earlier in this chapter.

Edge settings affect how the edges of your 3D models look. Edges are the lines or curves that border the faces. You can choose from three edge modes: Facet Edges, Isolines, or None. The Wireframe (3D) visual style uses isolines to give you a better sense of curves. The Hidden visual style uses facet edges to show just the edges and to provide a cleaner look. If you use isolines, you can choose the number of lines (the ISOLINES system variable). You can also decide if the isolines are always on top, which provides edges even to shaded objects.

Two edge modifiers, line extension and jitter, help to provide a hand-drawn look. Jitter adds additional lines, as if you're sketching. Line extension extends lines past their ends, as shown in Figure 22.24.

FIGURE 22.24

You can get a hand-drawn look with the jitter and line extension features.

 To set overhang, display the Visual Styles Manager, click the Line Extensions Edges button in the Edge Modifiers section, and change the Line Extensions value.

 To set jitter, display the Visual Styles Manager, click Jitter Edges in the Edge Modifiers section, and change the Jitter value.

Fast silhouette edges are the lines or curves around the edge of a model. The Hidden and Conceptual visual styles use fast silhouette edges, and you can increase their width for a bolder look. In the Visual Styles Manager, change the settings under the Silhouette Edges section.

Intersection edges display lines where solids intersect. Figure 22.25 shows a model with a smaller box intersecting with a larger box. The left side does not display an intersection edge between the two boxes; the right side does.

FIGURE 22.25

You can choose to display edges where solids intersect.

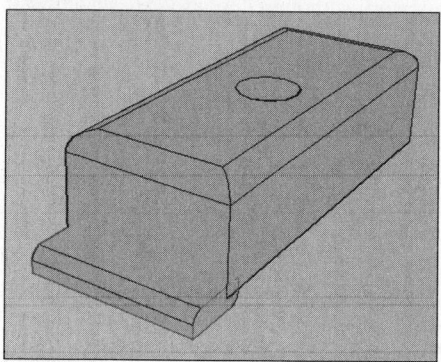
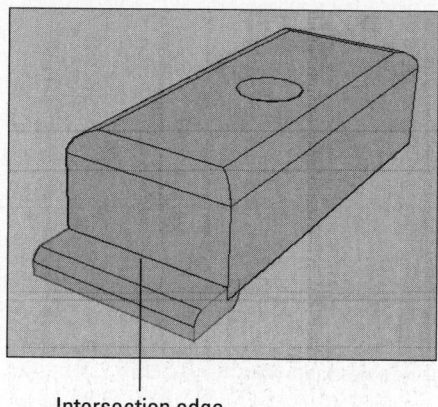

Intersection edge

When you're done designing your visual style, you can use the Apply Selected Visual Style to Current Viewport button to apply the visual style. The visual style also appears in the drop-down lists on the Home tab's View panel and the Render tab's Visual Styles panel, so you can choose it from either location. You can also use the Delete the Selected Visual Style button to delete your visual styles; however, you can't delete the styles that come with AutoCAD.

Using the shading options in AutoCAD LT

The SHADEMODE command in AutoCAD LT has only two options, 2D Wireframe and Hidden. The 2D Wireframe option allows you to turn off the shading that was set for one of the options available only in AutoCAD; you can use this when you open a drawing that was created in AutoCAD. However, AutoCAD LT has a SHADE command that provides the following options:

- **256 Color (0).** Displays shaded faces. Shading is flat, but curved faces give the impression of gradual shading because they're broken up into many faces, each a slightly different color.

- **256 Color Edge Highlight (1).** Similar to 256 Color, but highlights edges using the same color as your drawing background.

- **16 Color Hidden Line (2).** Looks like a hidden display. The non-hidden edges are in the object's color, and the faces are the color of the background of the drawing area.

- **16 Color Filled (3).** The reverse of 16 Color Hidden Line so that the faces are in the object's color, and non-hidden edges are the background color.

You control which shading method the SHADE command uses by changing the value of the SHADEDGE system variable. Type **shadedge** ↵ on the command line and then enter the number to the right of the shading method above. After setting the shading method, type **shade** ↵ on the command line.

In AutoCAD LT, you cannot edit your objects in Shaded mode, which is a better-looking version of the HIDE command. If you regenerate the drawing, the shading goes away.

Display materials, textures, and lights as you work

Materials, textures, and lights are used in rendering, which is covered in Chapter 25. You can display materials and textures that you've attached to objects, even as you work, although doing so may slow down performance. You can also display lights. To display these features, you need to use the Realistic visual style, or a visual style that uses the Real face style.

AutoCAD Only

This section applies to AutoCAD only. AutoCAD LT does not include materials, textures, or lights, which is part of the rendering capability of AutoCAD. ■

 To display materials and textures, choose Render tab ➪ Materials panel ➪ Materials and Textures drop-down list ➪ Materials / Textures On.

 To display lights that you have created, choose Render tab ➪ Lights panel (expanded) ➪ Default Lighting so that the button is selected. You can adjust the brightness and contrast of lighting by expanding the Lights panel; drag the Brightness and Contrast sliders.

Cross-Reference

If you don't see lights or materials, they may be off due to Adaptive Degradation. AutoCAD automatically turns off certain features, based on the capability of your graphics card and overall computer system. For more information, see Appendix A. ■

On the DVD

The drawing used in the following exercise on using and creating visual styles in a drawing, ab22-d.dwg, is in the Drawings folder on the DVD. This exercise is for AutoCAD only. AutoCAD LT doesn't offer these shading options. ■

STEPS: Using and Creating Visual Styles

1. Open ab22-d.dwg from the DVD.

2. Save it as ab22-03.dwg in your AutoCAD Bible folder. This drawing should display the 3D Wireframe visual style.

3. Choose Home tab ➪ View panel ➪ Visual Styles drop-down list ➪ 2D Wireframe. The background color and the UCS icon change.

4. This time, choose Hidden. Back lines disappear and the background is the same as for Wireframe.

5. Choose the Conceptual visual style. The colors of the model change to blue and green.

6. Choose the Realistic visual style. This time, if your computer system can support it, you see the bronze satin material that I attached to the drawing.

 7. On the View tab ➪ Visual Styles panel, click the dialog box launcher at the right side of the panel's title bar to open the Visual Styles Manager.

8. Click the Create New Visual Style button near the top of the Visual Styles Manager palette. In the Create New Visual Style dialog box, enter **MyRealistic** in the Name text box. In the Description text box, enter **No edges;silhouette**. You want to create a visual style that doesn't show edges within the model but displays a thick silhouette around its outside. Click OK.

9. Change the following settings:

   ```
   Material display: Material and textures
   Edge Settings-Show: None
   Silhouette Edges-Show: Yes
   Silhouette Edges-Width: 9
   ```

10. Click the Apply Selected Visual Style to Current Viewport button. You see the change in the model. The internal edges disappear, but there's a thicker edge around the outside.

11. Close or hide the Visual Styles Manager. Choose View tab ⇨ Visual Styles panel ⇨ Visual Styles drop-down list ⇨ Realistic. Then choose the MyRealistic visual style to see the difference. Your model should look like Figure 22.26.

FIGURE 22.26

The model with the MyRealistic custom visual style.

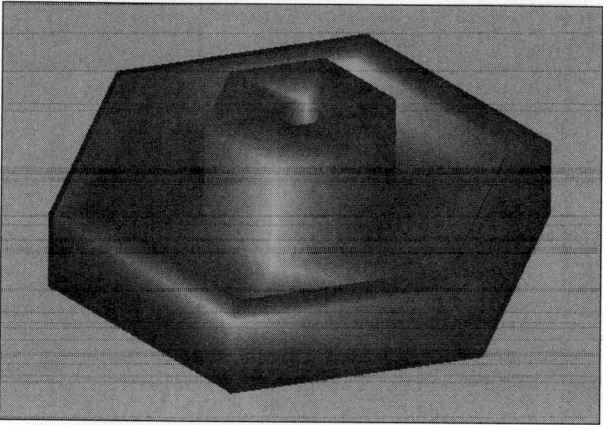

Laying Out 3D Drawings

Laying out a 3D drawing on a layout tab is an important aspect of viewing a 3D drawing, because the layout determines the final output of the drawing. AutoCAD offers three commands that help you lay out your 3D drawing in paper space layouts: SOLVIEW, SOLDRAW, and SOLPROF. (Chapter 17 explains layouts.) Another command flattens 3D drawings to convert them to 2D profiles.

AutoCAD Only

These three commands are available only in AutoCAD. ∎

Using SOLVIEW to lay out paper space viewports

SOLVIEW automates the process of creating floating viewports and orthogonal views (views at right angles from each other).

To start SOLVIEW, choose Home tab ⇨ Modeling panel (expanded) ⇨ Solid View. SOLVIEW has four options:

- **UCS** enables you to choose the UCS to work from, as well as set the scale, center, and clipping corners of a floating viewport. Use this option first. After you choose a UCS, type in a scale. You can change this later if you want. SOLVIEW then prompts you for the center of the view. Pick a point and wait until the 3D model regenerates. SOLVIEW continues to prompt you for a view center, letting you pick points until you like what you see. Press Enter to continue the prompts. The clipping corners are the corners of the viewport. At the `Enter view name:` prompt, type a name. SOLVIEW creates the first viewport.

  Choose a view name that describes the view, such as Top, Side, or East Elevation. This helps you when you start creating orthogonal views.

- **Ortho** creates orthogonal views. At the `Specify side of viewport to project:` prompt, pick one of the edges of the first viewport. Again, choose a view center and clip the corners to create the viewport. Type a name for this new view.

  If you don't see the model properly when you pick the view center, continue with the prompts, picking clipping corners where you want them. (This problem can happen when you have several separate 3D objects in your drawing.) Then pick the viewport (in model space with tile off) and do a Zoom Extents. You can then pan and zoom as you want.

- **Auxiliary** creates inclined views. At the `Specify first point of inclined plane:` prompt, pick a point in one of the viewports. At the `Specify second point of inclined plane:` prompt, pick another point in the same viewport. The two points are usually at an angle to create the inclined view. At the `Specify side to view from:` prompt, pick a point. You then pick a view center and clipping corners, and then specify a view name.

- **Section** creates cross-sections. At the `Specify first point of cutting plane:` prompt, pick a point in a viewport. At the `Specify second point of cutting plane:` prompt, pick a point on the opposite side of the model to create a cross-section. You then pick a side to view from, and enter the view scale, a view center, clipping corners, and a view name.

Figure 22.27 shows an example with a top view, an auxiliary view, and a section.

FIGURE 22.27

An example of using SOLVIEW.

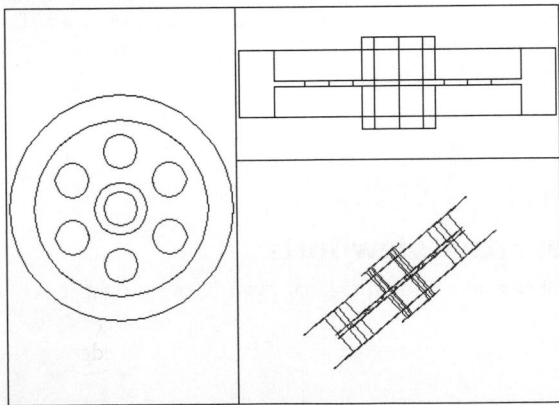

Using SOLDRAW to create hidden lines and hatching

 SOLDRAW uses the views created by SOLVIEW, and creates 2D profiles that include solid and hidden lines to represent the profiles and hatching for sectional views. You must use SOLVIEW before using SOLDRAW.

To use SOLDRAW, choose Home tab ⇨ Modeling panel (expanded) ⇨ Solid Drawing. SOLDRAW puts you into a paper space layout and prompts you to select objects, which means floating viewports. You can select all of them if you want. SOLDRAW then proceeds to automatically create the profile views. Figure 22.28 shows an example of the hatching created for a sectional view.

FIGURE 22.28

The result of using SOLDRAW on a sectional view.

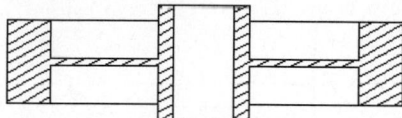

SOLDRAW uses hatch pattern defaults to define the hatch. You may have to change these settings by using HATCHEDIT.

Note

SOLVIEW creates a whole set of new layers in your drawing. SOLDRAW freezes your original layers, leaving visible only the layers that are needed to display the profile in that paper space viewport. SOLVIEW creates a special layer that you can use for dimensioning — one for each view that you create. For a view named `front`**, the layer is named** `front-dim`**. You can use these dimensioning layers to create dimensions in paper space.** ∎

Using SOLPROF to create profiles

 The SOLPROF command creates profiles like SOLDRAW, but you don't need to use SOLVIEW first. In addition, SOLPROF is more interactive than SOLDRAW. To start the command, choose Home tab ⇨ Modeling panel (expanded) ⇨ Solid Profile. SOLPROF prompts you to select objects.

Note

When you start SOLPROF, you must have already created a floating viewport, and you must be in model space. Double-click inside any viewport to enter model space. ∎

At the `Display hidden profile lines on separate layer? [Yes/No] <Y>:` prompt, type **Y** or **N** ↵. By specifying Yes, you give yourself the capability of freezing or turning off the layer that contains hidden parts of the model. You can also hide other 3D objects behind the one that you're profiling.

At the `Project profile lines onto a plane? [Yes/No] <Y>:` prompt, type **Y** or **N** ↵. If you choose Yes, SOLPROF creates 2D objects. If you choose No, SOLPROF creates 3D objects.

At the `Delete tangential edges? [Yes/No] <Y>:` prompt, type **Y** or **N** ↵. A tangential edge is the meeting of two contiguous faces. Most drafting applications don't require you to show tangential edges.

Figure 22.29 on the left shows the result of SOLPROF after freezing the layer that contains the original object; SOLPROF creates its own layers for the profile. Figure 22.29 on the right shows the result of SOLPROF after also freezing the layer that SOLPROF created, which contains the hidden parts of the model. In this case, the layer was named PH-159. Look for the *H* in the layer name, which stands for hidden. The last part of the layer name is the handle of the object that you're profiling, so it differs for each object.

FIGURE 22.29

A profile created with SOLPROF, before and after freezing the layer that contains the hidden parts of the model.

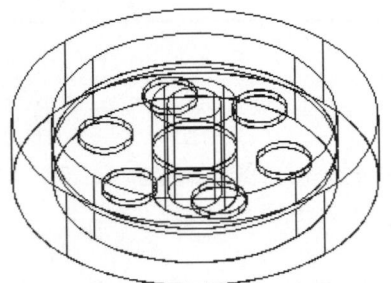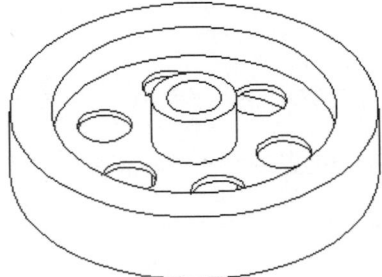

You can combine viewports created with SOLPROF and viewports created with SOLVIEW and SOLDRAW. For example, you can create two orthogonal views with SOLVIEW and SOLDRAW, and then add a viewport and use SOLPROF to create another view.

Tip

As soon as you have a separate layer for the hidden portion of the model, you can modify that layer's color and/or linetype to show the hidden lines in a contrasting color or linetype. ∎

Flattening 3D drawings

You may want to create a 2D representation of a 3D drawing. Some reasons to do this are for technical illustrations and to keep the core models of a drawing confidential. The FLATSHOT command takes all 3D objects in a drawing and makes 2D blocks from them. You can put objects that you don't want to include on off or frozen layers. This feature is available in AutoCAD only.

 Before you start, display your drawing in the desired view. If necessary, switch to parallel projection; the FLATSHOT command does not work reliably in perspective projection. Then choose Home tab ⇨ Section panel (expanded) ⇨ Flatshot. The Flatshot dialog box opens, shown in Figure 22.30, where you can specify settings.

In the Destination section, you decide where the 2D objects will go. You can insert them in the current drawing as a new block, replace an existing block, or export them to a new drawing. In the Foreground Lines section, you choose the color of the lines of the objects. Foreground lines are those that would not be hidden in Hidden visual style. In the Obscured Lines section, you decide how to treat lines that would be hidden in Hidden visual style. You can choose not to display them, for a hidden look, or use a different color or linetype. Click OK when you're done.

If you chose to insert a new block, place the block. If you chose to export to a new file, open that file. You will probably have to Zoom to Extents to see the block. Figure 22.31 shows the results, both with and without obscured lines.

FIGURE 22.30

Use the Flatshot dialog box to specify how the FLATSHOT command works.

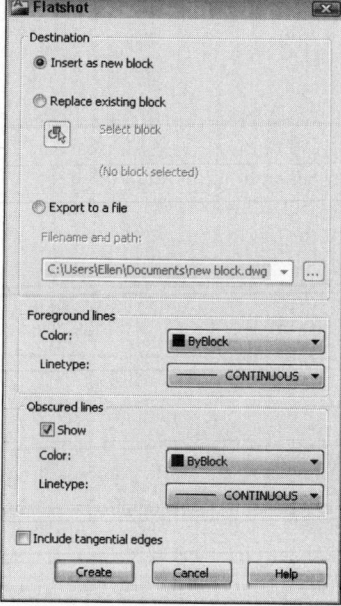

FIGURE 22.31

Flatshot can create a 2D representation of 3D objects with or without hidden lines.

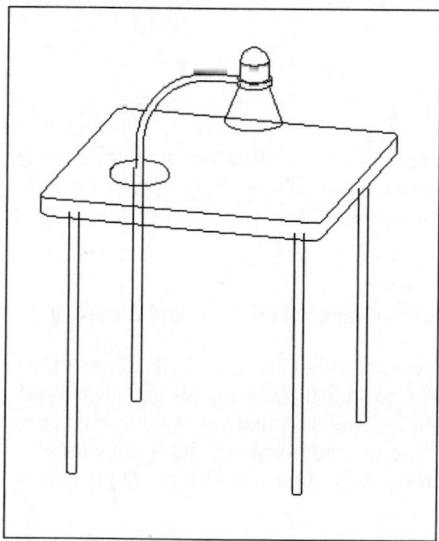
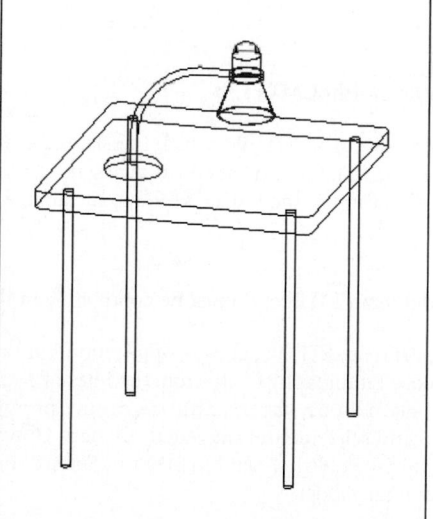

Note

The FLATTEN command is an Express Tools command that also creates 2D representations of 3D objects. In addition, it reduces elevation and thickness to 0. It is available only on the command line. ■

Printing in 3D

Stereolithography, or 3D printing, is a way of quickly creating prototypes. A 3D printer uses information from a drawing to deposit layer upon layer of a plastic, metal, or composite material, until the model is completed. Models can even be functional objects. In this way, 3D printing can allow you to see and test your 3D model. These models can also be used to show the customer what the final object will look like. Figure 22.32 shows a 3D printer and a sample model.

FIGURE 22.32

A 3D printer and a sample 3D model created with the 3D printing process.

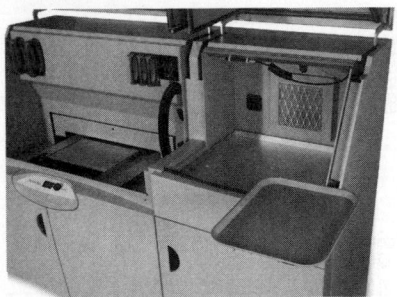 

Thanks to Z Corporation for this photo.

AutoCAD Only

This feature is not available in AutoCAD LT. ■

A 3D printer works from an STL file, which translates the drawing information into a format that the printer can understand. The STL file converts the drawing model to a faceted mesh representation consisting of a set of triangles. You can use the FACETRES system variable to control facet density.

Note

In order to export a model to an STL file, it must be completely in the positive range of the X, Y, and Z axes. ■

To export a model to an STL file, choose Application Button ⇨ Export ⇨ Other Formats. In the Export Data dialog box, choose Lithography (*.stl) from the Files of Type drop-down list. Name the file and click Save. At the Select solids or watertight meshes: prompt, select the objects that you want to include in the STL file and end selection to complete the export. However, you get additional options if you choose Application Button ⇨ Publish ⇨ Send to 3D Print Service. From there, you can get to a list of 3D printing services to print your model.

Summary

In this chapter, I covered all the ways to view your 3D drawing. You read about:

- Using the standard viewpoints for a quick look.
- Utilizing the DDVPOINT command to specify exact angles.
- Working with the ViewCube to change viewpoints.
- Creating a named 3D view with a camera.
- Adding a background to a named view.
- Using the tripod and compass for flexibility.
- Using the PLAN command to quickly return you to plan view.
- Displaying parallel and perspective projections.
- Applying 3D Orbit to view your model from any position. You can zoom and pan, create parallel and perspective views, and set clipping planes. You can also create a continuously moving orbit.
- Using ShowMotion to cycle through views.
- Walking and flying through a drawing. You can navigate through a drawing and save a movie file of the result. You can also save an animation of a motion path.
- Using the DVIEW command to let you create parallel and perspective views. You set the camera and target where you can create front and back clipping planes.
- Using the SteeringWheel, a feature that combines several navigational and view-related tools.
- Using and creating visual styles to determine how your drawing looks. Also, using the shading options in AutoCAD LT.
- Employing the three commands — SOLVIEW, SOLDRAW, and SOLPROF — that help you lay out views of a 3D drawing for plotting.
- Using the FLATSHOT command, which creates 2D blocks from 3D objects.
- Exporting to STL format for 3D printing.

In the next chapter, I explain how to create 3D surfaces.

Creating 3D Surfaces

I n this chapter, you learn to create all types of surfaces. In AutoCAD, you can draw four types of surfaces:

- **Polygonal meshes.** These surfaces use triangles and other polygons to define the surface and have been available for a long time. They are not the same as the newer mesh objects (smooth surfaces).

- **Smooth mesh surfaces.** These are also polygonal meshes, but the polygons are smaller, making the surface smoother and more flexible.

- **Procedural surfaces.** Procedural surfaces maintain properties based on how you created them. For example, if you use a spline as the basis for a surface, then editing the spline edits the surface accordingly.

- **NURBS (non-uniform ration b-spline) surfaces.** You can edit NURBS surfaces by moving and stretching their vertices.

New Feature

Procedural and NURBS surfaces are new for AutoCAD 2011. Also, a new Surface tab on the Ribbon consolidates commands for drawing surfaces. ■

Surfaces have a great advantage over 3D wireframe models because you can hide back surfaces and create shaded images for easier visualization of your models. Surfaces also enable you to create unusual shapes, such as topological maps or free-form objects. You cannot obtain information about physical properties — such as mass, center of gravity, and so on — from surfaces. Such information can be obtained only from 3D solids, which are covered in the next chapter.

Note

This chapter assumes that you are using the 3D Modeling Workspace. ■

IN THIS CHAPTER

Converting objects to surfaces

Drawing a revolved surface

Drawing surfaces with 3DFACE and PFACE

Creating 3D polygon meshes

Creating procedural surfaces

Creating plane surfaces

Creating extruded, ruled, lofted, and edge surfaces

Editing, converting, and analyzing procedural and NURBS surfaces

Working with surfaces, solids, and wireframes together

AutoCAD Only

This entire chapter applies to AutoCAD only. For information on surfaces that AutoCAD LT can create, see Chapter 21. ■

The left side of Figure 23.1 shows a lamp drawn with polygonal mesh surfaces. The back edges are hidden, so the lamp looks somewhat realistic. AutoCAD approximates curved surfaces by creating a mesh of planes at varying angles. You see the planes because AutoCAD displays them using a web of intersecting lines. AutoCAD defines the mesh by its *vertices* — where the lines intersect. The right side of Figure 23.1 shows a simple polygonal mesh with its vertices.

FIGURE 23.1

A lamp drawn with polygonal mesh surfaces is on the left. A mostly flat polygonal mesh is shown on the right.

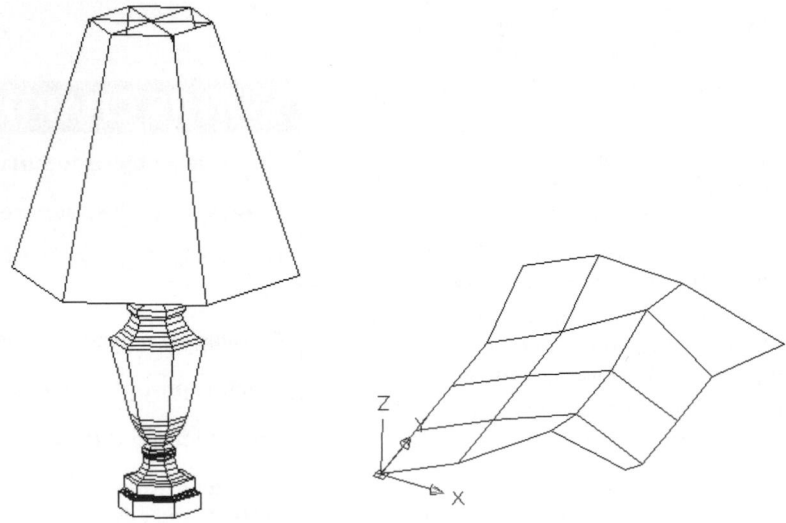

Drawing Surfaces with 3DFACE

Two-dimensional objects are often used to create three-dimensional models. In Chapter 21, I discuss how you can add a thickness to 2D solids (the SOLID command), wide polylines, and circles to make surfaces.

You can also use regions in 3D drawings. Although regions are 2D objects and cannot take a thickness, when you use the Hidden visual style, AutoCAD displays the region as a surface. When you regenerate the drawing to a wireframe display, the region appears as a wireframe again, losing its surface properties.

Another option is to use 3DFACE, which is a true 3D command. 3DFACE creates three- or four-sided surfaces that can be in any plane. You can place surfaces together to make a many-sided surface. While AutoCAD draws lines between these surfaces, you can make the lines invisible to create the effect of a seamless surface. You define the surface by specifying the points that create the corners of the surface. As a result, a 3D face cannot have any curves. 3DFACE only creates surfaces — you cannot give a thickness to a 3D face. However, you can create a 3D solid from a 3D face by using the EXTRUDE command. 3D solids are covered in the next chapter.

Using the 3DFACE command

To create a 3D face, type **3dface** ↵ on the command line. AutoCAD prompts you for first, second, third, and fourth points. You must specify points clockwise or counterclockwise, not in the zigzag fashion required by the SOLID command. When creating a 3D face:

- Press Enter at the `Specify fourth point or [Invisible] <create three-sided face>:` prompt to create a three-sided surface. Then press Enter again to end the command.

- Specify a fourth point to create a four-sided surface. AutoCAD repeats the `Specify third point or [Invisible] <exit>:` prompt. Press Enter to end the command.

- Continue to specify points to create surfaces of more than four sides. AutoCAD repeats the third- and fourth-point prompts until you press Enter — twice after a third point or once after a fourth point. Note that each additional set of prompts creates a separate surface object.

As you continue to add faces, the last edge created by the third and fourth points becomes the first edge of the new face so that adding a face requires only two additional points.

Tip

It often helps to prepare for a complex 3D face by creating 2D objects for some or all of the faces. You can then use Endpoint object snaps to pick the points of the 3D face. Place these 2D objects on a unique layer. You can also use point objects with a visible point style as a basis for 3D faces. ■

Making 3D face edges invisible

Making edges invisible makes a series of 3D faces look like one 3D face. Figure 23.2 shows three 3D faces with and without internal seams. You can control the visibility of 3D face edges in several ways.

FIGURE 23.2

You can make internal edges of a 3D face invisible.

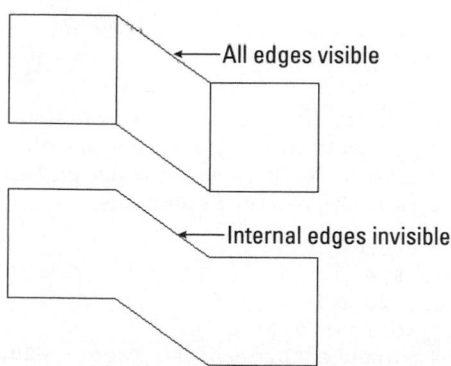

All edges visible

Internal edges invisible

Controlling visibility during 3D face creation

While you're drawing the 3D face, you can right-click and choose Invisible before each edge. Then specify the next point. However, it's sometimes difficult to predict exactly where to indicate the invisible edge.

Using the EDGE command

After creating the entire 3D face, you can use the EDGE command. The sole purpose of the EDGE command is to make 3D face edges visible and invisible — this is probably the easiest way to control the visibility of 3D face edges.

Type **edge** ↵ on the command line. At the `Specify edge of 3dface to toggle visibility or [Display]:` prompt, select a visible edge that you want to make invisible. AutoCAD repeats the prompt so that you can select additional edges. Press Enter to make the edges invisible. Although a visible edge might actually be two edges belonging to two adjacent 3D faces, EDGE makes them both invisible.

To make invisible edges visible, choose the Display option. AutoCAD displays all the edges in dashed lines and shows the `Enter selection method for display of hidden edges [Select/All] <All>:` prompt. Press Enter to display all the edges or use the Select option to select 3D faces (you can use windows for selection). Either way, you see the edges of the 3D face that you want to edit. AutoCAD then repeats the `Specify edge of 3dface to toggle visibility or [Display]:` prompt. You can now select the edge that you want to make visible. Press Enter to end the command and make the edge visible.

Note

You may need to use the 2D Wireframe visual style to see the effect of making edges invisible. However, a plot gives the correct result. ■

Using the SPLFRAME system variable

Set the SPLFRAME system variable to 1, and then regenerate the drawing to make all 3D face edges visible. (The SPLFRAME system variable also affects the display of spline-fit polylines, hence its name.) To return edges to their original settings, set SPLFRAME to 0 and do a REGEN.

On the DVD

The drawing used in the following exercise on drawing 3D faces, `ab23-a.dwg`, **is in the** `Drawings` **folder on the DVD.** ■

STEPS: Drawing 3D Faces

1. Open `ab23-a.dwg` from the DVD.

2. Save it as `ab23-01.dwg` in your `AutoCAD Bible` folder. This is a blank drawing with architectural units, based on `acad3D.dwt`. The visual style is set to 2D Wireframe. Turn on Ortho Mode. Object Snap should be on. Set running object snaps for Endpoint and Midpoint. This exercise assumes that Dynamic Input is on and set to the default of relative coordinates.

3. Type **3dface** ↵ on the command line. Follow the prompts:
   ```
   Specify first point or [Invisible]: 6,6 ↵
   Specify second point or [Invisible]: 20,0 ↵
   Specify third point or [Invisible] <exit>: 0,2' ↵
   Specify fourth point or [Invisible] <create three-sided face>: -20,0 ↵
   Specify third point or [Invisible] <exit>: ↵
   ```

4. Start the COPY command. Follow the prompts:
   ```
   Select objects: Select the 3D face.
   Select objects: ↵
   Specify base point or [Displacement/mOde] <Displacement>: Pick ❶ in
       Figure 23.3.
   ```

```
Specify second point or <use first point as displacement>: 0,0,1.5' ↵
Specify second point or [Exit/Undo]: 0,0,3' ↵
Specify second point or [Exit/Undo]: ↵
```

If necessary, zoom and pan so that you can see all three surfaces. Your drawing should look like Figure 23.3. You now have the top, bottom, and middle shelves of the cabinet.

FIGURE 23.3

The three 3D faces from an isometric viewpoint.

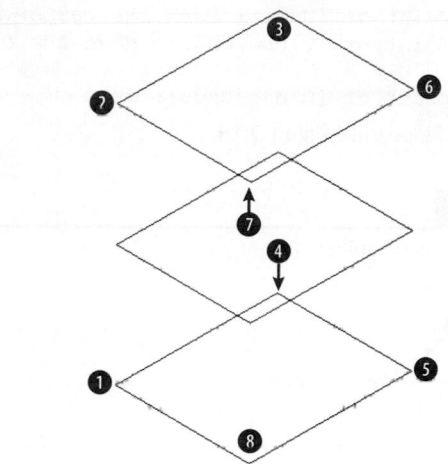

5. Start the 3DFACE command again. Follow the prompts:

```
Specify first point or [Invisible]: Pick the endpoint at ❶ in Figure
    23.3.
Specify second point or [Invisible]: Pick the endpoint at ❷.
Specify third point or [Invisible] <exit>: Pick the endpoint at ❸.
Specify fourth point or [Invisible] <create three-sided face>: Pick
    the endpoint at ❹.
Specify third point or [Invisible] <exit>: Pick the endpoint at ❺.
Specify fourth point or [Invisible] <create three-sided face>: Pick
    the endpoint at ❻.
Specify third point or [Invisible] <exit>: Pick the endpoint at ❼.
Specify fourth point or [Invisible] <create three-sided face>: Pick
    the endpoint at ❽.
Specify third point or [Invisible] <exit>: ↵
```

6. To draw the door of the cabinet, change the current layer to CONST. Start the LINE command and draw a line from ❷, shown in Figure 23.3, to 18<225. End the LINE command. Now start the COPY command and copy the line from ❷ to ❶. These two construction lines frame the door.

7. To make it easier to work on the door, choose View tab ➪ Coordinates panel ➪ 3-Point. Follow the prompts:

```
Specify new origin point <0,0,0>: Pick the left endpoint of the
    bottom construction line.
Specify point on positive portion of X-axis <-0'-5 3/4",-0'-6
    3/4",0'-0">: Pick ❶ in Figure 23.3.
```

```
Specify point on positive-Y portion of the UCS XY plane <-0'-7 7/16",-
    0'-6",0'-">: Pick the left endpoint of the top construction line.
```

If the grid is on, you may want to turn it off.

8. Start the LINE command again. Follow the prompts:

```
Specify first point: Choose the From object snap.
Base point: Pick the left endpoint of the top construction line.
<Offset>: @3,-3 ↵
Specify next point or [Undo]: Move the cursor to the right and type
    12 ↵.
Specify next point or [Undo]: Move the cursor down and type 30 ↵.
Specify next point or [Close/Undo]: Move the cursor to the left and
    type 12 ↵.
Specify next point or [Close/Undo]: c ↵
```

Your drawing should look like Figure 23.4.

FIGURE 23.4

The partially completed cabinet.

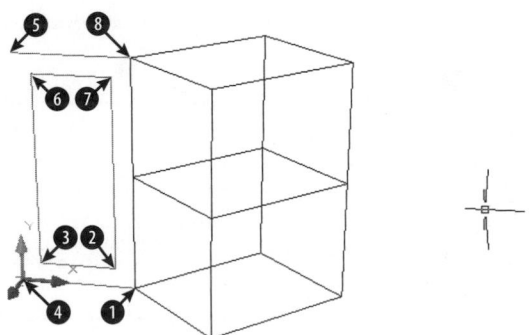

9. Change the current layer to 0. Start the 3DFACE command again. Follow the prompts:

```
Specify first point or [Invisible]: Pick the endpoint at ❶ in Figure
    23.4.
Specify second point or [Invisible]: Pick the endpoint at ❷.
Specify third point or [Invisible] <exit>: Pick the endpoint at ❸.
Specify fourth point or [Invisible] <create three-sided face>: Pick
    the endpoint at ❹. Notice the edge lines between ❶ and ❷ and
    between ❸ and ❹.
Specify third point or [Invisible] <exit>: Right-click and choose
    Invisible. Pick the endpoint at ❺.
Specify fourth point or [Invisible] <create three-sided face>: Pick
    the endpoint at ❻.
Specify third point or [Invisible] <exit>: Right-click and choose
    Invisible. Pick the endpoint at ❼.
Specify fourth point or [Invisible] <create three-sided face>: Pick
    the endpoint at ❽.
```

```
Specify third point or [Invisible] <exit>: Pick the endpoint at ❶.
Specify fourth point or [Invisible] <create three-sided face>: Pick
    the endpoint at ❷.
Specify third point or [Invisible] <exit>: ⏎
```

10. Type **edge** ⏎ on the command line. At the Specify edge of 3dface to toggle visibility or [Display]: prompt, pick the edge between ❶ and ❷ and then the edge between ❸ and ❹. (A Midpoint marker and SnapTip appear.) Press Enter. The edges disappear.

11. Choose View tab ⇨ Coordinates panel ⇨ UCS, World.

12. Type **ddvpoint** ⏎ to open the Viewpoint Presets dialog box. Set the From: X Axis angle to 200 degrees. Set the XY Plane angle to 35 degrees. Choose OK.

13. Choose Home tab ⇨ View panel ⇨ Visual Styles drop-down list ⇨ Hidden to see the result. You can clearly see through the window of the cabinet door.

14. Save your drawing. It should look like Figure 23.5.

FIGURE 23.5

The completed kitchen cabinet, including a window in the door.

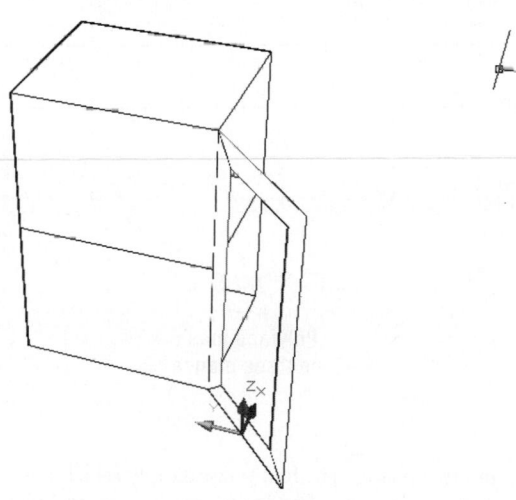

Drawing Surfaces with PFACE

PFACE draws surfaces called *polyface meshes,* which are a type of polyline. However, you cannot edit them with PEDIT. The best way to edit them is with grips. AutoCAD designed PFACE for the creation of surfaces using AutoLISP routines or other automated methods. Consequently, the input for polyface meshes is somewhat awkward. However, polyface meshes have the following advantages:

- You can draw surfaces with any number of sides, unlike 3D faces, which can have only three or four sides.
- The entire surface is one object.
- Sections that are on one plane do not show edges, so you don't have to bother with making edges invisible.
- You can explode polyface meshes into 3D faces.
- If you create a polyface mesh on more than one plane, each plane can be on a different layer or have a different color. This can be useful for assigning materials for rendering or other complex selection processes.

On the other hand, polyface meshes are difficult to create and edit. Figure 23.6 shows two polyface meshes, one on one plane and the other on three planes.

FIGURE 23.6

You can create many-sided polyface meshes on one plane, or on several different planes. After you switch to the Hidden visual style, the polyface mesh hides objects behind it.

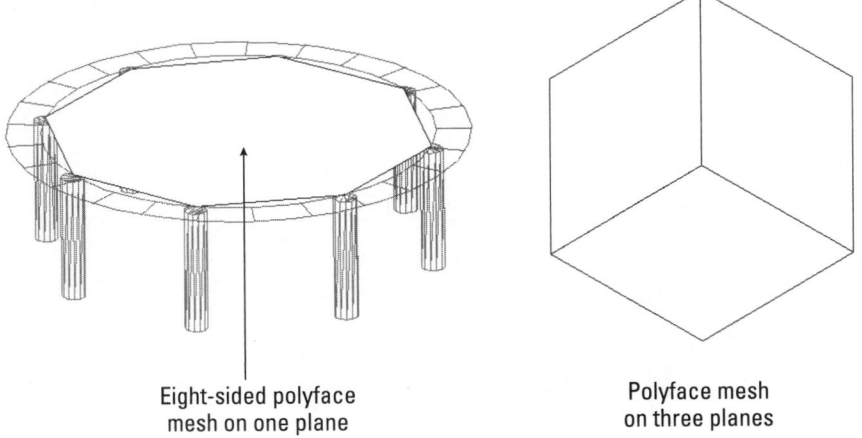

Eight-sided polyface
mesh on one plane

Polyface mesh
on three planes

The prompts for PFACE are divided into two phases. The first phase simply asks for vertices. The second phase asks you to specify which vertex makes up which face (or plane). The second phase is fairly meaningless for polyface meshes on one plane, but you have to specify the vertices anyway. Here are the steps:

1. Type **pface** ↵ on the command line.
2. At the Specify location for vertex 1: prompt, specify the first vertex.
3. Continue to specify vertices at the Specify location for vertex 2 or <define faces>: or Specify location for vertex 3 or <define faces>: prompt. Press Enter when you've finished.

4. At the Face 1, vertex 1: Enter a vertex number or [Color/Layer]: prompt, type which vertex starts the first face of the polyface mesh. It's usually vertex 1, so you type **1** ↵.

5. At the Face 1, vertex 2: Enter a vertex number or [Color/Layer] <next face>: prompt, type which vertex comes next on the first face. Continue to specify the vertices for the first face.

   If you're drawing a polyface mesh on one plane, continue to specify all the vertices in order, and then press Enter twice when you're done, to end the command.

   If you're drawing a polyface mesh on more than one plane, continue to specify the vertices on the first face (that is, plane) and press Enter. At the Face 2, vertex 1: Enter a vertex number or [Color/Layer]: prompt, type the first vertex of the second face (plane) and continue to specify vertices for the second face. Press Enter. Continue to specify vertices for all the faces. Press Enter twice to end the command.

Tip

In order to easily draw a polyface mesh with PFACE, draw 2D or point objects as a guide for picking vertices. Then you can use object snaps to pick the vertices. Also, for polyface meshes on more than one plane, draw a diagram that numbers the vertices. This helps you to specify which vertices make up which face. ■

During the second phase of the prompts, when PFACE asks you to define the faces, you can right-click and choose Layer or Color and specify the layer or color. Then specify the vertices that are to be on that layer or color.

On the DVD

The DVD contains an exercise on drawing polyface meshes. Look for it in the Bonus Exercise folder. ■

Creating Polygon Meshes with 3DMESH

The 3DMESH command creates polygon meshes. The 3DMESH command is used for creating irregular surfaces, vertex by vertex. The advantage of polygon meshes is that AutoCAD considers them to be polylines, and you can therefore edit them with the PEDIT command — although in a limited manner. 3D meshes are especially suitable for AutoLISP routines; in fact, AutoCAD supplies several. (I discuss these in the next section.) For regular drawing, you can get the same results with the newer smooth meshes, including solids (covered in Chapter 24). Smooth meshes have much better editing capabilities, so they're more flexible.

Using the 3DMESH command

Figure 23.7 shows two surfaces created with 3DMESH. The surface on the right has been smoothed by using PEDIT.

 To use 3DMESH, type **3dmesh** ↵ on the command line. AutoCAD then asks you for the Mesh M size and Mesh N size. M is the number of vertices going in the first direction. N is the number of vertices going in the other direction. Figure 23.8 shows a 3D Mesh with an M size of 5 and an N size of 3.

FIGURE 23.7

Two surfaces created with 3DMESH. The surface on the right has been smoothed, using the Smooth option of PEDIT.

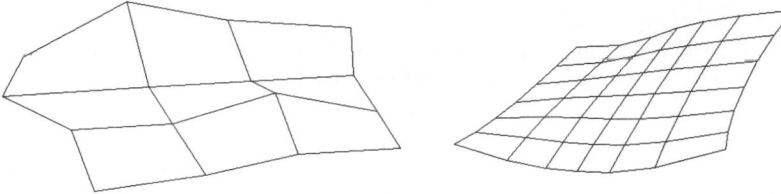

FIGURE 23.8

A 3D Mesh with an M size of 5 and an N size of 3, showing the vertex designations.

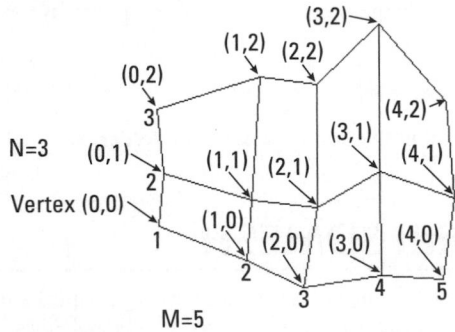

After you set the size of the 3D Mesh, you need to specify each vertex. For example, the 3D Mesh in Figure 23.8 has 15 vertices that you need to specify. AutoCAD prompts you for each vertex in order, starting with (0,0). Vertex (0,1) is the second vertex in the first column. Vertex (1,0) is the first vertex in the second column, starting from the bottom. It's a little confusing because AutoCAD starts the counting from 0 (zero), not 1. For the 3D Mesh in Figure 23.8, the last vertex is (4,2).

Note

In Figure 23.8, the 3D Mesh is five vertices wide and three vertices high as you look at it in plan view. However, you don't have to specify the vertices in the same direction. For the 3D Mesh in the figure, I started at the bottom left, continued to move up for (0,1) and (0,2), then moved to the right. However, you could start at the bottom left and move to the right for (0,1) and (0,2), and then go back to the left either above or below (0,0) — resulting in a 3D Mesh that is three vertices wide and five vertices high as you look at it in plan view. In other words, M and N can be in any direction. ∎

To smooth a polygon mesh, start the PEDIT command and select the polygon mesh. AutoCAD responds with the `Enter an option [Edit vertex/Smooth surface/Desmooth/Mclose/Nclose/Undo]:` prompt. Table 23.1 explains how to use these options.

TABLE 23.1

PEDIT options for 3D polygon meshes

Option	Description
Edit vertex	Displays the `Current vertex (0,0)`. `Enter an option -[Next/Previous/Left/Right/Up/Down/Move/REgen/eXit] <N>:` prompt. Use the Next, Previous, Left, Right, Up, and Down suboptions to move the X marker that displays the current vertex. When you're at the vertex that you want to move, use the Move suboption. REgen regenerates the 3D Mesh. Use eXit to return to the original prompt.
Smooth surface	Smoothes the surface according to one of three possible sets of equations — Quadratic, Cubic, or Bézier. Bézier results in the smoothest surface. Use the SURFTYPE system variable to set the type of smoothing. Set SURFTYPE to 5 to create a quadratic b-spline system, 6 to create a cubic b-spline surface, or 7 to create a Bézier surface. Cubic (6) is the default setting. To smooth a 3D Mesh, there must be more than three vertices in both the M and N directions.
Desmooth	Removes the smoothing on the 3D Mesh surface.
Mclose	Closes the surface in the M direction by connecting the last edge to the first edge.
Nclose	Closes the surface in the N direction by connecting the last edge to the first edge.
Undo	Undoes the last option.

You can use 3DMESH to create 3D topological surfaces. You may have a surveyor's drawing that marks measurement points. Open a new drawing, using the surveyor's drawing as an xref. In plan view, create a polygon mesh. For the vertices, pick the surveyor's measurement points. (You'll need to count them first to determine a regular grid for the M and N sizes.) Then select the polygon mesh to display its grip points. Select each grip in turn, and at the prompt, type (for example) @0,0,100.78 ↵ where the last coordinate is the measured height. When you're done, look at the surface in any nonplanar viewpoint to see the result.

Using the 3D command

AutoCAD includes several AutoLISP routines that use 3D meshes to create some standard shapes. These shapes are all options of the 3D command, which you enter on the command line. You can also type **ai_** followed by the name of the shape, such as **ai_box**. Table 23.2 shows the options and how to use them.

Cross-Reference
In Chapter 24, I cover the MESH command, which also creates standard shapes, except that they are smooth meshes. The MESH command offers more advanced editing options. ■

TABLE 23.2

3D Command Options

Example	Option	How to Use
	Box	At the Specify corner point of box: prompt, specify the lower-left corner of the base of the box. At the next three prompts, specify the length, width, and height, or use the Cube option. At the Specify rotation angle of box about the Z axis or [Reference]: prompt, specify an angle. AutoCAD rotates the box in the XY plane. Press Enter if you do not want to rotate the box. You can also use the Reference suboption, which works like the Reference option of the ROTATE command.
	Wedge	At the Specify corner point of wedge: prompt, specify the lower-left corner of the base of the wedge. At the next three prompts, specify the length, width, and height of the wedge. At the Specify rotation angle of wedge about the Z axis: prompt, specify an angle. AutoCAD rotates the wedge in the XY plane. Press Enter if you don't want to rotate the wedge.
	Pyramid	You can draw pyramids with three- and four-sided bases. You can top the pyramid with a point, a flat top, or, for four-sided bases, a ridge. At the Specify first corner point for base of pyramid: prompt, specify the first point (any point) on the base. Then specify the second and third corner points. At the Specify fourth corner point for base of pyramid or [Tetrahedron]: prompt, specify the fourth point on the base or choose the Tetrahedron option (creates a pyramid with a base of three points).
		If you chose the Tetrahedron option, at the Specify apex point of tetrahedron or [Top]: prompt, specify the apex (top point) or choose the Top option. AutoCAD prompts you for three top points. If you specified a fourth base point, at the Specify apex point of pyramid or [Ridge/Top]: prompt, specify the apex (top point) or choose the Ridge or Top option. If you choose the Ridge option, specify the two points for the ridge. If you choose the Top option, specify the four top points.
	Cone	You can create full or partial cones. At the Specify center point for base of cone: prompt, pick the center for the circle that makes the base of the cone. Then specify the radius for the circle at the base or choose the Diameter option to specify the diameter. At the Specify radius for top of cone or [Diameter] <0>: prompt, specify the radius of the top or choose the Diameter option and specify the diameter. If you accept the default of zero, you get a complete cone. If you specify a radius or diameter, you get a truncated cone. (You can specify the base's size to be larger than the top's size.) Specify the height. At the Enter number of segments for surface of cone <16>: prompt, specify the number of mesh segments. A higher number results in a smoother-looking cone.
	Sphere	Specify a center point. Then specify a radius or diameter. At the Enter number of longitudinal segments for surface of sphere <16>: prompt, type the number of north-south lines that you want. A higher number results in a smoother-looking sphere. At the Enter number of latitudinal segments for surface of sphere <16>: prompt, type the number of east-west lines that you want. A higher number results in a smoother-looking sphere. Remember that the center point is the center in all three dimensions. If you want to draw a ball on a table, it's easy to specify the center on the plane of the tabletop — but you end up with a ball that's half beneath the table!

Example	Option	How to Use
	DOme	Specify the center point of the circle that makes up the base of the dome. Then specify the radius or use the Diameter option to specify the diameter. At the `Enter number of longitudinal segments for surface of dome <16>:` prompt, type the number of north-south lines that you want. A higher number results in a smoother-looking dome. At the `Enter number of latitudinal segments for surface of dome <8>:` prompt, type the number of east-west lines that you want. A higher number results in a smoother-looking dome. The default is 8.
	DIsh	Specify the center point of the circle that makes up the base of the dish. Then specify the radius or diameter. At the `Enter number of longitudinal segments for surface of dish <16>:` prompt, type the number of north-south lines that you want. A higher number results in a smoother-looking dish. At the `Enter number of latitudinal segments for surface of dish <8>:` prompt, type the number of east-west lines that you want. A higher number results in a smoother-looking dish. As with spheres, remember that the center point is the center of the top of the dish, not its base.
	Torus	See Figure 23.9 for the parts of a torus. Specify the center of the torus. Then specify the radius or diameter of the torus. Next, specify the radius of the tube or use the Diameter option to define the diameter. At the `Enter number of segments around tube circumference <16>:` prompt, specify the number of segments around the tube. At the `Enter number of segments around torus circumference <16>:` prompt, specify the number of segments around the torus. As with a sphere, a torus is half above and half below the center point in the Z direction.
	Mesh	The Mesh option is similar to a planar surface, except that you can choose the number of mesh lines during the command. All you have to do is pick the four corners and the M and N mesh sizes. Specify the four corner points in clockwise or counterclockwise order. Then specify the M and N mesh sizes. The example shows a mesh with M=8 and N=4.

The parts of a torus.

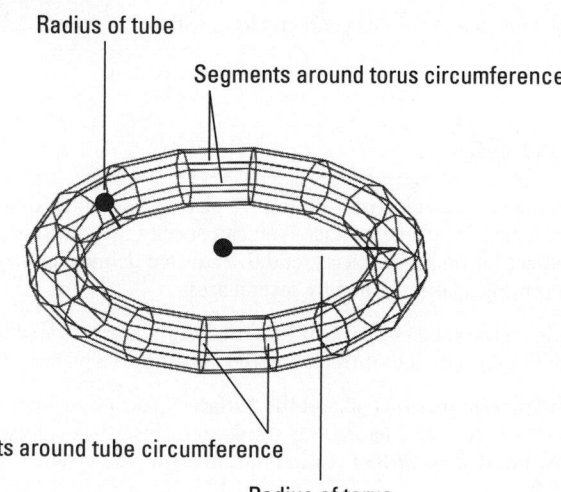

Radius of tube

Segments around torus circumference

Segments around tube circumference

Radius of torus

Drawing Procedural and NURBS Surfaces

Procedural surfaces (sometimes called analytic or explicit surfaces) contain analytic and history information, enabling them to be associative. As a result, when you edit a procedural surface, you can edit the basis of the surface, such as a spline, and the surface adjusts accordingly. For example, if you extrude an arc, you can edit the arc to change the surface.

By contrast, NURBS (non-uniform rational b-spline) surfaces are not associative. Instead, you edit them by moving or stretching their vertices. The vertices are defined in the U and V directions. (U and V are like X and Y, but don't have to match the XY directions of the User Coordinate System.)

New Feature

Procedural and NURBS surfaces are new for AutoCAD 2011. The new SURFACEMODELINGMODE system variable determines which type of surface you create. When off (0, the default), you create a procedural surface. When on (1), you create a NURBS surface.

The new SURFACEASSOCIATIVITY system variable toggles associativity. With this system variable on (set to 1), surfaces retain their connection to their source objects. The source objects are retained, regardless of the DELOBJ system variable's setting. ∎

To create a procedural surface, go to Surface tab ➪ Create panel and make sure that the NURBS Creation button is not selected. In addition, select the Surface Associativity button in the same location.

To create a NURBS surface, go to Surface tab ➪ Create panel ➪ NURBS Creation to turn on NURBS creation. (NURBS surfaces cannot be associative.)

Then use one of the following commands:

- PLANESURF
- REVOLVE
- EXTRUDE
- SWEEP
- LOFT
- NETWORK
- BLEND
- PATCH

These commands are covered over the next few sections of this chapter, along with other commands that create smooth mesh surfaces.

Creating Plane Surfaces

You can use the PLANESURF command to create a surface that is on the XY plane, and bounded by points that you specify. Choose Surface tab ➪ Create panel ➪ Planar Surface. You can specify two diagonal points that define a rectangle, or select a closed object (or multiple objects, end to end, that define a closed area). Figure 23.10 shows a planar surface, representing a lake, defined by several arcs.

The number of lines on the surface depends on the values of the SURFU and SURFV system variables. The default value for both is 6. You can use the Object option to turn closed 2D objects into a planar surface.

If the NURBS Creation button (Surface tab ➪ Create panel) is off and the Surface Associativity button is on (same location), you create a procedural surface. You can then modify the source objects — as long as they still create a closed area and are still end to end. If the NURBS Creation button is on, you create a NURBS surface.

FIGURE 23.10

A planar surface bounded by arcs.

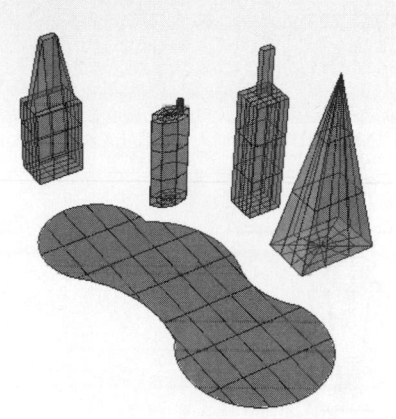

Tip

You can perform editing operations, such as union, subtraction, interference, intersection, and imprinting, on planar surfaces, as well as surfaces created with the REVOLVE, EXTRUDE, SWEEP, and LOFT commands. These last four commands are covered later in this chapter. I cover 3D editing in Chapter 24. ■

Revolved Surfaces

A common way to define a surface is to revolve an outline around an axis. You can create some very complex surfaces in this way. AutoCAD offers two commands to create surfaces from the revolution of an outline — REVSURF and REVOLVE.

Using the REVSURF command

The REVSURF command takes an object that defines an outline or profile — AutoCAD also calls it a *path curve* — and revolves it around an axis. The REVSURF command creates a smooth mesh object by default. Figure 23.11 shows two examples of revolved surfaces.

Note

You can create the older polygon mesh surface type, instead of a full-featured mesh object, by setting the MESHTYPE system variable's value to 0. Mesh objects are covered fully in Chapter 24. ■

The path curve must be one object — a line, arc, circle, polyline, ellipse, or elliptical arc. It can be open, like the path curves shown in Figure 23.11, or closed.

Tip

If you have several adjoining objects that you'd like to use as one path curve, you can use the PEDIT command to change lines and arcs to polylines and join them together. For more information, see Chapter 16. You can also use the JOIN command, which I cover in Chapter 10. ■

FIGURE 23.11

Two revolved surfaces.

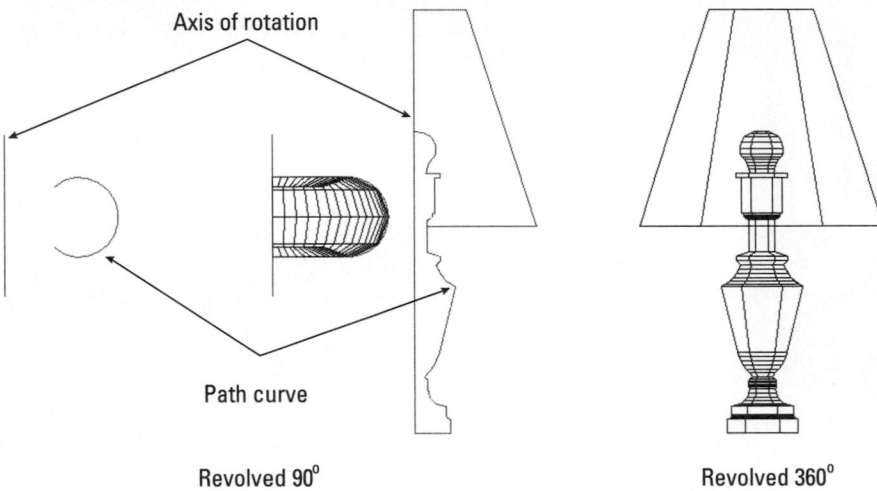

You can start the angle of rotation at any angle; it doesn't have to start on the plane of the path curve. You can rotate the path curve to any angle. Rotating the path curve 360 degrees closes the model.

When you rotate the path curve less than 360 degrees, you need to know which way to rotate. You can specify a positive (counterclockwise) or negative (clockwise) angle.

The point at which you pick the axis of rotation object affects the positive direction of rotation. Then you use the right-hand rule to determine which way the path curve will rotate around the axis. To do this, point your right thumb along the axis in the opposite direction from the endpoint closest to where you pick the axis. The direction in which your other fingers curl is the positive direction of rotation. Figure 23.12 shows the same model revolved in different directions. In the left model, the line of the axis was picked near the bottom endpoint. In the right model, the line of the axis was picked near the top endpoint.

You use the SURFTAB1 and SURFTAB2 system variables to determine how AutoCAD creates the mesh. AutoCAD calls this the *wireframe density*.

- SURFTAB1 affects how the M direction — the direction of revolution — is displayed.
- SURFTAB2 affects how the N direction — the path curve — is displayed.

The higher the setting, the more lines AutoCAD uses to display the model. However, if the path curve is a polyline with straight segments, AutoCAD just displays one line at each segment vertex.

In Figure 23.12, SURFTAB1 is 6 and SURFTAB2 is 12. To set these system variables, type them on the command line and specify the new value that you want.

Note

Although you count M and N mesh sizes by vertices, you specify SURFTAB1 and SURFTAB2 by the number of surface areas that you want to see. ■

FIGURE 23.12

From the viewer's point of view, the left revolved surface was rotated back 125 degrees, and the right revolved surface was rotated forward 125 degrees.

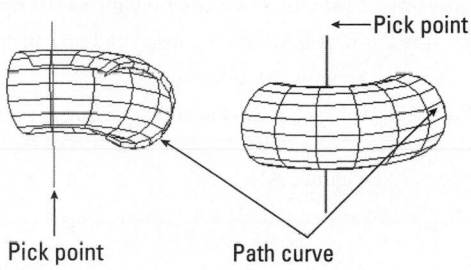

To create a revolved surface, follow these steps:

1. First create the path curve, which must be one object.
2. Draw the axis of revolution, usually a line.

3. Choose Mesh tab ➪ Primitives panel ➪ Modeling, Meshes, Revolved Surface to start the REVSURF command.
4. At the `Select object to revolve:` prompt, select the path curve object.
5. At the `Select object that defines the axis of revolution:` prompt, select the axis of revolution object.
6. At the `Specify start angle <0>:` prompt, press Enter to accept the default of 0 (zero) or type a start angle.
7. At the `Specify included angle (+=ccw, -=cw) <360>:` prompt, press Enter to revolve the surface 360 degrees or type a positive or negative angle.

You need to create the path curve and the axis in a different plane than the one you use when revolving them. You can draw the path curve and axis in one UCS and use REVSURF in another. If the object doesn't come out in the right direction, you can rotate the entire object when completed. Rotating objects in 3D is covered in the next chapter.

REVSURF retains the original path curve and axis objects. It helps to draw them in a different layer and color so that you can easily erase them afterward; otherwise, they're hard to distinguish from the revolved surface. Having the original objects on a separate layer also helps if you need to redo the revolved surface — you can more easily avoid erasing them when you erase the revolved surface.

On the DVD

The drawing used in the following exercise on drawing revolved surfaces, `ab23-b.dwg`, is in the `Drawings` folder on the DVD. ■

STEPS: Drawing Revolved Surfaces

1. Open `ab23-b.dwg` from the DVD.

2. Save it as ab23-02.dwg in your AutoCAD Bible folder. The path curve and axis are already drawn. This drawing was saved in the Conceptual visual style.

3. Choose Mesh tab ⇨ Primitives panel ⇨ Modeling, Meshes, Revolved Surface.

4. At the Select object to revolve: prompt, select the polyline to the right.

5. At the Select object that defines the axis of revolution: prompt, select the line.

6. At the Specify start angle <0>: prompt, press Enter.

7. At the Specify included angle (+=ccw, -=cw) <360>: prompt, press Enter to revolve the path curve in a full circle.

8. Save your drawing. It should look like Figure 23.13.

FIGURE 23.13

The revolved surface.

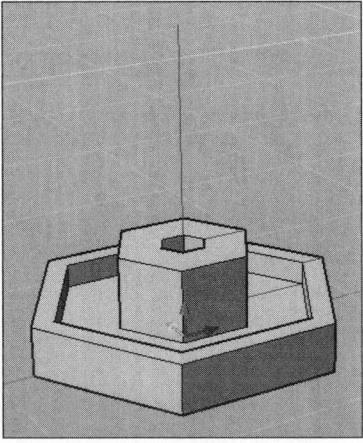

Using the REVOLVE command

The REVOLVE command allows you to select more than one object to revolve, something that you can't do with the REVSURF command. The prompts of the two commands ask for the same information, a profile and an axis, but in a slightly different way.

The REVOLVE command can create either a solid or a surface, based on the setting of the Closed Profiles Creation Mode. If you type the command on the command line, the mode is listed as either Solid or Surface and you can use the Mode option to change the setting. If you start the command from the Surface tab, you get a surface. If you start the command from the command line or the Solid tab, by default you get a solid — if a solid is possible. For a solid to be possible, the profile must be closed or the profile must be in one plane.

To use the REVOLVE command to create a surface, choose Surface tab ⇨ Create panel ⇨ Revolve. To create a procedural surface that maintains associativity, go to Surface tab ⇨ Create panel and make sure that the NURBS Creation button is off and the Surface Associativity button is on. I cover the REVOLVE command more fully in Chapter 24.

Figure 23.14 shows two examples of the REVOLVE command, one that creates a surface and the other that creates a solid. The arc is revolved around the line in each case, but when the line and the arc create a closed figure, the result can be a solid.

FIGURE 23.14

When the axis does not touch the arc, the REVOLVE command creates a surface. When the axis and the arc together create a closed figure, the command creates a solid.

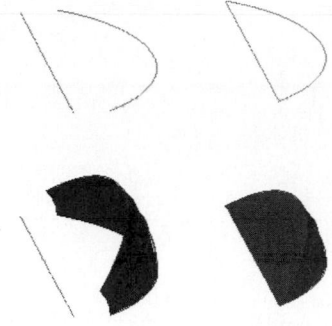

On the DVD

The drawing used in the following exercise on drawing procedural surfaces with the REVOLVE command, ab23-b.dwg, is in the Drawings folder on the DVD. ∎

STEPS: Drawing Procedural Surfaces with the REVOLVE command

1. Open ab23-b.dwg from the DVD. This is the same drawing used in the previous exercise.

2. Save it as ab23-03.dwg in your AutoCAD Bible folder. The path curve and axis are already drawn. This drawing was saved in the Conceptual visual style.

3. On the Surface tab, in the Create panel, make sure that the NURBS Creation button is deselected. At the same time, select the Surface Associativity button to the left.

4. Choose Surface tab ⇨ Create panel ⇨ Revolve. On the command line, check the Closed profiles creation mode; just above the prompt, you should see _su (for SUrface). If not, use the MOde option to choose the SUrface setting.

5. At the Select object to revolve or [MOde]: prompt, select the polyline to the right. Press Enter to end object selection.

6. At the Specify axis start point or define axis by [Object/X/Y/Z] <Object> prompt, press Enter to specify the Object option.

7. At the Select an object: prompt, select the red line.

8. At the Specify angle of revolution or [STart angle/Reverse/EXpression] <360>: prompt, press Enter to revolve the path curve in a full circle.

9. Save your drawing. It should look like Figure 23.15.

10. Select the red line that you used as an axis and click its middle grip to make it hot. Move your cursor to the left; because the model is a procedural surface, the hole at the center of the model gets larger. Move the cursor to the right slightly; the hole gets smaller. Press Esc to leave the model as is.

FIGURE 23.15

The procedural revolved surface.

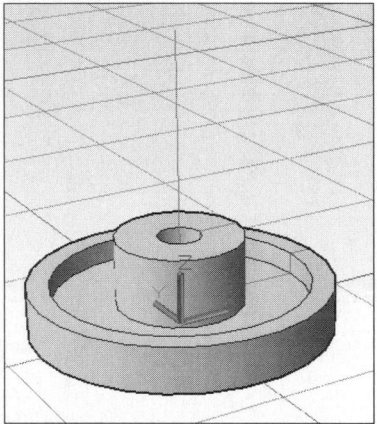

Drawing an Extruded Surface

A simple way to create a 3D object is to start with a 2D object and *extrude* it (thrust it out). In AutoCAD, extruding refers to creating a 3D object from a 2D object. Three commands, TABSURF, EXTRUDE, and SWEEP, allow you to extrude 2D objects to create surfaces.

Working with the TABSURF command

The TABSURF command takes an outline, or profile, called a *path curve,* and extrudes it along a vector that defines the direction and distance of the extrusion. The TABSURF command creates a smooth mesh object by default. Figure 23.16 shows two examples of extruded surfaces.

Note
You can create a polygon mesh surface, instead of a full-featured mesh object, by setting the MESHTYPE system variable's value to 0. Mesh objects are covered fully in Chapter 24. ∎

For the I-beam, you could have simply given the 2D polyline profile a thickness and achieved a similar result. However, you could not have done so with the extruded surface on the left, because the extrusion is not perpendicular to the XY plane that contains the 2D polyline profile. TABSURF can extrude a shape in any direction. When you select the vector object, your pick point determines the direction of the extrusion.

AutoCAD starts the extrusion from the end of the vector closest to the pick point. Use a non-planar view when using TABSURF to check that you've accurately defined the extrusion vector into the third dimension. Any of the preset isometric views are helpful.

FIGURE 23.16

Two extruded surfaces created by using TABSURF.

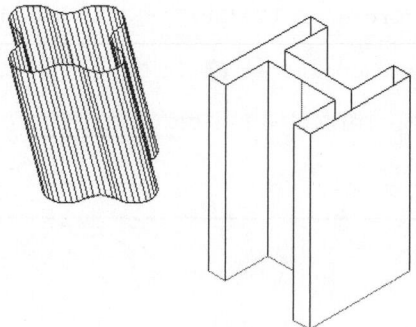

You use the SURFTAB1 system variable to control the number of lines AutoCAD uses to display the curve. If the curve is made up of polyline segments, AutoCAD displays one line at each segment vertex.

Caution

Note the I-beam in Figure 23.16. If you create an object by mirroring, stretching, and so on, you'll see extra tabulation lines at the separate segments in the polyline definition. If you want a clean look, you need to draw clean. You could use the original shape as a guide to draw a new polyline on top of the old one, and then erase the original. ■

To draw a tabulated surface, follow these steps:

1. Draw the object to extrude — a line, arc, circle, polyline, ellipse, or elliptical arc. This is the path curve.
2. Draw the vector, usually a line. If you use a 2D or 3D polyline, AutoCAD uses an imaginary line from the start point to the endpoint to determine the vector.

3. Choose Mesh tab ➪ Primitives panel ➪ Modeling, Meshes, Tabulated Surface.
4. At the Select object for path curve: prompt, select the path curve object.
5. At the Select object for direction vector: prompt, select the line that you're using for the vector.

On the DVD

The drawing used in the following exercise on drawing tabulated surfaces, ab23-c.dwg, is in the Drawings folder on the DVD. ■

Part IV: Drawing in Three Dimensions

STEPS: Drawing Tabulated Surfaces

1. Open ab23-c.dwg from the DVD.

2. Save it as ab23-04.dwg in your AutoCAD Bible folder. You see a tabletop. Its bottom is at a Z height of 30. The current elevation is 30. You're looking at the table from the SE isometric view. Object Snap should be on. Set running object snaps for Endpoint, Midpoint, and Center. The current layer is Const. The drawing is shown in Figure 23.17.

3. Start the CIRCLE command. Follow the prompts:

   ```
   Specify center point for circle or [3P/2P/Ttr (tan tan radius)]:
       Choose the From object snap.
   _from Base point: Pick the endpoint at ❶ in Figure 23.17.
   <Offset>: @-1,3 ↵
   Specify radius of circle or [Diameter]: .75 ↵
   ```

FIGURE 23.17

The tabletop.

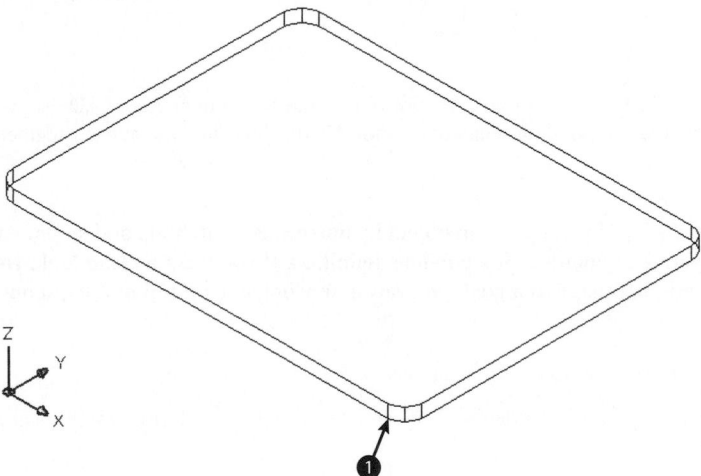

4. Start the LINE command. At the Specify first point: prompt, choose the Center object snap of the circle that you just drew. At the Specify next point or [Undo]: prompt, type 3,-3,-30 ↵ to draw a line flaring out from the circle and going down to the floor. End the LINE command.

5. Choose Mesh tab ➪ Primitives panel ➪ Modeling, Meshes, Tabulated Surface. At the Select object for path curve: prompt, select the circle. At the Select object for direction vector: prompt, select the line. (You can see only the top part of the line, but that's the part that you need to pick.) AutoCAD creates the tabulated surface.

6. Start the MIRROR command. Select the entire leg. Choose the Midpoint of the bottom edge of both long sides of the table for the two points of the mirror line.

7. Repeat the MIRROR line and select both legs. Mirror them by using the Midpoints of the bottom edge of the short sides of the table for the two points of the mirror line.

8. Do a Zoom Extents to see the entire table.

9. Save your drawing. It should look like Figure 23.18

FIGURE 23.18

The completed table.

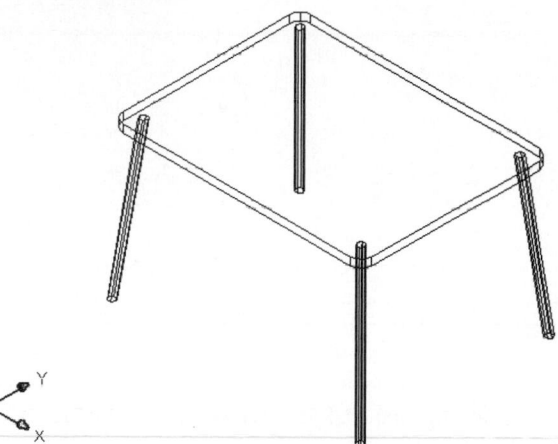

Working with the EXTRUDE command

 The EXTRUDE command is similar to the TABSURF command, but offers more options. The EXTRUDE command can create either a solid or a surface, based on the setting of the Closed Profiles Creation Mode. If you type the command on the command line, the mode lists either Solid or Surface and you can use the MOde option to change the setting. If you start the command from the Surface tab, you get a surface. If you start the command from the command line or the Solid tab, you get a solid — if a solid is possible. For a solid to be possible, the profile must be closed or the profile must be in one plane.

To create a procedural surface that maintains associativity, go to Surface tab ➪ Create panel and make sure that the NURBS Creation button is off and the Surface Associativity button is on.

To start the EXTRUDE command to create a surface, choose Surface tab ➪ Create panel ➪ Extrude. I discuss the EXTRUDE command more fully in Chapter 24.

Figure 23.19 shows an open 2D figure (an arc) and a closed figure (a line and an arc), and the results after using the EXTRUDE command.

FIGURE 23.19

On the left, the EXTRUDE command creates a surface from an arc. On the right, the command creates a solid from the closed figure of a line and an arc.

On the DVD

The drawing used in the following exercise on drawing NURBS surfaces with the EXTRUDE command, ab23-d. dwg, **is in the** Drawings **folder on the DVD.** ■

STEPS: Drawing NURBS Surfaces with the EXTRUDE Command

1. Open ab23-d.dwg from the DVD.

2. Save it as ab23-05.dwg in your AutoCAD Bible folder. You see a red keyhole shape, the base for a model. Object Snap should be on. Set running object snaps for Endpoint.

3. On the Surface tab, in the Create panel, make sure that the NURBS Creation button is on and the Surface Associativity button is off.

4. Choose Surface tab ⇨ Create panel ⇨ Extrude. On the command line, check the Closed profiles creation mode; just above the prompt, you should see _su (for SUrface). If not, use the MOde option to choose the SUrface setting.

5. At the Select objects to extrude or [Mode]: prompt, select the red base, which is a polyline, and press Enter to end selection.

6. At the Specify height of extrusion or [Direction/Path/Taper angle]: prompt, type 8 ↵. The model should look like Figure 23.20.

7. Select the face closest to you, at ❶ in Figure 23.20. Click the central grip to make it hot. At the prompt for a stretch point, type @5,0 ↵.

8. To extend the rest of the model, choose Surface tab ⇨ Edit panel ⇨ Surface Extend. At the Select surface edges to extend: prompt, select the end edges at ❷ and ❸ in Figure 23.20. Press Enter to end selection. (I cover this command later in this chapter.)

9. At the `Specify extend distance or [Modes]:` prompt, enter **m** ↵ to specify the extension mode.

10. At the `Extension mode [Extend/Stretch] <Extend>:` prompt, enter **s** ↵ to stretch the selected edges.

11. At the `Creation type [Merge/Append]:` prompt, enter **m** ↵ to extend the existing surface without creating a new one.

12. At the `Specify extend distance or [Modes]:` prompt, enter **@5,0** ↵. AutoCAD extends the edges to meet the new location of the end surface.

13. Save your drawing.

FIGURE 23.20

The extruded NURBS surface.

Sweeping objects along a path

Sweeping is similar to extruding, but you have more options. Like the EXTRUDE command, the SWEEP command can create both surfaces and solids, based on the setting of the Closed Profiles Creation Mode. If you type the command on the command line, the mode lists either Solid or Surface and you can use the MOde option to change the setting. If you start the command from the Surface tab, you get a surface. If you start the command from the command line or the Solid tab, you get a solid — if a solid is possible.

To create a procedural surface that maintains associativity, go to Surface tab ⇨ Create panel and make sure that the NURBS Creation button is off and the Surface Associativity button is on.

To start the SWEEP command to create a surface, choose Surface tab ⇨ Create panel ⇨ Sweep. I discuss the SWEEP command more fully in Chapter 24.

 Figure 23.21 shows two sweeps. On the left, an arc is swept along a helix, creating a surface. On the right, a circle is swept along the helix, creating a solid. You can scale the profile and twist it to create some very interesting models. To start the SWEEP command to create a surface, choose Surface tab ⇨ Create panel ⇨ Sweep. I cover the SWEEP command fully in the next chapter, where I discuss solids.

FIGURE 23.21

You can create interesting surfaces and solids by using the SWEEP command.

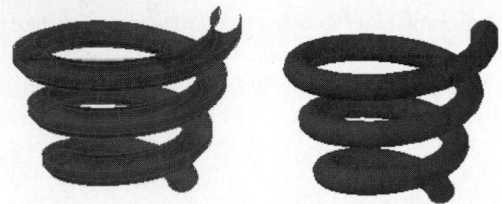

Drawing Surfaces Between Objects

If you have two or more existing objects, you may want to define the surface that would extend between these objects. Or, you may want to extrapolate a surface along two or more objects. You can use several commands to create these surfaces.

Creating ruled surfaces

Use the RULESURF command to create a surface that extends between two 2D objects. The objects can be lines, polylines (2D or 3D), circles, ellipses, elliptical arcs, splines, points, or helixes. The two objects must be either both open or both closed. Only one of the two can be a point.

Use the SURFTAB1 system variable to control the number of lines that AutoCAD uses to display the surface. Figure 23.22 shows some ruled surfaces.

Note

The RULESURF command creates a smooth mesh object by default. You can create a polyface or polygon mesh surface, instead of a full-featured mesh object, by setting the MESHTYPE system variable's value to 0. Mesh objects are covered fully in Chapter 24.

The pick points of the two objects affect the resulting curve. If you pick them both on the same side, you get the type of curves shown on the left in Figure 23.22. If you pick them on opposite sides, the curve intersects itself, as shown on the right in Figure 23.22. ■

Follow these steps to draw a ruled surface:

1. Draw the two objects for the ruled surface.
 2. Choose Mesh tab ⇨ Primitives panel ⇨ Modeling, Meshes, Ruled Surface.
3. At the Select first defining curve: prompt, choose the first object.
4. At the Select second defining curve: prompt, choose the second object.

On the DVD

The drawing used in the following exercise on drawing ruled surfaces, ab23-d.dwg, is in the Drawings folder on the DVD. ■

FIGURE 23.22

Ruled surfaces.

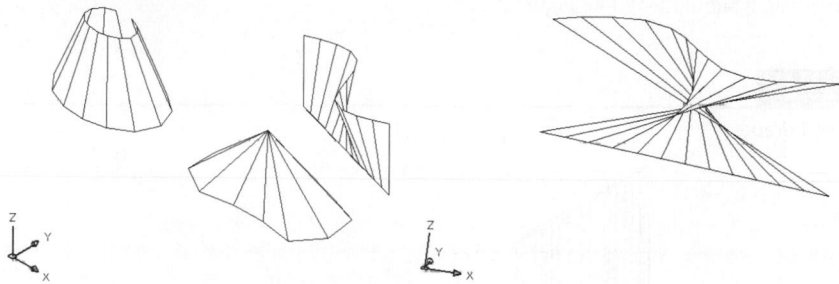

STEPS: Drawing Ruled Surfaces

1. Open ab23-e.dwg from the DVD.
2. Save it as ab23-06.dwg in your AutoCAD Bible folder. You see a spline, as shown in Figure 23.23. In this exercise, you use the spline to draw some drapes.

FIGURE 23.23

A spline.

3. Mirror the spline. For the mirror line, turn on Ortho Mode and use ❶ and ❷, as shown in Figure 23.23. Don't delete the original spline.
4. Start the COPY command and select both splines. At the Specify base point or [Displacement/mOde] <Displacement>: prompt, type **0,0,73** ↵ to copy the splines 73 units in the positive Z direction. Press Enter at the Specify second point or <use first point as displacement>: prompt.
5. Choose Home tab ➪ View panel ➪ Views 3D (3D Navigation) drop-down list ➪ SE Isometric.

 6. Choose Mesh tab ➪ Primitives panel ➪ Modeling, Meshes, Ruled Surface. At the Select first defining curve: prompt, choose the top-right spline near its right endpoint. At the Select second defining curve: prompt, choose the bottom-right spline near its right endpoint.

7. Repeat the RULESURF command. At the `Select first defining curve:` prompt, choose the top-left spline near its left endpoint. At the `Select second defining curve:` prompt, choose the bottom-left spline near its left endpoint.

8. Save your drawing. It should look like Figure 23.24.

FIGURE 23.24

The completed drapes.

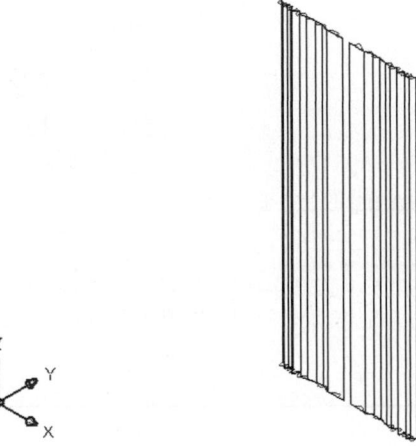

Lofting objects

The LOFT command lets you choose two or more 2D objects and creates a new surface or solid by interpolating through them. The LOFT command can create both surfaces and solids, based on the setting of the Closed Profiles Creation Mode. If you type the command on the command line, the mode lists either Solid or Surface and you can use the MOde option to change the setting. If you start the command from the Surface tab, you get a surface. If you start the command from the command line or the Solid tab, you get a solid — if a solid is possible.

To create a procedural surface that maintains associativity, go to Surface tab ➪ Create panel and make sure that the NURBS Creation button is off and the Surface Associativity button is on.

 Figure 23.25 shows two lofts. On the left is a surface created from four arcs. On the right is a solid created from four circles. To start the LOFT command to create a surface, choose Surface tab ➪ Create panel ➪ Loft. The LOFT command has a number of parameters that you need to set. I cover this command in detail in Chapter 24.

Using the EDGESURF command

For the EDGESURF command, you need four touching objects. The objects can be lines, arcs, splines, or polylines (2D or 3D). EDGESURF creates a smooth mesh that approximates a *Coon's surface patch mesh* — a surface defined by four edges. Figure 23.26 shows an edge surface.

FIGURE 23.25

You can create either a surface or a solid with the LOFT command.

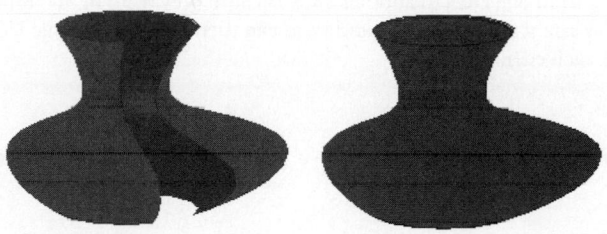

Note

You can create a polygon mesh surface, instead of a full-featured mesh object, by setting the MESHTYPE system variable's value to 0. Mesh objects are covered fully in Chapter 24. ∎

FIGURE 23.26

An edge surface created with the EDGESURF command.

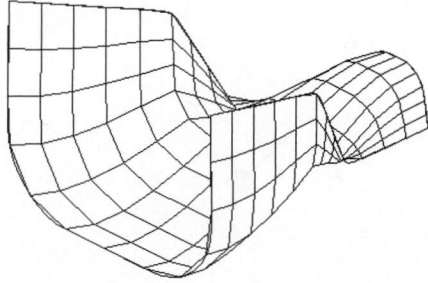

Use the SURFTAB1 and SURFTAB2 system variables to vary the displayed lines in each direction.

Follow these steps to create an edge surface:

1. Draw the four objects to create a boundary for the surface. They must touch, so use Endpoint object snaps to create them or to move them into place.

 2. Choose Mesh tab ⇨ Primitives panel ⇨ Modeling, Meshes, Edge Surface.

3. AutoCAD prompts you to select edges 1 through 4. You can select them in any order.

Creating the four edges involves moving from one UCS to another UCS because they're all in 3D. It helps to create a bounding box for your object by using the BOX command. You can then use the dynamic UCS feature to temporarily change UCSs for each edge.

On the DVD

The drawing used in the following exercise on drawing edge surfaces, ab23-e.dwg, is in the Drawings **folder on the DVD.** ■

STEPS: Drawing Edge Surfaces

1. Open ab23-f.dwg from the DVD.
2. Save it as ab23-07.dwg in your AutoCAD Bible folder. You see four curves in a bounding box, as shown in Figure 23.27. In this exercise, you use the curves to draw a dustpan.

> **FIGURE 23.27**
>
> The four curves are the basis for creating an edge surface.

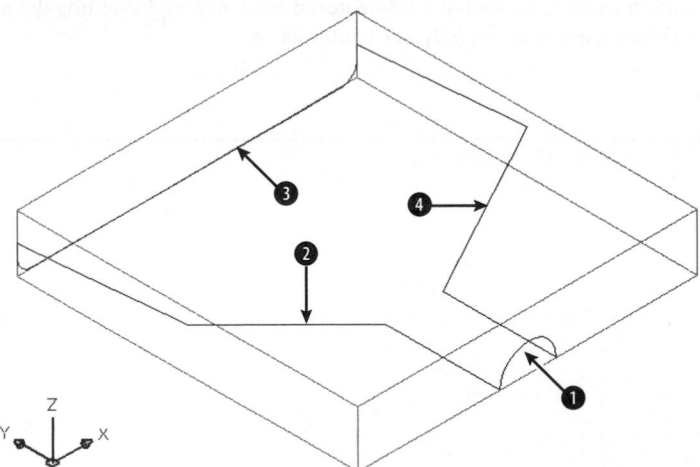

3. Freeze the Const layer.

4. Choose Mesh tab ⇨ Primitives panel ⇨ Modeling, Meshes, Edge Surface. At the prompts, select ❶, ❷, ❸, and ❹, shown in Figure 23.28.

5. Choose Home tab ⇨ View panel ⇨ Visual Styles drop-down list ⇨ Hidden to see the result.

6. Save your drawing. It should look like Figure 23.28. It's either a dustpan or a starship — your choice.

FIGURE 23.28

The completed dustpan — or starship.

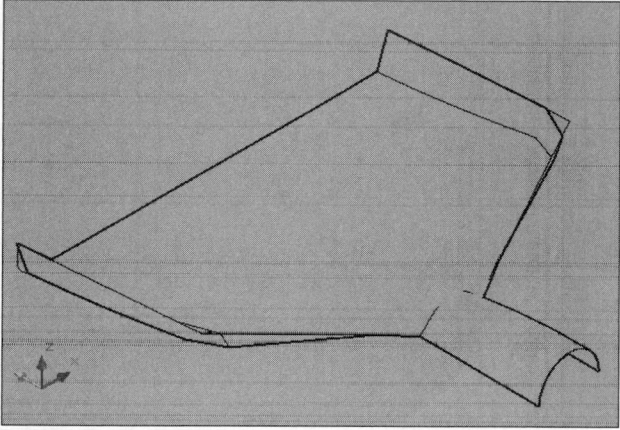

Using the SURFNETWORK command

The SURFNETWORK command creates a surface between a number of curves or the edges of surfaces or solids in two directions, called U and V. (U and V are like X and Y, but can be in any direction; they don't have to match the UCS.) Figure 23.29 shows some splines on the left, which were used to create the surface on the right.

New Feature

The SURFNETWORK command is new for AutoCAD 2011. ∎

FIGURE 23.29

The three splines in the U direction and two splines in the V direction create the network surface below.

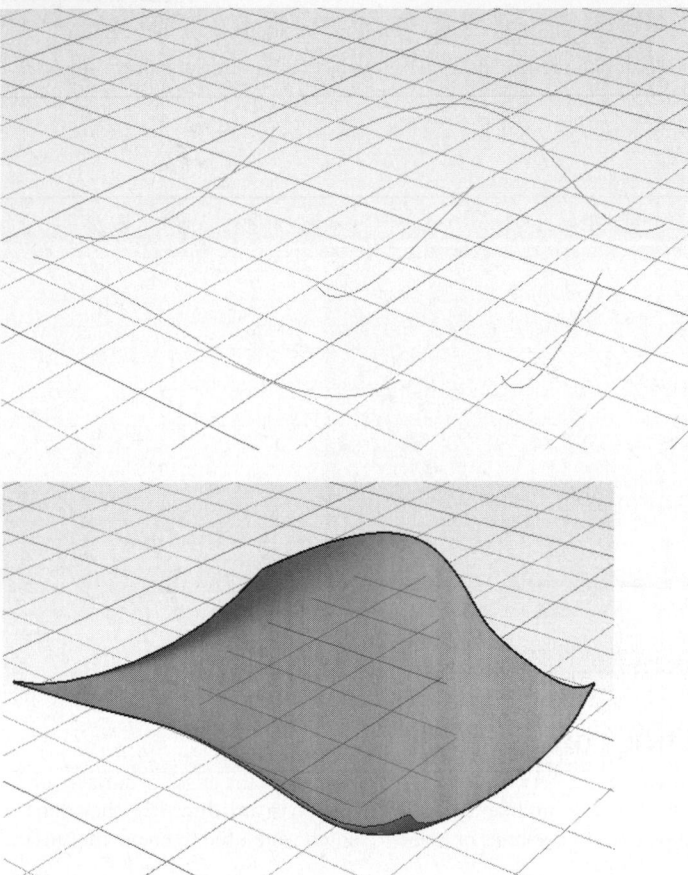

To create a procedural surface that maintains associativity, go to Surface tab ⇨ Create panel and make sure that the NURBS Creation button is off and the Surface Associativity button is on. To create a NURBS surface, the NURBS Creation button should be on and the Surface Associativity button off.

To create a surface using the SURFNETWORK command, follow these steps:

1. Create at least two curves or edges in one direction (the U direction) and then at least two perpendicular to the first (the V direction).

 2. Choose Surface tab ⇨ Create panel ⇨ Network Surface.

3. At the Select curves or surface edges in the first direction: prompt, select the edges. Press Enter to end selection.

4. At the Select curves or surface edges in second direction: prompt, select the edges. Press Enter to end selection.

On the DVD

The drawing used in the following exercise on drawing network surfaces, `ab23-g.dwg`, is in the `Drawings` folder on the DVD. ■

STEPS: Drawing Network Surfaces

1. Open `ab23-g.dwg` from the DVD.

2. Save it as `ab23-08.dwg` in your `AutoCAD Bible` folder. You see three splines in one direction and two in a perpendicular direction.

3. Choose Surface tab ⇨ Create panel ⇨ Surface Associativity. The NURBS Creation button to the right should not be selected. This will create a procedural surface.

 4. Choose Surface tab ⇨ Create panel ⇨ Network Surface.

5. At the `Select curves or surface edges in the first direction:` prompt, select the three edges that run approximately parallel to each other. Press Enter to end selection.

6. At the `Select curves or surface edges in second direction:` prompt, select the other two edges. Press Enter to end selection.

7. AutoCAD creates the network surface. Your drawing should look like Figure 23.30.

FIGURE 23.30

The network surface, shown in the Conceptual visual style.

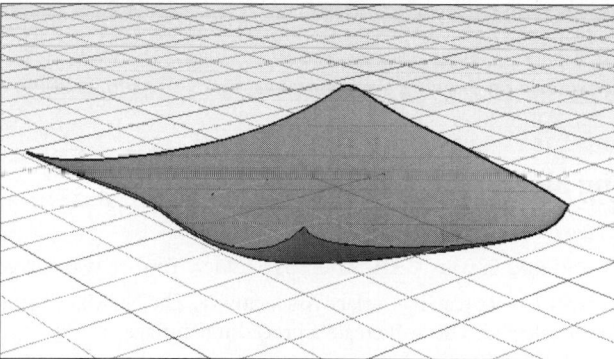

Connecting surfaces with the SURFBLEND command

The SURFBLEND command connects edges of two surfaces or surfaces and solids, and gives you options to specify the following properties of the blend:

- **Continuity.** Specifies how the two surfaces meet. You can choose G0 (Position, usually the sharpest edge), G1 (Tangent), or G2 (Curvature, a curved blend). The default is G0. Figure 23.31 shows a blend surface using each of these choices.

- **Bulge.** Determines the roundness of the blend. You can specify values from 0 to 1. The default is .5. Bulge only applies to blends that have G1 or G2 continuity.

New Feature

The SURFBLEND command is new for AutoCAD 2011. ■

Not all edges can be connected with a blend surface. The problem is usually the spatial relationship between the edges that you select.

To create a procedural surface that maintains associativity, go to Surface tab ⇨ Create panel and make sure that the NURBS Creation button is off and the Surface Associativity button is on. To create a NURBS surface, the NURBS Creation button should be on and the Surface Associativity button off.

To draw a blend surface, follow these steps:

1. Create at least two curves or edges in one direction (the U direction) and then at least two perpendicular to the first (the V direction).

2. Choose Surface tab ⇨ Create panel ⇨ Blend. (The tooltip says Surface Blend.)

3. At the Select first surface edges to blend: prompt, select the edges. Press Enter to end selection.

4. At the Select second surface edges to blend: prompt, select the edges. Press Enter to end selection.

5. At the Press Enter to accept the blend surface or [CONtinuity/Bulge magnitude]: prompt, use the drop-down grip or the CONtinuity option to specify G0, G1, or G2. Using the drop-down grips at both ends of the connection, you can choose a continuity for each point; if you use the prompt, you get a prompt for each edge. Use the Bulge magnitude option to determine the roundness of the connection. Press Enter to accept the blend and end the command.

On the DVD

The drawing used in the following exercise on drawing blend surfaces, ab23-h.dwg, is in the Drawings folder on the DVD. ■

STEPS: Drawing Blend Surfaces

1. Open ab23-h.dwg from the DVD.

2. Save it as ab23-09.dwg in your AutoCAD Bible folder. You see two curved surfaces.

3. Choose Surface tab ⇨ Create panel ⇨ Surface Associativity. The NURBS Creation button to the right should not be selected. This will create a procedural surface.

 4. Choose Surface tab ⇨ Create panel ⇨ Blend.

5. At the Select first surface edges to blend: prompt, select the upper edge of the leftmost surface. Press Enter to end selection.

6. At the Select second surface edges to blend: prompt, select the lower edge of the rightmost surface. Press Enter to end selection.

7. At the Press Enter to accept the blend surface or [CONtinuity/Bulge magnitude]: prompt, use the drop-down grips to change both edges to G2. Notice the difference in the curvature.

8. Type b ↵ to use the Bulge Magnitude option. Enter 1 ↵ twice to set each edge's bulge magnitude to 1. Notice how the bulge increases.

9. Press Enter to accept the surface and end the command. Your drawing should look like Figure 23.32.

FIGURE 23.31

The blend surface connects the holes in the two flat surfaces. From top to bottom, you see a continuity of G0, G1, and G2.

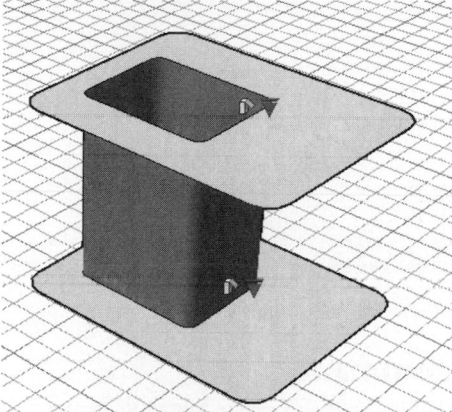

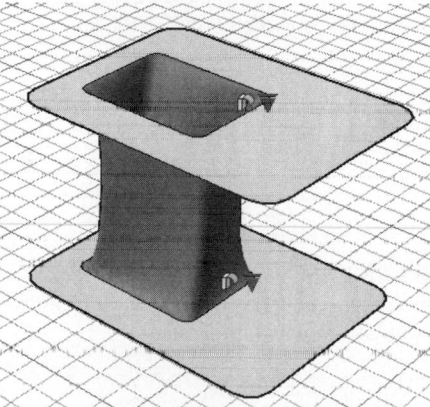

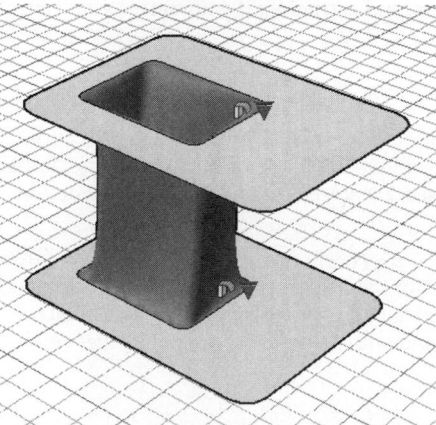

FIGURE 23.32

The blend surface.

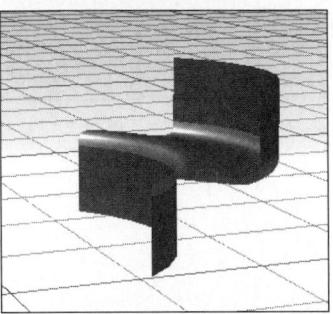

Patching holes with the SURFPATCH command

The SURFPATCH command patches holes. You can think of SURFPATCH as a way to put a roof over a closed surface with a hole in its middle. You can also use it to create a surface from a closed 2D object, such as a polyline, ellipse, circle, or spline; in this case, the result is similar to using the PLANESURF command with the Object option.

Like the SURFBLEND command, you can specify continuity and bulge. In addition, you can constrain the patch with curves or points, as shown on the right side of Figure 23.33.

New Feature

The SURFPATCH command is new for AutoCAD 2011. ■

To create a procedural surface that maintains associativity, go to Surface tab ⇨ Create panel and make sure that the NURBS Creation button is off and the Surface Associativity button is on. To create a NURBS surface, the NURBS Creation button should be on and the Surface Associativity button off.

To create a patch surface, follow these steps:

1. Draw surfaces that form a closed loop, such as the one shown on the left in Figure 23.33, which was created by drawing a rectangle, filleting its corners, and extruding. If you want to constrain the patch with curves or points, draw them as well.

 2. Choose Surface tab ⇨ Create panel ⇨ Patch.

3. At the Select surface edges to patch or <Select Curves>: prompt, select the surface edges. (In Figure 23.33, the surface has eight edges — four sides and four filleted corners.) Press Enter to end selection. To create a surface from a closed 2D object, use the Select Curves option and select the object.

4. At the Press Enter to accept the patch surface or [CONtinuity/Bulge magnitude/ CONStrain geometry]: prompt, press Enter to place the patch surface and end the command. Use the CONtinuity or Bulge Magnitude option, as explained previously for the SURFBLEND command. If you use the CONstrain geometry option, select the curves or points that you drew.

FIGURE 23.33

A closed loop surface, before and after patching. The patch uses G2 continuity to create a domed effect. On the bottom, the surface was constrained by a spline.

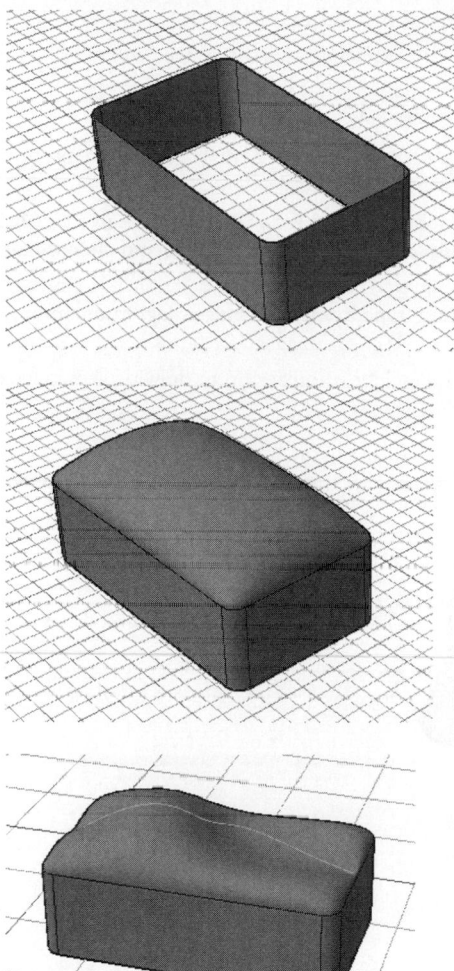

On the DVD

The drawing used in the following exercise on drawing patch surfaces, ab23-i.dwg, is in the Drawings folder on the DVD. ■

STEPS: Drawing Patch Surfaces

1. Open ab23-i.dwg from the DVD.

2. Save it as ab23-10.dwg in your AutoCAD Bible folder. You see a desk lamp. The top cylinder is a surface, which needs a cap that will be the on-off switch.

3. Choose Surface tab ➪ Create panel ➪ Surface Associativity. This will create a procedural surface. The NURBS Creation button to the right should not be selected.

4. Choose Surface tab ➪ Create panel ➪ Patch.

5. At the Select surface edges to patch or <Select Curves>: prompt, select the upper edge of the cylinder surface. Press Enter to end selection.

6. At the Press Enter to accept the patch surface or [CONtinuity/Bulge magnitude/ CONStrain geometry]: prompt, click the drop-down grip and choose Curvature (G2).

7. At the Press Enter to accept the patch surface or [CONtinuity/Bulge magnitude/ CONStrain geometry]: prompt, type **b** ↵ for the Bulge Magnitude option. Type **.75** ↵ to make the bulge higher.

8. Press Enter to accept the surface and end the command. Your drawing should look like Figure 23.34.

FIGURE 23.34

The patch surface represents the lamp's on-off switch.

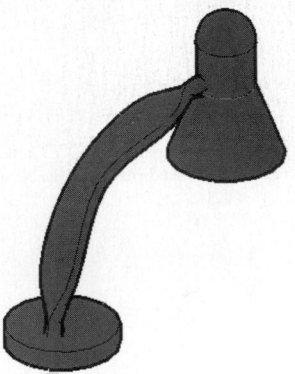

Editing and Analyzing Surfaces

How you edit a surface depends on the type of surface you created. The following lists the newer surfaces and their basic editing process:

- **Smooth meshes.** Use the editing tools on the Mesh tab (which I cover in Chapter 24). For example, you can smooth and crease meshes, as well as extrude, split, and merge faces.

- **Procedural surfaces.** Edit the objects you used to create the surface, and the surface adjusts. For example, if you extruded a spline, you can edit the spline to change the extruded surface.
- **NURBS surfaces.** Edit the vertices of the surface, using grip editing techniques. To display the vertices, choose Surface tab ⇨ Control Vertices panel ⇨ Show CV. In the same panel, you can hide, remove, add, and rebuild vertices.

Tip
You can turn procedural surfaces into NURBS surfaces, but not vice versa. So it makes sense to start out creating a procedural surface, do any necessary editing, and then convert to a NURBS surface. Use the CONVTONURBS command (Surface tab ⇨ Control Vertices panel ⇨ Convert to NURBS).

Creating surfaces with the SURFOFFSET command

You can consider the SURFOFFSET command both a surface creation and editing command, because it creates new surfaces from existing ones. It's very much like the 2D OFFSET command (which is usually considered an editing command). You can also offset regions. (I cover regions in Chapter 16.)

New Feature
The SURFOFFSET command is new for AutoCAD 2011.

To offset surfaces or regions, follow these steps:

1. Choose Surface tab ⇨ Create panel ⇨ Offset.
2. At the Select surfaces or regions to offset: prompt, select the surfaces or regions you want and press Enter to end selection. You see sets of arrows indicating the current direction of the offset.
3. At the Specify offset distance or [Flip direction/Both sides/Solid/Connect/ Expression] <0.0000>: prompt, enter an offset distance or use one of the options:
   - **Flip direction.** Switches the direction of the offset
   - **Both sides.** Offsets on both sides of the selected objects
   - **Solid.** Creates a solid from the original objects and their respective offsets, similar to the THICKEN command (covered later in this chapter).
   - **Connect.** Connects multiple offset surfaces, if they are connected. For example, if you have four lines that make up a rectangle (four separate objects) and extrude them, the SURFOFFSET command creates four separated surfaces without this option. Using the option extends the offset objects' edges to meet.
   - **Expression.** Lets you enter a formula or equation to specify the offset distance. A simple example is =4+10 to offset a distance of 14 units.

AutoCAD offsets the selected objects. Figure 23.35 shows an offset surface.

Cross-Reference
The SURFSCULPT command creates a solid from surfaces that enclose an area with no gaps. I cover this command in Chapter 24.

FIGURE 23.35

An offset surface.

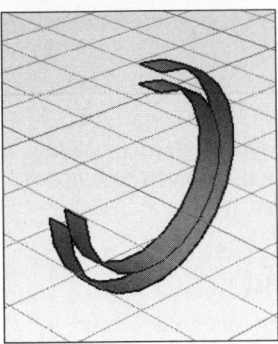

Trimming and extending surfaces

The SURFTRIM command is like a 3D TRIM command, trimming surfaces (or regions) that extend beyond another surface or object. It's a great clean-up tool. You can also use SURFUNTRIM to undo trims. The SURFEXTEND command is similar to the 2D LENGTHEN command, but is for surfaces.

New Feature

The SURFTRIM, SURFUNTRIM, and SURFEXTEND commands are new for AutoCAD 2011. ■

To trim a surface, follow these steps:

1. Choose Surface tab ➪ Edit panel ➪ Trim.
2. At the `Select surfaces or regions to trim or [Extend/PROjection direction]:` prompt, select the surface. Press Enter to end object selection.
   - Use the Extend option (which defaults to Yes) to specify whether the cutting edge can be extended for the purpose of the trim. If you set this option to No, the cutting edge must actually meet the surface you are trimming.
   - The PROjection direction option projects the cutting edge onto the surface, allowing you to trim objects that only appear to have a cutting edge. The default suboption, Automatic, trims as you would expect in 2D, but also extends in the Z direction. Use the View suboption to trim objects that appear to have a cutting edge from the current viewpoint. Use the Ucs suboption to project the cutting edge onto the XY plane of the current UCS. Use the None suboption to ensure trimming only when the cutting edge is on the surface you are trimming.
3. At the `Select cutting curves, surfaces or regions:` prompt, select the object that meets the first surface where you want to trim it. Press Enter to end selection.
4. At the `Select area to trim [Undo]:` prompt, pick the first surface (the one you want to trim) in the area that you want to trim (rather than the area that you want to keep).

   Figure 23.36 shows the process of trimming a surface with SURFTRIM.

FIGURE 23.36

Trimming a surface.

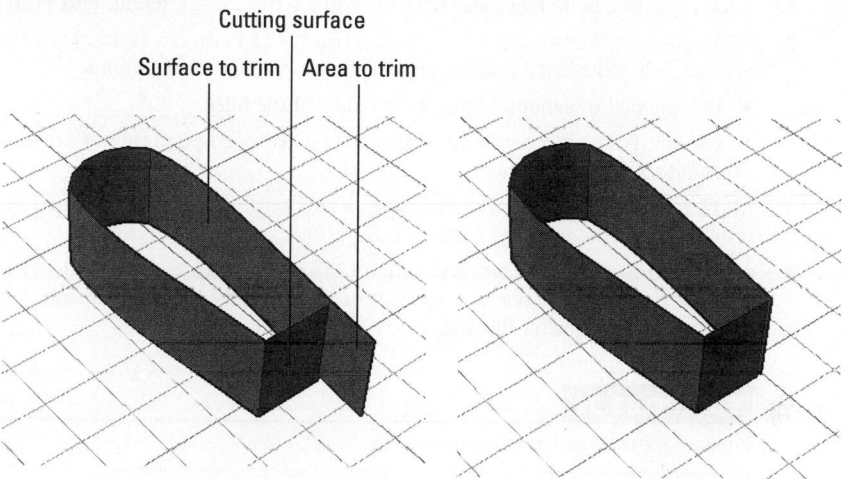

Cutting surface

Surface to trim | Area to trim

The SURFEXTEND command is like the 2D LENGTHEN command (which I cover in Chapter 10). However, you can choose to extend the existing surface or create a new surface that is appended to the original one. To extend a surface, follow these steps:

1. Choose Surface tab ⇨ Edit panel ⇨ Surface Extend. You see the current Mode and Creation settings.

2. At the `Select surface edges to extend:` prompt, select a surface edge. You cannot select a surface; you must select just its edge. Press Enter to end object selection.

3. At the `Specify extend distance [Expression/Modes]:`, enter a distance. You can use the Expression option to enter an equation or formula. Use the Modes option to specify one of two suboptions (or to access the Creation type option):

   - **Extend:** Extends the surface to continue its shape and direction
   - **Stretch:** Stretches the surface without continuing its shape and direction

4. At the `Creation type [Merge/Append] <Append>:` prompt, choose one of the two options:

   - **Merge:** Extends the surface so that the original surface is longer
   - **Append:** Adds a new surface adjacent to the original one

   AutoCAD extends the surface using the options you specified.

Filleting surfaces with the SURFFILLET command

New Feature

The SURFFILLET command is new for AutoCAD 2011. ■

Filleting surfaces is similar to filleting in 2D (which I cover in Chapter 10). You can also fillet two regions. To fillet a surface, follow these steps:

1. Choose Surface tab ⇨ Edit panel ⇨ Fillet. You see the current Radius and Trim Surface settings.
2. At the `Select first surface or region to fillet or [Radius/Trim surface]:` prompt, select the first surface or region, or use one of the suboptions:
   - Use the Radius suboption to set the radius of the fillet.
   - Use the Trim surface suboption to specify whether edges of the surface are trimmed. By default, they are trimmed.
3. At the `Select second surface or region to fillet or [Radius/Trim surface]:` prompt, select the second surface or region.
4. At the `Press Enter to accept the fillet surface or [Radius/Trim surfaces]:` prompt, press Enter to fillet the surfaces or regions and end the command. Figure 23.37 shows surfaces before and after filleting.

FIGURE 23.37

The surfaces were filleted in two places.

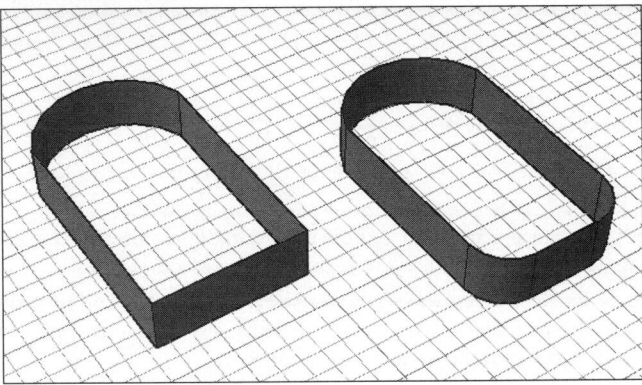

On the DVD

The drawing used in the following exercise on editing surfaces, ab23-j.dwg, is in the Drawings folder on the DVD. ■

STEPS: Editing Surfaces

1. Open ab23-j.dwg from the DVD.
2. Save it as ab23-11.dwg in your AutoCAD Bible folder. You see some construction lines that will be the basis for your model. Set a running object snap for Endpoint.
3. Choose Surface tab ⇨ Create panel ⇨ Extrude. At the `Select objects to extrude or [Mode]:` prompt, select all of the lines and press Enter to end selection.
4. At the next prompt, move the cursor up and type **6** ↵. You can see the result on the left side of Figure 23.38.

5. Choose Surface tab ⇨ Edit panel ⇨ Surface Extend. At the `Select surface edges to extend:` prompt, pick the edge at ❶ in Figure 23.38. Press Enter to end selection.

6. At the `Specify extend distance [Expression/Modes]:` prompt, type **m** ↵. Press Enter again to accept the current mode.

7. At the `Creation type [Merge/Append] <Append>:` prompt, type **m** ↵ to extend the original surface rather than add a new one.

8. At the `Specify extend distance [Expression/Modes]:` prompt, pick the endpoint at ❷.

9. Choose Surface tab ⇨ Edit panel ⇨ Trim.

10. At the `Select surfaces or regions to trim or [Extend/PROjection direction]:` prompt, select the surface at ❸. Press Enter to end selection.

11. At the `Select cutting curves, surfaces or regions:` prompt, select the surface at ❹ and press Enter to end selection.

12. At the `Select area to trim [Undo]:` prompt, select the first surface at ❺. Press Enter to end the command.

13. Choose Surface tab ⇨ Edit panel ⇨ Fillet. At the `Select first surface or region to fillet or [Radius/Trim surface]:` prompt, type **r** ↵ to set the radius. Type **3**↵.

14. At the `Select first surface or region to fillet or [Radius/Trim surface]:` prompt, pick the surface at ❸. At the `Select second surface or region to fillet or [Radius/Trim surface]:` prompt, pick the surface at ❹. Press Enter to accept the fillet and end the command.

15. Repeat the SURFFILLET command and fillet the surfaces at ❻ and ❼.

16. Choose Surface tab ⇨ Create panel ⇨ Offset. At the `Select surfaces or regions to offset:` prompt, select all of the surfaces, including the fillets, for a total of six objects. Press Enter to end selection.

17. At the `Specify offset distance or [Flip direction/Both sides/Solid/Connect/Expression] <0.0000>:` prompt, type **f** ↵ to move the direction arrows to the inside of the closed model.

18. The prompt repeats. Type **2** ↵ to offset the model by 2 units.

19. Choose View tab ⇨ Visual Styles panel ⇨ Visual Styles drop-down list ⇨ Conceptual. Your model should look like Figure 23.38.

FIGURE 23.38

The model shows the result after being extruded, extended, trimmed, filleted, and offset.

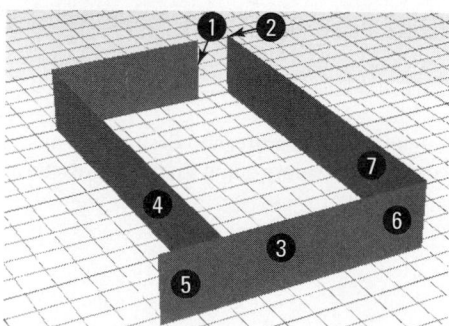
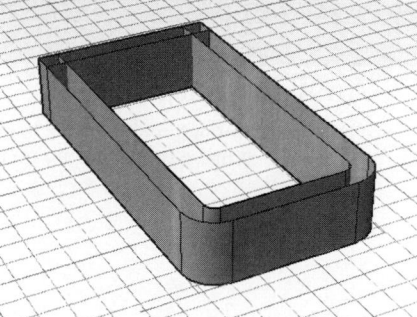

Projecting objects onto surfaces

The PROJECTGEOMETRY command projects 2D objects (points, lines, or curves) as well as 3D polylines and helixes onto a 3D solid or surface. It's similar to the IMPRINT command, which I cover in Chapter 24, but actually creates a surface on the face of the solid or surface. The object you project must be on or above the solid or surface. By setting the SURFACEAUTOTRIM system variable to 1, you can use the command as a way of trimming the 3D object.

New Feature

The PROJECTGEOMETRY command is new for AutoCAD 2011. ■

To start the PROJECTGEOMETRY command, choose Surface tab ⇨ Project Geometry panel and choose one of the following options:

- **Surface Projection UCS.** Projects the object along the Z axis of the current UCS. The object you are projecting must be directly above or below the receiving object.
- **Surface Projection View.** Projects the object along the line of the current viewpoint. The object you are projecting must look like it is above or below the receiving object.
- **Surface Projection Vector.** Projects the object along a line that you specify with two points. The object you are projecting must be in line with the two points and the receiving object.

Figure 23.39 shows an example of projecting a circle onto a surface, with the SURFACEAUTOTRIM system variable set to 1 (on). The example on the left used the UCS option; the example on the right used the View option.

FIGURE 23.39

Two examples of projecting geometry onto a surface — the UCS and the View options.

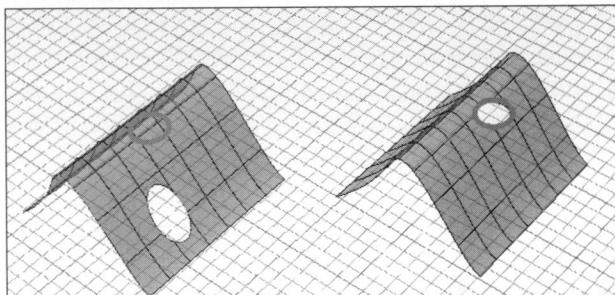

Analyzing surfaces

You can use surface analysis tools to check continuity, curvature, and draft angles of surfaces. These tools are helpful to make sure there are no unseen problems before going to the manufacturing stage.

New Feature

The surface analysis features are new for AutoCAD 2011. ■

AutoCAD offers three analysis tools:

- **Analysis Zebra.** Analyzes continuity by displaying parallel lines on the model.

- **Analysis Curvature.** Finds areas of high and low curvature by displaying a color gradient.

- **Analysis Draft.** Analyzes draft angle changes within a range that you specify by displaying a range of colors. Draft analysis is important for parts that are molded, to allow for easier removal from the mold.

To analyze surfaces, choose Surface tab ⇨ Analysis panel and choose one of the analysis types. For a more detailed configuration, choose Surface tab ⇨ Analysis panel ⇨ Analysis Options to open the Analysis Options dialog box, which contains a tab for each type of analysis. You can specify colors, ranges, and other settings.

Working with Multiple Types of Objects

Several commands convert one type of object to another or allow you to use multiple types of objects together. For example, you can convert 2D objects to surfaces and surfaces to solids.

Converting 2D objects to surfaces

Perhaps the simplest way to create a surface is to convert an existing object to a surface. The CONVTOSURFACE command allows you to do just that. You can convert the following objects to surfaces:

- 2D objects created with the SOLID command
- Regions
- Zero-width polylines with thickness and that don't create a closed figure
- Lines and arcs with thickness (covered in Chapter 21)

Caution

By default, the original objects are deleted. You can control this by using the DELOBJ system variable, which determines whether objects that are used to create other objects are deleted. To keep the original objects, change the value of DELOBJ to 0 (zero). (The default value is 3, which deletes the objects.) You can set the value to –2 to prompt you and allow you to decide if you want to delete the original objects. ■

To convert one of the supported objects to a surface, choose Mesh tab ⇨ Convert Mesh panel ⇨ Convert to Surface to start the CONVTOSURFACE command. Then select the object or objects that you want to convert.

Converting meshes to smooth surfaces

Objects that you create by using the PLANESURF, REVOLVE, EXTRUDE, SWEEP, and LOFT commands are called *smooth* surfaces to distinguish them from the older polygon or polyface mesh surfaces. You can control how mesh objects are converted to solids and smooth surfaces by using the SMOOTHMESHCONVERT variable. To set the system variable, choose Mesh tab ⇨ Convert Mesh panel ⇨ Smooth/Faceted drop-down list and choose one of the options. You can choose to create smoothed or flattened faces, and choose whether or not to merge coplanar faces. Then choose Mesh tab ⇨ Convert Mesh panel ⇨ Convert to Surface.

Thickening a surface into a solid

The THICKEN command allows you to add thickness to a surface and thereby turn it into a solid. You can only use it on surfaces created with the PLANESURF, EXTRUDE, SWEEP, LOFT, or REVOLVE command. However, you can start with a region, line, or arc — using CONVTOSURFACE, for example, to create a surface — and then use THICKEN to turn it into a solid.

To thicken a surface to a solid, follow these steps:

1. Choose Home tab ⇨ Solid Editing panel ⇨ Thicken.
2. Select the surface or surfaces that you want to thicken.
3. At the `Specify thickness <0.0000>:` prompt, enter a thickness. A positive number thickens in the positive direction of the axes; a negative number thickens in the negative direction.

Sculpting surfaces to create a solid

The SURFSCULPT command converts surfaces that create a completely enclosed volume and turn it into a solid. You can also use the command with solids and mesh objects (which I cover in Chapter 24).

New Feature

The SURFSCULPT command is new for AutoCAD 2011. ∎

To create a solid from surfaces that are enclosed, choose Surface tab ⇨ Edit panel ⇨ Surface Sculpt. At the `Select surfaces or solids to sculpt into a solid:` prompt, use a crossing window to select all of the surfaces. Press Enter to end selection. AutoCAD creates the solid.

Note

SURFSCULPT doesn't work with surfaces that have G1 or G2 continuity. For more information, see the earlier discussion on the SURFBLEND command. ∎

Extracting edges from a surface or a region

You can turn a surface or a region into a wireframe object by extracting its edges. To extract an edge, choose Home tab ⇨ Solid Editing panel ⇨ Edges drop-down list ⇨ Extract Edges. The XEDGES command works with 3D solids, mesh objects, regions, surfaces, and subobjects (edges and faces). You cannot convert polygon or polyface meshes. Figure 23.40 shows edges extracted from a lofted surface.

FIGURE 23.40

The XEDGES command can extract edges from a surface.

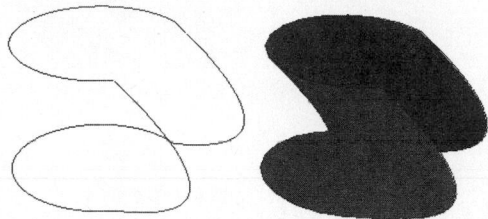

You can also select individual edges or faces to extract by pressing the Ctrl key and clicking the edges or faces that you want. Then use the XEDGES command to extract them.

Summary

In this chapter, you read all about 3D surfaces. You read about:

- Creating surfaces by using the 3DFACE command and controlling the visibility of the lines between the faces
- Creating polyface meshes
- Creating plane surfaces
- Drawing surfaces with 3D polygon meshes, including the basic shapes — box, wedge, pyramid, cone, sphere, dome, dish, and torus
- Making a surface by revolving a profile around an axis
- Extruding and sweeping a curve
- Creating a surface between two curves
- Making an edge surface from four curves
- Creating procedural and NURBS surfaces
- Editing and analyzing procedural and NURBS surfaces
- Working with multiple types of objects

In the next chapter, you discover how to create true solids and meshes (well, true electronic ones, at least) as well as how to edit in 3D.

Creating Solids and Editing in 3D

A lthough you can create great-looking models with surfaces, if you want truly realistic models, you need to create solids. After all, in real life, objects have solidity. Even a thin object such as a wastepaper basket or a drape has some thickness. Solids enable you to create more realistic models than surfaces. You can also combine or subtract solids and get information about their physical properties. Figure 24.1 shows a complex model created using solids.

AutoCAD Only

AutoCAD LT doesn't draw solids. For the 3D capabilities of AutoCAD LT, see Chapters 21 and 22. ∎

As I explain in Chapter 21, when working in 3D, you should use a 3D environment. This includes the following items:

- The 3D Modeling workspace, which you choose from the Workspace drop-down list on the Quick Access Toolbar in the upper-left corner of the screen. (I explain how to customize workspaces in Appendix A.)

New Feature

A new 3D Basics workspace is available in AutoCAD for simple 3D work. ∎

- The `acad3d.dwt` template (or `acadiso3d.dwt` or similar template) that turns on perspective view, the grid, and the Realistic or other 3D visual style. (I cover visual styles in Chapter 22.)
- The Ribbon, which combines many modeling commands and settings in one place.

To work with solids, you can use the Modeling and Solid Editing panels on the Home tab of the Ribbon. This entire chapter assumes that you're using the 3D Modeling workspace.

IN THIS CHAPTER

Drawing basic smooth solids

Creating extruded solids

Drawing swept, revolved, and lofted solids

Creating solids that you draw like polylines

Manipulating solids directly

Selecting sub-objects

Creating mesh shapes

Creating complex solids

Sectioning and slicing solids

Using editing commands in 3D

Editing solids

Determining solid properties

FIGURE 24.1

You can create complex and realistic models using solids.

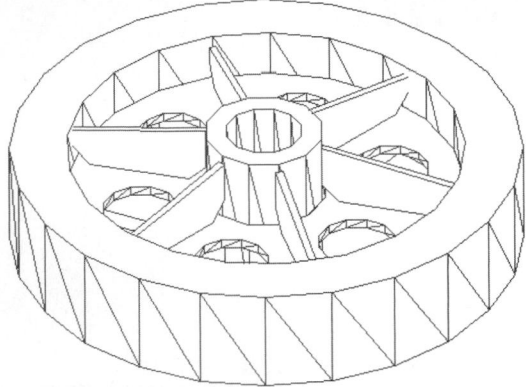

Thanks to Hans-Joachim Fach, Bremen, Germany, for this drawing.

Drawing Basic Smooth Solids

AutoCAD makes it easy to create most basic geometrical shapes. These shapes are easy to draw, because you can dynamically see the result as you draw.

Controlling the display of solids

The wireframe display of all the curved solids in a drawing is controlled by the ISOLINES system variable. The default, 4, provides a bare minimum of curved lines to let you view the outlines of the curve and results in the quickest display. Increasing the ISOLINES value improves the visual result but slows down the drawing display. Generally, you can find a happy medium based on the size of your drawing, the speed of your computer, and your personal preferences. The ISOLINES variable affects only wireframe display — it has no effect when you use another visual style. Figure 24.5 shows the effect of varying the ISOLINES setting. When you change the ISOLINES value, use the REGEN command to see the result on existing objects.

The FACETRES system variable is the 3D version of VIEWRES, and it determines the display of curved surfaces and solids that are shaded or rendered. You can set FACETRES from 0.01 to 10.0. Here you see a hidden sphere at FACETRES settings of 0.05 (left) and 5.0 (right). The default is 0.5, which is generally a happy medium.

The VSEDGES system variable controls the type of edges that models display. The default value of 1 displays lines. To show more edges, you can change VSEDGES to 2, which displays facets, as you see here on the left. If you are displaying your models with some visual style (anything but wireframe or hidden), you can set VSEDGES to 0, which displays no edges. This setting provides the cleanest look, as you see on the right.

Drawing a box

The box is one of the most commonly used 3D objects and is often the basis for more complex models. Figure 24.2 shows a solid box shown with the 3D Hidden visual style.

A solid box.

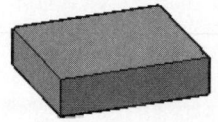

To draw a box, follow these steps:

1. Choose Home tab ➪ Modeling panel ➪ 3D Solid drop-down list ➪ Box.
2. At the `Specify first corner or [Center]:` prompt, specify any corner of the box, or right-click and choose Center to specify the 3D center of the box (not the center of the base).
3. If you specify the corner (the default), you then see the `Specify other corner or [Cube/Length]:` prompt.

   The default is to pick the opposite corner in the XY plane. This defines the base of the box. You can define the base just like you define any rectangle, by dragging and picking the opposite corner or by entering coordinates. At the `Specify height or [2Point]:` prompt, drag in the Z direction and pick a height or enter a height value. You can also pick two points to specify the height. This completes the box.

   If you use the Length option, AutoCAD asks you for a width and a height. If you use the Cube option, AutoCAD asks for one length and completes the box.
4. If you specify the center at the first prompt, you see the `Specify center:` prompt. Specify the center of the box. The `Specify corner or [Cube/Length]:` prompt appears.

   If you pick the corner of the box, AutoCAD then asks you for the height to complete the box.

   If you specify the length, AutoCAD then asks for a width and a height. If you use the Cube option, AutoCAD asks for a length and completes the box.

You can specify a negative length, width, or height to build the box in the negative direction. If you specify the center of the cube, don't forget that the center's Z coordinate is different from the corner's Z coordinate. AutoCAD always creates the box parallel to the XY plane.

Drawing a wedge

A wedge is a box sliced diagonally in half. The prompts are virtually the same as for the Box command. Figure 24.3 shows two wedges.

FIGURE 24.3

Two solid wedges.

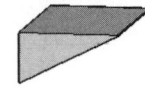

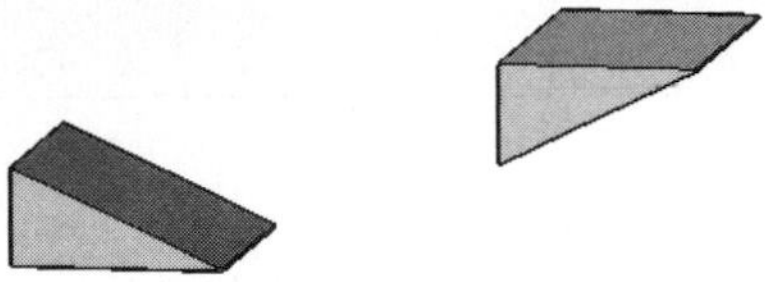

To create a wedge, follow these steps:

1. Choose Home tab ⇨ Modeling panel ⇨ 3D Solid drop-down list ⇨ Wedge.

2. At the `Specify first corner or [Center]:` prompt, specify any corner of the wedge or use the Center option to specify the 3D center of the wedge.

3. If you specify the corner (the default), you then see the `Specify other corner or [Cube/Length]:` prompt.

    The default is to pick the opposite corner in the XY plane — you can also define it by using coordinates. The command then asks you for the height in the Z direction. This completes the wedge.

    If you use the Length option, AutoCAD asks you for a width and a height.

    If you use the Cube option, AutoCAD asks for one length and completes the wedge. For positive lengths, the wedge slopes downward in the positive X direction. (However, if you have Dynamic Input on, the slope will follow the direction of the cursor.)

4. If you specify the center, you see the `Specify center:` prompt. Specify the center point. The `Specify corner or [Cube/Length]:` prompt displays.

    If you pick the corner of the wedge, the command asks for a height.

    If you specify the length, AutoCAD then asks for a width and a height. If you use the Cube option, AutoCAD asks for a length and completes the wedge.

Drawing a cone

You can draw cones with circular or elliptical bases. By specifying a negative height, you can create an inverted cone (like an ice-cream cone). By specifying the Axis endpoint (the apex), you can draw cones on an angle from the XY plane. You can also specify a top radius to create a truncated cone (sometimes called a frustum cone). Figure 24.4 shows some cones.

Follow these steps to draw a cone:

1. Choose Home tab ⇨ Modeling panel ⇨ 3D Solid drop-down list ⇨ Cone.

2. At the `Specify center point of base or [3P/2P/Ttr/Elliptical]:` prompt, specify the center of the base if you want a circular cone. Otherwise, use the 3P, 2P, or Ttr options to define a circular base. Use the Elliptical option to define an elliptical base.

    If you specified a center point, at the `Specify base radius or [Diameter]:` prompt, specify a radius or use the Diameter option to specify the diameter.

If you chose the Elliptical option, use the prompts to define the elliptical base. These prompts are like the prompts for the ELLIPSE command.

3. At the `Specify height or [2Point/Axis endpoint/Top radius]:` prompt, specify the height by dragging or entering a value. Use the 2Point option to specify the height by picking two points. The Axis endpoint option is another way to specify the height, and enables you to create an angled cone. (By default, the Axis endpoint is a relative coordinate, based on the center of the base.) The Top radius option creates a truncated cone.

FIGURE 24.4

Cones with varying heights and bases.

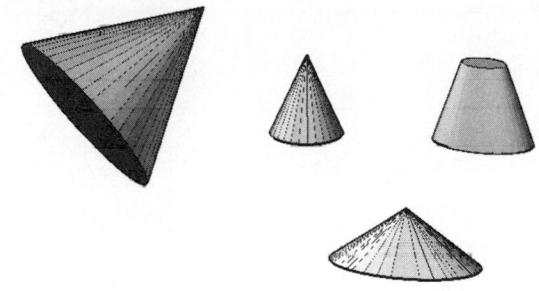

Drawing a sphere

Spheres are not used very often alone, but they can be the basis for more complex models — they certainly look pretty! Figure 24.5 shows two solid spheres. The left sphere uses the default ISOLINE value of 4. The right sphere uses an ISOLINE value of 8.

FIGURE 24.5

Two solid spheres, with ISOLINES set at 4 (left) and 8 (right).

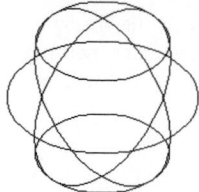 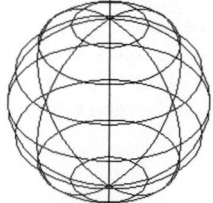

To draw a sphere, follow these steps:

1. Choose Home tab ⇨ Modeling panel ⇨ 3D Solid drop-down list ⇨ Sphere.
2. At the `Specify center point or [3P/2P/Ttr]:` prompt, specify the center of the sphere. If you want the sphere to lie on the XY plane, the Z coordinate of the center should be equal to the radius of the sphere. Use the 3P, 2P, or Ttr option to define a circle at the center of the sphere.

3. At the `Specify radius or [Diameter]:` prompt, drag and pick a point on the surface of the sphere or enter a value for the radius. You can use the Diameter option to specify the diameter instead.

Drawing a cylinder

Cylinders are very common in 3D drawing, both for building models and creating holes. Figure 24.6 shows three solid cylinders. The grid helps you to visualize the XY plane. You can draw cylinders with circular or elliptical bases. By specifying the center of the top of the cylinder separately, you can draw it at an angle.

FIGURE 24.6

Some solid cylinders.

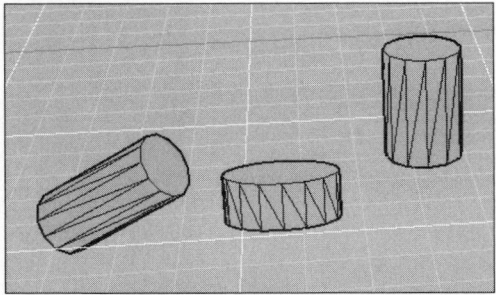

Follow these steps to draw a cylinder:

 1. Choose Home tab ⇨ Modeling panel ⇨ 3D Solid drop-down list ⇨ Cylinder.

2. At the `Specify center point of base or [3P/2P/Ttr/Elliptical]:` prompt, specify the center point for a circular cylinder or define the circle by using the 3P, 2P, or Ttr option. You can also choose the Elliptical option to define an ellipse as a base.

If you specified a center point, then at the `Specify base radius or [Diameter]:` prompt, specify a radius or use the Diameter option to specify the diameter.

If you chose the Elliptical option, use the prompts to define the elliptical base.

3. At the `Specify height or [2Point/Axis endpoint]:` prompt, specify the height by dragging, entering a value, or using the 2Point option. You can create a tilted cylinder by using the Axis endpoint option to specify the center of the other end of the cylinder. (By default, the Axis endpoint is a relative coordinate, based on the center of the base.)

Drawing a torus

A *torus* is a solid 3D donut. Figure 24.7 shows some examples with the parts of the torus labeled. You can make some unusual shapes by varying the torus and tube radii. If the torus radius is negative and the tube radius is larger than the absolute value of the torus radius (for example, –2 and 3), you create a lemon (or football) shape. If the tube radius is larger than the torus radius, you create a puckered ball (or apple) shape.

FIGURE 24.7

Varieties of the torus.

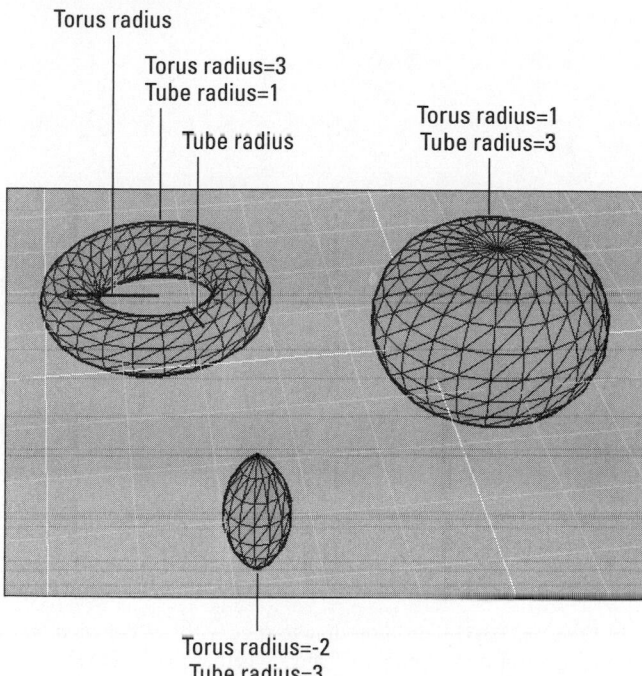

Torus radius

Torus radius=3
Tube radius=1

Tube radius

Torus radius=1
Tube radius=3

Torus radius=-2
Tube radius=3

To create a torus, follow these steps:

1. Choose Home tab ➪ Modeling panel ➪ 3D Solid drop-down list ➪ Torus.

2. At the `Specify center point or [3P/2P/Ttr]:` prompt, specify the center of the torus (the center of the hole). You can also use the 3P, 2P, or Ttr option to define a circle as the basis for the torus.

3. At the `Specify radius or [Diameter]:` prompt, specify the radius of the entire torus or use the Diameter option to specify the diameter.

4. At the `Specify tube radius or [2Point/Diameter]:` prompt, specify the radius of just the tube or use the Diameter option to specify the tube's diameter. You can use the 2Point option to pick two points that define the tube radius.

Drawing a pyramid

You can draw pyramids with a base of 3 to 32 sides. The prompts for the base are similar to the prompts for the POLYGON command. (For more information on the POLYGON command, see Chapter 6.) A pyramid can come to a point, or you can truncate it. You can also tilt the pyramid. Figure 24.8 shows three variations on the pyramid.

FIGURE 24.8

You can draw several types of pyramids.

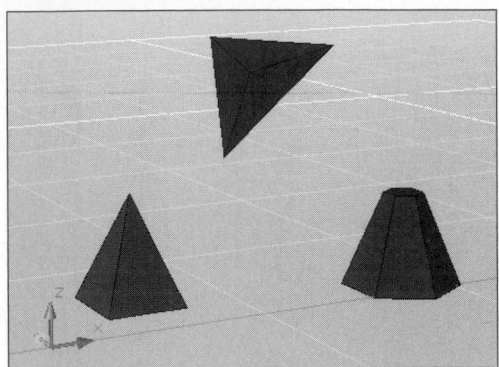

Follow these steps to draw a pyramid:

1. Choose Home tab ⇨ Modeling panel ⇨ 3D Solid drop-down list ⇨ Pyramid. The default number of sides is listed, as well as whether the base will be inscribed or circumscribed.

2. At the `Specify center point of base or [Edge/Sides]:` prompt, specify the center of the base. You can use the Edge option to define an edge, or the Sides option to specify the number of sides.

3. At the `Specify base radius or [Inscribed]:` prompt, drag to specify the radius or enter a value. You can use the Inscribed (or Circumscribed) option to change whether the radius is inscribed (based on the base points) or circumscribed (based on the base side midpoints).

4. At the `Specify height or [2Point/Axis endpoint/Top radius]:` prompt, drag to specify the height or enter a value. Use the 2Point option to specify the height by picking two points. Use the Axis endpoint to specify the tip. If it isn't directly over the base's center, you tilt the pyramid. Use the Top radius to truncate the pyramid; drag or enter a value for the top's radius and then enter the height of the pyramid.

On the DVD

The drawing used in the following exercise on drawing basic solids, `ab24-a.dwg`, is in the `Drawings` folder on the DVD. ∎

STEPS: Drawing Basic 3D Solids

1. Open `ab24-a.dwg` from the DVD.

2. Save the file as `ab24-01.dwg` in your `AutoCAD Bible` folder. Turn on Object Snap. Set running object snaps for Quadrant and Center. In this exercise, I assume that you have dynamic input on, set to the default of relative coordinates.

3. Choose Home tab ⇨ Modeling panel ⇨ 3D Solid drop-down list ⇨ Cylinder. Follow the prompts:
   ```
   Specify center point of base or [3P/2P/Ttr/Elliptical]: 7,6.5 ↵
   Specify base radius or [Diameter] <3.0000>: 3 ↵
   Specify height or [2Point/Axis endpoint] <1.0000>: Move the cursor
       upward and enter 1 ↵
   ```

4. Repeat the CYLINDER command. Zoom closer to the top end of the lamp's arm and change the viewpoint so that you can see the end circle more clearly. Follow the prompts:

```
Specify center point of base or [3P/2P/Ttr/Elliptical]: 2p ↵
Specify first end point of diameter: Choose the bottom quadrant of
    the top end of the lamp's arm.
Specify second end point of diameter: 3,0 ↵
Specify height or [2Point/Axis endpoint] <17.2980>: Move the cursor
    upward and enter 2.5 ↵.
```

5. Choose Home tab ⇨ Modeling panel ⇨ 3D Solid drop-down list ⇨ Sphere. Follow the prompts:

```
Specify center point or [3P/2P/Ttr]: 2p ↵
Specify first end point of diameter: Pick the left quadrant of the
    top of the cylinder that you just drew.
Specify second end point of diameter: Pick the right quadrant of the
    top of the cylinder that you just drew.
```

6. Choose Home tab ⇨ Modeling panel ⇨ 3D Solid drop-down list ⇨ Cone. Follow the prompts:

```
Specify center point of base or [3P/2P/Ttr/Elliptical]: Pick the
    center of the bottom of the cylinder.
Specify base radius or [Diameter] <1.5000>: Pick any quadrant on the
    edge of the cylinder's bottom edge.
Specify height or [2Point/Axis endpoint/Top radius] <4.0000>: t ↵
Specify top radius <3.0000>: 3 ↵
Specify height or [2Point/Axis endpoint] <4.0000>: Move the cursor
    downward and enter 4 ↵.
```

7. Choose View tab ⇨ Navigate panel ⇨ Zoom drop-down list ⇨ Extents.

8. Choose Home tab ⇨ View panel ⇨ Visual Styles drop-down list ⇨ Conceptual.

9. Save your drawing. It should look like Figure 24.9.

FIGURE 24.9

The desk lamp.

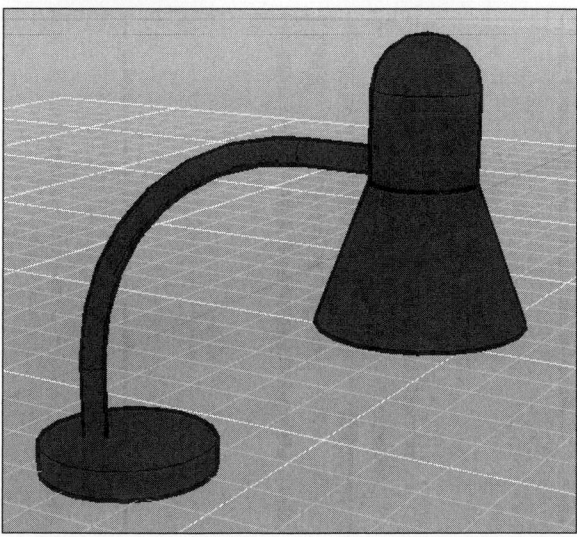

Creating Extruded Solids

The EXTRUDE command is similar to adding thickness to a 2D object (discussed in Chapter 21) or using the TABSURF command (see Chapter 23). You can also extrude the face of an existing solid, as I explain later in this chapter. You can extrude lines, arcs, elliptical arcs, 2D polylines, circles, ellipses, splines, 2D solids, planar surfaces, and regions. You can use the REGION command to create one object from several objects for this purpose. You can select several objects and extrude them at one time. Figure 24.10 shows several extruded solids.

New Feature

The EXTRUDE command can create either a solid or a surface, based on the setting of the Closed Profiles Creation Mode. If you type the command on the command line, the mode is listed as either Solid or Surface and you can use the MOde option to change the setting. If you start the command from the Surface tab, you get a surface. If you start the command from the command line or the Solid tab, you get a solid, When using the solid mode, you get a solid— if a solid is possible. For a solid to be possible, the profile must be closed or the profile must be in one plane. ■

FIGURE 24.10

Some extruded solids.

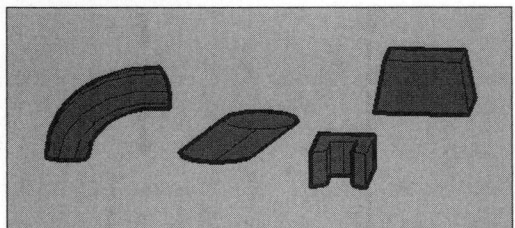

Managing objects used to make other objects

When you extrude a circle to make a cylinder, for example, what should happen to the circle? Do you want to delete it because you want to turn it into a cylinder, or do you want to keep it in case your cylinder isn't just right and you need to use the circle again? The DELOBJ system variable determines whether objects used by the EXTRUDE command (as well as the REVOLVE, LOFT, SWEEP, and others) to make other objects are retained. By default, certain source objects are deleted. Therefore, when you use a 2D object to make a solid, the 2D object is deleted.

The DELOBJ system variable has the following options:

- **0:** Retains all source objects.
- **1:** Deletes profile curves. For example, if you use a circle to create a cylinder, the circle is deleted. Cross-sections and guides used with the SWEEP command are also deleted. However, if you extrude along a path, the path is not deleted. This is the default option.
- **2:** Deletes all defining objects, including paths and guide curves.
- **3:** Deletes all defining objects, including paths and guide curves only if a solid is created.
- **-1:** Prompts to delete profile curves. This is like 1, but you get a prompt so you can choose.
- **-2:** Prompts to delete all defining objects. This is like 2, but you get a prompt.
- **-3:** Prompts to delete all defining objects if the result is a surface, but not if the result is a solid.

Tip

Put source objects on a separate layer. Set DELOBJ to 0 (zero) to keep objects used to create other objects, or to -2 to be prompted whenever a choice is possible. When you're done, turn off the layer containing your source objects. ∎

Using the EXTRUDE command

When you extrude an object, by default you extrude it perpendicular to the object. However, you can also taper the extrusion, as in the extruded rectangle on the right in Figure 24.10. A positive angle tapers the object inward. A negative angle tapers the object outward so it gets wider in the direction of the extrusion.

Note

Don't taper the object too much. If the taper angle results in the object coming to a point before its full height, AutoCAD cannot create the solid. ∎

You can extrude the object by specifying a height of extrude, a direction by specifying two points, or along a path. A path can be a line, circle, arc, ellipse, elliptical arc, polyline, spline, or even a helix. The path object must be in a different plane than the original object. Not all paths are suitable for extruding objects. In the following situations, the extrusion may not work. The path should not be:

- Too close to the original object's plane
- Too complex
- Too tightly curved or bent for the size of the original object

Here are the steps for creating an extruded solid:

1. Draw the object that you want to extrude. If you want to extrude along a path, draw the path object in a different plane from the source object.

2. Choose Home tab ⇨ Modeling panel ⇨ Solid Creation drop-down list ⇨ Extrude.

3. Select the object or objects to extrude.

4. At the `Specify height of extrusion or [Direction/Path/Taper angle/ Expression] <3.5226>:` prompt, specify the height of the extrusion (drag or enter a value). Use the Path option to extrude along a path object; just select the path object. The Direction option is similar to the Path option, except that you specify two points to indicate the path. Use the Taper angle option to enter a taper angle. Use the Expression option to help calculate the height of the extrusion.

New Feature

You can select an edge or other sub-object as the path. Also, the path does not have to be in one plane. In addition, use the new Expression option to enter a formula or equation to calculate the height of the extrusion. 4 * 0.125 is an example of an expression. ∎

On the DVD

The drawing used in the following exercise on creating extruded solids, `ab24-b.dwg`, is in the `Drawings` folder on the DVD. ∎

STEPS: Creating Extruded Solids

1. Open ab24-b.dwg from the DVD.

2. Save the file as ab24-02.dwg in your AutoCAD Bible folder. Make sure that Object Snap is on. Set running object snaps for Endpoint and Midpoint. This is a small mounting angle, shown in an edge view.

3. The angle is made up of lines and arcs. To extrude it, you need to change it into a polyline or region. To change it into a polyline, choose Home tab ⇨ Modify panel (expanded) ⇨ Edit Polyline. Follow the prompts:

```
Select polyline or [Multiple]: Select any object on the angle.
Object selected is not a polyline
Do you want to turn it into one? <Y> ↵
Enter an option [Close/Join/Width/Edit vertex/Fit/Spline/Decurve/
    Ltype gen/Reverse/Undo]: Right-click and choose Join.
Select objects: Use a window to select all the objects in the angle.
Select objects: ↵
Enter an option [Open/Join/Width/Edit vertex/Fit/Spline/Decurve/Ltype
    gen/Reverse/Undo]: Right-click and choose Enter.
```

4. Choose Home tab ⇨ Modeling panel ⇨ Solid Creation drop-down list ⇨ Extrude. The Closed Profiles Creation Mode should be set to Solid. (If not, use the MOde option and the SOlid suboption.) Select the mounting angle, and then press Enter to end object selection. At the Specify height of extrusion or [Direction/Path/Taper angle/Expression] <-1.0800>: prompt, move the cursor up and type 3 ↵.

5. Choose Home tab ⇨ View panel ⇨ Visual Styles drop-down list ⇨ Conceptual.

6. Save your drawing. It should look like Figure 24.11.

FIGURE 24.11

The completed mounting angle.

The mounting angle should have two holes in it. You would create the holes by using the SUBTRACT command, which I cover later in this chapter.

Drawing Swept Solids

The SWEEP command is similar to the EXTRUDE command, but it concentrates on using paths to define the direction of the extrusion.

The SWEEP command has some great tricks up its sleeve:

1. You can draw the source object on the same plane as the path. You don't even have to place the source object on the path. The SWEEP command figures out the center of the source object. (You can use the Base point option to specify the base point for the source object.)

2. You can twist the object along the path.

3. You can scale the source object.

4. If the source object is a closed object, like a circle, you get a solid; if it's open, you get a swept surface.

The DELOBJ system variable determines what happens to the original objects; for more information, see the explanation in the previous section. Figure 24.12 shows some swept solids.

FIGURE 24.12

You can create very interesting shapes by using the SWEEP command.

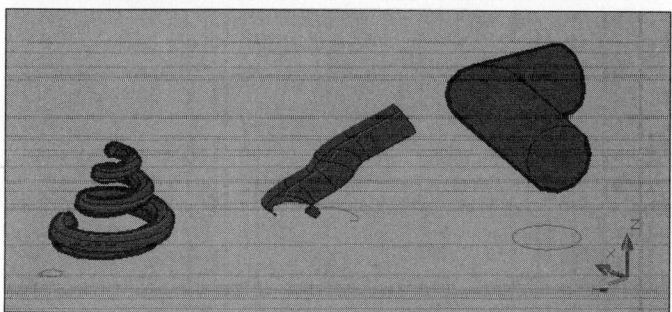

To create a swept solid or surface, follow these steps:

1. Draw the path that you want to sweep along.

2. In the same plane as the path, draw the object or objects that you want to sweep.

 3. Choose Home tab ➪ Modeling panel ➪ Solid Creation drop-down list ➪ Sweep.

New Feature

The SWEEP command can create either a solid or a surface, based on the setting of the Closed Profiles Creation Mode. For more information, see the explanation in the section on the EXTRUDE command. Also, the path can be an edge or other sub-object. ■

4. At the `Select objects to sweep or [MOde]:` prompt, select the object or objects that you drew.

5. At the `Select sweep path or [Alignment/Base point/Scale/Twist]:` prompt, select the path.

- Use the Alignment option if you don't want to align the object perpendicular to the path. By default, the SWEEP does so; for this reason, you don't have to set up the path and the object in different planes.

- Use the Base Point option to specify a base point on the objects to be swept, to determine the point on that object that actually lies along the path.

- Use the Scale option to scale the object before sweeping it.

- Use the Twist option to twist the object along the path. For example, if you specify 180°, the object twists that much from the beginning to the end of the path. This option has a suboption, Bank, that allows you to specify if you want the object to also rotate in the 3D direction when you use a 3D sweep path (a 3D polyline, 3D spline, or helix).

On the DVD

The drawing used in the following exercise on creating swept solids, `ab24-c.dwg`, is in the `Drawings` folder on the DVD. ■

STEPS: Creating Swept Solids

1. Open `ab24-c.dwg` from the DVD. This is the same drawing that was used for the exercise on drawing basic shapes; however, this time the desk lamp is missing its arm. A path is already drawn on the `const` layer.

2. Save the file as `ab24-03.dwg` in your `AutoCAD Bible` folder. If necessary, change the visual style to 3D Wireframe (choose Home tab ➪ View panel ➪ Visual Styles drop-down list ➪ 3D Wireframe).

3. Make the `const` layer current. Draw a circle anywhere with a radius of 0.375 (a diameter of 0.75).

4. Switch to the `object` layer.

 5. Choose Home tab ➪ 3D Modeling panel ➪ Solid Creation drop-down list ➪ Sweep. The Closed Profiles Creation Mode should be set to Solid. (If not, use the MOde option and the SOlid suboption.) Follow these prompts to sweep the circle along the arm (a polyline):

```
Select objects to sweep: Select the circle.
Select objects to sweep: ↵
Select sweep path or [Alignment/Base point/Scale/Twist]: Select the
    arm (the polyline).
```

6. Turn off the `const` layer.

7. Save your drawing. Look back to Figure 24.9 to see what the lamp looks like.

Drawing Revolved Solids

The REVOLVE command revolves a profile around an axis. You can revolve lines, arcs, elliptical arcs, 2D polylines, circles, ellipses, splines, 2D solids, planar faces, and regions.

The DELOBJ system variable affects whether the original objects are deleted. See the discussion on this system variable earlier in this chapter in the section "Managing objects used to make other objects."

New Feature

The REVOLVE command can create either a solid or a surface, based on the setting of the Closed Profiles Creation Mode. For more information, see the explanation in the section on the EXTRUDE command. The path can be an edge or other sub-object and the path does not have to be in one plane. Additionally, you can use the Reverse option to change the direction of the revolution and the EXpression option to enter a formula or equation to calculate the angle of revolution. 1.5708 * (180 / PI) is an example of an expression. ■

Figure 24.13 shows a solid created by revolving a rectangle around a line. (You can also create this solid by drawing two circles, extruding them into cylinders, and then subtracting the smaller cylinder from the larger one — it just depends on which technique you're more comfortable with.)

FIGURE 24.13

A solid created by revolving a rectangle around a line.

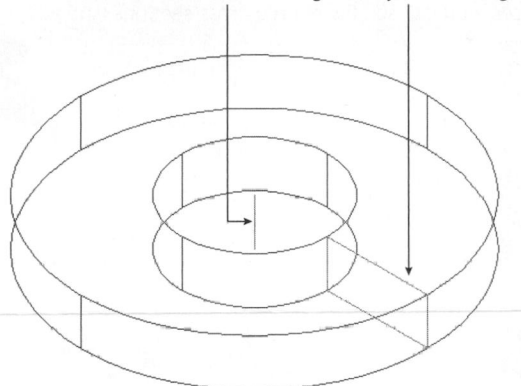

Axis of revolution   Original object (rectangle)

To create a revolved solid, follow these steps:

1. Choose Home tab ⇨ Modeling panel ⇨ Solid Creation drop-down list ⇨ Revolve.
2. At the Select objects to revolve or [MOde]: prompt, select one or more objects.
3. At the Specify axis start point or define axis by [Object/X/Y/Z] <Object>: prompt, you can pick two points to create an axis of revolution. You can also select an object as an axis. Use the X, Y, or Z option to revolve the object around the respective axis.
4. At the Specify angle of revolution or [STart angle/Reverse/EXpression] <360>: prompt, press Enter to revolve the object 360 degrees or type an angle, either positive or negative. You can use the STart angle option to specify a start and end angle; for example, you can start at 45 degrees and end at 90 degrees. Use the Reverse option to reverse the angle of revolution. The Expression option lets you calculate the angle of revolution based on a formula or equation.

You need to determine the positive direction of rotation if you're revolving less than 360 degrees. (Of course, it may be quicker to try one way and just do it the other way if it doesn't turn out right.) Here's how to figure it out:

1. First determine the positive direction of the axis. If you specify start and endpoints, the positive axis direction goes from the start point to the endpoint. If you pick an object, the positive axis direction goes from the pick point to the other endpoint. If you choose the X, Y, or Z axis, the positive direction is obvious.

2. Point your right thumb in the positive direction of the axis.

3. Look at the curl of your fingers on that hand. That's the positive direction of rotation.

Drawing Lofted Solids

The LOFT command creates a solid or surface that is interpolated from a series of profiles, or cross-sections. Figure 24.14 shows some lofted solids.

FIGURE 24.14

Two solid and two surface lofted objects. On one of the surfaces, you can see the source cross-sections (splines).

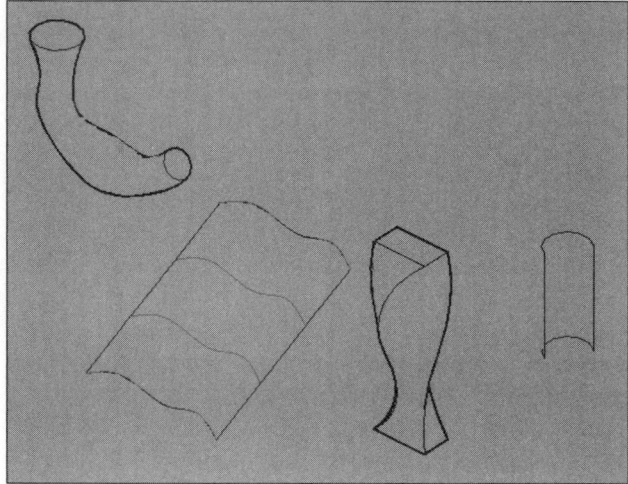

The difficult part of lofting is drawing and placing the source cross-sections to get the result that you want. To create a lofted surface or solid, follow these steps:

1. Draw a series of closed or open profiles. You can start with one and then copy it to nearby locations on the path that will run centrally along the lofted object. You can then modify the copies as necessary. These cross-sections become the basis for the lofted object. You need at least two cross-sections.

   - If you want to control the sides of the loft (generally for surfaces), draw guides on each side of your cross-sections. Guides must start at the first cross-section, end at the last cross-section, and intersect each cross-section.

   - If you want to specify a path through the middle of the loft, draw a path object. The path must intersect the plane of each cross-section. The resulting lofted model runs the length of the path.

 2. Choose Home tab ⇨ Modeling panel ⇨ Solid Creation drop-down list ⇨ Loft.

New Feature

The LOFT command can create either a solid or a surface, based on the setting of the Closed Profiles Creation Mode. For more information, see the explanation in the section on the EXTRUDE command. Also, the path can be an edge or other sub-object. ■

3. At the `Select cross-sections in lofting order or [Point/Join multiple edges/ MOde]:` prompt, choose each cross-section in order, and then end selection.

4. At the `Enter an option [Guides/Path/Cross sections only/Settings] <Cross sections only>:` prompt, press Enter to accept the default, which uses the cross-sections only to define the loft. Use the Guides option to select guides you have drawn. Use the Path option to select a path you have drawn. Choose Settings to display the Loft Settings dialog box. You use this dialog box to fine-tune the definition of the loft and specifically to control how the loft is curved at its cross-sections.

   - **Ruled.** Creates a straight (ruled) solid or surface between the cross-sections and sharp edges at the cross-sections.

   - **Smooth Fit.** Creates a smooth solid or surface between the cross-sections and sharp edges at the first and last cross-sections.

   - **Normal to.** Defines which cross-sections the solid or surface is perpendicular (normal) to — the start, end, both start and end, or all cross-sections.

   - **Draft Angles.** Controls the draft angle (the beginning and ending angles) at the first and last cross-sections. This is similar to specifying start and end tangents on a spline. A 0° angle is the default: normal to the cross-section's plane in the direction of the next cross-section. A 180° angle goes outward, away from the cross-section. You also define a magnitude, which is the relative distance that the solid or surface goes before bending to the next cross-section. In other words, if you use a 180° angle, a large magnitude creates a large bulge.

   - **Close Surface or Solid.** Closes the model.

   - **Periodic (smooth ends).** Creates a smooth closed surface when you choose Ruled or Smooth Fit.

   With all these options, you may need to experiment a little. Drag the Loft Settings dialog box to the side, and watch what happens as you change the settings. After you create a loft, you can select it and make changes in the Properties palette; again, you can see the results of your changes immediately.

On the DVD

The drawing used in the following exercise on creating lofted solids, ab24-d.dwg, is in the Drawings folder on the DVD. ■

STEPS: Creating Lofted Solids

1. Open ab24-d.dwg from the DVD. This is the same drawing that was used for the exercise on drawing swept solids; again, the desk lamp's arm is missing, but it has some cross-sections (on the const layer) that you can use to create a lofted solid. The object layer should be current.

2. Save the file as ab24-04.dwg in your AutoCAD Bible folder. If necessary, change the visual style to 3D Wireframe (choose Home tab ➪ View panel ➪ Visual Styles drop-down list ➪ 3D Wireframe).

 3. Choose Home tab ➪ Modeling panel ➪ Solid Creation drop-down list ➪ Loft. The Closed Profiles Creation Mode should be set to Solid. (If not, use the MOde option and the SOlid suboption.) Follow these prompts to loft the cross-sections along the arm:

```
Select cross sections in lofting order: Select the bottom-most cross-
   section (a circle).
Select cross sections in lofting order: Continue to select all the
   other cross-sections, one at a time, moving upward until you
   select the circle closest to the head of the lamp. Press Enter to
   end selection.
Enter an option [Guides/Path/Cross sections only/Settings] <Cross
   sections only>: c ↵
```

4. Turn off the const layer.

5. Change the visual style to Conceptual (choose Home tab ➪ View panel ➪ Visual Styles drop-down list ➪ Conceptual).

6. Save your drawing. Use the 3D Orbit override (Shift+mouse wheel) to change to a view that shows the arm more clearly. It should look like Figure 24.15.

FIGURE 24.15

The completed lamp with a lofted arm.

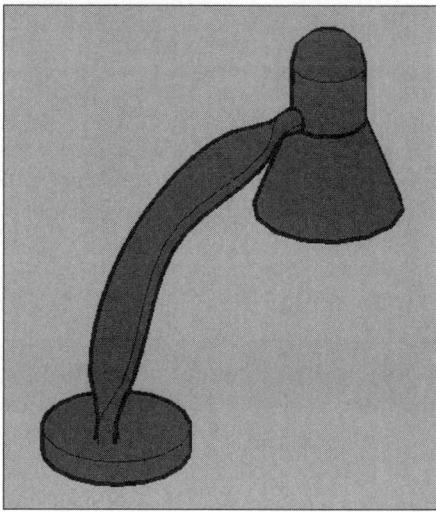

Drawing Polyline-Like Solids

The POLYSOLID command is helpful to architects who want to draw walls in 3D. Using POLYSOLID is like drawing a polyline with a width, or a multiline. You simply draw in plan view from point to point, but the result is a swept solid, using the width and height you specify. You can also convert existing 2D objects — lines, arcs, 2D polylines, and circles — into polysolids.

Figure 24.16 shows a simple layout, drawn by using polysolids.

FIGURE 24.16

You can draw walls by using the POLYSOLID command.

Follow these steps to draw a polysolid:

1. If you want to convert a 2D object, draw the object or open a drawing containing an existing 2D object.

2. Choose Home tab ⇨ Modeling panel ⇨ Polysolid.

3. At the `Specify start point or [Object/Height/Width/Justify] <Object>:` prompt, start by choosing the Height option.

4. At the `Specify height <8'-0">:` prompt, enter a height.

5. The original prompt returns. Choose the Width option. At the `Specify width <0'-6">:` prompt, enter a width.

6. Again the original prompt returns.

   - If you want to convert an existing object, choose the Object option (you can just press Enter because it's the default option). At the `Select object:` option, select the 2D object to complete the polysolid.

   - If you want to draw a new polysolid, specify the start point and continue to specify segments as you would for a polyline. After you specify the first point, you can use the Arc option to create arcs. The prompts are like those for the PLINE command, but you have fewer options. The arc starts tangent to the previous segment. You can specify the direction or the second point for more control.

You can use the Close option to close the polysolid. You can also use the Justify option to determine whether the polysolid is centered around the points you specify (the default), left-justified (your points are to the left side if you're drawing upward), or right-justified.

On the DVD

The drawing used in the following exercise on creating polysolids, `ab24-e.dwg`, is in the `Drawings` folder on the DVD. ■

STEPS: Creating Polysolids

1. Open `ab24-e.dwg` from the DVD. This drawing contains two polylines — one to turn into a polysolid and one to create a door gap.

2. Save the file as `ab24-05.dwg` in your `AutoCAD Bible` folder. If necessary, change the visual style to 3D Wireframe (choose Home tab ⇨ View panel ⇨ Visual Styles drop-down list ⇨ 3D Wireframe). The current layer should be `Walls`.

3. Set the value of the DELOBJ system variable to 0 (zero) so that you don't delete the source object.

4. Choose Home tab ⇨ Modeling panel ⇨ Polysolid. Follow the prompts:

   ```
   Specify start point or [Object/Height/Width/Justify] <Object>: h ↵
   Specify height <0'-4">: 8' ↵
   Specify start point or [Object/Height/Width/Justify] <Object>: w ↵
   Specify width <0'-0 1/4">: 6 ↵
   Specify start point or [Object/Height/Width/Justify] <Object>: ↵ to
       choose the Object option.
   Select object: Select the larger polyline.
   ```

5. Select the new polysolid and change its layer to `Walls`.

6. Zoom into the gap for the door. Repeat the POLYSOLID command. Follow the prompts:

   ```
   Specify start point or [Object/Height/Width/Justify] <Object>: j ↵
   Enter justification [Left/Center/Right] <Right>: r ↵
   Specify start point or [Object/Height/Width/Justify] <Object>: h ↵
   Specify height <8'-0">: 7' ↵
   Specify start point or [Object/Height/Width/Justify] <Object>: Pick
       the front endpoint on the left side of the gap.
   Specify next point or [Arc/Undo]: Pick the front endpoint on the
       right side of the gap.
   Specify next point or [Arc/Undo]: ↵
   ```

7. To create a gap for a side door, you need to create a surface and slice the solid with the surface. (I discuss slicing later in this chapter.) Switch to the 2D layer. Choose Home tab ⇨ Modeling panel ⇨ Solid Creation drop-down list ⇨ Extrude. Select the smaller polyline, end selection, and drag it so that it's higher than the polysolid wall you just created. This creates an extruded surface.

8. Choose Home tab ⇨ Solid Editing panel ⇨ Slice to start the SLICE command. (I discuss this command later in this chapter.) Follow the prompts:

   ```
   Select objects to slice: Select the first polysolid that you created.
   Select objects to slice: ↵
   Specify start point of slicing plane or [planar
   Object/Surface/Zaxis/View/XY/YZ/ZX/3points] <3points>: s ↵
   Select a surface: Select the extruded surface.
   Select solid to keep or [keep Both sides] <Both>: Pick anywhere on
       the main portion of the polysolid wall.
   ```

Note
If you find that this step doesn't work properly, undo it and redo the step, this time choosing the Both option. Then erase the smaller section of the polysolid in the door opening. ∎

9. Make the Walls layer current. Turn off the 2D layer.

10. Save your drawing. It should look like Figure 24.17. If you want, add a polysolid over the front door and rotate the front door to open it. You should also change the DELOBJ system variable back to its original value.

FIGURE 24.17

The polysolid walls with a door and a gap.

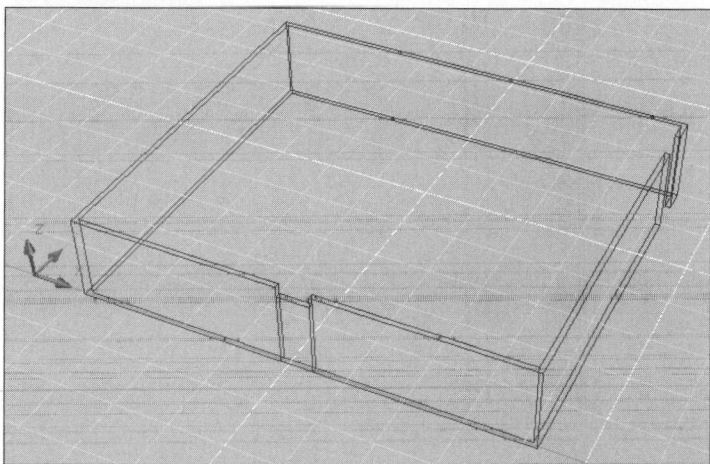

Manipulating Solids

You can directly manipulate solids and meshes (discussed later in this chapter) in several ways that don't involve executing a command. These methods are grip-editing, selecting sub-objects (faces, edges, and vertices), and using the Move, Rotate, and Scale tools (called *gizmos*).

Grip-editing solids
You can grip-edit solids in several ways. When you select them, they show grips that allow you to stretch them in all directions. Figure 24.18 shows the grips for a solid box. The triangular grips stretch objects in the direction of the arrow. The square grips also stretch objects, usually at a corner. One grip at the center just moves the object.

Cross-Reference
You can also use grips to move, rotate, scale, and mirror solids. I cover grip-editing in Chapter 10 for 2D drawings; the same principles apply for 3D drawings. ∎

FIGURE 24.18

You can stretch a 3D solid box in many directions.

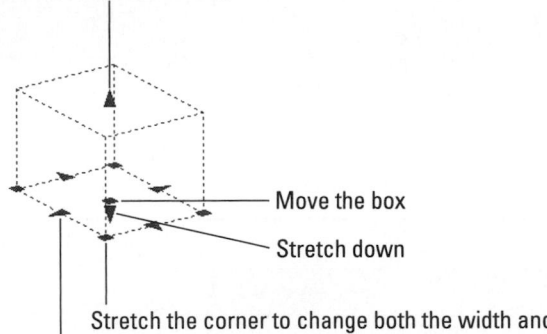

Stretch up to increase height

Move the box

Stretch down

Stretch the corner to change both the width and length

Stretch one side in the direction of the arrow

Selecting sub-objects

You can select *sub-objects* and edit them. A sub-object is the face, edge, or vertex of a solid. A subcomponent of a composite solid — one that you used UNION, SUBTRACT on — is also a sub-object. You can select more than one sub-object, whether on one solid or several solids.

To grip-edit a sub-object, follow these steps:

1. Press Ctrl.
2. Pass the cursor over a face, edge, or vertex. Faces and edges highlight, but vertices don't.
3. Click the grip that appears.
4. Drag the grip to grip-edit the solid.

You can press Ctrl and click to select a sub-object when you select objects for the MOVE, ROTATE, SCALE, or ERASE command. You can press Ctrl and drag a selection or crossing window to select multiple sub-objects.

If you want to select the back face of a solid, you can cycle through the faces by pressing and holding Ctrl and repeatedly pressing the Spacebar. Just as you can press Shift and pick to remove any object from a selection set, you can remove a sub-object from a selection set by pressing and holding Ctrl and pressing Shift while you pick a sub-object.

Note

To help make selecting sub-objects easier, you can create a filter that specifies which type of sub-object you want to select: face, edge, or vertex. Click Home tab ⇨ Subobject panel ⇨ Filter drop-down list and choose one of the options. You can also right-click before selecting any object and choose Subobject Selection Filter from the shortcut menu. ■

Figure 24.19 shows the process of grip-stretching an edge of a box.

Tip

The LEGACYCTRLPICK system variable lets you return to the older use of Ctrl+click, which was to cycle through overlapping objects for easier selection. By default, this system variable is set to 0, which allows you to select sub-objects on 3D solids. Change its value to 1 to use Ctrl+click to cycle through objects. When set to 1, you can't use Ctrl+click to select sub-objects. ∎

You can select sub-objects and edit them separately from the solid.

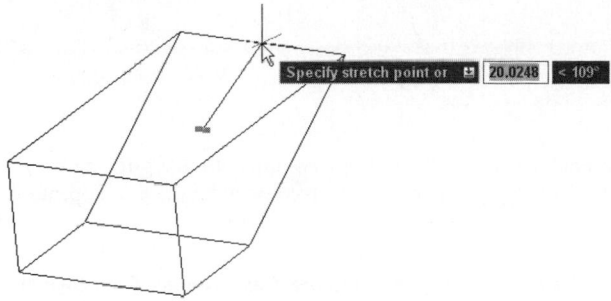

Moving, rotating, and scaling with the gizmos

When moving, rotating, and scaling in 3D, it's often hard to visualize the direction in which you want the object to go. Three tools (called *gizmos*) help with these tasks.

Using the Move gizmo and the 3DMOVE command

You can use the regular MOVE command to move objects in any direction, X, Y, or Z, but entering the coordinates can be awkward. Instead, you can use the Move gizmo, with or without executing the 3DMOVE command, to interactively move objects in 3D space. Figure 24.20 shows the Move gizmo.

To use the Move gizmo by itself, follow these steps:

1. Select an object, with no command active. If you have a 3D visual style active (anything except 2D Wireframe), the Move gizmo automatically appears. (By default, the Quick Properties palette appears nearby; close it if it interferes with your view.)

Note

The DEFAULTGIZMO system variable determines which gizmo appears by default. You can set this system variable by choosing Home tab ⇨ Subobject panel ⇨ Gizmo drop-down list, and choosing one of the gizmos. If one of the other gizmos appears, right-click the gizmo and choose Move from the shortcut menu. You can now use gizmos with sub-objects. If you don't want the Move gizmo to display automatically, set the GTAUTO system variable to 0 (zero). ∎

FIGURE 24.20

Use the Move gizmo to interactively move objects.

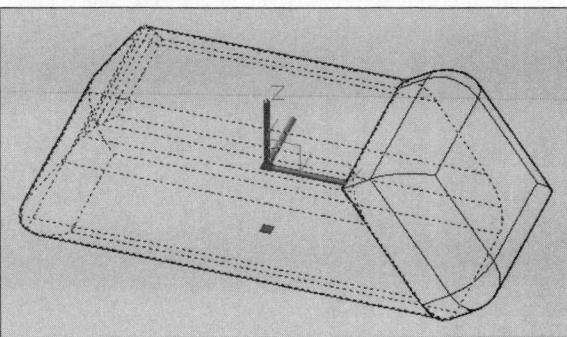

2. Pass the cursor over any grip (but not an arrow); the Move gizmo jumps to that grip. This temporarily places the origin of the UCS at that point and sets the base point for the move operation.

Note

In any 3D visual style, the X axis of the UCS icon is red, the Y axis is green, and the Z axis is blue. The Move gizmo uses the same colors to indicate the same directions. ■

3. You can now choose one of three setups to move the selected object:

- **To move the selected object in any direction.** Drag on the grip itself. This is no different from dragging without the Move gizmo.

- **To constrain the selected object along one axis.** Pass the cursor over that axis until it turns yellow and you see a line extending to the edge of the screen on either side, as shown in Figure 24.20. Click that axis; now you can move the object only along that axis line. Drag the object in the positive or negative direction along the line. You can use direct distance entry to move the object a specific distance, or just click where you want the grip to be.

- **To constrain the selected object along one plane.** Pass the cursor over the right-angle indicator at the intersection of any two axes, until it turns yellow. Click that right-angle indicator; now you can move the object only in that plane. Move the object in the desired direction. You can enter a relative coordinate or click where you want the grip to be.

Tip

Once you constrain the move, you can press the Spacebar to cycle among the three gizmos, retaining the directional constraint you specified. ■

 The 3DMOVE command also uses the Move gizmo, but adds prompts similar to the MOVE command. Follow these steps:

1. Choose Home tab ➪ Modify panel ➪ 3D Move and select objects, or select objects first and then start the command.

Note

If you're using the 2D Wireframe visual style, the command switches you temporarily to the 3D Wireframe visual style. When you're done, the 2D Wireframe visual style returns. ■

2. At the Specify base point or [Displacement] <Displacement>: prompt, the Move gizmo appears.

- To use the **base point/second point method**, specify a base point. You can now constrain movement to an axis or plane as described just previously in this section. Then specify a second point to move the object.

- To use the **displacement method**, enter a displacement as an X,Y or polar coordinate. At the Specify second point or <use first point as displacement>: prompt, press Enter to move the object and end the command. In this situation, you don't use the Move gizmo because you are specifying the movement by entering coordinates.

You have a chance to use the 3DMOVE command later in this chapter in the exercise on Extending Objects in 3D.

Using the Rotate gizmo and the 3DROTATE command

The Rotate gizmo lets you interactively rotate in 3D. You can rotate freely or constrain rotation around one axis. You can use it with or without the 3DROTATE command. To use it alone, follow these steps:

1. Select an object, with no command active. If you have a 3D visual style active (anything except 2D Wireframe), the Rotate gizmo automatically appears. (By default, the Quick Properties palette appears nearby; close it if it interferes with your view.)

Tip

If one of the other gizmos appears, right-click the gizmo and choose Rotate from the shortcut menu. In the previous explanation of the Move gizmo, I explain how to specify which gizmo appears by default. ∎

2. Pass the cursor over any grip (but not an arrow); the Rotate gizmo jumps to that grip. This temporarily places the origin of the UCS at that point and sets the base point for the move operation.

3. To constrain the selected object along one axis, pass the cursor over that axis's handle (a circle) until it turns yellow and you see a line extending to the edge of the screen on either side, as shown in Figure 24.21. Click that axis; now you can rotate the object only along that axis. Drag the object along the circle. You can enter a value to rotate the object a specific angle, or just click when the object is at the desired angle.

Tip

After you constrain the rotation, you can press the Spacebar to cycle among the three gizmos, retaining the directional constraint you specified. ∎

You can also use the 3DROTATE command. Follow these steps:

 1. Start the 3DROTATE command by choosing Home tab ➪ Modify panel ➪ 3D Rotate.

Note

If you are in 2D Wireframe visual style, this command temporarily changes you to 3D Wireframe. You need to be in a nonorthogonal view to use 3DROTATE. ∎

2. Select objects. The Rotate gizmo appears, as shown in Figure 24.21.

3. At the Specify base point: prompt, specify the base point for the rotation. The Rotate gizmo jumps to the base point.

FIGURE 24.21

The Rotate gizmo lets you constrain rotation to any axis in 3D space.

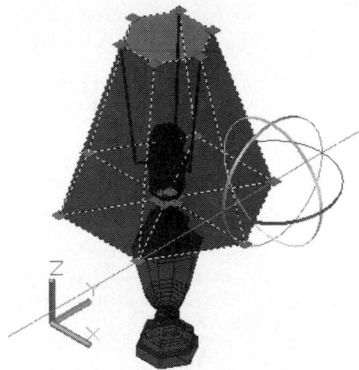

4. At the `Pick a rotation axis:` prompt, hover the cursor over the Ribbon that matches the axis around which you want to rotate. It turns yellow and you see an axis line, as shown in Figure 24.21. Click the yellow Ribbon.

5. At the `Specify angle start point or type an angle:` prompt, you can simply enter the rotation angle that you want, or pick two points to specify the angle.

I discuss another way to rotate, the ROTATE3D command, later in this chapter. There you'll find an exercise that uses the Rotate gizmo.

Using the Scale gizmo and the 3DSCALE command

The Scale gizmo, shown in Figure 24.22, lets you interactively scale in 3D. Most 3D objects you can scale uniformly along all three axes; however, you can scale meshes along one axis or a plane that you choose. I discuss meshes later in this chapter.

FIGURE 24.22

You can scale 3D objects with the Scale gizmo.

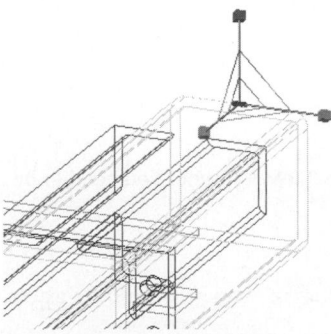

You can use the Scale gizmo with or without the 3DSCALE command. To use it alone, follow these steps:

1. Select an object, with no command active. If you have a 3D visual style active (anything except 2D Wireframe), the Scale gizmo automatically appears. (By default, the Quick Properties palette appears nearby; close it if it interferes with your view.)

Note

If one of the other gizmos appears, right-click the gizmo and choose Scale from the shortcut menu. In the previous explanation of the Move gizmo, I explain how to specify which gizmo appears by default. ∎

2. Pass the cursor over any grip (but not an arrow); the Scale gizmo jumps to that grip. This temporarily places the origin of the UCS at that point and sets the base point for the move operation. (Meshes only have one grip.)

Tip

To move the Scale gizmo to a location not on a grip, right-click and choose Relocate Gizmo. You can then use an object snap to specify any other location. ∎

3. For meshes only, you can constrain the scale along an axis or plane. Do one of the following:

   - **To constrain the selected object along one axis.** Pass the cursor over that axis until it turns yellow and you see a line extending to the edge of the screen on either side. Click that axis; now you can scale the object only along that axis. Drag the object along the axis and click when the object is at the desired size or enter a scale factor.

   - **To constrain the selected object along a plane.** Pass the cursor over one of the lines that join the axes. For example, to scale along the XY plane, pass the cursor over the line that runs from the X axis to the Y axis. The line turns yellow as do the axis names. Click that line; now you can scale the object only along the specified plane. Drag in the direction you want to scale or enter a scale factor.

Note

Once you constrain the scale, you can press the Spacebar to cycle among the three gizmos, retaining the directional constraint you specified. ∎

Tip

It can be hard to see the lines between the planes if the axes are facing away from you. If so, you can press Shift and drag with the mouse wheel to change the 3D view. ∎

You can also use the 3DSCALE command. Follow these steps:

 1. Start the 3DSCALE command by choosing Home tab ⇨ Modify panel ⇨ 3D Scale.

Note

If you are in 2D Wireframe visual style, this command temporarily changes you to 3D Wireframe. You need to be in a nonorthogonal view to use 3DSCALE. ∎

2. Select objects. The Scale gizmo appears, as shown in Figure 24.22.
3. At the `Specify base point:` prompt, specify the base point for the scale operation.

4. At the `Pick a scale axis or plane:` prompt, click an axis or plane line. Remember that you can only pick a scale axis or plane for mesh objects; you can only scale other 3D objects uniformly.

5. At the `Specify scale factor or [Copy/Reference]:` prompt, enter a scale factor or drag to the desired scale.

Working with Mesh Shapes

Meshes are 3D shapes that allow you to create *organic,* flexible models. Meshes can be either surfaces or solids. Meshes contain divisions that tile the mesh into faces. This division of the model into tiles is called *tessellation.* The tessellation divisions bound the edges of each face. You have detailed control over each face, edge, and vertex in the mesh. Figure 24.23 shows a solid mesh.

FIGURE 24.23

A solid mesh after moving and rotating some of the edges and faces.

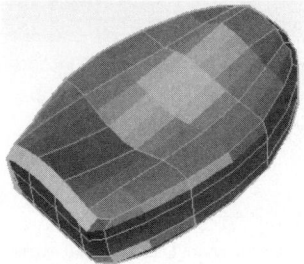

Creating meshes

Just as you can create basic smooth solids, called *primitives,* you can create mesh primitives. The same shapes are available and the prompts are almost identical. To create a mesh primitive, choose Mesh tab ➪ Primitives panel ➪ Mesh Creation drop-down list and choose one of the primitives. Then follow the prompts to complete the object. For more information on these prompts, see the "Drawing Basic Smooth Solids" section earlier in this chapter.

As mentioned in Chapter 23, by default, the REVSURF, RULESURF, EDGESURF, and TABSURF commands create meshes. These commands are also available in the Primitives panel of the Mesh tab.

Editing meshes

The power of meshes becomes apparent when you edit them; the editing tools allow you to mold shapes in ways that you can't with surfaces or smooth solids. The following sections explain how to edit meshes.

Using grips and gizmos to edit meshes

When you select a mesh, you see only one grip. However, by selecting sub-objects, you can easily use grips to stretch, move, rotate, scale, or mirror parts of the mesh. (See the "Selecting sub-objects" section earlier in this chapter for more information.) In this way, you can edit one or more faces, edges, and vertices. In the same way, you can use the Move, Rotate, and Scale gizmos to edit entire meshes or portions of them.

Adjusting mesh smoothness

 You can apply a smoothness value to a mesh to round its edges (the MESHSMOOTHMORE command). By default, you create a mesh with no smoothness and then add smoothness, if desired. Four levels of smoothness are available. To add smoothness, choose Mesh tab ⇨ Mesh panel ⇨ Smooth More. You can use this command until you get a message saying that you can't smooth the mesh any more. You can see a mesh's current Smooth level, and edit that level, in the Quick Properties palette or the Properties palette.

Figure 24.24 shows a mesh box in its original state and at Smooth levels 1 through 4.

FIGURE 24.24

You can smooth a mesh to create a molded look.

 Conversely, you can make a smoothed mesh less smooth (the MESHSMOOTHLESS command), but not less than its original shape. To unsmooth a mesh, choose Mesh tab ⇨ Mesh panel ⇨ Smooth Less. You can do this repeatedly until you see a message that you can't unsmooth the mesh any further.

Refining a mesh

When you *refine a mesh*, you increase the number of faces and, therefore, tessellations that the mesh contains. At the same time, each face becomes smaller, allowing you to make more localized changes to the mesh. You can refine an entire mesh or even an individual face. When you refine an individual face, you divide it into multiple faces. In order to refine a mesh, it must have a smoothness level of 1 or higher.

Refining an object resets its smoothness level to 0, but doesn't change its shape. Therefore, the object continues to look rounded, but you can't reduce its smoothness.

Refining an individual face subdivides the face into new faces, but does not reset the base level of smoothness. This method confines the changes to a smaller area and preserves system resources.

You can specify the number of tessellations that a mesh primitive has before you create it. To do so, choose Mesh tab ⇨ Primitives panel, and click the dialog box launcher arrow at the right end of the panel's title bar to open the Mesh Primitive Options dialog box (the MESHPRIMITIVEOPTIONS command). Choose the type of primitive from the list in the Mesh box and then enter the number of tessellation divisions for the length, height, and base. In the Preview box at the right, you can choose a smoothness level to see how that primitive will look at each level. It's easier to specify the tessellations that you need in advance than to change them later, and you don't need to smooth the model first.

Extruding a face

You can extrude an individual face. Select the face and choose Mesh tab ⇨ Mesh Edit panel ⇨ Extrude Face. At the `Specify height of extrusion or [Direction/Path/Taper angle] <2.0000>:` prompt, enter an extrusion height, or use one of the options. These are the same options used for the EXTRUDE command, which I cover earlier in this chapter.

Splitting a face

You can split a face into two parts, specifying the split path with object snaps or any other method of specifying coordinates. Split a face when you want to modify just part of it. To split a face, choose Mesh tab ⇨ Mesh Edit panel ⇨ Split Face. Then press Ctrl and select the face you want to split. Setting the filter in the Subobject panel's Filter drop-down list to Face can help you select the face more easily. Then specify the first and second split points. Specifying these points can be difficult, and you may have to try a few times to get the points you want.

Creasing a mesh

After smoothing a mesh, you may realize that you want part of the mesh to remain sharp, or *creased*. You can crease a face, edge, or vertex. To crease a sub-object, set the filter in the Subobject panel of the Mesh tab for that sub-object type. Then choose Mesh tab ⇨ Mesh panel ⇨ Add Crease (the MESHCREASE command). At the prompt, select the sub-objects that you want to crease.

At the `Specify crease value [Always] <Always>:` prompt, press Enter to always crease the sub-object. If you want the crease to apply only at lower smoothing levels, specify a level from 1 to 4. Then the sub-object loses its crease if you smooth above that level. You can select the sub-object and modify the crease value in the Properties palette.

Figure 24.25 on the left shows a mesh primitive box with the top face extruded. In the middle, you see the result after two smoothing operations. On the right, you see the result after creasing the top face of the extrusion.

FIGURE 24.25

To retain a face's sharpness after smoothing a mesh, you can add a crease to the face.

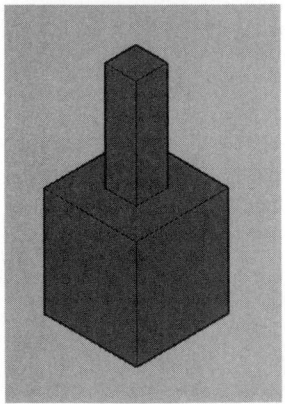
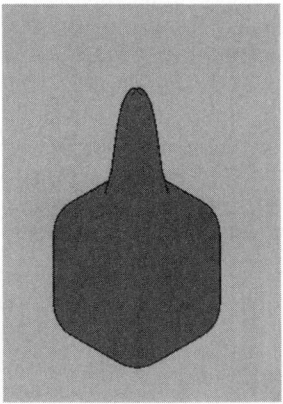

You can uncrease a sub-object; choose Mesh tab ⇨ Mesh panel ⇨ Remove Crease. You can also set the Crease value to 0 on the command line or None in the Properties palette.

Converting solids and meshes

You can convert smooth surfaces and solids to meshes, and vice versa. Each type of object has its own capabilities and you can take advantage of both by converting from one to the other. Previous sections have described how you can edit meshes. The following sections describe how you can edit smooth solids.

Converting smooth solids and surfaces to meshes

 You can convert existing 3D solids, 3D surfaces, 3D faces, polygon meshes, polyface meshes, regions, and closed polylines to mesh objects by using the Smooth Object tool. But before you do so, you should set options for the conversion. Choose Mesh tab ⇨ Mesh panel, and click the dialog box launcher arrow to the right of the panel's name to open the Mesh Tessellation Options dialog box, as shown in Figure 24.26. You can also use this dialog box to actually convert objects.

FIGURE 24.26

The Mesh Tessellation Options dialog box controls the results when you convert 3D solids and surfaces to meshes.

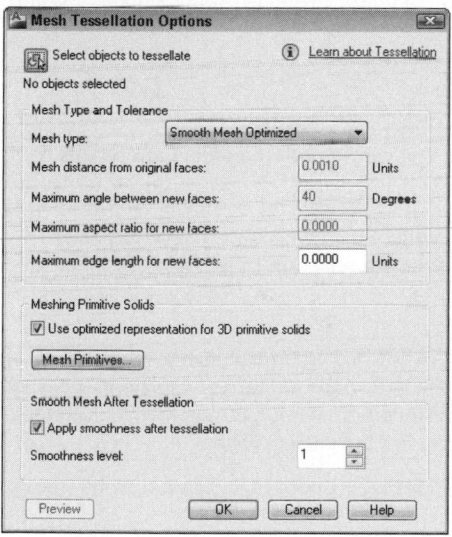

If you want to convert an object right away, click the Select Objects to Tessellate button to return to the drawing. Select the objects.

In the Mesh Type and Tolerance section, you have the following settings:

- **Mesh Type.** Choose a mesh type from the Mesh Type drop-down list. The default, Smooth Mesh Optimized, shapes the faces according to the shape of the mesh object. You can also specify mostly quadrilateral or triangle shapes. The latter two choices don't allow you to apply smoothness during conversion.

- **Mesh Distance from Original Faces.** Sets the maximum deviation of the faces from the shape of the original object. Smaller values result in a more accurate shape, but create more faces. This may slow down performance. The default value is 0.001.

- **Maximum Angle Between New Faces.** Sets the maximum angle between adjacent faces. If you increase the angle, you increase the density of mesh faces in high-curvature areas, and decrease the density in flatter areas. Increase the value if you need to create small details in your model. The default value is 40° and you can set values between 0 and 180.

- **Maximum Aspect Ratio for New Faces.** Sets the maximum height/width ratio for mesh faces. Use this feature to avoid long, skinny faces. The default value, 0, does not limit the aspect ratio. Values greater than 1 specify the maximum ratio that the height can exceed the width. Values less than 1 specify the maximum ratio that the width can exceed the height. A value of 1 creates faces that have the same height and width.

- **Maximum Edge Length for New Faces.** Sets the maximum length of a face's edge. The default value, 0, lets the size of the model determine the size of the faces.

You can check the Use Optimized Representation for 3D Primitive Solids check box to use the values in the Mesh Primitive Options dialog box, discussed in the "Refining a mesh" section earlier in this chapter. Click the Mesh Primitives button to open the Mesh Primitive Options dialog box and make changes there.

You can apply a smoothness level during conversion to a mesh. To do so, check the Apply Smoothness after Tessellation check box and specify the Smoothness Level. The default value is 1, which applies one level of smoothness.

Tip

For the most accurate results when converting, change this value to 0. You can smooth the object afterwards if you want. ■

Click OK to close the dialog box and specify the settings. If you selected an object, the conversion takes place. Otherwise, choose Mesh tab ➪ Mesh panel ➪ Smooth Object and select the object to convert that object according to the settings in the dialog box.

Converting meshes to smooth solids

After creating and editing meshes, you may want to convert them to smooth solids. As I explain in the next section, you can combine (union), subtract, intersect, and fillet smooth solids, something that you cannot do with meshes. To use these editing commands on meshes, you need to convert them.

 To convert a mesh to a solid, choose Home tab ➪ Solid Editing panel (expanded) ➪ Convert to Solid (the CONVTOSOLID command). Select the object or objects to execute the conversion.

Note

Choose Mesh tab ➪ Convert Mesh ➪ SmoothMeshConvert drop-down list (SMOOTHMESHCONVERT system variable) to specify whether you want smoothed or faceted solids and whether you want to optimize (merge) coplanar faces. The default option, Smooth, Optimized (0), creates a smooth model and optimizes coplanar faces. The Smooth, Not Optimized (1) option creates a smooth model but doesn't optimize faces. The Faceted, Optimized (2) option creates flattened faces and optimizes coplanar faces. The Faceted, Not Optimized (3) option creates flattened faces and does not optimize coplanar faces. ■

Tip

You can use the DELOBJ system variable (set it to 0) to retain the original mesh, in case you need to redo the operation later. By default, the value is 1, which deletes the original object. I describe all of the available DELOBJ values earlier in this chapter. ■

STEPS: Creating and Editing Meshes

1. Open a new drawing based on the `acad3d.dwt` template. If you're not in the 3D Modeling workspace, click the Workspace drop-down list on the Quick Access Toolbar and choose 3D Modeling. This exercise assumes that Dynamic Input settings are set to the default of relative coordinates. (For more information, see Chapter 4.)

2. Save it as `ab24-06.dwg` in your AutoCAD Bible folder.

3. Choose Mesh tab ⇨ Primitives panel and click the dialog box launcher arrow at the right end of the panel's title bar to open the Mesh Primitive Options dialog box. In the Tessellation Divisions section, change the Length value to **5** and click OK.

4. Choose Mesh tab ⇨ Primitives panel ⇨ Primitives drop-down list ⇨ Mesh Box. Follow these prompts:

   ```
   Specify first corner or [Center]: 5,5 ↵
   Specify other corner or [Cube/Length]: 85,25 ↵
   Specify height or [2Point] <28.9633>: 60 ↵
   ```

5. Choose Home tab ⇨ View panel ⇨ 3D Navigation drop-down list ⇨ SE Isometric. The box, shown in Figure 24.27, will become a camera. The units are in millimeters.

FIGURE 24.27

This mesh box will become a camera.

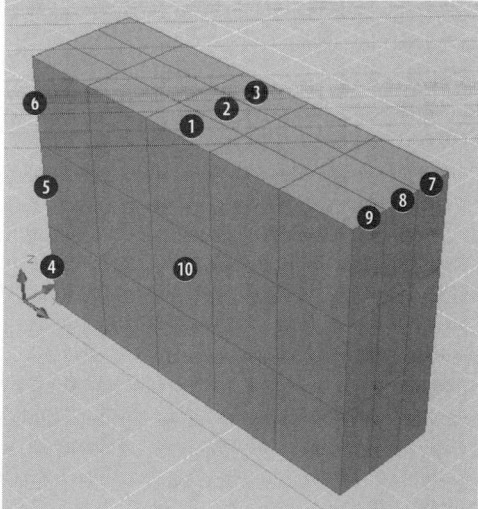

Thanks to Heidi Hewett and Guilermo Melantoni of Autodesk for the original concept of this camera and its modeling.

6. In the Subobject panel of the Mesh tab, choose Face from the Subobject Selection Mode drop-down list. Then choose Move Gizmo from the Default Gizmo drop-down list on the Subobject panel. These choices will help you edit the box.

7. Press the Ctrl key and click the faces at ❶, ❷, and ❸. You should see a red dot in each face and the Move gizmo should appear. Move the cursor over ❷ and the Move gizmo jumps to that point.

8. Move the cursor over the blue Z axis of the Move gizmo until it becomes yellow, and click. Drag upward a little, and then type **10** ↵. Press Esc to deselect the faces.

9. From the Subobject Selection Mode drop-down list, choose Edge. Then press Ctrl and select the three edges at ❹, ❺, and ❻. Move the cursor over the green Y axis of the gizmo until it turns yellow, and click. Drag outward from the camera body a little and then type **20** ↵ to create a grip for the camera. Press Esc to deselect the edges.

10. Press Ctrl and select the three edges at ❼, ❽, and ❾. Move the cursor over the blue Z axis until it turns yellow, and click. Then drag downward a little, and type **7** ↵. Press Esc to deselect the edges.

 11. From the Subobject Selection Mode drop-down list, choose No Filter. Click anywhere on the camera to select it. To round the model, choose Mesh tab ⇨ Mesh panel ⇨ Smooth More. Repeat to smooth the camera a second time. Press Esc to deselect the model.

12. Choose Face from the Subobject Selection Mode drop-down list. Press Ctrl and choose the face at ❿, which will be the lens. When the gizmo appears, right-click it and choose Scale to switch to the Scale gizmo. You want to scale the ZX plane. Place the cursor between the X and Z axes until they turn yellow, and click. It can be difficult to get the right plane; if so, right-click, and choose Set Constraint ⇨ ZX. At the prompt to specify the scale factor, type **1.5** ↵.

13. With the face still selected, pass the cursor over the Z axis until it turns yellow, and click. Then type **1.5** ↵ to scale in the Z direction.

14. To move the lens upwards, right-click the Scale gizmo and choose Move from the shortcut menu. Pass the cursor over the Z axis until it turns yellow, and click. Then drag upwards a little. Type **8** ↵.

15. To extrude the lens, with the lens face still selected, choose Mesh tab ⇨ Mesh Edit panel ⇨ Extrude Face. At the prompt, drag outward from the camera's body a little, and enter **5** ↵.

16. To work on the eyepiece at the back of the camera, choose Home tab ⇨ View panel ⇨ 3D Navigation drop-down list ⇨ NW Isometric.

17. Press Ctrl and click the top-center face on the back of the camera, where the eyepiece would be, to select that face.

18. Right-click the Move gizmo, and choose Scale. You want to scale this face in the ZX plane. Place the cursor between the X and Z axes on the gizmo to turn both axes yellow, and click; if this is hard, right-click and choose Set Constraint ⇨ ZX. At the prompt for a scale factor, enter **.5** ↵ to reduce the size of the face.

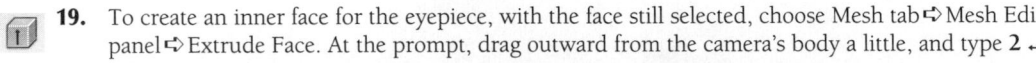 19. To create an inner face for the eyepiece, with the face still selected, choose Mesh tab ⇨ Mesh Edit panel ⇨ Extrude Face. At the prompt, drag outward from the camera's body a little, and type **2** ↵.

20. The extrusion creates a new, inner face. To push that new face out, select the innermost face and again extrude it outward, this time with a value of **1**.

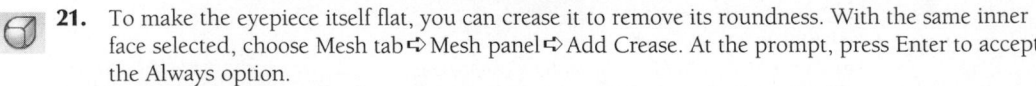 21. To make the eyepiece itself flat, you can crease it to remove its roundness. With the same inner face selected, choose Mesh tab ⇨ Mesh panel ⇨ Add Crease. At the prompt, press Enter to accept the Always option.

22. To make the eyepiece smaller, again select the inner face. If the Scale gizmo does not appear, right-click and choose Scale. As you did previously, select the ZX plane. At the prompt, enter **.7** ↵.

23. To push the eyepiece inward, right-click the Scale gizmo and choose Move to display the Move gizmo. Highlight the green Y axis (it becomes yellow) and click. Drag inward and enter **2** ↵. Press Esc to deselect the face and see the result.

24. You might want to work further on the camera in ways that require a smooth solid. For example, adding a hole for a strap would require the SUBTRACT command (explained in the next section of this chapter). First, go to Mesh tab ➪ Convert Mesh ➪ SmoothMeshConvert drop-down list, and check that the Smooth, Optimized option (the default) is selected. To convert the mesh to a smooth solid, choose Mesh tab ➪ Convert Mesh panel ➪ Convert to Solid. Select the camera and press Enter to end selection. Wait while AutoCAD executes the conversion. The final result should look like Figure 24.28.

FIGURE 24.28

The camera is now a smooth solid, ready for further editing.

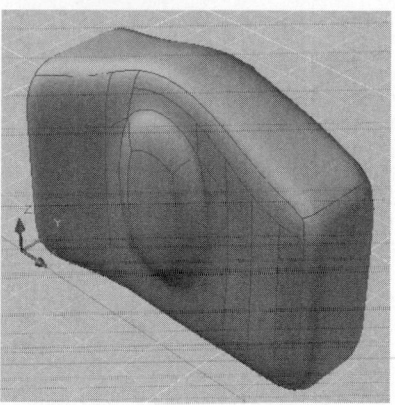
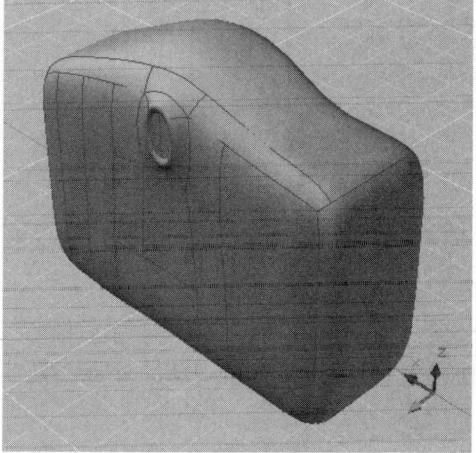

Creating Complex Solids

To create realistic objects, you usually need to edit the simple shapes that I have discussed in this chapter. You can create complex solids by adding them, subtracting them, or intersecting them. These processes are called *Boolean operations,* which in this context means using logical functions, such as addition or subtraction, on objects. You cannot perform Boolean operations on meshes; to do so, first convert them to smooth solids, as described in the previous section of this chapter.

Combining solids

You use the UNION command to add two solids together, making one solid. If the solids are touching, you get a new, unified solid. If the solids are not touching, but rather are completely separate, using UNION is similar to grouping, because you select them as one object. Figure 24.29 shows the union of two solids showing in the Hidden visual style.

Tip

You can also use the UNION command with 2D regions, either for 2D drawings or as a basis for a 3D model. ∎

To start the UNION command, choose Home tab ⇨ Solid Editing panel ⇨ Solid, Union. At the `Select objects:` prompt, select the objects that you want to unite.

FIGURE 24.29

The results of UNION on two solids.

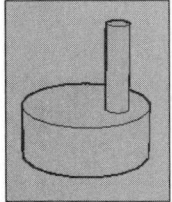

Caution

When you create complex solids, the original solids are not retained. Setting the DELOBJ system variable to 0 (zero) doesn't work because the original solids have been changed. If you want, you can copy the original objects to another location in the drawing, in case you need to use them again. You can also use UNDO if the result is not what you expected. ■

Subtracting solids

You use the SUBTRACT command to subtract one solid from another. This command is most commonly used to create holes. Figure 24.30 shows the result of subtracting a small cylinder from a larger one.

FIGURE 24.30

You can create holes by using the SUBTRACT command.

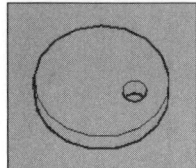

To subtract solids, follow these steps:

1. Choose Home tab ⇨ Solid Editing panel ⇨ Solid, Subtract.
2. At the following prompt, choose the solid (or region) that you want to subtract from (the one you want to keep):

   ```
   Select solids, surfaces, and regions to subtract from...
   Select objects:
   ```
3. At the following prompt, choose the solid (or region) that you want to subtract (the one you want to get rid of):

   ```
   Select solids, surfaces, and regions to subtract...
   Select objects:
   ```

Creating a solid from the intersection of two solids

You can also create a solid from the volume that two solids have in common. This volume is called their intersection. Figure 24.31 shows two solids before and after using the INTERSECT command. As you can see, you can create some very unusual models this way.

A box and a sphere before and after using the INTERSECT command.

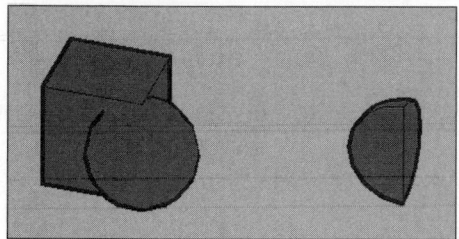

 To use the INTERSECT command, choose Home tab ⇨ Solid Editing panel ⇨ Solid, Intersect. Just select the objects in any order. AutoCAD creates the new solid. As explained for the UNION command, the command does not save your original objects.

Creating a solid from surfaces that enclose a volume

You can create a solid from surfaces that completely enclose a volume, creating an unbroken space, with the SURFSCULPT command.

New Feature

The SURFSCULPT command is new for AutoCAD 2011.

To create the solid, first draw solids that completely enclose a space on all sides. For example, you could draw a rectangle, then choose Surface tab ⇨ Create panel ⇨ Extrude and extrude the rectangle. Then you could choose Surface tab ⇨ Create panel ⇨ Planar Surface to create a surface at the bottom of the extruded rectangle and again at the top. These surfaces would enclose a volume on all six sides. Then choose Surface tab ⇨ Edit panel ⇨ Surface Sculpt and select the surfaces to create the solid.

Creating a new solid by using INTERFERE

INTERFERE is similar to INTERSECT, except that the original solids remain. AutoCAD creates a third solid from the volume that the two solids have in common. You can also use the INTERFERE command to highlight the common volume of several pairs of solids.

Figure 24.32 shows a solid that was created by using INTERFERE, as well as the Interference Checking dialog box, which opens after you select objects.

INTERFERE is useful when you have a number of interfering solids. This command enables you to divide the selection set of solids into two sets so that you can compare one against the other. For example, you can compare a box with three other solids by putting the box in one set and the other three solids in the other set.

FIGURE 24.32

When you use INTERFERE, the original solids remain intact.

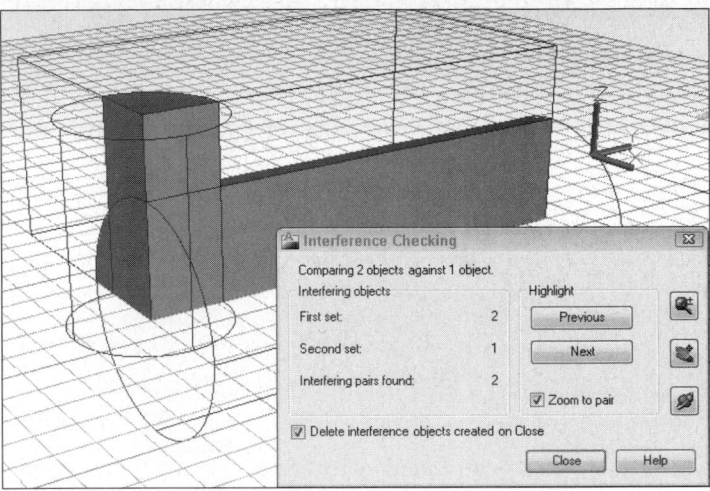

Tip

You can use INTERFERE for troubleshooting and visualizing a complex drawing. For example, you can use INTERFERE to determine which solids need to be subtracted from other solids. The new objects are created on the current layer. You can change the current layer before using INTERFERE to help you more clearly distinguish the new solid that you create. ■

To use INTERFERE, follow these steps:

1. Choose Home tab ⇨ Solid Editing panel ⇨ Interfere.

2. At the Select first set of objects or [Nested selection/Settings]: prompt, select objects. If you want to compare only two objects, you can put them both in the first set. Otherwise, select solids for the first set and press Enter to end object selection.

3. At the Select second set of objects or [Nested selection/checK first set] <checK>: prompt, select the second set of objects and press Enter to end object selection. If you don't want a second set, press Enter to check the solids. The Interference Checking dialog box opens and the display zooms in to the model, shading the interference and showing the rest of the model in wireframe, as shown in Figure 24.32.

4. If you have more than one interference, click the Next button to display the next one. You can use the Zoom Realtime, Pan Realtime, and 3D Orbit buttons to adjust your display. Then press Esc to return to the dialog box.

5. If you want to keep the interference solid after you close the dialog box, uncheck the Delete Interference Objects Created on Close check box.

6. Click Close when you're done.

On the DVD

The drawing used in the following exercise on creating complex solids, ab24-f.dwg, is in the Drawings folder on the DVD. ∎

STEPS: Creating Complex Solids

1. Open ab24-f.dwg from the DVD.

2. Save the file as ab24-07.dwg in your AutoCAD Bible folder. Make sure that Object Snap is on. Set running object snaps for Endpoint, Midpoint, and Center. This drawing is measured in millimeters. The solids have been created by drawing circles, using EXTRUDE, and moving the solids to the proper Z coordinate. The result is shown in Figure 24.33.

FIGURE 24.33

These solids are the basis for the model.

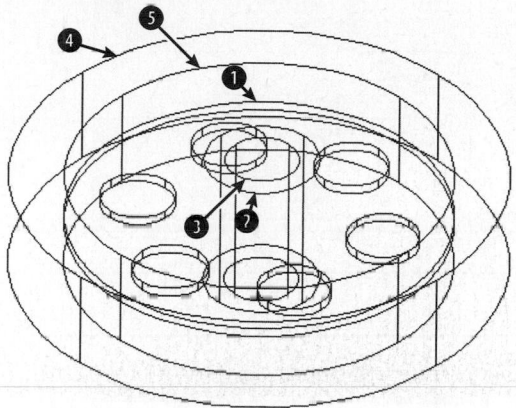

3. To create the six holes arrayed around the center plate, choose Home tab ⇨ Solid Editing panel ⇨ Solid, Subtract. Follow the prompts:

    ```
    Select solids, surfaces, and regions to subtract from...
    Select objects: Select the central plate at ❶ in Figure 24.33.
    Select objects: Right-click.
    Select solids, surfaces, and regions to subtract...
    Select objects: Select the six circles arrayed around the plate.
       Right-click to end selection.
    ```

4. To create the central tube, repeat the SUBTRACT command. Follow the prompts:

    ```
    Select solids, surfaces, and regions to subtract from...
    Select objects: Select the outer tube at ❷.
    Select objects: Right-click.
    Select solids, surfaces, and regions to subtract...
    Select objects: Select the inner tube at ❸. Right-click to end
       selection.
    ```

5. To "carve out" the central disk, again repeat the SUBTRACT command. Follow the prompts:

   ```
   Select solids, surfaces, and regions to subtract from...
   Select objects: Select the outer circle at ❹.
   Select objects: Right-click.
   Select solids, surfaces, and regions to subtract...
   Select objects: Select the inner circle at ❺. Right-click to end
       selection.
   ```

6. Change the visual style to Hidden (choose Home tab ⇨ View panel ⇨ Visual Styles drop-down list ⇨ Hidden). This enables you to check the effects of the subtraction operations. Your drawing should look like Figure 24.34.

FIGURE 24.34

The result of three subtraction operations.

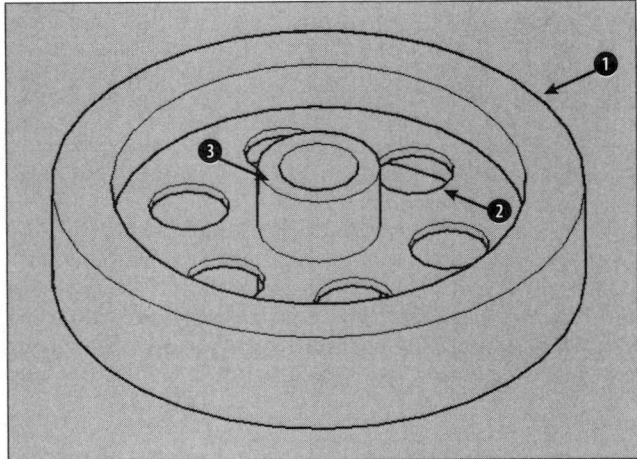

7. Choose Home tab ⇨ Solid Editing panel ⇨ Solid, Union. Select the three solids at ❶, ❷, and ❸, shown in Figure 24.34, and right-click to end selection.

8. Save your drawing.

Pressing or pulling a region

The PRESSPULL command finds closed areas, creates a region, and then lets you extrude or "press" a hole in that region. In addition to any enclosed area that you could hatch, you can press/pull segmented faces of 3D solids. For example, in Figure 24.35, you can press/pull the following:

- All the enclosed objects, such as the closed spline, the circle, and the rectangles.
- The area enclosed by the overlapping rectangles.
- The triangular area on the box created by drawing a line across the top face.
- The space in the middle of the four touching smooth solid (but not mesh) boxes, which does not contain any objects.

You can use the PRESSPULL command on any face of a solid. To use the command on a 2D object, you need to move the UCS to the plane of the boundary, as if you were hatching the area.

FIGURE 24.35

You can press or pull many types of enclosed areas.

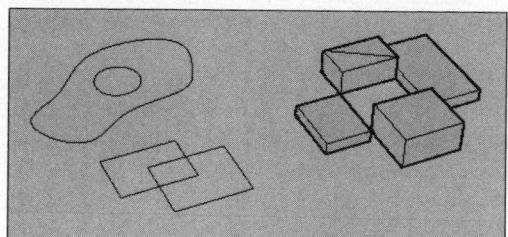

 To press/pull a closed area, choose Home tab ➪ Modeling panel ➪ Presspull. At the Click inside bounded areas to press or pull. prompt, click inside the enclosed area. You should see the following:

```
1 loop extracted.
1 Region created.
```

You can now move the cursor up or down in either direction to press or pull the region. You can click when you like what you see, or enter a value for the height. (You can usually click and drag in one action, but sometimes AutoCAD takes some time to calculate the region; in that case, click, wait a second, and then move the cursor up or down.)

Using solid history

Because AutoCAD doesn't retain source objects when you use the UNION, SUBTRACT, or INTERSECT command, it would be nice to have a way to modify the original objects separately. Solid history does just that.

Note

The SOLIDHIST system variable controls whether the history is maintained in the drawing. By default, this system variable is on, set to 1. ■

You can also display the object's history by selecting the object and setting the Show History item in the Properties palette to Yes. For example, if you used a cylinder to make a hole in a box by using the SUBTRACT command, when you show the history, you see the original cylinder again. This display lasts even when you deselect the object, until you change the setting in the Properties palette.

More important, you can use solid history to edit components of a complex solid. For example, you can move or resize a hole or one part of two objects that you combined. To work with one component of a complex solid, press the Ctrl key as you pass the cursor over the object. The individual component is highlighted. Click to display grips for grip-editing. I explain how to select individual components (sub-objects) and grip-edit solids earlier in this chapter.

The BREP command converts 3D solids into boundary representation (BREP) solids. This process deletes a solid's history and you can no longer grip-edit the solid or change its properties in the Properties palette. BREP is available on the command line only.

On the DVD

The drawing used in the following exercise on using PRESSPULL and solid history, ab24-g.dwg, is in the Drawings folder on the DVD. ■

STEPS: Using PRESSPULL and Solid History

1. Open ab24-g.dwg from the DVD.

2. Save the file as ab24-08.dwg in your AutoCAD Bible folder. This is the base of the lamp that was used for several exercises earlier in this chapter. There is a circle on the const layer at the top of the base. If necessary, change the visual style to Wireframe (choose Home tab ⇨ View panel ⇨ Visual Styles drop-down list ⇨ Wireframe).

3. Choose Home tab ⇨ Modeling panel ⇨ Presspull. At the Click inside bounded areas to press or pull. prompt, move the cursor inside the small circle until you see that it is highlighted. Click and drag downward through the thickness of the base (until you see it below the base — make it long) and then click. The cylinder jumps to the thickness of the base. You now have a hole in the base (for the arm).

4. Turn off the const layer.

5. Choose Home tab ⇨ Subobject panel ⇨ Filter drop-down list ⇨ Solid History. The Solid History option allows you to select the objects that were recorded when a solid was edited.

6. Press the Ctrl key and pass the cursor over the center of the new hole. When you see the long cylinder that you originally pressed, click. You now see some grips.

7. Click the grip at ❶, shown in Figure 24.36, and drag the hole to any new location. Then click.

8. Deselect the object.

9. Save your drawing.

FIGURE 24.36

You can drag a hole to another location because composite objects retain a record of their history.

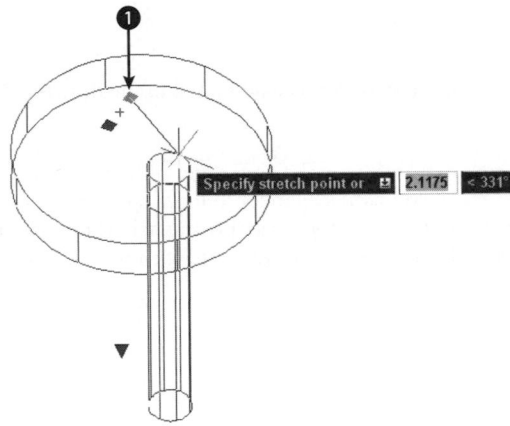

Sectioning and Slicing Solids

In many drawings, you need to show a cross-section of your models. A cross-section displays the inside of a 3D object. The SECTION, SECTIONPLANE, and SLICE commands create cross-section views of your 3D models.

Using the SECTION command

The SECTION command creates a 2D region from a cross-section of a 3D model along a plane that you specify. The original objects are left untouched. Figure 24.37 shows a region created by using the SECTION command.

The region created by using SECTION is shown with a dashed line.

Region created using SECTION

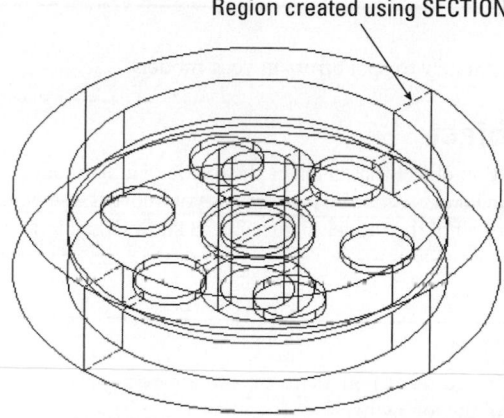

Tip

The SECTION command creates the region on the current layer. Switch to a layer with a contrasting color from the object's layer so that the region is clearly visible. ■

To use the SECTION command, enter **section** on the command line. Select the object that you want to section. AutoCAD displays the `Specify first point on Section plane by [Object/Zaxis/View/XY/YZ/ZX/3points] <3points>:` prompt. Use these options to define the plane of the cross-section. Table 24.1 explains how to use the options.

TABLE 24.1

SECTION Options

Option	Description
Object	Enables you to choose a circle, ellipse, arc, spline, or 2D polyline.
Zaxis	Defines the plane by defining a Z axis. The sectioning plane is then the XY plane perpendicular to the Z axis that you defined. You define the Z axis by first specifying a point on the sectioning plane. This point is the 0,0,0 point (for purposes of this command only) where the sectioning plane and the Z axis meet. Then you pick a point on the Z axis.
View	Defines the section plane parallel to the current view at the intersection of a point that you specify.
XY	Defines the section plane parallel to the XY plane at the intersection of a point that you specify.
YZ	Defines the section plane parallel to the YZ plane at the intersection of a point that you specify.
ZX	Defines the section plane parallel to the ZX plane at the intersection of a point that you specify.
3points	This is the default. Specify three points to define the section plane. Using object snaps is a good idea.

You can move the region that you create and view it separately to spot errors in your models.

Creating an interactive section object

The SECTIONPLANE command creates a movable section object that displays the inside of a 3D model. When you turn *live sectioning* on, you can see the resulting cross-section in real-time as you move the section plane. You can flip the section plane to show the other half of the model. Figure 24.38 shows a section object.

To create a section plane, follow these steps:

1. Choose Mesh tab ⇨ Section panel ⇨ Section Plane.
2. At the `Select face or any point to locate section line or [Draw section/Orthographic]:` prompt, do one of the following:
   - Pick a face of a 3D solid. Live sectioning is turned on.
   - Pick the first point of a section line. Then specify a second point at the `Specify through point:` prompt.
   - Use the Draw Section option to pick several points to create a section with corners (jogs). Live sectioning is turned off.
   - Use the Orthographic option to choose one of the orthographic directions. This creates a plane that applies to all 3D objects in your drawing. Live sectioning is turned on.
3. If Live sectioning is not on, you see just the section object's line. Select the section line, right-click, and choose Activate Live Sectioning.
4. Use the centerline end and center grips to move the section plane and adjust the sectioning of the object in real-time. You can use the flip arrow to view the other side of the object. Click the drop-down arrow to display a section boundary or section volume.

FIGURE 24.38

You can use the SECTIONPLANE command to see various sections of a model in real-time.

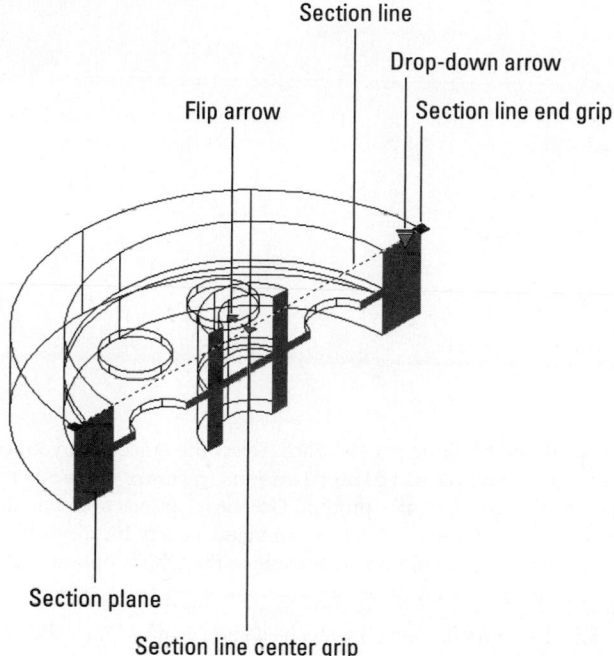

You can click the live section line and right-click to access section settings. To continue working, deactivate live sectioning and deselect the section plane line, which is quite unobtrusive.

The drop-down arrow lets you choose a section boundary or volume. The section boundary defines a plane perpendicular to the section option, underlying the visible part of the 3D model. The section volume defines a box encompassing the visible part of the model.

To specify settings for section planes, click the dialog box launcher arrow at the right end of the Section panel's title bar to open the Section Settings dialog box. Here you can activate live sectioning and specify how the intersection of the object and the section looks.

Using the SLICE command

The SLICE command slices a solid (but not a mesh) into two parts along a plane or surface. The original solids are modified but can be reunited with UNION. You can delete either part or keep both. Figure 24.39 shows the result of slicing a model, after one half of the model has been deleted. This can help you to identify problems in the construction of the model. For example, this slice reveals a fault with the model — the flat disk continues through the central tube — not the desired result. However, you can also use the SLICE command to construct your models. For example, in the exercise on drawing basic solids, the lamp top was a sphere. You could slice this sphere, because the lamp should only have a top half of the sphere.

FIGURE 24.39

The result of slicing a solid and retaining one of the resulting pieces.

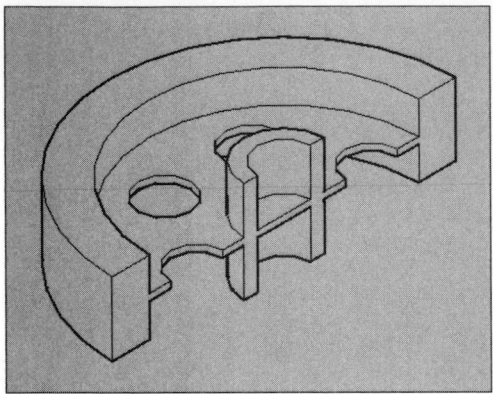

 To use the SLICE command, choose Home tab ⇨ Solid Editing panel ⇨ Slice. Select the object that you want to slice. AutoCAD displays the `Specify start point of slicing plane or [planar Object/Surface/Zaxis/View/XY/YZ/ZX/3points] <3points>:` prompt. Use these options to define the plane of the cross-section. The options are the same as for the SECTION command, except for the Surface option, and are explained in Table 24.1. (The Planar Object option is the same as the Object option in the SECTION command.)

The Surface option enables you to cut any lofted, extruded, swept, or revolved surface out of the solid. You can create some interesting shapes this way.

On the DVD

The drawing used in the following exercise on slicing solids, `ab24-07.dwg`, **is in the** `Results` **folder on the DVD.** ■

STEPS: Slicing Solids

1. If you did the exercise on creating complex solids, open `ab24-07.dwg` from your `AutoCAD Bible` folder; otherwise, open it from the `Results` folder of the DVD. If necessary, change the visual style to Wireframe. Object Snap should be on, with running object snaps for Endpoint, Midpoint, Center, and Quadrant. The drawing is shown in Figure 24.40.

2. Save your drawing as `ab24-09.dwg` in your `AutoCAD Bible` folder.

 3. Choose Home tab ⇨ Solid Editing panel ⇨ Slice. Follow the prompts:

```
Select objects: Select the solid model.
Select objects: Right-click.
Specify start point of slicing plane or [planar
Object/Surface/Zaxis/View/XY/YZ/ZX/3points] <3points>: ↵
Specify first point on plane: Pick the quadrant at ❶ in Figure
    24.40.
Specify second point on plane: Pick the quadrant at ❷.
Specify third point on plane: Pick the quadrant at ❸.
Specify a point on desired side of the plane or [keep Both sides]:
    Pick the model at ❹.
```

FIGURE 24.40

FIGURE 24.40

The 3D model for slicing.

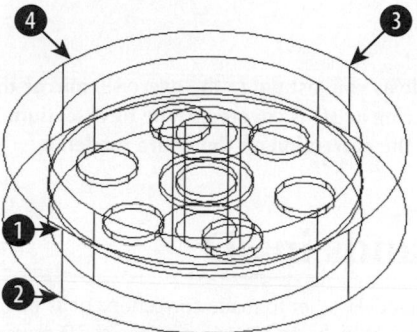

4. As mentioned earlier, the slicing reveals an error — the disk cuts through the central tube, as shown in Figure 24.41. To fix the error, zoom in so that the model takes up the entire screen.

5. Start the CYLINDER command. Follow the prompts:

```
Specify center point of base or [3P/2P/Ttr/Elliptical]: Pick the
    midpoint at ❶ in Figure 24.41.
Specify base radius or [Diameter] <3.2605>: Pick the endpoint at ❷.
Specify height or [2Point/Axis endpoint] <9.2711>: Move the cursor
    upward and enter 16 ↵.
```

FIGURE 24.41

The solid after slicing and deleting one half.

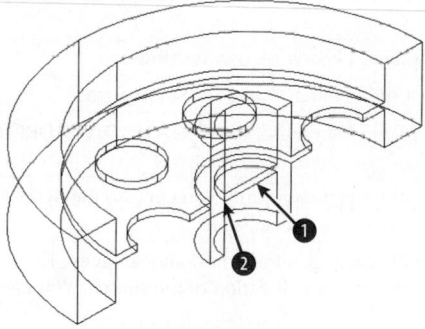

6. Choose Home tab ⇨ Solid Editing panel ⇨ Solid, Subtract. At the Select solids, surfaces, and regions to subtract from... Select objects: prompt, select the large solid and right-click to end object selection. At the Select solids, surfaces, and regions to subtract... Select objects: prompt, select the new cylinder that you just drew and right-click. AutoCAD subtracts the cylinder from the larger model.

825

7. Change the visual style to Hidden (choose Home tab⇨View panel⇨Visual Styles drop-down list⇨Hidden). Return to your previous view.

8. Save your drawing. If you're continuing on to the next exercise, keep the drawing open.

Note

To correct the model, you could subtract out the circle as you just did in the exercise, mirror the entire model, and use UNION to make the two halves whole. Mirroring in 3D is covered in the next section. You could also undo the slice as soon as you saw the error and make the correction on the entire model. ∎

Using Editing Commands in 3D

When you draw in 3D, you need to edit your models either to make corrections or as part of the construction process. A number of editing commands are exclusively for 3D or have special 3D options. In this section, you explore these special commands and options. Table 24.2 lists most of the 2D editing commands and how they're used in 3D drawings.

TABLE 24.2

Editing Commands in 3D

Command	Use in 3D Drawings
ERASE	Same as for 2D.
COPY	Same as for 2D.
MIRROR	Can be used on 3D objects as long as the mirror line is in the XY plane, including using grips. Otherwise, use MIRROR3D.
OFFSET	Can be used in 3D space, but only on 2D objects. You can also use the SURFOFFSET command with 3D surfaces.
ARRAY	Can be used on 3D objects in the XY plane. Otherwise, use 3DARRAY.
MOVE	Same as for 2D; can also use the 3DMOVE command and the Move gizmo.
ROTATE	Can be used on 3D objects in the XY plane. Otherwise, use ROTATE3D, or 3DROTATE. You can use the Rotate gizmo.
SCALE	Can be used on 3D objects. Scales in all three dimensions. You can use the 3DSCALE and the Scale gizmo. For meshes, you can choose the plane or axis to scale.
STRETCH	Can be used in 3D space, but only on 2D objects, wireframes, and surfaces. The results may not be what you expect because it is hard to visualize the direction of the stretch. You can stretch 3D objects with grips.
LENGTHEN	Can be used in 3D space, but only on 2D objects.
TRIM	Has special options for 3D, but works only on 2D objects, such as lines. You can also use the SURFTRIM and SURFUNTRIM commands with 3D surfaces.
EXTEND	Has special options for 3D, but works only on 2D objects, such as lines. You can also use the SURFEXTEND command with 3D surfaces.
BREAK	Can be used in 3D space, but only on 2D objects.

Command	Use in 3D Drawings
CHAMFER	Has special options for 3D. You can also use the CHAMFEREDGE command on 3D solids.
FILLET	Has special options for 3D. You can also use the FILLETEDGE command on 3D solids or the SURFFILLET command on 3D surfaces.
EXPLODE	Works on 3D objects — solids explode to surfaces, and surfaces explode to wireframes. Sometimes, you get regions. You can explode blocks containing 3D objects.
ALIGN	Works on 3D objects. You can also use the 3DALIGN command.

Mirroring in 3D

If the mirror line is on the XY plane, you can mirror any 3D object with the regular MIRROR command. If you want to mirror in any other plane, use MIRROR3D.

To use MIRROR3D, follow these steps:

1. Choose Home tab ⇨ Modify panel ⇨ 3D Mirror.
2. Select the object or objects that you want to mirror.
3. At the Specify first point of mirror plane (3 points) or [Object/Last/Zaxis/View/XY/YZ/ZX/3points] <3points>: prompt, choose one of the options to define the mirroring plane. These are the same options described in Table 24.1 for the SECTION command. The only additional option is Last, which uses the last defined mirroring plane.
4. At the Delete source objects? [Yes/No] <N>: prompt, press Enter to keep the original objects, or right-click and choose Yes to delete them.

On the DVD

The drawing used in the following exercise on mirroring in 3D, ab24-09.dwg, is in the Results folder on the DVD. ∎

STEPS: Mirroring in 3D

1. If you have ab24-09.dwg open from the previous exercise, use this drawing. If you don't have it open, open it from your AutoCAD Bible folder or from the Results folder of the DVD. If necessary, change the visual style to Wireframe. Make sure that Object Snap is on, and set a running object snap for Endpoint. The drawing is shown in Figure 24.42.
2. Save your drawing as ab24-10.dwg in your AutoCAD Bible folder.

3. Choose Home tab ⇨ Modify panel ⇨ 3D Mirror. Follow the prompts:

```
Select objects: Select the solid. Right-click to end object
    selection.
Specify first point of mirror plane (3 points) or
[Object/Last/Zaxis/View/XY/YZ/ZX/3points] <3points>: Pick ❶ in
    Figure 24.42.
Specify second point on mirror plane: Pick ❷.
Specify third point on mirror plane: Pick ❸.
Delete source objects? [Yes/No] <N>: Right-click and choose Enter.
```

4. Choose Home tab ⇨ Solid Editing panel ⇨ Solid, Union. Select both solids. Right-click to end object selection. AutoCAD unites them.

5. Save your drawing.

This 3D model was sliced and can now be mirrored.

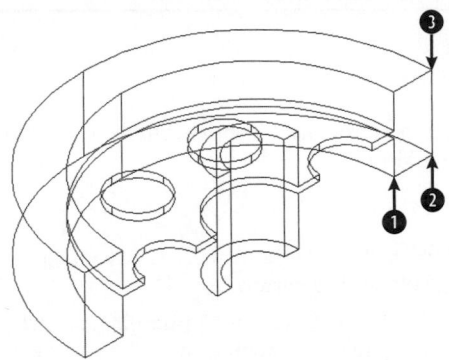

Arraying in 3D

You can array any 3D object by using the ARRAY command as long as you define the array in the current XY plane. The 3DARRAY command enables you to create a rectangular array with the normal rows and columns, but adding levels in the Z direction. For a 3D polar array, you define an axis of rotation instead of the 2D point used in the ARRAY command.

Creating 3D rectangular arrays

A 3D rectangular array has rows, columns, and levels. To create a 3D rectangular array, follow these steps:

1. Choose Home tab ⇨ Modify panel ⇨ 3D Array to start the 3DARRAY command.

2. Select the objects that you want to array.

3. At the `Enter the type of array [Rectangular/Polar] <R>:` prompt, right-click and choose Rectangular.

4. At the `Enter the number of rows (---) <1>:` prompt, type the total number of rows that you want. Rows are parallel to the X axis.

5. At the `Enter the number of columns (||||) <1>:` prompt, type the total number of columns that you want. Columns are parallel to the Y axis.

6. At the `Enter the number of levels (...) <1>:` prompt, type the total number of levels that you want. Levels are parallel to the Z axis.

7. At the `Specify the distance between rows (---):` prompt, type a unit distance or pick two points.

8. At the `Specify the distance between columns (||||):` prompt, type a unit distance or pick two points.

9. At the `Specify the distance between levels (...):` prompt, type a unit distance or pick two points.

On the DVD

The drawing used in the following exercise on creating a rectangular array in 3D, `ab24-h.dwg`, is in the `Drawings` folder on the DVD. ∎

STEPS: Creating a Rectangular Array in 3D

1. Open `ab24-h.dwg` from the DVD.

2. Save the file as `ab24-11.dwg` in your `AutoCAD Bible` folder. This is a drawing showing a sphere, a bead-like shape sometimes used for table legs. In this exercise, you create a 3D rectangular array to create four table legs.

3. Choose Home tab ⇨ Modify panel ⇨ 3D Array. Follow the prompts:

```
Select objects: Select the bead. Right-click to end object selection.
Enter the type of array [Rectangular/Polar] <R>: Right-click and
     choose Rectangular.
Enter the number of rows (---) <1>: 2 ↵
Enter the number of columns (|||) <1>: 2 ↵
Enter the number of levels (...) <1>: 20 ↵ (The bead is 1.5 inches
     high and the leg should be 30 inches high.)
Specify the distance between rows (---): 26 ↵ (This is the narrower
     distance between the legs.)
Specify the distance between columns (|||): 36 ↵ (This is the wider
     distance between the legs.)
Specify the distance between levels (...): 1.5 ↵ (You want the beads
     to touch along the leg.)
```

4. Do a Zoom Extents to see the result. (Now you would create the tabletop.)

5. Save your drawing. It should look like Figure 24.43.

FIGURE 24.43

The four legs of a table, created by using a 3D rectangular array.

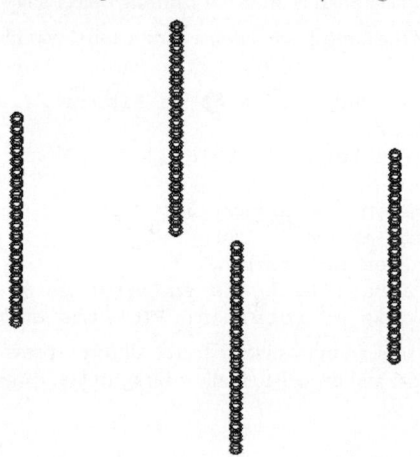

Creating 3D polar arrays

Instead of using a center point as you do in a 2D polar array, you define a center axis. To create a 3D polar array, follow these steps:

1. Choose Home tab ⇨ Modify panel ⇨ 3D Array to start the 3DARRAY command.

2. Select the objects that you want to array.

3. At the `Enter the type of array [Rectangular/Polar] <R>:` prompt, right-click and choose Polar.

4. At the `Enter the number of items in the array:` prompt, type the total number of items that you want.

5. At the `Specify the angle to fill (+=ccw, -=cw) <360>:` prompt, press Enter to array around a full circle or type any lesser angle.

6. At the `Rotate arrayed objects? [Yes/No] <Y>:` prompt, press Enter to accept the default or type **n** ↵ if you don't want to rotate the objects as they're arrayed.

7. At the `Specify center point of array:` prompt, specify the center point of the array. This is also the first point of the axis of rotation.

8. At the `Specify second point on axis of rotation:` prompt, specify any other point on the axis of rotation.

If you rotate less than a full circle, you need to determine the positive angle of rotation. The positive direction of the axis goes from the first point that you specify (the center point) to the second point. Point your right thumb in the positive direction and follow the curl of the fingers of that hand to determine the positive angle of rotation.

On the DVD

The drawing used in the following exercise on creating 3D polar arrays, `ab24-i.dwg`, is in the `Drawings` folder on the DVD. ∎

STEPS: Creating 3D Polar Arrays

1. Open `ab24-i.dwg` from the DVD.

2. Save the file as `ab24-12.dwg` in your `AutoCAD Bible` folder. You see part of a lamp, as shown in Figure 24.44. Make sure that Object Snap is on. Set a running object snap for Endpoint.

3. To array the bracket that supports the lampshade, choose Home tab ⇨ Modify panel ⇨ 3D Array. Follow the prompts:

   ```
   Select objects: Select the support at ❶ in Figure 24.44.
   Select objects: Right-click.
   Enter the type of array [Rectangular/Polar] <R>: Right-click and
       choose Polar.
   Enter the number of items in the array: 3 ↵
   Specify the angle to fill (+=ccw, -=cw) <360>: ↵
   Rotate arrayed objects? [Yes/No] <Y>: ↵
   Specify center point of array: Pick the endpoint at ❷.
   Specify second point on axis of rotation: Pick the endpoint at ❸.
   ```

4. One of the three supports cannot be seen in this view. To see all three, press Shift+mouse wheel to enter transparent 3D Orbit mode, and drag diagonally a bit until you can see all three supports.

5. Choose Home tab ⇨ View panel ⇨ 3D Navigation drop-down list ⇨ Top to return to plan view, and save your drawing.

FIGURE 24.44

A partially completed lamp.

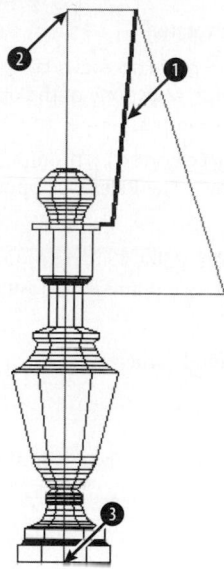

Rotating in 3D

You can rotate 3D objects in the XY plane with the ROTATE command. Use ROTATE3D when you need to rotate objects in any other plane. (The 3DROTATE command, which I discussed earlier in this chapter, offers interactive rotating in 3D.) When you use the ROTATE3D command, you need to specify the axis of rotation. The ROTATE3D options are shown in Table 24.3.

TABLE 24.3

ROTATE3D Options

Option	Description
Object	Enables you to choose a line, circle, arc, or 2D polyline. If you choose a circle or arc, AutoCAD rotates around a line that starts at the object's center and extends perpendicular to the object's plane.
Last	Uses the last defined axis of rotation.
View	Defines the axis of rotation parallel to the current view at the intersection of a point that you specify.
Xaxis	The axis of rotation is parallel to the X axis and passes through a point that you specify.
Yaxis	The axis of rotation is parallel to the Y axis and passes through a point that you specify.
Zaxis	The axis of rotation is parallel to the Z axis and passes through a point that you specify.
2points	This is the default. Specify two points to define the axis. It's a good idea to use object snaps.

Tip

Sometimes creating an object in the XY plane and then rotating it afterward is easier. In other words, you may create an object in the wrong plane on purpose and use ROTATE3D or 3DROTATE later to properly place it. ■

To use ROTATE3D, follow these steps:

1. Enter **rotate3d** ⏎ on the command line.
2. Select the object or objects that you want to rotate.
3. At the `Specify first point on axis or define axis by [Object/Last/View/` `Xaxis/Yaxis/Zaxis/2points]:` prompt, select one of the options explained in Table 24.3, and define the axis according to the option prompts.
4. At the `Specify rotation angle or [Reference]:` prompt, specify a positive or negative rotation angle or choose the Reference option. (The Reference option works like the Reference option for ROTATE. See Chapter 9.)

You need to determine the positive direction of rotation. Point your right thumb in the positive direction of the axis and follow the curl of your fingers. If you pick two points, the positive direction of the axis goes from the first pick point to the second pick point.

The 3DROTATE command and Rotate gizmo are covered earlier in this chapter.

On the DVD

The drawing used in the following exercise on rotating in 3D, ab24-j.dwg, is in the Drawings folder on the DVD. ■

STEPS: Rotating in 3D

1. Open ab24-j.dwg from the DVD.
2. Save the file as ab24-13.dwg in your AutoCAD Bible folder. You see the same lamp used in the previous exercise, but it has now been completed.
3. To insert the lamp in a plan view drawing of a house, you need to see it in plan view from the WCS. In other words, you should be looking down at the lamp. To do this, you need to rotate the lamp around the X axis. To visualize this, look at the UCS icon and imagine rotating the top of the lamp toward you around the horizontal (X) axis. To rotate the lamp, enter **rotate3d** ⏎ on the command line. Follow the prompts:

   ```
   Select objects: Start a crossing window to select the entire lamp.
   Select objects: Right-click to end selection.
   Specify first point on axis or define axis by [Object/Last/View/
       Xaxis/Yaxis/Zaxis/2points]: Right-click and choose Xaxis.
   Specify a point on the X axis <0,0,0>: Right-click.
   Specify rotation angle or [Reference]: 90 ⏎
   ```

4. Zoom to the extents of the drawing to see the entire lamp. The lamp is now rotated 90 degrees around the X axis in relation to the UCS, and you're looking at it from the top.
5. To get a better view, choose Home tab ➪ View panel ➪ 3D Navigation drop-down list ➪ SE Isometric. Change the visual style to Hidden (choose Home tab ➪ View panel ➪ Visual Styles drop-down list ➪ Hidden). The lamp should look like Figure 24.45.
6. Save your drawing.
7. To try the same rotation by using the 3DROTATE command, re-open ab24-j.dwg. You can save it again as ab24-13.dwg, because the result will be the same, or save it as ab24-13-1.dwg.

The lamp is now ready to place in a 3D drawing of a house.

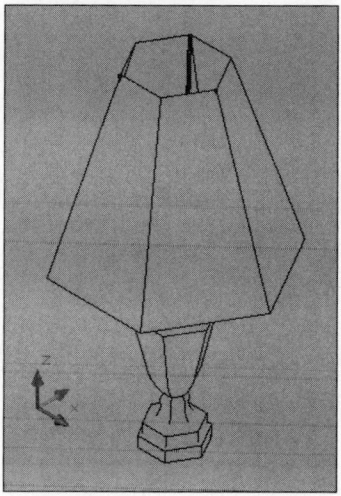

8. Change the visual style to Wireframe. Press Shift+mouse wheel and change the viewpoint so that you can see all three axes on the UCS icon.

9. Choose Home tab ⇨ Modify panel ⇨ 3D Rotate. At the `Select objects:` prompt, select the entire lamp and end selection.

10. At the `Specify base point:` prompt, specify the bottom corner of the lamp, using an Endpoint object snap.

11. At the `Pick a rotation axis:` prompt, hover over the red (X axis) Ribbon until it turns yellow, and click.

12. At the `Specify angle start point or type an angle:` prompt, enter **90** ↵.

13. Save your drawing.

Aligning in 3D

I have already covered the ALIGN and the 3DALIGN commands in Chapter 10. When you work in 3D, you can use these commands to move, rotate in the XY plane, and rotate in the Z direction — all in one command. In this exercise, you use the 3DALIGN command.

On the DVD

The drawing used in the following exercise on aligning in 3D, ab24-k.dwg, is in the Drawings folder on the DVD. ∎

STEPS: Aligning in 3D

1. Open ab24-k.dwg from the DVD.

2. Save the file as ab24-14.dwg in your AutoCAD Bible folder. You see part of the base assembly for an industrial washer, as shown in Figure 24.46. One sidebar needs to be moved and rotated into place. Make sure that Object Snap is on; set a running object snap for Endpoint.

FIGURE 24.46

Part of a base assembly for an industrial washer with a sidebar that needs to be moved and rotated into place. ■

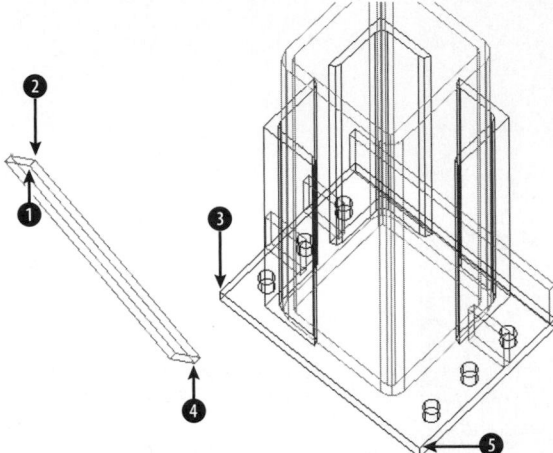

Thanks to Robert Mack of the Dexter Company, Fairfield, Iowa, for this drawing.

3. Notice that it's hard to tell which way the sidebar is facing because it's displayed in wireframe. Change the visual style to Hidden (choose Home tab ➪ View panel ➪ Visual Styles drop-down list ➪ Hidden). You can now see that ❶, shown in Figure 24.46, is facing away from you. Switch back to the Wireframe visual style.

4. Choose Home tab ➪ Modify panel ➪ 3D Align. Follow the prompts:

```
Select objects: Select the sidebar.
Select objects: Right-click.
Specify base point or [Copy]: Pick ❶ in Figure 24.46.
Specify second point or [Continue] <C>: Pick ❹.
Specify third point or [Continue] <C>: Pick ❷.
Specify first destination point: Pick ❸.
Specify second destination point or [eXit] <X>: Pick ❺.
Specify third destination point or [eXit] <X>: Pick any point further
    back than ❸ on the plate.
```

The smaller bars (shown in red in the drawing) provide several endpoints that you can easily locate.

5. AutoCAD aligns the sidebar. Save your drawing. It should look like Figure 24.47.

Tip

The trick when aligning in 3D is to properly visualize the parts. It helps to switch to Hidden visual style first, as you did in the exercise. Also, take the time to find the UCS and a viewpoint that make the points that you're specifying easy to see and pick. ■

Trimming and extending in 3D

You can use the TRIM and EXTEND commands to trim or extend 2D objects in 3D space. (I cover these commands for 2D drawing in Chapter 10.) AutoCAD provides the Project option for working in 3D space. The Project option has three sub-options:

FIGURE 24.47

The sidebar has been aligned with the rest of the model.

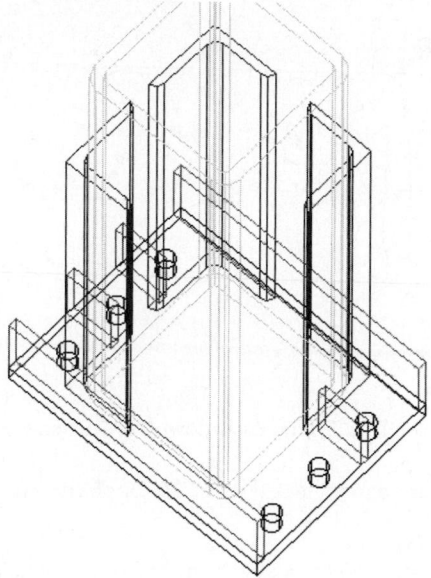

- **None.** AutoCAD trims or extends only objects that actually intersect or can intersect in 3D space.
- **UCS.** This is the default. AutoCAD projects objects onto the XY plane of the current UCS. Therefore, if two lines are on different Z coordinates, you can trim and extend one of them with reference to the other, even though they do not and cannot actually meet in 3D space.
- **View.** This projects objects parallel to the current view. Objects are trimmed or extended, based on the way they look on the screen. They need not (and probably won't) actually meet in 3D space.

You can also use the Extend option to trim or extend to implied intersections, as explained in Chapter 10. In the next exercise, you practice extending objects in 3D; trimming works similarly.

On the DVD

The drawing used in the following exercise on extending objects in 3D, ab24-1.dwg, is in the Drawings folder on the DVD. ■

STEPS: Extending Objects in 3D

1. Open ab24-1.dwg from the DVD.
2. Save the file as ab24-15.dwg in your AutoCAD Bible folder. You see a bushing, in 2D and 3D, as shown in Figure 24.48. The 3D bushing has been exploded into simple geometry — otherwise, you wouldn't be able to use it to extend the 2D lines. Set the Quadrant running object snap.
3. To turn the UCSORTHO system variable off, type **ucsortho** ↵ 0 ↵. (If its current value is 0, just press Enter at the Enter new value for UCSORTHO <0>: prompt.) You don't want the UCS to change when you change the view in Step 5.

FIGURE 24.48

A bushing in 2D and 3D. The 3D bushing has been exploded but still looks the same. It can now be used to extend lines.

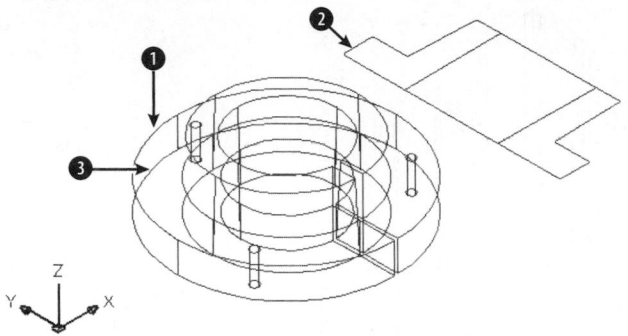

4. Choose Home tab ⇨ Modify panel ⇨ Trim/Extend drop-down list ⇨ Extend. Follow the prompts:

```
Select boundary edges ...
Select objects or <select all>: Pick the 3D bushing at ❶ in Figure
   24.48.
Select objects: Right-click.
Select object to extend or shift-select to trim or [Fence/Crossing/
   Project/Edge/Undo]: Right-click and choose Project.
Enter a projection option [None/Ucs/View] <Ucs>: Right-click and
   choose View.
Select object to extend or shift-select to trim or [Fence/Crossing/
   Project/Edge/Undo]: Pick the 2D bushing at ❷.
Select object to extend or shift-select to trim or [Fence/Crossing/
   Project/Edge/Undo]: Right-click and choose Enter.
```

5. Choose View tab ⇨ Views panel ⇨ 3D Navigation drop-down list ⇨ Top. You can now see that the 2D line doesn't actually meet the 3D bushing. By using the View option, you only extended the line in that view.

6. Choose View tab ⇨ Views panel ⇨ Previous View.

7. Repeat the EXTEND command. Follow the prompts:

```
Select boundary edges...Select objects or <select all>: Pick the
   bottom edge of the 3D bushing at ❸. (If you can't select the
   bottom edge, move your cursor around its circumference until you
   can.)
Select objects: Right-click.
Select object to extend or shift-select to trim or [Fence/Crossing/
   Project/Edge/Undo]: Right-click and choose Project.
Enter a projection option [None/Ucs/View] <View>: Right-click and
   choose None.
Select object to extend or shift-select to trim or [Fence/Crossing/
   Project/Edge/Undo]: Pick the same line that you picked in Step 4,
   but this time pick it closer to the 3D bushing, on the new length
   you created by extending it.
Select object to extend or shift-select to trim or [Fence/Crossing/
   Project/Edge/Undo]: Right-click and choose Enter.
```

8. Choose View tab ➪ Views panel ➪ 3D Navigation drop-down list ➪ Top. You can now see that the 2D line actually meets the 3D bushing.

9. Click Undo on the Quick Access Toolbar twice to undo the viewpoint change and the extend operation.

10. Choose Home tab ➪ Modify panel ➪ 3D Move. Select the entire 3D bushing. At the `Specify base point or [Displacement] <Displacement>:` prompt, right-click and choose Relocate Gizmo. Choose any quadrant at the base of the bushing. Then click the blue Z axis of the Move gizmo and move the cursor upward in the Z direction. (If a different gizmo appears, right-click and choose Move.) Type **2** ↵. If you miss any of the objects, pick them and move them, too. This moves the entire 3D bushing 2 units in the Z direction.

11. Start the EXTEND command again. Follow the prompts:

```
Select boundary edges...
Select objects or <select all>: Pick the 3D bushing at ❸ (the bottom
    ring). (You might have to click at a different location on the
    circumference of the bottom edge to select it.)
Select objects: Right-click.
Select object to extend or shift-select to trim or [Fence/Crossing/
    Project/Edge/Undo]: Right-click and choose Project.
Enter a projection option [None/Ucs/View] <View>: Right-click and
    choose Ucs.
Select object to extend or shift-select to trim or [Fence/Crossing/
    Project/Edge/Undo]: Pick the same line that you extended before,
    closer to its left endpoint.
Select object to extend or shift-select to trim or [Fence/Crossing/
    Project/Edge/Undo]: Right-click and choose Enter.
```

12. Choose View tab ➪ Views panel ➪ 3D Navigation drop-down list ➪ Top. It looks as if the 2D line now actually meets the 3D bushing.

13. Choose Home tab ➪ View panel ➪ 3D Navigation drop-down list ➪ Front. (Because UCSORTHO is off, the UCS does not change.) Now you can see that the 2D line doesn't meet the 3D bushing.

14. Type **ucsortho** ↵ 1 ↵ to return UCSORTHO to its previous setting, if you changed it in Step 3.

15. Save your drawing. It should look like Figure 24.49.

Filleting in 3D

You can fillet solids but not meshes. (In Chapter 23, I cover the SURFFILLET command, which fillets surfaces.) If you create a 3D object from lines, you can fillet the lines.

New Feature

The FILLETEDGE command fillets the edges of solids. Previously, you needed to use the FILLET command and select an edge; you can still use this command.

To use the FILLETEDGE command for solids, follow these steps:

1. Choose Solid tab ➪ Solid Editing panel ➪ Fillet Edge/Chamfer Edge drop-down list ➪ Fillet Edge. You see the current radius on the command line.

2. At the `Select select an edge or [Chain/Radius]:` prompt, use the Radius option to specify a radius, or select the edges of the solid that you want to fillet. Press Enter to end selection. You cannot deselect edges that you have already selected. AutoCAD displays the result using the current radius.

FIGURE 24.49

When you use the UCS option, the lines seem to touch the boundary edge when you view the bushing from the top, but they can have different Z coordinates.

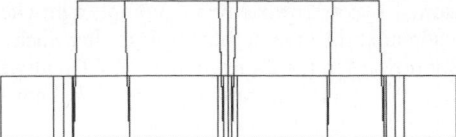

3. At the `Press Enter to accept the fillet or [Radius]:` prompt, press Enter to complete the command. You can also change the radius at this prompt by either using the Radius option or dragging on the fillet grip, which looks like an arrow. If you drag the grip, you need to click to finalize the result.

On the DVD

The drawing used in the following exercise on filleting solids, ab24-m.dwg, is in the Drawings folder on the DVD. ■

STEPS: Filleting Solids

1. Open ab24-m.dwg from the DVD.
2. Save the file as ab24-16.dwg in your AutoCAD Bible folder. This is a solid model of a mounting angle, as shown in Figure 24.50. It needs to be filleted. Turn Object Snap off.

3. Choose Solid tab ➪ Solid Editing panel ➪ Fillet Edge/Chamfer Edge drop-down list ➪ Fillet Edge.
4. At the `Select an edge or [Chain/Radius]:` prompt, type **r** ↵ to set the radius. Then type **.25** ↵.
5. At the `Select an edge or [Chain/Radius]:` prompt, type **.25** ↵.
6. At the `Select an edge or [Chain/Radius]:` prompt, pick ❶, ❷, and ❸. Press Enter to end selection. If you want, drag the fillet grip to adjust the fillet radius and click to finalize the result.
7. Press Enter to accept the fillet and end the command.
8. Save your drawing. It should look like Figure 24.51.

Chamfering in 3D

You can chamfer solids, but not meshes or surfaces. If you create a 3D object from lines, you can chamfer the lines.

FIGURE 24.50

The mounting angle needs filleting.

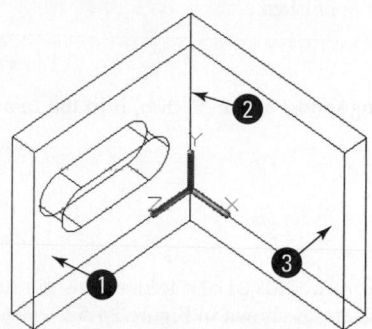

FIGURE 24.51

The filleted mounting angle.

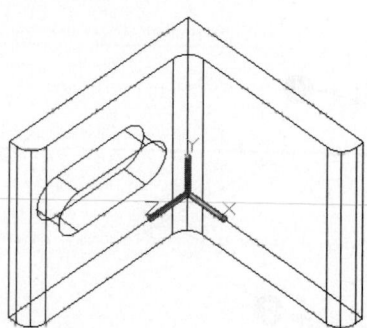

New Feature

The CHAMFEREDGE command chamfers the edges of solids. Previously, you needed to use the CHAMFER command; you can still use this command.

 To chamfer a solid, follow these steps:

1. Choose Solid tab ⇨ Solid Editing panel ⇨ Fillet/Chamfer drop-down list ⇨ Chamfer Edge. You see the Distance1 and Distance2 values on the command line.

2. At the `Select an edge or [Loop/Distance/]:` prompt, use the Distance option to specify the two distances or select an edge that you want to chamfer.

3. At the Select an edge that belongs to the same face or [Loop/Distance]: prompt, you can select additional edges around the same face as your first edge. Press Enter to end selection.

4. You can drag the chamfer grips (one for each distance) and then click to make adjustments. Press Enter to accept the chamfer when you're finished.

On the DVD

The drawing used in the following exercise on chamfering solids, ab24-n.dwg, is in the Drawings folder on the DVD. ∎

STEPS: Chamfering Solids

1. Open ab24-n.dwg from the DVD.

2. Save the file as ab24-17.dwg in your AutoCAD Bible folder. This is a simple box with dimensions of 233 × 102 × 12 millimeters, as shown in Figure 24.52.

FIGURE 24.52

You can chamfer this solid box to create a new shape.

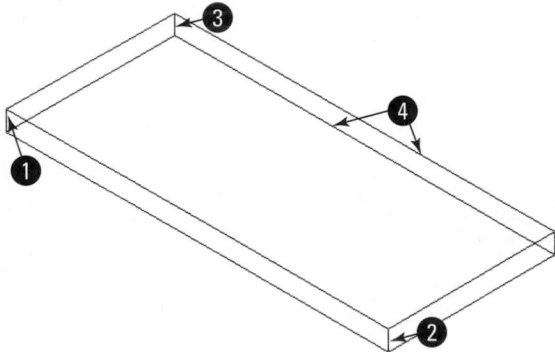

3. Choose Solid tab ➪ Solid Editing panel ➪ Fillet Edge/Chamfer Edge drop-down list ➪ Chamfer Edge. Follow the prompts:

```
Select an edge or [Loop/Distance]: Type d ↵ to specify the distances.
Specify Distance1 [or Expression] <0.5000>: 30 ↵
Specify Distance1 [or Expression] <0.5000>: 30 ↵
Select an edge or [Loop/Distance]: Pick ❶ in Figure 24.52.
Select an edge that belongs to the same face or [Loop/Distance]: ↵
Press Enter to accept the chamfer or [Distance]: ↵
```

You can't see the chamfer very well because of the viewpoint. You change the viewpoint at the end of the exercise.

4. Repeat the CHAMFEREDGE command. Do the exact same operation as in Step 3, but pick ❷.

5. Repeat the CHAMFEREDGE command. Follow the prompts:

```
Select an edge or [Loop/Distance]: Type d ↵ to specify the distances.
Specify Distance1 [or Expression] <0.5000>: 233 ↵
Specify Distance1 [or Expression] <0.5000>: 40 ↵
Select an edge or [Loop/Distance]: Pick ❶ in Figure 24.52.
Select an edge that belongs to the same face or [Loop/Distance]: ↵
Press Enter to accept the chamfer or [Distance]: ↵ (If the far edge
    doesn't take the long chamfer, click the edge at ❹.)
Press Enter to accept the chamfer or [Distance]: ↵
```

6. Choose Home tab ⇨ View panel ⇨ 3D Navigation drop-down list ⇨ Top. This shows you the shape in profile.

7. Save your drawing. It should look like Figure 24.53.

FIGURE 24.53

The completed solid.

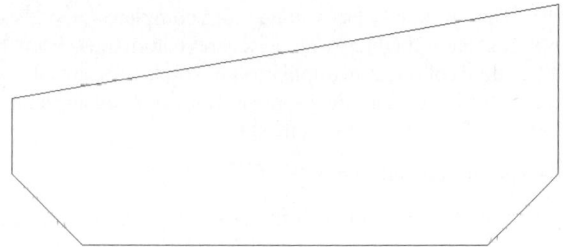

Exploding and converting 3D objects

The EXPLODE command has a particular effect that varies according to the type of 3D object. Table 24.4 lists the effects of exploding 3D objects.

TABLE 24.4

Using EXPLODE on 3D Objects

Object	Result
Smooth solids	Flat surfaces become regions; curved surfaces become surfaces.
Mesh solids	3D faces.
Swept, lofted, extruded, or rotated surfaces	These surfaces become 2D objects or other surfaces that you can explode again to 2D objects.
Polyface meshes	3D faces.
Polygon meshes	3D faces.
Polylines with thickness	Lines.

You can use the XEDGES command to convert smooth solids, mesh solids, surfaces, and regions to 2D wireframe objects. This is another kind of exploding. To use XEDGES, choose Home tab ⇨ Solid Editing panel ⇨ Edges drop-down list ⇨ Extract Edges. Then select objects. You can subselect faces and edges, as described earlier in this chapter, and use XEDGES on them.

 The CONVTOSOLID command, discussed earlier in this chapter in the context of converting meshes to smooth solids, also converts polylines with a uniform width, closed polylines with zero-width, and circles to solids if they have a thickness. These are all objects that look like solids anyway. Choose Home tab ⇨ Solid Editing panel (expanded) ⇨ Convert to Solid and select the objects. (I discuss the CONVTOSURFACE command in Chapter 23.)

The Express Tools' FLATTEN command converts a 3D drawing into a 2D drawing, and changes the thickness and elevation of objects to zero. Choose Express Tools ⇨ Modify panel (expanded) ⇨ Flatten Objects and select objects.

Using the SOLIDEDIT Command

The SOLIDEDIT command offers options to edit faces, edges, and complete smooth solids in specific ways. This command has so many options that it might as well be several commands. Many of the options are now out of date because of the methods of direct manipulation of solids introduced in AutoCAD 2007. However, the command still has value because it offers some options that are available nowhere else, or it makes certain edits easier. SOLIDEDIT doesn't work on meshes.

SOLIDEDIT offers three major types of solid editing:

- **Faces.** A number of options enable you to edit the faces of solids. You can extrude, move, rotate, offset, taper, delete, copy, and color (assign a color to) faces.
- **Edges.** You can color and copy edges.
- **Bodies.** The body options apply to solids as a whole. You can imprint, separate, shell, clean, and check solids.

The next three sections explain how to edit faces, edges, and bodies.

Editing faces

A face is a surface on a solid. A face can be either flat or curved. For example, a hole in a block is a face, and many of the face-editing operations work well to modify holes. Of course, you can edit an outer face of a surface as well. The SOLIDEDIT command supports several methods of selecting a face or faces:

- You can select sub-objects by using the Ctrl key, as described earlier in this chapter.
- You can click within the boundary of a face. AutoCAD selects the front-most face.
- You can click an edge to select its adjoining faces.

To make selecting the sub-object you want easier, choose Home tab ⇨ Subobject panel ⇨ Subobject Selection Mode drop-down list, and choose the type of sub-object that you want. If you don't get the face that you want at first, at the `Select faces or [Undo/Remove]:` prompt, right-click and choose Undo to undo your last selection operation. Right-click and choose Remove to select a face to remove from the selection set. (You can also press Shift and pick a face to remove it.) The prompt then includes an Add option that you can use to start adding faces again. Then press Enter to end face selection.

You may want to perform more than one operation on a face. After you complete an operation, you can right-click to open the shortcut menu and choose another operation. To exit the command, right-click and choose Exit twice or press Enter twice.

Extruding faces

Extruding a face is like extruding a 2D object. Instead, you can select a face (as described earlier in this chapter) and use the EXTRUDE command; the prompts are similar. If you just want to extrude a face, without tapering it, you can grip-edit the solid.

 To extrude a face by using SOLIDEDIT, choose Home tab ⇨ Solid Editing panel ⇨ Faces drop-down list ⇨ Extrude Faces. Then follow the prompts to specify a height and a taper. You can also use the Path option to extrude along an object. When you're done, press Enter twice to exit the command. For more information, see the "Using the EXTRUDE command" section earlier in this chapter.

AutoCAD extrudes the face. As you exit, AutoCAD performs a validation of the solid to make sure that the solid is a valid solid if the SOLIDCHECK system variable is on. By default, SOLIDCHECK is on (set to 1) and automatically checks solids when you edit them.

Moving faces

You can move a face when a solid is complex enough to have at least two separate elements — for example, a plate with a hole in it. You can then move the hole around wherever you want. You can also subselect the hole and move it by using its grips or the Move gizmo.

 To move a face, choose Home tab ⇨ Solid Editing panel ⇨ Faces drop-down list ⇨ Move Faces. Then follow the prompts as you would with the MOVE command. Press Enter twice to exit the command.

If you choose a face that cannot be moved, AutoCAD displays the Modeling Operation Error: No solution for an edge message.

Offsetting faces

You can offset a face when a solid has two separate elements, such as a wall with a window cut out of it. You can then resize the window by offsetting it. Offsetting a face increases all parts of the face equally by a distance that you specify.

Use a positive offset value to increase the volume of the solid. If your face is a solid axle in the middle of a disk, for example, and you offset the axle with a positive value, the axle gets bigger. However, if your face is a hole in the middle of a disk, a positive offset value makes the hole smaller because that makes the resulting solid bigger.

Use a negative offset value to decrease the volume of the solid. Using the same example, a negative offset value would make the axle smaller, but it would make the hole bigger.

To offset a face, follow these steps:

1. Choose Home tab ⇨ Solid Editing panel ⇨ Faces drop-down list ⇨ Offset Faces.
2. Select the face or faces that you want to offset and press Enter to end face selection.
3. At the Specify the offset distance: prompt, type a positive or negative distance. You can also pick two points to specify a positive offset.
4. Press Enter twice to exit the command.

AutoCAD offsets the face. If there is no room for the offset, AutoCAD displays the message Modeling Operation Error on the command line.

Deleting faces

You can delete a face of a solid. This is a great way to instantly get rid of a hole, axle, or window within a solid. You can delete faces to undo the effects of both the UNION and SUBTRACT commands. You can also remove filleted and chamfered faces. AutoCAD won't delete every face; for example, you can't turn a box into a tetrahedron by deleting the box's top face. Note that you can also subselect the face and press the Del key.

 To delete a face or faces, choose Home tab ⇨ Solid Editing panel ⇨ Faces drop-down list ⇨ Delete Faces. Select the face or faces and press Enter. AutoCAD deletes the face or faces that you selected. If your face(s) can't be deleted, you see the message Modeling Operation Error on the command line.

Rotating faces

You can rotate a face when a solid is complex enough to have at least two separate elements — for example, a box with a hole in it. The prompts for rotating are very similar to those for ROTATE3D, covered earlier in this chapter; you can select a sub-object and use that command, or the Rotate gizmo. To rotate a face by using SOLIDEDIT, choose Home tab ⇨ Solid Editing panel ⇨ Faces drop-down list ⇨ Rotate Faces. Select the face or faces that you want to rotate, using the selection method(s) described earlier. Follow the prompts, which are similar to those of the 3DROTATE command. Press Enter twice to exit the command.

If you choose a face that cannot be rotated, or if there isn't room on the solid for the rotation, AutoCAD lets you know with the message Modeling Operation Error on the command line. Note that you can also subselect the face and rotate it by using grip-editing.

Tapering faces

You can taper an entire simple solid, such as a box, or you can taper a face that is an element within a complex solid, such as a hole or an extruded face. Tapering angles the sides of the face. To determine the direction of the taper, that is, which end gets tapered, you specify a base point and a second point. The base point side of the solid is not tapered, and AutoCAD tapers the face in the direction from the base point toward the second point. You also specify the angle of the taper. A positive taper angle tapers the face inward; a hole is tapered outward. A negative taper angle tapers the face outward; a hole is tapered inward. In general, you should use small tapering angles. If the face tapers to a point before it reaches its existing height, then AutoCAD cannot complete the taper.

To taper a face, follow these steps:

1. Choose Home tab ⇨ Solid Editing panel ⇨ Faces drop-down list ⇨ Taper Faces. AutoCAD starts the SOLIDEDIT command and automatically enters the first two prompts of the command for you.

2. Select the face(s) that you want to taper. Press Enter to end face selection.

3. At the Specify the base point: prompt, pick the base point for the taper direction. Object snaps are a good idea.

4. At the Specify another point along the axis of tapering: prompt, specify a second point to indicate the direction of the taper. Again, use an object snap.

5. At the Specify the taper angle: prompt, specify an angle between –90° and +90°.

6. Press Enter twice to exit the command.

If AutoCAD can't taper the face, you see the message Modeling Operation Error on the command line.

Copying faces

You can copy any face, including a hole. AutoCAD creates regions or surfaces out of the face. However, if you copy a complex face, such as a hole that may consist of several regions, you can't turn it back into a solid again.

To copy a face, follow these steps:

1. Choose Home tab ⇨ Solid Editing panel ⇨ Faces drop-down list ⇨ Copy Faces.
2. Select the face(s) that you want to copy. Press Enter to end face selection.
3. At the `Specify a base point or displacement:` prompt, specify a base point. Object snaps are helpful.
4. At the `Specify a second point of displacement:` prompt, specify a second point to indicate the direction and distance for the copy.
5. Press Enter twice to exit the command.

Coloring faces

You can assign a color to a face of an object. You might want to color a face to make it easier to see. The color overrides the color setting for the solid's layer.

Note

When an object is assigned more than one material, priority goes to attachment by object, then by color, and finally by layer. If you attach a material to a solid by layer, and then attach a material to one of its faces (that you have colored) by color, both the solid and the face display their materials. For more information, see Chapter 25. ■

To color a face, follow these steps:

1. Choose Home tab ⇨ Solid Editing panel ⇨ Faces drop-down list ⇨ Color Faces.
2. Select the face or faces that you want to color. Press Enter to end face selection.
3. AutoCAD opens the Select Color dialog box. Choose a color and click OK.
4. Press Enter twice to exit the command.

Attaching a material to a face

You can assign a material to a face of an object. You would do this for the purpose of displaying the object with that material in your drawing, or for rendering. For more information on materials and how to add them to your drawing, see Chapter 25.

To add a material to a face, first add the material to the drawing (as I explain in Chapter 25). Then follow these steps:

1. Start the SOLIDEDIT command. Choose the Face option, then choose the mAterial option.
2. Select the face or faces that you want to use. Press Enter to end face selection.
3. At the `Enter new material name <ByLayer>:` prompt, type the name of the material as it appears in the Materials palette.
4. Press Enter twice to exit the command.

Editing edges

The two-dimensional place where two faces meet is an edge. You can perform only two editing operations on edges: You can copy them and color them.

When you copy an edge, you get a line, arc, circle, ellipse, or spline, depending on the shape of the solid's edge. To copy an edge, choose Home tab ⇨ Solid Editing panel ⇨ Edges drop-down list ⇨ Copy Edges. Select the edge or edges that you want to copy and follow the prompts, which are similar to those of the COPY command.

 You can color an edge to make it more visible. The color overrides the color setting for the solid's layer. To color an edge, choose Home tab ⇨ Solid Editing panel ⇨ Edges drop-down list ⇨ Color Edges. Select the edge or edges that you want to color, and choose the color that you want.

Editing bodies

Several of the SOLIDEDIT options apply to solids as a whole. The operations available are imprinting, cleaning, separating, shelling, and checking. These operations are discussed in the following sections.

Imprinting solids

You can imprint an arc, circle, line, 2D polyline or 3D polyline, ellipse, spline, region, or 3D solid on a solid. The object that you're imprinting must intersect a face on the solid. The shape made by the intersection of the object is left on the solid, as if you put ink on the edges of the object and stamped it on the solid. Figure 24.54 shows an example of imprinting.

FIGURE 24.54

The ellipse was drawn on the top of the solid. After imprinting and deleting the ellipse, the shape of half of the ellipse remains on the solid.

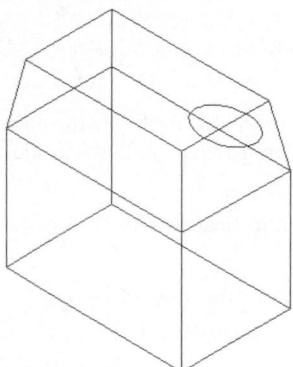 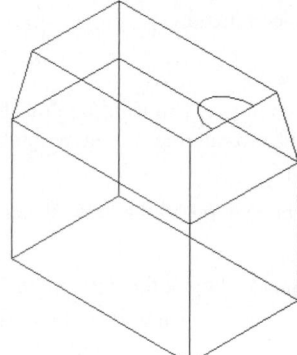

Cross-Reference

In Chapter 23, I cover the PROJECTGEOMETRY command, which is somewhat similar. ∎

To imprint a solid, follow these steps:

1. First create one of the stampable objects previously listed so that it intersects with a solid. If you draw in top view, check in an isometric view to make sure that the intersection is where you want it.

2. Choose Home tab ➪ Solid Editing panel ➪ Edges drop-down list ➪ Imprint.

3. At the `Select a 3D solid or surface:` prompt, select a solid. You can select only one.

4. At the `Select an object to imprint:` prompt, select the object that you want to imprint.

5. At the `Delete the source object [Yes/No] <N>:` prompt, type **y** ↵ or press Enter to indicate No.

6. AutoCAD repeats the `Select an object to imprint:` prompt. You can continue the command in the same way or press Enter if you're done.

7. Press Enter to exit the command.

AutoCAD imprints the solid. If you didn't delete the source object, you'll need to move it to see the result. You can subselect an imprint and delete it or edit it in any other way. You can also use an imprint to divide a face, and then use the PRESSPULL command to extrude or press that portion of the face.

Cleaning solids

After all the editing, you can end up with some pretty strange solids. Cleaning solids removes adjacent faces that share the same surface and other duplicate or unused edges, vertices, and geometry. Cleaning does not remove imprints.

To clean a solid, choose Home tab ➪ Solid Editing panel ➪ Body drop-down list ➪ Clean. At the `Select a 3D solid:` prompt, select a solid. AutoCAD cleans it.

Separating solids

You can separate a solid that is made up of nontouching sections. You would generally create such a solid from separate, nontouching solids, using the UNION command. The Separate option undoes the effect of the UNION command so that the solids become separate again.

To separate a solid, choose Home tab ➪ Solid Editing panel ➪ Body drop-down list ➪ Separate. At the `Select a 3D solid:` prompt, select the solid by picking any of its sections. AutoCAD separates the solids.

If your solid sections are even just touching, you get one of the odder AutoCAD messages: `The selected solid does not have multiple lumps.`

Shelling solids

When you shell a solid, you hollow out its inside, leaving a thin wall. Think of making a drinking glass from a truncated cone (or tapered cylinder) or a room from a solid box. To shell a solid, follow these steps:

1. Choose Home tab ➪ Solid Editing panel ➪ Body drop-down list ➪ Shell.

2. At the `Select a 3D solid:` prompt, select a solid.

3. At the `Remove faces or [Undo/Add/ALL]:` prompt, remove any face or faces that you don't want to shell. For example, if you're making a drinking glass from a truncated cone, you want to remove the larger circular face (the one you would drink out of) so that it will remain open. Otherwise, you end up with an enclosed solid that has a hollow interior. After you finish removing faces, press Enter. (The command line confirms `1 face found, 1 removed`, but there is no visual confirmation that AutoCAD has removed the correct face.)

4. At the `Enter the shell offset distance:` prompt, type the width of the wall that you want to create. A positive value creates a shell to the inside of the current solid. A negative value creates a shell to the outside of the current solid.

5. Press Enter twice to shell the solid and exit the command.

Checking solids

Checking ensures that your solid is a valid 3D solid object so that you can edit it without getting ACIS failure error messages. This might be a useful feature to put into an AutoLISP or VBA program, to make sure that it doesn't fail because of invalid solids.

 To check a solid, choose Home tab ⇨ Solid Editing panel ⇨ Body drop-down list ⇨ Check. At the `Select a 3D solid:` prompt, select a solid. Usually, AutoCAD replies with the message: `This object is a valid ShapeManager solid.`

On the DVD

The drawing used in the following exercise on editing solid bodies, `ab24-o.dwg`, is in the `Drawings` folder on the DVD. ■

STEPS: Editing Solid Bodies

1. Open `ab24-o.dwg` from the DVD.

2. Save the file as `ab24-18.dwg` in your `AutoCAD Bible` folder. This is a simple solid box with an ellipse drawn on part of its top face.

 3. Choose Home tab ⇨ Solid Editing panel ⇨ Edges drop-down list ⇨ Imprint. Follow the prompts:

```
Select a 3D solid or surface: Select the box.
Select an object to imprint: Select the ellipse.
Delete the source object [Yes/No] <N>: y ↵
Select an object to imprint: Right-click to complete the imprint and
    end the command.
```

Choose Home tab ⇨ Modeling panel ⇨ Presspull. Pull and move the cursor up. Enter **.2** ↵ on the command line or Dynamic Input tooltip.

 4. Choose Home tab ⇨ Solid Editing panel ⇨ Body drop-down list ⇨ Shell. Follow the prompts:

```
Select a 3D Solid: Select the box.
Remove faces or [Undo/Add/ALL]: Pick anywhere inside the top face.
Remove faces or [Undo/Add/ALL]: Right-click and choose Enter.
Enter the shell offset distance: .1 ↵
```

5. Press Enter twice to exit the command.

6. Choose Home tab ⇨ View panel ⇨ Visual Styles drop-down list ⇨ Hidden. You can now see the result of the shell operation.

7. Save your drawing. It should look like Figure 24.55.

FIGURE 24.55

The shelled box.

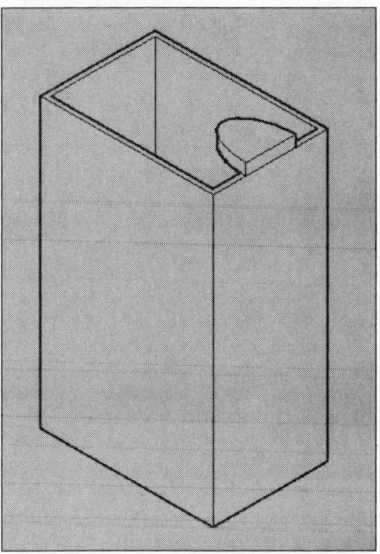

Listing Solid Properties

The MASSPROP command provides information about regions and solids that is useful for engineering applications. The bounding box, for example, is an imaginary box that contains the solid. The calculations are based on the relationship of the solid to the UCS. If you rotate the solid or change the UCS, you get different results. For example, after running MASSPROP to find the center of gravity (centroid) and axes of your model, move the UCS to the centroid and then run MASSPROP again to identify the moments of inertia, as shown in Figure 24.56.

For 2D regions, the area moment of inertia that MASSPROP generates can be used to calculate bending and twisting stresses. You could generate a 2D region of a solid model by using the SECTION command and then use the UCS command with the OBJECT option to set the UCS coplanar to the region. The MASSPROP command would then report the area moment of inertia.

AutoCAD assumes a density of 1 for all solids. You can then apply material density multipliers on the values that get reported.

To list a solid's properties, type **masprop** ↵ on the command line. Select the object that you want to list. AutoCAD opens the Text Window to display the calculations. At the Write analysis to a file? [Yes/No] <N>: prompt, press Enter to accept the No default, or right-click and choose Yes. AutoCAD prompts you for a filename and copies the data to that file.

Note

You can use the MEASUREGEOM command to get the volume of a 3D model. Enter measuregeom ↵ on the command line and use the Object option to select one or more objects. AutoCAD displays the volume. Use the eXit option (or type x ↵) to end the command. ∎

FIGURE 24.56

The results of the MASSPROP command.

```
Command: massprop

Select objects: 1 found

Select objects:

---------------    SOLIDS    ---------------

Mass:              5.3869
Volume:            5.3869
Bounding box:      X: -1.5177  --  1.4823
                   Y: -1.0000  --  1.0000
                   Z: -2.3111  --  2.8889
Centroid:          X: 0.0000
                   Y: 0.0000
                   Z: 0.0000
Moments of inertia: X: 16.7389
                   Y: 19.8802
                   Z: 9.8148
Products of inertia: XY: 0.0000
                   YZ: 0.0000
                   ZX: 0.2679
Radii of gyration: X: 1.7628
                   Y: 1.9211
                   Z: 1.3498
Principal moments and X-Y-Z directions about centroid:
Press ENTER to continue:
                   I: 16.7493 along [0.9993 0.0000 -0.0386
                   J: 19.8802 along [0.0000 1.0000 0.0000]
                   K: 9.8045 along [0.0386 0.0000 0.9993]

Write analysis to a file? [Yes/No] <N>: n
```

Summary

In this chapter, you learned how to create and edit solids. You read about:

- Drawing basic shapes
- Creating extruded, swept, revolved, and lofted solids from 2D profiles
- Drawing polysolids
- Manipulating solids by grip-editing, selecting sub-objects, and using the Move, Rotate, and Scale gizmos
- Creating and editing mesh solids
- Using UNION, SUBTRACT, and INTERSECT to create more-complex shapes
- Using the INTERFERE command to see the volume of interference between solids
- Pressing or pulling a solid
- Utilizing the SECTION, SLICE, and SECTIONPLANE commands to visualize and reshape solids
- Using the move grip tool and the 3DMOVE command
- Using the special 3D editing commands MIRROR3D, 3DARRAY, and ROTATE3D
- Using the 3DALIGN, TRIM, EXTEND, FILLETEDGE, and CHAMFEREDGE commands for 3D editing
- Exploding into surfaces and solids into 2D objects
- Using the SOLIDEDIT and IMPRINT command to edit faces, edges, and bodies
- Calculating a number of engineering functions and values for solids by using the MASSPROP and MEASUREGEOM commands

In the next chapter, I cover rendering 3D models.

Rendering in 3D

A lthough 3D drawings are more realistic than those that you create in 2D, they look very artificial — they lack realistic color, shading, and lighting, for example. Rendering enables you to display a 3D drawing more realistically. Some of the more advanced features let you create shadows, make objects transparent, add backgrounds, and map 2D images onto the surface of 3D models. You can shade and render 3D objects. Figure 25.1 shows a whimsical rendering that uses shadows and a background.

AutoCAD Only

AutoCAD LT does not offer any rendering features. This entire chapter applies only to AutoCAD. ∎

This entire chapter assumes that you're in the 3D Modeling (not the 3D Basics) workspace. Change the workspace by clicking the Workspace drop-down list on the Quick Access Toolbar or the Workspace Switching button on the status bar.

IN THIS CHAPTER
Understanding rendering
Creating lights and scenes
Working with materials
Using backgrounds
Rendering your drawing

FIGURE 25.1

This cog has been rendered with shadows and a background of clouds.

Understanding Rendering

Rendering is a much more sophisticated means of visualizing a drawing than using visual styles. AutoCAD offers many settings that allow you to fine-tune the results.

Learning the steps

Rendering is a multistep process. It generally requires a good deal of trial and error to get the exact results that you want. Here are the steps to render a drawing:

1. Start with trial rendering by using the default settings. The results let you know what settings need to be changed.

2. Create lights. AutoCAD has seven types of lights. I explain lights in the "Creating Lights" section later in this chapter.

3. Create materials. Materials are surface characteristics and include color and/or texture, reflection (shininess), transparency, refraction, and bump maps. These characteristics are explained later in this chapter in the "Working with Materials" section.

4. Attach materials to the objects in your drawing. You can attach materials by object or layer.

Cross-Reference
See Chapter 24 for information on how to attach a material to the face of a solid by using the SOLIDEDIT command. ■

5. Add a background or fog effect. I discuss these effects in the "Using backgrounds" section later in this chapter.

6. Fine-tune your rendering preferences, if desired. For example, you can render with a variety of output qualities.

7. Render the drawing.

The order of the steps is flexible. For example, you can create and attach materials before you add lights. Also, after you render, you'll probably see some room for improvement, so you may go back and make changes.

Doing a default rendering

Doing a default rendering often helps you to decide what materials and lights you need to create for your final rendering. It also reveals any problems with the models themselves. To render a drawing by using the default settings, choose Render tab ⇨ Render panel ⇨ Render drop-down list ⇨ Render.

One way to get a quick rendering is to choose Render tab ⇨ Render panel ⇨ Render drop-down list ⇨ Render Region, which executes the RENDERCROP command. You define a window, and the command does a default rendering within the area that you define.

Tip
Choose Render tab ⇨ Render panel and click the dialog box launcher at the right end of the panel's title bar (the RPREF command). In the Advanced Render Settings palette, use the Procedure drop-down list to choose Crop (the RENDERCROP command just mentioned) or Selection, to render just selected objects. You can also use the Destination drop-down list to choose to render in the current viewport rather than in the default separate window. These settings enable you to create quick draft renderings as you test your lights and materials. ■

On the DVD

The drawing used in the following exercise on creating a default rendering, `ab25-a.dwg`, is in the `Drawings` folder on the DVD. ∎

STEPS: Creating a Default Rendering

1. Open `ab25-a.dwg` from the DVD.

2. Save the file as `ab25-01.dwg` in your `AutoCAD Bible` folder.

 3. Choose Render tab⇨Render panel⇨Render drop-down list⇨Render. Watch as the Render window opens and renders the drawing.

4. Save your drawing. It should look like Figure 25.2. As you can see, the rendering is too dark and the objects need realistic materials.

FIGURE 25.2

An initial rendering, using default options and a crop window.

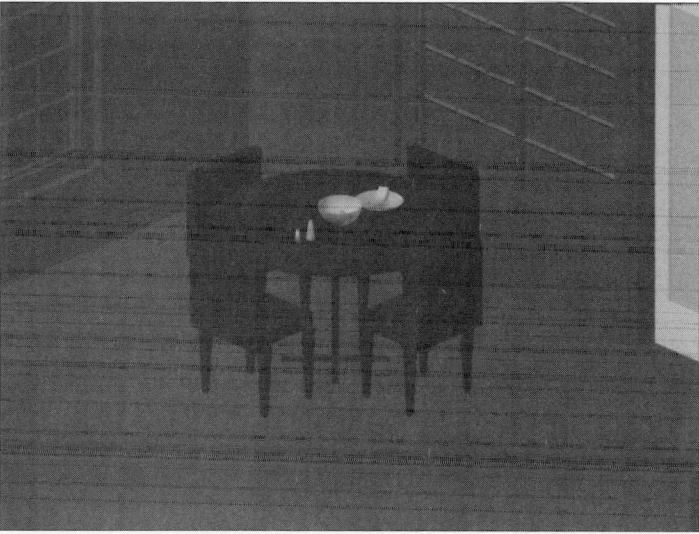

Thanks to Andrew Wilcox of Virtual Homes, Inc., Hammonds Plains, Nova Scotia, Canada, for this drawing.

Creating Lights

When you render by using the default options, AutoCAD uses default lighting that includes two light sources that fall on the objects in the view. However, the default lighting is rarely enough, nor is it realistic. AutoCAD offers seven types of lights to give you a great deal of flexibility in creating a realistic scene. If you plan to cast shadows in your rendering, the proper placement of lights is most important.

Note

The default lighting uses two lights that you must turn off to use the lights that you create. When you create a new light, AutoCAD displays a message asking if you want to turn off the default lighting. You can also choose Render tab ⇨ Lights panel (expanded) ⇨ Default Lighting to turn default lighting on and off. ∎

To create lights, choose one of the buttons from the Render tab ⇨ Lights panel ⇨ Lights drop-down list, or use the command line. (Several of the lights are available only from the command line.) If you execute the LIGHT command on the command line or in the Dynamic Input tooltip, you can choose one of the seven options to specify which type of light you want to create.

Note

AutoCAD offers precise photometry settings for lighting, including the ability to set light intensity using real-world values, such as candela, lumen, or lux. You can also choose the type of lighting (lamp color), such as fluorescent, halogen, or incandescent. To use the photometry feature, you need to set the LIGHTINGUNITS system variable to 1 or 2. A value of 1 enables photometric lighting with American lighting units, and a value of 2 enables it with International lighting units. Set the value of the LIGHTINGUNITS system variable in the Lighting section of the Units dialog box (Application Button ⇨ Drawing Utilities ⇨ Units), or choose Render tab ⇨ Lights panel (expanded) ⇨ Lighting Units drop-down list and choose one of the options. ∎

Setting the default light

The default lighting consists of two lights that uniformly light up the model from all directions. You can control brightness and contrast by using the sliders in the Render tab ⇨ Lights panel (expanded). If you have enabled photometric lighting by setting the lighting units of a drawing to American or International, the Midtones slider is available in addition to the Brightness and Contrast sliders. Remember that turning on your own lights turns off the default lighting.

Tip

Choose Render tab ⇨ Render panel (expanded) ⇨ Adjust Exposure (the RENDEREXPOSURE command) to open the Adjust Rendered Exposure dialog box, where you can control brightness, contrast, mid tones, exterior daylight, and processing of the background. This dialog box does a mini-rendering as you change the values, so that you can see their effect in real time. Lighting units must be set to American or International before the Adjust Rendered Exposure dialog box can be displayed. ∎

Creating a point light

A point light is equivalent to a typical light bulb or a candle. It comes from a specific location and radiates in all directions. A point light attenuates, meaning that the intensity lessens as the distance away from the light's source increases.

 To create a new point light, choose Render tab ⇨ Lights panel ⇨ Create Light drop-down list ⇨ Point. At the `Specify source location <0,0,0>:` prompt, specify the location of the light.

Use object snaps to specify the position of your lights. If there are no objects available, work out the position in advance and place an easily visible point object there; you can then snap to the point object by using the Node object snap. Other options are to type the absolute coordinates or use the From object snap to specify a coordinate, based on an existing geometric point on the model.

If you set the XY coordinates in plan view, be sure to set the proper Z coordinate as well. In an architectural drawing, you rarely want your lights to be coming from the floor! However, in a mechanical drawing, it might be appropriate to light your model from any angle.

Note

If you create an opaque lampshade and place a light inside it, light will get out only through the top and bottom. If you want light to filter through the lampshade, make it partially transparent. For more information, see "Working with Materials" later in this chapter. ■

The next prompt depends on the value of the LIGHTINGUNITS system variable, as follows:

- If the value is generic (0), you see the Enter an option to change [Name/Intensity/ Status/shadoW/Attenuation/Color/eXit] <eXit>: prompt.

- If the value is American (1) or Internaltional (2), you see the Enter an option to change [Name/Intensity factor/Status/Photometry/shadoW/Attenuation/filter Color/eXit] <eXit>: prompt.

These options are discussed in the next several sections. After you create the light, you can edit these settings in the Properties palette. When you finish specifying the light's properties, press Enter to exit the command and place the point light.

Name

When you create a light, a default name is automatically created — for example, Pointlight1. Use the Name option to change the name. At the Enter light name <Pointlight1>: prompt, enter a name. You then return to the options prompt. Press Enter to exit the command.

If you change the name, use a name that makes it clear that the light is a point light. Keep the name short; a simple sequence of P1, P2 is often sufficient. However, you could also use P-overhead and P-door or something similar.

Intensity/Intensity factor

Use the Intensity or Intensity factor option to set the intensity, or brightness, of the light. At the Enter intensity (0.00 - max float) <current>: prompt, enter a number. The default is 1; higher numbers make the light brighter. Note that you can also set the brightness by using the Photometry option if you are not using Generic lighting units.

Status

The Status option turns the light on and off. Choose either the oN or oFf option. You can turn lights on and off to create day and night scenes or to experiment with different lighting arrangements without having to delete or move lights.

Photometry

If photometry is enabled, use this option to specify the intensity and color of the light. There are two suboptions:

- **Intensity.** You can enter an intensity in candela (abbreviated as cd) units, or you can specify flux, the perceived power of the light, or illuminance, the total flux on a surface area. You can specify illuminance in lux (abbreviated as lx) or footcandle (fc) units.

- **Color.** You can enter a color name or a Kelvin temperature value. Use the ? option and then press Enter to see a list of names, such as Fluorescent, Coolwhite, Halogen, and others. (Press F2 to open the AutoCAD Text window, because the names scroll by too fast to see on the command line.)

Shadow

Shadows add greatly to the realism of your rendered image. They also add significantly to the rendering time. The Shadow option turns shadows on and off for that light and specifies the type of shadow. If you choose to create shadows, you can choose three types of shadows:

- **Sharp.** These are sometimes called ray-traced shadows. Use these shadows to reduce rendering time.

- **Soft Mapped.** Enter a map size from 64 to 4,096. Larger map sizes are more accurate but take longer to render. At the Enter softness (1-10) <1>: prompt, enter a number from 1 to 10. The shadow softness determines the number of pixels at the edge of the shadow that are blended into the rest of the image, thus creating the soft effect.

- **Soft Sampled.** Creates a penumbra (partial shadow) effect. You can specify values for three suboptions:

  - **Shape.** Specify the shape of the shadow and its dimensions. You can choose from Linear, Disk, Rect (rectangle), Sphere, and Cylinder. Then enter a distance or radius at the prompt to specify the size of the shadow.

  - **sAmples.** Specify a shadow sample size. The default is 16. A larger sampling size produces a more accurate shadow.

  - **Visibility.** You can choose whether or not to make the shape you used for the shadow visible in the drawing. Choose Yes or No (the default). If you choose Yes, you see the shape around the light in the rendering.

Tip

Because shadows add to rendering time, for your practice renderings while you're creating lights and materials, turn shadows off in the Advanced Render Settings palette (RPREF command). Scroll down to the Shadows section and click the Light bulb icon to toggle shadows on and off. When you're satisfied with the other settings, turn shadows on. ∎

Note

The 3DCONFIG command includes a Full-shadow Display suboption that allows you to turn shadows off. Also, the automatic adaptive degradation may affect shadows if your system is not powerful enough. For more information, see Appendix A. ∎

Attenuation

The Attenuation option sets the *attenuation,* which is the manner in which the light loses intensity as the distance from its source increases. The Attenuation Type suboption offers three choices:

- **None.** The light doesn't lose intensity.

- **Inverse Linear.** The light loses intensity in a linear manner, so that at 2 units from its source the light is half as intense, and at 4 units away the light is one quarter as intense.

- **Inverse Squared.** The light loses intensity at the square of the distance, so that at 2 units from its source the light is one quarter as intense and at 4 units away the light is one sixteenth as intense. Setting the attenuation to inverse square means that the intensity of the light drops off very quickly.

You can set a limit beyond which there is no light. The reason to do this is to improve rendering time. After a certain distance, it may make no difference if there is a little bit of light or no light, and limiting the light to that difference reduces the required calculations. Set the Use Limits suboption to On if you want to use limits. Then set the Attenuation Start Limit and Attenuation End Limit values. The default start limit is 0 (zero). The end limit is a distance from the center of the light.

Note

The software acceleration driver does not support the use of attenuation start and end limits in the drawing window, but the AutoCAD Device Manager (AcadDM10.hdi) driver does support attenuation end limits. ■

Color/Filter Color

You can give your light any color you want. Light colors are somewhat different from pigment colors, which are more familiar. The three primary light colors are red, green, and blue (RGB). Their mixtures are different, as well; for example, red and green make yellow. White light is the sum of all colors of light together. Black is the absence of any colors of light.

Rather than the RGB light color system, you can use the HLS (hue, lightness, saturation) system. Instead of mixing primary colors, you choose the color from a range of hues and then vary its lightness (brightness) and saturation (intensity).

When you use the Color option, you get the Enter true color (R,G,B) or enter an option [Index color/Hsl/colorBook] <255,255,255>: prompt.

- To enter RGB numbers, enter numbers from 0 to 255 for red, green, and blue. The default, 255,255,255, is white.

- To enter an ACI (AutoCAD Color Index) number, use the Index color suboption and enter a number from 1 to 255. These are the same numbers that you find on the Index Color tab of the Select Color dialog box.

- To use the HSL system, use the Hsl option and then enter an HSL color, which is also three numbers from 0 to 255.

- To specify a color-book color, use the colorBook option.

Tip

An easier way to assign a light color is to place the light without changing the color, select the light, and change the color in the Properties palette. When you choose Select Color from the Color drop-down list of the Properties palette, the Select Color dialog box opens, where you can see the color swatches for each color. (See Chapter 11 for a discussion of specifying colors and using color books.) ■

Creating a target point light

A target point light is like a point light, but you specify a target. This helps you control the direction of the light.

To create a target point light, enter **targetpoint** on the command line. At the Specify source location <0,0,0>: prompt, enter the source of the light. At the Specify target location <0,0,-10>: prompt, specify the target. By default, the target is 10 units less in the Z direction than the source. The rest of the prompts are the same as for a point light. You can change the source and target locations using the Properties palette after a light is placed.

Creating a spotlight

A spotlight differs from a point light in that it has a direction. As a result, you not only specify its location but also its target — two coordinates rather than one. In addition, a spotlight has a brighter center called the *hotspot*. Outside the center is a ring of lesser brightness called the *falloff*. Figure 25.3 shows the same scene used previously in this chapter, but with one overhead spotlight.

FIGURE 25.3

A rendering with one spotlight overhead. Here the hotspot angle is 45° and the falloff angle is 70°.

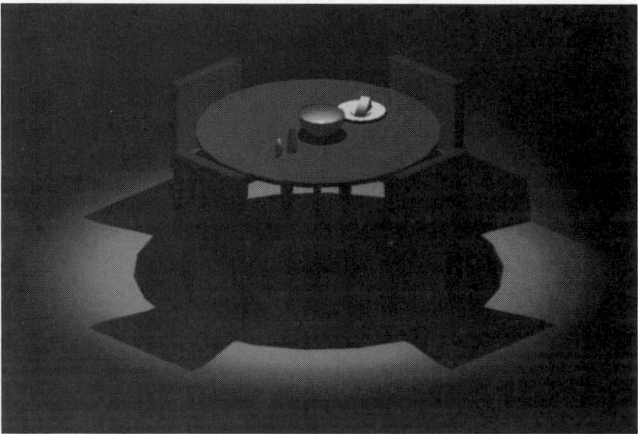

 To create a new spotlight, choose Render tab ⇨ Lights panel ⇨ Create Light drop-down list ⇨ Spot. At the `Specify source location <0,0,0>:` prompt, enter the spotlight's location. In most cases, you don't want the Z value to be 0 (zero). At the `Specify target location <0,0,-10>:` prompt, specify the light's target.

The prompt that you now see depends on the value of the LIGHTINGUNITS system variable (discussed earlier in this chapter), which turns the photometry feature on and off:

- If the value is generic (0), you see the `Enter an option to change [Name/Intensity/ Status/Hotspot/Falloff/shadoW/Attenuation/Color/eXit] <eXit>:` prompt.

- If the value is American (1) or International (2), you see the `Enter an option to change [Name/Intensity`

  `factor/Status/Photometry/Hotspot/Falloff/shadoW/Attenuation/filter-Color/eXit] <eXit>:` prompt.

All these options are the same as for a point light, except the Hotspot and Falloff options. (See the earlier section, "Creating a point light," for details.)

Set the hotspot and falloff angles for the spotlight. These angles emanate from the spotlight in the direction of the light's target. The maximum angle for both is 160 degrees. If the hotspot and falloff angles are the same, there is no falloff — the entire spotlight is bright. The defaults are 44 degrees for the hotspot and 50 degrees for the falloff. This does not leave very much falloff area. You may need to experiment to get the desired result. When you're done creating the spotlight, press Enter to exit the command.

Using Weblights

Photometric weblights provide a representation of the way a light's intensity varies in 3D space. You would use a weblight when you have data about the way a real light's intensity is distributed. The result is a very precise rendering of the effect of the light. However, this result is only approximate in the viewport.

In order to use weblights, you need to turn on the photometry feature by setting the value of the LIGHTINGUNITS system variable to 1 or 2. For more information on LIGHTINGUNITS, see "Creating Lights" earlier in this chapter.

You can insert weblights into your drawing by using the following commands:

- **Weblight.** Choose Render tab ⇨ Lights panel ⇨ Create Light drop-down list ⇨ Weblight. A weblight is similar to a spotlight, because it requires a target. The options are the same as for spotlights, except for an added Web option, which replaces the Hotspot and Falloff options.

- **Freeweb.** Enter **freeweb** ↵ on the command line. A freeweb light is similar to a point light, because it has only a source location. The options are the same as for point lights, except for an added Web option, which replaces the Hotspot and Falloff options.

The Web option lets you specify a file that contains light distribution information at various directions from the light in the IES (Illuminating Engineering Society) LM-63-1991 format. IES is a text-file format for describing this type of information. Light manufacturers provide these IES files (sometimes called photometric data) for their lights. You can also specify individual X, Y, and Z data for the light.

After you place a weblight, you can select it and use the Web File item in the Properties palette to load an IES file. By default, these web files are in the WebFiles folder. To find the exact location, choose Application Button ⇨ Options and click the Files tab. Double-click the Web File Search Path item. You can change that location or add additional locations.

Creating a Free spotlight

A free spotlight is like a spotlight, but it has no target. From this perspective, it's like a point light, but it has a hotspot and falloff, like a spotlight.

To create a free spotlight, enter **freespot** on the command line. At the Specify source location <0,0,0>: prompt, enter the location for the light. The rest of the prompts are the same as for a spotlight.

Creating a distant light

A distant light is similar to the sun. Its rays come from so far away that, for all practical purposes, they're parallel. A distant light does not attenuate (unless you're drawing a model on Pluto). Before inserting a distant light, it is recommended that you set the LIGHTINGUNITS system variable to 0 to turn off the photometric units, or lower the distant light's intensity.

To create a new distant light, choose Render tab ⇨ Lights panel ⇨ Create Light drop-down list ⇨ Distant. At the Specify light direction FROM <0,0,0> or [Vector]: prompt, specify the source of the light. At the Specify light direction TO <1,1,1>: prompt, specify the light direction. You can specify a point or use the vector system that I discuss in Chapter 22. If you use the Vector option, you only set the direction of the light. AutoCAD places the light outside the model, and there is no light glyph. The rest of the options are the same as for creating a point light, which I discuss earlier in this chapter. When you are finished specifying the light, press Enter to exit the command.

Simulating the sun

You can simulate the sun by specifying a geographic location for your model and setting specific properties for the sun. In this way, you can get very realistic lighting. When you use the sun tools, you are creating a special type of distant light.

Set the geographic location

 To set the geographic location, choose Render tab ➪ Sun & Location panel ➪ Set Location. You can then choose to import location information from KML or KMZ files or from Google Earth, or to enter location values. If you choose the latter, the Geographic Location dialog box opens, as shown in Figure 25.4. (I also discuss this command briefly in Chapter 22.)

FIGURE 25.4

Use the Geographic Location dialog box to specify the latitude and longitude for a specific location.

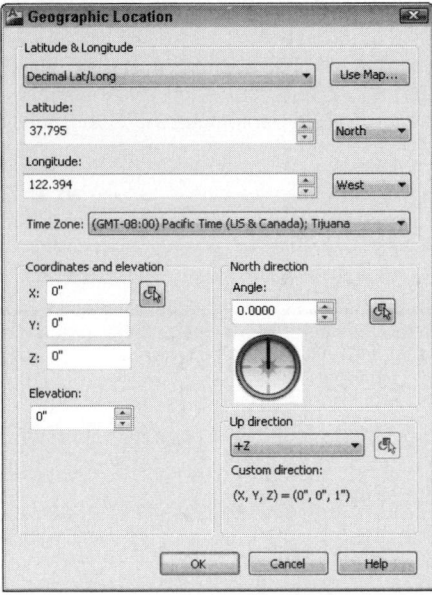

To specify the location, follow these steps in the Geographic Location dialog box:

1. If you know the latitude and longitude, choose the format, decimal or degrees (commonly known as degrees, minutes and seconds and formatted as DD.MMSS), in the uppermost drop-down list. Then enter them in the Latitude and Longitude sections, including the hemisphere (North or South and East or West). Then skip to Step 3. Alternatively, click Use Map to display the Location Picker dialog box, and choose the continent from the Region drop-down list. (India and Canada are separately listed among the continents.)

2. If your model is in a large city, select the Nearest Big City check box. The marker will then jump to the city nearest to the point you click. You can also choose a city from the Nearest City drop-down list. If you're not in a city, just click on the map.

Note

The time zone automatically adjusts to the location you chose. However, you can separately set the time zone by using the Time Zone drop-down list or the TIMEZONE system variable. ■

3. In the North Direction section, specify the angle that represents north in your drawing. Setting the north location is important to get accurate sun results. By default, north is the positive Y direction in the World Coordinate System (WCS). To change the default, type a new angle in the Angle text box, or click the compass face to specify the new angle. The positive Y axis is at 0 degrees, the positive X axis is at 90 degrees, and so on, clockwise.

4. Click OK. You may see a notice about the time zone, which is automatically calculated. Check the time zone and click Accept Updated Time Zone to close the notice.

Set sun properties

To set properties for the sun, such as the date and time, choose Render tab ⇨ Sun & Location panel and click the dialog box launcher at the right end of the panel's title bar (the SUNPROPERTIES command) to open the Sun Properties palette, as shown in Figure 25.5.

FIGURE 25.5

The Sun Properties palette keeps all the settings for the sun in one place.

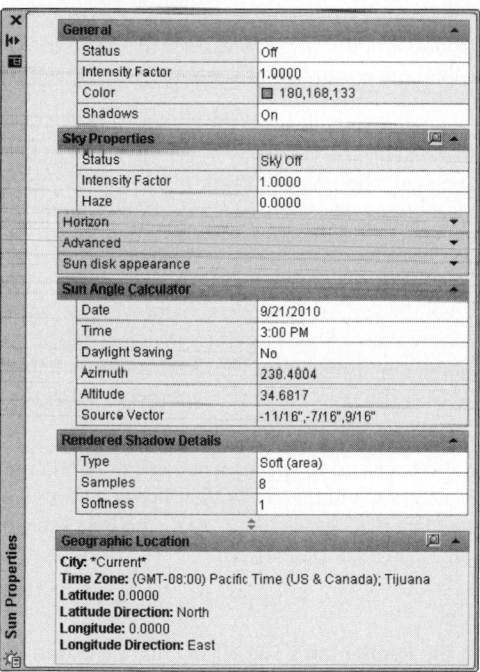

The first set of properties is the same as the options for the POINTLIGHT command. See the section "Creating a point light" earlier in this chapter for more details.

The next four sections only appear if you are using photometric lighting (which means that the LIGHTINGUNITS system variable is 1 or 2).

The Sky Properties section allows you to add a background and illumination effect for the sky when you render the drawing. You don't see any effect in the regular viewport. You can turn the sky off, choose just a sky background effect, or choose both the sky background and the illumination effect. You can add an intensity factor for the sky. The default value is 1. Changing the intensity to 2 will significantly brighten your sky.

Cross-Reference

To specify these sky properties for a background, turn on photometric lighting and create a new named view. At the bottom of the New View / Shot Properties dialog box, choose the Sun & Sky option. See Chapter 22 for more details on creating a new view with a background. ∎

The Haze setting creates a scattering effect. The default is 0.0 and the maximum is 15.0. A setting of 15.0 will create an effect of looking through haze.

The Horizon section controls the horizon, which is where the ground meets the sky. In order to see the horizon, you need a viewpoint that shows the horizon. If your viewport is too close to plan view, you won't see the horizon, because you'll be looking down instead of outward. You can set the following properties:

- **Height.** Sets the position of the ground plane relative to the zero value of the Z axis. Set this in real-world units. For example, 24 would be 2 feet high.
- **Blur.** Creates a blur at the junction between the ground and the sky. You can see this effect in your drawing (not only when you render), especially if the ground color contrasts with the sky color.
- **Ground Color.** Choose a color for the ground.

The Advanced section includes three "artistic" effects. First, you can choose a night color. You can also turn aerial perspective on. (It's off by default.) Aerial perspective is a bluing and slight blurring effect that creates the impression of distance. Finally, you can set the visibility distance, which is the distance at which 10% haze kicks in, reducing clarity. This setting also gives an impression of distance.

The Sun Disk Appearance section affects only the appearance of the sun, not the overall light. You can see the results of the changes you make here more clearly in the New View / Shot Properties dialog box. The Disk Scale item specifies a scale for the sun disk itself; a value of 1 is normal size. The Glow Intensity item changes the glow around the disk; 1 is the default value. The Disk Intensity value changes the intensity of the sun disk itself; again 1 is the default value.

The Sun Angle Calculator section allows you to enter a date and time and to specify whether or not you're using Daylight Savings Time. To change the date, click the Date item, and then click the Ellipsis button. A little calendar opens. Navigate to the desired date and double-click it. The calendar closes. Choose a time from the drop-down list. Choose Yes or No from the Daylight Savings drop-down list.

Note

You can also adjust the date and time using the two sliders found on the Render tab's Sun & Location panel on the ribbon. ∎

The next three settings are not changeable; they're based on the location you specified in the Geographic Location dialog box (or the values you previously chose for Date, Time, and Daylight Savings):

- The *azimuth* is the angle in the XY plane — North is located at 0 degrees. Use a positive angle to move clockwise from North, and a negative angle to move counterclockwise from North. Values can range from −180 to 180. (Both −180 and 180 would represent South.)

- The *altitude* is the angle from the XY plane. You can type in angles from −90 to 90. (An altitude of −90 would mean that the light was coming from beneath the model.)

- The *source vector* is the coordinates that represent the sun's direction. For more information on the vector system, see "Using the VPOINT command" in Chapter 22.

The Rendered Shadow Details section offers the same settings I discussed earlier in the "Creating a point light" section. However, when photometric lighting is on, the only shadow choice is Soft (Area), which creates sampled shadows. Shadows need to be on in the General section for these settings to be available.

Managing lights

 To keep track of and manage your lights, choose Render tab ⇨ Lights panel and click the dialog box launcher at the right end of the panel's title bar (the LIGHTLIST command). The Lights in Model palette is shown in Figure 25.6.

FIGURE 25.6

The Lights in Model palette lists all your lights.

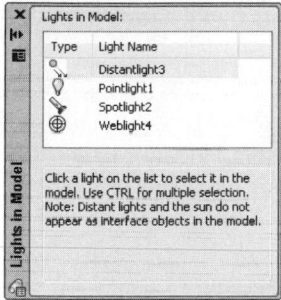

Lights can be difficult to select; they may be inside a lamp or high up, out of your current display. Distant lights don't have a glyph that you can click on to select them. The Lights in Model palette helps you select, modify, and delete lights. To select a light, choose it in the palette.

You can now edit the light either with grips or in the Properties palette. Figure 25.7 shows a selected spotlight. You can easily change the spotlight's location, target, hotspot, and falloff by using grips. To change its status (on or off), color, and other properties, use the Properties palette.

To delete a light, choose it in the Lights in Model palette and press Del. You can't delete the sun, you can only turn it off. (Good night!)

Note

You may have lights that you created in a release of AutoCAD prior to 2007 that you want to use in 2011 drawings. Use the CONVERTOLDLIGHTS command to convert your lights. You may have to adjust their intensity. To do so, select them and change the intensity in the Properties palette. In addition, the 3DCONVERSIONMODE system variable converts material and light definitions to the latest release. This system variable allows you to keep your definitions up-to-date with each new release. ∎

FIGURE 25.7

You can grip-edit a light by using the grips on the light glyph.

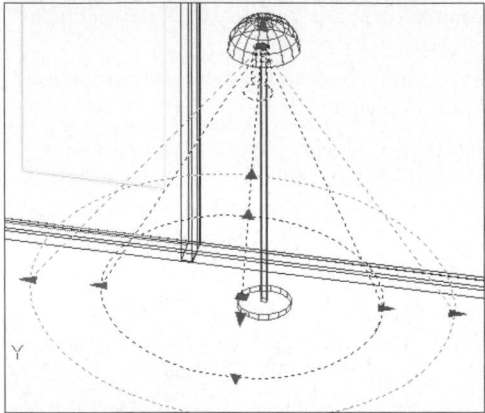

On the DVD

The drawing used in the following exercise on creating lights and shadows, `ab25-a.dwg`, **is in the** `Drawings` **folder on the DVD.** ∎

STEPS: Creating Lights and Shadows

1. Open `ab25-a.dwg` from the DVD. Object Snap should be on. Set running object snaps for Endpoint and Center. This exercise does not use the photometric feature; make sure that the value of the LIGHTINGUNITS system variable is set to 0.

2. Save the file as `ab25-02.dwg` in your `AutoCAD Bible` folder.

3. Choose Render tab ⇨ Lights panel ⇨ Create Light drop-down list ⇨ Point. At the Lighting – Viewport Lighting Mode message, click Turn Off Default Lighting (Recommended) to turn off default lighting.

4. Pan to the right until you see the floor lamp, as shown in Figure 25.8.

   Follow the prompts:
   ```
   Specify source location <0,0,0>: Pick the endpoint shown in Figure 25.8.
   Enter an option to change [Name/Intensity/Status/shadoW/Attenuation/
      Color/eXit]<eXit>: n ↵
   Enter light name <Pointlight1>: p1 ↵
   Enter an option to change [Name/Intensity/Status/shadoW/Attenuation/
      Color/eXit]<eXit>: i ↵
   Enter intensity (0.00 - max float) <1.0000>: 3 ↵
   Enter an option to change [Name/Intensity/Status/shadoW/Attenuation/
      Color/eXit]<eXit>: x ↵
   ```

5. Choose Render tab ⇨ Lights panel and click the dialog box launcher at the right end of the panel's title bar. In the Lights in Model palette, click the new p1 light listed there to select the light.

6. Right-click over the Lights in Model palette and choose Properties. On the Properties palette, click the Filter Color item and choose Yellow from the drop-down list. Click the Shadows item and choose On from the drop-down list (if it's not already on).

FIGURE 25.8

Picking the point light location.

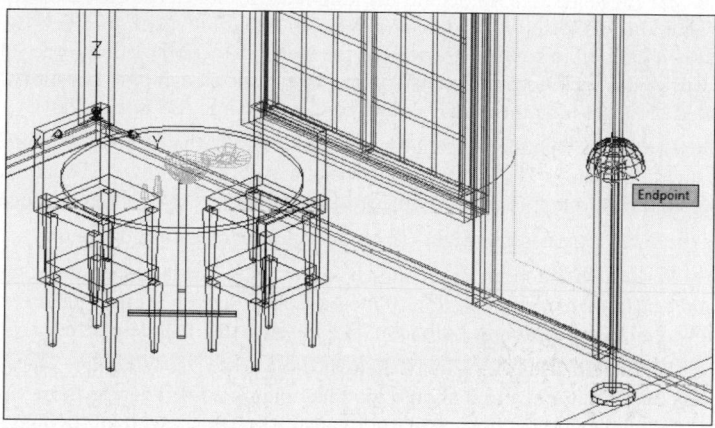

7. Choose View tab ➪ Views panel ➪ Previous View to return to your previous view.

 8. Choose Render tab ➪ Lights panel ➪ Create Light drop-down list ➪ Spot. Follow the prompts:

```
Specify source location <0,0,0>: Shift+right-click and choose From
     from the OSNAP list.
_from Base point: Use the Center object snap of the top edge of the
     round table.
<Offset>: @0,0,5' ↵ (This places the light 5 feet directly over the
     table, like a light hanging from the ceiling.)
Specify target location <0,0,-10>: Use the Center object snap of the
     top of the table.
Point to the edge of the round table.
Enter an option to change
[Name/Intensity/Status/Hotspot/Falloff/shadoW/Attenuation/Color/eXit]
     <eXit>: n ↵
Enter light name <Spotlight1>: s1 ↵
Enter an option to change
[Name/Intensity/Status/Hotspot/Falloff/shadoW/Attenuation/Color/eXit]
     <eXit>: f ↵
Enter falloff angle (0.00-160.00) <50>: 70 ↵
Enter an option to change
[Name/Intensity/Status/Hotspot/Falloff/shadoW/Attenuation/Color/eXit]
     <eXit>: h ↵
Enter hotspot angle (0.00-160.00) <3'-9">: 40 ↵
Enter an option to change
[Name/Intensity/Status/Hotspot/Falloff/shadoW/Attenuation/Color/eXit]
     <eXit>: w ↵
Enter [Off/Sharp/soFtmapped/softsAmpled] <Sharp>: f ↵
Enter map size [64/128/256/512/1024/2048/4096] <256>: ↵
Enter softness (1-10) <1>: 5 ↵
Enter an option to change
[Name/Intensity/Status/Hotspot/Falloff/shadoW/Attenuation/Color/eXit]
     <eXit>: x ↵
```

9. Choose Render tab ⇨ Sun & Location panel ⇨ Set Location. In the Geographic Location – Define Geographic Location dialog box, click Enter the Location Values. In the Geographic Location dialog box, set the latitude to 41.00 and the longitude to 91.57. The two drop-down list boxes to the right should read North for latitude and West for longitude. (The specified latitude and longitude indicates a location in southeast Iowa.) In the North Direction section, type **90** in the Angle text box. Click OK. Click Accept Updated Time Zone at the Geographic Location – Time Zone Updated message. (The time zone should be Central Time [US & Canada].)

10. Choose Render tab ⇨ Sun & Location panel and click the dialog box launcher at the right end of the panel's title bar. In the Sun Properties palette, set the date to 9/1 (September 1). Set the time to 8:00 in the morning. (You're having breakfast.) Set the Daylight Savings item to Yes.

11. Close the Sun Properties and Lights in Model palettes (or auto-hide them).

12. Choose Render tab ⇨ Render panel and click the dialog box launcher at the right end of the panel's title bar. In the Shadows section of the Advanced Render Settings palette, click the Specifies If Shadows Are Computed light bulb icon, making sure that it is deselected.

 13. Choose Render tab ⇨ Render panel ⇨ Render drop-down list ⇨ Render. The rendering should take less than a minute, and it should look like Figure 25.9. There is more than enough light this time — but remember, you wouldn't normally eat breakfast with all the lights on. Notice the effect of the yellow point light; it makes the blue floor and walls look green.

FIGURE 25.9

A rendering with lights but no shadows.

14. Display the Advanced Render Settings palette again if you closed it. Click the Specifies If Shadows Are Computed light bulb icon in the Shadows section. Click Render. Notice that the rendering takes much longer. Lots of shadows this time! This rendering also makes it clear that no light is coming through the windows. (See the "Working with Materials" section to learn how to make materials transparent.) The rendering should look like Figure 25.10.

15. Save your drawing. If you're continuing on to the next exercise, keep this drawing open.

FIGURE 25.10

The same rendering with shadows.

Working with Materials

Materials in AutoCAD are representations of actual materials on objects, such as glass, metal, fabric, wood, and others. Using materials is an important part of the rendering process and greatly affects the results. Materials interact with lights. For example, shiny materials reflect light differently than dull materials because shiny materials create highlights.

 You can display materials as you work. Although this requires more resources from your computer, you can see some results immediately, without rendering. Rendering always produces a more accurate result. To display materials, choose Render tab ⇨ Materials panel ⇨ Materials/Textures drop-down list ⇨ Materials / Textures On. You need to be in the Realistic visual style (or a custom visual style using the Realistic face style) to see the result.

Note

The Adaptive Degradation process may turn off materials automatically if your graphics card is not certified. You can turn the display of materials on manually by using the 3DCONFIG command. For more information, see Appendix A. ∎

Attaching a material from the Materials Browser

 The Materials Browser, as shown in Figure 25.11, lets you attach and manage materials. To open the Materials Browser, choose Render tab ⇨ Materials panel ⇨ Materials Browser. The Materials Browser is divided into two areas:

- **Document Materials:** The upper area of the Materials Browser lists the materials in the current drawing. You can use the Document Materials and Sort drop-down lists just above the material swatches to control how the materials in the current drawing are displayed in the Materials Browser.

- **Libraries:** The lower area of the Materials Browser provides access to materials in the available libraries, including the Autodesk Library and your own materials, called My Materials.

New Feature

AutoCAD 2011 introduces the Materials Browser, which allows you to use materials from the Autodesk Materials Library and the current drawing. The Materials Browser replaces the collection of material tool palettes on the Tool Palettes window in prior releases of AutoCAD. ■

FIGURE 25.11

The Materials Browser lets you manage materials in the current drawing and those stored in a materials library.

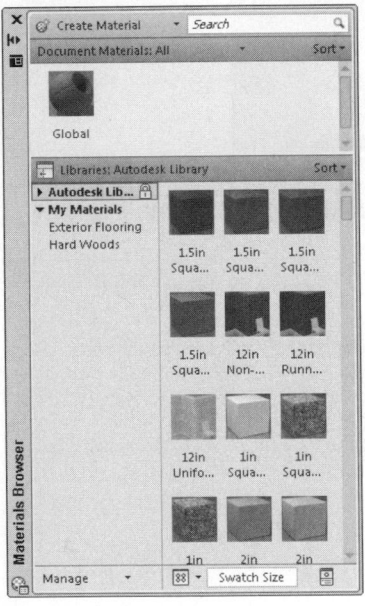

From the Materials Browser, you can manage the materials in the current drawing by doing the following:

- **Create a material.** Click the Create Material drop-down list at the top of the Materials Browser and choose a template to create a new material. Choose the Generic template to give you the most control over the definition of the new material. The Materials Editor palette opens so you can edit the properties of the new material.

- **Edit a material.** Right-click a material and choose Edit to display the material in the Material Editor palette.

- **Remove a material.** Right-click a material and choose Delete to remove the material definition from the current drawing.

- **Copy a material.** Right-click a material and choose Duplicate to create a duplicate copy of the material with a new name that you can then alter as needed.

- **Rename a material.** Right-click a material and choose Rename to change the name of the material in the current drawing.

- **Assign a material to an object.** Select the objects you want to apply the material to in the drawing. Right-click a material and choose Add to Selection. Press and hold the Ctrl key if you want to select a face on a 3D solid or mesh, or use subobject filtering (choose Home tab ⇨ Subobject panel ⇨ Subobject Filter drop-down list ⇨ Face). See the section, "Attaching and removing materials," for additional information.

- **Locate an object that has a material assigned to it.** Right-click a material and choose Select Objects Applied To. This selects the objects in the drawing that use the material.

- **Add a material to a library or current tool palette.** Right-click a material and choose the appropriate item from the Add To sub-menu.

- **Purge all unused materials.** Right-click a material and choose Purge All Unused Materials to remove the materials currently not assigned to any objects in the drawing.

Besides managing materials in the current drawing, you use the Materials Browser to organize and access materials stored in material libraries. AutoCAD comes with the Autodesk Library of materials. You can see which material libraries are available to you in the Libraries panel. Double-click a material library to see the categories contained in the library and select a category to see the materials it contains. You can manage a material library by doing the following:

- **Open a material library.** Click the Manage drop-down list at the bottom of the Materials Browser and choose Open Existing Library. In the Add Library dialog box, browse to and select the material library (ADSKLIB) file that you want to open. Click Open.

- **Create a material library.** You can create your own material library files, which allows you to easily share and archive your materials. Click the Manage drop-down list at the bottom of the Materials Browser and choose Create New Library. In the Create Library dialog box, browse to the location you want to store your material library at and enter a name for the library. Click Save. AutoCAD adds a Default category.

- **Remove a material library.** Select a library from the list that is not read-only. Click the Manage drop-down list at the bottom of the Materials Browser and choose Remove Library, or right-click a library and choose Remove Library.

- **Create or delete a category.** Categories help you organize your materials. Select a library from the list that is not read-only. Click the Manage drop-down list at the bottom of the Materials Browser and choose Create Category, or right-click a library and choose Create Category. Enter a name for the new category and press Enter. Select a category and choose Delete Category to remove the category. Click Delete to confirm the deletion of the category and its materials. To move materials to a category, drag them from the right-hand pane to the category.

- **Rename a category.** Select a category from a library that is not read-only. Click the Manage drop-down list at the bottom of the Materials Browser and choose Rename, or right-click the category and choose Rename. Enter a new name and press Enter.

Note

You can only edit the materials in the current drawing. If you need to make changes to a material stored in a library, add it to the current drawing and then edit it. After editing the material, add it to the library to update the old material with the revised material. ■

On the DVD

The drawing used in the following exercise on creating a new material library and attaching materials from the Materials Browser, ab25-02.dwg, is in the Results folder on the DVD. ■

STEPS: Creating a New Material Library and Attaching Materials from the Materials Browser

1. If you have ab25-02.dwg open, use this file. Otherwise, open it from your AutoCAD Bible folder or the Results folder on the DVD.

2. Save the file as ab25-03.dwg in your AutoCAD Bible folder.

3. Choose Render tab ➪ Materials panel ➪ Materials/Textures drop-down list ➪ Materials / Textures On.

4. Choose Render tab ➪ Materials panel ➪ Materials Browser.

5. Choose View tab ➪ Visual Styles panel ➪ Visual Styles drop-down list ➪ Realistic.

6. On the Materials Browser, double-click Autodesk Library and choose the Wood category.

7. On the bottom of the Materials Browser, click the Materials View drop-down list, to the right of the Swatch Size slider, and choose List View. Position the cursor between the column headers of Name and Type. When you see the double-arrow cursor, double-click to expand the Name column.

8. Locate the Maple - Stained Dark Polished material on the right side of the Materials Browser.

9. Select the table object in the drawing. Right-click the Maple - Stained Dark Polished material in the Materials Browser and choose Assign to Selection. The tabletop changes color, but still doesn't look very much like wood. In the next exercise, you'll fix that. Click in the drawing window and press Esc to deselect the table.

10. At the bottom of the Materials Browser, click Manage and choose Create New Library.

11. In the Create Library dialog box, browse to the AutoCAD Bible folder and enter **My Materials** in the File Name text box. Click Save.

12. Right-click the Maple - Stained Dark Polished material and choose Add To ➪ My Materials.

Using the Materials Editor palette

To manage and modify materials in the current drawing, choose Render tab ➪ Materials panel and click the dialog box launcher at the right end of the panel's title bar to open the Materials palette (the MATERIALS command), as shown in Figure 25.12. You can also click the Materials Editor button in the lower-right corner of the Materials Browser.

New Feature

The Materials Editor palette is a new feature in AutoCAD 2011 and is an improved version of the Materials palette that was in previous releases. The old Materials palette was split into the Materials Browser and Materials Editor palette. You use the Materials Editor palette to edit the properties of a material contained in the current drawing. ■

The top section of the Materials Editor palette displays a preview of the material that you are currently editing. To edit a material, you select it at the top of the Materials Browser.

FIGURE 25.12

The Materials Editor palette lets you create and edit materials. Note that the properties available vary with the material's template.

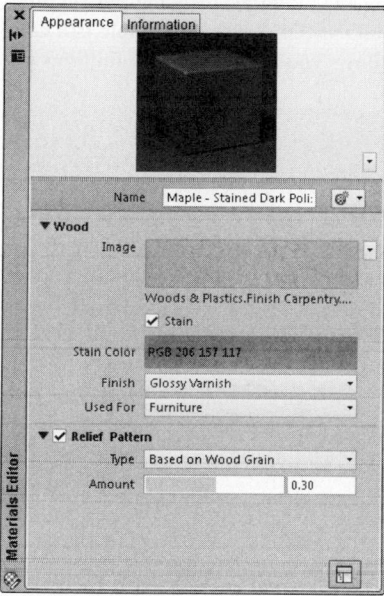

Tip

You can access the properties of a material on a tool palette by right-clicking the material in the Tool Palettes window and choosing Properties to open a dialog box for that material. ■

Creating your own materials

To create your own material, click the Create Material drop-down list on the right side of the Materials Editor palette or at the top of the Materials Browser. Then choose a material template. A new swatch appears in the Materials Browser and the material is now available for editing in the Materials Editor palette.

Note that you can also modify an existing material or copy an existing material and modify that copy from the Materials Browser. In fact, to get the results that you want, you often need to modify an existing material in some way. To copy a material, right-click it in the Materials Browser, and choose Duplicate.

You can also click the Create Material drop-down list in the Materials Editor palette, and choose Duplicate to create a copy of the material you are currently editing. The Materials Editor also allows you to choose Duplicate as Generic, which creates a new Generic material from the current material. The Generic material gives you much greater control over the appearance of the material by allowing you to access properties that are normally not exposed using the more specific material templates.

Note

You may have materials that you created in AutoCAD 2007 and previous releases that you would like to use. You must convert such materials to work with AutoCAD 2011. Use the CONVERTOLDMATERIALS command for this purpose. You may need to adjust the images and procedural-based textures for the materials by using the Texture Editor palette, as described later in this section. In addition, the 3DCONVERSIONMODE system variable can convert material and light definitions to the latest release. This system variable allows you to keep your definitions up-to-date with each new release. ■

Choose a material type

The first step is to choose a material type. Not all material templates allow you to specify a material type. A material type provides you with the ability to refine the material you created based on the original template you choose. For example, if you choose the Plastic template, you can define the type of plastic you want to create using the Type drop-down list; this makes it easy to get the material to look a specific way without worrying about a series of complex properties.

Choose a material color

The next step is to specify the properties for your new material. The properties available in the Materials Editor palette are determined by the material template you selected when you created the material. Figure 25.13 shows the properties for a material created with the Generic material template.

FIGURE 25.13

Use this section of the Materials Editor palette to specify colors and characteristics for your material.

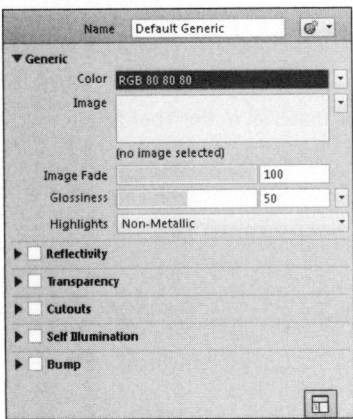

You assign a color to a material by clicking the color swatch, or clicking the down arrow to the right of the color swatch and choosing Edit Color. The Select Color dialog box opens. Specify the color you want to use for the material and click OK. You can choose to use the color an object is assigned in the drawing by clicking the down arrow to the right of the color swatch and choosing Color by Object.

Choose an image or procedural-based texture

You can further specify an image or procedural-based texture for your material if you need a material that is more than a single color. You commonly change the color or image of a material, not both. Click the down arrow to the right of the image swatch and choose Image to use a raster image file or one of the procedural-based textures listed. Choosing Image displays the Material Editor Open File dialog box, which allows you to select the image file you want to use for the material.

You can choose one of the following procedural-based textures for your material:

- **Checker.** Two-color checkerboard pattern.
- **Gradient.** Gradient pattern.
- **Marble.** Marble-like pattern that is defined by stone and vein colors.
- **Noise.** Randomly generated turbulence based on a combination of two colors or textures.
- **Speckle.** Randomly generated speckle pattern.
- **Tiles.** Brick and tile patterns.
- **Waves.** Randomly generated ripple or wave pattern.
- **Wood.** Wood grain-like pattern that is defined by main and grain colors.

After selecting an image file or a procedural-based texture, the Texture Editor palette opens, which allows you to control the appearance of the image or procedural-based texture. Figure 25.14 shows the Texture Editor palette. As you edit the properties in the Texture Editor palette, you can see the material update in real-time in both the Materials Browser and the Materials Editor palette.

FIGURE 25.14

You can define the settings for an image and procedural-based texture.

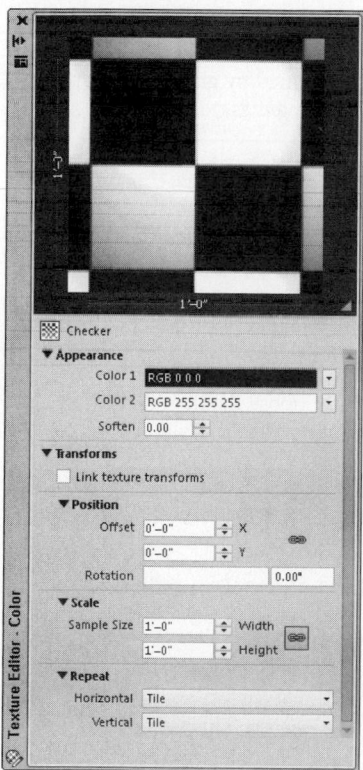

The Appearance section of the Texture Editor allows you to specify the image, colors, and other settings specific to the procedural-based texture you selected in the Materials Editor palette. Use the Transforms section to control the position, scale, and repeat (tiling) of the image or procedural-based texture. Check Link Texture Transforms under the Transforms section to have all textures of a material update when you make a change to the position, scale, or repeat values for a texture.

To edit an image or procedural-based texture assigned to a material, click the down arrow to the right of the image swatch and choose Edit Image to open the Texture Editor palette. Click the down arrow to the right of the image swatch and choose Remove Image to remove the assigned image or procedural-based texture.

Choosing properties specific to the material template

You can specify the properties specific to the material you are editing; these vary based on the material's template. For most materials, you can find these properties after the Color property, almost always in the upper section of the Materials Editor palette. Some examples of these properties are Sealant and Finish Bumps for Concrete, and Finish for Ceramic and Wood materials.

Adding other characteristics to a material

The lower sections of the Materials Editor palette allow you to add additional characteristics to your materials. You add these additional characteristics to a material by clicking the check box next to the ones you want to use. You can then edit the properties in each section. The following are the characteristics that you can add to a Generic material (there are others that are specific to materials such as Wood and Ceramic):

- **Reflectivity.** Controls the level of reflections and intensity of specular highlights.
- **Transparency.** Controls the level of transparency of the material. A value of 1 indicates the material is fully transparent, and 0 indicates it is fully opaque.
- **Cutouts.** Creates perforations in a material. Perforations are determined by grayscale interpretation; light areas are translated as opaque, while dark areas are translated as transparent.
- **Self illumination.** Marks an object to appear as if it emits light.
- **Bump.** Creates the effect of varying heights — bumps — on a material. The image or procedural-based texture is usually black and white.

Adjusting the mapping

The way in which a material, especially one with a texture, maps onto an object may not be suitable for that object's shape. For example, mapping a floral pattern onto a flat surface is different from mapping it onto the wall of a cylindrical shape. If the pattern has a direction, you may want to rotate it.

Use the MATERIALMAP command to fine-tune the mapping of a material. Choose Render tab ⇨ Materials panel ⇨ Material Mapping drop-down list, and choose one of the options (Box, Planar, Cylindrical, or Spherical) to specify which type of geometry you want to use. You can then move or rotate the texture, using the Move Grip or Rotate Grip tool.

On the DVD

The drawing used in the following exercise on modifying and creating materials, ab25-03.dwg, is in the Results folder on the DVD. ∎

STEPS: Modifying and Creating Materials

1. If you have ab25-03.dwg open from the previous exercise, use this file. Otherwise, open it from your AutoCAD Bible folder (if you did the exercise) or the Results folder of the DVD.

2. Save the file as `ab25-04.dwg` in your `AutoCAD Bible` folder.

3. If you can't see the beige color on the table top, choose Render tab ⇨ Materials panel ⇨ Materials/ Textures drop-down list ⇨ Materials / Textures On. Then choose View tab ⇨ Visual Styles panel ⇨ Visual Styles drop-down list ⇨ Realistic.

4. Choose Render tab ⇨ Materials panel ⇨ Materials Browser to open the Materials Browser. Right-click the Maple wood material and choose Edit.

5. In the Materials Editor palette, click the image swatch to open the Texture Editor palette.

6. In the Texture Editor palette, click the Transforms section to expand it. Expand the Scale section and enter **5** in the Width text box. This reduces the wood grain by 50 percent, because it tells AutoCAD that the image should be repeated every 5" instead of the default 10".

7. To create a material for the wedge of cheese on the plate, in the Materials Editor palette, click the Create Material drop-down list and then choose Generic. From the Swatch Shape drop-down list to the right of the Preview, choose Cube.

8. Use the following settings for the new material:
   - **Name.** Yellow Cheese.
   - **Color.** Click the color swatch. From the Index Color tab of the Select Color dialog box, choose Index Color 51, a light yellow. Click OK.
   - **Glossiness.** Drag the Glossiness slider down to about 20. Cheese isn't very shiny.
   - **Bump.** Click the check box next to Bump. In the Material Editor Open File dialog box, click Cancel. Click the down arrow to the right of the Image swatch under the Bump section and choose Noise. In the Texture Editor palette, click in the Size text box and enter **0.5**. Close or auto-hide the Texture Editor and Materials Editor palettes. Do not close the Materials Browser.

9. In the drawing window, select the wedge on the plate. In the Materials Browser, right-click the Yellow Cheese material swatch and choose Assign to Selection to attach the Yellow Cheese material.

Note

You may not be able to see the bump map in your drawing. To see it, choose Render tab ⇨ Render panel ⇨ Render drop-down list ⇨ Render. By default, the rendering appears in a separate application window. ■

10. Save your drawing.

Attaching and removing materials

After you import, create, and modify the materials that you need, you can attach them to objects. AutoCAD lets you attach materials by object or layer. In fact, these two options allow you to attach a material to the following:

- An entire object by selecting the object
- Any objects on a specified layer, including layers of objects within a block
- A face on an object (by subselecting the face)

I've already discussed how to attach materials from the Materials Browser in the "Attaching a material from the Materials Browser" section earlier in this chapter.

 To attach a material to all objects on a layer, you use the MATERIALATTACH command, which you can find by choosing Render tab ⇨ Materials panel (expanded) ⇨ Attach By Layer. The Material Attachment Options dialog box opens, as shown in Figure 25.15.

FIGURE 25.15

Use the Material Attachment Options dialog box to attach a material to all objects on a layer.

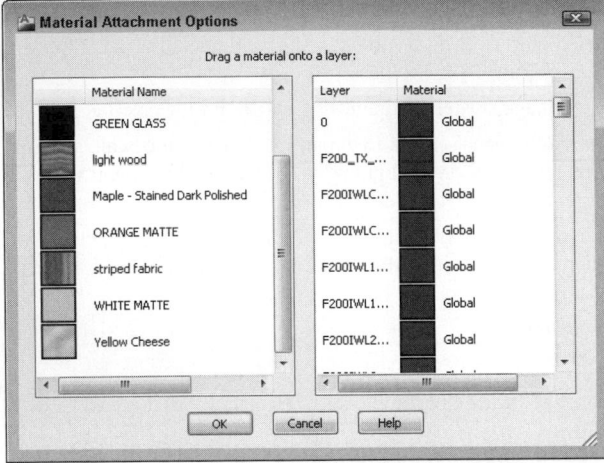

Drag any material from the left to a layer on the right to attach the material. To detach a material from a layer, click the Detach button (the X) that appears in the right-hand column.

Tip

Attaching materials by layer can be a very efficient method, but it requires some planning in advance. For example, if you have a block that is a chair, you can create it so that the legs are on one layer and the seat and back are on a different layer; then you can easily attach a wood-like material to the legs and a decorative pattern to the seat and back. ■

You can remove a material attached to an object by choosing Render tab ⇨ Materials panel (expanded) ⇨ Remove Materials. At the `Select objects:` prompt, select the object or face.

Using backgrounds

You can add a background to a rendering by saving a view that includes a background. In Chapter 22, I explain how to add a background by using the VIEW command. For example, you can place a picture of the sky in the background (see Figure 25.1 in this chapter).

Note

Releases of AutoCAD prior to 2007 included a scenes feature that allowed you to save views and light settings. Scenes are no longer available. The same is true of landscape objects, which included trees and other objects. ■

On the DVD

The files used in the following exercise on attaching materials and adding a background, ab25-b.dwg and bluesky.jpg, are in the Drawings folder on the DVD. ■

STEPS: Attaching Materials and Adding a Background

1. Open ab25-b.dwg from the DVD. Use Windows Explorer to copy bluesky.jpg from the Drawings folder of the DVD to your AutoCAD Bible folder.

2. Save the file as ab25-05.dwg in your AutoCAD Bible folder. This is the same drawing used earlier in the chapter, but all the materials have been imported and modified, and some materials have been attached to objects. Also, the table and chairs have been separated into appropriate layers.

3. If you're not in the Realistic visual style, choose View tab ➪ Visual Styles panel ➪ Visual Styles drop-down list ➪ Realistic.

 4. Choose Render tab ➪ Materials panel (expanded) ➪ Attach By Layer. In the Material Attachment Options dialog box, drag the light wood material from the Material Name list onto the LEGS layer. (To more easily find the layer, click the Layer heading in the right pane to alphabetize the layers.) Then drag the striped fabric material onto the CUSHIONS layer. Click OK.

5. In the drawing window, select the plate on the table. In the Materials Browser, right-click the GREEN GLASS material and choose Assign to Selection.

6. Choose View tab ➪ Views panel ➪ Named Views. In the View Manager, click New. In the New View / Shot Properties dialog box's View Name text box, enter **Render with background**. In the Background section, select Image from the drop-down list. The Background dialog box opens.

7. Click the Browse button. In the Select File dialog box, you may need to change the Files of Type drop-down list to All Image Files. Select bluesky.jpg (which you copied to your AutoCAD Bible folder in Step 1) and click Open.

8. In the Background dialog box, click Adjust Image. From the Image Position drop-down list, choose Stretch. You can see how the image improves. Click OK three times to return to the View Manager. Click Set Current and click OK to return to your drawing. You should see the image appear through the windows. (If not, you may need to render the drawing.)

9. Save your drawing. Keep it open if you're continuing to the next exercise.

Foggy landscapes

Fog is used to give a sense of distance by making objects in the distance less clear than those close up. To add a fog effect, choose Render tab ➪ Render panel (expanded) ➪ Environment to open the Render Environment dialog box. Choose On from the drop-down list in the Enable Fog field. You set the color (a gray color by default), near and far distances (where the fog starts and ends), and near and far percentages of fog (how much fog there should be at the near and far distances). You can also apply the fog to the background (the Fog Background setting), which turns the entire background the color of the fog. To use fog, you need to set front and back clipping on, using the 3DCLIP command. Move the front clipping plane in front of the nearest object and the back clipping plane behind the farthest object. You then need to render to see the results; you can't see them in the drawing viewport.

Doing the Final Render

You're finally ready for your final rendering. Preparing to render can be a long process. At this time, you may want to look at some of the more specialized settings for rendering in the Advanced Render Settings palette, as shown in Figure 25.16. To open the Advanced Render Settings palette (the RPREF command), choose Render tab ⇨ Render panel and click the dialog box launcher at the right end of the panel's title bar. Here I highlight some of the more common settings.

The Advanced Render Settings palette lets you set many rendering options. This figure shows about half of the available settings.

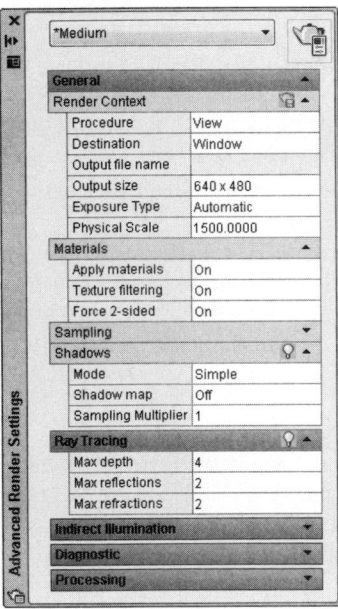

At the top of the Advanced Render Settings palette is the drop-down list of the render presets. Render presets are groups of settings that you can use when you don't want to customize the settings. You can choose from Draft, Low, Medium (the default), High, and Presentation. (You can customize the presets themselves, by choosing Render tab ⇨ Render panel ⇨ Render Presets drop-down list ⇨ Manage Render Presets [the RENDERPRESETS command]. You can also use the Render Presents drop-down list on the Render panel to set the current render present.) The choice you make depends on your situation — how much you need to see, whether you're doing a draft or final rendering, and the capabilities of your computer system, especially its graphics card and memory.

The **Render Context** section contains settings that relate to the rendering as a whole. This section allows you to choose how your model gets rendered. Here are your options:

- **Save File.** Click the Determines If File Is Written button if you want to save the resulting rendering to a file. Click the same button to cancel saving to a file.

- **Procedure.** You can render the current view, crop to a window, or render selected objects.

- **Destination.** You can render to the current viewport or to a separate window.

- **Output File Name.** If you chose to save a file, click this item, then click the Ellipsis button to navigate to a location, and enter a filename. You can save renderings as BMP, TIF, JPEG, PNG, TGA, or PCX files.

- **Output Size.** Choose an output size (in pixels) from the drop-down list or choose Specify Output Size to customize your size settings.

- **Exposure Type.** Choose Automatic or Logarithmic. Automatic exposure is the default output setting, and is the setting used with releases prior to AutoCAD 2009. The Logarithmic setting is useful when you want more control over exposure, but are not using photometric lighting.

- **Physical Scale.** This setting helps to reduce artifacts (imperfections) caused by changes in exposure. The default value is 1500. If you see artifacts, you need to experiment to find a value that works for you; the best value in a drawing with a sun will be different than in a drawing with just point lights.

The Materials section has settings relating to materials. You can specify the following:

- **Apply Materials.** Turns materials on and off.

- **Texture Filtering.** Samples textures by area to avoid aliasing, which results in artifacts, such as a jagged or moiré effect.

- **Force 2-Sided.** Renders both sides of faces, even those facing away from the view. You can turn this off to speed up rendering.

The Sampling section offers settings to control sampling, which is the precision with which the rendering deals with each pixel. A lower minimum sampling rate is quicker but less accurate. A 1/4 sampling rate (the default) makes one calculation for every four pixels. The maximum sampling rate applies when the neighboring pixels are different enough (have enough contrast) to require more precise sampling. The default is 1, which is one calculation per pixel. The contrast colors control the contrast values used to determine how much sampling to do, based on the minimum and maximum rates.

The Shadows section has a Light bulb button that turns shadows on and off. You can turn shadows off to speed up rendering. The Mode determines the order in which shadows are computed — Simple (randomly), Sorted (from an object to the light), and Segment (along the light ray). Shadow Map turns on shadow mapping. When this is off, shadows are ray-traced, which results in sharper and more accurate outlines. Shadow maps allow for soft shadows.

The Sampling Multiplier limits sampling for shadows throughout the drawing. Use this feature to create draft renders. Lower values mean less sampling; higher values produce more accurate results. Values range from 0 to 2.

The Ray Tracing section affects how the renderer calculates ray-traced shadows. The Light bulb button turns ray tracing on and off. The Max Depth setting controls how many reflections and refractions can be calculated. You can also individually set the maximum reflections and refractions that are calculated.

The Indirect Illumination section has three subsections — all relate to subtle light effects in addition to direct lights that you create. These settings control *radiosity,* the simulation of multiple reflections of light as they interact with each other, to create more natural lighting. For example, Global Illumination creates color bleeding, which occurs when the color of one surface affects the color of a nearby surface. Final Gather adds an additional calculation to eliminate dark corners and other artifacts, but adds greatly to rendering time. The Light Properties section has controls that affect lights that you create when you use indirect illumination. You can increase the accuracy and brightness of lights with these settings, but doing so increases rendering time.

The Diagnostic section helps troubleshoot the rendering results. You can turn on the display of a grid to help understand how the renderer is placing an object. You may have noticed that when you render, the rendering appears tile by tile. You can change the size of this tile, the order of the tiling, and the maximum memory used during the rendering process.

To render, choose Render tab ⇨ Render panel ⇨ Render drop-down list ⇨ Render. The model is rendered according to the settings in the Advanced Render Settings palette. You can also use the RENDER command on the command line by typing **-render** ↵. You can choose a render quality and output location.

On the DVD

The drawing used in the following exercise on creating a final rendering, ab25-05.dwg, is in the Results folder on the DVD. ∎

STEPS: Creating a Final Rendering

1. If you have ab25-05.dwg open, use this file. Otherwise, open it from your AutoCAD Bible folder if you did the previous exercise, or from the Results folder of the DVD.

2. Save the file as ab25-06.dwg in your AutoCAD Bible folder.

3. Choose Render tab ⇨ Lights panel and click the dialog box launcher at the right end of the panel's title bar. In the Lights in Model palette, choose P1. Display the Properties palette (Ctrl+1), change the intensity to 2, and press Enter. This is the type of adjustment you often make when doing the final rendering.

4. Choose Render tab ⇨ Render panel and click the dialog box launcher at the right end of the panel's title bar. In the Advanced Render Settings palette, under the Shadows section, change the Shadow Map setting to On. This results in softer shadows. (You can try it both ways to see the difference.)

5. Choose Render tab ⇨ Render panel ⇨ Render drop-down list ⇨ Render.

6. The Rendering window should open. Wait until AutoCAD finishes the rendering. Look at those shadows! Can you see the orange in the transparent green bowl? Note the sky image outside the window.

7. The rendering should look like Figure 25.17, only a lot better because you see it in color on your screen. Save your drawing.

Remember that rendering is a trial-and-error process. Don't expect to get it right the first time. You can probably see several areas that require improvement. At this point, you would go back and tweak the lights, materials, and so on until you were satisfied.

FIGURE 25.17

The final rendering with shadows, transparent objects, and a background.

On the DVD

AccuRender is a rendering program that offers additional rendering capabilities. Look for it in `Software\ Chapter 25.` ∎

Statistics

When you render to the render window, the right pane lists a number of statistics relating to your rendering. You can use these statistics to troubleshoot or compare results among renderings. The bottom pane shows your rendering history.

Saving rendered images

You can save your rendered images and re-display them at another time. You can also use saved rendered images in other applications and print them from those applications. Here are the steps to saving a rendering to an image file:

1. Render the image.
   - After rendering to a viewport, on the command line, type **saveimg** ↵.
   - After rendering to the render window, choose File ➪ Save from that window's menu.
2. In the Render Output File dialog box, choose a file type, enter a filename, and click Save. In the Render Output File dialog box, choose a file type from the File of Type drop-down list. Choose a location and enter a name for the file.
3. Depending on the image type that you choose, you'll see a dialog box offering options such as the number of colors and the quality. Choose the options you want and click OK to save the image.

You can import these saved rendered images back into your drawing. Figure 25.18 shows three floating viewports. One of the views shows the rendered image.

FIGURE 25.18

You can include your rendered images in your drawings.

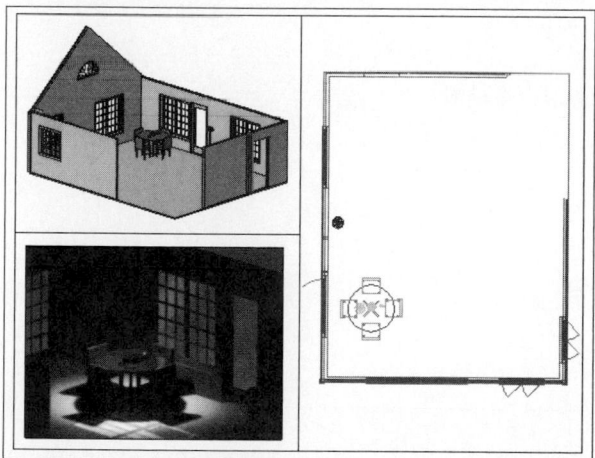

Cross-Reference

See Chapter 27 for detailed instructions on importing images. You can plot rendered viewports, as I explain in Chapter 17. ∎

Summary

In this chapter, I covered the process of rendering. You read about the following:

- Creating lights
- Managing, importing, and creating materials
- Attaching materials
- Using backgrounds
- Rendering a drawing

This chapter ends Part IV, "Drawing in Three Dimensions." Part V, "Organizing and Managing Drawings," explains how to manage drawings, work with other applications and file types, and use AutoCAD on the Internet.

Part V

Organizing and Managing Drawings

P art V is all about how to manage drawings. In Chapter 26, I discuss ways to keep control of your drawings, including features such as the DesignCenter, tool palettes, and the Communication Center. I also explain how to set and maintain standards, keep track of your drawings, handle errors and crashes, and work with prior AutoCAD releases. Finally, I thoroughly cover how to organize your drawings into sheet sets.

Chapter 27 explains how to interface with other applications and file formats, including raster (bitmap) images. Finally, Chapter 28 covers how to create electronic output, including placing your drawings on the Internet, using hyperlinks, and using the DWF and DWFx file formats.

Keeping Control of Your Drawings

W hen you create a drawing, you not only create objects, but you also
create a complex structure to support those objects. You create
named blocks, layers, layouts, text styles, dimension styles, multileader styles, table styles, and linetypes to help define those objects. And you
spend a lot of time creating them! All these named drawing components can be
reused and organized for greater efficiency, using the DesignCenter.

Tool palettes are a multifaceted solution that enables you to execute commands,
as well as to insert hatches and blocks. You can also insert tables, xrefs, images,
gradients, and more.

Having standards for named drawing components, such as layers and text styles,
is important for consistency and readability. AutoCAD offers a comprehensive
system for maintaining CAD standards. Security is also important, and AutoCAD
offers excellent features to help you with this. AutoCAD LT does not contain all
these features.

Sheet sets enable you to manage sets of drawings. You can automate the placement of viewports, as well as view and call out labels. You can plot or publish
sheet sets as one group. AutoCAD LT does not offer the sheet set feature.

You also need to keep track of your drawings and make sure that they're accessible. Archiving and repair procedures are important in any CAD environment.
This chapter covers all these topics to help you keep control of your drawings
and their content.

Accessing Drawing Components with the DesignCenter

I mention the DesignCenter many times in this book — for example, in Chapter 11
on layers and Chapter 18 on blocks. In this chapter, I cover the DesignCenter in
detail. You can use the DesignCenter to easily drag named drawing components

from one drawing to another. You can even drag raster images directly into your drawing. You can access this *drawing content* from drawings on your hard drive, on a network drive, or over the Internet. You never need to re-create them.

You can do the following with the DesignCenter:

- Browse and insert named drawing components, including blocks (and dynamic blocks), xrefs, layers, text styles, table styles, multileader styles, dimension styles, linetypes, and layouts. You can also access custom objects that are created by third-party applications.
- Create shortcuts to drawings and locations that you use most often.
- Search for drawings and named drawing components.
- Open drawings by dragging them into the drawing area.
- Create tools for your tool palettes.
- View and insert raster image files by dragging them into the drawing area.

Navigating with the DesignCenter

 To open the DesignCenter, choose View tab ➪ Palettes panel ➪ DesignCenter. As a shortcut, press Ctrl+2. The DesignCenter appears, as shown in Figure 26.1. Three tabs provide access to folders, open drawings, and history, where you can find content provided by Autodesk, manufacturers, and other users. You can add a fourth tab, DC Online, by installing the CAD Manager Control Utility and enabling the display of the tab.

Note

While the DC Online allows you to insert blocks from the Internet, the catalog is very limited. The Autodesk Seek Web site offers a large catalog of symbols and specifications that you can use in your drawing. Click The Autodesk Seek logo in the upper-right corner of DesignCenter or use the Content panel on the Insert tab. You can also use the SEEK command to open the Autodesk Seek Web site in your default Web browser and find content online. ■

FIGURE 26.1

The DesignCenter with the Folders tab displayed.

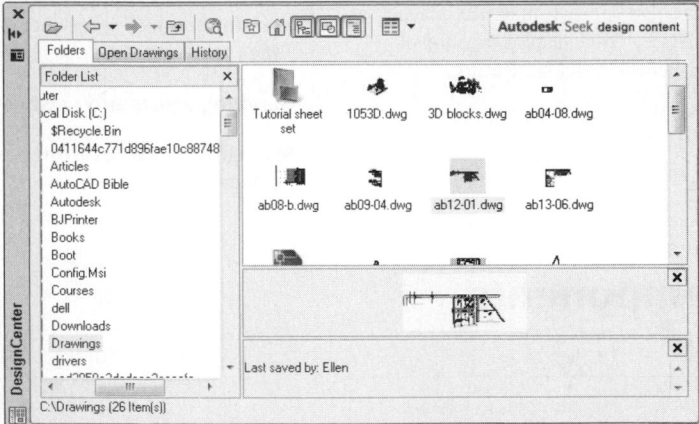

The Folders tab displays a tree view of any location — your hard drive, network, or the Internet — that you can access. This tree view is very similar to that of Windows Explorer. Click the plus sign next to a drive or folder to display its contents. Use the vertical scroll bar to display any location.

A selected drawing displays its named components in the content area on the right side of the palette. (Use the Views drop-down list to choose the type of display that you want.) You can also click the plus sign next to a drawing to display these components in the tree view. Then click a component type, such as blocks, to see a list of the blocks in the drawing, as shown in Figure 26.1. Click Preview on the DesignCenter toolbar to see a preview in the preview pane of blocks, drawings, and raster images. Click Description to display a description, if one is saved.

 After you narrow your search, you may want to click Tree View Toggle to toggle off the tree view, thus hiding the navigation pane. By default, the navigation pane displays your desktop, including the files and folders on your hard drive and network. To narrow your search, you can click two other tabs from the DesignCenter:

- The Open Drawings tab displays currently open drawings.
- The History tab displays the most recently opened drawings.

Finding named components and drawings

What do you do if you don't know the location of the drawing that you want? Suppose you know the name of the layer but not the name of the drawing that contains that layer. The DesignCenter includes a Search feature to help you.

 Choose Search from the DesignCenter toolbar to open the Search window, as shown in Figure 26.2. (You can also right-click in the Content area and choose Search.)

FIGURE 26.2

Use the Search window to locate drawings and drawing components.

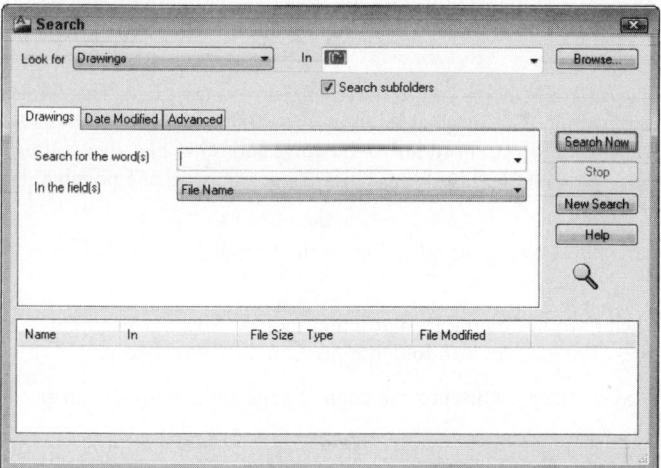

Here's how to use the Search window:

- Click the Look For drop-down list to choose what you're looking for. You can look for blocks, dimension styles, drawings, drawings and blocks, hatch pattern files, hatch patterns, layers, layouts, linetypes, multileader styles, table styles, text styles, and xrefs.

- Click the In drop-down list to specify the drive that you want to search. By default, the Search subfolders check box is checked so that the search looks in all folders and subfolders within the drive.

- Use the tabbed area to specify the name of the components that you want. The tab's name and content change, depending on what you chose in the Look For drop-down list. For example, if you chose Layers, the tab is called Layers and asks you for the name of the layer. If you're looking for drawings, you have three tabs to work with:

  - The **Drawings** tab enables you to look for a drawing by filename (the default), title, subject, author, or keywords. Choose one of these options in the In the Field(s) drop-down list. Then type the text that you want to look for in the Search for the Word(s) text box. You can use the wildcards * (to substitute for any number of characters) and ? (to substitute for any one character). Specifying a drawing's title, subject, and keywords is discussed later in this chapter.

  - The **Date Modified** tab enables you to search by the last date that the file was saved or modified. You can specify a range of dates, or look in the last x days or months.

  - The **Advanced** tab enables you to search for text in drawing descriptions, block names, attribute tags, and attribute values. You can also search here by drawing size.

- When you've created your specifications, click Search Now.

Cross-Reference

See Chapter 18 for information on creating block descriptions when you create a block. The main reason for creating a block description is to display it in the DesignCenter and use it in a search on the Advanced tab, as just described. ■

For more information on searching for drawings, see the section "Finding drawings" later in this chapter.

Using the Favorites folder

The Favorites folder is a Windows convention that helps you to find files that you use often. This folder contains shortcuts to actual files. The files remain in their original locations. You'll find an Autodesk subfolder within the Favorites folder where you can store shortcuts to drawings and other files that you use often. You can then easily open the Favorites folder and find these files. Favorites is one possible place to keep drawings that contain block libraries.

To add a shortcut to Favorites, right-click the drawing (or other file) in the DesignCenter and choose Add to Favorites.

 To access the drawings in Favorites, click Favorites on the DesignCenter toolbar. You can also right-click the Content pane and choose Favorites. The Favorites folder appears in the content pane.

To move, copy, or delete shortcuts from Favorites, right-click the content pane and choose Organize Favorites.

Accessing named drawing components

As soon as you have the item that you need in the content pane, you need to insert it into your drawing. If you used the Search window to locate a file, then you can also insert directly from the results that you find.

You can either drag the item onto the drawing area or right-click it and choose an option. Sometimes these two methods provide slightly different results. In this section, I explain how to insert drawing components into your drawing.

Inserting drawings

You can insert an entire drawing into your drawing. Choose the drawing's folder in the navigation pane so that the drawing appears in the content area. Drag the drawing's icon onto the drawing area. The command line prompts you for an insertion point, scale, and rotation angle, using the -INSERT command (the command-line version of the INSERT command).

If you right-click the drawing, you can choose to insert the drawing as a block, or attach it as an xref.

Opening drawings

You can open a drawing by using the DesignCenter. Display the drawing in the content pane, right-click it, and choose Open in Application Window. The drawing opens, keeping your current drawing open as well.

Inserting blocks

In Chapter 5, I explain that you can use the Units dialog box (choose Application Button ➪ Drawing Utilities ➪ Units) to set a unit, such as inches, for automatically scaling drawings when they're inserted from the DesignCenter.

You can insert blocks in two ways:

- If you drag the block's icon onto the drawing area, the drawing uses *Autoscaling*, which compares the current drawing's units with those of the block, and scales the block appropriately, using the value set in the Units dialog box. The block takes on the default scale and rotation.
- If you double-click the block's icon or right-click it and choose Insert Block, the Insert dialog box opens, where you can specify the insertion point, scale, and rotation. Right-click and choose Insert and Redefine Block to update an existing block definition and insert a reference of the block into the drawing.

Inserting raster images

A raster image is a bitmap graphic file. You can insert raster images directly into your drawing. To attach a raster image, drag its icon onto the drawing area. The command line prompts you for an insertion point, scale, and rotation angle. You can also double-click or right-click an image and choose Attach Image to display the Attach Image dialog box.

Cross-Reference

See Chapter 27 for more information on raster images, including determining which type of files you can import, attaching images, clipping images, and controlling how they're displayed. ∎

Tip

Knowing the appropriate scale of an image before inserting it is often difficult. When you move the cursor at the Specify scale factor or [Unit] <1>: prompt, you can see a bounding box that will help you visualize the resulting size of the image. ∎

Attaching an xref

To attach or overlay an xref, double-click or right-click its icon and choose Attach Xref to open the Attach External Reference dialog box. Choose either Attachment or Overlay in the Reference Type section. Specify an insertion point, scale, and rotation (or choose to specify them on-screen), and click OK.

If you drag the xref onto the drawing area, you see prompts on the command line that are similar to those of the INSERT command.

Inserting layers and styles

To insert a layer, layout, linetype, text style, table style, multileader styles, or dimension style into a drawing, drag its icon onto the drawing area. Of course, these items don't appear in your drawing area, but they're added to the drawing's database.

You can drag multiple items at one time. To select a contiguous group, click the first item, press and hold Shift, and click the last item. To select individual multiple items, click the first item, press and hold Ctrl, and click any other item that you want to insert. You can also double-click an item to insert it.

Caution

The insertion process does not check for duplicate layer names. If you try to insert a layer with the same name as a layer in your current drawing, you see a message: `Layer(s) added. Duplicate definitions will be ignored`**. You should check for duplicate layer names before trying to insert layers from the DesignCenter. ∎**

Controlling the DesignCenter display

The DesignCenter provides several controls that help you manage its display.

 A great feature of the DesignCenter is the preview pane. Click Preview and select the item in the content pane. You may or may not see a preview of a block. (A preview icon is created automatically when you use the Block Definition dialog box to create a block.) Usually, you'll see a preview of drawings and raster images. No previews exist for layers, linetypes, text styles, and so on.

Tip

If you have old blocks that don't have preview icons, use the BLOCKICON command and press Enter at the first prompt to automatically create preview icons of all the blocks in a drawing. ∎

 If you saved a description with a block, select the block in the content pane and click Description on the DesignCenter toolbar to see the description.

 To set the view, choose Views from the DesignCenter toolbar. The drop-down arrow lets you choose from four types of displays: large icons, small icons, list, and details.

If you make changes in the structure of a folder while the DesignCenter is open — for example, by deleting a drawing by using Windows Explorer — right-click the navigation or content pane and choose Refresh. The DesignCenter re-reads the data and refreshes the list.

To dock the DesignCenter, right-click the title bar and choose Allow Docking. Choose Anchor Left or Anchor Right to dock it to the left or right of your drawing window. To collapse the DesignCenter down to its title bar when you're not using it, right-click the title bar and choose Auto-Hide; whenever you move the mouse cursor off the DesignCenter, it collapses. Just move the cursor back onto the title bar to expand it again. You can anchor the DesignCenter at the same side as other palettes; its title bar becomes shorter to fit. When you expand it, it rolls down to its full length. To avoid unwanted docking, either uncheck Allow Docking on its title bar or press Ctrl as you drag. These instructions apply to all palettes in AutoCAD and AutoCAD LT.

On the DVD

The drawings used in the following exercise on using the DesignCenter, `ab26-a.dwg` and `ab26-b.dwg`, are in the `Drawings` folder on the DVD. ∎

STEPS: Using the DesignCenter

1. Open `ab26-a.dwg` from the DVD.

2. Save the file as `ab26-01.dwg` in your `AutoCAD Bible` folder. This drawing needs an updated set of layers and a titleblock. It is shown in Figure 26.3.

FIGURE 26.3

This drawing needs updated layers and a titleblock.

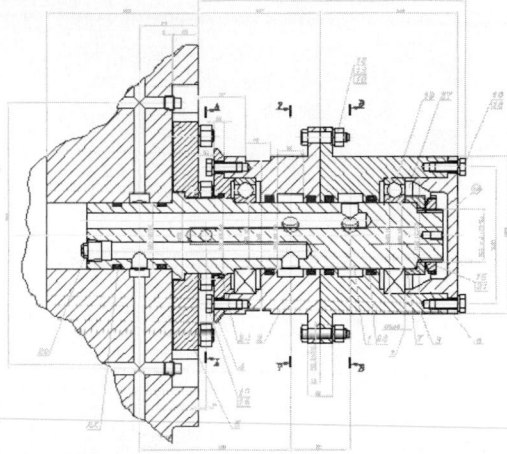

Thanks to Vladimir Sevastyanov of Ukraine for this drawing of a gyrating swivel that feeds oil to an uncoiling machine used in the cold rolling of metal.

3. Choose View tab ➪ Palettes panel ➪ DesignCenter. If the navigation pane is not displayed, click the Folders tab and then click Tree View Toggle on the DesignCenter toolbar.

4. In the navigation pane, locate `ab26-b.dwg` on the DVD. Click its plus sign.

5. Choose Blocks. The `ansi_d` block appears in the content pane. Double-click `ansi_d`. Uncheck all Specify On-screen check boxes and click OK.

6. Do a Zoom Extents.

7. In the navigation pane, click Layers for `ab26-b.dwg`.

8. In the content pane, click the first layer, press and hold Shift, and click the last layer to select all the layers. Drag them onto the drawing area to import the layers.

9. Save your drawing.

Accessing Drawing Content with Tool Palettes

The Tool Palettes window is a tabbed palette that can contain drawings, blocks, hatches, images, gradients, drawing objects, xrefs, tables, and commands. By default, the Tool Palettes window contains over 20 tabs in AutoCAD and 10 tabs in AutoCAD LT with sample content and commands. Each tab is considered a separate tool palette within the main Tool Palettes window. Figure 26.4 shows the default Tool Palettes window with the Draw tab on top. To open the Tool Palettes window, choose View tab ⇨ Palettes panel ⇨ Tool Palettes, or press Ctrl+3.

FIGURE 26.4

The standard Tool Palettes window has many tabs, each with a different category of commands or insertable content.

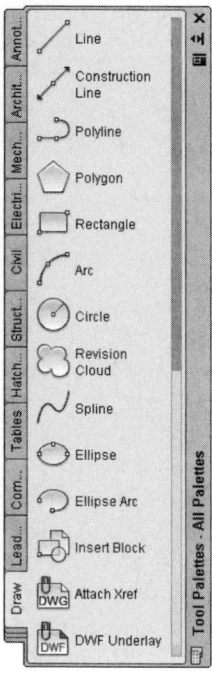

The tool palettes are meant to be customized with your own content. You can easily create new tabs with your own blocks and other types of content, objects, or commands. After you create the tab, you can drag the items into your drawing. A *tool* is any item on a tool palette, and is represented by an icon.

Note

Because there are so many tabs, several of the tabs overlap together at the bottom so that you can't see their titles. When you click these tabs, a menu pops up, listing the names of all the tabs. Click the tab that you want from the menu to display that tab. Materials used for rendering are on several palettes; other palettes contain visual style, light, and camera tools. ■

Creating a new tool palette

When you create a new tool palette, you add a tab to the Tool Palettes window. To create an empty tool palette, right-click in the Tool Palettes window and choose New Palette. A label appears so that you can name the tool palette. Type the name and press Enter. When you have a new tool palette, you're ready to add tools to the palette, as I explain in the following sections.

Cross-Reference
You can also create a new, empty tool palette by using the Customize dialog box. See Chapter 29 for details. ■

You can add descriptive text and separator bars to any tool palette. For example, you can include instructions that explain a tool and organize commands into groups by using separator bars. To add text or separators, right-click any tool palette and choose Add Text or Add Separator from the shortcut menu.

Adding content tools

The easiest way to create a new tool palette is from the DesignCenter, discussed in the previous section of this chapter. When you use this method, you simultaneously create not only the tool palette but also its contents. To create a new tool palette, follow these steps:

1. Open the DesignCenter.
2. In the tree view or content area, navigate to a folder, drawing file, block, raster image file, or hatch icon.
3. Right-click the item and choose Create Tool Palette.
   - If you select a folder or drawing, choose Create Tool Palette of Blocks.
   - If you select a hatch file (`*.pat`), choose Create Tool Palette of Hatch Patterns.

   After a few seconds, the new tool palette tab displays, showing each drawing, block, or hatch on the tab:
   - If you chose a folder, the tab includes all drawing files in the folder.
   - If you chose a drawing file, the tab includes all blocks in the drawing.
   - If you chose a block icon, the tab includes the block.
   - If you chose a hatch pattern file, the tab includes all hatch patterns in the PAT file. (See Chapter 31 for more information about creating hatch patterns in `.pat` files.)
   - If you chose a hatch icon, the tab includes the hatch pattern.

Another way to add content tools is to drag content directly from an open drawing. This method is the only way to add gradients to a tool palette, but it works with any other type of content as well. Just select the object, then click and drag it onto the tool palette. The tool palette assigns a name, but you can change it to anything you want. Right-click the tool and choose Rename. Type the new name and press Enter.

Tip
You can drag content over a tab that is not on top; that tab then becomes active so that you can add the content to it. ■

When you drag content from your drawing, you're creating a tool *by example*. The properties of the tool match those of the object in your drawing. For example, if you drag a hatch on layer `object` onto a tool and then use that tool to hatch a closed object in your drawing, you create a hatch on layer `object`.

Adding command tools

You can add commands to tool palettes. You choose your method depending on the amount of customization that you want and how you want to organize your commands. You can add commands by dragging objects from a drawing or by dragging commands from the Commands List pane in the Customize User Interface Editor (covered in Chapter 33).

Dragging objects from your drawing

You can drag drawing objects, such as circles, text, and so on onto a tool palette. AutoCAD creates a command tool that draws an object with the same properties as the original object. For example, if you regularly need to enter text on the Annotation layer by using the Annotation text style, select some existing text with those properties, and drag it onto a tool palette. The tool is now called simply MText. Right-click, choose Rename, and enter Annotation or another meaningful name. This command tool contains the properties of the object that you used.

Note

When you click the selected object to start dragging it, don't click it on the grip handles. When you click, after a moment you'll see the drag-and-drop arrow cursor, and then you can drag the object to the tool palette. To drag a table, you must drag-and-drop with the right mouse button; otherwise, you simply select one of the table cells. ∎

When you create certain types of command tools, the tool palette recognizes the command as one of a group of commands, and creates an entire group, or *flyout*, of command tools that all use the same properties as the original. This technique works with dimensions and common drawing geometry objects, such as lines and circles. Note, however, that the tool palettes include these flyouts by default.

Note

If you are using the AutoCAD Classic or AutoCAD LT Classic workspace, you can drag toolbar buttons onto a tool palette. Choose Manage tab ⇨ Customization panel ⇨ Tool Palettes or right-click in the Tool Palettes window and choose Customize Palettes. The Customize dialog box opens. One by one, drag the buttons that you want onto the tool palette. (The Customize dialog box doesn't seem to have any function here, but you can't drag buttons off of a toolbar without it.) ∎

Adding commands

You can add commands from the Command List pane of the Customize User Interface dialog box. Right-click the Tool Palettes window and choose Customize Commands to open the dialog box. Then drag any command from the dialog box to any tool palette tab.

Copying a tool

You can copy an existing tool to create a new tool, whether a content tool or a command tool. You can then change the tool properties. You can use this technique to create related, but slightly different, tools. For example, you could include a hatch on two different layers. You could also include variations of a dynamic block.

To copy a tool, right-click the tool and choose Copy from the shortcut menu. Then right-click again and choose Paste. The next section explains how to change tool properties.

Setting tool properties

Each tool on a tool palette has properties that you can set. The available properties vary slightly, depending on the type of tool. The properties specify how that tool is inserted into a drawing. Tools inherit their properties from the object that you dragged onto the tool palette. However, you can change the properties. To set the properties of a tool, right-click it and choose Properties to open the Tool Properties dialog box. Figure 26.5 shows the Tool Properties dialog box for a hatch pattern.

FIGURE 26.5

The Tool Properties dialog box for a hatch pattern.

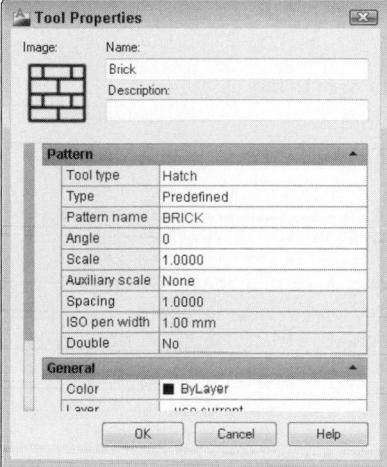

The middle section of the dialog box contains Insert, Attach, or Pattern properties (depending on the type of content), and the bottom section of the dialog box displays General properties.

To specify any property, click the rightmost column for that property. Either type a new value or choose from the drop-down list. After you're done, click OK to close the Tool Properties dialog box.

Tip

You can select multiple tools and change their common properties at one time. To select multiple tools, hold down the Ctrl key and click the tools that you want to change. ■

Adjusting the scale of inserted content

The tools that you create by dragging content from a drawing take their properties from that object, so they may contain an inherent scale. For example, your hatches, blocks, and xrefs have a certain size. If you need to adjust a scale, you can do so, based on one of the following:

- **Your overall dimension scale.** You set the dimension scale on the Fit tab of the Modify Dimension Style dialog box. The value is stored in the DIMSCALE system variable.
- **Your plot scale.** You set the plot scale in the Plot dialog box.

To set the scale of a hatch, block, or xref tool, right-click the tool and choose Properties. Click the Auxiliary Scale item. Then click the down arrow that appears at the right, and choose either Dimscale or Plot Scale. Click OK. From now on, the block or xref comes into your drawing at the scale that you've set in your drawing.

Moving, deleting, and renaming tools and tool palettes

You can change the order of tool palettes (tabs) in the Tool Palettes window, and you can change the order of tools on a palette.

- To move a tool on a palette, drag the tool. A horizontal or vertical cursor appears to show you where the tool will go.
- To move a palette, right-click the tab itself and choose Move Up or Move Down.

You can also move or copy a tool (drawing, block, or hatch) from one tool palette to another. Follow these steps:

1. Display the tool palette (tab) that contains the item that you want to move.
2. Right-click the item and choose Cut (to move it) or Copy (to copy it).
3. Display the tool palette (tab) where you want to place the item.
4. Right-click any blank area on the tab and choose Paste.

You can use this method to consolidate tabs or reorganize the tools on a tab.

To delete a tool palette, right-click the palette and choose Delete Palette. A warning message is displayed, explaining that you cannot recover the deleted tool palette unless you export it to a file; choose OK to delete the palette. To delete a tool on a tool palette, right-click the tool and choose Delete. Here, too, you need to confirm the deletion when a warning message appears; choose OK to delete the tool.

To export a tool palette, save it to a file. You can then share tool palettes with others. You import and export tool palettes in the Customize dialog box. See "Customizing Tool Palettes" in Chapter 29 for details.

To rename a tool palette, right-click the palette and choose Rename Palette. To rename a tool, right-click the tool and choose Rename. In both situations, type a new name and press Enter.

Updating tools

If the source of a tool changes, its icon does not automatically change to match. In this situation, the icon will not accurately represent its tool. To update an icon, use one of the following methods:

- Right-click the tool and choose Properties. Click the Source File (or Pattern Name) item, then use the Ellipsis button to choose any other file, block, or hatch pattern, and then immediately choose the correct item again. This technique updates the icon for the tool.
- Delete the tool and reinsert it.

If you change a block or dynamic block, you can update its image. Right-click the image and choose Update Tool Image from the shortcut menu.

Note

You can specify any image for a tool. Perhaps you want to create your own image. Most images are 32 x 32 pixels. To specify an image, right-click the tool and choose Specify Image. Choose the image you want, and click Open. To find the location of the `ToolPalette` folder, use the OPTIONS command to open the Options dialog box. On the Files tab, expand the Tool Palettes File Locations item. ■

If you move the source file for a tool, you need to update the tool with the new location:

1. Right-click the tool and choose Properties.
2. In the Tool Properties dialog box, use the Ellipsis button to choose the file again.
3. Click OK.

Setting tool palette options

To work most comfortably with the Tool Palettes window, you can adjust its display options. These options are the same as for the DesignCenter, discussed previously in this chapter. An additional option, Transparency, opens the Transparency dialog box. When the tool palette is transparent, you can see the drawing through it. You can specify the amount of transparency or turn it off. Then click OK.

Note
Palette transparency is available only when hardware acceleration is off (which it is by default). Hardware acceleration is governed by your computer's video card and helps to speed up the display. If you want to use the palette transparency feature, you must use software acceleration instead (and see if it affects your display speed). Choose Application Button⇨Options and click the System tab. In the 3D Performance section, click Performance Settings. In the Hardware and Performance Tuning section, click Manual Tune. In the Hardware Settings section, uncheck the Enable Hardware Acceleration check box. Click OK three times to close all the dialog boxes. Palette transparency is available only when the palette is not docked. Hardware acceleration is not available for AutoCAD LT. ■

Right-click any blank area of a tool palette and choose View Options to open the View Options dialog box. You can change the size and layout of the tool icons on a tool palette. Use the slider to change the size of the icons. You can choose to apply the changes to the current tool palette or to all tool palettes. Choose from the following display styles:

- **Icon only.** You see the icon displaying the drawing, block, or hatch, but no text.
- **Icon with text.** Text is displayed beneath each icon, and the icons are arranged in columns. This option displays much more on a tab than the list view.
- **List view.** You see one column of icons, with the text to the right of each icon.

Click OK when you're done.

Organizing tool palettes

You may have one set of tool palettes for architectural work and another for mechanical work. For whatever reason, you may want to display one set of tool palettes at one time and another set at another time. For this purpose, you organize tool palettes into groups. I explain how to create these groups in Chapter 29.

To display the various groups, right-click the title bar of the tool palette and choose the group that you want. Using groups helps to avoid clicking through too many tool palettes. After all, the point is instant access. However, you can always display all the palettes by right-clicking and choosing All Palettes.

Using a tool palette

Using a tool from a tool palette is as simple as dragging the tool onto the drawing area. The tool uses the properties specified in the Tool Properties dialog box (discussed previously in this section).

Tools know how to behave. Drag a gradient or hatch into an enclosed area and it automatically fills the area. Drag an xref onto a drawing and you get a prompt, at the command line, for the insertion point. Tools automatically use their properties so that you get a circle on its proper layer or a hatch with the proper scale.

If you want the flexibility to insert a block or hatch with more than one setting, you can insert another copy of the item onto a tool palette. For example, you can place two copies of a hatch pattern on a tool palette and set their properties to different spacing. You would then rename the tools to make the differences clear (for example, `lightning1` and `lightning 2`). You can also copy a tool and then modify it, as I explain in the section "Copying a tool" earlier in this chapter.

Tip

You can use the TPNAVIGATE command on the command line to display a tool palette or group, if you know its name. This command is especially useful for programming purposes. ∎

On the DVD

The drawings used in the following exercise on creating and using a tool palette, ab26-c.dwg and ab26-d.dwg, are in the Drawings folder on the DVD. ∎

STEPS: Creating and Using a Tool Palette

1. Open ab26-c.dwg from the DVD.
2. Save the file as ab26-02.dwg in your AutoCAD Bible folder. This drawing, shown in Figure 26.6, needs some blocks and a hatch pattern inserted. You'll also add a dimension.

FIGURE 26.6

This back porch needs some columns (which are blocks), some hatching, and a dimension.

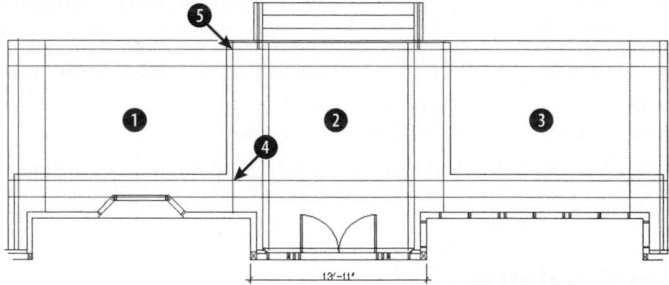

3. Choose View tab ⇨ Palettes panel ⇨ Tool Palettes.
4. Choose View tab ⇨ Palettes panel ⇨ DesignCenter. In the DesignCenter's Folder List, navigate to the Drawings folder of your DVD and click the plus sign to the left of ab26-d.dwg. Click the Blocks item to display the two blocks (post and post-structural) in the content pane on the right side of the DesignCenter.
5. Right-click any empty area of the tool palette, and choose New Palette. A label appears. Type **2d arch** and press Enter. You now have a new tool palette named 2d arch.

Note

If the tool palette is collapsed when the mouse cursor is not over it, right-click its title bar and choose Auto-Hide to uncheck this item. ∎

6. From the content pane of the DesignCenter, drag each of the blocks to the new tool palette. An icon appears on the tool palette for each block.
7. In the Folder List of the DesignCenter, navigate to acad.pat or acadlt.pat, which contains hatch patterns. Click acad.pat or acadlt.pat to display the hatch patterns in the content pane.

Note

To find the location of `acad.pat` or `acadlt.pat`, choose Application Button ⇨ Options and click the Files tab. Double-click the first item, Support File Search Path, to display the location of the support files. ∎

8. Drag User Defined, one of the hatch patterns, to the tool palette. (This hatch pattern is equivalent to choosing User Defined as the Hatch Type from the Hatch Creation tab on the Ribbon [or in the Hatch and Gradient dialog box]. See the section "Creating Hatches" in Chapter 16 for details.) The tool palette now has three items on it. Close or Auto-Hide the DesignCenter.

9. Right-click the User-Defined Hatch icon and choose Properties to open the Tool Properties dialog box. You want to specify settings so that this hatch pattern will look like scored concrete for the porch floor.

10. In the Tool Properties dialog box, make the following changes and then click OK:

   - For the Angle, type **45**.
   - For the Spacing, type **2'** (or **24**).
   - Click the Double item at the bottom of the Pattern section and then click the arrow at the right side of the row. Choose Yes from the drop-down list.
   - Click the Layer item in the General section and choose FLOOR from the drop-down list. (You may have to drag the bottom edge of the dialog box down to see the layer item.)

11. Right-click the hatch tool and choose Rename. Type **porch tile** and press Enter.

12. Drag the Porch Tile hatch icon to ❶, shown in Figure 26.6. Then do the same for ❷ and ❸. These areas are hatched, as shown in Figure 26.7.

13. Choose the Command Tool Samples tab and click the small arrow to the right on the Linear Dimension tool to see the flyout. (If you don't see the Command Tool Samples tab, click the overlapping tabs at the bottom of the palette window and choose Command Tool Samples from the list of tabs.) To place a linear dimension, click the main linear dimension icon. Follow the prompts:

```
Specify first extension line origin or <select object>: Pick the
     upper-left corner of the porch.
Specify second extension line origin: Pick the upper-right corner of
     the porch.
Specify dimension line location or [Mtext/Text/Angle/Horizontal/
     Vertical/Rotated]: Pick any location for the dimension line above
     the steps.
```

14. Choose View tab ⇨ Navigate panel ⇨ Zoom drop-down list ⇨ Window, and zoom into the central area of the drawing so that you can still see the double doors at the bottom and the steps at the top.

15. Switch back to the 2d arch tab and click the Post icon. At the `Specify insertion point:` prompt, pick the intersection at ❹, shown in Figure 26.6. Click the Post-Structural icon. At the prompt, pick the upper-right corner of the post block, as shown in Figure 26.7.

16. Click the Post icon. At the prompt, pick ❺, shown in Figure 26.6. Use the same technique to place the Post-Structural icon at the upper-right corner of the post block. (The posts would then need to be spaced and mirrored to the other side of the porch, but these tasks are not necessary for this exercise.)

17. Right-click the tool palette's title bar. If Allow Docking is checked, click Allow Docking to uncheck this item. If Auto-Hide is not checked, click Auto-Hide to enable this feature. Move the mouse off the tool palette. The tool palette collapses to its title bar. Move the tool palette to the right side of your screen.

18. If you're working on someone else's computer, you should delete the tool palette. Move the cursor over the palette to display it. Right-click any blank area and choose Delete Palette. Click OK to confirm the deletion.

19. Save your drawing. It should look like Figure 26.7.

FIGURE 26.7

The drawing now has hatches and blocks inserted from the tool palette. It also has a new dimension.

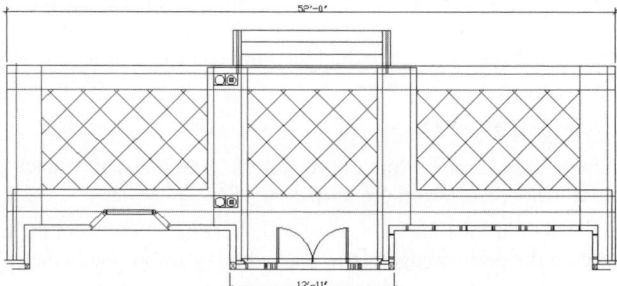

Setting Standards for Drawings

One person rarely has complete control over a drawing. You may xref in other drawings, or others may xref in your drawings. Several people may work on one drawing. You may send a drawing to a client who may work on it as well. Working on a drawing is usually a collaborative effort — and it can get out of control.

One way to maintain control is to set standards for drawings, and issue those standards so that everyone involved has access to them. If you don't have agreed-upon standards, you not only waste time changing layers, text styles, and so on, but your drawings become very complicated. You should set standards for the following:

- Drawing names and property summaries
- Blocks, including names, layers, and insertion points
- Layers, including uses, names, colors, linetypes, and lineweights
- Text styles, including uses, names, and properties
- Table styles
- Dimension styles and tolerances, if any
- Multileader styles
- Multiline styles
- Units settings
- Plot styles
- Layouts

In some cases, your standards are set by outside conventions. For example, the American Institute of Architects (AIA) and the Construction Standards Institute (CSI) publish layering standards for members.

Using the CAD Standards tools

The CAD Standards tools facilitate the process of checking drawings against standards. You can check the following in a drawing:

- Layers
- Text styles
- Linetypes
- Dimension styles

AutoCAD Only

The CAD Standards feature is not available in AutoCAD LT. ■

AutoCAD checks for both names (such as layer names) and properties (such as layer color and linetype).

Here's the general procedure for setting and maintaining standards with the CAD manager's tools:

1. Create a standards file (*.dws).
2. Associate the standards file with a drawing or template.
3. Test the drawing against its standards file.

You can test drawings against a standards file one by one (interactively) or as a group (batch auditing).

Creating a standards file

You use a standards file to set standards for drawings. A standards file has a filename extension of .dws. Unlike many of the support files used in AutoCAD, a standards file is not a text file; rather, it is similar to a drawing file. You create a standards file by creating a drawing that contains the standards — layers, linetypes, text styles, and dimension styles — that you want.

To create a standards file from scratch, follow these steps:

1. Choose Application Button ➪ New.
2. Choose a template, or click the Open button's down arrow and choose one of the Open with No Template options.
3. Create the layers, linetypes, dimension styles, and text styles that you want to place in the standards file.
4. Choose Application Button ➪ Save As ➪ AutoCAD Drawing Standards. In the File Name text box, type a name for the standards file.
5. In the Save In drop-down list, choose a location for the file.
6. Click Save to save the drawing standards file.

You can use an existing drawing for your standards file (in fact, this method is probably easier). However, be careful to purge all layers, linetypes, dimension styles, and text styles that you don't want. (I discuss the PURGE command in Chapter 11.)

Associating a standards file with a drawing

As soon as you have your standards file, you associate it with a drawing or template that you want to check, using the STANDARDS command.

Tip

If you use a template to start new drawings, open the template and associate the standards file with your template. Then every drawing that you start based on the template is associated with the standards file. ■

To associate a standards file with the current drawing, follow these steps:

1. Choose Manage tab ⇨ CAD Standards panel ⇨ Configure. (You can also type **standards** ↵.)
2. On the Standards tab of the Configure Standards dialog box, shown in Figure 26.8, click the + button.

FIGURE 26.8

Use the Configure Standards dialog box to associate a standards file with a drawing.

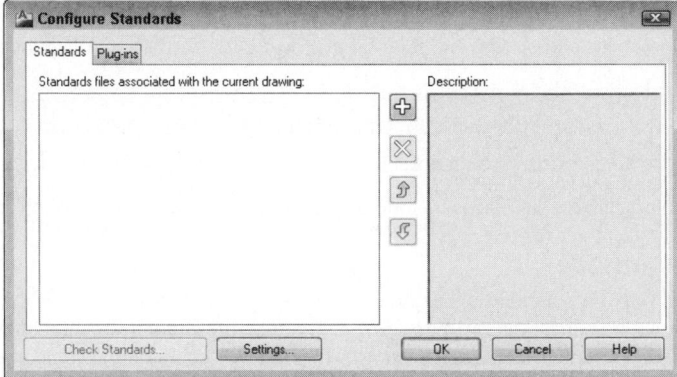

3. In the Select Standards File dialog box, choose the standards file that you want to use and click Open. You can associate more than one standards file with the drawing; continue to click the + button and choose more standards files.
4. Click the Plug-ins tab and click any standards that you don't want to check. All four standards types — Dimension Styles, Layers, Linetypes, and Text Styles — are initially checked. (The choices that you make persist for future standards checks until you change them.)
5. Click OK to close the Configure Standards dialog box and return to your drawing.

Checking a drawing against standards

To check a drawing against its associated standards file, choose Manage tab ⇨ CAD Standards panel ⇨ Check to start the CHECKSTANDARDS command and open the Check Standards dialog box, as shown in Figure 26.9.

Note

If you just finished associating a standards file with a drawing, you can click Check Standards in the Configure Standards dialog box. ■

The Check Standards dialog box lists all the problems — items in the drawing that don't match the standards file — that it finds, one by one. Here's the procedure for using this dialog box:

FIGURE 26.9

The Check Standards dialog box guides you through the process of checking a drawing against a standards file.

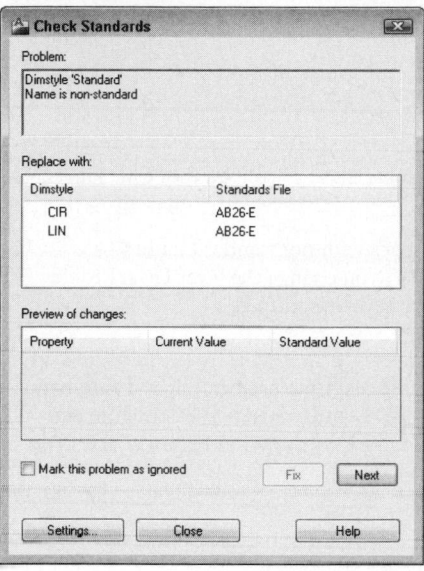

1. You see the first problem in the Problem section of the dialog box.
2. Use the Replace With section to choose a replacement for the nonstandard item. This section contains all eligible replacements according to the standards file.
3. Look at the Preview of Changes section to see how the replacement will affect your drawing.
4. To make the replacement and standardize your drawing, click the Fix button.

   To ignore the problem and go on to the next one, click the Next button.

   AutoCAD continues to display problems that you can fix or ignore. After you're done, you see the Check is complete message, along with a short report explaining how all the problems were handled, as shown in Figure 26.10. Click Close to close the message. You can click the Next button again to recheck the drawing.
5. Click Close to return to your drawing.

FIGURE 26.10

The completed standards check report.

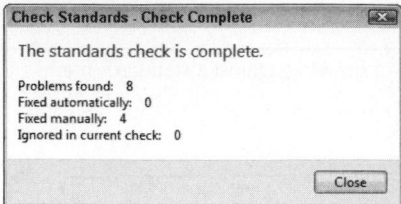

For information on *batch checking* (checking standards for many drawings at once), see the "Checking standards for multiple drawings" sidebar in this chapter.

When you fix nonstandard objects — for example, layers or linetypes with nonstandard names — AutoCAD purges these objects from the drawing. For example, after you change the layer Layer1 to the layer Notes, objects on Layer1 are changed to the layer Notes, and Layer1 is purged.

Specifying CAD standards settings

You can specify how the CAD standards feature functions to provide real-time notification and automatic repair. To specify CAD standards settings, choose Manage tab ⇨ CAD Standards panel ⇨ Configure and click the Settings button to open the CAD Standards Settings dialog box, as shown in Figure 26.11. (You can also click Settings from the Check Standards dialog box.)

FIGURE 26.11

Use the CAD Standards Settings dialog box to specify how you want CAD standards checking to work.

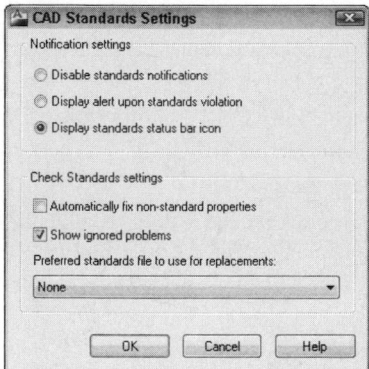

In the top section, Notification Settings, choose one of the following:

- **Disable standards notifications.** No real-time notification of standards violations. You can still check standards by using the Check Standards dialog box at any time.
- **Display alert upon standards violation.** Displays a message if your drawing is associated with a standards file and you make a change that puts the drawing in noncompliance with the standards file, as shown in Figure 26.12.

- **Display standards status bar icon.** Displays an icon on the AutoCAD status bar. The icon has an exclamation point if there is a nonstandard object in the drawing. A balloon appears to notify you that a standards violation has occurred. Click the Run Check Standards link or the icon to open the Check Standards dialog box so that you can fix the problems.

FIGURE 26.12

The alert message notifies you of a standards violation.

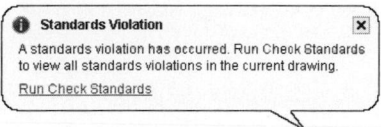

In the bottom section, Check Standards Settings, check Automatically Fix Non-standard Properties to automatically fix noncompliant drawings. Automatic fixing applies only to a situation where a drawing object has a name that matches a standard but has different properties. For example, if a standards file contains a layer named OBJ that has a blue color and the current drawing has an object on the OBJ layer that is red, the object will be changed to blue to match the color of the OBJ layer in the standards file.

Check Show Ignored Problems to display any problems that were not fixed in the standards check report.

From the Preferred Standards File to Use for Replacements drop-down list, choose a standards file to use by default in the Replace With section of the Check Standards dialog box. This standards file is used only if you choose to automatically fix nonstandard properties and the associated standards file, because the drawing does not provide a suitable replacement.

Using layer notification

Layers are an important part of maintaining drawings standards. Many people have strict rules about which layers are allowed in a drawing. Xrefs can be especially troublesome in this regard, because layers from the external drawings are added to your drawing. AutoCAD can notify you when new layers are added to a drawing. This notification is based on the layers existing when you open the drawing, not on a standards file.

 To set up layer notification, open the Layer Properties Manager and click the Settings button to open the Layer Settings dialog box, as shown in Figure 26.13.

By default, layer notification only applies when xrefs add new layers to a drawing, because xrefs are the most common means of adding layers without your knowledge. However, you can choose the Evaluate All New Layers option, especially if you use templates that already contain all the desired layers.

The Notify When New Layers Are Present check box and the other check boxes below it determine if and when you see a notification window. For example, if you choose to evaluate all new layers and specify notification when you save, when you add a layer and save the drawing, you see the notification bubble shown in Figure 26.14. Click the link in the bubble to open the Layer Properties Manager.

 You can uncheck the Notify When New Layers Are Present check box and still check for new layers by right-clicking the Unreconciled New Layers alert icon on the right side of the status bar and choosing View Unreconciled New Layers. The Layer Properties Manager opens.

FIGURE 26.13

Use the Layer Settings dialog box to specify when and how you receive notification about new layers in your drawing.

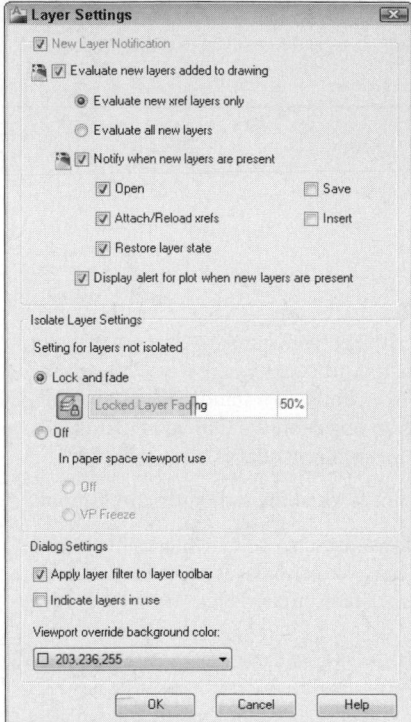

FIGURE 26.14

This bubble tells you that new layers have been added to the drawing.

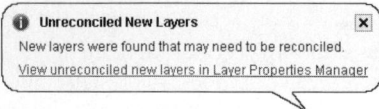

When you open the Layer Properties Manager in this way, you see only *unreconciled* layers. (AutoCAD activates the Unreconciled New Layers filter for your layers.) These are layers that have been added to the drawing (either consciously or via xrefs) but that you haven't yet reviewed. You can perform one of three actions:

- **Leave the layer unreconciled.**
- **Reconcile the layer.** Right-click the layer in the Layer Properties Manager and choose Reconcile Layer.
- **Delete the layer.**

Checking standards for multiple drawings

What do you do if you want to check standards for hundreds of drawings at once? For this scenario, AutoCAD has created Batch Standards Checking, shown here. Here's how to use the Batch Standards Checker:

1. From the Windows task bar, choose Start⇨All Programs⇨Autodesk⇨AutoCAD 2011⇨Batch Standards Checker. The Batch Standards Checker, shown in the following figure, appears.

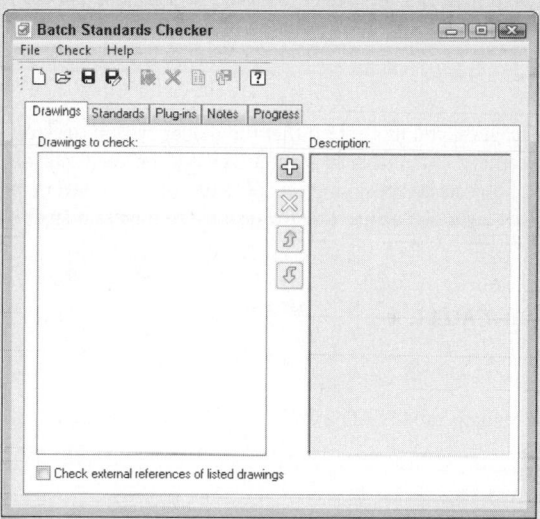

2. On the Drawings tab, click the + button and select the drawings that you want to include. Click Open. After you click Open, you can click the + button again and add drawings from a different folder. Use the Remove Drawing (Delete) button to delete drawings and the Move Up and Move Down buttons to change the order of the drawings. If you also want to check external references, check the Check External References of Listed Drawings check box. Note that you can't check password-protected drawings.

3. On the Standards tab, choose to check each drawing against its associated standards file if you have associated standards files for all your drawings. Otherwise, choose to check the drawings against the standards file(s) that you select. To select a standards file, click the + button, choose a standards file (.dws), and click Open.

4. On the Plug-ins tab, choose the standards that you want to check. This tab is the same as the Plug-ins tab of the Configure Standards dialog box, discussed earlier in this section.

5. Click Save on the Batch Standards Checker toolbar. In the Batch Standards Checker – File Save Dialog box, save the standards check file. A standards check file (.chx) contains information about which drawings and standards files you're using for the batch standards check. AutoCAD gives the file a default name, but you can change the name if you want.

6. To start checking the drawings, click Start Check on the Batch Standards Checker toolbar. (You can click Stop Check to stop the check at any time during its progress.) The Batch Standards Checker starts checking your drawings. You can click the Progress tab to see what is happening. When the checking is done, your Standards Audit Report is displayed.

Note

The layer notification settings are saved with the drawing, so each drawing can have its own settings. ■

When you create a template (as I explain in Chapter 2), after saving, the Template Options dialog box opens. Here you can decide if you want drawings created from that template to use reconciled or unreconciled layers. If you choose the default option, Save All Layers As Unreconciled, you can add layers without notification until you save the drawing. Saving the drawing creates a baseline, after which the notification starts. If you save layers as reconciled, then any new layers are considered unreconciled and you'll be notified about them according to your settings in the Layer Settings dialog box.

Translating layers

If you receive drawings from clients or colleagues, you might find that their layer system doesn't suit yours. Manually translating one set of layers to another to fit your layer standards could be a tedious job. The LAYTRANS command changes the layers of objects by specifying sets of "from" and "to" layers. For example, you can change all objects on layer1 to the layer objects. Use this feature to maintain layer standards.

AutoCAD Only

The Layer Translation feature is not available in AutoCAD LT. ■

Setting up the layer mapping

 To translate one layer to another, choose Manage tab ⇨ CAD Standards panel ⇨ Layer Translator. The Layer Translator, shown in Figure 26.15, opens.

FIGURE 26.15

The Layer Translator.

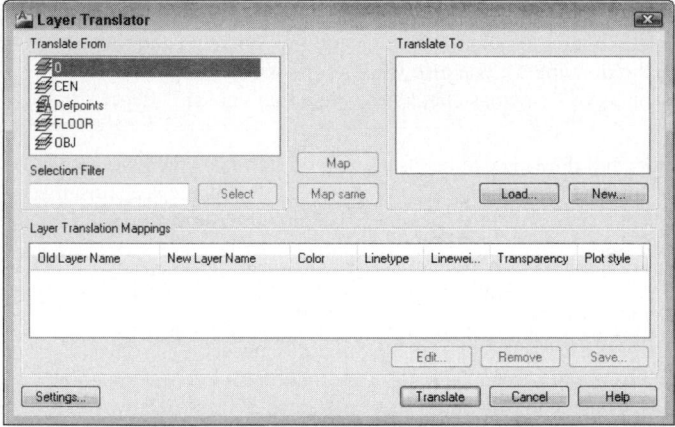

On the Translate From side of the dialog box, you see the layers in the drawing. (Layers with a white icon to their left are not being used. You can right-click them and choose Purge Layers to purge them from the drawing.) Select layers by clicking them. You can also select multiple layers. You can type a selection filter in the Selection Filter text box to select certain layers.

Cross-Reference

See the section "Filtering the layer list" in Chapter 11 for more information about filtering layer lists. ∎

To load existing layers, click Load. In the Select Drawing File dialog box, you can choose a drawing, a drawing template, or a drawing standards file. Click Open. The layers from that file now appear in the Translate To list. Select the layer to which you want to translate.

To define a new layer, click New. In the New Layer dialog box, type a name for the new layer and specify its color, linetype, lineweight, transparency, and plot style. Click OK.

To specify how layers are translated, *map* layers in the current drawing (listed in the Translate From list) to the layers to which you want to convert (listed in the Translate To list). Select a layer in the Translate From list, then select a layer in the Translate To list, and then click Map. The mapping appears below in the Layer Translation Mappings list. Finally, you're ready to translate your layers. Click Translate, and AutoCAD takes care of the rest. All objects on the Translate From layers are now on the Translate To layers. The translation process also purges unused layers from the drawing.

Tip

You can select more than one layer from the Translate From list by pressing Ctrl for each additional layer. You can select a contiguous group of layers by clicking the first layer in the group, holding Shift, and selecting the last layer in the group. Then from the Translate To list, select the layer that you want to map that group of layers to, and click Map. You can also quickly map all layers with the same name by choosing Map Same. ∎

Managing layer translations

After you create your mappings, you can edit, remove, or save them:

- To edit a mapping, select it and click Edit. In the Edit Layer dialog box, you can choose a new layer, color, linetype, lineweight, transparency, or plot style.

- To remove a mapping, select it and click Remove.

- To save a mapping, click Save. You can choose to save a mapping as a drawing standards file (.dws) or as an actual drawing file (.dwg). Type a filename, choose a location, and click Save. (If you don't save your layer mapping, AutoCAD prompts you to do so.)

- Click Settings to customize the translation process. Here are your options:

  - The first three options in the Settings dialog box force objects to take on their layer's assigned color, linetype, and transparency. Check these three settings to enforce consistency in your layer properties.

  - The Translate Objects in Blocks item determines whether layer mappings are applied to objects within blocks. See Chapter 18 for more about blocks.

  - Check Write Transaction Log to create a .log file in the same folder as the drawing that you're translating (the current drawing). The log file lists the details of the translation and can help you troubleshoot problems later.

  - Check Show Layer Contents When Selected to help you figure out which objects are on which layers. If you check this item and then select a layer translation in the Translate From or Layer Translation Mappings list, only objects on that layer are shown.

After you finish specifying the translation settings, click OK to close the Settings dialog box.

On the DVD

The drawings used in the following exercise on managing CAD standards, `ab26-e.dwg` and `ab26-e.dws`, are in the `Drawings` folder on the DVD. ■

STEPS: Managing CAD Standards

1. Open `ab26-e.dwg` from the DVD.

2. Save the file as `ab26-03.dwg` in your `AutoCAD Bible` folder.

3. Open the Layer Properties Manager palette by choosing Home tab ⇨ Layers panel ⇨ Layer Properties. Click the Settings button.

4. To try out the layer notification feature, click the Evaluate All New Layers option and check the Save check box. Click OK.

5. In the Layer Properties Manager palette, click the New Layer button. Leave the default properties unchanged.

6. Save the drawing. The Unreconciled New Layers bubble appears; you may need to move the mouse cursor over the drawing area. Click the link in the bubble to open the Layer Properties Manager palette, showing the new layer. Click the Delete Layer button to remove Layer 1.

7. Choose Home tab ⇨ Properties panel and click the Linetype drop-down list. Notice the Borderx2, Centerx2, Hiddenx2, and Phantom2 linetypes.

 8. Choose Manage tab ⇨ CAD Standards panel ⇨ Configure.

9. In the Configure Standards dialog box, click the + button. Find and choose `ab26-e.dws`, a drawing standards file, on the DVD. Click Open to associate `ab26-e.dws` with `ab26-03.dwg`.

10. In the same dialog box, click Check Standards to open the Check Standards dialog box.

11. The first standards problem, `Layer 'AME_FRZ' Name is non-standard`, is listed in the Problem box. Click the Next button to ignore this problem.

12. The next problem is `Layer 'CEN' Properties are non-standard`. Choose CEN from the Replace With list and click the Fix button.

13. Continue to make the following changes, clicking the Fix button after each one:

LINETYPE	BORDERX2	BORDER
LINETYPE	CENTERX2	CENTER
LINETYPE	PHANTOM2	PHANTOM
LINETYPE	HIDDENX2	HIDDEN
TEXTSTYLE	ZONE	ROMAND
TEXTSTYLE	TECHNIBOLD	ROMANS

14. The Check Standards – Check Complete dialog box appears with a summary of the standards check. Click Close.

15. Click Close.

16. Open the Linetype drop-down list again. The "x2" linetypes have been purged.

 17. Choose Manage tab ⇨ CAD Standards panel ⇨ Layer Translator.

18. On the right side of the Layer Translator dialog box, click Load. From the Files of Type drop-down list, choose Standards (*.dws). Choose ab26-e.dws, the same standards file that you used previously in this exercise, and click Open.

19. In the Translate From box, click CEN. Hold down the Ctrl key and click HAT.

20. In the Translate To box, click HID.

21. Click Map. This will map the layers CEN and HAT to the HID layer.

22. Click Translate to translate the mappings.

23. In the Layer Translator – Changes Not Saved dialog box, click Translate Only. All objects on the CEN and HAT layers are now on the HID layer.

24. Save your drawing.

The Communication Center

 The Communication Center feature notifies you about updates, product support, tips, articles, and so on. An icon to the right of the Search text box connects you to the Communication Center. ■

 To access the information for the first time, click the down arrow to the right of the Search text box at the upper-right corner of the application window and choose Search Settings, or click the InfoCenter Settings button at the top of the Communication Center results list to open the InfoCenter Settings dialog box. You can set the following:

- **General.** Specify your country and how often you want the Communication Center to check for new content.

- **Search Locations.** Specify which locations you want to include in the results when you enter a question in the search box. I discuss using the Search box in Chapter 3.

Note

In order to configure the Communication Center, you need to install Autodesk CAD Manager Tools. For more information, see Appendix A. You then need to choose Start➪(All) Programs➪Autodesk➪CAD Manager Tools➪CAD Manager Control Utility to configure the Communication Center panel. In the CAD Manager Control Utility dialog box, use the InfoCenter tab to enable the sections of the Communication Center. ■

- **Communication Center.** This item displays a CAD Manager Channel, a URL of an RSS news feed that a CAD Manager can use to make content available to AutoCAD users. You need to enable the CAD Manager Channel and enter the feed URL in the CAD Manager Control Utility.

- **Autodesk Channels.** If you have enabled information channels in the CAD Manager Control Utility, you can choose which Autodesk channels you want to see here. Available channels include Live Update maintenance patches, subscription announcements (for those users on AutoCAD's subscription program), articles and tips, featured technologies and content, and product support information.

- **Balloon Notification.** Choose if you want to see a balloon pop up to notify you of new content, and for which type of content.

- **RSS Feeds.** Use the New and Remove buttons to add and remove RSS feeds, respectively. RSS feeds are files that contain notification of new content, such as for blogs. You need to know the full URL of the RSS feed's file. (The URL of my AutoCAD Tips Newsletter RSS feed is www.ellenfinkelstein.com/pptblog/feed/.)

Click OK when you're done. After you specify the settings, click the Communication Center button to open the Communication Center window. From this window, you can click any link to access its source on the Internet.

Renaming named objects

Drawings contain many named objects, such as layers, text styles, dimension styles, and so on. Sometimes you need to rename these objects in order to maintain CAD standards and consistency. To rename objects, type **rename** ↵ on the command line to start the RENAME command. The Rename dialog box opens, as shown in Figure 26.16.

To rename objects, follow these steps:

1. Choose the type of object that you want to rename from the Named Objects list.

2. Choose the item that you want to rename from the Items list. This item appears in the Old Name text box.

3. In the Rename To text box, type the new name for the item.
   - If you want to change only one item, click OK to close the dialog box.
   - If you want to change more than one item, click Rename To. The dialog box remains open so that you can make other changes. Click OK after you're finished.

FIGURE 26.16

The Rename dialog box.

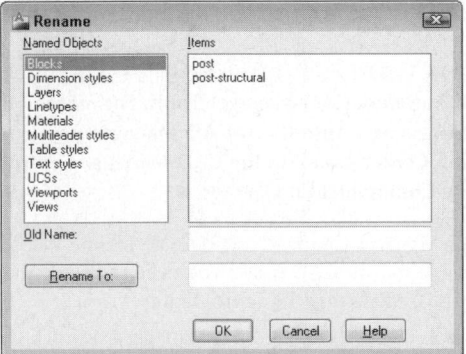

Working with Sheet Sets

Many AutoCAD users create sets of drawings that need to be delivered to a client. In an architectural setting, a set of drawings includes a cover page, floor plans, elevations, and sections, and may include additional sheets of sections, notes, and so on. In an engineering setting, a set of drawings may include a top view, a side view, and a section, in addition to schedules and other data. Organizing and managing all these drawings can be a huge task. Because the sheets are numbered and reference each other, one change can involve renumbering and re-referencing the entire set of drawings.

AutoCAD Only

The sheet set feature is available in AutoCAD only. ■

The sheet set feature offers a major rethinking of how you work with drawings. You still create your drawings in much the same way, but then you define *sheets* — paper space layouts — into sheet sets. You can do the following with sheet sets:

- **Number them.** Each sheet can have a number so that you can easily reorder them. Using fields, you can automate the process of placing the sheet number on each sheet. Changes in the sheet set order automatically change the number on the sheets (after reloading or regenerating the drawing).

- **Plot and publish them.** You can plot or publish the entire sheet set or any selection set of sheets, all at once.

- **Associate them with a template.** You can ensure that every sheet uses the same template, or organize them so that certain sheets use certain templates. By associating a standards file with the template, you can also ensure standards compliance.

- **Manage, open, and find them.** From the Sheet Set Manager, you can easily open or find any of the drawings in the set. You can also delete any sheet.

- **Transmit and archive them.** You can eTransmit the entire sheet set, along with any dependent files. You can also create an archive package for backup purposes.

- **Facilitate multiple-user access.** Although only one drawing can be open at a time, multiple people can have access to the sheet set information.

- **Create an index sheet.** You can create a table for an index sheet that lists all the sheets in the sheet set.

- **Automate the creation of viewports.** You can use named views in model space to create views in viewports on a paper space layout, and specify the scale as you place the viewport.

- **Automate the completion of text in a titleblock.** You can use fields to automatically place text in each titleblock of the sheet set.

- **Automate labeling and referencing.** Using fields, you can automate the process of creating sheet labels and callouts. Labels and callouts contain numbers that are updated when sheets are reordered. Callouts are hyperlinks so that you can immediately go to the view that the callout references.

As you can see, sheet sets are a tool for managing and automating many of the organizational tasks that you need to do every day if you work with groups of drawings.

Understanding sheet sets

The drawings that you need to deliver may have one drawing with three layouts, another with one layout, and a third with four layouts. You need to deliver sheets, which are layouts, but they can be hard to manage when some layouts are in one drawing, some in another, and so on.

When you work with sheet sets, you can pull content from resource drawings that have many layouts or a few, but you create new sheets, and each sheet is a drawing. For this reason, the sheet set structure creates new drawings, each with one layout.

You manage sheet sets and their individual sheets in the Sheet Set Manager, as shown in Figure 26.17. The Sheet Set Manager is a palette like the Properties palette. For example, you can auto-hide it in the same way. To open the Sheet Set Manager, choose View tab ⇨ Palettes panel ⇨ Sheet Set Manager, or press Ctrl+4.

FIGURE 26.17

The Sheet Set Manager is the home base for your sheet sets.

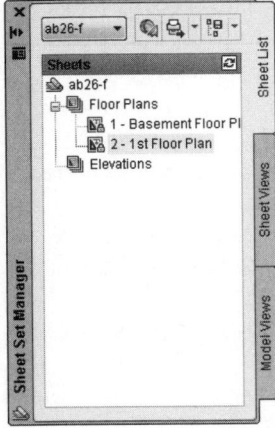

The Sheet Set Manager has three tabs:

- **Sheet List** contains the sheets that you create for the sheet set. You use this tab to manage and organize the sheet set. You can set properties for the sheet set, for subsets (categories), and for individual sheets. You can use this tab to add and remove sheets, and to import a layout from another drawing as a sheet. You can also use it to plot, publish, eTransmit, or archive an entire sheet set or a selection of sheets, to rename and renumber sheets, and to close the sheet set. You can also open any sheet, which is the same as opening the drawing. Figure 26.17 shows the Sheet List tab.

- **Sheet Views** contains a list of paper space views, which are viewports on a layout. A layout can have more than one viewport. You can create view categories, such as elevation and floor plan. You can display the view from this tab. You also use this tab to rename and renumber your views within a layout, as well as to place label blocks that label a view and callout blocks that reference other views. See Figure 26.18 on the left.

- **Model Views** lists the drawings that are the source of your sheets, as well as their model space views, as shown in Figure 26.18 on the right.

Tip

By hovering your cursor over an item in the Sheet Set Manager, you can preview and read details of sheet set layouts on a tooltip. Set preview and detail size preferences by right-clicking near the top of the palettes and choosing Tooltip Style. ∎

FIGURE 26.18

On the left, you see the Sheet Views tab, which displays the views on your sheets. On the right, you see the Model Views tab, which contains the source drawings for your sheet set.

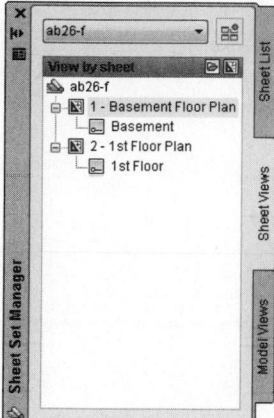
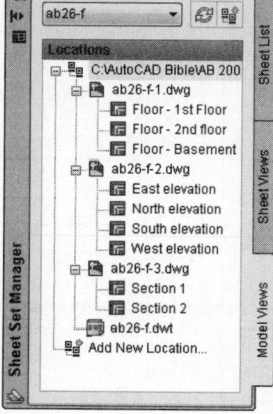

Creating a sheet set

Many AutoCAD users who work with multiple drawings create a folder structure to help organize the drawings. Sheet sets work the same way. You should start by creating a folder for your sheet set. If you want, you can create folders for categories. In the architectural example shown in Figures 26.17 and 26.18, the categories are Floor Plans, Elevations, and Sections. These become *subsets* in your sheet set. Finally, you should create a subfolder for your model space drawings, which are the drawings that you'll use to create the sheet set.

If you plan to use existing layouts as sheets, they should ideally have only one layout, especially if more than one person sometimes accesses drawings. Only one sheet in a drawing can be open at a time. Also, before you import existing layouts or create new sheets, you should first prepare your template — as I explain in the "Setting up sheet set references" section — especially if you plan to use the automatic numbering and referencing features of sheet sets.

To create a sheet set, open the Sheet Set Manager and choose New Sheet Set from the drop-down list at the top of the palette (the NEWSHEETSET command). The Create Sheet Set Wizard opens with the Begin page displayed, as shown in Figure 26.19.

You can choose to use an example sheet set that you've already created or that comes with AutoCAD, in order to use its structure. If you want to work with existing drawings, choose the Existing Drawings option. Then click Next. If you chose to use an example, the next screen allows you to choose the sheet set. Choose one and click Next. The following steps assume that you have chosen the Existing Drawings option.

On the Sheet Set Details page, shown in Figure 26.20, you name the sheet set, add an optional description, and specify the location of the file that contains the data for the sheet set; the default location is automatically entered for you but you can change it. Sheet set files have a .dst filename extension, and you can store them in the same folder as the sheets. Click the Ellipsis button to open the Browse for Sheet Set Folder dialog box. There you can navigate to a folder or create a new folder by clicking the Create New Folder button. Then click Open to return to the wizard.

FIGURE 26.19

The Create Sheet Set Wizard helps you to create sheet sets.

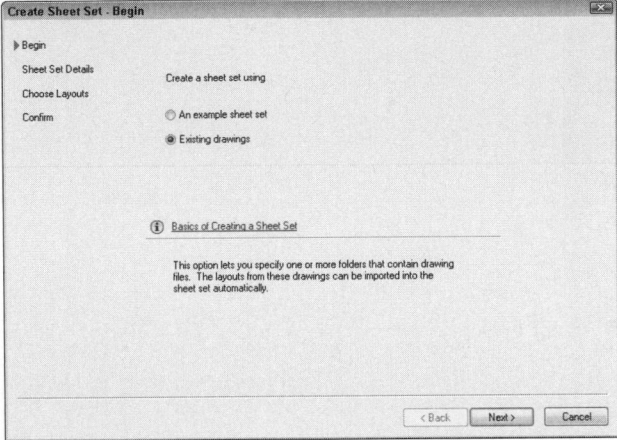

You can click the Sheet Set Properties button at this point to specify various settings, but you have access to these properties from the Sheet Set Manager, so you can skip the properties at this stage. Click Next.

FIGURE 26.20

You need to name the new sheet set and specify the location of its DST file.

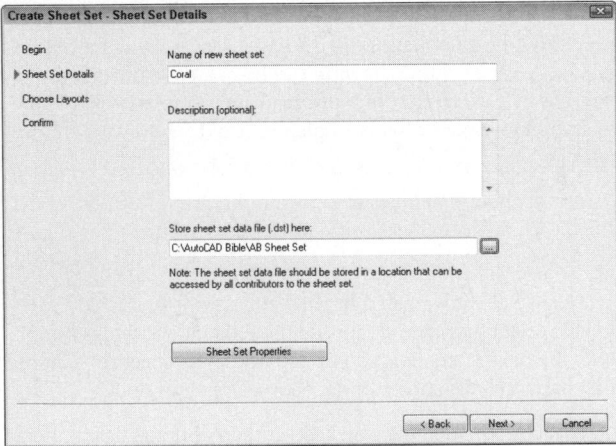

If you chose the Existing Drawings option on the first page, you now see the Choose Layouts page of the wizard. Click Browse to add existing drawings that have layouts that you want to include in the sheet set. If you've created only model space drawings and want to create new sheets instead of including layouts from these drawings, you can skip this page and click Next. However, if you have layouts that you've already set up, browse to a folder and click OK. You can continue to click Browse and add more folders if you want. You can then uncheck any folders that you don't want to include.

Click Import Options to open the Import Options dialog box. Here you can decide whether you want the sheet name to include the drawing name before the layout name. You can also choose to use your folder structure to create subsets. For example, if you have folders named Floor Plans, Elevations, and Sections, you could automatically create the subsets that you see in Figure 26.17. Click OK to close the Import Options dialog box and return to the wizard.

Click Next to display the Confirm page of the wizard. This pane summarizes the choices that you made in the wizard. If you want to change something, click Back. Otherwise, click Finish. You can change everything later except for the sheet set filename and location. Clicking Finish creates the DST file in the location that you chose.

The Sheet Set Manager now displays your new sheet set. If you didn't import any layouts, all you see is the Sheet List tab with the name of the sheet set. If you did import layouts, they're listed. You're now ready to set the properties of your sheet set.

Setting properties

Before you go any farther, you need to set the properties of your sheet set. These properties ensure that every aspect of the sheet set works the way that you want it to. You can separately set properties for the sheet set as a whole, for subsets, and for individual sheets. To set sheet set properties, right-click the name of the sheet set at the top of the Sheet List tab of the Sheet Set Manager, and choose Properties to open the Sheet Set Properties dialog box, as shown in Figure 26.21.

FIGURE 26.21

The Sheet Set Properties dialog box.

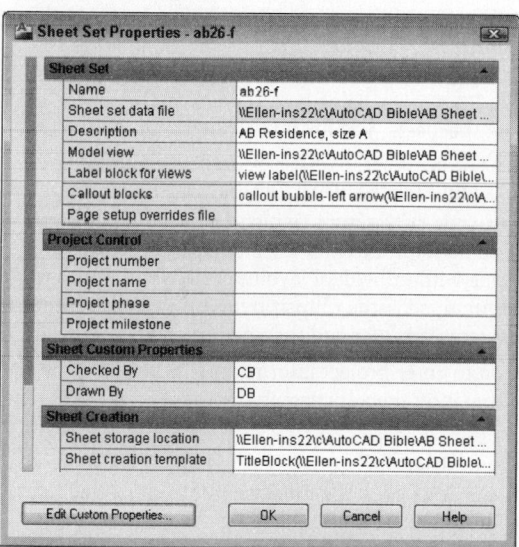

The Sheet Set Properties dialog box always contains the sheet set name and sheet set data file (DST) location. Complete the rest of the properties as follows:

- **Description.** Click this item and type a new description, or edit an existing description.
- **Model view.** Click this item to display the Ellipsis button. Click the button and then click Add to browse to a folder containing drawings that you want to use for your sheets. Click Open and then

click OK to return to the Sheet Properties dialog box. You can add more than one location. These drawings contain model space content that you want to place on layouts for your sheets. For easy organization, create a Model views folder inside the sheet set folder, and place your drawings there. The folders that you enter here appear on the Model Views tab of the Sheet Set Manager.

- **Label block for views.** A label block labels a view and usually includes the view name, view number, and scale. To choose a label block, click this item and click the Ellipsis button. In the Select Block dialog box, click the Ellipsis button to choose a drawing that contains the block that you want. (If your block is in your template, choose AutoCAD Drawing Template [*.dwt] from the Files of Type drop-down list.) Click Open. If the drawing contains only that block (in other words, if the drawing is the block that you want to use), choose the Select the Drawing File as a Block option. If the drawing contains several blocks, use the Choose Blocks in the Drawing File option. You then see a list of the blocks in the drawing. Choose the block that you want (you can choose only one label block) and click OK. If you want to use the automatic numbering and referencing feature of sheet sets, you need to set up this block, as I explain later in this chapter in the "Setting up sheet set references" section. If you want different blocks for different subsets, or if you don't use a label block, leave this item blank.

- **Callout blocks.** Callout blocks point to other drawings. For example, on a floor plan, a callout block marks the location of a section view that is on another sheet. To choose a callout block, click this item and click the Ellipsis button. In the List of Blocks dialog box, click the Add button. Then in the Select Block dialog box, click the Ellipsis button to choose a drawing from the Select Drawing dialog box that contains the blocks that you want. (For a template, choose AutoCAD Drawing Template [*.dwt] from the Files of Type drop-down list.) Click Open. If the drawing contains only that block (in other words, if the drawing is the block that you want to use), choose the Select the Drawing File as a Block option. If the drawing contains several blocks, use the Choose Blocks in the Drawing File option. You then see a list of the blocks in the drawing. You can choose multiple callout blocks, because many drawings contain variations of this type of block. Click OK twice to return to the Sheet Set Properties dialog box. If you want to use the automatic numbering and referencing feature of sheet sets, you need to set up this block, as I explain later in this chapter in the "Setting up sheet set references" section. If you want different blocks for different subsets, or if you don't use callout blocks, leave this item blank.

- **Page setup overrides file.** You may want to override page setups (which I explain in Chapter 17) if you imported layouts with varying setups. You may want to plot the entire sheet set with one page setup, rather than use page setups that came with individual layouts. You save these page setups in a sheet (drawing) template. Click this item, click the Ellipsis button that appears, choose a template, and click Open. You can create this template later and then go back and specify it.

- **Project control.** This feature provides a location to enter project information, including a project number, name, phase, and milestone. This information then appears in the Details section of the Sheet List tab of the Sheet Set Manager.

- **Sheet storage location.** This folder defines where sheets are stored. If you didn't specify this location when you created the sheet set, click this item, click the Ellipsis button, choose a folder, and click Open. Note that if the sheet set already contains sheets, changing this location doesn't move existing sheets; it only affects the location of new sheets that you create.

- **Sheet creation template.** Click this item and then the Ellipsis button. Then click the Ellipsis button in the Select Layout as Sheet Template dialog box. Choose a sheet (drawing) template (or a drawing or standards file) and click Open. You can then click a layout in the template. Click OK.

Caution

If you want to use the automatic numbering and referencing features of sheet sets, don't create any sheets before you've set up this template. ■

- **Prompt for template.** If you want your sheets to automatically use the template, this item should be set to No. If you sometimes vary your templates, set this item to Yes so that you can choose a different template when you want.

You can create custom properties. You create custom properties to automatically insert text in your title-block, using AutoCAD's field feature. After you create these properties, they become fields that you can insert. (See "Inserting Fields" in Chapter 13 for a discussion of fields.) A custom property can apply to a sheet set or an individual sheet. Common sheet set custom properties are client name, project name, or project address. A typical sheet set custom property would be the drawer's or proofer's initials, if more than one person works on the sheets in the sheet set.

To add custom properties, click the Edit Custom Properties button. In the Custom Properties dialog box, click Add. Then enter a name and a default value, and choose whether the property is for a sheet or a sheet set. (Adding a default value helps you test the fields when you set up your titleblock.) Click OK. Continue to click Add and define custom properties. When you're done, click OK to return to the Sheet Set Properties dialog box.

Caution

After you create custom properties, you can't change their name. To do so, you would need to delete and re-create the properties. ■

When you finish setting your sheet set properties, click OK to return to the Sheet Set Manager and your drawing.

Creating subsets

Subsets are categories that you can use to help you organize your sheets. They may or may not have corresponding folders where you keep sheets. To create a subset, right-click the sheet set name and choose New Subset. In the Subset Properties dialog box, name the subset and specify the location of the sheet drawings files for that subset as well as the template. The default location for both is the same as for the entire sheet set.

Note

In the Subset Properties dialog box, you can choose to include the subset when publishing the sheet set or to not publish the subset. See the "Plotting and publishing" section later in this chapter for more information. ■

After you've created a subset, you can change its properties by right-clicking the subset and choosing Properties from the shortcut menu.

When you create your sheets, you can set sheet properties in the same way, by right-clicking and choosing Properties.

Setting up sheet set references

One of the more exciting features of sheet sets is the ability to automate the completion of text in the title-block, as well as the numbering of sheets, titleblocks, and callout blocks. However, this feature is also fairly complex. You can omit this feature and still get significant benefits from sheet sets, such as the ability to plot the entire sheet set all at once and automate the creation of viewports. In this section, I explain how to configure the label and callout blocks so that the automation features work properly.

The secret of this feature is the use of fields, which I cover in Chapter 13 (in the "Inserting Fields" section). You can use the fields in two ways:

- Place the fields in Mtext, which you insert in your titleblock, label block, and callout blocks.
- Place the fields using attributes that you associate with these blocks. I cover attributes and blocks in Chapter 18.

The advantage of using attributes is that text cannot easily be changed. If you're a CAD Manager and want to reduce errors, you might choose to use attributes. Of course, if you already use attributes, you might find it simpler to continue to use them. On the other hand, you might want the increased flexibility and simplicity of Mtext, especially if you don't currently use attributes. One of the reasons for using attributes is to place text; using Mtext with fields works just as well to specify text placement.

Configuring titleblock text

There are many ways of creating a titleblock. In this section, I assume that you have a template that contains a titleblock that you've inserted on a layout. This template would also contain your text styles, table styles, dimension styles, layers, and so on.

Tip

To configure your template, don't open it directly. Instead, create a new sheet in your sheet set. This sheet will automatically be based on the template that you specified in the Sheet Set Properties dialog box. When you finish configuring this sheet, you will save it as a template. To create the sheet, right-click the sheet set name and choose New Sheet. Give the sheet a name that indicates that it will become a template, such as WillBeTemplate. This technique allows you to test your fields as you work, because the sheet is part of the sheet set (unlike a template that you open directly). Thanks to Heidi Hewett of Autodesk for this tip. ■

At this point, you should look at your titleblock and determine any custom properties that you need, as I explained in the previous section. You should set up these properties before you go on.

Create a new sheet on the Sheet List tab of the Sheet Set Manager. Double-click the sheet to open it. You should now see your template with its titleblock. If the titleblock text is part of a block, whether Mtext or attributes, explode the titleblock.

Tip

Don't try to edit attributes or blocks by using the Block Attribute Manager (BATTMAN command) or the REFEDIT command, because the existing block's text will not be updated with the new field values. Instead, explode the block, change the text to fields, and redefine the block. Thanks to Heidi Hewett of Autodesk for this tip. ■

Double-click the Mtext or attribute text to open the In-Place Text Editor or the Edit Attribute Definition dialog box. To replace the text with a field, follow these steps:

1. Select the text.
2. Right-click and choose Insert Field to open the Field dialog box.
3. Choose one of the following fields:
   - **CurrentSheetCategory.** The view category for the current sheet.
   - **CurrentSheetCustom.** Custom properties that apply to individual sheets.

- **CurrentSheetDescription.** The description that you entered for a sheet.
- **CurrentSheetIssuePurpose.** The purpose property for a sheet.
- **CurrentSheetNumber.** The sheet number.
- **CurrentSheetNumberandTitle.** The sheet number and name.
- **CurrentSheetRevisionDate.** The revision date for the current sheet.
- **CurrentSheetRevisionNumber.** The revision number for the current sheet.
- **CurrentSheetSet.** The name of the sheet set.
- **CurrentSheetSetCustom.** Custom properties that apply to the sheet set.
- **CurrentSheetSetDescription.** The sheet set description that you specified.
- **CurrentSheetSetProjectMilestone.** The milestone value from the Project Control section of the Sheet Set Properties dialog box.
- **CurrentSheetSetProjectName.** The project name from the Project Control section of the Sheet Set Properties dialog box.
- **CurrentSheetSetProjectNumber.** The project number from the Project Control section of the Sheet Set Properties dialog box.
- **CurrentSheetSetProjectPhase.** The project phase value from the Project Control section of the Sheet Set Properties dialog box.
- **CurrentSheetSetSubSet.** The name of the subset that the current sheet is in.
- **CurrentSheetTitle.** The name of the sheet.
- **Sheet Set.** The name of the sheet set.
- **CreateDate.** Places the current date. (Unlike the Date field, this field doesn't update each time you open or regenerate the drawing.)

You may find other fields that are useful for your titleblock.

4. Choose a format from the Format list.
5. If you chose one of the custom fields, choose the specific field from the Custom Property Name drop-down list.

Note

You should immediately see the value of your field, either in your drawing or in the Edit Attribute Definition dialog box. ∎

6. Click OK. Repeat Steps 1 through 5 to continue to add fields for the entire titleblock in this way.
7. Choose Application Button ⇨ Save As. From the Files of Type drop-down list, choose AutoCAD Drawing Template (*.dwt). Specify the location that you want for your sheet set template. (The Template folder has a SheetSets subfolder that you can use.) Click Save. Usually, you're overwriting an existing template, so confirm the overwrite. Enter a description in the Template Description dialog box and click OK.
8. You can now delete the sheet from the sheet set. Deleting a sheet doesn't delete the drawing. Right-click the sheet and choose Remove Sheet. Click OK to confirm. The drawing is still open.
9. The template is now open on your screen. If you exploded the titleblock, you need to redefine the block. If you're using attributes for your text, you need to include the text as attribute definitions.
10. Select all the objects in your titleblock. Choose Insert tab ⇨ Block panel ⇨ Create. In the Block Definition dialog box, enter the name of your titleblock block in the Name text box. Click OK.

You can now immediately define label and callout blocks directly in the template. If you don't need these blocks, skip the next section and close the template.

Configuring label and callout blocks

Label blocks can automatically display the sheet number, sheet name, and scale. Callout blocks can automatically display the view number (often called the detail number), as well as the sheet number. In addition, callout blocks can contain a hyperlink to the view that they reference so that users can immediately display that view. You can see an example of label and callout blocks in Figure 26.23.

To set up your label and callout blocks, the simplest solution is probably to work directly in the template. When you're done, you'll delete the inserted blocks to keep only their definitions. If you want to store these blocks in a separate drawing, open the drawing. Follow these steps:

1. Choose Insert tab ⇨ Block panel ⇨ Insert and choose your label block. Click OK and specify any insertion point.

2. Explode the block.

3. Double-click the text that contains the view number. (This is often called the detail number and will number a floating viewport containing one view of the drawing.) The In-Place Text Editor opens (the Edit Attribute Definition dialog box opens if the text is an attribute).

4. Select the text. (In the Edit Attribute Definition dialog box, select the text in the Default text box.) Right-click and choose Insert ⇨ Field. The Field dialog box opens.

5. From the Field Names list, choose SheetSetPlaceholder. From the Placeholder Type list, choose ViewNumber.

6. Repeat Steps 3 through 5 for the view name and the view scale, using the ViewTitle and the ViewportScale types of the SheetSetPlaceholder field, respectively.

7. To redefine the block, select all the objects, choose Insert tab ⇨ Block panel ⇨ Create, and type the titleblock name in the Name text box. When the label block is automatically inserted into the drawing, its insertion point will be at the lower-left corner of the view, so you need to define the base point of the block slightly above the block's left edge. Click OK, and then click Yes to confirm the redefinition of the block.

Tip

You can use the Block Editor to edit the block. Then you don't have to explode or redefine the block. ■

Note

If your text is composed of attributes, choose Insert tab ⇨ Attributes panel ⇨ Manage to open the Block Attribute Manager. Choose each field, click Edit, check the Preset check box, and click OK twice to return to your drawing. You want attributes that are fields to be preset because you'll define their value by using the Sheet Set Manager; you don't want the Edit Attributes dialog box to pop up to ask for a value whenever you insert a titleblock. You can also select the attribute, open the Properties palette, and change the Preset item's value to Yes. ■

8. If you didn't choose the Delete option in the Block Definition dialog box, delete the block. The block definition stays in the template's database and will be available to any drawing that you base on that template.

9. Repeat Steps 1 through 8 for your callout blocks. For these blocks, you use the SheetSetPlaceholder field with the ViewNumber and SheetNumber field types. However, for callout blocks, be sure to

check the Associate Hyperlink check box in the Field dialog box, so that the callout bubble will link to the view (detail) that it references.

10. Save the template and close it.

You're now ready to use your sheet set.

Adding and managing sheets

After you've configured your sheet set properties, you're ready to use your sheet set. The first step is to specify the value of any custom properties that you have defined so that they'll appear in your titleblock text property. On the Sheet List tab, right-click the sheet set name and choose Properties. Click Edit Custom Properties and set the values that you want.

You can now add sheets. Each sheet will be a separate drawing with one layout tab. To add a sheet, follow these steps:

1. Display the Sheet List tab of the Sheet Set Manager.
2. Right-click the sheet set name and choose New Sheet.
3. In the New Sheet dialog box, give the sheet a number and a name.
4. The name of the drawing is automatically completed, using both the number and the name of the sheet.

Tip

You can delete the number in front of the sheet name. Otherwise, if you change the order of your sheets, the drawing filename won't change, and your filenames get out of sync. ■

5. Click OK. The new sheet appears on the Sheet List tab.
6. If you created sheet properties, right-click the sheet name and choose Properties. Change the values of any custom properties that are specific for that sheet.

Tip

You can import a layout as a sheet by displaying the layout and dragging from the layout tab to the Sheet List tab of the Sheet Set Manager. ■

Tip

You can quickly preview and easily switch between all open drawings and layouts by choosing Quick View Drawings from the status bar. To make the thumbnails larger or smaller, hold down the Ctrl key while using your mouse wheel's scroll feature. ■

To organize your sheets, you can create subsets. A subset is just an organizational tool, although you can create a folder structure that matches your subsets. You can also assign different templates to sheets in different subsets. To add a subset, right-click the sheet set name and choose New Subset. You can also right-click an existing subset and choose New Subset to create a nested subset. In the Subset Properties dialog box, name the subset. You can also assign a template and folder location, and control if the sheets in the subset are published. Click OK.

On the Sheet List tab, you can also do the following with sheets:

- **Move sheets.** You can place sheets in a different order by dragging them. You can drag multiple sheets to a new location or subset.
- **Remove sheets.** Right-click any sheet and choose Remove Sheet. You can also select multiple sheets to remove all the selected sheets. Click OK to confirm.
- **Change a sheet's name and number.** Right-click a sheet and choose Rename & Renumber. Type a new number, a new name, or both, and click OK. Note that renumbering a sheet doesn't change its order on the Sheet List. Two sheets can have the same number. You can use any numbering system that you want.

Note

When changing a sheet's name, you have an option to also change the name of the associated drawing file to match the new sheet name. ■

- **Change sheet properties.** Right-click a sheet and choose Properties. Make any changes that you want in the Sheet Properties dialog box and click OK.
- **Import a sheet.** You can create a sheet by importing a layout tab of an existing drawing. On the Sheet List tab, right-click the sheet set name and choose Import Layout as Sheet. In the Import Layouts as Sheets dialog box, click the Browse for Drawings button. Navigate to a drawing and click Open. Then choose the layouts in that drawing that you want to import. Click the Import Checked button.

Note

To import a layout as a sheet, you must have displayed a layout tab in that drawing; otherwise, you get a message that the drawing does not contain any initialized layouts. To remedy the situation, open the drawing, click the layout tab, and save the drawing. Then close the drawing. You can now import the layout into your sheet set. ■

On the DVD

The drawings and files used in the following exercise on creating and configuring a sheet set, ab26-f-1.dwg, ab26-f-2.dwg, ab26-f-3.dwg, and ab26-f.dwt, are in the Drawings folder on the DVD. ■

STEPS: Creating and Configuring a Sheet Set

Note: This is a long exercise. You should leave yourself 45 to 60 minutes to complete it.

1. Open Windows Explorer. (Right-click the Windows Start button and choose Explore.) In the folder pane, locate and click the AutoCAD Bible folder that you created for the exercises in this book. From the menu, choose File ➪ New ➪ Folder, or Organize ➪ New Folder (in Windows Vista or Windows 7), and name the new folder AB 2011 Sheet Set.
2. Click the new AB 2011 Sheet Set folder and again create a new folder. Name the new folder Model View Drawings.
3. Copy ab26-f-1.dwg, ab26-f-2.dwg, ab26-f-3.dwg, and ab26-f.dwt (a template file) from the DVD of this book to the Model View Drawings folder.
4. Open a new drawing, based on any template. (You need a drawing open to create a new sheet set, but not to open an existing one.)
5. Choose View tab ➪ Palettes panel ➪ Sheet Set Manager. From the drop-down list at the top, choose New Sheet Set to open the Create Sheet Set Wizard.

6. On the Begin page, choose Existing Drawings and click Next.

7. In the Name of New Sheet Set text box, type **ab26-f**. In the Description text box, type **AB Residence, size A**. (You wouldn't normally use size A sheets for architectural drawings, but using this size enables you to print the sheets on your printer if you don't have a plotter available.) In the Store Sheet Set Data File (`.dst`) Here box, click the Ellipsis button and navigate to the `AutoCAD Bible\AB 2011 Sheet Set` folder that you created in Step 1. Click Open and then click Next.

8. On the Choose Layouts page, click Next. You're going to create the sheets from scratch rather than import them. (You will use the existing drawings for the model view, but you won't use them as the sheets themselves.)

9. On the Confirm page, read the information. If it's correct, click Finish. (Otherwise, click Back and make any corrections that you want.)

10. Click the Sheet List tab of the Sheet Set Manager if it isn't already on top. You should see your sheet set listed. Right-click the sheet set name and choose Properties from the shortcut menu.

11. In the Sheet Set Properties dialog box, set the following items:

    - **Model view.** Click the Ellipsis button. Click Add. Navigate to the `AutoCAD Bible\AB 2011 Sheet Set\Model View Drawings` folder that you created in Step 2. Click Open. Click OK to return to the Sheet Set Properties dialog box.

    - **Label block for views.** Click the Ellipsis button. In the Select Block dialog box, click the Ellipsis button again. If necessary, choose AutoCAD Drawing Template (`*.dwt`) from the Files of Type drop-down list. Navigate to the `AutoCAD Bible\AB 2011 Sheet Set\Model View Drawings` folder and choose `ab26-f.dwt`. Click Open. Choose the Choose Blocks in the Drawing File option. Choose the `view label` block. Click OK.

    - **Callout blocks.** Click the Ellipsis button. In the List of Blocks dialog box, click Add. In the Select Block dialog box, click the Ellipsis button. If necessary, choose AutoCAD Drawing Template (`*.dwt`) from the Files of Type drop-down list. Navigate to the `AutoCAD Bible\AB 2011 Sheet Set\Model View Drawings` folder and choose `ab26-f.dwt`. Click Open. Choose the Choose Blocks in the Drawing File option. Choose the `Callout button-left arrow` block. Click OK twice.

    - **Sheet creation template.** Click the Ellipsis button. In the Select Layout as Sheet Template dialog box, click the Ellipsis button. If necessary, choose AutoCAD Drawing Template (`*.dwt`) from the Files of Type drop-down list. Navigate to the `AutoCAD Bible\AB 2011 Sheet Set\Model View Drawings` folder and choose `ab26-f.dwt`. Click Open. (If the template contained more than one layout, you would choose the layout of the template that you want to use.) Click OK.

    - **Prompt for template.** Choose No from the drop-down list if this value is set to Yes.

12. Click Edit Custom Properties. Click Add. In the Add Custom Property dialog box, add the following custom properties:

    - Customer Name, with a value of CustomerName, sheet set
    - Customer Address 1, with a value of CustomerAddress1, sheet set
    - Customer Address 2, with a value of CustomerAddress2, sheet set
    - Drawn By, with a value of DB, sheet
    - Checked By, with a value of CB, sheet

    Click OK to close the Custom Properties dialog box. Click OK again to close the Sheet Set Properties dialog box and return to your drawing.

13. Right-click the sheet set name and choose New Subset. In the Subset Properties dialog box, type **Floor Plans** in the Subset Name field and click OK. Repeat this process to add subsets for Elevations and Sections.

14. To configure the titleblock text, right-click the sheet set name and choose New Sheet. Because you'll later save this sheet as a template and then delete it, number it XX and name it WILL BE TEMPLATE. (This technique helps you to confirm your fields.) Delete the XX from the front of the filename and click OK.

15. Double-click the new sheet to open it. You should see the template's titleblock.

16. Double-click the text CustomerName to open the In-Place Text Editor. Select the text, right-click, and choose Insert Field. Choose SheetSet from the Field Category drop-down list to filter the fields that you see on the Field Names list. Choose CurrentSheetSetCustom (check the field name carefully, because there are many similar fields), set the format to Title case, and choose Customer Name from the Custom Property Name drop-down list. Click OK. You now see the text surrounded by the gray field box. Click outside of the In-Place Text Editor to close it. In the same way, set the following other fields:

- **CustomerAddress1.** CurrentSheetSetCustom, Title case, Customer Address 1
- **CustomerAddress2.** CurrentSheetSetCustom, Title case, Customer Address 2
- **DB.** (Drawn By) CurrentSheetCustom, Uppercase, Drawn By
- **CB.** (Checked By) CurrentSheetCustom, Uppercase, Checked By
- **P-01.** CurrentSheetNumber, Uppercase

You can now see the values of all the fields in the titleblock.

17. The Layout tab takes on the name of the sheet, which is WILL BE TEMPLATE. If your drawing window displays the Layout tab, double-click the Layout tab to rename it. If your drawing window doesn't display the Layout tab (the default), first right-click the layout's button on the status bar and click Display Layout and Model Tabs. In the Sheet Set – Rename Layout dialog box, click Rename Layout Only. Name the Layout tab **Titleblock** and press Enter.

18. Choose Application Button ➪ Save As ➪ AutoCAD Drawing Template. Navigate to your AutoCAD Bible\AB 2011 Sheet Set\Model View Drawings folder. Name the template ab26-f. dwt and click Save. Click Yes to replace the existing template. Click OK to accept the description. (Because you have now changed the template, if you want to do the exercise again, you must recopy the template from the DVD.)

19. You no longer need the WILL BE TEMPLATE sheet. Right-click the sheet and choose Remove Sheet. Click OK to confirm. (Removing the sheet does not remove the drawing or templates.)

20. The template is still open. Make sure that the current layer is 0.

21. To configure the label and callout blocks, choose Insert tab ➪ Block panel ➪ Insert and choose the view label block from the Name drop-down list. Make sure that only the Insertion Point Specify On-Screen check box is checked, and click OK. Pick any insertion point. If the Edit Attributes dialog box opens, click OK. If the attribute prompts appear on the command line (and in the Dynamic Input tooltip), press Enter until the command is completed.

22. In the same way, insert the callout bubble-left arrow block.

23. Select the view label block and choose Insert tab ➪ Block panel ➪ Block Editor. In the Edit Block Definition dialog box, with the view label block highlighted, click OK.

24. Double-click the V# text inside the circle. The Edit Attribute Definition dialog box opens. Select the text in the Default text box. Right-click in the Default text box and choose Insert Field. In the Field dialog box, choose SheetSetPlaceholder as the Field Name and ViewNumber as the

Placeholder Type. (If you use view numbers that include letters, choose Uppercase as the Format.) Click OK twice to return to the Block Editor.

Note

You don't see the gray field box yet, because you haven't yet inserted the attribute as part of a block. ■

25. Use the same procedure to add SheetSetPlaceholder fields for VIEWNAME (use the ViewTitle type and Title case format) and SCALE (use the ViewportScale type and choose the format that you want). Press Enter to end the DDEDIT command.

26. Select the attributes. Display the Properties palette and change the Preset item's value to Yes.

27. Click Save Block in the Open/Save panel on the Block Editor tab and click Close Block Editor in the Close panel to return to your drawing.

28. Repeat Steps 23 through 27 for the `callout bubble-left arrow` block. For the top text, use the ViewNumber placeholder type. For the bottom text, use the SheetNumber placeholder type. This time, be sure to check the Associate Hyperlink check box in the Field dialog box.

29. Delete both blocks. Then save and close the template.

30. Before you create new sheets, specify the values of the sheet set level custom properties. Right-click the sheet set name on the Sheet List tab of the Sheet Set Manager and choose Properties. The Sheet Set Custom Properties section lists the sheet set properties that you created earlier. (You might have to scroll down in the Sheet Set Properties dialog box to see them.) For Customer Name, type **AB Residence**. For Customer Address 1, enter any address. For Customer Address 2, enter any city, state, and ZIP or postal code. Click OK to return to your drawing.

31. On the Sheet List tab of the Sheet Set Manager, right-click the Floor Plans subset and choose New Sheet. Number the new sheet 1 and name it Basement Floor Plan. Delete the number 1 from the filename and click OK. In the same way, create a sheet 2 named 1st Floor Plan, and a sheet 3 named 2nd Floor Plan.

32. In the same way, add four new sheets to the Elevations subset:

- 4: East Elevation
- 5: North Elevation
- 6: West Elevation
- 7: South Elevation

33. In the same way, add two new sheets to a new Sections subset: a sheet 8 called Internal Sections and a sheet 9 called External Sections.

34. Right-click each sheet that you've created and choose Properties. Change the values for the DB and CB sheet properties to any initials.

35. Leave AutoCAD and the Sheet Set Manager open for the next exercise.

Using a sheet set

When your sheet set is configured and you've created your sheets, you're ready to use your sheet set. You can create viewports on your sheets, insert callout blocks, plot or publish sheets, archive and eTransmit sheets, and create a table that lists all the sheets.

Creating viewports from named views

A major feature of a sheet set is the ability to create viewports on your sheets. You do this by creating named views in model space in your resource drawings. Then you place the view onto a layout to create a viewport. (For information on named views, see the section "Creating Named Views" in Chapter 8. For coverage of viewports, see the section "Creating a Layout in Paper Space" in Chapter 17.) When you place the view, you can specify the scale that you need.

If you don't already have the named view that you need, click the Model Views tab and double-click the drawing containing the content that you need. This opens the drawing. (If necessary, click the plus sign next to the resource location to display the available drawings.) Click the Model button on the status bar (or the Model tab if it's displayed), define the named view, and then save and close the drawing.

The Model Views tab now lists the named view under the drawing. (Again, you may have to click the plus sign next to the drawing to display the view.)

To create a viewport based on a named view, follow these steps:

1. Click the Sheet List tab. Double-click the sheet on which you want to place a viewport, to open the drawing with the layout displayed.

2. Click the Model Views tab.

3. Right-click the named view that you want to use, and choose Place on Sheet.

4. Move the cursor onto the drawing area. The command line displays the `Specify insertion point:` prompt, and you can see the view on the layout. AutoCAD calculates a standard scale, based on the size of the layout and the size of the view.

5. To change the scale, right-click in the drawing area. A list of scales appears. Choose the scale that you want.

6. Click to specify the insertion point that you want, and place the viewport. If you've specified a label block, the block automatically appears with its insertion point at the lower-left corner of the view.

Use this procedure to place viewports on all your sheets. Your views now appear on the Sheet Views tab. If you want to place callout or label blocks that use the ViewNumber field, you need to number these views. Right-click a view on the Sheet Views tab and choose Rename & Renumber. Enter a number and a name and click OK. To see the result in an existing field, regenerate the drawing to update the fields.

Inserting callout blocks

If you've set up callout blocks, as I describe in the "Configuring label and callout blocks" section earlier in this chapter, now is the time to place them. A callout block references another sheet that contains a detail or a different view. Follow these steps:

1. On the Sheet List tab of the Sheet Set Manager, double-click the sheet on which you want to place the callout block, to open the layout.

2. Click the Sheet Views tab, which contains all the model views that you have on your layouts, and right-click the view that you want to reference. Choose Place Callout Block and choose the block. (If you see a Select Blocks submenu item, choose it, choose the block that you want, and click OK to select the block that you want to use. This makes the block available on the menu. Then right-click the view again, choose Place Callout Block, and choose the block.)

3. At the prompt, pick an insertion point to place the block. The block should display the correct view (detail) and sheet number.

Plotting and publishing

Automation of plotting and publishing is one of the advantages of sheet sets. You can plot or publish an entire sheet set or just part of it, directly from the Sheet Set Manager.

To plot the entire sheet set, click the sheet set name and choose Publish ⇨ Publish to Plotter. Your sheet set plots according to the settings in the template. To apply page-setup overrides, choose Publish Using Page Setup Override.

To publish the sheet set, click the sheet set name and choose Publish to DWF. If you plan to publish to DWF format, choose Sheet Set Publish Options from the Publish drop-down list. The Sheet Set Publish Options dialog box opens, where you can specify options for publishing to DWF. For example, you can decide whether you want to publish to single-sheet or multi-sheet DWF format. You can also specify a password and decide how much data you want to make available. For more information about the PUBLISH command and the DWF format, see Chapter 28.

Note

The PUBLISHCOLLATE system variable determines whether a sheet set is published as a single plotting job or as separate jobs for each sheet. The default value, 1, publishes the sheets as a single job. However, to publish sheets as a single job, all sheets must be the same size, and you need to choose the Publish Using Page Setup Override option from the Publish drop-down list on the Sheet List tab of the Sheet Set Manager. Change the value to 0 if you might need to have other plotting jobs interrupt the sheet set. You can also publish the sheet set in reverse order; choose Publish in Reverse Order from the Publish drop-down list. On the same menu, you have options to add a plot stamp, manage plot setups, and open the PUBLISH dialog box. ■

To plot or publish a subset or sheet, right-click the subset or sheet and use the options on the shortcut menu.

Note

You can include or exclude subsets and sheets when publishing the rest of the set by using the Include for Publish setting. Right-click the sheet set name and choose Publish ⇨ Edit Subset and Sheet Publishing Settings. In the Publish Sheets dialog box, choose the sheets and subsets that you want to publish. Click OK. The Sheet Set Manager now displays a No-Plot icon next to each sheet that you chose not to publish.

You can override the Include for Publish settings for subsets. Right-click the subset name and choose Publish ⇨ Publish Sheets in Subset and click on either Publish by Sheet 'Include for Publish' Setting or the Do Not Publish Sheets option. You have similar controls on a per-sheet basis. Right-click the sheet name and choose Publish ⇨ Include for Publish and click either Yes or No. To avoid a missing sheet, be careful when overriding the Include for Publish settings, especially when others may be plotting your drawings and are unaware of your overrides. ■

 You can create selection sets of sheets and save them. Then you can plot or publish the selection set of sheets. To create a selection set of sheets, select the sheets that you want to include and click Sheet Selections ⇨ Create. Name the selection set and click OK. After that, you can choose the selection set from the Sheet Selections drop-down list to select the sheets that you need. Then you can choose to plot or publish them.

Archiving and eTransmitting sheet sets

Archive your sheet sets to save them in ZIP format (by default). You can use the ZIP file for transmittal or backup purposes. (For more information about the archiving process, see the discussion on eTransmitting drawings in Chapter 28.) To archive a sheet set, follow these steps:

1. Right-click the sheet set name and choose Archive.
2. In the Archive a Sheet Set dialog box, you can add notes that will go in the archive report, use the tabs to review the files that will be included, view the archive report, and modify current archive settings. Then click OK.
3. Choose a location for the archive file and click Save.

You create a transmittal when you want to e-mail your sheet set along with all necessary dependent drawings and files. I cover eTransmitting drawings in Chapter 28. To eTransmit a sheet set, follow these steps:

1. Right-click the sheet set name and choose eTransmit.

2. In the Create Transmittal dialog box, you can add notes, use the tabs to review the files that will be included, view the transmittal report, and choose a transmittal setup that you've saved. Click OK.

3. Choose a location for the file and click Save.

Creating a list of sheets

A sheet set often has an index sheet that contains a table of contents. Using AutoCAD's table feature, you can automatically generate a table that lists all the sheets in the sheet set or just a subset. To create a table listing the sheets, follow these steps:

1. Create a new sheet. You can number it sheet 1 or sheet 0.

2. Double-click the sheet to open its drawing.

3. Right-click the sheet set name and choose Insert Sheet List Table to open the Sheet List Table dialog box, as shown in Figure 26.22.

FIGURE 26.22

Use the Sheet List Table dialog box to create a table that lists the sheets in a sheet set or a subset.

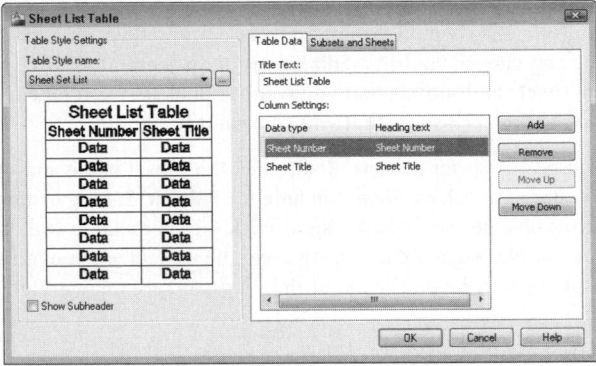

4. From the Table Style Name drop-down list, choose any table style that you've saved in your template. You can click the Ellipsis button to open the Table Style dialog box and define a table style.

5. Check the Show Subheader check box if you want to show your sheets divided by subsets.

6. In the Title Text text box, enter a name to appear as the title of the table. You may want to use the name of the sheet set here, rather than the default text.

7. In the Column Settings section, specify what data you want to show and how you want to title each column. On the left, you can choose the data from the drop-down lists. On the right, you can change the text. For example, for the Sheet Title item, you may want the title to appear as "Sheet Name." Click Add to add a new column, or click Remove to remove a column. You can also change the order of the columns.

8. On the Subsets and Sheet tab, check the sheets that you want to include in the table. By default, all the sheets in the set should be included. Uncheck any sheets that you don't want to appear in the table.

Note

To make sure that the table automatically picks up changes to the sheet set, you must check the sheet set name and the subset names. AutoCAD does not update changes to unchecked sheets or subsets. ■

9. Click OK.

If you make any changes in your sheet set, such as adding or renumbering sheets, you should update the table. Select the table by clicking on any outside border, right-click, and choose Update Data Table Links.

On the DVD

The drawings and files used in the following exercise on using a sheet set, ab26-f-1.dwg, ab26-f-2.dwg, and ab26-f-3.dwg, are in the Drawings folder on the DVD. The ab26-f.dwt file is in the Results folder. (It's called ab26-f.dwt after exercise.dwt because it contains the results of the previous exercise. Ideally, you should do the previous exercise and use the template that you saved in that exercise.) ■

STEPS: Using a Sheet Set

1. You should do the previous exercise before doing this exercise to set up and configure your sheet set and the blocks. If the Sheet Set Manager is not open, choose View tab ⇨ Palettes panel ⇨ Sheet Set Manager, click Open, and open the ab26-f sheet set from the AutoCAD Bible\AB 2011 Sheet Set folder.

2. Click the Model Views tab of the Sheet Set Manager. Click the plus sign next to the folder name at the top to display the list of the three drawings in the Model View Drawings folder. Click the plus sign next to each drawing to display their model space named views.

3. Click the Sheet List tab. Double-click 1 - Basement Floor Plan. You see the titleblock displayed with all the titleblock fields completed.

4. Change the current layer to Viewport.

5. Click the Model Views tab again. Expand the ab26-f-1.dwg item in the Sheet Set Manager, right-click Floor - Basement, and choose Place on Sheet. Move the cursor onto the drawing area. (You may want to auto-hide the Sheet Set Manager at this point.) Right-click and choose 1/16"=1'. Place the viewport all the way to the left of the layout. (The view doesn't fit perfectly, but that's okay for this exercise.) The result should look like Figure 26.23, except without the callout block. (If you want, continue to place the floor-plan views on the floor-plan sheets, matching the first- and second-floor views to the sheets. You can also do the same for the four elevation views.)

6. On the Sheet List tab, double-click the External Sections sheet to open it. Make Viewport the current layer. Click the Model Views tab. Expand the ab26-f-3.dwg item in the Sheet Set Manager, right-click the Section 2 view, and choose Place on Sheet. In the drawing area, right-click and choose 1/16"=1' and pick a point for the view.

7. Click the Sheet Views tab to see the views that you've placed. To number these views, expand each sheet, right-click each view and choose Rename & Renumber. Because you're placing only one view on a sheet, number each view 1 and click OK.

FIGURE 26.23

The basement floor plan.

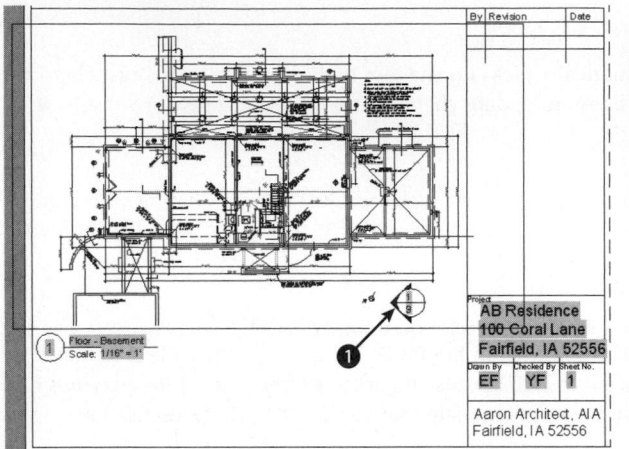

8. To place a callout bubble on the basement floor plan that references the Exterior Section sheet, click the Quick View Drawings button on the status bar, and choose that drawing from the thumbnails that appear. Click the Sheet Views tab. This tab now lists the views that you just placed. Right-click the `Section 2` view (the one that you're pointing to) and choose Place Callout Block ➪ `callout bubble-left arrow`. At the prompt, pick ❶, shown in Figure 26.23. The fields in the callout block show the correct view and sheet numbers.

 9. If you have a printer or plotter available, click the Sheet List tab. Select the Basement Floor Plan and Exterior Sections sheets. Click the Sheet Selections button and choose Create. Name the selection **basement-exterior sections** and click OK.

10. Choose Publish ➪ Publish to Plotter. The two sheets are plotted.

Note

If you have any difficulty plotting/printing, you may need to change the page setup to point to your plotter or printer. ∎

11. To create a table that lists all the sheets, first create a new sheet. On the Sheet List tab, right-click the sheet set name and choose New Sheet. Number it 0 and name it Index Sheet. Delete the 0 from the filename and click OK.

12. Double-click the new sheet's name to open it.

13. Right-click the sheet set name and choose Insert Sheet List Table. From the Table Style Name drop-down list, choose Sheet Set List. (This table style was saved with the template.) The Show Subheader check box should be checked. In the Title Text box, type **AB26-f Sheets**. For the column settings, set up the following columns. If necessary, click Add to add a column.

Sheet Number	Sheet No.
Sheet Title	Sheet Name
Drawing Author	By

14. Click OK to return to your drawing. Pick an insertion point for the table.

15. Save and close any open drawings.

Organizing Your Drawings

Some offices keep track of thousands of drawings. You must not only track your drawings' names and other properties, but also make sure that you don't lose them! Archiving and finding drawings are important procedures in any CAD environment.

Archiving drawings

You should use the Autosave feature to regularly save a backup of the drawing to the hard drive. The default time is set to 10 minutes, but automatic backups can still be useful. Choose Application Button ⇨ Options, click the Open and Save tab, and change the Automatic Save setting. Click OK. Of course, you shouldn't rely on Autosave; instead, save your drawing frequently by clicking the Save button on the Quick Access Toolbar.

The Autosave time counts from the most recent time you saved your drawing. Therefore, if you manually save more often than every 10 minutes, the feature doesn't create an Autosave file.

Backing up to the hard drive doesn't provide sufficient security. Hard drives can fail. Every time you exit AutoCAD or AutoCAD LT, you should back up every drawing that you worked on to some type of external storage medium. Backing up drawings for storage is called *archiving*.

On the DVD

On the DVD, I include an AutoLISP program, `save2d.lsp`, which backs up to the `d:` drive without leaving your drawing. (You can change it to back up to any drive.) This enables you to back up while working on a drawing. See the `Software\Chapter 01` folder of the DVD. This program works with AutoCAD only. ∎

You'll probably want to invest in one of the many types of removable backup systems. These come in six main types:

- **Tape drives** (internal or external) are cheap and good for entire hard-drive backups.
- **Disk cartridge drives** offer the convenience of a floppy disk but with more capacity.
- **Read/write DVD-ROM or DVD drives** enable you to write to a DVD-ROM or DVD.
- **Flash drives** are easy to use, and you can take them home with you because they're so small.
- **External hard drives** can back up your entire hard drive, and you can take them with you if you travel or need to take them off-site.
- **Optical drives** have the longest life (at least 30 years) and resist accidental erasure.

If your drawings are *really* important to you, back them up twice and store one backup set off-site. This way, if some disaster strikes your office, you haven't lost everything. Remote backup services provide this type of archiving for you, and you can access your files through the Internet.

The secret to backing up is to create a schedule and then stick to it. For example, you may do a complete hard-drive backup once a week, and do drawing backups at the end of each day. Many software backup programs exist that let you choose what you want to back up and reduce the process to the click of a button. Each situation is different, but take the time to think about your needs, create a system, and let everybody know about it. Then do it.

Finding drawings

Let's say your client calls and says, "I want to see the apartment building on Fourth Street that you did three years ago." How do you find the drawing? One low-tech way is to keep a book of 8½ × 11" plots. Using the PUBLISH command (which I explain in Chapter 28), you can plot out a week's drawings overnight and put them in a book. Amazingly, it doesn't take that long to leaf through even a few hundred pages. (You usually have *some* idea of when you did the drawing.)

Tip

Use the PLOTSTAMP command to label each drawing. Or place the drawing name and date written in large text on a separate layer in the drawing. Set the Plot property of the layer to Not Plottable while you work and for regular plotting. Set it to Plottable for your batch plots. Then even when it is reduced, you'll know the drawing name when you look at the drawing in the book. ■

A number of third-party drawing management programs are available. Some of these enable you to view and manage drawings created in other CAD programs as well. Some also manage workflow by letting you route drawings to team members.

Here's a short selection of the many drawing management programs that are available:

- **AutoEDMS.** www.acssoftware.com
- **Synergis-Adept.** www.synergissoftware.com/
- **Blue Cielo.** www.cyco.com
- **Columbus.** www.oasys-software.com

You can store and manage drawings online. Web-based services, such as Autodesk Buzzsaw (www.buzzsaw.com), let you store drawings online, view them, mark them up, organize and track them, and access them.

Before backing up drawings, purge any unused layers, blocks, text styles, and so on to reduce file size. (I cover the PURGE command in Chapter 11.)

If you know that a drawing is on the hard drive, then you can use the Find function from within AutoCAD or AutoCAD LT. Click Open on the Quick Access Toolbar. In the Select File dialog box, choose Tools ⇨ Find to open the Find dialog box, as shown in Figure 26.24. Use the Name & Location tab to set criteria according to the filename, file type, and location. Use the Date Modified tab to set criteria by the date that the file was saved.

Tip

You can use the Windows' Search feature to search for text inside drawings. ■

To search for drawings with the Windows' Search feature, choose Start ⇨ Search in Windows XP. In the Search window, enter the word or phrase that you want to look for in the Containing Text text box, and click Search Now. In Windows Vista or Windows 7, open Windows Explorer and use the Search box in the upper-right corner. Using this technique, you can find not only MText and other text objects but also names of layers and other named objects that match your search word or phrase.

FIGURE 26.24

You can use the Find dialog box to set criteria for finding drawings.

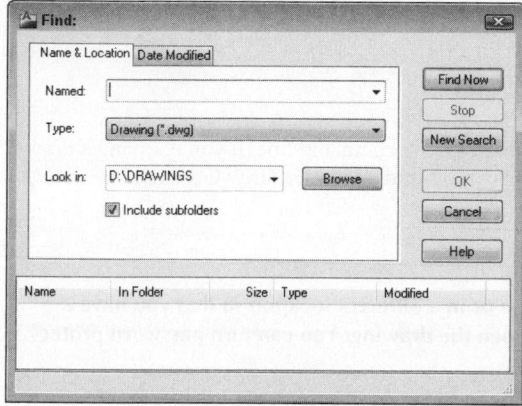

Specifying drawing properties

You can specify drawing properties that you can use in the DesignCenter and even in Windows Explorer. These properties are therefore available to people who can access your drawings but who don't have AutoCAD or AutoCAD LT.

To specify drawing properties, choose Application Button ⇨ Drawing Utilities ⇨ Drawing Properties to open the Properties dialog box.

On the Summary tab, you can specify a title, subject, author, and keywords. You can also write comments. At the bottom of the dialog box, you can specify a base for relative hyperlinks in the drawing. For example, you could use www.companyname.com as the base. AutoCAD or AutoCAD LT would then attach this base to the beginning of links in the drawing.

You can also use the Custom tab to create custom properties and give them values. This lets you create a simple database of your drawings that you can search by using the DesignCenter's Find dialog box. When you're done, click OK.

To access a drawing's properties in Windows Explorer, navigate to the drawing and right-click it. Choose Properties from the shortcut menu.

AutoCAD Only

The Express Tools contain a command, PROPULATE (on the command line, type propulate ↵), which automatically creates or updates Property data for one or more drawings. ■

Maintaining Security

In these days of collaboration and interconnectivity, maintaining security is an important issue. Two features help you to keep your designs secure: password protection and digital signatures.

Password protection

Password protection ensures that unauthorized people don't open your drawings. You create a password when you save a drawing.

AutoCAD Only

AutoCAD LT does not offer password protection. ■

To create a password for a drawing, type **securityoptions** ↵ on the command line. If you're saving a drawing for the first time, you can also click the Tools drop-down list and choose Security Options. The Security Options dialog box opens.

Caution

Before adding a password, save the drawing under another name or in a different location so that you have a copy. If you lose or forget the password, you won't be able to open the drawing. You can turn password protection off for network installations of AutoCAD. ■

To password-protect a drawing:

1. Type a password in the text box.
2. If you also want to encrypt drawing properties that identify the drawing, such as the title, author, subject, and keywords, check the Encrypt Drawing Properties check box.
3. Click OK.
4. The Confirm Password dialog box appears. Retype the password.
5. Click OK.

You can also change or remove a password:

1. Open the Security Options dialog box.
2. Type a new password or delete the current password. Click OK.
3. If you type a new password, reconfirm the password and click OK.

The dialog box displays the current encryption type. To specify a different encryption, click Advanced Options. Choose a new encryption type from the list and a key length, and then click OK.

When a password-protected drawing is opened, the Password dialog box appears. To open the drawing, type the password and click OK.

Digital signatures

A digital signature uses software that confirms who signed the drawing and that it has not been changed, as well as nonrepudiation (so that signers cannot claim that they never signed the drawing). To use a digital signature, you need to purchase a digital ID. You can use digital IDs in both AutoCAD and AutoCAD LT.

Generally, you would use a digital signature when you send a drawing to someone else. That person can then verify that the drawing is from you and has not been changed. If the person sends the drawing back to you, you can verify that the person has not changed the drawing, because changing the drawing invalidates the digital signature.

To attach a digital signature to a drawing, follow these steps:

1. Choose Application Button ➪ Options and click the Open and Save tab. Click Security Options and then click the Digital Signature tab.

2. Check the Attach Digital Signature after Saving Drawing check box and choose a digital signature.

3. To place a time stamp on the drawing, choose one of the options from the Get Time Stamp From drop-down list.

4. To add a comment (that appears when the drawing is opened), type the text in the Comment text box.

5. Click OK.

When a digitally signed drawing is opened, the Digital Signature Contents dialog box appears, verifying the digital signature and the fact that the drawing has not been changed since it was signed. Click Close to close the dialog box.

Note that making any changes to the drawing invalidates the digital ID. If you make changes or try to save a drawing with an attached digital signature, a message appears asking you whether you want to continue. When you re-open the drawing, the Digital Signature Contents dialog box appears, displaying the fact that the digital signature is invalid.

A drawing with a valid digital signature has a checkmark attached to its icon in Windows Explorer. The drawing itself also sports an icon in the status bar.

Note

Users who don't have the Digital Signature feature can download the Digital Signature Verifier, a free application to verify digital signatures on signed drawings. The Digital Signature Verifier is available from the Autodesk Web site at `http://usa.autodesk.com/adsk/servlet/item?siteID=123112&id=877495`. **(You can also go to** `www.autodesk.com` **and do a search on Digital Signature Verifier.)** ■

Keeping Track of Referenced Files

A drawing references several types of outside files, and you often need to keep track of these files, especially when you send a drawing to someone else or move it to another computer. Also, the referenced files may be moved, even if the drawing stays in the same place. Without these outside files, the drawing is not complete.

AutoCAD Only

AutoCAD LT does not include the Reference Manager. ■

Outside files include the following:

- Other drawings (xrefs, DWF, PDF, and DGN underlays)
- Text fonts
- Shape files
- Images
- Plot configurations

The Reference Manager not only lists referenced files, but also enables you to change saved reference paths so that the drawing can find the needed files. You don't even need to open the AutoCAD drawing, because the Reference Manager is a stand-alone application.

Cross-Reference

The External References palette helps you manage xrefs. For more information, see Chapter 19. ■

To open the Reference Manager, choose Start ➪ [All] Programs ➪ Autodesk ➪ AutoCAD 2011 ➪ Reference Manager. The Reference Manager is shown in Figure 26.25.

FIGURE 26.25

The Reference Manager.

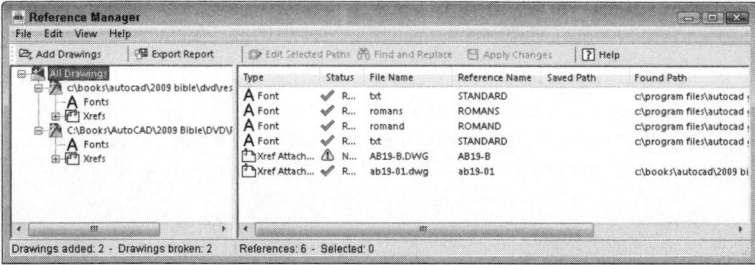

To add drawings to the Reference Manager, click Add Drawings and select the drawings. If a drawing has xrefs, you see a message asking whether you want to add the xrefs. To add them, click Yes.

The left pane of the Reference Manager contains a tree view of the drawings that you've added and external references, if any. The right pane is a Reference list and displays the specific external files associated with the added files. You can choose View ➪ Options in the Reference Manager to customize how the Reference Manager displays files.

Note

Reference Manager does not find text fonts that are not used in a text style, TrueType fonts that are not saved in the Windows `Fonts` folder, OLE links, hyperlinks, database file links, PMP files, and external references to URLs on the Web. ■

To modify the path of an external reference so that a drawing can find it, follow these steps:

1. Close any drawings or files that you might need to access.
2. Choose a drawing in the left pane.
3. Right-click the external reference in the Reference list that you want to change, and choose Edit Selected Paths. (You can also choose Edit Selected Paths from the Reference Manager toolbar.)

Tip

You can also choose Find and Replace to change all references that use a certain saved path, and replace them with a new path. Use this feature when you have a large number of drawings that need paths to changed referenced files. ■

4. Type in a new path, or use the Ellipsis button to browse to the location. Click OK.
5. From the Reference Manager toolbar, choose Apply Changes. A summary message appears to confirm that the drawing has been updated.

To create a list of references, choose Export Report. In the Export Report dialog box, choose the file type that you want to create from the Files of Type drop-down list. You can create the following file types:

- Comma-separated values report file (`*.csv`)
- Extensible Markup Language report file (`*.xml`)
- Microsoft Excel Workbook (`*.xls`)

Choose a name and a location for the file and then click Save.

AutoCAD Only

The Express Tools contain a command, REDIR (on the command line, type redir ↵), that redefines paths for xrefs, images, shapes, and fonts. ■

Handling Errors and Crashes

Although AutoCAD 2011 and AutoCAD LT 2011 are stable, nothing can eliminate the occasional crash. Knowing how to re-open a drawing after a crash can save hours of work.

Taking care of temporary files

When AutoCAD or AutoCAD LT is loaded, it opens one or more temporary files as part of its normal functioning. Note the following two points regarding these files:

- You need to leave room on your hard drive for these files — 50MB is a good starting point.
- Never erase current temporary files if you're on a network, because someone else might be using them.

Caution

Never erase temporary files (they have an extension of `.ac$`) while AutoCAD or AutoCAD LT is open. Normally, they're erased when you close a drawing. Others are erased when you close the program. ■

However, if the program or your entire computer crashes, you may be left with one or more `.ac$` files. A good guideline for erasing `.ac$` files is to only erase those from yesterday or earlier. Leave today's alone.

Tip

If you don't see the date and time of the files in Windows Explorer, choose View ➪ Details. ■

You can also specify where you want these temporary files. You might want to place them on a hard drive with more room. If you're on a network, you might want to place them on your local drive so that there is less traffic back and forth on the network. To find or change the current location, follow these steps:

1. Choose Application Button ➪ Options. Click the Files tab.
2. Click the plus sign next to Temporary Drawing File Location to display the current location.
3. If you want to change the location, click Browse.
4. In the Browse for Folder list, find and choose the desired folder and click OK.
5. Click OK to close the Options dialog box.

Repairing corrupted drawing files

The most common cause for a corrupted drawing file is a program crash, but power surges and system crashes can also be causes. If AutoCAD or AutoCAD LT detects an error in a file during loading, it attempts to fix the problem automatically. In many cases, it is successful.

When it isn't, you can try the AUDIT and RECOVER commands. These commands search the database for errors and try to fix them. If they cannot fix an error, they simply move on, letting you recover at least part of the file.

If you have a drawing open and see an error message that AutoCAD or AutoCAD LT can't read the file or part of it, follow these steps:

1. Choose Application Button ⇨ Drawing Utilities ⇨ Audit.
2. At the `Fix any errors detected? [Yes/No] <N>:` prompt, type **y** ↵ to fix any errors.
3. Watch the screen as it displays messages for errors.

Use RECOVER when you can't even load the drawing. Follow these steps:

1. Open a new drawing.
2. Choose Application Button ⇨ Drawing Utilities ⇨ Recover ⇨ Recover.
3. In the Select File dialog box, choose the corrupted drawing file and click Open. The recovery process starts and displays the results in the Text window.

Tip

The RECOVERALL command lets you select a drawing and run RECOVER on that drawing as well as all associated xref files. (See Chapter 19 for more on xrefs.) ∎

The DWGCHECK system variable controls how your drawings open when they have errors. Look up this system variable in Help to find a setting that gives you the information and control that you need. Here are some other tips for opening a recalcitrant drawing:

- Open a new drawing and choose Insert tab ⇨ Block panel ⇨ Insert. Click Browse and insert the problem drawing as a block. (See Chapter 18 for more information on blocks.) Then use the AUDIT command.
- Open a new drawing and choose Insert tab ⇨ Reference panel ⇨ Attach. Locate and attach the problem drawing as an external reference. (See Chapter 19 for more information on external references.) Then use the AUDIT command.
- If the drawing crashes just when it looks like it has almost loaded, try again; however, this time, press Esc repeatedly until the loading is complete. This procedure aborts the regeneration of the drawing, which may be causing the crash due to corrupt objects. Then use the AUDIT command.
- If you can open the drawing but objects are not displayed, try the following:
  - Choose Application Button ⇨ Save As and save it as a new drawing.
  - Use the WBLOCK command to save the drawing as a new file.
  - Save the drawing as a DXF file. (See Chapter 27 for more on the DXF file format.)
  - Choose Application Button ⇨ Save As or save as a DXF format, but to an earlier version of AutoCAD or AutoCAD LT.

Thanks to Darren Young of Minnesota CADWorks, Inc., (www.mcwi.com) for these suggestions.

Using backup drawings

If you can't repair a drawing, perhaps you have an archived copy that you can use. If not, AutoCAD and AutoCAD LT automatically create backup drawings that have the same name as your drawings, but with a .bak filename extension. You can change the extension to .dwg and open it. You may also find one of the .ac$ drawings. You can also try changing the extension of this file to .dwg.

Tip

If your computer doesn't show filename extensions for BAK and AC$ drawings, open Windows Explorer and choose Tools ⇨ Folder Options. Click the File Types tab. Choose BAK from the list of extensions. Then click the Advanced button and check the Always Show Extension check box. Click OK. Do the same for the AC$ extension. Click OK (or Close). In Windows Vista and Windows 7, choose Start ⇨ Control Panel ⇨ Classic View ⇨ Folder Options. Click View tab, and clear Hide Extensions for Known File Types. Click OK to display the file extensions for all files. ■

If you want to troubleshoot a persistent crash, try turning on the log file. Choose Application Button ⇨ Options and choose the Open and Save tab. Check Maintain a Log File. This log file lists all your activity and can be used to try to determine what actions caused a crash. You can also customize the log file's location by using the Files tab of the Options dialog box. In the same location, you can turn on or off the saving of backups.

AutoCAD Only

The Express Tools contain a command, MOVEBAK (on the command line, type movebak ↵), that moves backup files (*.bak) to a folder that you specify, and thereafter saves the backup files in that folder every time you save your drawing. ■

Recovering from a crash

Yes, AutoCAD does occasionally crash. You may see a message with a Continue button, which you can click to try to continue working on your drawing. If not, the Drawing Recovery Manager tries to make recovering from a crash easy by displaying available backup drawings for you. You see a Drawing Recovery message explaining the process of recovering a crashed drawing.

The Drawing Recovery Manager palette then opens, where you see a list of drawings that are available for recovery. You can select one to see it in the drawing area. You can easily and quickly choose any one of these and open them to see which one you want to continue working with. AutoCAD automatically deletes old drawing recovery files.

After a crash, the AutoCAD Error Report window opens so that you can send information to Autodesk about the crash. This information helps Autodesk design AutoCAD to be more stable.

Managing Drawings from Prior Releases

When you upgrade to a new release, you need to understand how to work with drawings from earlier releases. Also, you may need to send drawings to clients or colleagues who have an earlier release. AutoCAD 2011 uses the same format as 2010, and the same goes for AutoCAD LT. Therefore, AutoCAD 2011 and AutoCAD LT 2011 save in the 2010 format. You cannot open a 2011 drawing in releases 2009 and earlier. You can save your AutoCAD 2011 drawings in the following earlier drawing formats:

- AutoCAD 2007/AutoCAD LT 2007 Drawing (*.dwg). This format includes AutoCAD and AutoCAD LT 2008 and 2009.
- AutoCAD 2004/AutoCAD LT 2004 Drawing (*.dwg). This format includes AutoCAD and AutoCAD LT 2005 and 2006.
- AutoCAD 2000/LT 2000 Drawing (*.dwg). This format includes 2000, 2000i, and 2002.
- AutoCAD R14/LT98/LT97. This is the earliest version you can save to in DWG format.
- AutoCAD R12/LT 2 DXF (*.dxf). To go back earlier than AutoCAD R14/AutoCAD LT 97, you need to save to DXF format. See Chapter 27 for more about the DXF format.

Choose Application Button ⇨ Save As and choose the file type in the Save As Type drop-down list. Then click Save.

Summary

In this chapter, I covered various methods for managing drawings. You read about the following:

- Using the DesignCenter to access drawing components
- Using tool palettes to access drawings, blocks, and hatches
- Maintaining CAD standards, including checking a drawing against a standards drawing and translating layers
- Understanding the Communication Center
- Renaming named objects
- Working with sheet sets
- Organizing your drawings, including archiving drawings, finding them, and setting properties for them
- Maintaining security of your drawings with a password and digital signatures
- Using the Reference Manager to keep track of external files referenced in a drawing
- Handling errors and crashes
- Managing drawings from prior releases

In the next chapter I cover how to use AutoCAD or AutoCAD LT with other applications.

Working with Other Applications

Your drawing is not a world unto itself. Many times, you need to work with files or data from other applications. Here are some possibilities:

- Working for a client who uses another CAD program
- Placing an image of a logo into your titleblock
- Inserting a drawing into a report
- Inserting a spreadsheet into your drawing
- Using a satellite photo as a basis to create a map

You have several ways of working with other applications:

- You can import another file format so that the entire file is brought into your drawing.
- You can export to another file format so that the entire drawing can be imported into another application.
- You can export to an image format that others can view.
- You can import a *raster* image (bitmap) without changing any file format. A raster image is made up of dots, called *pixels,* as opposed to vectors. AutoCAD and AutoCAD LT are vector programs.
- You can import, or export to, a DXF file, which is a way of interchanging drawings between AutoCAD or AutoCAD LT and other CAD programs.

As you can imagine, the possibilities are endless. This chapter explains how to work with other applications.

Importing and Exporting Other File Formats

You can export to several other file formats, thereby enabling you to save the file in another format. You can also import several formats. This section explains how to do both.

Exporting drawings

You usually export objects to an image format and then use that format in another application. You may also export a drawing to import it into another CAD program. The method you use depends on the type of format that you want. Table 27.1 shows the file formats that AutoCAD and AutoCAD LT can create. Except as noted, you are prompted to select objects to export.

TABLE 27.1

Export File Formats

Format	Description
WMF	Windows Metafile Format — a Windows vector format.
ACIS	A solid modeling file format stored as `.sat` files, in text (ASCII) form (AutoCAD only).
STL	Exports a single solid in a format usable with stereolithography (AutoCAD only).
BMP	Windows bitmap — a raster format.
EPS	Encapsulated PostScript — a format used by certain printers to create high-quality text and images. Exports all objects (AutoCAD only).
DXF	Drawing Interchange Format is a text format for CAD drawings that most CAD programs accept. You can choose from Releases 2010, 2007, 2004, 2000, and 12 DXF file formats. Exports the entire drawing.
DXB	Another format for transferring CAD drawings, but in binary format (not ASCII). Used less often than the DXF format.
DWF/DWFx	Design Web Format — a format for placing a drawing on a Web site.
DGN	Format of Bentley Microstation drawings. You can export the entire drawing as a Version 7 or 8 DGN file.
FBX	Interchange file that allows you to share 2D and 3D objects between multiple programs. Useful when working with multiple Autodesk products and sharing data between them, such as exchanging models between AutoCAD and Autodesk 3ds Max.
JPG	Joint Photographic Expert Group — a raster (bitmap) format commonly used on the Web. It can be compressed, but will lose some detail. Often used for photographs because it supports many colors.
TIF	Tagged Image File Format — a raster (bitmap) format often used for scanned images. Provides good quality.
PNG	Portable Network Graphics — a raster (bitmap) format that supports many colors and also compresses well without losing detail. It also supports transparency.
PDF	Adobe Acrobat Portable Document Format.

Cross-Reference

For more information on the DWF and DWFx file formats, see the next chapter. The DWF and DWFx formats are a way to share your drawings with others either directly or on the Internet. ∎

Exporting to DXF format

The DXF (drawing interchange file) format is a text file that contains all the information in a 2D drawing. Because most CAD programs accept this format, you can export to DXF and send the file to someone else who can then import it into another CAD program. Figure 27.1 shows the part of a DXF file that defines a line. Not only are objects defined, but all layers, linetypes, and other settings are defined as well. The file lists codes that specify a certain type of data (for example, the X coordinate of a line's endpoint), followed by the values for the codes (for example, 7.55).

FIGURE 27.1

Most CAD programs accept the DXF file format.

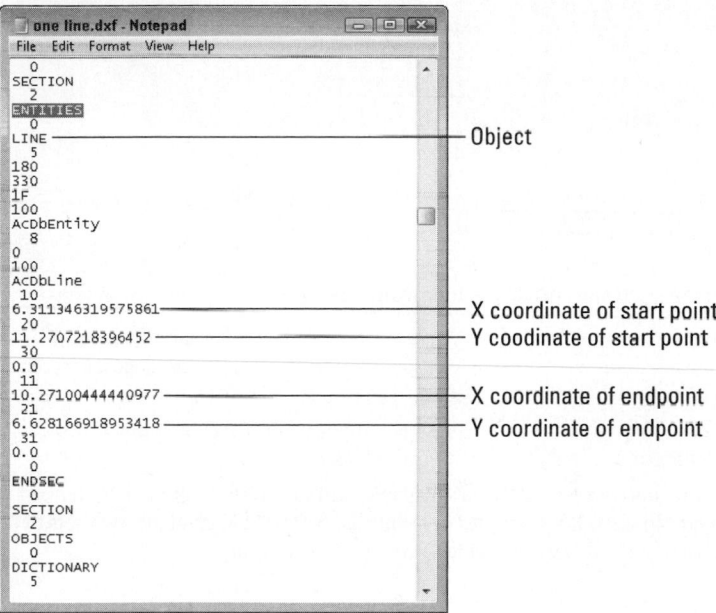

To create a DXF file, choose Application Button ➪ Save As. Choose one of the DXF formats in the Files of Type drop-down list. You can save in DXF formats for Releases 12, 2000 (which includes Releases 2000i and 2002), 2004 (which includes Releases 2005 and 2006), 2007 (which includes Releases 2008 and 2009), and 2010 (which includes Release 2011). Click Save.

Exporting to DGN format

Some users work with companies that use Bentley Microstation, another CAD product. It creates DGN files. The DGNEXPORT command allows you to translate your drawing file (and any xrefs) according to your preferences. (I cover xrefs in Chapter 19.) To export a drawing to DGN format, choose Application Button ⇨ Export ⇨ DGN to open the Export DGN File dialog box.

Choose the version you want from the Files of Type drop-down list, choose a location and filename, and click Save. The Export DGN Settings dialog box opens, as shown in Figure 27.2.

FIGURE 27.2

The Export DGN Settings dialog box lets you fine-tune your DGN export.

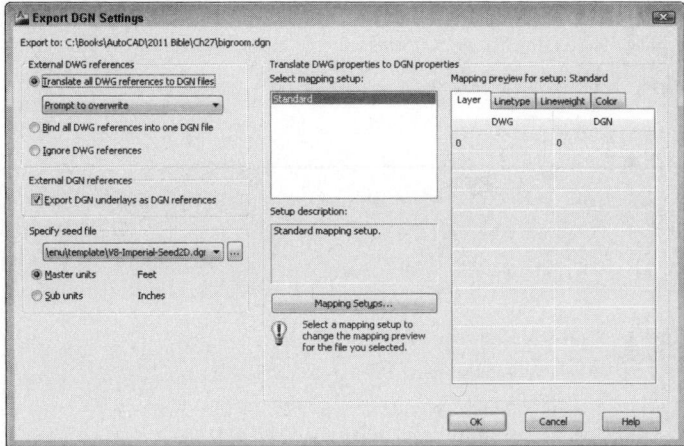

In the Export DGN Settings dialog box, you can specify the following settings:

- **External DWG References.** You specify whether you want to translate external references in AutoCAD DWG format into DGN references. You can keep them as external references, combine them into one drawing, or ignore them.

- **External DGN References.** You may have DGN drawings in your AutoCAD drawing as underlays. You can choose whether or not to include DGN underlays.

- **Specify Seed File.** You can choose a seed file from available samples in the Template folder or from another location. You can also choose master or subunits. A DGN file can have two sets of measurement units ¾ master and sub. Choose which units you want to use.

Note

A seed file for a DGN file is similar to a drawing template file. It contains settings such as the measurement units (imperial or metric), the Origin, and whether the file is 2D or 3D. ∎

- **Translate DWG Properties to DGN Properties.** You can specify *mapping setups* to define how layers, linetypes, lineweights, and colors are translated during the export. The default setup is called Standard. To create a new mapping setup, click the Mapping Setups button to open the DGN Mapping Setups dialog box. Click New to create a new mapping setup. Name the setup and click Continue to complete the process.

You can check the results of a setup by clicking the four tabs in the Export DGN Settings dialog box.

Keep in mind that some objects and properties are not translated properly. Examples are:

- 3D solids and surfaces
- Annotative properties
- Layer property overrides by viewport
- Custom AutoCAD objects (such as those created by related Autodesk products or third-party applications)
- Objects with Z values other than 0, when you use a 2D seed file

Exporting to PDF format

Many AutoCAD and AutoCAD LT users like to use the DWF format to share drawings when they don't want to send the drawing itself — whether for security reasons or because a colleague doesn't have the program. DWF files display the drawing in a free viewer or on the Web, and they support zooming, panning, layers, named views, and so on. I cover the DWF format in Chapter 28.

However, non-CAD users, such as clients, may not want to install software to view DWF files, or they may simply feel more comfortable with an Adobe Acrobat PDF (Portable Document Format) file. The Adobe Acrobat Reader, which is the viewer for PDF files, is widely available and free.

Note

The DWFx format creates files whose 2D data conform to Microsoft's XPS format. This format is an image format similar to PDF. Windows Vista and Windows 7 come with an XPS reader, so people with either version of Windows will be able to view the new DWF files without a separate reader. People with Windows XP and Microsoft .NET Framework 3.0 will also be able to view DWFx files. ■

To export to the PDF format, you can use the PLOT command and plot to a file by using a plotter configuration (PC3) file. (See Chapter 17 and Appendix A for more information.) Follow these steps:

1. Display the drawing that you want to export.
2. Start the PLOT command.
3. In the Printer/Plotter section of the Plot dialog box, click the Name drop-down list and choose DWG To PDF.pc3.
4. To adjust PDF settings, click Properties and make changes in the Plotter Configuration Editor. For example, you can merge overlapping lines. Click OK, and then choose whether you want the changes to apply to the current plot or to all plots using that configuration file.
5. Make any other adjustments that you want to make in the Plot dialog box and click OK.
6. In the Browse for Plot File dialog box, name the PDF file (or accept the default) and choose a location.
7. Click Save.

Tip

Another option is to choose Output tab ⇨ Export to DWF/PDF panel ⇨ Export drop-down menu ⇨ PDF. This starts the EXPORTPDF command. The Save As PDF dialog box opens, offering a number of options. For example, you can click the Options button and choose whether to include layer information, and password-protect the file. ■

When you're done, you can view your drawing in the Adobe Acrobat Reader.

Cross-Reference

The PUBLISH command, covered in Chapter 28, can also create single-sheet or multi-sheet PDF files. You can publish from a sheet set, as I explain in Chapter 26, and create a multi-sheet PDF file of the sheets. Finally, you can insert a PDF as an underlay; for more information, see Chapter 19. ■

Exporting to other file formats

To export to JPG, PNG, or TIF format, use the JPGOUT, PNGOUT, or TIFOUT command, respectively, on the command line. Then choose a folder, click Save, and select objects at the prompt.

When you want to export a drawing to another file format, whether to create an image file or import that file into another application, you export the drawing. WMF, which is a vector image file, is probably the most commonly used format. You can also export to a BMP file. To export a drawing to another format (except for JPG, PNG, and TIF), follow these steps:

1. Choose Application Button ➪ Export ➪ Other Formats to open the Export Data dialog box.
2. Choose the file format that you want in the Files of Type drop-down list.
3. Find the desired folder by using the Save In drop-down list and the Folder box, and change the filename in the File Name text box if desired.
4. Click Save.

Note

You can also export to 3D DWF format (AutoCAD only). See Chapter 28 for more information on DWF files. ■

Controlling the display of exported WMF files

The WMFBKGND system variable controls the background of WMF files that you export, whether using the Export Data dialog box, copying and pasting, or dragging and dropping. When the value of this system variable is Off (the default), the background color of the file is transparent, so that it doesn't interfere with the background on which it is pasted. You can set it to On so that the background is the same as that of the drawing background.

The WMFFOREGND system variable works in tandem with the WMFBKGND system variable. It controls the foreground (line) color of objects when you export WMF files. WMFFOREGND takes effect only when you set WMFBKGND to 0, which makes the background color transparent. A value of 0, the default, swaps foreground and background colors, if necessary, to make the foreground color (the objects) darker than the background color. A value of 1 does the opposite — the foreground color is lighter than the background color.

On the DVD

The drawing used in the following exercise on exporting a WMF file, ab27-a.dwg, is in the Drawings folder on the DVD. ■

STEPS: Exporting a WMF File

1. Open ab27-a.dwg from the DVD.
2. Save the file as ab27-01.dwg in your AutoCAD Bible folder. You can see it in Figure 27.3.

The Easy Cotton Mills logo.

3. Choose Application Button ⇨ Export ⇨ Other Formats. The Files of Type drop-down list should say Metafile (*.wmf). The filename automatically reads ab27-01.wmf.

4. If necessary, locate your AutoCAD Bible folder. Click Save.

5. At the Select objects: prompt, make a window around the red rectangle to include all three objects. End object selection to end the command and create the WMF file.

Importing files

To import WMF, SAT, or DGN files, choose Insert tab ⇨ Import panel ⇨ Import in AutoCAD only. These are the WMFIN, ACISIN, and DGNIMPORT commands respectively. If you are using AutoCAD LT, you need to use the appropriate command on the command line. Find the file in the dialog box and click Open. Generally, the command line then prompts you for an insertion point, X and Y scale factors, and a rotation angle, just as for block insertion.

In the following exercise, you practice importing a WMF file.

On the DVD

The file used in the following exercise on importing a WMF file, ab27-01.wmf, is in the Results folder on the DVD. If you did the previous exercise, you can also find the file in your AutoCAD Bible folder. ∎

STEPS: Importing a WMF File

1. Open a new drawing by using the acad.dwt or acadlt.dwt template.

2. Save the file as ab27-02.dwg in your AutoCAD Bible folder.

3. Enter **wmfin** ↵ on the command line. From the Files of Type drop-down list, choose Metafile (*.wmf).

4. If you did the previous exercise, locate your AutoCAD Bible folder in the Import WMF dialog box. Choose ab27-01.wmf. If you didn't do the previous exercise, find ab27-01.wmf in the Results folder of the DVD. In the Import WMF dialog box, choose Tools ⇨ Options. Check Wire Frame (No Fills), uncheck Wide Lines, if necessary, and click OK. Click Open.

5. At the Specify insertion point or [Basepoint/Scale/X/Y/Z/Rotate]: prompt, pick any point near the top of your screen. Notice that the insertion point is at the top-left corner of the image.

6. Press Enter to accept the defaults for X and Y scales and rotation angle. Notice that you've lost the solid fill in the logo. The red rectangle came in fine. Also, you may see an added rectangle around the extents of the image where the extents of the screen were when the WMF file was created.

7. Pick the image. Notice that everything is selected with one grip at the insertion point. Choose Home tab ⇨ Modify panel ⇨ Explode.

8. Choose Home tab ⇨ Properties panel ⇨ List, and pick any part of the logo. Press Enter. Notice from the listing that the logo is now made up of polylines. Repeat the LIST command with the text. It has been converted to a TEXT object. (If the text was based on an SHX font, it would be converted to polylines.) Because WMF files convert to drawing objects, you can edit them, but they may require a good deal of cleanup to attain a pleasing result.

9. Start the WMFIN command, and select Metafile (*.wmf) from the Files of Type drop-down list. Choose ab27-01.wmf. Click Tools ⇨ Options to open the WMF In Options dialog box. This time, check Wide Lines, uncheck Wire Frame (No Fills), and click OK. In the Import WMF dialog box, click Open to import the file. Pick in a different location in your drawing, and accept the defaults.

10. Explode the inserted image. (You may have to pick it at its edge.) Erase the rectangle and the remaining line at the right. Now you have an image that is very close to the original. The text comes in with the Bookman Old Style font (or the font that you used — the same font as the original), although the spacing is not exact. Also, the logo now has its solid fill. It should look like Figure 27.4.

11. Save your drawing.

FIGURE 27.4

An imported WMF file.

Importing a DGN file

If someone sends you a file in DGN (Bentley Microstation) format, you can import this file by choosing Application Button ⇨ Open ⇨ DGN (the DGNIMPORT command). In the Import DGN File dialog box, select the file, and click Open. The Import DGN Settings dialog box opens, where you can specify the following settings:

- **Select a design model from the DGN file.** A design model is like AutoCAD's model space. A DGN drawing may have multiple model spaces. You can only import one at a time; if you need more than one, you need to import them separately.

- **External DGN References.** You can choose to ignore any xrefs, translate all xrefs into individual files, or keep the references as DGNs and use them as underlays. (See Chapter 19 for more information about DGN underlays.)

- **Conversion units.** The DGN has a master unit and a subunit (such as feet and inches or meters and millimeters). The dialog box displays the units, and you choose which one to import as one unit. For example, if you choose to import the file using master units of feet, it will appear $\frac{1}{12}$ the size of the same drawing using subunits (inches). Be sure to measure and make sure that you choose the right units.

- **Explode text nodes to text elements.** Text nodes are multiple lines of text in one object, such as AutoCAD's Mtext. Text elements would be single lines of text, such as Dtext. If you want to keep the file looking the same as the original, especially around curves and arcs, then you should check this option.
- **Translate DGN properties to DWG properties.** You specify how layers, linetypes, lineweights, and colors will appear after import. You can save these property settings for use during both import and export of DGN files.

Click OK when you're done, to import the drawing.

Cross-Reference
You can attach PDF, DWF, DWFx, and DGN files (Microstation drawings) to your drawing. When you attach a file, you are not importing it; rather, you are just displaying it along with your drawing. These files are similar to xrefs, so I discuss them in Chapter 19, where I cover xrefs. ■

Inserting a DXF file
If someone sends you a file in DXF format, it probably contains a drawing that was created in another CAD program. You can open that drawing in AutoCAD or AutoCAD LT. You can import a DXF file in two ways:

- To import a DXF file into a new drawing, choose Application Button ➪ Open, choose DXF in the Files of Type drop-down list, choose the DXF file, and click Open.
- To insert a DXF file into an existing drawing, choose Insert tab ➪ Block panel ➪ Insert. In the Insert dialog box, click Browse. Then choose DXF in the Files of Type drop-down list, choose the DXF file, and click Open.

Working with Raster Images

You can easily attach scanned images, digital photographs, and other image files into your drawings. You can use these images to insert a logo, show a photo or artist's rendering of your model, and for many other uses. Although raster (bitmap) images are generally much larger files than vector drawings, you can easily zoom and pan throughout your drawing. You can usually plot these raster images, as well. Table 27.2 shows the raster formats that AutoCAD 2011 supports.

TABLE 27.2

Raster Formats Supported by AutoCAD 2011

File Type	File Extension	Comments
BMP	.bmp, .dib, .rle	Windows and OS/2 bitmap
CALS1	.gp4, .mil, .rst, .cg4, .cal, .cals	Mil-R-Raster 1
FLIC	.flc, .fli	Autodesk Animator FLIC
GeoSPOT	.bil	GeoSPOT (used in GIS applications); HDR and PAL files with correlation data must be in the same folder
IG4	.ig4	Image Systems Group 4

continued

TABLE 27.2	*(continued)*	
File Type	**File Extension**	**Comments**
JFIF or JPEG	`.jpg`	Joint Photographic Experts Group
PCX	`.pcx`	Paintbrush
PICT	`.pct, .pict`	Macintosh picture
PNG	`.png`	Portable Network Graphic
RLC	`.rlc`	Run-Length Compressed
TARGA	`.tga`	True Vision Raster-Based Data Format
TIF	`.tif, .tiff`	Tagged Image File Format

Attaching images

You can easily attach an image into your drawing and manipulate it in a number of ways. To attach an image, choose Insert tab ⇨ Reference panel ⇨ Attach to open the Select Reference File dialog box.

Locate the image that you want to attach and click Open. The Attach Image dialog box opens, as shown in Figure 27.5; this dialog box lets you specify how to attach the image. You can specify the insertion point, scale, and rotation in the dialog box or on-screen. This dialog box is very similar to the Insert dialog box that you use when inserting drawings and blocks. (See Chapter 18.)

Tip

You can specify a relative path (rather than the full path) for an image. A relative path stores only the relationship between the drawing and the image. Choose Relative Path from the Path Type drop-down list. If you put the image in the same folder as the drawing, only the drawing name is stored. Using a relative path and placing the image in the same folder as the drawing is ideal when you need to share drawings with people who don't have the same folder structure as you. ■

FIGURE 27.5

The Attach Image dialog box.

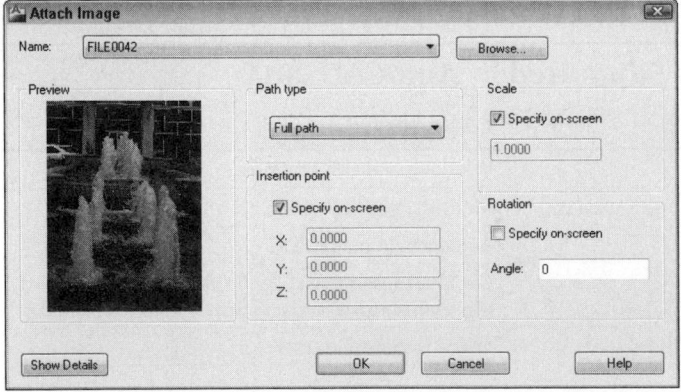

Click Show Details to open the bottom of the dialog box. Here the dialog box lists the resolution (number of pixels) per drawing unit and the size in pixels, as well as the size in drawing units. The Current AutoCAD Unit is based on the specification in the Units dialog box. (See Chapter 5 for more information.) This information is helpful in deciding how to scale an image. Click OK to insert the image.

Note

Raster images usually don't scale up very well. If you enlarge them too much, the image looks grainy. However, the higher the resolution, the better the image will look when enlarged. You can also use the DesignCenter to insert raster images, as described in Chapter 26. ■

AutoCAD Only

The Express Tools contain a command, IMAGEEDIT (enter imageedit ↵ on the command line), that opens a selected image in a specified image-editing application. Use the IMAGEAPP command to specify the editor that the IMAGEEDIT command should use to open the image. ■

Managing images

As with xrefs, you may need a way to keep track of your images, especially if you attach many of them. Choose Insert tab ⇨ Reference panel and click the dialog box launcher button on the right side of the panel's title bar to open the External References palette, as shown in Figure 27.6. The External References palette enables you to manage the images (as well as external drawing references, and PDF, DWF [and DWFx], and DGN underlays) in your drawing. You can attach images from this palette, as well.

New Feature

When you select an item in the External References palette, AutoCAD selects its corresponding reference in the drawing, and vice versa. You can turn off this behavior by setting the ERHIGHLIGHT system variable to 0. ■

FIGURE 27.6

The External References palette.

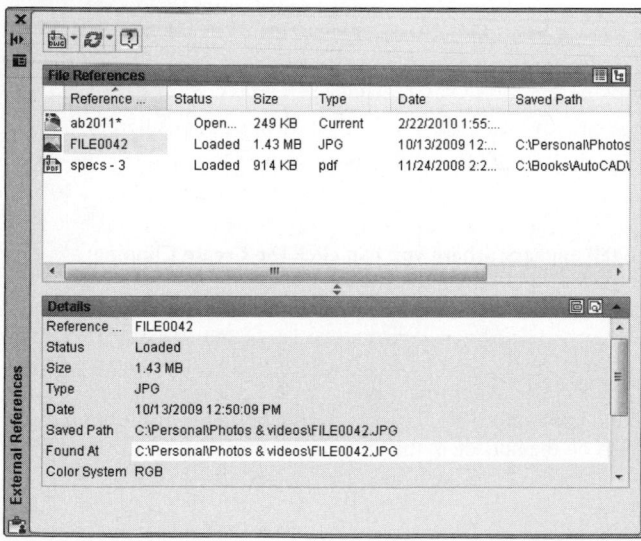

You can use the List View and Tree View buttons at the top-right corner of the File References pane to view your images as a *flat* list or a hierarchical (tree) format. Use the Details and Preview buttons at the top-right corner of the bottom pane to view either file details or a preview. Here are the other options:

- Choose **Attach Image** from the Attach drop-down list at the top of the palette (or right-click any item) to attach an image, opening the Select Reference dialog box (refer to Figure 27.5). You can also attach a drawing, DWF, DGN, or PDF file from this drop-down list.

- Right-click any item and choose **Detach** to delete it from your drawing and all references to it in the drawing database.

- Right-click any item and choose **Unload** to remove the display of the item but retain the reference to it. Later, you can reload the image to redisplay it.

- Right-click any item and choose **Reload** to redisplay an item after you've unloaded it or made changes to it.

Tip

You can attach rendered images that you've saved as PCX, JPG, JPEG, PNG, TIF, TGA, or BMP files. A great way to do this is to create a floating viewport in paper space for the rendered image, letting your clients see not only the regular drawing, but also the rendered result on one sheet of paper. (Figure 25.17 in Chapter 25 was created this way.) Remember that you can plot shaded and rendered images. See Chapter 17 for details. ∎

Clipping images

A powerful feature of AutoCAD lets you clip images just as you clip external references. Large images can slow down your drawing display. You may also simply find it distracting to see parts of an image that you don't need for your work. For example, if you attach an aerial photograph of a city block but want only one house, being able to clip around the house and not display the rest of the image is a great advantage.

Tip

You can use the same procedure described here to clip an xref (see Chapter 19), a PDF, a DWF (see Chapter 28), or a DGN file. ∎

To clip an image, follow these steps:

1. Attach an image.
2. Choose Insert tab ⇨ Reference panel ⇨ Clip (the CLIP command).
3. At the `Select Object to clip:` prompt, select the image. Pick the image at its border.
4. At the prompt, press Enter to accept the default of creating a new clipping boundary.

Tip

An alternative is to select the image first. The Image tab appears, where you can click the Create Clipping Boundary button. ∎

5. At the `Specify clipping boundary or select invert option [Select polyline/Polygonal/Rectangular/Invert clip] <Rectangular>:` prompt, press Enter to create a rectangular clip, choose Polygonal to create a multisided boundary, or Select Polyline to convert a closed polyline to a clipping boundary. You can also choose Invert Clip to invert the clipping of the image, showing the image that is on the outside of the boundary rather than on the inside.

- To use a closed polyline as a polygonal boundary, select the closed polyline that you want to use as the clipping boundary.

- For a rectangular boundary, pick a first point and the opposite corner to create the boundary.

- For a polygonal boundary, specify the first point and then use the `Specify next point or [Undo]:` prompt to pick points until you've completed the boundary. You can use the Undo option to undo the last pick, or the Close option (which appears after you pick three points) to close the final boundary. AutoCAD creates a rubber-band boundary as you pick points so that you can see the result. Press Enter when you're done.

Tip

You can modify a clipped image's boundary by using its grips. Select the clipped image to displays its grips. Use the square grips to resize the clipping boundary and click the arrow grip to invert the clipping boundary. ■

At the `Enter image clipping option [ON/OFF/Delete/New boundary] <New>:` prompt, you can also use the following options:

- Choose ON to turn on a boundary that you previously turned off.

- Choose OFF to turn off a boundary and redisplay the entire image.

- Choose Delete to delete the clipping boundary.

Note

Images are 2D objects. The clipping boundary must be parallel to the plane of the image. ■

Controlling image display

You can control several aspects of image display, using the commands detailed in this section. Control the image display to adjust the properties that control how the image looks.

Image display

The ADJUST command lets you change the brightness, contrast, and fade of an image. Select the image by picking its border. The Image tab appears. In the Adjust panel, use the Contrast, Fade, and Brightness sliders to adjust the image.

You can also adjust an image's display by selecting an image, right-clicking, and choosing Image ⇨ Adjust from the shortcut menu. The Image Adjust dialog box opens. This dialog box enables you to dynamically change the brightness, contrast, and fade of the image, using the slider bars or text boxes. You immediately see the results in the preview box. Choose Reset to return the image to its original status.

Image quality

To adjust image quality, use the IMAGEQUALITY command on the command line. AutoCAD displays the `Enter image quality setting [High/Draft] <High>:` prompt. Choose either High or Draft. This command affects the display of all the images in a drawing. Plotting is always at high quality. Use this command when a high-quality image slows down performance. A regen is not necessary after you change this setting.

Image transparency

If the image format that you're using supports transparent pixels, you can use the TRANSPARENCY command to create a transparent background for your image. This works for bi-tonal or grayscale images. (*Bi-tonal* images have only a foreground color and a background color.) By default, transparency is turned off.

To turn transparency on, select the image. The Image tab appears, where you can click the Background Transparency button. Click it again to turn transparency off. You may need to do a regen. Other objects in your drawing will now be visible through the background of your image.

New Feature

You can also put an image on a layer that has a transparency value. For more information about transparency as an object property, see Chapter 11. ■

Image frame

The FRAME system variable controls the frame that surrounds all images in a drawing. (It also works for DWFs, PDFs, DGNs, and xrefs.) Choose Insert tab ➪ Reference panel ➪ Frame drop-down list and then choose the setting that you want to apply. Choose one of three settings:

- **Hide Frames.** Turns off the frame, both in the drawing display and when plotting.
- **Display and Plot Frames.** Turns on the frame, both in the drawing display and when plotting.
- **Display but Don't Plot Frames.** Displays the frame in the drawing, but doesn't plot it. This is the default value.

FRAME can have a fourth value, *Frames Vary*, which denotes that one of the individual frame settings is different from the FRAME system variable. You can override the frame settings used for images by changing the value of the IMAGEFRAME system variable to 0 (not visible or plotted), 1 (displayed and plotted), or 2 (displayed but not plotted).

Turning off the frame often improves the way the image looks. However, you select an image by clicking its frame. Therefore, using the Hide Frames value means that you cannot select the image, except when using commands specific to images, such as TRANSPARENCY, ADJUST, and CLIP.

When an image has a border, the border displays the properties of the layer that was current when you attached the image.

Draw order

The DRAWORDER command changes the display order of objects, including raster and OLE objects. (OLE is discussed later in this chapter.) This command is very helpful when working with raster and OLE objects, where you may or may not want to hide the other objects in your drawing. You can move an object to the top or bottom or change its order in relation to another object — above or below it. To change an object's display order, choose Home tab ➪ Modify panel ➪ Draw Order drop-down list and choose one of the options. At the prompt, select the objects you want. Draw order settings are saved with the drawing.

Tip

The TEXTTOFRONT command controls the order of both text and dimensions. Use this command to ensure that text is always on top and never obscured by other objects. In Chapter 13, I explain how to use a background mask to make text more legible. ■

On the DVD

The drawing used in the following exercise on working with raster images, ab27-b.dwg, and the images ab27-b.tif and ab27-b1.bmp, are in the Drawings folder on the DVD. This exercise works with AutoCAD only. ∎

STEPS: Working with Raster Images

1. Open ab27-b.dwg from the DVD.

2. Save the file as ab27-03.dwg in your AutoCAD Bible folder.

3. Enter **plan** on the command line and press Enter twice to view the model from the top (plan view).

4. Choose Insert tab ⇨ Reference panel ⇨ Attach.

5. In the Select Reference File dialog box, choose ab27-b.tif from the DVD. Click Open. In the Attach Image dialog box, click Show Details. Notice that the image is 1 × 0.61 units. Compared to the house, it is tiny.

6. In the Attach Image dialog box, uncheck Specify On-Screen for the Scale factor (if it's checked), and change the scale factor to 5. Click OK.

7. At the Specify insertion point <0,0>: prompt, pick any point on the left side of the screen. The image is still tiny, but that's okay. Choose View tab ⇨ Zoom drop-down list ⇨ Window and define a window to zoom closely into the image, as shown in Figure 27.7.

8. Click the border of the image; the Image tab appears. In the Adjust panel, change the Contrast to 60 and the Brightness to 40.

9. With the image still selected, choose Create Clipping Boundary in the Clipping panel of the Image tab. Follow the prompts:

   ```
   Specify clipping boundary or select invert option [Select polyline/
       Polygonal/Rectangular/Invert clip] <Rectangular>: ↲
   Specify first corner point: If Object Snap is on, turn it off. Pick
       ❶ in Figure 27.7.
   Specify opposite corner point: Pick ❷.
   ```

FIGURE 27.7
_____

Clipping the raster image.

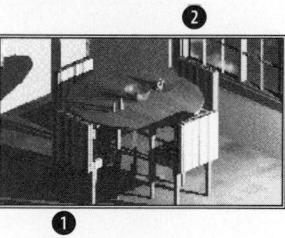

10. If necessary, zoom out so that you have room to insert another image. Choose Insert tab ⇨ Reference panel ⇨ Attach and attach ab27-b1.bmp (located on the DVD) with a scale factor of 5. Insert it below the first image.

11. Click the Layout1 button on the status bar (or the Layout1 tab) to enter paper space, which has three floating viewports. Double-click the bottom-left viewport. Enter **plan** on the command line and press Enter twice. You should now see the images as a small dot to the left of the house. Use Zoom Window to zoom into the rendered table. Your drawing should now look like Figure 27.8.

The drawing with a rendered view in one viewport.

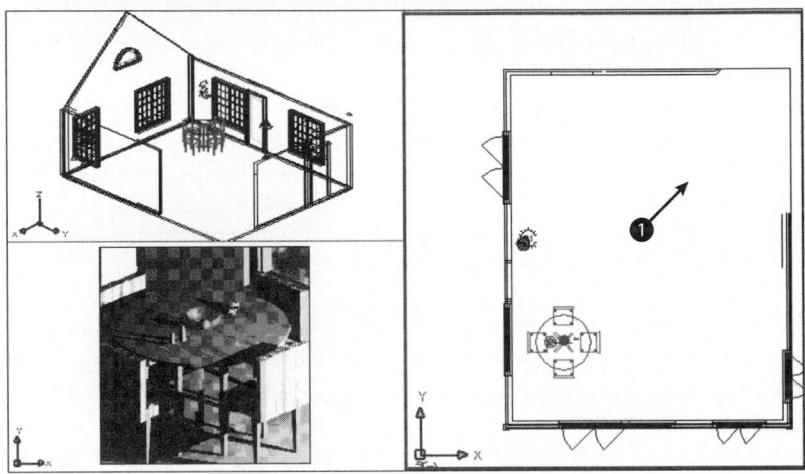

12. Click the right viewport. If necessary, pan the house to the right until you can see the two images that you attached. Move the Cottonmill Houses image to ❶, shown in Figure 27.8. Use the SCALE command to scale it, using a base point at its lower-left corner and a scale factor of 25. Move it until it fits nicely in the upper-right corner of the floor plan. Pan again to center the house in the viewport. (If it disappears, do a Zoom Extents.)

13. Click the Insert tab ⇨ References panel ⇨ Frames drop-down list and choose Hide Frames. AutoCAD removes the frames from the two images.

14. Save your drawing.

Pasting, Linking, and Embedding Objects

To maximize the data that you have in other documents, you can insert objects from other applications into your drawing. For example, you may have a description of your drawing in a word-processing application or in a table in a spreadsheet. You can use the Windows Clipboard to share data between applications.

Cross-Reference

In Chapter 18, I explain how to use the Windows Clipboard to copy and move material from one drawing to another. Chapter 13 includes a discussion of several techniques for importing text into your drawing. ■

You can insert data (text or images) created with other applications into a drawing in three ways:

- **Embed** the object if you want to be able to return to the source application to edit the object. When you double-click the object, the source application opens so that you can edit the object.

- **Paste** the object when you don't need any connection with the source application.

- **Link** the object when you want to retain a permanent link to the source file so that when the source file is changed, the drawing data changes accordingly.

You can use the Clipboard to move material from one application to another and take advantage of the special options for pasting, linking, and embedding data. Linking and embedding are often referred to as Object Linking and Embedding, or OLE. You can also use drag-and-drop between applications.

Embedding objects into a drawing

You have three ways to embed data from other applications. Each method has its advantages and disadvantages.

Here's the first way:

 1. From your drawing, choose Insert tab ⇨ Data panel ⇨ OLE Object to open the Insert Object dialog box, as shown in Figure 27.9. This starts the INSERTOBJ command. (The entries listed in this dialog box depend on the applications that you have installed on your computer.)

FIGURE 27.9

The Insert Object dialog box.

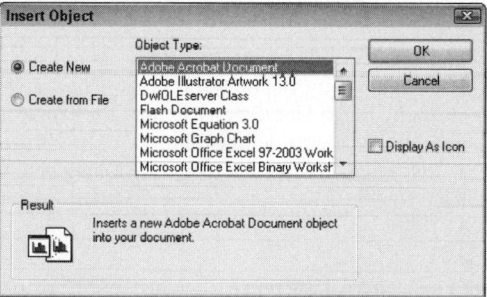

2. Do one of the following:

- If you want to create a new file in the other application, choose Create New, choose the application that you want to use from the Object Type list, and click OK. The other application opens so that you can create the new data. When you're done, choose File ⇨ Update (or Application Button ⇨ Update) from the other application's menu. (This menu item can vary, depending on the application.) Close the application and return to your drawing. If the OLE Properties dialog box appears, specify how you want the object to appear, and click OK. The new file is inserted.

- If you want to choose an existing file, choose Create from File. Click Browse to find the file. Click Open. You return to the Insert Object dialog box, where you can choose Link to link the data (described in the next section of this chapter). Choose OK. The file appears at the top-left corner of your screen with handles that you can use to move and/or resize the object.

Here's the second way:

1. Open the source application, select the data, and copy it to the Clipboard. Leave the source application open.
2. If your drawing is open, switch to it by choosing its button on the task bar. Otherwise, open it.
3. In your drawing, choose Home tab ➪ Clipboard panel ➪ Paste drop-down list ➪ Paste Special.
4. In the Paste Special dialog box, choose the first option, which lets you embed the object as an object of the source application. Click OK.
5. You can now close the other application.

The third way to insert data is to use drag-and-drop:

1. Open the drawing where you want to embed the data.
2. Open the source application and select the data.
3. Press Ctrl and click the selected data again, holding down the mouse button.
4. Drag the data to the AutoCAD or AutoCAD LT button on the Windows task bar and continue to hold down the mouse button until your drawing displays.
5. Drag the data to the desired location in your drawing.

Using INSERTOBJ gives you the option of creating a new file on the spot in the other application. You don't have to keep the other application open when you return to your drawing. Note that you cannot create a link if you're creating a new file.

Using the Clipboard enables you to insert part of a file — for example, part of a spreadsheet — which can be a great advantage. You need to keep the other application open until you paste the object into your drawing.

You can control the size of text and the plot quality of OLE objects. Choose Application Button ➪ Options and click the Plot and Publish tab, where you can set the default OLE plot quality. To change the plot quality, select the OLE object and change the quality in the Plot Quality item of the Properties palette. Text is automatically scaled to approximate the size in the original application. To change the text size, select the OLE object and right-click. Choose OLE ➪ Text Size. In the OLE Text Size dialog box, you can change the text size in the Text Height text box. Click OK.

OLE objects have a few limitations:

- If they're contained in a block or an external reference, they may not be displayed or plotted.
- In certain cases, OLE objects can be printed out only on Windows system printers. You can usually configure your plotter to be the system printer.
- OLE objects don't rotate with your drawing when you use a PLOT rotation. To work around this, you can use the system printer's Landscape setting.
- OLE objects don't display or plot if displayed in a rotated viewport. If you need an OLE object to be displayed in a viewport, you should not rotate the viewport.

Tip

If you don't mind a few steps, you can sometimes get good results importing large Excel spreadsheets by way of Microsoft Word, as follows: In Excel, use Save As to save the spreadsheet in Text (Tab delimited) format. Insert the file into Word (choose Text Files from the Open dialog box's Files of Type drop-down list). Select the entire file and choose Table ➪ Convert ➪ Text to Table. Change the Page Setup to accommodate the large size of the table, using a custom paper size. Format the table if you want. Copy it to the Clipboard. In your drawing, choose Home tab ➪ Utilities panel ➪ Paste drop-down list ➪ Paste. ■

Tip

If you try to use HIDE on a 3D model that contains OLE objects, the OLE objects disappear! The solution is to insert them in paper space. You can then hide the 3D model in one floating viewport and display the OLE object in another. ∎

Using Paste Special

When you copy data to the Clipboard, it's stored in several formats, depending on the type of data. You can then choose which format you want to use when you paste it into your drawing, using the PASTESPEC (Paste Special) command. Choosing the right format can make a big difference, by enabling you to edit the data in your drawing as you wish.

Pasting data into your drawing

To paste data by using PASTESPEC, open the source application, select the data, and copy it to the Clipboard. Leave the source application open.

If your drawing is open, choose its button on the task bar. If not, open it. In your drawing, choose Home tab ⇨ Clipboard panel ⇨ Paste drop-down list ⇨ Paste Special. This opens the Paste Special dialog box. The choices that you see in the As box of the Paste Special dialog box depend on the type of data that you copied. In most cases, you can paste as an object of the source application, as a picture (metafile), as a bitmap, and as text. Table 27.3 shows the options that are available when you paste in a range of cells from a spreadsheet.

TABLE 27.3

Paste Special Data Types

Data Type	Characteristics
Object of Source Application	The object is inserted at the top-left corner of your drawing. You cannot explode the object, but you can select it and then resize it or move it by using its handles. This is an embedded object — if you double-click it, the source application opens, letting you edit the object by using the source application's tools.
Picture (Metafile or Enhanced Metafile)	The object is inserted at the top-left corner of your drawing. You cannot explode the object, but you can select it and then resize it or move it by using its handles. You cannot edit the object. It maintains good quality when scaled up.
Bitmap	The object is inserted at the top-left corner of your drawing. You cannot explode the object, but you can select it and then resize it or move it by using its handles. You cannot edit the object.
AutoCAD Entities	You see prompts for an insertion point, scale factor, and rotation angle. You can explode the object into drawing objects. (Objects were once called *entities* in AutoCAD and AutoCAD LT.) Text objects maintain their original font and formatting.
Image Entity	You see prompts for an insertion point, scale factor, and rotation angle. The object is inserted as approximately a 1 × 1-unit square. It is a kind of bitmap. You can explode it, but then you lose the image!
(Unicode) Text	The object is inserted at the top-left corner of your drawing. You can explode it, but the text then loses the original formatting and font.

The best choice depends on the type of data that you're pasting. For a spreadsheet, the Picture, Bitmap, and Image Entity choices aren't useful, but they would be quite appropriate if you were pasting in an image.

Pasting drawing objects into another application

You can also copy drawing objects to the Clipboard and paste them into another application, such as a word-processing document, a spreadsheet, or a presentation program. Figure 27.10 shows a PowerPoint slide that includes a model from an AutoCAD drawing. To paste drawing objects into another application, select the objects that you want to copy. Choose Home tab ⇨ Clipboard panel ⇨ Copy Clip (or press Ctrl+C). Load the other application (in this case PowerPoint), create a document or file (in this case a slide), and paste the drawing object.

FIGURE 27.10

Placing part of a drawing on a PowerPoint slide.

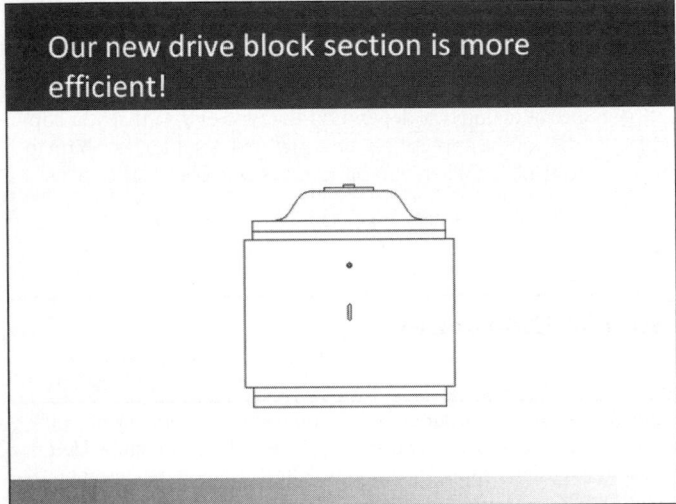

Inserting AutoCAD as an ActiveX Component into PowerPoint

When you insert or paste AutoCAD objects into another document, such as a Word document or PowerPoint presentation, the objects are static images. What if you could display your AutoCAD drawing dynamically, with zooming and panning? You could then show your intended audience all the detail you want.

It turns out that you can. You can use the DWF format (covered in more detail in Chapter 28) and insert it into any version of Word, Excel, or PowerPoint that supports ActiveX components. Viewers need the free Autodesk Design Review, which they can download at www.autodesk.com/designreview. Here are instructions for PowerPoint:

1. Create the DWF file. (See Chapter 28 for instructions.)

2. In PowerPoint, choose a slide layout that gives you room for the DWF file.

3. Choose Insert ➪ Object. (See below for instructions if you have PowerPoint 2007.)

4. Click Create New and then choose Autodesk DWF Viewer Control. Click OK. On your slide, you see a box with handles.

5. If you want, resize or move the box. (If you deselect the box, it may disappear. Click inside the box to select it again.)

6. Right-click the box and choose Autodesk DWF Viewer Control Object ➪ Properties.

7. In the Autodesk DWF Viewer Control Properties dialog box, on the SourcePath tab, type the path to the DWF file or click browse to browse to the file. Click OK.

8. In your PowerPoint presentation, enter Slide Show view. You can now pan, zoom, turn layers on and off, print, and so on from within your presentation.

In PowerPoint 2007, you need to make sure that ActiveX settings in the Trust Center (Office button ➪ PowerPoint Options) are not disabled. Then you need to display the Developer tab. (Choose Office button ➪ PowerPoint Options and use the Popular category.) On the Developer tab, in the Controls group, click More Controls. Choose Autodesk DWF Viewer Control, and click OK. Drag a rectangle on the slide. Right-click the rectangle and continue from Step 6.

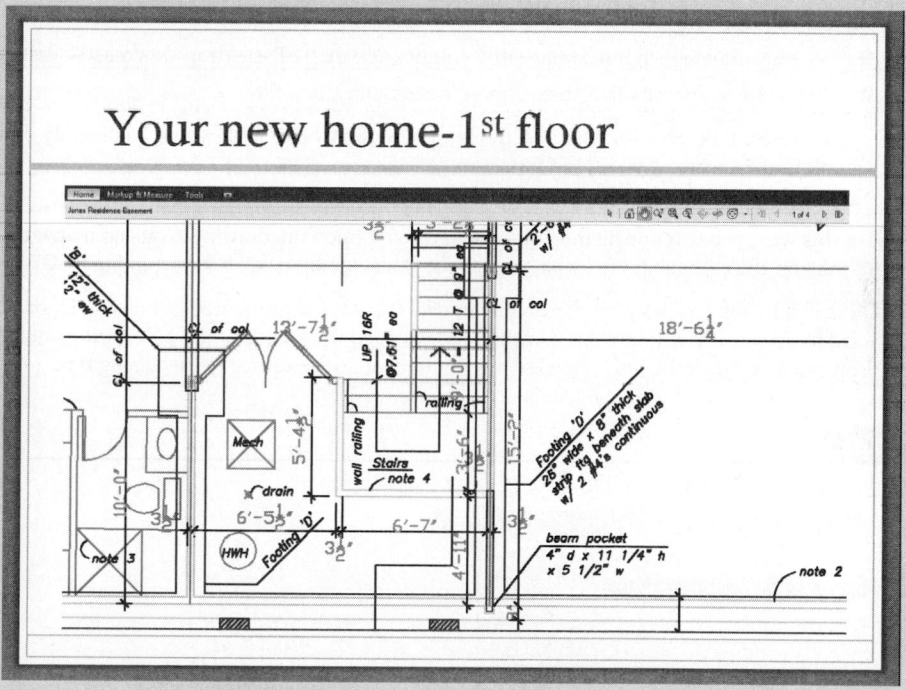

Tip

You can hide a 3D view and copy and paste the view into another application. However, you cannot copy and paste a rendered view. To bring a rendered view into another application, save it as an image and import it. Chapter 25 covers saving rendered images. You can freeze any layers that you don't want to include, such as dimension and text layers. ∎

Linking data

You can insert data from a spreadsheet or text document and maintain a link to the original file, so that if the original file changes, the inserted data is updated as well, very similar to xrefs. For example, you could use this feature to place a schedule of doors and windows in an architectural drawing or a bill of materials in a mechanical drawing. You have two ways to link data.

Cross-Reference

You can also create a link to an Excel spreadsheet. You can even change the Excel spreadsheet from within AutoCAD. In other words, you have a link in both directions. For more information, see Chapter 13. ∎

First, you can link data by using INSERTOBJ, as described earlier in this chapter. Second, you can use the Clipboard by following these steps:

1. Open the source application, select the data, and copy it to the Clipboard.
2. If your drawing is open, display it. If not, open it.
3. In your drawing, choose Home tab ⇨ Clipboard panel ⇨ Paste drop-down list ⇨ Paste Special.
4. In the Paste Special dialog box, choose Paste Link. Click OK.

When you create a link, you don't have all the format options that you do when you simply paste. You can create a link in the source application's format only.

When you open a drawing containing a link, a message appears, asking whether you want to update the links. In this way, you can update the links whenever you open the drawing. You can manage links by typing **olelinks** on the command line, which opens the Links dialog box, as shown in Figure 27.11.

The Links dialog box enables you to manually update the links at any time by choosing Update Now. You may want to do this if you know that someone has changed the source of the link during your drawing session. You can also break the link, open the source, or change the source in this dialog box.

FIGURE 27.11

Use the Links dialog box to manage your links.

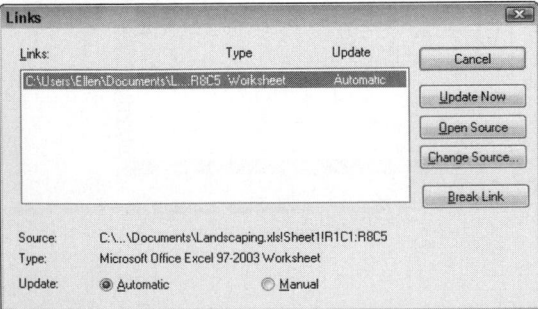

Remember that if you give a drawing to someone else, you also need to include any attached images or embedded objects. If the person does not have the source application for an embedded object, you can paste it in as an image.

On the DVD

The drawing, ab27-c.dwg, and the file, ab27-c.xls, used in the following exercise on pasting, linking, and embedding objects are in the Drawings folder on the DVD. ■

To do the following exercise, you need a spreadsheet application. I use Microsoft Excel in this exercise.

STEPS: Pasting, Linking, and Embedding Objects

1. Open ab27-c.dwg from the DVD.
2. Save the file as ab27-04.dwg in your AutoCAD Bible folder.
3. Choose Insert tab ➪ Data panel ➪ OLE Object. Choose Create New and choose your worksheet application from the list. Click OK. Your worksheet program opens.
4. Create the worksheet shown in Figure 27.12. Adjust the width of the columns to fit the data.

FIGURE 27.12

Create this worksheet to insert into your AutoCAD drawing.

	A	B	C	D
1	Tag	Part No.	Description	
2	11	9075-052-002	Collar-Shaft	
3	17	9029-072-001	Bracket-Tube Assembly	
4	19	9081-114-001	Channel Motor Mtg. Rod	
5				

5. In the spreadsheet application, choose File ➪ Update (or Application Button ➪ Update) and then choose File ➪ Exit (or Application Button ➪ Exit). The worksheet appears in the drawing, as shown in Figure 27.13.

FIGURE 27.13

The spreadsheet inserted into the drawing.

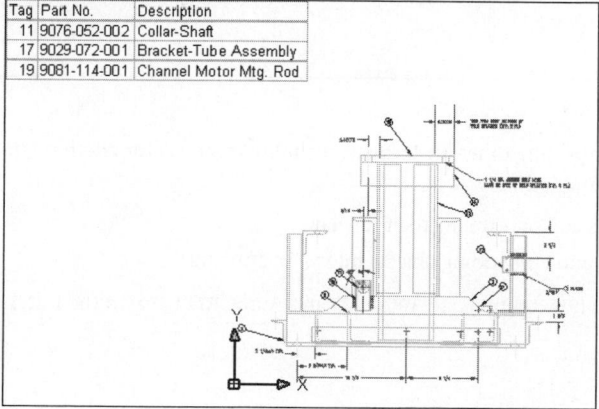

Tag	Part No.	Description
11	9076-052-002	Collar-Shaft
17	9029-072-001	Bracket-Tube Assembly
19	9081-114-001	Channel Motor Mtg. Rod

6. Open your spreadsheet application and open `ab27-c.xls` from the DVD. Select the data in the last three columns, as shown in Figure 27.14. Copy it to the Clipboard.

FIGURE 27.14

Selecting part of a file to insert into your drawing.

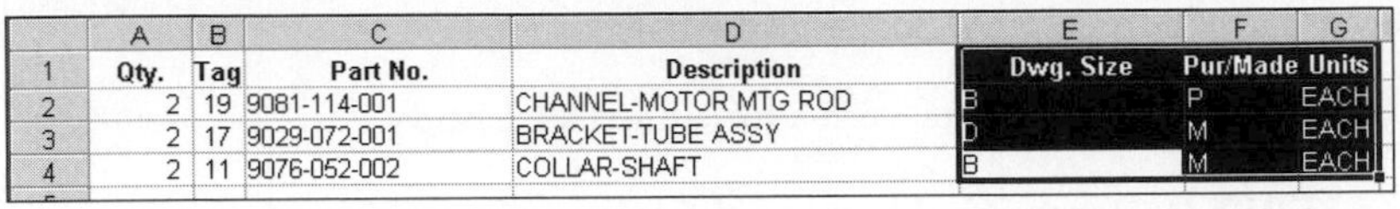

	A	B	C	D	E	F	G
1	Qty.	Tag	Part No.	Description	Dwg. Size	Pur/Made	Units
2	2	19	9081-114-001	CHANNEL-MOTOR MTG ROD	B	P	EACH
3	2	17	9029-072-001	BRACKET-TUBE ASSY	D	M	EACH
4	2	11	9076-052-002	COLLAR-SHAFT	B	M	EACH

7. Leave your spreadsheet open and click the AutoCAD or AutoCAD LT button on the Windows task bar. Choose Home tab ⇨ Clipboard panel ⇨ Paste drop-down list ⇨ Paste Special. Although you could insert this as an Excel Worksheet (or object from your spreadsheet application), to try another method, choose AutoCAD (LT) Entities and click OK. Pick an insertion point near the right of the existing OLE object.

8. The spreadsheet is inserted as a table object, but is very small. Click outside the table to close the In-Place Text Editor. Zoom in on the table. Click the lower-right corner of the table and drag its handle down and to the right until the table is the same height as the spreadsheet to its left.

9. Click inside the upper-left cell, press Shift, and click inside the lower-right cell. Display the Properties palette (Ctrl+1) and change the Text Height to .6800. Change the Text Style to WMF-Arial0. (This text style was created when you imported the spreadsheet, to match the original text in the spreadsheet.) Change the Alignment to Middle Center.

10. Choose Home tab ⇨ Clipboard panel ⇨ Paste drop-down list ⇨ Paste Special again. Choose Paste Link. Now you can paste in your spreadsheet's format as an AutoCAD (LT) Entities (which creates a linked table). Click OK. Pick an insertion point. Pick the lower-right corner of the spreadsheet and drag its handle down and to the right to enlarge the table.

11. Note that the first row of data has a "P" in the `Pur/Made` column. Return to your spreadsheet and change cell F2 (which now says P) to M, and press Enter. Go back to your drawing and note that the P has changed to an M. Because the data are linked, any changes made to the spreadsheet are updated in your drawing.

12. Save your drawing. Close your spreadsheet program without saving the change that you made.

Summary

In this chapter, you read about the following:

- Importing and exporting other file formats, including both vector and bitmap (raster) formats
- Working with DXF files
- Managing images and controlling their display
- Pasting, linking, and embedding objects into your drawing

The next chapter discusses how to integrate AutoCAD and AutoCAD LT with the Internet.

Creating Electronic Output

A utoCAD and AutoCAD LT offer many ways to integrate your drawings with the Internet. You can open drawings from a Web site, hyperlink objects to anywhere on the Web, and publish drawings in PNG, JPG, DWF, or DWFx format on a Web site. When you access a Web site (perhaps your company's intranet), you can find blocks or other data, and drag them into your drawing. This chapter covers all the ways to connect your drawings with the Internet.

You can share your 3D drawings in the 3D DWF or 3D DWFx format. The DWF and DWFx formats are not only for use on the Internet; your colleagues can also view your DWF and DWFx files by using Autodesk Design Review.

Sending Drawings

You can instantly send your drawings to others on your team or to your clients, by either faxing or e-mailing them, just as you fax and e-mail other documents. You can fax a drawing if the recipient doesn't have AutoCAD or AutoCAD LT and wants to quickly see the drawing on paper. (Later in this chapter, I explain how someone can use Autodesk Design Review to view AutoCAD or AutoCAD LT drawings.)

You can also send a drawing to an FTP site. Another option is to create a PDF file from the drawing and then e-mail the PDF file. Use e-mail if the recipient has AutoCAD or AutoCAD LT; however, you may need to edit the drawing. I explain how to create a PDF file from a drawing in Chapter 27.

Using eTransmit

The eTransmit feature packs together all associated files with your drawing so that you can e-mail it to colleagues, clients, customers, and so on. To start a transmission, choose Application Button ➪ Send ➪ eTransmit. The Create Transmittal dialog box opens, shown in Figure 28.1, with the Files Tree tab on top and all the file items expanded.

FIGURE 28.1

The Create Transmittal dialog box enables you to create a transmittal file that you can attach to an e-mail message. The transmittal file contains a drawing, along with its associated files.

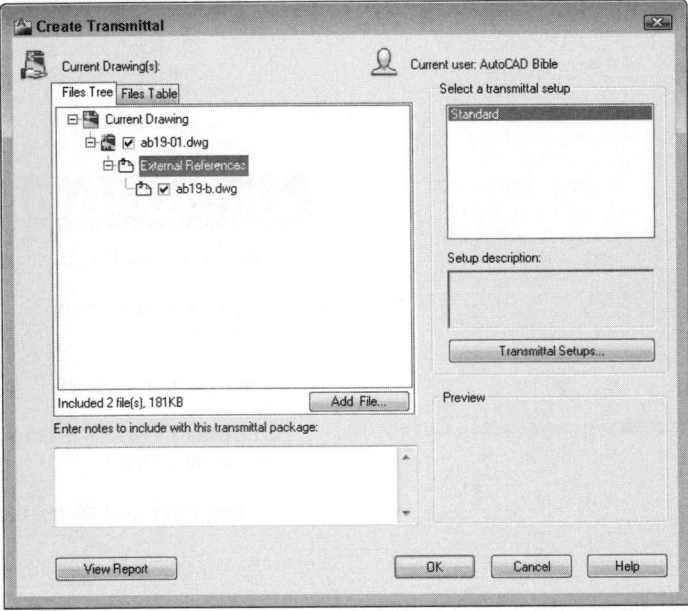

You can write a note to the recipient in the Notes section. The content of the Notes section becomes part of the transmittal report, a separate file that is included in the EXE or ZIP file. If you send an e-mail message, the note becomes the body of the message.

Specifying transmittal settings

If you have a saved transmittal setting, choose it from the Select a Transmittal Setup box and click OK. Otherwise, click Transmittal Setups to open the Transmittal Setups dialog box. To create a new setup, click New, name the setup, and click Continue. To modify an existing setup, select the setup and click Modify. In both cases, you end up in the Modify Transmittal Setup dialog box, as shown in Figure 28.2.

FIGURE 28.2

Use the Modify Transmittal Setup dialog box to specify how to structure your transmittal.

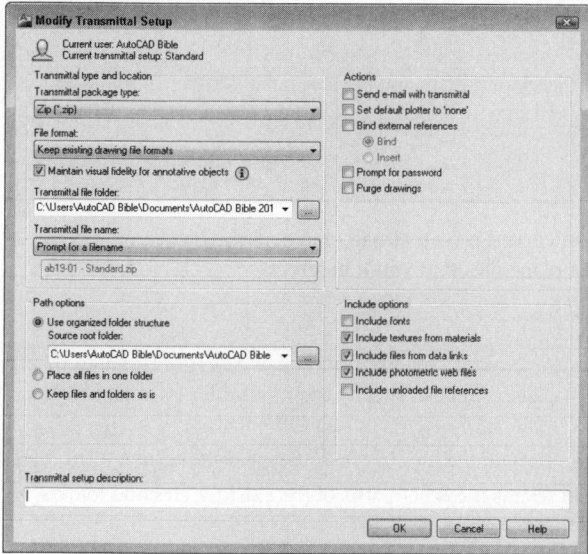

From the Transmittal Package Type drop-down list, choose one of the following types of transmittals:

- **Folder (set of files).** Creates a folder that includes all the files in the transmittal. The files are not compressed.
- **Self-extracting executable** (`*.exe`). Creates a compressed EXE file. Recipients can double-click the file to decompress and extract the files.

Caution

Some people won't open EXE or ZIP files for fear of computer viruses, so you might need to notify your recipient in advance that you're sending an EXE or ZIP file. Also, some e-mail programs block EXE and ZIP attachments. You might also consider using a secure FTP site or a project collaboration Web portal like Autodesk Buzzsaw to work around these limitations. ■

- **Zip** (`*.zip`). Creates a compressed ZIP file.

From the File Format drop-down list, you can choose to save files in earlier release formats if you want. From the Transmittal File Folder drop-down list, choose a location to save the transmittal files, or click Browse to specify another location. You can leave this item blank to save the files in the same folder as the first drawing on the list in the Create Transmittal dialog box. If you're transmitting a sheet set (AutoCAD only), the transmittal file goes in the same folder as the drawing set data (DST) file.

For drawings with annotative objects, you can check or uncheck the Maintain Visual Fidelity for Annotative Objects check box. This sets the SAVEFIDELITY system variable, which determines what happens when someone views the drawing in earlier releases. By default, this system variable is on (the check box is checked), which saves each scale representation as a separate object on a separate layer. This allows users in previous versions to choose which version they want by turning off layers or deleting objects. If you work in model space and don't need layouts to look the same as in 2011, you should uncheck this check box to avoid creating all the additional layers and objects when sharing with users using AutoCAD 2007 or earlier.

If you create an EXE or ZIP file, you can use the Transmittal File Name drop-down list to choose how you want to name the file. You can choose to be prompted for a filename, have eTransmit assign a name and overwrite any existing file with that name, or have eTransmit assign a name and increment the filename (add a number) to avoid overwriting an existing file.

Tip
Because you often don't need the transmittal file after you've sent it (you already have all the files), you can put it in the `Windows\Temp` **file or another location where you place files that you'll delete.** ∎

Choose one of the following Path options:

- The Use Organized Folder Structure option creates a hierarchical folder structure based on the structure of the files in the transmittal package. You can specify the root folder for this structure. When the recipient opens the transmittal package, all these folders are created.

- The Place All Files in One Folder option puts all the files in one folder that the recipient specifies.

- The Keep Files and Folders As Is option retains the exact paths of the existing files and folders, which is best when working with files that contain xrefs.

Use the following Actions options to define which actions to use when creating the transmittal package:

- The Send E-mail with Transmittal check box opens your e-mail program and creates a new message with the files and notes as attachments and as the body of the message, respectively. Using this feature makes sending your drawings very easy.

- The Set Default Plotter to 'None' check box removes the plotter information from the drawings, because it's probably not useful to your recipient.

- The Bind External References check box binds xrefs to their host drawings.

- The Prompt for Password check box opens a dialog box (after you save the transmittal file) where you can specify a password. Be sure to tell your recipient the password.

- The Purge Drawings check box removes all unused named objects in the drawing before adding a drawing to the transmittal package. Named objects include layers, blocks, text styles, and so on.

Use the following Include options to define which types of files to include when creating the transmittal package:

- The Include Fonts check box includes the AutoCAD fonts in the transmittal. If your drawing only uses fonts included in a normal installation of AutoCAD or AutoCAD LT, you can probably assume that your recipients have them. You can include TrueType fonts, but make sure that you can redistribute them as they are often licensed and proprietary.

- The Include Textures from Materials check box includes texture files that you have used as the basis for materials. Materials are used in rendering. (See Chapter 25 for more information on rendering.)

- The Include Files from Data Links check box includes Excel or CSV files that you have linked to in the drawing. (See Chapter 13 for a discussion of data links.)

- The Include Photometric Web Files check box includes Web files that contain photometric data. (See Chapter 25 for more information.)
- The Include Unloaded File References check box includes unloaded xrefs, images, and underlays. (See Chapter 19 for more information.)

The Include Unloaded File References option allows you to remove unloaded xrefs, images, and underlays from the drawings before sending them to others. At the bottom of the dialog box, you can add a description for the transmittal. Then click OK. The Transmittal Setups dialog box reappears, where you can choose the transmittal setup that you want. Then click Close.

You're now back in the Create Transmittal dialog box. Click the Files Table tab to see the files that will be included in your transmittal. The normal files are acad.fmp or acadlt.fmp (the font map that specifies font substitutions), SHX files (usually compiled fonts), TTF files (TrueType fonts), and any xrefs, raster images, or standards files that are attached to the drawing.

Caution

The eTransmit feature does not include files referred to by hyperlinks. Therefore, if you want hyperlinks to work, you need to add the referenced files. ■

To add files, click Add File, navigate to the desired file, select it, and click Open. To see the Transmittal Report, click the View Report button. The report includes your notes and instructions to the recipient for using the associated files. For example, there are instructions for where to place SHX files and xrefs. Choose Save As to create an additional copy of the report for your own records.

When you're done, click OK. If you checked Send E-mail with Transmittal, your e-mail program opens, and you can send an e-mail message and the files. Either way, eTransmit creates the type of transmittal files that you requested.

Opening Drawings from the Web

You can access drawings, blocks, and so on from the Internet in the same way that you currently access them on your hard drive or network. Sharing drawings around the world can be as easy as opening a drawing on your hard drive. You have two methods for bringing objects from the Internet into your drawings.

Using the Browse the Web – Open dialog box

You can directly open a drawing from the Web within the Select File dialog box (click Open on the Quick Access Toolbar) by using the Search the Web button. As long as you have an active connection to the Internet, the Browse the Web – Open dialog box opens and functions as a browser. In this way, you can access drawings and other files over the Internet.

Using i-drop to drag objects into a drawing

An i-drop-enabled Web site displays the i-drop cursor when you pass the cursor over an image, as shown in Figure 28.3. This cursor indicates that you can drag the object represented by the image into your drawing. For more information on creating i-drop-enabled Web sites, go to http://idrop.autodesk.com. The Publish to Web feature, covered later in this chapter, also contains i-drop capability.

FIGURE 28.3

Dragging an object from an i-drop-enabled Web site.

Thanks to Eric Stover of Autodesk for permission to display this i-drop example from the Autodesk i-drop Web site.

If you drag with the right mouse button, a prompt asks you whether you want to save associated blocks or data when you drag with the right mouse button. Also, inserted blocks automatically include a hyperlink to the source of the content.

Creating Object Hyperlinks

You can hyperlink objects in your drawing to files or Web sites that may be located anywhere on the Internet, a network, or your own hard drive. A hyperlink creates a permanent connection between your drawing and other files that may provide supporting documentation or additional information.

When you follow a hyperlink, the appropriate application is opened with the specified file. For example, a Web site is opened in your Web browser, or a word-processing document is opened in your word-processing application.

Creating a hyperlink

Before you create your hyperlink, consider the environment in which it will be used. The file or Web page that you're linking to must be available for the hyperlink to work. For example, if you send a drawing with hyperlinks to a colleague, be sure to include the files to which the hyperlinks refer. If you're posting the drawing on a Web site as a DWF or DWFx file, you need to upload the files that the hyperlinks refer to, along with the DWF or DWFx file.

Here's how you create a hyperlink:

1. Select one or more objects in your drawing. The hyperlink will be attached to these objects.
2. Choose Insert tab ⇨ Data panel ⇨ Hyperlink (or press Ctrl+K) to open the Insert Hyperlink dialog box, as shown in Figure 28.4. If you start the command first, select objects at the prompt.

FIGURE 28.4

The Insert Hyperlink dialog box attaches hyperlinks to objects in your drawing.

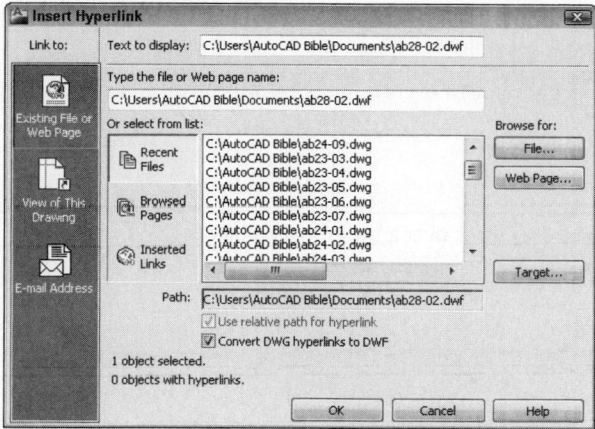

3. Use the Link To list to choose the type of hyperlink that you want to create. The central portion of the dialog box changes, depending on which of these options you choose: a Web page, named view, or e-mail address.

   - **Existing File or Web Page.** Creates a hyperlink to another file (on your own computer, network, intranet, or the Internet) or a Web page. You can choose from Recent Files, Browsed Pages, or Inserted Links.

   - **View of This Drawing.** Creates a hyperlink to a named view, camera, or layout in the open drawing. (I explain cameras in Chapter 22. A camera is a type of 3D named view.) You can use this option to help viewers navigate to detail views or schedules (tables of data) in the drawing.

   - **E-mail Address.** Opens the viewer's e-mail program and starts a new message to the specified address.

4. To help you specify the file or Web page, click either the File or Web Page button at the right side of the dialog box. To specify a named view in a drawing, click the Target button. In the Select Place in Document dialog box, click the plus sign next to the layout and select a view. Click OK.

5. In the Text to Display text box, type a short description of the hyperlink. The description is displayed as the tooltip. If you don't create a description, when you pass the cursor over the hyperlink, the tooltip lists the URL or filename. If the URL or filename is confusing, use a description instead.

6. Uncheck the Use Relative Path for Hyperlink check box if you want to use the entire path that you placed in the Type of File or Web Page Name text box. A relative path uses a base as a given, and requires you to specify only the part of the path after the base. Use relative paths when the hyperlinked file is in the same folder as the drawing.

Note

You can set the base path by using the HYPERLINKBASE system variable. By default, the base is the folder of the current drawing. ■

7. Uncheck the Convert DWG Hyperlinks to DWF check box if you don't want to convert drawing hyperlinks to DWF or DWFx hyperlinks. For example, if this box is checked, a hyperlink to `mydrawing.dwg` becomes a hyperlink to `mydrawing.dwf`. If you plan to create a DWF or DWFx file from the drawing that you're hyperlinking to, leave this check box checked.

8. Click OK to create the hyperlink.

Check the hyperlink by passing the cursor over the object to which you attached the hyperlink. You see the Web cursor, as shown in Figure 28.5.

FIGURE 28.5

The Web cursor appears when you pass the cursor over a hyperlinked object.

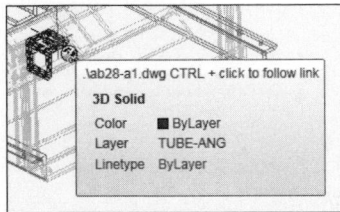

Using a hyperlink

After you create a hyperlink, you can use it at any time to open the associated file or to move to the associated location within the drawing. To open a file associated with a hyperlink, Ctrl+click any hyperlinked object. Remember that you can't just click a hyperlink as you do on a Web site, because that just selects the object in your drawing. Make sure that the hyperlink icon appears before you click, because pressing Ctrl and clicking is also a way to select edges and faces of 3D solids, as well as meshes.

Editing a hyperlink

To edit any feature of a hyperlink, select the hyperlinked object and choose Insert tab ⇨ Data panel ⇨ Hyperlink. You can also right-click and choose Hyperlink ⇨ Edit Hyperlink. The Edit Hyperlink dialog box opens. This dialog box is the same as the Insert Hyperlink dialog box and lets you edit the hyperlink. Click OK when you're done.

On the DVD

The files used in the following exercise on creating hyperlinks, `ab28-a.dwg`, `ab28-a1.dwg`, **and** `ab28-a2.dwg`, **are in the** `Drawings` **folder on the DVD.** ■

STEPS: Creating Hyperlinks

1. Open `ab28-a.dwg` from the DVD.

2. Save the file as `ab28-01.dwg` in your `AutoCAD Bible` folder. This is a 3D drawing of a base assembly frame for an industrial washer, as shown in Figure 28.6.

FIGURE 28.6

The base assembly frame.

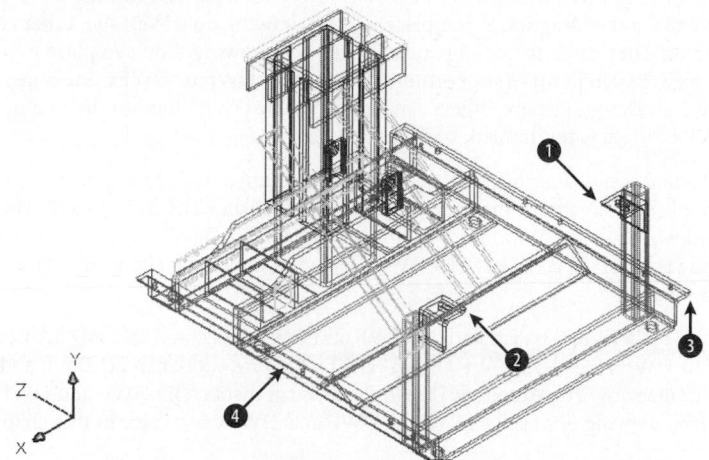

Thanks to Robert Mack of the Dexter Company, Fairfield, Iowa, for this drawing.

3. Copy ab28-a1.dwg and ab28-a2.dwg from the DVD to your AutoCAD Bible folder. (You can use Windows Explorer to drag the files.)

4. Choose Insert tab ⇨ Data panel ⇨ Hyperlink. At the Select objects: prompt, pick ❶ and ❷, shown in Figure 28.6, and press Enter. The Insert Hyperlink dialog box opens.

5. Click File. Choose ab28-a1.dwg in your AutoCAD Bible folder. Click Open. Click OK in the Insert Hyperlink dialog box.

6. Repeat the HYPERLINK command. This time attach ❸ and ❹, shown in Figure 28.6, to ab28-a2.dwg in your AutoCAD Bible folder. Click OK to close the dialog box.

7. Ctrl+click the hyperlink at ❶. The ab28-a1.dwg file should open. Close it. In the same way, test the hyperlink at ❷. Do the same with the hyperlinks at ❸ and ❹.

8. Save your drawing. Keep it open if you're going on to the next exercise.

AutoCAD Only

The Express Tools contain three commands to help you find and change URLs that you create with hyperlinks. SHOWURLS (choose Express Tools tab ⇨ Web panel ⇨ URL Options drop-down list ⇨ Show URLs) lists all the hyperlinks in your drawing, can show you the objects to which they are linked, and enables you to edit them. CHURLS (choose Tools tab ⇨ Web panel ⇨ URL Options drop-down list ⇨ Change URLs) prompts you to select a hyperlinked object so that you can change the hyperlink. REPURLS (choose Tools tab ⇨ Web panel ⇨ URL Options drop-down list ⇨ Find and Replace URLs) replaces the existing hyperlink URL of a selected hyperlinked object. ■

Publishing Drawings

You can save drawings as DWF (Design Web Format) or DWFx files. You can use DWF files as a way to deliver files to clients and colleagues. If you place a DWF drawing on a Web site, others can view the drawing in their browser. They can also zoom, pan, and print the drawing. You can place hyperlinks in your drawing so that viewers can jump to supporting data, to other DWF or DWFx drawings, or to other Web sites. Using Autodesk Design Review, others can view DWF or DWFx files on their computer; as a result, the DWF or DWFx format is not limited to use on a Web site.

The DWFx file format is based on Microsoft's XML Paper Specification (XPS), which allows anyone to view the 2D geometry of the file without the need for software other than the XPS Viewer. The XPS Viewer comes with Windows Vista and Windows 7, and you can install it on Windows XP. You can use Autodesk Design Review to view the 3D geometry of a DWFx file, view metadata, change the visibility of objects on a layer, and much more.

You can publish 2D DWF and DWFx, and 3D DWF and DWFx files in AutoCAD. (AutoCAD LT does not create 3D DWF or DWFx files.) 3D DWF and 3D DWFx files are similar to 2D DWF and DWFx files, but they have some limitations. The Autodesk Design Review can display 3D DWF and DWFx files and includes a 3D Orbit viewing option. I explain 3D DWF and DWFx files later in this chapter.

Understanding DWF and DWFx files

DWF and DWFx files are a simplified version of a drawing that can contain multiple pages which can be layouts from the same drawing or multiple drawings. You can include as many drawings as you want, including the layouts you've created for each drawing; however, very large numbers of layouts may create a file that is too large to open and view.

The DWF and DWFx formats have several advantages:

- **They are a vector format.** Viewers can zoom in closely and see the details clearly.
- **2D DWF and DWFx files are 2D representations, similar to a plot.** The actual objects are not available to the viewer. They cannot edit the drawing, and you can restrict access to object information such as layers, object coordinates, and so on. This feature maintains security for the creator of the drawing.
- **3D DWF and DWFx files do not expose the actual objects.** Viewers can view the model from any angle but cannot access object information.
- **DWF and DWFx files are compressed while being transmitted.** Their small size reduces the time it takes to download and view them.
- **The Autodesk Design Review enables people without AutoCAD or AutoCAD LT to view your drawings.** You can also post DWF and DWFx files on a Web site.
- **Viewers of 2D DWF and DWFx files can zoom to named views.** Some drawing information is available. For both 2D and 3D DWF and DWFx files, you can choose to allow viewers to turn layers on and off, see block properties and attributes, and display sheet set information. You have full control over whether you want to enable this information.
- **2D DWF and DWFx files support hyperlinks to other drawings, data, or files.** You can provide the viewer with supporting schedules, and so on. (3D DWF and DWFx files don't support hyperlinks.)

Creating 2D DWF and DWFx files

To create a 2D DWF or DWFx file from a set of drawings, you use the PUBLISH command to do the following:

- Create the drawing set; that is, the list of drawings and layouts to include in the DWF or DWFx file.
- Specify a page setup for each drawing.
- Save the list of drawings or load an existing list.

The PUBLISH command creates the multipage DWF or DWFx format. The PUBLISHTOWEB command, which creates DWF and DWFx files (but can also create JPEG or PNG files), is different — it uses a wizard and a template to format a Web page containing images of your drawings. The PUBLISHTOWEB command is covered later in this chapter. Before using the PUBLISH command, save your drawing.

Starting the PUBLISH command

 Start the PUBLISH command by choosing Output tab ⇨ Plot panel ⇨ Batch Plot. The Publish dialog box opens, as shown in Figure 28.7. You see the model and layout tabs of the current or all open drawings displayed.

FIGURE 28.7

The PUBLISH command opens the Publish dialog box, listing the model and layout tabs of the current or all open drawings.

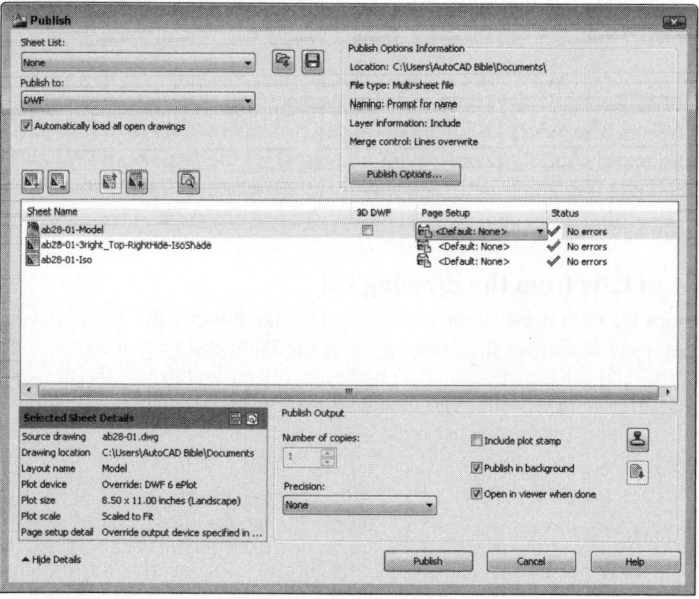

Adding drawings to the drawing list

The next step is to add any other drawings and layouts that you want to include in the drawing list. The PUBLISH command streamlines the process of defining scale and plot area for each drawing by using the page setup information defined with the layouts. Because layouts include this information, you can quickly create drawing sets for many drawings without individually deciding how to plot each drawing. You can specify a saved page setup for individual drawings for more control. (For more information on page setups and layouts, see Chapter 17.)

Note

By default, the Publish dialog box initially lists all sheets, models, and layouts for all open drawings. To list only the sheets of the current drawing, uncheck the Automatically Load All Open Drawings check box in the Publish dialog box or change the value of the PUBLISHALLSHEETS system variable to 0. ∎

You can add new drawings and layouts to the drawing list, using any of the following methods:

- Drag drawings directly from Windows Explorer. You can add large numbers of drawings this way — in any folder, click the first drawing, press and hold Shift, and click the last drawing.

- Click Add Sheets and choose drawings from the Select Drawings dialog box.
- Click Load Sheet List and choose a saved drawing list from the Load List of Sheets dialog box.

To save a drawing list, click Save Sheet List. The Save List As dialog box opens. Change the name if you want, choose a location, and click Save. Drawing lists have a .dsd extension. (DSD stands for Drawing Set Description.)

Tip

You can use the +PUBLISH command, a variant of the PUBLISH command that enables you start with a saved DSD file instead of the current, or all open, drawings. The Select List of Sheets dialog box opens. Choose a DSD file and click Select. You can use the –PUBLISH command (AutoCAD only) with a saved DSD file to publish DWF files from a script file. You then get a prompt for the DSD file. The process automatically generates a log file (with the name of the drawing list and an extension of .csv) that you can look at in case there are errors. ∎

Removing model space or layout tabs from the drawing list

By default, the model tab and layout tabs for each drawing are all included in the drawing list. If you don't want to see the model tab for drawings, right-click over the drawing list in the Publish dialog box and choose Include Model When Adding Sheets if it has a checkmark. Likewise, you can right-click the drawing list and choose Include Layouts When Adding Sheets. After you change this setting, new drawings that you add to the drawing set will not include the tab that you unchecked.

Editing the drawing list

After you have the drawings and layouts that you want, you can modify the list in several ways:

- **Change the sheet name.** The sheet names are generated automatically from the drawing and layout names, but you might want to use a different name. Click the drawing's row and then click the sheet name one time. Enter a new name.

Tip

If you aren't in the habit of renaming your layout tabs, you might find that your sheet names are rather unhelpful. `Handwheel-Layout1` doesn't explain very much. To rename a layout tab, right-click it and choose Rename. In the In-Place Editor, enter a new name and press Enter. (You need to display layout tabs to rename a layout. If you don't see tabs, right-click the Layout button on the status bar and choose Display Layout and Model Tabs.) ■

- **Page setup.** If you've specified a page setup, you can assign it to any drawing. (You can apply model page setups to model listings and layout page setups to layout listings.) Click the drawing's page setup and then click the down arrow that appears. From the drop-down list, you can choose a page setup from the drawing or import a page setup.

- **Change sheet order.** The sheet order defines how the sheets in the DWF file will be listed in the viewer. Choose a sheet and use the Move Sheet Up and Move Sheet Down buttons.

 - **Remove sheets.** To remove one or more items from the list, select them and click Remove Sheets.

Defining the output

When your list is complete, you decide on the output. From the Publish To drop-down list of the Publish dialog box, you can choose four types of output:

- **Plotter Named in Page Setup.** Choose this option to plot all the layouts in the list. This is essentially a batch plot. Each item in the drawing set is plotted to the plotter named in its page setup, including the default page setup. The folder setting is used if you've saved a plotter configuration file that plots drawings to a file.

- **DWF.** Choose this option to create a DWF file that can be viewed with Autodesk Design Review.

Note

By default, the name of the DWF, DWFx, or PDF file is the same as the name of the drawing (and in the same location). You can change the location of the file by clicking the Publish Options button and then specifying a new location in the Location field. ■

- **DWFx.** Choose this option to create a DWFx file that can be viewed with the XPS Viewer or Autodesk Design Review. ■

- **PDF.** Choose this option to create a PDF file that can be viewed with Adobe Acrobat, Adobe Acrobat Reader, or another viewer that can open and display PDF files. For more information on plotting PDF files, see Chapter 27.

Caution

Note that plotting, or your last setting, is the default option. Be careful, or you may end up plotting when you want to publish. ■

Setting publish options

Click the Publish Options button to open the Publish Options dialog box, where you can specify how the DWF or DWFx file will be published. You can do the following:

- Specify the location of the DWF or DWFx file.

- Choose the type of DWF or DWFx file — single-sheet or multi-sheet. You would use a single-sheet format for people using an older viewer that doesn't support the multi-sheet format.

- Specify the filename now, or ask to be prompted when you click the Publish button.
- Include layer information. If you include layer information, the viewer can turn layers on or off.
- Specify if overlapping lines are merged or overwritten.
- Create a password.
- Include block information, including a template file for extracting attributes. (You can only create these drawing templates with AutoCAD, not AutoCAD LT.) See Chapter 18 for more about block template files.
- Include sheet set and sheet information if you are publishing a sheet set (AutoCAD only).
- For 3D DWF or 3D DWFx files, list files by their xref hierarchy and include materials (AutoCAD only).

Publishing

When you've created your drawing list and defined your output, you're ready to publish. Click the Publish button. You may see a message asking whether you want to save the list of sheets. Choose Yes or No. When the publishing process is completed, you see the Plot and Publish Complete notification bubble at the lower-right corner of your screen. (I explain this bubble in Chapter 17.)

You can customize several settings for DWF or DWFx files, such as the resolution and background color (for example, black or white). You can also create your own ePlot plotter configuration file. For more information, see the "Customizing DWF and DWFx settings" sidebar.

Creating DWF files from other applications

You can create a DWF file from a Microsoft Word document, an Excel spreadsheet, or any other Windows application by using Autodesk DWF Writer. You can download the Autodesk DWF Writer for free from `www.autodesk.com/dwfwriter`. The Autodesk DWF Writer works as a printer driver. For example, in Microsoft Word, choose Office button ⇨ Print (or File ⇨ Print) and choose Autodesk DWF Writer for 2D from the Printer Name drop-down list. Then click OK to create a DWF file from your current document. You can view this document in Autodesk Design Review, as I explain in the section "Viewing DWF and DWFx drawings" later in this chapter.

Auto-publishing

The AUTOPUBLISH command is a way to quickly publish to a DWF, DWFx, or PDF file. To specify the settings that this command uses, choose Application Button ⇨ Options and click the Plot and Publish tab. In the Auto Publish section, click the Automatic Publish Settings button. There you can specify settings similar to those you set by clicking the Publish Options button in the Publish dialog box, as previously described.

The AUTODWFPUBLISH system variable turns the AutoPublish feature on and off. When you turn this system variable on (set its value to 1), AutoCAD executes the AUTOPUBLISH command every time you save or close the drawing. You can also turn this system variable on in the Auto Publish section of the Plot and Publish tab of the Options dialog box by checking the Automatic Publish check box. Turn on AUTODWFPUBLISH if you always need to keep DWF, DWFx, or PDF files synchronized with your drawings.

Customizing DWF and DWFx settings

You can modify the PC3 file that defines the DWF or DWFx file to specify certain settings that you might want, including compression, resolution, and whether to include layer information. The DWF file format follows the specification of the DWF6 ePlot.pc3 file. For safety, it's good to make a backup of the PC3 file before modifying it. To find the PC3 file, choose Application Button ➪ Print ➪ Manage Plotters. Double-click DWF6 ePlot.pc3 to change the settings for creating DWF files, or DWFx ePlot (XPS Compatible).pc3 to change the settings for creating DWFx files. Right-click the file and choose Copy. Right-click in the file listing and choose Paste. Rename the copy (perhaps DWF6 ePlot-original.pc3). If you don't like the results of your editing, delete the DWF6 ePlot.pc3 file and remove -original from the name of the copy.

To modify the PC3 file for creating a DWF file, follow these steps:

1. Choose Application Button ➪ Print ➪ Manage Plotters.
2. Double-click DWF6 ePlot.pc3 or DWFx ePlot (XPS Compatible).pc3.
3. Click the Device and Document Settings tab and choose Custom Properties.
4. In the middle of the dialog box, click the Custom Properties button to open the DWF6 ePlot Properties dialog box.

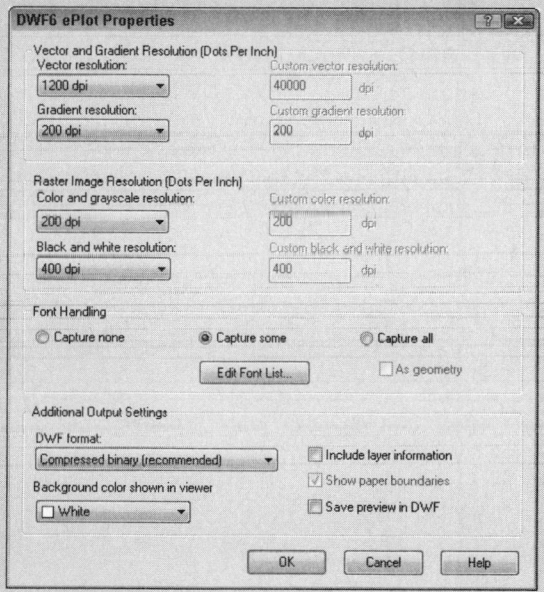

When you finish specifying the properties for the DWF or DWFx file format, click OK. If you see a message asking whether you want to apply the changes for the current plot only (which creates an override of the configuration file but doesn't change it) or to save the changes to the file (which changes the configuration file, although you can always change it back), respond as desired.

On the DVD

The drawing used in the following exercise on creating a 2D DWF file, ab28-01.dwg, is in the Results folder on the DVD. If you did the previous exercise, you also have this file in your AutoCAD Bible folder. ■

STEPS: Creating a 2D DWF File

1. If you did the previous exercise, use ab28-01.dwg. If not, open it from the Results folder on the DVD and save it to your AutoCAD Bible folder. Although this drawing is a 3D drawing, you can make a 2D DWF file from it, especially if you want to preserve the hyperlinks.

2. Close any other drawings that you may have open. Choose Output tab ⇨ Plot panel ⇨ Batch Plot.

3. Choose ab28-01-Model and click Remove Sheets.

4. In the Publish To drop-down list, choose DWF. Click Publish to create the DWF file.

5. In the Specify DWF File dialog box, enter **ab28-02.dwf** and **AutoCAD Bible** for the file location. Click Select.

6. A Publish – Save Sheet List dialog box opens and asks whether you want to save the current list of sheets. Click No. If you see the Processing Background Job message telling you that your job is processing in the background, click Close.

Creating 3D DWF and DWFx files

You use the PUBLISH command to create 3D DWF or DWFx files in the same way that you create 2D DWF or DWFx files, as explained previously in this chapter. (AutoCAD LT doesn't contain this feature.) You don't need to specify that the file is a 3D drawing. You can also use the 3DDWF command to create a 3D DWF or DWFx file and immediately open it in the Autodesk Design Review. This method has fewer options but is quicker. You can also choose Application Button ⇨ Export ⇨ 3D DWF and choose 3D DWF (*.dwf) or 3D DWFx (*.dwfx) from the Files of Type drop-down list.

Either way, a dialog box opens where you can specify the name and location of the file. To set a few options, choose Tools ⇨ Options. The 3D DWF Publish dialog box opens, as shown in Figure 28.8.

FIGURE 28.8

The 3D DWF Publish dialog box sets options for 3D DWF and DWFx files.

Choose whether you want to publish all objects or just selected objects, and how you want to organize xrefs in the drawing — either along with other objects or by their xref hierarchy. You can also choose to publish materials that you've attached to objects or layers. Then click OK to return to the Export 3D DWF dialog box. Specify a location and name for the DWF or DWFx file and click Save. A message appears asking whether you want to view the file. Click Yes to open the file in Autodesk Design Review.

The 3D DWF and DWFx files (for AutoCAD only) are similar to 2D DWF and DWFx files, but the following items are not displayed:

- Images and other inserted (OLE) objects
- Hyperlinks
- Bold and italic fonts
- Gradients
- Certain rendering features, such as lights, shadows, and certain types of materials
- Rays and xlines
- Named views and cameras
- Hidden edges

Using the Publish to Web Wizard

The Publish to Web feature creates HTML pages that display your drawings in DWFx, DWF, JPEG, or PNG format. Through the use of templates, you can upload drawings without getting involved in Web-design issues.

To publish drawings to the Web, first prepare your drawings and decide how many you want to publish. Then follow these steps:

1. Type **publishtoweb** ⏎ at the command prompt to open the Begin page of the Publish to Web Wizard.

2. Choose to create a new Web page or edit an existing one. Then click Next.

3. On the Create Web Page screen, shown in Figure 28.9, type a filename for the Web page. (This action creates a folder with this name and places all the files for the Web page in the folder.) Then click the ellipsis button (...) to navigate to where you want to create this file. If you already store Web page files on your system, you can use the same location. Finally, add a description that will appear on the Web page. Click Next.

4. On the Select Image Type screen, choose the type of image that you want to create, whether DWFx, DWF, JPEG, or PNG. As you choose each type from the drop-down list, a description appears on the screen. For JPEG and PNG, also click the image size that will appear on the Web page. Click Next.

5. On the Select Template screen, choose a template that structures your Web page, and click Next. You have four choices:

- **Array of Thumbnails.** Creates a set of thumbnail images. Clicking any image displays a larger image.

- **Array plus Summary.** Creates a set of thumbnail images. Adds information from the Summary tab of the Drawing Properties dialog box, displayed when the mouse cursor is over a thumbnail. (Choose Application Button ⇨ Drawing Utilities ⇨ Drawing Properties to create summary information.)

- **List of Drawings.** Creates a list of drawings and a frame displaying a drawing image. Users select a drawing from the list to update the image in the frame.

- **List plus Summary.** Creates a list of drawings, an image frame, and summary information from the Summary tab of the Drawing Properties dialog box, displayed when the mouse cursor is over a thumbnail. (Choose Application Button ⇨ Drawing Utilities ⇨ Drawing Properties to create summary information.)

FIGURE 28.9

On the Create Web Page screen, specify where you want to create your Web page on your own computer system, and create a description of the page.

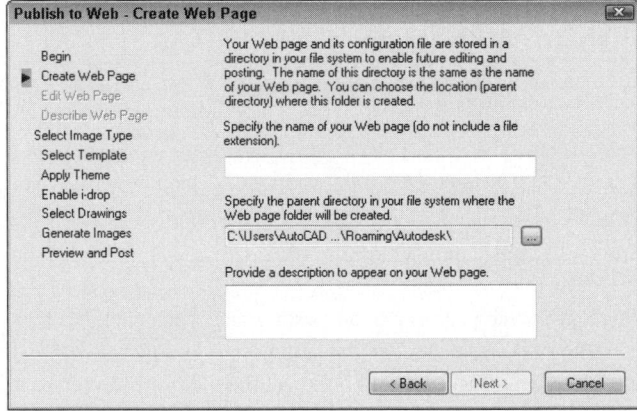

6. On the Apply Theme screen, choose one of the preset themes that control colors and fonts on your Web page. You see an example in the preview pane. Click Next.

7. On the Enable i-drop screen, choose whether you want to create an i-drop Web page so that users can drag actual drawings from the Web page into a drawing. Click Next.

8. On the Select Drawings screen, shown in Figure 28.10, choose the drawings that you want to publish. If the drawing is open, you can select it from the Drawing drop-down list. Select each drawing, choose a layout (or model) from the Layout drop-down list, type a label, and type a description to appear on the Web page. Then click Add. (If the drawing is not open, click the ellipsis button, navigate to the drawing, and click Open. Enter a label and description and then click Add.) Click Next.

9. On the Generate Images screen, choose to regenerate either all images or only those that have changes. (There is no difference if you're creating a new Web page.) Click Next and wait for the plotting process to complete.

FIGURE 28.10

On the Select Drawings screen, add each drawing that you want to include on the Web page, and specify a layout, label, and description for each.

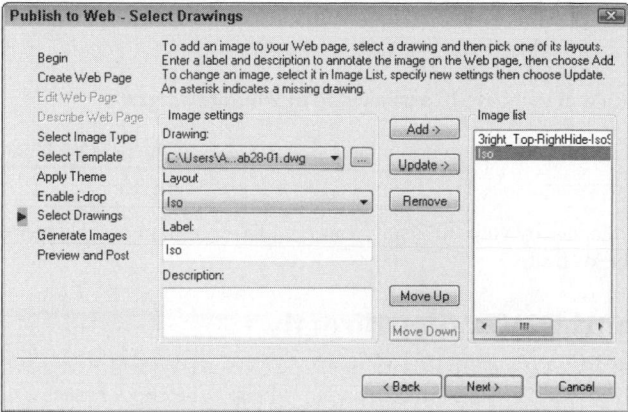

10. On the Preview and Post screen, click Preview to preview what the Web page will look like. Your Web browser opens and displays a fully functional Web page, including links, if any. Figure 28.11 shows an example.

FIGURE 28.11

A preview of some drawings using the Array of Thumbnails template and DWF files. You can click on any thumbnail to see the full-size DWF file. Note the i-drop icons.

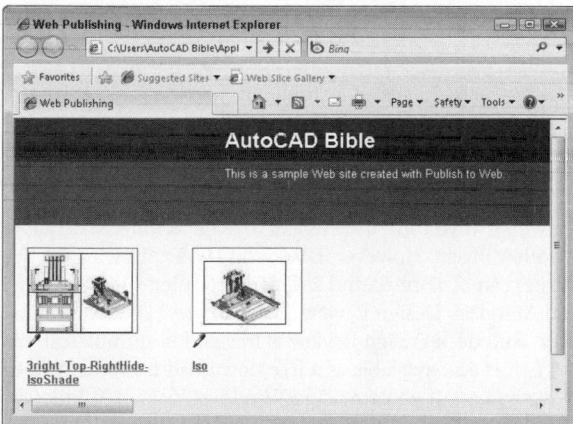

11. Click Post to post your new Web page. The Posting Web dialog box opens, which is like the Save As dialog box. In the Save In drop-down list, choose the desired location. To use FTP to post directly to a server, choose FTP locations or choose FTP from the Places list. (If you're saving to an intranet, you'll choose a location designated by your network administrator.) Double-click the

FTP location and wait until you see the folder structure of your Web site. If you want, double-click one of the folders to save there. (The Publish to Web process creates a number of files. You probably don't want them all in the root of your Web site.) Click Save. You should see a File Upload dialog box showing the progress of the file transfer. If everything goes well, you'll see a success message that posting has been successfully completed.

Note
Remember to also upload any files that you have hyperlinked to in your drawing. ■

12. If you want, click Send Email to notify people of the URL to the new Web page.

13. To find your new page, look for a file named `acwebpublish.htm`.

You can always upload the files by yourself, using your own FTP program or whatever other means you usually use to post to the Web site.

Posting DWF and DWFx files directly

You don't need to use the Publish to Web Wizard to place DWF or DWFx files on a Web site. You can upload 2D and 3D DWF and DWFx files directly, and give people the URL or place a link to them on another page. You can also create JPG or PNG images on your own, as I explained in Chapter 27, and use them to display an image of the DWF or DWFx file.

Editing Web pages

You can edit your Web page — for example, you can delete existing drawings and add new ones. Start the Publish to Web command and choose Edit Existing Web Page on the first screen. Click Next and choose the Web page that you want to edit by choosing a PTW (Publish to Web) file. Click Next again. From this point on, you can change any existing information.

On the Select Drawings screen, click Update to update a drawing that has changed since the last time that you created the Web page. Click Remove to remove a drawing. To add a new drawing, follow the same procedures described in the previous section.

To change the order of the drawings, select a layout from the list and click Move Up or Move Down until you have the results that you want. Continue through the wizard and re-post your drawings.

Viewing DWF and DWFx drawings

The final step is to view the drawings. If you use the Publish to Web Wizard to create JPEG or PNG files, you simply view them like any other image. However, DWF and DWFx drawings, whether viewed locally on a computer or from a Web site, can be panned and zoomed and offer other viewing options as well. To view a DWF drawing, you need Autodesk Design Review. You can view DWFx files in Autodesk Design Review or Microsoft XPS Viewer. Autodesk Design Review is free and is automatically installed when you install AutoCAD or AutoCAD LT. It is also available as a free download from the Autodesk Web site at `www.autodesk.com/designreview`. If you are using Windows Vista or Windows 7, the XPS Viewer comes installed, but if you are using Windows XP, you can download and install it for free. To learn more about the XPS viewer, you can visit the Microsoft Web site at `www.microsoft.com/xps`.

The XPS Viewer offers only basic viewing features, such as scrolling and changing the zoom percentage used. To view 3D DWFx files and the metadata saved with a DWFx file, you need Autodesk Design Review; you also get better viewing tools with Autodesk Design Review.

Autodesk Design Review can function in two ways:

- **As a stand-alone reader,** it opens like any other program. (You can generally find it by choosing Start ➪ [All] Programs ➪ Autodesk ➪ Autodesk Design Review 2011.) Choose File ➪ Open to open a DWF or DWFx file. You can also double-click the DWF or DWFx file in Windows Explorer. Use the reader in this way to view DWF or DWFx files without using AutoCAD or AutoCAD LT.

- **As an ActiveX component,** Autodesk Design Review functions within Microsoft Internet Explorer. Use the reader within Internet Explorer when you've posted DWF or DWFx files on a Web site. When you enter the URL in the browser, the DWF or DWFx file appears. (The ActiveX doesn't work in the Firefox Web browser. Instead, the browser offers to download the file or open it, using Autodesk Design Review.)

Note

Autodesk has a working solution for opening DWF files in Firefox. While it is not finalized yet, Autodesk has released it for you to try and provide feedback. You can download the Firefox Add-on for Autodesk Design Review at `http://labs.autodesk.com/utilities/firefox_adr/`**. Autodesk Labs is kind of window into projects that Autodesk is working on and are available for everyone to try, not quite like the closed Beta program (**`http://beta.autodesk.com`**) that Autodesk also runs. ■**

If you send DWF or DWFx files to clients or colleagues, you can send them the link to the Install file for Autodesk Design Review as well.

If you're given a DWF or DWFx file with a password, a dialog box opens, requesting the password before the DWF or DWFx file is displayed.

Using view options

To view any sheet in the DWF or DWFx file, choose it from the list at the left, or use the Next Page and Previous Page buttons on the viewer's toolbar. Choose the Views tab on the right side to display any named views that were saved with the drawing. You can use saved views to help a customer focus on certain details and provide information about the views that you saved.

By default, layer information is not included in the DWF or DWFx format. As explained earlier in this chapter, you can include layer information if you want. If the DWF or DWFx file includes layer information, viewers can choose the Layers tab on the right side, where they can choose to click the On or Off toggle next to a layer.

Viewers have complete freedom to pan and zoom however they want. Note that if you're sending a DWF or DWFx file to a client who doesn't use AutoCAD or AutoCAD LT, the controls may not be obvious, so you may need to provide an explanation. The controls are as follows:

- Fit to Window is equivalent to a Zoom Extents. The button looks like the Zoom Extents button.
- Zoom Rectangle does a Zoom Window.

- The 2D Navigation Wheel works just like the one in AutoCAD or AutoCAD LT.
- For 3D DWF and DWFx files only, the Orbit option functions somewhat like the 3D Orbit feature. (See Chapter 22 for an explanation of 3D Orbit.) Drag to tumble the model in any direction, as shown in Figure 28.12. Press Ctrl as you drag to constrain the tumbling to the vertical direction. Press Shift as you drag to tumble only horizontally. Press Ctrl and Shift together as you drag to constrain the view to rolling.
- For 3D DWF and DWFx files only, the viewer can use the ViewCube, which works like the one in AutoCAD. You can switch to a present view or rotate the current view. (See Chapter 22 for information on the ViewCube.)

Tip

The Orbit option works better if you first use the Zoom Rectangle option. Otherwise, the model tends to disappear from view as you drag. ■

FIGURE 28.12

You can use the Orbit option to tumble a 3D DWF file in any direction.

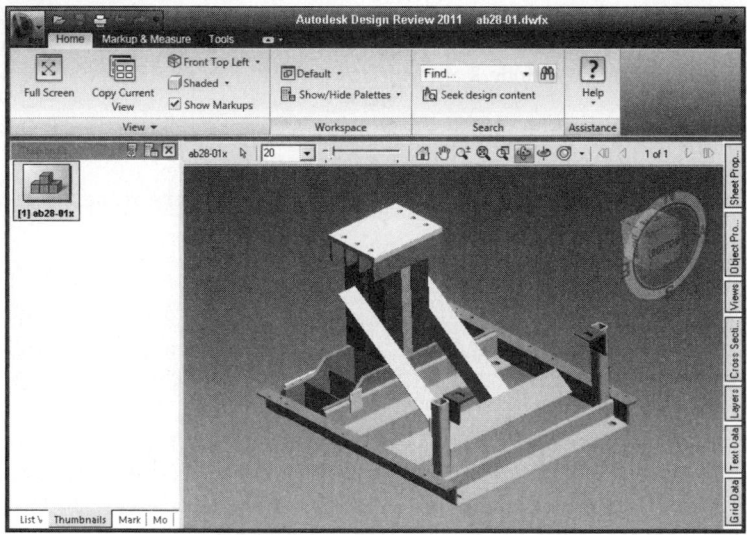

- Zoom enables you to zoom. Drag up to zoom in, and drag down to zoom out.
- Pan enables you to pan. Drag in any direction to pan in that direction.

A mouse with an IntelliMouse wheel works just as it would in AutoCAD or AutoCAD LT. Zoom in by scrolling forward, and zoom out by scrolling backward. Press the wheel and drag to pan.

If the DWF or DWFx file has hyperlinks, when your cursor passes over a URL area, you can click to follow the link, as shown in Figure 28.13.

FIGURE 28.13

Passing over a URL in a DWF file.

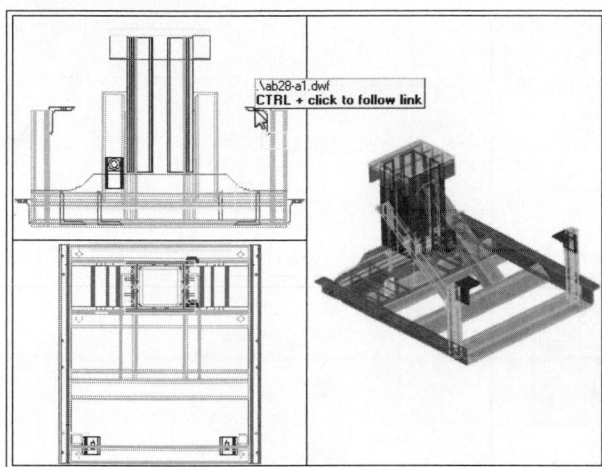

Printing and plotting

You can print/plot drawings from Autodesk Design Review. The print options are somewhat like those in Microsoft Word because they take into account the fact that a DWF or DWFx file can have many pages. Click the Print button on the Quick Access Toolbar to open the Print dialog box, as shown in Figure 28.14.

The Print dialog box offers the following features:

- **Printer.** In the Printer section, choose the printer or plotter that you want to use. Click Properties to specify how the printer/plotter functions. The features depend on the device that you choose. You can also select the Print to File check box to print to a file. Check Always Use This Printer if you typically use a printer other than the default Windows printer when using Autodesk Design Review.

- **Paper.** Choose the page size from the drop-down list. The available paper sizes vary, depending on your printer or plotter.

- **Print Range.** You can choose to print all pages, or you can specify the pages. You can also choose Full Page or Current View from the View drop-down list. (Remember that 3D DWF and 3D DWFx files can only have one page.)

- **Page Handling.** Choose the number of copies you want to print and whether you want to collate them.

- **Scaling and Alignment.** You can fit to the page or specify a scale. If you scale, you can tile or clip the pages. If you clip them, you can align to one corner of the paper or center the drawing.

- **Orientation.** Choose Portrait or Landscape.

- **Print Color.** You can choose to print the sheets or markups in color, black and white (2D DWF and DWFx files only), or grayscale.

- **Advanced.** Click Advanced to convert the data that is selected for printing into a bitmap; this can help to speed up printing, but it may use more memory. This option only affects 2D DWF and DWFx files.

FIGURE 28.14

The Print dialog box helps you to print or plot drawings from Autodesk Design Review.

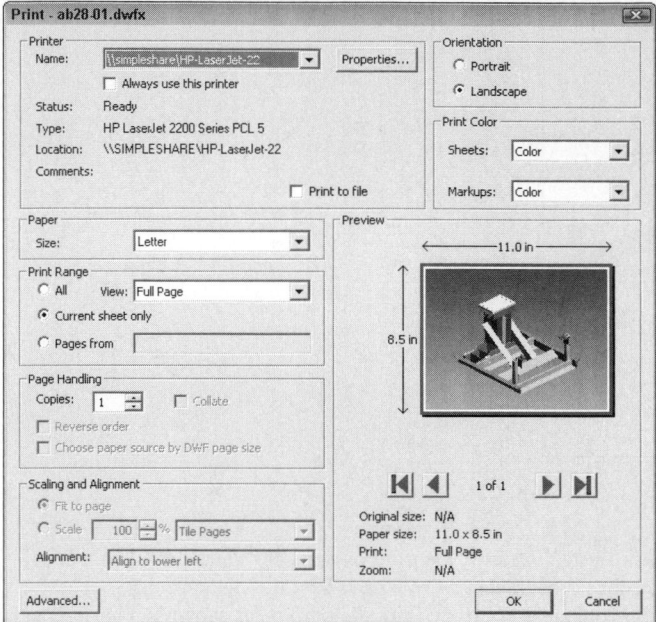

The Preview pane lets you visualize what the output will look like. If you choose All or multiple pages in the Print Range section, you can use the arrows to scroll through each page in a multipage DWF file.

Click OK to print. If you choose a size that doesn't fit on one sheet of paper, you see a message saying that the drawing may print across several pages.

On the DVD

The file used in the following exercise on viewing a DWF drawing, ab28-02.dwf, is in the Results folder of the DVD. ■

STEPS: Viewing a DWF Drawing

1. If you didn't do the exercise on creating a 2D DWF file, copy ab28-02.dwf from the DVD to your AutoCAD Bible folder. Open Windows Explorer and navigate to ab28-02.dwf. Double-click the file to open it in Autodesk Design Review.

Note

If the DWF file were on a Web site, you would view it by typing the URL in your browser. ■

2. Autodesk Design Review opens automatically and displays the DWF file that was created in the previous exercise. From the Contents item on the left pane of the Autodesk Design Review, choose the second sheet, labeled [2] ab28-01-Iso (11.0 x 8.5 in), as shown in Figure 28.15.

FIGURE 28.15

The DWF file as seen in Autodesk Design Review.

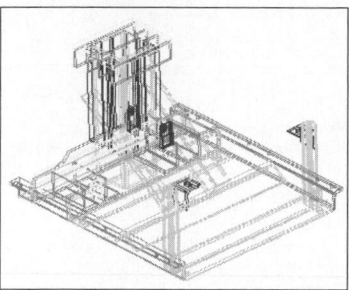

3. Right-click in the drawing to open the shortcut menu. Choose Zoom Rectangle. Drag a window to zoom in. Choose Pan from the shortcut menu, and pan to the left. Choose Fit in Window from the shortcut menu to return to the previous view.

4. To print the drawing to the system printer, click Print on the Quick Access Toolbar. In the Print dialog box, click the All option in the Print Range section. Click OK.

5. Close Autodesk Design Review.

Summary

In this chapter, you discovered how to integrate your drawings with the Internet. You read about the following:

- Faxing, e-mailing, and eTransmitting drawings
- Opening drawings from anywhere on the Internet
- Creating hyperlinks in your drawings
- Using the PUBLISH command to create DWF and DWFx files
- Creating 3D DWF and 3D DWF files
- Using the Publish to Web Wizard to create Web pages with DWFx, DWF, JPEG, or PNG images
- Utilizing Autodesk Design Review to view DWF and DWFx files

This chapter ends Part V, "Organizing and Managing Drawings." Part VI, "Customizing AutoCAD and AutoCAD LT," shows you the inner workings of AutoCAD and AutoCAD LT so that you can work in the way that best suits your needs. Chapter 29 explains how to create customized command shortcuts and toolbars.

Part VI

Customizing AutoCAD and AutoCAD LT

In Part VI, you discover how to make AutoCAD work the way you want. Customizing AutoCAD can speed up your work, make it easier, create standards for all drawings where you work, and automate often-used or repetitive tasks. You can customize the process of issuing commands as well as customize toolbars and tool palettes (Chapter 29), create macros and slide shows with script files (Chapter 30), create your own linetypes and hatch patterns (Chapter 31), create your own fonts and other shapes (Chapter 32), and customize AutoCAD's ribbon and menus (Chapter 33).

Customizing Commands, Toolbars, and Tool Palettes

C ustomizing AutoCAD and AutoCAD LT can increase your efficiency and productivity. The time spent in preparation will be paid back many times. Before you start customizing, you need to know some basics that apply to almost all customization tasks. After you understand these basics, the process becomes much easier.

Overall, AutoCAD LT offers less customizability than AutoCAD; however, most of the features in this chapter apply to both AutoCAD and AutoCAD LT.

Working with Customizable Files

The capability to customize AutoCAD and AutoCAD LT is based on the fact that many of the support files are text files that you can edit yourself. The menu customization and tool palettes are in XML files that you customize by using the Customize User Interface Editor and the Customize dialog box. Table 29.1 lists the most important files and their functions.

Figure 29.1 shows a portion of one of these files, `acad.pgp`, which lists command shortcuts, or aliases. The equivalent file for AutoCAD LT is `acadlt.pgp`. The files listed in the table can be located in one of AutoCAD's support file search paths (Application Button ⇨ Options, click the Files tab and then expand the Support File Search Path node). Others can be located by looking in the paths defined on the Files tab of the Options dialog box.

Tip
Use the Search text box from the Start menu or within Windows Explorer to help you locate a file. Each company sets up AutoCAD differently, so the Windows Search feature can be an invaluable tool when looking for customized files. ∎

IN THIS CHAPTER

Understanding the basics of customization

Creating keyboard shortcuts for commands

Customizing toolbars

Customizing the Quick Access Toolbar

Customizing tool palettes

FIGURE 29.1

You can edit the `acad.pgp` file to create keyboard shortcuts for AutoCAD commands.

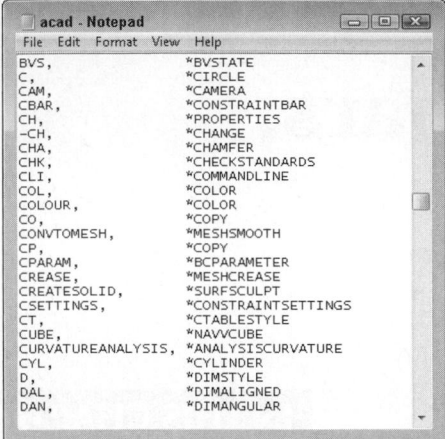

TABLE 29.1

Customizable Files

AutoCAD Filename	AutoCAD LT Filename	Function
sample.cus	sample.cus	Custom dictionary file. You can add words to the custom dictionary for use with the SPELL command.
acad.pgp	acadlt.pgp	Program parameters file. This file is generally used to create keyboard shortcuts (called aliases) for commands.
acad.cuix	acadlt.cuix	Customization file. You modify this file by using the Customize User Interface Editor. This file replaces the CUI files used in the 2006 through 2009 releases of AutoCAD and AutoCAD LT.
acad.mnl	N/A	AutoLISP routines used by AutoCAD's main menu. If you create your own menus, you can have an MNL file with the same name as your menu for AutoLISP routines (AutoCAD only).
acad2011.cfg	acadlt2011.cfg	Configuration file for storing digitizer and other settings. Usually, you should use the Options dialog box to make these selections, instead of manually editing this file. See Appendix A for more information about this file.
acad.dcl	acadlt.dcl	Dialog Control Language (DCL) file. This file describes dialog boxes. You usually don't edit this file, but you can write your own DCL files to create dialog boxes you display with AutoLISP. You would not create custom DCL files for AutoCAD LT because it lacks support for AutoLISP.
acad.lin and acadiso.lin	acadlt.lin and acadltiso.lin	Linetype definition file. You can also create your own linetype definition (LIN) files or add your own definitions to one of the standard linetype files.

AutoCAD Filename	AutoCAD LT Filename	Function
acad.lsp and acaddoc.lsp	N/A	AutoCAD's AutoLISP files. You create these files from scratch. You can edit or add to these files to automatically load AutoLISP routines. Other customizable LSP files are discussed in Chapter 35 (AutoCAD only).
acad.mln	N/A	AutoCAD's multiline library file (AutoCAD only).
acad.pat and acadiso.pat	acadlt.pat and acadltiso.pat	AutoCAD's hatch pattern file. You can also create your own.
*.pc3	*.pc3	Plot configuration files. You can also create your own. A PC3 file contains all configuration settings for a plotter. This is not a text file; you customize it by using a dialog box. For more information, see Chapter 17 and Appendix A.
acad.fmp	acadlt.fmp	Font mapping file. Use this file to specify substitute fonts, whether or not the original fonts are available on your system.
acad.psf	acadlt.psf	PostScript support file. It is used for the PSOUT and PSFILL commands. PSFILL is in AutoCAD only.
acad.slb	acadlt.slb	Slide library file, used for hatch pattern examples in customization files. You can use this file or create your own slide libraries. This is not a text file; see Chapter 30 for an explanation of how to create a slide library.
*.scr	*.scr	A script file that you create and name. Script files are macros of commands and options that run automatically.
*.shp	*.shp	A shape file that you create and name. Shape files usually hold fonts, but can hold other shapes as well. A shape file is then compiled into a file with an SHX extension for more efficient use.
acad.rx	N/A	A list of ObjectARX (a programming interface for AutoCAD) applications that load automatically (AutoCAD only). You must create this file, if you are going to load ObjectARX files, by using this method.
mtextmap.ini	mtextmap.ini	Font mapping for the appearance of text in the MTEXT editor.
*.adsklib	N/A	A material library file that you create to store custom materials used when rendering 3D objects (AutoCAD only). For more information on materials and rendering, see Chapter 25.
acad.unt	acadlt.unt	A file that defines every conceivable type of unit.

Editing customizable files

To customize AutoCAD or AutoCAD LT, you edit a text file, use the Customize User Interface Editor, or use the Customize dialog box. To edit files in text-only (ASCII) format, you need a text editor, which is like a word processor but does not place any formatting codes in the file. For most of the ASCII files, you can use Notepad, which comes with Windows. All major word processors let you save documents as text documents — just remember not to click that Save button until you've specified the right file format. Files that are not in ASCII format generally have an interface, such as a dialog box, in the program for editing them.

Backing up customizable files

Before editing any preexisting files, back them up. The system of editing user interface elements, such as menus and toolbars, in a dialog box helps to protect your system from errors that you might make when customizing, but if you want to undo all your changes, you need a backup. You should back up in three stages:

- Back up the original file as it came out of the box. Keep a disk with all the customizable files that you might ever edit in their original form.

- After you edit the file, back it up before each editing session. This way you always have your most recent version of the file. If you make a mistake, it's easy to copy that file on top of the one with the mistake and put everything back to normal.

- After you edit a file, back it up again so that you have it in case your hard drive crashes, or you need to reinstall AutoCAD or AutoCAD LT.

Note

To find `acad.cuix` or `acadlt.cuix`, choose Application Button⇨Options and click the Files tab. Open the Customization Files item, and then open the Main Customization File item. The location of this file is listed there. ■

This means that you should have two disks, one with the original customizable files and one with your most recent versions of them. At the very least, these disks should contain the following files:

- `acad.lin` and `acadiso.lin`/`acadlt.lin` and `acadltiso.lin`
- `acad.lsp` and `acaddoc.lsp` (AutoCAD only)
- `acad.mln` (AutoCAD only)
- `acad.mnl` (AutoCAD only)
- `acad.cuix`/`acadlt.cuix`
- `acad.pat` and `acadiso.pat`/`acadlt.pat` and `acadltiso.pat`
- `acad.pgp`/`acadlt.pgp`

You may also want to back up drawing templates that you've created.

Tip

If you get into trouble, you can find an original copy of many of the customizable files at `C:\Program Files\Autodesk\AutoCAD 2011\UserDataCache\Support` for AutoCAD and `C:\Program Files\Autodesk\AutoCAD LT 2011\UserDataCache\Support` for AutoCAD LT (if you used the default installation location). ■

You'll use these disks not only when you make a mistake, but also whenever you need to reinstall AutoCAD or AutoCAD LT, whether due to hard-drive failure, a virus on your system, the replacement of your old computer with a new one, or some other reason. Also, when you upgrade AutoCAD or AutoCAD LT to the next release, you can usually continue to work with your familiar, customized files.

Cross-Reference

In Appendix A, I discuss the Migrate Custom Settings dialog box that appears when you install or upgrade AutoCAD or AutoCAD LT. This dialog box helps you to bring existing customizable files into your new installation of AutoCAD or AutoCAD LT. ■

Using the command-line form of commands

For many customization tasks, you need to work with commands. When you create a *script file*, which is a series of commands, or when you edit the menu file, you need to type out the commands that you want to execute. In these cases, the customizable files can only contain the command-line form of the commands. As a result, you need to learn a whole new way of working — the old-fashioned way, by typing commands on the command line.

Tip

If you're not sure of the command name but you know the menu or toolbar item, execute the command from a user interface and then press Esc. You see the command name on the command line. ■

A number of commands have a non-dialog-box version. Many commands can be executed in their command-line version by placing a hyphen (-) before the command name. For some commands that have no command-line equivalent, you can use system variables to create the same effect. Table 29.2 lists command-line versions of commands that you can use for customization.

TABLE 29.2

Command-Line Forms of Commands

Command	Command-Line Form	Command	Command-Line Form
3DCONFIG	-3DCONFIG (AutoCAD only)	ACTSTOP	-ACTSTOP (AutoCAD only)
3DOSNAP	-3DOSNAP (AutoCAD only)	ACTUSERMESSAGE	-ACTUSERMESSAGE (AutoCAD only)
ARCHIVE	-ARCHIVE (AutoCAD only)	ARRAY	-ARRAY
ATTACH	-ATTACH	ATTDEF	-ATTDEF
ATTEDIT	-ATTEDIT	ATTEXT	-ATTEXT
BEDIT	-BEDIT	BLOCK	-BLOCK
BOUNDARY	-BOUNDARY	COLOR	-COLOR
COPYTOLAYER	-COPYTOLAYER	CVREBUILD	-CVREBUILD (AutoCAD only)
DATAEXTRACTION	-DATAEXTRACTION (AutoCAD only)	DDPTYPE	PDMODE, PDSIZE
DDVPOINT	VPOINT	DGNADJUST	-DGNADJUST (AutoCAD only)
DGNATTACH	-DGNATTACH	DGNEXPORT	-DGNEXPORT
DGNIMPORT	-DGNIMPORT	DIMINSPECT	-DIMINSPECT
DIMSTYLE	-DIMSTYLE	DSETTINGS	ORTHO, SNAP, GRID, ISOPLANE, AUTOSNAP, SNAPTYPE, DYNMODE, DYNPROMPT

continued

TABLE 29.2 (continued)

Command	Command-Line Form	Command	Command-Line Form
DWFADJUST	-DWFADJUST (AutoCAD only)	DWFATTACH	-DWFATTACH
EATTEXT	-EATTEXT (AutoCAD only)	ETRANSMIT	-ETRANSMIT
GROUP	-GROUP	HATCH	-HATCH
HATCHEDIT	-HATCHEDIT	HYPERLINK	-HYPERLINK
IMAGE	-IMAGE	IMAGEADJUST	-IMAGEADJUST
INSERT	-INSERT	INTERFERE	-INTERFERE (AutoCAD only)
LAYDEL	-LAYDEL	LAYER	-LAYER
LAYMCH	-LAYMCH	LAYMRG	-LAYMRG
LINETYPE	-LINETYPE	LWEIGHT	-LWEIGHT
MLEDIT	-MLEDIT (AutoCAD only)	MTEXT	-MTEXT
OBJECTSCALE	-OBJECTSCALE	OPENSHEETSET	-OPENSHEETSET (AutoCAD only)
OSNAP	-OSNAP	PAN	-PAN
PARAMETERS	-PARAMETERS	PARTIALOAD	-PARTIALOAD (AutoCAD only)
PDFADJUST	-PDFADJUST	PDFATTACH	-PDFATTACH
PLOT	-PLOT	PLOTSTAMP	-PLOTSTAMP
PLOTSTYLE	-PLOTSTYLE	POINTCLOUDATTACH	-POINTCLOUDATTACH (AutoCAD only)
PROPERTIES	CHANGE, CHPROP, -COLOR, -LAYER, -LINETYPE, CELTYPE, CELTSCALE, ELEV, THICKNESS	PSETUPIN	-PSETUPIN
PUBLISH	-PUBLISH (AutoCAD only), +PUBLISH	PURGE	-PURGE
REFEDIT	-REFEDIT	RENAME	-RENAME
RENDER	-RENDER (AutoCAD only)	SCALELISTEDIT	-SCALELISTEDIT
STYLE	-STYLE	TABLE	-TABLE
TEXT	-TEXT	TOOLBAR	-TOOLBAR
UNITS	-UNITS	VIEW	-VIEW
VISUALSTYLES	-VISUALSTYLES (AutoCAD only)	VPORTS	-VPORTS
WBLOCK	-WBLOCK	WSSAVE	-WSSAVE
XBIND	-XBIND	XREF	-XREF

In addition, you can use the dimension variables to format dimensions in place of using the DIMSTYLE command, which opens the Dimension Style Manager dialog box. Chapter 15 discusses the DIMSTYLE command.

The FILEDIA system variable determines whether a dialog box opens for commands, such as SAVEAS and OPEN, that request filenames. When FILEDIA is set to 1, the default dialog boxes open. The CMDDIA system variable affects the display of command-related dialog boxes or in-place editors for such commands as LEADER and QLEADER.

Note
Even if FILEDIA is set to 1, if a script or AutoLISP/ObjectARX program is active, the command prompt is used rather than a dialog box. You can still set the FILEDIA system variable to 0, but be sure to change it back again at the end of your script or program. (Scripts, but not AutoLISP or ObjectARX programs, are available in AutoCAD LT.) ∎

Documenting your files

Placing comments in customized files to explain how you customized them is standard practice. Although your customizations may seem obvious at the time, if you go back to a file later, you may not understand what you were trying to accomplish. Also, other people may need some explanation.

You can place comments in many of the customizable files by placing a semicolon (;) before any line of text.

Now that you know the basics of customizing files, you can move on to creating keyboard shortcuts and customizing toolbars.

Creating Shortcuts for Commands

You can create keyboard shortcuts for commands, thereby enabling you to enter commands on the command line without remembering and typing the full command name. Shortcuts are stored in the `acad.pgp` file for AutoCAD and the `acadlt.pgp` file for AutoCAD LT. To open the PGP file, choose Manage tab ⇨ Customization panel ⇨ Edit Aliases.

You can use this file for three purposes:

- To create shortcuts to Windows programs (AutoCAD only)
- To create shortcuts to DOS commands (AutoCAD only)
- To create keyboard shortcuts for AutoCAD and AutoCAD LT commands

The auto-complete feature completes commands that you start to type in the Dynamic Input tooltip or on the command line. Type as many letters as you know, and then press Tab or Shift+Tab to cycle through all the commands that start with those letters.

Cross-Reference
You can also create keyboard shortcuts, such as Ctrl+G or F11, for commands. See Chapter 33 for more information. The shortcuts in `acad.pgp` and `acadlt.pgp` use only letters and numbers. ∎

Creating shortcuts to Windows programs

In AutoCAD, you can use the `acad.pgp` file to create shortcuts to Windows programs. For example, you may often open Notepad while customizing files. The `acad.pgp` file includes the following three shortcuts to Windows programs:

```
EXPLORER, START EXPLORER, 1,,
NOTEPAD,  START NOTEPAD, 1,*File to edit: ,
PBRUSH,   START PBRUSH,  1,,
```

AutoCAD Only

The AutoCAD LT `acadlt.pgp` file does not support shortcuts to Windows programs. ■

The first column is the command name that you type at the command line. The second column is the command that you want Windows to execute. The number 1 specifies to start the application but not to wait until you've finished using it. This lets you return to your drawing at any time. After the 1, you can finish with two commas. However, notice that the Notepad entry has `*File to edit:` before the last comma. This is a prompt that you see on the command line. Type the name of the file to edit, and Windows opens it in Notepad. (You need to type in the complete path of the file.) To open Notepad without a file, press Enter at the `*File to edit:` prompt.

Creating keyboard shortcuts to commands

Most of the `acad.pgp` or `acadlt.pgp` files contain aliases, or keyboard shortcuts, for common commands. You can change these or add your own. After you become used to them, it's often faster to type shortcuts at the command line than to click the Ribbon button or menu item, especially if your hands are already on the keyboard. You cannot include a command option in the `acad.pgp` file. To do that, you need to create a Ribbon button, a menu item (accessible from the menu bar), a toolbar button, or an AutoLISP routine. Remember that the menu bar and toolbars are not displayed in the default AutoCAD and AutoCAD LT workspaces.

AutoCAD Only

The Express Tools contain an Alias Editor that enables you to edit the `acad.pgp` file through a dialog box interface. Choose Express Tools tab ➪ Tools panel ➪ Command Aliases. ■

On the DVD

`Quickkey` is an expanded replacement for `acad.pgp` that supports commands with their options, such as ZOOM Previous. Look in `\Software\Chapter 29\Quickkey`. ■

The format for creating an alias is as follows:

```
Shortcut,*Full command name
```

Refer to Figure 29.1 for some examples of command aliases. Note that the space between the columns is not necessary — it simply improves readability.

Note

The `acad.pgp` and `acadlt.pgp` files contain a special User Defined Command Aliases section at the end for creating your own aliases. Aliases in this section override aliases in the main section. ■

You can use an alias transparently if the command itself can be used transparently. Aliases in script files or menus can fail when used on an installation of AutoCAD that doesn't have those aliases defined. Note that you cannot use control or function keys in command aliases in the PGP file.

Caution

If you're working on someone else's computer, don't do the following exercise without that person's permission. It isn't good computer etiquette to modify other people's files without asking first. ∎

STEPS: Customizing the PGP File

1. Start AutoCAD or AutoCAD LT.
2. Prepare and insert a backup medium, such as a flash drive or CD-RW. Do one of the following:
   - If you have AutoCAD, type **explorer** ⏎. After opening a preliminary window, the acad.pgp shortcut opens Windows Explorer.
   - If you have AutoCAD LT, open Windows Explorer by right-clicking the Windows Start button and choosing Explore.

Note

To find the location of `acad.pgp` **or** `acadlt.pgp`, **choose Application Button⇨Options and click the Files tab. Double-click Support File Search Path to display the location of the support files. ∎**

3. Find `acad.pgp` or `acadlt.pgp`, click it, and drag it to the drive for your backup medium (in the Folders window). Windows copies `acad.pgp` or `acadlt.pgp` to the backup medium. If you haven't already backed up your other customizable files and you're using AutoCAD, copy `acad.lin`, `acad.lsp`, `acad.mln`, `acad.mnl`, `acad.cuix`, and `acad.pat` to the backup medium as well. If you're using AutoCAD LT, back up the `acadlt.lin`, `acadlt.cuix`, and `acadlt.pat` files.
4. In AutoCAD or AutoCAD LT, choose Manage tab⇨Customization panel⇨Edit Aliases to open `acad.pgp` or `acadlt.pgp`.
5. In AutoCAD only, scroll down roughly two screens until you see the three Windows commands, as shown in Figure 29.2. Place the cursor at the end of the PBRUSH line and press Enter.

FIGURE 29.2

The Windows commands in the acad.pgp file.

```
; Examples of external commands for Windows
; See also the (STARTAPP) AutoLISP function for
an alternative method.

EXPLORER,   START EXPLORER, 1,,
NOTEPAD,    START NOTEPAD,  1,*File to edit: ,
PBRUSH,     START PBRUSH,   1,,
```

6. In AutoCAD only, type the following and press Enter (the uppercase format and spaces are used to match the format of the rest of the file):

```
WORDPAD,    START WORDPAD,  1,,
```

7. Look at the next section of `acad.pgp` or `acadlt.pgp`. Read the guidelines for creating new aliases.

8. Scroll down until you see the following two lines:

```
CH,      *PROPERTIES
-CH,     *CHANGE
```

The alias for the CHANGE command follows the guideline of using a hyphen to distinguish command-line versions of commands. Suppose you have trouble finding that hyphen quickly (you end up typing =ch instead). You want to change the alias to cg (with no hyphen).

9. Scroll down to the end of the file until you see the User Defined Command Aliases section. Place the cursor at the very end of the file and press Enter. Type the following and press Enter (don't worry about the spaces; I've matched the spacing of the `acad.pgp` or `acadlt.pgp` file):

```
CG,      *CHANGE
```

10. Choose File ⇨ Save.

11. Close Notepad. Generally, `acad.pgp` or `acadlt.pgp` is accessed only when you load a new or existing drawing. However, you can use the REINIT command to reload the file at any time. Type **reinit** ↵. The Re-initialization dialog box opens, as shown in Figure 29.3.

The Re-initialization dialog box.

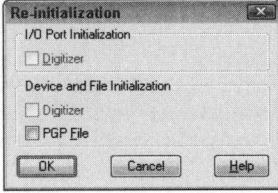

12. Check the PGP File check box and click OK. In your drawing, draw a line anywhere on the screen.

13. Type **cg** ↵. The CHANGE command starts. Select the line, right-click to end selection, and pick a new endpoint location. The endpoint of the line changes accordingly.

14. If you are using AutoCAD, type **wordpad** ↵. The WordPad application is started.

15. Do not save your drawing.

On the DVD

The edited `acad.pgp` and `acadlt.pgp` files are on the DVD in the `Results` folder. Although you made only two changes, if you want, you can copy the `acad.pgp` or `acadlt.pgp` file from the DVD over your original `acad.pgp` or `acadlt.pgp` file. Of course, you can make additional changes to suit your needs. ∎

Customizing Toolbars

 The Customize User Interface Editor, shown in Figure 29.4, combines the tools that you need to manage most aspects of the user interface, including the Quick Access Toolbar, Ribbon, toolbars, menus, keyboard shortcuts, and more. To open the Customize User Interface Editor, choose Manage tab ⇨ Customization panel ⇨ User Interface to start the CUI command.

In this section, I explain how to use the Customize User Interface Editor to customize toolbars, including the Quick Access Toolbar. You can create toolbars, create custom commands, design toolbar buttons, delete toolbars that are no longer needed, customize existing toolbars, and add or remove commands from the Quick Access Toolbar. Note that the default workspace for AutoCAD and AutoCAD LT, 2D Drafting & Annotation, shows only one toolbar, the Quick Access Toolbar.

In the default workspace, the Ribbon replaces toolbars, except for the Quick Access Toolbar. You can customize the Quick Access Toolbar so that the commands that you use most frequently are easily accessible. The Classic workspace includes the traditional menus and toolbars from previous releases. You can add toolbars to any workspace.

Note

The CUI files used in the 2006 through 2009 releases of AutoCAD and AutoCAD LT were replaced by the CUIx file format starting with the 2010 release. You can migrate your customization from a CUI file to a CUIx file using the Customize User Interface Editor. ■

Tip

To display a toolbar, click the Customize button (the drop-down arrow) on the right end of the Quick Access Toolbar, and choose Show Menu Bar. From the menu bar, choose Tools ⇨ Toolbars ⇨ AutoCAD (or AutoCAD LT), and click the toolbar that you want to display from the list of toolbars. You can also choose View tab ⇨ Windows panel ⇨ Toolbars drop-down list ⇨ AutoCAD (or AutoCAD LT), and click the toolbar that you want to display from the list of toolbars. ■

Cross-Reference

For information on customizing the Ribbon and other aspects of the user interface, see Chapter 33. Note that when you apply a change to the user interface, all aspects of the interface are updated, including the Workspaces feature, which provides a way to create and save multiple interface displays. Therefore, you may find that various toolbars, palettes, and so on suddenly open when you return to your drawing. To learn how to control workspaces, see Appendix A. ■

Tip

Typing quickcui opens a simplified view of the Customize User Interface Editor. You can also access this simplified view by right-clicking toolbars or tool palettes, and choosing Customize (or Customize Commands). This view lets you easily drag commands onto a toolbar or tool palette. Click the right arrow at the bottom of the dialog box to expand it to its full size. ■

FIGURE 29.4

The Customize User Interface Editor with the Dimension toolbar item selected.

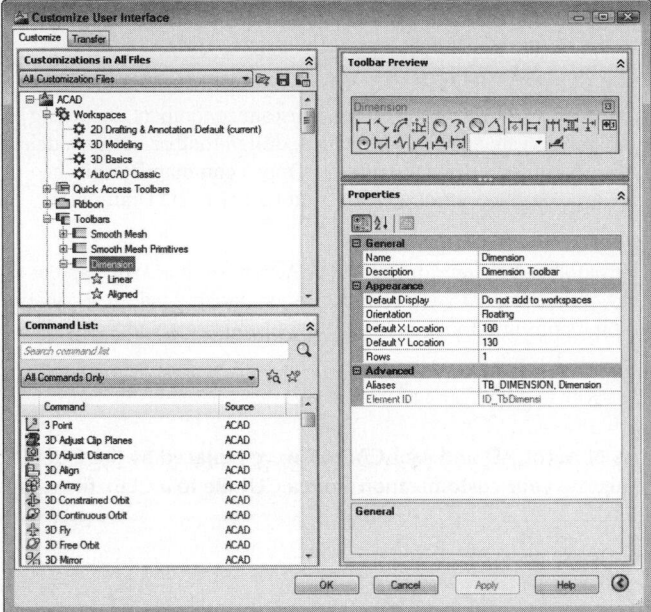

Customizing classic toolbars

How many times have you found yourself typing a command because you couldn't quickly find an equivalent button on a toolbar, or because it was on a flyout that required too many clicks to access? In addition, think of how often you start a command with a toolbar button, only to return to the keyboard to type in a simple option.

You can customize the toolbars to make your work easier and faster. You can create new toolbars from scratch, or edit existing ones. You can even create your own toolbar buttons. When you create a toolbar button, you can attach any sequence of commands to it, such as a complex macro, the command name defined by an action macro (AutoCAD only), or even an AutoLISP expression (AutoCAD only).

Although classic toolbars do not appear in the default workspace in AutoCAD or AutoCAD LT, you may want to use the Classic workspace, which includes toolbars, or add a toolbar to the default workspace or a custom workspace. Therefore, the skills for customizing toolbars are very useful.

Removing buttons from an existing toolbar

You can customize any existing toolbar by removing buttons that you rarely use. To remove buttons from a toolbar, follow these steps:

1. Choose Manage tab ⇨ Customization panel ⇨ User Interface to start the CUI command and display the Customize User Interface Editor.

2. In the Customizations In pane, with All Customization Files selected in the drop-down list, double-click the Toolbars item to expand the list of all the toolbars.

3. Double-click the toolbar that you want to work with to expand its list of buttons.

4. Right-click the button that you want to remove, and choose Remove from the shortcut menu.

Creating a new toolbar

You may want to create your own toolbar from scratch that contains buttons for commands that you use often. To avoid changing the main customization file, you should use the `custom.cuix` file. If this is not loaded by default, you can find it in the `Support` folder with the main customization file. This file is a separate *partial customization file*. Using a partial customization file helps you to keep your customization files separate from the standard customization file (`acad.cuix` or `acadlt.cuix`). For more information on partial customization files, see Chapter 33.

To create a new toolbar, first choose `custom.cuix` from the drop-down list at the top of the Customizations In pane of the Customize User Interface Editor. Then right-click the Toolbars item and choose New Toolbar.

Tip

You can also create a new partial customization file. On the Transfer tab of the Customize User Interface Editor, choose New File from the Customizations In drop-down list on the right. From the drop-down list, choose Save As. In the Save As dialog box, name the new file. Make sure that you use a name that is different from all other customization files. To use the file, go to the Customize tab and choose Main Customization File from the drop-down list in the Customizations In pane. Then click the Load Partial Customization File button to the right of the drop-down list. In the Open dialog box, locate the partial CUIx file and click Open. Again choose Main Customization File from the drop-down list. You should now see the new file listed if you expand the Partial Customization Files item. ■

A new toolbar appears under the Toolbars item, named Toolbar1. You can immediately rename this toolbar or right-click it and choose Rename. If you click Apply, a small, new toolbar appears on the screen. You may need to reposition the Customize User Interface Editor to see the new toolbar.

The new toolbar is just a baby, but with some nurturing, by adding buttons to it, it grows automatically.

Adding buttons

After you've created a new toolbar, you need to add buttons to it. One method is to add a command from the Command List pane of the Customize User Interface Editor. Follow these steps:

1. On the Customize tab, in the Customizations In pane, choose All Customization Files from the drop-down list.

2. If you are working in a partial customization file, double-click the Partial Customization Files item to expand it.

3. Expand the Toolbars item to display the list of toolbars.

4. Select the toolbar that you want to add buttons to.

5. From the Categories drop-down list of the Command List pane, choose All Commands or a category that displays the command that you want to add.

6. Drag the command from the list to the toolbar item in the Customizations In pane until you see an arrow pointing to the toolbar.

When you create a new toolbar, it appears in the Toolbar Preview pane. You can drag commands from the Command List to the preview of the toolbar. (However, for the first button, you need to use the method just described.) Also, to quickly add a new button to an existing toolbar, you can right-click the toolbar and choose Customize from the bottom of the list of toolbars. The simplified view of the Customize User Interface Editor opens, listing all the commands. You can then drag the command you want to the desired location on the toolbar.

Tip
To check the results of your customization before closing the Customize User Interface Editor, click Apply and then move the editor so that it doesn't cover the new toolbar. If you are satisfied, click OK to close the editor. ■

You can also move a button from one toolbar to another. In the Customize User Interface Editor, expand the toolbar that contains the button that you want to move. Then drag the button to your new toolbar or to any other toolbar. This moves the button, deleting it from the original toolbar.

To copy a button from another toolbar, use the same technique as for moving a button, but hold down the Ctrl key as you drag a button from one toolbar to another toolbar. This procedure leaves the first toolbar intact. You can also copy a button by right-clicking over the button, choosing Copy, and then pasting it into the desired location.

Tip
To help organize your toolbars, you can add separator spaces. With the toolbar expanded, right-click the button above where you want to add the space and choose Insert Separator. You can also drag buttons to change their order, either in the Customizations In pane or in the Toolbar Preview pane. ■

Creating a custom command

You can also create your own commands from scratch, which you display on a toolbar as a button. This involves creating a custom command macro and then choosing or designing a button icon. Follow these steps to create a custom command:

1. In the Customizations In pane, double-click the Toolbars item and choose the toolbar that you want to work with.

2. In the Command List pane, click the Create a New Command button. The Properties pane shows the properties of the new command, as shown in Figure 29.5.

3. In the Name text box, replace the default name (Command1) with your own name. This name appears as the title for a tooltip, so don't make it too long.

4. Type a helpful description in the Description text box. This text appears in a tooltip to further explain the function of the command.

FIGURE 29.5

You define a toolbar button in the Properties pane of the Customize User Interface Editor.

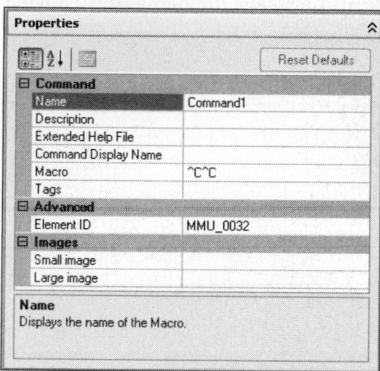

5. Write the macro in the Macro text box. The ^c^c cancels any other command that may be active when you use the command. After that, place any valid command string or action macro name as it would be typed on the command line, or even an AutoLISP expression. Both action macros and AutoLISP are available only in AutoCAD.

Cross-Reference
You need to use menu syntax for the macro. I explain the details of creating command strings in Chapter 33, where I cover customizing menus in depth. ■

6. From the Categories drop-down list, choose Custom Commands. Drag the new command onto a toolbar.
7. Select the button in the Command List pane. In the Button Image pane, choose a button icon from the list of button icons, or click Edit to create a custom image for your button, as explained in the next section.
8. Click Apply to save the changes and keep the Customize User Interface Editor displayed, or click OK to save the changes and close it.

Using the Button Editor
The Button Editor, shown in Figure 29.6, enables you to make your own button icons. In the Customizations In pane of the Customize User Interface Editor, select the toolbar command that you want to work with. Open the Button Editor by clicking Edit in the Button Image pane of the Customize User Interface Editor. You must choose one of the provided buttons before you can create or edit an existing button image.

Note

To help you find the right button to edit, each button in the Button Image pane shows a tooltip with the name of its image file. When you click an image, the larger preview also displays the name of the image file. ■

FIGURE 29.6

The Button Editor lets you design your own toolbar buttons.

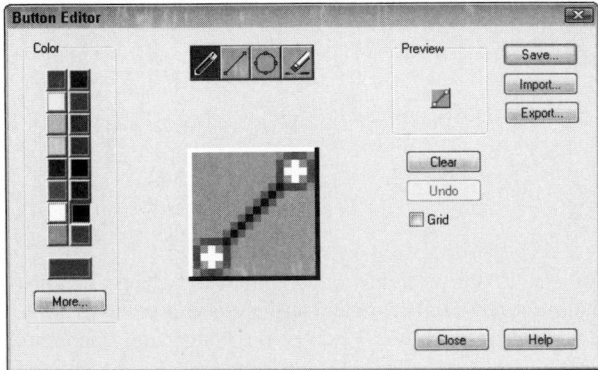

The center of the editing area shows an enlarged view of the button. You see the button's actual size to the right of the editing area of the dialog box. Check the Grid check box to show a grid of pixels — this is just a drawing aid. Choose a color from the color palette and then choose one of the four tools at the top of the dialog box:

- The Pencil tool draws any shape. To draw, click anywhere to draw pixel by pixel, or drag across the editing area.
- Click and drag the Line tool to draw a straight line.
- The Circle tool draws circles and ellipses. You click the center and drag out to the circumference to indicate the radius.
- The Erase tool erases. You can click to erase pixel by pixel, or drag to erase a series of pixels.

Here are the other features of the Button Editor:

- Click Clear to clear the editing area and start from scratch.
- Click Import to load an existing button image that is stored externally of the CUIx file for editing. Button images are stored as BMP files in the CUIx package file.
- Click Undo to undo your most recent action.
- Click Save to save the custom image to a BMP file under a new name in the CUIx file.
- Click Export to save the button image as a BMP file that is stored outside of the CUIx file. The default location is the Icons folder, which you can find by choosing Application Button ⇨ Options, clicking the Files tab, expanding Customization Files and then clicking the Custom Icon Location.
- Click Close to exit the Button Editor.
- Click More to select a standard index color or true color.

If you edited an existing button and saved the changes, then you're done. However, if you saved your button image under another filename, you need to associate the new file with the toolbar button. In the Properties pane, click the Small Image text box, and then select the image from the palette of images or click the Ellipsis (...) button. If you click the Ellipsis button, browse to the BMP file and choose it. Click Open. This action imports the BMP file into the CUIx file and its name appears in the Small Image text box. You can now click Apply, or if you want to return to your drawing, click OK.

Tip

You can import BMP images into the palette of images in the Button Image pane. Right-click the image palette and choose Import Image. After browsing to the image and importing it, you can assign it to any command. ■

If you think you might ever want to display large toolbar buttons, do the same for the Large Image text box. By default, when you create a button image, the Both option button is selected in the Button Image pane, so you create both a small and a large image. To display large toolbar buttons, choose Application Button ⇨ Options and click the Display tab. In the Window Elements section, check the Use Large Buttons for Toolbars check box.

Creating flyouts

Flyouts are toolbars that expand from a toolbar button. You can use the Customize User Interface Editor to create your own flyouts, or you can use one of the existing flyouts. To use an existing flyout, just drag one toolbar onto another one. Expand the Toolbars item in the Customizations In pane. Then expand the toolbar that you want to work with. In the same pane, locate the toolbar that you want to turn into a flyout, and drag it to any location on the expanded toolbar.

To create your own flyout from scratch, follow these steps:

1. Expand the Toolbars item in the Customizations In pane.
2. Right-click any toolbar and choose New Flyout.
3. Right-click the new flyout (named Toolbar1 by default) and choose Rename. Type a name for the flyout.
4. From the Command List pane, drag commands to the flyout, using the same technique as described in the "Adding buttons" section earlier in this chapter.

Removing custom commands

You can remove custom commands that you added to the customization file and no longer use. To remove a custom command, follow these steps:

1. Choose Manage tab ⇨ Customization panel ⇨ User Interface to display the Customize User Interface Editor.
2. In the Command List pane, from the Categories drop-down list, choose Custom Commands.
3. From the Command list, right-click the custom command that you want to delete, and choose Delete from the shortcut menu.

Note

If you try to delete a command that is in use, you see a message stating that the command can't be deleted, and the location of the command is highlighted in the Customizations In pane. ■

Customizing the Quick Access Toolbar

Being able to access the commands that you use frequently is important, and the Quick Access Toolbar allows you to do just that. The Quick Access Toolbar is located in the upper-left corner of the application window, just to the right of the Application button, and above or below the Ribbon when it is displayed. The current workspace determines which commands are accessible from the Quick Access Toolbar. By default, you can create, open, save, and plot a drawing, undo or redo your most recent actions, as well as switch between workspaces.

Creating and displaying a Quick Access Toolbar

You can create custom Quick Access Toolbars to display the commands that you might frequently use and want to access, no matter which toolbars or Ribbon panels are currently displayed. After you create a new Quick Access Toolbar, you must assign it to the Quick Access Toolbars node of a workspace in order to display it in the application window. Follow these steps:

1. Choose Manage tab ⇨ Customization panel ⇨ User Interface to display the Customize User Interface Editor.

2. In the Customizations In pane, right-click the Quick Access Toolbars item and choose New Quick Access Toolbar.

3. Right-click the new toolbar (named Quick Access Toolbar 2 by default) and choose Rename. Type a name for the toolbar and press Enter.

4. From the Command List pane, drag the commands that you want to display on the new Quick Access Toolbar.

5. From the Customizations In pane, expand the Workspaces item and select the workspace for which you want to display the new Quick Access Toolbar when it is current.

6. In the Workspace Contents pane, click Customize Workspace.

7. From the Customizations In pane, expand the Quick Access Toolbars item (if necessary) and check the Quick Access Toolbar you want to display when the workspace is current.

8. In the Workspace Contents pane, click Done.

You can remove commands that you no longer use from a Quick Access Toolbar. Right-click the command in the Customize User Interface Editor, or the Quick Access Toolbar, and choose Remove from Quick Access Toolbar.

Adding a drop-down list

Drop-down lists on a Quick Access Toolbar allow you to group multiple commands under a single button. They are just like a flyout on a classic toolbar, but the drop-down list on a Quick Access Toolbar is not a reference to another toolbar. To control the appearance and behavior of a drop-down list, select it in the Customizations In pane, and use the Properties pane.

To add a drop-down list, right-click the Quick Access Toolbar in the Customizations In pane of the Customize User Interface Editor, and choose New Drop-Down. Rename the drop-down list, and then change its appearance and behavior from the Properties pane. After you have defined the drop-down list, add commands to it from the Command List pane like you would for a toolbar. If you want to assign a default command to the drop-down list, drag a command from the Command List pane to the Primary Command node under the drop-down list.

STEPS: Customizing Quick Access Toolbars

1. Open Windows Explorer. Copy acad.cuix (for AutoCAD) or acadlt.cuix (for AutoCAD LT) to a flash drive, a CD-RW, or your AutoCAD Bible folder as a backup. If you use a folder on your hard drive, be sure to press the Ctrl key as you drag the file so that you copy it instead of moving it. If you don't do this step, you won't have a way to undo the changes that you make to the menu file.

Note

To find the location of *these files*, choose Application Button ⇨ Options and click the Files tab. Double-click the Customization Files item, and then double-click the Main Customization File item to display the location of the menu file. ■

2. Start a new drawing by using any template. Save the file as ab29-01.dwg in your AutoCAD Bible folder.

3. Choose Manage tab ⇨ Customization panel ⇨ User Interface to display the Customize User Interface Editor. In the Customizations In pane, you should see All Customization Files in the drop-down list. If not, select it from the drop-down list.

4. From the Command List drop-down list, choose All Commands. Find the Donut item and drag it to the right side of the Quick Access Toolbar in the application window.

5. From the Categories drop-down list in the Command List pane, choose the Modify category and find Polyline Edit. (This is the PEDIT command.) Drag it to the right of the Donut button.

Tip

To find a command in the long list, click any command and type the first letter of the command you want. The list jumps to the first command with that letter. You can then scroll down and quickly find the command you want. ■

6. With All Commands displayed in the Categories List, drag the Visual Styles, Hidden command (for AutoCAD) or the Hide command (for AutoCAD LT) to the right side of the Quick Access Toolbar.

7. To create a custom command, click the Create a New Command button to the right of the All Commands drop-down list. You see the new command listed as Command1 in the Properties pane.

8. Complete the Properties pane, as shown in Figure 29.7. Type the macro as follows after the ^C^C (which is already there), being careful to also include the spaces:

```
pedit \w .1 ;
```

9. From the Categories drop-down list, choose Custom Commands. Drag the pline_tenth command to the Quick Access Toolbar. The button is blank because you haven't yet assigned it a button image.

10. With the pline_tenth command still selected, in the Button Image pane, click the PEDIT icon. (It looks similar to the icon in Figure 29.8; its tooltip is RCDATA_16_PEDIT.) Then choose Edit to open the Button Editor.

The completed Properties pane for the custom command.

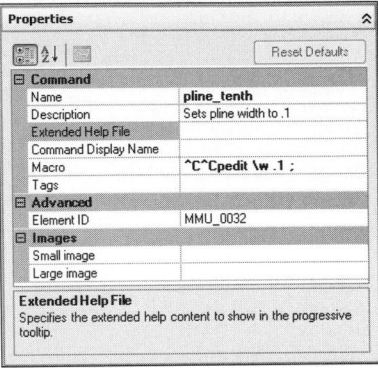

11. You want to change the button so that it looks as if a zero-width polyline is being changed to a wider polyline, because that's what the macro does. Click the red color. Choose the Pencil tool (by default, it is already chosen). Click the Grid check box to help you work. Click (or drag) the point of the Pencil tool in each box, using Figure 29.8 as a guide. (Figure 29.8 shows the button in black and white.) When you're done, click Save.

Tip

If you make a mistake, it's easy to correct it. If you place a red pixel over an existing black pixel, choose black and redraw the black pixel. If you place a red pixel in a wrong spot, choose the Erase tool and click the pixel. ∎

12. In the Save Image dialog box, type **pline_tenth** in the Image Name text box and click OK. (Note that the file is saved in the main customization file by default.) Click Close.

You can create a new button in the Button Editor.

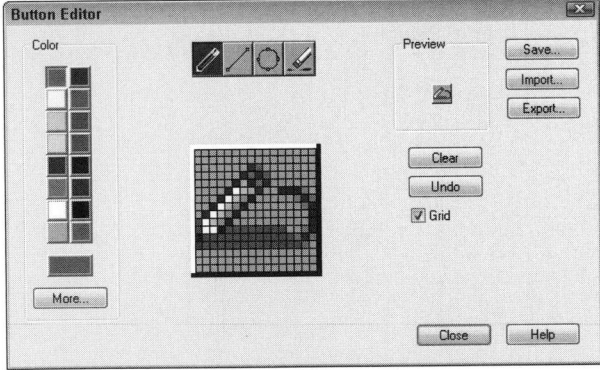

Undoing changes to the user interface

To undo the changes that you made, you need to take two steps. To unload a partial customization file that you have loaded or created, right-click it from the Partial Customization Files item in the Customizations In pane and choose Unload <file name>. This file is separate from the main customization file, so it doesn't affect the main customization file directly. The previous exercise didn't create a partial customization file.

To undo the changes that you made to the main customization file (acad.cuix or acadlt.cuix), copy the original file over the new one. To find the location of this file, choose Application Button ➪ Options and click the Files tab. Double-click the Customization Files item, and then double-click the Main Customization File item.

13. To assign the icon to the button, in the Button Image pane, click the Both item, and then scroll down to the bottom of the button image palette and choose the icon where it appears as the last button.

14. Click Apply. If necessary, move the dialog box so that you can see the Quick Access Toolbar. If it seems okay, click OK to close the Customize User Interface Editor. (If not, continue to make changes in the dialog box.) The pline_tenth button updates to the new icon. The Quick Access Toolbar should look like Figure 29.9.

FIGURE 29.9

The Quick Access Toolbar contains four additional buttons.

15. Choose Home tab ➪ Draw panel ➪ Polyline and draw any series of polyline segments. Choose the pline_tenth button from the Quick Access Toolbar. At the Select polyline or [Multiple]: prompt, pick the polyline. Its width changes to 0.1. (If it doesn't work, return to the Customize User Interface Editor and check the macro.)

16. Save your drawing.

Tip

You can reset one of the customization files that are installed with AutoCAD. Right-click the top item in the Customizations In pane or a customization file from the Partial Customization Files item, and choose Reset. ■

Close AutoCAD. In Windows Explorer, locate the backup copy that you made in Step 1 of the previous exercise. Expand the location of the current main customization file. Press Ctrl and drag the backup file to the current file of the same name.

When you open AutoCAD again, it will load the backup copy of the main customization file.

Here's how the pedit macro that you used in the previous exercise works:

1. Pedit issues the PEDIT command. The space after pedit is equivalent to pressing Enter after you've typed the command on the command line. The PEDIT command then displays the Select polyline or [Multiple]: prompt.

2. The backslash (\) is a special character that pauses the macro for your input. When you select the polyline, the macro continues, displaying the `Enter an option [Close/Join/Width/Edit vertex/Fit/Spline/Decurve/Ltype gen/Reverse/Undo]:` prompt.

3. The w then specifies the Width option. The space following it is like pressing Enter. The PEDIT command then displays the `Specify new width for all segments:` prompt.

4. The macro then specifies 0.1. The space after it is like pressing Enter again. The PEDIT command then issues the `Enter an option [Close/Join/Width/Edit vertex/Fit/Spline/Decurve/Ltype gen/Reverse/Undo]:` prompt.

5. The macro then uses a semicolon, which is used to specify pressing Enter at the end of a menu macro. This ends the command.

Customizing Tool Palettes

Tool palettes give you quick access to blocks, xrefs, hatches, and commands. I cover tool palettes in Chapter 26. You can perform some customization directly on the tool palettes themselves. Here I explain the procedure for customizing the tool palettes by using the Customize dialog box.

To customize tool palettes, choose Manage tab ⇨ Customization panel ⇨ Tool Palettes to display the Customize dialog box, as shown in Figure 29.10. The current tool palettes are listed. Remember that each tab on the Tool Palettes window is considered a separate tool palette.

Use the Customize dialog box to customize tool palettes as follows:

- **Change the order of the tool palette tabs.** Select one of the tabs in the Tool Palettes list and drag it up or down. You can also move the tabs directly on the tool palette by right-clicking the tab name and choosing Move Up or Move Down.

- **Create a new tool palette.** Right-click and choose New Palette. Enter a name and press Enter. To create a new tool palette on the palette itself, right-click anywhere on the palette and choose New Palette.

- **Rename a tool palette.** Click the palette's name to select it, and then click it again so that you see a border around the name. Enter a new name and press Enter. To rename a tool palette on the palette itself, right-click on the tab's name and choose Rename Palette.

- **Delete a tool palette.** Select the tool palette, right-click and choose Delete. In the Confirm Palette Deletion dialog box, which warns you that deletion is permanent unless you first export the tool palette, click OK to delete the tool palette. You can also right-click any tool palette and choose Delete Palette.

- **Import a tool palette or group.** Right-click a palette or group and choose Import. In the Import Palette dialog box, locate the XTP file. Click Open.

- **Export a tool palette group.** Right-click a palette or group and choose Export. In the Export Palette dialog box, choose the location for the file. You can change the name if you want. The tool palette is saved as an XTP file. Click Save.

- **Organize tool palettes into groups.** In the Palette Groups area, right-click and choose New Group. Enter a name for the group and press Enter. From the Palettes list on the left side of the dialog box, drag one or more tool palettes under the group name on the right, as you see in Figure 29.10.

Note that the tool palettes come with blocks and hatches, as well as some visual styles, lights, and cameras (AutoCAD only).

The Customize dialog box.

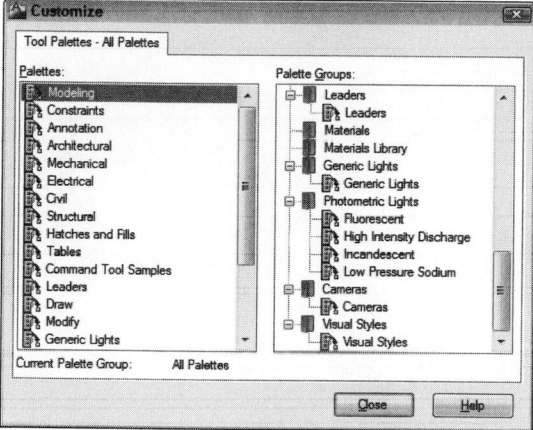

Summary

In this chapter, I covered the basics of customizing AutoCAD and AutoCAD LT. You started to customize by:

- Creating command shortcuts (aliases) in the `acad.pgp` or `acadlt.pgp` file
- Using the Customize User Interface Editor to create custom commands for use on the Quick Access Toolbar and other toolbars
- Customizing the Quick Access Toolbar so that the commands that you need frequently are accessible
- Creating your own toolbars that can contain any command sequence that you need
- Customizing tool palettes, including importing, exporting, and creating groups

In the next chapter, you read about how to create macros with script files.

Creating Macros and Slide Shows

S cript files are like macros that you create in your word processor or spreadsheet. They automatically execute a series of commands. You can use script files to automate plotting, set up a drawing, clean up a drawing, create a slide show, or do any repetitive task. By running a script file on a number of drawings, you can complete a time-consuming task in a fraction of the time.

You can also record actions on the screen and save them as a macro. Doing so saves you the time of figuring out the exact command-line sequences.

If you need to put together just a few commands that you might use another time for other drawings, you may want to consider creating either a menu item, or a toolbar or ribbon button. Chapter 29 explains how to customize toolbars, and Chapter 33 explains how to customize the ribbon and menus.

Creating Macros with Script Files

A script file contains a list of commands and options. To create a script file, you need to think out the commands that you want to execute, as well as their options and prompts. Then you create the text for the script file. Script files have the following characteristics:

- They must use the .scr filename extension.
- They are text-only (ASCII) files.
- They must use command-line syntax only (which can include AutoLISP expressions if you are creating a script for AutoCAD only and not AutoCAD LT).

Creating the script file

You can create the script file by using a text editor, such as Notepad. For early practice with script files, type each command on its own line. A blank space is equivalent to pressing Enter. End each line by pressing Enter, without extra blank spaces. If you need two returns, one after another, at the end of a line, use a blank line for the second return. Every space is meaningful; getting those spaces and blank lines right is probably the hardest part of creating a script file. One technique is to start your script files in a word-processing program that can display nonprinting characters (blank spaces and returns). You can either save the script file in text format or copy it into Notepad. Some tips to help you create successful script files with the least aggravation are as follows:

- Before creating the script file, go through the steps once, using only the command line. Turn off the Dynamic Input feature for this purpose, because it doesn't always include all the command-line content; click the Dynamic Input (or DYN) button on the status bar.

- If the script includes commands that open a dialog box that asks for files, set the system variable FILEDIA to zero (off) before experimenting with the commands that you'll use in the script file. This setting lets you practice the keystrokes without opening dialog boxes. You can also practice using the version of the command with the hyphen in front of it (such as -layer); however, in most cases, you don't need the hyphen in the actual script file.

Note
Script files automatically run as if FILEDIA were off, even if it's set to 1 (on). The FILEDIA system variable determines whether dialog boxes appear for commands that let you open or select files. ∎

- For commands that require inputting text such as layer names or filenames, enclose the names in quotation marks. Then for the next use of Enter, press Enter and go to the next line in the script instead of using a space. Otherwise, AutoCAD may misinterpret a space as a space in the layer name or filename, rather than an Enter.

- Place comments in your script file to explain what you're doing. A comment is any line that starts with a semicolon.

- Keep Notepad open as you work. When you've completed a set of keystrokes that you want, open the AutoCAD Text Window (press F2), select the command string that you want, right-click, choose Copy, switch back to Notepad, right-click on a blank line, and choose Paste. Then cut out all the prompts, leaving only the keyboard entry. You'll probably have to readjust the spaces between the words.

- You can press End to check for blank spaces at the end of a line. Pressing Ctrl+End moves the cursor to the end of the document; this is useful for checking for extra spaces and lines at the end of a script.

Remember, you can open Notepad from within AutoCAD by typing **Notepad** at the command line. At the File to edit: prompt, press Enter to open a new file. (In AutoCAD LT, you need to start Notepad from the Windows Start menu.)

Another option is to write down what you type at the command line. As you write, use an underscore to represent each space. It's very hard to remember that you left three spaces between two words unless you see three underscores. Of course, when you create the script file, you must use spaces, not underscores.

As soon as you complete the script file, save it with any name that is meaningful to you, plus an extension of .scr.

Here's an example of a script file that draws a series of circles:

```
circle 2,2 1.5
circle 6,2 1.5
circle 10,2 1.5
circle 14,2 1.5
```

This script file starts the CIRCLE command, specifies a center point, and specifies a radius, four times. The results are shown in Figure 30.1.

FIGURE 30.1

Running a script file created this drawing.

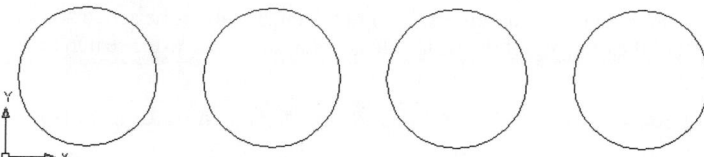

Running a script file

You can run a script file from within a drawing. Use this technique when you want the script to apply only to that drawing. However, you can also start a script within a drawing, and then close the drawing and continue on to open and run the same script in other drawings.

You can also run a script file when loading AutoCAD or AutoCAD LT. You would do this when you want the script file to apply to more than one drawing. For example, you could use script files in the following situations when:

- You want to use a script file to set up every drawing that you open. Although the script file applies to only one drawing at a time, you use it on a different drawing each time.

- You want to use a script file to clean up a list of drawings in one batch, such as thawing all layers on all the drawings in a folder.

Running a script file from within a drawing

If you want the script to apply only to the current drawing, then start the script from within your drawing. To run a script from within a drawing, follow these steps:

 1. Choose Manage tab ➪ Applications panel ➪ Run Script. This opens the Select Script File dialog box.

2. Choose the script file that you want.

3. Click Open. AutoCAD or AutoCAD LT runs the script file.

Running a script when starting AutoCAD or AutoCAD LT

To run a script when starting AutoCAD or AutoCAD LT, change the target expression that Windows uses to start AutoCAD or AutoCAD LT. The easiest way to do this is to use the shortcut to AutoCAD or AutoCAD LT on your desktop and modify the target there. Right-click the AutoCAD or AutoCAD LT shortcut and choose Properties. Click the Shortcut tab.

The Target text box displays the command expression that Windows uses to start AutoCAD or AutoCAD LT. Don't make any change to the current expression — just add to it. If you're using AutoCAD LT, substitute `acadlt.exe` for `acad.exe` and your AutoCAD LT program location in the following examples. The format for starting a script file is:

```
drive:\path\acad.exe drive:\path\drawingname.dwg /b script_file
```

For example, if your current target reads `C:\Program Files\Autodesk\AutoCAD 2011\acad.exe` and you want to open a drawing named `ba-349.dwg` in `c:\drawings` and run a script file named `pre-plot.scr`, your target should read:

```
"C:\Program Files\Autodesk\AutoCAD 2011\acad.exe" c:\drawings\ba-349.
    dwg /b pre-plot
```

You don't need to add the `.scr` extension after the script filename. If you have long file and folder names that contain spaces, you must enclose them in quotation marks, both in the target and in the actual script file. You need to include the full path of the drawing. If the script file is not in the support-file search path, include the entire path. For example:

```
"C:\Program Files\Autodesk\AutoCAD 2011\acad.exe" "c:\aec\drc\Dobbs
    Ferry Apts.dwg" /b c:\aec\drc\cleanup
```

If you want to start a new drawing, you might want to specify a template. In the preceding format, replace the drawing filename with:

```
/t template_name
```

Cross-Reference

In Appendix A, I explain more about changing the target expression to open AutoCAD or AutoCAD LT the way you want. ■

When you've finished typing your additions in the Target text box, click OK. Now, when you start AutoCAD or AutoCAD LT, the drawing or template opens, and the script starts.

From within a script file, you can open (and close) other drawings. In this way, you can run a script file on as many drawings as you want. Figure 30.2 shows a script file, `multi-cleanup.scr`, that you could use when loading AutoCAD or AutoCAD LT. The target is set to `Apt 1A.dwg`.

FIGURE 30.2

A script file that cleans up three drawings.

```
chprop all  c bylayer

-layer f no-plot

qsave
close
open "f:\aec\Apt 1B"
chprop all  c bylayer

-layer f no-plot

qsave
close
open "f:\aec\Apt 1C"
chprop all  c bylayer

-layer f no-plot
qsave
```

Note

Use the CLOSE command to close each drawing after your script file has finished working on it. If you don't, you may end up with 100 drawings open at once, and probably a major computer crash as well! ∎

Here's how `multi-cleanup.scr` works:

1. The CHPROP command selects all objects and sets their color to BYLAYER.
2. The -LAYER command freezes the layer named `no-plot`.
3. The script file saves the drawing.
4. The script file closes the drawing and opens the next drawing.
5. This process is repeated until the last drawing is edited and saved. The last drawing is left open.

You create a script file that is similar to `cleanup.scr` in the "Creating and Using a Script File" section.

Tip

It's helpful to leave the last drawing open so that when you return to see the results, you can see that the last drawing has been properly edited. You then feel pretty sure that all the previous drawings were similarly edited. ∎

Notice the quotation marks around the filenames in the script file. These are necessary because the drawing filenames include spaces.

In the following exercise, you practice creating and using a script file similar to the multi-cleanup script file used in the previous example, but for only one drawing.

On the DVD

The drawing used in the following exercise on creating and using a script file, `ab30-a.dwg`, is in the `Drawings` folder on the DVD. ∎

STEPS: Creating and Using a Script File

1. Open `ab30-a.dwg` from the DVD.
2. Save the file as `ab30-01.dwg` in your `AutoCAD Bible` folder.
3. In Windows XP, choose Start ➪ Run. Type **notepad** and click OK. If you are using Windows Vista or Windows 7, choose Start and click in the Search field. Type **notepad** and press Enter.
4. In Notepad, type the following, replacing the underscores with spaces. Note that there should be two spaces between `all` and `c`. Press Enter after the `qsave` line.

```
chprop_all__c_bylayer

-layer_f_no-plot

qsave
```

5. Choose File menu ➪ Save As. In the Save As dialog box, save the file as `cleanup.scr` in your `AutoCAD Bible` folder. Close Notepad.

   The script file changes the color property of all objects to ByLayer and freezes the no-plot layer. Notice that the drawing has some text that has been set to a blue color (maybe to make it more readable). The titleblock is on the no-plot layer.

6. In AutoCAD, choose Manage tab ➪ Applications panel ➪ Run Script.

7. In the Select Script File dialog box, find `cleanup.scr` in your `AutoCAD Bible` folder and click Open. The script runs, changing the text's color to ByLayer (green) and freezing the no-plot layer. It also saves the drawing.

   If the script file doesn't work, press F2 to open the AutoCAD Text Window and see where the file got hung up. This will help you see where to correct the script file. Re-open it and make the correction. Save the file, close it, and try again.

8. Save your drawing.

Recording Actions

You can record actions that you perform in a drawing, such as starting commands, using options, and selecting objects, and save them as a macro. You don't need to know any programming. Then you can play the macro to facilitate automating often-repeated tasks.

AutoCAD Only

The Action Recorder is not available in AutoCAD LT. ■

This feature can relieve you of time-consuming script development. You can edit macros and even create prompts and explanatory messages for users in the Action Tree window, which lists the individual components of the macro.

Creating an action macro

In order to get the most out of the Action Recorder, you need to plan in advance, and experiment. You may want to run through the actions first, before recording. Often, using the command-line form of a command is the best plan, just as it is for scripts. Here are the steps for recording an action macro:

1. Set up the conditions that you want to apply for the macro. The macro does not record all drawing settings. You can include settings in the macro by using the SETVAR command. For more information, see Chapter 12.

2. Choose Manage tab ➪ Action Recorder panel ➪ Record.

3. Carry out the actions you want to include in the macro. A red circle follows the cursor to remind you that you are recording.

4. Choose Manage tab ➪ Action Recorder panel ➪ Stop.

5. The Action Macro dialog box opens. There you do the following:

   • Enter a name for the macro in the Action Macro Command Name text box. The name can be up to 31 letters/numbers, with no spaces. You can use hyphens and underscores.

   • Enter a description in the Description text box.

   • Choose if you want to restore the drawing view as it was before playback. By default, the command restores the view only if the macro asks for user input, because this offers the opportunity for users to change the view.

   • Choose if you want to scan the macro for inconsistencies between the current drawing state and the drawing state when you recorded the macro. This option is on by default, and helps avoid problems due to differences in settings.

6. Click OK.

The Action Tree window appears beneath the Action Recorder panel, showing the exact sequence of commands in the macro, as shown in Figure 30.3.

FIGURE 30.3

The Action Tree window shows you the contents of the macro.

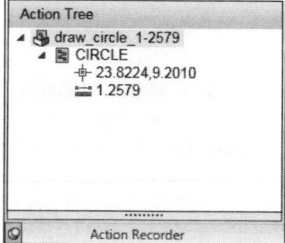

Note

Macros are saved with an ACTM filename extension in the `Support\Actions` **folder of your AutoCAD installation. To find the exact location on your system, choose Application Button⇨Options, and click the Files tab. Expand the Action Recorder Settings item, and then expand the Actions Recording File Location item. ■**

Editing an action macro

When you have completed recording and naming your macro, you can add pauses for user input or user messages. For example, if you draw a circle, the macro records the specified center point and radius, but you can add a pause for the user to specify the center of the circle anywhere in the drawing when the macro is played back. To add a pause for user input, right-click the item in the macro that you want to replace, and choose Pause for User Input. In the example of drawing a circle, you would right-click the item showing the center point of the circle.

Pausing for input is not the only way to specify points in a drawing for use in a macro; you can insert a base point to establish an absolute coordinate point to use for following actions by choosing the Insert Base Point option from the right-click menu of the Action Tree window.

Note

An action macro stores coordinates as absolute coordinates. This means that the macro records the exact coordinates that you specified when recording the macro. However, by default, the macro treats all coordinates except for the first one as relative to the first coordinate of the macro. Let's say that your macro draws a square, and then a circle inside the square. If you add a prompt for user input for the first corner of the square, the circle will be inside the square, no matter where you place the square. To change this default, right-click any item containing coordinates, and choose the Relative to Previous item on the shortcut menu to deselect it. ■

You can add a user message to provide an explanation of the actions in a macro at any point. To add a user message, right-click the item of the macro at the point where you want the message to appear, and choose Insert User Message. You then enter the message you want displayed in the Insert User Message dialog box. To edit the message, right-click the user message item, and choose Edit Message.

You can also edit a recorded value. To do so, right-click it, and choose Edit. You can then change its value. You can also delete any item; to do so, right-click it and choose Delete. Keep in mind that if an item is necessary for the command, then you can't delete it. For example, you can't delete the item that sets the radius of a circle, because a circle needs a radius.

Managing a macro file

You can rename a macro by right-clicking its name in the Action Tree window and choosing Rename. To delete a macro, right-click the macro's name, and choose Delete.

 Along with managing action macros from the Action Tree window, you can use the Action Macro Manager, which allows you to manage multiple action macro files at once. Choose Manage tab ⇨ Action Recorder panel ⇨ Manage Action Macros. From the Action Macro Manager, you can copy, modify the properties for, rename, and delete action macro files.

Playing back a macro

To use the macro, choose Manage tab ⇨ Action Recorder panel and choose the macro that you want to play from the Actions drop-down list. Then click the Play button. If you added any pauses for user input, the cursor will change during playback and you'll see a prompt to input a value.

Tip
You can also type an action macro's name on the command line to start it. ∎

Creating Slide Shows

You can create an image from the display on your screen and save it as a slide. You can use several of these images to create a slide show. You can then use script files to direct the timing and order of the slide show. You first save a view of a drawing as a slide, create a slide library from the slides, and then show the slides one after another automatically.

Cross Reference
You can use the ShowMotion feature to create shots of views and show them one after another. For more information, see Chapter 8. ∎

Tip
You can save any drawing as an image file and import it into a presentation program. You can add text and special effects to create a professional slide show. For more information, see Chapter 27. ∎

Creating slides

Creating a slide is like capturing a screen shot of your drawing. AutoCAD or AutoCAD LT makes a simplified vector file from the current viewport in model space, or from all viewports in paper space layouts. You can create a slide of a *wireframe* or hidden display. However, you cannot make a slide of a shaded or rendered display.

To create a slide, follow these steps:

1. Display the view of the drawing that you want to save as a slide.
2. Type **mslide** ↵.
3. In the Create Slide File dialog box, choose a location and name for the slide. Its file extension will automatically be .sld.
4. Click Save.

Viewing slides

After you have created your slides, you will want to look at them! To view a slide, follow these steps:

1. Type **vslide** ↵.
2. In the Select Slide File dialog box, choose the slide that you want to view.
3. Click Open to display the slide.

Do a Redraw to return to your drawing. You cannot draw in or edit a slide.

On the DVD

The drawing used in the following exercise on creating and viewing slides, ab30-b.dwg, is in the Drawings folder on the DVD. ■

STEPS: Creating and Viewing Slides

1. Open ab30-b.dwg from the DVD.
2. Save the file as ab30-02.dwg in your AutoCAD Bible folder.
3. On the command line, type **hide** ↵ to hide the drawing.
4. On the command line, type **mslide** ↵. In the Create Slide File dialog box, click the Save In drop-down list and select your AutoCAD Bible folder, if it isn't already selected. In the File Name text box, change the name from its default of ab30-02.sld to ab30-02a.sld. Click Save.
5. On the command line, type **ddvpoint** ↵. Change the value in the From XY Plane text box to 60, and then click OK. Use the HIDE command to restore the hidden view.
6. Repeat the MSLIDE command. This time, save the slide as ab30-02b.sld.
7. On the command line, type **ddvpoint** ↵ again. Change the value in the From XY Plane text box to 90 and click OK. Use the HIDE command to restore the hidden view.
8. Repeat the MSLIDE command and save the slide as ab30-02c.sld.
9. Choose View tab ⇨ Views panel ⇨ Previous View until you see the message No previous view saved.
10. On the command line, type **vslide** ↵. In the Select Slide File dialog box, choose the first slide, ab30-02a.sld. Click Open. AutoCAD displays the slide.
11. Repeat the VSLIDE command and display ab30-2b.sld. Do the same with ab30-02c.sld.
12. On the command line, type **redraw** ↵.
13. Save your drawing.

Using scripts to create slide shows

You can create a script file that displays slides one after another, resulting in a slide show. You can use three special script file commands for this purpose:

- DELAY *nnnn* pauses the script for the number of milliseconds that you specify. For example, DELAY 3000 pauses the script for 3 seconds.
- RSCRIPT repeats the script from the beginning. Use this command to create a continuously running script. To stop the script (whether repeating or not), press Esc or Backspace, or start a command from the user interface.
- RESUME restarts a script file after you've stopped it.

The VSLIDE command, which displays a slide, can also be used to preload the next slide into memory. You use this command to preload a slide while viewers are looking at the previous slide. This reduces the waiting time between slides. To use this feature, put an asterisk (*) before the filename in the VSLIDE command. The next VSLIDE command detects that a slide has been preloaded and displays it without asking for the slide name. Here's how it works:

```
vslide ab30-02a
vslide *ab30-02b
delay 3000
vslide
vslide *ab30-02c
delay 3000
vslide
rscript
```

This script file does the following:

Line 1 displays ab30-02a.sld.

Line 2 preloads ab30-02b.sld.

Line 3 waits 3 seconds, displaying ab30-02a.sld.

Line 4 displays ab30-02b.sld.

Line 5 preloads ab30-02c.sld.

Line 6 waits 3 seconds, displaying ab30-02b.sld.

Line 7 displays ab30-02c.sld.

Line 8 repeats the script from the beginning.

Note

The Dynamic Input feature sometimes interferes with a slide show. If so, turn off Dynamic Input (click the DYN button on the status bar) before running the slide show. ∎

STEPS: Creating a Slide Show

1. Open Notepad and type the following script:
```
vslide ab30-02a
vslide *ab30-02b
delay 3000
```

```
vslide
vslide *ab30-02c
delay 3000
vslide
delay 3000
rscript
```

2. Remember to press Enter at the end of the last line. Save the file as ab30-02.scr in your AutoCAD Bible folder. Close Notepad.

3. To ensure that AutoCAD can find the slide files, place your AutoCAD Bible folder in the support-file search path. To do this, choose Application Button ⇨ Options and click the Files tab. Click Support File Search Path and then click Add. Click Browse and find your AutoCAD Bible folder. Click OK twice.

4. In any drawing, choose Manage tab ⇨ Applications panel ⇨ Run Script. Locate ab30-02.scr in your AutoCAD Bible folder and click Open. The slide show runs. Notice that the last slide still takes a while to display.

5. Let the slide show run through twice. The last slide displays a little more quickly the second time. Press Esc to stop the slide show.

6. Don't save your drawing.

Tip

When running a slide show, you might want to maximize the screen area by reducing menu, ribbon, and command-line space. You can use the CLEANSCREENON and CLEANSCREENOFF commands (press Ctrl+0) to toggle the user interface components on and off. You can also hide (and redisplay) the command-line window by pressing Ctrl+9. ■

Creating Slide Libraries

You can organize your slides into slide libraries. Slide libraries have an .slb file extension. One reason for creating slide libraries is to create image tiles when you're creating a custom image tile menu. If you're using AutoCAD, then you can see an example of an image tile menu by entering the following AutoLISP code at the command line:

```
(menucmd "I=ACAD.image_3dobjects") ↵
(menucmd "I=ACAD.*") ↵
```

These image tiles are created with slides organized into libraries.

To view slides in a library, use the following format:

```
library(slidename)
```

For example, you can place the three slides that you used in the preceding exercise in a slide library called 3dmodel.slb. You can then use the following command sequence in the script file to preload the second slide (the second line of the script file):

```
vslide *3dmodel(ab30-02b)
```

To create a slide library, you need to use the DOS prompt. You use the SLIDELIB utility, which you can find in your AutoCAD 2011 or AutoCAD LT 2011 folder.

To get to the DOS prompt, choose Start ⇨ (All) Programs ⇨ Accessories ⇨ Command Prompt.

Follow these steps to create a slide library:

1. Create a text file (you can use Notepad) that contains the names of the slide files. Include the paths of the slide files if they're not in the support-file search path. Place each slide filename on a new line. Save the file as `ab30sld.lst`.

Tip

SLIDELIB can read a listing that was created by using DOS's `dir` **command with the** `/b` **parameter, which creates a simple listing of just the filenames. Therefore, you can place all the slide files in a folder and redirect the** `dir` **listing to a file. For example, you can create a list named** `ab30sld.lst` **by typing the following at the DOS prompt:** ■

```
dir *.sld /b >ab30sld.lst
```

This creates the list in the same folder as the slide files.

2. Assuming that you're still in the same folder where you created the slide file list and you want to create a library called `ab30sld.slb` in the same folder, type the following at the DOS prompt (substituting the actual path to your AutoCAD or AutoCAD LT program, and the `AutoCAD Bible` folder):

```
"c:\Program Files\Autodesk\AutoCAD 2011\slidelib" "c:\AutoCAD Bible\
    ab30sld" < "c:\AutoCAD Bible\ab30sld.lst"
```

Note

SLIDELIB cannot accept filenames with spaces, but it can handle long filenames, provided that you use a character, such as an underscore, where you might normally have a blank space. ■

Summary

This chapter explained how to create script files to automate repetitive commands. You read about the following:

● Creating script files that contain commands, options, and values in command-line format

● Running script files from within a drawing or when loading AutoCAD or AutoCAD LT

● Using the Action Recorder to automate the process of creating macros

● Creating slides from the display in your viewport and creating a script file that displays several slides, one after another, thus resulting in a slide show

● Organizing your slides into slide libraries

In the next chapter, you read about how to create your own linetypes and hatch patterns.

Creating Your Own Linetypes and Hatch Patterns

AutoCAD and AutoCAD LT come with a large number of linetypes and hatch patterns. However, when these do not serve your particular needs, you can create your own linetypes and hatch patterns. You can then use them in your drawings in the same way that you use the linetypes and hatch patterns that come with the software.

Linetypes are useful whenever you don't want a continuous linetype. They apply not only to lines, but also to polylines, arcs, ellipses, wireframes, and solids — in fact, to most objects. You use hatch patterns to fill in closed (or almost closed) areas. Hatch patterns often represent textures or materials.

Creating Linetypes

There are two types of linetypes: simple and complex. Simple linetypes consist of only dashes and dots. Complex linetypes usually have dashes and/or dots, but also contain text and/or shapes.

The default linetype file is `acad.lin` for AutoCAD and `acadlt.lin` for AutoCAD LT. You can add your own linetype definitions to this file or create your own linetype files. Linetype files are text files and must have a `.lin` file extension. Of course, be sure to make a backup copy of `acad.lin` or `acadlt.lin` before you edit it. You commonly use Notepad to edit a linetype file.

New Feature
Complex linetypes now support the ability to keep the text or shape upright. As a result, when you draw a line segment from right to left or apply a linetype to a curve, the text is not upside down but always displays at an easy-to-read angle. To keep text or a shape upright, use the new U (upright) rotation option in the definition of the linetype. ■

Creating simple linetypes

In the syntax for creating simple linetypes, each linetype is defined by using two lines of text. The first line contains the linetype name and an optional description, formatted as follows:

```
*linetype name[, description]
```

Here are some points to remember:

- Always start the definition with an asterisk.
- The name and description of a linetype is limited to 279 characters total. However, descriptions longer than 45 characters are hard to read in the Linetype Manager and other dialog boxes and drop-down lists.
- If you include a description, precede it with a comma.

The second line of the linetype syntax is its definition. With simple linetypes, you're limited to dashes, dots, and spaces, which are measured in units and specified as follows:

- A dash is indicated by a positive number.
- A dot is indicated by a 0.
- A space is indicated by a negative number.
- Each item is separated by a comma, there are no spaces; you must have a minimum of 2 dashes, dots, or spaces items and can have up to a total of 12.
- Each line must start with the letter A.

The following definition creates a line with two dashes of 0.25 units, followed by two dots, all separated by spaces of 0.1 units.

```
*seeingdouble, Future hedge line
A,.25,-.1,.25,-.1,0,-.1,0,-.1
```

The result is shown in Figure 31.1.

FIGURE 31.1

The seeingdouble linetype.

If you feel confident, you can even create linetypes on the fly, using the command-line form of the LINETYPE command. Type **-linetype** ↵ and use the Create option. Follow the prompts and type the linetype definition on the command line. If you make a mistake, you must open the linetype file in a text editor to make your corrections.

Tip

If your linetype definition will include both dashes and dots, you'll get the best results when you start the linetype definition with a dash. Starting the definition with a dash is a matter of aesthetics, perhaps, but such a line connects better to other lines. ∎

STEPS: Creating a Simple Linetype

1. Create a drawing by using the `acad.dwt` or `acadlt.dwt` template.

2. Save your drawing as `ab31-01.dwg` in your `AutoCAD Bible` folder.

3. In Windows XP, choose Start ⇨ Run. Type **notepad** and click OK to open Notepad. In Windows Vista or Windows 7, choose Start and type **notepad** ↵ in the Start Search box.

4. Type the following:

   ```
   *3dotsandadash, temporary fencing
   A,.5,-.25,0,-.1,0,-.1,0,-.25
   ```

5. Press Enter after the last line. Save the file as `ab31-01.lin` in your `AutoCAD Bible` folder and close Notepad.

6. In your drawing, choose Home tab ⇨ Layers panel ⇨ Layer Properties, and click the New Layer icon. Name the new layer `tfence`. Set its color to red.

7. Click Continuous in the Linetype column to open the Select Linetype dialog box. Click Load.

8. In the Load or Reload Linetypes dialog box, click File. In the Select Linetype File dialog box, find `ab31-01.lin` in your `AutoCAD Bible` folder, choose it, and click Open.

9. Back in the Load or Reload Linetypes dialog box, choose `3dotsandadash` and click OK.

10. Again, in the Select Linetype dialog box, choose `3dotsandadash` and then click OK. The layer `tfence` now shows the correct linetype. Click Set Current and then close or auto-hide the Layer Properties Manager.

11. Start the LINE command and turn on Ortho Mode. Draw any line to see the linetype. Save your drawing. The linetype should look like Figure 31.2.

FIGURE 31.2

The 3dotsandadash linetype.

Creating complex linetypes

A complex linetype includes either shapes or text in the linetype definition. Complex linetype definitions are similar to those for simple linetypes, except that they add a definition for a shape or text. Figure 31.3 shows an example of each type.

Shapes are covered in the next chapter. At this point, you only need to know that shapes are contained in files with the file extension `.shx`.

FIGURE 31.3

Complex linetypes include shapes or text.

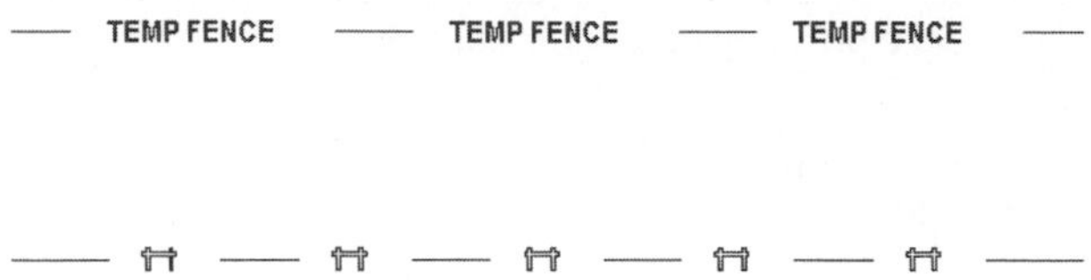

The first line of the linetype definition is the same as for simple linetypes. The second line of the definition can contain all the same features as those for a simple linetype. However, you add the special shape or text definition in square brackets:

- **Syntax for shapes.** [shapename,shxfilename,details]
- **Syntax for text.** ["text string",textstyle,details]

details refers to an optional series of rotation, scale, and offset specifications that you can add to the definition. Table 31.1 describes these specifications.

The following complex linetype definition uses a shape and has no details:

```
*TEMPFENCE, FENCE SHAPE AND DASH
A,.5,-.25,[FENCE,"C:\AUTOCAD BIBLE\FENCE.SHX"],-.5
```

The specification for the shape is simply part of the rest of the definition that includes a dash and spaces before and after the shape. The shape is enclosed in both commas and square brackets. The first part of the shape definition is the name of the shape (which is defined in the shape's definition file), and the second part is the name of the shape file. In this case, the shape file is not in the support-file search path, so the entire path needs to be specified. Don't forget to use quotation marks around the shape filename if the folder name or filename contains spaces.

Tip

Note that the space after the shape (created with the –.5 code) is larger than the space before it (created with the –.25 code). You need to allow for the space that the shape takes up. This is largely a matter of trial and error, but if you know the shape definition well, you can make a good estimate. If you need to go back and change the line-type definition, don't forget to reload the linetype (using the Load option). ■

The following complex linetype definition uses text and has no details:

```
*TFENCE, DASH & TEXT
A,.5,-.25,["TEMP FENCE",FENCE],-1.5
```

Again, the specification for the text is placed within a linetype definition that includes a dash and spaces. The first part of the text definition is the text string, which is always in quotation marks. The second part of the definition is the text style. As with the previous linetype definition containing a shape, the space after the text is larger than the space before in order to leave enough room for the text. You must define the text style in the drawing before you load the linetype.

Table 31.1 lists the details that you can add to both the shape and text parts of complex linetype definitions.

TABLE 31.1

Optional Details for Shapes and Text in Complex Linetype Definitions

Detail	Syntax	Description
Upright rotation	U=##	Rotates the shape or text so it is always at an upright or near-upright angle (can be read from the bottom or right sides of the drawing when published), keeping the text in the linework from appearing upside down or backwards. Typically, you use an angle of 0 to make sure the shape or text is rotated uniformly.
Relative rotation	R=##	Rotates the shape or text relative to the angle of the line that you draw.
Absolute rotation	A=##	Rotates the shape or text based on the World Coordinate System, regardless of the angle of the line. Because the default is a relative rotation of 0, you can use absolute rotation to keep the text facing upright, regardless of the direction of the line.
Scale	S=##	Scales the text or shape. This scale is multiplied by any scale that is contained in a shape definition or height in a text style. If you use a text style with a height of 0, this scale number defines the text's height.
X offset	X=##	A positive number moves the shape or text toward the endpoint of the line. A negative number moves the shape or text toward the start point of the line. You can use an X offset to place a shape or text along a continuous linetype. You can also use an X offset to adjust the spacing of a shape or text between dashes, instead of changing the spaces before or after the dashes.
Y offset	Y=##	Moves the shape or text perpendicular to the direction of the line. A positive number moves the shape or text up if the line is drawn from left to right. Uses a Y offset to center text and shapes along a linetype.

* Although using an absolute rotation of 0 might sound like a good idea for complex linetypes with text, if you use the linetype at varying angles or on curves, you may find that the text shifts to an undesirable location due to the text's justification point.

Here is a definition that includes a shape with a scale and a Y offset:

```
*TEMPFENCE, FENCE SHAPE AND DASH
A,.5,-.25,[FENCE,"C:\AUTOCAD BIBLE\FENCE.SHX",U=0, S=.025,Y=-.07],-.5
```

This shape definition scales the shape to 0.025 of its original size. This results in the linetype shown in Figure 31.4. Of course, in order to scale the shape, you need to know its original size. You can use the SHAPE command to insert a shape and get an idea of what it looks like. In this case, the shape's original definition is much too large for a linetype and needs to be scaled down.

FIGURE 31.4

The TEMPFENCE linetype.

The shape definition also moves the shape in the minus Y direction by 0.07 units. This centers the shape nicely within the linetype.

Caution

When you create drawings using shapes or custom fonts, as in the case of complex linetypes, you need to include the shape files or font files when you distribute the drawings to others. You will also want to make sure that text style effects such as oblique angle do not cause legibility issues with your linetypes. ■

By including more involved shapes in a complex linetype and not much else, you can create a linetype that is mostly a series of shapes displayed one after the other. You can create some interesting effects in this way.

You can find several complex linetypes at the end of the acad.lin or acadlt.lin linetype definition file. Look at their definitions and try them out to get ideas for your own complex linetypes. The Express Tools installation (in AutoCAD only) has a command, MKLTYPE, that automatically creates linetypes, even complex ones. Choose Express Tools tab ➪ Tools panel (expanded) ➪ Make Linetype.

Cross-Reference

In Chapter 32, I explain more about creating custom shapes. You can use the MKSHAPE command to create custom shapes. Choose Express Tools tab ➪ Tools panel (expanded) ➪ Make Shape. ■

Note

To find the location of acad.lin or acadlt.lin, choose Application button ➪ Options and click the Files tab. Double-click the first item, Support File Search Path, to display the location of the support files. ■

On the DVD

The drawing used in the following exercise on creating a complex linetype, ab31-a.dwg, is in the Drawings folder on the DVD. ■

STEPS: Creating a Complex Linetype

1. Open ab31-a.dwg from the DVD.

2. Save the file as ab31-02.dwg in your AutoCAD Bible folder. This drawing is a simple plan for a trailer park.

3. Choose Home tab ➪ Annotation panel (expanded) ➪ Text Style. Click New and type **TVCABLE** for the Style Name. Click OK. In the Font Name drop-down list, choose Arial. Click Apply and then click Close.

4. In Windows, open Notepad, and type the following:

   ```
   *TV, Buried television cable
   A,.5,-.5,["TV",TVCABLE,U=0,S=.3,X=-.1,Y=-.15],-.75
   ```

5. Press Enter after the last line. Save the file in your AutoCAD Bible folder as ab31-02.lin.

6. Open the Layer Properties Manager. Choose Buried_cable and click its Continuous linetype in the Linetype column. In the Select Linetype dialog box, choose Load. Click File. Find ab31-02.lin in your AutoCAD Bible folder, choose it, and click Open.

7. In the Load or Reload Linetypes dialog box, choose TV and click OK. Do the same in the Select Linetypes dialog box. Click Set Current. Close or auto-hide the Layer Properties Manager.

8. Choose Home tab ⇨ Properties panel ⇨ Linetype drop-down list, and choose Other. In the Linetype Manager, click Show Details to display the Details section. Change the Global Scale Factor to 192. Click OK.

9. Draw some lines or polylines. Zoom in to see the linetype more clearly. Figure 31.5 shows the resulting linetype.

10. Save your drawing.

FIGURE 31.5

The TV linetype.

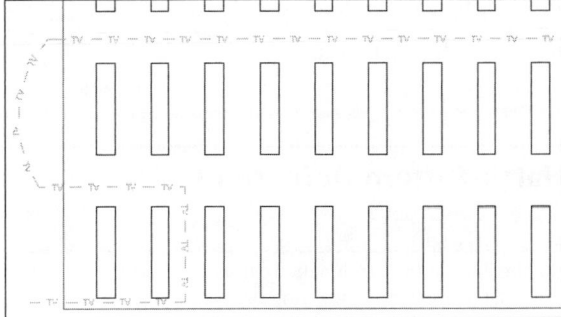

Creating Hatch Patterns

Hatch patterns are sets of line patterns that are used to fill an enclosed area. Although the part of the hatch pattern definition that defines each line is similar to a linetype definition, you also need to specify the angle and spacing of the lines. You cannot include text or shapes in hatch patterns.

Hatch patterns are stored in files with a file extension of .pat. The acad.pat or acadlt.pat file includes a large number of hatch patterns. You can add to or edit this file, or create your own .pat file. As always, don't forget to make a copy of acad.pat or acadlt.pat before you edit it. When creating your own .pat file, remember the following:

- If you aren't adding patterns to acad.pat or acadlt.pat, you can put only one hatch pattern in a custom .pat file. The filename and pattern name must be the same.

- You can insert comments in your .pat file after a semicolon.

- You must press Enter after the end of the last line of the hatch definition.

Note

To find the location of acad.pat or acadlt.pat, choose Application Button ⇨ Options and click the Files tab. Double-click the Support File Search Path item to display the location of the support files. ■

The syntax for hatch patterns is as follows:

```
*pattern-name[, description]
angle, x-origin,y-origin, delta-x,delta-y [, dash1, dash2, ...]
```

Here are some general points for hatch-pattern definitions:

- The pattern name cannot have spaces, but you can create a custom hatch pattern in which the filename and pattern name have a space.
- The description is optional; if you include one, precede it with a comma.
- Add the dash specifications only for noncontinuous lines.
- You can have more than one definition line (the second line in the syntax I just showed), creating sets of hatch definitions that combine to create the hatch pattern.
- Each definition line can be no more than 80 characters.
- You can include a maximum of six dash specifications (which include spaces and dots).
- You can add spaces in the definition lines for readability.

Table 31.2 describes the features of a hatch-pattern definition.

TABLE 31.2

Hatch-Pattern Definitions

Specification	Explanation
Angle	Defines the angle of the lines in the hatch pattern. If you also specify an angle on the Hatch Creation tab or in the Hatch and Gradient dialog box (when you are placing the hatch), the two angles are added. For example, if a hatch pattern defines lines at 105 degrees and you specify a hatch angle of 30 degrees, you end up with lines running at 135 degrees.
X-origin	Specifies the X coordinate of the base point of the hatch pattern. Your hatch probably won't go through 0,0; however, this point lines up sets of lines in hatch patterns, as well as aligning hatch patterns in different areas. Because all hatch patterns are calculated from the base point, they're always aligned, no matter where they actually appear in the drawing.
Y-origin	Specifies the Y coordinate of the base point of the hatch pattern.
Delta-x	Specifies the offset of successive lines. This applies only to dashed lines and is measured along the direction of the lines. Specifying a delta-x staggers each successive line by the amount that you specify so that the dashes don't line up.
Delta-y	Specifies the distance between lines, measured perpendicular to the direction of the lines. This applies to both continuous and dashed lines.
Dash	Defines a noncontinuous line, using the same system as linetype definitions: positive for a dash, negative for a space, and 0 for a dot.

The hatch pattern shown in Figure 31.6 is the simplest form of hatch pattern.

Although you could specify this simple hatch pattern on the Hatch Creation tab or in the Hatch and Gradient dialog box by specifying a user-defined hatch with an angle and spacing, the example that follows shows the syntax clearly. The lines are at an angle of 105 degrees; the hatch pattern starts at 0,0; and the spacing between the lines is 0.5 units. The lines are continuous.

```
*ftrailer, proposed future trailers
105, 0,0, 0,0.5
```

FIGURE 31.6

The `ftrailer` hatch pattern with continuous lines.

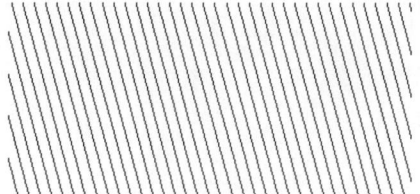

By adding one level of complexity, you can make the lines in the hatch pattern noncontinuous, as follows:

```
*ftrailer, proposed future trailers
105, 0,0, 0,0.5, .5,-.25,0,-.1,0,-.25
```

Note that this definition uses the maximum of six dash specifications (the dash, space, dot, space, dot, and space).

A close-up of this hatch pattern is shown in Figure 31.7.

FIGURE 31.7

The `ftrailer` hatch pattern with a dash and two dots.

If you add a delta-x of 0.25, the lines in the pattern are staggered by 0.25 units, along the direction of the lines, as shown in this code and in Figure 31.8:

```
*ftrailer, proposed future trailers
105, 0,0, 0.25,0.5, .5,-.25,0,-.1,0,-.25
```

You might wonder why the pattern staggers downward after adding a positive delta-x. The answer is that the direction of the lines (in this case, 105 degrees) becomes the X axis for this calculation. Figure 31.9 shows a zoomed-in display of the hatch pattern around 0,0, which is the base point. The hatch pattern is being generated up and to the left. The first line starts at 0,0, and the second line starts to the left by 0.5 units (the delta-y) and up by 0.25 units (the delta-x), as shown by the dimensions.

FIGURE 31.8

The `ftrailer` hatch pattern with an added delta-x.

FIGURE 31.9

Calculating how the delta-x and delta-y affect a hatch pattern.

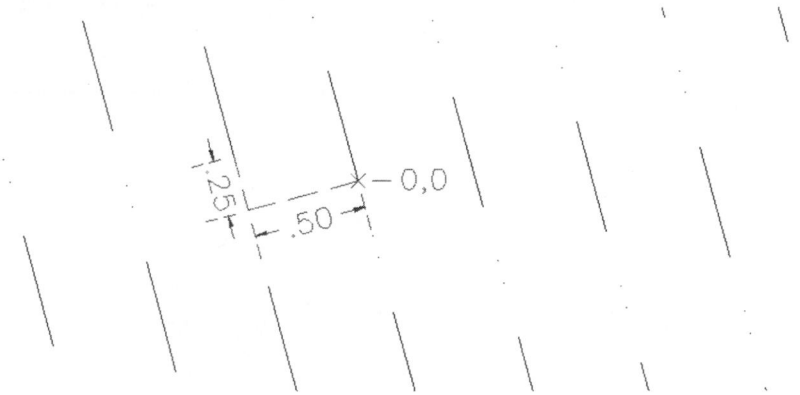

Finally, you can add additional definition lines. One of the definition lines should start at 0,0, but the others may start anywhere. Here is the definition for the pattern in Figure 31.10. It actually creates the shape of the trailers. Although you see the rectangular shape, the hatch pattern is created from four separate lines, two at 0 degrees and two at 90 degrees. Note that the two 0-degree lines are the same, except that they start at different base points. The same is true for the two 90-degree lines.

```
*trail, whole trailers-proposed
0, 0,0, 0,2, .5,-1
90, 0,0, 0,1.5, .5,-.25,0,-.25,.5,-.5
90, .5,0, 0,1.5, .5,-.25,0,-.25,.5,-.5
0, 0,1.5, 0,2, .5,-1
```

FIGURE 31.10

The `trail` hatch pattern looks like trailers.

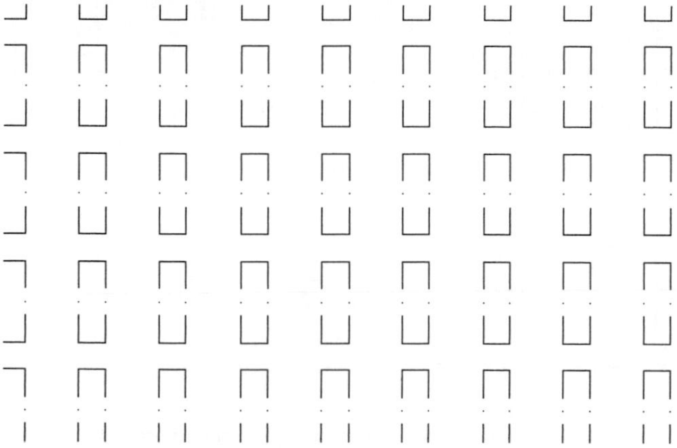

STEPS: Creating and Using a Hatch Pattern

1. Create a drawing by using the acad.dwt (or acadlt.dwt) template.

2. Save the file as ab31-03.dwg in your AutoCAD Bible folder.

3. In Windows, choose Start ⇨ Run. Type **notepad** and click OK. Notepad opens. In Windows Vista or Windows 7, choose Start and type **notepad** in the Start Search text box and press Enter.

4. Type the following:

```
*lightning, interwoven lightning
90, 0,0, 0,.5, .5,-.25
0, -.25,.5, 0,.75, .25,-.25
90, -.25,.5, 0,.5, .5,-.25
```

5. Press Enter after the last line. Save the file as lightning.pat in your AutoCAD Bible folder. Close Notepad.

6. If you haven't already done so, you need to add your AutoCAD Bible folder to the support-file search path. Choose Application Button ⇨ Options, and click the Files tab. Click the plus sign to the left of Support File Search Path. Choose Add. Choose Browse. Find your AutoCAD Bible folder and click OK. Click OK again to close the Options dialog box.

7. Choose Home tab ⇨ Draw panel ⇨ Rectangle. At the first prompt, type **0,0** ↵. At the Specify other corner point or [Area/Dimensions/Rotation]: prompt, type **10,6** ↵.

8. Choose Home tab ⇨ Draw panel ⇨ Hatch.

9. Choose Hatch Creation tab ⇨ Hatch Pattern panel ⇨ Hatch Pattern. Scroll to the bottom of the list and select Lightning.

10. Choose Hatch Creation tab ⇨ Boundaries panel ⇨ Select Boundary Objects and select the rectangle in your drawing. Press Enter. The rectangle fills with the lightning hatch, as shown in Figure 31.11.

FIGURE 31.11

The lightning hatch pattern.

11. Save your drawing.

Check out the `acad.pat` or `acadlt.pat` file for some ideas on how to create your own hatch-pattern definitions.

Summary

In this chapter, you discovered how to create your own linetypes and hatch patterns. You read about the following:

- Creating simple linetypes that contain only dashes, dots, and spaces
- Making complex linetypes that include shapes and text
- Constructing your own hatch patterns that are made up of sets of lines

In the next chapter, you read about how to create shapes and fonts.

Creating Shapes and Fonts

S hapes are text files that define a shape, or figure, that you can insert into your drawing. Shapes are similar to blocks in that you create, store, and insert them. They are different from blocks in the following ways:

- Shapes are much harder to create.

- Shapes are compiled into a format that conserves storage space, memory, and regeneration time.

- You can use shapes to create fonts, and you can insert them into linetypes.

- Like fonts, shape files are support files. If you distribute a drawing, then be sure to include any font or shape files that the drawing uses.

You can use shapes for simple outlines that you need to quickly insert many times. Some examples are shapes that are inserted into complex linetypes and font characters.

AutoCAD Only
AutoCAD LT doesn't offer the ability to create or insert shapes, but you can include shapes in complex linetypes that you might create. For information on complex line types, see Chapter 31. Shapes display in an AutoCAD LT drawing if originally inserted with AutoCAD. This entire chapter applies to AutoCAD only. ■

The Express Tools (in AutoCAD only) contain a command, MKSHAPE, which makes shapes for you. Choose Express Tools tab ➪ Tools panel (expanded) ➪ Make Shape. You simply draw the objects, and use the command to name the shape. You can then immediately use the SHAPE command to insert the shape.

IN THIS CHAPTER
Creating shapes

Creating fonts

Creating Shapes

Shape files are used for both shapes and fonts. You create them with a text editor and save them with the .shp file extension. You then use the COMPILE command (on the command line), which opens the Select Shape or Font File dialog box. Choose the .shp file and click Open. AutoCAD automatically compiles the file into a new file with the same name but with the .shx file extension. It then displays a message on the command line that the compilation has succeeded.

Using shape files

After you have compiled a shape file, you must load it with the LOAD command before you can place it in a drawing. The Select Shape File dialog box opens. Choose the SHX file and click Open. Font files don't have to be loaded because they're automatically referenced by text styles that use the font files.

To insert a shape, use the SHAPE command prompts as follows:

Enter shape name or [?]: Type the name of the shape, or type ? ↵ to get a list of loaded shapes.

Specify insertion point: Pick a point on the screen. AutoCAD drags the shape as you move the cursor.

Specify height <1.0000>: This functions like a scale factor. For example, type .5 ↵ to insert the shape at one half its original size.

Specify rotation angle <0>: Type a rotation angle.

Creating shape files

Shape files and font files are essentially the same. In this section, I explain how to create shapes. At the end of the chapter, I explain the few distinctions necessary to create a font file.

As with many customizable files, you use a text editor to create shape files. You can add comments by preceding them with a semicolon. A shape definition has the following syntax:

```
*shapenumber,#ofspecs,SHAPENAME
spec1,spec2,...,0
```

The definition must start with an asterisk. Each line cannot contain more than 128 characters. Table 32.1 explains the parts of this shape definition.

TABLE 32.1

The Parts of a Shape Definition

Item	Explanation
Shapenumber	You can use any number from 1 to 258 for a total of 258 shapes (and up to 32768 for Unicode fonts). Each shape in a file must have a unique number. The shape numbers 256, 257, and 258 are typically reserved for the symbols Degree_Sign, Plus_Or_Minus_Sign, and Diameter_Symbol. For Unicode fonts, the reserved shape numbers are U+00B0, U+00B1, and U+2205, respectively.
#ofspecs	This is the number of specifications in the second line of the definition, including the mandatory 0 at the end. Numbers grouped by parentheses are not counted as a single specification, but instead each number in parentheses is counted as one specification byte. For example, (0,-8,-127) counts as 3 specifications.

Item	Explanation
SHAPENAME	You must use uppercase for the shape name. This is the name you use with the SHAPE command or in a complex linetype.
spec1...	This is a code that defines the actual shape. Each specification code defines a part of the shape, such as a line segment or an arc. Together, all the specifications draw the shape.
0	The definition must end with a 0.

Using length and direction codes

You can use two sets of codes to define a shape. The first set, the length and direction codes, only allows you to draw straight line segments. You use this system to create specifications in the three-character hexadecimal format.

- The first character is 0, which tells AutoCAD that the next two characters are hexadecimal values.
- The second character is a length in units. The maximum is 15 units. The number values can range from 0 to 9. For values from 10 to 15, use A to F. Keep in mind that the length is measured along the nearest X or Y distance. Therefore, diagonal lengths are not true lengths.
- The third character is a direction code. Figure 32.1 shows how this code works. Use the code that represents the desired direction of the line from the start point.

FIGURE 32.1

The direction codes.

```
6   5  4  3   2
7 ·  ·  ·  ·  · 1
8 ·  ·  ·  ·  · 0
9 ·  Start point  · F

A   B  C  D   E
```

Here is the code for the shape shown in Figure 32.2:

```
*2,4,PENNANT
044,02F,029,0
```

FIGURE 32.2

The PENNANT shape.

   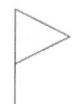

Here's how this shape works:

- 2 is the shape's unique number.
- 4 is the number of bytes (specifications) on the second line of the definition.
- PENNANT is the shape's name.
- 044 draws the pole, a line that is 4 units in the vertical direction.
- 02F draws the top line of the pennant, a line that is approximately 2 units in the F direction. (See the following note.)
- 029 draws the bottom line of the pennant, a line that is approximately 2 units in the 9 direction. (See the following note.)

Note
Although the length of the two diagonal lines was specified as 2, they're actually about 2.22 units long because the line endpoints snapped to the nearest imaginary grid point. ■

Using supplemental shape codes
The length and direction codes have a number of limitations:

- You can draw in only 16 directions.
- The maximum length of a line is 15 units.
- You can draw only straight line segments.
- The shape has to be continuous; you cannot lift the "pen" up and start in a new place.

The second set of codes, called the supplemental shape codes, brings additional flexibility (and complexity) to your shapes. Table 32.2 lists these codes, which can be in either hexadecimal or decimal format.

TABLE 32.2

Supplemental Shape Codes

Hexadecimal Code	Decimal Code	Explanation
000	0	Specifies the end of the shape definition.
001	1	Starts draw mode (puts the "pen" down).
002	2	Ends draw mode (lifts the "pen" up) so that you can move to a new location.
003	3	Divides the vector lengths by the specification that follows, as in 3,5 to divide the lengths by 5. This scales down the shape. You should reverse this at the end of the shape by using the 4 code.
004	4	Multiplies the vector lengths by the specification that follows, as in 4,2 to multiply the lengths by 2. This scales up the shape. You should reverse this at the end of the shape by using the 3 code.
005	5	Saves the current position so that you can return to it later in the shape definition. You must use (restore) every position that you save (with a maximum of four).

Hexadecimal Code	Decimal Code	Explanation
006	6	Restores the last saved position.
007	7	Draws another shape that is defined within the shape file whose number follows. For example, use 7,230 to draw shape 230. When the other shape is complete, AutoCAD returns to the current shape definition.
008	8	Draws a line specified by X and Y displacements that follow the code. For example, 8,(8,–12) draws a line whose endpoint is 8 units to the right and 12 units down from the current coordinate. You can add parentheses to your shape codes for readability.
009	9	Draws multiple X,Y displacements. You end this code with a displacement of 0,0. For example, 9,(8,–12),(1,0),(0,12),(–8,0),(0,0) draws four X,Y displacements. You can add parentheses to your shape codes for readability.
00A	10	Draws an octant arc specified by its radius (ranging from 1 to 255), and a second code in the syntax (–)0SC. In the second code, the minus sign is optional, and indicates a clockwise arc, the 0 is mandatory, the S specifies the starting octant, and the C specifies the number of octants that the arc covers. An octant is an eighth of a circle. Figure 32.3 shows the octant codes that you must use for the starting octant. For example, 10,(2,014) indicates an arc with a radius of 2 that is drawn counterclockwise from octant 1 and covers 4 octants (ending at octant 5). This is a semicircle.
00B	11	Draws a fractional arc that is not limited by octants specified by the five following codes in the syntax: `start_offset,end_offset,high_radius,radius,(-)0SC` The start offset specifies how far past an octant the arc begins and is calculated as follows: (starting degrees – degrees of the last octant passed) * 256/45. The end offset specifies how far past an octant the arc ends and is calculated as follows: (ending degrees – degrees of the last octant passed) * 256/45. For both the start and the end of the arc, the last octant passed is specified in degrees, not the numbers in Figure 32.3, and is always a multiple of 45. The high radius is 0 unless the radius is more than 255. If your radius is larger, the high radius is the maximum number of 256 multiples in the value of the radius (for example, 2, if your radius is 600). The difference (the radius minus 256 times the high radius value, or 88 if your radius is 600) is placed in the radius specification. The radius is just the radius of the arc. The (–)0SC part of the code is the same as for code 10 (00A), except that S is the octant that the arc starts in and C is the number of octants that the arc covers.

continued

TABLE 32.2 *(continued)*

Hexadecimal Code	Decimal Code	Explanation
00C	12	Draws an arc using a system of X,Y displacement and bulge using the syntax X-displacement, Y-displacement, and bulge. These three codes can range from –127 to +127. The X and Y displacements just specify the endpoint of the arc. The bulge equals ((2 * H/D) * 127) where D is the *chord length* (the distance from the start point to the endpoint) and H is the height measured from the midpoint of the chord to the circumference of the arc. The bulge should be negative if the arc is drawn clockwise.
00D	13	Draws multiple arcs using the X,Y displacement and bulge system. End the arcs with (0,0). You can use 0 for a bulge to place a line segment in the midst of several arcs.
00E	14	This code is used only for text fonts that can be used in the vertical orientation (where each letter is drawn under the previous letter). When the vertical orientation is chosen, the specifications after this code are used. Use this code to move the starting and ending point of letters to a point appropriate for vertical orientation (that is, on top of and below the letter). See the "Creating Fonts" section later in this chapter for more information.

FIGURE 32.3

The codes for octant arcs.

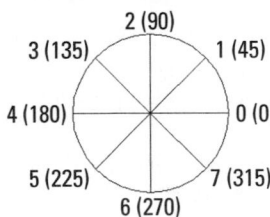

The most common use for shapes is to create fonts. Here are a few examples:

```
*3,22,ALEF
010,07E,010,2,8,(-6,5),1,8,(-2,-4),01C,2,8,(5,2),1,8,(2,4),014,0
```

This is a squared-off aleph, the first letter of the Hebrew alphabet, as shown in Figure 32.4. Displaying non-Roman fonts is a common use for shapes.

Planning in advance is almost essential. A common technique is to draw the shape in a drawing on a grid set to 1-unit spacing. You can use only integers in your shape codes, so you must often scale the shape up so that the smallest line segment is 1 unit.

FIGURE 32.4

A squared-off aleph.

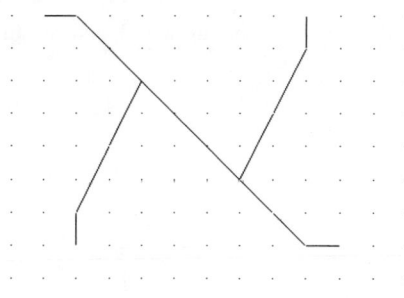

Here's how the code for the aleph works:

- The shape starts at the top left. The code 010 is a hexadecimal length and direction code that specifies a line with a length of 1 unit and a direction of 0 degrees.
- The second code, 07E, is also a hexadecimal length and direction code. It specifies a line with a length of 7 units in the E direction (315 degrees). Although the line is not actually 7 units long, its X (and in this case Y) distance is 7.
- The third code, 010, is the same as the first code and ends the first set of line segments.
- The fourth code, 2, lifts up the pen so that you can move to the start of the next line.
- The fifth code, 8, indicates that the following two codes will be an X,Y displacement.
- The sixth and seventh codes (-6,5) are placed in parentheses for readability. They move the pen (while it is up) −6 units in the X direction and +5 units in the Y direction from the end of the last line to the start of the next line. (Count the grid dots to find it.)
- The eighth code, 1, puts the pen down so that you can draw.
- The ninth code, 8, is the same as the fifth code.
- The tenth and eleventh codes (-2,-4) draw the first segment of the second line so that the endpoint is −2 units in the X direction and −4 units in the Y direction from the start point.
- The twelfth code, 01C, is a hexadecimal code and finishes the second line with a 1-unit line segment in the C direction (270 degrees).
- The thirteenth code, 2, lifts up the pen again.
- The fourteenth code, 8, is the same as the fifth code.
- The fifteenth and sixteenth codes (5,2) move the pen (which is up) +5 units in the X direction and +2 units in the Y direction.

- The seventeenth code, 1, puts the pen down again.
- The eighteenth code, 8, is the same as the fifth code.
- The nineteenth and twentieth codes (2,4) draw a line whose endpoint is 2 units in the X direction and 4 units in the Y direction from its start point.
- The twenty-first code, 014, is a hexadecimal length and vector code that draws a 1-unit line in the 4 (90-degree) direction.
- The twenty-second code, 0, ends the shape definition.

Here's another example, a script aleph, as shown in Figure 32.5:

```
*4,10,S-ALEF
06C,2,8,(6,5),1,10,(3,016),0
```

FIGURE 32.5

A script aleph.

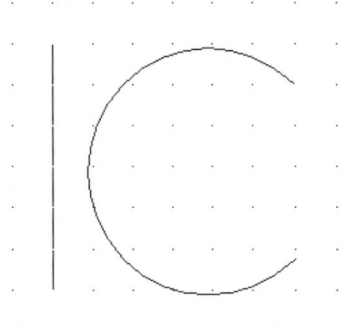

Here's the explanation of the code for the script aleph:

- The first code, 06C, creates the line on the left, starting at the top and making it 6 units long.
- The second code, 2, lifts up the pen.
- The third code, 8, specifies an X,Y displacement, with the pen up.
- The fourth and fifth codes (6,5) move the pen 6 units to the right and 5 units up, to the start of the arc.
- The sixth code, 10, introduces an octant arc.
- The seventh and eighth codes (3,016) specify an arc with a radius of 3 units that starts at octant 1 and covers 6 octants (to octant 7). (See Figure 32.3 to review the octant codes.)
- The last code, 0, ends the definition.

On the DVD

The drawing used in the following exercise on creating a shape, ab32-a.dwg, is in the Drawings folder on the DVD. ■

STEPS: Creating a Shape

1. Open ab32-a.dwg from the DVD.

2. Save the file as ab32-01.dwg in your AutoCAD Bible folder. This drawing shows an upper-case P, with dashed lines to indicate spaces before and after the letter, as shown in Figure 32.6. This is the type of drawing that you might use as a basis for creating a shape definition.

An uppercase P.

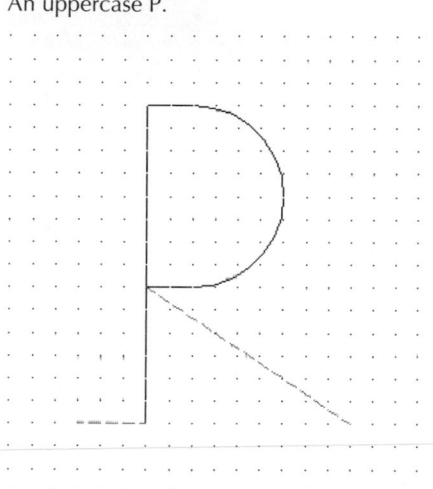

3. Type **notepad** ↵ on the command line and press Enter at the File to edit: prompt to open a new file.

4. Type the following in Notepad:

```
*80,15,UCP
2,030,1,0E4,020,12,(0,-8,-127),028,2,8,(9,-6),0
```

5. Press Enter at the end of the last line. Choose File ⇨ Save in Notepad and save the file in your AutoCAD Bible folder as ab32-01.shp. Close Notepad.

6. In AutoCAD, type **compile** ↵. Double-click ab32-01.shp. AutoCAD compiles the .shp file. AutoCAD confirms on the command line that the compilation succeeded. (Press F2 to open the AutoCAD Text Window if necessary.)

7. Type **load** ↵ and choose `ab32-01.shx`. Click Open. Type **shape** ↵. To insert the shape, follow the prompts:

```
Enter shape name or [?]: ucp ↵
Specify insertion point: Pick any point.
Specify height <1.0000>: ↵
Specify rotation angle <0>: ↵
```

8. Save your drawing. It should look like Figure 32.7.

FIGURE 32.7

The picture and shape of the letter P.

Editing shape files

You don't often get a shape right the first time, and you don't see the result until after you've compiled, loaded, and inserted the shape. Editing shape files involves the following steps:

1. Erase all copies of the shape.
2. Purge the `.shx` file by using the PURGE command and choosing Shapes in the dialog box. (You may sometimes need to purge more than once.) This step removes the existing shape definition from the drawing. If you forget this step, when you try to insert the corrected shape, AutoCAD uses the old definition!
3. Edit the `.shp` file. Don't forget to change the `#ofspecs` value in the first line if necessary. Save the file.
4. Recompile the `.shp` file with the COMPILE command.
5. Reload the `.shx` file with the LOAD command.
6. Reinsert the shape by using the SHAPE command.

Creating Fonts

AutoCAD's support for TrueType fonts makes so many fonts available that the need to create your own is certainly less than with earlier versions. However, you might want to add special symbols to some existing fonts, especially if you often use these symbols within text.

Font files use the same codes to define the characters as shape files use. They have the following unique characteristics:

- The shapenumber part of the definition must correspond to the ASCII code value for the character you're defining. To find these codes, look at the sample fonts in the Help file (from the InfoCenter toolbar, click the drop-down list to the right of the Help button on the far right and then choose Help). On the Help landing page, click Customization Guide from the left side. Then in the middle of the page, click Create Shape Definition Files under Shapes and Shape Fonts. Click Sample Files. Fonts generally use either hexadecimal or decimal format.

- The shapename part of the definition is lowercase and is usually used to label the character. For example, it uses ucp for uppercase *p* and lcr for lowercase *r*. The sample files mentioned in the preceding item use these codes.

- The file must include a special shape identifier UNIFONT that defines the entire font, using the following syntax:

  ```
  *UNIFONT,4,font-name
  above,below,modes,0
  ```

  The above value specifies how far above the baseline that uppercase letters extend. The below value specifies how far below the baseline that lowercase letters, such as *p* or *q*, extend. Together, these two values define the size of the characters. AutoCAD uses these values to scale letters when you define a text height for the font. Modes should be 0 for a horizontal font and 2 for a font that supports both horizontal and vertical orientations. For example, a header for a font named arch with capital letters 21 units high and lowercase letters that extend 7 units below the line could be:

  ```
  *UNIFONT,4,arch
  21,7,0,0
  ```

- You must define the line feed (LF), which drops down one line without drawing so that lines of text can be placed beneath each other. The line feed is ASCII code 10.

- You need to create a start point and endpoint with the pen up to create spacing between letters. See the previous exercise for an example.

As with all shapes, you probably want to use AutoCAD to draw all the characters on a grid with a spacing of 1. Decide on the height of the letters and be consistent.

Big fonts and Unicode fonts

The Japanese and Chinese written languages use fonts with thousands of characters, because each character represents a word. AutoCAD uses big fonts to support these languages. It is beyond the scope of this book to go into detail about how to create these fonts, but a short explanation is useful. Big font files use special codes to allow for the larger number of shapes. Big fonts allow up to 65,535 shape numbers.

Unicode fonts support the ISO10646 standard, which uses 16-bit encoding to support many languages in one font file. If you open one of the .shp files, you'll see characters for all the letters that may have accents in French, Spanish, and so on. All the fonts in AutoCAD are now compliant with this standard.

The advantage of Unicode fonts is that characters that you type appear the same in all systems and countries. This is important if you exchange drawings with clients or colleagues in other countries. Unicode fonts use a special header that includes two extra codes.

Unicode special characters can be inserted by typing **\u+** and the hexadecimal Unicode value in the font file. (For this reason, Unicode font files use hexadecimal shape numbers.) For example, the hexadecimal code for the plus/minus sign is 00B1. If you type **\u+00b1** and press Enter (using TEXT in this example), you get the plus/minus sign. (It works with multiline text, too.)

If you don't need the additional capabilities of big fonts or Unicode fonts, you can create fonts without them.

Summary

In this chapter, you read about how to create shapes. You discovered how to:

- Use shape files when you need to insert a shape many times, while using as little storage space as possible
- Create fonts by using shape files with a few special codes that define both the font as a whole and each character

In the next chapter, I explain how to customize menus.

Customizing the Ribbon and Menus

Although the ribbon and menu are designed to be useful for most people, the whole point of customization is that everyone has different needs. You can probably draw more efficiently and faster by customizing the user interface to suit your own individual requirements. Not only can you add commands, but you can also add items consisting of a series of commands that run like a macro. If you're using AutoCAD, you can even add AutoLISP routines. You may want to create specialized items that are used only for one drawing — for example, to help clients view a drawing. User interface customization includes the ribbon, menus, mouse or puck buttons, toolbars (covered in Chapter 29), rollover tooltips, shortcut menus, image-tile menus, keyboard shortcuts, temporary override keys, the double-click function, and the Quick Properties palette. The only limits are your imagination and the time that you can devote to customization.

Working with the Customization File

The AutoCAD or AutoCAD LT user interface is contained in a file that you don't edit directly; instead, you use the Customize User Interface, or CUI, Editor to modify the menu.

Starting with AutoCAD 2010 and AutoCAD LT 2010, a new packaged file format was introduced for the menu file. If you're upgrading from a release earlier than AutoCAD 2010 or AutoCAD LT 2010, you'll see that in place of the CUI, MNU, MNS, or MNC files is one file, `acad.cuix` or `acadlt.cuix`. The packaged file format contains all the bitmap image files used for the custom commands in the customization file that you create that are not stored in a DLL file.

Understanding the Customization file

The main customization file is `acad.cuix` in AutoCAD, and `acadlt.cuix` in AutoCAD LT. You can either customize this file or load another customization file.

Caution

Don't even think about customizing until you've backed up at least `acad.cuix` or `acadlt.cuix`. It is possible to corrupt the customization file. ∎

Tip

If you get into a problem with your customization file, then you can restore your most recently saved file by right-clicking the customization group's name at the top of the Customizations In pane and choosing Restore ACAD.CUIX (or ACADLT.CUIX). You can also go back to the original customization file that came with the program by right-clicking the customization group name and choosing Reset ACAD.CUIX (or ACADLT.CUIX). Another way to find the original customization file is to look in `C:\Program Files\Autodesk\AutoCAD 2011 (AutoCAD LT 2011)\UserDataCache\Support` (if you used the default installation location). ∎

In addition to the main customization file, AutoCAD and AutoCAD LT use these other files:

- `custom.cuix`. This file is specifically meant to be used for your menu customization. It is a *partial* customization file, which means that you use it to add on to the main customization file. For example, you can add a toolbar and a menu that you use with the regular menu.

- `acad.mnr` or `acadlt.mnr`. This file contains the bitmap images used by the commands in the customization file, such as toolbar icons and icons on ribbon panels, but stored in a special way that allows AutoCAD to load them faster.

- `acad.mnl`. This file contains AutoLISP routines used by the menu and is automatically loaded when the customization file is loaded (AutoCAD only).

You can create your own *full* (main or enterprise) or partial customization files, using any name that you want. You'll have the best results if you place all your customization files in the same folder as the main customization file.

Note

To find the location of `acad.cuix` or `acadlt.cuix`, choose Application Button ➪ Options and then click the Files tab. Expand the Customization Files item, and then expand the Main Customization File item. Browse to that location in Windows Explorer. ∎

Loading and unloading customization files

There are two types of customization files: partial and full. A partial customization file usually has only one or two ribbon panels, menus, or toolbars. You can then load this partial customization file along with your main customization file. If your customization file consists of simply adding a few items, then you may want to create a partial customization file and add it to your current main customization file. In this way, you don't need to alter the customization in your main customization file. While the customization in the main customization file is not altered, a reference to your partial customization file is added to the main customization file, though, so it is loaded when the main customization file is loaded.

On the other hand, you may also want to have complete alternate interfaces, in which case you can customize the main customization file. Perhaps two different people work on one computer and have different customization needs. For example, you may find it useful to have one customization file for architectural drawings, another for mechanical drawings, and a third for electrical schematics.

Loading and unloading a customization file

Using your own customization file is a good way to keep the original file safe, in case you want to go back to it. Generally, you start by making a copy of the default main customization file, `acad.cuix` or `acadlt.cuix`.

You can copy a customization file (or any file, for that matter) in Windows Explorer. Right-click the file and choose Copy. Then right-click in any blank space in the Explorer window and choose Paste. The new file appears at the bottom of the list of files. Click the file to select it, and then click it again to change its name. Enter the new name, and then press Enter.

Each loaded customization file must have a unique name. If you want to work with your own customization file, you first need to unload the current customization file. Use the CUILOAD command on the command line both to unload and load a customization file. The Load/Unload Customizations dialog box opens, as shown in Figure 33.1. Choose the customization file that you want to unload, and click Unload.

FIGURE 33.1

The Load/Unload Customizations dialog box.

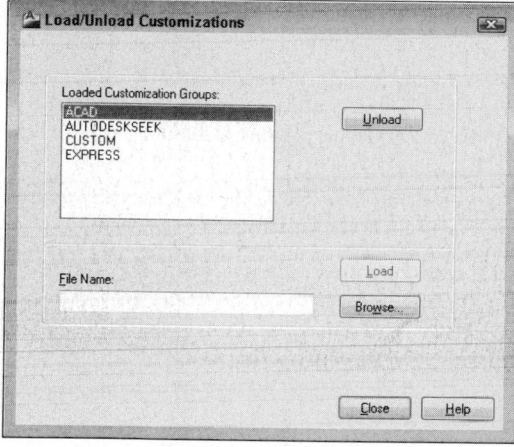

To load a customization file, follow these steps:

1. At the command line, type **cuiload** and press Enter.
2. In the Load/Unload Customizations dialog box, choose the current customization file and click Unload.
3. Click the Browse button.
4. In the Select Customization File dialog box, browse to and select the customization file you want to load. Click Open.
5. In the Load/Unload Customizations dialog box, click Load.
6. Click Close to close the dialog box.

Tip

You can determine the current main customization file by choosing Application Button⇨Options, clicking the Files tab, and then expanding the Customization Files and Main Customization File item. ■

7. Choose Manage tab ⇨ Customization panel ⇨ User Interface (or type **cui** ↵ on the command line or in the Dynamic Input tooltip).

8. In the Customizations In pane, the drop-down list should show All Customization Files or Main Customization File. The top item in the pane lists the current main customization group name. It may still show the customization file that you unloaded; in that case, right-click it and choose Rename. Enter the name of the customization file that you loaded, and press Enter to match the customization group name to the filename.

By default, when you start AutoCAD or AutoCAD LT, the last customization file that you used, the name of which is stored in the Windows registry, is loaded. If you want to use a new customization file while in AutoCAD or AutoCAD LT, unload the current customization file and load the new one.

Loading and unloading partial customization files

You can use custom.cuix, a partial customization file, that comes with AutoCAD (or AutoCAD LT) or create your own partial customization file. To create a new partial customization file, follow these steps:

1. On the Transfer tab of the Customize User Interface Editor, click the Create a New Customization File button to the right of the Customizations In drop-down list.

2. From the drop-down list, choose Save As. Enter a name for the new file in the Save As dialog box. Make sure that you use a name that is different from all other customization files.

3. To use the file, go to the Customize tab and choose Main Customization File from the drop-down list in the Customizations In pane. Then click the Load Partial Customization File button to the right of the drop-down list. In the Open dialog box, locate the partial customization file and click Open.

4. Choose Main Customization File again from the drop-down list. You should now see the new file listed under the expanded Partial Customization Files item at the bottom of the tree view.

You can load more than one partial customization file along with the main customization file. For example, you might have one partial customization file for 2D work and another for 3D work; sometimes, you might want both of them.

You can load and unload partial customization files in two ways:

- Use the CUILOAD command as explained in the previous section.

- Use the CUI command to open the Customize User Interface Editor. To load a file, click the Load Partial Customization File button in the Customizations In pane. Select the file and click Open. In the Customize User Interface Editor, click Apply.

After you have loaded a partial customization file, check to make sure that it has been loaded. In the Customize User Interface Editor, choose Main Customization File from the top drop-down list. Expand the Partial Customization Files item in the Customizations In pane, and make sure that your partial customization file is listed.

To unload a partial customization file, use one of these methods:

- Use the CUILOAD command. Follow the instructions for unloading a main customization file, described in the previous section.

- In the Customize User Interface Editor, right-click the file from the Partial Customization Files item and choose Unload.

Transferring customization between files

You can also move customization items between customization files, using the Transfer tab of the Customize User Interface Editor. You can transfer items from a loaded customization file to any customization file. You can also transfer items between both full and partial customization files.

When you display the Transfer tab, the main customization file is listed in the left pane. To open another file, click the Open Customization File button in the right pane, choose the file that you want to use, and click Open.

In each pane, expand the element that you want to transfer. For example, if you want to transfer menus, expand the Menus item on each side. You then see the actual menus in each file that is listed. To transfer an item, drag it from one pane to the other. Make sure that you are dragging to the same type of item, that is, menu to menu or ribbon panel to ribbon panel.

When you're done, click OK to close the Customize User Interface Editor.

Customizing the Interface

When you first start customizing a customization file, the process may seem overwhelming. However, even small changes can be very useful. Start simple and take it from there.

Customization files include many types of customizable content, as follows:

- Toolbars let you choose commands from buttons and change settings from drop-down lists. I discuss customizing toolbars in Chapter 29. Chapter 29 also covers customizing the Quick Access toolbar, which is above the ribbon.
- Ribbon panels also let you choose commands from buttons, as well as specify settings using special controls. You can add or remove buttons, drop-down lists, rows, sub-panels, and fold panels.

New Feature

Ribbon panels in AutoCAD 2011 or AutoCAD LT 2011 allow you to add fold panels to help organize and display buttons and controls. A fold panel resizes a set of buttons or controls horizontally as you add or remove panels from the ribbon. ■

- Ribbon tabs let you organize and display ribbon panels on the ribbon.
- Ribbon contextual tab states allow you to display ribbon tabs based on a set of predefined states that the drawing editor might be in (an object being selected or a command being active).
- Menus are the drop-down lists of items that are at the top of the AutoCAD and AutoCAD LT application window when the Classic workspace is current.
- Keyboard shortcuts come in two varieties. Shortcut keys, such as Ctrl+C for the COPYCLIP command, which execute commands, and temporary override keys.
- Temporary override keys (which I explain how to use in Chapter 4) are another kind of keyboard shortcut, but they temporarily override settings, such as Object Snap and Ortho Mode.
- Shortcut menus appear when you click the right mouse button. (See Chapter 3 and Appendix A for more information on right-clicking.)
- Double-click actions control what happens when you double-click an object.

- The Quick Properties palette shows the properties of objects that you select. You can control which properties appear on this panel. Rollover tooltips are similar, but they appear when you hover the cursor over an object, without selecting it.
- Button menus control the buttons on your mouse.
- Tablet menus control the menu that can be overlaid on a digitizing tablet.
- Tablet buttons control the multiple buttons on a puck that you use with a digitizing tablet.
- The screen menu is AutoCAD's original menu that used to appear at the right side of your screen. (This section does not exist in AutoCAD LT.) By default, it is not displayed, but it still exists in the customization file. In AutoCAD, you can display it by choosing Application Button ⇨ Options, clicking the Display tab, and checking the Display Screen Menu check box.
- Image-tile menus create dialog boxes with images.

Looking at a ribbon panel

The best way to start customizing the user interface is to look at a ribbon panel and its corresponding representation in the Customize User Interface Editor. Each type of user interface content has its own unique features, but certain features apply to most, if not all, user interface elements.

Figure 33.2 shows the AutoCAD Draw panel of the Home tab in the 2D Drafting & Annotation workspace.

FIGURE 33.2

The AutoCAD Draw panel of the Home tab as it appears in the 2D Drafting & Annotation workspace.

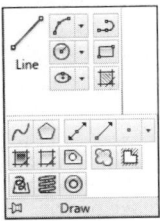

Figure 33.3 shows the same panel as it is displayed in the Customize User Interface Editor. Compare this list to the panel shown in Figure 33.2.

In Figure 33.3, the LINE command is selected, and the right side of the Customize User Interface Editor shows the information relating to that command. Commands assigned to a ribbon panel have the following elements:

- **Name.** The name is what you actually see on the ribbon panel when the button is set to display labels. When working with menus, the ellipsis (...) after the name provides a visual cue that this item opens a dialog box. You can use an ampersand (&) to underscore the following letter. You can then press the Alt key with the underscored letter to execute the menu item (instead of clicking the menu item with your mouse). KeyTips on ribbon panel items are similar to an ampersand (&) in a menu item. The mouse buttons, tablet buttons, tablet menus, shortcut menus, and double-click actions do not display the name, but the name is required.
- **Button Style.** This controls the direction of the icon and its label, if the label is displayed, and its size. This property is unique to commands on ribbon panels and Quick Access toolbars, but it does not change the display of the button on the Quick Access toolbar.

- **Group Name.** This is used to group commands together when placed on a drop-down list with grouping enabled. This property is unique to commands on ribbon panels and Quick Access toolbars.

- **Command Name.** This is the name of the command. Usually, it's the same as the display name.

- **Description.** For ribbon panels, drop-down lists, shortcut menus, and toolbars, the description appears on the status bar when you hover the cursor over the menu item or button. The other menu elements don't use the description, although some of them let you enter one.

- **Extended Help File.** You can create an expanded tooltip that contains instructions for using the command. The expanded tooltip appears when you hover the cursor over a command on a toolbar, ribbon panel, or Quick Access toolbar. Here you would put the filename and ID for that content.

- **Command Display Name.** This text contains the name of the AutoCAD or AutoCAD LT command used in the macro. This text value is displayed at the bottom of a tooltip.

- **Macro.** The macro is the command that the item executes. In the next section, I explain how to write menu macros. This can be a simple command, any group of commands, or an AutoLISP expression if you're using AutoCAD. The following conventions are recommended:

  - Add an apostrophe (') before commands that can be used transparently. (Otherwise, the commands won't work transparently when chosen from the menu.)

  - All other commands start with ^C^C, which is equivalent to pressing Esc twice. This cancels any other command that may be active. One Esc is generally enough, but occasionally two are necessary. (In rare situations, more might be needed.)

  - The underscore is used before each command. This allows translation of the command into other languages. For example, your menus would automatically be translated into the equivalent French command in France!

FIGURE 33.3

The Home 2D - Draw panel in the Customize User Interface Editor.

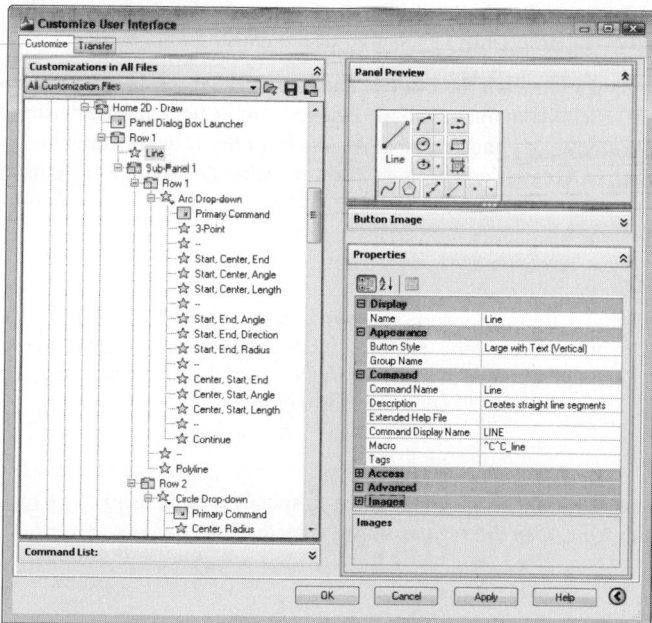

- **Tags.** You can add keywords to facilitate searching for the command in the application menu's search box.

- **KeyTip.** This character sequence is used to access ribbon tabs and panels, and the Quick Access toolbar from the keyboard. Press Alt to display the KeyTips for the items on the ribbon, application menu, and Quick Access toolbar. You see KeyTips only when the menu bar is not displayed (MENUBAR system variable set to 0); otherwise, Alt allows you to access the menu bar by using the keyboard.

- **Tooltip Title.** This controls the alternate title displayed for the command if it is the most recent command used from a drop-down list. This property is unique to commands on drop-down lists, which are displayed on a ribbon panel or Quick Access toolbar.

- **Element ID.** This is a unique identifier that the program assigns automatically. In previous releases, it was used to link flyouts and toolbar buttons to their status bar help, and to link a keyboard shortcut to a menu item. You can still use this identifier for programming purposes. You cannot change the ID of an existing command, but you should add one for new commands that you create.

- **Images.** Ribbon and toolbar buttons and some menu items have images. Most people use only the small image, but you can specify large images on the Display tab of the Options dialog box (Application Button ⇨ Options). You can choose an image from the Button Image pane, or create your own image by using the Button Editor. I cover the Button Editor in Chapter 29.

Drop-down and shortcut lists (the entire lists, not their items) also have aliases that you use when referring to the list. You can add an alias by clicking the Ellipsis button to the right of the alias item.

Note

In Windows XP, by default, the underscores appear only when you press Alt on your keyboard and the ribbon is hidden. You then type the underscored letter to open the menu. To choose a menu item, type its underscored letter. To disable this behavior and display the underscores all the time, choose Start ⇨ Control Panel and choose Display. If you have Windows XP, choose the Appearance tab and click the Effects button. Then uncheck the Hide Underlined Letters for Keyboard Navigation Until I Press the Alt Key check box.

In Windows Vista, choose Personalization from the Control Panel and click Ease of Access in the lower-left corner. In the Ease of Access Center, click Make the Keyboard Easier to Use. Check the Underline Keyboard Shortcuts and Access Keys check box. In Windows 7, choose Ease of Access from the Control Panel and click Change How Your Keyboard Works. In the Ease of Access Center, check the Underline Keyboard Shortcuts and Access Keys check box. Click Save. ■

Writing macros

The macro is the heart of a custom command. To enter a macro, click the text box to the right of the Macro item and start typing. If your macro is long, click the Ellipsis button at the right of the text box to open the Long String Editor dialog box. You need to know a number of special characters and conventions in order to write menu macros. Table 33.1 lists some of the most common ones.

Note

Because the backslash pauses for user input, you cannot use it to specify a path, as in `C:\Program Files\Autodesk\AutoCAD 2011\Support`. Use the regular slash (/) instead. ■

TABLE 33.1

Special Characters for Menu Macros

Character	Description
;	Equivalent to pressing Enter. The end of a line in a menu macro is also equivalent to pressing Enter. Use the semicolon when you need two returns at the end of a line, or when you want to indicate pressing Enter. Some commands, such as TEXT, also require a return to complete. You can also use ^M.
Space	Similar to pressing Enter, except when entering text (to create a text object) that contains spaces (such as between words). Use between the command and its options. Note that you can even use a space on the command line for most commands.
\	Pauses for user input, such as picking a point or typing a value.
+	Used at the end of a line to continue the macro on the next line.
*	Placed at the beginning of a macro (before the ^C^C), this character repeats the macro until you end it by pressing Esc or choosing another menu item. For example, the POINT command works this way.
^R	Indicates using the latest version of the command that follows in the macro. When ^R is not used, the oldest version of the command is used instead; this applies to commands that have changed from one release to another. For example, macros that use the LAYOUT and SOLIDEDIT commands work this way.
^P	Turns on and off (toggles) the display of the menu macro, including menu prompts, on the command line.

Here is one macro from the Draw panel (hidden in a flyout) — Arc Drop-down: Start, Center, Angle — that uses the backslash and the space:

```
^C^C_arc \_c \_a
```

Here's how this command works:

^C^C	Cancels any previous command.
_arc	Starts the ARC command (enables translation to another language version of AutoCAD or AutoCAD LT).
Space	Equivalent to pressing the Spacebar, which is the same as pressing Enter after typing **arc** on the command line. The command line displays the `Specify start point of arc or [Center]:` prompt.
\	The backslash pauses the macro to let you specify a start point.
_c	Chooses the Center option, and enables translation to another language.
Space	Equivalent to pressing the Spacebar, which is the same as pressing Enter after typing c on the command line (for the Center option). The command line displays the `Specify center point of arc:` prompt.
\	The backslash pauses the macro to let you specify a center point.
_a	Chooses the Angle option. Because this is at the end of the command, you don't need to specify a pause. The user specifies an angle and presses Enter, thus ending the command and drawing the arc.

The backslash allows for only one input, except when used with the SELECT command. Therefore, you can use the SELECT command in menu macros to collect a selection set, and then use another command with the Previous option to act on the entire selection set. For example:

```
^C^Cselect \move previous ;.1,0 ;
```

This macro cancels any existing command, starts the SELECT command, and lets you select as many objects as you want. You end object selection by pressing Enter. Then the macro automatically moves those objects to the right by 0.1 unit. Using the All selection option is another way to select more than one object in a menu macro.

Here are a few more examples of macros from earlier chapters:

- You could place this macro on a drop-down list to make a selected polyline 0.1 unit wide:

  ```
  ^C^Cpedit \w .1 ;
  ```

- You could use the following macro to automatically draw four circles with the specified centers and radius.

  ```
  ^C^Ccircle 2,2 1.5 circle 6,2 1.5 circle 10,2 1.5 circle 14,2 1.5
  ```

- You could use this macro to clean up a drawing. It uses CHPROP to select all the objects in a drawing, and it uses the Color option to change their color to ByLayer. Then it uses the LAYER command to freeze the layer named no-plot and saves the drawing.

  ```
  ^C^Cchprop all  c bylayer  -layer f no-plot  qsave
  ```

Customizing the ribbon

You can customize the ribbon by adding or deleting buttons, rows, sub-panels, fold panels, panels, and tabs. You can add existing commands or create a custom command. I discuss how to create custom commands in Chapter 29. You add commands to a panel; you can't add commands to a tab. If you want a new panel, you add it and then add commands to it. Also, you can add a tab and add panels to that tab. After you create a tab, you can display it on the ribbon by assigning it to a workspace or a contextual tab state.

Understanding ribbon panels

Ribbon panels are containers for commands, drop-down lists, and so on. They have a structure that enables you to lay out buttons so that they are easy to find and are well organized. Ribbon panels can contain the following elements:

- **Panel Separators.** Each panel has a top portion that is visible by default, and an expanded portion that you see only when you click the panel's title bar at the bottom. You would place commonly used commands above the panel separator, and less common commands below it. Each panel comes with a panel separator that you cannot remove, indicated by the <SLIDEOUT> item in the Customizations In pane on the panel.

- **Rows.** You place commands in rows. A panel can have rows above and below the panel separator.

- **Sub-panels.** Sub-panels create separate sections in the ribbon panel. You use them to offset and group commands. For example, in the Draw panel (shown in Figures 33.2 and 33.3), Sub-Panel 1 follows the LINE command, setting it off by itself and grouping the rest of the commands in the ribbon panel. Sub-panels are optional.

- **Fold panels.** Fold panels are similar to sub-panels, in that you use them to group commands on a ribbon panel. The difference is that you have much greater control over the size of a fold panel. Each fold panel looks to see how much space is available on the ribbon and, based on its assigned priority, resizes horizontally to maximize the space available. Fold panels are optional.

New Feature

Fold panels are new in AutoCAD 2011 and AutoCAD LT 2011. ∎

- **Drop-down lists.** You can add drop-down lists; they are used to organize multiple similar commands so they take up the space of one command.
- **Separators.** You can add separators to separate commands. You can create two styles of separators: line and spacer.

Except for panel separators, you add these items by right-clicking in the appropriate location and choosing the item that you want. For example, you can right-click any row and add a new row, sub-panel, drop-down list, fold panel, or separator. To control how an item behaves or is displayed on the ribbon, select the item and use the Properties panel on the right side of the Customize User Interface Editor.

Adding a command to a ribbon panel

To add a command to a ribbon panel, follow these steps:

1. Choose Manage tab ⇨ Customization panel ⇨ User Interface to open the Customize User Interface Editor.

Tip

To be able to see the tab that you want to work on, display that tab and then enter cui on the command line or in the Dynamic Input tooltip, instead of using the button on the Manage tab. ∎

2. At the top of the Customizations In pane of the dialog box, expand the Ribbon item from the tree view. Then expand the Panels item and the panel that you want to contain the command. Finally, expand the row that you want to add the command to. You might need to expand a sub-panel or fold panel as well. Note that many of the panels have 2D and 3D versions; pick the one that you'll be working with.

3. Choose the command that you want to add from the Command List pane. (If necessary, display that pane by clicking the double-down arrow to the right of the Command List title.) You can choose an existing or a custom command. Chapter 29 explains more about how to use this pane, including how to find commands easily.

4. Drag the command to the desired row. If it isn't in the proper location within the row, drag it again to where you want it to be using the visual indicators.

Tip

You can then click the panel and see a preview in the Panel Preview pane. ∎

5. Click Apply to apply the change. You can move the Customize User Interface Editor to see if you like the result.

6. Click OK to close the Customize User Interface Editor.

Tip

You can copy an entire toolbar to a ribbon panel by right-clicking the toolbar in the Customize User Interface Editor and choosing Copy to Ribbon Panels. You can use this technique to convert custom toolbars that you created to ribbon panels. ∎

AutoCAD 2008 and AutoCAD LT 2008 allowed you to customize the dashboard panel by creating or modifying control panels. AutoCAD 2009 and AutoCAD LT 2009 did not allow you to migrate your control panels to the ribbon, but AutoCAD 2011 and AutoCAD LT 2011 do. You migrate a control panel by clicking Open Customization File on the Transfer tab, and then opening the CUI file that contains the control panels you want to migrate. Expand the Dashboard Panels item and right-click the control panel to migrate and choose Copy to Ribbon Panels. Click Yes. Expand the Ribbon and Panels item, and drag the converted control panel to the Panels item of one of the loaded customization files.

Adding a ribbon panel to a tab

You may want to create your own ribbon panel. You start by creating the ribbon panel and adding commands to it. Then you add the panel to a tab.

To create a ribbon panel, follow these steps:

1. Choose Manage tab ➪ Customization panel ➪ User Interface to open the Customize User Interface Editor.
2. At the top of the Customizations In pane, expand the Ribbon item and right-click the Panels item and choose New Panel. A new panel appears, selected.
3. Enter a name for the panel and press Enter.
4. You can now add commands to the panel, as described previously.

When your new ribbon panel is complete, drag the panel to the desired tab. You may find it helpful to collapse the Command List pane first by clicking its double-down arrow.

Adding a tab to the ribbon

1. At the top of the Customizations In pane, expand the Ribbon item, right-click Tabs, and choose New Tab. A new tab appears, selected.
2. Enter a name for the new tab and press Enter. You now need to add ribbon panels to the tab.
3. Expand the Panels items and select the panels that you want to add to the tab. You can select more than one panel by pressing and holding Ctrl as you click each new panel. You may find it helpful to collapse the Command List pane first by clicking its double-down arrow.
4. Right-click any of the selected panels, and choose Copy. This copies the panels, instead of moving them.
5. Right-click the new tab, and choose Paste to add a reference to the selected panels on the tab.

Contextual states are used to specify the state that AutoCAD should be in before the ribbon tab is displayed, such as a command being active, the drawing editor being idle, or an object being selected. When talking about the ribbon, contextual states relate to a predefined list of commands that might be active or a specific type of object that is selected. Contextual tab states are not workspace specific like ribbon tabs.

Adding a tab to a contextual tab state

1. At the top of the Customizations In pane, expand the Ribbon and Contextual Tab States items.
2. Expand the Tabs item and select the tabs that you want to add to the contextual tab state. You can select more than one tab by pressing and holding Ctrl as you click each tab. You may find it helpful to collapse the Command List pane first by clicking its double-down arrow.
3. Click and drag any of the selected tabs and drop them on the contextual tab state in which you want to assign them.

Tip

Instead of dragging ribbon tabs to a contextual tab state, you can select the ribbon tabs you want to add and press Ctrl+C. Then, to add the ribbon tabs, select the contextual tab state and press Ctrl+V. ■

4. Select one of the tabs you just assigned to the contextual tab state.

5. In the Properties pane, choose a display type for the ribbon tab under the Contextual Display Type field. You can select Merged to merge the ribbon tab with all displayed ribbon tabs, or choose to display it as its own ribbon tab by selecting Full.

Note

You can control the display behavior of context tabs with the Ribbon Contextual Tab State Options dialog box. To display the Ribbon Contextual Tab State Options dialog box, open the Options dialog box and click the Selection tab. Then click the Contextual Tab States button in the Ribbon Options section. (Choose Application Button⇨ Options to display the Options dialog box.) ■

Customizing the Menu bar and shortcuts menus

The Menus item of the Customize User Interface Editor controls the menus, which appear along the top of the AutoCAD or AutoCAD LT application window when the Classic workspace is current. You can customize existing menus or add your own menus to a customization file. You can create a partial customization file with one or more menus or work with just the main customization file. Adding a command to a menu is very similar to adding a command to a toolbar (see Chapter 29) or ribbon panel (see the discussion earlier in this chapter).

Here are the basic procedures for creating menus:

- To add a menu, right-click the Menus item in the Customizations In pane and choose New Menu. The menu appears at the bottom of the list of menus. You can immediately edit the default name. Press Enter.

Note

The name of a menu appears as the menu title. Keep these fairly short to keep the menu titles from running into each other. Don't place spaces in menu title names — it becomes hard to distinguish where one menu ends and the next one starts. ■

- To add a command (an item) to a menu, drag the command from the Command List pane to the menu's name. If you already have items on the menu, you can drag above or below an existing item. You can also duplicate an existing command on a menu: Right-click the item in the Customizations In pane and choose Duplicate. To make sure that all commands are available, choose All Customization Files from the Customizations In pane drop-down list, and choose All Commands from the Categories drop-down list. For information on creating custom commands, see Chapter 29.

Tip

To find any command that you're looking for, use the Find Command or Text button at the top of the Command List pane. The Find and Replace dialog box opens. Enter some text and click Find Next. Commands also show a tooltip of their macro in the Command List pane. There's also a Search Command List text box at the top of the Command List pane. You can type in text to display only matching commands in the list. ■

- To add a separator below any item, right-click that item and choose Insert Separator from the shortcut menu. The separator helps to organize a menu into logical sections.
- To delete an item, right-click the item and choose Remove.

Note

You can display the menu bar by setting the system variable MENUBAR to a value of 1 or by clicking the Customize button on the right side of the Quick Access toolbar and choosing Show Menu Bar. ■

Creating sub-menus

Sub-menus help you to organize your menu so that related commands stay together. Figure 33.4 shows the Ellipse sub-menu on the Draw menu, as shown on the menu bar.

FIGURE 33.4

The AutoCAD Draw menu with the Ellipse sub-menu displayed.

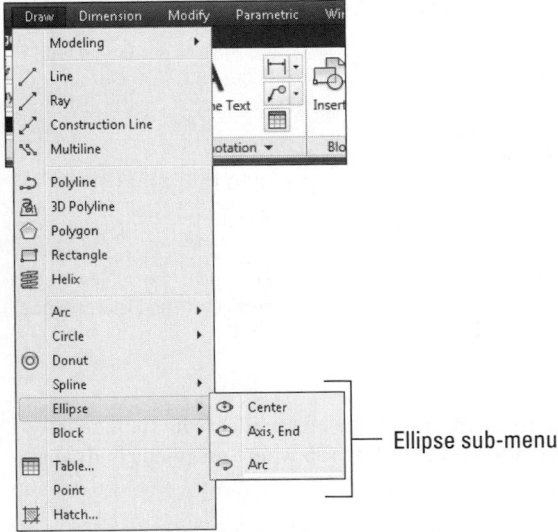

To add a sub-menu, right-click any menu item and choose New Sub-menu. Name the sub-menu the same way that you would name a menu. You also add commands to a sub-menu in the same way that you add commands to a menu.

STEPS: Customizing the Ribbon and Menu

1. If you haven't already done so, back up the customization files. (These are `acad.cuix`, `acad.mnr`, and `acad.mnl`, or `acadlt.cuix` and `acadlt.mnr`.) You will use the backup files at the end of this exercise to undo the changes you make.

Caution

Don't continue with this exercise until you've completed Step 1. If you're working on someone else's computer, ask permission before doing this exercise. To find the location of your customization files, choose Application Button ➪ Options and click the Files tab. Double-click Customization Files ➪ Main Customization File. ■

2. Open a drawing by using the `acad.dwt` or `acadlt.dwt` template.

3. The workspace should be set to 2D Drafting & Annotation. If it isn't, select 2D Drafting & Annotation from the Workspace drop-down list on the Quick Access toolbar.

4. Display the Home tab. Click the Modify panel's title to expand the panel. Notice the Set to ByLayer button at the top left of the expanded panel. This executes the SETBYLAYER command. You would like to have this command more easily accessible and on the Layers panel. You can't put a single command in a partial customization file, so you need to change the main customization file.

5. Type **cui** ↵ on the command line or in the Dynamic Input tooltip.

6. In the Customizations In pane, expand the Ribbon and Panels items, and then expand the Home – Layers item. Expand Row 1. You want to place the SETBYLAYER command after the `Layer, Layer Off` command, which displays as the `Off` item in the row.

7. To find the command, click the Find Command or Text button to the right of the All Commands drop-down list. (The command is not listed under SETBYLAYER.) In the Find and Replace dialog box, enter **setbylayer** in the Find What text box and click Find Next. The `Change to ByLayer` item highlights in the Command List and you can see the Properties panel of the item as well, which shows the correct command. Click Close in the Find and Replace dialog box.

8. Drag the `Change to ByLayer` command from the Command List pane beneath the `Off` item in the Customizations In pane. If it pops to the top of Row 1, drag it back down again.

9. Click Apply and wait for the customization files to save your changes. Drag the dialog box down so that you can see the Layers panel. You should now see the SETBYLAYER command at the top right of the Layers panel.

 10. Now you want to add some items to the menu. To create a new partial customization file, click the Transfer tab of the Customize User Interface Editor, and click the Create a New Customization File button in either pane.

11. In the Save As dialog box, enter **ab1** in the File Name text box. Browse to your `AutoCAD Bible` folder, and click Save. If the Save As dialog box is not displayed, select Save As from the drop-down list next to the Create a New Customization File button.

 12. Click the Customize tab. The drop-down list in the Customizations In pane should show All Customization Files. Then click the Load Partial Customization File button to the right of the drop-down list. In the Open dialog box, locate the `ab1.cuix` file and click Open. (If you see a Warning about Workspaces message, click OK.)

13. Choose All Customization Files from the drop-down list. Expand the Partial Customization Files item; you now see `AB1` listed. Double-click the `AB1` item to expand it.

14. Right-click the Menus item and choose New Menu. Enter **AB1** ↵ to rename the menu.

15. To create a sub-menu, right-click the new AB1 menu and choose New Sub-menu. Enter **&Special Edits** ↵ to rename the sub-menu. (The ampersand allows you to open the menu by pressing Alt+S.)

 16. To create the first custom menu item, click the Create a New Command button in the Command List pane. In the Properties pane, enter the following:

```
Name: Move .1 right
Description: Moves objects .1 unit to the right
Macro (after ^C^C): _select;\_move;_previous;;.1,0;;
Element ID: AB_001a
```

In the Command List pane, choose the `Move .1 right` command, which is now highlighted, and drag it to the `Special Edits` sub-menu. As you do this, you should see a small, left-pointing arrow. When you release the mouse button, the command should appear just below the sub-menu.

17. To allow keyboard access, click the Name property for the `Move .1 right` command in the Properties pane and type **&** in front of the name.

18. To create another custom command, again click Create a New Command in the Command List pane. In the Properties pane, enter the following:

Name: **Pedit .1**
Description: **Sets polyline width to .1**
Macro (after ^C^C): **_pedit;\w;.1;;**
Element ID: **AB_001b**

Drag the new command below the previous custom command.

19. To allow keyboard access, click the Name property for the `Pedit .1` command in the Properties pane and type **&** in front of the name.

20. To add an existing command to the main part of the menu (not the sub-menu), you need to display all the customization files. From the drop-down list under the Customizations In pane, choose All Customization Files. Then expand the Partial Customization Files item (at the bottom of the pane) to see the AB1 partial customization file. Expand Menus, then AB1.

21. From the Command List pane, choose `Change to ByLayer` (the same command you used earlier in this exercise), and drag it up to the AB1 item.

22. Click the Save All Current Customization Files button in the Customizations In pane. Your pane should look like Figure 33.5.

FIGURE 33.5

The new partial customization file in the Customize User Interface Editor.

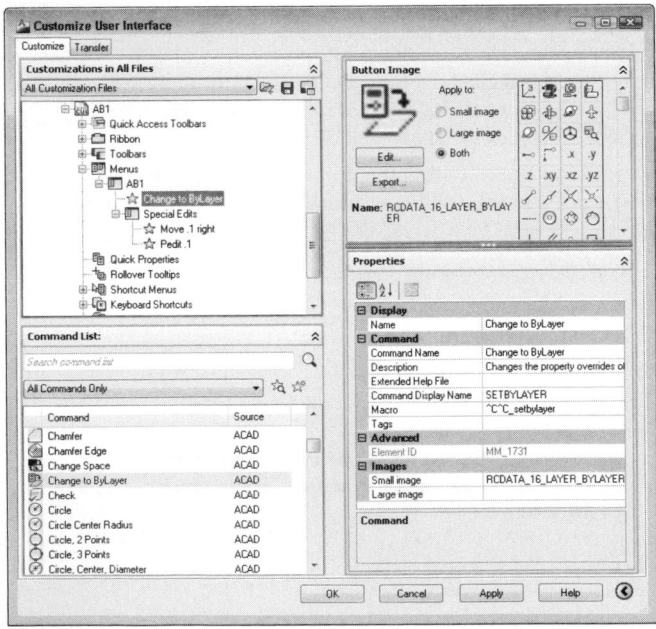

23. Click OK to close the Customize User Interface Editor.

24. Choose AB1 on the menu bar and click the Special Edits sub-menu to expand it. It should look like Figure 33.6.

The AB1 menu, including the Special Edits sub-menu.

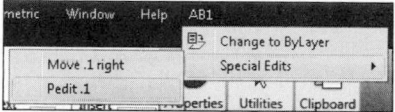

Note

If the AB1 menu doesn't appear, type cuiload ⏎. Unload and then reload AB1. Also, you may need to re-display your current workspace, which you can do from the Workspace drop-down list on the Quick Access toolbar or the Workspace Switching button on the status bar. Make sure that the MENUBAR system variable is set to a value of 1 or you are using the AutoCAD Classic or AutoCAD LT Classic workspace. ■

25. Open ab33-a.dwg from the DVD. Save it as ab33-01.dwg in your AutoCAD Bible folder.

26. To try out the menu, choose AB1 ➪ Special Edits ➪ Move .1 Right. At the Select objects: prompt, pick the vertical red line and right-click to end object selection. The menu macro moves the line 0.1 unit to the right.

27. Choose AB1 ➪ Special Edits ➪ Pedit .1. At the Select polyline or [Multiple]: prompt, choose the green polyline. The polyline becomes 0.1-unit wide.

28. To try out the SETBYLAYER command that you placed in the Layers panel of the ribbon, click the Change to ByLayer button there. At the Select objects or [Settings]: prompt, enter **all** ⏎. Press Enter twice to change objects that are ByBlock to ByLayer and to include blocks in the change to ByLayer.

29. Enter **cuiload** ⏎ and unload AB1. Close the Load/Unload Customizations dialog box. Then display the Customize User Interface Editor again, right-click the ACAD (or ACADLT) item at the top of the Customizations In pane, and choose Restore ACAD.CUIX (or ACADLT.CUIX) to undo the recent changes made to the main customization file or Reset ACAD.CUIX (or ACADLT.CUIX) to return the main customization file to its pristine state when it was first installed.

30. Save your drawing.

Note

If some of the items don't work properly, edit the macros and try again.■

Customizing shortcut menus

Shortcut menus appear at the cursor. In addition to the Object Snap menu, which appears when you press and hold Shift and then right-click, and the Grips menu, which appears when there is a hot grip and you right-click, there are several other shortcut menus. You access a shortcut menu by using the buttons on your mouse or puck. You can customize shortcut menus that are specific to a command or to a selected object. For example, if you right-click when a polyline is selected, the shortcut menu includes a Polyline sub-menu. However, if you right-click when a spline is selected, the shortcut menu includes a Spline sub-menu instead. Because the appropriate shortcut menu appears depending on the context, that is, the object that is selected, shortcut menus are *context-sensitive*. For this reason, they are sometimes called context menus. You can create your own context menus.

To create a shortcut menu, you specify the following:

- **Name.** Although no name appears at the top of a shortcut menu (unlike a menu), a name is required.
- **Description.** The description is optional. The description would only appear if you turned the shortcut menu into a sub-menu, which you can do by dragging a shortcut menu in the Customize User Interface Editor to an item under Menus.
- **Aliases.** Aliases are used to reference the shortcut menu from elsewhere in the customization file. Aliases are assigned automatically, but you need to add an alias in a special format if you create your own shortcut menu. To specify the alias, click in the Aliases text box, and then click the Ellipsis button to open the Aliases dialog box. Click at the end of the current line and press Enter to start a new line. Enter the new alias in the format appropriate for that type of shortcut menu, and then click OK to close the dialog box. See the next two sections for a description of these formats.
- **Element_ID.** An ID is required, but is assigned automatically. Change this if you want to refer to the shortcut menu in program code that you write.

You can create two kinds of context-sensitive menus: object and command menus. AutoCAD and AutoCAD LT only use the context-sensitive menus defined in the main customization file.

Note

If you've turned on time-sensitive right-clicking, remember to hold down the right mouse button long enough to open the shortcut menu. See Chapter 3 for details. ■

Object menus

The Edit mode shortcut menu appears when you right-click in the drawing area while one or more objects are selected but no command is active, as shown in Figure 33.7. Note that this menu includes the most common editing commands.

You can create *object menus* that are specific to a type of object. You might want to add certain commands that you use often with that type of object. The commands that you add to an object menu are appended to the Edit mode shortcut menu so that the result is a menu that contains the Edit mode shortcut menu, plus any additional commands that you've added for that type of object.

To create an object menu, you must assign the menu an alias of either OBJECT_objectname (used when one object of a type is selected) or OBJECTS_objectname (used when more than one object of a type is selected). The object name is the DXF name of the object, with the following five exceptions:

- BLOCKREF for a block insertion with no attributes
- ATTBLOCKREF for a block insertion with attributes
- DYNBLOCKREF for a dynamic block insertion with no attributes
- ATTDYNBLOCKREF for a dynamic block insertion with attributes
- XREF for an xref

FIGURE 33.7

The Edit mode shortcut menu.

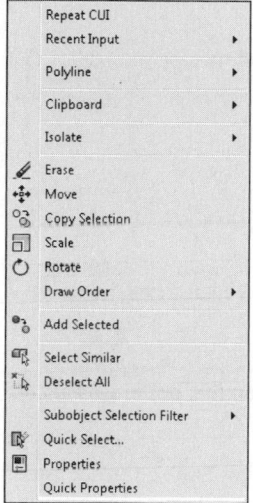

	Repeat CUI
	Recent Input ▶
	Polyline ▶
	Clipboard ▶
	Isolate ▶
✍	Erase
✛	Move
⊙	Copy Selection
⬚	Scale
↻	Rotate
	Draw Order ▶
⊙	Add Selected
⬚	Select Similar
⬚	Deselect All
	Subobject Selection Filter ▶
⬚	Quick Select...
⬚	Properties
	Quick Properties

Tip

To find out the object name of an object in AutoCAD, type the following on the command line:

```
(cdr (assoc 0 (entget (car (entsel))))) ↵
```

That's five closing parentheses at the end. AutoCAD then prompts you to select an object. As soon as you do, you see the object's name on the command line. See Chapters 34 and 35, which cover AutoLISP and Visual LISP, for an explanation of the parts of this AutoLISP expression. AutoLISP is not available for AutoCAD LT. In AutoCAD LT, you can create a drawing with only the one object whose name you want to know, and save it as a DXF file. Scroll down to the ENTITIES section in the DXF file to find the object's name. See Chapter 27 for more information about DXF files. ■

For example, to create an object menu that appears when one or more circles are selected, create an object shortcut menu with an alias of OBJECTS_CIRCLE. Open the Customize User Interface Editor and look at the shortcut menus in `acad.cuix` or `acadlt.cuix` for examples to help you create your own menus.

Command menus

The Command mode shortcut menu appears when you right-click in the drawing area while a command is active. You can create command menus that are specific to a command. The contents of the menu are appended to the Command mode shortcut menu; the result is a menu that contains the Command mode shortcut menu, plus any additional commands that you've added for that command. The default main customization file doesn't include any specific command menus. To create a command menu, you must assign the menu an alias COMMAND_commandname, where commandname is any valid command, including any custom or third-party command. After you name the menu, you can add commands to it that you would like to have available in the middle of the command just by right-clicking. Here are a couple of possibilities:

- For the LINE command, you might want to add the PLINE command to the shortcut menu so that you can change your mind mid-command and create a polyline rather than a line. Of course, you can execute the PLINE command with one pick from the Draw panel, but the shortcut menu is closer.
- For the ROTATE command, you might want to add the ALIGN command, in case you realize that you need to align an object instead of just rotating it.

Customizing mouse buttons and tablet buttons

You can add as many commands as your input device has buttons. To add a button, in the Customize User Interface Editor, right-click one of the items under the Mouse Buttons section, such as Click or Shift+click, and choose New Button.

To add a command to a button, drag the command from the Command List pane to the mouse button section.

Note
You should only customize the mouse buttons and tablet buttons in the main customization file, not in partial customization files. ■

Expand the Mouse Buttons Click item to see the default settings for up to 10 buttons. Button 1 is not listed, because it's always the pick button. If you have a number of buttons on your pointing device, you can leave these macros as they are or change them to suit your needs.

Tip
You can pan and zoom with the IntelliMouse. The MBUTTONPAN system variable controls the middle (third) button or wheel on your pointing device. By default, it's set to 1, which supports panning and zooming. Set it to 0 to support the definition in the customization file. ■

The following exercise shows you how you can customize even a two-button device. Because you may be working on someone else's computer, the exercise undoes the customization at the end.

STEPS: Customizing the Buttons Menu

1. Back up your menu files. (By default, these are `acad.cuix` for AutoCAD and `acadlt.cuix` for AutoCAD LT.)

Caution
Don't continue this exercise until you've completed Step 1. If you're working on someone else's computer, ask permission before doing this exercise. ■

2. To make a duplicate of `acad.cuix` or `acadlt.cuix`, right-click the file in Windows Explorer and choose Copy from the shortcut menu. Right-click again and choose Paste. Windows places a copy of the file in the same folder.

Note
To find the location of your menu files, choose Application Button ➪ Options and click the Files tab. Double-click Customization Files ➪ Main Customization File to display the location of the menu files. ■

3. Click the copied customization file and rename it ab2.cuix. Press Enter.

4. Open a drawing by using any template. On the command line or in the Dynamic Input tooltip, type **cuiload** ↵. In the Load/Unload Customizations dialog box, choose ACAD (or ACADLT) and click Unload.

5. Click Browse. In the Select Customization File dialog box, choose ab2.cuix and click Open. Back in the Load/Unload Customizations dialog box, click Load. All of your user interface elements reappear. Click Close to return to your drawing.

6. On the command line or in the Dynamic Input tooltip, type **cui** ↵. In the Customizations In pane of the Customize User Interface Editor, right-click ACAD *(or ACADLT)* and choose Rename. Type **ab2** ↵ to change the customization name to match the filename.

7. If you use a system mouse, double-click the Mouse Buttons item, and then double-click the Ctrl+Click item. If you use a digitizing tablet or other non-system input device, double-click Legacy, double-click Tablet Buttons, and then double-click the Ctrl+Click item. Click the Button 2 item (the right mouse button on a two-button mouse).

8. In the Command List pane, click the Create a New Command button. In the Name text box of the Properties pane, enter **Toggle Snap Mode** ↵. This lets you turn Snap on and off by using Ctrl plus the right button on your pointing device. Change the current macro to ^B.

Note

If your menu doesn't list a button for Ctrl+Click, then right-click this item and choose New Button. ■

9. Find the new Toggle Snap Mode command in the Command List pane's list of commands and drag it to the Button 2 item. You should see a small left-facing arrow pointing directly to the Button 2 item.

10. Double-click Ctrl+Shift+Click in the Customizations In pane and click the Button 2 item. Again click the Create a New Command button in the Command List pane. In the Name text box of the Properties pane, type **Toggle Ortho Mode** ↵. This lets you turn Ortho Mode on and off by using Ctrl+Shift+right-click. In the Macro text box, type ^O ↵.

11. Find the new Toggle Ortho Mode command in the Command List pane's list of commands and drag it to the Ctrl+Shift+Click Button 2 item. You should see a small left-facing arrow pointing directly to the Button 2 item.

12. Click OK to return to your drawing.

13. Press and hold Ctrl and right-click the button. The Snap Mode button on the status bar turns on (highlighted in blue). Move your cursor around to verify that Snap is on. (If the cursor doesn't snap to points, then PolarSnap is on. Right-click Snap Mode on the status bar and choose Grid Snap On.)

14. Hold Ctrl+Shift and right-click the button. Ortho Mode turns on if it's currently off or turns off if it's currently on.

15. Hold Ctrl+Shift and right-click the button again to toggle Ortho Mode again.

16. To return to your original menu, enter **cuiload** ↵ on the command line or in the Dynamic Input tooltip to open the Load/Unload Customizations dialog box. Choose AB2 and click Unload. Click Browse, choose acad.cuix (or acadlt.cuix), and click Open. Click Load, and then click Close.

17. Again, try using Ctrl+right-click and Ctrl+Shift+right-click. The button no longer works as before. Instead, both key combinations open the Object Snap shortcut menu.

Don't save your drawing.

Customizing image-tile menus

Image-tile menus are menus that contain slides. The image tile displays the contents of the slides. The main use of image-tile menus is to insert blocks. You could use tool palettes in the same way, and tool palettes are easier to create. I cover slides in Chapter 30 and tool palettes in Chapter 29. AutoCAD LT doesn't include any image-tile menus, but you can create them. Image-tile menus are not easy to create, and you can probably use a tool palette instead. They're an old user interface technology. Before you create your own image-tile menus, you need to create the slides. In order that they fit into the image tiles properly, you should create a floating viewport that is 3 units wide by 2 units high (or any multiple thereof, to maintain the proportion), center the drawing so that it takes up most of the viewport, and create the slide. Then create the slide library, as explained in Chapter 30.

To create a new image-tile menu, follow these steps:

1. Open the Customize User Interface Editor.
2. Double-click the Legacy item in any loaded customization file to expand it.
3. Right-click the Image Tile Menus item and choose New Image Tile Menu.
4. Name the image-tile menu. The name will appear at the top of the dialog box.
5. Add a description if you want.
6. Add an alias. You will need to use this alias in the command macro that will be used to display the image-tile dialog box.
7. Either drag an existing command to the new image-tile menu, or create a custom command and drag that to the menu.
8. In the Slide Library text box, enter the slide library name. The slide library is the name of the SLB file that contains the slides.
9. In the Slide Label text box, enter the label that you want to appear in the image-tile dialog box, which should also be the name of the slide (SLD) file.

You display an image-tile menu from another customization file. To display the 3D Objects image-tile menu (which is no longer available from the user interface), use the following macro:

```
$I=ACAD.image_3dobjects $I=ACAD.*
```

This special format *swaps* to the 3D Objects image-tile menu and displays it. The customization group name (ACAD in the previous example) is not necessary if both the image-tile menu that you're referring to and the customization file that you're loading it from are the same. You can create a partial customization file that displays an image-tile menu. Therefore, you need to add a command somewhere to display your image-tile menu. For example, if your image-tile menu's alias is MyBlocks, you could use the following macro:

```
$I=MyBlocks $I=*
```

When you're done, click OK to close the Customize User Interface Editor. Choose the new command that references the image-tile menu, and the image-tile dialog box appears. AutoCAD or AutoCAD LT automatically creates the dialog box. If it has more than 20 items, AutoCAD or AutoCAD LT creates Previous and Next buttons as well. To use one of the images, choose it either from the listing or from the image tiles and click OK.

Customizing tablet menus

Tablet menus are straightforward. Figure 33.8 shows the default tablet arrangement. You can print out this tablet drawing; download `tablet.dwg` from www.autodesk.com/autocad-samples if you are using AutoCAD, or `tablet_overlay.dwg` from www.autodesk.com/autocadlt-samples if you are using AutoCAD LT, and compare it to the Tablet Menus item in the Legacy section. The entire first section, Tablet Menu 1, is left blank for you to configure. Although this tablet menu section lists 25 rows and 25 columns, to match `Tablet.dwg`, use 9 rows and 25 columns. If you configure this tablet menu area (using the TABLET command) to contain 9 rows and 25 columns, you can place your own macro in each of these boxes.

FIGURE 33.8

The standard digitizer tablet menu and its four parts.

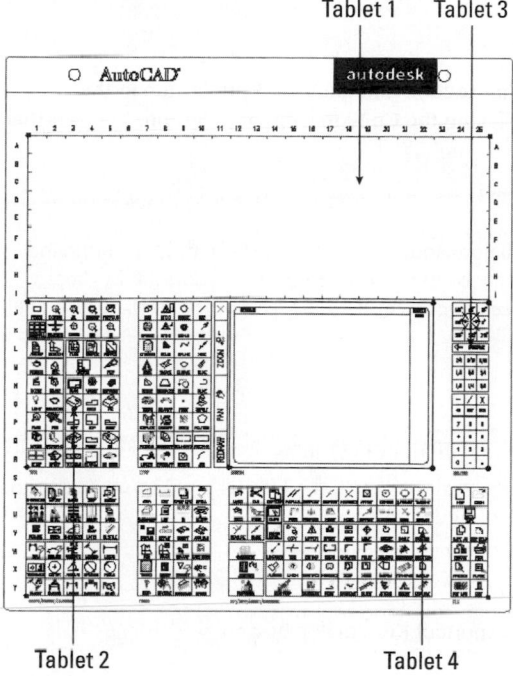

Tablet 1   Tablet 3

Tablet 2   Tablet 4

Cross-Reference
For information on digitizing drawings and calibrating a tablet, including an exercise, see Chapter 16. ■

The syntax of the Tablet menu is very simple; you just need a name and the macro itself, although you can add a description.

Note
If you customize the tablet menu, don't forget to also open `tablet.dwg` **(for AutoCAD) or** `tablet_overlay.dwg` **(for AutoCAD LT). Make the corresponding changes, and print it out to overlay on your digitizer.** ■

Working with the Screen menu
I don't cover the Screen menu because it's rarely used. If you're interested in customizing it, click the Screen Menu item under the Legacy item and click the Learn More about Screen Menus link. AutoCAD LT doesn't

contain a Screen menu. If you or your company is still using the Screen Menu, I recommend moving to tool palettes or the ribbon, as Autodesk has indicated that the Screen Menu will be removed in a future release.

Creating keyboard shortcuts

The Keyboard Shortcuts section has two subsections. Shortcut keys are a way to speed up your work. You can add keyboard shortcuts for commands that you use often. Temporary override keys are keyboard combinations that temporarily affect commonly used drafting settings, such as Object Snap and Ortho Mode. Note that keyboard shortcuts are different from aliases, which I explain in Chapter 29.

Tip

To print a list of shortcut keys or temporary overrides, click either section and click the Print button in the Shortcuts pane. You can also copy the list to the clipboard by clicking the Copy to Clipboard button. You can then paste the list into another document. ■

Working with shortcut keys

You can create a keyboard shortcut for any command. Before adding a keyboard shortcut for a command, check to see that one doesn't already exist. In the Customize User Interface Editor, expand the Keyboard Shortcuts item, and then the Shortcut Keys section to see the current list. To create a new keyboard shortcut, follow these steps:

1. Open the Customize User Interface Editor.
2. Expand the Keyboard Shortcuts item.
3. From the Command List, drag a command to the Shortcut Keys item.
4. In the Properties pane, click the Key(s) text box, and then click the Ellipsis button to the right to open the Shortcut Keys dialog box, as shown in Figure 33.9.

FIGURE 33.9

You assign shortcut keys to commands in the Shortcut Keys dialog box.

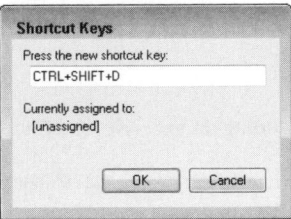

5. Click in the Press New Shortcut Key text box and press the keyboard combination that you want to use on your keyboard. Table 33.2 lists the keys that you can use to create shortcuts. When you include a *modifier,* such as Ctrl or Ctrl+Alt, with another key, you need to hold down the modifier or modifiers as you press the key. If the keyboard combination is already assigned to another command, then you see that command below the text box. If you want, you can choose another combination, or keep the one that you chose, thus overriding the original shortcut.
6. Click OK to close the dialog box.
7. Click OK to close the Customize User Interface Editor and try out your new keyboard shortcut.

Caution

You should not reassign the commonly used Windows shortcuts, such as Ctrl+C (to copy data to the Clipboard), Ctrl+V (to paste data from the Clipboard), and so on. ∎

TABLE 33.2

Allowable Modifier and Key Combinations for Keyboard Shortcuts

Modifier	Key
Ctrl	Any letter, number, or function key
Ctrl+Alt	Any letter, number, or function key
Shift	Any letter, number, or function key
Shift+Alt	Any letter, number, or function key
Ctrl+Shift	Any letter, number, or function key
Ctrl+Shift+Alt	Any letter, number, or function key

To remove a keyboard shortcut, right-click the shortcut in the Shortcut Keys section of the Customize User Interface Editor and choose Remove.

Working with temporary override keys

Temporary override keys are keyboard combinations that toggle drafting settings, such as Object Snap settings. AutoCAD and AutoCAD LT define most of these for you, which is helpful, because the required macros are complex. Most of them also have keyboard combinations, but several don't, and you can easily add them. I explain how to use the existing temporary override keys in Chapter 4.

To see the current temporary override keys, open the Customize User Interface Editor. In the Customizations In pane, double-click the Keyboard Shortcuts item, and then the Temporary Override Keys item. Select any individual temporary override to see its properties in the Properties pane. Keyboard combinations can include function keys, or the Shift key with any letter, number, or function key. Some of the temporary overrides have two or three keyboard combinations, one for the left hand, one for the right hand, and perhaps a function key.

To create a new temporary override key, follow these steps:

1. In the Customize User Interface Editor, expand the Keyboard Shortcut item in the Customizations In pane.

2. Right-click the Temporary Override Keys item and choose New Temporary Override. Enter a new name for the temporary override. This name doesn't have to be unique. In fact, if you want a temporary override to have two keyboard combinations, you need to create two temporary overrides with the same name and macro.

3. In the Properties pane, enter a description, if you want one. Enter a macro in the Macro 1 (Key Down) text box. You can also enter a second macro in the Macro 2 (Key Up) box, which is executed when the keyboard combination is released. Most temporary overrides don't have a macro here; in this case, releasing the keys restores the settings prior to using the temporary override.

Tip

To make a copy of an existing temporary override (in order to add a second key combination), copy the existing macro and paste it into the Macro 1 (Key Down) text box of your new temporary override. ∎

4. Click the Key(s) text box and then click the Ellipsis button. In the Shortcut Keys dialog box, click in the Press New Shortcut Key text box and press the keyboard combination that you want to use on your keyboard. The message below the text box indicates whether the keyboard combination is assigned. To accept the keyboard combination, click OK.

Note

Make sure that Caps Lock is off; otherwise, you won't be able to add a Shift to your temporary override. ■

You can now use your temporary override.

Customizing the double-click behavior

When you double-click an object, you usually see either the Properties palette or a specific dialog box that helps you edit that object. In Chapter 10, I explain this process. You can now customize what happens when you double-click an object.

To see the current double-click settings, open the Customize User Interface Editor and expand (or, appropriately, double-click) the Double Click Actions item. You see a list of objects. Expand any object and select the item beneath it. In the Properties pane, you see the current action, usually a command, in the Macro text box.

For example, if you choose the Block object, the item beneath is labeled Block – Double Click, and you can see that it executes the -BEDIT command, which opens the Block editor.

To change the double-click behavior for an object, follow these steps:

1. Start the CUI command to open the Customize User Interface Editor.
2. Expand the Double Click Actions item and expand an object type.
3. Select the item beneath the object.
4. In the Properties pane, change the current macro and press Enter. You can also drag a command from the Command List.

Right-click the Double Click Actions item and choose New Double Click Action to create a new double-click action. Change the Object Name text box to the value of the object's DXF name that you want the double-click action to respond to. For information on how to determine an object's DXF name, see the "Object menus" section earlier in this chapter.

Note

You can disable all double-click actions for editing by unchecking the Double Click Editing check box on the User Preferences tab of the Options dialog box (Application Button ➪ Options). This controls the DBLCLKEDIT system variable. ■

Customizing the Quick Properties palette and rollover tooltips

The Quick Properties palette appears when you select an object. Rollover tooltips appear when you hover the cursor over an object without selecting it. You can customize which types of objects display the Quick Properties palette and rollover tooltips, and which properties appear, so that you see the information you need right away.

To specify which objects display the Quick Properties palette, open the Customize User Interface Editor and click the Quick Properties item in the Customizations In pane. The right side of the dialog box changes to display a list of object types and properties. When no object is selected, you see only general properties that apply to all objects, such as color, layer, and linetype. Choose any object type, shown in Figure 33.10, to see additional properties that are specific to that object.

FIGURE 33.10

The Quick Properties item with the Line object selected shows a list of the properties that will display when you select a line.

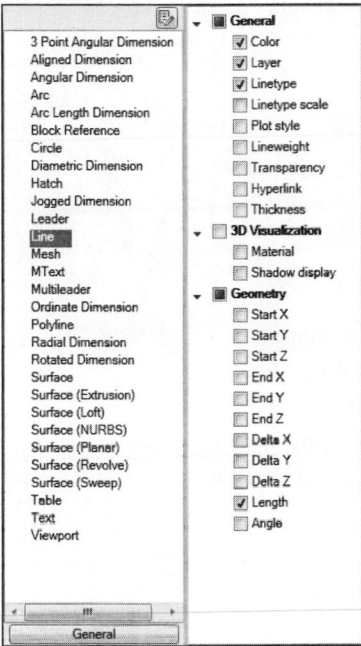

The general properties listed when no object is selected in the object list apply to all objects, even objects not on the object list. For example, a spline is not on the list by default. Therefore, if you select a spline, you'll see only Color and Layer properties, which are the default general properties for all objects. By adding an object to the list, you can specify which additional properties you want to see for that object type.

To edit the object types, click the Edit Object Type List button at the top of the list of objects to open the Edit Object Type List dialog box. There you can check or uncheck objects. Click OK to close the dialog box. Then select the object from the object list and check the properties you want to see from the properties list on the right.

For any object, you can add or remove properties that will appear by selecting the object from the object list and checking or unchecking objects.

You can customize rollover tooltips in exactly the same way. Click the Rollover Tooltips item in the Customizations In pane and make the changes as just described for the Quick Properties palette.

In addition, you can synchronize the rollover tooltips with your Quick Properties settings, or vice versa. To do so, right-click the Quick Properties or Rollover Tooltips item, and choose one of the following:

- Apply Rollover Tooltips Settings to Quick Properties palette.
- Apply Quick Properties Settings to Rollover Tooltips.

Choose one of the options and click Apply.

Summary

In this chapter, you read about how to customize the user interface to suit your situation and speed up your everyday work. Specifically, you learned the following:

- How to load and unload main and partial customization files
- How to write menu macros
- All about customizing the ribbon and menus on the menu bar
- How to create custom shortcut menus
- How to customize mouse and tablet buttons
- How to create image-tile menus
- About customizing the tablet menu
- How to create keyboard shortcuts, including shortcut keys and temporary override keys
- How to customize what happens when you double-click an object
- How to customize the Quick Properties palette and rollover tooltips

This chapter ends Part VI, "Customizing AutoCAD and AutoCAD LT." Part VII challenges you to go farther in your customization of AutoCAD by starting to program with AutoLISP and Visual Basic for Applications.

Part VII

Programming AutoCAD

Part VII invites you to go the distance and start programming AutoCAD with AutoLISP, Visual LISP, and Microsoft Visual Basic (VB.NET). AutoLISP is a powerful programming language that lets you quickly create your own commands and routines that are tailored to your needs. Visual LISP adds an easy-to-use interface to AutoLISP programming.

.NET is a framework you can use with many programming languages, such as VB.NET and C#, to develop stand-alone (EXE) applications and add-ins for AutoCAD. You can create custom commands and AutoLISP functions for AutoCAD. One of the programming languages that can be used with the .NET Framework is Microsoft Visual Basic (VB.NET), which supports both ActiveX/COM and .NET application programming interfaces (APIs). Many Windows applications support the use of ActiveX/COM to allow communication with other applications. For example, you can create a macro in Microsoft Excel that can manipulate objects in an AutoCAD drawing file. Due to page overruns, this chapter is on the DVD.

Unfortunately, AutoCAD LT doesn't support either AutoLISP or .NET development. Therefore, this entire part applies only to AutoCAD.

Understanding AutoLISP and Visual LISP Basics

utoLISP is a programming language supported by AutoCAD that can greatly enhance your productivity by automating often-used or repetitive tasks. AutoLISP provides a glimpse into the inner workings of AutoCAD and can serve as an excellent steppingstone to learning more advanced automation methods, such as .NET and ObjectARX. An AutoLISP routine gives you complete control over its interaction with the user and what it does after it's loaded.

AutoCAD Only

AutoCAD LT does not support AutoLISP. This entire chapter is for AutoCAD only. ■

You can type AutoLISP expressions on the command line in response to prompts, or you can save your code to a file that you can load and use when needed. AutoLISP offers wide and varied possibilities for shortcuts.

AutoLISP intimidates many AutoCAD users, but the many benefits well justify the time that you invest to learn this full-featured programming language. Best of all, you do not need to learn all the complexities of AutoLISP to see productivity gains from its use.

You can find a tremendous number of AutoLISP routines on the Internet. Many CAD Web sites offer huge libraries of AutoLISP routines as free downloads. (For more details, see Appendix B.) Many CAD offices have created AutoLISP routines to expedite some common tasks.

LISP stands for *List Processing* (not Lists in Silly Parentheses, as some say!). As you see in the next chapter, the understanding of lists is crucial to using AutoLISP.

Most AutoLISP routines define a command name, which you then type at the command line in AutoCAD to run the routine. Some routines include a dialog box to help you choose options and specifications.

IN THIS CHAPTER

Understanding AutoLISP programming and the Visual LISP environment

Working with the Visual LISP editor

Getting help in Visual LISP

Creating your own AutoLISP expressions

Using AutoLISP on the command line

Introducing Visual LISP

Visual LISP (VLISP) is an integrated development environment (IDE) that provides an easy-to-use editor to help you create code, debug errors, and test programs. You can write AutoLISP code in Notepad or any ASCII text editor, but the Visual LISP editor offers many advantages:

- Syntax checker, color coding, and highlighting to help correct syntax errors
- File compilation for security and faster execution
- Debugger, with support for stepping through source code to find errors
- Inspect and Watch windows for querying a value or examining a variable during execution
- Context-sensitive help
- Management of multiple file applications from a project window
- Console history, which makes it possible to recall previously entered information

Opening Visual LISP

 To display the Visual LISP editor and to start the VLIDE command, choose Manage tab ➪ Applications panel ➪ Visual LISP Editor. At any time, you can switch to the Visual LISP authoring environment by using this method. Figure 34.1 shows the Visual LISP screen with an AutoLISP file open.

FIGURE 34.1

An AutoLISP file open in its own window in the Visual LISP editor.

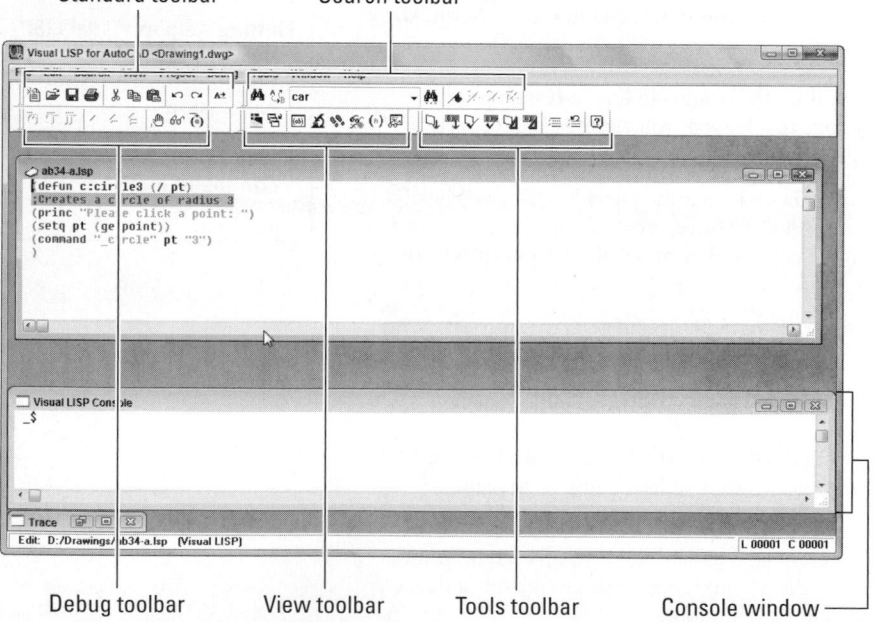

Opening and loading an AutoLISP file with Visual LISP

As soon as you're in the Visual LISP environment, you can create a new AutoLISP file or open an existing file. To edit or view a file in the Visual LISP text editor, follow these steps:

1. Choose File ⇨ Open File.
2. In the Open File to Edit/View dialog box, locate and choose the file that you want to open.
3. Click Open. Visual LISP opens the file in its own window, as shown in Figure 34.1.

When you open a file, the title bar of its window displays a blank paper icon to show that the file has not been changed. If you make any changes to the file, Visual LISP adds a pencil to the image to show that you've edited the file.

Loading an AutoLISP file

To use the AutoLISP program in AutoCAD, you must load it. You can load it from within Visual LISP or from within AutoCAD.

 If you have a file open in Visual LISP, choose Load Active Edit Window from the Tools toolbar or choose Tools ⇨ Load Text in Editor.

If you're in AutoCAD, you can load AutoLISP files into AutoCAD in two main ways. One method is at the command line. To load `circle3.lsp` from the command line, type **(load "circle3")** ↵. The parentheses are required, as they indicate that you're entering an AutoLISP expression. AutoLISP requires the quotation marks because you're specifying a filename. AutoCAD responds with `C:CIRCLE3` because `circle3` is the name of the command that `circle3.lsp` defines.

When you enter the statement to load `circle3.lsp`, AutoCAD searches all the support paths for a file called `circle3.lsp`. At installation time, AutoCAD automatically configures the support-file search path to include the path of `AutoCAD 2011\Support`. For a full list of folders in the support-file search path, choose Application Button ⇨ Options and click the Files tab. Double-click the Support File Search Path item.

Note

AutoLISP files have the extension of `.lsp`**. However, for security and speed, you can compile AutoLISP routines as** `.fas` **or** `.vlx` **project application files. AutoCAD loads** `.vlx` **first, then** `.fas`**, and** `.lsp` **files last. For example, if you have both a** `redline.vlx` **file and a** `redline.lsp` **file, AutoCAD loads the** `redline.vlx` **file. If, however, the** `.lsp` **file is newer than the** `.fas` **file, AutoCAD will load the** `.lsp` **file. If an AutoLISP file is associated with a menu, it has a** `.mnl` **extension. For more information, see Chapter 33. ■**

If your file is not in a folder in AutoCAD's support-file search path, then you must specify the full path name. To specify the full path to a routine, you would enter:

```
(load "c:/Program Files/Autodesk/AutoCAD 2011/Support/circle3") ↵
```

or

```
(load "c:\\Program Files\\Autodesk\\AutoCAD 2011\\Support\\circle3") ↵
```

The backslash (\) has special meaning in AutoLISP, so you need to use two of them or a regular slash (/) when specifying a path. (The backslash character tells AutoLISP to interpret the following character as a special control code. For example, to use a double quote in an AutoLISP expression, precede it with a backslash.)

You can also load AutoLISP routines with the APPLOAD command by choosing Manage tab ⇨ Applications panel ⇨ Load Application. AutoCAD opens the Load/Unload Applications dialog box. By choosing AutoLISP Files (*.lsp) from the Files of Type drop-down list, you can limit the list to only LSP files, as shown in Figure 34.2.

Note

You can load LSP files by adding them to the LISP Files node in the Customizations In pane of the Customize User Interface (CUI) Editor. For information on the CUI Editor, see Chapter 33. ■

FIGURE 34.2

The Load/Unload Applications dialog box.

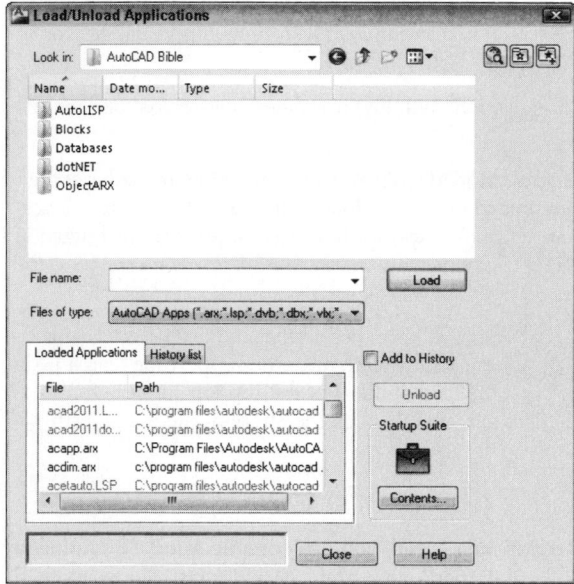

If you check the Add to History check box, AutoCAD lists previously loaded applications in the dialog box — just click the History List tab. Locate and choose the file you want to load, and click Load.

Tip

If you want to use a routine regularly, you can add it to the Startup Suite, which loads it whenever you start AutoCAD. Locate the AutoLISP file in the Load/Unload Applications dialog box and drag it to the Startup Suite area of the dialog box. ■

Using an AutoLISP routine in AutoCAD

After you load an AutoLISP routine, you can use it. How you use the routine depends on the routine. If the program defines a function that is a command, you can type the command's name on the command line like any other AutoCAD command. Most routines contain prompts to guide you in their use. If the routine defines a standard function, you must type the name of the function between parentheses.

On the DVD
The AutoLISP file used in the following exercise on loading and using an AutoLISP routine, circle3.lsp, is in the Drawings folder on the DVD. ∎

STEPS: Loading and Using an AutoLISP Routine

1. Use Windows Explorer to copy circle3.lsp from the DVD to your AutoCAD Bible folder, or to a folder that you added to the support-file search path.
2. Create a new drawing by using any template.

3. Choose Manage tab ➪ Applications panel ➪ Visual LISP Editor. The Visual LISP editor opens.
4. If any AutoLISP files are displayed in the main area, click their Close boxes.
5. Choose Open File on the Standard toolbar. In the Open File to Edit/View dialog box, navigate to the folder where you saved circle3.lsp and double-click it. It appears in a new window within the Visual LISP editor.

6. Choose Load Active Edit Window from the Tools toolbar. The Visual LISP Console window confirms that circle3.lsp has been loaded.
7. Choose Activate AutoCAD from the View toolbar. Visual LISP returns you to AutoCAD.
8. Now that circle3.lsp has been loaded, at the command prompt, type **circle3** ↵.
9. At the Please click a point: prompt, pick any point on-screen. You see a 3-unit radius circle with its center at the point that you picked.
10. Save your drawing in your AutoCAD Bible folder as ab34-01.dwg.

Tip
You can also load AutoLISP routines by dragging and dropping LSP files into the drawing window from Windows Explorer. ∎

Looking at an AutoLISP routine

To examine the contents of the circle3.lsp file, open it in the Visual LISP editor. Figure 34.3 shows the circle3 routine. At this point, ignore the color formatting, which is discussed later in this chapter.

FIGURE 34.3

The circle3 AutoLISP routine.

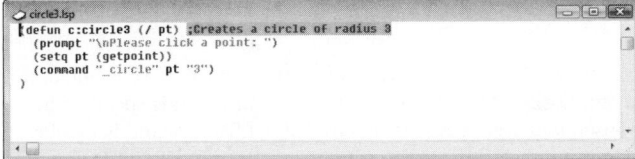

This figure illustrates several general characteristics of AutoLISP routines:

- As in many programming languages, indentation is used in AutoLISP to make it easier to read the code. It has no effect on the operation of the routine.

- The returns at the end of each line also make it easier to read and understand the code. All five lines could be placed on a single line, and the program would work exactly the same way.

- All AutoLISP statements are placed in parentheses. Therefore, whenever you open a parenthesis, you must close it. Every AutoLISP routine must have the same number of left and right parentheses. The physical location of a right parenthesis is not relevant; it can be placed on a new line or positioned several spaces away from the left parenthesis. In both cases, the pair is interpreted the same way.

- You interpret AutoLISP from the innermost parenthetical elements first. For example, on line 3 of the code shown in Figure 34.3, (getpoint) is done first, and then the result is used for the (setq pt (getpoint)) expression. This is analogous to mathematics, as in the expression (3 + (5 × 4)), where 5 × 4 is computed first, and the result is added to 3.

- At the end of the first line is a comment, ;Creates a circle of radius 3. The program ignores any text preceded by a semicolon. Use this technique to place explanations in your routines to help you and others understand what the routine is doing.

The following explains the routine in Figure 34.3 line by line:

- Line 1 begins with an open parenthesis that is balanced with the one on line 5. This pair of parentheses delineates the body of the function. The line begins with defun, which stands for *define function,* and the function is called c:circle3. When you prefix the function with c:, you can use it in AutoCAD by just entering **circle3** at the command line like any other AutoCAD command. (The c: stands for command and has no relation to your hard drive, which is also usually called c:.) You could use just circle3, but you would have to type **(circle3)** at the command line to use the routine. The last item on Line 1 is (/ pt). The pt after the slash means that pt is a *local variable.* A variable stores a value for later use in the routine. A local variable is used only in its own routine and is not retained for use in other routines. If you replaced (/ pt) with simply ( ), the pt variable would be available to other AutoLISP routines as well.

- Line 2 is the simplest line in this routine. It simply prints the statement Please click a point: at the command line. Anything in the quotes after prompt will be printed on the AutoCAD command line. The statement is used as a prompt to tell the user to pick a point. Putting \n before the prompt puts it on a new line and is for readability purposes.

- Line 3 is typical of AutoLISP routines that contain nested parentheses. Remember to read from the innermost parenthetical element outward. Thus, reading from the innermost parenthetical element, you have first (getpoint). This simply means to get a point. Any of the AutoCAD input methods work, such as clicking in the drawing area, typing coordinates, or using object snaps. Reading outward you have (setq pt (getpoint)). The setq function assigns a value to a specified variable. The value returned by getpoint is assigned to the variable pt. Therefore, if you enter the coordinates 2,2 by typing or picking them in the drawing area, the variable pt equals 2,2.

- Line 4 reads (command "_circle" pt "3"). The command function in AutoLISP is one of the easier functions to understand. It simply executes whatever AutoCAD command is specified in the quotes that follow, using all subsequent arguments. When the CIRCLE command is invoked in AutoCAD, it asks for the center point first and then the radius. Line 4 starts the CIRCLE command, uses for the center point whatever is assigned to the variable pt, and sets the radius to 3 units.

Note

An underscore precedes the CIRCLE command so that it can be translated into other language versions of AutoCAD. Without the underscore, the CIRCLE command will not be recognized by a non-English version of AutoCAD. For example, CIRCLE in the French version is CERCLE. By using the underscore, the French version of AutoCAD will understand the use of the CIRCLE command. It functions as a built-in language translator for AutoCAD. ■

Using the Visual LISP editor

The Visual LISP editor contains a number of tools that make your programming life simpler. These tools represent the difference from the old way of writing AutoLISP code, which involved creating text files in an ASCII text editor. The visual way involves working with tools that help you format and complete your code. Some of the more useful tools include:

 • **Format Edit Window.** Choose Format Edit Window on the Tools toolbar (or choose Tools ➪ Format Code in Editor) to indent code (and comments) so that it's more readable. Indenting code helps you to understand the levels of nested parentheses more clearly.

 • **Format Selection.** Select the code that you want to format. Then choose Format Selection on the Tools toolbar (or choose Tools ➪ Format Code in Selection) to indent only the selected code.

 • **Check Edit Window.** Choose Check Edit Window from the Tools toolbar (or choose Tools ➪ Check Text in Editor) to perform a preliminary evaluation prior to loading the file. This evaluation checks the code for unbalanced parentheses, invalid function definition formatting (an attempt to redefine a built-in or protected function), and many other common errors. Visual LISP opens the Build Output window to show you the results.

 • **Check Selection.** Select the code that you want to check. Choose Check Selection from the Tools toolbar (or choose Tools ➪ Check Selection) to perform a preliminary evaluation on selected code. Visual LISP opens the Build Output window to show you the results.

• **Parentheses Matching.** The most common error for an AutoLISP programmer is incorrect parentheses matching. Visual LISP enables you to jump between matching parentheses and to quickly check your current nesting level as you develop your application. While you can choose Edit ➪ Parentheses Matching ➪ Match Forward or Match Backward, you'll find that the keyboard shortcuts distract you less from the code that you're viewing. To find a matching right parenthesis, press Ctrl+]. To find a left matching parenthesis, press Ctrl+[.

Tip

You can highlight all the code between matching parentheses. To highlight from left to right, place the cursor in front of a left parenthesis and press Ctrl+Shift+] or simply double-click. To highlight from right to left (backwards), place the cursor after a right parenthesis and press Ctrl+Shift+[or double-click. ■

 • **Load Selection.** You've already seen how to load the code in the active window. You can also load selected code. Select the code that you want to load and choose Load Selection from the Tools toolbar (or choose Tools ➪ Load Selection).

 • **Comment Block.** In Figure 34.3, you see an example of a comment. Visual LISP supports several comment styles, which Chapter 35 covers. Visual LISP simplifies the addition of a three-semicolon comment. To place a three-semicolon comment, highlight the text that you want to change into a comment and click Comment Block on the Tools toolbar (or choose Edit ➪ Extra Commands ➪ Comment Block). See Chapter 35 for more information on creating comments.

• **Uncomment Block.** To remove a three-semicolon comment, click Uncomment Block on the Tools toolbar (or choose Edit ⇨ Extra Commands ⇨ Uncomment Block).

Another feature of Visual LISP is the Console window. The Console window usually resides at the bottom of the Visual LISP window. The Console window is similar to the AutoCAD command line. Just as you can enter AutoLISP expressions on the AutoCAD command line, as explained later in this chapter, you can also enter AutoLISP expressions in the Console window and see the results. Each line uses a _$ prompt.

A nice feature of the Console window is that Visual LISP remembers everything that you enter. You can retrieve it by pressing Tab for a forward history or Shift+Tab for a backward history.

Closing a file and Visual LISP

To close a file within Visual LISP, click its Close button. (You can also press Ctrl+F4.) To exit Visual LISP, click its Close button or press Alt+F4. As with AutoCAD, Visual LISP warns you about saving your changes.

On the DVD

The file used in the following exercise on using the Visual LISP editor, `ab34-a.lsp`, is in the `Drawings` folder on the DVD. ■

STEPS: Using the Visual LISP Editor

1. From AutoCAD, choose Manage tab ⇨ Applications panel ⇨ Visual LISP Editor to open Visual LISP.

2. Choose Open File on the Standard toolbar, and open `ab34-a.lsp` from the DVD. Save the file as `ab34-01.lsp` in your `AutoCAD Bible` folder.

 3. Choose Format Edit Window on the Tools toolbar. Visual LISP automatically formats the code.

4. Select the line of the code that reads:

   ```
   (command "_circle" pt "3")
   ```

 5. Choose Comment Block. Visual LISP places three semicolons before the text and shades it. Choose Uncomment Block. Visual LISP returns the code to its previous state.

 6. Choose Check Edit Window on the Tools toolbar. Visual LISP opens the Build Output window and issues the `Check done` message.

 7. Click anywhere in the edit window to activate it. Choose Load Active Edit Window on the Tools toolbar. AutoCAD loads the routine.

8. In the Visual LISP Console window, type **(c:circle3)** and press Enter. Visual LISP returns you to AutoCAD and starts the routine. Pick a point. When you're done, you're automatically returned to the Visual LISP editor.

9. Click the text editor window and choose Save File on the Standard toolbar. Click the Close button at the top-right corner of the text editor window to close the AutoLISP file.

10. Click the Close button at the top-right corner of your screen to close Visual LISP.

Getting Help in Visual LISP

Visual LISP offers two ways for you to get help while writing AutoLISP code: context-sensitive help on any term that you select, and the overall Help system.

 To get help on any AutoLISP function in your code, select the function (either in the text editor window or in the Console window) and choose Help on the Tools toolbar.

To open the entire Visual LISP Help system, choose Help ➪ Visual LISP Help Topics on the Visual LISP menu or press F1 when the Visual LISP editor is active. Visual LISP displays the main Help landing page.

All these help features can be a bit overwhelming, but for AutoLISP and Visual LISP you basically have three choices:

- **AutoLISP Reference.** This guide is equivalent to the Command Reference in AutoCAD's Help system. Here you'll find an alphabetical list of all AutoLISP functions.
- **AutoLISP Developer's Guide.** This guide is equivalent to the AutoCAD User's Guide. It contains all the basic topics that you need to know to program in Visual LISP.
- **AutoLISP Tutorial.** This is a tutorial that creates a garden path.

Working with AutoLISP Expressions

As with any programming language, AutoLISP has its own functions and syntax. This section explains how to start writing AutoLISP code. One big advantage to AutoLISP is that you can test your code immediately, unlike the case with languages that you need to compile first. For compiled languages, such as C++ and VB.NET, every time a code change is made, the code must be recompiled and re-linked before you can see the changes in AutoCAD.

Understanding AutoLISP syntax

In AutoLISP's syntax, an operator always comes first, followed by a number of operands. An operator can be thought of as a function that does something, and the operands are the elements on which the function operates. Place a space between each component of the statement.

Another way to describe the syntax of AutoLISP is that, within each set of parentheses, the first item is a function, and what follows are parameters or arguments to that function.

Working with numbers and text

Table 34.1 lists the basic arithmetic functions. You can use these functions on anything that has a value. For example, if you create a variable with a value of 2, you can use that variable with the arithmetic functions.

You can find more operators in the AutoLISP Function Synopsis under the Appendixes topic of the AutoLISP Developer's Guide, under Basic Functions ➪ Arithmetic Functions.

Some fundamental arithmetic operations can provide a feel for the fundamentals. If you type (+ 2 3) ↵ on the AutoCAD command line (being careful to put a blank space after the + and the 2), AutoLISP responds with 5. This syntax of having the operator (the plus sign) come before the operands (2 and 3) is different from that of many languages but is important to understand in AutoLISP.

TABLE 34.1

Basic Arithmetic Functions

Function	Description
+	Addition
–	Subtraction
*	Multiplication
/	Division
Sqrt	Square root

To nest expressions, simply add another set of parentheses to enclose the nested expression. For example, when you enter (* 5 (+ 2 3)), AutoCAD responds with 25. The nested expression is evaluated from the innermost parenthesis pair out; first 2 and 3 are added, and then that sum is multiplied by 5.

Working with floating-point numbers (numbers with decimal points) is as easy as working with integers. If you type (/ 7.3 5.84) ↵, then AutoLISP responds with 1.25.

Note
If you're using a number less than 1, you must include the leading 0, as in (+ 2.5 0.5). ■

Working with text is as easy as working with numbers. In AutoLISP, a *string* is simply a series of text characters. Table 34.2 lists some common string functions.

TABLE 34.2

Basic String Functions

Function	Description
strcat	Concatenates (attaches) strings to one another.
substr	Returns (provides you with) a substring (a portion) of a string. The first argument is the string, the second is an integer that specifies the position of the first character that you want, and the third (optional) is the number of characters that you want.
strlen	Calculates string length; returns the number of characters, including spaces in the string.

Here are two examples:

```
(strcat "Today is " "a good day" ".")
"Today is a good day."
(substr "Today is a good day." 12 4)
"good"
```

strcat stands for *string concatenate* and appends one string with another. Any number of strings can come after the strcat function. (There are three strings enclosed in quotes in the above strcat example.)

substr stands for *substring*, and in the above example it returns the four characters starting at position 12.

Note

The first character of the string for substr is number 1. However, other functions that process elements of a list (such as nth) count the first element as 0. ∎

Table 34.3 offers you a few more functions that work with numbers and strings.

TABLE 34.3

AutoLISP Functions for Numbers and Strings

Function	Description
abs	Returns the absolute value of the argument. (abs -76) returns 76.
ascii	Returns the ASCII code of a character. (ascii "B") returns 66.
chr	Returns the text string for an ASCII code. (chr 66) returns "B". (Stands for character.)
atoi	Converts a string to an integer. (atoi "2.7") returns 2. (Stands for ASCII to integer.)
atof	Converts a string to a real number. (atof "7.6") returns 7.6. (Stands for ASCII to float, as in floating point — that is, a real number.)
itoa	Converts an integer to a text string. (itoa 76) returns "76". (Stands for integer to ASCII.)
rtos	Converts a real number to a text string, enclosed in quotes. You can add a mode (1=scientific, 2=decimal, 3=engineering, 4=architectural, 5=fractional) and a precision. Otherwise, rtos uses the current settings. (rtos 87.3 2 2) returns "87.30". (rtos stands for real to string.)
=	Equal to. Returns T for true if all arguments are numerically equal. (= 3 3.0) returns T. If the arguments are not equal, it returns nil.
/=	Not equal to. Returns T if all arguments are not numerically equal. (/= 5 6) returns T. If they are equal, it returns nil.
<	Less than. Returns T if each argument is numerically less than the next argument. Otherwise returns nil.
>	Greater than. Returns T if each argument is numerically greater than the next argument. Otherwise returns nil.
>=	Greater than or equal to. Returns T if each argument is numerically greater than or equal to the next argument. Otherwise returns nil.
<=	Less than or equal to. Returns T if each argument is numerically less than or equal to the next argument. Otherwise returns nil.

Using AutoLISP on the Command Line

You can use AutoLISP on the fly in AutoCAD because it is *interpreted*. By typing an expression on the command line, you get the result immediately. An interpreted language is one in which a single source statement is translated to machine language and executed, and then each subsequent source statement is operated on in the same way. This enables interactive entry of AutoLISP code into AutoCAD.

The output of an AutoLISP expression can be used in response to AutoCAD prompts as well. For example, you can type (+ 1 7) at the Diameter/<Radius>: prompt of the CIRCLE command for a circle with a radius of 8 units. This capability to place AutoLISP expressions into AutoCAD commands is a very powerful tool.

If you leave out a closing parenthesis, AutoCAD returns (_> when you press Enter. This tells you that one open parenthesis has not been closed. If two open parentheses remain to be closed, AutoCAD responds with ((_>. Just type the correct number of closing parentheses at the command line and press Enter. AutoCAD accepts the expression.

STEPS: Working with Numbers and Text on the Command Line

1. Open a new drawing by using any template.

2. Type **circle** ↵. Follow the prompts:

```
Specify center point for circle or [3P/2P/Ttr (tan tan radius)]: Pick
    any point.
Specify radius of circle or [Diameter]: (- 5 3) ↵
```

AutoCAD draws a circle with a radius of 2.

3. Type **(strcat "This is an example of " "regular text.")** ↵. Don't forget the space between *of* and the quotation mark. When the two phrases are put together, this creates the space between *of* and *regular*. AutoCAD returns "This is an example of regular text."

4. Press the up-arrow key. AutoCAD repeats the last line. Press the left-arrow key to move to the right of the last *r* in *regular,* and press Backspace to delete the word *regular.* Type **italic** ↵. AutoCAD returns the new string concatenation.

5. Save the drawing in your AutoCAD Bible folder as ab34-02.dwg.

Note
When you create AutoLISP expressions on the command line or in the Console window, they aren't saved with the drawing. They have the same status as any input that you type at the command line. ∎

Creating AutoLISP Files

If you want to use your AutoLISP expressions more than a couple of times, you should save them in a file. Create the routine in Visual LISP and choose Save File.

Tip
A common practice is to consolidate all AutoLISP routines in one folder to make it easier to store and find them. To do this, you can create a folder called LISP in any drive or folder where you keep files that you create, and then choose Application Button ⇨ Options. On the Files tab, expand the Support File Search Path and click Add. Add the path by typing it directly in the edit box or by clicking Browse and navigating to it. ∎

Because AutoCAD can open multiple drawings, you need to organize your AutoLISP routines based on whether you want them to apply to all drawings or just the first drawing that you open.

AutoCAD offers two LSP files that you can use for your AutoLISP routines:

- acad.lsp. Use this file for routines that customize the initialization of AutoCAD. acad.lsp is not automatically loaded for every consecutive drawing. For example, if you want to load a special menu for only a specific drawing, you could put the routine in acad.lsp. (You can choose to load acad.lsp with every drawing. Choose Application Button ⇨ Options and click on the System tab. In the General Options section, check the Load acad.lsp with Every Drawing check box.)

- **acaddoc.lsp.** Use this file for routines that customize the initialization of individual drawings. This file is loaded every time a drawing is opened. If you have custom routines you want available in each drawing you open, put the AutoLISP routines in **acaddoc.lsp.**

Each drawing contains its own AutoLISP environment. AutoLISP files that you load in one drawing, along with their variables, won't be accessible to another drawing. To share functions, use (vl-load-all "filename") rather than (load "filename"), where filename is the name of the AutoLISP file. This enables you to "populate" each open drawing, as well as any new drawing that you may create. The vl-load-all function is equivalent to placing an AutoLISP routine in acaddoc.lsp.

Note

If you have routines that you access from the user interface, such as a menu item or Ribbon button, place the routines in an AutoLISP Menu (MNL) file that has the same name as the customization (CUIx) file that uses them. MNL files are loaded with each new or opened drawing in the same way that acaddoc.lsp is loaded. ■

 To create a new Visual LISP file, open the Visual LISP editor (choose Manage tab ⇨ Applications panel ⇨ Visual LISP Editor) and choose New File on the Standard toolbar. Visual LISP opens an untitled document, as shown in Figure 34.4. You can now start typing code in the new document. When you start typing, you immediately notice that your code looks different than it would if you had typed it in an ASCII text editor — it's in color! Visual LISP distinguishes certain features in your code, and colors it accordingly. Table 34.4 lists the colors and their meanings.

FIGURE 34.4

A new AutoLISP document in the Visual LISP editor.

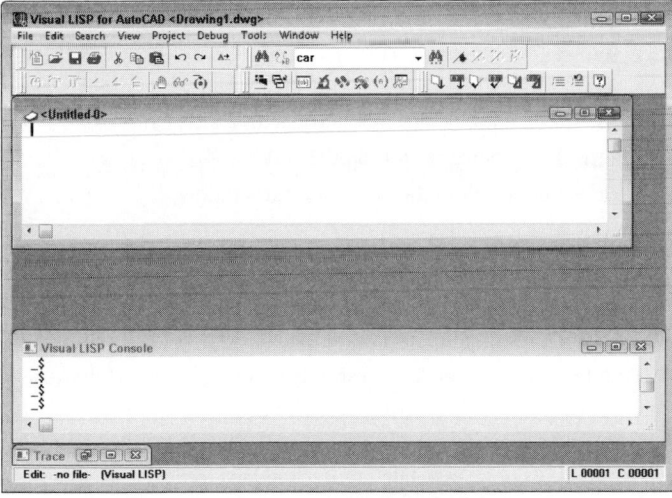

If you want, you can customize these colors. From the Visual LISP menu, choose Tools ⇨ Window Attributes ⇨ Configure Current. In the Window Attributes dialog box, choose an element from the drop-down list and pick a color from the color swatches. You can also change the left margin and the tab width in this dialog box.

TABLE 34.4	

Visual LISP Editor Coloring System

Color	AutoLISP Syntax Element
Blue	Built-in functions and protected symbols
Magenta	Text strings
Green	Integers
Teal	Real numbers
Purple on gray background	Comments
Red	Parentheses
Black	Unrecognized items, such as variables that you've created

STEPS: Creating a New Visual LISP File

1. Start a new drawing by using any template. You shouldn't have any other drawings open.
2. Choose Manage tab ⇨ Applications panel ⇨ Visual LISP Editor.

3. Choose New File from the Standard toolbar.
4. Type the following:

```
draws a horizontal line 3 units long
(defun c:line3 (/ pt)
(prompt "\nPlease pick a point: ")
(setq pt (getpoint))
(command "_line" pt "@3,0" "")
)
```

5. Select the first line of text and choose Comment Block from the Tools toolbar.
6. Choose Format Edit Window from the Tools toolbar to format the code.
7. Choose Check Edit Window and look at the result in the Build Output window.
8. Click the Visual LISP Editor to activate it again.
9. Choose Load Active Edit Window to load the routine.
10. Choose Activate AutoCAD from the View toolbar.
11. On the command line or at the Dynamic Input tooltip, type **line3** ↵.
12. At the Please pick a point: prompt, use any method to specify a point. AutoCAD draws a horizontal line 3 units long.
13. Use the Windows task bar to return to the Visual LISP editor.
14. Click the Visual LISP editor to activate it. Choose Save File on the Standard toolbar. Save the routine as ab34-02.lsp in your AutoCAD Bible folder.
15. Close the Visual LISP editor by clicking its Close button. Do not save your drawing.

Summary

This chapter covers the fundamentals of AutoLISP programming and the Visual LISP environment. You read about:

- How to open the Visual LISP editor and load and use AutoLISP files
- How to use AutoLISP on the command line
- What AutoLISP routines look like
- How to get help in Visual LISP
- The basic structure of AutoLISP syntax, as well as how to work with numbers and text

In the next chapter, you examine how to create variables, work with AutoCAD commands and system variables, modify AutoCAD objects (or entities, as they're often still called in AutoLISP), and work with the fundamental units of AutoLISP, known as lists.

Exploring AutoLISP Further

AutoLISP offers many features that enable you to create sophisticated programs. These include variables, functions, and conditional statements. You can use these features to easily create drawing objects. You can retrieve information about drawing objects and then modify them. As a result, getting input from the user makes your programs more interactive.

AutoCAD Only

AutoCAD LT does not support AutoLISP. This entire chapter is for AutoCAD only. ■

Creating Variables

You can't do anything very useful in programming without using variables. A *variable* is a symbolic name that a program operates on. An important part of the usefulness of variables is that you can assign values to them. You use the setq function to name and assign a value to a variable.

The following example sets the value of 3 to a variable named `radius`.

```
(setq radius 3)
3
```

You can try this example in Visual LISP in the Console window. If you want to use this variable on the AutoCAD command line, precede it with an exclamation point (!). For example:

```
Command: !radius
3
```

The exclamation point before a variable evaluates the value that is stored in the variable and returns it to the command line. When you use a variable in the

IN THIS CHAPTER

Creating variables and functions

Working with AutoCAD commands and system variables

Working with lists

Setting conditions and creating loops

Managing drawing objects

Getting input from the user

Console window that you've already set, you don't need the exclamation point. The Console treats everything that you type there as an AutoLISP expression.

Assigning strings to a variable is as easy as assigning numerals to a variable:

```
(setq name "Robin")
"Robin"
```

You can also nest AutoLISP expressions by placing one expression inside the other.

```
(setq radius (+ 2 1))
3
```

As explained in the previous chapter, AutoLISP evaluates LISP expressions from the innermost set of parentheses outward. In the above example, AutoLISP evaluates (+ 2 1) first and then assigns the result to the variable radius.

STEPS: Using AutoLISP Variables from within AutoCAD

1. Start a new drawing by using the acad.dwt template.
2. Type **(setq radius (+ 2 1))** ↵. AutoLISP returns 3.
3. Start the CIRCLE command. Specify any center point. At the Specify radius of circle or [Diameter]: prompt, type **!radius** ↵. AutoCAD draws a circle with a radius of 3 units.
4. Type **(setq color "green")** ↵. AutoLISP returns "green".
5. Type **-color** ↵. At the Enter default object color [Truecolor/COlorbook] <BYLAYER>: prompt, type **!color** ↵.
6. Draw a circle. The circle is green because the current color is now green.
7. Save your drawing in your AutoCAD Bible folder as ab35-01.dwg.

Working with AutoCAD Commands

Accessing AutoCAD commands from within AutoLISP is a powerful way to automate commonly used functions. By combining access to commands from AutoLISP with variables as described in the previous section, you gain a great deal of flexibility.

Accessing AutoCAD commands

In Chapter 34, when you looked at an AutoLISP routine (see Figure 34.3), you saw an example of the command function. You use the command function in AutoLISP to execute AutoCAD commands. This function treats all subsequent arguments as if they were typed at the command line interactively. When programming with the command function in AutoLISP, exactly duplicate what you would do at the command line. For example, to draw a line, you follow the steps shown in the following table. The second column shows how you would perform the same action in an AutoLISP routine.

Enter **line** at the command line	"line" (or "_line").
Specify the start point for the line	Use a variable, actual coordinates, or pause for user input.
Specify the endpoint	Use a variable, actual coordinates, or pause for user input.
Press Enter to end the LINE command	Use an empty set of double quotation marks to represent pressing Enter either within a command or to end a command.

For example, if you're using the variables startpt and endpt for the start point and endpoint of a line, here's how you would access the LINE command in an AutoLISP expression using the command function:

```
(command "_line" startpt endpt "")
```

Creating functions

Functions always begin with the defun function. You can define three principal types of functions:

- The type that you have been using thus far precedes the command name defined by defun with c:, which is interpreted by AutoCAD as a command and enables you to use the function by name at the AutoCAD command line. The function becomes useable like any other AutoCAD command.

- You can also create a function definition without preceding the name with c:. This type is most valuable when it's called by other AutoLISP routines. If you need to execute it at the command line, you must enclose the function name in parentheses. Similarly, you can execute functions prefixed with a c: as an AutoLISP expression by enclosing the functions in parentheses, as in (c:circle3).

- The third type is s::startup. By defining a function (usually in acaddoc.lsp, which is loaded into every drawing) with the name s::startup, every AutoLISP function in the routine will automatically execute after the drawing has fully initialized. The reason for the s::startup function is to ensure that AutoLISP routines that use the command function run only after AutoCAD fully initializes the components that can execute commands.

When you create an s::startup function, you need to decide where to put it. Chapter 34 briefly explained the difference between acad.lsp and acaddoc.lsp. The need for two files arose because AutoCAD includes MDI (Multiple Document Interface), which enables you to open more than one drawing at a time. For more information, see the "Automatically loading LSP files" sidebar. s::startup is a great function for enhancing productivity. In this way, you can automate whatever general setup operations you normally do at the beginning of a drawing session, or for every drawing that you open.

Automatically loading LSP files

AutoCAD automatically loads four AutoLISP files. Two files, acad2011.lsp and acad2011doc.lsp, are specific to AutoCAD 2011. Autodesk recommends that you reserve these files for AutoCAD use. The acad2011.lsp file is loaded only once per AutoCAD session when you first load AutoCAD, while the acad2011doc.lsp file is loaded each time a drawing is opened or created.

The other two automatically loaded AutoLISP files are reserved for you, the user. These files are acad.lsp, which is loaded once per AutoCAD session, and acaddoc.lsp, which is loaded every time a drawing is opened or created. What this means to you is that you can place different initialization routines in each file — one for AutoCAD initialization (acad.lsp), and the other for the initial drawing as well as future drawings. You can place an s::startup function in both acad.lsp and acaddoc.lsp. However, be aware that placing different s::startup functions in both files effectively disables the s::startup function defined in acad.lsp.

You must create both acad.lsp and acaddoc.lsp. However, after you create any AutoLISP routine and save it under either name, you can add additional routines to the same file. AutoCAD automatically loads these files, as long as they exist in the support file search path.

Note

You can change the value of the ACADLSPASDOC system variable to 1 to load `acad.lsp` into every drawing that you open, rather than just the first drawing that you open in an AutoCAD session. ∎

Here's an AutoLISP routine that uses both the defun and command functions:

```
(defun c:redline (/ startpt endpt)
  (terpri)
  (setq startpt (getpoint "Select the redline start point:"))
  (terpri)
  (setq endpt (getpoint startpt "Select the redline end point:"))
  (command "_line" startpt endpt "")
  (command "_chprop" "_last" "" "_color" "red" "")
)
```

Here's an explanation of this routine:

- The first line of this routine defines a function called `redline`. Because `redline` is preceded by `c:`, you can type **redline** at the command line when using it within AutoCAD. As you may remember from the discussion of the `circle3` routine, the expression (/ startpt endpt) means that `redline` has two local variables that are available only to this routine. These variables are used in the next two lines. Place local variables after the forward slash.

- The `terpri` function, on the second and fourth lines, tells AutoCAD to print a blank line at the command line. You can use this function to improve readability of the prompts. Otherwise, two or more prompts run together on one line.

- Reading the third line from the innermost parenthesis pair outward, AutoCAD obtains the red line's start point from the user with the prompt `Select the redline start point:` and sets the variable `startpt` equal to that start point's value. Similarly, the fifth line obtains the red line's endpoint and sets the variable `endpt` to that value. By first getting the start point, you see a rubber-band effect between the start and endpoints that you specify.

- Line 6 uses the AutoLISP command function. It issues the LINE command, specifies the start point and endpoint, and uses a set of empty double quotation marks to represent pressing Enter to end the LINE command.

- Line 7 uses the same syntax for the CHPROP command. It does the following: issues the CHPROP command; selects the line that you just created by using the Last Selection option; ends object selection by using the empty set of double quotation marks; specifies the Color option; and sets the color to red. Another empty set of double quotation marks ends the command.

- Line 8 ends the `redline` routine with a closing parenthesis.

To use this routine, you would follow these steps:

1. Open Visual LISP and start a new file.
2. Type the routine.
3. Save the routine as `redline.lsp` and place it in AutoCAD's `Support` folder or any other folder that you may have created for AutoLISP routines and added to AutoCAD's support-file search path.
4. Load the routine.
5. Switch to AutoCAD.

6. On the command line, type **redline** ↵.

7. In response to the prompts for the start point and endpoint of the redline, choose any two points in the drawing area. AutoCAD draws a red line between the two selected points.

On the DVD

The file `redline.lsp` is in the `\Results` folder on the DVD. Feel free to copy it to your system and play around with it. For example, using your knowledge of the `circle3` routine discussed in Chapter 34, you could create a red circle. ∎

Here is another example of an AutoLISP routine that defines an s::startup function. It uses several of the features that I've been discussing in this chapter.

```
(defun s::startup ()
  (setq old_osmode (getvar "osmode"))
  (setvar "osmode" 0)
  (command "_rectang" "_width" "0.1" "0,0" "10,10")
  (command "_text" "8,1" "0.2" "0" "name")
  (command "_text" "8,0.7" "0.2" "0" "date")
  (command "_text" "8,0.4" "0.2" "0" "revision")
  (command "_zoom" "_extents")
  (setvar "osmode" old_osmode)
)
```

This routine creates a simple title block and border each time you open a new drawing. It turns object snaps off (the OSMODE system variable) so that all the text doesn't snap to the same location. But first it saves the current OSMODE value. At the end, the routine returns OSMODE to its original setting.

In order to use this routine — or one of your own — you can add it to the end of `acaddoc.lsp`. AutoCAD 2011 does not come with this file, so the first time that you want to use it, you must create it.

Caution

Before using the s::startup function, be sure that an s::startup function does not already exist. Other applications that you may have purchased or downloaded may include an s::startup file. Adding a second s::startup could possibly interfere with the operation of these other applications. On the command line, type (s::startup) ↵. If the text `"; error: no function definition: S::STARTUP"` is displayed, no AutoLISP file that is currently loaded defines an s::startup routine. If one exists, open an AutoLISP file in Notepad, choose Edit⇨Find, and type s::startup in the Find What text box. Click Find Next. Then add the body of your s::startup function (minus the first line, which already exists) to the end of the existing s::startup routine and save the file. ∎

Creating functions with arguments

You can create functions that accept arguments, sometimes called parameters. An *argument* is a value that must be supplied with the function. The function then uses the value of that argument in its operation.

Earlier in this chapter, I explained that local variables are placed in parentheses after a forward slash. Arguments go in the same set of parentheses, but before the forward slash. If there are no local variables, you don't need the forward slash. Here is an example of a function with one argument:

```
(defun chg2red (selected_object)
...
)
```

To actually use this routine in AutoCAD or within another AutoLISP routine, use the format (chg2red selected_object). The argument is sent to the chg2red routine by adding the argument after the function name, all enclosed in parentheses.

Whenever you use the chg2red function within a routine, you must follow it by its argument. You can obtain the argument by using a variable whose value you've set in the routine, by obtaining a value through user input, or by typing in a specific value when you use the function.

Caution

You should not create functions which define a command that requires arguments. Instead of using arguments, you need to get input from the user. User input is discussed later in this chapter. ■

The following exercise uses a function that is called from within the routine.

On the DVD

The file used in the following exercise on using AutoLISP functions and commands, ab35-a.lsp, is in the Drawings folder on the DVD. ■

STEPS: Using AutoLISP Functions and Commands

1. Start a new drawing by using any template.
2. Use Windows Explorer to copy ab35-a.lsp from the DVD to AutoCAD's Support folder, or any folder that you've created for AutoLISP routines and added to AutoCAD's support-file search path. This file is shown in Figure 35.1.

FIGURE 35.1

An AutoLISP routine to change an object's color to red.

```
(defun chg2red (selected_object)
       (command "_chprop" selected_object "" "_color" "red" "")
)
(defun c:chgcolor (/ selected)
       (terpri)
       (setq selected (entsel "Select an object to change to red:"))
       (chg2red selected)
)
```

3. Choose Manage tab ➪ Applications panel ➪ Visual LISP Editor. In Visual LISP, open ab35-a.lsp. The routine appears in the Edit window.
4. Choose Load Active Edit Window.
5. Choose Activate AutoCAD.
6. Draw any object.
7. At the command line, type **chgcolor** ↵.
8. At the Select an object to change to red: prompt, select the object that you drew in Step 6. Watch its color change to red.

Don't save the routine or your drawing.

Here's how the routine works:

- This routine defines a function, chg2red, which is not preceded by c:. It has one argument, selected_object.

- What AutoLISP actually ran when you typed **chgcolor** in Step 7 is the function c:chgcolor on the fourth line of the routine. In the last AutoLISP statement in that function — (chg2red selected) — the variable selected is derived from the previous step as a result of the operation entsel (entity select).

- The variable selected is the argument passed to the function chg2red. The function chg2red now knows what object to operate on.

- The function chg2red then uses the CHPROP command to change the object's color to red.

Note

To call a function at the command line, you would need to type (func arg) where func is the name of the function defined in a loaded AutoLISP routine (in this case, it is chg2red) and arg is an argument (in this case, it must be an entity name). Entity names are discussed later in this chapter. ∎

Working with system variables

AutoCAD has a wide variety of system variables to control the drawing environment. Thankfully, the creators of AutoLISP enabled the AutoLISP programmer to automate setting and retrieving AutoCAD system variables.

Don't confuse the terms *variable* and *system variable*. A variable is a value that is stored for use in a routine. A system variable is an AutoCAD setting that changes how AutoCAD works.

To set or retrieve AutoCAD system variables, you use two functions, setvar and getvar, which can be used on AutoCAD system variables. (You can use setvar only on system variables that are not read-only.) Here's how they work:

- setvar stands for *set variable*. You use setvar to change a system variable. Place the system variable in quotes, followed by the new value, as in (setvar "cmdecho" 0).

- getvar stands for *get variable*. It enables you to obtain the value of any system variable. As soon as you have the value, you can set it to a variable. This is often done so that you can return a system variable to its previous value if you've changed it during a routine. Place the system variable in quotes, as in (getvar "cmdecho").

Although you can use setvar and getvar on many system variables, here are two system variables that are often changed in an AutoLISP routine:

- In all the AutoLISP routines created thus far, AutoCAD's command responses could be seen scrolling off the command-line window. The CMDECHO system variable determines whether you see prompts and input during the functioning of AutoLISP's command function. By default, echoing is on (set to 1). If you set it to 0, you do not see prompts and input, and the functioning of the AutoLISP routine looks cleaner and runs slightly faster.

- The FILEDIA system variable turns on and off the display of dialog boxes that enable you to choose files. Turning off this system variable enables you to work with files on the command line in AutoLISP routines.

On the DVD

The file used in the following exercise on using AutoLISP to work with system variables, `ab35-a.lsp`, **is in the** `Drawings` **folder on the DVD.** ■

STEPS: Using AutoLISP to Work with System Variables

1. If you did the previous exercise and copied `ab35-a.lsp` to AutoCAD's `Support` folder (or another folder that you created for AutoLISP routines, and added to AutoCAD's support-file search path), open it from that folder. If you did not do the previous exercise, copy `ab35-a.lsp` from the DVD to AutoCAD's `Support` folder, or another folder in AutoCAD's support-file search path.

2. Start a new drawing by using the `acad.dwt` template. Choose Manage tab ⇨ Applications panel ⇨ Visual LISP Editor, to open Visual LISP. Click Open and open `ab35-a.lsp`. Edit it to read as follows:

```
(defun chg2red (selected_object)
  (command "_chprop" selected_object "" "_color" "red" "")
)
(defun c:chgcolor (/ selected old_cmdecho)
  (setq old_cmdecho (getvar "cmdecho"))
  (setvar "cmdecho" 0)
  (terpri)
  (setq selected (entsel "Select an object to change to red:"))
  (chg2red selected)
  (setvar "cmdecho" old_cmdecho)
)
```

3. Save the file as `ab35-01.lsp` in the same location.

4. Choose Load Active Edit Window to load the routine.

5. Draw any object.

6. At the command line, type **chgcolor** ↵.

7. At the `Select an object to change to red:` prompt, select the object that you drew in Step 5. You no longer see the prompts scrolling by. The object that you select turns red, and AutoCAD immediately displays the command prompt.

Don't save your drawing.

Here's how this routine works. This discussion assumes that you have already read the discussion of the previous routine, which was very similar.

- First, you added a new variable, `old_cmdecho`, to the `chgcolor` function.

- In the following line, you set this variable to the current value of the CMDECHO system variable. You obtained this current value by using getvar.

- You then used setvar to set the AutoCAD system variable CMDECHO to 0.

- You may need to see the commands echoed for debugging purposes, so it would prove best to return CMDECHO to the value that it was set to before running the routine. Therefore, in the last line, you use setvar again to reset CMDECHO to the variable `old_cmdecho`, which stored the original value of CMDECHO.

As a result of these changes, the `chgcolor` program always sets the CMDECHO system variable back to the value it had before being run as long as the program finishes.

1108

Working with Lists

Lists are the primary structures that you work with while programming in AutoLISP. As you work in this chapter, you'll begin to understand the use of lists to modify objects (also called *entities*) in the AutoCAD database, and in a variety of other contexts with AutoLISP. AutoCAD represents all object data in a list that contains many smaller lists, but the lists are simple to use and manipulate.

Using lists for coordinates

A list is always enclosed in parentheses with spaces between the elements of the list. One common use for lists is for coordinates, as shown in the following example:

```
(1.0 3.5 2.0)
```

This list represents the X,Y,Z coordinates 1.0,3.5,2.0. You often need to extract one or more of the elements in a list. Table 35.1 shows the common list-extraction functions, using the example list (1.0 3.5 2.0).

TABLE 35.1

Basic List-Extraction Functions

Function	Pronunciation	Example Output	Description
car	Car	1.0	Returns the first element in a list
cdr	Could-er	(3.5 2.0)	Removes the first element from a list
cadr	cad-er	3.5	Returns the second element in a list
caddr	ca-did-der	2.0	Returns the third element in a list

For more flexibility, you can use the nth function. Use the nth function to access any element in a list by passing two arguments that specify the number of the element (items are numbered starting from 0) and the list that you want.

The name of the list is usually a variable set with setq:

```
(setq corner (list 1.0 3.5 2.0))
```

In this example, (nth 0 corner) returns 1.0 because 1.0 is the first item in the list corner.

The list function creates a list. If all the items in a list are constant values (not variables), you can use the quote function to create a list. You can use a single quote (the same as an apostrophe on the keyboard) as a shortcut for the quote function. The following two functions are equivalent:

```
(setq corner (list 1.0 3.5 2.0))
(setq corner '(1.0 3.5 2.0))
```

Many more AutoLISP list-extraction functions are detailed in the AutoLISP Function Synopsis Appendix of the AutoLISP Developer's Guide. Look under Basic Functions; then List Manipulation Functions. However, you can go a long way by remembering the functions listed here.

Creating dotted pairs

A *dotted pair* is a special type of list that contains only two elements. Some AutoLISP functions do not accept dotted pairs as an argument, but they're used to represent AutoCAD database objects. To construct a dotted pair, use the cons function:

```
(cons 40 4.5)
```

This example returns (40 . 4.5). This list type is known as a dotted pair because it contains exactly two elements, and the elements are separated by a period or dot.

STEPS: Working with AutoLISP Lists

1. Start a new drawing by using the acad.dwt template.
2. Choose Manage tab ➪ Applications panel ➪ Visual LISP Editor, to open Visual LISP.
3. In the Visual LISP Console window, type **(setq endpt '(3.5 2.0 1.4))** ↵. AutoLISP returns (3.5 2.0 1.4).
4. Continue in the Visual LISP Console. Type **(car endpt)** ↵. AutoLISP returns 3.5.
5. Type **(cadr endpt)** ↵. AutoLISP returns 2.0.
6. Type **(cdr endpt)** ↵. AutoLISP returns (2.0 1.4).
7. Type **(nth 1 endpt)** ↵. AutoLISP returns 2.0.

Don't save your drawing.

Setting Conditions

Often, you want to execute a procedure based on a certain condition. One way of doing this is with the if statement, which does one thing if a specified condition is true and another thing if it's false. In other words, the operation is conditioned on the truth of a certain statement.

Looping is an important part of programming. Frequently, you want to execute a procedure over and over until the routine has finished operating on all the target objects or items. Looping sets up the condition that determines when the operation starts, the number of objects upon which the routine operates, and when the operation ends.

Conditional statements

Conditional statements enable program flow to be determined, based on the outcome of a given decision. These decisions result in the return of either T, meaning true, or nil, meaning false. To try out the following statements, type them in the Visual LISP Console window. For instance, for the statement

```
(< 3 5)
T
```

AutoLISP returns T for true, having determined that 3 is less than 5. For the statement

```
(> 3 5)
nil
```

AutoLISP returns `nil` for false, having determined that 3 is not greater than 5. For the statement

```
(= 3 5)
nil
```

AutoLISP returns `nil`, because 3 is not equal to 5. Because conditional statements return either `T` or `nil`, you can use the if statement. The general syntax of the if statement is (`if conditional-test if-true if-false`). You can also use the if statement with other functions that return a value; `nil` is always evaluated as the if-false potion of the if statement while `T` or any other value is evaluated as the if-true portion.

For example, you may want to find circles whose radius is less than 0.25. In this case, you could use the following if statement. In this example, `radius` is a variable that has been previously set.

```
(if (< radius 0.25)
 (princ "\nThe radius is less than .25")
 (princ "\nThe radius is not less than .25")
 )
```

The conditional test is (`< radius 0.25`). The if-true statement is (`princ "\nThe radius is less than .25"`). The if-false statement is (`princ "\nThe radius is not less than .25"`). This if statement is equivalent to saying, "If the radius is less than .25, print 'The radius is less than .25', but if not, print 'The radius is not less than .25.'"

You can leave out the if-false statement. In this case, AutoLISP executes the if-true statement if the conditional statement is true and does nothing if it's false, and continues on to the rest of the program. In the following exercise, you see both types of if statements, one nested inside the other.

STEPS: Using the if Statement

1. Start a new drawing by using the `acad.dwt` template.
2. Open Visual LISP, start a new file, and type the following:

```
(defun c:compare2three (/ entered_num)
  (setq entered_num (getint "\nEnter an integer: "))
  (if (< entered_num 3)
    (princ "\nThe entered number is less than 3.")
    (if (= entered_num 3)
      (princ "\nThe entered number is equal to 3.")
      (princ "\nThe entered number is greater than 3.")
      )
    )
  (princ)
  )
```

The getint function gets an integer from the user and is covered later in this chapter. The princ function prints a text string on the command line. The \n before the `Enter an integer:` prompt starts a new line; it's similar to using (`terpri`). Using (`princ`) at the end of a routine is also covered later in this chapter.

3. Choose Check Edit Window. If you see any error message in the Build Output window, check your typing, make any necessary corrections, and try again.
4. Save the file as `ab35-02.lsp` in a folder that is in the support-file search path, or in `AutoCAD 2011\Support`.
5. Choose Load Active Edit Window and then choose Activate AutoCAD.

6. To try out the if statement, type **compare2three** ↵. At the Enter an integer: prompt, type **5** ↵. AutoCAD displays: The entered number is greater than 3.

7. Repeat the COMPARE2THREE command. At the Enter an integer: prompt, type **3** ↵. AutoCAD displays: The entered number is equal to 3.

8. Repeat the COMPARE2THREE command. At the Enter an integer: prompt, type **2** ↵. AutoCAD displays: The entered number is less than 3.

Don't save your drawing.

Loop statements

Looping provides the capability to execute a step or a number of steps a given number of times, based on an evaluation that you make in your application. One way to do this is with the while function.

The format of the while function is:

```
(while conditional-test-if-true
        then-perform-following-code-until-condition-is-false)
```

One method that can be useful with a while conditional-test-if-true statement is to include a *counter* for the while expression. A counter counts how many times an operation is executed. You can then end the operation when the counter reaches a certain number. To create a counter, set a variable (perhaps named "counter") to the number at which you want to start. Then write the code for one pass through the looping statement. Then set the counter to the next higher number, using an expression, such as the following:

```
(setq counter (+ 1 counter))
```

The routine then loops back over the statements until the counter reaches the value that you set.

Here's a simple example:

```
(defun c:process (/ counter)
  (setq counter 1)
  (while (< counter 6)
    (princ "\nProcessing number ")
    (princ counter)
    (terpri)
    (setq counter (+ 1 counter))
  )
)
```

In this example, the process function starts by setting the variable counter to 1. Then you start the while statement and specify that the counter must be less than 6. Within the while statement, you print the text string "Processing number" and then the value of the counter variable. You use (terpri) so that each text string starts on a new line. Then you set the counter to the next higher number. Each time through the while loop, the value of the counter is incremented by 1. Without the increment statement, line 3 would always evaluate to true, and the while loop would never exit because the counter would always be 1.

If you accidentally program an infinite loop like this, you can stop the execution of your AutoLISP routine by pressing Esc, pressing Ctrl+Break, or choosing Debug⇨Abort Evaluation from the Visual LISP menu.

In the preceding example, the while loop continues as long as the counter is less than 6. When the counter reaches 6, the while function stops. The while statement returns the last value of the routine, so AutoCAD prints 6 on the last line. Figure 35.2 shows the result.

FIGURE 35.2

The result of the process function.

```
Command: process
Processing number 1
Processing number 2
Processing number 3
Processing number 4
Processing number 5
6
```

When using while, you may want to combine several operations under the condition. The if function normally evaluates one then expression if the test expression is true. Suppose you want an if expression that processes various tasks if the test condition is true. An if expression, as previously mentioned, processes a "do-if-true" and "do-if-false." Therefore, to process more than one "do-if-true" expression, you need to separate the "do-if-true" processes from the "do-if-false" processes. To accomplish this, use progn (short for *program nest*) to include (or nest) all items that you want executed when the test is true. In general, progn evaluates all the statements within its parentheses and returns the last evaluation as if it were one statement, as the following example demonstrates.

In the following example, you see the same if statements used in an earlier example. However, after the second if statement, you want your routine to print two lines if the entered number equals 3. You can do this by enclosing the two lines of code (plus a terpri) within a progn statement:

```
(defun c:compare2three (/ entered_num)
  (setq entered_num (getint "\nEnter an integer: "))
  (if (< entered_num 3)
    (princ "\nThe entered number is less than 3.")
    (if (= entered_num 3)
      (progn
        (princ "\nThe entered number is equal to 3.")
        (terpri)
        (princ "\nThis is the one we are looking for.")
      )
      (princ "\nThe entered number is greater than 3.")
    )
  )
  (princ)
)
```

On the DVD

The file used in the following exercise on using while, if, progn, and a counter, ab35-b.lsp, is in the Drawings folder on the DVD. ∎

STEPS: Using while, if, progn, and a Counter

1. Start a new drawing with any template.
2. Open Visual LISP.
3. Click Open File on the Visual LISP Standard toolbar, and open ab35-b.lsp from the DVD.

4. Save the file as `ab35-03.lsp` in `AutoCAD 2011\Support` or any folder in the support-file search paths. Figure 35.3 shows this routine.

FIGURE 35.3

The print0to10 routine.

```
(defun c:print0to10 (/ counter halfway)
  (setq counter 0                          ; initial value of counter
        halfway 5                          ; initial value of halfway
  )
  (terpri)
  (while (< counter 11)                    ; as long as counter is less than 11
    (if (= counter halfway)
      (progn                               ; process this if the variable halfway is 5
        (princ "Hey The halfway mark is: ")
        (princ halfway)
        (terpri)
      )
      (progn                               ; otherwise just show the present counter value
        (princ "The Counter value is: ")
        (princ counter)
        (terpri)
      )
    )
    (setq counter (+ counter 1))           ; Increment the value of counter
  )
)
```

5. Load `ab35-03.lsp`. Return to AutoCAD.

6. Type **print0to10** ↵. Press F2 to open the AutoCAD Text Window and see the result, as shown in Figure 35.4.

FIGURE 35.4

The result of the print0to10 function.

```
Command: print0to10

The Counter value is: 0
The Counter value is: 1
The Counter value is: 2
The Counter value is: 3
The Counter value is: 4
Hey The halfway mark is: 5
The Counter value is: 6
The Counter value is: 7
The Counter value is: 8
The Counter value is: 9
The Counter value is: 10
11
```

Don't save your drawing.

Managing Drawing Objects

The real power of AutoLISP is in manipulating drawing objects. This section reveals how many of the AutoLISP routines perform their magic. You can find information about an object and then use that information to change the object. You can also create selection sets of objects.

Getting information about an object

Every object in the AutoCAD database has an entity name. This name enables you to reference that object anywhere in your AutoLISP application. To see an example of an entity name, type the following after starting a new drawing:

```
(command "_line" "3,3" "5,5" "")
(entlast)
```

AutoLISP responds with an Entity name such as <Entity name: 2ed0520>.

The numbers will probably differ on your system, but using the information returned from entlast enables you to programmatically get or set a variety of options on any given database object by referencing its entity name.

The entget (entity get) function is the key to making modifications to the drawing database. The entget function takes an entity name as an argument. After drawing the line in the preceding steps, type the following:

```
(setq myline (entget (entlast)))
```

AutoLISP responds with:

```
((-1 . <Entity name: 15ac558>) (0 . "LINE") (330 . <Entity name:
   15ac4f8>)(5 . "2B") (100 . "AcDbEntity") (67 . 0)
(410 . "Model") (8 . "0")(100 . "AcDbLine") (10 3.0 3.0 0.0) (11 5.0
   5.0 0.0) (210 0.0 0.0 1.0))
```

This is a representation of how the line is stored in the AutoCAD drawing database. AutoLISP returns a large list that contains multiple smaller lists. Each of the smaller lists is referred to as a group indexed by the first element. The entity name is in group −1. Each of the initial numbers in the small lists represents a different quality of the line. These numbers are called *object group codes*. The object group codes used most often are listed in Table 35.2.

TABLE 35.2

Commonly Used AutoCAD Object Group Codes

Group Code	Description
−1	Entity name
0	Entity type
1	Text value
8	Layer
10	Start point (or center)
11	Endpoint (or alignment point)
38	Elevation
39	Thickness
40	Radius (or height of text)
62	Color
67	Paper space flag

Note

As you can see from the 10, 11, and 40 codes, the meaning of the group codes can change, depending on the type of object that it's used for. ■

You can also use Visual LISP to examine an AutoCAD object. Begin by choosing View ⇨ Browse Drawing Database ⇨ Browse Selection. At this point, Visual LISP will display a pickbox in your drawing so that you can select an object.

After you end object selection, you're returned to Visual LISP, where you see the Inspect dialog box. Select the name of the entity and right-click while the cursor is over the selected text. Choose Inspect to see information about the object. Figure 35.5 shows information about a line.

FIGURE 35.5

Getting information about a drawing object from Visual LISP.

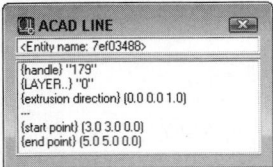

Not all these group codes are present in the line that you drew. For instance, group 62 (color) is absent in the list returned by Visual LISP. Every time you draw a line, you don't explicitly set its color. As a result, it defaults to the current color. In the same way, AutoLISP doesn't explicitly set every attribute of every group. In this case, the color is ByLayer and the current layer is 0. Visual LISP returned (8 . "0") in the preceding list to signify that the line is on layer 0.

There are many other group codes in addition to the ones listed in Table 35.2, and they can be found in the AutoCAD Help system. From Visual LISP, choose Help ⇨ Visual LISP Help Topics. From the Help Landing page, click DXF Reference. (Because the group codes are also used for DXF files, they're found in the DXF Reference.) Click Common Group Codes for Entities or a specific entity that you want to look up under the Entities section. In many cases, one group code can have different meanings, depending on the entity in which it appears. For example, in the list representing the line that you drew, group 10 is represented by (10 3.0 3.0 0.0), which means that the start point of the line is at X = 3.0, Y = 3.0, Z = 0.0. If group 0 were a circle instead, the coordinates of group 10 would specify the center point of the circle.

To manipulate a given attribute of an object, two important functions are assoc and subst:

- assoc returns a list that finds the entry associated with an item in a list. It takes two arguments: the item in the list and the list itself. For example, if you specify the group code (such as 10) as the first argument, it returns the code's value (which would be the start point of a line). Or, if a list named myobject contains three groups, as in ((0 . "group 0") (1 1.0 2.0) (3 4.2 1.5 6.75)), then (assoc 1 myobject) would return (1 1.0 2.0).

- subst substitutes a value for every occurrence in a list. The subst function takes three arguments. To make the substitution, the first argument specifies what to substitute with, the second argument specifies what to substitute for, and the third argument specifies on what list to perform this operation.

To manipulate the start point of your line, first get the start point:

```
(setq startpt (assoc 10 myline))
```

AutoLISP responds:

```
(10 3.0 3.0 0.0)
```

To modify the start point of your line, use:

```
(setq new_startpt '(10 6.5 1.0 0.0))
(setq myline (subst new_startpt startpt myline))
```

AutoLISP responds:

```
((-1 . <Entity name: 15ac558>) (0 . "LINE") (330 . <Entity name:
    15ac4f8>)(5 . "2B") (100 . "AcDbEntity") (67 . 0)
(410 . "Model") (8 . "0")(100 . "AcDbLine") (10 6.5 1.0 0.0) (11 5.0
    5.0 0.0) (210 0.0 0.0 1.0))
```

In this case, new_startpt is substituted for the existing startpt in the object myline. No changes to the line are yet apparent. To commit the change, you need the entmod function.

Modifying objects

The key to modifying objects is the entmod (entity modify) function. The list returned by AutoLISP can be modified and then passed to entmod as an argument to update the AutoCAD database. Continuing with the previous example, if you enter:

```
(entmod myline)
```

AutoLISP responds:

```
((-1 . <Entity name: 15ac558>) (0 . "LINE") (330 . <Entity name:
    15ac4f8>) (5 . "2B") (100 . "AcDbEntity") (67 . 0)
(410 . "Model") (8 . "0") (100. "AcDbLine") (10 6.5 1.0 0.0)
(11 5.0 5.0 0.0) (210 0.0 0.0 1.0))
```

The AutoCAD database is changed as well, and the start point of your line is now at X = 6.5, Y = 1.0, Z = 0.0.

Creating selection sets

A selection set is created with the ssget (selection set get) function. This prompts the user with the familiar Select objects: prompt. Table 35.3 shows commonly used selection-set functions.

TABLE 35.3

Common AutoCAD Selection-Set Functions

Function	Description
ssget	Obtains a selection set from the user.
sslength	Returns the number of objects in a selection set. It takes one argument, which is the selection set.
ssname	Returns the entity name of a given object in a selection set. It takes two arguments: the selection set and the number of the object in the selection set. The first item number is 0, the second is 1, and so on.

You can use a maximum of 128 selection sets at any given time. To release a selection set back to AutoLISP so that it can be used again, set the selection set to nil, as in (setq ss nil).

For example, you can enter the following in a new drawing:

```
(command "_circle" "3,3" "2")
nil
(command "_circle" "4,4" "3")
nil
(command "_line" "7,2" "6,6" "3,4" "5,5" "")
nil
(setq mysset (ssget))
Select objects: all ↵
5 found
Select objects: ↵
<Selection set 1>
```

Now mysset is set to the selection set specified by all, which includes the three line segments and the two circles. To see how many objects you have in your selection set, type the following, either on the command line or in the Visual LISP Console window:

```
(sslength mysset)
5
```

You now know that you have five objects in your selection set. The first object is number 0, and the fifth object is number 4. To see what the first object is, enter the following:

```
(ssname mysset 0)
<Entity name: 3fe0550>
```

To get the database data on the object, enter:

```
(entget (ssname mysset 0))
```

A list of group codes is returned, and looks similar to the following:

```
((-1 . <Entity name: 3fe0550>) (0 . "LINE") (330 . <Entity name:
    16014f8>)(5 . "30") (100 . "AcDbEntity") (67 . 0) (410 . "Model")
    (8 . "0")(100 . "AcDbLine") (10 3.0 4.0 0.0) (11 5.0 5.0 0.0)
    (210 0.0 0.0 1.0))
```

By stepping through each of the entity names returned by ssname from 0 to 4, you can manipulate each of the objects in the selection set.

STEPS: Creating Selection Sets

1. Start a new drawing by using the acad.dwt template, and type the following in a new file in the Visual LISP edit window. Don't enter the numbers on the left. Save it as ab35-04.lsp in your AutoCAD 2011\Support folder or any folder in the support-file search path.

```
1   (defun c:listsset (/ mysset counter)
2     (setq mysset (ssget))
3     (setq counter 0)
4     (while (< counter (sslength mysset))
5       (terpri)
```

```
6        (princ (cdr (assoc 0 (entget (ssname mysset counter)))))
7        (setq counter (+ counter 1))
8    )
9   (princ)
10 )
```

2. Load ab35-04.lsp.

3. Activate AutoCAD and draw any number of objects on-screen — at least two different types of objects.

4. Type **listsset** ↵. AutoCAD prompts you to select objects (because of the ssget function).

5. Select all the objects in your drawing. The routine prints the type of each object that you selected. (Press F2 to open the AutoCAD Text Window to see the entire results.) Figure 35.6 shows the results. Of course, your results will be different because you probably drew different types of objects.

FIGURE 35.6

One possible result of the listsset routine.

```
Command: listsset

Select objects: all
5 found

Select objects:

LWPOLYLINE
CIRCLE
TEXT
LINE
LINE
```

Here's a breakdown of the routine in Step 1:

- **Line 1** creates a function and declares two variables, mysset and counter.
- **Line 2** sets the mysset variable equal to the selection set that the user provides by using ssget.
- **Line 3** sets the counter variable to 0, because selection sets work on a zero-based index (the first item is 0).
- **Line 4** starts a while loop. Working from the innermost set of parentheses, you first obtain the number of objects in the mysset selection set, using sslength. Then you specify that the while loop will continue as long as the counter is less than the number of objects in the mysset selection set. In other words, when the routine has cycled through all the objects in the selection set, it stops.
- **Line 5** uses terpri to start a new line before printing out the object type of the selected object.
- **Line 6** prints the object type of the selected object. Working from the innermost set of parentheses, the routine first obtains the name of the object in the mysset selection set whose number is equal to the variable counter. The routine then gets that object by using entget. The routine then gets the name of that object by using assoc with the 0 group code. The result is a dotted-pair list whose second item is the name of the object. The cdr function eliminates the first item in the dotted-pair list, leaving just the name of the object, which is what you want. The routine then prints the result.
- **Line 7** increments the counter by one to repeat the while loop for the next object.

- **Line 8** closes the while loop.
- **Line 9** exits the routine quietly. (I discuss exiting quietly later in the chapter.)
- **Line 10** closes the entire function.

Getting Input from the User

Many of your AutoLISP routines may often depend on user input. To satisfy this need, AutoCAD has a family of functions prefaced with the word get. You have seen requests for user input while using commands; LINE or CIRCLE, for example, request input in the forms of points or distances. You have seen getvar for obtaining system variable information. Table 35.4 shows some other useful get functions.

Basic User-Input Functions

Function	Description
getdist	Returns the distance between two points
getint	Returns an integer
getreal	Returns a real number (which can be a non-integer, negative, and so on)
getstring	Returns a text string

Within the command function, you can use the pause variable to pause and enable user input, such as picking a point or typing a value. For example, the expression (command "circle" pause "3") pauses to let the user specify a center point and then creates a circle with a radius of 3.

Notice the function entsel in the next exercise. This is a type of shorthand for ssget. Use it when you want to limit the user to selecting a single object. entsel returns an entity name and the coordinates of your pick point in a dotted-pair list. Therefore, you can use car before entsel to get the entity name for entget.

There is also a new argument for getstring, T. If you use this argument and it isn't nil, users can place spaces in the input. Using this argument enables users to type a text value that includes more than one word. Without the T, AutoLISP would interpret a space as equivalent to pressing Enter.

STEPS: Getting User Input

1. Start a new drawing by using the acad.dwt template.
2. Start Visual LISP, open a new file, and enter the following routine. Don't enter the numbers on the left. Save it as ab35-05.lsp in AutoCAD 2011\Support or a folder that you've added to the support-file search path.

```
1   (defun c:chgmytext (/ src_object new_ht new_str)
2     (setq src_object (entget (car (entsel))))
3     (setq new_ht (getreal "\nWhat is the new height? "))
4     (setq new_str (getstring T "\nWhat is the new text value? "))
5     (setq src_object
6       (subst (cons 40 new_ht) (assoc 40 src_object) src_object)
7     )
```

```
8     (setq src_object
9       (subst (cons 1 new_str) (assoc 1 src_object) src_object)
10    )
11    (entmod src_object)
12  (princ)
13 )
```

3. Choose Format Edit Window from the Visual LISP Tools toolbar.

4. Load ab35-05.lsp.

5. Create some text by using the TEXT command and run chgmytext on it. AutoCAD changes the text object's height and content to the values that you input in response to the prompts.

Don't save your drawing.

Here's a breakdown of the routine in Step 2:

- **Line 1** defines the function and declares three local variables.
- **Line 2** uses entsel to let the user select one object. As explained earlier, car enables you to get just the entity name. entget gets this entity name so that you can modify it. Finally, this line sets the resulting entity data equal to the variable src_object.
- **Line 3** prompts the user for a new height for the text and sets the entered number equal to the new_ht variable.
- **Line 4** prompts the user for a new text value (a new string) and sets the entered text value equal to the new_str variable.
- **Line 5** starts the process of substituting the new values for the old values. Here the routine starts to set the new value for src_object.
- **Line 6** uses subst to substitute the new text height for the old text height for the object src_object. (Group code 40 represents text height.)
- **Line 7** closes the setq function.
- **Line 8** is the same as line 5. You'll be repeating the process of lines 5 through 7 for the new text (string) value.
- **Line 9** uses subst to substitute the new text value for the old text value. (Group code 1 represents the text value.)
- **Line 10** closes the setq function.
- **Line 11** uses entmod on src_object to make the change in the drawing database.
- **Line 12** exits quietly.
- **Line 13** closes the entire function.

Putting on the Finishing Touches

You have a number of finishing touches that you should add to a routine before you can call it complete. All AutoLISP expressions return a value, and the last expression returns its value on the command line. You've noticed the princ function at the end of several routines. princ returns a blank line and, therefore, ensures that no extraneous evaluation return values are echoed on the command line. Using the princ function in this way is called *exiting cleanly* or *exiting quietly*.

Most of the AutoLISP programs covered thus far do not include much in the way of error handling. A function called equal is used on line 5 of the final routine in the next exercise. equal is different than = in that equal returns true only if two expressions are equal (each of the two objects tested for equality are evaluated before checking whether they're equal). A simple rule of thumb is to use equal for list comparisons and = for numeric and string comparisons.

In the routine in the next exercise, if you select an object that is not a text object, the program jumps to line 20 and prints the error message You must select a text object.

A similar type of error handling is to enclose the selection of objects in an if function. The if function's test condition has to exist in order for the if function to work. Therefore, if the user doesn't select an object, the test evaluates as false. You can place an error message as the if-false part of the if function to catch this type of error.

This type of error handling is crucial to making your AutoLISP programs look finished and function properly.

Another way to finish off your routine is to add comments. Start with a comment at the beginning that states the purpose and function of the routine. This helps others understand what the routine does and can help you as well when you look at the routine again a few months later! Comments are prefaced with a semicolon.

Continue to make comments throughout your code. A lack of comments can make even the most useful code useless. Most professional programmers fully comment and document a function's purpose and behavior by placing comments within the code.

Visual LISP supports several commenting styles. When you click Format Edit Window on the Tools toolbar, Visual LISP uses these styles to automatically format your code. Here's how they work:

- ;;; **Triple semicolon.** When you type a comment with three semicolons, Visual LISP places the comment at the left margin. You can use a triple semicolon comment at the beginning of your routine to describe its overall purpose and what it does.

- ;; **Double semicolon.** Visual LISP indents a comment with two semicolons at the current nesting level, flush with the next level of parentheses. You can use this type of comment to explain the next line or lines of code.

- ; **Single semicolon.** By default, Visual LISP indents a comment with one semicolon by 40 spaces. Choose Tools ⇨ Environment Options ⇨ Visual LISP Format Options to open the Format Options dialog box, shown in Figure 35.7, and change this value if you want. You can use this type of comment for running comments at the right side of your code. Because they're indented, they stand out from the body of your code.

- ;| |; **Inline comment.** Place an inline comment within any line of code so that it has code both before and after it. An inline comment is formatted as follows: ;|This is a comment|;. You use the pipe symbol (usually over the backslash) along with the semicolon. You can use an inline comment to explain a small section of code within a line, or to span comments over several lines without adding a semicolon before each line.

- ;_ **End-of-line comment.** Place an end-of-line comment at the end of any line of code. An end-of-line comment is formatted as follows: ;_ This is an end-of-line comment. You use the underscore symbol along with the semicolon. You can use an end-of-line comment to explain which function is matched to which closing parenthesis. This is especially useful for conditional functions where one closing parenthesis can be several lines from the opening parenthesis.

FIGURE 35.7

Use the Format Options dialog box to format margins and indentation in the Visual LISP editor.

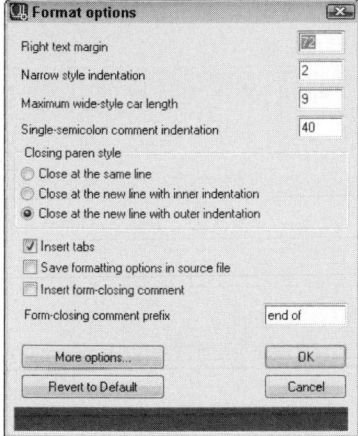

STEPS: Putting on the Finishing Touches

1. Load the application that was completed in the previous exercise. If you didn't do the previous exercise, enter the text of the chgmytext routine from that exercise in Visual LISP's edit window, and save it as ab35-05.lsp in AutoCAD 2011\Support or in a folder that you've added to the support-file search path. Then load it with any drawing that you open in AutoCAD.

2. Now run chgmytext and choose an object that is not a text object (such as a circle) in response to the Select object: prompt. Answer the prompts for new height and new text values.

   If the selected object is a circle, you see its radius change to match the value that you specified to be the new text height. This is definitely not what you intended when writing this program.

3. Modify the program so that it reads as follows, and save it as ab35-06.lsp:

```
;;;modifies text height and content (value)
(defun c:chgmytext (/ src_object new_ht new_str)
  (terpri)
  (setq src_object (entget (car (entsel))))
  (if (equal (assoc 0 src_object) '(0 . "TEXT"))
    (progn
      (prompt "\nWhat is the new height for the text? ")
      (setq new_ht (getreal))
      (prompt "\nWhat is the new text value? ")
      (setq new_str (getstring))
      (setq src_object
        (subst (cons 40 new_ht) (assoc 40 src_object) src_object)
      )
      (setq src_object
        (subst (cons 1 new_str) (assoc 1 src_object) src_object)
      )
```

```
        (entmod src_object)
      )
      (princ "\n You must select a text object. ")
      )
    (princ)
  )
```

4. Load `ab35-06.lsp`. Start `chgmytext` and try out the routine again with a circle or other non-text object.

Don't save your drawing.

Summary

In this chapter, you learned:

- How to create variables
- How to create AutoLISP functions
- How to work with AutoCAD commands and system variables
- About extending AutoLISP's power by using lists and looping
- How to modify and get information about drawing objects
- How to create selection sets
- About obtaining user input
- Tools for finishing off your AutoLISP routines by adding some error handling, making sure that the routine exits quietly, and adding helpful comments about the routine's function

In the next chapter, you read about some of the more-advanced features of Visual LISP.

Exploring Advanced AutoLISP Topics

This chapter builds on the previous two chapters and introduces you to a few advanced AutoLISP topics, including global and local variables, ActiveX, and debugging.

AutoCAD Only

AutoCAD LT does not support AutoLISP, so this entire chapter is for AutoCAD only. ■

Understanding Global and Local Variables

IN THIS CHAPTER

Understanding global and local variables

Working with Visual LISP ActiveX functions

Debugging code

Using the Error Trace window

Using the Watch window

In this section, you read how global and local variables are accessed within a function, as well as some common syntax. You also discover what can happen when global variables are not properly documented.

Chapter 35 explained that a *variable* is a symbolic name that you can use in a given function. An important part of using variables is being able to assign values to them. There are two types of variables, global and local.

A *global* variable is exposed, or available, to all AutoLISP functions that are loaded into your drawing. A global variable retains its value after the function that defined it is finished. You use a global variable when you want its value to be available while a drawing is open, as opposed to just one function. This allows you to retain a fixed value that might be used and assigned by different functions, or for debugging. Any variable that you don't specifically define as a local variable is a global variable.

A *local* variable is temporarily assigned a value during a function's execution. After the function completes executing, the local variable value is discarded. AutoLISP can now use the memory that was taken up by that local variable.

You use a local variable when you want to be sure that you don't have variable values floating around and interfering with other functions. Local variables are also easier to debug because they affect only the code within their function. In general, most of your variables should be local. You create a local variable and declare it in the defun statement after the slash and a space, as in this example:

```
(defun list-objects ( / counter sset)...
```

Caution

Global variables can be tricky. For example, they can easily cause bugs. This is because their values persist and can be hard to debug because the values are hard to find. A common syntax for global variables is to prefix and suffix the variable with an asterisk, as in *aGlobal*. In this way, you can easily identify global variables in your code. Keep your use of global variables to a minimum, and carefully document those that you do use. Failure to follow these simple rules could result in undesirable and difficult-to-trace bugs. ■

STEPS: Using Global and Local Variables

1. Start a new drawing by using the acad.dwt template. You should not have any other drawing open.

2. Open the Visual LISP editor.

3. In the Console window, type the following line and then press Ctrl+Enter. You use Ctrl+Enter in the Console window to enter in code of more than one line. This line declares one local variable:

```
(defun local-variable (/ var1)
```

4. Type the second line of code in the Console window as follows:

```
(setq var1 "I'm local")) ↵
```

This sets the local variable to the string that you typed. The Console returns the name of the function:

```
LOCAL-VARIABLE
```

5. Before you test this function, you can check out the current value of the local variable, var1. Type **var1** ↵ in the Visual LISP Console. The Console returns:

```
nil
```

As you can see, the value is nil.

6. Test the local-variable function to check the value that it sets to the var1 variable. In the Console window, type **(local-variable)** ↵. The Console returns:

```
"I'm local"
```

You now know that the local-variable function definitely assigns the value of "I'm local" to the variable var1.

7. To create a global variable, type **(setq var1 "I'm global")** ↵ in the Console window. The Console returns:

```
"I'm global"
```

You know that the value of var1 is now "I'm global".

8. Test the local variable again by typing **(local-variable)** in the Console window. The Console returns "I'm local" because it executes the local-variable function.

9. Test the variable var1 to see what its value is now. In the Console window, type **var1** ↵. The Console returns "I'm global". The local variable was not retained when the function used the variable because the variable was local to the function. However, the global variable's value persisted.

Working with Visual LISP ActiveX Functions

ActiveX is an interface that exposes objects to the user, a programmer, or an application. AutoLISP supports ActiveX, giving you more information and flexibility in working with your drawings. You can also use ActiveX to work with objects in other Windows applications that support ActiveX. ActiveX is a *programming interface* that is used within a programming language that supports it. For example, you can also use ActiveX with VB.NET (see the next chapter), C++, and C#.

Cross-Reference

In ActiveX, objects are structured in a hierarchy. You need to understand this structure before working extensively with ActiveX. For information on this hierarchical structure, see ActiveX and VBA Reference on the AutoCAD Help Landing page (online only, not locally installed) or from C:\Program Files\Common Files\Autodesk Shared\acadauto.chm. ■

ActiveX enables you to get information about objects (called *get functions*) and modify them (called *put functions*). The following section reviews how you can create functions in AutoLISP that emulate the get and put functionality of ActiveX functions.

Reviewing AutoLISP retrieval and modification

In this section, you look at developing a small routine, written in AutoLISP, that mimics ActiveX properties and methods. This will help you to compare how AutoLISP works compared to ActiveX.

To understand Visual LISP's ActiveX features, you need to know how AutoCAD exposes an object's properties in AutoLISP. The following examples work with a line that is 10 units long and that was created by using the following AutoLISP function:

```
;;; This function creates a line using the AutoLISP
;;; command function and returns nil.
(defun make-aLine ()
  (command "_line" "5,5" "15,5" "")
)
```

Note

The uppercase letter (in the function name) is used for readability, but you can type all lowercase letters if that's easier for you. ■

After loading it, you can use this function (that is, draw the line) by typing the following in the Visual LISP Console window:

(make-aLine)

As explained in Chapter 35, to retrieve the last object that was created (the line), you use entlast, as shown in the following code fragment. The next expression assigns the value of the last created entity, as an entity name, to the variable LineEntity. To try this out, type the following code in the Console window:

(setq LineEntity (entlast))

Visual LISP responds with the entity name. As soon as you receive the entity name, you can use entget to retrieve the object property list of the line. The following code fragment places the property list value in the variable `LinePropertyList`. If you type the following in the Console window and press Enter, Visual LISP responds with the property list:

```
(setq LinePropertyList (entget LineEntity))
```

Here is an example of a property list, which is formatted for readability:

```
((-1 . <Entity name: 1456d60>)
 (0 . "LINE")
 (330 . <Entity name: 1456cf8>)
 (5 . "2C")
 (100 . "AcDbEntity")
 (67 . 0)
 (410 . "Model")
 (8 . "0")
 (100 . "AcDbLine")
 (10 5.0 5.0 0.0)
 (11 15.0 5.0 0.0)
 (210 0.0 0.0 1.0))
```

As you can see, entget returns an entity's properties as a collection of lists, all which have a distinctive number at their first position. Some of these group codes (also commonly known as DXF fields, because you can also find them in DXF files) were listed in Table 35.2 in Chapter 35. For this exercise, you just need to remember that the group 10 code is associated with the start point of a line.

Having the entity list and knowing which values to retrieve, you can use the AutoLISP function assoc, which returns an associated item from a property list.

To retrieve the start point of the line, you would use the following code, which you can type in the Console window:

```
(setq StartofLineList (assoc 10 LinePropertyList))
```

The Console returns the list that is associated with the group 10 code, including the group code and the coordinates:

```
(10 5.0 5.0 0.0)
```

Because the only value that you require is the start point of the line object, use the function cdr to remove the first element of the list, as shown in the following code.

```
(setq StartofLine (cdr (assoc 10 LinePropertyList)))
```

This code returns only the start point coordinate:

```
(5.0 5.0 0.0)
```

This review of how to retrieve a value from an AutoCAD object shows that retrieving information from an associated list is relatively straightforward. But how about retrieving more than one property at a time? As you can see from the preceding example, you'd have to repeat the same body of code many times over to retrieve any information. Knowing this, you could write a simple *interface function*, putting together all the steps that I have just explained, to retrieve any group code — not just the group 10 code — from an object.

Note

An interface function is a function that hides a complex behavior from the user. The user needs to provide only basic information, but the function uses the information in several steps to obtain the desired result. ■

An example of an interface function is shown in the following lines:

```
;;; Returns any group code value if it is present in the entity
;;; the required parameters are an entity name and a group code.
(defun Get-A-Group-Code (EntityName GroupCode)
   (cdr (assoc GroupCode (entget EntityName)))
   )
```

After you create this function and load it, you can test it out in the Console window as follows, using the LineEntity variable that was previously defined:

```
(Get-A-Group-Code LineEntity 10) ↵
(5.0 5.0 0.0)
```

As you can see, the function returns only the value of the group 10 code.

You can refine this small interface by defining a separate group 10 code function, such as the following. The only required parameter is an entity name. The group code is included in the call to Get-A-Group-Code. You could do the same for a group 11 code, if you want.

```
(defun Get-Group-10-Code (anEntityName)
   (Get-A-Group-Code anEntityName 10)
   )
```

After loading, test the function, as follows:

```
(Get-Group-10-Code LineEntity) ↵
```

Visual LISP returns the start point of the line:

```
(5.0 5.0 0.0)
```

These examples summarize how you would create a simple function to get the start point of a line by using AutoLISP. What if you need to change an object's property? You can do this by using the functions cons, subst, and entmod, which Chapter 35 covers.

cons constructs a list. Use it when you want to create new values for a group code within an entity list, as in the following example, which you can type in the Console window:

```
(setq NewStartPoint (cons 10 '( 0.0 0.0 0.0 ))) ↵
```

Visual LISP returns the following:

```
(10 0.0 0.0 0.0)
```

Using the variables NewStartPoint and LinePropertyList, you can substitute the newly created group 10 code. You do this by using the subst function. The following code substitutes the new group 10 code that is represented by the variable NewStartPoint for the 10 association in LinePropertyList in the list called LinePropertyList.

```
(Setq LinePropertyList
   (subst NewStartPoint (assoc 10 LinePropertyList) LinePropertyList)
)
```

To test this out, type the preceding code in the Console window. To see the new start point, you need to scroll all the way to the right. The list (nicely formatted here) now has a new group 10 value (the start point), shown on the third-to-last line that follows:

```
((-1 . <Entity name: 1456d60>)
 (0 . "LINE")
 (330 . <Entity name: 1456cf8>)
 (5 . "2C")
 (100 . "AcDbEntity")
 (67 . 0)
 (410 . "Model")
 (8 . "0")
 (100 . "AcDbLine")
 (10 0.0 0.0 0.0)
 (11 15.0 5.0 0.0)
 (210 0.0 0.0 1.0))
```

To reflect the modification of this line in AutoCAD, you can now use the function entmod by typing it in the Console window, as follows. This code actually changes the start point of the line. (You can return to AutoCAD to check it out.)

```
(entmod LinePropertyList) ↵
```

As you can see from this example, getting object properties and modifying them can be a tedious and time-consuming process. Here is an example of an interface function that modifies any group code that is contained in any object.

```
1   (defun put-group-code-value (Entityname Groupcode Value /
2                                   PropertyList)
3     (setq PropertyList (entget EntityName))
4     (setq PropertyList
5         (subst
6           (cons GroupCode Value)
7           (assoc GroupCode PropertyList)
8           PropertyList
9         )
10    )
11    (entmod PropertyList)
12  )
```

This function combines all the preceding steps into one function. Here's how it works:

- **Lines 1 and 2** define the function with three arguments: the entity name, a group code, and a new value for the group code. It also declares a local variable, PropertyList, which is the property list of the object.
- **Line 3** sets the property list equal to the entget of the entity name.
- **Line 4** starts the process of setting the same property list to the new value.

- **Lines 5 through 8** execute the substitution. They substitute the new group, created by (cons GroupCode Value), for the current group value, created with the assoc function, in the property list named PropertyList.

- **Line 9** closes the subst function.

- **Line 10** closes the second setq function.

- **Line 11** modifies the drawing database by using entmod.

- **Line 12** closes the defun function.

Using the preceding function, you now have a much simpler interface for modifying any group code. Next, you use the function Put-Group-Code-Value to modify the group 10 code of the line object.

After entering and loading the preceding function, you can test the function by typing the following in the Console window:

```
(Put-Group-Code-Value LineEntity 10 '(5.0 5.0 0.0))
```

This function changes the start point of the line to 5,5,0.

Using the same logic to write the get functions, you can now define a separate group 10 code modifier function. You can do the same for any group code.

```
(defun Put-Group-10-Code (EntityName Value)
   (Put-Group-Code-Value EntityName 10 Value)
)
```

After entering and loading this function, type the following in the Console window to change the start point of the line to 15,–5,0.

```
(Put-Group-10-Code LineEntity '(15.0 -5.0 0.0))
```

Activate AutoCAD to check that the line has been changed.

Using ActiveX with Visual LISP

ActiveX enables you to retrieve and modify objects similar to the method used in the previous section of this chapter, but it requires some preparation. The following section explains how you can use ActiveX functions to create, retrieve, and modify an object.

Retrieving and modifying object information with ActiveX

Visual LISP enables you to retrieve and modify most AutoCAD objects by using AutoCAD's ActiveX interface. That is to say, AutoCAD exposes most of its objects to ActiveX-enabled applications. This includes Visual LISP as ActiveX objects, which expose their properties, including put (modify) and get (retrieve) functions.

Using Visual LISP to communicate with AutoCAD is very straightforward. You must first load all the ActiveX functions, using the vl-load-com function within Visual LISP. You need to use the vl-load-com function only once each time that you open AutoCAD, because vl-load-com loads the ActiveX functions for the entire drawing session. (However, using vl-load-com more than once doesn't cause any harm.) To use the ActiveX interface, enter the following in the Visual LISP Console window:

```
(vl-load-com)
```

After the ActiveX interface is loaded, you can interrogate the line that you created previously, but first you need to convert the entity name into a vla-object. A vla-object is no different from an entity name, except that the ActiveX object exposes certain properties that its AutoLISP counterpart does not. To convert the entity name into a vla-object, you use the function vlax-ename->vla-object, as shown here:

```
(setq vla-line (vlax-ename->vla-object (entlast)))
```

Visual LISP returns the following (your object name will be different):

```
#<VLA-OBJECT IAcadLine2 03612b14>
```

As you can see by the return value of vlax-ename->vla-object, the value of the variable vla-line contains a vla-object. At this point, you can visually inspect the variable by selecting it and choosing View⇨Inspect from the Visual LISP editor. Although you see the line's property in a dialog box, you can also "dump" its properties and values to the Console window by using the vlax-dump-object Visual LISP function as follows:

```
(vlax-dump-object vla-line)
```

This causes Visual LISP to display the following:

```
; IAcadLine2: AutoCAD Line Interface
; Property values:
;   Angle (RO) = 1.5708
;   Application (RO) = #<VLA-OBJECT IAcadApplication 00af9594>
;   Delta (RO) = (0.0 10.0 0.0)
;   Document (RO) = #<VLA-OBJECT IAcadDocument 038be900>
;   EndPoint = (15.0 5.0 0.0)
;   EntityTransparency = "ByLayer"
;   Handle (RO) = "89"
;   HasExtensionDictionary (RO) = 0
;   Hyperlinks (RO) = #<VLA-OBJECT IAcadHyperlinks 01011d44>
;   Layer = "0"
;   Length (RO) = 10.0
;   Linetype = "ByLayer"
;   LinetypeScale = 1.0
;   Lineweight = -1
;   Material = "ByLayer"
;   Normal = (0.0 0.0 1.0)
;   ObjectID (RO) = 2130009736
;   ObjectName (RO) = "AcDbLine"
;   OwnerID (RO) = 2130009336
;   PlotStyleName = "ByLayer"
;   StartPoint = (15.0 -5.0 0.0)
;   Thickness = 0.0
;   TrueColor = #<VLA-OBJECT IAcadAcCmColor 01015170>
;   Visible = -1
T
```

Note

If you are using a 64-bit release of AutoCAD, the ObjectID and OwnerID properties are listed as ObjectID32 and OwnerID32. ∎

You'll probably have to resize the window to see all these properties. Notice the similarities between the named properties shown here, such as EndPoint and StartPoint, and the line's group codes that you retrieved by using AutoLISP. As you can see, one of the advantages of using an ActiveX-enabled object is that ActiveX exposes more information to the programmer than standard AutoLISP does. One of the benefits of using ActiveX is its interface. Previously, you queried and modified a line object's start point and endpoint by using the group 10 and 11 codes. Using ActiveX to query the start point and endpoint is very straightforward. However, ActiveX returns these points in a data type called a *variant* that you need to convert to the familiar coordinate format.

To get the start point of an object, use the vla-get-startpoint function. In the current example, the line has been set to `vla-line`, so you would type the following expression:

```
(setq Starting (vla-get-startpoint vla-line)) ↵
```

Visual LISP responds as follows:

```
#<variant 8197 ...>
```

To convert the start point from the variant data type to a useable coordinate format, you would type the following line:

```
(safearray-value (vlax-variant-value Starting))
```

Visual LISP responds with a coordinate:

```
(15.0 -5.0 0.0)
```

To modify the StartPoint property of a line to (0,0,0), you would use the following expression:

```
(vla-put-startpoint vla-line (vlax-3d-point '(0.0 0.0 0.0)))
```

You can return to AutoCAD to check out the line. To verify the new StartPoint, you can also use the vla-get-startpoint function:

```
(safearray-value (vlax-variant-value (vla-get-StartPoint vla-line)))
```

Visual LISP returns the start point of the line:

```
(0.0 0.0 0.0)
```

As you can see, this is very similar to the small routine that was developed in AutoLISP earlier in this chapter.

STEPS: Retrieving and Modifying Objects with ActiveX

1. To start a new drawing session, open AutoCAD. If AutoCAD is already open, close and re-open it.
2. Start a new drawing by using the `acad.dwt` template.
3. Draw any line. Neither the start point nor the endpoint should be 0,0,0.
4. Open the Visual LISP editor.
5. In the Console window, type (**vl-load-com**) ↵ to load the ActiveX functions.
6. To convert the entity name into a `vla-object`, type (**setq vla-line (vlax-ename->vla-object (entlast)))** ↵.
7. To view the line's properties, type (**vlax-dump-object vla-line**) ↵.
8. To get the start point of the line, type (**setq Starting (vla-get-startpoint vla-line)**) ↵.

9. To convert the start point from the variant data type to coordinate format, type **(safearray-value (vlax-variant-value Starting))** ↵.

10. To change the line's start point to 0,0,0, type **(vla-put-startpoint vla-line (vlax-3d-point '(0.0 0.0 0.0)))** ↵.

11. Choose Activate AutoCAD on the Visual LISP View toolbar to check out the line. Its start point is now 0,0,0.

Creating objects with ActiveX

This section looks at functions that create objects. When you work with ActiveX, you need to retrieve objects in their hierarchical order. The AutoCAD application is at the top of the object hierarchy, followed by the current drawing. The drawing is then broken up into objects that represent both graphical and non-graphical objects, such as model and paper space. Some of the common objects that you work with are:

- **Acad-object.** Represents the AutoCAD application.
- **ActiveDocument.** Represents the current drawing.
- **ModelSpace/PaperSpace.** Represents the type of space that you want to use within the current drawing.

In AutoLISP, you first retrieve the AutoCAD application, then your drawing, and finally the space (model or paper). Here you take the simple line command used earlier in this chapter and convert it by using ActiveX:

```
;;; This function creates a line using Visual LISP
;;; ActiveX and returns the line object as a vla-object.
(defun ax-make-aLine ()
  (vla-AddLine
    (vla-get-ModelSpace              ; retrieve the model
                                     ; space object
      (vla-get-ActiveDocument        ; get the current
                                     ; active document
        (vlax-get-acad-object)       ; get the acad object
      )
    )
    (vlax-3d-point '(5 5 0))         ; starting point
    (vlax-3d-point '(15 5 0))        ; ending point
  )
)
```

You can type this code in the Visual LISP editor and load it. To try it out, type the following in the Console window:

(ax-make-aLine)

Visual LISP responds with the following:

```
#<VLA-OBJECT IAcadLine2 03614934>
```

This might seem a little cumbersome — as if it might be a lot of work to create a line — but it's actually quite flexible.

To locate other ActiveX functions that create objects, you need to look in the AutoCAD ActiveX and VBA Reference. In Visual LISP, choose Help ⇨ Visual LISP Help Topics. From the Help Landing page, click

ActiveX and VBA Reference, and then click Methods. You immediately see an alphabetical list of the functions that begin with the letter *A* displayed. Here are all the ActiveX methods that add drawing objects. To use the ActiveX method with Visual LISP, add vla- before the method. For example, to add a circle, you would use vla-addcircle.

Tip
You immediately know whether the function is correct, because it turns from black to blue as you enter it. ∎

Debugging Code

Because few people can write perfect code on their first try, there's always a need to *debug* code. Debugging is simply the process of trying to locate and correct mistakes. This section looks at some simple examples, using some of the debugging tools that Visual LISP has to offer.

In the first example, you define a function that is guaranteed to fail. You can type this code in the Visual LISP editor and load it:

```
;;; The function below will produce an error
;;; because strcat concatenates strings.
(defun Error-Prone-Code ()
  (strcat "This will never print the number: " 1)
)
```

Before you continue, you need to choose Debug ⇨ Break On Error. When you select this menu option, Visual LISP enables you to jump to the error in your source code automatically.

Using the function `Error-Prone-Code` produces an error because `strcat` concatenates strings, as the following demonstrates. You can type this at the Console window:

```
(Error-Prone-Code) ↵
```

Visual LISP responds with the following:

```
; error: bad argument type: stringp 1
```

 After you receive the error, choose Last Break on the Visual LISP Debug toolbar. Visual LISP places you in the line of the code where the error occurred.

How can you find the source of the problem in a routine? To answer this question, you often need to perform some detective work. Visual LISP provides a wealth of debugging tools, which you can leverage when you encounter an unplanned "enhancement" or bug.

STEPS: Finding the Last Break

1. Start a new drawing using the `acad.dwt` template.
2. Start Visual LISP and start a new file.
3. In the Visual LISP editor, type the following:

```
;;; The function add-3-numbers will not produce
;;; an error if all its arguments are numbers.
(defun add-3-numbers (num1 num2 num3)
  (+ num1 num2 num3)
)
```

4. Choose Load Active Edit Window on the Visual LISP Tools toolbar.

5. In the Console window, type the following:

```
(add-3-numbers 1 2 3) ↵
```

Visual LISP returns 6.

6. However, if you substitute a string for one of its arguments, an error occurs. Type the following in the Console window:

```
(add-3-numbers 1 "a" 3) ↵
```

Visual LISP returns the following:

```
; error: bad argument type: numberp: nil
```

7. Choose Debug ⇨ Break on Error. Look again to confirm that Break on Error is checked.

8. Choose Last Break on the Visual LISP Debug toolbar. Visual LISP places you in the function add-3-numbers, with (+ num1 num2 num3) as the cause of the error.

To continue after turning on Break on Error, click Reset on the Debug toolbar.

Using the Error Trace window

Any time an error occurs, you can use the last break along with the Visual LISP Error Trace window. To display the Error Trace window, choose View ⇨ Error Trace to see an error list, as shown in Figure 36.1.

FIGURE 36.1

To help you debug your code, the Error Trace window displays every function call before the error, as well as where the error occurred.

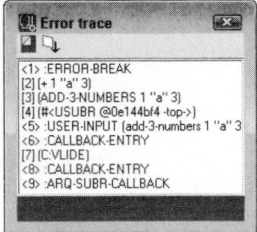

The item numbered <5> in Figure 36.1 is what you entered in the Console window. The item labeled [2] (+ 1 "a" 3) is where the error occurred, while <1> :ERROR-BREAK signaled the function's termination because of the error.

Visual LISP enables you to find the source *position* (the line of code that produced the error) and the *call source point* (the position in your code where the function was called) for the error. To find them, right-click the third item in the Error Trace window. From the shortcut menu, you can choose either Source Position or Call Source Point. Jumping to the position in your code where the function was called is extremely handy when debugging a large application.

Working with breakpoints

Sometimes when you choose Last Break to highlight an error, you find that a great deal of code is high-lighted, which is not very helpful for finding the error. This is where break points come in handy. *Break points* are locations in your code, specified by you, that signal Visual LISP to stop and wait until you're ready to continue processing the code. Visual LISP executes your code and stops at each break point to wait for your instructions. Break points enable you to break down your code into smaller pieces and watch what's going on piece by piece so that you can more easily find the error.

To place a break point, position your cursor to the left of an opening parenthesis or to the right of a closing parenthesis, and press F9. Visual LISP places a temporary red mark in your code.

After creating your break points, you need to reload your code to tell Visual LISP about your break points. Then try to execute the function again. Notice that the Debug toolbar buttons become available. Visual LISP executes your code up to the first break point.

You can use the Debug toolbar to help find your error. The first three buttons offer three different ways to move through your code:

 • **Step Into.** Use this button to "step in" one expression from the innermost nested expression (from opening to closing parentheses) to the outermost, one at a time.

 • **Step Over.** Use this button to ignore the nested expressions; that is, step over the highlighted expression.

 • **Step Out.** Use this button to move to the end of the function. You can ignore the entire function that is being debugged.

To remove break points, choose View ⇨ Breakpoints Window. The Breakpoints dialog box opens, as shown in Figure 36.2.

FIGURE 36.2

Use the Breakpoints dialog box to remove, show, or disable break points.

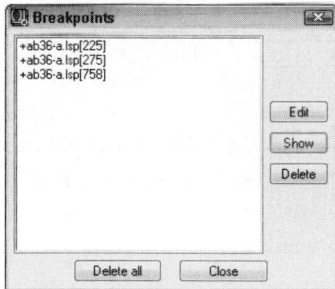

In the Breakpoints dialog box, you can do the following:

• Delete all break points by clicking Delete all.
• Delete individual break points by choosing a break point and clicking Delete.

- Jump to a break point by choosing a break point and clicking Show. Visual LISP places a blinking cursor at the break point.
- Edit a break point by choosing a break point and clicking Edit. Visual LISP then lets you disable, delete, or show the break point.

On the DVD

The file used in the following exercise on working with break points, ab36-a.lsp, is in the Drawings folder on the DVD. ■

STEPS: Working with Break Points

1. Open AutoCAD and start a new drawing using any template.
2. Start the Visual LISP editor. Open ab36-a.lsp from the DVD. Choose File ⇨ Save As and save it as ab36-01.lsp in the AutoCAD 2011\Support folder or in another folder that you've added to the support-file search path.
3. Choose Load Active Edit Window from the Visual LISP Tools toolbar.
4. Read through the code. This routine creates a vertical list of numbers. The foreach function steps through each item in a list. The comments explain why it contains a bug.
5. If you didn't do the previous exercise, choose Debug ⇨ Break on Error. (Don't do anything if the Break on Error item is already checked.)
6. Type the following in the Console window:

   ```
   (list-beautify-with-bug '(1 2 3 4 5)) ↵
   ```

   The Console returns the following:

   ```
   (1
   ; error: bad argument type: FILE 1
   ```

7. Choose Last Break on the Visual LISP Debug toolbar to jump to the error in the source code.
8. To place a break point in the code, place the cursor after (princ (chr 40)). Press F9. Visual LISP marks the break with a red box.
9. Place another break point after (princ (car aList)). Finally, place a third break point after the closing parenthesis on the line that follows (princ item 1). Your code should look like Figure 36.3.

10. After the code produces an error, you need to reset. Click Reset on the Visual LISP Debug toolbar.
11. Click the Visual LISP editor and reload the function into Visual LISP. (Choose Load Active Edit Window on the Visual LISP Tools toolbar.)
12. Type the same expression that produced the error in the Console window:

    ```
    (list-beautify-with-bug '(1 2 3 4 5)) ↵
    ```

13. Visual LISP highlights the expression (princ (chr 40)). Choose Step Into on the Debug toolbar. Visual LISP highlights (princ (car aList)).
14. Choose Step Into. Now only (car aList) is highlighted.
15. Choose Step Into until you reach the error, (princ item 1).
16. Edit (princ item 1) so that it reads (princ item).
17. Click Reset again.

FIGURE 36.3

Your code should look like this after you place three break points.

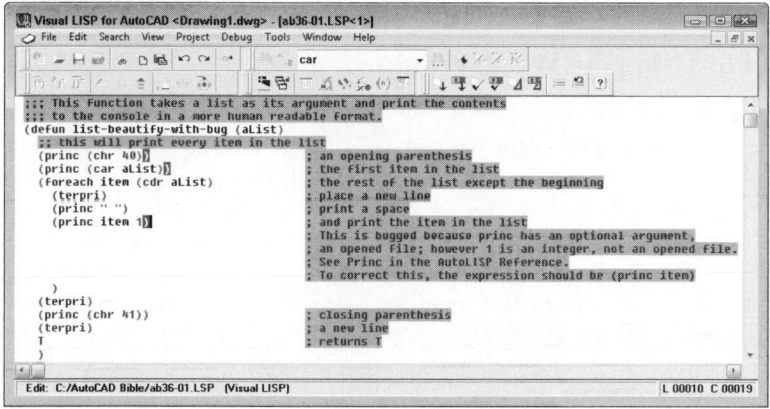

18. Choose Debug ⇨ Clear All Breakpoints. Click Yes to confirm.

19. Activate the Editor window and reload the function.

20. In the Console window, type (**list-beautify-with-bug** '(1 2 3 4 5)) ↵.

21. Activate the Editor window and save the file.

On the DVD

If you have difficulty fixing this bug, you can find the "repaired" version in the Results **folder on the DVD, with the filename** list-beautify-without-bug.lsp. ∎

Using the Watch window

The Watch window enables you to examine expressions and variable values as they're being evaluated. To watch a variable, select it in the code and choose Debug ⇨ Add Watch, or press Ctrl+W. Visual LISP opens the Watch window listing the expression or variable and displaying its value after an equal sign. If you select an expression or nothing is selected and you press Ctrl+W, the Add Watch dialog box opens. If it is not already displayed, enter the expression that you want to watch and click OK. For example, if you add a watch for (princ (chr 40)), the Watch window displays (PRINC (CHR 40)) = "(" because (princ (chr 40)) is another way of telling AutoLISP to print a left parenthesis. After the Watch window is open, you can add expressions or variables by selecting them and choosing Add Watch on the Watch window toolbar.

If you have a routine with arguments, you can execute the function with various arguments and see the results on your watched expressions and variables in the Watch window.

Furthermore, you can add any expression to the Watch window and alter the contents of any variable while debugging a function.

On the DVD

The file used in the following exercise on using the Watch window, `ab36-01.lsp`, is in the `Results` folder on the DVD. ■

STEPS: Using the Watch Window

1. Open AutoCAD and start a new drawing using the `acad.dwt` template.

2. Start the Visual LISP editor. Open `ab36-01.lsp` from the `Results` folder of the DVD. If you did the previous exercise, you can open it from your `AutoCAD Bible` folder.

3. Select the expression `(princ (chr 40))`. Choose Debug➪Add Watch. Click OK in the Add Watch dialog box. Visual LISP opens the Watch window and displays the expression, as well as its value.

4. To add a variable to the Watch window, select `item` to the right of the foreach function and choose Add Watch in the Watch window. The Watch window should look like Figure 36.4.

FIGURE 36.4

The Watch window shows an expression and a variable, and displays their values.

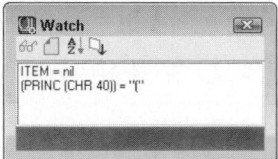

5. Add a break point after `(princ item)` by placing the cursor there and pressing F9.

6. Choose Load Active Edit Window from the Visual LISP Tools toolbar.

7. To examine the Watch window display as the function `list-beautify-with-bug` is evaluated, type the following in the Console window:

   `(list-beautify-with-bug '(1 2 3 4 5))` ↵

8. The `(princ item)` expression should be highlighted. Choose Step Into on the Visual LISP Debug toolbar. The `item` variable in the Watch window should now display its current value. Continue to click Step Into, watching the value of `item` increase in the Watch window each time you step through the cycle.

9. In the Console window, type **aList** ↵ after the last prompt. This is a variable argument that is used in the function `list-beautify-with-bug`. The Console returns:

   `(1 2 3 4 5)`

   As you can see, you can interrogate any variable while debugging the function.

10. To add a new expression to the Watch window, select the variable `aList` and press Ctrl+W.

11. To change the value of `aList`, return to the Console window and type the following:

    `(setq aList (list 6 7 8 9 10))` ↵

The Console responds as follows:

```
(6 7 8 9 10)
```

Notice the change in the Watch window.

12. To remove the break point, choose View ⇨ Breakpoints Window to open the Breakpoints dialog box. Click Delete All to delete the break point. Visual LISP automatically closes the dialog box.

13. Click Reset on the Visual LISP Debug toolbar.

14. Close the Watch window and the Visual LISP editor without saving the file.

As you can see, Visual LISP is not just an editor; it's a full-featured, integrated development environment for AutoLISP.

Summary

In this chapter, you examined some of the advanced features of AutoLISP and Visual LISP. You read about:

- Global and local variables
- Some of the features of ActiveX
- How to use some of Visual LISP's debugging features, including the Error Trace window, break points, and the Watch window

In the next chapter, you read about the basics of Microsoft Visual Basic (or VB.NET), another programming language that you can use with AutoCAD.

Part VIII

Appendixes

The three appendixes in Part VIII provide important additional information. Although these appendixes are especially useful when you first start to use AutoCAD 2011 or AutoCAD LT 2011, they offer a great deal of information for ongoing use as well.

Appendix A runs you through the process of installing and configuring AutoCAD and AutoCAD LT to suit your personal needs. Many new features appear in the Options dialog box that I cover here. I also explain the importance of workspaces here.

Appendix B lists numerous additional resources, where you can find information on AutoCAD and AutoCAD LT, including discussion groups, Web sites, and blogs. Appendix C explains what is on the DVD and how to use the files there.

Installing and Configuring AutoCAD and AutoCAD LT

Installing AutoCAD and AutoCAD LT, once something to avoid as long as possible, is now a breeze. For all practical purposes, all that you need to do is to put the DVD into your DVD drive and follow the instructions. Nevertheless, I provide some helpful tips and comments in this appendix. As with all software that comes with an installation program, you should close all other applications before starting, including antivirus software.

In this appendix, I also cover many ways to configure AutoCAD and AutoCAD LT so that these programs function best for your circumstances.

Installing AutoCAD and AutoCAD LT

The installation process involves some preparation, the actual installation, and finally authorization.

Preparing to install

Before you install, make sure that your system meets the minimum, and preferably the recommended, requirements:

- **Operating system.** Windows XP (Home or Professional) with Service Pack 2; Windows Vista (Enterprise, Business, Ultimate, or Home Premium) with Service Pack 1; Windows 7 (Enterprise, Business, Ultimate, or Home Premium).

  AutoCAD and AutoCAD LT are also offered as 64-bit versions that are available for Windows XP Professional x64 Edition with Service Pack 2, Windows Vista 64-bit with Service Pack 1, and Windows 7 64-bit.

- **Processor speed (32-bit).** Intel Pentium 4 or AMD Athlon Dual Core, 1.6 GHz or higher with SSE2 for Windows XP or 3.0 GHz for Windows Vista and Windows 7, but I would recommend 2.0 GHz as a minimum for 2D. For 3D work, 3.0 GHz or higher is recommended.

- **Processor speed (64-bit).** AMD Athlon 64 or Opteron with SSE2, Intel Pentium 4, or Xeon with Intel EM64T support and SSE2.
- **RAM (memory).** 2GB for 2D work and 2GB or more for 3D work; however, 512MB is acceptable for AutoCAD LT running on Windows XP, or 1GB if you are running Windows Vista.
- **Video.** 1024 × 768 VGA or higher with true color. For 3D work in AutoCAD, you should use a screen resolution of 1280 × 1024 with 32-bit color, and at least 128MB of RAM on a Direct3D capable, workstation-class graphics card. Autodesk certifies specific graphics cards for use with AutoCAD's 3D features. To see which cards are certified, use the 3DCONFIG command (AutoCAD only). In the Adaptive Degradation and Performance Tuning dialog box, click the Check for Updates button to go to a Web page on Autodesk's Web site that lists graphics cards and their test results.

  Using the 3DCONFIG command, you can specify either hardware or software acceleration.

Note

If your graphics card is not certified, your computer won't explode, but it could crash when using some effects, display artifacts (extra visual effects), or fail to display some features, such as materials and lights. ∎

- **Hard drive.** 1 to 2GB free for installation depending on whether you are installing AutoCAD or AutoCAD LT on a Windows 32- or 64-bit operating system; for permanent storage, about 1GB for 2D features on a 32-bit release of Windows or 1.5GB on a 64-bit release of Windows; 2GB for 3D features, and 550MB for AutoCAD LT.
- **Pointing device.** Mouse, trackball, digitizer puck, or other device.
- **3D mouse.** As a secondary input device to a pointing device, you can use a 3Dconnexion device to navigate 2D and 3D drawings (in AutoCAD only).
- **DVD drive.** Any speed (for installation only).
- **Browser.** Internet Explorer 7.0 or later minimum; in most cases, you can use other browsers as well. Internet Explorer is recommended for Web-based Help.
- **Optional equipment.** A printer or plotter; a digitizing tablet; a network interface card if you're using the network version of AutoCAD, or Internet-enabled features of AutoCAD or AutoCAD LT.

In order to install AutoCAD or AutoCAD LT, you may need administrator permission to write to the folder where you're installing AutoCAD, the system registry, and the Windows System folder.

Note

AutoCAD 2011 and AutoCAD LT 2011 can coexist with earlier releases of both programs. When you install, the Migrate Custom Settings feature detects if you have an earlier release on your computer and guides you through the process of migrating custom features. Nevertheless, if you have customized files that you want to keep, it's always good to back them up before installation. To read the installation documentation before starting to install, insert the AutoCAD 2011 or AutoCAD LT 2011 DVD into the DVD drive and click Read the Documentation. The Home page for Help is displayed. You can also read the ReadMe file at the end of installation. ∎

Starting installation

You're now ready to install AutoCAD 2011 or AutoCAD LT 2011. Here are the steps:

1. Place the DVD in your DVD drive. In most cases, the setup procedure starts automatically. If it does not, choose Start ➪ Run. In the text box, type **d:\setup** ↵ where **d** is your DVD drive. (In Windows Vista or Windows 7, choose Start and type in the Start Search text box.)

2. When the Welcome screen appears, click the type of installation that you want:
   - **Install Products.** One seat (location) standard installation.
   - **Create Deployments.** Set configurations to distribute to client workstations.
   - **Install Tools and Utilities.** Administrative, reporting, and network licensing tools (AutoCAD only). The CAD Manager Tools are also here (and included in AutoCAD LT as well). See the section later in this chapter on the tools and utilities.

3. The Install screen provides links to all the installation tasks and information that you need, as shown in Figure A.1. In these steps, I clicked Install Products (for a stand-alone installation).

Note
Some plotter manufacturers, such as Hewlett-Packard, offer a special driver that optimizes the plotter for use with AutoCAD. Check the manufacturer's Web site for the latest driver. ■

FIGURE A.1
The initial screen of the Installation Wizard.

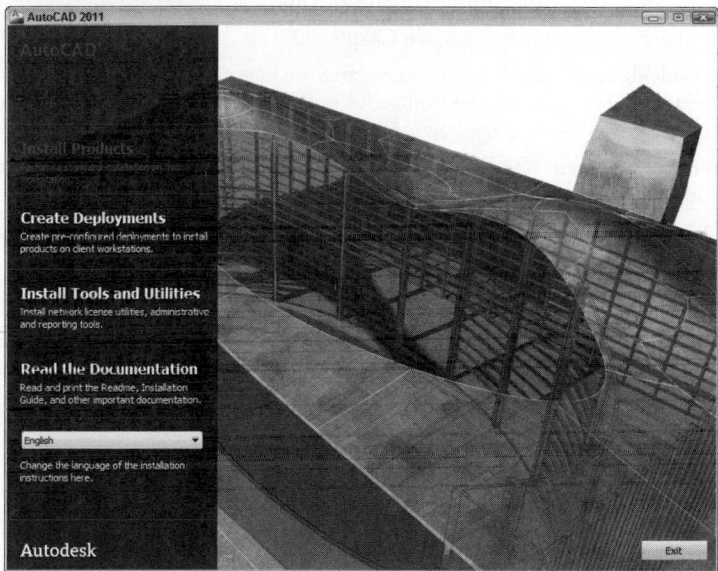

4. On the next screen, select the products you want to install. The choices are AutoCAD 2011 or AutoCAD LT 2011, Autodesk Design Review 2011, and Autodesk Material Library 2011 Medium Image Library (AutoCAD only). If your product offers more than one language option, choose the language option you want to use. Click Next.

5. Read the software license agreement. Click the Print button if you want to print the agreement. Click "I Accept" and then click Next.

6. On the User and Product Information screen, enter your name and organization along with the serial number and product key. In AutoCAD only, this information is permanent and you can't change it without uninstalling AutoCAD. In AutoCAD LT, you can change this information on the

System tab of the Options dialog box (OPTIONS command). If you do not have a serial number and product key, select "I want to try this Product for 30 Days". Click Next.

7. On the Begin Installation screen, you review the installation settings. To use these default values, click Install and wait while the software installs. To change them, select the product you want to change from the Select the Product to Configure drop-down list and click the Configure button.

8. If you choose to configure, on the Select the License Type screen, select a license type: stand-alone or network license. Click Next. On the Select the Installation Type screen, select the installation type: typical or custom. You can also choose to install the Express Tools (highly recommended) if you are installing AutoCAD. In addition, you can choose to create a desktop shortcut and specify the install location for AutoCAD or AutoCAD LT. If you choose a custom installation, you can choose which of the following items you want by checking or unchecking their check box. Then click Next.

- **CAD Standards.** For more information, see Chapter 26 (AutoCAD only).
- **Database.** External database connectivity. For more information, see Chapter 20 (AutoCAD only).
- **Dictionaries.** For more information, see Chapter 13.
- **Drawing encryption.** Password protection. For more information, see Chapter 26 (AutoCAD only).
- **Express Tools.** Supplemental commands (AutoCAD only).
- **Fonts.** For more information, see Chapter 13.
- **Autodesk Seek.** Allows you to access and use content from Autodesk Seek in your drawings. Autodesk Seek is an online resource for building product information, including 3D models, 2D drawings, visual images, and product specification data.
- **Welcome Screen.** A utility that you see at startup, providing access to learning videos and resources.
- **License Transfer Utility.** Tools to transfer a stand-alone license among computers.
- **Migrate Custom Settings.** A utility to help you keep your custom settings when you upgrade.
- **Initial Setup.** A utility which allows you to do some very basic customization of the program before you start it the first time.
- **Reference Manager.** Manages external files connected to a drawing. For more information, see Chapter 27 (AutoCAD only).
- **Samples.** Sample drawings that you can use for your reference.
- **Tutorials.** Mostly programming tutorials (AutoCAD only).

You can go back later and add items if you decide that you need an item that you didn't initially install. When you're done, click Next. On the Include Service Pack screen, specify any service packs from Autodesk.com or a local/network drive that you might want to install with the product. Click Next. On the Configuration Complete screen, click Configuration Complete. You return to the Begin Installation pane. Click Install. This takes a few minutes. You can take a break or watch the status bar that appears during the process.

9. You're now done, and you have an opportunity to read the README file — always a good idea — by checking the appropriate check box. Click Finish. The README file opens if you have asked for it. (If you want to read it later, in AutoCAD or AutoCAD LT, click the Help button located to the right of InfoCenter. Then choose Readme from the Home page.)

Note

You may see a dialog box asking you to restart your computer. Because you shouldn't have any other applications open, you can do so immediately. ■

Don't forget to reenable your antivirus software.

You're done! You can now choose Start ➪ (All) Programs ➪ Autodesk ➪ AutoCAD 2011 or AutoCAD LT 2011 to see the submenu. The submenu includes some or all of the following items:

- **Attach Digital Signatures.** A security feature for attaching a digital signature to a drawing (see Chapter 26).

- **AutoCAD 2011 or AutoCAD LT 2011.** Starts AutoCAD or AutoCAD LT.

- **Batch Standards Checker.** Checks CAD standards for a group of drawings (see Chapter 26; AutoCAD only).

- **License Transfer Utility.** Helps you move a license from one computer to another.

- **Reference Manager.** Manages and reports on xrefs, images, and other files associated with a drawing (see Chapter 26; AutoCAD only).

- **Migrate Custom Settings.** Contains the Migrate From a Previous Release item that launches the Migrate Custom Settings dialog box to help you keep your custom settings from a previous release as you upgrade. This stand-alone application usually runs automatically when you start the program the first time. From the sub-menu, you can also select items that allow you to import and export custom settings between different computers running the same release. You can export settings and files for use on another computer. You can then import those settings to the destination computer.

Installing the VBA enabler

AutoCAD 2011 does not come with the VBA feature installed; you need to download it and install it separately. This is part of a long-term plan to transition to .NET and VSTA (Visual Studio Tools for Applications), Microsoft technologies that software companies can incorporate into their products for programming customization. Microsoft has stopped supporting VBA for third-party developers and has not made it available for 64-bit computers; hence the transition plan.

You can download a VBA enabler for free from Autodesk at www.autodesk.com/vba-download. Installing this enabler allows VBA code to function as before.

Note

You may see a dialog box asking you to restart your computer. Because you shouldn't have any other applications open, you can do so immediately. ∎

Installing network licenses and CAD Manager tools

If you have multiple licenses, you may want to use the network license utilities. Network licenses allow you to more flexibly manage multiple sets of AutoCAD. At the first screen of the Installation Wizard, choose Install Tools and Utilities. Here you can install the Autodesk Network License Manager and Autodesk Asset Locator. There's also a reporting utility, SAMreport-Lite, for tracking network license usage.

The Autodesk CAD Manager Tools feature allows CAD Managers to control certain general features of AutoCAD and AutoCAD LT, including which content is available in the Communication Center and if DesignCenter Online is accessible from the DesignCenter palette. This feature is therefore essential for stand-alone installations as well.

Check the items that you want to install and click Next. Then follow the instructions, which vary according to your choices. For information about network licensing, click the Documentation link on the installation screen and open the Network Licensing Guide. There are also guides for stand-alone installations.

Changing an installation

After you install AutoCAD or AutoCAD LT, you can add features by using the following procedure:

1. Choose Start ➪ Settings ➪ Control Panel (or Start ➪ Control Panel) and double-click Add/Remove Programs or Programs and Features (depending on your version of Windows). If you're not using the Classic view, you need to choose Add or Remove Programs, and then Programs and Features (depending on your version of Windows).

2. In the dialog box, choose AutoCAD 2011 or AutoCAD LT 2011 and then click Change, Change/Remove, or Uninstall/Change (depending on your version of Windows).

3. The software Setup Initialization feature starts. Click Add or Remove Features.

4. In the dialog box, check a feature, or uncheck an existing feature. Click Next.

5. Click Next again. The software is updated.

6. Click Finish.

You may be prompted to restart your computer.

Authorizing AutoCAD and AutoCAD LT

As with earlier releases, for security purposes, Autodesk requires that you activate AutoCAD and AutoCAD LT. (Certain customers, such as subscription customers, are exempt from the activation process.) When you first open AutoCAD or AutoCAD LT, the Activation dialog box opens. Click Activate to authorize the program or click Try to start using the program without activating it. If you click Activate, you will first enter your serial number. You receive this number with your product or subscription. Then enter your product key, which also comes with your product or subscription. Click Next. If you are registering online (the default option), the Registration – Activation Confirmation page should be displayed. Click Finish. If you are not registering online, click Next. Choose Request an Activation Code Using an Offline Method and click Next. Follow the instructions on screen. Click Close when done. You can use the product for 30 days while waiting for the activation code. When you get it, choose the I have an Activation Code from Autodesk option and either paste it from the Clipboard or type it in.

AutoCAD or AutoCAD LT is now ready to use. By default, your system is configured to use the current system pointing device and the current system printing device. You can further configure AutoCAD and AutoCAD LT by using the Options dialog box and Initial Setup. The Options dialog box and Initial Setup are covered later in this appendix.

Note

The Express Tools menu, toolbars, ribbon tab, and ribbon panels are automatically included when you choose to install Express Tools. Express Tools includes three toolbars, a menu, and a ribbon tab with several panels. To display the menu and toolbars, select AutoCAD Classic from the Workspace drop-down list on the Quick Access toolbar, and right-click in any toolbar area that doesn't contain a toolbar. Choose Express and then choose a toolbar from the sub-menu. The ribbon tab and its panels are part of the default workspace, so you see them automatically. This applies to AutoCAD only.

If your Express Tools don't appear, you may need to activate them. Enter expresstools ↵ on the command line. If the Express menu doesn't appear, enter expressmenu ↵. ■

When you first open AutoCAD or AutoCAD LT, if you have an earlier release of AutoCAD or AutoCAD LT on your system, the Migrate Custom Settings dialog box opens. This gives you a chance to keep many of your custom settings. Choose the options that you want to keep.

Also when you start AutoCAD or AutoCAD LT for the first time, the Welcome Screen appears. From the Welcome Screen, you can view videos that demonstrate how to use some of the core features that are used for 2D drafting and 3D modeling (AutoCAD only). The Welcome Screen also contains links to the New Features Workshop, Learning Path resources page, additional videos and tutorials, and online Help. If you choose to not show the Welcome Screen at startup, you can always access it by clicking the drop-down arrow of the Help button to the right of InfoCenter and choosing Welcome Screen. Both the Welcome Screen and New Features Workshop display short videos that demonstrate the basics of using the program and which new features are now available.

Configuring and Using Workspaces

A *workspace* is a configuration of toolbars, menus, ribbon tabs, and palettes. You can create workspaces so that you can quickly switch from one configuration to another. For example, when you are creating, organizing, and saving blocks, you might want the DesignCenter and Tool Palettes window displayed.

AutoCAD comes with four workspaces: AutoCAD Classic, 2D Drafting & Annotation, 3D Basics, and 3D Modeling. AutoCAD LT comes with two workspaces, 2D Drafting & Annotation and AutoCAD LT Classic. For both programs, 2D Drafting & Annotation is the default workspace and it displays the ribbon. In many cases, you will want to change these workspaces to suit your drawing needs.

Creating and modifying a workspace

The easiest way to create a workspace is to start with the workspace closest to the one that you want to use, display toolbars, menus, ribbon tabs, and palettes the way you want them, and then choose Save Current As from the Workspace drop-down list on the Quick Access toolbar, as shown in Figure A.2. In the Save Workspace dialog box, name the workspace and then click Save. You can use this same method to modify an existing workspace. Make the changes and choose the current workspace in the Name drop-down list of the Save Workspace dialog box. Click Save, and then click Replace when asked whether you want to replace the workspace.

FIGURE A.2

The Workspace drop-down list makes changing and saving workspaces easy.

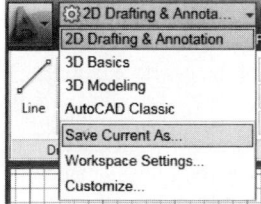

If you want to make sure that you don't forget anything, you can use the Customize User Interface Editor. This method lets you pick and choose from the complete list of Quick Access toolbars, menus, legacy toolbars, ribbon tabs, and palettes. Follow these steps:

1. Type **cui** ↵ to open the Customize User Interface Editor.

2. In the Customizations in All Files pane, double-click the Workspaces item to expand it.

3. To create a new workspace, right-click the Workspaces item and choose New Workspace. Then choose the new workspace to specify its settings. To edit an existing workspace, choose that workspace. The Workspace Contents pane appears to the right.

Tip
You can create a new workspace based on an existing workspace by right-clicking the workspace you want to duplicate under the Workspaces node, and choosing Duplicate. ■

4. In the Workspace Contents pane, click the Customize Workspace button. All the Quick Access toolbars, ribbon tabs, toolbars, and menus in the Customizations In pane now have check boxes next to them.

5. To add (display) or remove (hide) the Quick Access toolbar, ribbon tabs, toolbars, and menus, expand those items. Check or clear check boxes to specify the Quick Access toolbar, ribbon tabs, toolbars, and menus that you want to display or hide for that workspace. Don't forget to expand the Partial Customization Files item so that you can specify the Quick Access toolbar, ribbon tabs, toolbars, and menus for those files as well. As you add or remove items, they appear or disappear from the list in the Workspace Contents pane.

6. To specify the details of how each item should appear, click the item to show its properties in the Properties pane, where you can edit such properties as the location of a toolbar, its orientation (floating or docked), and its X and Y position. You can't edit menu properties.

7. To specify palette settings, which don't appear in the Customizations in All Files pane, double-click the Palettes item in the Workspace Contents pane. Choose any palette to edit its properties in the Properties pane.

8. To save your changes, click the Customize Workspace button at the top of the Workspace Contents pane.

9. Click OK to close the Customize User Interface Editor.

Switching between workspaces

To switch between workspaces, click the Workspace drop-down list on the left side of the Quick Access toolbar, and choose one of the workspaces.

If you make changes to the interface display, such as displaying a toolbar, this change does not automatically become part of the workspace. However, AutoCAD remembers the last state of the interface, and if you close and re-open AutoCAD, that toolbar is displayed.

You can specify that you want to save changes that you make to the interface display to the workspace. Select Workspace Settings from the Workspace drop-down list to open the Workspace Settings dialog box. Choose the Automatically Save Workspace Changes option and click OK. If you want to choose which changes are saved, keep the default Do Not Save Changes to Workspace option, and manually modify the current workspace, replacing the current one, as explained in the previous section. You can also use the Workspace Settings dialog box to organize the list of workspaces by changing their order in the list and adding separators to group certain workspaces together. Use the My Workspace drop-down list in the dialog box to assign a workspace to the My Workspace button on the Workspaces toolbar. You can control

AutoCAD's settings (but not AutoCAD LT's) with profiles, which are different from workspaces. I discuss profiles later in this appendix.

Using Initial Setup

Initial Setup, shown in Figure A.3, allows you to perform basic customization of AutoCAD or AutoCAD LT. You can specify which industry best describes the type of drawings you work on, configure the user interface by choosing which task-based tools you want to use, and choose the default drawing template you want when creating a new drawing. You can start Initial Setup by choosing Application Button ⇨ Options. In the Options dialog box, click the User Preferences tab, and then click the Initial Setup button.

On the initial page, choose the industry that best describes your work. The industry you choose helps to identify Web content that is relevant to you on Autodesk's Web site, determine which tool palette group to display in the Tool Palette Window, and specify the default drawing template when creating a new drawing. Click Next.

Initial Setup allows you to do some basic customization of AutoCAD or AutoCAD LT.

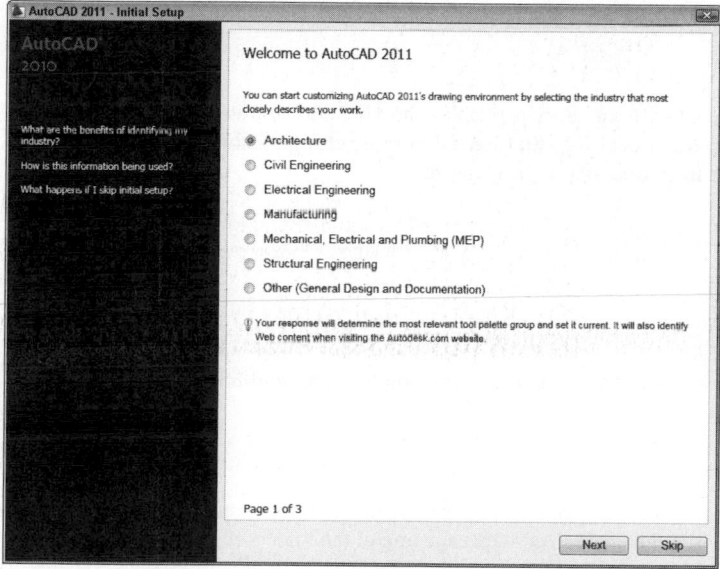

On the Optimize Your Default Workspace page (AutoCAD only), check which task-based tools you would like to add to your default workspace. You can choose from 3D modeling, rendering, review and mark up, and sheet set tools. Click Next. On the Specify a Drawing Template File page, choose the default drawing template you want to use when creating a new drawing. AutoCAD assigns the template you select to the QNEW command. You can also set this by going to the Options dialog box, clicking the Files tab, expanding the QNEW node, and using the Default Template File Name item. Click Finish to close Initial Setup.

When you complete Initial Setup, you have a new current workspace named Initial Setup Workspace. If you are using AutoCAD, you also have a new user profile named Initial Setup Profile to store the changes made with Initial Setup.

Configuring AutoCAD and AutoCAD LT

AutoCAD and AutoCAD LT have many options and settings that you can modify to suit your particular needs. Because you usually configure the software once when you first install, and only go back to these settings occasionally, it is easy to forget them. Knowing the available options is worthwhile; sometimes these options can make your life so much easier.

Customizing the status bar

You can customize what appears in the status bar of the application window. For example, if you never use lineweights, you can remove the Show/Hide Lineweight button on the status bar.

To customize the status bar, click the down arrow at the right end of the status bar or right-click in an empty area on the status bar to display the status bar menu. Click any item to hide the item if it's checked or to display the item if it isn't checked. For each additional item, you need to click the down arrow or right-click again to re-open the menu.

Configuring options

You configure many features of the application by using the Options dialog box. Choose Apply to configure a setting and keep the dialog box open. Choose OK to configure a setting and close the dialog box.

Note

In the Options dialog box, items that are saved with the drawing display the blue and yellow drawing icon next to them. These settings change when you open other drawings that have different settings. Other settings are saved in the Windows Registry and do not change from drawing to drawing. ■

Take the time to browse through all the tabs in the Options dialog box so that you know what is available. You change many of these settings only rarely after the initial run-through. Choose Application Button ⇨ Options to open the Options dialog box.

Tip

A quick way to access the Options dialog box is to right-click in the drawing or command-line area with no objects selected, and choose Options. ■

The Files tab

The Files tab lets you configure search paths, as well as specify filenames and locations. You'll probably most often use the Support File Search Path, which contains a listing of the folders that AutoCAD uses to search for customization files, fonts, linetypes, and hatch patterns. Rather than add your customized linetypes, hatches, and so on to an existing support folder, you can create a folder especially for these files and add the folder to the Support File Search Path.

The default location for support files is the first listing under the Support File Search Path item. This location may vary, depending on your operating system. However, you can also use Program Files\
Autodesk\AutoCAD 2011\Support or Program Files\Autodesk\AutoCAD LT 2011\Support,
which is listed as one of the support locations.

As you position the cursor over an item in the main listing of the dialog box, you see an explanation in a tooltip for that item. To edit the item, double-click the item or click the plus sign to the left of the item. You can then click a subitem and remove it, or click Add to add a subitem. Click Browse to find a folder or file rather than type it. Some other commonly used settings on the File tab are:

- **Project Files Search Path.** The search path for xrefs (AutoCAD only).
- **Automatic Save File Location.** Where the software automatically saves files if you don't.
- **Template Settings.** Default locations for various templates. You can set the default template for the QNEW command here. When you do so, clicking the New button on the Quick Access toolbar automatically opens a new drawing with this template.

New Feature

The Help Location node under Help and Miscellaneous File Names specifies the location of the Home page for the locally installed HTML-based Help system. ■

The Display tab

The Display tab, shown in Figure A.4, contains settings related to the display that you see on your screen.

FIGURE A.4

The Display tab of the Options dialog box.

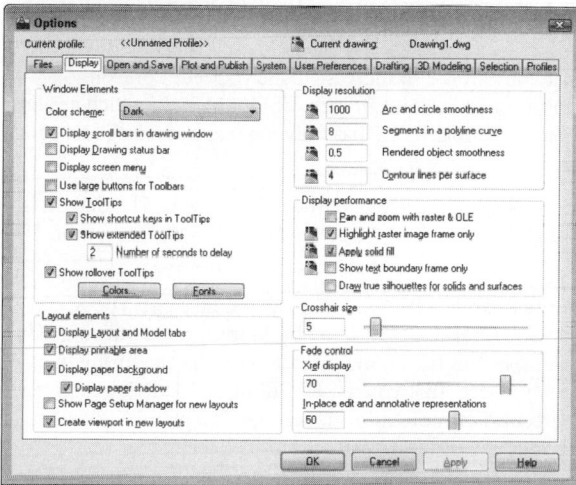

The Window Elements section determines whether you see scroll bars, the screen menu, large toolbar buttons, tooltips, and rollover tooltips. (The screen menu is not available in AutoCAD LT.) You can also set the colors and fonts for the various screen elements. For example, by clicking Colors, you can change the background color of the Model and layout tabs.

Note

AutoCAD 2011 contains separate background settings for 3D environments, with separate settings for parallel and perspective projections. ■

The Layout Elements section controls the display settings for paper space layouts. Most are checked by default. You can set the following items:

- The Display Layout and Model Tabs option determines if you see the tabs at the bottom of the drawing area. If you uncheck this box, you see the Model and Layout buttons on the status bar.

You can switch between these settings without using the Options dialog box by right-clicking the tabs or buttons.

- Uncheck the Display Printable Area option to hide the dashed line that you usually see around a layout. The dashed line represents the margin of the paper and, therefore, shows you the printable area.

- Uncheck the Display Paper Background option to avoid seeing the edge of the paper and the gray background. This setting makes a layout tab look very much like the model tab. If this item is checked, you can uncheck the Display Paper Shadow item to get rid of the shadow effect that makes the paper look like it's slightly above the surface of the gray background.

- Check the Show Page Setup Manager for New Layouts option to display the Page Setup Manager when you click a new layout tab. (See Chapter 17 for information on the Page Setup Manager.) This item is unchecked by default.

- Uncheck the Create Viewport in New Layouts option to display layouts with no viewport. This setting is useful if you always want to set up your own viewport configurations.

The Display Resolution section sets arc and circle smoothness (also accessible by using the VIEWRES command), the number of segments in a polyline curve (the SPLINESEGS system variable), rendered object smoothness (the FACETRES system variable), and contour lines per surface (the ISOLINES system variable). The last two items are not available in AutoCAD LT, because they apply to 3D objects.

The Display Performance section offers settings that you can use to increase display speed. For example, several settings affect the way AutoCAD displays raster images. You can turn off FILLMODE, which applies solid fill in wide polylines, donuts, and hatched objects. AutoCAD LT has only the text boundary and solid fill items.

The Crosshair Size section sets the size of the crosshairs as a percentage of the entire screen. The default is 5. You can type a new number in the text box or drag the slider bar. To create crosshairs that cover the entire screen, use a setting of 100.

The Fade Control section controls the fading intensity of xrefs when you display or edit them. The Xref Display setting controls how much an attached drawing (xref) fades into the background of a drawing. The In-place Edit and Annotative Representations setting specifies the fading intensity for objects during in-place reference editing. This setting affects how much objects that you are *not* editing are faded, compared to objects that you *are* editing. The default is 50 percent. For more information, see Chapter 19. This last setting applies to both AutoCAD and AutoCAD LT, but in AutoCAD LT, you can only change it via the XFADECTL system variable.

The Open and Save tab

The Open and Save tab, shown in Figure A.5, contains settings related to opening the program and files, as well as saving drawings.

The File Save section specifies the default drawing type and whether or not a thumbnail preview image is saved. You can see this preview when you want to open a new drawing and set the view to Preview. You can separately specify thumbnails for sheet sets.

You can control whether the drawings you create support large objects. If large-object compatibility is not enabled, then AutoCAD 2011 allows you to create large 3D objects and drawings that can't be saved to a previous release. If you work with users that use a release prior to AutoCAD 2010 or AutoCAD LT 2010, check the Maintain Drawing Size Compatibility check box (or set the LARGEOBJECTSUPPORT system variable to 0).

The Open and Save tab.

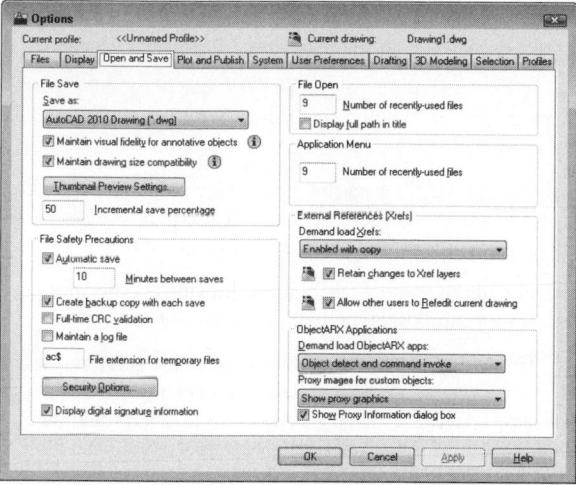

Note

Annotative scaling was introduced in AutoCAD 2008 and AutoCAD LT 2008 and is not supported in earlier releases. As a result, there is an option to specially preserve those scales when opening the file in older versions of AutoCAD and AutoCAD LT. When you check Maintain Visual Fidelity for Annotative Objects, each scale representation of your annotative objects is saved as a separate block on a separate layer. These layers are automatically frozen according to which annotation scale is current (visible). If you don't use this option, the older drawing will only have objects from the annotative scale on the Model tab. More objects could appear in model space (depending on the ANNOALLVISIBLE system variable) and paper space viewports in varying sizes. This option is checked by default to facilitate using annotative objects in earlier releases. This option does not affect DWG or DXF files saved to the AutoCAD 2010 format. ■

Setting the Incremental Save percentage enables you to control when AutoCAD or AutoCAD LT saves the entire drawing, as opposed to just your changes — an incremental save. The default is 50 percent, which avoids too many long, full saves.

In the File Safety Precautions section, set the default time between automatic saves. The other settings in this section are:

- **Create Backup Copy with Each Save.** By default, AutoCAD and AutoCAD LT create backup drawings whenever you save a drawing. Backup drawings have the same name as your drawing, but with an extension of .bak. Although you probably spend some time erasing these drawings, they can be very useful if a drawing becomes corrupted. You can change their extension to .dwg and open them as drawing files. However, you can also turn off this feature. Unfortunately, you can't control where the backup files are stored unless you use the MOVEBAK command that is available when the Express Tools are installed. Express Tools are available in AutoCAD only.

- **Full-Time CRC Validation.** Check this item if data that you import is becoming corrupted and you suspect a hardware problem. A cyclic redundancy check performs a validation during the importing process and can help you troubleshoot this problem (AutoCAD Only).

- **Maintain a Log File.** Keeps a log file that records the contents of the text window. Each time you work in AutoCAD, the new material is added to the end of the existing log file, so you should periodically edit or delete material from the log file. Use the Files tab to control the log file location.
- **File Extension for Temporary Files.** Sets the filename extension for temporary files that are created while you're working. By default, the extension for these files is .ac$. Use the Files tab to control the temporary file location.

Use the Security Options button to set options for passwords and digital signatures. See Chapter 26 for more details. AutoCAD LT doesn't include the password feature.

In the File Open section, you can set how many of the most recently used drawings you want to see at the bottom of the File menu. The default is nine, which is also the maximum setting. You can also choose whether or not you want to see the full path on the File menu listing and on the application window title bar.

In the Application Menu section, you can set how many of the most recently used drawings you want to see displayed in the Recent Documents list. The default is nine, and 50 is the maximum setting.

In the External References (Xrefs) section, you can turn on and off demand loading of external references. When the Retain Changes to Xref Layers setting is checked (which it is by default), any changes that you made to xref layer properties and states (such as freezing a layer) are saved. When you re-open the drawing containing the xref, these changes are retained. Finally, you can set whether the current drawing can be edited in-place when someone else is referencing it. The last setting applies to both AutoCAD and AutoCAD LT, but in AutoCAD LT you must use the XEDIT system variable. For more information, see Chapter 19.

In the ObjectARX Applications section (AutoCAD only), you have settings related to ObjectARX applications and proxy graphics created by ObjectARX applications. ObjectARX is a programming interface for creating applications that work with AutoCAD. By default, the application is loaded when you either use one of the application's commands or open a drawing containing a custom object created by the application. You can further restrict when the application is loaded to reduce demands on memory. In the Proxy Images for Custom Objects drop-down list, you can control how custom objects created by an ObjectARX application are displayed.

The Plot and Publish tab

The Plot and Publish tab, shown in Figure A.6, contains settings related to plotting and publishing, including plot-style table settings. Later in this appendix, I explain how to configure a plotter.

In the Default Plot Settings for New Drawings section, you set the default plotter/printer for new drawings and whether or not to use the same settings that you used the last time you plotted. As soon as you create plot settings for a drawing, those settings are saved with the drawing. Click Add or Configure Plotters for access to the Add-A-Plotter Wizard and existing plot configuration files. If you use a template, the plot settings in the template take precedence over the settings here.

The Plot to File section sets the default location for the file when you plot to a file. The Background Processing Options section determines whether plotting and publishing occur in the background (so that you can continue to work) or in the foreground. By default, background plotting is off for plotting and on for publishing (using the PUBLISH command). The Plot and Publish Log File section specifies whether to create a log file specifically for plotting and publishing operations.

In the Auto Publish section, you can set options for automatically creating DWF, DWFx, or PDF files every time you save or close a drawing. You do this to make sure that your DWF, DWFx, or PDF files are always up-to-date with your drawings. Click the Automatic Publish Settings button to open the Auto Publish Settings dialog box. I describe these settings in Chapter 28. Then check the Automatic Publish check box.

Appendix A: Installing and Configuring AutoCAD and AutoCAD LT

FIGURE A.6

The Plot and Publish tab.

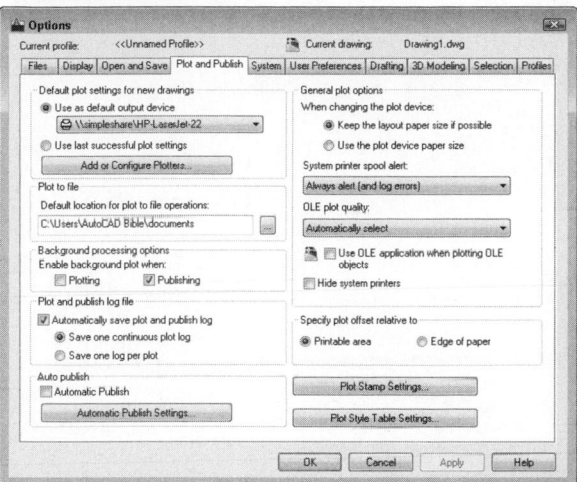

In the General Plot Options section, you can choose whether to keep the paper size specified on the layout tab or use the plotter's default paper size when you change plotters. You can also decide whether AutoCAD alerts you and creates an error log when the drawing is spooled through a system printer because of a port conflict.

In the same section, you can set a value for the quality of plotted OLE objects. You can choose from Monochrome, Low Graphics, High Graphics, and Automatically Select. The default is Automatically Select. Check the Use OLE Application When Plotting OLE Objects check box for the best quality when plotting OLE objects. Check the Hide System Printers check box to repress the display of Windows system printers on the list of printers in the Plot and Page Setup dialog boxes, so that you can't inadvertently print to your printer rather than to your plotter.

The Specify Plot Offset Relative To section determines how plot offsets (which you set in the Plot or Page Setup dialog box) work. Click the Plot Stamp Settings button to specify what you want to include if you add a plot stamp when plotting.

Click the Plot Style Table Settings button to decide whether to use color-dependent or named plot styles for new drawings, and choose a default plot-style table. You can also set default plot styles for layer 0 and objects. Click the Add or Edit Plot Style Tables button to go to the Plot Styles folder where the plot-style tables are stored. You can then double-click the Add-A-Plot Style Table Wizard to create a new table or open an existing table for editing. For more information on plotting and plot-style tables, see Chapter 17.

The System tab

The System tab contains a number of settings that affect how your computer works with AutoCAD or AutoCAD LT, as well as some general settings. Figure A.7 shows the System tab.

In the 3D Performance Settings section (AutoCAD only), click the Performance Settings button to open the Adaptive Degradation and Performance Tuning dialog box, as shown in Figure A.8.

FIGURE A.7

The System tab.

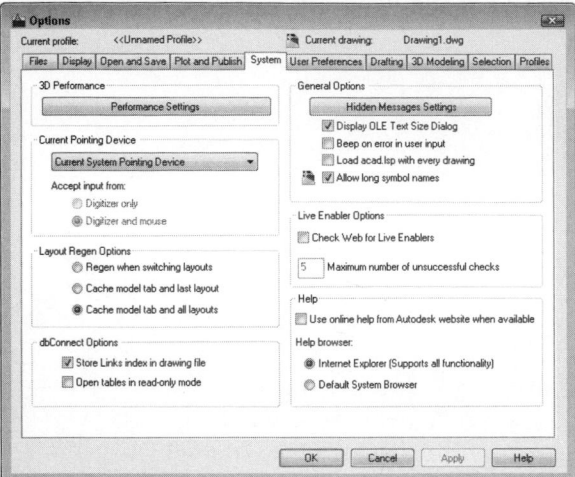

FIGURE A.8

The Adaptive Degradation and Performance Tuning dialog box allows you to specify how AutoCAD displays 3D features in relation to your computer system's capabilities.

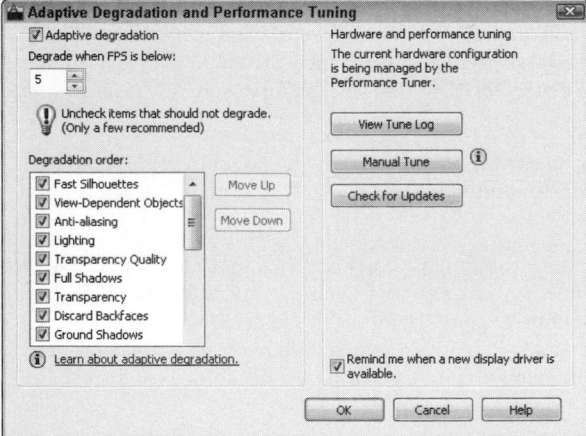

Note

AutoCAD 2011 analyzes your computer system and degrades the display, based on the settings in this dialog box. For example, if your graphics card is not certified, materials and textures do not display by default. (You can easily turn them on. See Chapter 22 for more information.) ∎

On the left side of the dialog box, you can turn Adaptive Degradation off by unchecking the check box at the top. Then you can set the level at which degradation starts to function. By default, this is five frames per second, which refers to the speed at which your monitor refreshes the display. In the Degradation Order box, you can do two things:

- **Uncheck items that you don't want to degrade.** For example, you may always want to see materials and textures.
- **Change the order of degradation.** Items at the top degrade first. Select an item and click the Move Up or Move Down button to change the order.

You may need to see the results you get before making these decisions.

The right side of the dialog box contains information about performance tuning. Click View Tune Log to see the Performance Tuner Log window. Here you can see if your graphics card is certified, which just means that Autodesk has tested it and recommends it. The bottom of the window shows the effects on specific features, such as current acceleration driver, enhanced 3D performance, the Gooch shader, and full-shadow display.

Click the Manual Tune button to change the settings. For example, you can choose to enable *hardware acceleration,* even if your graphics card is not certified. Hardware acceleration means that your graphics card's capabilities are used. (When hardware acceleration is turned off, AutoCAD uses *software acceleration* to try to display the screen properly.) Autodesk says that you do this at your own risk, but you may find that this works for you. For example, you may have an excellent graphics card, but Autodesk may not have tested and certified it yet. You can also turn off specific features, such as full-shadow display, which involve intensive computer capabilities. If your card cannot support a specific feature, you can have AutoCAD reproduce the effect during plotting by checking the Emulate Unsupported Hardware Effects in Software When Plotting check box.

New Feature

There are two new hardware acceleration effects that AutoCAD 2011 supports: Smooth Display and Advanced Material Effects. Smooth Display applies anti-aliasing to the drawing window, smoothing out the jagged display of angled lines and objects with curves. Advanced Material Effects controls the display in the drawing window of materials assigned to objects. ■

In the lower section of the dialog box, you can adjust features that don't require hardware acceleration, such as the display of backward-facing faces of solids, transparency, and tessellation lines (the apparent smoothness of curved objects created by using many short lines or triangles). The Tessellation cache is useful if you are displaying 3D objects in more than one viewport. You can also reset the setting to their recommended values. Click OK when you're done.

So, how do you know which graphics cards are certified? Click the Check for Updates button in the Adaptive Degradation and Performance Tuning dialog box to go to Autodesk's Web site and see a list of recommended cards. When you're done with the Adaptive Degradation and Performance Tuning dialog box, click OK to return to the Options dialog box.

In the Current Pointing Device section of the Options dialog box, you choose Wintab Compatible Digitizer ADI 4.2 if you have a digitizer. If you have a digitizing device, you can choose to accept input from only the digitizer, or both the digitizer and the mouse.

Note

If you're installing a digitizer, follow the instructions provided by the digitizer manufacturer to configure Windows for the Wintab driver. You need to configure the digitizer to work with Windows. ■

In the Layout Regen Options section (AutoCAD only), you can choose to cache (save in memory) the model and layout tabs to avoid regenerations when you switch among the tabs.

In the dbConnect Options section (AutoCAD only), you can choose whether to store the index of database links in the drawing file to enhance performance during Link Select functions. You can also choose to open database tables in read-only mode; however, you won't be able to edit them.

AutoCAD LT has a User Name section that contains your name and organization. This is derived from the information that you provided at installation. You can change this name. The REVDATE command, which is available only in AutoCAD LT, uses this name to place a time stamp on your drawing.

In the General Options section, you can do the following:

- Bring back dialog boxes that have a Don't Display This Warning Again check box (that you checked). Click the Hidden Message Settings button to choose from dialog boxes that you checked.

- Turn off the display of the OLE Text Size dialog box when inserting OLE objects into AutoCAD drawings.

- Tell AutoCAD to beep (or to remain silent) when it detects an invalid entry.

- Determine whether AutoLISP loads `acad.lsp` into every drawing that you open. By default, this box is not checked, meaning that only `acaddoc.lsp` is loaded into every drawing (AutoCAD only).

- Disable long names for layers, dimension styles, blocks, linetypes, text styles, layouts, UCS names, views, and viewport configurations for compatibility with prior releases and customization.

In the Live Enabler Options section, you can decide when you want to check for object enablers. Object enablers let the user display and use custom objects in drawings, even when the application that created them is unavailable. For example, if you send a customer who is using Release 2000 a drawing with associative dimensions, that customer can use an object enabler to view those dimensions.

In the Help section, you control whether you use the locally installed HTML Help system or the latest Help files for AutoCAD directly from Autodesk's Web site.

New Feature

Autodesk has switched to using HTML files instead of a compiled CHM file for the Help system in AutoCAD. While it has a different look and feel from the CHM files present in earlier releases, it does provide access to additional information that you would otherwise have to visit multiple sites to access. ∎

Clear the Use Online Help from Autodesk Website When Available check box to use the locally installed files if you have a slow connection to the Internet. You can find the location of the locally installed HTML Help files under Help and Miscellaneous File Names⇨Help Location on the Files tab of the Options dialog box. Under Help Browser, select either Internet Explorer or the default Web browser on your system (if you have installed Mozilla Firefox or Google Chrome). Some features of the online Help system might not work properly with Web browsers other than Internet Explorer.

While the locally installed files are similar to the online Help files, additional content is displayed for each topic when viewing AutoCAD's Help files from the Autodesk Web site. The additional content comes from resources such as the Discussion Groups on Autodesk.com and Autodesk's Knowledge Base.

The User Preferences tab

The User Preferences tab, shown in Figure A.9, offers a variety of preference settings. In the Windows Standard Behavior section, you can turn double-click editing on or off. Double-click editing determines what happens when you double-click an object. (You can customize this process in the Customize User

Interface Editor, as I explain in Chapter 33.) You can also disable the shortcut menus that appear when you right-click in the drawing or command area. A right-click is then equivalent to pressing Enter.

FIGURE A.9

The User Preferences tab.

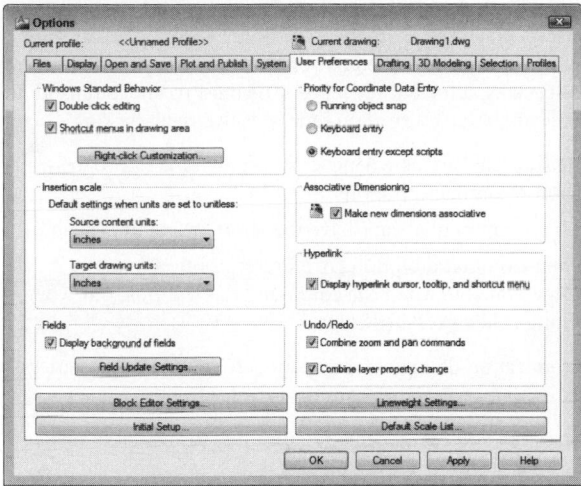

You can customize what happens when you right-click. Click Right-Click Customization to open the dialog box shown in Figure A.10.

FIGURE A.10

The Right-Click Customization dialog box.

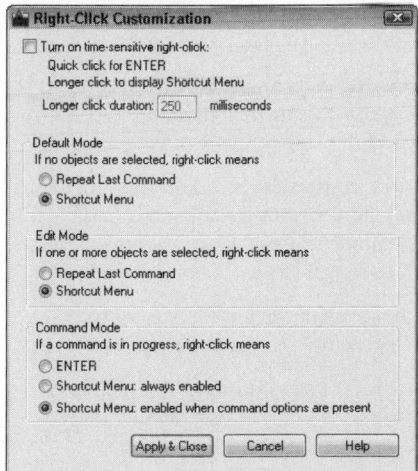

At the top of the Right-Click Customization dialog box, you can turn on the time-sensitive right-click feature.

With time-sensitive right-clicking, a quick right-click is equivalent to pressing Enter. For example, it repeats the last command, or ends the LINE command (and other commands that require Enter to end). A longer right-click (hold your finger on the mouse slightly longer) opens the shortcut menu. You can specify the length of time required for the longer right-click, which is 250 milliseconds by default.

In the Default Mode section, if you haven't turned on time-sensitive right-clicking, then you can choose the Repeat Last Command option if you don't want to use shortcut menus. In the Edit Mode section, you can choose the Repeat Last Command option to disable the shortcut menus only when one or more objects are selected, but no command is in progress. When you do this, right-clicking automatically repeats the most recent command. In the Command Mode section, you have three choices if you haven't turned on time-sensitive right-clicking:

- Choose the ENTER option to disable the shortcut menus whenever a command is in progress. You then have to use the keyboard to choose command options.
- Choose the Shortcut Menu: Always Enabled option to always have the shortcut menu available.
- Choose the Shortcut Menu: Enabled When Command Options Are Present option as an in-between option. The shortcut menu is now available when the command has options, but when the command has no options, right-clicking is like pressing Enter.

Click Apply & Close to close the Right-Click Customization dialog box and return to the User Preferences tab of the Options dialog box.

In the Insertion Scale section of the User Preferences tab, you can specify default units for inserted objects (*source contents units*) and drawings (*target drawing units*) when dragging objects into a drawing from the DesignCenter or i-drop, or using commands like INSERT or XATTACH. When you don't use the INSUNITS system variable (saved in your drawing), this setting determines the units to apply. You can choose anything from inches to parsecs!

In the Fields section, you can turn on and off the gray background behind fields. (The background doesn't plot; it just indicates to you that the text is a field.) Click the Field Update Settings button to specify when fields are automatically updated. By default, they update when you open, save, plot, eTransmit, or regenerate a drawing.

Click the Block Editor Settings button to open the Block Editor Settings dialog box, where you can control the display in the Block Editor.

In the Authoring Objects section, you control the color of parameters and grips in the Block Editor along with orientation of labels for parameters. The Parameter Font section controls the text and font style for parameter labels, while the Parameter and Grip Size section controls parameter and grip size.

The Constraint Status section controls the colors assigned to geometric constraints based on the constraints' current status. The three settings in the lower-left corner of the Block Editor Settings dialog box control the display of constrained objects, parameters with value sets, and the action bar. Click Reset Values to restore the default values in the Block Editor Settings dialog box. Click OK to return to the Options dialog box.

Click the Initial Setup button to open Initial Setup and perform some basic customization of AutoCAD or AutoCAD LT. For more information on Initial Setup, see the "Using Initial Setup" section earlier in this chapter.

In the Priority for Coordinate Data Entry section, you specify which has priority: running object snaps or keyboard entry. By default, keyboard entry has priority except in scripts, so you can use running object snaps when picking points on the screen, but override them when you want to type in coordinates.

In the Associative Dimensioning section, choose whether you want new dimensions to be *associative* and thus automatically adjusting as their associated objects change size.

In the Hyperlink section, you can disable the hyperlink cursor (which appears when you pass the cursor over a hyperlink) and the hyperlink shortcut menu, as well as the hyperlink tooltip that appears when you pass the cursor over a hyperlink.

The Undo/Redo section allows you to combine consecutive zooms and pans into a single operation that can be undone with the U or UNDO command. You may perform several zooms and pans together, but you probably don't want to step backward through each one individually. You can also combine consecutive layer property changes made with the Layer Properties Manager into a single operation. Both these features are on by default.

Click the Lineweight Settings button to open the Lineweight Settings dialog box. For more information on lineweights, see Chapter 11.

In the Lineweight Settings dialog box, you can select a lineweight from the Lineweights list to set it current. There are three standard lineweight styles: ByLayer, ByBlock, and Default. The Default value is 0.01 inches or 0.25 mm. All new layers have a default setting of Default. You can also set any specific width that you want. In the Units for Listing section, choose Millimeters or Inches. The default is Millimeters, probably because pen widths for pen plotters are traditionally defined in millimeters. Checking the Display Lineweight check box is equivalent to clicking the Show/Hide Lineweight button on the status bar. In the Default drop-down list, you can change the default lineweight that new layers automatically use.

With the Adjust Display Scale slider, you can control how lineweights are displayed on the Model tab. (Lineweights on a paper space layout are displayed in real-world units.) On the Model tab, lineweights are displayed in pixels, using a proportion of pixel width to real-world unit value. Depending on the resolution of your monitor, you may want to adjust the display scale to better see different lineweights.

Tip

You can see the results of any display scale change immediately in the Lineweights list on the left of the dialog box. Scroll down to the bottom to see the difference for wider lineweights. ∎

Click Apply & Close to return to the User Preferences tab of the Options dialog box. Click the Default Scale List button to open the Default Scale List dialog box. Here you can customize the list of scales so that you always have the scales that you need (and don't have the scales that you never use). I discuss the scale list in Chapter 5.

The Drafting tab

The Drafting tab, shown in Figure A.11, includes AutoSnap and AutoTrack settings. In the AutoSnap Settings section, you can disable the marker (that visually indicates each object snap), the magnet (that draws the cursor to the object snap), and the tooltip (that says which object snap you've found). By default, the aperture is not displayed with AutoSnap markers because the combination can be confusing. You can also choose a color for the AutoSnap marker. Click the Colors button to change the color of the AutoSnap marker item. You can also change the marker size by dragging the control bar.

In the Object Snap Options section, you can turn off the option to ignore hatch objects. By default, you cannot snap to hatch objects. If you want to snap to hatch objects, uncheck the check box. You can also choose the Replace Z Value with Current Elevation option (AutoCAD only) to specify that object snaps use the current elevation for the Z value instead of the Z value of the object snap's point on the object.

You can also specify how the Dynamic UCS feature works with object snaps (AutoCAD only). By default, when you're in a Dynamic UCS, you don't snap to object snaps with negative Z values, so you can easily draw on the temporary XY plane. Uncheck the Ignore Negative Z Object Snaps for Dynamic UCS option to enable snapping to all object snaps.

FIGURE A.11

The Drafting tab.

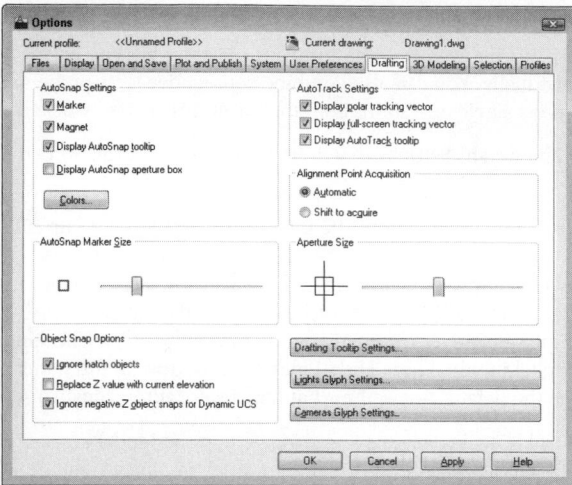

In the AutoTrack Settings section, you control the visual elements for AutoTracking:

- Uncheck the **Display Polar Tracking Vector** check box to disable the vector that appears when you move the cursor along a polar angle. You still see the tooltip.

- Uncheck the **Display Full-Screen Tracking Vector** check box to see only a localized vector when using object snap tracking — the vector appears between the acquired points, instead of crossing the entire screen.

- Uncheck the **Display AutoTrack Tooltip** check box to disable the tooltip that tells you which object snaps you've tracked.

In the Alignment Point Acquisition section, you can require pressing the Shift key to acquire points. You might do this if you find yourself acquiring points by accident, which can result in annoying tracking vectors.

You can set the aperture size for picking an object snap. However, the aperture box is off by default. (You can turn it on in the AutoSnap Settings section, as previously described.)

Click the Drafting Tooltip Settings button to open the Tooltip Appearance dialog box. Here you can set the color, size, and transparency for tooltips. You can also choose to apply these settings to all tooltips or only to the Dynamic Input tooltip.

Click the Light Glyph Settings button (AutoCAD only) to open the Light Glyph Appearance dialog box, where you can determine how light glyphs look. You can change their color and size.

Click the Camera Glyph Settings button (AutoCAD only) to open the Camera Glyph Appearance dialog box. Here, too, you can change the size and color of the glyphs.

The 3D Modeling tab

This tab, available in AutoCAD only, contains settings specific to 3D modeling. The 3D Modeling tab is shown in Figure A.12.

FIGURE A.12

The 3D Modeling tab.

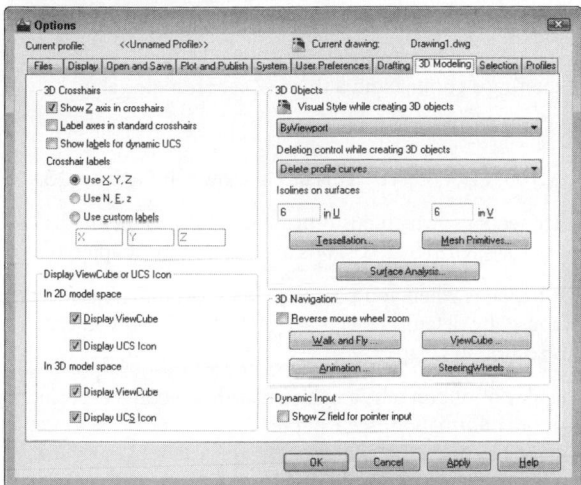

In the 3D Crosshairs section, you can specify the look of the 3D crosshairs. You can choose to show the Z axis (on by default) and to label the axes. If you show labels, you can customize them. You can also show labels for a Dynamic UCS.

In the Display ViewCube or UCS Icon section, you can decide when you want to see the UCS icon and ViewCube (AutoCAD only). Some people don't want the UCS icon in 2D model space, for example, but want it on for 3D work.

New Feature

You can now display the ViewCube tool in the 2D wireframe visual style and not just 3D visual styles. ■

In the 3D Objects section, you can set a separate visual style while you are creating 3D solids and extruded solids and surfaces. By default, the current visual style (ByViewport) is used, but you may want a special one for the creation process.

The Deletion Control While Creating 3D Objects drop-down list sets the DELOBJ system variable, which I discuss in Chapter 24.

The two text boxes under the Isolines on Surfaces label control the SURFU and SURFV system variables, which I cover in the "Creating Plane Surfaces" section of Chapter 23. These set the default number of isolines on surfaces.

Click the Tessellation and Mesh Primitives buttons to change the settings used to convert objects to 3D mesh objects and to create mesh primitive objects (AutoCAD only). For more information, see Chapter 24.

New Feature

Click the Surface Analysis button to display the Analysis Options dialog box. Use the settings in the Analysis Options dialog box to control the display settings for the ANALYSISZEBRA, ANALYSISCURVATURE, and ANALYSISDRAFT commands (AutoCAD only). For more information, see Chapter 23. ■

The 3D Navigation section contains settings related to 3D Navigation. You can reverse the direction that you scroll the mouse wheel to zoom in and out to match other software that may be the opposite of AutoCAD. You can set walk and fly settings, ViewCube, animation, and SteeringWheels settings here. I cover these settings in Chapter 22.

In the Dynamic Input section, you can display a Z field for pointer input. If you leave this item unchecked (the default), you can always display it by simply entering a comma and a third (Z) coordinate value.

The Selection tab

The Selection tab contains settings that control how you select objects. This tab is shown in Figure A.13.

The options in the Selection Modes and Pickbox Size sections, which customize object selection, are discussed in detail in Chapter 9. The options in the Grips and Grip Size sections are covered in Chapter 10.

The Selection Preview section lets you specify what happens when you pass the cursor over an object to see what object you would select if you clicked your mouse. By default, objects are highlighted and you can customize the look of this highlighting. I cover this section in Chapter 9.

The Ribbon Options section lets you control the display of ribbon tabs associated with selecting a specific type of object or starting a specific command. For more information, see Chapter 33.

FIGURE A.13

The Selection tab.

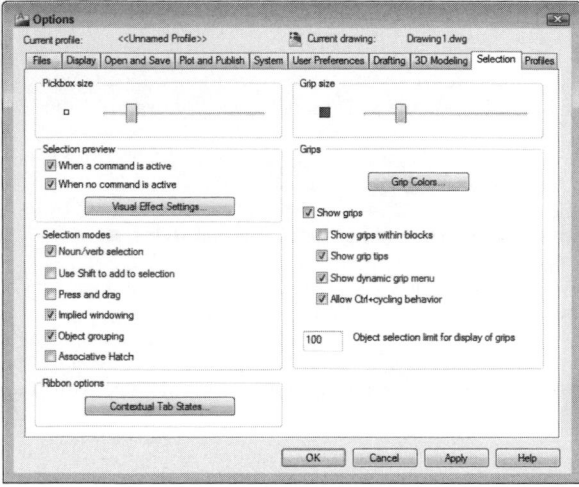

The Profiles tab

The Profiles tab, shown in Figure A.14, enables you to create user profiles. AutoCAD LT does not offer this feature (or the tab). A profile is a group of settings, most of which you set in the Options dialog box. It can include all settings that are saved in the Windows Registry. Settings that are saved in the current drawing (indicated in the Options dialog box by the blue and yellow drawing icon) are not included in a profile. If you share your system with someone else and you each want to store different settings, or if you want different settings for different projects, you can create a profile and make it current when you open AutoCAD.

FIGURE A.14

The Profiles tab with the default and one custom profile.

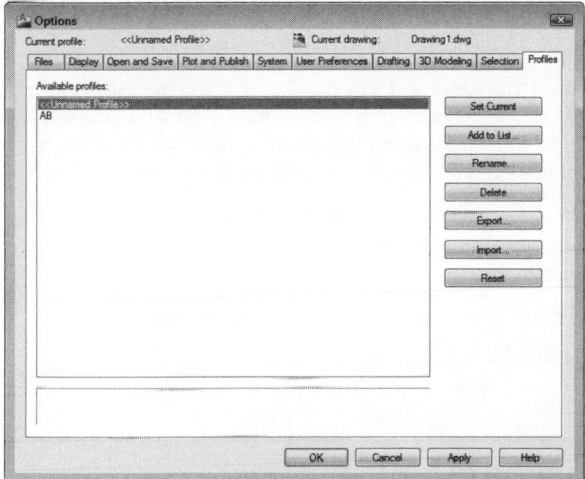

Whatever settings you create with the Options dialog box are automatically part of the default profile, which starts out with the unexciting name of Unnamed Profile. Here's how you create a new profile:

1. Click Add to List to open the Add Profile dialog box. Type in a profile name and description and click Apply & Close. This adds a new profile that is a duplicate of the current profile.

2. On the Profiles tab, click the new profile and choose Set Current.

3. Go through the other tabs and make the changes that you want. Be sure to click Apply on each tab.

4. Click OK to close the Options dialog box.

Whenever you make changes in AutoCAD settings that affect the Windows Registry, those changes become part of the current profile.

To use the profile or another profile, choose Application Button ⇨ Options and click the Profiles tab. Choose the profile and click Set Current, or double-click the profile. Click OK to return to your drawing. You see the results immediately. Of course, some settings are not visible but make themselves evident in other ways, such as right-click functioning and the creation of a log file.

Tip

To start AutoCAD with a specific profile, you can specify a profile by using a command-line switch, as explained in the next section. You can also export a profile (click the Export button) to share it with colleagues or use it on another computer. To use an exported profile, click the Import button on the Profiles tab of the Options dialog box. ∎

Starting AutoCAD Your Way

When you choose the AutoCAD icon to open AutoCAD, Windows notwithstanding, you execute a statement similar to the one that old-timers once typed at the DOS prompt. This is called a *command-line statement.* By

default, it looks something like c:\Program Files\Autodesk\AutoCAD 2011\acad.exe or c:\
Program Files\Autodesk\AutoCAD LT 2011\acadlt.exe. Your exact command-line statement
depends on where you installed AutoCAD or AutoCAD LT.

Using command-line switches

You can add parameters, called *switches,* to the end of this command line to control what happens when
you start the program. Always add a space between the acad.exe or acadlt.exe command and a
switch. Before any switch, you can add the name of a drawing to open that drawing. You need quotation
marks around any path or drawing name that contains spaces. Table A.1 lists the available command-line
switches and their functions.

You can combine switches. For example, the following command-line statement opens the drawing "Union
Hill Apts" in the front view and runs the setup script.

```
C:\Program Files\Autodesk\AutoCAD 2011\acad.exe "c:\drawings\Union
    Hill Apts.dwg" /v front /b setup
```

TABLE A.1

Command-Line Switches

Switch	Example	Function
/b	"c:\drawings\ Union Hill Apts. dwg" /b setup	Runs a script file on the default drawing or the one you are opening. The example opens a drawing (here named "Union Hill Apts") and runs a script (here named "setup"). You need to specify the full drawing path.
/c	/c c:\steve\ steve.cfg	Specifies the location and, optionally, the filename of the hardware configuration file that you want to use. Configuration files are discussed in the next section.
/ld	/ld balloon.dbx	Loads an ARX or DBX file (AutoCAD only).
/nohardware	/nohardware	Disables hardware acceleration (AutoCAD only).
/nologo		Starts AutoCAD or AutoCAD LT without displaying the splash screen at startup.
/nossm	/nossm	Opens AutoCAD without the Sheet Set Manager (AutoCAD only).
/p	/p steve	Specifies an existing profile to use when starting AutoCAD. This profile is used only for the current session. You can also change profiles by using the Profile tab of the Options dialog box. Use quotation marks around the name if it contains spaces (AutoCAD only).
/pl	/pl garage.dsd	Publishes a drawing set description (DSD) file (AutoCAD only).
/r	/r	Resets AutoCAD to the default configuration (acad2011.cfg) for the default system pointing device (AutoCAD only).
/s	/s c:\steve	Specifies support folders for fonts, menus, AutoLISP files, linetypes, and hatch patterns. Use this when you want to use support files that are not in AutoCAD's support-file search path. You can specify up to 15 folders, separated by semicolons without spaces (AutoCAD only).
/set	/set ab26-f	Opens AutoCAD and the named sheet set (here called "ab26-f") (AutoCAD only).

Switch	Example	Function
/t	/t a-tb	Opens a new drawing based on a template file (here named "a-tb").
/v	`"c:\drawings\ Union Apts" /v front`	Opens a drawing and immediately displays the specified view (here named "front"). The full drawing path is required.
/w	/w ab_3d	Opens AutoCAD or AutoCAD LT with the specified workspace.

To change the command-line switch, follow these steps:

1. Right-click the shortcut to AutoCAD or AutoCAD LT on your desktop.
2. Choose Properties.
3. Click the Shortcut tab.
4. In the Target text box, add your switches to the end of the current command-line statement.
5. Click OK.

Understanding configuration files

Every time you open AutoCAD, a configuration file is created. By default, this file (acad2011.cfg for AutoCAD or acadlt2011.cfg for AutoCAD LT) is an ASCII file containing mostly hardware-configuration information for your mouse and digitizer.

If you use multiple pointing devices — for example, a large and a small digitizer — you may want to create more than one configuration file to make it easy to switch from one configuration to another.

You should not edit the configuration file; instead, let AutoCAD create it for you. The problem is that AutoCAD assumes one configuration file and overwrites the previous one whenever you make changes that affect the file — such as adding a pointing device.

Remember that you can use the /c command-line switch to specify a configuration file. To create a new file, follow these steps:

1. Use Windows Explorer to back up your current configuration file under a new name, such as acad2011-orig.cfg.

Note
To find the location of acad2011.cfg, choose Application Button ⇨ Options and click the Files tab. Double-click Help and Miscellaneous Files, and then double-click Configuration File (AutoCAD only). ∎

2. Open AutoCAD and make the pointer change that you want on the System tab of the Options dialog box. (If you're installing a new digitizer, follow the manufacturer's instructions to install the digitizer.) Click OK.
3. Close AutoCAD.
4. In Explorer, find the new acad2011.cfg file that AutoCAD created. Change its name, using something meaningful, such as LargeDigitizer.cfg.
5. If you want to keep the original acad2011.cfg file, change its name back to acad2011.cfg.

You now have two configuration files. (You can create more if you want.) To use them, you can change the command-line switch as needed, but there's an easier way, as explained in the next section.

Creating multiple configurations

This appendix has discussed three different ways to create session configurations:

- Profiles
- Configuration files
- Command-line switches

You can use command-line switches to specify a profile and a configuration file, as well as to configure AutoCAD in other ways, such as opening a drawing with a certain template or running a script file when you open a drawing.

If you regularly use these features, you should create multiple configurations to make it easy to open AutoCAD the way that you want by doing the following:

- Create the profiles and configuration files that you need.
- Make as many shortcuts as you need.

Note

To create a new shortcut, use Explorer to find `acad.exe` (usually in `AutoCAD 2011`) or `acadlt.exe` (usually in `AutoCAD LT 2011`). Right-click it and choose Create Shortcut from the menu. Drag this to your desktop and rename it. ■

- Change the command-line switches to specify the profiles and configuration files that you want, and add any other command-line switches that you need.

For example, here are command lines for two separate AutoCAD desktop shortcuts. You could make similar command lines for AutoCAD LT.

```
C:\Program Files\Autodesk\AutoCAD 2011\acad.exe /t acad /nologo
C:\Program Files\Autodesk\AutoCAD 2011\acad.exe /p steve /c steve.cfg
    /t arch
```

The first command-line statement opens drawings by using the `acad.dwt` template and doesn't display the logo. It also uses the default profile and configuration file.

The second command-line statement opens drawings by using the `arch.dwt` template and displays the logo. It also uses the `steve` profile and the `steve` configuration file.

You could also have each configuration run different script files. This technique takes some time to set up, but after it's done, it saves you time and reduces errors each time you open AutoCAD or AutoCAD LT.

Configuring a Plotter

Windows supports many printers. To add a printer supported by Windows, choose one of the following:

- Start ➪ Settings ➪ Printers and Faxes
- Start ➪ Control Panel ➪ Printers
- Start ➪ Devices and Printers

Click (or double-click) Add Printer. A printer added in this way is called a *Windows system printer*.

The Windows system printer drivers are great for small desktop printers because that's their intended use, but they aren't optimized for pen plotters or large-format plotters. For this purpose, AutoCAD and

AutoCAD LT come with *non-system drivers*. These drivers are specially designed for CAD and usually provide you with more options than if you choose the default Windows system printer settings. You cannot use them with other Windows applications.

Using the Plotter Manager

To configure a non-system plotter, use the Plotter Manager. (You can also use the Plotter Manager to create custom settings for a system printer.) You have several ways to open the Plotter Manager:

- From Windows, choose Start ⇨ Settings ⇨ Control Panel (or Start ⇨ Control Panel) and double-click Autodesk Plotter Manager. (If you're not using the Classic view, click Printer, or Printers and Other Hardware, to see the shortcut for the Autodesk Plotter Manager.)

- From within AutoCAD or AutoCAD LT, choose Output tab ⇨ Plot panel ⇨ Plotter Manager.
- From within AutoCAD or AutoCAD LT, choose Application Button ⇨ Print ⇨ Manage Plotters.
- From within AutoCAD or AutoCAD LT, choose Application Button ⇨ Options. On the Plot and Publish tab, click Add or Configure Plotters.

The Plotter Manager has a wizard (double-click Add-A-Plotter Wizard) that guides you through the process of configuring a printer. Follow the instructions on each page, which vary based on your previous choices.

For more information, see the "Use Plotters and Printers" section in the Help system. On the application title bar, click the Help button and then choose Driver and Peripheral Guide from the Home page.

During the process of configuring a plotter, you can import a PCP or PC2 configuration file that was created with an earlier release.

The result of configuring a plotter is a plotter configuration file that has a filename extension of .pc3. These PC3 files are saved in the Plotters folder. (To find the PC3 files, choose Application Button ⇨ Options and click the Files tab. Double-click Printer Support File Path and then double-click Printer Configuration Search Path.) You can share plotter configuration files with colleagues or copy them to another computer, such as a notebook computer. You can configure more than one plotter. You can also create more than one configuration for a single plotter. To use a PC3 file, choose it from the Name drop-down list under the Printer/Plotter section of the Plot dialog box.

At the end of the Plotter Manager Wizard, you can click Edit Plotter Configuration to change the default settings for your plotter. You can also click Calibrate Plotter to test that the plotter plots accurately.

Editing a plotter configuration

You can edit a plotter configuration and change its original settings. You can access the file in several ways:

- As just mentioned, click Edit Plotter Configuration at the end of the Plotter Manager Wizard.
- From within AutoCAD or AutoCAD LT, choose Application Button ⇨ Print ⇨ Page Setup or Output tab ⇨ Plot panel ⇨ Page Setup Manager. Click Modify. In the Page Setup dialog box, choose the plotter that you want and click Properties.
- From Windows Explorer, double-click a PC3 file. The location of the PC3 files is listed on the Files tab of the Options dialog box, under Printer Support File Path ⇨ Printer Configuration Search Path.

A PC3 file is not an ASCII file. When you open a PC3 file, you see the Plotter Configuration Editor dialog box, as shown in Figure A.15.

The General tab lists basic information about the plotter. This tab does not contain any options that you can configure, although you can add a description of the plotter and its settings.

The Ports tab enables you to choose to plot through a port (the usual situation), plot to a file, or use AutoSpool to plot to a printer spooler. If more than one port is available, then you can choose and configure the port.

The Device and Document Settings tab contains plotting options, depending on your plotter.

FIGURE A.15

The Plotter Configuration Editor is the place to change settings related to your printer or plotter.

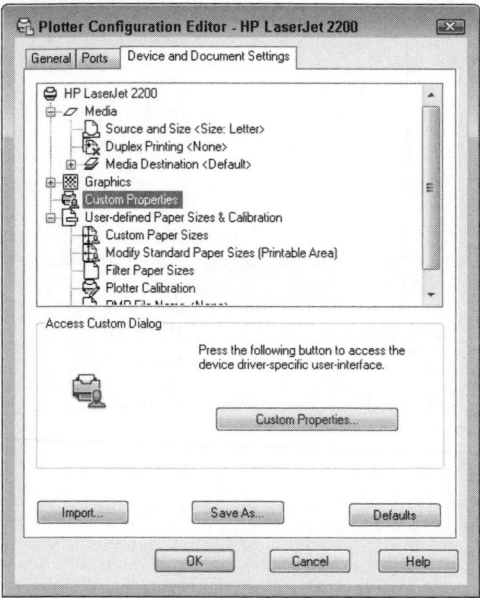

As you select an item from the top part of the Plotter Configuration Editor, the appropriate options become available on the bottom of the dialog box. You can configure the following (your plotter will probably show different options):

- **Media.** The source and size of the paper.

- **Physical Pen Configuration.** Correction for filled areas (for extra accuracy), pen optimization for faster plotting, pen color, pen speed, and pen width.

- **Graphics.** Color depth (the number of colors), monochrome, resolution, and dithering.

- **Custom Properties.** Vary by plotter. For Windows system printers, you might find settings such as draft printing and grayscale (for color printers).

- **Initialization Strings.** Rarely used nowadays. If you're plotting to an unsupported plotter, you may be able to prepare the plotter for printing, set options, and restore the plotter to its original state by using ASCII text initialization strings.

- **User-Defined Paper Sizes and Calibration.** Calibrate a plotter, create custom paper sizes, and change the plottable area of standard paper sizes. You can filter out unused paper sizes by unchecking sizes that you don't want to display. You can choose to apply the changes only to the current plot or to the configuration file.

When you finish making changes, click OK to save the changes to the PC3 files. You can also click Save As to create a new PC3 file. Click Defaults to return all settings to their defaults.

AutoCAD and AutoCAD LT Resources

A side from this book, you have many other resources for learning about AutoCAD. These resources range from AutoCAD's New Features Workshop to Web sites, and include everything else in between.

On the DVD

This book's DVD contains a document containing clickable links for the Internet resources in this appendix. Look in the Links folder. ■

Discovering AutoCAD and AutoCAD LT

AutoCAD and AutoCAD LT are not programs that you can easily pick up as you work with them. You'll need some formal education, whether by using this book, taking a course, or using a combination of methods.

Using AutoCAD and AutoCAD LT Help resources

AutoCAD's own Help resources are a good place to start when you have a question. In Chapter 3, I explain how to use Help. You can also try the New Features Workshop, which includes explanations and demonstrations that are related to the new 2011 features. Click the Help (?) button's down arrow (at the right side of the AutoCAD title bar), and choose New Features Workshop.

Learning from your reseller

You're supposed to learn AutoCAD from your reseller. Most resellers offer some training when you purchase AutoCAD. However, the amount of training and follow-up support varies greatly, and so does the price. If you have more than one AutoCAD reseller nearby, check not only the cost of AutoCAD but also the cost of training.

IN THIS APPENDIX

Learning AutoCAD or AutoCAD LT

Accessing technical support

Joining Autodesk user groups

Finding Internet resources

Unlike AutoCAD, AutoCAD LT is often sold online without any training. Keep in mind that AutoCAD LT is not a simple program either, and some training will definitely help you get more out of the program.

Resellers usually offer upgrade seminars and courses when you upgrade. If you're already using AutoCAD or AutoCAD LT, you may be able to take a course that focuses on the new features.

If you're going to use third-party applications that work with AutoCAD or other Autodesk products, check how much experience the reseller has with these products and what kind of support the reseller offers.

Autodesk has an Autodesk Training Center program that certifies trainers. Your reseller may or may not be an Autodesk Training Center; remember to ask. Premier Training Centers offer additional training in certain disciplines, thus offering solutions that are more specialized to their customers.

Taking a course

You may be able to take a course in AutoCAD at a local college or Autodesk Training Center. Many universities and community colleges offer courses in AutoCAD. Such courses may fit your schedule because they're often offered in the evening, over a period of several weeks. Of course, that may not work if you need to get up and running very quickly. I haven't heard of courses on AutoCAD LT. AutoCAD LT courses are less common, but you can check out your local colleges. However, a course on AutoCAD would certainly help you to learn AutoCAD LT.

Autodesk holds a once-a-year conference, called Autodesk University, which offers classes that are taught by top AutoCAD experts. For more information, go to au.autodesk.com.

Autodesk sells short, self-paced courses on both AutoCAD and AutoCAD LT. From the Autodesk home page (www.autodesk.com), hover over Services & Support, and then choose Courseware from the menu. You can find other training-related links under the same menu.

If you are a Subscription member, you have access to special courses. For more information about the Subscription program, go to www.autodesk.com and hover over Services & Support and choose Subscription.

Learning from other users

If you work in an office with several AutoCAD or AutoCAD LT users, you'll find that they're usually happy to share information and tips with you. This won't generally get you started from scratch, but it's great for rounding out your knowledge.

Reading magazines and newsletters

Cadalyst (www.cadalyst.com) covers AutoCAD as well as other CAD programs. It is published in both print and Web versions, and includes many helpful articles. In addition, *Cadalyst* has an extensive Web site that I discuss later as a Web resource.

AUGI has a couple of great publications, including *AUGIWorld* magazine. You can find out more at www.augi.com. A free registration is required. Then click the Publications link.

If you're interested in the CAD industry in general, try Ralph Grabowski's weekly *upFront.eZine*, which you can subscribe to by sending the e-mail message "subscribe upfront" to editor@xyzpress.com.

I offer an e-mail newsletter, *AutoCAD Tips Newsletter*. It contains tips, tutorials, and techniques. You can sign up at www.ellenfinkelstein.com/acad_submit.html.

Accessing Technical Support

Autodesk has always referred customers to their reseller for technical support. As with training, you should check out the provisions of the technical support. Some resellers charge for each phone call, while others provide free support to all customers for as long as Autodesk supports the product.

However, Autodesk offers its own support. For an overview of support options, hover over Services & Support and choose Support & Documentation from the Autodesk home page (www.autodesk.com), then select one of the links to the right of AutoCAD or AutoCAD LT. The Knowledge Base link allows you to access a large number of technical documents that answer many common questions. You can also access additional documentation and the product's online help.

The Autodesk Web site offers discussion groups. From Autodesk's home page, hover over Communities, choose Discussion Groups, and then choose AutoCAD or AutoCAD LT under Product Forums. You can ask questions and receive answers from other users as well as from Autodesk employees.

Autodesk User Groups

Autodesk User Groups (AUGs) meet regularly, offer courses and seminars, bring in speakers, and generally offer the types of resources that all AutoCAD users need. The AUGI Web site is at www.augi.com. Go there to see if there is a group in your area.

AUGI also offers its own technical support and training. You can find a lot of information and educational resources there, as well as AutoCAD and AutoCAD LT forums, which have their own easy entrance via the AutoCAD Community at www.augi.com/autocad/.

Internet Resources

The Internet sports hundreds of CAD-related Web sites. Here are some of the most prominent:

- The Autodesk Web site, at www.autodesk.com, contains a lot of product and support resources on AutoCAD and other Autodesk products. At www.autodesk.com/autocad, AutoCAD's home page, you can find a great deal of information about AutoCAD, including training and upgrade information. For information on AutoCAD LT, go to www.autodesk.com/autocadlt.

- The *Cadalyst* Web site, at www.cadalyst.com, shown in Figure B.1, is another important resource. Here you can find news, events, links, products, downloads, and so on. The *Cadalyst* files, at cadtips.cadalyst.com, offer all the AutoLISP code that the magazine has published since 1993.

- The CAD Depot, at www.caddepot.com, has a great collection of freeware and shareware, articles, news, and links. To find downloads applicable to AutoCAD LT, you can perform a search on AutoCAD LT.

- TenLinks.com, at www.tenlinks.com, is a wide-ranging directory and news source, with a daily e-mail newsletter.

FIGURE B.1

The *Cadalyst* Web site.

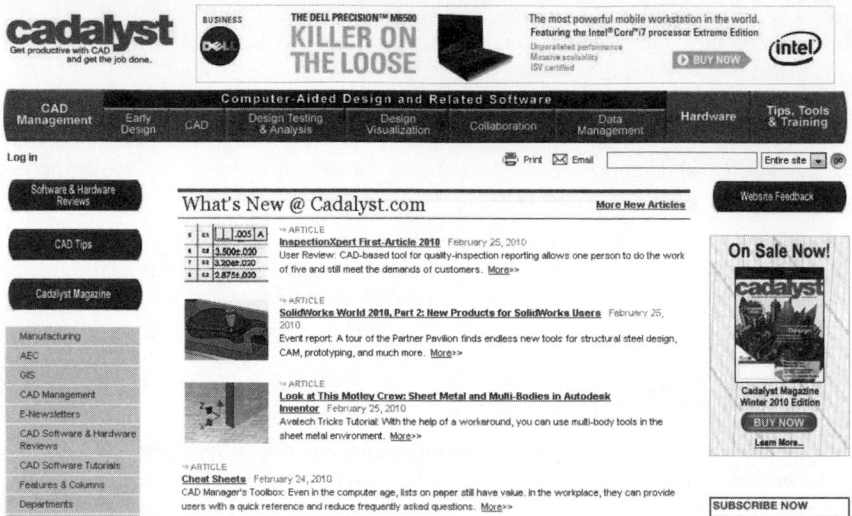

- CADwire.net, at `www.cadwire.net`, offers news, articles, and directories.
- CADInfo.net, at `www.cadinfo.net`, has software libraries, links, and articles on various CAD-related topics.

The Web has many, many more AutoCAD sites, but most of them are more specialized. Table B.1 lists some useful sites. If you don't have this list when you access the Internet, just type **AutoCAD** into any major search engine. One Web site will lead to another until you find what you need. Enjoy!

TABLE B.1

Useful AutoCAD Web Sites

Name	URL	Description
AUGI	`www.augi.com`	AutoCAD User Group International. This site includes a lot of information on AutoCAD, connections to local groups, and a newsletter.
Better Than Nothing AutoLISP	`home.pacifier.com/~nemi`	Leonid Nemirovsky's AutoLISP routines are useful and are free to download. I put several of them on the DVD-ROM of this book. Leonid wrote two (`It.lsp` and `Idt.lsp`) at my request, for which I'm grateful.
CAD Forum	`www.cadforum.cz/ cadforum_en/`	This site offers loads of tips on both AutoCAD and AutoCAD LT.
CADTutor	`www.cadtutor.net`	Free tutorials and articles on AutoCAD.

Appendix B: AutoCAD and AutoCAD LT Resources

Name	URL	Description
Dotsoft	www.dotsoft.com	Terry Dotson's site offers AutoCAD-related software for sale, along with a lot of freebies and tips. I've put some of his free software on the DVD of this book.
EllenFinkelstein.com	www.ellenfinkelstein.com	My site contains information about the latest AutoCAD features, tips, tutorials, and links. You can sign up for the AutoCAD Tips Newsletter or read my AutoCAD Tips Blog.
HyperPics	www.hyperpics.com	Lee Ambrosius's site offers AutoCAD and AutoCAD LT tips and tricks, with a lot of information on customization.
ManuSoft	www.manusoft.com	This site offers a good collection of software for AutoCAD — some for free, others to buy.
upfront.eZine	www.upfrontezine.com	You can find the archives of Ralph Grabowski's ezine, and purchase his eBooks.

A number of AutoCAD blogs have sprung up — and more keep coming. If you want the latest news, tips, and information, try one of these:

- **AutoCAD Tips Blog** (my own) at www.ellenfinkelstein.com/acadblog
- **Between the Lines** by Autodesk employee Shaan Hurley at autodesk.blogs.com/between_the_lines
- **RobiNZ CAD Blog** by Robin Capper at rcd.typepad.com/rcd
- **Beyond the UI** by Lee Ambrosius (contributor to, and technical editor of, this book) at hyperpics.blogs.com/beyond_the_ui
- **Lynn Allen's Blog** by Autodesk employee Lynn Allen at blogs.autodesk.com/lynn
- **AutoCAD Insider** by Autodesk employee Heidi Hewitt at blogs.autodesk.com/autocadinsider
- **Beth's CAD Blog** by Beth Powell at bethscadblog.blogspot.com
- **CAD Panacea** by R. K. McSwain at www.cadpanacea.com
- **CAD-a-Blog** by Brian Benton at cadablog.blogspot.com
- **JTB World Blog** by Jimmy Bergmark at jtbworld.blogspot.com
- **Mistress of the Dorkness** by Melanie (Stone) Perry at mistressofthedorkness.blogspot.com
- **CADman-Do** by David Cohn at cadman-do.blogspot.com
- **The CAD Geek** by Donnie Gladfelter at www.thecadgeek.com/blog
- **The Lazy Drafter** by Todd Shakelford at lazydrafter.blogspot.com
- **CAD-e-Corner** by Ward Romberger at cadecorner.blogspot.com
- **blog nauseam** by Steve Johnson at www.blog.cadnauseam.com
- **Daily AutoCAD** by Erhan and Orhan Toker at www.dailyautocad.com
- **Kate's CAD Tips for LT** by Autodesk employee Kate Morrical at blogs.autodesk.com/ltunlimited

- **The LT Side of Things** by Erik Deyo at `ltsideofthings.blogspot.com`
- **It's Alive in the Labs** by Scott Sheppard at `blogs.autodesk.com/labs`
- **BLAUGI** by Autodesk User Group International at `augi.typepad.com`
- **Through the Interface** by Autodesk employee Kean Walmsley at `blogs.autodesk.com/through-the-interface`

What's on the DVD

he *AutoCAD 2011 and AutoCAD LT 2011 Bible* DVD contains all the drawings and files that you need to do the exercises in the book, as well as the
results of those exercises. In addition, I've tried out many useful shareware programs and AutoLISP routines to see whether they work with AutoCAD
2011 and AutoCAD LT 2011, and then selected those that I felt would be most
useful. AutoCAD LT doesn't support AutoLISP routines. You can also find a document of links to Internet resources. I hope that you find this DVD a valuable
addition to your AutoCAD arsenal.

Cross-Reference
The drawings on the DVD are also available on the publisher's Web site at
`www.wiley.com/go/autocad2011bible`**. Click the Downloads link.** ■

This appendix provides you with information on the contents of the DVD that
accompanies this book. (Electronic versions of this book do not include a DVD.
To obtain the drawings for the exercises, see the Web site.) For the latest information, please refer to the README file located at the root of the DVD. Here is
what you'll find:

- System requirements for the DVD
- Using the DVD with Windows
- What's on the DVD
- Troubleshooting

IN THIS APPENDIX
Using the DVD
Accessing the software
Troubleshooting tips

System Requirements

Make sure that your computer meets the minimum system requirements listed in
this section. If your computer doesn't match up to most of these requirements,
you may have a problem using the contents of the DVD:

- Windows XP, Windows Vista, or Windows 7
- PC with a Pentium processor running at 200 MHz or faster

- At least 64MB of total RAM installed on your computer; for best performance, I recommend at least 128MB
- Ethernet network interface card (NIC) or modem with a speed of at least 28,800 bps
- A DVD drive

For system requirements for AutoCAD 2011 and AutoCAD LT 2011, see Appendix A.

Using the DVD with Microsoft Windows

You can copy certain items from the DVD to your hard drive. Follow these steps:

1. Insert the DVD into your computer's DVD drive.
2. The DVD interface will appear. The interface provides a simple point-and-click way to explore the contents of the DVD. Click one of the buttons to continue.

If the DVD interface does not appear, follow these steps to access the DVD:

1. Click the Start button on the left end of the task bar.
2. Choose Run from the menu that pops up. (In Windows Vista and Windows 7, skip this step.)
3. In the dialog box that appears, type **d:\setup.exe**. (If your DVD drive is not drive d, use the appropriate letter in place of d.) This brings up the DVD interface described in the preceding set of steps. (In Windows Vista or Windows 7, type **d:\setup.exe** in the Start Search text box.)

What's on the DVD

The following sections provide a summary of the software and other materials that you'll find on the DVD.

Using the Drawings folder

I've placed all the files that you need for the exercises in the Drawings folder of the DVD. Almost all these files are named as in the following examples: ab15-a.dwg, ab15-b.dwg, ab15-c.dwg, and so on. In these examples, the number 15 corresponds to the chapter number, and the letters correspond to the first, second, and third drawings that you need to open.

A few files have other names, such as bluesky.jpg and others. In each case, I provide you with the name of the file to open in the exercise's steps. You can easily find these files with Windows Explorer, because Explorer automatically alphabetizes the files. (If they aren't alphabetized, click the Name column. If Explorer alphabetizes them in reverse order, click Name one more time.)

Using the Results folder

The Results folder offers you the results of all the exercises. You may want to check your work in the exercises against these results. You may also sometimes use the result of one exercise as the basis for a second exercise. In this situation, if you haven't done the previous exercise, you can access the resulting file from the Results folder and use it for the next exercise. If you have any difficulty opening a drawing from the Results folder, copy it to your hard drive and remove its read-only attribute, as described in the "Changing the Windows Read-Only attribute" sidebar.

Changing the Windows Read-Only attribute

You can use the exercise drawings directly from the DVD, but you might get better results by copying them to your hard drive. The exercises instruct you to do this.

To use the software from the DVD, copy the files to a folder in AutoCAD's support-file search path.

Occasionally, you might run into the problem of not being able to access files on the DVD after you copy the files to your computer. After you copy or move a file from the DVD to your hard drive or another storage medium (such as a Zip drive), you may see the following error message when you attempt to open or save a file with its associated application:

```
[Application] is unable to open the [file].
Please make sure the drive and file are writable.
```

Windows recognizes all files on a DVD drive as read-only. Normally, this makes sense, because a DVD is a read-only medium — that is, you can't write data back to the disc. However, when you copy a file from a DVD to your hard drive or to a Zip drive, Windows may not automatically change the file attribute from read-only to writable. Installation software normally takes care of this chore for you, but when the files are to be manually copied to your disk, you may have to change the file attribute yourself. Luckily, this is easy:

1. Choose Start ⇨ (All) Programs ⇨ Accessories ⇨ Windows Explorer.
2. Highlight the filename(s).
3. Right-click the highlighted filename(s) to display a shortcut menu.
4. Choose Properties to display the Properties dialog box.
5. Click the Read-Only check box so that it's no longer checked.
6. Click OK.

You should now be able to use the file(s) with the specific application without seeing the annoying error message.

Using the Links folder

Appendix B contains numerous links to AutoCAD resources. The Links folder contains these resources as live links to make it easy for you to navigate to them with a single click.

Using the Videos folder

I have created a few video tutorials for you, to help you visualize some of the more difficult concepts. I've also created a video tutorial for the Quick Start chapter, because I know that beginners use this chapter. I hope that these videos will help you learn some of AutoCAD's features more quickly.

Using the Bonus Exercise and Bonus Chapter 37 folders

I took one exercise out of Chapter 23, because it covers an old technology, but you can find it on the DVD in the Bonus Exercise folder. The exercise is called "Bonus exercise on drawing polyface meshes." Due to space constraints, Chapter 37 is on the DVD, in the Bonus Chapter 37 folder. This chapter covers programming AutoCAD with VB.NET.

Using the Software folder

I have assembled an excellent collection of software that works with AutoCAD 2011. The Software folder is divided into subfolders by chapter. Not all chapters have software, so subfolders appear only for the chapters that have software. This makes it easy for you to find software by function. For example, you can find software for text objects by looking in the Chapter 13 subfolder because Chapter 13 covers text. Table C.1, at the end of this appendix, lists the software alphabetically so that you can review it at a glance. Within each chapter's subfolder, you'll find subfolders for each program or AutoLISP routine. There are a couple of block libraries and these also work in AutoCAD LT.

I'm very pleased to include 30-day trial versions of AutoCAD 2011 and AutoCAD LT 2011 with this book. These trial versions are in the Software folder. You cannot install them directly from the DVD. Double-click the EXE file. In the WinZip Self-Extractor dialog box that opens, click the Unzip button to decompress the file onto your own hard drive. When this process is completed, the installation process should automatically start; if not, double-click setup.exe in the folder you unzipped to.

Note

Trial versions of the current release are also available from Autodesk's Web site. For AutoCAD, go to www. autodesk.com/autocad-trial. **For AutoCAD LT, go to** www.autodesk.com/autocadlt-trial. ■

To find out in detail what each software program or AutoLISP routine does, read the text (TXT) file if there is one. It provides details about what the software does and how to install it. Sometimes details are at the beginning of the LSP file. You can open and read it.

Software can be of the following types:

- Shareware programs are fully functional, free, trial versions of copyrighted programs. If you like particular programs, register with their authors for a nominal fee and receive licenses, enhanced versions, and technical support.

- Freeware programs are free, copyrighted games, applications, and utilities. You can copy them to as many computers as you like — for free — but they offer no technical support.

- GNU software is governed by its own license, which is included inside the folder of the GNU software. There are no restrictions on distribution of GNU software. See the GNU license at the root of the CD for more details.

- Trial, demo, or evaluation versions of software are usually limited either by time or functionality (such as not letting you save a project after you create it).

Using Adobe Reader

Adobe Reader is included on the DVD to enable you to read any PDF files that may be on the DVD. You can find it in the \Software\Adobe Reader folder. Follow these steps to install the software:

1. Start Windows Explorer and open the Software\Adobe Reader folder on the DVD.
2. In the Software\Adobe Reader folder, locate the EXE file and double-click it.
3. Follow the instructions on-screen to install the software.
4. To read a PDF file, start Windows Explorer and double-click the PDF file.

Using AutoLISP routines

AutoLISP routines are easy to install. (AutoCAD LT does not support AutoLISP.) Follow these steps:

1. Copy the LSP file to AutoCAD's Support folder or to a folder that you've placed in AutoCAD's support-file search path.

Note

To add a folder to AutoCAD's support-file search path, choose Application Button ⇨ Options, and click the plus sign (+) next to Support File Search Path on the Files tab. Choose Add. Type in a folder path or choose Browse to locate one. ∎

2. In AutoCAD, type (**load** *"filename"*) where *filename* is the name of the LSP file. You don't need the `.lsp`, but don't forget the parentheses or the quotation marks. Alternatively, choose Manage tab ⇨ Applications panel ⇨ Load Application to use a dialog box. AutoCAD responds with the name of the last function that was defined in the routine.

3. Type the name of the function to use the AutoLISP routine.

If no text file explains how to use the program, brief instructions may be displayed on the command line. If not, type the name of the file, such as **atc**, and press Enter.

Using VBA programs

To load a VBA program, copy it to a folder in AutoCAD's support-file search path. (AutoCAD LT does not support VBA.) Choose Manage tab ⇨ Applications panel (expanded) ⇨ Load Project. Locate the VBA program (a DVB file), select it, and click Open. AutoCAD displays a message telling you that the VBA program contains macros and allows you to disable them. Of course, the VBA program doesn't work if you disable the macros. If you want, you can check the file with a virus-checker first. To enable the macros, choose Enable Macros. AutoCAD loads the VBA program.

To use a VBA program, choose Manage tab ⇨ Applications panel ⇨ Run VBA Macro. Select the VBA program and click Run.

Note

VBA is no longer included when you first install AutoCAD. Before you can use any of the VBA-related commands or Visual LISP functions, you must enable it by visiting Autodesk's Web site at `www.autodesk.com/avb-download`**. Follow the directions to download and install the VBA component. When installed, VBA works just like it did in previous releases. You need to install the VBA component before you can load and run macros contained in a DVB file.** ∎

Using .NET programs

.NET programs are easy to install. (AutoCAD LT does not support .NET.) Follow these steps:

1. Copy the DLL file to AutoCAD's `Support` folder or to a folder that you've placed in AutoCAD's support-file search path.

2. In AutoCAD, type **netload** and select the DLL file in the Choose .NET Assembly dialog box. Click Open.

3. Type the name of the command or function to use the .NET program.

For more information on creating and loading .NET programs, see Chapter 37.

Using a setup or install file

If you see a setup or install file (such as `setup.exe`), use it to install the software. You can also install everything from within the DVD interface.

Applications

The applications in Table C.1 are in the \Software folder on the *AutoCAD 2011 and AutoCAD LT 2011 Bible* DVD. The Chapter column lets you know which subfolder to look in. These subfolders correspond to the chapters of the book. Where possible, I also give you a Web site where you can find more information.

TABLE C.1

The DVD Software

Name	Type	Chapter	Description
AccuRender, from Robert McNeel & Associates	Evaluation	25	Advanced rendering program. For more information, go to www.mcneel.com.
Adobe Reader, from Adobe Systems, Inc.	Freeware		View electronic content in PDF format. For more information, go to www.adobe.com.
Ar1, from Leonid Nemirovsky	Freeware	16	Creates a label of the area of an enclosed polyline. For more information, go to home.pacifier.com/~nemi.
Arcsum, from Dotsoft	Freeware	12	Lists the total length of a selection set of arcs. For more information, see www.dotsoft.com.
Attstrip, from Dotsoft	Freeware	18	Removes all attributes from selected blocks. For more information, see www.dotsoft.com.
AutoCAD 2011, from Autodesk, Inc.	30-day trial		AutoCAD® 2011 software boosts efficiency with customizable and extensible user interface enhancements that increase overall drafting productivity by decreasing the number of steps required to reach a command. Newly designed, innovative features simplify working with layers and help make new users productive as quickly as possible. Easy-to-use navigation tools facilitate working with 3D models.
AutoCAD LT 2011, from Autodesk, Inc.	30-day trial		AutoCAD LT® 2011 software, the world's number one–selling 2D drafting and detailing product, is a powerful solution for designers who need full DWG native file format compatibility without 3D capabilities or advanced customization. An updated user interface helps increase productivity not only by accelerating routine tasks, but also by making commands easier to find and working with layers more straightforward, so that new users can become productive as quickly as possible.
Br	Freeware	10	Draws a break symbol. For more information, go to home.pacifier.com/~nemi.
GeomCurves, from Eugeny Kalney	Shareware	16	Creates a variety of mathematically defined curves.
Idt, from Leonid Nemirovsky	Freeware	13	Lets you specify spacing between lines of dtext. For more information, go to home.pacifier.com/~nemi.
Insrot, from DotSoft	Freeware	18	Inserts rotated blocks while maintaining horizontal attributes. For more information, see www.dotsoft.com.
It, from Leonid Nemirovsky	Freeware	13	Lets you specify spacing between lines of text. For more information, go to home.pacifier.com/~nemi.

Appendix C: What's on the DVD

Name	Type	Chapter	Description
Layerhtm, from DotSoft	Freeware	11	Displays a copy of the Layer Properties Manager dialog box in your browser so that you can print it. For more information, see `www.dotsoft.com`.
Linesum, from DotSoft	Freeware	12	Provides the total length of selected lines. For more information, see `www.dotsoft.com`.
Mhatch, from DotSoft	Freeware	16	Creates solid fills for a selection of closed objects. For more information, see `www.dotsoft.com`.
Mmt, from Leonid Nemirovsky	Freeware	13	Merges two Mtext objects. For more information, go to `home.pacifier.com/~nemi`.
Mpe-Arch	Freeware	18	A collection of electrical symbols for architectural drawings.
North, from DotSoft	Freeware	18	A collection of North symbols for architectural drawings. For more information, see `www.dotsoft.com`.
Pend, from Leonid Nemirovsky	Freeware	10	Creates a pipe break symbol in a line. For more information, go to `home.pacifier.com/~nemi`.
Polydis, from DotSoft	Freeware	12	Reports the length of a selected polyline. For more information, see `www.dotsoft.com`.
Psp1, from Leonid Nemirovsky	Freeware	17	Automates the setting of scales for paper space, creating viewports, and switching between viewports and corresponding views in model space. For more information, go to `home.pacifier.com/~nemi`.
Quickkey, from DotSoft	Freeware	29	"Super-Alias" replacement for `acad.pgp` that supports command options like ZOOM Previous. For more information, see `www.dotsoft.com`.
Save2d, from the author	Freeware	1	Saves a drawing to the `d:` drive, if you have a writable CD or DVD in that drive.
Sfld, from Leonid Nemirovsky	Freeware	13	Creates custom fields. For more information, go to `home.pacifier.com/~nemi`.
Stmplot, from Leonid Nemirovsky	Freeware	17	Adds drawing information to plots. For more information, go to `home.pacifier.com/~nemi`.
Txtexprt, from DotSoft	Freeware	13	Exports Text objects to a text file. For more information, see `www.dotsoft.com`.
Txtstack, from DotSoft	Freeware	13	Adjusts spacing between lines of single-line text. For more information, see `www.dotsoft.com`.
Wb, from Leonid Nemirovsky	Freeware	18	Creates a list of blocks in a folder, and wblocks the blocks to that folder. For more information, go to `home.pacifier.com/~nemi`.
Wblockm, from DotSoft	Freeware	18	Creates individual drawings (write blocks) of all the blocks in a drawing, in a folder that you specify. For more information, see `www.dotsoft.com`.
WinRAR, from Softronic Oy (Rarsoft)	Trial Version		A compression and decompression program. For more information, go to `www.rarlab.com`.

Troubleshooting

If you have difficulty installing or using any of the materials on the companion DVD, try the following solutions:

- **Turn off any antivirus software that you may have running.** Installers sometimes mimic virus activity and can make your computer incorrectly believe that a virus is infecting it. (Be sure to turn the antivirus software back on later.)

- **Close all running programs.** The more programs that you're running, the less memory is available to other programs. Installers also typically update files and programs; if you keep other programs running, installation may not work properly.

- **Reference the README file.** Please refer to the README file located at the root of the DVD for the latest product information at the time of publication.

- **If you are trying to use an AutoCAD drawing, copy it to your local hard drive and remove its Read-Only attribute, as described in the sidebar, "Changing the Windows Read-Only attribute."**

There is no way to install the DVD as a whole; you can only install individual software applications on the DVD or copy drawing files. For AutoLISP software, see information in the "Using the Software folder" section of this appendix.

Customer Care

If you have trouble with the DVD, please call the Wiley Product Technical Support phone number at 877-762-2974. Outside the United States, call 1-317-572-3993 or fax 317-572-4002. You can also contact Wiley Product Technical Support at www.wiley.com/techsupport. John Wiley & Sons will provide technical support only for installation and other general quality control items. For technical support on the applications themselves, consult the program's vendor or author.

To place additional orders or to request information about other Wiley products, please call 877-762-2974.

Index

Index

Index

Index

B

Index

Index

Index

Index

Index

Index

Index

Index

Index

Index

Index

Index

Index

Index

Index

Index

Index

Index

Index